Business Communications

Process & Product

8th Edition

Mary Ellen Guffey | Dana Loewy

CENGAGE
Learning

Australia • Brazil • Japan • Korea • Mexico • Singapore • Spain • United Kingdom • United States

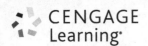

Business Communications; Process & Product; 8th Edition

Business Communications; Process & Product; 8th Edition
Mary Ellen Guffey | Dana Loewy

Senior Manager, Student Engagement:

Linda deStefano

Janey Moeller

Manager, Student Engagement:

Julie Dierig

Marketing Manager:

Rachael Kloos

Manager, Production Editorial:

Kim Fry

Manager, Intellectual Property Project Manager:

Brian Methe

Senior Manager, Production and Manufacturing:

Donna M. Brown

Manager, Production:

Terri Daley

> For product information and technology assistance, contact us at
> **Cengage Learning Customer & Sales Support, 1-800-354-9706**
>
> For permission to use material from this text or product,
> submit all requests online at **cengage.com/permissions**
> Further permissions questions can be emailed to
> **permissionrequest@cengage.com**

This book contains select works from existing Cengage Learning resources and was produced by Cengage Learning Custom Solutions for collegiate use. As such, those adopting and/or contributing to this work are responsible for editorial content accuracy, continuity and completeness.

Compilation © 2014 Cengage Learning

ISBN-13: 978-1-305-29719-7

ISBN-10: 1-305-29719-9

WCN: 01-100-101

Cengage Learning

5191 Natorp Boulevard
Mason, Ohio 45040
USA

Cengage Learning is a leading provider of customized learning solutions with office locations around the globe, including Singapore, the United Kingdom, Australia, Mexico, Brazil, and Japan. Locate your local office at:
international.cengage.com/region.

Cengage Learning products are represented in Canada by Nelson Education, Ltd.
For your lifelong learning solutions, visit **www.cengage.com/custom.**
Visit our corporate website at **www.cengage.com.**

Printed in the United States of America

Business Communication: Process and Product

Dr. Mary Ellen Guffey
Emerita Professor of Business
Los Angeles Pierce College
m.e.guffey@cox.net

Dr. Dana Loewy
Business Communication Program
California State University, Fullerton
dloewy@fullerton.edu

Dear Business Communication Student:

The Eighth Edition of ***Business Communication: Process and Product*** prepares you for a career in an increasingly digital and global workplace. My coauthor Dr. Dana Loewy and I have substantially revised our award-winning book to show how the explosive growth of social media networks and mobile technology is changing the workplace.

We have retained all of the features that have made ***BC:PP*** so successful over the years. In addition to solid instruction in writing skills, which employers continue to demand, the Eighth Edition brings you innumerable enhancements, a few of which are highlighted here:

Dana Loewy and Mary Ellen Guffey

Photographer: Barbara D'Allessandro

- **Expanded online resources.** The premium website, available at www.cengagebrain.com, offers one convenient place for you to review chapter concepts and practice developing your skills. You will find chapter quizzes, downloadable documents to revise, flashcards, and unparalleled resources to achieve success in the course.

- **Integrated coverage of communication technologies.** The Eighth Edition provides you with integrated coverage and applications of the latest digital technologies and mobile devices, emphasizing best practices for texting, instant messaging, blogging, wikis, and social media.

- **Stunning new design and graphics.** This edition's innovative design, with its engaging infographics and figures, presents concepts in an appealing format that strengthens your comprehension and engagement.

- **Comprehensive PowerPoint slides.** Available at the premium website (www.cengagebrain.com), our professionally designed slide shows help you quickly grasp and retain important chapter concepts.

- **Strengthened coverage of soft skills.** This edition delivers up-to-date guidance on acceptable workplace attire, professional behavior, and business etiquette for today's digital workplace.

- **Intriguing Reality Checks.** Valuable insights from business professionals demonstrate career relevance and offer advice to help you succeed in your career.

As always, we welcome your comments and suggestions as you use the No. 1 business communication book in this country and abroad.

Cordially,

Mary Ellen Guffey and Dana Loewy

Digital Tools with Guffey/Loewy

The premium student website is packed with resources to practice your new skills and improve your grade.

Mastering workplace communication is now easier than ever. Access numerous, robust study resources that complement your textbook at **www.cengagebrain.com**, and improve your business communication grade.

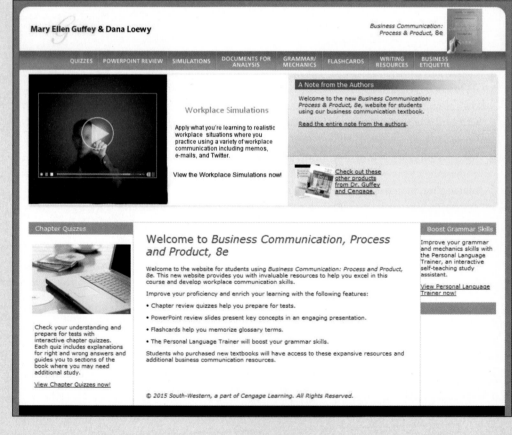

Access these resources to improve your grade:

CHAPTER REVIEW QUIZZES

Quizzing capabilities allow you to brush up on important chapter concepts throughout the course or just prior to exams. Each quiz question includes feedback that further improves your understanding of important topics.

POWERPOINT REVIEWS

PowerPoint slides review important concepts from each chapter and help you comprehend and retain these concepts as you prepare for exams or internalize your learning.

DOCUMENTS FOR ANALYSIS

Avoid having to do the extra work rekeying documents by downloading them from the premium website. Or use these documents for additional practice, beyond instructor requirements.

PERSONAL LANGUAGE TRAINER

Personal Language Trainer is a comprehensive learning resource that ensures mastery of the grammar/mechanics required in the business communication course. Take a diagnostic quiz to assess your current knowledge base. Complete warmup activities and exercises to brush up on problem areas. Then test your knowledge with a comprehensive test that helps you track your progress.

SPEAK RIGHT!/SPELL RIGHT!

Improve your pronunciation and spelling skills by utilizing these interactive language resources.

FLASHCARDS

Improve your vocabulary by using these interactive, online study aids.

WORKPLACE SIMULATIONS

Polish your communication skills by solving realistic workplace problems, and gain practice using the latest workplace technology.

WRITING RESOURCES

This handy resource includes references and links to online writing resources to help you more easily complete writing assignments. Specifically, access Online Writing Labs, MLA and APA formats, a list of nearly 100 report topics, and other valuable writing resources.

How do you access the Guffey/Loewy premium website?

- To register a product using the access code found in your textbook, go to **www.cengagebrain.com**.
- Register as a new user or log in as an existing user if you already have an account with Cengage Learning or CengageBrain.com.
- Follow the prompts.

Note: If you did not buy a new textbook, the access code may have been used. You can either buy a new book or purchase access to the Guffey/Loewy Premium website at **www.cengagebrain.com**.

Brief Contents

Contents

Chapter 3
Intercultural Communication 80

© iStockphoto.com/Anton Seleznev

Unit 2
The Writing Process in the Digital Age

Chapter 4
Planning Business Messages 120

© Multi-bits/The Image Bank/Getty Images

Chapter 5
Organizing and Drafting Business Messages   150

© Yuri Arcurs/Shutterstock.com

Chapter 6
Revising Business Messages   176

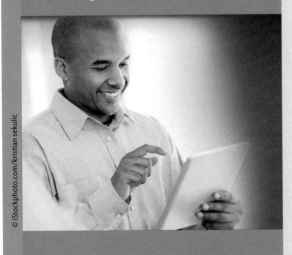

© iStockphoto.com/kristian sekulic

Unit 3
Workplace Communication

Chapter 7
Short Workplace Messages and Digital Media 204

© Betsie Van der Meer/Stone/Getty Images

Chapter 8
Positive Messages 244

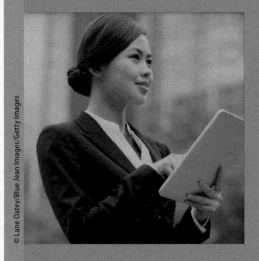

© Lane Oatey/Blue Jean Images/Getty Images

Chapter 9
Negative Messages 284

© iStockphotos.com/Jacob Wackerhausen

Chapter 10
Persuasive and Sales Messages 326

© Warren Goldswain/Shutterstock.com

Unit 4
Reports, Proposals, and Presentations

Chapter 11
Reporting in the Digital-Age Workplace 372

© Xavier Arnau/the Agency Collection

Chapter 12
Informal Business Reports 418

© iStockphoto.com/Neustockimages

Chapter 13
Proposals, Business Plans, and Formal Business Reports 464

© Tony Metaxas/Asia Images/Getty Images

Chapter 14
Business Presentations 500

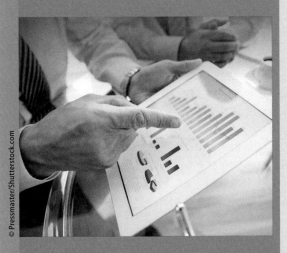

© Pressmaster/Shutterstock.com

Unit 5
Employment Communication

Chapter 15
The Job Search and Résumés in the Digital Age 542

© Sam Edwards/OJO Images/Getty Images

Chapter 16
Interviewing and Following Up 586

© iStockphoto.com/sturti

Appendixes

End Matter

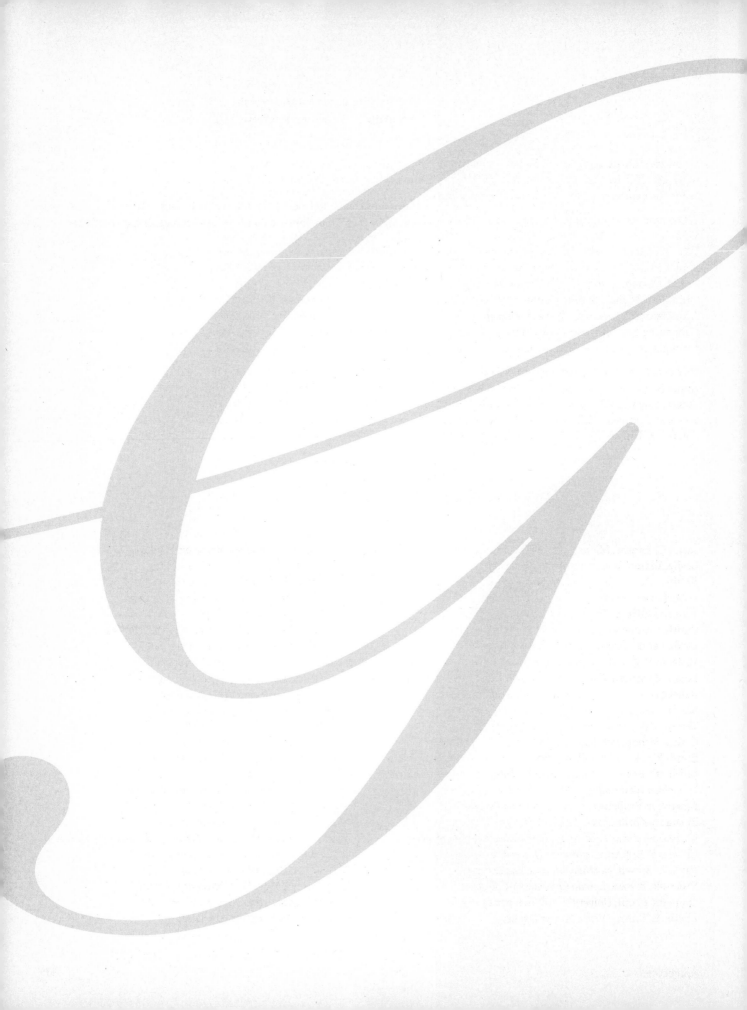

Appreciation for Support

No successful textbook reaches a No. 1 position without a great deal of help. We are exceedingly grateful to the reviewers and other experts who contributed their pedagogic and academic expertise in shaping *Business Communication: Process and Product.*

We extend sincere thanks to many professionals at Cengage Learning, including Jack W. Calhoun, Senior Vice President, Global Product Manager, Higher Education; Erin Joyner, Vice President, General Manager, Social Science & Qualitative Business; Jason Fremder, Senior Product Manager; Mary Emmons, Senior Content Developer; Kristen Hurd, Senior Brand Manager; John Rich, Senior Media Developer; Shirley Stacy, Senior Art Director; Tamborah Moore, Senior Content Project Manager, and Deanna Ettinger, Senior Rights Acquisitions Specialist. We are also grateful to the publishing professionals at LEAP Publishing Services, especially Malvine Litten, who ensured premier quality and accuracy throughout the publishing process.

Our heartfelt appreciation also goes to the following for their expertise in creating exceptional instructor and student support materials: Carolyn M. Seefer, Diablo Valley College; Steven Chen, California State University, Fullerton; Joyce Staples, Bellevue College; Jane Flesher, Chippewa Valley Technical College; Susan Guzmán-Treviño, Temple College; Jane Johansen, University of Southern Indiana; and John Donnellan, University of Texas, Austin.

Mary Ellen Guffey
Dana Loewy

Grateful Thanks to Reviewers

Janet G. Adams, *Minnesota State University, Mankato*
Leslie Adams, *Houston Baptist University*
Kehinde A. Adesina, *Contra Costa College*
Asberine Parnell Alford, *Suffolk Community College*
Virginia Allen, *Joliet Junior College*
Cynthia Anderson, *Youngstown State University*
Linda Landis Andrews, *University of Illinois, Chicago*
Vanessa D. Arnold, *University of Mississippi*
Lois J. Bachman, *Community College of Philadelphia*
Rebecca Barksdale, *University of Central Florida*
Sandra Berill, *Arkansas State University*
Teresa L. Beyer, *Sinclair Community College*
Cathie Bishop, *Parkland College*
Randi Blank, *Indiana University*
Elizabeth Bowers, *Orange Coast College and Golden West College*
Martha E. Bradshaw, *Southeastern Louisiana Univ.*
Bernadine Branchaw, *Western Michigan University*
Maryanne Brandenburg, *Indiana University of Pennsylvania*
Charles P. Bretan, *Northwood University*
Paula E. Brown, *Northern Illinois University*
Vivian R. Brown, *Loredo Community College*
Domenic Bruni, *University of Wisconsin Oshkosh*
Phyllis C. Bunn, *Delta State University*

Mary Ann Burris, *Pueblo Community College*
Roosevelt D. Butler, *College of New Jersey*
Jane Campanizzi-Mook, *Franklin University*
James F. Carey, *Onondaga Community College*
Leila Chambers, *Cuesta College*
Patricia H. Chapman, *University of South Carolina*
Judie C. Cochran, *Grand Canyon University*
Marjorie Coffey, *Oregon State University*
Randy E. Cone, *University of New Orleans*
James Conley, *Eastern Michigan University*
Billie Miller Cooper, *Cosumnes River College*
Linda W. Cooper, *Macon State College*
Jane G. Corbly, *Sinclair Community College*
Martha Cross, *Delta State University*
Linda Cunningham, *Salt Lake Community College*
Lajuan Davis, *University of Wisconsin-Whitewater*
Fred DeCasperis, *Siena College*
Guy Devitt, *Herkimer County Community College*
Linda Di Desidero, *University of Maryland University College*
John Donnellan, *University of Texas at Austin*
J. Yellowless Douglas, *University of Florida*
Bertha Du-Babcock, *City University of Hong Kong*
Dorothy Drayton, *Texas Southern University*
Kay Durden, *University of Tennessee*

Anna Easton, *Indiana University*
Lorena B. Edwards, *Belmont University*
Donald E. English, *Texas A&M University*
Margaret Erthal, *Southern Illinois University*
Donna R. Everett, *Morehead State University*
Gwendolyn Bowie Ewing, *Southwest Tennessee Community College*
Anne Finestone, *Santa Monica Community College*
Peggy B. Fisher, *Ball State University*
Terry M. Frame, *University of South Carolina*
Gen Freese, *Harrisburg Area Community College*
Kerry J. Gambrill, *Florida Community College*
Judith L. Graham, *Holyoke Community College*
Carolyn G. Gray, *The University of Texas, Austin*
Diane Gruber, *Arizona State University West*
Susan Guzmán-Treviño, *Temple College*
David Hamilton, *Bemidji State University*
Bill Hargrave, *University of West Georgia*
Paul Hegele, *Elgin Community College*
Susan A. Heller, *Reading Area Community College*
K. Virginia Hemby, *Middle Tennessee State University*
Rovena L. Hillsman, *California State University, Sacramento*
Kenneth Hoffman, *Emporia State University*
Shirley Houston, *University of Nebraska*
Warren B. Humphrey, *University of Central Florida*
Robert G. Insley, *University of North Texas*
Edna Jellesed, *Lane Community College*
Glen J. Jenewein, *Portland Community College*
Kathy Jesiolowski, *Milwaukee Area Technical College*
Carolyn Spillers Jewell, *Pembroke State University*
Pamela R. Johnson, *California State University, Chico*
Eric Johnstone, *Montana State University*
Cheryl L. Kane, *University of North Carolina Charlotte*
Diana K. Kanoy, *Central Florida Community College*
Tina S. Kazan, *University of Illinois, Chicago*
Carolyn E. Kerr, *University of Pittsburgh*
Sonia Khatchadourian, *University of Wisconsin-Milwaukee*
Margaret S. Kilcoyne, *Northwestern State University*
G. Scott King, *Sinclair Community College*
Suzanne P. Krissler, *Orange County Com. College*
Linda L. Labin, *Husson College*
Gary E. Lacefield, *University of Texas at Arlington*
Richard Lacy, *California State University, Fresno*
Suzanne Lambert, *Broward Community College*
Marilyn L. Lammers, *California State University, Northridge*
Lorita S. Langdon, *Columbus State Community College*
Joyce N. Larsen, *Front Range Community College*
Marianna Larsen, *Utah State University*
Barbara Lea, *West Valley College*
Claire E. Legowski, *North Dakota State University*
Mary E. Leslie, *Grossmont College*
Kathy Lynn Lewis-Adler, *University of North Alabama*
Kristie J. Loescher, *The University of Texas at Austin*
Jennifer Cook Loney, *Portland State University*
Mary Jean Lush, *Delta State University*

Sonia Maasik, *University of California, Los Angeles*
Bruce MacBeth, *Clarion University of Pennsylvania*
Georgia E. Mackh, *Cabrillo College*
Andrew Madson, *Milwaukee Area Technical College*
Anna Maheshwari, *Schoolcraft College*
Maureen L. Margolies, *University of Cincinnati*
Leon Markowicz, *Lebanon Valley College*
Thomas A. Marshall II, *Robert Morris College*
Jeanette Martin, *University of Mississippi*
John F. Mastriani, *El Paso Community College*
Cynthia H. Mayfield, *York Technical College*
Susan Smith McClaren, *Mt. Hood Community College*
Beryl C. McEwen, *North Carolina A&T State University*
Marya McFadden, *California State University Northridge*
Nancy McGee, *Davenport University*
Diana McKowen, *Indiana University*
Mary C. Miller, *Ashland University*
Marci Mitchell, *South Texas Community College*
Nancy B. Moody, *Sinclair Community College*
Danne Moore, *Shawnee State University*
Wayne A. Moore, *Indiana University of Pennsylvania*
Paul W. Murphey, *Southwest Wisconsin Technical College*
Lin Nassar, *Oakland Community College*
Beverly H. Nelson, *University of New Orleans*
Matt Newby, *Heald College*
John P. Nightingale, *Eastern Michigan University*
Ed Nagelhout, *University of Nevada*
Jeanne E. Newhall, *Middlesex Community College*
Alexa B. North, *State University of West Georgia*
Nancy Nygaard, *University of Wisconsin-Milwaukee*
Rosemary Olds, *Des Moines Area Community College*
James S. O'Rourke IV, *University of Notre Dame*
Smita Jain Oxford, *University of Mary Washington*
Ed Peters, *University of Texas at Arlington*
Melinda Phillabaum, *Indiana University*
Richard David Ramsey, *Southeastern Louisiana University, Hammond*
Betty Jane Robbins, *University of Oklahoma*
Janice Rowan, *Rowan University*
Calvin R. Parks, *Northern Illinois University*
Pamela A. Patey, *Riverside Community College*
Shara Toursh Pavlow, *University of Miami*
William Peirce, *Prince George's Community College and University of Maryland University College*
Joan Policano, *Onondaga Community College*
Paula J. Pomerenke, *Illinois State University*
Jean Anna Sellers, *Fort Hays State University*
Deborah Von Spreecken, *Anoka-Ramsey Community College*
Karen Sterkel Powell, *Colorado State University*
Gloria Power, *Delgado Community College*
Richard P. Profozich, *Prince George's Community College*
Carolyn Mae Rainey, *Southeast Missouri State University*
Richard David Ramsey, *Southeastern Louisiana University*
Richard G. Raspen, *Wilkes University*
Virginia L. Reynolds, *Cleveland State University*

Ruth D. Richardson, *University of North Alabama*
Joseph H. Roach, *Middlesex County College*
Terry D. Roach, *Arkansas State University*
Betty Jane Robbins, *University of Oklahoma*
Linda Sarlo, *Rock Valley College*
Christine A. Saxild, *Mt. Senario College*
Joseph Schaffner, *State University of New York at Alfred*
Annette Schley, *North Seattle Community College*
Betty L. Schroeder, *Northern Illinois University*
Carolyn M. Seefer, *Diablo Valley Community College*
Marilyn Simonson, *Lakewood Community College*
Sue C. Smith, *Palm Beach Community Collage*
Kathleen M. Sole, *University of Phoenix*
Charles L. Snowden, *Sinclair Community College*
Gayle A. Sobolik, *California State University, Fresno*
Jeanette Spender, *Arkansas State University*
Jan Starnes, *The University of Texas at Austin*
Judy Steiner-Williams, *Indiana University*
Ted D. Stoddard, *Brigham Young University*
Susan Switzer, *Central Michigan University*
Roni Szeliga, *Gateway Technical College*
Leslie S. Talley, *University of Central Florida*

Barbara P. Thompson, *Columbus State Community College*
Sally J. Tiffany, *Milwaukee Area Technical College*
Lori M. Townsend, *Niagara County Community College*
Mary L. Tucker, *Ohio University*
Richard F. Tyler, *Anne Arundel Community College*
Deborah Valentine, *Emory University*
Doris A. Van Horn Christopher, *California State University, Los Angeles*
David Victor, *Eastern Michigan University*
Lois Ann Wagner, *Southwest Wisconsin Technical College*
John L. Waltman, *Eastern Michigan University*
Marion Webb, *Cleveland State University*
Beverly A. Westbrook, *Delta College*
Carol Smith White, *Georgia State University*
Carol M. Williams, *Pima County Community College*
Debbie J. Williams, *Abilene Christian University*
Jane D. Williams, *J. Sargeant Reynolds Community College*
Rosemary B. Wilson, *Washtenaw Community College*
Beverly C. Wise, *State University of New York, Morrisville*
William E. Worth, *Georgia State University*
Myron D. Yeager, *Chapman University*
Karen Zempel, *Bryant and Stratton College*

About the Authors

Dr. Mary Ellen Guffey

A dedicated professional, Mary Ellen Guffey has taught business communication and business English topics for over thirty-five years. She received a bachelor's degree, *summa cum laude*, from Bowling Green State University; a master's degree from the University of Illinois, and a doctorate in business and economic education from the University of California, Los Angeles (UCLA). She has taught at the University of Illinois, Santa Monica College, and Los Angeles Pierce College.

Now recognized as the world's leading business communication author, Dr. Guffey corresponds with instructors around the globe who are using her books. She is the founding author of the award-winning *Business Communication: Process and Product,* the leading business communication textbook in this country. She also wrote *Business English,* which serves more students than any other book in its field; *Essentials of College English*; and *Essentials of Business Communication,* the leading text/workbook in its market. Dr. Guffey is active professionally, serving on the review boards of the *Business Communication Quarterly* and the *Journal of Business Communication*, publications of the Association for Business Communication. She participates in national meetings, sponsors business communication awards, and is committed to promoting excellence in business communication pedagogy and the development of student writing skills.

Dr. Dana Loewy

Dana Loewy has been teaching business communication at California State University, Fullerton since 1996. She enjoys introducing undergraduates to business writing and honing the skills of graduate students in managerial communication. Most recently, she has also taught various German courses and is a regular guest lecturer at Fachhochschule Nürtingen, Germany. In addition to completing numerous brand-name consulting assignments, she is a certified business etiquette consultant. Dr. Loewy has collaborated with Dr. Guffey on recent editions of *Business Communication: Process & Product* as well as on *Essentials of Business Communication*.

Dr. Loewy holds a master's degree from Bonn University, Germany, and earned a PhD in English from the University of Southern California. Fluent in several languages, among them German and Czech, her two native languages, Dr. Loewy has authored critical articles in many areas of interest—literary criticism, translation, business communication, and business ethics. Before teaming up with Dr. Guffey, Dr. Loewy published various poetry and prose translations, most notably *The Early Poetry* of Jaroslav Seifert and *On the Waves of TSF*. Active in the Association for Business Communication, Dr. Loewy focuses on creating effective teaching/learning materials for undergraduate and graduate business communication students.

Unit 1
Communication Foundations

0:05 / 12:50 ● 720p

Business Communication in the Digital Age

OBJECTIVES

After studying this chapter, you should be able to

1 Explain how communication skills fuel career success, and understand why writing skills are vital in a digital workplace embracing social media.

2 Identify the tools for success in the hyperconnected 21st-century workplace, and appreciate the importance of critical-thinking skills in the competitive job market of the digital age.

3 Describe significant trends in today's dynamic, networked work environment, and recognize that social media and other new communication technologies require excellent communication skills, particularly in an uncertain economy.

4 Examine critically the internal and external flow of communication in organizations through formal and informal channels, explain the importance of effective media choices, and understand how to overcome typical barriers to organizational communication.

5 Analyze ethics in the workplace, understand the goals of ethical business communicators, recognize and avoid ethical traps, and choose the tools for doing the right thing.

Intel Blazes the Social Media Trail

Zooming in

Technology giant Intel is known for being on the cutting edge of an industry that epitomizes innovation. Its many products power computers, phones, and even car security systems. However, its sophisticated use of social media has made Intel a leader in a wholly separate sphere: strategic communication with customers.

From blogs to wikis to social media networks, Intel's social media presence permeates the Internet. Its Facebook presence is especially effective. Ekaterina Walter, a member of Intel's Social Media Center of Excellence team, explains some of the reasons for that success. Wall posts are written to enhance "news feed optimization,"[1] which encourages more viewers to join Intel's Facebook conversation, says Walter. "The higher the engagement with you (which are 'likes' and comments), the more likely it is that your page will be picked up by the Facebook algorithm and make it to the news feed," she adds.[2]

Posts go beyond sharing information, however. The page contains humorous videos, offers good wishes during the holidays, and thanks "friends" when they compliment an Intel product. Contributors customize every post and stick to a strict editorial calendar.

Whichever social media mode is used, Intel's 100,100 employees in 65 countries must undergo training before participating.[3] In addition, the Intel Social Media Guidelines provide the firm's core social media principles, and, not surprisingly, offer writing advice. Authors are urged to compose in the first person so readers are clear about who is responsible for each message. They are reminded that social media is a conversation. "Talk to your readers like you would talk to real people in professional situations . . . avoid overly pedantic language," the guidelines recommend.[4] Likewise, writers must be considerate, cautious not to post in haste, and willing to revise. Content should add value and be "thought-provoking."[5]

Intel demonstrated its leadership when it made its Social Media Guidelines available on the Internet. Doing so at a time when many other firms were banning employees from using social media is just another example of Intel's trailblazing ethos.

You will learn more about Intel and be asked to complete a relevant task at the end of this chapter.

Critical Thinking

- Why is a natural writing style more appropriate for social media than a formal writing style?

- Why is reading and revising especially important when using social media?

- How are an organization's values reflected in its business practices?

Communicating in the Digital World

You may wonder what kind of workplace you will enter when you graduate and which skills you will need to be successful in it. Expect a fast-paced, competitive, and highly connected digital environment. Communication technology provides unmatched mobility and connects individuals anytime and anywhere in the world. Today's communicators interact using multiple electronic devices and access information stored in remote locations, "in the cloud." This mobility and instant access explain why increasing numbers of workers must be available practically around the clock and respond quickly. Intel and other technology-savvy businesses have recognized the power of social media networks and seek to engage their customers and other stakeholders where they meet online. Communication no longer flows one way; rather, electronic media have empowered the public to participate and be heard.

In this increasingly complex, networked digital environment, communication skills matter more than ever.[6] Such skills are particularly significant at a time when jobs are scarce and competition is keen. However, job candidates with exceptional communication skills immediately stand out. In this chapter you will learn about communication skills in the digital era and about the changing world of work. Later you will study tools to help you negotiate ethical minefields and do the right thing. Each section covers the latest information about communicating in business. Each section also provides tips that will help you function effectively and ethically in today's fast-moving, information-driven workplace.

LEARNING OBJECTIVE 1
Explain how communication skills fuel career success, and understand why writing skills are vital in a digital workplace embracing social media.

Communication Skills: Your Pass to Success

Over the last decade, employer surveys have consistently shown that strong communication skills are critical to effective job placement, performance, career advancement, and organizational success.[7] In making hiring decisions, employers often rank communication skills among the most desirable competencies.[8]

Interviewers for defense contractor BAE Systems may request a writing sample to "literally see if the candidate can write," but also to find out whether the applicant can organize and share ideas, explains Curt Gray, senior vice president of human resources and administration. UPS requires its workers to write clear and concise messages and "to investigate, analyze and report their findings in a professional manner," says Matt Lavery, managing director of corporate talent acquisition.[9] In a Fortune poll, 1,000 executives cited writing, critical-thinking, and problem-solving skills along with self-motivation and team skills as their top choices in new-hires.[10]

Writing skills can be your ticket to work—or your ticket out the door, according to a business executive responding to a significant survey. This much-quoted study of 120 American corporations by the National Commission on Writing found that two thirds of salaried employees have some writing responsibility. However, about one third of them do not meet the writing requirements for their positions.[11] "Businesses are crying out—they need to have people who write better," said Gaston Caperton, executive and College Board president.

Writing has been variously called a "career sifter," a "threshold skill," and "the price of admission,"[12] indicating that effective writing skills can be a stepping stone to great job opportunities, or, if poorly developed, may derail a career. Writing is a marker of high-skill, high-wage, professional work, according to Bob Kerrey, university president and chair of the National Commission on Writing. If you can't express yourself clearly, he says, you limit your opportunities for many positions.[13]

When we discuss communication skills, we generally mean reading, listening, nonverbal, speaking, and writing skills. In addition, workers today must be media savvy and exercise good judgment when posting messages on the Internet and writing e-mails. To be successful, they must guard their online image and protect the reputation of their employers. In this book we focus on the listening, nonverbal, speaking, and writing skills necessary in a digital workplace. Chapters are devoted to each of these skills. Special attention is given to writing skills because they are difficult to develop and increasingly significant in e-communication.

Writing in the Digital Age

If you are like many young adults, you may think that your daily texts, instant messages, Facebook posts, blog entries, e-mails, and more are not "real writing." A Pew Internet & American Life study found that teens and young adults consider their frequent e-communication to be very different from the traditional writing they learn in school.[14] Perhaps young people understand that their digital writing is largely casual, but that employers expect more formal, thoughtful, informative, and error-free messages. In any case, the respondents in the study rightly believe that solid writing skills are a necessity in today's networked digital world.

Long gone are the days when business was mostly conducted face-to-face and when administrative assistants corrected spelling and grammar for their bosses. Although interpersonal skills still matter greatly, writing effectively is critical. Ever since the digital revolution swept the workplace, most workers write their own messages. New communication channels appeared, including the Web and e-mail, followed by instant messaging, blogs, and social media networks. Figure 1.1 displays the emergence of new communication technology and the rapid growth of Internet users over the last two decades. So far, the number of Internet users has roughly doubled every five years.

Communication technology connects individuals anytime and anywhere in the world.

© artsstock/Photos.com

NOTE: Because this is a well-researched textbook, you will find small superscript numbers in the text. These announce information sources. Full citations are located in the Notes section at the end of each chapter. This edition uses a modified American Psychological Association (APA) reference citation format.

Figure 1.1 Timeline: Communication Technology and Social Media

2000 | | | | | 2005 | | | | | 2010 | | | | 2015

1998
Google
MSN

1999
Napster
Blogger

2000
GPS III
Geocaching
ThumbDrive

2001
StumbleUpon
Wikipedia
iTunes
iPod

2002
Blackberry
Palm OS
Treo

2003
Skype
Second Life
RSS 2.0
MySpace
LinkedIn

2004
Facebook
World of Warcraft
Digg
Flickr

2005
YouTube
Vimeo

2006
Blu-ray Disc

2007
iPhone
Netbooks
Kindle
Hulu

2008
Android
Dropbox
WiMax networks
USB 3.0

2009
IPTV

2010
iPad
WiMax
Smartphones
Pinterest

2011
Cloud computing
Technology
convergence
Semantic Web

RESPONSE TIME: Weeks > Days > Hours > Minutes > Seconds

NUMBER OF INTERNET USERS: 361 Million   >   500 Million   >   1.15 Billion   >   2.3 Billion

© Cengage Learning 2015

Writing matters more than ever because the online media require more of it, not less.[15] An important poll by Hart Research Associates supports this view. The participating employers admitted that their expectations of employees have increased because the challenges on the job are more complex than in the past. The executives also said that employees today need a broader range of skills as well as higher levels of knowledge in their fields.[16] "Communicating clearly and effectively has NEVER been more important than it is today. Whether it's fair or not, life-changing critical judgments about you are being made based solely on your writing ability," says management consultant Victor Urbach. "Having excellent command of your online digital persona will enable you to quickly surpass those who present themselves weakly in the new competitive arena. Since you probably won't get a second chance, what kind of digital first impression will you choose to make?"[17] Developing these skills in this course will help you stand out.

It's Up to You: Communication Skills Can Be Learned

By enrolling in a business writing class, you have already taken the first step toward improving or polishing your communication skills. The goals of this course and this book include teaching you basic business communication skills, such as how to write an effective e-mail or a clear business letter and how to make a memorable presentation in person or using various digital media. Thriving in the challenging digital work world depends on many factors, some of which you cannot control. However, one factor that you do control is how well you communicate. You are not born with the abilities to read, listen, speak, and write effectively. These skills must be learned. This book and this course may well be the most important in your entire college curriculum because they will equip you with the skills most needed in today's fast-paced digital workplace.

© Pablo Scapinachis/Shutterstock.com

Job candidates with exceptional communication skills instantly stand out. Communication skills are critical to career success.

"To succeed in today's workplace, young people need more than basic reading and math skills. They need substantial content knowledge and information technology skills; advanced thinking skills, flexibility to adapt to change; and interpersonal skills to succeed in multi-cultural, cross-functional teams."[18]

—J. WILLARD MARRIOTT, JR., *Chairman and CEO, Marriott International, Inc.*

LEARNING OBJECTIVE 2

Identify the tools for success in the hyperconnected 21st-century workplace, and appreciate the importance of critical-thinking skills in the competitive job market of the digital age.

The Digital Revolution and You: Tools for Success in the 21st-Century Workplace

If you are a young adult, chances are that you check for Facebook posts, smartphone texts, tweets, or e-mails first thing in the morning and repeatedly throughout the day to stay connected with your friends and family. Most likely you write and create digital documents with computers and other Internet-enabled electronic devices in today's networked environment without thinking much about the technology enabling you to do all this. Information technology has changed how we work, play, and communicate in distinct ways. It has never been easier to access and share information via various digital media from a vast network of sources and to distribute it nearly instantly and to widespread audiences.[19] What hasn't changed is that communication skills need time and effort to develop.

To achieve literacy in the digital age means not only using multimedia applications and snazzy late-model gadgets but also thinking critically about new media. It means using technology thoughtfully and in a professional manner to achieve success in such a hyperconnected digital world.

The 21st-century economy depends mainly on information and knowledge. Previously, in the Industrial Age, raw materials and physical labor were the key ingredients in the creation of wealth. Today, however, individuals in the workforce offer their knowledge, not their muscles. Knowledge workers (a term first coined by management guru Peter Drucker) get paid for their education and their ability to learn.[20] More recently, we are hearing the term *information worker* to describe those who produce and consume information in the workplace.[21] Regardless of the terminology, knowledge and information workers engage in mind work. They must make sense of words, figures, and data. At the same time, the knowledge available in the "digital universe" is more than doubling every year, according to computing pioneer George Dyson.[22]

In this light it may not surprise you that jobs in the information technology sector are likely to jump 24 percent in the next seven years.[23] Moreover, despite a bleak U.S. labor market, hundreds of thousands of jobs in science, technology, engineering, and math remain unfilled.[24] Experts also worry about domestic "talent shortages" in skilled manufacturing.[25] In such a demanding environment, continuous, lifelong learning will make you more competitive and valuable to future employers. An adaptable, highly skilled workforce is well equipped to weather even the deepest recessions and the threat of outsourcing.

Why Should You Care?

As a knowledge worker in the digital age, you can expect to be generating, processing, and exchanging information. You will need to be able to transmit it effectively across various communication channels and multiple media. You might be called upon to use e-mail, electronic slide presentations, wikis, podcasts, or Facebook and other social media in a

It has never been easier to access and share information via various digital media from a vast network of sources and to distribute it instantly to widespread audiences.

professional setting. With added job responsibilities, you will be expected to make sound decisions and solve complex problems. Interviewers at global giant Siemens probe job applicants for the ability "to quickly distill the key issues and relationships in complex situations," says Mike Panigel, senior vice president of human resources.[26]

In a study conducted by the Society for Human Resource Management and *The Wall Street Journal*, human resources professionals identified problem solving and critical thinking as top workplace skills today, right behind adaptability and flexibility.[27] You are learning to think, read, and ask questions in a networked world, accessed with computers, tablets, smartphones, e-readers, and more. The avalanche of information that engulfs you daily requires you to evaluate all sources critically because information flows at a great speed, across various media, and in many directions. With potentially a global audience watching, you can choose to project a positive, professional image, or you can publish misinformation and embarrassing falsehoods.[28]

REALITY CHECK: Wanted! 21st-Century Skills

In the media-driven world of the 21st century, workers must process vast amounts of information fast and judge accurately whether the information is reliable. "It's important that students know how to manage it, interpret it, validate it, and how to act on it."[29]

—**KAREN BRUETT,** *higher education expert, former Dell executive*

Thinking Critically in the Digital Age

Whether you work in *m-commerce* (mobile technology businesses), *e-commerce* (Internet-based businesses), or *brick-and-mortar commerce*, nearly three out of four jobs will involve some form of mind work. Jobs that require thinking, brainpower, and decision-making skills are likely to remain plentiful. To be successful in these jobs, you will need to be able to think critically, make decisions, and communicate those decisions.

Management and employees work together in such areas as product development, quality control, and customer satisfaction. All workers, from executives to subordinates, need to think creatively and critically. Even in factory production lines, workers are part of the knowledge culture. Toyota's management philosophy of continuous improvement by engaged and empowered workers is much admired around the world.[30] One of the secrets of Toyota's success, said Takis Athanasopoulos, former chief executive of the Japanese carmaker's European operations, "is that the company encourages every worker, no matter how far down the production line, to consider himself a knowledge worker and to think creatively about improving his particular corner of the organization."[31]

When your boss or team leader says, "What do you think we ought to do?" you want to be able to supply good ideas and demonstrate that you can think critically. This means having opinions that are backed by reasons and evidence. Faced with a problem or an issue, most of us do a lot of worrying before separating the issues or making a decision. Figure 1.2 provides a three-point plan to help you think critically and solve problems competently. As you can probably see, understanding the problem is essential and must come first. Generating and selecting the most feasible ideas is the intermediate step. Finally, the problem-solving model prompts you to refine, justify, and implement the solution. At the end of each chapter in this text, you will find activities and problems that will help you develop and apply your critical-thinking skills.

Managing Your Career Well

In a dynamic, highly competitive world of work, not even the most talented college graduate can afford to send out résumés, kick back, and wait to be discovered. You will need to be proactive and exercise greater control over your career than college graduates before you did. Like most workers today, you will not find nine-to-five jobs, predictable pay increases, lifetime

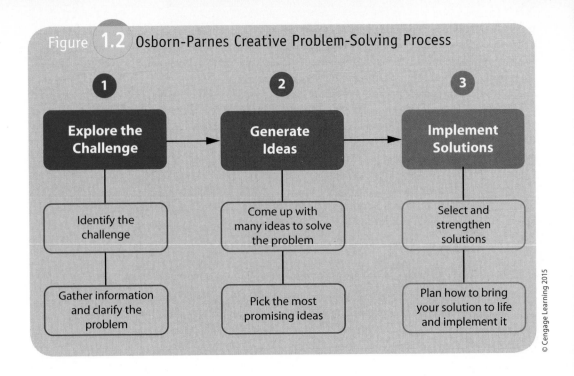

© Cengage Learning 2015

Figure 1.2 Osborn-Parnes Creative Problem-Solving Process

1

Explore the Challenge

Identify the challenge

Gather information and clarify the problem

2

Generate Ideas

Come up with many ideas to solve the problem

Pick the most promising ideas

3

Implement Solutions

Select and strengthen solutions

Plan how to bring your solution to life and implement it

security, and even conventional workplaces.[32] Don't presume that companies will provide you with a clearly defined career path or planned developmental experiences. In the private sector, you can expect to work for multiple employers, moving back and forth between work and education and between work and family responsibilities.[33]

To keep up with evolving technologies and procedures, you can look forward to constant training and lifelong learning. Whether you are currently employed or about to enter today's demanding workplace, you must be willing to continually learn new skills that supplement the strong foundation of basic skills you are acquiring in college.

In addition, in the networked professional environment of the digital era, you must manage and guard your reputation—at the office and online. How you present yourself in the virtual world, meaning how well you communicate and protect your "brand," may very well determine how successful your career will be. Thoughtful blog posts, astute comments on LinkedIn and Facebook, as well as competent e-mails will help you make a positive impression.

Succeeding in a Volatile, Competitive Job Market

In an unstable economy and a tight job market, you may rightly worry about finding work.[34] In one of its much-noted Job Outlook studies, the National Association of Colleges and Employers (NACE) investigated what makes the "perfect" job candidate in a gloomy economy. First, a prospective employee must meet the employer's fundamental criteria, including having the required major, course work, and GPA. By the way, nearly 70 percent of employers in the study reported that they screened candidates by grade point average, with 3.0 (a B average) considered the cutoff point. If a candidate passes these hurdles, then employers look for communication skills, a strong work ethic, the ability to work in a team, and initiative.[35] Similar results from another employer survey are summarized in Figure 1.3.

Considering that employers in the United States spend more than $3 billion annually on improving writing on the job, your potential competitive advantage becomes clear. Facing about $950 per employee in training costs, companies desperately seek excellent communicators in a market in which at least a third of the applicants come without the requisite skills.[36] If you are able to communicate effectively about work that is increasingly complex and intellectually demanding, you will be more likely to secure employment even in a tough market. Job candidates needing remediation in basic skills will be last on the list of potential new-hires.

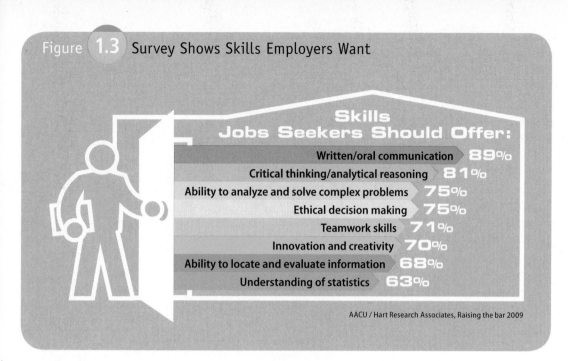

Figure 1.3 Survey Shows Skills Employers Want

Skills
Jobs Seekers Should Offer:

Written/oral communication ▷ **89%**
Critical thinking/analytical reasoning ▷ **81%**
Ability to analyze and solve complex problems **75%**
Ethical decision making ▷ **75%**
Teamwork skills **71%**
Innovation and creativity **70%**
Ability to locate and evaluate information ▷ **68%**
Understanding of statistics **63%**

AACU / Hart Research Associates, Raising the bar 2009

Trends and Challenges Affecting You in the Information Age Workplace

Today's digital workplace is changing profoundly and rapidly. As a businessperson and especially as a business communicator, you will undoubtedly be affected by many trends. Some of those trends include new communication technologies such as social media, expectations of around-the-clock availability, and global competition. Other trends include flattened management hierarchies, team-based projects, a diverse workforce, and the mobile or virtual office. The following overview reveals how communication skills are closely tied to your success in a constantly evolving networked workplace.

Social Media and Changing Communication Technologies

Although interacting with others on Facebook, YouTube, Skype, or Twitter may seem a daily necessity to you, social media are still relatively new and untried communication channels for some businesses. Other organizations, however, are completely "plugged in" and have created a positive presence with the help of both old and new media. Quite logically, social media networks first attracted industries built on communication and technology, such as traditional media outlets and information technology firms. New communication technologies also quickly took hold among marketers, in public relations, and in advertising. Even so, many businesses relying on traditional media seem to be waiting to figure out how the new media might benefit them[37] to justify the huge investments that are needed.

However, even the most reluctant late adopters of technology eye the explosive growth of social media networks in the last decade with some interest. After all, online communities continue to draw huge numbers of people from all over the world, as Figure 1.4 illustrates. Since its inception in 2004, Facebook alone has ballooned into a massive global force of more than 1 billion users. Figure 1.5, on page 11, shows some of the current statistics, which tend to become obsolete by the time they are printed.

Twitter has demonstrated the power of crowds during political crises in Iran and during the Arab Spring. The more than 145 million users of the microblogging site today clock an average 90 million "tweets" per day.[38] Ordinary citizens can organize protests and boycotts within hours, even minutes. Bad customer-service experiences

LEARNING OBJECTIVE 3
Describe significant trends in today's dynamic, networked work environment, and recognize that social media and other new communication technologies require excellent communication skills, particularly in an uncertain economy.

Figure **1.4** Some Twitter and YouTube Facts

The user statistics for YouTube and Twitter alone attest to the growing popularity of social media.

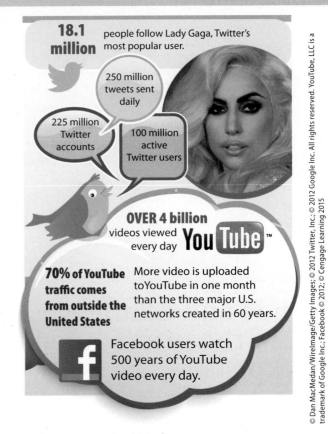

can lead to lifelong grudges.[39] In short, word of mouth, positive and negative, can travel instantly at the speed of a few mouse clicks.

Tech-savvy companies are embracing digital tools to connect with consumers, invite feedback, and improve their products and services. They may announce promotions and events in blog posts, in tweets, on their company websites, and in online communities. Above all, plugged-in businesses realize that to manage public perceptions, they need to be proactive but also respond quickly and deftly within the social media when a crisis hits. They need to go where their customers are and attempt to establish and keep a loyal following online. It has never been easier to interact so fast with so many people at once.

At the very least, even if they still pass on social media, nearly all businesspeople today in some way rely on the Internet to collect information, serve customers, and sell products and services. Figure 1.6 on pages 12 and 13 illustrates many new office and communication technologies you will meet in today's workplace. To make the most of the new resources, you, as a skilled business communicator, must develop a tool kit of new communication skills. You will want to know how to select the best communication channel, how to use each channel safely and effectively, and how to incorporate the latest technologies and search tools efficiently. All of these topics are covered in later chapters.

Anytime, Anywhere: 24/7/365 Availability

Although the dizzyingly fast connectedness across time zones and vast distances offers businesses and individuals many advantages, it also comes with a darker side. As you rise on the career ladder, you may be expected to work long hours without extra compensation and be available practically anytime and anywhere, should a crisis strike at work. In the last two decades, the line between work and leisure has become increasingly blurry. In many industries information workers are expected to remain tethered to their workplaces with laptops, tablets, and smartphones around the clock and on weekends.

Figure **1.5** Internet and Facebook User Statistics

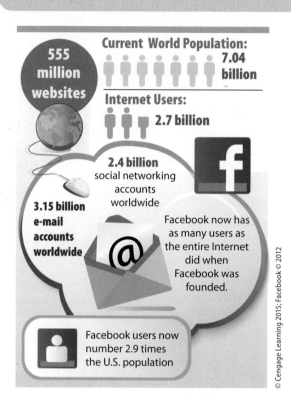

© Cengage Learning 2015; Facebook © 2012

Since its inception in 2004, Facebook alone has ballooned into a massive global force of more than 1 billion users.

The physical office is extending its reach, sometimes overreaching, perhaps. Compared to workers in other industrialized nations such as Japan and most European countries, Americans put in the longest hours (about 50 percent more). They also receive the shortest paid vacations. In contrast, workers in the European Union enjoy four to six weeks of paid time off per year. Most are also protected from overtime exceeding 48 hours per week.[40] A different picture emerges in the United States. As the digital revolution reached the masses in the 2000s, articles in major U.S. publications such as *The New York Times* decried the 24/7 work climate, citing its negative effects on workers' health and personal lives.[41] The perceived work–life imbalance became a hot topic. Be that as it may, the office of the future is mobile and always "on."

In a global economy in which corporations own far-flung operations around the world, a networked information-driven workforce never goes "off duty." Similarly, the organization essentially "never sleeps," according to one expert. The 24/7 workplace operates around the clock, he says, with managers, staff, and teams always staying connected to share information when needed and address issues when they arise.[42] Managers exert power beyond the physical office. Moreover, the nature of information work in the digital age demands that participants stay on until the project is finished, not when the clock strikes five or six at the end of the day. As your work responsibilities grow, you can expect not only to be accessible 24/7 but also to feel the significant impact of globalization.

The Global Marketplace and Competition

The rise of new communication technologies, the removal of trade barriers, advanced forms of transportation, and saturated local markets—all of these developments have encouraged companies to move beyond familiar territories to emerging markets around the world. Small, medium, and large companies in the United States and abroad have expanded overseas. Teenagers in Singapore, Latvia, South Korea, Australia, and the United States alike flock in droves to popular store openings by Swedish clothing retailer H&M. British food retailer Fresh & Easy is gaining a foothold in a crowded marketplace in the United States.

Figure **1.6** Communication and Collaborative Technologies

Communication Technologies
Reshaping the World of Work

Becoming familiar with modern communication technology can help you be successful on the job. Today's digital workplace is changing dramatically as a result of innovative software, social media networks, superfast broadband and wireless access, and numerous technologies that allow workers to share information, work from remote locations, and be more productive in or away from the office. With today's tools, you can exchange ideas, solve problems, develop products, forecast future performance, and complete team projects any time of the day or night anywhere in the world.

Cloud Computing and Web 2.0

Increasingly, applications and data are stored in remote locations online, "in the cloud." *Cloud computing* means that businesses and individuals no longer need to maintain costly hardware and software in-house; instead, they can pay for digital storage space and software applications offered by providers online. Photo- and video-sharing sites such as Picasa or Flickr keep your photos "in the cloud." Similarly, Dropbox, a popular file-synchronization service, and online backup provider Carbonite allow users to edit and sync files online independent of the device used to access them. The term Web 2.0 means that websites and Web applications have moved from "read only" to "read-write," thus enabling users to participate, collaborate, and network in unprecedented ways.

Telephony: VoIP

Savvy businesses are switching from traditional phone service to voice over Internet protocol (VoIP). This technology allows callers to communicate using a broadband Internet connection, thus eliminating long-distance and local telephone charges. Higher-end VoIP systems now support unified voice mail, e-mail, click-to-call capabilities, and softphones (phones using computer networking). Free or low-cost Internet telephony sites, such as the popular Skype, are also increasingly used by businesses although their sound and image quality is often uneven.

Voice Recognition

Computers equipped with voice recognition software enable users to dictate up to 160 words a minute with accurate transcription. Voice recognition is particularly helpful to disabled workers and to professionals with heavy dictation loads, such as physicians and attorneys. Users can create documents, enter data, compose and send e-mails, browse the Web, and control the desktop—all by voice.

Open Offices

Widespread use of laptop computers, tablets and other smart devices, wireless technology, and VoIP have led to more fluid, flexible, and open workspaces. Smaller computers and flat-screen monitors enable designers to save space with boomerang-shaped workstations and cockpit-style work surfaces rather than space-hogging corner work areas. Smaller breakout areas for impromptu meetings are taking over some cubicle space, and digital databases are replacing file cabinets. Mobile technology allows workers to be fully connected and productive on the go.

Voice Conferencing

Telephone "bridges" allow two or more callers from any location to share the same call. *Voice conferencing* (also called *audioconferencing*, *teleconferencing*, or just plain *conference calling*) enables people to collaborate by telephone. Communicators at both ends use enhanced speakerphones to talk and be heard simultaneously.

Smart Mobile Devices and Convergence

A new generation of light-weight, handheld devices provide phone, e-mail, Web browsing, and calendar options anywhere there is a cellular or wi-fi network. Tablets and smartphones such as Android devices and the iPhone now allow you to tap into corporate data-bases and intranets from remote locations. Increasingly businesses are issuing smartphones to their workforce, abandoning landlines completely. At the same time, the need for separate electronic gadgets is waning as digital smart devices are becoming multi-functional and highly capable. With streaming video on the Web, connectivity between TVs and computers, and networked mobile devices, technology is converging, consolidating into increasingly powerful devices.

Videoconferencing

Videoconferencing allows participants to meet in special conference rooms equipped with cameras and television screens. Individuals or groups see each other and interact in real time, although they may be far apart. Faster computers, rapid Internet connections, and better cameras now enable 2 to 200 participants to sit at their computers or mobile devices and share applications, spreadsheets, presentations, and photos.

Electronic Presentations

Business presentations in PowerPoint or Keynote can be projected from a laptop, tablet, or posted online. Sophisticated presentations may include animations, sound effects, digital photos, video clips, or hyperlinks to Internet sites. In some industries, PowerPoint slides ("decks") are replacing or supplementing traditional hard-copy reports.

Presence Technology

Presence technology makes it possible to locate and identify a computing device as soon as users connect to the network. This technology is an integral part of communication devices including smartphones, laptop computers, tablets, and GPS devices. Collaboration is possible wherever and whenever users are online.

Web Conferencing

With services such as GoToMeeting, WebEx, and Microsoft LiveMeeting, all you need is a computer or a smart device and an Internet connection to hold a meeting (*webinar*) with customers or colleagues in real time. Although the functions are constantly evolving, Web conferencing currently incorporates screen sharing, chats, slide presentations, text messaging, and application sharing.

Social Media

Broadly speaking, the term *social media* describes technology that enables participants to connect and participate in social

networks online. For example, tech-savvy companies and individuals send *tweets*, short messages of up to 140 characters, to other users to issue up-to-date news about their products, to link to their blogs and *websites*, or to announce events and promotions. The micro-blogging service Twitter also allows businesses to track what is being said about them and their products. Similarly, businesses use social networks such as Facebook to interact with customers and to build their brands.

Collaboration with Blogs, Podcasts, and Wikis

Businesses use *blogs* to keep customers and employees informed and to receive feedback. Company news can be posted, updated, and categorized for easy cross-referencing. An audio or video file streamed online or downloaded to a digital music player is called a *podcast*. A *wiki* is a website that allows multiple users to collaboratively create and edit pages. Information can get lost in e-mails, but wikis provide an easy way to communicate and keep track of what is said.

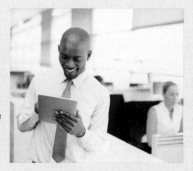

If necessary, multinational companies even adjust their products to different palates. For example, Kraft Foods now drenches its familiar Oreo cookie in chocolate to sell well in China,[43] and Wal-Mart courts Chinese shoppers with exotic fruits and live seafood.[44] PepsiCo has extended its rivalry with Coca-Cola to India. McDonald's has built its biggest venue ever in London for the Olympics; it is also the world's busiest,[45] ahead of the former record-breaking restaurant in Moscow at Pushkin Square.[46] Many traditional U.S. companies are global players now and generate more profit abroad than at home.

Doing business in faraway countries means dealing with people who may be very different from you. They may practice different religions, follow different customs, live different lifestyles, and rely on different approaches in business. Now add the complications of multiple time zones, vast distances between offices, and different languages. No wonder global communicators can stumble. Take, for example, the blunder committed by Nike in China, where the company used a commercial released in several countries. The TV ad showed the American NBA player LeBron James competing against Chinese heroes and defeating a Chinese martial art master. The Chinese government found the ad to be offensive and banned it for disrespecting Chinese culture and offending national dignity.[47]

Successful communication in new markets requires developing new skills and attitudes. These include cultural awareness, flexibility, and patience. Because these skills and attitudes may be difficult to achieve, you will receive special communication training to help you deal with intercultural business transactions.

Shrinking Management Layers

In traditional companies, information flows through many levels of managers. In response to intense global competition and other pressures, however, innovative businesses have for years been cutting costs and flattening their management hierarchies. This flattening means that fewer layers of managers separate decision makers from line workers. In flat organizations, in which the lines of communication are shorter, decision makers can react more quickly to market changes.

When GE Capital, General Electric's financial services arm, split into four business units, the reorganization spearheaded by the post–Jack Welch CEO, Jeffrey Immelt, met with skepticism. GE Capital's former chairman Denis Nayden exited, and the four unit heads started reporting directly to the CEO. The organization became flatter. Immelt reasoned that he wanted more immediate contact with the financial services teams.[48] He also believed that the greater number of direct reports would provide clarity for investors. GE Capital is thriving after weathering several crises over the last decade.[49] Restructured companies organize work with horizontal teams that allow various areas to interact more efficiently.

An important factor in the flattening of management hierarchies was movement away from mainframe computing. As recognized by Thomas Friedman in his bestselling book *The World Is Flat*, the combination of the personal computer, the microprocessor, the Internet, fiber optics, and, more recently, wireless networks "flipped the playing field."

REALITY CHECK: Keeping the Organization Flat—A Core Value at Google

"I work with employees around the world to figure out ways to maintain and enhance and develop our culture and how to keep the core values we had in the very beginning—a flat organization, a lack of hierarchy, a collaborative environment—to keep these as we continue to grow and spread them and filtrate them into our new offices around the world."[50]

—STACY SAVIDES SULLIVAN, *chief culture officer and head of HR at Google*

Courtesy of Google, Inc.

Management moved away from command and control to connecting and collaborating horizontally.[51] This means that work is organized to let people use their own talents more wisely.[52]

Today's flatter organizations, however, also pose greater communication challenges. In the past, authoritarian and hierarchical management structures did not require that every employee be a skilled communicator. Managers simply passed along messages to the next level. Today, however, frontline employees as well as managers participate in critical thinking and decision making. Nearly everyone is a writer and a communicator.

Collaborative Environments and Teaming

Teamwork has become a reality in business. Many companies have created cross-functional teams to empower employees and boost their involvement in decision making. Such stable teams of people have learned to work well together over time. To generate new products, Johnson & Johnson started forming small teams and charged each with tackling a cosmetic problem. The acne team, composed of scientists along with marketing and production people, focused on finding ways to help teenagers zap zits. A pigmentation team struggled to create products that evened out skin tone.[53] Traditional teams helped turn around Simmons Bedding Company a decade ago by reducing waste in operations, boosting sales, and improving the relationships with dealers. Customer satisfaction and employee morale also soared.[54]

However, the complex and unpredictable challenges in today's workplace require rapid changes in course and greater flexibility, says Harvard management professor Amy Edmondson. She argues that the new era of business requires a new strategy she calls *teaming*: "Teaming is teamwork on the fly: a pickup basketball game rather than plays run by a team that has trained as a unit for years."[55] This means that instead of traditional standing teams, organizations are now forming ad-hoc teams to solve particular problems. Such project-based teams disband once they have accomplished their objectives. Although the challenges of making such diverse and potentially dispersed teams function well are many, teaming is here to stay.

A sizable chunk of our future economy may rely on "free agents" who will be hired on a project basis. This practice is reminiscent of filmmaking, in which creative talent gathers to work on a feature film; after the wrap, the crew disperses to tackle the next movie, each with a whole new team. In one of its reports, accounting firm PricewaterhouseCoopers envisions a future workplace in which companies hire a network of independent contractors for short-term projects,[56] a far cry from today's full-time and relatively steady jobs.

Whether companies form standing or ad-hoc teams, individuals must work together and share information. Working relationships can become strained when individuals don't share the same location, background, knowledge, or training. Some companies even hire communication coaches to help teams get along. Such experts work to develop interpersonal, negotiation, and collaboration techniques. However, companies would prefer to hire new workers who already possess these skills. That is why so many advertisements for new employees say "must possess good communication skills"—which you are learning in this book and this course.

REALITY CHECK: **What Teams Can Learn From Bees**

"Bees . . . use a marvelous system of dancing competitions to decide where to get their pollen. According to our data, it's as true for humans as for bees: How we communicate turns out to be the most important predictor of team success, and *as important as all other factors combined*, including intelligence, personality, skill, and content of discussions."[57]

—**COMPUTER SCIENTIST ALEX "SANDY" PENTLAND,** *MIT Media Lab*

Courtesy of Alex "Sandy" Pentland

Growing Workforce Diversity

In addition to pervasive communication technology, advanced team management, and distant work environments, today's workplace is changing in yet another area. The U.S. workforce is becoming increasingly diverse. As shown in Figure 1.7, the white non-Hispanic population of the United States is expected to drop from 69 percent in 2000 to 60 percent in 2020. Hispanics will climb from 13 percent to 19 percent, while African Americans will hold steady at around 13 percent relative to the growing total U.S. population. Asians and Pacific Islanders will rise from 4 percent to 6 percent.[58]

Women attain higher education in greater numbers than men do; about 36 percent of women ages 25 to 29 pursue bachelor's degrees, as opposed to 28 percent of men.[59] However, in many industries and in executive positions, they are still the minority. According to the National Science Foundation, the gender gap is most pronounced in business and industry, where women fill only 21 percent of jobs, followed by the high-tech industry (25 percent), and science and engineering (27 percent).[60] The U.S. Bureau of Labor Statistics projects that overall women will account for 47 percent of the labor force by 2020, up slightly from 46.7 in 2010.[61]

In addition to increasing numbers of women and minorities, the workforce will see a big jump in older workers. By 2020, the number of workers aged fifty-five and older will grow to a quarter of the labor force, more than double their number in 1998.[62] To this competition for information-age jobs, add the influx of skilled immigrants. Despite barriers to immigration, some experts predict that by 2030 roughly 500 million people will legally work outside their home countries. This means that twice as many migrants, up from 250 million today, will seek economic opportunities abroad, displaced by armed conflict, natural disasters, and climate change.[63] As a result of these and other demographic trends, businesses must create work environments that value and support all people.

Communicating in this diverse work environment requires new attitudes and skills. Acquiring these new employment skills is certainly worth the effort because of the benefits diversity brings to consumers, work teams, and business organizations. A diverse staff is better able to read trends and respond to the increasingly diverse customer base in local and world markets. In the workplace, diversity also makes good business sense.

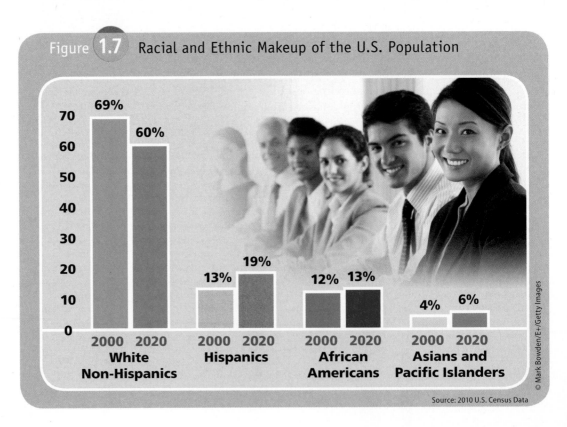

Figure 1.7 Racial and Ethnic Makeup of the U.S. Population

© Mark Bowden/E+/Getty Images

Source: 2010 U.S. Census Data

Most employees today can only dream of the virtual office. Meet the "work shifter," a new type of teleworker who operates anytime and anywhere with a smart device and a wireless connection. Business professionals aren't the only work shifters. Stanford Cardinal football players use iPad-based digital playbooks to learn their sport wherever they may be—the dorm, the food court, or out on the commons. The playbooks sync wirelessly with coaches' notes and training videos, and players use live messaging apps to discuss plays and strategies. What skills do work shifters need to collaborate effectively in a remote environment?[64]

© darren baker/Photos.com

Teams made up of people with various experiences are more likely to create the products that consumers demand. Customers also want to deal with companies that respect their values. They are more likely to say, "If you are a company whose ads do not include me, or whose workforce does not include me, I will not buy from you." Learning to cooperate and communicate successfully with diverse coworkers should be a major priority for all businesspeople.

Virtual and Nonterritorial Offices

You may have heard people refer to the "virtual office," a workspace that's mobile and decentralized. Today's physical work environments are changing profoundly. Thanks largely to advances in high-speed and wireless Internet access, millions of workers no longer report to nine-to-five jobs that confine them to offices. They have flexible working arrangements so they can work at home, on the road, and at the customer's place of business. Meet the "work shifter," a new breed of telecommuter or, more broadly, teleworker, who remains outside the traditional office the majority of the time. The "anytime, anywhere" office the work shifter needs requires only a smartphone and a wireless connection.[65]

Teleworkers now represent almost 20 percent of the U.S. working adult population.[66] Reliable data tracking office "road warriors" are lacking, but as many as 52 million employees—nearly a third of the U.S. workforce—could likely work from remote locations in the near future.[67]

To save on office real estate, a number of companies such as American Express and drug maker GlaxoSmithKline provide "nonterritorial" workspaces. Also known as "mobile platforms" and "hot desks," these unassigned workspaces are up for grabs. The first to arrive gets the best desk and the corner window.[68] Increasingly, work shifters and home office workers resort to "coworking" as an alternative to holding business meetings at the local coffee shop or in the living room. Coworkers are professionals who share a communal office space on an as-needed basis. Although most coworking spaces provide monthly memberships, some offer day passes.[69] Even in more traditional offices, employees work in open-plan spaces with flexible workstations, shared conference rooms, and boomerang-shaped desks that save space and discourage territorial behavior while encouraging casual interaction as well as spontaneous collaboration.

Open Office Rules

© Cengage Learning 2015

Rules for sharing open workspace

1. Don't hang around.
2. Limit chitchat.
3. Don't sneak up on anyone.
4. Don't eavesdrop or otherwise spy on others.
5. Speak in a soft voice.
6. Wear headphones.

Open, nonterritorial workspaces require a new kind of etiquette. Some companies have instituted rules on sharing office space.

LEARNING OBJECTIVE **4**

Examine critically the internal and external flow of communication in organizations through formal and informal channels, explain the importance of effective media choices, and understand how to overcome typical barriers to organizational communication.

Information Flow and Media Choices in Today's Business World

You may want to connect with friends and family for a specific reason or just for fun. However, businesspeople almost always communicate strategically—that is, purposefully, hoping to achieve a particular outcome. Business communication functions can be summarized in three simple categories: (a) to inform, (b) to persuade, and/or (c) to promote goodwill. Most business messages have one of these functions as their purpose. Informing or sharing information is perhaps the most common communication function in all organizations today. On the job you will have a dizzying array of media to help you share information and stay connected both internally and externally. You will need to know which medium is most suitable to accomplish your goal and be able to distinguish between formal and informal channels.

The Networked Workplace in a Hyperconnected World

Social media and other sophisticated information technology coupled with flatter hierarchies have greatly changed the way people communicate internally and externally at work. One major shift is away from one-sided, slow forms of communication such as hard-copy memos and letters to interactive, instant, less paper-based communication. Speeding up the flow of communication in organizations are e-mail, instant messaging (IM), texting, and interacting with social media such as Facebook, Twitter, and LinkedIn. To stay connected on the go, business communicators rely on smart electronic devices.

Mobility and Interactivity. Mobility has revolutionized the way we communicate on the job. Internet access is ever-present, whether provided by cellular phone companies or wireless networks. Wireless access is increasingly blanketing entire office buildings, airports, hotels, restaurants, school and college campuses, cities, and other public spaces.

Other forms of interactive and mobile communication in the contemporary workplace include intranets (secured local area networks within organizations), corporate websites, audio and video podcasting, videoconferencing, and Web chats. The latter is rapidly becoming the preferred communication channel for online customer service. Consumers shopping online or inquiring about billing or technical support use the company website and "chat" with customer-service representatives in real time by typing their questions. Live service agents respond with typed replies.

Smart Devices. The revolution in communication technology that we now take for granted and have come to depend on is fueled by smart mobile electronics. They include smartphones, tablets, and notebook PCs and are predicted to grow three times as fast as the overall mobile market by 2015.[70] Whether used to inform, communicate, or entertain, more and more smart devices are sharing features, functions, and platforms.[71] Smart devices allow many users to bypass desktop computers and notebooks entirely. Since Apple's launch of the phenomenally successful iPad, more and more knowledge workers rely on their tablets on the job, citing e-mail (77 percent) as the most common workplace use. Tablets are also popular for calendar management, note taking, and presentations.[72]

Smartphone owners now outnumber users of basic mobile phones. Nearly half of U.S. adults use smartphones,[73] once the domain of businesspeople, the wealthy, young adults, and other early adopters. Ahead of the popular iPhone, the Android platform has taken the smartphone market by storm worldwide. Forecasts estimate that low-cost Android handsets will grab 80 percent of the smartphone market in Africa, India, and China by 2015.[74] Thus, millions of people will access the Internet by mobile phone not only in industrialized nations but also in the emerging regions of the world.

> The revolution in communication technology that we now take for granted and have come to depend on is fueled by smart mobile electronics.

Internal and External Communication

Despite the range of interactive technologies, businesspeople are still working with two basic forms of communication: oral and written. Each has advantages and disadvantages, as summarized in Figure 1.8. These general rules apply whether the communication is directed at audiences inside the organization or outside.

Internal communication includes exchanging ideas and messages with superiors, coworkers, and subordinates. When those messages must be written, you will probably choose e-mail—the most prevalent communication channel in the workplace today. Some of the functions of internal communication are to issue and clarify procedures and policies, inform management of progress, develop new products and services, persuade employees or management to make changes or improvements, coordinate activities, and evaluate and reward employees. Brief messages and status updates may be conveyed by text message or IM especially when the writer is traveling.

External communication is also handled by e-mail in most routine cases. When you are communicating externally with customers, suppliers, the government, and the public, e-mail correspondence is generally appropriate. Hard-copy letters sent by traditional "snail mail" are becoming increasingly rare, especially under time constraints. However, some businesses do create signed paper documents to be faxed, or they scan and e-mail them. External functions

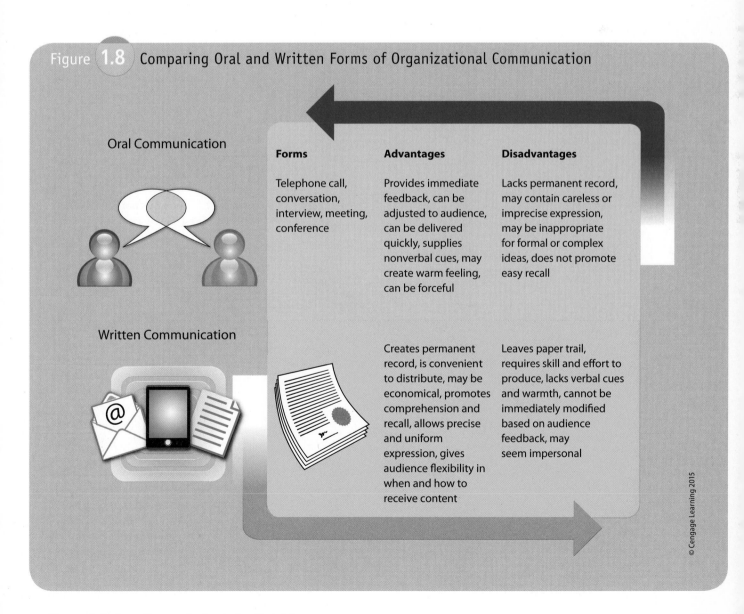

Figure 1.8 Comparing Oral and Written Forms of Organizational Communication

Oral Communication

Forms	Advantages	Disadvantages
Telephone call, conversation, interview, meeting, conference	Provides immediate feedback, can be adjusted to audience, can be delivered quickly, supplies nonverbal cues, may create warm feeling, can be forceful	Lacks permanent record, may contain careless or imprecise expression, may be inappropriate for formal or complex ideas, does not promote easy recall

Written Communication

	Creates permanent record, is convenient to distribute, may be economical, promotes comprehension and recall, allows precise and uniform expression, gives audience flexibility in when and how to receive content	Leaves paper trail, requires skill and effort to produce, lacks verbal cues and warmth, cannot be immediately modified based on audience feedback, may seem impersonal

© Cengage Learning 2015

involve answering inquiries about products or services, persuading customers to buy products or services, clarifying supplier specifications, issuing credit, collecting bills, responding to government agencies, and promoting a positive image of the organization.

Media Richness and Social Presence

Business communicators must be able to choose from a wide range of options those communication channels most suitable "to get the job done"—that is, most likely to elicit the desired outcome. How to choose the appropriate medium in organizations to avoid ambiguity, confusing messages, and misunderstandings has long been studied by researchers. Media richness theory and the concept of social presence are particularly useful for evaluating the effectiveness of old and new media in a given situation.

Media Richness.   Daft and Lengel's media richness theory attempts to classify media in organizations according to how much clarifying information they are able to convey from a sender to a recipient.[75] The more helpful cues and immediate feedback the medium provides, the richer it is; face-to-face and on the telephone, managers can best deal with complex organizational issues. For routine, unambiguous problems, however, media of lower richness, such as memos, reports, and other written communication, usually suffice. Figure 1.9 displays contemporary and traditional media based on their richness and, hence, their likely communication effectiveness.

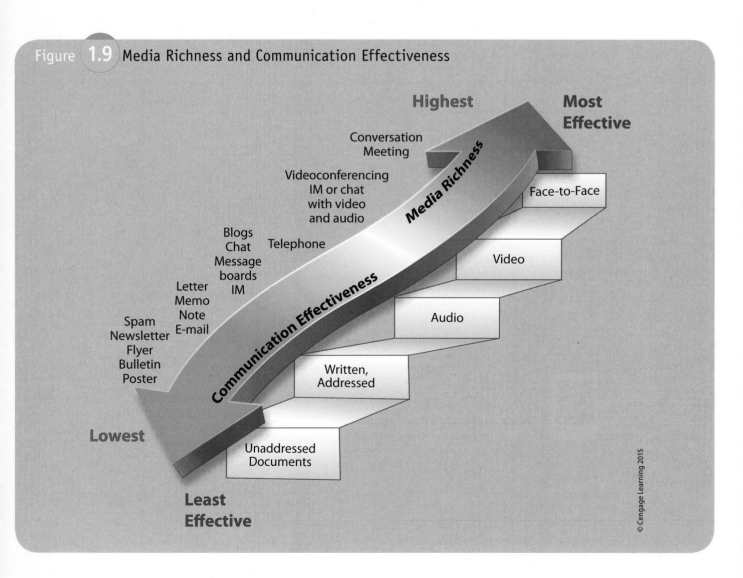

Figure 1.9 Media Richness and Communication Effectiveness

© Cengage Learning 2015

Ideally, senders would choose the richest medium necessary to communicate the message to the recipient with as little ambiguity as possible. Because a rich medium (such as a face-to-face conversation) is not always available, communicators must often use leaner media (for example, e-mail) that may not be as effective in reducing ambiguity and decreasing the risk of miscommunication. Just think how hard it is to know whether a text or an e-mail is sarcastic.

Social Presence. *Social presence* has come to mean the degree to which people are engaged online and ready to connect with others. As proposed by Short, Williams, and Christie,[76] however, social presence is the degree of "salience" (being there) between a sender and receiver using a communication medium. Media with high social presence convey warmth and are personal. Social presence is greatest face-to-face, and less so in mediated and written communication, such as phone conversations and text messages. Likewise, social presence is greater in synchronous communication (live chat, IM) than in asynchronous communication (e-mail, forum post) that is rather impersonal.

Face-to-face we receive many more signals than just speech. For example, nonverbal cues, emotional disposition, and voice inflection help us interpret a message correctly. In real time, we can ask the author of a message to clarify—something we cannot do as easily when the message arrives with a delay and is enabled by technology. You could say that social presence means how much awareness of the sender is conveyed along with the message. Communication can succeed as long as the chosen communication medium offers enough social presence to complete the task.[77]

Formal Communication Channels

Information within organizations flows through formal and informal communication channels. A free exchange of information helps organizations respond rapidly to changing markets, boost efficiency and productivity, build employee morale, serve the public, and take full advantage of the ideas of today's knowledge workers. Official information within an organization typically flows through formal channels in three directions: downward, upward, and horizontally, as shown in Figure 1.10.

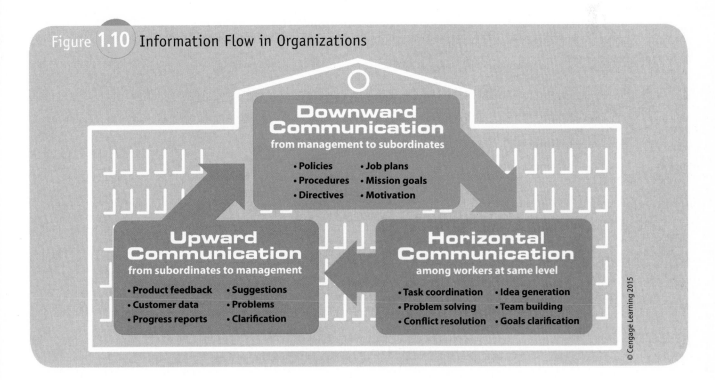

Figure **1.10** Information Flow in Organizations

© Cengage Learning 2015

Formal channels of communication generally follow an organization's chain of command. That is, a message originates with executives and flows down through managers to supervisors and finally to lower-level employees. Many organizations have formulated communication policies that encourage regular open communication through newsletters, the corporate intranet, official messages, company-provided social networks, and blogs. Free-flowing, open communication invigorates organizations and makes them successful. Barriers, however, can obstruct the flow of communication, as summarized in Figure 1.11, and must be overcome if the organization is to thrive.

Improving Downward Information Flow.   To improve communication and to compete more effectively, many of today's companies have restructured and reengineered themselves into smaller operating units and work teams. Rather than being bogged down with long communication chains, management speaks directly to employees. In addition to shorter chains of communication, management can improve the downward flow of information through company publications, announcements, meetings, videos, podcasts, and other channels. Instead of hoarding information at the top, today's managers recognize the importance of letting workers know how well the company is doing and what new projects are planned.

Improving Upward Information Flow.   To improve the upward flow of communication, some companies are (a) hiring communication coaches to train employees, (b) asking employees to report customer complaints, (c) encouraging regular meetings with staff, (d) providing a trusting, nonthreatening environment in which employees can comfortably share their observations and ideas with management, and (e) offering incentive programs that encourage employees to collect and share valuable feedback. Companies are also building trust by setting up hotlines for anonymous feedback to management and by installing ombudsman programs. An *ombudsman* is a mediator who hears employee complaints, investigates, and seeks to resolve problems fairly.

Improving Horizontal Information Flow.   To improve horizontal communication, companies are (a) training employees in teamwork and communication techniques, (b) establishing reward systems based on team achievement rather than individual achievement, and (c) encouraging full participation in team functions. However, employees must also realize that they are personally responsible for making themselves heard, for really understanding what other people say, and for getting the information they need. Developing those business communication skills is exactly what this book and this course will do for you.

Figure 1.11 Barriers Blocking the Flow of Communication in Organizations

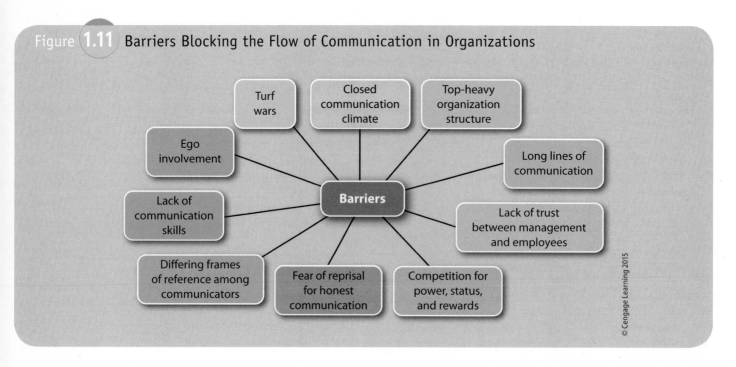

© Cengage Learning 2015

Informal Communication Channels

Most organizations today share company news through consistent, formal channels such as e-mail and staff meetings. However, as many as 20 percent do not provide consistent channels to share company news.[78] Even within organizations with consistent formal channels, people still gossip about company news. The *grapevine* is an informal channel of communication that carries organizationally relevant gossip. This powerful but informal channel functions through social relationships; people talk about work when they are lunching, working out, golfing, and carpooling, as well as in e-mails, texts, and blogs. At one time gossip took place mostly around the water cooler. Today, however, gossip travels much more rapidly online.

Using the Grapevine Productively.   Researchers studying communication flow within organizations know that the grapevine can be a powerful, pervasive source of information. In some organizations it can account for as much as two thirds of an employee's information. Is this bad? Well, yes and no. The grapevine can be a fairly accurate and speedy source of organization information. Studies in the past have demonstrated accuracy ratings of 80 percent or more for many grapevine transmissions.[79] However, grapevine information is often incomplete because it travels in headlines: *Vice President Sacked* or *Jerk on the Fourth Floor Promoted*. When employees obtain most of their company news from the grapevine, management is not releasing sufficient information through formal channels.

Managers can use the grapevine productively by doing the following: (a) respecting employees' desire to know, (b) increasing the amount of information delivered through formal channels, (c) sharing bad as well as good news, (d) monitoring the grapevine, and (e) acting promptly to correct misinformation.[80] Employees who know the latest buzz feel like important members of the team. Nevertheless, the office grapevine is probably here to stay because sensitive rumors publicized online have cost many workers their jobs.

As opposed to the "offline" grapevine, online consumer-generated media such as forums, Internet discussion boards, blogs, Facebook posts, and tweets provide a very public glimpse of what employees and the public are thinking. High-profile leaks travel fast, and their accuracy can be verified more easily than rumors in an offline grapevine. Companies such as Intel that actively monitor social media are better able to correct inaccuracies and misperceptions. To counter a negative YouTube video going viral with more than 2 million views, Hewlett-Packard quickly responded on its blog and in Internet forums. The company's excellent crisis communication reassured its audiences and won praise.[81] Through formal and informal channels of communication, smart companies keep employees and the public informed.

Responding Ethically to Office Gossip.   To many of us, gossip is fun and even entertaining. It encourages social bonding and makes us feel close to others who share our trust. We feel a part of the group and that we can influence others when we share a significant tidbit. We might even argue that gossip is good because it can help people learn how to behave and how to respond to social miscues faster and less awkwardly than if they made the mistakes themselves. For example, you're not likely to wear that new revealing camisole after hearing the scathing remarks being circulated about a similar one worn by Lacy in the Marketing Department.

However, not all gossip is harmless. Someone known as an office gossip can be viewed as untrustworthy and unpromotable. Even more damaging, malicious gossip spread in e-mails, via text messages, or on social media sites can be used in defamation cases. It can also become evidence against employers in supporting charges of harassment or maintaining a hostile work environment. Unfounded gossip can ruin careers and harm companies. In addition, employers look upon gossip as a productivity drain. The time spent gossiping reduces the time spent working.

How can you respond ethically to gossip or reduce its occurrence? Workplace ethics expert Nan DeMars offers several helpful pointers, reproduced here from her Office Ethics website:

- **Run, don't walk, away from anyone who starts to gossip.** Even if you don't contribute to the conversation, just being present indicates consent.

- **End rumors about others.** If you overhear something that is untrue, step up and say so. People will respect your integrity.

- **Attack rumors about yourself.** Be aggressive and determine who originated the remark, if possible. Always follow up with documentation explaining what really happened.
- **Keep confidences.** Become known as someone who is close-mouthed.
- **Limit the personal tidbits you share about yourself and keep them on the light side.** Too much information may be blown out of proportion and/or become tempting to someone else to expand. Trust only those who have demonstrated and earned your confidence.
- **Avoid any form of coworker belittlement.** Today's coworker may be tomorrow's senior vice president.
- **Build coworkers up; don't tear them down.** If you must use the grapevine, use it to praise coworkers. They will remember.[82]

LEARNING OBJECTIVE **5**
Analyze ethics in the workplace, understand the goals of ethical business communicators, recognize and avoid ethical traps, and choose the tools for doing the right thing.

Ethics in the Workplace Needed More Than Ever

Ethics is once again a hot topic in business circles. On the heels of the banking crisis and the collapse of the real estate market, a calamitous recession followed, caused largely, some say, by greed and ethical lapses. With the passage of the Sarbanes-Oxley Act, the government required greater accountability. As a result, businesses are now eager to regain public trust by building ethical environments. Many have written ethical mission statements, installed hotlines, and appointed compliance officers to ensure strict adherence to their high standards and the law.

In addition, individuals are more aware of their personal actions and accountability. After watching executive assistant Doug Faneuil, who was forced to testify against his boss and their biggest client, Martha Stewart, people realized that they cannot lie, even to protect their jobs or their bosses. It's unacceptable to excuse an action with "the company made me do it." Figure 1.12 exhibits the results of a workplace ethics survey showing a hopeful downward trend in unethical workplace behavior.

The recent financial mess and economic tailspin forced many to wonder what caused the severe economic crisis. Who or what was to blame? Some observers claim that business organizations suffered from an ethics deficit; they were too intent on short-term profits and cared little about the dangerous risks they were taking. Executives and managers were

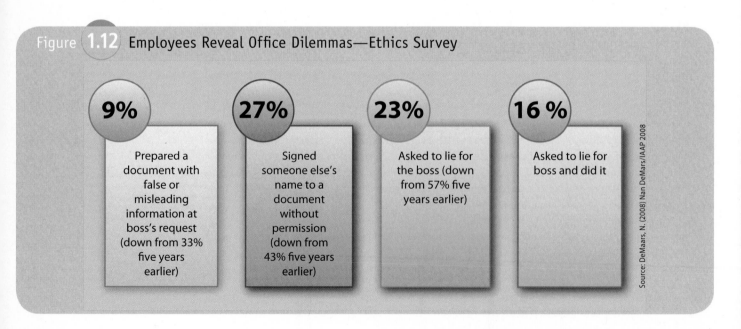

Figure **1.12** Employees Reveal Office Dilemmas—Ethics Survey

9%
Prepared a document with false or misleading information at boss's request (down from 33% five years earlier)

27%
Signed someone else's name to a document without permission (down from 43% five years earlier)

23%
Asked to lie for the boss (down from 57% five years earlier)

16 %
Asked to lie for boss and did it

Source: DeMaars, N. (2008) Nan DeMars/IAAP 2008

so self-centered that they failed to see themselves as caretakers of their own institutions. Critics also extended their blame to business schools for not doing a better job of teaching ethics.[84] Still others complained that the financial debacle was caused by greedy individuals who were interested only in personal gain at all costs. Ethical lapses and a relaxed regulatory climate conspired to create the perfect storm that ripped through the economy.

Although the financial mess was not directly created by any single factor, many believe that it would not have occurred if those involved had acted less selfishly and more ethically. The entire topic of ethics in business has captured the spotlight as a result of the financial crisis and economic downturn. The topic of ethics could fill entire books. However, we will examine aspects that specifically concern you as a business communicator in today's workplace.

Defining Ethics

Ethics refers to conventional standards of right and wrong that prescribe what people should do. These standards usually consist of rights, obligations, and benefits to society. They also include virtues such as fairness, honesty, loyalty, and concern for others. Ethics is about having values and taking responsibility. Ethical individuals are expected to follow the law and refrain from theft, murder, assault, slander, and fraud. Figure 1.13 depicts some of the influences that form our awareness of ethics and help us develop a value system that guides our ethical decisions. In the following discussion, we examine ethics in the workplace, study goals of ethical business communicators, and learn tools for doing the right thing.

As a business communicator, you should understand basic ethical principles so that you can make logical decisions when faced with dilemmas in the workplace. Professionals in any field must deal with moral dilemmas on the job. However, just being a moral

Figure **1.13** The Context of Ethical Decision Making

Various influences shape an individual's value system and affect ethical decision making. Most of us exist in a family, workplace, one or several communities, and society at large. Each of these environments may emphasize different norms. Not surprisingly, sometimes the various rules and beliefs clash, causing ethical dilemmas that need to be resolved.

© Cengage Learning 2015

person and having sound personal or professional ethics may not be sufficient to handle the ethical issues that you may face in the workplace. Consider the following ethical dilemmas:

- **E-mail message**   You accidentally receive a message outlining your company's restructuring plan. You see that your coworker's job will be eliminated. He and his wife are about to purchase a new home. Should you tell him that his job is in danger?

- **Customer e-mail**   You are replying to an e-mail from to a customer who is irate over a mistake you made. Should you blame it on a computer glitch, point the finger at another department, or take the blame and risk losing this customer's trust and possibly your job?

- **Progress report**   Should you write a report that ignores problems in a project, as your boss asks? Your boss controls your performance evaluation.

- **Sales report**   Should you inflate sales figures so that your team can meet its quarterly goal? Your team leader strongly urges you to do so, and you receive a healthy bonus if your team meets its goal.

- **Presentation**   You are rushing to prepare a presentation. On the Web you find perfect wording and great graphics. Should you lift the graphics and wording but change a few words? You figure that if it is on the Web, it must be in the public domain.

- **Proposal**   Your company urgently needs a revenue-producing project. Should you submit a proposal that unrealistically suggests a short completion schedule to ensure that you get the job?

- **Résumé**   Should you inflate your grade point average or give yourself more experience or a higher job title than your experience warrants to make your résumé more attractive? The job market is very competitive.

On the job you will face many dilemmas, and you will want to react ethically. Determining the right thing to do, however, is not always an easy task. No solid rules guide us. For some people, following the law seems to be enough. They think that anything legal must also be ethical or moral. Most people, however, believe that ethical standards rise to a higher level. What are those standards? Although many ethical dilemmas have no "right" answer, one solution is often better than another. In deciding on that solution, keep in mind the goals of ethical business communicators.

Doing What Ethical Communicators Do

Taking ethics into consideration can be painful in the short term. In the long term, however, ethical behavior makes sense and pays off. Dealing honestly with colleagues and customers develops trust and builds strong relationships. The following guidelines can help you set specific ethical goals. Although these goals hardly constitute a formal code of conduct, they will help you maintain a high ethical standard.

Abiding by the Law.   Know the laws in your field and follow them. Particularly important for business communicators are issues of copyright law. Under the concept of fair use, individuals have limited rights to use copyrighted material without requiring permission. To be safe, you should assume that anything produced privately after 1989—including words, charts, graphs, photos, and music—is copyrighted. More information about copyright law and fair use appears in Chapter 11 on page 399. By the way, don't assume that Internet items are in the public domain and free to be used or shared. Internet items are covered by copyright laws. A Swedish court convicted four men running Pirate Bay, an Internet file-sharing service,[85] and two higher courts since upheld the guilty verdict. If you are in accounting, financial management, investing, or corporate management, you should be aware of the restrictions set forth by the Sarbanes-Oxley Act. Whatever your field, become familiar with its regulations.

Telling the Truth.   Ethical business communicators do not intentionally make statements that are untrue or deceptive. In the corporate scandals of the last decade, some executives landed in jail or lost their jobs for lying. Accused of selling stock based on insider information, Martha Stewart was actually jailed for lying about it. Hewlett-Packard CEO Patricia Dunn lost her job after authorizing "pretexting," which is pretending to be someone else, to investigate phone records. A high-profile football coach resigned after the discovery that he had lied about his academic and athletic background. These big-time lies made headlines, and you may see no correlation to your life. On a personal level, however, we all may lie and deceive in various ways. We say things that are not so. We may exaggerate to swell the importance of our assertions.

Labeling Opinions.   Sensitive communicators know the difference between facts and opinions. Facts are verifiable and often are quantifiable; opinions are beliefs held with confidence but without substantiation. It is a fact, for example, that women are starting businesses at two times the rate of men.[86] It is an opinion, though, that the so-called "glass ceiling" has held women back, forcing them to start their own businesses. Such a cause-and-effect claim would be difficult to prove. It is a fact that many corporations are spending billions of dollars to be socially responsible, including using ethically made products and developing eco-friendly technology. It is an opinion that consumers are willing to pay more for a pound of coffee if they believe that the seller used ethical fair-trade production standards.[87] Assertions that cannot be proved are opinions, and stating opinions as if they were facts is unethical and, well, foolish.

Being Objective.   Ethical business communicators recognize their own biases and strive to keep them from distorting a message. Suppose you are asked to investigate laptop computers and write a report recommending a brand for your office. As you visit stores, you discover that an old high school friend is selling Brand X. Because you always liked this individual and have faith in his judgment, you may be inclined to tilt your recommendation in his direction. However, it is unethical to misrepresent the facts in your report or to put a spin on your arguments based on friendship. To be ethical, you could note in your report that you have known the person for ten years and that you respect his opinion. In this way, you have disclosed your relationship as well as the reasons for your decision. Honest reporting means presenting the whole picture and relating all facts fairly.

Communicating Clearly.   Ethical business communicators feel an obligation to write clearly so that receivers understand easily and quickly. Some states have even passed "plain English" (also called "plain language") laws requiring businesses to write policies, warranties, and contracts in language comprehensible to average readers. Under former chairman Arthur Levitt, the Securities and Exchange Commission issued *A Plain English Handbook* explaining how to create clear SEC disclosure documents. Persistent lobbying efforts by plain-language advocacy groups at the federal level culminated in the Plain Writing Act in October 2010. The law mandates that government agencies use unadorned prose in documents addressing the public. Plain English means short sentences, simple words, and clear organization. Communicators who intentionally obscure the meaning with long sentences and difficult words are being unethical.

Using Inclusive Language.   Ethical business communicators use language that includes rather than excludes. They avoid expressions that discriminate against individuals or groups on the basis of their sex, ethnicity, disability, race, sexual orientation, or age. Language is discriminatory when it stereotypes, insults, or excludes people. You will learn more about how to use inclusive, bias-free language in Chapter 4.

Giving Credit.   Ethical communicators give credit for ideas by (a) referring to originators' names within the text; (b) using quotation marks; and (c) documenting sources with endnotes, footnotes, or internal references. You will learn how to do this in Chapter 11 and Appendix C. Don't suggest that you did all the work on a project if you had help. In school or on the job, stealing ideas, words, graphics, or any other original material is unethical.

In addition to legal and regulatory restrictions in their fields, many professionals uphold their own rigorous rules of conduct; for example, physicians, psychologists, and accountants follow standards of professional ethics much higher than the restrictions imposed by law. Similarly, members of the International Association of Business Communicators have developed a code of ethics with 12 guidelines (articles) that spell out criteria for determining what is

"We have found that much unethical conduct that goes on, whether in social life or work life, happens because people are unconsciously fooling themselves. They overlook transgressions—bending a rule to help a colleague, overlooking information that might damage the reputation of a client—because it is in their interest to do so."[88]

—MAX H. BAZERMAN AND ANN E. TENBRUNSEL, *business ethicists, coauthors of* Blind Spots

right and wrong for members of its organization. Search for *IABC Code of Ethics for Professional Communicators* on the Web.

Overcoming Obstacles to Ethical Decision Making

Even when business communicators are aware of their goals and want to do the right thing, a number of obstacles can prevent them from doing so. Businesses are downsizing staff and reducing resources. Employees may feel pressured to increase productivity by whatever means. Knowingly or not, managers under pressure to make profit quotas may send the message to workers that it's OK to lie, cheat, or steal to achieve company goals. These and other rationalizations can motivate unethical actions. In making ethical decisions, business communicators commonly face five traps that can make arriving at the right decision more difficult.

The False Necessity Trap.   People act from the belief that they are doing what they must do. They convince themselves that they have no other choice, when in fact it's generally a matter of convenience or desire. Consider the Beech-Nut Corporation's actions when it discovered that its supplier was providing artificial apple juice. Beech-Nut canceled its contracts but continued to advertise and sell the adulterated "apple" juice as a 100 percent natural product in its baby food line. Falling into the false necessity trap, Beech-Nut felt it had no choice but to continue the deception. Similarly, a twenty-three-year-old applicant was desperate for a retail job in a dwindling market. The retailer required a personality test. With a little digging on the Internet, he found an unauthorized answer key and scored well.[89] He apparently justified cheating on the test by telling himself that he really needed this job and the only way to score highly was to cheat.

The Doctrine-of-Relative-Filth Trap.   Unethical actions sometimes look good when compared with worse behavior by others. What's a little fudging on an expense account compared with the pleasure cruise the boss took and charged as a business trip? How about using IM and Twitter at your desk to keep in touch with friends? Perhaps you will steal a little time at work to do some much-needed research on a hybrid car you are considering buying. After all, the guys in Engineering told you that they spend hours online checking sport scores, playing games, and conducting recreational Web surfing. While you are on the subject, how about Chelsea who spends hours communicating with Facebook contacts on her tablet computer? Your minor infractions seem insignificant compared with what others are doing.

The Rationalization Trap.   In falling into the rationalization trap, people try to explain away unethical actions by justifying them with excuses. Consider employees who "steal" time from their employers by taking long lunch and coffee breaks, claiming sick leave when not ill, and completing their own tasks on company time. It's easy to rationalize such actions: "I deserve an extra-long lunch break because I can't get all my shopping done on such a short lunch hour" or "I'll just write my class report at the office because the computer printer is much better than mine, and they aren't paying me what I'm worth anyway."

The Self-Deception Trap.   Applicants for jobs often fall into the self-deception trap. They are all too willing to inflate grade point averages or exaggerate past accomplishments to impress prospective employers. One applicant, for example, claimed experience as a broker's assistant at a prestigious securities firm. A background check revealed that he had interviewed for the securities job but was never offered it. Another applicant claimed that he held a summer job in which he was "responsible for cross-corporate transferal of multidimensional client receivables." In other words, he moved boxes from sales to shipping. Self-deception can lead to unethical and possibly illegal behavior.

The Ends-Justify-the-Means Trap. Taking unethical actions to accomplish a desirable goal is a common trap. Consider a manager in a Medicare claims division of a large health insurance company who coerced clerical staff into working overtime without pay. The goal was to reduce a backlog of unprocessed claims. Despite the worthy goal, the means of reaching it was unethical.

Choosing Tools for Doing the Right Thing

It's easy to fall into ethical traps because of natural self-interests and the desire to succeed. In composing messages or engaging in other activities on the job, business communicators can't help being torn by conflicting loyalties. Do we tell the truth and risk our jobs? Do we show loyalty to friends even if it means bending the rules? Should we be tactful or totally honest? Is it our duty to make a profit or to be socially responsible?

Acting ethically means doing the right thing given the circumstances. Each set of circumstances requires analyzing issues, evaluating choices, and acting responsibly. Resolving ethical issues is never easy, but the task can be made less difficult if you know how to identify key issues. The five questions in Figure 1.14 may help you resolve most ethical dilemmas. The checklist begins by asking whether an action is legal. You should go forward only if the action complies with the law. If it does, then test the ethical soundness of your plan by asking the remaining questions: Would you proceed if you were on the receiving end of the action, and can you rule out better options? Even if the answer is *yes,* consider then how a trusted mentor or your family, friends, and coworkers would view your decision.

Perhaps the best advice in ethical matters is contained in the Golden Rule: Treat others the way you wish to be treated yourself. The principle of reciprocity has a long tradition and exists in most religions and cultures. This simple maxim can go a long way toward resolving conflict. The ultimate solution to all ethics problems is treating others fairly and doing what is right to achieve what is good. In succeeding chapters you will find additional discussions of ethical questions as they relate to relevant topics.

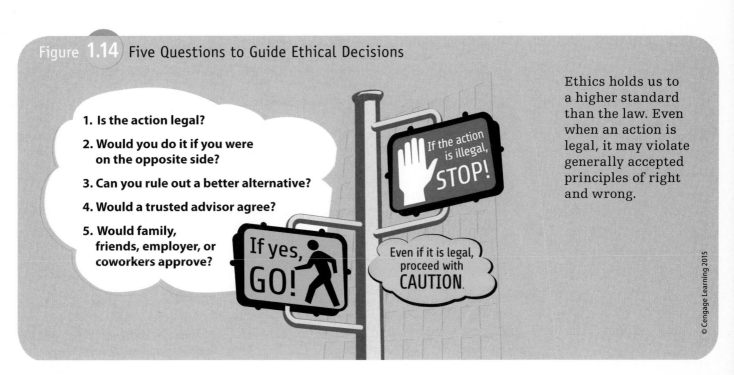

Figure 1.14 Five Questions to Guide Ethical Decisions

1. Is the action legal?
2. Would you do it if you were on the opposite side?
3. Can you rule out a better alternative?
4. Would a trusted advisor agree?
5. Would family, friends, employer, or coworkers approve?

If the action is illegal, STOP!

If yes, GO!

Even if it is legal, proceed with CAUTION.

Ethics holds us to a higher standard than the law. Even when an action is legal, it may violate generally accepted principles of right and wrong.

© Cengage Learning 2015

Zooming in

Your Turn: Applying Your Skills at Intel

Intel's social media strategist Ekaterina Walter has been called a "thought leader."[83] She tweets comments to support entrepreneurs and offers tips on Facebook to struggling small businesses as a way to promote Intel. Such engagement allows Intel to connect with its consumers in a personal way. Sometimes, however, posts invite hostile responses.

YOUR TASK. As an intern in Intel's Social Media Center for Excellence, you have discovered an offensive Facebook post that used vulgar language about Intel's use of minerals mined in Congo. You are aware that the firm's Social Media Guidelines contain policies about how to deal with such comments, but you cannot remember which one pertains to this particular situation. With a fellow intern, you reexamine the Guidelines and find what you think is the appropriate response. You know to notify a superior, so you and your colleague compose an e-mail to Ms. Walter that informs her of the situation. Tell her when and where you saw the post. Mention the suitable policy for dealing with such a post to show you have done your homework. Refer to Chapter 7 for information about how to draft an e-mail.

Summary of Learning Objectives

Go to
www.cengagebrain.com
and use your access code to unlock valuable student resources.

1 Explain how communication skills fuel career success, and understand why writing skills are vital in a digital workplace embracing social media. In a fast-paced, competitive, and highly connected digital workplace, communication skills matter more than ever before. Communication technology has provided unprecedented mobility, and workers are increasingly expected to be plugged in after hours and wherever they may travel. Today's workers write more, not less, and excellent oral and written communication skills are the top qualities that employers seek. Such skills are critical to job placement, performance, career advancement, and organizational success. Especially in a recession, excellent communication skills can set you apart from other candidates. Communication skills include reading, listening, nonverbal, speaking, and writing skills. Ever since the digital revolution swept the workplace, most workers write their own messages and increasingly use new communication channels such as social media. Excellent writing skills are particularly important because messages today travel more rapidly, more often, and to greater numbers of people than ever before. Writing skills are not inherent; they must be learned.

2 Identify the tools for success in the hyperconnected 21st-century workplace, and appreciate the importance of critical-thinking skills in the competitive job market of the digital age. Accessing and sharing various digital media from a vast network of sources and distributing them nearly instantly to widespread audiences have never been easier. In today's demanding digital workplace, you can expect to be a knowledge worker. You must learn to think critically and develop opinions backed by reasons and evidence. You are learning to think, read, and ask questions in a networked world, accessed with electronic devices on the go. Because technologies and procedures are constantly evolving, you must be flexible and willing to engage in lifelong learning. You should expect to take charge of your career as you work for multiple employers. Knowledge workers who communicate well tend to find employment and advance even in a tough market.

3 Describe significant trends in today's dynamic, networked work environment, and recognize that social media and other new communication technologies require excellent communication skills, particularly in an uncertain economy. The trends affecting today's workers include new communication technologies such as social media, expectations of around-the-clock availability, and global competition. Other trends are flattened management hierarchies, team-based projects, a diverse workforce, and the mobile or virtual office operating practically 24/7/365. These trends require new skills and attitudes. Teamwork is a reality in business; workers must collaborate and share information. The workplace in the United States is becoming increasingly diverse with growing numbers of women, minorities, and older workers. Teleworking from remote locations and nonterritorial workspaces are impossible without the productive use of communication technologies. Businesspeople need to have strong communication skills to make decisions, exchange information effectively, and stay connected across time zones and vast distances.

4 Examine critically the internal and external flow of communication in organizations through formal and informal channels, explain the importance of effective media choices, and understand how to overcome typical barriers to organizational communication. Whether informing, persuading, or promoting goodwill, businesspeople communicate to achieve a particular objective. Internal and external office communication has accelerated thanks to new communication technologies. The mobile digital workplace is unthinkable without e-mail, IM, company intranets, corporate websites, audio and video podcasting, videoconferencing, and Web chats. Internal communication includes exchanging ideas and messages with superiors, coworkers, and subordinates. External communication involves customers, suppliers, government agencies, and the public. Media richness and social presence are concepts that help classify the communication media most suitable to avoid ambiguity in a given workplace interaction. Formal channels of communication follow an organization's hierarchy of command. Informal channels of communication, such as the grapevine, deliver unofficial news—both personal and organizational—among friends and coworkers. Smart communicators avoid office gossip.

5 Analyze ethics in the workplace, understand the goals of ethical business communicators, recognize and avoid ethical traps, and choose the tools for doing the right thing. Ethics describes standards of right and wrong prescribing what people should do. These standards consist of rights, obligations, and benefits to society. They include virtues such as fairness, honesty, loyalty, and more. Ethical standards rise to a level higher than the law. The goals of ethical business communicators include abiding by the law, telling the truth, labeling opinions, being objective, communicating clearly, using inclusive language, and giving credit. Obstacles to ethical decision making include the false necessity trap, the doctrine-of-relative-filth trap, the rationalization trap, the self-deception trap, and the ends-justify-the means trap. When faced with a difficult decision, the following questions serve as valuable tools in guiding you to do the right thing: (a) Is the action legal? (b) Would you do it if you were on the opposite side? (c) Can you rule out a better alternative? (d) Would a trusted advisor agree? and (e) Would your family, friends, employer, or coworkers approve?

Chapter Review

1. Explain why writing has been called a "career sifter," a "threshold skill," or "the price of admission." (Obj. 1)

2. What does the expression *communication skills* include? (Obj. 1)

3. What type of employee is required in today's dynamic world of work, and what new job requirements have emerged? (Obj. 1)

4. What kind of digital-age literacy does the hyperconnected workplace of today require? (Obj. 2)

5. Who are knowledge workers? Why are they hired? (Obj. 2)

6. What types of jobs will probably remain plentiful in the future, and how can you prepare for them? (Obj. 2)

7. How are tech-savvy companies using social media and other digital tools? (Obj. 3)

8. What does it mean that the office of the future is mobile and always "on"? (Obj. 3)

9. Why do fewer layers of management mean greater communication challenges for frontline workers? (Obj. 3)

10. How has technology changed the way businesses communicate internally and externally? (Obj. 4)

11. Why is information-rich oral communication considered more effective than written communication transmitted by "leaner" media? Why doesn't everyone exclusively use the richest media to communicate? (Obj. 4)

12. Compare formal and informal channels of communication within organizations. Which is more valuable to employees? (Obj. 4)

13. How can you control or respond ethically to office gossip? (Obj. 5)

14. What are seven goals of ethical business communicators? (Obj. 5)

15. When you are faced with a difficult ethical decision, what questions should you ask yourself? (Obj. 5)

Critical Thinking

1. Do you consider your daily texting, Facebook updates, blog entries, e-mails, and other informal writing to be "real writing"? How might such writing differ from the writing done in business? (Obj. 1)

2. Sharing various digital media impulsively can lead to embarrassment and worse. Have you or has someone you know ever regretted posting a comment, photo, or other digital media online? (Obj. 2)

3. How do you feel about the work–life balance in today's 24/7 "anytime, anywhere" digital workplace? Do you anticipate negative effects on your health and personal life? (Obj. 3)

4. Critics complain that e-mail and other mediated communication are reducing the number of face-to-face interactions at work and that this is bad for business. Do you agree or disagree? (Obj. 4)

5. **Ethical Issue:** Josh in the Accounting Department tells you that he heard from a reliable source that 15 percent of the staff will be fired within 120 days. You would love to share this juicy news with other department members, for their own defense and planning. Should you? Why or why not?

Activities

1.1 Social Media Inventory (Objs. 1–4)

Communication Technology **Social Media** **Web**

The millennials, those born after 1985, do not remember a time without computer technology and cellular phones in wide use. People born in the 1990s have only known a society that depends on the Internet and mobile technology. Social media are second nature to most of these young people, who seem to be inseparably attached to their smart devices.

You too may live, learn, work, play, network, and shop in the digital world. Even if you are not crazy about the latest gadgets and gizmos, your daily life depends on technology as your cell phone, iPod, TV, DVD player, and other electronics couldn't work without it and are increasingly networked.

YOUR TASK. Take stock of your Internet, social media, and other technology use. First establish useful criteria—for example, categories such as consumer electronics, social networking sites, preferred modes of communication with friends and family, and so forth. Within each category, list the technology you use most frequently. For instance, for social media networks, indicate your use of Facebook, Twitter, Pinterest, YouTube, Hulu, LinkedIn, and more. How do you use each? Estimate how often you access these sites per day and indicate the tools you use (smartphone, tablet, or laptop). How much do you text every day? Your instructor may ask you to list your responses in writing or verbally; you may want to share your results individually or in teams.

1.2 Writing Inventory (Objs. 1–3)

Communication Technology **E-mail** **Social Media**

What, no more term papers? Students blog instead? While employers are desperate to hire job seekers with solid communication skills, the debate over how best to prepare students for writing in the digital age is raging across the country. A professor at Duke University now wants to replace the old-style term paper with the blog. Cathy N. Davidson finds the academic paper requiring that the writer make a point, explain it, and defend it deeply offensive. She wants to make writing fun, practical, and relevant and believes that the blog is the ticket.[90]

Professor Davidson has plenty of detractors. "Writing term papers is a dying art, but those who do write them have a dramatic leg up in terms of critical thinking, argumentation and the sort of expression required not only in college, but in the job market," says Douglas B. Reeves, a columnist for the *American School Board Journal*. "It doesn't mean there aren't interesting blogs. But nobody would conflate interesting writing with premise, evidence, argument and conclusion," he says. The author of a recent survey of student engagement concurs with this criticism: "She's right," William H. Fitzhugh says of Professor Davidson. "Writing is being murdered. But the solution isn't blogs, the solution is more reading. We don't pay taxes so kids can talk about themselves and their home lives."

According to the National Survey of Student Engagement, 82 percent of college freshmen and more than half of seniors weren't asked to do a single paper of 20 pages or more. Most of their writing assignments were for papers of one to five pages. Another study estimated that 80 percent of high school students were not asked to write a history term paper of more than 15 pages. How much writing have you been asked to do in high school and college?

YOUR TASK. In an e-mail or a memo to your instructor, reflect on your writing experience. See Appendix B for memo formats and Chapters 7 and 8 for tips on preparing a professional e-mail message. Consider the arguments in this controversy pitting what has been dubbed "old literacy" against "new literacy." Explain to your instructor how much and what kind of writing you had to do in high school and in college. How long were typical assignments? What subjects did you discuss? What is your take on the controversy? Should term papers really be replaced by blog entries?

1.3 Assessing Communication Skills Online: Evaluate Your Skills (Objs. 1–3)

Web

This course can help you dramatically improve your business communication skills. How much do you need to improve? This assessment exercise enables you to evaluate your skills with specific standards in four critical communication skill areas: writing, reading, speaking, and listening. How well you communicate will be an important factor in your future career—particularly if you are promoted into management, as many college graduates are.

YOUR TASK. For each of the following skills, either here or online at **www.cengagebrain.com,** select a number from 1 (indicating low ability) to 5 (indicating high ability) that best reflects your perception of yourself. Be honest in rating yourself. Think about how others would rate you. When you finish, see a rating of your skills. Complete this assessment online to see your results automatically!

Writing Skills	Low				High
1. Possess basic spelling, grammar, and punctuation skills.	1	2	3	4	5
2. Am familiar with proper e-mail, memo, letter, and report formats for business documents.	1	2	3	4	5
3. Can analyze a writing problem and quickly outline a plan for solving the problem.	1	2	3	4	5
4. Am able to organize data coherently and logically.	1	2	3	4	5
5. Can evaluate a document to determine its probable success.	1	2	3	4	5

Reading Skills					
1. Am familiar with specialized vocabulary in my field as well as general vocabulary.	1	2	3	4	5
2. Can concentrate despite distractions.	1	2	3	4	5
3. Am willing to look up definitions whenever necessary.	1	2	3	4	5
4. Am able to move from recreational to serious reading.	1	2	3	4	5
5. Can read and comprehend college-level material.	1	2	3	4	5

Speaking Skills					
1. Feel at ease in speaking with friends.	1	2	3	4	5
2. Feel at ease in speaking before a group of people.	1	2	3	4	5
3. Can adapt my presentation to the audience.	1	2	3	4	5
4. Am confident in pronouncing and using words correctly.	1	2	3	4	5
5. Sense that I have credibility when I make a presentation.	1	2	3	4	5

Listening Skills					
1. Spend at least half the time listening during conversations.	1	2	3	4	5
2. Am able to concentrate on a speaker's words despite distractions.	1	2	3	4	5
3. Can summarize a speaker's ideas and anticipate what's coming during pauses.	1	2	3	4	5
4. Provide proper feedback such as nodding, paraphrasing, and asking questions.	1	2	3	4	5
5. Listen with the expectation of gaining new ideas and information.	1	2	3	4	5

Total your score in each section. How do you rate?

22–25	Excellent! You have indicated that you have exceptional communication skills.
18–21	Your score is above average, but you could improve your skills.
14–17	Your score suggests that you have much room for improvement.
5–13	You recognize that you need serious study, practice, and follow-up reinforcement.

Where are you strongest and weakest? Are you satisfied with your present skills? The first step to improvement is recognition of a need. The second step is making a commitment to improve. The third step is following through, and this course will help you do that.

1.4 Collaborating on the Opening Case Study (Objs. 1–5)

Team **Web**

Each chapter contains a two-part case study of a well-known company. To help you develop collaboration and speaking skills as well as to learn about the target company and apply the chapter concepts, your instructor may ask you to do the following.

YOUR TASK. Individually or as part of a three-student team during your course, work on one of the 16 case studies in the textbook. Answer the questions posed in both parts of the case study, look for additional information in articles or on websites, complete the application assignment, and then make a five- to ten-minute presentation to the class with your findings and reactions.

1.5 Introducing Yourself (Objs. 1, 2)

Communication Technology **E-mail** **Social Media**

Your instructor wants to know more about you, your motivation for taking this course, your career goals, and your writing skills.

YOUR TASK. Send an e-mail or write a memo of introduction to your instructor. See Appendix B for memo formats and Chapters 7 and 8 for tips on preparing an e-mail message. In your message include the following:

a. Your reasons for taking this class

b. Your career goals (both temporary and long-term)

c. A brief description of your employment, if any, and your favorite activities

d. An assessment and discussion of your current communication skills, including your strengths and weaknesses

Alternatively, your instructor may ask you to (a) create a profile for LinkedIn, the business-oriented social networking site or (b) develop a profile within a learning-management system (e.g., Blackboard, Moodle, or WebCT) to introduce yourself to your classmates. If yours is a small class, your instructor may challenge you to compose your introduction in Twitter posts of 140 or fewer characters (see Chapter 6 for tips on writing tweets and other microblogging messages).

1.6 Small-Group Presentation: Introducing Team Members (Objs. 1, 2)

Team

Many business organizations today use teams to accomplish their goals. To help you develop speaking, listening, and teamwork skills, your instructor may assign team projects. One of the first jobs in any team is selecting members and becoming acquainted.

YOUR TASK. Your instructor will divide your class into small groups or teams. At your instructor's direction, either (a) interview another group member and introduce that person to the group or (b) introduce yourself to the group. Think of this as an informal interview for a team assignment or a job. You will want to make notes from which to speak. Your introduction should include information such as the following:

a. Where did you grow up?

b. What work and extracurricular activities have you engaged in?

c. What are your interests and talents? What are you good at doing?

d. What have you achieved?

e. How familiar are you with various computer technologies?

f. What are your professional and personal goals? Where do you expect to be five years from now?

To develop listening skills, team members should practice good listening techniques (see Chapter 2) and take notes. They should be prepared to discuss three important facts as well as remember details about each speaker.

1.7 Communication Skills: Employer Wish List (Obj. 1)

Team **Web**

What do employers request when they list job openings in your field?

YOUR TASK. Individually or in teams, check the listings at an online job board such as Monster, CollegeRecruiter, CareerBuilder, or CollegeGrad. Use your favorite search engine to locate their sites. Follow the instructions to search job categories and locations. Also check college resources and local newspaper listings of job openings. Find five or more job listings in your field. If possible, print the results of your search. If you cannot print, make notes on what you find. Examine the skills requested. How often do the ads mention communication, teamwork, and computer skills? What tasks do the ads mention? Discuss your findings with your team members. Prepare a list of the most frequently requested skills. Your instructor may ask you to submit your findings and/or report to the class.

1.8 Writing Skills: But My Job Won't Require Writing! (Objs. 1–3)

Team

Some job candidates experience a disconnect between what they expect to be doing in their career fields and what they actually will do.

YOUR TASK. In teams or in class, discuss the accuracy of the following statements. Are they myths or facts?

a. No one really writes anymore. They just text and send e-mails.

b. Because I'm in a technical field, I will work with numbers, not words.

c. Secretaries will clean up my writing problems.

d. Technical writers do most of the real writing on the job.

e. Today's sophisticated software programs can fix any of my writing mistakes.

f. I can use forms and templates for most messages.

1.9 Wanted: A Jack- or Jill-of-All-Trades

Web

Want to "future-proof" your career? Read employer and worker surveys to discover your potential competitive advantages. Know current trends and be able to adapt to changing demands in the labor market. Learn from the mistakes of others to secure a job even in a tough economy. One good source of such data is the annual *EDGE Report* by Robert Half International and CareerBuilder. This survey of 501 hiring managers and 505 workers is one of many that provide clues as to how to make yourself valuable to recruiters.[91] Here are excerpts:

Employers complain: Qualified applicants are in short supply, 47 percent of managers said; 44 percent of résumés come from unqualified applicants.

Most desirable hire: Thirty-six percent of hiring managers want "A multitasker who thrives on a variety of projects"—that is, a flexible team member capable of taking on "hybrid" roles (multiple responsibilities, even absorbing some of the duties of former colleagues); 31 percent of recruiters desire "a go-getter who takes initiative"; while 21 percent wish for "A creative thinker who solves problems."

Where the critical jobs are now: 1. Customer service, 2. Sales, 3. Marketing/creative, 4. Technology, and 5. Public relations/communication

Future opportunities after an economic rebound: 1. Technology, 2. Customer service, 3. Sales, 4. Marketing/creative, and 5. Business development

Employers are slow to hire: Finding a comparable position after job loss takes more than three months.

Perks workers expect when the economy picks up: Technology upgrades, 79 percent; tuition reimbursement or subsidized training, 61 percent; flexible schedules, 47 percent. Twenty-seven percent desire telecommuting.

Another important study focuses on the economic value of bachelor's degrees. The authors confirm the commonly held belief that college graduates make a lot more over a lifetime than those with high school diplomas (a whopping 84 percent more!), but the researchers see huge variations in incomes. The median highest earning major is 314 percent ahead of the median lowest earning one. This range extends from $29,000 for counseling psychology to $120,000 for petroleum engineering. The study's authors conclude: "In some ways, then, a student's choice of undergraduate college major can be almost as important as deciding whether to get a bachelor's degree at all."[92] Although you shouldn't choose a major solely based on financial rewards, lifetime earnings and future opportunities should be part of your considerations.

YOUR TASK. Being prepared for an uncertain future is important, as we have seen in this chapter. Discuss these results in small groups or in class. Relate them to your own situation. Your instructor may ask for a written response to these data. If you choose to download these or similar reports, view the data most applicable to your future goals and career plans.

1.10 Taking the Pulse of Today's Workforce

Not only business organizations, but you too can benefit from knowing what current employees think and how happy they are on the job. A recent report by the Society for Human Resource Management[93] provides a glimpse into the attitudes of today's workers. In a slow economy, it does not come as a surprise that workers cite job security (63 percent) as the chief factor affecting their job satisfaction, followed by "opportunities to use skills and abilities" (62 percent). Financial stability of the organization (55 percent) and the relationship with the immediate supervisor (55 percent) tied for third place. The other factors in the top five are compensation/pay (54 percent) ahead of benefits, communication between employees and management, and the work itself (all at 53 percent, tying for fifth place). The sluggish economy has made workers less willing to look for new jobs, as 64 percent of employees report.

However, the authors of the study caution that reported job satisfaction does not mean that workers are connected and committed to their employers. On average, employees were moderately engaged (3.6) on a scale of 1 to 5, where 1 is highly disengaged and 5 is highly engaged. To bridge this disconnect, the HR experts suggest that employers communicate effectively with employees, counter rumors, and promote trust. They propose upward communication to gather feedback from employees through peer-led focus groups.

YOUR TASK. What would it take for you to be happy with your job? Which aspects of your work now or in the future will ensure that you will be a committed and engaged employee? Discuss these and similar questions in small groups or in class. Your instructor may ask for a written response to this survey or require that you do further research.

1.11 Customer Service: Tech Skills Not Enough (Objs. 1–3)

◆ Communication Technology ◆ ◆ Social Media ◆ ◆ E-mail ◆
◆ Team ◆ ◆ Web ◆

"One misspelled word and customers begin to doubt the validity of the information they are getting," warned Mary Jo Lichtenberg, former director of training, quality, and career development at CompUSA, in Plano, Texas. One of her big problems was training service agents with weak language skills. "Just because agents understand technically how to troubleshoot computers or pieces of software and can walk customers through solutions extremely well over the telephone doesn't mean they can do the same in writing," she complained. "The skill set for phone does not necessarily translate to the skill set needed for writing e-mail."[94] As more customers choose e-mail, Web chat sessions, and even social networking sites such as Facebook to obtain service and voice complaints, numerous service reps are finding it necessary to brush up their writing skills.

YOUR TASK. In teams, discuss what communication skills are necessary for customer-service agents troubleshooting computer and software problems as well as other companies offering chat, e-mail, and social media customer support. How are the skill sets different for answering phones and for writing e-mail responses? What suggestions could you make to a trainer preparing customer-service reps for chat and e-mail responses?

1.12 Oral or Written Communication: How Rich Must the Media Be? (Obj. 4)

◆ Communication Technology ◆ ◆ Social Media ◆ ◆ E-mail ◆

YOUR TASK. First decide whether the following messages need to be communicated orally or in writing. After consulting the media-richness diagram in Figure 1.9 on page 20, consider how rich the medium must be in each communication situation to convey the message most appropriately and reliably. You may want to choose channels such as e-mail, letter, report, texting, instant messaging, telephone call, live chat, teleconferencing, face-to-face conversation, or team meeting. Describe the advantages and disadvantages of each choice.

a. You are returning with the senior auditor from a client visit to company headquarters, where you must attend an important department meeting. It looks as though you will be at least 15 minutes late. What are your options?

b. Working at 8 a.m. in your Boston office, you need to get in touch with your counterpart at your company's West Coast office and ask a few clarifying formatting questions about a report on which the two of you are collaborating.

c. John, the information technology vice president, must tell employees about a new company social media policy. He has two employees in mind who particularly need this information.

d. As soon as possible, you need to learn from Daryle in Document Imaging whether she can make copies of a set of engineering blueprints. If she cannot, you need her advice on where you can get it done.

e. As a manager in your Human Resources department, you must terminate three employees in a company-wide initiative to reduce costs.

f. It wasn't your fault, but an order for printed checks for a long-time customer was mishandled. The checks are not ready, and the customer is angry.

g. As chairman of the Employee Benefits Committee, you have worked with your committee for two months evaluating several health plan options. You are now ready to convey the recommendations of the committee to management.

1.13 Information Flow: What's Good and Bad About Gossip at Work? (Obj. 5)

Ethics ▸ **E-mail** ▸ **Team**

Jon Bender, a managing partner at PrincetonOne, an executive search firm, was surprised to receive a nasty, gossipy e-mail about himself. He was obviously not the intended receiver. Instead of shooting back an equally incendiary message, he decided to talk with the sender. He said, "You're upset. Let's talk about it, but it's not appropriate in an e-mail."[95]

YOUR TASK. In groups, discuss Mr. Bender's response to gossip about himself. Did he do the right thing? How would you have reacted? Although gossip is generally considered unacceptable and a negative force, it can be a tool for managers and employees. Make a list of at least four benefits and four negative consequences of workplace gossip. Be prepared to explain and defend each item.

1.14 Attitudes Toward Ethics: Making Concessions on the Job (Obj. 5)

Ethics

Consider this statement from a young respondent in a recent survey of ethical decision making among young public relations professionals:

> At this point in my life, a job is a job, and in terms of ethics, I'll do what I have to do to keep my job; my personal feelings will take a back seat. With the economy so bad, it's just one of those things. I can't afford to let my personal feelings complicate my career.[96]

Do you agree that personal ethics must not get in the way of one's career? Under what circumstances would you hold your tongue and keep your head down at work?

YOUR TASK. Discuss this view with your classmates and instructor in the light of what you read in this chapter.

1.15 Ethical Dilemma: Applying Tools for Doing the Right Thing (Obj. 5)

Ethics ▸ **Team**

As a business communicator, you may face various ethical dilemmas in your career. Many factors can determine your choice of an action to take.

YOUR TASK. Study the seven dilemmas appearing on pages 25–26. Select four of them and apply the tools for doing the right thing on page 29 in choosing an appropriate action. In a memo to your instructor or in a team discussion, explain the action you would take for each dilemma. Analyze your response to each question (Is the action you are considering legal? How would you see the problem if you were on the opposite side? and so forth).

1.16 Ethical Dilemma: Rival Chicken Chains Tempt Ethics in Taste Test (Obj. 5)

Ethics ▸ **Team**

Kentucky Fried Chicken (KFC) is best known for its fried chicken. Right? Recently, however, it has become more health conscious and launched a new product—grilled chicken. In doing so, it ruffled the feathers of chicken rival, El Pollo Loco, a fast-food chain in Western states. For years El Pollo Loco has staked out the "healthful chicken" territory by claiming that its grilling technique offers a delicious and wholesome alternative to traditional fast food. "Marinated in a special blend of herbs, spices, and fruit juices and then flame-broiled over an open grill right before your eyes," El Pollo's chicken is both "healthful and great tasting."[97]

After KFC rolled out its Kentucky grilled chicken campaign, El Pollo Loco CEO Steve Carley challenged KFC to a taste test. Fast-food chicken lovers could call an 800 number to say whether they preferred the taste of KFC to El Pollo Loco grilled chicken. The 800-number taste test was sponsored by El Pollo Loco.[98]

YOUR TASK. Assume you work for KFC, and you are convinced that your new grilled chicken tastes great. In fact, you think that its blend of secret spices makes it far superior to El Pollo Loco's citrus-marinated grilled chicken. One of your KFC coworkers feels the same way and urges you to join him and other KFC employees in calling the El Pollo 800 number to register your preference. You didn't hear about any restrictions regarding who could enter the taste test. Should you call? Apply the tools for doing the right thing that you studied in this chapter. Be prepared to defend your position in a team or class discussion.

Chat About It

In each chapter you will find five discussion questions related to the chapter material. Your instructor may assign these topics for you to discuss in class, in an online chat room, or on an online discussion board. Some of the discussion topics may require outside research. You may also be asked to read and respond to postings made by your classmates.

Topic 1: Which tips and suggestions in this chapter for functioning effectively and ethically in today's workplace do you think might be the most helpful to you in your current or future career?

Topic 2: In your chosen career, what sorts of continuing education do you think you might need to stay employed or to be promoted?

Topic 3: This chapter discusses how Nike' ad featuring LeBron James was banned by the Chinese government, which considered the ad to be offensive to national dignity. Can you think of another popular ad that might not work in China as well as one that might work there?

Topic 4: With so many ways to stay connected (e-mail, voice mail, text messaging, and so on) and with many people feeling over-whelmed because of this high degree of connectedness, what are some ways to give yourself a break from always being on call while still being fair to people who need to contact you?

Topic 5: Some experts believe that although computer technology is improving our lives in many ways, it might be impairing our ability to think critically by putting answers at our fingertips. What do you think?

C.L.U.E. Grammar & Mechanics | *Review 1*

Each chapter includes an exercise based on Appendix A, Grammar and Mechanics Guide: Competent Language Usage Essentials (C.L.U.E.). This appendix is a business communicator's condensed guide to language usage, covering 50 of the most used and abused language elements. It also includes a list of frequently misspelled words as well as a list of confusing words. In the first ten chapters, each exercise will focus on a specific set of grammar/mechanics guidelines. In the last six chapters, exercises will review all the guidelines plus spelling and confusing words.

Note: In addition to the C.L.U.E. exercises in the textbook, you will find similar C.L.U.E. exercises at **www.cengagebrain.com** under the Grammar/Mechanics tab. The online exercises parallel the sentences in this textbook and test the same principles. However, the online exercises provide feedback and explanations.

SENTENCE STRUCTURE

Study sentence structure in Guides 1–3 of Appendix A beginning on page A-2. Some of the following numbered word groups have sentence faults. On a sheet of paper, indicate whether each word group is (a) correctly punctuated (b) a fragment, (c) a comma splice, or (d) a run-on. If incorrect, write a correct version. Also, identify the fault and the relevant guide. Avoid adding new phrases or rewriting in your own words. When finished, compare your responses with the key beginning on page Key-1.

EXAMPLE: The message was meant to inform, however it confused instead.

REVISION: The message was meant to **inform; however,** it confused instead. [c, Guide 3, Comma splice]

1. Because you will be entering a fast-paced, competitive, and highly connected digital environment. Communication and technology skills are critical to your career success.

2. Such skills are particularly significant now. When jobs are scarce and competition is keen.

3. During a recession many candidates vie for fewer jobs, however candidates with exceptional communication skills will immediately stand out.

4. Although we cannot predict the kinds of future jobs that will be available, they will undoubtedly require brainpower and education.

5. In traditional companies decisions must move through many levels of managers, in flat organizations decisions can be made more quickly.

6. Millions of workers no longer report to nine-to-five jobs. Thanks largely to advances in high-speed and wireless Internet access.

7. Knowledge workers must be able to explain their decisions they must be critical thinkers.

8. The grapevine can be a powerful source of information. Although it increasingly operates informally through social media.

9. Ethical companies experience less litigation, and they also are the target of less government regulation.

10. Ethics is a hot topic and trend in the workplace, however making ethical decisions is not always easy.

Notes

[1] Quoted in Stelzner, M. (2012, August 2). The inside scoop on how Intel manages its Facebook page. Retrieved from http://www.socialmediaexaminer.com/intel-case-study/

[2] Ibid.

[3] Intel Social Media Guidelines. http://www.intel.com/content/www/us/en/legal/intel-social-media-guidelines.html

[4] Ibid.

[5] Ibid.

[6] Canavor, N. (2012). *Business writing in the digital age*. Los Angeles: Sage; see also National Writing Project with DeVoss, D. N., Eidman-Aadahl, E., & Hicks, T. (2010). *Because digital writing matters*. San Francisco: Jossey-Bass.

[7] The National Leadership Council for Liberal Education & America's Promise. Association of American Colleges and Universities. (2007).

College learning for the new global century. Retrieved from http://www.aacu.org/leap/documents/GlobalCentury_final.pdf; Casner-Lotto, J., Wright, M., & Barrington, L. (2006, October). Are they really ready to work? Employers' perspectives on the basic knowledge and applied skills of new entrants to the 21st century U.S. workforce. Retrieved from: http://www.p21.org/storage/documents/FINAL_REPORT_PDF09-29-06.pdf; College Board: The National Commission on Writing. (2004, September). Writing: A ticket to work... Or a ticket out: A survey of business leaders. Retrieved from http://www.collegeboard.com/prod_downloads/writingcom/writing-ticket-to-work.pdf

[8] The National Association of Colleges and Employers. (2011, October 26). Job outlook: The candidate skills/qualities employers want. Retrieved from

http://www.naceweb.org/s10262011/candidate_skills_employer_qualities; The Association of American Colleges and Universities/Hart Research Associates. (2009, November). Raising the bar: Employers' views on college learning in the wake of the economic downturn. Retrieved from http://www.aacu.org/leap/documents/2009_EmployerSurvey.pdf

[9] Kay, A. (2011, May 30). What employers want: 5 more skills to cultivate. *USA Today*. Retrieved from http://www.usatoday.com/money/jobcenter/workplace/kay/2011-05-30-skills-employers-want-part-ii_N.htm

[10] The MetLife Survey of the American Teacher: Preparing students for college and careers. (2011, May). Retrieved from http://www.metlife.com/assets/cao/contributions/foundation/american-teacher/MetLife_Teacher_Survey_2010.pdf

[11] College Board: The National Commission on Writing. (2004, September). Writing: A ticket to work...Or a ticket out: A survey of business leaders. Retrieved from http://www.collegeboard.com/prod_downloads/writingcom/writing-ticket-to-work.pdf

[12] College Board: The National Commission on Writing. (2004, September). Writing: A ticket to work...Or a ticket out: A survey of business leaders, p. 3. Retrieved from http://www.collegeboard.com/prod_downloads/writingcom/writing-ticket-to-work.pdf; O'Rourke, IV, J. S. (2013). Management communication: A case-analysis approach (5th ed.). Boston: Prentice Hall, p. 9; Canavor, N. (2012). Business writing in the digital age. Los Angeles: Sage, p. 3.

[13] College Board: The National Commission on Writing. (2004, September). Writing: A ticket to work...Or a ticket out: A survey of business leaders. Retrieved from http://www.collegeboard.com/prod_downloads/writingcom/writing-ticket-to-work.pdf

[14] Pew/Internet & College Board: The National Commission on Writing. (2008, April 24). Writing, technology, and teens. Retrieved from http://www.collegeboard.com/prod_downloads/prof/community/PIP_Writing_Report_FINAL.pdf

[15] Canavor, N. (2012). Business writing in the digital age. Los Angeles: Sage, pp. 1-3; National Writing Project with DeVoss, D. N., Eidman-Aadahl, E., & Hicks, T. (2010). Because digital writing matters. San Francisco: Jossey-Bass, pp. 1-5.

[16] The Association of American Colleges and Universities/Hart Research Associates. (2009, November). Raising the bar: Employers' views on college learning in the wake of the economic downturn, p. 5-6. Retrieved from http://www.aacu.org/leap/documents/2009_EmployerSurvey.pdf

[17] Quoted in Canavor, N. (2012). Business writing in the digital age. Los Angeles: Sage, p. 4.

[18] Casner-Lotto, J., Wright, M., & Barrington, L. (2006, September). Are they really ready to work? Employers' perspectives on the basic knowledge and applied skills of new entrants to the 21st century U.S. workforce, p. 24. Retrieved from http://www.p21.org/storage/documents/FINAL_REPORT_PDF09-29-06.pdf

[19] National Writing Project with DeVoss, D. N., Eidman-Aadahl, E., & Hicks, T. (2010). Because digital writing matters. San Francisco: Jossey-Bass, p. 7.

[20] Drucker, P. (1989, May). New realities, new ways of managing. Business Month, pp. 50-51.

[21] White, C. (2008, October 29). Knowledge and information workers: Who are they? Retrieved from http://www.b-eye-network.com/view/8897

[22] Kelly, K. (2012, February 17). Q&A: Hacker historian George Dyson sits down with Wired's Kevin Kelly. Wired Magazine (March 2012). Retrieved from http://www.wired.com/magazine/2012/02/ff_dysonqa/all/1

[23] Fox, A. (2010, January). At work in 2020. HR Magazine, p. 20.

[24] Ibid., p. 21.

[25] Deloitte & Manufacturing Institute. (2011, September). Boiling point? The skills gap in U.S. manufacturing. National Association of Manufacturers. Retrieved from http://www.nam.org/~/media/A07730B2A798437D98501E798C2E13AA.ashx

[26] Kay, A. (2011, May 30). What employers want: 5 more skills to cultivate. USA Today. Retrieved from http://www.usatoday.com/money/jobcenter/workplace/kay/2011-05-30-skills-employers-want-part-ii_N.htm

[27] Society for Human Resource Management and WSJ.com/Careers. (2008, June). Critical skills needs and resources for the changing workforce. Retrieved from http://www.shrm.org/Research/SurveyFindings/Articles/Documents/08-0798CriticalSkillsFigs.pdf

[28] National Writing Project with DeVoss, D. N., Eidman-Aadahl, E., & Hicks, T. (2010). Because digital writing matters. San Francisco: Jossey-Bass, p. 150.

[29] Quoted in Wallis, C. (2006, December 10). How to bring our schools out of the 20th century. Time Magazine U.S. Retrieved from http://www.time.com/time/magazine/article/0,9171,1568480,00.html

[30] Understanding Kaizen & the continuous improvement process. (2010). Process Improvement Japan. Retrieved from http://www.process-improvement-japan.com/continuous-improvement-process.html

[31] Survey: Thinking for a living. (2006, January 21). The Economist (US). Retrieved from http://search.proquest.com

[32] Fox, A. (2010, January). At work in 2020. HR Magazine, p. 23. Retrieved from http://search.ebscohost.com

[33] O'Toole, J. & Lawler, E. E., III. (2006, July). The new American workplace. New York: Palgrave Macmillan, p. 17.

[34] Shierholz, H., & Edwards, K. A. (2011, April 20). The class of 2011: Young workers face a dire labor market without a safety net. Economic Policy Institute, Briefing Paper 306. Retrieved from http://www.epi.org/publication/bp306-class-of-2011

[35] Koncz, A. (2009, January 29). Employers cite qualities, attributes of "perfect" job candidate. [NACE Web press release]. Retrieved from http://www.naceweb.org

[36] College Board: The National Commission on Writing. (2004, September). Writing: A ticket to work... Or a ticket out: A survey of business leaders, pp. 13, 18. Retrieved from http://www.collegeboard.com/prod_downloads/writingcom/writing-ticket-to-work.pdf

[37] Kaplan, A. M., & Haenlein, M. (2010). Users of the world, unite! The challenges and opportunities of social media. Business Horizons, 53, 67-68. Retrieved from http://michaelhaenlein.com/Publications/publications.htm

[38] Kietzman, J. H., Hermkens, K., McCarthy, I. P., & Silvestre, B. S. (2011). Social media? Get serious! Understanding the functional building blocks of social media. Business Horizons, 54, 242. Retrieved from http://beedie.sfu.ca/profiles/JanKietzmann

[39] Roberts, I. (2011, March 30). Consumer boycotts: How bad brand experience can turn into lifelong grudges. Retrieved from http://experiencematters.criticalmass.com

[40] Cooper, C. L. (2011, May 25). America can learn from Europe on work-life balance. CNNOpinion. Retrieved from http://articles.cnn.com/2011-05-25/opinion/cooper.vacation.europe_1_holiday-entitlement-work-life-working-time-directive?_s=PM:OPINION

[41] Piazza, C. F. (2007, January 23). 24/7 workplace connectivity: A hidden ethical dilemma. SCU White Paper, p. 1. Retrieved from www.scu.edu/ethics/practicing/focusareas/business/connectivity.pdf

[42] Ibid.

[43] Jargon, J. (2008, May 1) Kraft reformulates Oreo, scores in China. The Wall Street Journal, p. B1.

[44] Heller, L. (2006, August 7). Customer experience evolves in China. Retailing Today, 45(14), 42. Retrieved from http://search.proquest.com

[45] Wallop, H. (2011, July 20). McDonald's Olympic restaurant will be biggest in the world. The Telegraph. Retrieved from http://www.telegraph.co.uk

[46] Smithers, R. (2012, June 25). McDonald's pops-up its biggest ever restaurant for Olympics. The Guardian. Retrieved from http://www.guardian.co.uk/business/2012/jun/25/mcdonalds-london-olympic-games-restaurant

[47] Singh, N. (2012). Localization strategies for global e-business. Cambridge, MA: Cambridge University Press, p. 88.

[48] Rajan, R. G., & Wulf, J. (2006, November). The flattening firm: Evidence from panel data on the changing nature of corporate hierarchies. Review of Economics and Statistics, 88(4), 3. Retrieved from http://www.nber.org/papers/w9633

[49] Protess, B. (2012, January 20). Once a millstone, GE Capital is now a profit center. Dealbook, The New York Times. Retrieved from http://dealbook.nytimes.com/2012/01/20/once-a-millstone-ge-capital-now-a-profit-center

[50] Mills, E. (2007, April 27). Newsmaker: Meet Google's culture czar. Retrieved from http://news.cnet.com/Meet-Googles-culture-czar/2008-1023_3-6179897.html%5D

[51] Friedman, T. L. (2005). The world is flat. New York: Garrar, Straus and Giroux, pp. 178-179.

[52] Malone, T. W. (2004). The future of work. Cambridge, MA: Harvard Business School Press, p. 32.

[53] Weintraub, A. (2007, June 18). J & J's new baby. BusinessWeek, p. 48.

[54] Edmondson, A. C. (2012, April). Teamwork on the fly. Harvard Business Review. Retrieved from http://hbr.org/2012/04/teamwork-on-the-fly/ar/1

[55] Ibid.

[56] Fox, A. (2010, January). At work in 2020. HR Magazine, p. 21. Retrieved from http://search.ebscohost.com

[57] Pentland, A. (2012, March 20). The hard science of teamwork. Harvard Business Review. [Blog]. Retrieved from http://blogs.hbr.org/cs/2012/03/the_new_science_of_building_gr.html

[58] Ortman, J. M., & Guarneri, C. E. (2009). United States population projections: 2000-2050. Retrieved from U.S. Census Bureau http://www.census.gov/population/www/projections/analytical-document09.pdf

[59] de Vise, D. (2011, August 18). Women enjoy college more than men, survey says. The Washington Post. Retrieved from http://www.washingtonpost.com/blogs/college-inc/post/women-enjoy-college-more-than-men-survey-says/2011/08/18/gIQAJCBQNJ_blog.html

[60] Fox, A. (2010, January). At work in 2020. HR Magazine, p. 22. Retrieved from http://search.ebscohost.com

[61] Toosi, M. (2012, January). Labor force projections to 2020: A more slowly growing workforce. Office of Occupational Statistics and Employment Projections, Bureau of Labor Statistics, p. 56. Retrieved from http://www.bls.gov/opub/mlr/2012/01/art3full.pdf

[62] Bureau of Labor Statistics, U.S. Department of Labor. (2012, March 29). Occupational outlook handbook, 2012-13 edition, Projections Overview. Retrieved from http://www.bls.gov/ooh/about/projections-overview.htm; Toosi, M. (2012, January). Labor force projections to 2020: A more slowly growing workforce. Office of Occupational Statistics and Employment Projections, Bureau of Labor Statistics, p. 56. Retrieved from http://www.bls.gov/opub/mlr/2012/01/art3full.pdf

[63] David Arkless, president of global corporate and government affairs at Manpower, Inc., in London quoted in Fox, A. (2010, January). At work in 2020. HR Magazine, p. 21. Retrieved from http://search.ebscohost.com

[64] Proefrock, P. (2010, April 27). Professional space and coworking. Retrieved from http://www.workshifting.com/2010/04/professional-space-and-coworking.html; Gemmell, K. (2012, August 6); Cardinal go digital with playbook. ESPN. Retrieved from http://espn.go.com/blog/stanford-football/post/_/id/6803/cardinal-go-digital-with-playbook

[65] Holland, K. (2008, September 28). The anywhere, anytime office. The New York Times, p. 14 BUY.

[66] Telework 2011: A WorldatWork special report, p. 3. Retrieved from www.worldatwork.org/waw/adimLink?id=53034

[67] Lister, K. (2010, February 21). How many people actually telecommute? Retrieved from http://www.workshifting.com/2010/02/how-many-people-actually-telecommute.html

[68] Silverman, R. E., & Sidel, R. (2012, April 17). Warming up to the officeless office. *The Wall Street Journal*. Retrieved from http://online.wsj .com/article/SB100014240527023048184045773497833161465976.html; Holland, K. (2008, September 28). The anywhere, anytime office. *The New York Times*, p. 14 BU Y.

[69] Proefrock, P. (2010, April 27). Professional space and coworking. Retrieved from http:// www.workshifting.com/2010/04 /professional-space-and-coworking.html

[70] Smartphones, tablets, and notebook PCs to grow at 25.7% CAGR through 2015. (2012, February 1). [In-Stat press release]. Retrieved from http://www.instat.com .asp?ID=3334&sku=IN1105075SI

[71] Ibid.

[72] Tablets make their way into the workplace: Email and note taking are most popular business uses. (2012, February 14). [In-Stat press release]. Retrieved from http://www.instat.com /press.asp?ID=3340&sku=IN1205312ID

[73] Murthy, S. (2012, March 1). Smartphone owners now outnumber basic phone users. Retrieved from http://mashable.com/2012/03/01 /smartphones-outnumber-basic-mobile-phone

[74] Low-cost Android smartphones will seize 80% of market in Africa, India, and China. (2012, February 15). [In-Stat press release]. Retrieved from http://www.instat.com/press .asp?ID=3342&sku=IN1104911WH

[75] Daft, R. L., & Lengel, R. H. (1983, May). Information richness: A new approach to managerial behavior and organization design. [Technical report], p. 13. Retrieved from http://www.dtic.mil/cgi-bin /GetTRDoc?AD=ADA128980; Daft, R. L. & Lengel, R. H. (1986). Organizational information require- ments, media richness and structural design. *Management Science 32*(5), 560. Retrieved from http://search.ebscohost.com

[76] Short, J., Williams, E., & Christie, B. (1976). *The social psychology of telecommunications*. London, England: John Wiley.

[77] Discussion based in part on Kaplan, A., & Haenlein, M. (2010). Users of the world unite! The chal- lenges and opportunities of social media. *Business Horizons, 53*, 59-69. Retrieved from http://michaelhaenlein.com/Publications /publications.htm

[78] Steelcase Inc. (2007, August 9). Steelcase Workplace Index Survey examines "water cooler" conversations at work. Retrieved from http://www.prnewswire.com

[79] Steelcase Inc. (2007, August 9). Steelcase Workplace Index Survey examines 'water cooler' conversa- tions at work. Retrieved from http://www .prnewswire.com. See also Wademan Dowling, D. (2009, April 24). The truth about office rumors. *Harvard Business Review*. Retrieved from http://blogs.hbr.org/dowling/2009/04 /the-truth-about-office-rumors.html and DiFonzo, N. (2009). *The water cooler effect: An indispensable guide to understanding and harnessing the power of rumors*. New York: Penguin, pp. 151, 174-175, 180.

[80] Goman, C. K. (2006, June). I heard it through the grapevine. Paper presented at the International Association of Business Communicators, Vancouver, Canada.

[81] The *Marketing News* Staff. (2010, March 15). Digital dozen. Retrieved from http://www .marketingpower.com/resourceLibrary /Publications/MarketingNews/2010/3_15_10 /Digital%20Dozen.pdf

[82] DeMars, N. (2008). What you can do when you're the latest topic on the rumor mill. Retrieved from http://www.office-ethics.com/columns /gossip.html

[83] Israel, S. (2012, April 17). Social media's thought leaders: Intel's Ekaterina Walter. *Fortune*. Retrieved from www.forbes.com.

[84] Gentile, M. C. (2009, February 5). Business schools: A failing grade on ethics. *BusinessWeek*. Retrieved from http://www.businessweek.com

[85] Pfanner, E. (2009, April 18). Four convicted in Internet piracy case. *The New York Times*, p. B1.

[86] Women-owned businesses in the 21st century. (2010, October). U.S. Department of Commerce, Economics and Statistics Administration. Retrieved from http://www.esa.doc.gov /sites/default/files/reports/documents /women-owned-businesses.pdf

[87] Trudel, R., & Cotte, J. (2008, May 12). Does being ethical pay? *The Wall Street Journal*, p. R4.

[88] Bazerman, M. H., & Tenbrunsel, A. E. (2011, April 20). Stumbling into bad behavior. *The New York Times*. Retrieved from http://www.nytimes .com/2011/04/21/opinion/21bazerman.html

[89] O'Connell, V. (2009, January 7). Test for dwindling retail jobs spawns a culture of cheating. *The Wall Street Journal*, p. A1.

[90] Activity based on Richtel, M. (2012, January 20). Blogs vs. term papers. *The New York Times*. Retrieved from http://www.nytimes.com

[91] Activity based on Robert Half International & CareerBuilder. (2009). The EDGE Report: A preview of the post-recession job market. Retrieved from http://www.rhi.com /EDGEReport2009 and Carnevale, A. P., Strohl, J., & Melton, M. (2011). What's it worth? The economic value of college majors. Georgetown University Center on Education and the Workforce. Retrieved from http://www .georgetown.edu/grad/gppi/hpi/cew/pdfs /whatsitworth-complete.pdf

[92] Carnevale, A. P., Strohl, J., & Melton, M. (2011). What's it worth? The economic value of college majors. Georgetown University Center on Education and the Workforce, p. 5. Retrieved from http://www9.georgetown.edu/grad/gppi /hpi/cew/pdfs/whatsitworth-complete.pdf

[93] 2011 Employee job satisfaction and engagement: Gratification and commitment at work in a sluggish economy. (2011). Society for Human Resource Management. Retrieved from http://www.weknownext.com/docs /11-0618_Job_Satisfaction_FNL.pdf

[94] Do your reps' writing skills need a refresher? (2002, February). *Customer Contact Management Report*, p. 7.

[95] Armour, S. (2007, September 7). Did you hear the real story about office gossip? *USA Today*, p. 1B.

[96] Curtin, P. A., Gallicano, T., & Matthews, K. (2011, Spring). Millennials' approaches to ethical decision making: A survey of young public relations agency employees. *Public Relations Journal, 5*(2), 11.

[97] El Pollo Loco. (n.d.) Healthier dining. Retrieved from http://www.elpolloloco.com/Food /HealthyDining.aspx

[98] Jargon, J. (2008, May 9). Rival chicken chain calls out KFC. *USA Today*, p. B5.

Professionalism:
Team, Meeting, Listening, Nonverbal, and Etiquette Skills

OBJECTIVES

After studying this chapter, you should be able to

1 Understand the importance of teamwork in today's digital-era workplace, and explain how you can contribute positively to team performance.

2 Discuss effective practices and technologies for planning and participating in face-to-face meetings and virtual meetings.

3 Explain and apply active listening techniques.

4 Understand how effective nonverbal communication can help you advance your career.

5 Improve your competitive advantage by developing professionalism and business etiquette skills.

© Joshua Hodge Photography/the Agency Collection/Getty Images

Teamwork Keeps TBS on Top

Zooming in

Turner Broadcasting System programming reaches millions of households worldwide. The Atlanta-based media organization employs nearly 11,000 people in 150 locations worldwide.

TBS, with its 100 channels that include HBO, CNN, and TNT, relies on its workforce to stay on top of the ever-evolving world of television. To accomplish its mission, the organization has made teamwork one of its core values. According to its "Principles That Guide Us": "Office walls and organization charts are good for some things, but collaboration isn't one of them. Sharing information and ideas always makes us faster, smarter, and stronger."[1]

Nowhere is that mantra more evident than in the company's Animation, Young Adults & Kids Media division, overseer of Cartoon Network. The division's chief marketing officer, Brenda C. Freeman, manages 140 employees who work together to create programming that is watched in nearly 100 million U.S. homes.[2] Freeman has helped expand the division beyond airing classic cartoons such as *Scooby Doo—Where Are You!* to include original animated shows such as *Dexter's Laboratory*, live-action programming, and online games. She acknowledges that during a recent repositioning effort to expand the network's brand beyond cartoons, teamwork was essential.

"Collaboration between key departments allows for creative, out-of-the-box solutions to business objectives," Freeman explained.[3] She said that during the reorganization, TBS used its internal creative team to come up with the new branding and positioning rather than hiring an outside agency. "To make such a fundamental change in strategy, you need to make sure the entire organization is part of the solution."[4]

The team approach TBS has embraced as part of its corporate culture requires a high level of communication. Freeman explains that she elicits the most out of her team when she does not constrain people to "boxes in an organizational chart." She prefers a matrix approach to maximize the team's synergy. "It requires more constant communication," she says. "But that helps cross and forge bridges."[5]

You will learn more about Turner Broadcasting System and be asked to complete a relevant task at the end of this chapter.

Critical Thinking

- What are some of the main benefits teamwork brings to an organization?

- How can a team improve an organization's efficiency?

- What are some individual team member traits that reduce a team's effectiveness?

Adding Value to Professional Teams

LEARNING OBJECTIVE **1**
Understand the importance of teamwork in today's digital-era workplace, and explain how you can contribute positively to team performance.

Most businesses seek employees who can get along and deliver positive results that increase profits and boost their image. As a budding business professional, you have a stake in acquiring skills that will make you a strong job applicant and a valuable employee.

What Do Digital-Age Employers Want?

Employers are typically interested in four key areas: education, experience, hard skills, and soft skills. Hard skills refer to the technical skills in your field. Soft skills, however, are increasingly important in the knowledge-based economy of the digital era. Desirable competencies include not only oral and written communication skills but also active listening skills, appropriate nonverbal behavior, and proper business etiquette. In addition, employers such as Turner Broadcasting System want efficient and productive team members. They want managers and employees who are comfortable with diverse audiences, listen actively to customers and colleagues, make eye contact, and display good workplace manners. These soft skills are immensely important not only to be hired but also to be promoted.

Hiring managers naturally expect you to have technical expertise in your field and know the latest communication technology. Such skills and an impressive résumé may get you in the door. However, your long-term success depends on how well you communicate with your boss, coworkers, and customers and whether you can be an effective and contributing team member. Even in technical fields such as accounting and finance, employers are looking for soft skills. Staffing firm Robert Half surveyed chief financial officers and found that 65 percent "would hire someone with fewer technical skills if the candidate had particularly strong soft skills, such as communication and interpersonal abilities."[6]

REALITY CHECK: Tech Skills Are Not Enough

Financial professionals such as accountants "must be able to produce financial reports and perform complex calculations, as well as explain the meaning behind the numbers. This requires a broader skill set, which includes strong written, verbal and interpersonal capabilities."[7]

—**PAUL McDONALD,** *senior executive director, Robert Half International*

Courtesy of Paul McDonald

As we discussed in Chapter 1, the workplace is changing. Collaboration is the rule today, and an overwhelming majority of white-collar professionals (82 percent) need to partner with others to complete their work.[8] Far beyond meeting and conference rooms, workers collaborate all the time not only at their desks, but also in hallways and new flexible unassigned work environments suitable for spontaneous and informal collaboration. They may meet in rooms equipped with the latest technology tools or virtually via the Internet or smartphones. Tech companies—for example, Cisco, Pixar, and Skype—have redesigned their workspaces to meet this growing need for collaboration.[9] Needless to say, workers must have solid soft skills to be successful in this environment.

This chapter focuses on developing team, meeting, listening, nonverbal, and etiquette skills. These are some of the professional skills that employers seek in the hyperconnected, competitive work environment of the digital age.

Why Form Teams?

Today's workplace is teeming with teams. You might find yourself a part of a work team, project team, customer support team, supplier team, design team, planning team, functional team, or cross-functional team. You might be assigned to a committee, task force, steering group, quality control circle, flat team, hierarchical team, advisory team, action team, or some other group. All of these teams are formed to accomplish specific goals.

Businesses are constantly looking for ways to do jobs better at less cost. They are forming teams for the following reasons:

- **Better decisions.** Decisions are generally more accurate and effective because group members contribute different expertise and perspectives.
- **Faster response.** When action is necessary to respond to competition or to solve a problem, small groups and teams can act rapidly.
- **Increased productivity.** Because they are often closer to the action and to the customer, team members can see opportunities for improving efficiency.
- **Greater buy-in.** Decisions arrived at jointly are usually better received because members are committed to the solution and are more willing to support it.
- **Less resistance to change.** People who have input into decisions are less hostile, aggressive, and resistant to change.
- **Improved employee morale.** Personal satisfaction and job morale increase when teams are successful.
- **Reduced risks.** Responsibility for a decision is diffused on a team, thus carrying less risk for any individual.

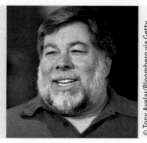
Despite the current popularity of teams, however, they are not a panacea for all work-place problems, particularly if such groups are dysfunctional. Harvard professor J. Richard Hackman claims that research "consistently shows that teams underperform despite all their extra resources."[11] This team expert and more recent studies suggest that organizations must strike a balance between solo effort—in highly creative endeavors—and collective action. "The most spectacularly creative people" are often introverted and prefer to work alone, which is when they do their best and most innovative work.[12] However, in most models of future organizations, teams—not individuals—function as the primary performance units.

Collaborating in Virtual Teams

The days when you could expect to work with a colleague who sat near you are long gone. Today you can expect to collaborate with fellow workers in other cities and even in other countries. Such collaborations are referred to as *virtual teams*. This is a group of people who, aided by information technology, must accomplish shared tasks largely without face-to-face contact across geographic boundaries, sometimes on different continents and across time zones.[13]

Although Yahoo and Best Buy have recently reversed their acclaimed work-at-home policies, virtual teams are here to stay. Consultant Jessica Lipnack concurs: "The 9:00 to 5:00 office, as we have known it, is more often than not—not. Many of us attend meetings in our pajamas, talk with people halfway around the globe, use insomnia to catch up online, worry about head-set not car-seat comfort, and partner with people we have never [met]—and may never meet—face-to-face." Software corporation SAP is headquartered in Walldorf, Germany, but it has established research and development centers in India, China, Israel, and the United States to save costs and to take advantage of global know-how. Each unit is highly specialized. Depending on the competence needed, employees from different locations form virtual teams that pool their expertise to complete particular assignments.[14] These teams must coordinate their work and complete their tasks across time and geographic zones. As you can see, work is increasingly viewed as *what you do* rather than a place you go.

In some organizations remote coworkers may be permanent employees from the same office or may be specialists called together for special projects. Regardless of the assignment, virtual teams can benefit from shared views, skills, and diversity.

Understanding the Four Phases of Team Development

Although formed for various purposes, teams normally go through predictable phases as they develop. The psychologist B. A. Tuckman identified four phases: *forming, storming, norming,* and *performing*, as Figure 2.1 illustrates.[16] Some groups get lucky and move quickly from forming to performing. But most struggle through disruptive, although ultimately constructive, team-building stages.

Forming.   During the first stage, individuals get to know each other. They often are overly polite and feel a bit awkward. As they search for similarities and attempt to bond, they begin to develop trust in each other. Members discuss fundamental topics such as why the team is necessary, who "owns" the team, whether membership is mandatory, how large the team should be, and what talents members can contribute. A leader functions primarily as a traffic director. Groups and teams should resist the efforts of some members to dash through the first stages and race to the performing stage. Moving slowly through the stages is necessary to build a cohesive, productive unit.

Storming.   During the second phase, members define their roles and responsibilities, decide how to reach their goals, and iron out the rules governing how they interact. Unfortunately, this stage often produces conflict, resulting in *storming*. A good leader, however, should step in to set limits, control the chaos, and offer suggestions. The leader will be most successful if she or he acts like a coach rather than a cop. Teams composed of dissimilar personality types may take longer to progress through the storming phase. Tempers may flare, sleep may be lost, leaders may be deposed. But most often the storm passes, and a cohesive group emerges.

Norming.   Once the sun returns to the sky, teams and groups enter the *norming* stage. Tension subsides, roles are clarified, and information begins to flow among members. The group periodically checks its agenda to remind itself of its progress toward its goals. People are careful not to shake the hard-won camaraderie and formation of a single-minded purpose. Formal leadership is unnecessary because everyone takes on leadership functions. Important data are shared with the entire group, and mutual interdependence becomes typical. The group or team begins to move smoothly in one direction. Figure 2.1 shows how a team might proceed through the four phases while solving a problem and reaching a decision.

Performing.   In Tuckman's team growth model, some groups never reach the final stage of *performing*. For those that survive the first three phases, however, the final stage is gratifying. Group members have established routines and a shared language. They develop loyalty and a willingness to resolve all problems. A "can-do" mentality pervades as they progress toward their goal. Fights are clean, and members continue working together without grudges. Best of all, information flows freely, deadlines are met, and production exceeds expectations.

Figure 2.1   Four Phases of Team Development in Decision Making

Forming
- Select members.
- Become acquainted.
- Build trust.
- Form collaborative culture.

Storming
- Identify problems.
- Collect and share information.
- Establish decision criteria.
- Prioritize goals.

Norming
- Discuss alternatives.
- Evaluate outcomes.
- Apply criteria.
- Prioritize alternatives.

Performing
- Select alternative.
- Analyze effects.
- Implement plan.
- Manage project.

© Cengage Learning 2015

Examining Positive and Negative Team Member Traits

Team members who are committed to achieving the group's purpose contribute by displaying positive behavior. How can you be a good team member? The most effective groups have members who are willing to establish rules and abide by them. Effective team members are able to analyze tasks and define problems so that they can work toward solutions. They offer information and try out their ideas on the group to stimulate discussion. They show interest in others' ideas by listening actively. Helpful team members also seek to involve silent members. They strive to resolve differences, and they encourage a warm, supportive climate by praising and agreeing with others. When they sense that agreement is near, they review significant points and move the group toward its goal by synthesizing points of understanding.

Not all groups, however, have members who contribute positively. Negative behavior is shown by those who constantly put down the ideas and suggestions of others. They insult, criticize, and aggress against others. They waste the group's time with unnecessary recounting of personal achievements or irrelevant topics. The team clown distracts the group with excessive joke-telling, inappropriate comments, and disruptive antics. Also disturbing are team members who withdraw and refuse to be drawn out. They have nothing to say, either for or against ideas being considered. To be a productive and welcome member of a group, be prepared to perform the positive tasks described in Figure 2.2. Avoid the negative behaviors.

Combating Groupthink

Conflict is normal in team interactions, and successful teams are able to resolve it using the methods you just learned. But some teams avoid conflict. They smooth things over and in doing so may fall victim to *groupthink*. This is a term coined by theorist Irving Janis to describe faulty decision-making processes by team members who are overly eager to agree with one another.[17] Apparently, when we deviate from a group, we fear rejection. Scientists variously call this natural reluctance "the pain of independence"[18] or describe it as "the hazards of courage."[19]

Several conditions can lead to groupthink: team members with similar backgrounds, a lack of systematic procedures, a demand for a quick decision, and a strong leader who favors a specific outcome. Symptoms of groupthink include pressure placed on any member who argues against the group's mutual beliefs, self-censorship of thoughts that stray from the group's agreement, collective efforts to rationalize, and an unquestioned belief in the group's moral authority. Teams suffering from groupthink fail to check alternatives, are biased in collecting and evaluating information, and ignore the risks of the preferred choice. They may also neglect to work out a contingency plan in case the preferred choice fails.[20]

Effective teams avoid groupthink by striving for team diversity—in age, gender, background, experience, and training. They encourage open discussion, search for relevant

Figure 2.2 Positive and Negative Group Behaviors

Positive Group Behaviors
- Setting rules and abiding by them
- Analyzing tasks and defining problems
- Contributing information and ideas
- Showing interest by listening actively
- Encouraging members to participate

Negative Group Behaviors
- Blocking the ideas of others
- Insulting and criticizing others
- Wasting the group's time
- Making improper jokes and comments
- Failing to stay on task
- Withdrawing, failing to participate

© Cengage Learning 2015

information, evaluate many alternatives, consider how a decision will be implemented, and plan for contingencies in case the decision doesn't work out.

Reaching Group Decisions

The way teams reach decisions greatly affects their morale and commitment, as well as the implementation of any team decision. In U.S. culture the majority usually rules, but other methods, five of which are discussed here, may be more effective. As you study these methods, think about which would be best for routine decisions and which would be best for dealing with emergencies.

- **Majority.** Group members vote and a majority wins. This method results in a quick decision but may leave an alienated minority uncommitted to implementation.
- **Consensus.** Discussion continues until all team members have aired their opinions and, ultimately, agree. This method is time-consuming; however, it produces creative, high-quality discussion and generally elicits commitment by all members to implement the decision.
- **Minority.** Typically, a subcommittee investigates and makes a recommendation for action. This method is useful when the full group cannot get together to make a decision or when time is short.
- **Averaging.** Members haggle, bargain, wheedle, and negotiate to reach a middle position, which often requires compromise. With this method, the opinions of the least knowledgeable members may cancel the opinions of the most knowledgeable.
- **Authority rule with discussion.** The leader, boss, or manager listens to team members' ideas, but the final decision is his or hers. This method encourages lively discussion and results in participatory decision making. However, team members must have good communication skills. This method also requires a leader who is willing to make decisions.

Defining Successful Teams

The use of teams has been called the solution to many ills in today's workplace.[21] Someone even observed that as an acronym TEAM means "Together, Everyone Achieves More."[22] Many teams, however, do not work well together. In fact, some teams can actually increase frustration, lower productivity, and create employee dissatisfaction. Experts who have studied team workings and decisions have discovered that effective teams share some or all of the following characteristics.

Stay Small and Embrace Diversity.   Teams may range from 2 to 25 members, although 4 or 5 is optimal for many projects. Teams smaller than ten members tend to agree more easily on a common objective and form more cohesive units.[23] For the most creative decisions, teams generally have male and female members who differ in age, ethnicity, social background, training, and experience. The key business advantage of diversity is the ability to view a project and its context from multiple perspectives. Many of us tend to think that everyone in the world is like us because we know only our own experience. Teams with members from different ethnicities and cultures can look at projects beyond the limited view of one culture. Many organizations are finding that diverse teams can produce innovative solutions with broader applications than homogeneous teams can.

Agree on Purpose.   An effective team begins with a purpose. Working from a general purpose to specific goals typically requires a huge investment of time and effort. Meaningful discussions, however, motivate team members to buy in to the project. When the Great Lakes Coast Guard faced the task of keeping commerce moving when the lakes and rivers froze, it brought all the stakeholders together to discuss the mission. The U.S. Coast Guard, the Canadian Coast Guard, and the maritime industry formed a partnership to clear and flush ice from the Great Lakes and connecting rivers during winter months. Agreeing on the purpose was the first step in developing a concerted team effort. Preseason planning and daily phone conferences cemented the mission and gained buy-in from all stakeholders.[24]

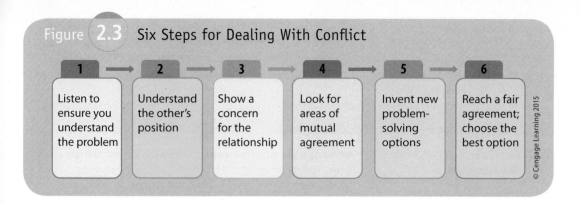

Figure 2.3 Six Steps for Dealing With Conflict

1	2	3	4	5	6
Listen to ensure you understand the problem	Understand the other's position	Show a concern for the relationship	Look for areas of mutual agreement	Invent new problem-solving options	Reach a fair agreement; choose the best option

© Cengage Learning 2015

Agree on Procedures.   The best teams develop procedures to guide them. They set up intermediate goals with deadlines. They assign roles and tasks, requiring all members to contribute equivalent amounts of real work. They decide how they will reach decisions using one of the strategies discussed earlier. Procedures are continually evaluated to ensure movement toward the attainment of the team's goals.

Confront Conflict.   Poorly functioning teams avoid conflict, preferring sulking, gossiping, or bickering. A better plan is to acknowledge conflict and address the root of the problem openly using the six-step plan outlined in Figure 2.3. Although it may feel emotionally risky, direct confrontation saves time and enhances team commitment in the long run. To be constructive, however, confrontation must be task oriented, not person oriented. An open airing of differences, in which all team members have a chance to speak their minds, should center on the strengths and weaknesses of the various positions and ideas—not on personalities. After hearing all sides, team members must negotiate a fair settlement, no matter how long it takes.

Communicate Effectively.   The best teams exchange information and contribute ideas freely in an informal environment often facilitated by technology. Team members speak and write clearly and concisely, avoiding generalities. They encourage feedback. Listeners become actively involved, read body language, and ask clarifying questions before responding. Tactful, constructive disagreement is encouraged. Although a team's task is taken seriously, successful teams are able to inject humor into their face-to-face interactions.

Collaborate Rather Than Compete.   Effective team members are genuinely interested in achieving team goals instead of receiving individual recognition. They contribute ideas and feedback unselfishly. They monitor team progress, including what's going right, what's going wrong, and what to do about it. They celebrate individual and team accomplishments.

Accept Ethical Responsibilities.   Teams as a whole have ethical responsibilities to their members, to their larger organizations, and to society. Members have a number of specific responsibilities to each other. As a whole, teams have a responsibility to represent the organization's view and respect its privileged information. They should not discuss with outsiders any sensitive issues without permission. In addition, teams have a broader obligation to avoid advocating actions that would endanger members of society at large.

Share Leadership.   Effective teams often have no formal leader. Instead, leadership rotates to those with the appropriate expertise as the team evolves and moves from one phase to another. Many teams operate under a democratic approach. This approach can achieve buy-in to team decisions, boost morale, and create fewer hurt feelings and less resentment. In times of crisis, however, a strong team member may need to step up as a leader.

The following checklist summarizes effective techniques for developing successful teams.

Developing Team Effectiveness

© Daniilantiq/Shutterstock.com

- **Establish small teams.** Smaller teams function more efficiently and more effectively than larger teams.

- **Encourage diversity.** Innovative teams typically include members who differ in age, gender, ethnicity, and background. Team members should possess the necessary technical expertise, problem-solving skills, and interpersonal skills.

- **Determine the purpose, procedures, and roles.** Members must understand the task at hand and what is expected of them. Teams function best when operating procedures are ironed out early and each member assumes a specific role.

- **Acknowledge and manage conflict.** Conflict is productive when it motivates a team to search for new ideas, increase participation, delay premature decisions, or discuss disagreements. Keep conflict centered on issues rather than on people.

- **Cultivate effective communication skills.** Productive team members articulate ideas clearly and concisely, recognize nonverbal cues, and listen actively.

- **Advance an environment of open communication.** Teams are most productive when members trust each other and feel free to discuss all viewpoints openly in an informal atmosphere.

- **Encourage collaboration and discourage competition.** Sharing information in a cooperative effort to achieve the team purpose must be more important than competing with other members for individual achievement.

- **Share leadership.** Members with the most expertise should lead at various times during the project's evolution.

- **Strive to make fair decisions.** Effective teams resolve problems without forcing members into a win–lose situation.

- **Lighten up.** The most successful teams take their task seriously, but they are also able to laugh at themselves and interject humor to enliven team proceedings.

- **Continually assess performance.** Teams should establish checkpoints along the way to determine whether they are meeting their objectives and adjust procedures if progress is unsatisfactory.

LEARNING OBJECTIVE **2**

Discuss effective practices and technologies for planning and participating in face-to-face meetings and virtual meetings.

Planning and Participating in Face-to-Face and Virtual Meetings

As you prepare to join the workforce, expect to attend meetings—lots of them! Estimates suggest that workers on average spend four hours a week in meetings and consider more than half of that time as wasted.[25] Managers spend even more time in meetings. Studies of executives in Europe and the United States reveal that nearly 60 percent of managers devote 21 to 60 percent of their workweeks to meetings with the average meeting lasting nearly three hours.[26] In one survey, managers considered over a third of meeting time unproductive and reported that two thirds of meetings fell short of their stated objectives.[27]

Meetings consist of three or more people who assemble to pool information, solicit feedback, clarify policy, seek consensus, and solve problems. However, as growing numbers of employees work at distant locations, meetings have changed. People are meeting regularly, but not always face-to-face. To be able to exchange information effectively and efficiently, you should know how to plan and participate in face-to-face as well as other kinds of meetings.

Making Face-to-Face Meetings Productive

As inevitable and commonplace as meetings are, most workers dread them. Nearly 50 percent of respondents in a recent Salary.com survey named "too many meetings" as the biggest waste of time at work.[29] One writer called them "the black holes of the workday"[30]; another complained that "long-winded colleagues consume all available oxygen, killing good ideas by asphyxiation."[31] In spite of their bad reputation, if meetings are well run, workers actually desire more, not fewer, of them.[32] Our task, then, as business communicators is to learn how to make them more efficient, satisfying, and productive.

Although meetings are disliked, they can be career-critical. At meetings, judgments are formed and careers are made or blunted.[33] Therefore, instead of treating them as thieves of your valuable time, try to see them as golden opportunities to demonstrate your leadership, communication, and problem-solving skills. So that you can make the most of these opportunities, this section outlines techniques for planning and conducting successful meetings.

Deciding Whether a Meeting Is Necessary

A face-to-face meeting provides the most nonverbal cues and other signals that help us interpret the intended meaning of words. Thus, an in-person meeting is the richest of available media. No meeting should be called unless it is important, can't wait, and requires an exchange of ideas. If people are merely being informed, send an e-mail, text message, memo, or letter. Leave a telephone or voice mail message, but don't call a costly meeting. Remember, the real expense of a meeting is the lost productivity of all the people attending. To decide whether the purpose of the meeting is valid, consult the key people who will be attending. Ask them what outcomes they desire and how to achieve those goals. This consultation also sets a collaborative tone and encourages full participation.

Selecting Participants. The purpose of the meeting determines the number of participants, as shown in Figure 2.4. If the meeting purpose is motivational, such as an awards

Figure **2.4** Meeting Purpose and Number of Participants

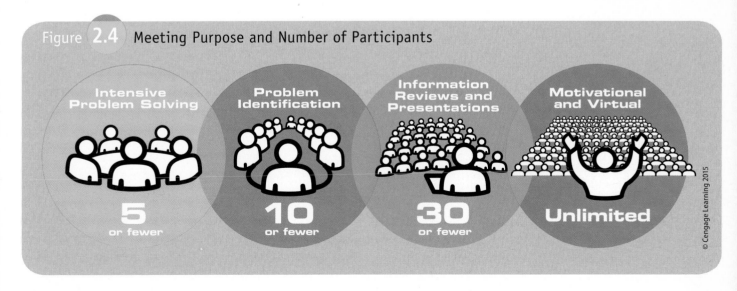

© Cengage Learning 2015

ceremony for sales reps of cosmetics giant Avon, then the number of participants is potentially unlimited. However, to make decisions, the best number is five or fewer participants, as studies at 3M Corporation suggest.[34] Others believe that six to eight is the optimal meeting size.[35]

Ideally, decision makers and people with the information necessary to make the decision should attend. Also attending should be people who will be responsible for implementing the decision and representatives of groups who will benefit from the decision. Let's consider Timberland. After being acquired by VF Corporation, the outdoor apparel maker is continuing its signature employee volunteer program. Company leaders might meet with managers, employee representatives, and community leaders to decide how best to "green" a community center, improve school grounds, or frame houses for families of tornado victims.[36]

Distributing Advance Information.   At least two days in advance of a meeting, distribute an agenda of topics to be discussed. Also include any reports or materials that participants should read in advance. For continuing groups, you might also include a copy of the minutes of the previous meeting. To keep meetings productive, limit the number of agenda items. Remember, the narrower the focus, the greater the chances for success. A good agenda, as illustrated in Figure 2.5, covers the following information:

- Date and place of meeting
- Start time and end time
- Brief description of each topic, in order of priority, including the names of individuals who are responsible for performing some action
- Proposed allotment of time for each topic
- Any premeeting preparation expected of participants

Figure 2.5 Typical Meeting Agenda

AGENDA
Quantum Travel International
Staff Meeting
September 4, 2015
10 to 11 a.m.
Conference Room

I. Call to order; roll call

II. Approval of agenda

III. Approval of minutes from previous meeting

		Person	Proposed Time
IV.	Committee reports		
	A. Website update	Jared	5 minutes
	B. Tour packages	Lakisha	10 minutes
V.	Old business		
	A. Equipment maintenance	John	5 minutes
	B. Client escrow accounts	Alicia	5 minutes
	C. Internal newsletter	Adrienne	5 minutes
VI.	New business		
	A. New accounts	Garth	5 minutes
	B. Pricing policy for Asian tours	Minh	15 minutes

VII. Announcements

VIII. Chair's summary, adjournment

Using Digital Calendars to Schedule Meetings. Finding a time when everyone can meet is often difficult. Fortunately, digital calendars now make the task quicker and more efficient. Two of the most popular digital calendar programs are Google Calendar and Yahoo Calendar. Microsoft Outlook also provides a calendar program, as shown in Figure 2.6. Online calendars enable you to make appointments, schedule meetings, and keep track of daily activities. To schedule meetings, you enter a new meeting request, and add the names of attendees. You select a date, enter a start and end time, and list the meeting subject and location. Then the meeting request goes to each attendee. Later you check the attendee availability tab to see a list of all meeting attendees. As the meeting time approaches, the program automatically sends reminders to attendees.

Getting the Meeting Started. To avoid wasting time and irritating attendees, always start meetings on time–even if some participants are missing. For the same reasons, don't give a quick recap to anyone who arrives late. Open the meeting with a three- to five-minute introduction that includes the following:

- Goal and length of the meeting
- Background of topics or problems
- Possible solutions and constraints
- Tentative agenda
- Ground rules to be followed

Typical ground rules are communicating openly, being supportive, listening carefully, participating fully, confronting conflict frankly, and following the agenda. More formal groups follow parliamentary procedures based on Robert's Rules. The next step is to assign one attendee to take minutes and one to act as a recorder. The recorder uses a computer and projector or stands at a flipchart or whiteboard to list the main ideas being discussed and agreements reached.

Figure 2.6 Using Calendar Programs

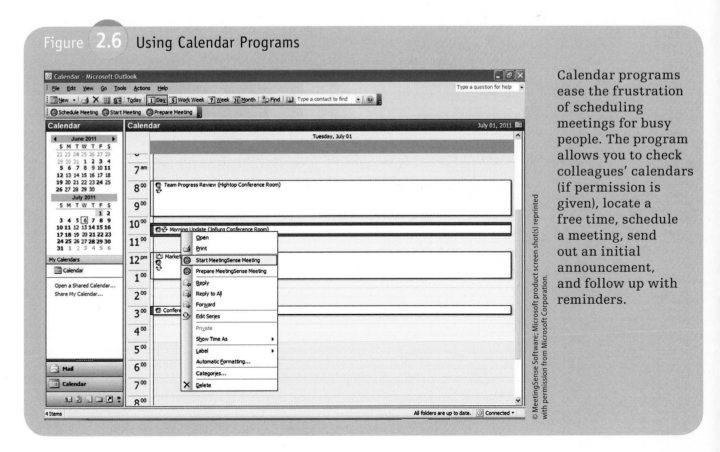

Calendar programs ease the frustration of scheduling meetings for busy people. The program allows you to check colleagues' calendars (if permission is given), locate a free time, schedule a meeting, send out an initial announcement, and follow up with reminders.

Moving the Meeting Along.

After the preliminaries, the leader should say as little as possible. Like a talk show host, an effective leader makes "sure that each panel member gets some air time while no one member steals the show."[37] If the group has one member who monopolizes, the leader might say, "Thanks, Michelle, for that perspective, but please hold your next point while we hear how Ryan would respond to that." This technique also encourages quieter participants to speak up.

To avoid allowing digressions to sidetrack the group, try generating a "parking lot" list. This is a list of important but divergent issues that should be discussed later. Another way to handle digressions is to say, "Folks, we're drifting astray here. Please forgive me for pressing on, but let's return to the central issue of . . . ." It is important to adhere to the agenda and the schedule. Equally important, when the group seems to have reached a consensus, is to summarize the group's position and check to see whether everyone agrees.

Participating Actively and Productively.

Meetings are an opportunity for you to showcase your abilities and boost your career. To get the most out of the meetings you attend, try these techniques:[38]

- **Arrive early.** You show respect and look well organized when you arrive a little early.
- **Come prepared.** Bring the agenda and any distributed materials. Study the topics and be ready with questions, comments, and good ideas.
- **Have a positive attitude.** Use positive body language; speak energetically.
- **Contribute respectfully.** Wait your turn to speak; raise your hand to be recognized.
- **Wait for others to finish.** Show respect and good manners by not interrupting.
- **Keep your voice calm and pleasant, yet energetic.** Avoid showing anger as this focuses attention on your behavior rather than on your ideas.
- **Give credit to others.** Gain allies and enhance your credibility by recognizing others in front of peers and superiors.
- **Use your cell phone, tablet, and laptop only for meeting-related tasks.** Focus your attention on the meeting, not on answering e-mails or working on your computer.
- **Help summarize.** Assist the meeting leader by reviewing points you have noted.
- **Express your views IN the meeting.** Build trust by not holding postmeeting "sidebars" that involve criticism and judgments.
- **Follow up.** Send the signal that you are efficient and caring by completing the actions assigned to you.

REALITY CHECK: How Smart Are Smartphones and Tablets at Meetings?

During today's meetings attendees may bring smartphones and tablets to take notes. Because these devices are usually associated with gaming and texting, it's smart to explain. Matt Eventoff, founder of Princeton Public Speaking, gives this advice: "As soon as you take the device out, tell the other attendees, 'I use my iPad or phone to take notes.' That way, no one will question whether you're paying attention."

—**MATT EVENTOFF,** *owner, Princeton Public Speaking, a communication training business*

Handling Conflict in Meetings.

As you learned earlier, conflict is natural and even desirable. However, it can also cause awkwardness and uneasiness. In meetings, conflict typically develops when people feel unheard or misunderstood. If two people clash, the best approach is to encourage each to make a complete case while group members give their full attention. Let each one question the other. Then, the leader should summarize what was said, and the participants should offer comments. The group may modify a recommendation or suggest alternatives before reaching consensus on a direction to follow.

Ending and Following Up.   End the meeting at the agreed time or sooner. The leader should summarize all decisions, assigned tasks, and deadlines. It may be necessary to ask attendees to volunteer for completing action items. All participants should understand what was accomplished. One effective technique that encourages full participation is "round-robin." Everyone takes turns summarizing briefly his or her interpretation of what was decided and what happens next. Of course, this closure technique works best with smaller groups. The leader should conclude by asking the group to set a time for the next meeting. He or she should assure the group that a report will follow. Finally, the leader should thank participants for attending.

If minutes were taken, they should be distributed within a couple of days of the meeting. Software programs, such as that shown in Figure 2.7, enable you to follow a structured template that includes brief meeting minutes, key points and decisions, and action items. The leader needs to ensure that decisions are executed. The leader may need to call participants to remind them of their assignments and also to solicit help if necessary.

Using Effective Practices and Technologies in Virtual Meetings

One of the major trends in today's workplace is the rise of virtual meetings instead of face-to-face meetings. *Virtual meetings* are gatherings of participants who are connected technologically. As travel costs rise and companies slash budgets, many organizations are cutting back on meetings that require travel.[39] In addition, more and more people work together but are not located in the same spot. Instead of meeting face-to-face, people have found other ways to exchange ideas, brainstorm, build consensus, and develop personal relationships. They may meet in audioconferences using telephones or in videoconferences using the Internet. Steady improvement in telecommunications networks, software, and computer processing continues to fuel the shift to virtual meetings. These meetings have many purposes, including training employees, making sales presentations, coordinating team activities, and talking to customers.

Saving travel costs and reducing employee fatigue are significant reasons for the digital displacement of business travel. Darryl Draper, a Subaru customer-service training manager,

Figure 2.7 E-Mail Meeting Minutes

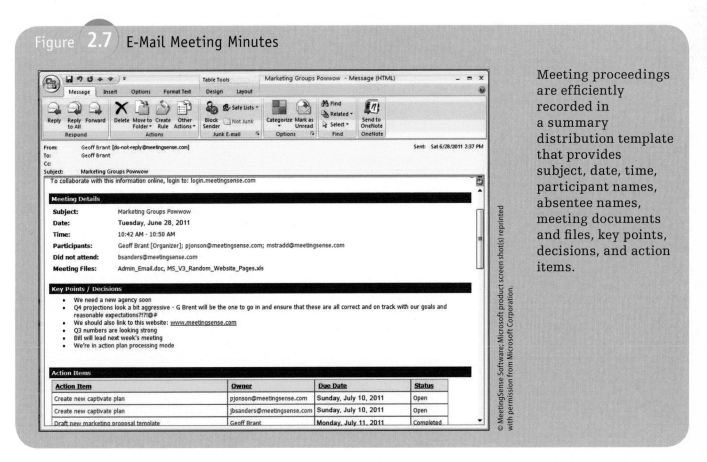

Meeting proceedings are efficiently recorded in a summary distribution template that provides subject, date, time, participant names, absentee names, meeting documents and files, key points, decisions, and action items.

© MeetingSense Software; Microsoft product screen shot(s) reprinted with permission from Microsoft Corporation.

formerly traveled nine months of the year. Now she does nearly all of her training online. She estimates that, when traveling, she reached about 100 people every six months at a cost of $300 a person. Now she reaches 2,500 people every six months at a cost of 75 cents a person.[40]

Virtual meetings are possible through the use of a number of efficient tools including audioconferencing, videoconferencing, and Web conferencing.

Audioconferencing. Among the simplest collaboration tools is *audioconferencing* (also called *teleconferencing, conference calling,* or *phone conferencing*). One or more people use a handset or an enhanced speakerphone to confer with others by telephone. To make a call, a company engages a telecommunications carrier and participants dial a given number. They enter a pass code and are admitted to a conference bridge. Participants at both ends can speak and be heard simultaneously. Thanks to mobile devices, people can participate in audioconferences wherever they receive a signal, even at the beach. Although audioconferencing is not as glitzy as other communication tools, it is a mainstay in the teleconferencing industry because of its low cost.

Videoconferencing. If meeting participants need to see each other or share documents, they may use *videoconferencing.* This tool combines video, audio, and communication networking technologies for real-time interaction.

At the high end of videoconferencing systems are *telepresence rooms.* These rooms typically are equipped with three huge curved screens, custom lighting, and advanced acoustics. Sharper than the best high-definition television sets, images may be magnified to scrutinize even the microcircuitry on new electronic products. Multiple high-definition monitors deliver life-size images so real that the next time you see a participant, you feel as if you've met that person before, says one proponent.[41] Although the price tag may reach $350,000 per room, companies such as Cisco Systems figure it saves $100 million in yearly travel costs. What's more, Cisco's reduced travel cuts greenhouse gas emissions from travel by 10 percent.[42] More conventional videoconference rooms may cost $5,000 to $80,000 a room. Whether using high- or low-end conferencing tools, participants do not have to journey to distant meetings; rather, they can interact in real time. Organizations reduce travel expenses, travel time, greenhouse gases, and employee fatigue.

Web Conferencing. *Web conferencing* is similar to videoconferencing but may work with or without the transmission of pictures of the participants. Attendees use their computers to access an online virtual meeting room where they can present PowerPoint slides or share spreadsheets or Word documents, just as they might do in a face-to-face meeting. Web conferencing is particularly useful for team meetings, training, and sales presentations.

Enterprise-level videoconferencing systems are transporting professionals to a futuristic world of virtual face-to-face meetings. Telepresence rooms like the one pictured here feature high definition, multiple-screen systems with such low delay that participants can carry on conversations and read the body language of people half way around the world. The benefits of videoconferencing are so wide-ranging that telepresence applications are replacing business travel, doctor's visits, and even courtroom appearances. What are the advantages of videoconferencing compared to face-to-face meetings?

© Monty Rakusen/Cultura/Getty Images

Features of Web conferencing programs typically include slideshow presentations, live or streaming video, tours of websites in which users may participate, meeting recording, whiteboard with annotation capabilities, screen sharing, and text chat. GoToMeeting, a reasonably priced commercial conferencing tool, enables people to launch meetings by sending instant messages to attendees, who click on an embedded link to join the group. WebEx offers a richer Web conferencing tool, including whiteboarding and other advanced functions.

It's even possible to participate in conferences using your iPhone or other smartphone while having breakfast on the way to work—or poolside.

Skype, a virtually free conferencing tool popular with students and expatriates, is also used by businesspeople. It allows conferencing with or without a camera. All that is needed is a laptop, tablet, or a smartphone; a microphone; and an optional webcam. Constantly evolving, Web conferencing is changing the way businesspeople work together. Figure 2.8 shows how athletic gear company Sportster Marketing used Web conferencing to meet virtually and design a new sports watch.

Planning Virtual Meetings and Interacting Professionally.   Although the same good meeting management techniques discussed for face-to-face meetings prevail, additional skills and practices are important in virtual meetings. A major problem when participants are not facing each other is that any small infraction or miscue can be blown out of proportion. Words and tone can be easily misinterpreted. In addition, bandwidth and technology glitches can derail virtual meetings. The following suggestions from experienced meeting facilitators will help you ace virtual meetings.[43]

Premeeting Considerations.   To conduct successful virtual meetings or teleconferences, address a number of premeeting issues. Most important, decide what technology will be used. Be sure that everyone is able to participate fully using that technology. If someone can't see what is happening on screen, the entire meeting can be disrupted and delayed. Some participants may need coaching before the session begins. Set the time of the meeting, preferably using Coordinated Universal Time (UTC) so that participants in different time zones are not confused. Be particularly mindful of how the meeting schedule affects others. Avoid spanning a lunch hour, holding someone overtime, or making someone arrive extra early.

Figure 2.8 Understanding Web Conferencing

1. **E-Mail Contact**
Enter
www.meet

Alan T., president of Sportster Marketing, an athletic gear company in Seattle, WA, sends an email to Meghan R., chief designer at NexxtDesign in Venice, CA, to discuss a new sports watch. The e-mail includes the meeting date and time and a link to launch the session.

2. **Virtual Meeting**
sketch #1

When the Web conference begins, participants see live video of each other's faces on their screens. They look at photos of sports watches, share ideas, sketch designs on a shared "virtual whiteboard," and review contract terms.

3. **Design Collaboration**
design: sportster 1
Enter   Enter   Enter

NexxtDesign artists and Sportster Marketing managers use peer-to-peer software that allows them to share spaces on each other's computers. The software enables them to take turns modifying the designs, and it also tracks all the changes.

© Cengage Learning 2015

For global meetings decide what language will be used. If that language may be difficult for some participants, think about using simple expressions and repeating major ideas. Before the meeting distribute any materials that will be shared. If documents will be edited or marked during the meeting, be sure participants know how to use the online editing tools. Finally, to avoid panic at the last minute, encourage participants to log in 15 minutes early. Some programs require downloads and installations that can cause immense frustration if not done early.

Ground Rules for Virtual Meetings.   During virtual meetings, establishing a few ground rules achieves the best results. Before beginning, explain how questions may be asked and answered. Many meeting programs allow participants to "raise their hands" with an icon on a side panel of the computer screen. Then they can type in their question for the leader and others to see. Unless the meeting involves people who know each other well, participants in audioconferences should always say their names before beginning to comment.

One of the biggest problems of virtual meetings is background noise from participants' offices or homes. You might hear dogs barking, telephones ringing, and toilets flushing. Meeting planners disagree on whether to require participants to put their phones on mute. Although the mute button reduces noise, it also prevents immediate participation and tends to deaden the conference. If you decide to ask participants to mute their phones, make it part of your ground rules and include a reminder at the beginning of the session. In addition, remind the group to turn off all phones, alarms, and electronic reminders. As a personal ground rule, don't multitask—and that includes texting and checking e-mail—during virtual meetings. Giving your full attention is critical.

Techniques for Collaborating Successfully in Virtual Meetings.   Collaborating successfully in virtual meetings requires managing limitations. For example, when individuals meet face-to-face, they usually can recognize blank looks when people do not understand something being discussed. But in virtual meetings participants and presenters cannot always see each other. "[Participants] will lose place, lose focus, and lose attention to the meeting," one meeting expert noted.[44] He also warned that participants won't tell you if are lost. As a result, when presenting ideas at a virtual meeting, you should be as precise as possible. Give examples and use simple language. Recap and summarize often. Confirm your understanding of what is being discussed. If you are a presenter, project an upbeat, enthusiastic, and strong voice. Without eye contact and nonverbal cues, the best way to keep the attention of the audience is through a powerful voice.

To encourage participation and avoid traffic jams with everyone talking at once, experts suggest a number of techniques. Participants soon lose interest if the leader is the only one talking. Therefore, encourage dialogue by asking questions of specific people. Often you will learn not only what the person is thinking but also what others feel but have not stated. Another technique that promotes discussion and gives everyone a chance to speak is "round-robin," which you learned about earlier. Go through the list of participants inviting each to speak for 30 seconds without interruption. If individuals have nothing to say, they may pass when their names are called. Leaders should avoid asking vague and leading questions such as, *Does everyone agree?* Remote attendees cannot answer easily without drowning out each other's responses.

One final suggestion involves building camaraderie and trust. For teams with distant members, it helps to leave time before or after the scheduled meeting for small talk. A few moments of chat build personal bonds and establish a warm environment. Even with larger, unfamiliar groups, you can build trust and interest by dialing in early and greeting others as they join the group.

Virtual meetings are the wave of the future. Learning to plan and participate in them professionally will enhance your career as a business communicator. The following checklist summarizes helpful techniques for both face-to-face and virtual meetings.

Planning and Participating in Productive Meetings

Before the Meeting

- **Consider alternatives.** Unless a topic is important and pressing, avoid calling a meeting. Perhaps an e-mail message, telephone call, or announcement would serve the purpose.

- **Invite the right people.** Invite people who have information and authority to make the decision and implement it.

- **Distribute an agenda.** Prepare an agenda that includes the date and place of the meeting, the starting and ending time, a brief description of each topic, the names of the people responsible for any action, and a proposed time allotment for each topic.

- **Use a calendar program.** If available, use calendaring software to set a meeting date, issue invitations, and send the agenda.

- **Train participants on technology.** Especially for virtual meetings, be sure participants are comfortable with the conferencing software.

During the Meeting

- **Start on time and introduce the agenda.** Discuss the goal and length of the meeting, provide backgrounds of topics for discussion, suggest possible solutions and constraints, propose a tentative agenda, and clarify the ground rules for the meeting.

- **Appoint a secretary and a recorder.** Ask one attendee to take notes of the proceedings, and ask another person to record discussion topics on a flipchart or whiteboard.

- **Encourage participation.** Ensure that all participants' views are heard and that no one monopolizes the discussion. Avoid digressions by steering the group back to the topics on the agenda. In virtual meetings be sure participants identify themselves before speaking.

- **Confront conflict frankly.** Encourage people who disagree to explain their positions completely. Then restate each position and ask for group comments. The group may modify a recommendation or suggest alternatives before agreeing on a plan of action.

- **Summarize along the way.** When the group seems to reach a consensus, summarize and see whether all members agree.

Ending the Meeting and Following Up

- **Review meeting decisions.** At the end of the meeting, consider using "round-robin" to be sure everyone understands what has been decided. Discuss action items, and establish a schedule for completion.

- **Distribute minutes of the meeting.** A few days after the meeting, distribute the minutes. Use an e-mail template, if available, to share meeting minutes.

- **Remind people of action items.** Follow up by calling people to see whether they are completing the actions recommended at the meeting.

© Daniilantiq/Shutterstock.com

Listening in the Workplace

"No one ever listened himself out of a job," observed President Calvin Coolidge many years ago. His words are even more significant today as listening skills are part of the professional traits that employers seek when looking for well-rounded job candidates.

Now, you may be thinking, everyone knows how to listen. Most of us believe that listening is an automatic response to noise. We do it without thinking. Perhaps that explains why so many of us are poor listeners. In this section we explore the importance of listening, the kinds of listening required in the workplace, and improving listening skills. Although many of the tips for improving your listening skills will be effective in your personal life, our discussion centers primarily on workplace and employment needs.

As you learned earlier, workers are communicating more than ever before, largely because of the Internet, social media, teamwork, global competition, and an emphasis on customer service. A vital ingredient in every successful workplace is high-quality communication, and three quarters of high-quality communication involves listening.[45]

Listening skills are important for career success, organization effectiveness, and worker satisfaction. Numerous studies and experts report that good listeners make good managers and that good listeners advance more rapidly in their organizations.[46] Studies of Fortune 500 companies report that soft skills such as listening, writing, and speaking are most likely to determine hiring and career success.[47] Listening is especially important in the workplace because we spend so much time doing it. Although estimates vary, most workers spend 30 to 45 percent of their communication time listening.[48] Executives spend 60 to 70 percent of their communication time listening.[49]

Poor Listening Habits

Although executives and employees devote the bulk of their communication time to listening, research suggests that they're not very good at it. In fact, most of us are poor listeners. Some estimates indicate that only half of the oral messages heard in a day are completely understood.[50] Experts say that we listen at only 25 percent efficiency. In other words, we ignore, forget, distort, or misunderstand 75 percent of everything we hear.

Poor listening habits may result from several factors. Lack of training is one significant factor. Few schools give as much emphasis to listening as they do to the development of reading, speaking, and writing skills. In addition, our listening skills may be less than perfect because of the large number of competing sounds and stimuli in our lives that interfere with concentration. Finally, we are inefficient listeners because we are able to process speech much faster than others can speak. Although most speakers talk at about 125 to 175 words per minute, listeners can listen at 450 words per minute.[51] The resulting lag time fosters daydreaming, which clearly reduces listening efficiency.

Most of us can probably recall a situation in which smart portable electronics created a distraction, making listening difficult.

Types of Workplace Listening

On the job you can expect to be involved in many types of listening. These include listening to supervisors, to colleagues, and to customers. If you are an entry-level employee, you will probably be most concerned with listening to superiors. But you also must develop skills for listening to colleagues and team members. As you advance in your career and enter the ranks of management, you will need skills for listening to subordinates. Finally, the entire organization must listen to customers, employees, government agencies, all stakeholders, and the public at large to compete in today's service-oriented economy.

Listening to Supervisors.   One of your most important tasks will be listening to instructions, assignments, and explanations about how to do your work. You will be listening to learn and to comprehend. To focus totally on the speaker, be sure you are not distracted by noisy surroundings or other tasks. Don't take phone calls, and don't try to complete another job while listening with one ear. Show your interest by leaning forward and striving for good eye contact.

Above all, take notes. Don't rely on your memory. Details are easy to forget. Taking selective notes also conveys to the speaker your seriousness about hearing accurately and completely. Don't interrupt. When the speaker finishes, paraphrase the instructions in your own words. Ask pertinent questions in a nonthreatening manner. Don't be afraid to ask "dumb" questions, if it means you won't have to do a job twice. Avoid criticizing or arguing when you are listening to a supervisor. Your goals should be to hear accurately and to convey an image of competence.

Listening to Colleagues and Teammates.   Much of your listening will take place during interactions with fellow workers and teammates. In these exchanges two kinds of listening are important. *Critical listening* enables you to judge and evaluate what you are hearing. You will be listening to decide whether the speaker's message is fact, fiction, or opinion. You will also be listening to decide whether an argument is based on logic or emotion. Critical listening requires an effort on your part. You must remain objective, particularly when you disagree with what you are hearing. Control your tendency to prejudge. Let the speaker complete the message before you evaluate it. *Discriminative listening* is necessary when you must discern, understand, and remember. It means you must identify main ideas, understand a logical argument, and recognize the purpose of the message.

Listening to Customers.   As the U.S. economy becomes increasingly service oriented, the new management mantra has become "Customers rule." Many organizations know that listening to customers results in increased sales and profitability as well as improved customer acquisition and retention. The simple truth is that consumers feel better about companies that value their opinions—views that are amplified with unprecedented speed and reach by social media. Listening is an acknowledgment of caring and is a potent retention tool. Customers want to be cared about. By doing so, companies fulfill a powerful human need.

How can organizations improve their customer listening techniques? Because employees are the eyes and ears of the organization, smart companies begin by hiring staff members who genuinely care about customers. Organizations intent on listening also train their employees to listen actively and to ask gentle, probing questions to ensure clear understanding. As you can see in Figure 2.9, employees trained in listening techniques are far more likely to elicit customer feedback and promote goodwill than untrained employees are.

Figure 2.9   Listening to Customers: Comparing Trained and Untrained Listeners

Untrained Listeners	Trained Listeners
✗ Tune out some of what the customer is saying because they know the answer	✓ Defer judgment; listen for the customer's feelings and assess the situation
✗ Focus on style; mentally dismiss grammar, voice tone, and speaking style	✓ Pay most attention to content, not to appearances, form, or other surface issues
✗ Tend to listen mainly for facts and specific bits of information	✓ Listen completely, trying to really understand every nuance
✗ Attempt to take in everything being said, including exaggerations and errors ("fogging"), only to refute each comment	✓ Listen primarily for the main idea and avoid replying to everything, especially sidetracking issues
✗ Divide their attention among two or more tasks because listening is automatic	✓ Do one thing at a time, realizing that listening is a full-time job
✗ Tend to become distracted by emotional words, have difficulty controlling anger	✓ Control their anger and refuse to fight fire with fire
✗ Interrupt the customer	✓ Are silent for a few seconds after speakers finish to let them complete their thought
✗ Give few, if any, verbal responses	✓ Give affirming statements and invite additional comments

© Cengage Learning 2015

Improving Workplace Listening

Listening on the job is more difficult than listening in college classes in which experienced professors present well-organized lectures and repeat important points. Workplace listening is more challenging because information is often exchanged casually or under time pressure. It may be disorganized, unclear, and cluttered with extraneous facts. Moreover, your fellow workers are usually friends. Because they are familiar with you, they may not be as polite and respectful as they are with strangers. Friends tend to interrupt, jump to conclusions, and take each other for granted.

Listening in groups or listening to nonnative speakers further complicates the listening process. In groups, more than one person talks at once, and topics change rapidly. Group members are monitoring both verbal and nonverbal messages to learn what relates to their group roles. Listening to nonnative speakers often creates special challenges. Chapter 3 presents suggestions for communicating across cultures.

Ten Keys to Building Powerful Listening Skills

Despite the complexities and challenges of workplace listening, good listeners on the job must remember that their goal is to listen carefully and to *understand* what is being said so that they can do their work well. The following recommendations can help you improve your workplace listening effectiveness.

1. **Control external and internal distractions.** Move to an area where you can hear without conflicting noises or conversations. Block out surrounding physical distractions. Internally, try to focus totally on the speaker. If other projects are on your mind, put them on the back burner temporarily. When you are emotionally charged, whether angry or extremely happy, it is a good idea to postpone any serious listening.

2. **Become actively involved.** Show that you are listening closely by leaning forward and maintaining eye contact with the speaker. Don't fidget or try to complete another task at the same time you are listening. Listen to more than the spoken words. How are they said? What implied meaning, reasoning, and feelings do you hear behind the spoken words? Does the speaker's body language (eye contact, posture, movements) support or contradict the main message?

3. **Separate facts from opinions.** Facts are truths known to exist; for example, *Microsoft is located in Redmond, Washington.* Opinions are statements of personal judgments or preferences; for example, *Microsoft stock is always a good investment.* Some opinions are easy to recognize because speakers preface them with statements such as, *I think, It seems to me,* and *As far as I'm concerned.*[52] Often, however, listeners must evaluate assertions to decide their validity. Good listeners consider whether speakers are credible and speaking within their areas of competence. They do not automatically accept assertions as facts.

4. **Identify important facts.** Speakers on the job often intersperse important information with casual conversation. Unrelated topics pop up—ball scores, a customer's weird request, a computer glitch, the boss's extravagant new sports car. Your task is to select what's crucial and register it mentally. What step is next in your project? Who does what? What is your role?

5. **Avoid interrupting.** While someone else has the floor, do not interrupt with a quick reply or opinion. Don't signal nonverbal disagreement such as negative head shaking, rolling eyes, sarcastic snorting, or audible sighs. Good listeners let speakers have their say. Interruptions are not only impolite, but also prevent you from hearing the speaker's complete thought. Listeners who interrupt with their opinions sidetrack discussions and cause hard feelings.

6. **Ask clarifying questions.** Good listeners wait for the proper moment and then ask questions that do not attack the speaker. Instead of saying, *But I don't understand how you can say that,* a good listener seeks clarification with statements such as, *Please help me understand by explaining more about . . . .* Because questions can put you in the driver's seat,

think about them in advance. Use *open questions* (those without set answers) to draw out feelings, motivations, ideas, and suggestions. Use *closed questions* (those that require a choice among set answers) to identify key factors in a discussion.[53] By the way, don't ask a question unless you are ready to be quiet and listen to the answer.

7. **Paraphrase to increase understanding.** To make sure you understand a speaker, rephrase and summarize a message in your own words. Be objective and nonjudgmental. Remember, your goal is to understand what the speaker has said—not to show how mindless the speaker's words sound when parroted. Remember, too, that other workplace listeners will also benefit from a clear summary of what was said.

© Everett Collection Inc/Alamy

REALITY CHECK: Listen and Learn

Celebrated media proprietor and talk show host Oprah Winfrey owes much of her success to the artful practice of listening and responding: "Communicating with people is how I always developed any kind of value about myself." She is well-known for her ability to block out external distractions, become actively involved, listen empathically without interrupting, paraphrase her guests' ideas, and ask clarifying questions to draw out deep meanings and issues that underlie their everyday lives.[54]

8. **Capitalize on lag time.** While you are waiting for a speaker's next idea, use the time to review what the speaker is saying. Separate the central idea, key points, and details. Sometimes you may have to supply the organization. Use lag time to silently rephrase and summarize the speaker's message. Another effective trick for keeping your mind from drifting is to try to guess what a speaker's next point will be. Most important, keep your mind focused on the speaker and his or her ideas—not on all the other work waiting for you.

9. **Take notes to ensure retention.** A wise person once said that he would rather have a short pencil than a long memory. If you have a hallway conversation with a colleague and don't have a pen or smart electronic device handy, make a mental note of the important items. Then write them down as soon as possible. Even with seemingly easily remembered facts or instructions, jot them down to ease your mind and also to be sure you understand them correctly. Two weeks later you will be glad you did. Be sure you have a good place to store notes about various projects, such as file folders, notebooks, or digital files.

10. **Be aware of gender differences.** Men tend to listen for facts, whereas women tend to perceive listening as an opportunity to connect with the other person on a personal level.[55] Men tend to use interrupting behavior to control conversations, while women generally interrupt to communicate assent, to elaborate on an idea of another group member, or to participate in the topic of conversation. Women listeners tend to be attentive, provide steady eye contact, remain stationary, and nod their heads.[56] Male listeners are less attentive, provide sporadic eye contact, and move around. Being aware of these tendencies will make you a more sensitive and knowledgeable listener. To learn more about gender differences in communication, see the Career Coach box in Chapter 3.

Communicating Nonverbally

LEARNING OBJECTIVE 4
Understand how effective nonverbal communication can help you advance your career.

Understanding messages often involves more than merely listening to spoken words. Nonverbal cues also carry powerful meanings. Nonverbal communication includes all unwritten and unspoken messages, both intentional and unintentional. Eye contact, facial expressions, body movements, space, time, distance, appearance—all of these nonverbal cues influence the way a message is interpreted, or decoded, by the receiver. Many of the nonverbal messages that we send are used intentionally to accompany spoken words. When Stacy slaps her monitor and shouts "This computer just crashed again!" we interpret

© Daniilantiq/Shutterstock.com

- **Stop talking.** Accept the role of listener by concentrating on the speaker's words, not on your response.

- **Work hard at listening.** Become actively involved; expect to learn something.

- **Block out competing thoughts.** Concentrate on the message. Don't daydream during lag time.

- **Control the listening environment.** Move to a quiet area where you won't be interrupted by calls, texts, or visitors. Check to be certain that listeners can hear speakers.

- **Maintain an open mind.** Know your biases and try to correct for them. Be tolerant of less-abled and different-looking speakers. Provide verbal and nonverbal feedback. Encourage the speaker with comments such as, *Yes, I see, OK,* and *Uh huh.* Ask polite questions, and look alert by leaning forward.

- **Paraphrase the speaker's ideas.** Silently repeat the message in your own words, sort out the main points, and identify supporting details. In conversation sum up the main points to confirm what was said.

- **Listen between the lines.** Observe nonverbal cues and interpret the feelings of the speaker: What is really being said?

- **Distinguish between facts and opinions.** Know the difference between factual statements and opinions stated as assertions.

- **Capitalize on lag time.** Use spare moments to organize, review, anticipate, challenge, and weigh the evidence.

- **Use memory devices.** If the information is important, develop acronyms, links, or rhymes to help you remember it.

- **Take selective notes.** If you are hearing instructions or important data, record the major points; then, revise your notes immediately or verify them with the speaker.

the loudness of her voice and the act of slapping the machine as an intentional emphasis of her words. But people can also communicate nonverbally even when they don't intend to. What's more, not all messages accompany words. When Jeff hangs on to the speaker's rostrum and barely looks at the audience during his presentation, he sends a nonverbal message of fear and lack of confidence.

The nonverbal message in such a situation speaks louder than the words uttered. In one experiment speakers delivered a positive message but averted their eyes as they spoke. Listeners perceived the overall message to be negative. Moreover, listeners thought that gaze aversion suggested nonaffection, superficiality, lack of trust, and nonreceptivity.[57] The lesson to be learned here is that effective communicators must be certain that all their nonverbal messages reinforce their spoken words and their professional goals. To make sure that you're on the right track to nonverbal communication competency, let's look at the specific forms of nonverbal communication.

Forms of Nonverbal Communication

Instead of conveying meaning with words, nonverbal messages carry their meaning in a number of other forms ranging from facial expressions to body language and even clothes. Each of us sends and receives thousands of nonverbal messages daily in our business and personal lives. Although the following discussion covers many forms of nonverbal communication, we will be especially concerned with workplace applications. As you learn about the messages sent by eye contact, facial expressions, posture, gestures, as well as the use of time, space, territory, and appearance, think about how you can use these nonverbal cues positively in your career.

Eye Contact.   The eyes have been called the "windows to the soul." Even if communicators can't look directly into the soul, they consider the eyes to be the most accurate predictor of a speaker's true feelings and attitudes. Most of us cannot look another person straight in the eyes and lie. As a result, in our culture we tend to believe people who look directly at us. We have less confidence in and actually distrust those who cannot maintain eye contact. Sustained eye contact suggests trust and admiration; brief eye contact signifies fear or stress. Prolonged eye contact, however, can be intrusive and intimidating. One successful CEO says that he can tell from people's eyes whether they are focused, receptive, or distant. He also notes the frequency of eye blinks when judging a person's honesty.[58]

> Good eye contact enables the message sender to determine whether a receiver is paying attention, showing respect, responding favorably, or feeling distress.

Good eye contact enables the message sender to determine whether a receiver is paying attention, showing respect, responding favorably, or feeling distress. From the receiver's perspective, good eye contact reveals the speaker's sincerity, confidence, and truthfulness. Because eye contact is a learned skill, however, you must be respectful of people who do not maintain it. You must also remember that nonverbal cues, including eye contact, have different meanings in different cultures. Chapter 3 presents more information about the cultural influence of nonverbal cues.

Facial Expressions.   The expression on a communicator's face can be almost as revealing of emotion as the eyes. Researchers estimate that the human face can display over 250,000 expressions.[59] Although a few people can control these expressions and maintain a "poker face" when they want to hide their feelings, most of us display our emotions openly. Raising or lowering the eyebrows, squinting the eyes, swallowing nervously, clenching the jaw, smiling broadly—these voluntary and involuntary facial expressions supplement or entirely replace verbal messages. In the workplace, maintaining a pleasant expression with frequent smiles promotes harmony.

Posture and Gestures.   An individual's general posture can convey anything from high status and self-confidence to shyness and submissiveness. Leaning toward a speaker suggests attraction and interest; pulling away or shrinking back denotes fear, distrust, anxiety, or disgust. Similarly, gestures can communicate entire thoughts via simple movements. But remember that these nonverbal cues may have vastly different meanings in different cultures. An individual who signals success by forming the thumb and forefinger into a circle would be in deep trouble in Germany or parts of South America. The harmless OK sign is actually an obscene reference in those areas.[60]

In the workplace you can make a good impression by controlling your posture and gestures. When speaking, make sure your upper body is aligned with the person to whom you're talking. Erect posture sends a message of confidence, competence, diligence, and strength. During the Microsoft antitrust trial, CEO Bill Gates slouched in his chair and rocked back and forth as he pondered questions and responded. Body language experts thought his childlike, rhythmic rocking did not help his case.[61] Women are advised to avoid tilting their heads to the side when making an important point. This gesture diminishes the main thrust of the message.[62]

Time.   How we structure and use time tells observers about our personality and attitudes. For example, when Maritza Perez, a banking executive, gives a visitor a prolonged interview, she signals her respect for, interest in, and approval of the visitor or the topic being discussed. By sharing her valuable time, she sends a clear nonverbal message. Likewise, when David Ing twice arrives late for a meeting, it could mean that the meeting has low priority to David, that he is a self-centered person, or that he has little self-discipline. These are assumptions that typical Americans might make. In other cultures and regions, though, punctuality is viewed differently. In the workplace you can send positive nonverbal messages by being on time for meetings and appointments, staying on task during meetings, and giving ample time to appropriate projects and individuals.

ETHICS CHECK:

Impressing Your Instructor

Projecting a professional image begins in your business communication classroom and in other courses in which your instructors evaluate your work and your participation. Imagine how a professor perceives students who skip classes, arrive late, forget homework, yawn with their tonsils showing, chew gum or eat, play with their electronic toys, and doodle during class. What message does such nonverbal behavior send?

Space. How we arrange things in the space around us tells something about ourselves and our objectives. Whether the space is a dorm room, an office, or a department, people reveal themselves in the design and grouping of furniture within that space. Generally, the more formal the arrangement, the more formal and closed the communication environment. An executive who seats visitors in a row of chairs across from his desk sends a message of aloofness and a desire for separation. A team leader who arranges chairs informally in a circle rather than in straight rows or a rectangular pattern conveys her desire for a more open, egalitarian exchange of ideas. A manager who creates an open office space with few partitions separating workers' desks seeks to encourage an unrestricted flow of communication and work among departments.

Territory. Each of us has certain areas that we feel are our own territory, whether it is a specific spot or just the space around us. Your father may have a favorite chair in which he is most comfortable, a cook might not tolerate intruders in her kitchen, and veteran employees may feel that certain work areas and tools belong to them. We all maintain zones of privacy in which we feel comfortable. Figure 2.10 categorizes the four zones of social interaction among Americans, as formulated by anthropologist Edward T. Hall. Notice that we North Americans are a bit standoffish; only intimate friends and family may stand closer than about 1½ feet. If someone violates that territory, we feel uncomfortable and defensive and may step back to reestablish our space. In the workplace be aware of the territorial needs of others and don't invade their space.

Appearance of Business Documents. The way a letter, memo, or report looks can have either a positive or a negative effect on the receiver. Envelopes through their postage, stationery, and printing can suggest routine, important, or junk mail. Letters and reports can look neat, professional, well organized, and attractive—or just the opposite. Sloppy, hurriedly written documents convey negative nonverbal messages regarding both the content and the sender. Among the worst offenders are e-mail messages.

Although they seem like conversation, e-mails are business documents that create a permanent record and often a bad impression. Sending an e-mail full of errors conveys a damaging nonverbal message. It says that the writer doesn't care enough about this message to take the time to make it read well or look good. The receiver immediately doubts the credibility of the sender. How much faith can you put in someone who can't spell, capitalize, or punctuate and won't make the effort to communicate clearly?

In succeeding chapters you will learn how to create documents that send positive nonverbal messages through their appearance, format, organization, readability, and correctness.

Appearance of People. The way you look—your clothing, grooming, and posture—telegraphs an instant nonverbal message about you. Based on what they see, viewers make quick judgments about your status, credibility, personality, and potential. Business communicators who look the part are more likely to be successful in working with supervisors, colleagues,

Figure **2.10** Four Space Zones for Social Interaction

Intimate Zone
(1 to 1½ feet)

Personal Zone
(1½ to 4 feet)

Social Zone
(4 to 12 feet)

Public Zone
(12 or more feet)

© iStockphoto.com/morganl

© iStockphoto.com/Dean Mitchell

© iStockphoto.com/Catherine Yeulet

© Kablonk Royalty-Free/Inmagine

© Cengage Learning 2015

and customers. Because appearance is such a powerful force in business, some aspiring professionals are turning for help to image consultants (who charge up to $500 an hour!).

What do image consultants say? They suggest investing in appropriate, professional-looking clothing and accessories. Remember that quality is more important than quantity. Avoid flashy garments, clunky jewelry, garish makeup, and overpowering colognes. Pay attention to good grooming, including a neat hairstyle, body cleanliness, polished shoes, and clean nails. Project confidence in your posture, both standing and sitting.

One of the latest fads is body art in the form of tattoos and piercings. Once seen primarily on bikers, prisoners, and sailors, inked images increasingly adorn the bodies of Americans today. The Food and Drug Administration estimates that as many as 45 million Americans have at least one tattoo. A Pew Research study found the highest rate of tattoos in eighteen- to twenty-nine-year-olds (38 percent).[63] Think twice, however, before displaying "tats" and piercings at work. Conspicuous body art may make you feel distinctive and slightly daring, but it could derail a professional career.

A less risky trend is the movement toward one or more days per week of casual dress at work. Be aware, though, that casual clothes change the image you project and also may affect your work style. See the accompanying Career Coach box regarding the pros and cons of casual apparel.

In the preceding discussion of nonverbal communication, you learned that each of us sends and responds to thousands of nonverbal messages daily in our personal and work lives. You can harness the power of silent messages by reviewing Figure 2.11 and by studying the tips in the checklist at the top of page 67.

Figure **2.11** Sending Positive Nonverbal Signals in the Workplace

CAREER COACH:

Perils of Casual Apparel in the Workplace

Your choice of work clothes sends a strong non-verbal message about you. It also affects the way you work. Some surveys suggest that the pendulum is swinging back to more conservative attire in the workplace,[64] although employers and employees have mixed feelings about what to wear to work.

What Critics Are Saying

Some employers oppose casual dress because, in their opinion, too many workers push the boundaries of what is acceptable. They contend that absenteeism, tardiness, and flirtatious behavior have increased since dress-down policies began to be implemented. Relaxed dress codes also lead to reduced productivity and lax behavior. Image counselor Judith Rasband claimed that the general casualization of America has resulted in an overall decline in civility. "Manners break down, you begin to feel down, and you're not as effective," she said.[65] Others fear that casual attire undermines the authority and credibility of executives, particularly females and minorities.[66] Moreover, customers are often turned off by casually attired employees.[67]

What Supporters Are Saying

Supporters argue that comfortable clothes and relaxed working environments lift employee morale, increase employee creativity, and improve internal communication. Employees appreciate reduced clothing-related expenses, while employers use casual dress as a recruitment and retention tool. Because employees seem to love casual dress, nine out of ten employers have adopted casual-dress days for at least part of the workweek—even if it is just on Fridays during the summer.

What Employees Need to Know

The following suggestions, gleaned from surveys and articles about casual-dress trends in the workplace, can help you avoid casual-attire blunders.

- For job interviews, dress conservatively or call ahead to ask the interviewer or the receptionist what is appropriate.

- Find out what your company allows. Ask whether a dress-down policy is available. Observe what others are wearing on casual-dress days.

- If your company has no casual-attire policy, volunteer to work with management to develop relevant guidelines, including illustrations of suitable casual attire.

- Avoid wearing the following items: T-shirts, sandals, flip-flops, shoes without socks, backless dresses, tank tops, shorts, miniskirts, spandex, athletic shoes, hiking boots, baseball caps, and visors.[68]

- When meeting customers, dress as well as or better than they do.

LEARNING OBJECTIVE 5
Improve your competitive advantage by developing professionalism and business etiquette skills.

Developing Professionalism and Business Etiquette Skills

Good manners and a businesslike, professional demeanor are among the top soft skills that employers seek in job candidates. Employers are far more likely to hire and promote a courteous and professional job candidate than one who lacks these skills and traits. But can you really learn how to be courteous, civil, and professional? Of course! This section gives you a few pointers.

CHECKLIST ▶▶

Techniques for Improving Nonverbal Communication Skills in the Workplace

- **Establish and maintain eye contact.** Remember that in North America appropriate eye contact signals interest, attentiveness, strength, and credibility.

- **Use posture to show interest.** Encourage interaction by leaning forward, sitting or standing erect, and looking alert.

- **Reduce or eliminate physical barriers.** Move out from behind a desk or lectern; arrange meeting chairs in a circle.

- **Improve your decoding skills.** Watch facial expressions and body language to understand the complete verbal and nonverbal message being communicated.

- **Probe for more information.** When you perceive nonverbal cues that contradict verbal meanings, politely seek additional clues (*I'm not sure I understand, Please tell me more about . . .,* or *Do you mean that . . . ?*).

- **Interpret nonverbal meanings in context.** Make nonverbal assessments only when you understand a situation or a culture.

- **Associate with people from diverse cultures.** Learn about other cultures to widen your knowledge and tolerance of intercultural nonverbal messages.

- **Appreciate the power of appearance.** Keep in mind that the appearance of your business documents, your business space, and yourself sends immediate positive or negative messages to others.

- **Observe yourself on video.** Ensure that your verbal and nonverbal messages are in sync by recording and evaluating yourself making a presentation.

- **Enlist friends and family.** Ask friends and family members to monitor your conscious and unconscious body movements and gestures to help you become a more effective communicator.

Professionalism Leads to Success

Not everyone who seeks a job is aware of the employer's expectations. Some new-hires have no idea that excessive absenteeism or tardiness is grounds for termination. Others are surprised to learn that they are expected to devote their full attention to their duties when on the job. One young man wanted to read *Harry Potter* novels when things got slow. Many employees don't realize that they are sabotaging their careers when they sprinkle their conversation with *like, you know,* and uptalk (making declarative statements sound like questions).

Projecting and maintaining a professional image can make a real difference in helping you obtain the job of your dreams. Once you get that job, you are more likely to be taken seriously and much more likely to be promoted if you look and sound professional. Do not send the wrong message with unwitting or unprofessional behavior. Figure 2.12 reviews seven areas you will want to check to be sure you are projecting professionalism.

Gaining an Etiquette Edge

An awareness of courtesy and etiquette can give you a competitive edge in the job market. Etiquette, civility, and goodwill efforts may seem out of place in today's fast-paced, high-tech offices. However, when two candidates have equal qualifications, the one who appears to be more polished and professional is more likely to be hired and promoted.

Figure 2.12 Projecting Professionalism When You Communicate

Unprofessional   Professional

Unprofessional		Professional
Uptalk, a singsong speech pattern, making sentences sound like questions; *like* used as a filler; *go* for *said*; slang; poor grammar and profanity.	**Speech habits**	Recognizing that your credibility can be seriously damaged by sounding uneducated, crude, or adolescent.
Messages with incomplete sentences, misspelled words, exclamation points, IM slang, and mindless chatter; sloppy messages signal that you don't care, don't know, or aren't smart enough to know what is correct.	**E-mail**	Employers like to see subjects, verbs, and punctuation marks. They dislike IM abbreviations. They value conciseness and correct spelling, even in brief e-mail messages and texts.
E-mail addresses such as *hotbabe@outlook.com, supasnugglykitty@yahoo.com,* or *buffedguy@gmail.com.*	**Internet**	E-mail addresses should include a name or a positive, businesslike expression; they should not sound cute or like a chat room nickname.
An outgoing message with strident background music, weird sounds, or a joke message.	**Voicemail**	An outgoing message that states your name or phone number and provides instructions for leaving a message.
Soap operas, thunderous music, or a TV football game playing noisily in the background when you answer the phone.	**Telephone presence**	A quiet background when you answer the telephone, especially if you are expecting a prospective employer's call.
Using electronics during business meetings for unrelated purposes or during conversations with fellow employees; raising your voice (cell yell); forcing others to overhear your calls.	**Cell phones, tablets**	Turning off phone and message notification, both audible and vibrate, during meetings; using your smart devices only for meeting-related purposes.
Sending and receiving text messages during meetings, allowing texting to interrupt face-to-face conversations, or texting when driving.	**Texting**	Sending appropriate business text messages only when necessary (perhaps when a cell phone call would disturb others).

© Cengage Learning 2015

As workloads increase and face-to-face meetings decline, bad manners and incivility are becoming alarmingly common in the American workplace.[69] One survey showed that 71 percent of workers said they had been insulted, demeaned, ignored, or otherwise treated discourteously by their coworkers and supervisors.[70] Employers, of course, suffer from the resulting drop in productivity and exodus of talent. Employees, too, suffer. They worry about incidents, think about changing jobs, and cut back their efforts on the job. It is not hard to understand why employers are looking for people who are courteous, polite, respectful, and well-mannered.

Good manners convey a positive image of an organization. People like to do business with those who show respect and treat others politely. Most of us also like to work in a pleasant environment. Considering how much time Americans spend at work, you realize that it makes sense that people prefer an agreeable environment to one that is rude and uncivil.

Etiquette is more about attitude than about formal rules of behavior. Attitude is a desire to show others consideration and respect. It includes a desire to make others feel comfortable. You don't have to become an etiquette nut, but you might need to polish your social competencies a little to be an effective businessperson today. Here are a few simple pointers:

- **Use polite words.** Be generous with words and phrases such as *please, thank you,* and *you're welcome.*

- **Express sincere appreciation and praise.** Tell coworkers how much you appreciate their efforts. Remember that written and specific thank-you notes are even better than saying thanks.

- **Be selective in sharing personal information.** Avoid talking about health concerns, personal relationships, or finances in the office.

- **Don't put people down.** If you have a reputation for criticizing people, your coworkers will begin to wonder what you are saying behind their backs.

- **Respect coworkers' space.** Turn down the ringer on your business phone, minimize the use of speakerphones, and turn your personal cell phone down or off during business hours. Avoid wearing heavy perfumes or bringing strong-smelling food.

- **Rise above others' rudeness.** Don't use profanity or participate in questionable joke-telling.

- **Be considerate when sharing space and equipment with others.** Clean up after yourself.

- **Choose the high road in conflict.** Avoid letting discussions degenerate into shouting matches. Keep a calm voice tone and focus on the work rather than on personality differences.

- **Disagree agreeably.** You may not agree with everyone, but you should respect their opinions.

To strengthen your etiquette skills, visit *Dr. Guffey's Guide to Business Etiquette and Workplace Manners* at **www.cengagebrain.com**. You will find the author's tips on topics such as networking manners, coping with cubicles, managers' manners, business gifts, dealing with angry customers, and gender-free etiquette. Your instructor may give you etiquette quizzes to test your skills from this online material.

Your Turn: Applying Your Skills at TBS

You landed a 12-week paid "Students Work" internship at Turner Broadcasting System. Your facility with Microsoft Office was a deciding factor in securing the position. Because of your expertise, your manager has asked you to put together a PowerPoint presentation to highlight the organization's commitment to collaboration and diversity. She also wants some general information about the benefits of teamwork in the workplace.

YOUR TASK. Visit the TBS website **http://www.tbs. com** to research its policies and value statements on collaboration. Then create a PowerPoint presentation of no more than ten slides that highlights TBS's policy and that provides an overview of the information you've learned about teamwork in Chapter 2. See Chapter 14 for advice on preparing PowerPoint slides.

Summary of Learning Objectives

Go to
www.cengagebrain.com
and use your access code
to unlock valuable student
resources.

1 Understand the importance of teamwork in today's digital-era workplace, and explain how you can contribute positively to team performance. Employers seek workers who have strong communication, team, listening, nonverbal, and etiquette skills. Team skills are especially important because many organizations are forming teams to compete in today's fast-paced, global economy. Virtual teams are groups of people who work independently with a shared purpose across space, time, and organization boundaries using technology. Teams typically go through four stages of development: forming, storming, norming, and performing. Open discussion of conflict prevents *groupthink*, a condition that leads to faulty decisions. In resolving conflict, you should listen, understand the other's point of view, show a concern for the relationship, look for common ground, invent new problem-solving options, and reach a fair agreement. Successful teams are small, diverse, and able to agree on their purpose, procedures, and method of conflict resolution. They use good communication techniques, collaborate rather than compete, accept ethical responsibilities, and share leadership.

2 Discuss effective practices and technologies for planning and participating in face-to-face meetings and virtual meetings. Workplace meetings are called only when urgent two-way communication is necessary. Leaders should start the meeting on time and keep the discussion on track. Conflict should be confronted openly by letting each person present his or her views fully. Leaders should summarize what was said, end the meeting on time, and distribute minutes afterwards. To participate actively, attendees should arrive early, come prepared, have a positive attitude, and contribute respectfully. In virtual meetings people who cannot be together physically connect with technology. Such meetings save travel time, trim costs, and reduce employee fatigue. *Audioconferencing* enables people to use an enhanced speakerphone to confer with others by telephone. *Videoconferencing* combines video and audio for real-time interaction in special telepresence rooms. *Web conferencing* enables participants to share documents and converse in real time.

3 Explain and apply active listening techniques. Experts say that we listen at only 25 percent efficiency. While listening to supervisors on the job, take notes, avoid interrupting, ask pertinent questions, and paraphrase what you hear. When listening to colleagues and teammates, listen critically to recognize facts and listen discriminately to identify main ideas and to understand logical arguments. When listening to customers, defer judgment, pay attention to content rather than form, listen completely, control emotions, give affirming statements, and invite additional comments. Keys to building powerful listening skills include controlling external and internal distractions, becoming actively involved, separating facts from opinions, identifying important facts, refraining from interrupting, asking clarifying questions, paraphrasing, taking advantage of lag time, taking notes to ensure retention, and being aware of gender differences.

4 Understand how effective nonverbal communication can help you advance your career. Nonverbal communication includes all unwritten and unspoken messages, both intentional and unintentional. Nonverbal communication takes many forms including eye contact, facial expressions, posture, and gestures, as well as the use of time, space, and territory. To improve your nonverbal skills, establish and maintain eye contact, use posture to show interest, reduce or eliminate physical barriers, improve your decoding skills, probe for more information, avoid assigning nonverbal meanings out of context, associate with people from diverse cultures, and appreciate the power of appearance.

5 Improve your competitive advantage by developing professionalism and business etiquette skills. You are more likely to be hired and promoted if you project professionalism in the workplace. This includes avoiding speech habits that make you sound uneducated, crude, or adolescent. Professionalism also is reflected in writing carefully worded e-mails and other messages and having a businesslike e-mail address, as well as good voice mail, cell phone, and telephone manners. To gain a competitive etiquette edge, use polite words, express sincere appreciation and praise, be selective in sharing personal information with work colleagues, avoid criticizing people, respect coworkers' space, rise above others' rudeness, be considerate when sharing space, choose the high road in conflict, and disagree agreeably.

Chapter Review

1. What are soft skills, and why are they increasingly important in the knowledge-based economy of the digital era? (Obj. 1)

2. Name at least five reasons that explain why organizations are forming teams. (Obj. 1)

3. What are virtual teams, and how can they reduce misunderstandings among participants? (Obj. 1)

4. What are the four phases of team development as identified by psychologist B. A. Tuckman? (Obj. 1)

5. What is the best approach to address conflict in meetings? (Obj. 2)

6. How is videoconferencing different from Web conferencing? (Obj. 2)

7. List five behaviors you consider most important to participate actively in workplace meetings. (Obj. 2)

8. What techniques can make virtual meetings as effective as face-to-face meetings? (Obj. 2)

9. Is listening automatic? How much time do we spend listening in the workplace? (Obj. 3)

10. According to experts, we ignore, forget, distort, or misunderstand 75 percent of everything we hear. Why are we such poor listeners? (Obj. 3)

11. What are ten techniques for improving workplace listening? Be prepared to describe each. (Obj. 3)

12. Which forms of nonverbal communication or nonverbal cues send silent messages about us? (Obj. 4)

13. List ten techniques for improving nonverbal communication skills in the workplace. Be prepared to discuss each. (Obj. 4)

14. How is projecting a professional image related to career success? (Obj. 5)

15. What five specific behaviors do you think would be most important in giving you an etiquette edge in your business career? (Obj. 5)

Critical Thinking

1. Author and teamwork critic Susan Cain claims that research "strongly suggests that people are more creative when they enjoy privacy and freedom from interruption." In her book *Quiet: The Power of Introverts in a World That Can't Stop Talking*, in articles, and public appearances, Cain cautions against the current emphasis on teamwork in the workplace. Cain cites studies by the psychologists Mihaly Csikszentmihalyi and Gregory Feist, according to whom "the most spectacularly creative people in many fields are often introverted. . . . They are not joiners by nature."[71] How would you, as a critical thinker, respond to these statements? (Obj. 1)

2. Evaluate the following humorous analogy between the murder of a famous Roman emperor and the deadening effect of meetings: "This month is the 2,053rd anniversary of the death of Julius Caesar, who pronounced himself dictator for life before running the idea past the Roman Senate. On his way to a meeting, he was met by a group of senators who, wishing to express their unhappiness with his vocational aspirations, stabbed him to death. Moral of the story: Beware of meetings."[72] Is the comparison fitting? What might the author of the article have wanted to convey? (Obj. 2)

3. Why do executives and managers spend more time listening than do workers? (Obj. 3)

4. What arguments could you give for or against the idea that body language is a science with principles that can be interpreted accurately by specialists? (Obj. 4)

5. **Ethical Issue:** After much discussion and even conflict, your workplace team has finally agreed on Plan B, but you are firmly convinced that Plan A is a much better option. Your team is presenting Plan B to the whole department and company executives are present. A vice president asks you for your opinion. Should you (a) keep your mouth shut, (b) try to persuade the team to adopt Plan A, (c) explain why you believe Plan A is a better plan, (d) tell the VP and all present that Plan B is not your idea, or (e) discuss one or two points you can agree on in Plan B?[73] (Objs. 1, 2, 5)

Activities

2.1 Soft Skills: Which Competencies Are Most Desirable? (Obj. 1)

⟨ Web ⟩

YOUR TASK. Check job listings in your field at an online job board. Visit a job board such as Monster, CollegeRecruiter, CareerBuilder, Yahoo Careers, or Indeed. Follow the instructions to search job categories and locations. Study many job listings in your field. Then prepare a list of the most frequently requested soft skills in your area of interest. Next to each item on the list, indicate how well you think you would qualify for the skill or trait mentioned. Your instructor may ask you to submit your findings and/or report to the class. If you are not satisfied with the job selection at any job site, choose another job board.

2.2 Soft Skills: Personal Strengths Inventory (Obj. 1)

When hiring future workers, employers look for hard skills, which are those we learn such as mastery of software applications or accountancy procedures, and soft skills. Soft skills are personal characteristics, strengths, or other assets a person possesses. Studies have divided soft skills into four categories:

- Thinking and problem solving
- Oral and written communication
- Personal qualities and work ethic
- Interpersonal and teamwork

YOUR TASK. Using the preceding categories to guide you, identify your own soft skills, paying attention to those attributes you think a potential employer would value. Prepare lists of at least four items in each of the four categories. For example, as evidence of problem solving, you might list a specific workplace or student problem you recognized and solved. You will want to weave these words and phrases into cover letters and résumés, which are covered in Chapter 15.

2.3 Reaching Group Decisions: Majority, Consensus, or What? (Obj. 1)

Team

YOUR TASK. In small groups decide which decision strategy is best for the following situations:

a. A team of 15 employees must decide whether to choose the iPad or an Android tablet for their new equipment. Some team members dislike Apple's closed system and would prefer the more open Android platform. However, Apple offers more apps.

b. Company employees numbering 900 or more must decide whether to adopt a floating holiday plan proposed by management or stay with the current plan. A yes-or-no vote is required.

c. The owner of your company is meeting with all managers to decide which departments will be allowed to move into a new facility.

d. Appointed by management, an employee team is charged with making recommendations regarding casual Fridays. Management feels that too many employees are abusing the privilege.

e. Members of a business club must decide which members will become officers.

f. A group of town officials and volunteers must decide how to organize a town website and social media presence. Only a few members have technical expertise.

g. An employee committee of three members (two supervisors and the manager) must decide on promotions within a department.

h. A national professional organization with thousands of members must decide on the site for its next convention.

2.4 Resolving Workplace Conflicts: Apply a Plan (Obj. 1)

Team

Although conflict is a normal part of every workplace, if unresolved, it can create hard feelings and reduce productivity.

YOUR TASK. Analyze the following scenarios. In teams, discuss each scenario and apply the six-step procedure for dealing with conflict outlined in Figure 2.3. Choose two of the scenarios to role-play, with two of your team members taking roles.

a. Meghan, an accountant, cannot complete her report until Matt, a salesman, provides her with all the necessary numbers and documentation. Meghan thinks that Matt is a procrastinator who forces her to deliver a rush job thus causing her great stress and increasing the likelihood of error. Matt believes that Meghan is exerting pressure on both of them and setting unrealistic deadlines. As the conflict is intensifying, productivity decreases.

b. A company policy manual is posted and updated at the company intranet, an internal website. Employees must sign that they have read and understand the manual. A conflict arises when team member Brian insists that employees should sign electronically. Fellow team member Erika thinks that a paper form should be signed by employees so that better records may be kept.

c. The author of a lengthy report refuses to collaborate with another colleague on future projects because she feels that the review of her document completed by the peer was superficial, short, and essentially useless. The report author is angry at the lack of attention her 25-page paper received.

d. Two management team members disagree on a new company social media policy. One wants to ban personal visits to Facebook and Twitter totally. The other thinks that an outright ban is impossible to implement and might raise the ire of employees. He is more concerned with limiting Internet misuse, including visits to online game, pornography, and shopping sites. The management team members agree that they need a social media policy, but they disagree on what to allow and what to prohibit.

e. A manager and his assistant plan to attend a conference together at a resort location. Six weeks before the conference, the company announces a cutback and limits conference support to only one person. The assistant, who has developed a presentation specifically for the conference, feels that he should be the one to attend. Travel arrangements must be made immediately.

f. Customer-service rep Jackie comes to work one morning and finds Alexa sitting at Workstation 2. Although the customer-service reps have no special workstations assigned to them, Jackie has the longest seniority and has always assumed that Workstation 2 is hers. Other workstations were available, but the supervisor told Alexa to use Workstation 2 that morning because she didn't know that Jackie would be coming in. When Jackie arrives and sees her workstation occupied, she becomes angry and demands that Alexa vacate "her" station.

2.5 Workplace Conflict: The Perils of Groupthink (Obj. 1)

"Conflict can be good because you get the devil's advocate position," says Mary Osswald, senior manager at Kamehameha Schools, Honolulu, Hawaii. "Conflict usually comes because someone doesn't want change or they don't agree with how you're making change. It certainly inspires better conversation and more thought about what's being done and why it's being done. It forces the project to evolve."[74]

The absence of conflict is not always a good sign, Ms. Osswald believes: "If you have a project with no conflict, you might have just as much of a leadership problem as if you were experiencing massive conflict. Ms. Osswald suspects groupthink is at work: "It's very unlikely everybody always agrees with how the project activities are progressing. If you have zero conflict, my thought is you've got a bunch of 'yes men' who are keeping their mouths shut and simply doing what they think the leaders want."

YOUR TASK. Do you agree with Mary Osswald's views on workplace conflict and groupthink? Look back at your teamwork experience and consider tensions that arose. How were they addressed and settled? Have you worked on teams that were conflict-free? Were you ever afraid to speak up? Could negative situations have been salvaged with the tips suggested in this chapter? Discuss these and similar questions in small groups or in front of the class. If asked, provide a written assessment of your views on workplace conflict.

2.6 Groupthink: Fastest Decision May Not Be Best (Obj. 1)

You are a member of a team charged with recommending a vendor to perform an upgrade of your firm's computer systems. Greg, the group leader, suggests the company where his sister works, claiming it will give your firm a good price. Lucinda says she will go along with whatever the group decides. Estéban announces he has another meeting in five minutes. Paul says he would like to solicit bids from several companies before recommending any one firm, but Greg dismisses that idea saying, "The sooner we make a recommendation, the sooner we improve our computer systems. My sister's firm will make our job a top priority and besides, it's local. Let's support a company in our own community." The committee urges Paul to drop the idea of putting the job out to bid, and the group makes a unanimous decision to recommend the firm of Greg's sister.

YOUR TASK. In class discussion answer the following questions:

a. What aspects of groupthink were at work in this committee?

b. What conditions contribute to groupthink?

c. What can groups do to avoid groupthink?

2.7 Meeting Malaise: Beyond Contempt (Obj. 2)

[Team]   [Web]

"Meetings are indispensable when you don't want to do anything," observed the late economist John Kenneth Galbraith. This sentiment was echoed by Stanford professor Thomas Sowell who declared: "People who enjoy meetings should not be in charge of anything." Finally, management guru Peter Drucker claimed: "Meetings are a symptom of a bad organization. The fewer meetings, the better."

Much venomous ink has been spilled decrying meetings, but they won't go away because—despite their potential shortcomings—many workplace gatherings are necessary.

YOUR TASK. Examine the preceding quotations and perhaps other statements deriding meetings. Are they exaggerations or accurate assessments? If the assertions of wastefulness are true, what does that mean for the health of organizations conducting large numbers of meetings? Individually or as a team, search the Web for information in defense of meetings. (a) Begin by discussing your own and classmates' experience with workplace meetings. (b) Interview your parents, other relatives, and friends about meetings. (c) Finding gripes is easy, but search the Web for advice on making meetings more effective. What information beyond the tips in this book can you find? In a class discussion or individually—perhaps in writing or in an electronic slide presentation if your instructor directs—introduce your findings.

2.8 Evaluating Meetings: Productive or Not? (Obj. 2)

[Communication Technology]   [E-mail]   [Web]

A poll of senior executives revealed that 45 percent thought that employees could be more productive if meetings were banned at least one day a week.[75] Clearly, these executives would like to see their meetings improved. Now that you have studied how to plan and participate in productive meetings, you should be able to judge whether meetings are successful and why.

YOUR TASK. Attend a structured meeting of a college, social, business, or other organization. Compare the way the meeting is conducted with the suggestions presented in this chapter. Why did the meeting succeed or fail? Alternatively, if you have experience with virtual collaboration and networking, you may want to evaluate this particular type of technology-facilitated meeting. In class discussion, an e-mail, or memo (see Chapters 4 and 8) to your instructor, discuss your analysis.

2.9 Stand-Up Meetings: Keeping Business Meetings Short and Sweet (Obj. 2)

[Communication Technology]   [E-mail]   [Team]

Here is an idea to shorten tedious meetings: Ban sitting down! A growing number of tech companies hold mandatory morning meetings where nonwork chatter is frowned upon and all participants must stand. Called "the huddle" in one company and "a daily scrum" in another firm, these regular stand-up meetings last no longer than 15 minutes. At one company if someone starts rambling, an employee holds up a rubber rat. A Microsoft development team determines the next speaker by tossing around a rubber chicken called Ralph. Other gimmicks include passing around a 10-pound medicine ball to literally keep the meeting moving. At one company, latecomers must pay a small fine, run a lap around the office building, or sing a nursery rhyme such as "I'm a Little Teapot." Other methods to speed up the proceedings include holding meetings just before lunch or gathering in cold stairwells.

The idea of stand-up meetings is spreading in the wake of Agile, a method in software development that involves compressing lengthy projects into short segments. This approach also includes speedy daily updates of colleagues about three things: what was accomplished since the previous meeting, what will be done today, and what stands in the way of finishing the job. It turns out that the practice of holding meetings standing up dates back to some military commanders in World War I. A researcher who conducted a study of stand-up meetings found that they were about a third shorter than sit-down meetings while the quality of decision making did not suffer at all. A recent survey of more than 6,000 global tech workers found that 78 percent held daily stand-up meetings.

YOUR TASK. As a team, brainstorm all possible applications of quick stand-up meetings. What types of businesses could benefit from such meetings? How would you ensure on-time arrival, participation and order during the meeting, and turn-taking? What type of sanctions would you impose for violations? If your instructor directs, write an e-mail (see Chapter 4) to persuade your current or past boss to adopt stand-up meetings.

2.10 Virtual Meetings: Improving Distance Meeting Buy-In (Obj. 2)

> Communication Technology   Team   Web

Marina Elliot works at the headquarters for a large HMO that contracts with physician groups in various locations across the nation. Her position requires her to impose organizational objectives and systems on smaller groups that often resist such interference. Marina recently needed to inform regional groups that the home office was instituting a systemwide change to hiring practices. To save costs, she set up a Web conference between her office in Charlotte and others in Chicago, Denver, and Seattle. Marina set the meeting for 10 a.m. Eastern Standard Time. At the designated date and hour, she found that the Seattle team was not logged in and she had to delay the session. When the Seattle team finally did log in, Marina launched into her presentation. She explained the reasons behind the change in a PowerPoint presentation that contained complex data she had not distributed prior to the conference. Marina heard cell phone ringtones and typing in the background as she spoke. Still, she pushed through her one-hour presentation without eliciting any feedback.

YOUR TASK. In teams, discuss ways Marina might have improved the Web conference. Prepare a list of recommendations from your team.

2.11 Virtual Meetings: Connecting by Skype to Clarify an Order (Obj. 2)

> Communication Technology   Social Media   Web

Paramount Fitness Corporation, a commercial strength equipment manufacturer in California, contracts with several distributors overseas who exclusively sell Paramount weight machines to gyms and fitness studios, not to the general public. The representative in the UK, Mr. Rowan Been, has sent a confusing order by e-mail containing incorrect item numbers and product names as well as inconsistent quantities of items. Mr. Been doesn't respond to telephone calls or e-mail requests for clarification. You remember that you conversed with Mr. Been by Skype and notice to your delight that your distributor is online.

YOUR TASK. By Skype, call a classmate designated to play Mr. Been and request clarification of the rather large order. Improvise the details of the order and complete a Skype call to your peer (with or without camera) applying the tips for virtual meetings in this book. Alternatively, your instructor may introduce a short background fact sheet or script for each participant, guiding your conversation and defining your roles and the particulars of the order. To use Skype with or without a camera, select a laptop, computer lab desktop computer, smartphone, iPod Touch, or iPad. This exchange can occur in the classroom or computer lab where the image can be projected onto a screen. The person playing the remote Skype partner should leave the room and connect from a quiet place outside. Fellow students and your instructor will evaluate your virtual meeting with Mr. Been.

2.12 Web Conferencing: Take a Quick Tour (Obj. 2)

> Communication Technology   Web

Your office team finds it increasingly difficult to find times to meet. Tyler is frequently on assignment traveling across the country. Melissa wants to work from home since her baby arrived. Others are in and out of the office as their schedules demand. Team leader Susan asks you to check out WebEx and report how it works to the team.

YOUR TASK. Visit the WebEx site and view its video called "Quick Tour." Take notes and report what you learn. Does it sound as though WebEx would work for your team? In class discussion or in a memo, describe how WebEx works.

2.13 Rating Your Listening Skills (Obj. 3)

> Web

You can learn whether your listening skills are excellent or deficient by completing a brief quiz.

YOUR TASK. Take *Dr. Guffey's Listening Quiz* at **www.cengagebrain.com**. What two listening behaviors do you think you need to work on the most?

2.14 Listening: Recognizing Good Habits (Obj. 3)

> Team

You have probably never paid much attention to listening. However, now that you have studied it, you have become more conscious of both good and bad listening behavior.

YOUR TASK. For one week focus on the listening behavior of people around you—at work, at school, at home. Make a list of five good listening habits that you see and five bad habits. Identify the situation and participants for each item on your list. Who is the best listener you know? What makes that person a good listener? Be prepared to discuss your responses in class, with your team, or in a memo to your instructor.

2.15 Listening: An In-Person or Virtual Social Media Interview

> Communication Technology   Social Media   Team

How much and to whom do businesspeople listen?

YOUR TASK. Interview a businessperson about his or her work-place listening. Connect with a worker in your circle of friends, family, and acquaintances; in your campus network; prior or current employment; or via an established LinkedIn or Facebook contact. Come up with questions to ask about listening, for example: (a) How much active listening do you practice daily? (b) To whom do you listen on the job? (c) How do you know that others are listening or not listening to you? (d) Can you share anecdotes of poor listening that led to negative outcomes? (e) Do you have tips for better listening?

2.16 Listening and Nonverbal Cues: Skills Required in Various Careers (Objs. 3, 4)

> Team

Do the listening skills and behaviors of individuals differ depending on their careers?

YOUR TASK. Your instructor will divide you into teams and give each team a role to discuss, such as business executive, teacher, physician, police officer, attorney, accountant, administrative assistant, mentor, or team leader. Create a list of verbal and nonverbal cues that a member of this profession would display to indicate that he or she is listening. Would the cues and behavior change if the person were trying to listen discriminatively versus critically? How?

2.17 Nonverbal Communication: Body Language (Obj. 4)

YOUR TASK. What attitudes do the following body movements suggest to you? Do these movements always mean the same thing? What part does context play in your interpretations?

a. Whistling, wringing hands

b. Bowed posture, twiddling thumbs

c. Steepled hands, sprawling sitting position

d. Rubbing hand through hair

e. Open hands, unbuttoned coat

f. Wringing hands, tugging ears

2.18 Nonverbal Communication: Universal Sign for *I Goofed* (Obj. 4)

Team

In an effort to promote tranquility on the highways and reduce road rage, motorists submitted the following suggestions. They were sent to a newspaper columnist who asked for a universal nonverbal signal admitting that a driver had "goofed."[76]

YOUR TASK. In small groups consider the pros and cons of each of the following gestures intended as an apology when a driver makes a mistake. Why would some fail?

a. Lower your head slightly and bonk yourself on the forehead with the side of your closed fist. The message is clear: *I'm stupid. I shouldn't have done that.*

b. Make a temple with your hands, as if you were praying.

c. Move the index finger of your right hand back and forth across your neck—as if you were cutting your throat.

d. Flash the well-known peace sign. Hold up the index and middle fingers of one hand, making a V, as in victory.

e. Place the flat of your hands against your cheeks, as children do when they have made a mistake.

f. Clasp your hand over your mouth, raise your brows, and shrug your shoulders.

g. Use your knuckles to knock on the side of your head. Translation: *Oops! Engage brain.*

h. Place your right hand high on your chest and pat a few times, like a basketball player who drops a pass or a football player who makes a bad throw. This says, *I'll take the blame.*

i. Place your right fist over the middle of your chest and move it in a circular motion. This is universal sign language for *I'm sorry.*

j. Open your window and tap the top of your car roof with your hand.

k. Smile and raise both arms, palms outward, which is a universal gesture for surrender or forgiveness.

l. Use the military salute, which is simple and shows respect.

m. Flash your biggest smile, point at yourself with your right thumb, and move your head from left to right, as if to say, *I can't believe I did that.*

2.19 Verbal Versus Nonverbal Signals (Obj. 4)

To show the power of nonverbal cues, the president of a large East Coast consulting company uses the following demonstration with new employees. Raising his right hand, he touches his pointer finger to his thumb to form a circle. Then he asks new employees in the session to do likewise. When everyone has a finger–thumb circle formed, the president tells each person to touch that circle to his or her chin. But as he says this, he touches his own finger–thumb circle to his cheek. What happens? You guessed it! About 80 percent of the group follow what they see the president do rather than following what they hear.[77]

YOUR TASK. Try this same demonstration with several of your friends, family members, or work colleagues. Which is more effective—verbal or nonverbal signals? What conclusion could you draw from this demonstration? Do you think that nonverbal signals are always more meaningful than verbal ones? What other factors in the communication process might determine whether verbal or nonverbal signals would be more important?

2.20 Nonverbal Communication: Signals Sent by Casual Attire (Obj. 4)

Communication Technology **E-mail** **Social Media**
Team **Web**

Although many employers allow casual attire, not all employers and customers are happy with the results. To learn more about the implementation, acceptance, and effects of casual-dress programs, select one of the following activities, all of which involve some form of interviewing.

YOUR TASK.

a. In teams, gather information from human resources directors to determine which companies allow casual or dress-down days, how often, and under what specific conditions. The information may be collected by personal interviews, e-mail, telephone, or instant messaging.

b. In teams, conduct inquiring-reporter interviews. Ask individuals in the community how they react to casual dress in the workplace. Develop a set of standard interview questions.

c. In teams, visit local businesses on both casual days and on traditional business dress days. Compare and contrast the effects of business dress standards on such factors as the projected image of the company, the nature of the interactions with customers and with fellow employees, the morale of employees, and the productivity of employees. What generalizations can you draw from your findings?

2.21 Nonverbal Communication: Comparing and Contrasting *Casual* and *Business Casual* (Obj. 4)

E-mail **Team** **Web**

Although many business organizations are adopting business casual attire or even plain casual dress, most people cannot reliably define the two. Your boss asks your internship team to use the Web to find out exactly what *business casual* means and how it compares to casual attire.

YOUR TASK. Using a good search engine such as Google, explore the Web for *business casual dress code*. A few websites actually try to define the term and give examples of appropriate clothing. Visit many sites and decide whether they are reliable enough to use as sources of accurate information. Download or print several relevant pages. Get together with your team and compare notes. Then write an e-mail or memo to your boss explaining what men and women should and shouldn't wear on *business casual* days.

2.22 The Silent Language of Tattoos: How Much Self-Expression on the Job? (Obj. 4)

Communication Technology ⟩ **E-mail** ⟩ **Social Media** ⟩ **Team**

Tattoos and piercings have gained in popularity among young Americans over the last two decades. Current findings by Pew Research Center suggest that nearly 40 percent of eighteen- to twenty-nine-year-olds and about one third of thirty- to forty-five-year-olds sport a tattoo.[78] Employment services firm Challenger, Gray & Christmas reports that job candidates among the millennials, also called Generation Y, do not particularly try to hide their body art. About 25 percent of this generation also show off piercings in places other than their earlobes.

CEO John Challenger suggests that a generational shift accounts for the changing mores: "Those making hiring decisions are younger and not as adherent to traditions about workplace appearance." Career expert Andrea Kay agrees, but she warns that acceptance among hiring managers varies by industry. She says that recruiters in the technology and retail fields may be more forgiving than those in banking and law. Tattoos and piercings send a strong message, and Kay cautions that if they make people at work uncomfortable, such decorations are detrimental. She has the following advice for job seekers: "People have adjusted their thinking in what is acceptable, but it still comes down to the impression you want to make on the people you're dealing with in your business." Many workplaces today have policies covering body adornment, some requiring employees with customer contact to conceal such decorations.

YOUR TASK. In teams or in class, discuss tattoos as a form of self-expression in the workplace. Gauge the attitudes toward tattoos and piercings in your class. Consider the limits to self-expression on the job. Think about casual clothing or blogging and tweeting about your employer. What is different? What are some of the similarities among these various forms of self-expression? What types of nonverbal cues do body adornments send? Summarize your discussion orally or in an e-mail to your instructor. Alternatively, your instructor may ask you to post your responses to a Blackboard discussion board or some other forum that allows individual postings.

2.23 Nonverbal Communication Around the World (Obj. 4)

Intercultural ⟩ **Web**

Gestures play an important role when people communicate. Because culture shapes the meaning of gestures, miscommunication and misunderstanding can easily result in international situations.

YOUR TASK. Use the Web to research the meanings of selected gestures. Make a list of ten gestures (other than those discussed in the text) that have different meanings in different countries.

Consider the fingertip kiss, nose thumb, eyelid pull, nose tap, head shake, and other gestures. How are the meanings different in other countries?

2.24 Guide to Business Etiquette and Workplace Manners: Sharpening Your Skills (Obj. 5)

Business communicators feel more confident and make better impressions when they are aware of current business etiquette and proper workplace manners. But how do you know what is the right thing to do? You can gauge your current level of knowledge and sharpen your etiquette skills with a little effort.

YOUR TASK. At **www.cengagebrain.com** find *Dr. Guffey's Guide to Business Etiquette and Workplace Manners.* Take the preview test and then study the 17 business etiquette topics presented. Your instructor may give you one or more posttests to learn whether you fully understand the implications of the workplace manners discussed.

2.25 Business Etiquette: Breaking the Smartphone Habit in Meetings (Obj. 5)

Communication Technology ⟩ **Social Media** ⟩ **Team**

Not long ago it was almost a status symbol for professionals to "lay [their] BlackBerrys or iPhones on a conference table before a meeting—like gunfighters placing their Colt revolvers on the card tables in a saloon."[79] Businesspeople would compulsively eyeball their smartphones and tablets to read e-mail, search Google, and check Facebook or Twitter during meetings. In fact, in a Robert Half Management survey, 85 percent of executives stated that meeting participants who read and respond to e-mail on their mobile devices are a common sight. However, the tide is turning. Increasingly, many professionals are tired of disruptions caused by electronic gadgets during meetings.

Etiquette consultants concur: "Electronic devices are like the smoking of the '90s," says Pamela Eyring, president of the Protocol School of Washington. "Companies are aggravated and losing productivity." Businesses hire her to enact formal policies and to teach workers "why it's not a good idea to be texting while your boss is speaking at the podium," Eyring says.[80] Nancy Flynn, executive director of the ePolicy Institute and author of *The Handbook of Social Media,* has this suggestion: "Require employees to turn off mobile devices during business-related meetings, seminars, conferences, luncheons and any other situation in which a ringing phone or tapping fingers are likely to disrupt proceedings or interrupt a speaker's or participant's train of thought."

Flynn notes that banning electronic devices in meetings is not just about interruptions: "You don't want employees shooting video via a smartphone during a meeting in which company secrets are discussed, then uploading the video to YouTube or sharing it with a competitor, reporter or other third party."[81]

YOUR TASK. Organizations are only beginning to establish policies on smartphone use in meetings. Assume that your team has been asked to develop such a policy. Your boss can't decide whether to ask your team to develop a short policy or a more rigorous one. Unable to make a decision, he asks for two statements: (a) a short statement that treats employees as grownups who can exercise intelligent judgment and (b) a more complete set of guidelines that spell out exactly what should and should not be done.

Chat About It

In each chapter you will find five discussion questions related to the chapter material. Your instructor may assign these topics for you to discuss in class, in an online chat room, or on an online discussion board. Some of the discussion topics may require outside research. You may also be asked to read and respond to postings made by your classmates.

Topic 1: Do you agree with the statement that it's harder to convince potential employers that you possess a soft skill than it is to convince potential employers that you possess a hard skill? How would you convincingly present your strongest soft skill on a résumé or in a job interview?

Topic 2: Suppose you are working on a team that has one or two dominant individuals who make most of the decisions and who sometimes don't consider your ideas. Instead of giving up and not participating, what could you do that would be more helpful to the team and to your career?

Topic 3: Psychologists say that we fear rejection when deviating from group consensus; we try to avoid the "hazards of courage" and may consequently fall victim to groupthink. Recall a past or present team experience. Can you relate to feeling "the pain of independence" when going against the majority opinion?

Topic 4: Consider a situation in your family, in your circle of friends, in high school, at college, during an internship, or at work that shows the potential risks of poor listening skills. How could the resulting misunderstandings or other negative consequences have been prevented? Which techniques would have helped avert the undesirable outcome?

Topic 5: A realtor who missed out on a $12,000 commission because he was serving on a sequestered jury where cell phone use was prohibited has no regrets. He considers it rude to answer a phone during a meeting with a client and purposely leaves his phone in the car to avoid temptation.[82] What events would justify remaining permanently tethered to your mobile phone? What types of situations would warrant turning off or at least ignoring your electronic devices?

C.L.U.E. Grammar & Mechanics | *Review 2*

Verbs

Review Guides 4–10 in Appendix A, Grammar and Mechanics Guide, beginning on page A-3. On a separate sheet, revise the following sentences to correct any errors in verb use. For each error that you locate, write the guide number that reflects this usage. If a sentence is correct, write *C*.

NOTE: Remember that you can complete a similar C.L.U.E. review exercise with feedback at **www.cengagebrain.com.**

EXAMPLE: If I was in charge, I would have handled the matter differently.

REVISION: If I **were** in charge, I would have handled the matter differently. [Guide 5]

1. Although three team members proofread the report, no one seen the error.

2. During job interviews one of the most frequently requested soft skills are writing proficiency.

3. Jeremy said he wished he was president for just one day.

4. Better decisions and faster response time explains why companies are using teams.

5. Either the team leader or the manager are going to schedule the meeting.

6. Conflict and disagreement is normal and should be expected in team interactions.

7. Everything in the company's e-mails and written records were made public during the trial.

8. A committee of faculty and students are examining strategies to improve campus interviewing.

9. Each of the employees was given the opportunity to chose a team to join.

10. The appearance of e-mail messages, memos, and reports have a negative or positive effect on receivers.

Notes

1 Turner Broadcasting System. (n.d.). Operating principles: Principles that guide us. Retrieved from http://www.turner.com/company#/company/values

2 Turner Broadcasting System. (n.d.). Cartoon Network. Retrieved from http://www.turner.com/brands#/brands/cartoon-network

3 Lott, A., ed. (2010, February). Team player. *Black Enterprise*. Retrieved from http://www.blackenterprise.com

4 Ibid.

5 Ibid.

6 Chapman, J. (2008, January 19). Number crunching alone insufficient for today's financial professionals. Robert Half Inc. Retrieved from http://www.hr.com/en/articles/number-crunching-alone-insufficient-for-today%E2%80%99s-fi_fbiq84ks.html

7 Paul McDonald quoted in CFOs seek soft skills: Number crunching alone insufficient for today's financial professional, suggests survey. (2008, December 18). *PR Newswire*. Retrieved from http://www.prnewswire.com/news-releases/cfos-seek-soft-skills-number-crunching-alone-insufficient-for-todays-financial-professionals-suggests-survey-58769972.html

8 Lechner, A. (2012, April 18). Better teamwork through better workplace design. *Harvard Business Review*. Retrieved from http://blogs.hbr.org/cs/2012/04/better_teamwork_through_office.html

9 Lechner, A. (2012, April 18). Better teamwork through better workplace design. *Harvard Business Review*. Retrieved from http://blogs.hbr.org/cs/2012/04/better_teamwork_through_office.html

10 Cain, S. (2012, January 13). The rise of the new groupthink. *The New York Times*. Retrieved from http://www.nytimes.com/2012/01/15/opinion/sunday/the-rise-of-the-new-groupthink.html?pagewanted=all

11 Coutu, D. (2009, May). Why teams don't work. *Harvard Business Review, (87)*5, 100. Retrieved from http://search.ebscohost.com

12 Cain, S. (2012, January 13). The rise of the new groupthink. *The New York Times*. Retrieved from http://www.nytimes.com/2012/01/15/opinion/sunday/the-rise-of-the-new-groupthink.html?pagewanted=all

13 Zofi, Y. S. (2012). *A manager's guide to virtual teams.* New York: American Management Association, p. 1.

14 Siebdrat, F., Hoegl, M., & Ernst, H. (2009, Summer). How to manage virtual teams. *MIT Sloan Management Review, 50*(4), p. 64. Retrieved from http://search.ebscohost.com

15 Isaacson, W. (2012, April). The real leadership lessons of Steve Jobs. *Harvard Business Review*. Retrieved from http://hbr.org/2012/04/the-real-leadership-lessons-of-steve-jobs/ar/1

16 Discussion of Tuckman's model based on Robbins, H. A., & Finley, M. (1995). *Why teams don't work.* Princeton, NJ: Peterson's/Pacesetter Books, Chapter 22.

17 Discussion of conflict and groupthink based on Toledo, R. (2008, June). Conflict is everywhere. *PM Network*. Retrieved from http://search.ebscohost.com; McNamara, P. (2003, August/September). Conflict resolution strategies. *OfficePro*, p. 25; Weiss, W. (2002, November). Building and managing teams. *SuperVision*, p. 19; Eisenhardt, K. (1997, July/August). How management teams can have a good fight. *Harvard Business Review*, pp. 77-85; Brockmann, E. (1996, May). Removing the paradox of conflict from group decisions. *Academy of Management Executives*, pp. 61-62; and Beebe, S., & Masterson, J. (1999). *Communicating in small groups.* New York: Longman, pp. 198-200.

18 Emory University neuroscientist Gregory Berns quoted in Cain, S. (2012, January 13). The rise of the new groupthink. *The New York Times*. Retrieved from http://www.nytimes.com/2012/01/15/opinion/sunday/the-rise-of-the-new-groupthink.html?pagewanted=all

19 J. Richard Hackman quoted in Coutu, D. (2009, May). Why teams don't work. *Harvard Business Review, (87)*5, 105. Retrieved from http://search.ebscohost.com

20 Janis, I. L. (1982). *Groupthink: Psychological studies on policy decisions and fiascoes.* Boston: Houghton Mifflin. See also Miranda, S. M., & Saunders, C. (1995, Summer). Group support systems: An organization development intervention to combat groupthink. *Public Administration Quarterly, 19*, 193-216. Retrieved from http://search.ebscohost.com

21 Amason, A. C., Hochwarter, W. A., Thompson, K. R., & Harrison, A. W. (1995, Autumn). Conflict: An important dimension in successful management teams. *Organizational Dynamics, 24*, 1. Retrieved from http://search.ebscohost.com

22 Parnell, C. (1996, November 1). Teamwork: Not a new idea, but it's transforming the workplace. *Executive Speeches, 63*, 46. Retrieved from http://search.ebscohost.com

23 Holtzman, Y., & Anderberg, J. (2011). Diversify your teams and collaborate: Because great minds don't think alike. *The Journal of Management Development, 30*(1), 79. doi: 10.1108/02621711111098389; Katzenbach, J., & Smith, D. (1994). *Wisdom of teams.* New York: HarperBusiness, p. 45.

24 Callahan, D. (2009, April 21). Breaking the ice; success through teamwork and partnerships. Retrieved from http://greatlakes.coastguard.dodlive.mil/2009/04/breaking-the-ice-success-through-teamwork-and-partnerships

25 Phillips, A. (2012, May 9). Wasted time in meetings costs the UK economy £26 billion. http://www.businessrevieweurope.eu/business_leaders/wasted-time-in-meetings-costs-the-uk-economy-26-billion; Herring, H. B.

(2006, June 18). Endless meetings: The black holes of the workday. *The New York Times*. Retrieved from http://www.nytimes.com

26 Loechner, J. (2009, May 12). Meeting optimization too. Retrieved from http://www.mediapost.com; Hollon, J. (2007, November 5). Meeting malaise. *Workforce Management, 68*(19). Retrieved from http://search.ebscohost.com

27 Rogelberg, S. G., Shanock, L. R., & Scott, C. W. (2012). Wasted time and money in meetings: Increasing return on investment. *Small Group Research, 43*(2), 237. doi: 10.1177/1046496411429170

28 Francisco, J. (2007, November/December). How to create and facilitate meetings that matter. *The Information Management Journal*, p. 54. Retrieved from http://search.ebscohost.com

29 Gouveia, A. (2012). Wasting time at work 2012. Retrieved from http://www.salary.com/wasting-time-at-work-2012

30 Herring, H. B. (2006, June 18). Endless meetings: The black holes of the workday. *The New York Times*. Retrieved from http://www.nytimes.com

31 Shellenbarger, S. (2012, May 16). Meet the meeting killers—In the office, they strangle ideas, poison progress; how to fight back. *The Wall Street Journal*. Retrieved from http://search.proquest.com

32 Rogelberg, S. G., Shanock, L. R., & Scott, C. W. (2012). Wasted time and money in meetings: Increasing return on investment. *Small Group Research, 43*(2), 237. doi: 10.1177/1046496411429170

33 Wuorio. J. (2010). 8 ways to show speaking skills in a meeting. Microsoft Business. Retrieved from http://www.microsoft.com/business/en-us/resources/management/leadership-training/8-ways-to-show-speaking-skills-in-a-meeting.aspx?fbid=O3xpKd4lO4M

34 Bruening, J. C. (1996, July). There's good news about meetings. *Managing Office Technology, 41*(7), 24-25. Retrieved from http://find.galegroup.com

35 Francisco, J. (2007, November/December). How to create and facilitate meetings that matter. *The Information Management Journal*, p. 54. Retrieved from http://search.ebscohost.com

36 Timberland responsibility. (2012). Retrieved from http://responsibility.timberland.com/service/?story=3; Marquis, C. (2003, July). Doing well and doing good. *The New York Times*, p. BU2.

37 Schabacker, K. (1991, June). A short, snappy guide to meaningful meetings. *Working Women*, 73.

38 Based on the following: Master the meeting madness. (2008). *Briefings bonus, communication briefings*; and Egan, M. (2006, March 13). Meetings can make or break your career. *Insurance Advocate, 117*, p. 24.

39 Lohr, S. (2008, July 22). As travel costs rise, more meetings go virtual. *The New York Times*. Retrieved from http://www.nytimes.com

40 Ibid.

41 Yu, R. (2009, June 23). Videoconferencing eyes growth spurt. *USA Today*, p. 3B.

42 Lohr, S. (2008, July 22). As travel costs rise, more meetings go virtual. *The New York Times*. Retrieved from http://www.nytimes.com

43 Schlegel, J. (2012). Running effective meetings: Types of meetings. Salary.com. Retrieved from http://www.salary.com/running-effective-meetings-6; Cohen, M. A., Rogelberg, S. G., Allen, J. A., & Luong, A. (2011). Meeting design characteristics and attendee perceptions of staff/team meeting quality. *Group Dynamics: Theory, Research, and Practice, 15*(1), 100-101; Schindler, E. (2008, February 15). Running an effective teleconference or virtual meeting. *CIO*. Retrieved from www.cio.com. See also Brenowitz, R. S. (2004, May). Virtual meeting etiquette. Article 601, *Innovative Leader*. Retrieved from http://www.winstonbrill.com

44 Schindler, E. (2008, February 15). Running an effective teleconference or virtual meeting. *CIO*. Retrieved from www.cio.com. See also Brenowitz, R. S. (2004, May). Virtual

meeting etiquette. Article 601, *Innovative Leader*. Retrieved from http://www.winstonbrill.com

45 Robbins, H., & Finley, M. (1995). *Why teams don't work*. Princeton, NJ: Peterson's/Pacesetter Books, p. 123.

46 Pellet, J. (2003, April). Anatomy of a turnaround guru. *Chief Executive*, 41; Mounter, P. (2003). Global internal communication: A model. *Journal of Communication Management*, 3, 265; Feiertag, H. (2002, July 15). Listening skills, enthusiasm top list of salespeople's best traits. *Hotel and Motel Management*, 20; Goby, V. P., & Lewis, J. H. (2000, June). The key role of listening in business: A study of the Singapore insurance industry. *Business Communication Quarterly*, 63, 41-51; Cooper, L. O. (1997, December). Listening competency in the workplace: A model for training. *Business Communication Quarterly*, 60, 75-84; and Penley, L. E., Alexander, E. R., Jerigan, I. E., & Henwood, C. I. (1997). Communication abilities of managers: The relationship to performance. *Journal of Management*, 17, 57-76.

47 Awang, F., Anderson, M. A., & Baker, C. J. (2003, Winter). Entry-level information services and support personnel: Needed workplace and technology skills. *The Delta Pi Epsilon Journal*, 48; and American Management Association. (1999, August). The challenges facing workers in the future. *HR Focus*, p. 6.

48 Harris, T. W. (1989, June). Listen carefully. *Nation's Business*, p. 78.

49 Steil, L. K., Barker, L. I., & Watson, K. W. (1983). *Effective listening: Key to your success* Reading, MA: Addison-Wesley; and Harris, J. A. (1998, August). Hear what's really being said. *New Zealand Management*, 45, 18.

50 Nelson, E., & Gypen, J. (1979, September/October). The subordinate's predicament. *Harvard Business Review*, 133.

51 International Listening Association. (2009). Listening and speech rates. Retrieved from http://www.listen.org

52 Wolvin, A., & Coakley, C. G. (1996). *Listening* (5th ed.). New York: McGraw-Hill, pp. 136-137.

53 Effective communication. (1994, November). *Training Tomorrow*, 32-33.

54 Based on Marshall, L. (1998, November). The intentional Oprah. *InStyle*, p. 341.

55 Wood, J. T. (2003). *Gendered lives: Communication, gender, and culture* (5th ed.). Belmont, CA: Wadsworth, pp. 119-120; Anderson, K. J., & Leaper, C. (1998, August). Meta-analyses of gender effects on conversational interruption: Who, what, when, where, and how. *Sex Roles: A Journal of Research*, 225; and Booth-Butterfield, M. (1984). She hears: What they hear and why. *Personnel Journal*, 44, 39.

56 Tear, J. (1995, November 20). They just don't understand gender dynamics. *The Wall Street Journal*, p. A12; and Wolfe, A. (1994, December 12). She just doesn't understand. *New Republic*, 26-34.

57 Burgoon, J., Coker, D., & Coker, R. (1986). Communication explanations. *Human Communication Research*, 463-494.

58 Tarsala, M. (1997, November 7). Remec's Ronald Ragland: Drawing rivals to his team by making their concerns his. *Investor's Business Daily*, A1.

59 Birdwhistel, R. (1970). *Kinesics and context.* Philadelphia: University of Pennsylvania Press.

60 What's A-O.K. in the U.S.A. is lewd and worthless beyond. (1996, August 18). *The New York Times*, p. E7.

61 Zielinski, D. (2001, April). Body language. *Presentations*, 15, 36-42. Retrieved from http://search.ebscohost.com

62 Body speak: What are you saying? (2000, October). *Successful Meetings*, 49-51.

63 Schepp, D. (2010, July 26). People@work: How to job hunt with tattoos. *Daily Finance*. Retrieved from http://www.dailyfinance.com/2010/07/26/tattoos-job-hunt-interviews-career

[64] Finney, P. (2007, October 23). Redefining business casual. *The New York Times*. Retrieved from http://search.ebscohost.com; see also Osterman, R. (2006, March 20). Casual loses its cool in business: More employers are trying to tighten up workplace clothing standards. *Sacramento Bee*. Retrieved from http://search.ebscohost.com; and Business casual: Out of style? (2005, May). *HR Focus*, 9. Retrieved from http://search.ebscohost.com

[65] Wilkie, H. (2003, Fall). Professional presence. *The Canadian Manager*, 14; and Kaplan-Leiserson, L. (2000, November). Casual dress/back to business attire. *Training & Development*, 38-39.

[66] Kennedy, M. M. (1997, September-October). Is business casual here to stay? *Executive Female*, 31.

[67] Wood, N., & Benitez, T. (2003, April). Does the suit fit? *Incentive*, p. 31.

[68] Business casual out of style. (2005, May). *HR Focus*, *82*, 16. Retrieved from http://search.ebscohost .com; Egodigwe, L. (2003, March). Here come the suits. *Black Enterprise*, *33*, 59. Retrieved from http://search.ebscohost.com; and Summerson, C. (2002, November 18). The suit is back in business. *BusinessWeek*, p. 130.

[69] Chao, L. (2006, January 17). Not-so-nice costs. *The Wall Street Journal*, p. B1.

[70] Rubin, C. (2010, July 12). The high cost of rudeness in the workplace. *Inc.* Retrieved from http://www.inc.com/news/articles/2010/07 /how-rudeness-affects-the-workplace.html; Yu, W. (2012, January 3). Workplace rudeness has a ripple effect. *Scientific American*. Retrieved from http://www.scientificamerican.com /article.cfm?id=ripples-of-rudeness; Jayson, S. (2011, August 9). Incivility a growing problem at work, psychologists say. *USA Today*. Retrieved from http://www.usatoday.com /news/health/wellness/story/2011/08 /Incivility-a-growing-problem-at-work -psychologists-say/49854130/1

[71] Cain, S. (2012, January 13). The rise of the new groupthink. *The New York Times*. Retrieved from http://www.nytimes.com/2012/01/15/opinion /sunday/the-rise-of-the-new-groupthink .html?pagewanted=all

[72] Gulley, P. (2009, March). 'Til we meet again: Nothing like a good old-fashioned business meeting to turn a crisis from bad to worse. *Indianapolis Monthly*, *32*(8). Retrieved from http://search .ebscohost.com

[73] Based on Ferguson. (2004). *Professional ethics and etiquette* (2nd ed.). New York: Ferguson.

[74] Scenario based on Hollingsworth, C. (2010, December). The peace process. *PM Network*, *24*(12), 63. Retrieved from http://search.zebscohost.com

[75] Office Team poll. (2008, June 23). Meetings and productivity. Graphic appearing in *USA Today*, p. 1.

[76] What's the universal hand sign for "I goofed"? (1996, December 16). *Santa Barbara News-Press*, p. D2.

[77] Bell, A. H. (1999, September). Using nonverbal cues. *Incentive*, *173*, 162. Retrieved from http://search.ebscohost.com

[78] Scenario based on Schepp, D. (2010, July 26). People@work: How to job hunt with tattoos. DailyFinance.com. Retrieved from http://www.dailyfinance.com/story/careers /tattoos-job-hunt-interviews-career/19566567

[79] Williams, A. (2008, June 24). At meetings, it's mind your BlackBerry or mind your manners. *The New York Times*, pp. A1, A3.

[80] O'Brien Coffey, J. (2011, September). How to manage smartphones at meetings. *Executive Travel Magazine*. Retrieved from http://www .executivetravelmagazine.com/articles /how-to-manage-smartphones-at-meetings

[81] Ibid.

[82] Ibid.

3

Intercultural Communication

OBJECTIVES

After studying this chapter, you should be able to

1 Understand the powerful effects of globalization and the major trends fueling it.

2 Define *culture*, name its primary characteristics, and explain the five key dimensions of culture: context, individualism, time orientation, power distance, and communication style.

3 Discuss strategies for enhancing intercultural effectiveness, reflect on nonverbal intercultural communication, assess how social media affect intercultural communication, and apply techniques for successful oral and written interactions across cultures.

4 Grasp the complexities of ethics across cultures, including business practices abroad, bribery, prevailing customs, and methods for coping.

5 Explain the advantages and challenges of workforce diversity, and address approaches for improving communication among diverse workplace audiences.

© iStockphoto.com/Anton Seleznev

Intercultural Lessons for the World's Largest Retailer

Walmart was forced to withdraw from its first European market, Germany, amid a loss of $1 billion. "The company's culture does not travel, and Walmart does not understand the German customer," said the CEO of a large local competitor six years before the retail behemoth exited the German market.[1] *The New York Times* wrote that Walmart's foray into its first European market had become "a template for how not to expand into a country."[2] Aside from underestimating its discounter competitors and the legal environment, most of Walmart's blunders seemed to be cultural. Top executives didn't speak German, and greeters with Midwestern folksiness were lost on German employees and local shoppers.[3] A court overturned Walmart's policy against dating coworkers, and Walmart's antiunion stance fell flat in a country where unions and corporations collaborate closely.

How has Walmart fared in Asia? Cultural differences and fierce local competition forced the world's largest retailer to leave Korea to stem heavy losses. "Why would you buy a box of shampoo bottles?" asked Lee Jin Sook, a Seoul housewife. Koreans favor smaller packages and walk or take the subway to shop daily at a variety of stores.[4] Consumers in this and other Asian countries don't buy in bulk. Moreover, Walmart's no-frills warehouse stores and high racks frustrated diminutive shoppers, who had to borrow ladders.

What about Japan and China? Although retailers Tesco and Carrefour have already exited Japan, Walmart is holding on to its supermarket chain Seiyu despite facing similar problems as its competitors[5] and besides struggling with mistrust and public resentment.[6] Walmart's Chinese Supercenters thrived at first because the company did try to cater to local tastes by offering, for example, green tea tastings, live fish, and freshly baked Chinese sweets.[7] Now, however, Walmart's market share in China is plummeting as domestic chains opt for small neighborhood stores that sell key goods the consumers want.

Says one analyst: "Instead of adjusting to the local competition by shrinking store sizes or selling higher margin products, Walmart is doing little to change its business model." He faults the retailer and other U.S. companies for not localizing their business models and management to keep up with new domestic players.[8] Can Walmart do better in its future international endeavors?

You will learn more about Walmart and be asked to complete a relevant task at the end of this chapter.

Critical Thinking

- In its international expansion policy, Walmart at first followed the advice of Harvard business professor Theodore Levitt. His famous book *The Globalization of Markets* advocated standardization, not localization. "Gone are accustomed differences in national or regional preference," Levitt wrote. Whereas conventional multinational companies adapted to "superficial and even entrenched differences within and between nations," truly global firms sought to "force suitably standardized products and practices on the entire globe."[9] Should companies stick to a standardized approach or adapt to local markets?

- What domestic and global changes are taking place that encourage the international expansion of companies such as Walmart?

- What other U.S. businesses can you name that have merged with foreign companies or expanded to become multinational? Have you heard of any notable successes or failures?

The Growing Importance of Intercultural Communication

The "global village" predicted many years ago is here, making intercultural communication skills ever more important. Especially in North America, but also around the world, the movement toward a global economy has swelled to a torrent. To drive profits, many organizations are expanding overseas. If you visit a European or Asian city, you will see many familiar U.S. chains such as The Gap, Subway, Abercrombie & Fitch, Guess, Starbucks, Apple, and KFC. To be immediately competitive, some companies formed multinational alliances. For example, Walmart, the U.S. super discounter, joined forces with Seiyu, Japan's fifth-largest food and retail chain.

However, as Walmart also learned, expanding companies sometimes stumble when they cross borders and are forced to confront obstacles never before encountered. Significant obstacles involve confusion and clashes resulting from intercultural differences. You may face such intercultural differences in your current or future jobs. Your employers, coworkers, or customers could very well be from other countries and cultures. You may travel abroad for your employer or on your own. Learning more about the powerful effect that culture has on behavior will help you reduce friction and misunderstanding in your dealings with people from other cultures. Before examining strategies for helping you overcome intercultural obstacles, let's take a closer look at globalization and the trends fueling it.

Markets Go Global

Doing business beyond borders is now commonplace. Coca-Cola battles Pepsi in India, and Frito-Lay pushes its potato chips in China.[10] Finnish mobile phone maker Nokia ranks as the most trusted brand in India.[11] Newell Rubbermaid offers stylish Pyrex cookware to European chefs; and McDonald's, KFC, and Starbucks serve hungry customers around the world.

Not only are familiar businesses expanding their markets beyond their borders, but acquisitions, mergers, alliances, and buyouts are obscuring the nationality of many companies. The quirky Vermont ice cream purveyor Ben & Jerry's is a division of Dutch multinational Unilever,[12] and Bridgestone Americas is owned by a Japanese conglomerate. The Arco gas station chain is a subsidiary of the third-largest energy company in the world, British Petroleum. Last, "Your Neighborhood Grocery Store," Trader Joe's, is owned by Germany's top discounter, Aldi.[13]

Many home-grown companies with famous brands—such as Ford, Firestone, Coca-Cola, AT&T, Colgate, and JP Morgan—are now controlled by global enterprises.[14] A prime example is 7-Eleven. Originating in the United States, it is now a subsidiary of Seven-Eleven Japan. It ranks as the highest-grossing retailer in Japan and has nearly twice as many outlets there as it has in the United States.[15]

To succeed in today's interdependent global village, multinational companies are increasingly finding it necessary to adapt to other cultures. Selling laundry products in Europe, Unilever learned that Germans demand a product that is gentle on lakes and rivers. Spaniards wanted cheaper products that get shirts white and soft, and Greeks preferred small packages that were cheap and easy to carry home.[16] When upscale sandwich chain New York NY Fresh Deli opened a franchise in Dubai, it had to replace all salad dressings that contained vinegar. Considered a spirit, vinegar and other alcoholic beverages can be served only in hotels and to non-Muslims.[17] As Figure 3.1 shows, Starbucks has established itself very successfully in China by adjusting its brand to the local market and is poised to enter India.

Dunkin' Donuts catered to local palates in Singapore with wasabi cheese, in Korea with red bean, and in China with dry pork and seaweed-flavored donuts.[18] In India a few years ago, mobile phone giant Nokia offered a device that combined a phone, flashlight, radio, and alarm clock. This device was a big hit in a country with regular power outages.[19]

But not all overseas expansion thrives. Best Buy, the world's largest consumer electronics retailer, failed in China when it did not adjust to shoppers' preferences.[20] Chinese tech shoppers were familiar with small stores crammed with products from each manufacturer bunched together and sold by that maker's clerks. The Best Buy strategy of comparison shopping did not sit well with these shoppers, and Best Buy pulled out.[21] Similarly, Home Depot, America's do-it-yourself center, closed all of its big-box China stores after years of losses. It failed to recognize that in China, where cheap labor abounds, "the market trend is more of a do-it-for-me culture."[22]

Figure **3.1** Starbucks—A Global Brand That Understands Localization

As market researcher Shaun Rein puts it, Starbucks is a truly global brand because it has successfully adapted to a very different market and modified its model to fit China while remaining faithful to its core values. It remains to be seen whether the coffee chain can replicate its global success in India, another traditionally tea-loving culture.

© iStockphoto.com/maomaotou

Starbucks' Triumph in China

Introduced flavors appealing to local tastes, such as green-tea flavored coffee drinks

500 outlets in China: more profitable per store than the U.S.

Offers dine-in service and a comfortable environment with air conditioning

China: Starbucks' largest market outside the U.S.

$ premium pricing strategy

Superb service equal to 5-star hotels

Even consumers who prefer competing coffee products prefer Starbucks for its service.

Starbucks' annual turnover is much lower than the 30% common in China because of good benefits, work environments, and career options.

Outlets: meeting places for executives and gatherings of friends

Carrying a cup: a little personal luxury, a status symbol, a way to show sophistication

Coffee conquering tea cultures

Coffee consumption has nearly doubled over last 10 years.

Coffee, a "sexy" beverage to enjoy.

Coffee has become the "in" thing.

Neutral place to go and sit, hang out

Starbucks enters India

Competition

Growth of **café culture**, not so much of coffee

© AP Images/Rajanish Kakade

Instead of traditional coffee, young Indians favor Café Coffee Day's cold, sweet milkshakes and teas.

Lavazza of Italy and Coffee Bean & Tea Leaf have outlets in India.

O⊠ering a Starbucks-like experience

A small cappuccino costs $1 at Café Coffee Day, India's largest café chain.

© Cengage Learning 2015

Rein, S. (2012, February 13). Why Starbucks succeeds in China. CNBC guest blog. Retrieved from http://www.cnbc.com/id/46186635/Rein_Why_Starbucks_Succeeds_in_China

Bajaj, V. (2012, January 30). After a year of delays, the first Starbucks is to open in tea-loving India This fall. The New York Times. Retrieved from http://www.nytimes.com/2012/01/31/business/global/starbucks-to-open-first-indian-store-this-autumn.html

Major Trends Fuel Globalization

Although some companies fail, a vast number of domestic and international businesses are rushing to expand around the world. What is causing this dash toward the globalization of markets and blurring of national identities? Many companies, such as Walmart, are increasingly looking overseas as domestic markets mature. They can no longer expect double-digit

REALITY CHECK: Regional, Cultural Differences Still Matter

"The flattening of the world has not flattened unique cultural and national characteristics, or the idiosyncratic preferences of customers."[23]

—**MARTIN ROLL,** *brand advisor, Martin Roll Company - www.martinroll.com*

sales growth at home. As summarized in Figure 3.2, aside from shrinking domestic markets, several trends fuel global expansion including favorable trade agreements, growing numbers of middle-class consumers in emerging nations, transportation advancements, and increasingly sophisticated information and communication technologies.

Favorable Trade Agreements. A significant factor in the expansion of global markets is the passage of favorable trade agreements. The General Agreement on Tariffs and Trade (GATT) promotes open trade globally, and the North American Free Trade Agreement (NAFTA) expands free trade among Canada, the United States, and Mexico. NAFTA has created one of the largest and richest free-trade regions on earth. Additional trade agreements are causing markets to expand. At this writing the United States has 12 Free Trade Agreements (FTAs) in force with 18 countries.[24] These agreements significantly open global markets to imports and exports.

Robust Middle Classes in Emerging Economies. Parts of the world formerly considered developing now boast robust middle classes. Once known only for cheap labor, many countries with emerging economies are now seen as promising markets. Estimates suggest that 70 percent of world growth over the next few years will come from emerging markets. The brightest spots are expected to be Brazil, Russia, India, and China.[25] By 2020 more than half the world's middle class is predicted to be in Asia.[26] Consumers in these emerging economies crave everything from cola to smartphones and high-definition TVs. What's more, many countries such as China and India have become less suspicious of foreign investment and free trade, thus fostering vigorous globalization.

Advancements in Transportation and Logistics. Of paramount importance in explaining the explosive growth of global markets are amazing advancements in transportation and logistics technology. Supersonic planes carry goods and passengers to other continents overnight.

Figure 3.2 Trends Fueling Globalization

Produce shoppers in Japan can choose from the finest artichokes, avocados, and apples only hours after they were picked in California. Americans enjoy bouquets of tulips, roses, and exotic lilies soon after harvesting in Holland and Colombia. Fruits and vegetables such as strawberries and asparagus, once available only in season, are now enjoyed nearly year-round.

Breakthroughs in transportation technology also push the drive toward globalization. For example, digital wireless sensor telemetry keeps shippers informed of vital information en route.[27] Senders can track the destination, the speed of movement, and even the temperature of a shipment's environment. This technology expands markets by enabling senders to monitor shipments and learn of delays or harmful conditions for the goods being shipped.

Growing Reach of Information and Communication Technologies. Probably the most significant factor fueling globalization is the development of information and communication technologies. These technologies, known as ICT (Information and Communication Technologies), have changed the way we live and do business. ICT includes the Internet, wireless networks, smartphones, mobile electronic devices, and other communication media. High-speed, high-capacity, and relatively low-cost communications have opened new global opportunities that make geographic location virtually irrelevant for many activities and services. Workers have access to company records, software programs, and colleagues whether they're working at home, in the office, or at the beach.

Rotation Curation: From Social Media to Cultural Networking

Plugged In

© iStockphoto/Thinkstock

Would you want to tweet for your country? A recent Twitter as well as Instagram trend could lead to an opportunity to be the voice of the nation. Would you consider rotation curation? It's a social media experiment (or a *movement,* if you want to believe its boosters at **#RotationCuration**) that started when the country of Sweden in late 2011 decided to entrust its official Twitter account **@Sweden** to a different "average" citizen each week to tweet about anything he or she might want to share. Anything! As *The New York Times* and others observed, Sweden may have gotten more than it had bargained for when the various Swedish twitterers began airing very personal and even inappropriate tweets to the world.

The most notorious so far has been 27-year-old Sonja Abrahamsson, who joked about AIDS and Down syndrome, asked baffling questions about Jews, and freely shared with the world her grievously inappropriate parenting. Another Swedish representative crossed the line of propriety with outrageous, sexually tinged content. The oldest curator so far was sixty; the youngest, eighteen years old. The rotation curation project is the brainchild of a public relations agency hired by the Swedish government tourism agency to represent what Sweden stands for, "being progressive, democratic, creative." To show just how progressive the Swedish society is, the PR agency had decided to give control of the Twitter account to ordinary Swedes. Even in the face of mounting criticism, the Swedish government did not censor its citizen representatives, requiring only that they not be criminals and label their political opinions as their own.

What qualifies candidates, who must be nominated by others for the job? They are expected to be interesting, English-tweeting, experienced Twitter users who engage in "their normal Twitter behavior" and do so "with some dignity," although the latter is only a suggestion. Eric Isberg, the youngest Swede speaking for 9 million people, at one point posted mouth-watering photos of his school lunch on Twitter and conveyed the compliments of his readers all around the world to the overjoyed cook. However, when asked about the significance of a Swedish patriotic holiday or where his followers might be able to watch the transit of Venus in Stockholm, he was stumped. Eric Isberg's mother told the media that the officials "were very brave to trust him."

After Sweden, other entities, official or not, followed suit—for example, the city of Leeds, England (**@People ofLeeds**); Australia (**@WeAreAustralia**); the United States (**@TweetWeekUSA**); Mexico (**@CuratorsMexico**); and the expatriate Basque community (**@BasquesAbroad**). More cities, counties, neighborhoods, states, and cultural projects caught on. During the crisis in Syria, **@TweetWeekSyria** became the first political rotation curation project; and **@iamclimate**, the first issue-driven rotation curation project.[28] See Activity 3.14 for discussion questions and applications of rotation curation.

The world's new economic landscape enables companies to conduct business anytime, anywhere, and with any customer.[29] As discussed in Chapters 1 and 2, technology is making a huge difference in the workplace. Wireless connectivity, portable electronic devices, teleconferencing, instant messaging, intranets as well as social media, wikis, and blogs streamline business processes and improve access to critical company information. Managers in Miami or Milwaukee can use high-speed data systems to swap marketing plans instantly with their counterparts in Milan or Munich. Fashionistas can snap a digital photo of a garment on a runway in Europe and immediately transmit it to manufacturers in Hong Kong and Jakarta, Indonesia. Further expanding the concept of a global village, social networking sites such as Facebook and Twitter enable users from all over the world to communicate as if they lived next door.

The changing landscape of business and society clearly demonstrates the need for technology savvy and connectedness around the world. Career success and personal wealth depend on the ability to use technology effectively. As the accompanying Plugged In feature demonstrates, communication technology must be used cautiously and professionally.

REALITY CHECK: Do We Need Immigration?

Immigration to the United States is currently decreasing, although the foreign-born population has grown 10 million over the last decade.[30] Some experts fear future labor shortages and a decline in U.S. competitiveness. According to the latest U.S. Census, 40 states have fewer children than in 2000, and states that don't—Texas, for example—owe their growth to immigrants: "The new engines of growth in America's population are Hispanics, Asians and other minorities."[31]

—**BILL FREY,** *demographer and sociologist*

Domestic Workforce Is Becoming Increasingly Diverse

As world commerce mingles more and more, another trend gives intercultural communication increasing importance: people are on the move. Lured by the prospects of peace, prosperity, education, or a fresh start, people from many cultures are moving to countries promising to fulfill their dreams. For generations the two most popular destinations have been the United States and Canada.

Because of increases in immigration over time, foreign-born people comprise an ever-growing portion of the total U.S. population. Over the next 40 years, the population of the United States is expected to grow by nearly 50 percent, from about 308.7 million in the year 2010 to as many as 458 million people in 2050. Two thirds of that increase will be the result of higher fertility rates among immigrants and their offspring.[32]

This influx of immigrants is reshaping American and Canadian societies. Earlier immigrants were thought to be part of a "melting pot" of ethnic groups. Today, they are more like a "tossed salad" or "spicy stew," with each group contributing its own unique flavor. Instead of the exception, cultural diversity is increasingly the norm. As we seek to accommodate multiethnic neighborhoods, multinational companies, and an intercultural workforce, we can expect some changes to happen smoothly. Other changes will involve conflict and resentment, especially for people losing their positions of power and privilege. Learning to accommodate and manage intercultural change is an important part of the education of any business communicator.

Culture **and Communication**

LEARNING OBJECTIVE **2**
Define *culture*, name its primary characteristics, and explain the five key dimensions of culture: context, individualism, time orientation, power distance, and communication style.

Comprehending the verbal and nonverbal meanings of a message is difficult even when communicators share the same culture. When they come from different cultures, special sensitivity and skills are necessary. True, global business, new communication technologies, the Internet, and social media span the world, shrinking distances. However, cultural differences still exist and can cause significant misunderstandings.

For our purposes, *culture* may be defined as the complex system of values, traits, morals, and customs shared by a society. Culture is a powerful operating force that molds the way we think, behave, and communicate. The objective of this chapter is to broaden your view of culture and open your mind to flexible attitudes so that you can avoid frustration when cultural adjustment is necessary.

Characteristics of Culture

Every country or region within a country has a unique common heritage, joint experience, or shared learning. This shared background creates the culture of a region, country, or society. Despite globalization, interculturalism, and extensive social networking, we should expect to make adjustments and adopt new attitudes. However, first we must understand some basic characteristics of culture.

Culture Is Learned.   Rules, values, and attitudes of a culture are learned and passed down from generation to generation. For example, in many Middle Eastern and some Asian cultures, same-sex people may walk hand-in-hand in the street, but opposite-sex people may not do so. In Arab cultures conversations are sometimes held nose to nose. However, in Western cultures if a person stands too close, one may react as if violated: *He was all over me like a rash.* Cultural rules of behavior learned from your family and society are conditioned from early childhood.

Cultures Are Inherently Logical.   The rules in any culture reinforce that culture's values and beliefs. They act as normative forces. For example, in Japan the original Barbie doll was a failure for many reasons, one of which was her toothy smile.[33] This is a country where women cover their mouths with their hands when they laugh so as not to expose their teeth. Exposing one's teeth is not only immodest but also aggressive. Although current cultural behavior may sometimes seem silly and illogical, nearly all

© Rolf Bruderer/Blend Images/Jupiterimages

Professionals need to learn important dos and don'ts when conducting business across cultures. In Argentina, it is common for businesspeople to touch others during personal conversations; in Saudi Arabia, men and women must avoid all physical contact. In Latin America, businesspeople wear attire that is bright and colorful; in Asian countries, professionals wear neutral colors and exhibit strict modesty. In Russia, it is customary to drink a toast to new business relationships; in the Middle East, such toasts are taboo. Why is it important for communicators to understand and respect cultural differences?[34]

serious rules and values originate in deep-seated beliefs. Rules about exposing teeth or how close to stand are linked to values about sexuality, aggression, modesty, and respect. Acknowledging the inherent logic of a culture is extremely important when encountering behavior that differs from one's own cultural norms.

Culture Is the Basis of Self-Identity and Community.   Culture is the basis for how we tell the world who we are and what we believe. People build their identities through cultural overlays to their primary culture. When North Americans make choices in education, career, place of employment, and life partner, they consider certain rules, manners, ceremonies, beliefs, languages, and values. These considerations add to their total cultural outlook and are major expressions of their self-identity.

Culture Combines the Visible and Invisible.   To outsiders, the way we act—those things that we do in daily life and work—are the most visible parts of our culture. On the surface, we recognize numerous signs of culture including the words we use, our body language and gestures, the way we dress, and our outward behavior. Under the surface, however, lie unspoken rules governing what is seen. These unspoken and often unconscious rules are determined by our beliefs and values, attitudes and biases, feelings and fears, and upbringing. The invisible structure of culture vastly outnumbers the visible, as illustrated by the iceberg concept shown in Figure 3.3.

Culture Is Dynamic.   Over time, cultures change. Changes are caused by advancements in technology and communication, as discussed earlier. Local differences are modified or slowly erased. Change is also caused by events such as migration, natural disasters, and wars. The American Civil War, for instance, produced far-reaching cultural changes for both the North and the South. Another major event in the United States was the exodus of people from farms. When families moved to cities, major changes occurred in the way family members

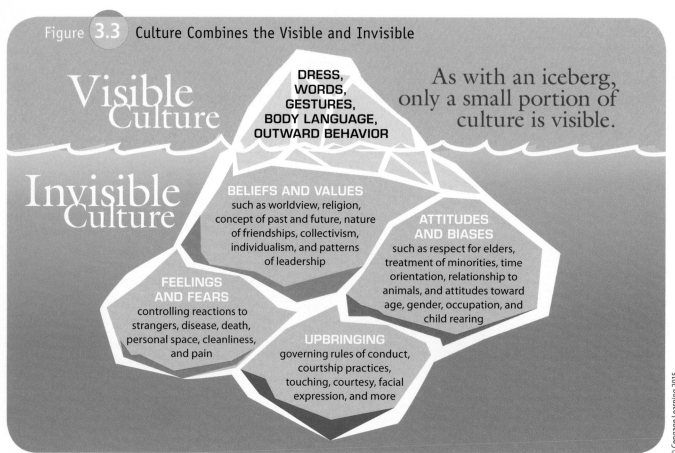

Figure **3.3** Culture Combines the Visible and Invisible

Visible Culture

DRESS, WORDS, GESTURES, BODY LANGUAGE, OUTWARD BEHAVIOR

As with an iceberg, only a small portion of culture is visible.

Invisible Culture

BELIEFS AND VALUES such as worldview, religion, concept of past and future, nature of friendships, collectivism, individualism, and patterns of leadership

ATTITUDES AND BIASES such as respect for elders, treatment of minorities, time orientation, relationship to animals, and attitudes toward age, gender, occupation, and child rearing

FEELINGS AND FEARS controlling reactions to strangers, disease, death, personal space, cleanliness, and pain

UPBRINGING governing rules of conduct, courtship practices, touching, courtesy, facial expression, and more

© Cengage Learning 2015

Chapter 3: Intercultural Communication

interacted. Attitudes, behaviors, and beliefs change in open societies more quickly than in closed societies.

Dimensions of Culture

The more you know about culture in general and your own culture in particular, the better able you will be to adopt an intercultural perspective. In this book, it is impossible to describe fully the infinite facets of culture, but we can outline some key dimensions of culture identified by social scientists.

So that you will better understand your culture and how it contrasts with other cultures, we will describe five key dimensions of culture: context, individualism, time orientation, power distance, and communication style.

High and Low Context.   Context is probably the most important cultural dimension and also the most difficult to define. It is a concept developed by cultural anthropologist Edward T. Hall. In his model, context refers to the stimuli, environment, or ambience surrounding an event. Communicators in low-context cultures (such as those in North America, Scandinavia, and Germany) depend little on the context of a situation and shared experience to convey their meaning. They assume that messages must be explicit, and listeners rely exclusively on the written or spoken word. In high-context cultures (such as those in Japan, China, and Middle Eastern countries), much is left unsaid because the listener is assumed to be already "contexted" and does not require much background information.[35] To identify low- and high-context countries, Hall arranged them on a continuum, as shown in Figure 3.4.[36]

Low-context cultures tend to be logical, analytical, and action oriented. Business communicators stress clearly articulated messages that they consider to be objective, professional, and efficient. High-context cultures are more likely to be intuitive and contemplative. Communicators in high-context cultures pay attention to more than the spoken or written words. They emphasize interpersonal relationships, nonverbal expression, physical setting,

Figure 3.4 Comparing Low- and High-Context Cultures

Higher Context

Asian • Arabian • South European • African • South American • Central European • Australian • American • Northern European • German • Swiss

Lower Context

- Tend to prefer direct verbal interaction
- Tend to understand meaning at one level only
- Are generally less proficient in reading nonverbal cues
- Value individualism
- Rely more on logic
- Say *no* directly
- Communicate in highly structured, detailed messages with literal meanings
- Give authority to written information

- Tend to prefer indirect verbal interaction
- Tend to understand meanings embedded at many sociocultural levels
- Are generally more proficient in reading nonverbal cues
- Value group membership
- Rely more on context and feeling
- Talk around point, avoid saying *no*
- Communicate in sometimes simple, sometimes ambiguous messages
- Understand visual messages readily

© Cengage Learning 2015

and social setting. For example, a Japanese communicator might say *yes* when he really means *no*. From the context of the situation, the Japanese speaker would indicate whether *yes* really means *yes* or whether it means *no*. The context, tone, time taken to answer, facial expression, and body cues would convey the meaning of *yes*.[37] Thus, in high-context cultures, communication cues are transmitted by posture, voice inflection, gestures, and facial expression. Establishing relationships is an important part of communicating and interacting.

In terms of thinking patterns, low-context communicators tend to use *linear logic*. They proceed from Point A to Point B to Point C and finally arrive at a conclusion. High-context communicators, however, may use *spiral logic*, circling around a topic indirectly and looking at it from many tangential or divergent viewpoints. A conclusion may be implied but not argued directly. For a scale ranking low- and high-context cultures, see Figure 3.4.

Individualism and Collectivism.   An attitude of independence and freedom from control characterizes individualism. Members of low-context cultures, particularly Americans, tend to value individualism. They believe that initiative and self-assertion result in personal achievement. They believe in individual action and personal responsibility, and they desire a large degree of freedom in their personal lives.

Members of high-context cultures are more collectivist. They emphasize membership in organizations, groups, and teams; they encourage acceptance of group values, duties, and decisions. They typically resist independence because it fosters competition and confrontation instead of consensus. In group-oriented cultures such as those in many Asian societies, for example, self-assertion and individual decision making are discouraged. "The nail that sticks up gets pounded down" is a common Japanese saying.[38] Business decisions are often made by all who have competence in the matter under discussion. Similarly, in China managers also focus on the group rather than on the individual, preferring a consultative management style over an autocratic style.[39]

Many cultures, of course, are quite complex and cannot be characterized as totally individualistic or group oriented. For example, European Americans are generally quite individualistic, whereas African Americans are less so, and Latinos are closer to the group-centered dimension.[40]

Time Orientation.   North Americans consider time a precious commodity to be conserved. They correlate time with productivity, efficiency, and money. Keeping people waiting for business appointments is considered a waste of time and also rude.

In other cultures time may be perceived as an unlimited and never-ending resource to be enjoyed. A North American businessperson, for example, was kept waiting two hours past a scheduled appointment time in South America. She wasn't offended, though, because she was familiar with South Americans' more relaxed concept of time.

Although Asians are punctual, their need for deliberation and contemplation sometimes clashes with an Americans' desire for speedy decisions. They do not like to be rushed. A Japanese businessperson considering the purchase of American appliances, for example, asked for five minutes to consider the seller's proposal. The potential buyer crossed his arms, sat back, and closed his eyes in concentration. A scant 18 seconds later, the American resumed his sales pitch to the obvious bewilderment of the Japanese buyer.[41]

Power Distance.   One important element of culture is power distance, first introduced by influential social psychologist Geert Hofstede. The Power Distance Index measures how people in different societies cope with inequality; in other words, how they relate to more powerful individuals. In high power distance countries, subordinates expect formal hierarchies and embrace relatively authoritarian, paternalistic power relationships. In low power distance cultures, however, subordinates consider themselves as equals of their supervisors. They confidently voice opinions and participate in decision making. Relationships between high-powered individuals and people with little power tend to be more democratic, egalitarian, and informal.

As you probably guessed, in Western cultures people are more relaxed about social status and the appearance of power.[42] Deference is not generally paid to individuals merely because of their wealth, position, seniority, or age. In many Asian cultures, however, these characteristics are important and must be respected. Walmart, facing many hurdles in breaking into the Japanese market, admits having had difficulty training local employees to speak up to their bosses. In the Japanese culture, lower-level employees do not question management. Deference and respect are paid to authority and power. Recognizing this cultural pattern,

Marriott Hotel managers learned to avoid placing a lower-level Japanese employee on a floor above a higher-level executive from the same company.

Communication Style.   People in low- and high-context cultures tend to communicate differently with words. To Americans and Germans, words are very important, especially in contracts and negotiations. People in high-context cultures, on the other hand, place more emphasis on the surrounding context than on the words describing a negotiation. A Greek may see a contract as a formal statement announcing the intention to build a business for the future. The Japanese may treat contracts as statements of intention, and they assume changes will be made as projects develop. Mexicans may treat contracts as artistic exercises of what might be accomplished in an ideal world. They do not necessarily expect contracts to apply consistently in the real world. An Arab may be insulted by merely mentioning a contract; a person's word is more binding.[43]

North Americans tend to take words literally, whereas Latinos enjoy plays on words; and Arabs and South Americans sometimes speak with extravagant or poetic figures of speech that may be misinterpreted if taken literally. Nigerians prefer a quiet, clear form of expression; and Germans tend to be direct but understated.[44]

In communication style North Americans value straightforwardness, are suspicious of evasiveness, and distrust people who might have a "hidden agenda" or who "play their cards too close to the chest."[45] North Americans also tend to be uncomfortable with silence and impatient with delays. Some Asian businesspeople have learned that the longer they drag out negotiations, the more concessions impatient North Americans are likely to make.

As you can see, high-context cultures differ from low-context cultures in many dimensions. These differences can be significant for companies engaging in international business.

Becoming Interculturally Proficient

LEARNING OBJECTIVE **3**
Discuss strategies for enhancing intercultural effectiveness, reflect on nonverbal intercultural communication, assess how social media affect intercultural communication, and apply techniques for successful oral and written interactions across cultures.

Being aware of your own culture and how it contrasts with others is an important first step in achieving intercultural proficiency. Another step involves recognizing barriers to intercultural accommodation and striving to overcome them. Some of these barriers occur quite naturally and require conscious effort to surmount. You might be thinking, why bother? Probably the most important reasons for becoming interculturally competent are that your personal life will be more satisfying and your work life will be more productive, gratifying, and effective.

Strategies for Improving Your Intercultural Effectiveness

Remember that culture is learned. Developing cultural competence often involves changing attitudes. Through exposure to other cultures and through training, such as you are receiving in this course, you can learn new attitudes and behaviors that help bridge gaps between cultures. Following are some suggestions to help you boost your intercultural savvy.

Building Cultural Self-Awareness.   Begin to think of yourself as a product of your culture, and understand that your culture is just one among many. Try to stand outside and look at yourself. Do you see any reflex reactions and automatic thought patterns that are a result of your upbringing? These may be invisible to you until challenged by difference. Remember, your culture was designed to help you succeed and survive in a certain environment. Be sure to keep what works and yet be ready to adapt as environments change. Flexibility is an important survival skill.

Curbing Ethnocentrism.   The belief in the superiority of one's own race is known as *ethnocentrism*, a natural attitude inherent in all cultures. If you were raised in North America, many of the dimensions of culture described previously probably seem "right" to you. For example, it is only logical to think that time is money and you should not waste it. Everyone knows that, right? That is why an American businessperson in an Arab or Asian country might feel irritated at time spent over coffee or other social rituals before any "real" business is transacted. In these cultures, however, time is viewed differently. Moreover, personal relationships must be established and nurtured before credible negotiations may proceed.

An assorted group of business professionals attending a diversity training class in Hartford, Connecticut, are asked for epithets they free-associate with the word *Muslim*. They call out: *poor, uneducated immigrant, Arab, foreigner,* and *terrorist*.[46]

Goodwill Ambassadors. Aida Mansoor, wife of cardiologist Reza Mansoor, began teaching seminars explaining Islam immediately after September 11, 2001. Originally from Sri Lanka, the couple reluctantly embraced their role as ambassadors of their faith: "We were terrified, but we decided either we face this now or we pack up and leave," says Reza Mansoor. "If we were going to stay, we had to explain our faith. What was the other choice? To live in a country without self-respect or dignity?" Yet even in a diverse, tolerant city such as Hartford, Mansoor has fielded jokes about her hijab, the Islamic head scarf she wears, and endured hate mail sent to her mosque.

Reacting to Discrimination. To illustrate the daily reality of Muslims in America, Mansoor shows her classes an experiment staged by a TV station: A bagel shop employee ostensibly refuses to serve a Muslim woman wearing a hijab. The camera reveals the other customers' reactions. Three people thank the clerk for standing up to "un-American terrorists." However, several customers leave in protest, and one man tells the clerk with tears in his eyes: "Every person deserves to be treated with respect, dignity."

Facts Versus Prejudice. A recent survey shows that 46 percent of the Muslim population in the United States boast a college education, nearly 70 percent are younger than forty, and 12.4 percent are engineers. A majority of the world's Muslims are not Arabs; they live in India, many regions of Asia, Russia, and parts of Europe and Africa. Although the exact number is difficult to establish, experts generally agree that the United States is home to about 2 million Muslims, most of whom are U.S. citizens and oppose violence. See Activity 3.16 for discussion questions and tasks for overcoming prejudice.

Ethnocentrism causes us to judge others by our own values. We expect others to react as we would, and they expect us to behave as they would. Misunderstandings naturally result. A North American smiling broadly, joking, and presenting excitedly a proposed project to German business partners will be perceived as lacking credibility. In turn, German businesspersons who respond soberly and ask direct, probing questions will appear rude and humorless. These knee-jerk ethnocentric responses can be reduced through knowledge of other cultures and the development of increased intercultural sensitivity.

Political conflict can reinforce ethnocentric gut-level reactions that are often fueled by ignorance and fear. Without a doubt, the fear of terrorism today is real and justified. Since the terrorist attacks on September 11, 2001, Americans feel threatened on their own soil. Radical Islam and the subsequent wars in Iraq and Afghanistan have fueled anti-Arab and anti-Muslim sentiments in general. Battling prejudice and even hate may be a tall order for diversity training in the workplace as the Ethical Insights box shows.

Understanding Generalizations and Stereotyping.   Most experts recognize that it is impossible to talk about cultures without using mental categories, representations, and generalizations to describe groups. These categories are sometimes considered *stereotypes*. Because the term *stereotype* has a negative meaning, intercultural authors Varner and Beamer suggested that we distinguish between *stereotype* and *prototype*.

A *stereotype* is an oversimplified behavioral pattern applied uncritically to groups. Although they may be exaggerated and overgeneralized beliefs when applied to groups of people, stereotypes are not always entirely false.[47] Often they contain a grain of truth. When a stereotype develops into a rigid attitude and when it is based on erroneous beliefs or preconceptions, however, then it should be called a *prejudice*.

Varner and Beamer recommended using the term *prototype* to describe "mental representations based on general characteristics that are not fixed and rigid, but rather are open to new definitions."[48] Prototypes, then, are dynamic and change with fresh experience. Prototypes based on objective observations usually have a considerable amount of truth in them. That is why they can be helpful in studying culture. For example, South American businesspeople often talk about their families before getting down to business. This prototype is generally accurate, but it may not universally apply, and it may change over time.

Some people object to making any generalizations about cultures whatsoever. It is wise to remember, however, that whenever we are confronted with something new and unfamiliar, we naturally strive to categorize the data to make sense out of them. In categorizing these new data, we are making generalizations. Significant intellectual discourse and science would be impossible without generalizations. Unfounded generalizations about people and cultures, of course, can lead to bias and prejudice. However, for our purposes, when we discuss cultures, it is important to be able to make generalizations and describe cultural prototypes.

Being Open-Minded.   One desirable attitude in achieving intercultural proficiency is that of *tolerance*. Closed-minded people cannot look beyond their own ethnocentrism. But as global markets expand and as our own society becomes increasingly multiethnic, tolerance becomes especially significant. Some job descriptions now include statements such as, *Must be able to interact with ethnically diverse personnel*.

To improve tolerance, you will want to practice *empathy*. This means trying to see the world through another's eyes. It means being less judgmental and more eager to seek common ground. BMW Group and the United Nations Alliance of Civilizations jointly award projects around the world that promote international understanding and the overcoming of religious and cultural boundaries. A pair of recent finalists, a Palestinian school principal and an Israeli school principal, joined forces to counter the political turmoil in Jerusalem with their peace-building project billed "an ark of tolerance and understanding." To bridge the divide, students of both schools collaborate on local environmental protection activities and study each other's language. Says Rana Khalaf, the Palestinian principal: "Learning the other language is another way to break down prejudices and reduce fears as well as to strengthen the feeling of fellowship." Khalaf believes that "by initiating and implementing a joint project, divided communities can find a way to grow together again."[49]

Being tolerant also involves patience. If a nonnative speaker is struggling to express an idea in English, Americans must avoid the temptation to finish the sentence and provide the word that they presume is wanted. When we put words into their mouths, our foreign friends often smile and agree out of politeness, but our words may in fact not express their thoughts. Remaining silent is another means of exhibiting tolerance. Instead of filling every lapse in conversation, North Americans, for example, should recognize that in Asian cultures people deliberately use periods of silence for reflection and contemplation.

Saving Face.   In business transactions North Americans often assume that economic factors are the primary motivators of people. It is wise to remember, though, that strong cultural influences are also at work. *Saving face*, for example, is important in many parts of the world. *Face* refers to the image a person holds in his or her social network. Positive comments raise a person's social standing, but negative comments lower it.

People in low-context cultures are less concerned with face. Germans and North Americans, for instance, value honesty and directness; they generally come right to the point and "tell it like it is." Mexicans, Asians, and members of other high-context cultures, on the other hand, are more concerned with preserving social harmony and saving face. They are indirect and go to great lengths to avoid giving offense by saying *no*. The Japanese, in fact, have 16 different ways to avoid an outright *no*. The empathic listener recognizes the language of refusal and pushes no further. Accepting cultural differences and adapting to them with tolerance and empathy often results in a harmonious compromise.

Successful Nonverbal Intercultural Communication

Verbal skills in another culture can generally be mastered if one studies hard enough. But nonverbal skills are much more difficult to learn. Nonverbal behavior includes the areas described in Chapter 2, such as eye contact, facial expressions, posture, gestures, and the use of time, space, and territory. Fortunately, you can learn techniques to boost your intercultural competence.

How Nonverbal Cues Affect Communication.   The messages sent by body language and the way we arrange time and space have always been open to interpretation. Does a raised eyebrow mean that your boss doubts your statement, or just that she is seriously considering it?

ETHICS CHECK:

The World's Worst Tourists: The "Ugly American" Is Back

The demanding, ethnocentric traveler who finds fault with all that is different abroad is no longer French. Only a few years ago, tourists from France topped the list of least liked visitors in one study.[50] But a recent survey among 5,600 travelers from five countries puts Americans first as the worst. The Irish believe the British are the worst travelers, while the British picked the Germans as the tourists to hate. Americans rank the Dutch, Irish, Swiss, and Australians among the best foreign visitors.[51] What may account for such perceptions?

Does that closed door to an office mean that your coworker is angry, or just that he is working on a project that requires concentration? Deciphering nonverbal communication is difficult for people who are culturally similar, and it is even more troublesome when cultures differ.

In Western cultures, for example, people perceive silence as negative. It suggests rejection, unhappiness, depression, regret, embarrassment, or ignorance. The English expression, "The silence was deafening," conveys its oppressiveness. However, the Japanese admire silence and consider it a key to success. A Japanese proverb says, "Those who know do not speak; those who speak do not know." Silence is equated with respect and wisdom.[52]

Although nonverbal behavior is ambiguous within cultures and even more problematic between cultures, it nevertheless conveys meaning. If you've ever had to talk with someone who does not share your language, you probably learned quickly to use gestures to convey basic messages. Because gestures can create very different reactions in different cultures, one must be careful in using and interpreting them. In some societies it is extremely bad form to point one's finger, as in giving directions. Other hand gestures can also cause trouble. The thumbs-up symbol may be used to indicate approval in North America, but in Iran and Ghana it is a vulgar gesture.

As businesspeople increasingly interact with their counterparts from other cultures, they become more aware of these differences. Numerous lists of cultural dos and don'ts have been compiled. However, learning all the nuances of nonverbal behavior in other cultures is impossible; such lists are merely the tip of the cultural iceberg (see Figure 3.3). Striving to associate with people from different cultures can further broaden your intercultural savvy.

Techniques for Achieving Intercultural Competence. In improving effectiveness and achieving intercultural competence, one expert, M. R. Hammer, suggested that three processes or attitudes are effective. *Descriptiveness* refers to the use of concrete and specific feedback. As you will learn in Chapter 4 in regard to the process of communication, descriptive feedback is more effective than judgmental feedback. For example, using objective terms to describe the modest attire of Muslim women is more effective than describing it as unfeminine or motivated by the oppressive and unequal treatment of females.

Figure 3.5 Basic Expressions in Other Languages

ENGLISH
hello
please
thank you
yes
no
goodbye
sorry

ARABIC
as-salam alaykum
min fadhlik
shukran
aiwa/na'am
la
ma'a salama
asef(a)

FRENCH
bonjour
s'il vous plaît
merci
oui
non
au revoir
pardon

GERMAN
guten Tag
bitte
danke
ja
nein
auf Wiedersehen
Entschuldigung

ITALIAN
buon giorno
per favore
grazie
sì
no
arrivederci
scusa

JAPANESE
konnichiwa
onegai shimasu
arigato goizamasu
hai
iie [ee-yeh]
sayonara
sumimasen

NORWEGIAN
god dag
vær så snill
takk
ja
nei
ha det
beklager

RUSSIAN
zdravstvujte
požalujsta
spasiba
da
net [nyet]
do svidanija
izvinite

SPANISH
buenos días
por favor
gracias
sí
no
adiós
perdón

A second attitude is what Hammer called *nonjudgmentalism*. This attitude goes a long way in preventing defensive reactions from communicators. Most important in achieving effective communication is *supportiveness*. This attitude requires us to support others positively with head nods, eye contact, facial expressions, and physical proximity.[53]

From a practical standpoint, when interacting with businesspeople in other cultures, you would be wise to follow their lead. If they avoid intense eye contact, don't stare. If no one is putting his or her elbows on a table, don't be the first to do so. Until you are knowledgeable about the meaning of gestures, it is probably a good idea to keep yours to a minimum. Learning the words for *please, yes,* and *thank you,* some of which are shown in Figure 3.5, is even better than relying on gestures.[54] Achieving intercultural competence in regard to nonverbal behavior may never be totally attained, but sensitivity, nonjudgmentalism, and tolerance go a long way toward improving interactions.

How Technology and Social Media Affect Intercultural Communication

Much has been made of the unprecedented hyperconnectivity facilitated by social media and communication technology today. Certainly, users can interact instantly across time zones and vast distances. With minimal resources, they can also potentially reach out to more individuals and groups all over the world than ever before in history. Not surprisingly, social media may potentially bridge cultural differences as well as reinforce them, depending on their users. New communication technology offers the potential for intercultural engagement. It is being adopted by global businesses at varying degrees, revealing each culture's values and norms.

REALITY CHECK: Twitter—A Hub for Intercultural Engagement

"Twitter is like the ticker tapes you see in Times Square. It's entertainment and it's a voyeuristic medium."[55]

—**HALLEY SUITT TUCKER,** *blogger and founder of BoOkBoX*

Social Networking: Bridging Cultural Divides? What we make of the potential for connectedness and intercultural communication online is as much up to us as it would be at a dinner party where we don't know any of the other guests. "Digital media is an amplifier. It tends to make extroverts more extroverted and introverts more introverted," says Clay Shirky, social media expert at New York University.[56] At the same time, the online environment may deepen feelings of isolation; it can make social presence and interpersonal contact more difficult because all contact is mediated electronically.[57]

In real life, as online, we instinctively tend to gravitate toward people who seem similar to us, believes Gaurav Mishra, a social media strategist from India: "[H]uman beings have a strong tendency to prefer the familiar, so we pay attention to people with a shared context and treat the rich Twitter public stream as background noise."[58] Twitter and other social media can boost intercultural communication; however, we must be willing to reach out across the boundaries that separate us. Shared causes can mobilize social media users halfway across the globe, as Invisible Children, Inc.'s *Kony 2012* film proves. Conducted mostly via YouTube, Twitter, and Facebook, this viral campaign exposing a brutal dictator became hugely popular.[59] Similarly, the public around the world witnessed firsthand, real-time accounts of the Arab Spring and the Syrian Revolution on Twitter and other social networks.

The majority of social media pundits agree that Twitter in particular offers a rich opportunity for intercultural engagement. They credit the diversity of Twitter users and the open design of the microblogging platform for inviting intercultural exploration.[60] Zendesk customer advocate Justin Flitter says that Twitter makes it easier to connect with others across cultural divides: "Accents, tone, body language and other subtleties are reduced when it's just text on screen." Because people are sharing interests, they overcome potential barriers such as Twitter jargon and cultural context, Flitter believes.[61]

Social Networking: Erasing Cultural Differences or Deepening Them? Despite the equalizing influence of globalization, regional and cultural differences persist, as those who design media for markets in other countries know. Asian users may prefer muted pastel colors and anime-style graphics that North Americans would find unusual. Conversely, Korean and Japanese employees may balk at being compelled to post photos of themselves on company intranet pages. They opt for avatars or pictures of pets instead, possibly as an expression of personal modesty or expectations of privacy, whereas North Americans believe photos promote cohesion and make them seem accessible.[62]

Some have argued that social networks such as Facebook are predominantly infused by Anglo-Saxon culture (the United States, the UK, and Canada) and might not be as successful elsewhere.[63] However, 80 percent of Facebook users are located outside the United States and Canada. They converse in 70 languages on the site.[64] Aside from language, regional differences on Facebook and Twitter seem minor.

Global Businesses and Social Media Use. A study of the top 100 corporations of *Fortune* Global 500 companies by Burson-Marsteller, a global public relations firm, revealed that 65 percent are building relationships with stakeholders on Twitter, 54 percent manage Facebook fan pages, 50 percent use YouTube channels, and 33 percent maintain corporate blogs.[65]

Burson-Marsteller also analyzed media use in various countries and found intercultural differences. Chinese Internet users flock to discussion boards (BBS), social networks, video sharing, and online games. While private and multinational companies have embraced social media, state-owned enterprises are lagging far behind. Koreans too prefer the relative anonymity of homegrown online discussion boards and avoid non-Korean social networks other than YouTube. Brazilian companies are avid Twitter users but have avoided Brazil's popular social network Orkut as well as Facebook for fear of appearing intrusive and losing control of the conversation. Although Japanese people boast cutting-edge electronics and an always-on culture, they hesitate to share their thoughts and exploits publicly. Domestic social networks such as Mixi compete successfully with YouTube and Twitter, but Japanese companies prefer websites and online ads when addressing Japanese audiences.[66]

It remains to be seen whether social networking will slowly erase many of the cultural differences present today or whether distinct national, even local, networks will emerge. In the United States some Internet users are flocking to so-called "unsocial" networks—smaller, closed, privacy-controlled social media tools such as Pinterest, Path, Google+, and more.[67] As Americans are adopting portable electronics at a blistering rate, applications more suited for mobile devices than current powerhouse Facebook may soon become potent rivals.[68] More discussion of social media and communication technology follows in subsequent chapters and especially in Chapter 7.

Improving Conversations in Intercultural Environments

Although it is best to speak a foreign language fluently, many Americans lack that skill. Fortunately, global business transactions are increasingly conducted in English. English has become the language of technology, the language of Hollywood, and the language of business even for traditionally non-English-speaking countries. English is so dominant that when Koreans go to China, English is the language they use to conduct business.[69] However, Americans and others who communicate with nonnative speakers are more likely to be understood if they observe a few polite and helpful suggestions.

Enhancing Oral Communication. Americans abroad make a big mistake in thinking that nonnative speakers of English can always follow the conversation. Comprehension can be fairly superficial. Even when they use English, foreign nationals appreciate your learning greetings and a few phrases in their language. It's also wise to speak slowly, use simple English, opt for short sentences, and avoid long, complex words. Following are additional suggestions to improve oral intercultural communication:

- **Observe eye messages.** Be alert to a glazed expression or wandering eyes. These tell you that the listener is lost.

- **Encourage accurate feedback.** Ask probing questions, and encourage the listener to paraphrase what you say. Do not assume that a *yes*, a nod, or a smile indicates comprehension.
- **Accept blame.** If a misunderstanding results, graciously accept the blame for not making your meaning clear.
- **Listen without interrupting.** Curb your desire to finish sentences or to fill out ideas for the speaker. Keep in mind that North Americans abroad are often accused of listening too little and talking too much.
- **Smile when appropriate.** The smile is often considered the single most understood and most useful form of communication. However, in some cultures excessive smiling may seem insincere.
- **Follow up in writing.** After conversations or oral negotiations, confirm the results and agreements with written messages. For proposals and contracts, hire a professional translator.

Improving Written Communication.   In sending letters, e-mails, and other documents to businesspeople in other cultures, try to adjust your writing style and tone. For example, in cultures where formality and tradition are important, be scrupulously polite. Don't even think of sharing the latest joke. Humor translates very poorly and can cause misunderstanding and negative reactions. Familiarize yourself with customary channels of communication. Are letters, e-mails, and faxes common? Would a direct or indirect organizational pattern be more effective? What's more, forget about trying to cut through "red tape": In some cultures bureaucracy is widely accepted. The following additional suggestions can help you prepare successful written messages for intercultural audiences.

- **Use short sentences and short paragraphs.** Sentences with fewer than 20 words and paragraphs with fewer than 8 lines are most readable.
- **Observe titles and rank.** Use last names, titles, and other signals of rank and status. Send messages to higher-status people and avoid sending copies to lower-rank people.
- **Avoid ambiguous expressions.** Include relative pronouns (*that, which, who*) for clarity in introducing clauses. Stay away from contractions (especially ones like *Here's the problem*). Avoid idioms and figurative clichés (*once in a blue moon*), slang (*my presentation really bombed*), acronyms (*ASAP,* for *as soon as possible*), abbreviations (*DBA,* for *doing business as*), jargon (*input, bottom line*), and sports references (*play ball, slam dunk, ballpark figure*). Use action-specific verbs (*purchase a printer* rather than *get a printer*).
- **Strive for clarity.** Avoid words that have many meanings (the word *light* has 18 different meanings). If necessary, clarify words that may be confusing. Replace two-word verbs with clear single words (*return* instead of *bring back; delay* instead of *put off; maintain* instead of *keep up*).
- **Use correct grammar.** Be careful about misplaced modifiers, dangling participles, and sentence fragments. Use conventional punctuation.
- **Cite numbers carefully.** In international trade learn and use the metric system. In citing numbers use figures (*12*) instead of spelling them out (*twelve*). Always convert dollar figures into local currency. Avoid using figures to express the month of the year. In North America, for example, June 12, 2014, might be written as 6/12/14, whereas in Europe the same date might appear as 12.6.14.

An Intercultural E-Mail Message That Misses the Mark

Figure 3.6 illustrates an ineffective intercultural message. The writer uses a casual, breezy tone in a message to a Chinese company when a formal tone would be more appropriate. In addition, the e-mail includes slang and ambiguous expressions that would almost surely confuse readers for whom English is not a first language.

In the effective version in Figure 3.7, the writer adopts a formal but pleasant, polite tone, striving for complete sentences and correct grammar. The effective e-mail message avoids

Figure **3.6** Ineffective Intercultural E-Mail Message

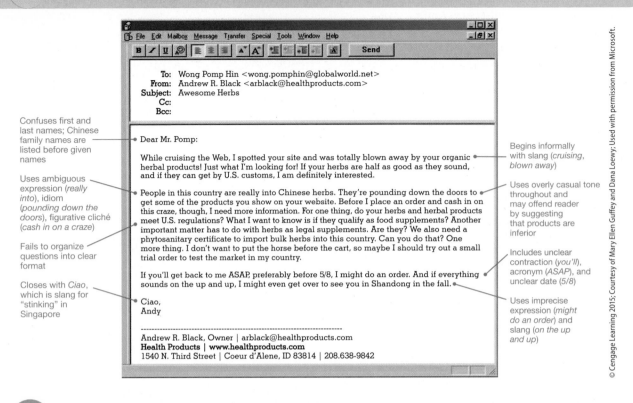

Confuses first and last names; Chinese family names are listed before given names

Begins informally with slang (*cruising*, *blown away*)

Uses ambiguous expression (*really into*), idiom (*pounding down the doors*), figurative cliché (*cash in on a craze*)

Uses overly casual tone throughout and may offend reader by suggesting that products are inferior

Fails to organize questions into clear format

Closes with *Ciao*, which is slang for "stinking" in Singapore

Includes unclear contraction (*you'll*), acronym (*ASAP*), and unclear date (*5/8*)

Uses imprecise expression (*might do an order*) and slang (*on the up and up*)

Figure **3.7** Effective Intercultural E-Mail Message

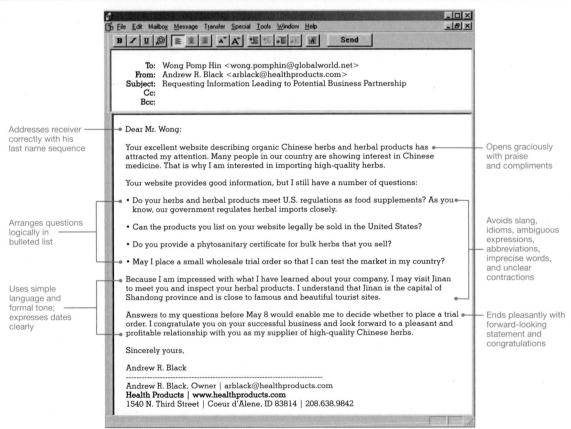

Addresses receiver correctly with his last name sequence

Opens graciously with praise and compliments

Arranges questions logically in bulleted list

Avoids slang, idioms, ambiguous expressions, abbreviations, imprecise words, and unclear contractions

Uses simple language and formal tone; expresses dates clearly

Ends pleasantly with forward-looking statement and congratulations slang (*on the up and up*), idioms, imprecise words (*I might do an order*), unclear abbreviations (*ASAP*), and confusing dates (*5/8*). To further aid comprehension, the writer organizes the message into a bulleted list with clear questions.

As the world economies continue to intermingle and globalization spreads, more businesspeople are adopting Western ways. Although Japanese writers may open letters with a seasonable greeting (*Cherry trees will soon be blooming*), it is unnecessary for a U.S. correspondent to do so.[70]

The following checklist summarizes suggestions for improving communication with intercultural audiences.

Culture and Ethical Business Practices

LEARNING OBJECTIVE **4**
Grasp the complexities of ethics across cultures, including business practices abroad, bribery, prevailing customs, and methods for coping.

When you do business around the world, whose values, culture, and, ultimately, laws do you follow? This perplexing problem faces conscientious organizations and individuals in a global economy. Do you heed the customs of your country or those of the host country? Some

CHECKLIST ≫
Achieving Intercultural Proficiency

© Daniilantiq/Shutterstock.com

- **Examine your own culture.** Culture is learned. Study your customs, biases, and views and how they differ from those in other societies. Thus you may better understand and accept the values and behavior of other cultures.

- **Explore other cultures.** Education can help you alter cultural misconceptions, reduce fears, and minimize misunderstandings. Knowledge of other cultures opens your eyes and enriches your life.

- **Curb ethnocentrism.** Avoid judging others by your personal views. Overcome the view that other cultures are incorrect, defective, or primitive. Try to develop an open mind-set.

- **Treat each individual you meet as a *prototype*.** Be open to question and adjust your perceptions of other cultures. Generalizations are natural and unavoidable, but beware of stereotypes and prejudice. Most people like to be treated as unique individuals, not typical representatives of an entire group.

- **Observe nonverbal cues in your culture.** Become more alert to the meanings of eye contact, facial expressions, posture, gestures, and the use of time, space, and territory. How do they differ in other cultures?

- **Embrace nonjudgmentalism.** Strive to accept unfamiliar behavior as different, rather than as right or wrong. However, try not to be defensive in justifying your own culture. Strive for objectivity.

- **Be aware of culture when using communication technology.** Don't expect that individuals from other cultures think and act the same way you do; at the same time, try to reach out to others over common interests.

- **Use plain English.** Speak and write in short sentences using simple words and standard English. Eliminate puns, slang, jargon, acronyms, abbreviations, and any words that cannot be easily translated.

- **Encourage accurate feedback.** In conversations ask probing questions and listen attentively without interrupting. Do not assume that a *yes* or a smile indicates agreement or comprehension.

- **Adapt to local preferences.** Shape your writing to reflect the document styles of the reader's culture, if appropriate. Express currency in local figures. Write out months of the year for clarity.

observers claim that when American businesspeople venture abroad, they're wandering into an ethical no-man's land, a murky world of payola where transactions often demand gratuities to oil the wheels of business.[71]

Doing Business Abroad

As companies do more and more business around the globe, their assumptions about ethics are put to the test. Businesspeople may face simple questions regarding the appropriate amount of money to spend on a business gift or the legitimacy of payments to agents and distributors to "expedite" business. They may also encounter out-and-out bribery, child-labor abuse, environment mistreatment, and unscrupulous business practices. In the wake of the banking crisis, in a lingering recession, the ethics of U.S. businesses are increasingly being scrutinized. Violators of laws or company policies can land in big trouble. However, what ethical standards do these companies follow when they do business abroad?

Today most companies that are active in global markets have ethical codes of conduct. These codes are public documents and can usually be found on company websites. They are an accepted part of governance. The growing sophistication of these codes results in ethics training programs that often include complicated hypothetical questions. Ethics trainers teach employees to solve problems by reconciling legal requirements, company policies, and conflicting cultural norms.[72]

Businesses in other countries are also adopting ethics codes and helping employees live up to the standards. Alan Boeckman, CEO of Fluor, the multinational construction firm, has worked very hard to rid his company of corruption. The battle against bribery in an industry in which corruption is rampant hasn't been easy. Yet the company experienced success after installing a company lawyer as head of compliance.[73] After investing $4 billion in Russia, Swedish furniture powerhouse IKEA halted further expansion. Safety inspectors, expecting bribes, were withholding permission for additional stores outside Moscow. The company cited "zero tolerance on corruption" and refused to pay up. Bribery in Russia serves the personal enrichment of law enforcement and other authorities to the tune of $300 billion annually.[74]

Transparency International, a Berlin-based watchdog group, compiled a ranking of corruption in many countries. Based on polls and surveys of businesspeople and journalists, the index shown in Figure 3.8 presents a look at the perceptions of corruption.[75] Gauging corruption precisely is impossible. However, this graph reflects the feelings of individuals doing business in the countries shown. Of the countries selected for this graph, the least corrupt were New Zealand, Denmark, Finland, Sweden, and Singapore. The most corrupt were Iraq, Afghanistan, Myanmar, North Korea, and Somalia.

The United States ranked between Chile, Qatar, and France near the bottom of the top 25.

Antibribery Laws

The United States is not highest on the index of least corruptible countries. However, it has taken the global lead in fighting corruption. Over three decades ago, the U.S. government passed the Foreign Corrupt Practices Act of 1977. It prohibits payments to foreign officials for the purpose of obtaining or retaining business. But the law applied only to U.S. companies. Therefore, they were at a decided disadvantage when competing against less scrupulous companies from other nations. U.S. companies complained that they lost billions of dollars in contracts every year because they refused to bribe their way to success.

Most other industrialized countries looked the other way when their corporations used bribes. They considered the "greasing of palms" just a cost of doing business in certain cultures. Until 1999 German corporations were even allowed to deduct bribes as a business expense— as long as they got receipts. A few years ago, the engineering giant Siemens was slapped with

Figure 3.8 Corruption Perceptions Index: Highly Clean or Highly Corrupt?

Highly Clean

This index of selected countries represents a compilation of polls and surveys put together by Transparency International. The purpose of this Berlin-based watchdog organization is curbing the corruption that stunts the development of poor countries. The index relates to perceptions of corruption as seen by businesspeople, risk analysts, and the general public. It ranges between 10 (highly clean) and 0 (highly corrupt).

Country	Rank	Index
New Zealand	1	9.5
Denmark	2	9.4
Sweden	4	9.3
Singapore	5	9.2
Norway	6	9.0
Netherlands	7	8.9
Australia	8	8.8
Canada	10	8.7
Luxembourg	11	8.5
Hong Kong	12	8.4
Iceland	13	8.3
Germany/Japan	14	8.0
United Kingdom	16	7.8
Belgium	19	7.5
Bahamas	21	7.3
Chile/Qatar	22	7.2
United States	24	7.1
France	25	7.0
Spain	31	6.2
Portugal	32	6.1
Poland	41	5.5
South Korea	43	5.4
Hungary/Kuwait	54	4.6
Saudi Arabia	57	4.4
South Africa	64	4.1
Italy	69	3.9
Brazil	73	3.8
China	75	3.6
Greece	80	3.4
Bulgaria	86	3.3
India	95	3.1
Mexico	100	3.0
Iran	120	2.7
Philippines	129	2.6
Pakistan	134	2.5
Russia	143	2.4
Venezuela	172	1.9
Iraq	175	1.8
Afghanistan	180	1.5

Highly Corrupt

Source: Transparency International, 2011.

© Cengage Learning 2015

billion-dollar fines in Germany and in the United States for systematically paying off foreign officials. In total, its corrupt practices cost the company $2.6 billion for fines and internal reforms.[76]

In the United States, bribery is a criminal offense, and American corporate officials found guilty are fined and sent to jail. For example, Chiquita Brands has been the subject of lengthy litigation and fines for its activities in Colombia. The company made "protection payments" to right-wing paramilitaries as well as a left-wing army, ostensibly to protect its employees.[77] Domestically, the Sarbanes-Oxley Act is a tool in the anticorruption battle. It forbids off-the-book bribes. However, American law does permit payments that may ease the way for routine government actions, such as expediting a visa request. Such payments are reportedly capped at about $500.[78]

More attention is now being paid to the problem of global corruption. With increased global interdependence, corruption is increasingly seen as costly as well as unethical. It has been estimated that moving from a "clean" government like that of Singapore to one as corrupt as Mexico's would have the same effect on foreign direct investment as an increase in the corporate tax rate of 50 percent.[80] Many of the world's industrialized countries formally agreed in 1999 to a new global treaty promoted by the Organization for Economic Cooperation and Development (OECD). This treaty bans the bribery of foreign government officials. Today, bribery is illegal almost everywhere in the world.[81]

Deciding Whose Ethics to Follow

Although world leaders seem to agree that bribing officials is wrong, many other shady areas persist. Drawing the lines of ethical behavior here at home is hard enough. When faced with a cultural filter, the picture becomes even murkier. Most people agree that mistreating children is wrong. But in some countries, child labor is not only condoned but also considered necessary for families to subsist. Although most countries want to respect the environment, they might also sanction the use of DDT because crops would be consumed by insects without it.

In some cultures "grease" payments to customs officials may be part of their earnings—not blackmail. In parts of Africa, a "family" celebration at the conclusion of a business deal includes a party for which you are asked to pay. This payment is considered a sign of friendship and lasting business relationship, not a personal payoff. In some Third World countries, requests for assistance in developing technologies or reducing hunger may become part of a business package.[82]

The exchanging of gifts is another tricky subject. In many non-Western cultures, the gift exchange tradition has become a business ritual. Gifts not only are a sign of gratitude and hospitality but also generate a future obligation and trust. Americans, of course, become uneasy when gift giving seems to move beyond normal courtesy and friendliness. If it even remotely suggests influence peddling, they back off. Many companies suggest $50 as a top limit for gifts.

Whose ethics should prevail across borders? Unfortunately, no clear-cut answers can be found. Americans are sometimes criticized for being ethical "fanatics," wishing to impose their "moralistic" views on the world. Also criticized are ethical "relativists," who contend that no absolute values exist.[83]

Ethical Decision Making Across Borders

Instead of trying to distinguish "good ethics" and "bad ethics," perhaps the best plan is to look for practical solutions to the cultural challenges of global business interaction. Following are suggestions that acknowledge different values but also respect the need for moral initiative.[84]

- **Broaden your view.** Become more sensitive to the values and customs of other cultures. Look especially at what they consider moral, traditional, practical, and effective.

- **Avoid reflex judgments.** Don't automatically judge the business customs of others as immoral, corrupt, or unworkable. Assume they are legitimate and workable until proved otherwise.

- **Find alternatives.** Instead of caving in to government payoffs, perhaps offer nonmonetary public service benefits, technical expertise, or additional customer service.

- **Refuse business if options violate your basic values.** If an action seriously breaches your own code of ethics or that of your firm, give up the transaction.

- **Embrace transparency.** Conduct all relations and negotiations as openly as possible.

- **Don't rationalize shady decisions.** Avoid agreeing to actions that cause you to say, *This isn't really illegal or immoral, This is in the company's best interest*, or *No one will find out.*

- **Resist legalistic strategies.** Don't use tactics that are legally safe but ethically questionable. For example, don't call *agents* (who are accountable to employers) *distributors* (who are not).

When faced with an intercultural ethical dilemma, you can apply the same five-question test you learned in Chapter 1, Figure 1.14. Even in another culture, these questions can guide you to the best decision.

1. Is the action legal?

2. Would you do it if you were on the opposite side?

3. Can you rule out a better alternative?

4. Would a trusted advisor agree?

5. Would family, friends, an employer, or coworkers approve?

REALITY CHECK: Diversity Encourages Unique Contributions That Benefit the Group

"Our research suggests that the mere presence of social diversity makes people with independent points of view more willing to voice those points of view, and others more willing to listen."[85]

—**KATHERINE PHILLIPS,** *professor, Kellogg School of Management, Northwestern University*

Courtesy of Katherine Phillips

Workforce Diversity: Benefits and Challenges

LEARNING OBJECTIVE **5**
Explain the advantages and challenges of workforce diversity, and address approaches for improving communication among diverse workplace audiences.

While North American companies are expanding global operations and adapting to a variety of emerging markets, the domestic workforce is also becoming more diverse. This diversity has many dimensions—race, ethnicity, age, religion, gender, national origin, physical ability, sexual orientation, and other qualities. No longer, say the experts, will the workplace be predominantly Anglo oriented or male. As discussed in Chapter 1, by 2020 many groups now considered minorities (African Americans, Hispanics, Asians, Native Americans) are projected to become 36 percent of the U.S. population. Between 2040 and 2050, these same groups will reach the "majority–minority crossover," the point at which they will represent the majority of the U.S. population.[86] Women will comprise nearly 50 percent of the workforce. Moreover, latest U.S. Census data suggest that the share of the population over sixty-five will jump from 13 percent now to almost 20 percent in 2030. Trends suggest that many of these older people will remain in the workforce. Because of technological advances, more physically challenged people are also joining the workforce.

Diversity and Its Advantages

As society and the workforce become more diverse, successful interactions and communication among the various identity groups bring distinct advantages in three areas.

A diverse staff is better able to read trends and respond to the increasingly diverse customer base in local and world markets.

Consumers. A diverse staff is better able to read trends and respond to the increasingly diverse customer base in local and world markets. Diverse consumers now want specialized goods and services tailored to their needs. Teams made up of people with different experiences are better equipped to create products that these markets require. Consumers also want to deal with companies that respect their values and reflect themselves. "We find that more and more of our clients are demanding that our partners and staff—involved in securing new business as well as delivering the work—reflect diversity within their organizations," said Toni Riccardi. She represents PricewaterhouseCoopers, the world's largest accounting firm.[87] Sharing this view is Theo Fletcher, vice president of security, compliance, and diversity at IBM's Integrated Supply Chain Group. He said, "It is important that we have a supply base that looks like our employee base and that looks like the market we are trying to attract."[88]

Work Teams. As you learned in Chapter 2, employees today work in teams. Team members with different backgrounds may come up with more creative and effective solutions than homogeneous teams. Adrian Savage, a management consultant, believes that a diverse staff is more likely to see opportunities that a homogeneous group would miss. Small businesses in particular can be closed to outsiders and run a greater risk of becoming inflexible than they would if they left their comfort zones.[89] At PepsiCo, work teams created new products inspired by diversity efforts. Those products included guacamole-flavored Doritos chips and Gatorade Xtremo aimed at Hispanics, as well as Mountain Dew Code Red, which appeals to African Americans. One Pepsi executive said that companies that "figure out the diversity challenge first will clearly have a competitive advantage."[90]

Business Organizations. Companies that set aside time and resources to cultivate and capitalize on diversity will suffer fewer discrimination lawsuits, fewer union clashes, and less government regulatory action. Most important, though, is the growing realization among organizations that diversity is a critical bottom-line business strategy to improve employee relationships and to increase productivity. Consultant Fred Miller points out that almost 80 percent of Fortune 500 companies have created some kind of diversity program because, among other things, diversity drives sales. The government and corporations increasingly contract only with suppliers who can show "cultural readiness." "The world is changing," says Miller. "If it's not on your doorstep now, it will be soon. You can't wait. Reaction time must be instantaneous."[91] Developing a diverse staff that can work together is one of the biggest challenges facing business organizations today.

Diversity and Discord

Diversity can be a positive force within organizations. However, all too often it can also cause divisiveness, discontent, and clashes. Many of the identity groups, the so-called workforce "disenfranchised," have legitimate gripes.

Women complain of the *glass ceiling*, that invisible barrier of attitudes, prejudices, and "old boy networks" blocking them from reaching important corporate positions. Some women feel that they are the victims of sexual harassment, unequal wages, sexism, and even their style of communication. See the Career Coach box to learn more about gender talk and gender tension. On the other hand, men, too, have gender issues. One manager described gender discrimination in his office: "My boss was a woman and was very verbal about the opportunities for women to advance in my company. I have often felt she gave much more attention to the women in the office than the men."[92]

Older employees feel that the deck is stacked in favor of younger employees. Minorities complain that they are discriminated against in hiring, retention, wages, and promotions. Physically challenged individuals feel that their limitations should not hold them back, and they fear that their potential is often prejudged. People of different religions feel uncomfortable working alongside each other. A Jew, for example, may be stressed if he has to help train a Palestinian. Similarly, a manager confessed, "I am half Jewish on my father's side. Very often someone will make a comment about Jews and I am always faced with the decision of speaking up or not."[93]

He Said, She Said: Gender Talk and Gender Tension

Has the infiltration of gender rhetoric done great damage to the workplace? Are men and women throwing rotten tomatoes at each other as a result of misunderstandings caused by stereotypes of "masculine" and "feminine" attitudes?[94]

Deborah Tannen's book *You Just Don't Understand: Women and Men in Conversation*, as well as John Grey's *Men Are From Mars, Women Are From Venus*, caused an avalanche of discussion (and some hostility) by comparing the communication styles of men and women.

Gender theorists suggest that one reason women can't climb above the glass ceiling is that their communication style is less authoritative than that of men. Compare the following observations (greatly simplified) from gender theorists:

	Women	Men
Object of talk	Establish rapport, make connections, negotiate inclusive relationships	Preserve independence, maintain status, exhibit skill and knowledge
Listening behavior	Attentive, steady eye contact; remain stationary; nod head	Less attentive, sporadic eye contact; move around
Pauses	Frequent pauses, giving chance for others to take turns	Infrequent pauses; interrupt each other to take turns
Small talk	Personal disclosure	Impersonal topics
Focus	Details first, pulled together at end	Big picture
Gestures	Small, confined	Expansive
Method	Questions, apologies; "we" statements; hesitant, indirect, soft speech	Assertions; "I" statements; clear, loud, take-charge speech

Improving Communication Among Diverse Workplace Audiences

Harmony and acceptance do not happen automatically when people who are dissimilar work together. This means that organizations must commit to diversity. Harnessed effectively, diversity can enhance productivity and propel a company to success. Mismanaged, it can become a tremendous drain on a company's time and resources. How companies deal with diversity will make all the difference in how they compete in an increasingly global environment. The following suggestions can help you and your organization find ways to improve communication and interaction.

- **Seek training.** Especially if an organization is experiencing diversity problems, awareness-raising sessions may be helpful. Spend time reading and learning about workforce diversity and how it can benefit organizations. Look upon diversity as an opportunity, not a threat. Intercultural communication, team building, and conflict resolution are skills that can be learned in diversity training programs.

- **Understand the value of differences.** Diversity makes an organization innovative and creative. Sameness fosters an absence of critical thinking called groupthink, discussed in Chapter 2. Case studies, for example, of the *Challenger* shuttle disaster suggest that groupthink prevented alternatives from being considered. Even smart people working collectively can make dumb decisions if they do not see the situation from different perspectives.[95] Diversity in problem-solving groups encourages independent and creative thinking.

- **Don't expect conformity.** Gone are the days when businesses could say, "This is our culture. Conform or leave."[96] Paul Fireman, former CEO of Reebok, stressed seeking people who have new and different stories to tell. "And then you have to make real room for them, you have to learn to listen, to listen closely, to their stories. It accomplishes next to nothing to employ those who are different from us if the condition of their employment is that they become the same as us. For it is their differences that enrich us, expand us, provide us the competitive edge."[97]

- **Make fewer assumptions.** Be careful of seemingly insignificant, innocent workplace assumptions. For example, don't assume that everyone wants to observe the holidays with a Christmas party and a decorated tree. Celebrating only Christian holidays in December and January excludes those who honor Hanukkah, Kwanzaa, and the Lunar New Year. Moreover, in workplace discussions don't assume anything about others' sexual orientation or attitude toward marriage. For invitations, avoid phrases such as *managers and their wives*. *Spouses* or *partners* is more inclusive. Valuing diversity means making fewer assumptions that everyone is like you or wants to be like you.

- **Build on similarities.** Look for areas in which you and others not like you can agree or at least share opinions. Be prepared to consider issues from many perspectives, all of which may be valid. Accept that there is room for different points of view to coexist peacefully. Although you can always find differences, it is much harder to find similarities. Look for common ground in shared experiences, mutual goals, and similar values.[98] Concentrate on your objective even when you may disagree on how to reach it.

Your Turn: Applying Your Skills at Walmart

A few years ago, at its Sustainability Summit in Sao Paolo, Brazil, Walmart announced plans to address some of the world's most pressing environmental problems. With its global clout, Walmart set ambitious goals to become "a more sustainable, responsible company . . . building meaningful, long-term change."[99] The retailer wanted its suppliers to use less packaging, cut phosphates in detergent 70 percent, and reduce the use of plastic bags by 50 percent by 2013. More recently, Walmart also pledged to increase its use of renewable energy, expand its offering of locally grown produce, and boost the diversity of its employees.[100]

These proposals are part of Walmart's global effort to impose sustainability and efficiency targets on each of the 15 countries in which the company currently operates. In China, the Bentonville giant held an earlier summit with more than 1,000 suppliers to address social problems specific to that emerging economy. Businesses and the Chinese government agreed to (a) comply with environmental laws, (b) improve energy efficiency and the use of natural resources, (c) increase quality standards, and (d) make manufacturing more transparent.[101]

Two additional initiatives were launched most recently. One was designed to support women around the world by sourcing from women-owned businesses domestically and abroad. Second, Walmart pledged to introduce healthier, more affordable food to Americans by deploying the "Great for You" icon, so that customers could readily identify healthier fare in the stores.[102] Andrew Winston, an expert on green business, wrote in his blog: "Wal-Mart is changing the world for the better and is setting the new pace in corporate sustainability. The rest of the business world—let alone the politicians still debating action on climate—can only try to keep up."[103]

YOUR TASK. As a junior member of a joint task force at McKinsey & Co., a consulting firm advising Walmart, you are working to improve the image of the global retailer. Despite several praiseworthy initiatives, Walmart is still viewed by many with suspicion. Stories in the media detailing discrimination lawsuits and corrupt practices in Mexico have not been helpful. As a team, discuss the global impact of Walmart's sustainability effort. Create a communication strategy: How should Walmart spread the news about its sustainability policies to reach the broader public and young people in particular? Consider the use of social media such as Facebook, Twitter, Pinterest, and so forth. Your team may be asked to explain its decision to the class or to write a summary of the pros and cons of each option. Be prepared to support your choice.

Summary of Learning Objectives

1 **Understand the powerful effects of globalization and the major trends fueling it.** A shrinking domestic market and four other major trends explain the need for developing intercultural communication techniques and competency. First, globalized markets free of trade barriers mean that you can expect to be doing business with people from around the world. Second, advancements in transportation technology are making the world smaller and more intertwined. Third, communication and information technologies extend the global reach of business. Fourth, these trends are giving rise to new middle classes in emerging economies. Meanwhile, the domestic workforce is becoming increasingly diverse as immigrants from other cultures continue to settle in North America, and their offspring outnumber the descendants of non-Hispanic whites.

2 **Define *culture*, name its primary characteristics, and explain the five key dimensions of culture: context, individualism, time orientation, power distance, and communication style.** *Culture* is the complex system of values, traits, morals, and customs shared by a society. Significant characteristics of culture include the following: (a) culture is learned, (b) cultures are inherently logical, (c) culture is the basis of self-identity and community, (d) culture combines the visible and invisible, and (e) culture is dynamic. Members of low-context cultures (such as those in North America, Scandinavia, and Germany) depend on words to express meaning, whereas members of high-context cultures (such as those in Japan, China, and Arab countries) rely more on context (social setting, a person's history, status, and position) to communicate meaning. Other key dimensions of culture include individualism, time orientation, power distance, and communication style.

3 **Discuss strategies for enhancing intercultural effectiveness, reflect on nonverbal intercultural communication, assess how social media affect intercultural communication, and apply techniques for successful oral and written interactions across cultures.** To function effectively in a global economy, we must acquire knowledge of other cultures and be willing to change our attitudes, but first we need to become aware of our own cultural assumptions and biases. Culture is learned. *Ethnocentrism* refers to the belief that one's own culture is superior to all others and holds all truths. Overcoming stereotypes and developing tolerance often involve practicing *empathy*, which means trying to see the world through another's eyes. We can minimize nonverbal miscommunication by recognizing that meanings conveyed by body language such as eye contact, posture, gestures, use of time, space, and territory are largely culture dependent. Becoming aware of your own nonverbal behavior and what it conveys is the first step in broadening your intercultural competence. Communicating in social networks, people tend to seek out those who are like them; the extent to which they reach out across boundaries depends on whether they are outgoing or introverted. In improving oral messages, use simple English, speak slowly and enunciate clearly, observe eye messages, encourage accurate feedback, accept blame, listen without interrupting, smile, and follow up important conversations in writing. To improve written messages, try to accommodate the reader in organization, tone, and style. Use short sentences and short paragraphs, observe titles and rank, avoid ambiguous expressions, strive for clarity, use correct grammar, and cite numbers carefully.

4 **Grasp the complexities of ethics across cultures, including business practices abroad, bribery, prevailing customs, and methods for coping.** In doing business abroad, businesspeople should expect to find differing views about ethical practices. Although deciding whose ethics should prevail is tricky, the following techniques are helpful: Broaden your understanding of values and customs in other cultures, and avoid reflex judgments regarding the morality or corruptness of actions. Look for alternative solutions, refuse business if the options violate your basic values, and conduct all relations as openly as possible. Don't rationalize shady decisions. Resist legalistic strategies, and apply a five-question ethics test when faced with a perplexing ethical dilemma.

5 Explain the advantages and challenges of workforce diversity, and address approaches for improving communication among diverse workplace audiences. A diverse workforce can benefit consumers, work teams, and business organizations. However, diversity can also cause discord among identity groups. Business communicators should be aware of and sensitive to differences in the communication techniques of men and women. To promote harmony and communication in diverse workplaces, many organizations develop diversity training programs. You should understand and accept the value of differences. Don't expect conformity, make fewer assumptions about others, and look for common ground.

Chapter Review

1. Which important trends fuel globalization? (Obj. 1)

2. Which significant changes in the workforce can we expect over the next 40 years? (Obj. 1)

3. List the five main characteristics of culture. (Obj. 2)

4. Describe five major dimensions of culture. (Obj. 2)

5. Name four or more strategies for bridging the gap between cultures and achieving intercultural proficiency. (Obj. 3)

6. Describe three processes or attitudes that will help you achieve intercultural competence, according to M. R. Hammer. (Obj. 3)

7. Does social networking help bridge cultural divides? (Obj. 3)

8. Describe five specific ways you can improve oral communication with someone who speaks another language. (Obj. 3)

9. Describe at least five ways you can improve written communication with someone who speaks another language. (Obj. 3)

10. What categories of ambiguous expressions should be avoided because they could confuse readers for whom English is not a first language? (Obj. 3)

11. Are there laws forbidding bribery in the United States, and are they effective in stopping corruption? (Obj. 4)

12. Why is gift giving to customers and business partners problematic, and what is the recommended limit in most U.S. companies? (Obj. 4)

13. List seven techniques for making ethical decisions across borders. (Obj. 4)

14. Name three groups that benefit from workforce diversity and explain why. (Obj. 5)

15. Describe five guidelines for improving communication among diverse workplace audiences. (Obj. 5)

Critical Thinking

1. English is becoming the world's business language because the United States is a dominant military and trading force. Why should Americans bother to learn about other cultures? (Objs. 1, 2, and 5)

2. A *stereotype* is an oversimplified perception of a behavioral pattern or characteristic applied to entire groups. For example, the Swiss are hardworking, efficient, and neat; Germans are formal, reserved, and blunt; Americans are loud, friendly, and impatient; Canadians are polite, trusting, and tolerant; Asians are gracious, humble, and inscrutable. In what way are such stereotypes harmless or harmful? (Objs. 2, 3)

3. It is quite natural to favor one's own country over a foreign one. To what extent can ethnocentrism be considered a normal reaction, and when could it become destructive and unproductive? Provide examples to support your answer. (Objs. 2, 3)

4. Some economists and management scholars argue that statements such as *diversity is an economic asset* or *diversity is a new strategic imperative* are unproved and perhaps unprovable assertions. Should social responsibility or market forces determine whether an organization strives to create a diverse workforce? Why? (Obj. 5)

5. **Ethical Issue:** You know that it's not acceptable to make ethnic jokes, least of all in the workplace, but a colleague of yours keeps invoking the worst ethnic and racial stereotypes. How do you respond? Do you remain silent and change the subject, or do you speak up? What other options do you have in dealing with such a coworker? Consider whether your answer would change if the offender were your boss. (Objs. 4, 5)

Activities

3.1 Minding One's Intercultural Social Media Manners (Objs. 1–3)

Intercultural **Social Media**

Consider your worst, most embarrassing intercultural blunder and then imagine it amplified a thousandfold or millionfold for everyone to see. Social networking is instant and, once unleashed, it can't be throttled back. What follows is a partial list of extremely awkward social media slip-ups with intercultural implications.[104]

YOUR TASK. Consider the gravity of each offense; individually or in groups discuss each for its "take-away," the lesson to be learned from it. Contribute your own intercultural blunders that you or someone you know has experienced. Explain lessons learned.

a. Kenneth Cole used the violent uprising in Egypt to peddle its clothing line in this ill-considered tweet from its corporate Twitter account **@KennethCole:** "Millions are in uproar in #Cairo. Rumor is they heard our new spring collection is now available online at **http://bit.ly/KCairo** –KC."

b. As if to prove that humor is not universally shared, nor is it always in good taste, comedian Gilbert Gottfried tweeted this lame joke in the wake of the tsunami in Japan: "Japan called me. They said 'maybe those jokes are a hit in the U.S., but over here, they're all sinking.'" At the time, Gilbert was the spokesperson for insurer Aflac.

c. Home improvement chain Lowe's allowed a discussion on its Facebook page to get out of hand after withdrawing its advertising from a TLC reality show about Muslim families. The 23,000 comments on Facebook that followed were mostly critical of the company, but some praised the home improvement giant. Only when the media picked up the story did the company respond to offensive and racist posts by deleting all the messages and explaining its late intervention as "respect for the transparence of social media."

d. Australian airline Qantas tried to lure its customers with gift packs to describe their "dream luxury in-flight experience." However, this promotion coincided with grounded flights in response to ongoing strikes, and the passengers took to venting and griping, not praising.

e. Red Cross social media specialist Gloria Huang sent out the following tweet from the organization's Twitter account **@RedCross:** "Ryan found two more 4 bottle packs of Dogfish Head's Midas Touch beer.... when we drink we do it right #gettngslizzerd." The late-night tweet stayed up for an hour. Huang's boss, Wendy Harman, fielded calls in the middle of the night and took the tweet down.

3.2 Analyzing Intercultural Gaffes (Objs. 1–3)

Intercultural

As business organizations become increasingly global in their structure and marketing, they face communication problems resulting from cultural misunderstandings.

YOUR TASK. Based on what you have learned in this chapter, describe several broad principles that could be applied in helping the individuals involved understand what went wrong in the following events. What suggestions could you make for remedying the problems?

a. Alert Driving, a firm that provides online driving training courses to companies with vehicle fleets, expanded into more than 20 countries before realizing that its product had cultural flaws. In Japan its product was poorly translated and failed to address geographic nuances, but the company's Japanese customers were slow to voice dissatisfaction. As a result, the company had to spend about $1 million to revamp its product line after it was already in the market. What cultural trait caused the delay in negative feedback?[105]

b. The owners of the British food company Sharwood spent millions of dollars launching a new curry sauce called *Bundh*. The firm was immediately deluged with calls from Punjabi speakers who said the new product sounded like their word for "backside." How important is it for companies to test product names?[106]

c. During a festive dinner for a delegation from Singapore visiting the government of the Czech Republic, the conversation turned to the tasty main course they were eating. One of the Czech hosts explained to the inquiring foreign guests that they were enjoying a Czech specialty, rabbit, known for its light white meat. The Singaporeans' faces mirrored shock, embarrassment, and irritation. As inconspicuously as possible, they put down their silverware. Only later did the Czech delegation learn that rabbit is a pet in Singapore much like the house cat in European or North American households.[107]

d. The employees of a large U.S. pharmaceutical firm became angry over the e-mail messages they received from the firm's employees in Spain. The messages weren't offensive. Generally, these routine messages just explained ongoing projects. What riled the Americans was this: every Spanish message was copied to the hierarchy within its division. The Americans could not understand why e-mail messages had to be sent to people who had little or nothing to do with the issues being discussed. However, this was accepted practice in Spain.[108]

e. As China moves from a planned to a market economy, professionals suffer the same signs of job stress experienced in Western countries. Multinational companies have long offered counseling to their expatriate managers. Locals, however, frowned on any form of psychological therapy. When China's largest bank hired Chestnut Global Partners to offer employee counseling services, Chestnut learned immediately that it could not talk about such issues as conflict management. Instead, Chestnut stressed workplace harmony. Chestnut also found that Chinese workers refused one-on-one counseling. They preferred group sessions or online counseling.[109] What cultural elements were at work here?

3.3 Mastering International Time (Objs. 1–3)

Communication Technology **Intercultural** **Web**

Assume you are a virtual assistant working from your home. As part of your job, you schedule webcasts, online chats, and teleconference calls for businesspeople who are conducting business around the world.

YOUR TASK. To broaden your knowledge of time zones, respond to the following questions.

a. What does the abbreviation UTC indicate? (Use Google and search for *UTC definition.*)

b. Internationally, time is shown with a 24-hour clock (sometimes called "military time"). What time does 13.00 indicate? (Use Google; search for *24-hour clock.*) How is a 12-hour clock different from a 24-hour clock? With which are you most familiar?

c. You must schedule an audioconference for a businessperson in Indianapolis, Indiana, who wants to talk with a person in Osaka, Japan. What are the best business hours (between 8 a.m. and 5 p.m.) for them to talk? (Many websites provide time zone converters. For example, try searching for *time and date.* Several websites display time and date in any time zone on Earth.)

d. What are the best business hours for an online chat between an executive in Atlanta and a vendor in Singapore?

e. When is a businessperson in Arizona most likely to reach a contact in Belgium on Skype during office hours? Your instructor may select other cities for you to search.

3.4 Twitter Opening up Countries and Cultures (Objs. 1, 3)

E-mail **Intercultural** **Social Media** **Web**

Perhaps you are one of a growing number of younger people who tweet regularly. Twitter and other social media have become primary news sources for many adults under age thirty, Pew Internet Project found when it studied the viral campaign Kony 2012. This 30-minute indictment of brutal Ugandan warlord Joseph Kony, released by the group Invisible Children, has become one of the most watched videos of all time on YouTube (currently at 97 million views and counting) and Vimeo (18 million plays). It was by far the top story on Twitter and thus again confirmed social media's power to galvanize people across the globe.[110] During the Arab Spring and the uprising in Libya, social media also allowed uncensored news to emerge at a time when reporting by traditional media was severely limited. Shocking Twitter pictures of natural disasters such as the tsunami in Japan or the Colorado wildfires can also be spread instantly to millions by citizen reporters with smartphones.

Time magazine called Twitter the "medium of the movement" for its role in Iranian protests following a suspect election. Twitter has been one of the fastest-growing phenomena on the Internet, in the words of *The New York Times.* Tweets from Iran emerged as free, unfiltered real-time news items from protesters and witnesses documenting government repression. Although officials could technically cut both Internet connections and the SMS network, never again will a dictator be able to impose a complete information monopoly. Even if some of the information may be unreliable and unverifiable, tweets are the latest means of instant cross-border, globe-spanning communication and a high-speed alternative to traditional mainstream media.[111]

YOUR TASK. You don't need to register with Twitter to search for and view tweets in your Internet browser, but you should open a Twitter account to enjoy the full benefits of the free service. Signing up is quick and intuitive. You will be able to follow not only friends and family, but also news, business updates, film reviews, and sports, or receive and share other up-to-the-minute messages.

Start by viewing *trending topics.* Some may be business related. A few may be international in scope. Use the search box to type any current international or business event to see what "twitterers" are saying about it. For instance, check out the tweets of CNN's Christiane Amanpour or those of another well-known journalist; for example, Nick Gillespie or George Will. In the classroom, discuss the usefulness of Twitter as you see it. Your instructor may ask you to prepare an e-mail or memo identifying and summarizing three trending business topics. In your opinion, how accurately do the tweets convey the trend? Can trends be summarized in 140 characters? You will learn more about Twitter and other highly mobile new media in Chapter 7.

3.5 Learning About the Global Economy (Obj. 1)

Intercultural

Fred W. Smith, CEO of FedEx, said, "It is an inescapable fact that the U.S. economy is becoming much more like the European and Asian economies, entirely tied to global trade."

YOUR TASK. Read your local newspapers for a week and peruse national news periodicals (*Time, Newsweek, BusinessWeek, U.S. News, The Wall Street Journal,* and so forth) for articles that support this assertion. Your instructor may ask you to (a) report on many articles or (b) select one article to summarize. Report your findings orally or in a memo to your instructor. This topic could be expanded into a long report for Chapters 12 or 13.

3.6 Intercultural Divide at Resort Hotel in Thailand (Objs. 1–3)

Intercultural **Team**

The Laguna Beach Resort Hotel in Phuket, Thailand, nestled between a tropical lagoon and the sparkling Andaman Sea, is one of the most beautiful resorts in the world. (You can take a virtual tour by using your favorite browser and searching for *Laguna Beach Resort Phuket.*) When Brett Peel arrived as the director of the hotel's kitchen, he thought he had landed in paradise. Only on the job six weeks, he began wondering why his Thai staff would answer *yes* even when they didn't understand what he had said. Other foreign managers discovered that junior staff managers rarely spoke up and never expressed an opinion that was contrary to those of senior executives. What's more, guests with a complaint thought that Thai employees were not taking them seriously because the Thais smiled at even the worst complaints. Thais also did not seem to understand deadlines or urgent requests.[112]

YOUR TASK. In teams decide how you would respond to the following questions. If you were the director of this hotel, would you implement a training program for employees? If so, would you train only foreign managers, or would you include local Thai employees as well? What topics should a training program include? Would your goal be to introduce Western ways to the Thais? At least 90 percent of the hotel guests are non-Thai.

3.7 Trek Bicycle Goes Global (Objs. 1, 3, and 5)

Intercultural **Social Media** **Web**

Despite doping, in winning the Tour de France seven times, Lance Armstrong brought international prestige to Waterloo, Wisconsin. That is the home of Trek Bicycle, manufacturer of the superlightweight carbon bikes Armstrong has ridden to victory over the years. The small town of Waterloo (population 2,888) is about the last place you would expect to find the world's largest specialty bicycle maker. Trek started its global business in a red barn smack in the middle of Wisconsin farm country. It employs 1,500 people in Waterloo and serves 2,000 stores in the United States alone and 4,000 dealers worldwide in 65 countries. Nearly 50 percent of the sales of the high-tech bicycles come from international markets. Future sales abroad look promising as Trek expands into Chinese and Indian markets. In Asia, bicycles are still a major means of transportation. To accommodate domestic and international consumers, Trek maintains a busy international website. Enter the search term *Trek Bicycle*. Also, visit Trek Bicycles' Facebook fan page.

Like many companies, Trek encountered problems in conducting intercultural transactions. For example, in Mexico, cargo was often pilfered while awaiting customs clearance. In Singapore a buyer balked at a green bike helmet, explaining that when a man wears green on his head it means his wife is unfaithful. In Germany, Trek had to redesign its packaging to reduce waste and meet environmental requirements. Actually, the changes required in Germany helped to bolster the company's overall image of environmental sensitivity.

YOUR TASK. Based on principles you studied in this chapter, name several lessons that other entrepreneurs can learn from Trek's international experiences.[113]

3.8 Interpreting Intercultural Proverbs (Objs. 2, 3)

⟨ E-mail ⟩ ⟨ Intercultural ⟩

Proverbs, which tell truths with metaphors and simplicity, often reveal fundamental values held by a culture.

YOUR TASK. Discuss the following proverbs and explain how they relate to some of the cultural values you studied in this chapter. In an e-mail or memo to your instructor, provide additional proverbs and explain what they mean. What additional proverbs can you cite, and what do they mean?

North American proverbs

An ounce of prevention is worth a pound of cure.

The squeaky wheel gets the grease.

A bird in the hand is worth two in the bush.

He who holds the gold makes the rules.

Japanese proverbs

A wise man hears one and understands ten.

The pheasant would have lived but for its cry.

The nail that sticks up gets pounded down.

German proverbs

What is bravely ventured is almost won.

He who wants to warm himself in old age must build a fireplace in his youth.

Charity sees the need, not the cause.

3.9 Negotiating Traps (Objs. 2, 3)

⟨ Intercultural ⟩

Businesspeople often have difficulty reaching agreement on the terms of contracts, proposals, and anything that involves bargaining. They have even more difficulty when the negotiators are from different cultures.

YOUR TASK. Discuss the causes and implications of the following common mistakes made by North Americans in their negotiations with foreigners.

a. Assuming that a final agreement is set in stone

b. Lacking patience and insisting that matters progress more quickly than the pace preferred by the locals

c. Thinking that an interpreter is always completely accurate

d. Believing that individuals who speak English understand every nuance of your meaning

e. Ignoring or misunderstanding the significance of rank

3.10 Learning About Other Countries (Objs. 2, 4)

⟨ Intercultural ⟩ ⟨ Web ⟩

When meeting business people from other countries, you will feel more comfortable if you know the basics of business etiquette and intercultural communication, such as greetings, attire, or dos and don'ts. On the Web you will find many resources, some more reliable than others.

YOUR TASK. Visit the websites of Executive Planet and the International Business Center, or use a browser to search for *International Business Etiquette*. On the International Business Center website, for example, click the button *Hofstede resource pages*. This website provides analysis based on the renowned Dutch psychologist's five dimensions of culture applied to each country. Peruse both websites and answer the following questions:

a. How do people greet each other in Australia, India, Japan, Korea, the Netherlands, and Spain?

b. In what countries is it important to keep a certain distance from the person you are greeting?

c. In what countries is a kiss an appropriate greeting?

3.11 Learn to Speak a Foreign Language or Just a Few Phrases With Livemocha or Busuu (Objs. 2, 3)

⟨ E-mail ⟩ ⟨ Intercultural ⟩ ⟨ Social Media ⟩ ⟨ Web ⟩

The social Web has taken the world by storm; therefore, it's not surprising that social networks have formed around various interests and human pursuits. At least two major social networks have united people eager to learn or practice a foreign language online. The two major ones are Livemocha and Busuu. Both social networks offer some free basic instruction and premium fee-based content in a number of popular languages.

YOUR TASK. Compare the two online language learning communities. Consider these and similar questions: How many languages do they support? How do they operate, and how much do they cost? What features do they offer? How many users do they have? Learn a few phrases in a language that interests you and report back to class. Your instructor may ask you to summarize your findings in writing, either in an e-mail or in an online post.

3.12 Checking in With Facebook (Objs. 1, 3)

⟨ Intercultural ⟩ ⟨ Social Media ⟩ ⟨ Team ⟩ ⟨ Web ⟩

With over 1.06 billion monthly active users, Facebook is currently the largest social networking site. It is still growing, not in the United States, but globally, mainly in Latin America, Japan, India, and some African countries. You may be surprised to hear that Brazil contributed 16 million new users within a mere six months, a 46 percent increase. Argentina's presence grew by almost 1.5 million, and Mexicans made up 4.6 million new users. The growth is currently stalling in the United States, where Facebook users decreased 1 percent. In

Asia, Japanese Facebook users grew a whopping 85 percent and Vietnam added 52 percent new users over a recent six-month period, while China's Facebook use declined almost 4 percent.

YOUR TASK. As a team or alone, visit any of the Facebook tracking websites—for example, Inside Facebook, a platform for developers and marketers, Socialbakers, or Internet World Stats. Study the tables listing the top countries in various categories. Which country is currently the fastest-growing country in absolute numbers? Find out which country has the largest presence on Facebook outside the United States. Do not rely solely on absolute numbers, but compare population penetration rates, the ratio between Facebook use and population.

Even if you don't speak another language, visit at last one non-English Facebook site and evaluate surface similarities and differences. Chances are that you will recognize some familiar features. Discuss similarities and differences in class. If you speak a foreign language, can you spot any customization that suggests adaptation to local preferences and customs?

As you will learn in Chapter 15, Facebook is also playing an increasing role in recruiting and other business applications.

3.13 Iceland and Norway: The Most Connected Countries in the World?

Intercultural) (Social Media) (Web)

The American Internet? Think again. Yes, the precursors of the Internet that emerged from the sciences and the military were U.S.-based. Early websites were almost always in English and meant for Americans.

Perhaps it's the cold climate, but Iceland—one of the least densely populated countries in the world—is also the most connected one, closely followed by Norway.

A look at per capita use of the Internet reveals that Scandinavian countries—Iceland, Norway, Sweden, Denmark, and Finland—lead the world and rank up to 19.5 percentage points ahead of the United States.

Asia has the most Internet users in absolute numbers (over 1 billion), followed by Europe (over 500 million) and North America (276 million). However, Internet users from Asia, the most populous continent, comprise a rather modest 26.2 percent. Europe shows a penetration of 61.3 and North America of 78.6 percent.

YOUR TASK. Examine Figure 3.9 and relate the percentage of Internet use to the country. For example, in China 38.4 percent of the people have Internet access up from 22.4 percent two years earlier. Consider these or similar questions: Is this figure likely to increase in the future? How can you explain the low Internet penetration for Asia as a whole? Why do you think North European nations are so Internet friendly? Which regions have experienced the strongest growth in two years? What conclusions can you draw about Internet use worldwide? Discuss your observations in small groups or in class. Your instructor may ask you to submit your conclusions in writing. You may also be asked to conduct more research for a short report. Statistics about Internet use worldwide abound, along with more recent numbers showing global social media use.

Figure 3.9 Internet Use Around the World

Country	Current Population	Internet Users 2011	Internet Users 2009	% Population Penetration 2011	% Population Penetration 2009
Iceland	311,058	304,129	273,930	97.8	90.0
Norway	4,691,849	4,560,572	3,993,400	97.2	86.0
Sweden	9,088,728	8,441,718	7,295,200	92.9	80.7
Denmark	5,529,888	4,923,824	4,408,100	89.0	80.4
Finland	5,259,250	4,661,265	5,244,749	88.6	83.0
South Korea	48,754,657	40,329,660	36,794,800	82.7	76.1
Canada	34,030,589	27,757,540	21,700,000	81.6	80.0
Japan	126,475,664	191,228,736	94,000,000	80.0	73.8
United States	313,232,044	245,203,319	227,190.989	78.3	74.7
China	1,336,718,015	513,100,000	298,000,000	38.4	22.4
Total North America	**347,394,870**	**276,067,546**	**251,000,000**	**78.6**	**74.4**
Total Europe	**816,426,346**	**500,723,686**	**393,000,000**	**61.3**	**48.9**
Total Asia	**3,879,740,877**	**1,016,799,076**	**658,000,000**	**26.2**	**17.4**
Total Africa	**1,037,524,058**	**139,875,242**	**69,000,000**	**13.5**	**5.6**
TOTAL WORLD	**6,930,055,154**	**2,267,233,742**	**1,596,270,108**	**32.7**	**23.8**

Source: Internet World Stats—www.internetworldstats.com, 2011 and 2009.

© Cengage Learning 2015

Chapter 3: Intercultural Communication

3.14 Rotation Curation: Cultural Networking at Its Best?

Review the Plugged In feature on page 85 about rotation curation for the country of Sweden.

YOUR TASK. Consider the subject matter the Swedish citizen "curators" addressed in their tweets. Should they be free to post whatever they want, or should some (tougher) guidelines apply? If you believe in restrictions, what kind of rules would you champion? Is tweeting from an *official* account—one that represents an organization, a cause, or even a country—different from using a personal Twitter account? How about rules for posting on Facebook, Pinterest, or other social media accounts? Which causes might be suitable for rotation curation? Could businesses benefit? If you were chosen to represent your country, how would you view your responsibilities? How would you approach your posts? What topics might you want to choose? Ponder, too, whether you would be comfortable tweeting in another language as the curators representing **@Sweden** do, required as they are to post in English.

3.15 Examining Cultural Stereotypes (Objs. 2, 3)

As you have learned in this chapter, generalizations are necessary as we acquire and categorize new knowledge. As long as we remain open to new experiences, we won't be stymied by rigid, stereotypical perceptions of other cultures. Almost all of us are at some point in our lives subject to stereotyping by others, whether we are immigrants, minorities, women, members of certain professions, Americans abroad, and so forth. Generally speaking, negative stereotypes sting. However, even positive stereotypes can offend or embarrass because they fail to acknowledge the differences among individuals.

YOUR TASK. Think about a nation or culture about which you have only a hazy idea. Jot down a few key traits that come to mind. For example, you may not know much about the Netherlands and the Dutch people. You can probably think of gouda cheese, wooden clogs, Heineken beer, tulips, and windmills. Anything else? Then consider a culture with which you are very familiar, whether it is yours or that of a country you visited or studied. In one column, write down a few stereotypical perceptions that are positive. Then, in another column, record negative stereotypes you associate with that culture. Share your notes with your team or the whole class, as the instructor may direct. How do you respond to others' descriptions of your culture? Which stereotypes irk you and why? For a quick fact check and overview at the end of this exercise, google the *CIA World Factbook* or *BBC News Country Profiles*.

3.16 Exploring Negative Stereotypes and Prejudice (Obj. 3)

Review the Ethical Insights feature on page 92, Overcoming Prejudice.

YOUR TASK. Organize a debate or class discussion focused on these questions: How can we explain the different reactions of the bagel shop customers to the store clerk's refusal to serve the Muslim woman? What do they indicate? Why didn't Aida Mansoor and the woman in the TV scenario choose to be less conspicuous by shedding the hijab? What are the effects of prejudice, especially in the workplace?

3.17 Analyzing a Problem International E-Mail (Obj. 3)

American writers sometimes forget that people in other countries, even if they understand English, are not aware of the meanings of certain words and phrases.

YOUR TASK. Study the following e-mail[114] to be sent by a U.S. firm to a potential supplier in another country. Identify specific weaknesses that may cause troubles for intercultural readers.

> Dear Koichi:
>
> Because of the on-again/off-again haggling with one of our subcontractors, we have been putting off writing to you. We were royally turned off by their shoddy merchandise, the excuses they made up, and the way they put down some of our customers. Since we have our good name to keep up, we have decided to take the bull by the horns and see if you would be interested in bidding on the contract for spare parts.
> By playing ball with us, you are sure to score big with your products. So please give it your best shot and fire off your price list ASAP. We will need it by 3/8 if you are to be in the running.
>
> Yours,

3.18 Make Yourself at Home: Ambiguous Expressions Invite New Friends (Obj. 3)

To end conversations, North Americans often issue casual invitations to new acquaintances and even virtual strangers, such as *Visit me when you come to New York,* or *Come on over anytime.* However, nonnative speakers and visitors may misinterpret such casual remarks. They may embarrass their hosts and suffer disappointment by taking the offhand invitation literally and acting on it. Those interacting across cultures would be wise to avoid using expressions that have multiple meanings.

YOUR TASK. Assume you are a businessperson engaged in exporting and importing. As such, you are in constant communication with suppliers and customers around the world. In messages sent abroad or in situations with nonnative speakers of English at home, what kinds of ambiguous expressions should you avoid? In teams or individually, list three to five original examples of idioms, slang, acronyms, sports references, abbreviations, jargon, and two-word verbs. Which phrases or behavior could be taken literally by a person from a different culture?

3.19 Greasing Palms Abroad: *Baksheesh, Mordida,* and *Kumshah* (Obj. 4)

In the Middle East, bribes are called *baksheesh*. In Mexico, they are *mordida*; and in Southeast Asia, *kumshah*. Although it takes place in many parts of the world, bribery is not officially sanctioned by any country. In the United States, the Foreign Corrupt Practices Act prohibits giving anything of value to a foreign official in an effort to win or retain business. However, this law does allow payments that may be necessary to expedite or secure "routine governmental action." For instance, a company could make small payments to obtain permits and licenses or to process visas or work orders. Also allowed are payments to secure telephone service and power and water supplies, as well as payments for the loading and unloading of cargo.

YOUR TASK. In light of what you have learned in this chapter, how should you act in the following situations? Are the actions legal or illegal?[115]

a. Your company is moving toward final agreement on a contract in Pakistan to sell farm equipment. As the contract is prepared, officials ask that a large amount be included to enable the government to update its agriculture research. The extra amount is to be paid in cash to the three officials you have worked with. Should your company pay?

b. You have been negotiating with a government official in Niger regarding an airplane maintenance contract. The official asks to use your Diner's Club card to charge $2,028 in airplane tickets as a honeymoon present. Should you do it to win the contract?

c. You are trying to collect an overdue payment of $163,000 on a shipment of milk powder to the Dominican Republic. A senior government official asks for $20,000 as a collection service fee. Should you pay?

d. Your company is in the business of arranging hunting trips to East Africa. You are encouraged to give guns and travel allowances to officials in a wildlife agency that has authority to issue licenses to hunt big game. The officials have agreed to keep the gifts quiet. Should you make the gifts?

e. Your firm has just moved you to Malaysia, and your furniture is sitting on the dock. Cargo handlers won't unload it until you or your company pays off each local dock worker. Should you pay?

f. In Mexico your firm has been working hard to earn lucrative contracts with the national oil company, Pemex. One government official has hinted elaborately that his son would like to do marketing studies for your company. Should you hire the son?

3.20 Investigating Gifts, Gratuities, and Entertainment Limits (Obj. 4)

Ethics **Intercultural** **Team** **Web**

You are one of a group of interns at a large company. As part of your training, your director asks your team to investigate the codes of conduct of other companies. In particular, the manager asks you to find comparison information on gifts, gratuities, and kickbacks.

YOUR TASK. Search the Web for sections in codes of conduct that relate to gifts, gratuities, entertainment, and kickbacks. From three companies or organizations (such as Blue Cross Blue Shield, 3M Corporation, or a university), investigate specific restrictions. What do these organizations allow and restrict? Prepare a list summarizing your findings in your own words.

3.21 Investigating Gender Talk (Obj. 5)

Review the Career Coach feature on page 105 about gender talk and gender tension.

YOUR TASK. In small groups or in a class discussion, consider these questions: Do men and women have different communication styles? Which style is more appropriate for today's team-based management? Do we need a kind of communicative affirmative action to give more recognition to women's ways of talking? Should men and women receive training encouraging the interchangeable use of these styles depending on the situation?

3.22 Encouraging Gender Diversity in Corporations (Obj. 5)

Communication Technology **E-mail** **Intercultural**

Despite strides by some global companies toward greater diversity, a recent Alliance for Board Diversity (ABD) study reported that women and minorities are still underrepresented in U.S. corporate boardrooms. The alliance led by research firm Catalyst found that men held 82 percent of board seats at Fortune 100 companies (white men occupied 70 percent). Men's share on boards in Fortune 500 companies was higher at 85 percent (white men held nearly 75 percent).[116] ABD called a 1.1 percentage point gain for women over six years since its last census "not appreciable."[117] Also, white men held as many as 95.5 percent of board chair positions, the top jobs in the Fortune 500. Ilene Lang, chair of ABD and CEO of Catalyst, suggested that greater diversity benefits corporations: "More diverse boards, on average, are linked with better financial performance."[118] The most recent *Women Matter* report published by consulting firm McKinsey & Company concurs and confirms its own earlier findings: "[T]he link between the presence of women in executive committees and better financial performance is still valid."[119]

A Ceram Business School study in France found that across all industries, corporations with the highest proportion of female managers saw their share prices fall the least at the height of the Great Recession. "Feminisation of management seems to protect against financial crisis," the study's author, Michael Ferrary, concluded. Ferrary credits female managers' aversion to risk and long-term perspective for balancing the more risk-taking behavior of their male colleagues. He says that in uncertain times financial markets favor stable and risk-averse companies.[120] He calls for greater gender diversity because it fosters a more diverse culture and leads to the exploration of more varied business opportunities. He believes that reducing gender inequality is not only socially responsible but also profitable for a company.[121] According to a *Financial Times* editorial, lack of gender diversity "now sends negative signals of a conservative mind-set, an inability to look beyond a tried circle of directors and a proneness to damaging group-think."[122]

How can greater gender diversity be accomplished? European countries such as Germany, the UK, France, Italy, and the Netherlands are taking radical measures. They are threatening to impose mandatory quotas within the next five years unless public companies increase the percentage of women on their corporate boards to as much as 40 percent. Critics counter that rigid quotas could jeopardize the very goal of greater diversity, unduly affect smaller companies, and encourage the appointment of token women just to satisfy the requirement. Rather, they suggest that politicians and business leaders pursue voluntary targets and appeal to investors to step up the pressure on companies to change.[123]

YOUR TASK. Individually or in groups discuss whether the United States should rely on the marketplace to effect change, or whether the government should speed change along. If your instructor directs, summarize your thoughts in a concise e-mail message or a post on Blackboard, Moodle, or another online discussion board or in a chat room. Alternatively, plan a message to investors encouraging them to diversify their boards of directors to include more women and minorities.

3.23 What Makes a "Best" Company for Minorities? (Obj. 5)

 Web

In its ranking of the 50 Best Companies for Minorities, *Fortune* listed the following suggestions for fostering diversity: [124]

- Make an effort to hire, retain, and promote minorities.
- Interact with outside minority communities.
- Hold management accountable for diversity efforts.
- Create a culture in which people of color and other minorities feel that they belong.
- Match a diverse workforce with diversity in an organization's management ranks and on its board.

YOUR TASK. Assume that you work for a company like the ones described in **Activity 3.22** and that you believe your organization would be better if it were more diverse. Because of your interest in this area, your boss says he would like you to give a three- to five-minute informational presentation at the next board meeting. Your assignment is to present what the leading minority-friendly companies are doing. You decide to prepare your comments based on *Fortune* magazine's list of the 50 best companies for minorities, using as your outline the previous bulleted list. You plan to provide examples of each means of fostering diversity. Your instructor may ask you to give your presentation to the entire class or to small groups.

Chat About It

In each chapter you will find five discussion questions related to the chapter material. Your instructor may assign these topics for you to discuss in class, in an online chat room, or on an online discussion board. Some of the discussion topics may require outside research. You may also be asked to read and respond to postings made by your classmates.

Topic 1: Discuss the advantages and disadvantages of learning a foreign language. Is learning a foreign language necessary when English is the language of business? If you were to learn a foreign language, which would you choose and why?

Topic 2: Consider the social networks you use daily. Could they help you connect with people outside your immediate circle of friends or family and reach out to people from other, perhaps unfamiliar cultures? Would you find it useful? Would you agree that people behave the same on social media networks as they do in real life and that some users are more outgoing than others? Name specific examples.

Topic 3: Name a time when you were aware of ethnocentrism in your own actions or those of friends, family members, or colleagues. In general terms, describe what happened. What made you think the experience involved ethnocentrism?

Topic 4: Do some research to determine why Transparency International ranked New Zealand, Denmark, Finland, Sweden, and Singapore as the least corrupt countries or why it ranked Haiti, Iraq, Afghanistan, Myanmar, North Korea, and Somalia as the most corrupt countries.

Topic 5: In your own experience, how accurate are characterizations that gender theorists make about differences between men and women? Support your views.

C.L.U.E. Grammar & Mechanics | *Review 3*

Pronouns
Review Guides 11–18 about pronoun usage in Appendix A, Grammar and Mechanics Guide, beginning on page A-6. On a separate sheet, revise the following sentences to correct errors in pronouns. For each error that you locate, write the guide number that reflects this usage. Some sentences may have two errors. If the sentence is correct, write *C*. When you finish, check your answers on page Key-1.

EXAMPLE: My friend and me are both looking for jobs.

REVISION: My friend and **I** are both looking for jobs. [Guide 12]

1. Send all instructions to my manager and I; he and I will study them carefully.
2. Except for Mark and I, all the sales reps attended the team meeting.
3. In promoting it's shoes to kids in Rome, Nike featured a Brazilian soccer star.
4. Most of we consumers remember when fruits and vegetables were available only in season.
5. The senior project manager and I are on call tonight, so please direct all calls to him or myself.
6. Every employee has a right to see their personnel folder.
7. Lunches will be delivered to whomever ordered them.
8. Most reservations were made in time, but your's and her's missed the deadline.
9. Just between you and me, who do you think will be our new manager?
10. It must have been her who sent the e-mail to Jason and me.

Notes

[1]Metro's chief executive, Hans-Joachim Koerber, in Hall, A., & Bawden, T. (2006, July 29). Wal-Mart pulls out of Germany at cost of $1bn. *The Times Online*. Retrieved from http://business .timesonline.co.uk/tol/business/industry _sectors/retailing/article694345.ece

[2]Landler, M., & Barbaro, M. (2006, August 2). No, not always. *New York Times*, p. 1. Retrieved from http://www.nytimes.com

[3]Ibid.

[4]Ibid.

[5]Wal-Mart to augment Japan operations via acquisitions. (2011, September 8). Retrieved from http://www.istockanalyst.com /finance/story/5404859/wal-mart-wmt-to -augment-japan-operations-via-acquisitions

[6]Holstein, W. (2007). Why Wal-Mart can't find happiness in Japan. *Fortune*, *156*(3), pp. 73-78. Retrieved from http://search.proquest.com

[7]Based on McGee, S. (2007, June 29). What's on the shelves in China's Wal-Marts? *MSN Money*. Retrieved from http://moneycentral.msn.com /home.asp

[8]Rein, S. (2012, January 16). Why global brands fail in China. CNBC guest blog. Retrieved from http://www.cnbc.com/id/46009614 /Rein_Why_Global_Brands_Fail_in_China

[9]Smith, J. (2007). The perils of prediction. *World Trade*, *20*(1), 39-44. Retrieved from http://search .ebscohost.com

[10]Martens, C. (2010, Sep. 9).Top ten Lay's chip flavors in China. Retrieved from http://www.foodchannel.com/articles/article /top-ten-lays-chips-flavors-in-china

[11]Nokia most trusted brand in India. (2011, Jan. 19). Retrieved from http://articles.economictimes. indiatimes.com/2011-01-19/news/28429397_1 _brand-trust-sachin-tendulkar-survey

[12]McLean, D. (2010, March 24). Ben & Jerry's new CEO promises to keep it in Vermont. Retrieved from http://www.usatoday.com/money /industries/food/2010-03-24-ben-and-jerrys -ceo-solheim_N.htm

[13]von Zeppelin, C. (2010, July 28). Billionaire owner of Trader Joe's, Theo Albrecht, dies. Retrieved from http://www.forbes.com/sites /billions/2010/07/28/billionaire-owner-of -trader-joes-theo-albrecht-dies

[14]The most famous American brands now in foreign hands. (2010, October 8). Retrieved from http://www.huffingtonpost.com/2010/10/08 /american-brands-in-foreig_n_755900 .html#s152955&title=Budweiser

[15]Seven-Eleven Japan. (2011). Retrieved from http://www.sej.co.jp/company/en/n_stores.html

[16]Browning, E. S. (1992, April 23). In pursuit of the elusive Euroconsumer. *The Wall Street Journal*, p. B1; and Wheatley, M. (1995). The branding of Europe. *Management Today*, 66. Retrieved from http://search.ebscohost.com

[17]Brooks, S. (2006, December). Tomorrow, the world. *Restaurant Business*, *105*(12), pp. 26-32. Retrieved from http://search.ebscohost.com

[18]Sterpa, M. (2010). The most unusual Dunkin' Donuts from around the world. Retrieved from http://www.buzzfeed.com/mjs538/the-most -unusual-dunkin-donuts-from-around-the-wor

[19]Gunther, M. (2010, July 26). The world's new economic landscape. *Fortune*, p. 106.

[20]Rein, S. (2011, March 7). Why Best Buy failed in China. CNBC.com. Retrieved from http://www .cnbc.com/default.aspx?id=41882157&Why _Best_Buy_Failed_in_China=print&1=display mode&1098=print&1

[21]Longid, F., ed. (2011, February 21). Best Buy shuts China stores to focus on more profitable brand. Retrieved from http://www .bloomberg.com/news/2011-02-22

/best-buy-s-china-stores-shut-as-retailer -focuses-on-more-profitable-brand.html

[22]Burkitt, L. (2012, Sept. 15-16). Home Depot: Chinese prefer 'Do it for me.' *The Wall Street Journal*, p. B1.

[23]Longid, F., ed. (2011, February 21). Best Buy shuts China stores to focus on more profitable brand. Retrieved from http://www.bloomberg.com /news/2011-02-22/best-buy-s-china-stores-shut -as-retailer-focuses-on-more-profitable-brand .html

[24]U.S. Free Trade Agreements. (2012, May 15). Export .gov. Retrieved from http://export.gov/FTA /index.asp; Free Trade Agreements. (2012). Office of the United States Trade Representative. Retrieved from http://www.ustr.gov /trade-agreements/free-trade-agreements

[25]Ernst & Young. Six major trends shaping the business world: Emerging markets increase their global power. Retrieved from http://www .ey.com/GL/en/Issues/Business-environment /Six-global-trends-shaping-the-business-world —Emerging-markets-increase-their-global-power

[26]Kharas, H. (2011, November 5). Can the Asian middle class come of age? Retrieved from http://www.brookings.edu/opinions/2011/0612 _asian_middle_class_kharas.aspx

[27]Vossos, T. (2011, April 3). The effect of advancements in transportation technology on global business. Retrieved from http://www.ehow .com/info_8160779_effects-transportation -technology-global-business.html

[28]Scenario based on Twitter evolves. (n.d.). Rotation Curation. Retrieved from http://rotationcuration .com; About. (n.d.). Rotation curation. Retrieved from http://rotationcuration.com; Lyall, S. (2012, June 12). Swedes' Twitter voice: Anyone, saying (blush) almost anything. *The New York Times*. Retrieved from http://www.nytimes .com/2012/06/11/world/europe/many-voices -of-sweden-via-twitter.html; Haberman, S. (2012, June 12). Sweden Twitter experiment goes painfully awry. Mashable. Retrieved from http://mashable.com/2012/06/12 /sweden-twitter; Arons, R. (2012, June 19). The pleasing irreverence of @Sweden. *The New Yorker*. Retrieved from http://www.newyorker .com/online/blogs/culture/2012/06/sonja -abrahamsson-twitter-sweden.html?printable =true&currentPage=all

[29]Gunther, M. (2010, July 26). The world's new economic landscape. *Fortune*, p. 105.

[30]Kotkin, J., & Ozuna, E. (2012, Winter). America's demographic future. *Cato Journal*, 38(1), 59. http://www.cato.org/pubs/journal/cj32n1 /cj32n1-5.pdf

[31]Bill Frey cited in Kotkin, J., & Ozuna, E. (2012, Winter). America's demographic future. *Cato Journal*, 38(1), 60. http://www.cato.org/pubs /journal/cj32n1/cj32n1-5.pdf

[32]Ortman, J. M., & Guarneri, C. E. (2009). United States population projections: 2000 to 2050. Retrieved from http://www.census.gov/population /projections; U.S. Census 2010. (2011, March 24). 2010 Census shows America's diversity. Retrieved from http://2010.census.gov/news/releases /operations/cb11-cn125.html; U.S. Department of Labor. (2007). Futurework: Trends and challenges for work in the 21st century. Retrieved from http://www.dol.gov/oasam/programs /history/herman/reports/futurework/report .htm#.ULhdaWeQOWY

[33]Pollack, A. (1996, December 22). Barbie's journey in Japan. *The New York Times*, p. E3. Retrieved from http://www.nytimes.com

[34]Photo essay based on Tulshyan, R. (2010, March 18). Quirkiest cultural practices from around the world. Forbes. Retrieved from http://www .forbes.com

[35]Hall, E. T., & Hall, M. R. (1990). *Understanding cultural differences*. Yarmouth, ME: Intercultural Press, pp. 183-184.

[36]Figure based on Chaney, L. H., & Martin, J. S. (2011). *Intercultural business communication* (5th ed.). Upper Saddle River, NJ: Prentice Hall, Chapter 5; J. Chung's analysis appearing in Chen, G. M., & Starosta, W. J. *Foundations of intercultural communication*. Boston: Allyn and Bacon, 1998, p. 51; and O'Hara-Devereaux, M. & Johansen, R. (1994). *Globalwork: Bridging distance, culture, and time*. San Francisco: Jossey-Bass, p. 55.

[37]Chaney, L. H., & Martin, J. S. (2011). *Intercultural business communication* (5th ed.). Upper Saddle River, NJ: Prentice Hall, p. 93.

[38]Daft, R. L., & Marcic, D. (2011). *Understanding management*, 7th ed. Mason, OH: South-Western, Cengage Learning, p. 93; Zunker, V. (2008). *Career, work, and mental health*. Thousand Oaks, CA: Sage, p. 140.

[39]Chen, M.-J., & Miller, D. (2010, November). West meets East: Toward an ambicultural approach to management. *Academy of Management Perspectives*, *24*(4), 19ff. Retrieved from http://search.ebscohost.com; Sheer, V. C., & Chen, L. (2003, January). Successful Sino-Western business negotiation: Participants' accounts of national and professional cultures. *The Journal of Business Communication*, *40*(1), 62; see also Luk, L., Patel, M., & White, K. (1990, December). Personal attributes of American and Chinese business associates. *The Bulletin of the Association for Business Communication*, 67.

[40]Gallois, C., & Callan, V. (1997). *Communication and culture*. New York: Wiley, p. 24.

[41]Copeland, J. (1990, December 15). Stare less, listen more. American Airlines. *American Way*, p. 32.

[42]Gallois, C., & Callan, V. (1997). *Communication and culture*. New York: Wiley, p. 29.

[43]Copeland, L., & Griggs, L. (1985). *Going international*. New York: Penguin, p. 94.

[44]Ibid., p. 108.

[45]Ibid., p. 12.

[46]Ethical Insight based on Saslow, E. (2009, June 3). As the myths abound, so does Islamic outreach. *The Washington Post*, p. C1. Retrieved from http://www.dowjones.com/factiva

[47]Chen, G. M., & Starosta, W. J. (1998). *Foundations of intercultural communication*. Boston: Allyn and Bacon, p. 40.

[48]Varner, I., & Beamer, L. (2001). *Intercultural communication in the global workplace*. Boston: McGraw-Hill Irwin, p. 18.

[49]BMW Group. (2010, November 18). The intercultural innovation award. Retrieved from http://www.bmwgroup.com/e/0_0_www _bmwgroup_com/verantwortung/gesellschaft /lifeaward/ausschreibung2010/_pdf/profils _finalists_engl.pdf

[50]Tandy, J., & Mackenzie, J. (2009, July 9). French tourists seen as world's worst: Survey. Reuters .com. Retrieved from http://www.reuters.com

[51]Clabaugh, J. (2012, March 12). Worst tourists are Americans, say Americans. *Washington Business Journal*. Retrieved from http://www.bizjournals .com/washington/news/2012/03/02/worst -tourists-are-americans-say.html; and Tandy, J., & Mackenzie, J. (2009, July 9). French tourists seen as world's worst: Survey. Retrieved from http://www.reuters.com

[52]Martin, J. S., & Chaney, L. H. (2006). *Global business etiquette*. Westport, CT: Praeger, p. 69.

[53]Hammer, M. R. (1993). Quoted in Chen and Starosta's *Foundations of intercultural communication*. Boston: Allyn & Bacon, p. 247.

[54]Chaney, L. H., & Martin, J. S. (1995). *Intercultural business communication*. Englewood Cliffs, NJ: Prentice Hall Career and Technology, p. 67.

[55]Carter, J. F. (2010, October 14). Why Twitter influences cross-cultural engagement. Mashable Social Media. Retrieved from http://mashable.com/2010/10/14/twitter-cross-cultural

[56]Klass, P. (2012, January 9). Seeing social media more as portal than as pitfall. The New York Times. Retrieved from http://www.nytimes.com/2012/01/10/health/views/seeing-social-media-as-adolescent-portal-more-than-pitfall.html

[57]Aragon, S. R. (2003, Winter). Creating social presence in online environments. New Directions for Adult and Continuing Education, 100, 59.

[58]Carter, J. F. (2010, October 14). Why Twitter influences cross-cultural engagement. Mashable Social Media. Retrieved from http://mashable.com/2010/10/14/twitter-cross-cultural

[59]Choney, S. (2012, March 13). Kony video proves social media's role as youth news source. MSNBC.com. Retrieved from http://www.technolog.msnbc.msn.com/technology/technolog/kony-video-proves-social-medias-role-youth-news-source-pew-455365

[60]Carter, J. F. (2010, October 14). Why Twitter influences cross-cultural engagement. Mashable Social Media. Retrieved from http://mashable.com/2010/10/14/twitter-cross-cultural

[61]Ibid.

[62]McGrath, C. (2009, August 5). Five lessons learned about cross-cultural social networking. ThoughtFarmer. Retrieved from http://www.thoughtfarmer.com/blog/2009/08/05/5-lessons-cross-cultural-social-networking/#comments

[63]Masterson, M. (2009, January 27). Can social software "work" in Germany? Enterprise 2.0 blog. Retrieved from http://enterprise20blog.com/2009/01/27/can-social-software-work-in-germany

[64]Market trends. (2012, January). Broadband strategies toolkit. Retrieved from http://broadbandtoolkit.org/1.4

[65]Burson-Marsteller. (2010). Global media check-up. Retrieved from http://www.slideshare.net/kornfeind/burson-marsteller-2010-global-social-media-checkup-10241454

[66]Ibid.

[67]Kunz, B. (2012, April 19). Facebook, Google must adapt as users embrace "unsocial" networks. Bloomberg Businessweek. Retrieved from http://www.businessweek.com

[68]Jackson, E. (2012, June 5). Will Facebook exist in five years? [Video]. Retrieved from http://www.businessweek.com/videos/2012-06-05/will-facebook-exist-in-five-years

[69]Weber, G. (2004, May). English rules. Workforce Management, 47-50; Desai, D. (2008). Globalization and the English skills gap. Chief Learning Officer, 7(6), 62-63. Retrieved from http://search.ebscohost.com; and Dvorak, P. (2007, November 5). Plain English gets harder in global era. Wall Street Journal. Retrieved from http://search.ebscohost.com

[70]Martin, J. S., & Chaney, L. H. (2006). Global business etiquette. Westport, CT: Praeger, p. 191.

[71]Finney, P. B. (2005, May 17). Shaking hands, greasing palms. The New York Times, p. C1.

[72]Berenbeim, R. (2000, May). Global ethics. Executive Excellence, p. 7.

[73]Kimes, M. (2009, February 16). Fluor's corporate crime fighter. Fortune, p. 26. Retrieved from http://search.ebscohost.com

[74]Meyer, H. (2011, March 7). Corruption halts IKEA in Russia. The Age. Retrieved from http://www.theage.com.au/world/corruption-halts-ikea-in-russia-20110306-1bji5.html; see also Bush, J. (2009, July 2). Why IKEA is fed up with Russia. BusinessWeek.com. Retrieved from http://www.businessweek.com/magazine/content/09_28/b4139033326721.htm

[75]The 2011 Corruption Perceptions Index, Transparency International. Retrieved from http://www.transparency.org/policy_research/surveys_indices/cpi

[76]Schubert, S., & Miller, T. C. (2008, December 21). Where bribery was just a line item. New York Times, p. BU1. Retrieved from http://search.proquest.com

[77]Going after Chiquita. (2008, March 24). BusinessWeek, p. 10.

[78]Finney, P. B. (2005, May 17). Shaking hands, greasing palms. The New York Times, p. C1.

[79]PricewaterhouseCoopers International. (2008, January). Confronting corruption: The business case for an effective anti-corruption programme. Retrieved from http://www.pwc.com/gx/en/forensic-accounting-dispute-consulting-services/business-case-anti-corruption-programme.jhtml

[80]Wei, S-J. (2003, March 12). Corruption in developing countries. Global Economics. Retrieved from http://www.brookings.edu/research/speeches/2003/03/12development-wei

[81]Alvarez, S. (2006, December). Global integrity: Transparency International's David Nussbaum is fighting for a world that is free of bribery and corruption. Internal Auditor, 63(6), 53. Retrieved from http://www.dowjones.com/factiva

[82]Hodgson, K. (1992, May). Adapting ethical decisions to a global marketplace. Management Review, 56. Retrieved from http://www.dowjones.com/factiva/. See also Digh, P. (1997, April). Shades of gray in the global marketplace. HR Magazine, p. 42. Retrieved from http://search.ebscohost.com

[83]Solomon, C. M. (1996, January). Put your ethics to a global test. Personnel Journal, 66-74. See also Smeltzer, L. R., & Jennings, M. M. (1998, January). Why an international code of business ethics would be good for business. Journal of Business Ethics, 57-66. See also Barker, T. S., & Cobb, S. L. (2000). A survey of ethics and cultural dimensions of MNCs [multinational companies]. Competitiveness Review, 10(2), 123. Retrieved from http://search.ebscohost.com

[84]Hodgson, K. (1992, May). Adapting ethical decisions to a global marketplace. Management Review, 54. Retrieved from http://www.dowjones.com/factiva; See also Franke, G. R. (2008, March). Culture, economic development, and national ethical attitudes. Journal of Business Research, 61(3). Retrieved from http://search.ebscohost.com

[85]Phillips, K. (2009, June 2). Diversity helps your business—But not the way you think. Forbes. Retrieved from http://www.forbes.com/2009/06/02/diversity-collaboration-teams-leadership-managing-creativity.html

[86]Ortman, J. M., & Guarneri, C. E. (2009). United States population projections: 2000-2050, p. 4. Retrieved from http://www.census.gov/population/projections; see also 2000 U.S. Census figures, as reported by Little, J. S., & Triest, R. K. (2001). Proceedings from the Federal Reserve Bank of Boston Conference Series. The impact of demographic change on U.S. labor markets. Seismic shifts: The economic impact of demographic change. Retrieved from http://www.bos.frb.org/economic/conf/conf46/conf46a.pdf

[87]Hansen, F. (2003, April). Tracing the value of diversity programs. Workforce, p. 31.

[88]Carbone, J. (2005, August 11). IBM says diverse suppliers are good for business. Purchasing, p. 27. Retrieved from http://search.ebscohost.com

[89]Krotz, J. L. (2011). Business benefits of diversity. Microsoft Small Business Center. Retrieved from http://www.microsoft.com/business/en-us/resources/management/recruiting-staffing/diversity-pays-off-for-everyone.aspx?fbid=pMjis7yNs4-

[90]Terhune, C. (2005, April 19). Pepsi, vowing diversity isn't just image polish, seeks inclusive culture. The Wall Street Journal, p. B4.

[91]Krotz, J. L. (2011). Business benefits of diversity. Microsoft Small Business Center. Retrieved from http://www.microsoft.com/business/en-us/resources/management/recruiting-staffing/diversity-pays-off-for-everyone.aspx?fbid=pMjis7yNs4-

[92]Andre, R. (1995, June). Diversity stress as morality stress. Journal of Business Ethics, 489-496.

[93]Andre, R. (1995, June). Diversity stress as morality stress. Journal of Business Ethics, 489-496.

[94]Career Coach (He Said, She Said) based on Basow, S. A., & Rubenfeld, K. (2003, February). Troubles talk: Effects of gender and gender-typing. Sex Roles: A Journal of Research, 183. Retrieved from http://www.springerlink.com/content/rm75xx843786037q/fulltext.pdf; Wood, J. T. (2002). Gendered lives. Belmont, CA: Wadsworth, p. 119; Tear, J. (1995, November 20). They just don't understand gender dynamics. The Wall Street Journal, p. A12. Retrieved from http://www.dowjones.com/factiva; Roiphe, A. (1994, October). Talking trouble. Working Woman, pp. 28-31; Stuart, C. (1994, February). Why can't a woman be more like a man? Training Tomorrow, pp. 22-24; and Wolfe, A. (1994, December 12). She just doesn't understand. New Republic, 211(24), pp. 26-34.

[95]Schwartz, J., & Wald, M. L. (2003, March 9). Smart people working collectively can be dumber than the sum of their brains. Appeared originally in The New York Times. Retrieved from http://www.mindfully.org/Reform/2003/Smart-People-Dumber9mar03.htm

[96]Capowski, G. (1996, June). Managing diversity. Management Review, p. 16.

[97]Makower, J. (1995, Winter). Managing diversity in the workplace. Business and Society Review, pp. 48-54.

[98]White, M. D. (2002). A short course in international marketing blunders. Novato, CA: World Trade Press, p. 46.

[99]Walmart. (2012). Beyond 50 years: Building a sustainable future. 2012 global responsibility report. Retrieved from http://www.walmartstores.com/sites/responsibility-report/2012/pdf/WMT_2012_GRR.pdf

[100]Ibid.

[101]Based on Walmart Brazil mobilizes suppliers and announces sustainability pact. (2009, June 23). Facts & News/Walmart.com. Retrieved from http://walmartstores.com/FactsNews/NewsRoom/9223.aspx; Winston, A. (2009, July 14). Wal-Mart Brazil thinks green. BusinessWeek/Harvard Business Online. Retrieved from http://www.businessweek.com; and Aston, A. (2009, May 14). Wal-Mart: Making its suppliers go green. BusinessWeek Online. Retrieved from http://www.businessweek.com/magazine/content/09_21/b4132044814736.htm

[102]Walmart. (2012). Beyond 50 years: Building a sustainable future. 2012 global responsibility report. Retrieved from http://www.walmartstores.com/sites/responsibility-report/2012/pdf/WMT_2012_GRR.pdf

[103]Winston, A. (2009, July 14). Wal-Mart Brazil thinks green. BusinessWeek/Harvard Business Online. Retrieved from http://www.businessweek.com

[104]Scenario based on Berens, C. (n.d.). Top 12 social media blunders of 2011. Inc. Retrieved from http://www.inc.com/ss/caitlin-berens/top-12-social-media-blunders-2011#3 and on Wasserman, T. (2011, February 16). Red Cross does PR disaster recovery on rogue tweet. Mashable.com. Retrieved from http://mashable.com/2011/02/16/red-cross-tweet

[105]Maltby, E. (2010, January 19). Expanding abroad? Avoid cultural gaffes. The Wall Street Journal, p. B5.

[106]Hookway, J. (2012, June 5). Ikea's products make shoppers blush in Thailand. The Wall Street Journal, p. A16.

[107]Špaček, L. (2008). Nová velká kniha etikety. Prague: Mladá Fronta, p. 260.

[108]Cottrill, K. (2000, November 6). The world according to Hollywood. Traffic World, p. 15.

[109]Conlin, M. (2007, April 23). Go-go-going to pieces in China. BusinessWeek, p. 88.

[110]Pew Research Center's Internet & American Life Project. (2012, March 15). The viral Kony 2012

video, p. 1. Retrieved from http://pewinternet.org/~/media//Files/Reports/2012/The_Viral_Kony_2012_Video.pdf

[111]Nasr, O. (2009, June 15). Tear gas and Twitter: Iranians take their protests online. CNN.com. Retrieved from http://edition.cnn.com/2009/WORLD/meast/06/14/iran.protests.twitter/; Grossman, L. (2009, June 17). Iran protests: Twitter, the medium of the movement. *Time*. Retrieved from http://www.time.com/time/world/article/0,8599,1905125,00.html; and Sarno, D. (2009, March 6). Twittergates: Twitter's @billgates isn't really Bill Gates. Los Angeles Times.com. Retrieved from http://latimesblogs.latimes.com/technology/2009/03/latest-twitter.html

[112]Thapanachai, S. (2003, October 6). Awareness narrows cross-cultural gap in Thai management training courses. *Bangkok Post*. Retrieved from http://www.dowjones.com/factiva

[113]Dawson, D. (2005, March 1). At the top and still climbing. High Performance Composites.

Retrieved from http://www.compositesworld.com/articles/at-the-top-and-still-climbing.aspx; and Wucker, M. (1998, December/January). Keep on trekking. *Working Woman*, pp. 32-36.

[114]Based on Knotts, R., & Thibodeaux, M. S. (1992). Verbal skills in cross-culture managerial communication. *European Business Review, 92*(2), v-vii.

[115]Martin, K., & Walsh, S. M. (1996, October). Beware the Foreign Corrupt Practices Act. *International Commercial Litigation*, 25-27; and Lay-person's guide to Foreign Corrupt Practices Act (FCPA). (n.d.). United States Department of Justice. Retrieved from http://www.usdoj.gov/criminal/fraud/fcpa/

[116]Alliance for Board Diversity. (2011, July 21). Missing pieces: Women and minorities on Fortune 500 boards. Updated datasheet. Retrieved from http://theabd.org/ABD_datasheet.pdf

[117]Ibid.

[118]Vannucci, C. (2011, July 28). U.S. firms slow to raise women directors, study finds.

Bloomberg. com. Retrieved from http://www.bloomberg.com/news/2011-05-02/u-s-companies-fail-to-increase-women-directors-study-finds.html

[119]McKinsey & Company. (2010, October). Women matter 2010. Retrieved from http://www.mckinsey.com/locations/paris/home/womenmatter.asp

[120]Ferrary, M. (2009, March 2). Why women managers shine in a downturn. *Financial Times*. Retrieved from http://www.ft.com/cms/s/0/0993d9e0-f284-11df-a2f3-00144feab49a,s01=1.html#axzz1LCrlq3Jk

[121]Ibid.

[122]Hill, A. (2010, November 17). Companies that fail the Lagarde test must act. *Financial Times*. Retrieved from http://www.ft.com/cms/s/0/0993d9e0-f284-11df-a2f3-00144feab49a,s01=1.html#axzz1LCrlq3Jk

[123]Ibid.

[124]Daniels, C. (2004, June 28). 50 best companies for minorities. *Fortune*, p. 138.

Unit 2

The Writing Process in the Digital Age

decision

ethic

vision

integrity

Leadership

contribution

communication

motivation

influence

responsibility

© Dusit/Shutterstock.com

CHAPTER 4

Planning Business Messages

OBJECTIVES

After studying this chapter, you should be able to

1 Understand the nature of communication and its barriers in the digital age.

2 Summarize the 3-x-3 writing process and explain how it guides a writer.

3 Analyze the purpose of a message, anticipate its audience, and select the best communication channel.

4 Employ expert writing techniques such as incorporating audience benefits, the "you" view, conversational but professional language, a positive and courteous tone, bias-free language, plain language, and vigorous words.

5 Understand how teams approach collaborative writing projects and what collaboration tools support team writing.

120

© Multi-bits/The Image Bank/Getty Images

TOMS Founder Blake Mycoskie Inspires Doing Good With a Powerful Message

Blake Mycoskie, founder of TOMS Shoes, had a simple idea: sell a pair of shoes today; give away a pair of shoes tomorrow.[1] That message has turned into a communication mantra for the entrepreneur, whose trademark canvas shoes have propelled him, his ideas, and his brand into a global phenomenon.

The story began in 2006 when Mycoskie visited Argentina and was moved by the many children he witnessed suffering from a disease they contracted when going barefoot. He was soon selling his version of the plain Argentine *alpargata* shoe to finance giving free shoes to needy children. Within a few years, the TOMS brand was selling in hundreds of U.S. outlets including Nordstrom, Macy's, and Whole Foods. Mycoskie's philanthropy won him the 2009 Secretary of State's Award for Corporate Excellence (ACE). The company distributed its one millionth pair of free shoes in 2010.[2]

Mycoskie's success in creating a product specifically to do good in the world is part of a powerful communication message that resonates with many consumers. To promote that message, TOMS has been savvy in using audience awareness and well-chosen media channels available in this exciting digital age.

Perhaps one of the company's most innovative strategies has been its active engagement of young people, especially college students, through internships and campus programs. TOMS actively invites enthusiastic students to become part of the company and its message. Interns participate in various functions at the Santa Monica, California, headquarters. One recent intern in the TOMS online content department explains the importance of planning in creating Web content. "Content isn't just randomly pushed through at random times; it actually involves a lot of strategy and planning to maximize our efforts and our reach," intern Andrew Kirschner writes in a blog post.[3]

Creating effective content certainly involves careful planning. It also requires the writer to be aware of the audience's needs, to write with a clear purpose, to hone words and phrases through careful editing, and to proofread to ensure the professionalism today's consumers demand. In short, from interns to managers, all professionals are more effective when they write using a process.

You will learn more about TOMS and be asked to complete a relevant task at the end of this chapter.

Critical Thinking

- In planning your business messages, how can you alter your writing to effectively engage audiences of various ages or education levels?

- Why do even experienced writers use a writing process?

- Why is it so important to know your purpose before beginning to write?

Understanding the Nature of Communication

LEARNING OBJECTIVE 1
Understand the nature of communication and its barriers in the digital age.

The digital revolution with electronic transmission of messages has profoundly changed the way we live our lives, do business, and communicate. Staff members and college interns at TOMS use Facebook, Twitter, blogs, e-mail, and other digital media to communicate and create content as part of their effort to engage fans and expand business. Not only the media but also the volume of messages is changing for organizations involved in doing business in the digital age.

People are sending more and more messages, and they are using exciting new avenues of interaction as the world becomes increasingly interconnected. However, even as we have gotten used to e-mail, instant messaging, texting, Twitter, and other interactive media, the nature of communication remains unchanged. No matter how we create or send our messages, the basic communication process consists of the same elements. It starts with an idea that must be transmitted.

In its simplest form, **communication** may be defined as the *transmission of information and meaning from a sender to a receiver*. The crucial element in this definition is *meaning*. The process is successful only when the receiver understands an idea as the sender intended it. How does an idea travel from one person to another? It involves a sensitive process, shown in Figure 4.1. This process can easily be sidetracked resulting in miscommunication. The process of communication, however, is successful when both the sender and receiver understand the process and how to make it work effectively. In our discussion we will be most concerned with professional communication in the workplace so that you can be successful as a business communicator in your career.

Sender Has Idea

The communication process begins when the sender has an idea. The form of the idea may be influenced by complex factors surrounding the sender. These factors may include mood, frame of reference, background, culture, and physical makeup, as well as the context of the situation and many other factors. Senders shape their ideas based on their own experiences and assumptions. A manager sending an e-mail announcement to employees asking them to conserve energy assumes that they will be receptive. On the other hand, a direct-mail advertiser promoting a new magazine assumes that receivers will give only a quick glance to something perceived as junk mail. To communicate most effectively, a sender must begin by clarifying the idea and purpose. What exactly does the sender want to achieve? How is the message likely to be received? When senders know their purpose and anticipate the expected response, they are better able to shape successful messages.

Figure 4.1 The Communication Process

The Communication Process

1 Sender has idea
2 Sender encodes message
3 Sender selects channel, transmits message
4 Receiver decodes message
5 Feedback returns to sender

To communicate effectively:

Sender should
- Clarify idea
- Decide on purpose of message
- Analyze idea and how it can best be presented
- Anticipate effect on receiver

Sender should
- Consider receiver's background, communication skills, experience, culture, context
- Choose concrete words and appropriate symbols
- Encourage feedback

Sender should
- Consider importance of message, feedback required, interactivity
- Choose a channel that the receiver prefers
- Think of ways to reduce channel noise and distractions
- Be aware of competing messages

Receiver should
- Avoid prejudging message
- Strive to understand both verbal and nonverbal cues
- Ignore distractions
- Create receptive environment
- Expect to learn

Receiver should
- Craft clear and complete response that reveals comprehension of message meaning
- Begin the cycle again when the receiver becomes the sender with the same concerns

© Cengage Learning 2015

Sender Encodes Idea

The next step in the communication process involves *encoding*. This means converting the idea into words or gestures that will convey meaning. A major problem in communicating any message verbally is that words have different meanings for different people. Recognizing how easy it is to be misunderstood, skilled communicators choose familiar, concrete words. In choosing proper words and symbols, senders must be alert to the receiver's communication skills, attitudes, background, experiences, and culture. Including a smiley face in an e-mail announcement to stockholders may turn them off.

International messages require even more care. In Great Britain the press called a new recycling program a *scheme*, which seriously offended the New York–based sponsor of the program, RecycleBank. In the United States, *scheme* connotes deceit. In Britain, however, it carries no such negative meaning.[4] The most successful messages use appropriate words, gestures, and symbols selected specifically to match the situation. Good messages also encourage feedback and make it easy for the receiver to respond.

Sender Selects Channel and Transmits Message

The medium over which the message travels is the *channel*. Messages may be delivered by computer, wireless network, smartphone, social media, letter, memorandum, report, announcement, picture, spoken word, fax, Web page, or some other channel. Today's messages are increasingly carried over digital networks with much opportunity for distraction and breakdown. Receivers may be overloaded with incoming messages or unable to receive messages clearly on their devices. Only well-crafted messages may be accepted, understood, and acted on. Anything that interrupts the transmission of a message in the communication process is called *noise*. Channel noise may range from a weak Internet signal to sloppy formatting and typos in e-mail messages. Noise may even include the annoyance a receiver feels when the sender chooses an improper channel for transmission or when the receiver is overloaded with messages and information.

Receiver Decodes Message

The individual to whom the message is intended is the *receiver*. Translating the message from its symbol form into meaning involves *decoding*. Only when the receiver understands the meaning intended by the sender—that is, successfully decodes the message—does communication take place. Such success is often difficult to achieve because of a number of barriers that block the process.

No two people share the same life experiences or have the same skills. Decoding can be disrupted internally by the receiver's lack of attention or by bias against the sender or by competing messages. It can be disrupted externally by loud sounds or illegible words. Decoding can also be sidetracked by semantic obstacles, such as misunderstood words or emotional reactions to certain terms. A memo that refers to women in the office as "chicks" or "babes," for example, may disturb its receivers so much that they fail to focus on the total message. On the receiving end, successful decoding is more likely to be achieved when the receiver creates a receptive environment and ignores distractions. Alert receivers strive to understand both verbal and nonverbal cues, avoid prejudging the message, and expect to learn something.

Feedback Returns to Sender

The verbal and nonverbal responses of the receiver create *feedback*, a vital part of the communication process. Feedback helps the sender know that the message was received and understood. Senders can encourage feedback by asking questions such as, *Am I making myself clear?* and, *Is there anything you don't understand?* Senders can further improve feedback by timing the delivery appropriately and by providing only as much information as the receiver can handle. Receivers improve the communication process by providing clear and complete feedback. In the business world, one of the best ways to advance understanding is by paraphrasing the sender's message with comments such as, *Let me try to explain that in my own words.* The best feedback tends to be descriptive rather than evaluative. Here's a descriptive response: *I understand you want to grow square watermelons because they fit into refrigerators more easily.*

An innovative entrepreneurial idea to market square watermelons draws both judgmental and evaluative feedback.

Here's an evaluative response: *Your business ideas are always goofy!* An evaluative response is judgmental and doesn't tell the sender whether the receiver actually understood the message. When the receiver returns feedback, this person then becomes the sender of a new cycle of communication with all of the same concerns as the original sender.

Barriers That Create Misunderstanding

The communication process is successful only when the receiver understands the message as intended by the sender. It sounds quite simple. Yet it's not. How many times have you thought that you delivered a clear message, only to learn later that your intentions were misunderstood? Most messages that we send reach their destinations, but many are only partially understood.

You can improve your chances of communicating successfully by learning to recognize barriers that are known to disrupt the process. Some of the most significant barriers for individuals are bypassing, differing frames of reference, lack of language skill, and distractions.

Bypassing. An important barrier to clear communication involves words. Each of us attaches a little bundle of meanings to every word, and these meanings are not always similar. Bypassing happens when people miss each other with their meanings.[6] Let's say your boss asks you to "help" with a large customer mailing. When you arrive to do your share, you learn that you are expected to do the whole mailing yourself. You and your boss attached different meanings to the word *help*. Bypassing can lead to major miscommunication because people assume that meanings are contained in words. Actually, meanings are in people. For communication to be successful, the receiver and sender must attach the same symbolic meanings to their words. One study revealed a high likelihood of miscommunication when people use common but vague words such as *probably, always, never, usually, often, soon,* and *right away*. What do these words really mean?[7]

Differing Frames of Reference. Another barrier to clear communication is your *frame of reference*. Everything you see and feel in the world is translated through your individual frame of reference. Your unique frame is formed by a combination of your experiences, education, culture, expectations, personality, and other elements. As a result, you bring your own biases and expectations to any communication situation. Because your frame of reference is different from everyone else's, you will never see things exactly as others do. American managers eager to reach an agreement with a Chinese parts supplier, for example, were disappointed with the slow negotiation process. The Chinese managers, on the other hand, were pleased that so much time had been taken to build personal relationships with the American managers. Wise business communicators strive to prevent miscommunication by being alert to both their own frames of reference and those of others.

REALITY CHECK: Are You a 10?

When interviewing candidates for employment, this executive asks one important question: "How good of a writer are you, on a scale of 1 to 10?"[8]

—**JACK DANGERMOND,** *founder, Esri, geographic mapping software*

Lack of Language Skill. No matter how extraordinary the idea is, it won't be understood or fully appreciated unless the communicators involved have good language skills. Each individual needs an adequate vocabulary and skill in oral and written expression. Using unfamiliar words, jargon, and unrecognizable abbreviations can seriously impede the transmission of meaning. Consider the following message posted on LinkedIn regarding social media and search engines: *Although SEO is part of SEM, you can't just lump in SMM and PR under the SEO banner!* Translation: *Although search engine optimization (SEO) is part of search engine marketing (SEM), you can't just lump social media marketing (SMM) and public relations (PR) under the search engine optimization (SEO) banner!* You will learn more about using plain language and familiar words later in this chapter.

Despite the growing number of multitaskers in society, studies have found that people who combine texting, video, phone, and other activities perform tasks significantly worse than nonmultitaskers. According to researchers, our brains can do two things at once, but they can't do them very well. In particular, recall, focus, and attention become impaired by information overload. The findings have broad implications for such multitasking behaviors as texting and driving, homework and Facebooking, and e-mailing while working. How can communicators win the attention of audiences in the digital age?[9]

Distractions.   Other barriers include emotional interference, physical distractions, and digital interruptions. Shaping an intelligent message is difficult when one is feeling joy, fear, resentment, hostility, sadness, or some other strong emotion. To reduce the influence of emotions on communication, both senders and receivers should focus on the content of the message and try to remain objective. Physical distractions such as faulty acoustics, noisy surroundings, or a poor mobile connection can disrupt oral communication. Similarly, sloppy appearance, poor printing, careless formatting, and typographical or spelling errors can disrupt written messages. What's more, technology doesn't seem to be helping. In this digital age, knowledge workers are increasingly distracted by multitasking, information overload, conflicting demands, and being constantly available digitally. Clear communication requires focusing on what is important and shutting out interruptions.[10]

Overcoming Communication Obstacles

Careful communicators can conquer barriers in a number of ways. Half the battle in communicating successfully is recognizing that the entire process is sensitive and susceptible to breakdown. Like a defensive driver anticipating problems on the road, a good communicator anticipates problems in encoding, transmitting, and decoding a message. Effective communicators also focus on the receiver's environment and frame of reference. They ask themselves questions such as, *How is that individual likely to react to my message?* or, *Does the receiver know as much about the subject as I do?*

Misunderstandings are less likely if you arrange your ideas logically and use words precisely. Mark Twain was right when he said, "The difference between an almost-right word and the right word is like the difference between lightning and the lightning bug." But communicating is more than expressing yourself well. A large part of successful communication is listening. Management advisor Peter Drucker observed that "too many executives think they are wonderful with people because they talk well. They don't realize that being wonderful with people means listening well."[11]

Effective communicators create an environment for useful feedback. In oral communication this means asking questions such as, *Do you understand?* and, *What questions do you have?* as well as encouraging listeners to repeat instructions or paraphrase ideas. As a listener it means providing feedback that describes rather than evaluates. In written communication it means asking questions and providing access: *Do you have my phone numbers in case you have questions?* or, *Here's my e-mail address so that you can give me your response immediately.*

> Like a defensive driver anticipating problems on the road, a good communicator anticipates problems in encoding, transmitting, and decoding a message.

LEARNING OBJECTIVE **2**

Summarize the 3-x-3 writing process and explain how it guides a writer.

Using the 3-x-3 Writing Process as a Guide

Today's new media and digital technologies enable you to choose from innumerable communication channels to create, transmit, and respond to messages. Nearly all communication, however, revolves around writing. Whether you are preparing a message that will be delivered digitally, orally, or in print, that message requires thinking and writing. Many of your messages will be digital. A **digital message** may be defined *as one that is generated, stored, processed, and transmitted electronically by computers using strings of positive and nonpositive binary code (0s and 1s)*. That definition encompasses many messages, including e-mail, Facebook posts, tweets, and other messages. For our purposes, we will focus primarily on messages exchanged on the job. Because writing is central to all business communication, this chapter presents a systematic plan for preparing business messages in the digital age.

Defining Your Business Writing Goals

One thing you should immediately recognize about business writing is that it differs from other writing you have done. In preparing high school or college compositions and term papers, you probably focused on discussing your feelings or displaying your knowledge. Your instructors wanted to see your thought processes, and they wanted assurance that you had internalized the subject matter. You may have had to meet a minimum word count. Business writing is definitely not like that! It also differs from personal texts you may exchange with your friends and family. Those messages enabled you to stay connected and express your feelings. In the workplace, however, you will want your writing to be:

- **Purposeful.** You will be writing to solve problems and convey information. You will have a definite strategy to fulfill in each message.
- **Economical**. You will try to present ideas clearly but concisely. Length is not rewarded.
- **Audience oriented.** You will concentrate on looking at a problem from the perspective of the audience instead of seeing it from your own.

REALITY CHECK: Why Is Business Writing So Bad?

Writing for the *Harvard Business Review*, David Silverman, blasts "an educational system that rewards length over clarity." Students learn to overwrite, he says, in hopes that at least some of their sentences "hit the mark." Once on the job, they continue to act as if they were paid by the word, a perception that must be unlearned.[12]

—**DAVID SILVERMAN**, *entrepreneur and business teacher*

Courtesy of David Silverman

These distinctions actually ease your task. You won't be searching your imagination for creative topic ideas. You won't be stretching your ideas to make them appear longer. Writing consultants and businesspeople complain that many college graduates entering industry have a conscious—or perhaps unconscious—perception that quantity enhances quality. Wrong! Get over the notion that longer is better. Whether you are presenting your ideas in print, online, or in person, conciseness and clarity are what count in business.

The ability to prepare purposeful, concise, and audience-centered messages does not come naturally. Very few people, especially beginners, can sit down and draft an effective e-mail message, letter, or report without training. However, following a systematic process, studying model messages, and practicing the craft can make nearly anyone a successful business writer or speaker.

Introducing the 3-x-3 Writing Process

Regardless of what you are writing, the process will be easier if you follow a systematic plan. The 3-x-3 writing process breaks the entire task into three phases: *prewriting, drafting,* and *revising,* as shown in Figure 4.2.

Figure **4.2** The 3-x-3 Writing Process

1 Prewriting

Analyze
- What is your purpose?
- What do you want the receiver to do or believe?
- What channel should you choose: face-to-face conversation, group meeting, e-mail, memo, letter, report, blog, wiki, tweet, etc.

Anticipate
- Profile the audience.
- What does the receiver already know?
- Will the receiver's response be neutral, positive, or negative? How will this affect your organizational strategy?

Adapt
- What techniques can you use to adapt your message to its audience?
- How can you promote feedback?
- Strive to use positive, conversational, and courteous language.

2 Drafting

Research
- Gather data to provide facts.
- Search company files, previous correspondence, and the Internet.
- What do you need to know to write this message?
- How much does the audience already know?

Organize
- Organize direct messages with the big idea first, followed by an explanation in the body and an action request in the closing.
- For persuasive or negative messages, use an indirect, problem-solving strategy.

Draft
- Prepare a first draft, usually quickly.
- Focus on short, clear sentences using the active voice.
- Build paragraph coherence by repeating key ideas, using pronouns, and incorporating appropriate transitional expressions.

3 Revising

Edit
- Edit your message to be sure it is clear, concise, conversational, readable.
- Revise to eliminate wordy fillers, long lead-ins, redundancies, and trite business phrases.
- Develop parallelism.
- Consider using headings and numbered and bulleted lists for quick reading.

Proofread
- Take the time to read every message carefully.
- Look for errors in spelling, grammar, punctuation, names, and numbers.
- Check to be sure the format is consistent.

Evaluate
- Will this message achieve your purpose?
- Does the tone sound pleasant and friendly rather than curt?
- Have you thought enough about the audience to be sure this message is appealing?
- Did you encourage feedback?

© Cengage Learning 2015

To illustrate the writing process, let's say that you own a popular local McDonald's franchise. At rush times, you face a problem. Customers complain about the chaotic multiple waiting lines to approach the service counter. You once saw two customers nearly get into a fistfight over cutting into a line. What's more, customers often are so intent on looking for ways to improve their positions in line that they fail to examine the menu. Then they are undecided when their turn arrives. You want to convince other franchise owners that a single-line (serpentine) system would work better. You could telephone the other owners. However, you want to present a serious argument with good points that they will remember and be willing to act on when they gather for their next district meeting. You decide to send a persuasive e-mail that you hope will win their support.

Prewriting. The first phase of the writing process prepares you to write. It involves *analyzing* the audience and your purpose for writing. The audience for your message will be other franchise owners, some highly educated and others not. Your purpose in writing is to convince them that a change in policy would improve customer service. You think that a single-line system, such as that used in banks, would reduce chaos and make customers happier because they would not have to worry about where they are in line.

Prewriting also involves *anticipating* how your audience will react to your message. You are sure that some of the other owners will agree with you, but others might fear that customers seeing a long single line might go elsewhere. In *adapting* your message to the audience, you try to think of the right words and the right tone that will win approval.

REALITY CHECK: Writing Matters

At investment banker Morgan Stanley, writing skills count. New-hires are often challenged when they have to adapt their writing for multiple audiences, say Keisha Smith. She points out that some tend to write long e-mails when only a short list is needed. Managers look over new-hires' e-mails before they are sent.[13]

—KEISHA SMITH, *Global Head of Recruiting, Morgan Stanley*

Drafting.   The second phase involves researching, organizing, and then drafting the message. In *researching* information for this message, you would probably investigate other kinds of businesses that use single lines for customers. You might check your competitors. What are Wendy's and Burger King doing? You might do some calling to see whether other franchise owners are concerned about chaotic lines. Before writing to the entire group, you might brainstorm with a few owners to see what ideas they have for solving the problem.

Once you have collected enough information, you would focus on *organizing* your message. Should you start out by offering your solution? Or should you work up to it slowly, describing the problem, presenting your evidence, and then ending with the solution? The final step in the second phase of the writing process is actually *drafting* the letter. At this point many writers write quickly, realizing that they will polish their ideas when they revise.

Revising.   The third phase of the process involves editing, proofreading, and evaluating your message. After writing the first draft, you will spend considerable time *editing* the message for clarity, conciseness, tone, and readability. Could parts of it be rearranged to make your point more effectively? This is the time when you look for ways to improve the organization and tone of your message. Next, you will spend time *proofreading* carefully to ensure correct spelling, grammar, punctuation, and format. The final phase involves *evaluating* your message to decide whether it accomplishes your goal.

Pacing the Writing Process

The time you spend on each phase of the writing process varies depending on the complexity of the problem, the purpose, the audience, and your schedule. On average, you should expect to spend about 25 percent of your time prewriting, 25 percent drafting, and 50 percent revising, as shown in Figure 4.3.

These are rough guides, yet you can see that good writers spend most of their time on the final phase of revising and proofreading. Much depends, of course, on your project, its importance, and your familiarity with it. What is critical to remember, though, is that revising is a major component of the writing process even if the message is short. What is critical to remember is that revising is a major component of the writing process even if the message is short.

It may appear that you perform one step and progress to the next, always following the same order. Most business writing, however, is not that rigid. Although writers perform the tasks described, the steps may be rearranged, abbreviated, or repeated. Some writers revise every sentence and paragraph as they go. Many find that new ideas occur after they have begun to write, causing them to back up, alter the organization, and rethink their plan. Beginning business writers often follow the writing process closely. With experience, though, they will become like other good writers and presenters who alter, compress, and rearrange the steps as needed.

ETHICS CHECK:

Buying Words

Websites with playful names such as Cramster (now called Chegg Homework Help), Course Hero, Koofers, and Spark Notes provide ready-made solutions, test answers, and essays for students. Do such sites encourage cheating and undermine the mental sweat equity of day-to-day learning?

Figure 4.3 Scheduling the Writing Process

Prewriting
25%

Drafting
25%

Revising
50%

Although the writing process looks like a linear set of steps, it actually is recursive, enabling writers to revise their work continually as they progress. However, careful planning can avoid wasted time and frustration caused by rethinking and reorganizing during drafting.

© Cengage Learning 2015

Analyzing and Anticipating the Audience

LEARNING OBJECTIVE 3
Analyze the purpose of a message, anticipate its audience, and select the best communication channel.

Surprisingly, many people begin writing and discover only as they approach the end of a message what they are trying to accomplish. If you analyze your purpose before you begin, you can avoid having to backtrack and start over. The remainder of this chapter covers the first phase of the writing process: analyzing the purpose for writing, anticipating how the audience will react, and adapting the message to the audience.

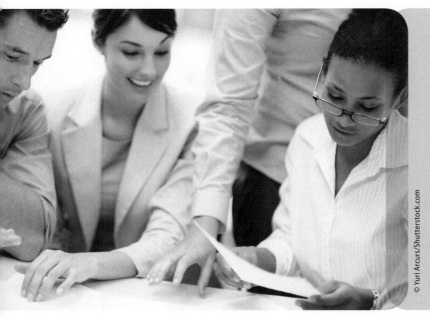

One would imagine that executives at Amazon use only the latest digital communication technologies to share information during meetings. However, instead of reading from interactive whiteboards and Kindles, CEO Jeff Bezos and his leadership team spend the first 30 minutes of strategy meetings reading paper memos and jotting comments in the margins. According to Bezos, memos are ideal because they have a narrative structure that allows for a logical development of ideas. What do business writers need to think about when preparing written materials for meetings?[14]

© Yuri Arcurs/Shutterstock.com

Determining Your Purpose

As you begin to compose a workplace message, ask yourself two important questions: (a) Why am I sending this message? and (b) What do I hope to achieve? Your responses will determine how you organize and present your information.

Your message may have primary and secondary purposes. For college work your primary purpose may be merely to complete the assignment; secondary purposes might be to make yourself look good and to earn an excellent grade. The primary purposes for sending business messages are typically to inform and to persuade. A secondary purpose is to promote goodwill. You and your organization want to look good in the eyes of your audience.

Many business messages do nothing more than *inform*. They explain procedures, announce meetings, answer questions, and transmit findings. Such messages are usually developed directly, as will be discussed in Chapter 5. Some business messages, however, are meant to *persuade*. These messages sell products, convince managers, motivate employees, and win over customers. Persuasive messages are often developed indirectly, as will be presented in Chapter 5 and subsequent chapters.

Anticipating and Profiling the Audience

A good writer anticipates the audience for a message: What is the reader or listener like? How will that person react to the message? Although one can't always know exactly who the receiver is, it is possible to imagine some of that person's characteristics. A copywriter at Lands' End, the shopping and Internet retailer, pictures his sister-in-law whenever he writes product descriptions for the catalog.

Profiling your audience is a pivotal step in the writing process. The questions in Figure 4.4 will help you profile your audience.

How much time you devote to answering these questions depends on your message and its context. An analytical report that you compose for management or an oral presentation before a big group would, of course, demand considerable time profiling the audience. An e-mail message to a coworker or a message to a familiar supplier might require only a few moments of planning.

Preparing a blog on an important topic to be posted to a company website would require you to think about the local, national, and international audiences that might read that message. Similarly, posting brief messages at microblogging sites such as Facebook, Twitter,

Figure 4.4 Asking the Right Questions to Profile Your Audience

Primary Audience

- Who is my primary reader or listener?
- What are my personal and professional relationships with this person?
- What position does this person hold in the organization?
- How much does this person know about the subject?
- What do I know about this person's education, beliefs, culture, and attitudes?
- Should I expect a neutral, positive, or negative response to my message?

Secondary Audience

- Who might see or hear this message in addition to the primary audience?
- How do these people differ from the primary audience?
- Do I need to include more background information?
- How must I reshape my message to make it understandable and acceptable to others to whom it might be forwarded?

© Cengage Learning 2015

and Tumblr should make you think about who will read the messages. How much of your day and life do you want to share? Will customers and business partners be reading your posts?

No matter how short your message is, though, spend some time thinking about the people in your audience so that you can tailor your words to them. Remember that your receivers will be thinking, *What's in it for me?(WIIFM)* One of the most important writing tips you can take away from this book is recognizing that every message you write should begin with the notion that your audience is thinking *WIIFM*.

Making Choices Based on the Audience Profile

Profiling your audience helps you make decisions about shaping the message. You will discover what language is appropriate, whether you are free to use specialized technical terms, whether you should explain the background, and so on. Profiling the audience helps you decide whether your tone should be formal or informal. Profiling helps you consider whether the receiver is likely to respond positively or negatively to your message, or be neutral about it.

Another consideration in profiling your audience is the possibility of a secondary audience. For example, let's say you start to write an e-mail message to your supervisor, Sheila, describing a problem you are having. Halfway through the message, you realize that Sheila will probably forward this message to her boss, the vice president. Sheila will probably not want to summarize what you said; instead, she may take the easy route and merely forward your e-mail. When you realize that the vice president may see this message, you decide to back up and use a more formal tone. You remove your inquiry about Sheila's family, you reduce your complaints, and you tone down your language about why things went wrong. Instead, you provide more background information, and you are more specific in identifying items the vice president might not recognize. Analyzing the task and anticipating the audience help you adapt your message so it will be effective for both primary and secondary receivers.

Selecting the Best Channel

After identifying the purpose of your message, you will want to select the most appropriate communication channel. In this digital age, the number of channels continues to expand, as shown in Figure 4.5. Your decision to send an e-mail message, schedule a videoconference, post a note on the company intranet, or use some other channel depends on some of the following factors:

- Importance of the message
- Amount and speed of feedback and interactivity required
- Necessity of a permanent record
- Cost of the channel
- Degree of formality desired
- Confidentiality and sensitivity of the message
- Receiver's preference and level of technical expertise

In addition to these practical issues, you will also consider how "rich" the channel is. As discussed in Chapter 1, the richness of a channel involves the extent to which a channel or medium recreates or represents all the information available in the original message. A richer medium, such as a face-to-face conversation, permits more interactivity and feedback. A leaner medium, such as a letter or an e-mail, presents a flat, one-dimensional message. Richer media enable the sender to provide more verbal and visual cues as well as to tailor the message to the audience.

Choosing the wrong medium can result in a message that is less effective or even misunderstood. If, for example, marketing manager Rodney must motivate the sales force to increase sales in the fourth quarter, he is unlikely to achieve his goal if he merely posts an announcement on the office bulletin board, writes a memo, or sends an e-mail. Rodney could be more persuasive with a richer channel, such as individual face-to-face conversations or a group meeting to stimulate sales. For sales reps on the road, a richer medium would be a

Figure **4.5** Comparing Rich and Lean Communication Channels

Ten Levels of Richness in Today's Workplace Communication Channels—Richest to Leanest

FACE-TO-FACE CONVERSATION
Richest medium. Best for persuasive, bad-news, and personal messages

VIDEO CHAT
Best for group interaction and consensus building when members are dispersed

IM
Best for short online messages that need a quick response

MEMO
To distribute interoffice information, especially when e-mail is unavailable

REPORT
To deliver considerable data internally or externally

1   2   3   4   5   6   7   8   9   10

TELEPHONE
Best choice when two people cannot meet in person

E-MAIL
Best for routine messages that do not require immediate feedback

LETTER
For external messages that require formality, sensitivity, or a written record

BLOG
To share ideas with a wide Internet audience and encourage responses

WIKI
To provide a repository for digital information that can be easily changed

Richest   Leanest

© Cengage Learning 2015

videoconference. In choosing channels, keep in mind two tips: (a) Use the richest media available, and (b) employ richer media for more persuasive or personal communications.

LEARNING OBJECTIVE **4**

Employ expert writing techniques such as incorporating audience benefits, the "you" view, conversational but professional language, a positive and courteous tone, bias-free language, plain language, and vigorous words.

Using Expert Writing Techniques to Adapt to Your Audience

After analyzing the purpose and anticipating the audience, writers begin to think about how to adapt a message to the task and the audience. Adaptation is the process of creating a message that suits the audience. Skilled communicators employ a number of expert writing techniques, such as those illustrated in the two versions of an e-mail in Figure 4.6. These techniques include featuring audience benefits, cultivating a "you" view, sounding conversational but professional, and using positive, courteous expression. Additional adaptive techniques include using bias-free language and preferring plain language with familiar but vigorous words.

Spotlighting Audience Benefits

Focusing on the audience sounds like a modern idea, but actually one of America's early statesmen and authors recognized this fundamental writing principle over 200 years ago. In describing effective writing, Ben Franklin observed, "To be good, it ought to have a tendency to benefit the reader."[15] These wise words have become a fundamental guideline for today's business communicators. Expanding on Franklin's counsel, a contemporary communication consultant gives this solid advice to his business clients: "Always stress the benefit to the audience of whatever it is you are trying to get them to do. If you can show them how you are going to save them frustration or help them meet their goals, you have the makings of a powerful message."[16] Remember, WIIFM!

Adapting your message to the receiver's needs means putting yourself in that person's shoes. It's called *empathy*. Empathic senders think about how a receiver will decode a message. They try to give something to the receiver, solve the receiver's problems, save the receiver's

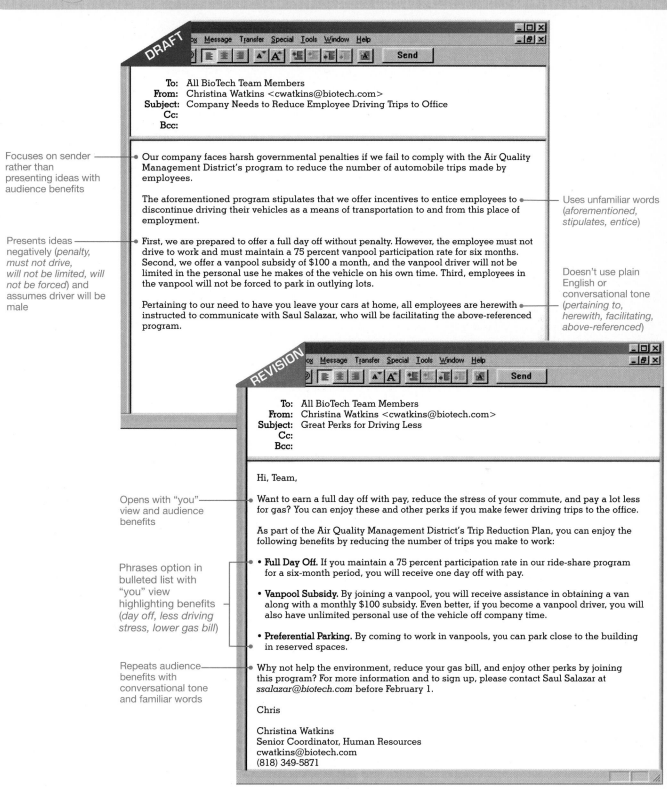

DRAFT

To: All BioTech Team Members
From: Christina Watkins <cwatkins@biotech.com>
Subject: Company Needs to Reduce Employee Driving Trips to Office
Cc:
Bcc:

Focuses on sender rather than presenting ideas with audience benefits

Our company faces harsh governmental penalties if we fail to comply with the Air Quality Management District's program to reduce the number of automobile trips made by employees.

The aforementioned program stipulates that we offer incentives to entice employees to discontinue driving their vehicles as a means of transportation to and from this place of employment.

Uses unfamiliar words (*aforementioned, stipulates, entice*)

Presents ideas negatively (*penalty, must not drive, will not be limited, will not be forced*) and assumes driver will be male

First, we are prepared to offer a full day off without penalty. However, the employee must not drive to work and must maintain a 75 percent vanpool participation rate for six months. Second, we offer a vanpool subsidy of $100 a month, and the vanpool driver will not be limited in the personal use he makes of the vehicle on his own time. Third, employees in the vanpool will not be forced to park in outlying lots.

Pertaining to our need to have you leave your cars at home, all employees are herewith instructed to communicate with Saul Salazar, who will be facilitating the above-referenced program.

Doesn't use plain English or conversational tone (*pertaining to, herewith, facilitating, above-referenced*)

REVISION

To: All BioTech Team Members
From: Christina Watkins <cwatkins@biotech.com>
Subject: Great Perks for Driving Less
Cc:
Bcc:

Hi, Team,

Opens with "you" view and audience benefits

Want to earn a full day off with pay, reduce the stress of your commute, and pay a lot less for gas? You can enjoy these and other perks if you make fewer driving trips to the office.

As part of the Air Quality Management District's Trip Reduction Plan, you can enjoy the following benefits by reducing the number of trips you make to work:

Phrases option in bulleted list with "you" view highlighting benefits (*day off, less driving stress, lower gas bill*)

- **Full Day Off.** If you maintain a 75 percent participation rate in our ride-share program for a six-month period, you will receive one day off with pay.

- **Vanpool Subsidy.** By joining a vanpool, you will receive assistance in obtaining a van along with a monthly $100 subsidy. Even better, if you become a vanpool driver, you will also have unlimited personal use of the vehicle off company time.

- **Preferential Parking.** By coming to work in vanpools, you can park close to the building in reserved spaces.

Repeats audience benefits with conversational tone and familiar words

Why not help the environment, reduce your gas bill, and enjoy other perks by joining this program? For more information and to sign up, please contact Saul Salazar at *ssalazar@biotech.com* before February 1.

Chris

Christina Watkins
Senior Coordinator, Human Resources
cwatkins@biotech.com
(818) 349-5871

money, or just understand the feelings and position of that person. Which version of each of the following messages is more appealing to the audience?

Sender Focus	Audience Focus
All employees are instructed herewith to fill out the enclosed questionnaire completely and immediately so that we can allocate our training resource funds to employees.	By filling out the enclosed questionnaires, you can be one of the first employees to sign up for our training resource funds.
Our warranty becomes effective only when we receive an owner's registration.	Your warranty begins working for you as soon as you return your owner's registration.
We are proud to announce our new real-time virus scanner that we think is the best on the market!	Now you can be sure that all your computers will be protected with our real-time virus scanner.

Developing the "You" View

Notice that many of the previous audience-focused messages included the word *you*. In concentrating on receiver benefits, skilled communicators naturally develop the "you" view. They emphasize second-person pronouns (*you, your*) instead of first-person pronouns (*I/we, us, our*). Whether your goal is to inform, persuade, or promote goodwill, the catchiest words you can use are *you* and *your*. Compare the following examples.

"I/We" View	"You" View
We are requiring all employees to respond to the attached survey about health benefits.	Because your ideas count, please complete the attached survey about health benefits.
I need your account number before I can do anything.	Would you mind giving me your account number so that I can locate your records and help you solve this problem?
We have shipped your order by UPS, and we are sure it will arrive in time for your sales promotion December 1.	Your order will be delivered by UPS in time for your sales promotion December 1.

Although you want to focus on the reader or listener, don't overuse or misuse the second-person pronoun *you*. Readers and listeners appreciate genuine interest; on the other hand, they resent obvious attempts at manipulation. The authors of some sales messages, for example, are guilty of overkill when they include *you* dozens of times in a direct-mail promotion. What's more, the word can sometimes create the wrong impression. Consider this statement: *You cannot return merchandise until you receive written approval.* The word *you* appears twice, but the reader may feel singled out for criticism. In the following version, the message is less personal and more positive: *Customers may return merchandise with written approval.*

Another difficulty in emphasizing the "you" view and de-emphasizing *we/I* is that it may result in an overuse of the passive voice. For example, to avoid *We will give you* (active voice), you might write *You will be given* (passive voice). The active voice in writing is generally preferred because it identifies who is doing the acting. You will learn more about active and passive voice in Chapter 5.

In recognizing the value of the "you" attitude, however, you don't have to sterilize your writing and totally avoid any first-person pronouns or words that show your feelings. You can convey sincerity, warmth, and enthusiasm by the words you choose. Don't be afraid of phrases such as *I'm happy* or *We're delighted,* if you truly are. When speaking face-to-face, you can show sincerity and warmth with nonverbal cues such as a smile and a pleasant voice tone. In letters, e-mail messages, memos, and other digital messages, however, only expressive words and phrases can show your feelings. These phrases suggest hidden messages that say *You are important, I hear you,* and *I'm honestly trying to please you.*

Sounding Conversational but Professional

Most of the business messages you write replace conversation. Thus, they are most effective when they convey an informal, conversational tone instead of a formal, pretentious tone. Just how informal you can be depends greatly on the workplace. At Google, casual seems to be preferred. In a short message to users describing changes in its privacy policies, Google recently wrote, "We believe this stuff matters."[18] In more traditional organizations, that message probably would have been more formal. The dilemma for you, then, is knowing how casual to be in your writing. We suggest that you strive to be conversational but professional, especially until you learn what your organization prefers.

E-mail, instant messaging, chat, Twitter, and other short messaging channels enable you and your coworkers to have spontaneous conversations. Don't, however, let your messages become sloppy, unprofessional, or even dangerous. You will learn more about the dangers of e-mail and other digital channels later. At this point, though, we focus on the tone of the language.

To project a professional image, you want to sound educated and mature. The overuse of expressions such as *totally awesome, you know,* and *like,* as well as reliance on unnecessary abbreviations (*BTW* for *by the way*), make a businessperson sound like a teenager. Professional messages do not include texting-style abbreviations, slang, sentence fragments, and chitchat. We urge you to strive for a warm, conversational tone that avoids low-level diction. Levels of diction, as shown in Figure 4.7, range from unprofessional to formal.

Your goal is a warm, friendly tone that sounds professional. Although some writers are too casual, others are overly formal. To impress readers and listeners, they use big words, long sentences, legal terminology, and third-person constructions. Stay away from expressions such as

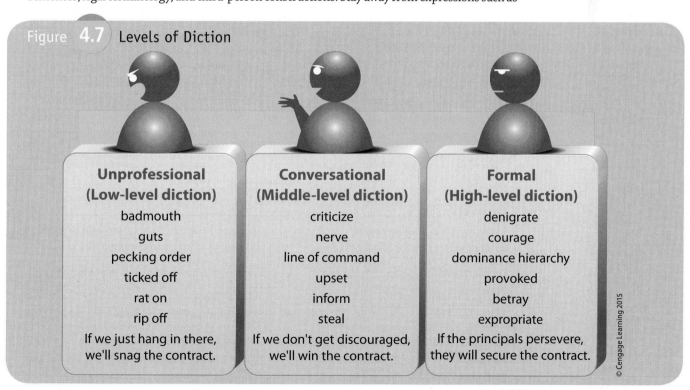

Figure 4.7 Levels of Diction

Unprofessional (Low-level diction)	Conversational (Middle-level diction)	Formal (High-level diction)
badmouth	criticize	denigrate
guts	nerve	courage
pecking order	line of command	dominance hierarchy
ticked off	upset	provoked
rat on	inform	betray
rip off	steal	expropriate
If we just hang in there, we'll snag the contract.	If we don't get discouraged, we'll win the contract.	If the principals persevere, they will secure the contract.

© Cengage Learning 2015

the undersigned, the writer, and *the affected party.* You will sound friendlier with familiar pronouns such as *I, we,* and *you.* The following examples illustrate a professional yet conversational tone:

Unprofessional	Professional
Hey, boss, Gr8 news! Firewall now installed!! BTW, check with me b4 announcing it.	Mr. Smith, our new firewall software is now installed. Please check with me before announcing it.
Look, dude, this report is totally bogus. And the figures don't look kosher. Show me some real stats. Got sources?	Because the figures in this report seem inaccurate, please submit the source statistics.

Overly Formal	Conversational
All employees are herewith instructed to return the appropriately designated contracts to the undersigned.	Please return your contracts to me.
Pertaining to your order, we must verify the sizes that your organization requires prior to consignment of your order to our shipper.	We will send your order as soon as we confirm the sizes you need.

Being Positive Rather Than Negative

You can improve the clarity, tone, and effectiveness of a message if you use positive rather than negative language. Positive language generally conveys more information than negative language does. Moreover, positive messages are uplifting and pleasant to read. Positive wording tells what *is* and what *can be done* rather than what *isn't* and what *can't be done.* For example, *Your order cannot be shipped by January 10* is not nearly as informative as *Your order will be shipped January 15.* An office supply store adjacent to an ice cream parlor in Portland, Maine, posted a sign on its door that reads: *Please enjoy your ice cream before you enjoy our store.* That sounds much more positive and inviting than *No food allowed!*[19]

Using positive language also involves avoiding negative words that create ill will. Some words appear to blame or accuse your audience. For example, opening a letter to a customer with *You claim that* suggests that you don't believe the customer. Other loaded words that can get you in trouble are *complaint, criticism, defective, failed, mistake,* and *neglected.* Also avoid phrases such as *you apparently are unaware of, you did not provide, you misunderstood,* and *you don't understand.* Often you may be unconscious of the effect of these words. Notice in the following examples how you can revise the negative tone to create a more positive impression.

Negative	Positive
This plan definitely cannot succeed if we don't obtain management approval.	This plan definitely can succeed if we obtain management approval.
You failed to include your credit card number, so we can't mail your order.	We look forward to completing your order as soon as we receive your credit card number.
Your letter of May 2 claims that you returned a defective headset.	Your May 2 letter describes a headset you returned.
Employees cannot park in Lot H until April 1.	Employees may park in Lot H starting April 1.
You apparently are unaware of our new mailing address for deposits because you used the old envelopes.	Enclosed are envelopes with our new mailing address for your deposits.

Expressing Courtesy

Maintaining a courteous tone involves not just guarding against rudeness but also avoiding words that sound demanding or preachy. Expressions such as *you should, you must,* and *you have to* cause people to instinctively react with *Oh, yeah?* One remedy is to turn these demands into rhetorical questions that begin with *Will you please . . . .* Giving reasons for a request also softens the tone.

Even when you feel justified in displaying anger, remember that losing your temper or being sarcastic will seldom accomplish your goals as a business communicator: to inform, to persuade, and to create goodwill. When you are irritated, frustrated, or infuriated, keep cool and try to defuse the situation. In dealing with customers in telephone conversations, use polite phrases such as *I would be happy to assist you with that, Thank you for being so patient,* and *It was a pleasure speaking with you.*

Less Courteous	More Courteous and Helpful
Can't you people get anything right? This is the second time I've written!	Please credit my account for $340. My latest statement shows that the error noted in my letter of May 15 has not yet been corrected.
Stewart, you must complete all performance reviews by Friday.	Stewart, will you please complete all performance reviews by Friday.
You should organize a car pool in this department.	Organizing a car pool will reduce your transportation costs and help preserve the environment.
Am I the only one who can read the operating manual?	Let's review the operating manual together so that you can get your documents to print correctly next time.

As a new or young employee who wants to fit in, don't fail to be especially courteous to older employees (generally, those over thirty) and important people in superior positions.[20] To make a great impression and show respect, use good manners in person and in writing. For example, don't be presumptuous by issuing orders or setting the time for a meeting with a superior. Use first names only if given permission to do so. In your messages be sure to proofread meticulously even if the important person to whom you are writing sends careless, error-filled messages.[21]

Employing Bias-Free Language

In adapting a message to its audience, be sure your language is sensitive and bias free. Few writers set out to be offensive. Sometimes, though, we all say things that we never thought might be hurtful. The real problem is that we don't think about the words that stereotype groups of people, such as *the boys in the mail room* or *the girls in the front office*. Be cautious about expressions that might be biased in terms of gender, race, ethnicity, age, or disability.

Generally, you can avoid gender-biased language by choosing alternate language for words involving *man* or *woman*, by using plural nouns and pronouns, or by changing to a gender-free word (*person* or *representative*). Avoid the *his or her* option whenever possible.

REALITY CHECK: Changing Perceptions With People-First Language

In a letter to the editor, a teacher criticized an article in *USA Today* on autism because it said "autistic child" rather than "child with autism." She championed "people-first" terminology, which avoids defining individuals by their ability or disability.[22] Can language change perceptions?

Courtesy of IndependenceFirst/ Designer Clay Altman

It's wordy and conspicuous. With a little effort, you can usually find a construction that is graceful, grammatical, and unself-conscious.

Specify age only if it is relevant, and avoid expressions that are demeaning or subjective (such as *spry old codger*). To avoid disability bias, do not refer to an individual's disability unless it is relevant. When necessary, use terms that do not stigmatize disabled individuals. The following examples give you a quick look at a few problem expressions and possible replacements. The real key to bias-free communication, though, lies in your awareness and commitment. Be on the lookout to be sure that your messages do not exclude, stereotype, or offend people.

Gender Biased	Improved
female doctor, woman attorney, cleaning woman	doctor, attorney, cleaner
waiter/waitress, authoress, stewardess	server, author, flight attendant
mankind, man-hour, man-made	humanity, working hours, artificial
office girls	office workers
the doctor . . . he	doctors . . . they
the teacher . . . she	teachers . . . they
executives and their wives	executives and their spouses
foreman, flagman, workman, craftsman	lead worker, flagger, worker, artisan
businessman, salesman	businessperson, sales representative
Each employee had his picture taken.	Each employee had a picture taken. All employees had their pictures taken. Each employee had his or her picture taken.

Racially or Ethnically Biased	Improved
An Indian accountant was hired.	An accountant was hired.
James Lee, an African American, applied.	James Lee applied.

Age Biased	Improved
The law applied to old people.	The law applied to people over sixty-five.
Sally Kay, 55, was transferred.	Sally Kay was transferred.
a sprightly old gentleman	a man
a little old lady	a woman

Disability Biased	Improved
afflicted with arthritis, suffering from arthritis, crippled by arthritis	has arthritis
confined to a wheelchair	uses a wheelchair

Preferring Plain Language and Familiar Words

In adapting your message to your audience, use plain language and familiar words that you think audience members will recognize. Don't, however, avoid a big word that conveys your idea efficiently and is appropriate for the audience. Your goal is to shun pompous and pretentious language. Instead, use "GO" words. If you mean *begin,* don't say *commence* or *initiate*. If you mean *pay*, don't write *compensate*. By substituting everyday, familiar words for unfamiliar ones, as shown here, you help your audience comprehend your ideas quickly.

Unfamiliar	Familiar
commensurate	equal
interrogate	question
materialize	appear
obfuscate	confuse
remuneration	pay, salary
terminate	end

At the same time, be selective in your use of jargon. *Jargon* describes technical or specialized terms within a field. These terms enable insiders to communicate complex ideas briefly, but to outsiders they mean nothing. Human resources professionals, for example, know precisely what's meant by *cafeteria plan* (a benefits option program), but most of us would be thinking about lunch. Geologists refer to *plate tectonics*, and physicians discuss *metastatic carcinomas*. These terms mean little to most of us. Use specialized language only when the audience will understand it. In addition, don't forget to consider secondary audiences: Will those potential receivers understand any technical terms used?

Using Precise, Vigorous Words

Strong verbs and concrete nouns give receivers more information and keep them interested. Don't overlook the thesaurus (or the thesaurus program on your computer) for expanding your word choices and vocabulary. Whenever possible, use specific words, as shown here.

Imprecise, Dull	More Precise
a change in profits	a 25 percent hike in profits
	a 10 percent plunge in profits
to say	to promise, confess, understand
	to allege, assert, assume, judge
to think about	to identify, diagnose, analyze
	to probe, examine, inspect

The checklist at the top of page 140 reviews important elements in the first phase of the 3-x-3 writing process. As you review these tips, remember the three basics of prewriting: analyzing, anticipating, and adapting.

Sharing the Writing in Teams

LEARNING OBJECTIVE 5
Understand how teams approach collaborative writing projects and what collaboration tools support team writing.

As you learned in Chapter 2, many of today's workers collaborate in teams to deliver services, develop products, and complete projects. It is almost assumed that today's progressive organizations will employ teams in some capacity to achieve their objectives. Because much of a team's work involves writing, you can expect to be putting your writing skills to work as part of a team.

When Is Team Writing Necessary?

Collaboration on team-written documents is necessary for projects that (a) are big, (b) have short deadlines, and (c) require the expertise or consensus of many people. Businesspeople sometimes also collaborate on short documents, such as memos, letters, information briefs, procedures, and policies. More often, however, teams work together on big documents and presentations.

CHECKLIST ▶▶|
Adapting a Message to Its Audience

- **Identify the message purpose.** Why are you writing and what do you hope to achieve? Consider both primary and secondary audiences.

- **Select the most appropriate channel.** Consider the importance, feedback, interactivity, cost, formality, sensitivity, and richness of the options.

- **Profile the audience.** What is your relationship with the receiver? How much does the receiver know or need to know?

- **Focus on audience benefits.** Phrase your statements from the reader's view. Concentrate on the "you" view.

- **Avoid gender, racial, age, and disability bias.** Use bias-free words (*businessperson* rather than *businessman*, *manager* rather than *Hispanic manager*, *new employee* rather than *new twenty-two-year-old*

employee, uses a wheelchair rather than *confined to a wheelchair*).

- **Be conversational but professional.** Strive for a warm, friendly tone that is not overly formal or familiar. Avoid slang and low-level diction.

- **Express ideas positively rather than negatively.** Instead of *We can't ship until June 1*, say *We can ship on June 1*.

- **Use short, familiar words.** Avoid big words and technical terms unless they are appropriate for the audience (*end* not *terminate*).

- **Search for precise, vigorous words.** Use a thesaurus if necessary to find strong verbs and concrete nouns (*announces* instead of *says*, *brokerage* instead of *business*).

Why Are Team-Written Documents Better?

Team-written documents and presentations are standard in most organizations because collaboration has many advantages. Most important, collaboration usually produces a better product because many heads are better than one. In addition, team members and organizations benefit from team processes. Working together helps socialize members. They learn more about the organization's values and procedures. They are able to break down functional barriers, and they improve both formal and informal chains of communication. Additionally, they "buy in" to a project when they are part of its development. Members of effective teams are eager to implement their recommendations.

How Are Team-Written Documents Divided?

With big writing projects, teams may not actually function together for each phase of the writing process. Typically, team members gather at the beginning to brainstorm. They iron out answers to questions about the purpose, audience, content, organization, and design of their document or presentation. They develop procedures for team functioning, as you learned in Chapter 2. Then, they often assign segments of the project to individual members.

In Phase 1 of the writing process, teams work together closely as they discuss the project and establish their purpose. In Phase 2 members generally work separately when they conduct research, organize their findings, and compose a first draft. During Phase 3, some teams work together to synthesize their drafts and offer suggestions for revision. Other teams appoint one person to proofread and edit and another to prepare the final document. The revision and evaluation phase might be repeated several times before the final product is ready for presentation. Sharing the entire writing process, illustrated in Figure 4.8, means that all team members contribute their skills during the three phases.

Figure 4.8 Sharing the Writing of Team Documents

Three Phases in Team Writing

Phase 1
Prewriting
Team members work closely to determine purpose, audience, content, and organization.

Phase 2
Drafting
Team members work separately to collect information and compose first draft.

Phase 3
Revising
Team members work together to synthesize and edit, but individuals may do the final formatting and proofreading.

What Digital Collaboration Tools Support Team Writing?

One of the most frustrating tasks for teams is writing shared documents. Keeping the various versions straight and recognizing who made what comment can be difficult. Fortunately, digital collaboration tools are constantly being developed and improved. They range from simple to complex, inexpensive to expensive, locally installed to remotely hosted, commercial to open source, and small to large. Digital collaboration tools are especially necessary when team members are not physically in the same location. Even when members are nearby, they may use collaboration tools such as the following:

- **E-mail.** Despite its many drawbacks, e-mail remains a popular tool for online asynchronous (intermittent data transmission) collaboration. As projects grow more complex and involve more people who are not working near each other, however, e-mail becomes a clumsy, ineffective tool, especially for collaborative writing tasks.

- **Instant messaging and texting.** Because they ensure immediate availability, instant messaging and texting allow members to clear up minor matters immediately. They also may be helpful in initiating a quick group discussion.

- **Wikis.** A *wiki* is a website that allows multiple users to create, revise, and edit their own documents as well as contribute ideas to others. As illustrated in Figure 4.9, a wiki facilitates teamwork because members can make comments and monitor the progress of a project. Perhaps the best part of a wiki is that it serves as an ongoing storehouse of information that can be used for reference. Wikis avoid the danger of losing track of information in e-mails and separate documents. You'll learn more about wikis in Chapter 7.

- **Track Changes and other tools.** MS Word includes **Track Changes** and **Comment** features that enable collaborators working on the same document to identify and approve edits made by team members. See the accompanying Plugged In box for more information about using these collaboration tools.

- **Web and telephone conferencing.** When teams need to share information and make decisions in real time, conferencing tools such as WebEx and GoToMeeting work well. Telephone conferencing tools also enable teams to work together when they can't be together.

- **Google Docs and other collaboration software.** For simple projects, collaboration software such as Google Docs permits teams to work on text documents, spreadsheets, and presentations either in real time or at different times. Multiple team members can edit and share Web pages, MS Word documents, or PDF (portable document format) files.

Figure 4.9   Team Collaboration Using a Wiki

Team members contribute ideas and information to a Web-based wiki where others may revise, edit, and comment. The wiki serves as a storehouse of project or organizational information that is immediately accessible to all.[23]

© Cengage Learning 2015; http://www.wikipedia.org

Another popular collaboration tool is Dropbox, which offers cross-platform file sharing and online backup. For more complex projects, teams may use enterprise-level software such as MS SharePoint, which has a huge learning curve, requires technical support, and is relatively expensive. Less expensive enterprise collaboration tools include Basecamp, Box, Huddle, and Socialtext.[24]

How to Edit Team Writing Without Making Enemies

When your team is preparing a report or presentation and members create different sections, you will probably be expected to edit or respond to the writing of others. Remember that no one likes to be criticized, so make your statements specific, constructive, and helpful. The following suggestions will help you edit team writing without making enemies:

- Begin your remarks with a positive statement. What can you praise? Do you like the writer's conversational tone, word choice, examples, directness, or conciseness?
- Do you understand the writer's purpose? If not, be specific in explaining what you don't understand.
- Is the material logically organized? If not, how could it be improved?
- What suggestions can you make to improve specific ideas or sections?
- Make polite statements such as, *I would suggest . . . , You might consider . . ., How about doing this . . . .*

Using Track Changes and Other Editing Tools to Revise Collaborative Documents

Plugged In

Collaborative writing and editing projects are challenging. Fortunately, Microsoft Word offers useful tools to help team members edit and share documents electronically. Two simple but helpful editing tools are **Text Highlight Color** and **Font Color**. These tools, which are found on the **Home** tab in MS 2010 Office suite, enable reviewers to point out errors and explain problematic passages through the use of contrast. However, some projects require more advanced editing tools such as **Track Changes** and **Comment**.

Track Changes. To suggest specific editing changes to other team members, **Track Changes** is handy. The revised wording is visible on screen, and deletions show up in callout balloons that appear in the right-hand margin (see Figure 4.10). Various team members suggest revisions that are identified and dated. The original writer may accept or reject these changes. **Track Changes** is located on the **Review** tab.

Comment. Probably the most useful editing tool is the **Comment** function, also shown in Figure 4.10. This tool allows users to point out problematic passages or errors, ask or answer questions, and share ideas without changing or adding text. When more than one person adds comments, the comments appear in different colors and are identified by the writer's name and a date/time stamp. To use this tool in Word 2010, click **New Comment** from the drop-down **Review** tab. Then type your comment, which can be seen in the Web or print layout view (click **View** and **Print Layout** or **Web Layout**).

Completing a Document. When a document is finished, be sure to accept or reject all changes on the **Review** tab, a step that removes the tracking information.

Figure **4.10** Track Changes and Comment Features in a Team Document

Team members can collaborate on shared documents with the **Track Changes** and **Comment** features in MS Word. Notice that **Track Changes** displays balloons to show deletions, comments, formatting changes, and the people who made the changes. See the Plugged In box for information on how **Track Changes** and **Comment** features are useful when individuals collaborate on team documents.

Your Turn: Applying Your Skills at TOMS

College students have been a large part of the success of TOMS. The company's website even features its own student network, Campus Clubs. Students who want to raise awareness about "conscious consumerism" and social responsibility join to generate buzz about the TOMS message. One of the ways TOMS does this is by sponsoring an event, One Day Without Shoes. Last year the company sponsored over 1,000 events in more than 25 countries.

The way it works is simple. Individuals go barefoot for one day. When asked why, they explain the impact of being shoeless on young children: diseases contracted from soil-transmitted germs, painful sores and infections, absence from schools that require children to wear shoes. The idea behind One Day Without Shoes is to raise awareness about shoeless children's plight so that more people will eventually act to change the situation.

YOUR TASK. In a team of three to five classmates, draft an e-mail that encourages your fellow students to join you for a One Day Without Shoes event at your college. Pick a specific day for the event and provide information about where the students can learn more about TOMS. As you work in your team, consider editing the document by using **Track Changes** in Word.

Summary of Learning Objectives

Go to
www.cengagebrain.com
and use your access code to unlock valuable student resources.

1 Understand the nature of communication and its barriers in the digital age. Although people are sending more messages and using new technologies in this digital age, the basic communication process still consists of the same basic elements. The sender encodes (selects) words or symbols to express an idea in a message. It travels verbally over a channel (such as an e-mail, website, tweet, letter, or smartphone call) or is expressed nonverbally with gestures or body language. "Noise" such as loud sounds, misspelled words, or other distractions, may interfere with the transmission. The receiver decodes (interprets) the message and may respond with feedback, informing the sender of the effectiveness of the message. Miscommunication may be caused by barriers such as bypassing, differing frames of reference, lack of language skills, and distractions.

2 Summarize the 3-x-3 writing process and explain how it guides a writer. Business writing should be purposeful, economical, and audience oriented. Following the 3-x-3 writing process helps writers create efficient and effective messages. Phase 1 of the 3-x-3 writing process (prewriting) involves analyzing the message, anticipating the audience, and considering ways to adapt the message to the audience. Phase 2 (drafting) involves researching the topic, organizing the material, and drafting the message. Phase 3 (revising) includes editing, proofreading, and evaluating the message. A writing process helps a writer by providing a systematic plan describing what to do in each step of the process.

3 Analyze the purpose of a message, anticipate its audience, and select the best communication channel. Before drafting, communicators must decide why they are creating a message and what they hope to achieve. Although many messages only inform, some must also persuade. After identifying the purpose, communicators visualize both the primary and secondary audiences, which helps them choose the most appropriate language, tone, and content for a message. Senders should remember that receivers will usually be thinking, *What's in it for me?(WIIFM)*. Senders select the best channel by considering the importance of the message, the amount and speed of feedback required, the necessity of a permanent record, the cost of the channel, the degree of formality desired, the confidentiality and sensitivity of the message, and the receiver's preference and level of technical expertise.

4 Employ expert writing techniques such as incorporating audience benefits, the "you" view, conversational but professional language, a positive and courteous tone, bias-free language, plain language, and vigorous words. The term *audience benefits* involves looking for ways to shape the message from the receiver's, not the sender's, view. Skilled communicators look at a message from the receiver's perspective applying the "you" view without attempting to manipulate. Expert writing techniques also include using conversational but professional language along with positive language that tells what can be done rather than what can't be done. (*The project will be successful with your support* rather than *The project won't be successful without your support*). A courteous tone means guarding against rudeness and avoiding sounding preachy or demanding. Writers should also avoid language that excludes, stereotypes, or offends people (*lady lawyer, spry old gentleman,* and *confined to a wheelchair*). Finally, plain language, familiar terms, strong verbs, and concrete nouns improve readability and effectiveness.

5 Understand how teams approach collaborative writing projects and what collaboration tools support team writing. Large projects or team efforts involving the expertise of many people often require team members to collaborate. During Phase 1 (prewriting) of the writing process, teams usually work together in brainstorming and working out their procedures and assignments. During Phase 2 (drafting) individual members research and write their portions of the project report or presentation. During Phase 3 (revising) teams may work together to combine and revise their drafts. Teams may use digital collaboration tools such as e-mail, instant messaging, texting, wikis, word processing functions such as **Track Changes**, Web conferencing, Google Docs, or other software to collaborate effectively.

Chapter Review

1. Define *communication*. When is it successful? (Obj. 1)
2. Describe the five steps in the process of communication. (Obj. 1)
3. Name four barriers to communication and be prepared to explain each. What other barriers have you experienced? (Obj. 1)
4. Define *digital message*. (Obj. 2)
5. In what ways is business writing different from school essays and private messages? (Obj. 2)
6. Describe the components in each stage of the 3-x-3 writing process. Approximately how much time is spent on each stage? (Obj. 2)
7. What does *WIIFM* mean? Why is it important to business writers? (Obj. 3)
8. How does profiling the audience help a business communicator prepare a message? (Obj. 3)

9. What seven factors should writers consider in selecting an appropriate channel to deliver a message? (Obj. 3)
10. Why is positive wording more effective in business messages than negative wording? (Obj. 4)
11. What is the "you" view? When can the use of *you* backfire? (Obj. 4)
12. What are three ways to avoid biased language? Give an original example of each. (Obj. 4)
13. When are team-written documents necessary? (Obj. 5)
14. How do teams collaborate during the three phases of the writing process? (Obj. 5)
15. What is a wiki, and why is it superior to e-mail in collaborating on writing projects? (Obj. 5)

Critical Thinking

1. Has digital transmission changed the innate nature of communication? (Obj. 1)
2. Why do you think employers prefer messages that are not written like high school and college essays? (Obj. 2)
3. Why should business writers strive to use short, familiar, simple words? Does this "dumb down" business messages? (Obj. 4)

4. A wise observer once said that bad writing makes smart people look dumb. Do you agree or disagree, and why? (Objs. 1–4)
5. **Ethical Issue:** A student in a business communication class refused to join a team report-writing project because he said he hated situations in which he would end up doing all the work with credit going to the team. What counseling should the instructor give?

Activities

4.1 Audience Benefits and the "You" View (Obj. 4)

YOUR TASK. Revise the following sentences to emphasize the perspective of the audience and the "you" view.

a. We have prepared the enclosed form that may be used by victims to report identity theft to creditors.

b. To help us process your order with our new database software, we need you to go to our website and fill out the customer information required.

c. We are now offering RapidAssist, a software program we have developed to provide immediate technical support through our website to your employees and customers.

d. We find it necessary to restrict parking in the new company lot to those employee vehicles with "A" permits.

e. To avoid suffering the kinds of monetary losses experienced in the past, our credit union now prohibits the cashing of double-endorsed checks presented by our customers.

f. Our warranty goes into effect only when we have received the product's registration card from the purchaser.

g. Unfortunately, the computer and telephone systems will be down Thursday afternoon when we will be installing upgrades to improve both systems.

h. As part of our company effort to be friendly to the environment, we are asking all employees to reduce paper consumption by communicating by e-mail and avoiding printing.

4.2 Conversational but Professional (Obj. 4)

YOUR TASK. Revise the following to make the tone conversational yet professional.

a. Pertaining to your request, the above-referenced items (printer toner and supplies) are being sent to your Oakdale office, as per your telephone conversation of April 1.

b. Kindly inform the undersigned whether or not your representative will be making a visitation in the near future.

c. It's totally awesome that we still snagged the contract after the customer amped up his demands, but our manager pushed back.

d. BTW, dude, we've had some slippage in the schedule but don't have to dump everything and start from scratch.

e. To facilitate ratification of this agreement, your negotiators urge that the membership respond in the affirmative.

f. R head honcho wz like totally raggety bkuz I wz sick n stuff n mist the team meet. Geez!

4.3 Positive and Courteous Expression (Obj. 4)

YOUR TASK. Revise the following statements to make them more positive.

a. Plans for the new community center cannot go forward without full community support.

b. We must withhold authorizing payment of your contractor's fee because our superintendent claims your work was incomplete.

c. If you do not fill in all of the blanks in the application form, we cannot issue a password.

d. It is impossible for the builder to pour the concrete footings until the soil is no longer soggy.

e. Although you apparently failed to consult the mounting instructions for your Miracle Wheatgrass Extractor, we are enclosing a set of clamps to fasten the device to a table. A new set of instructions is enclosed.

f. We regret to announce that the special purchase price on iPads will be available only to the first 25 buyers.

4.4 Bias-Free Language (Obj. 4)

YOUR TASK. Revise the following sentences to reduce gender, racial, ethnic, age, and disability bias.

a. Every employee must wear his photo identification on the job.

b. The conference will offer special excursions for the wives of executives.

c. Does each salesman have his own smartphone loaded with his special sales information?

d. A policeman is responsible for covering his territory.

e. Serving on the panel are a lady veterinarian, an Indian CPA, two businessmen, and a female doctor.

4.5 Plain Language and Familiar Words

YOUR TASK. Revise the following sentences to use plain language and familiar words.

a. We are offering a pay package that is commensurate with other managers' remuneration.

b. The seller tried to obfuscate the issue by mentioning closing and other costs.

c. Even after officers interrogated the suspect, solid evidence failed to materialize.

d. In dialoguing with the owner, I learned that you anticipate terminating our contract.

4.6 Precise, Vigorous Words (Obj. 4)

YOUR TASK. From the choices in parentheses, select the most precise, vigorous words.

a. Management is predicting a (change, difference, drop) in earnings after the first of the year.

b. Experts (predict, hypothesize, state) that the economy will (change, moderate, stabilize) by next year.

c. We plan to (acknowledge, announce, applaud) the work of outstanding employees.

d. After (reading, looking at, studying) the report, I realized that the data were (bad, inadequate, inaccurate).

e. The comments responding to his blog were (emotional, great, really different).

4.7 Document for Analysis: Applying Expert Writing Techniques to a Poor E-Mail Message (Objs. 4, 5)

◄ Communication Technology ► ◄ E-mail ► ◄ Team ►

YOUR TASK. Analyze the following demanding e-mail message to be sent by the vice president to all employees. In teams or individually, discuss the tone and writing faults in this message. Your instructor may ask you to revise the message so that it reflects some of the writing techniques you learned in this chapter. How can you make this message more courteous, positive, and precise?

Focus on conciseness, familiar words, and developing the "you" view. Consider revising this e-mail as a collaboration project using Word's **Track Changes** and **Comment** feature.

To:	All Staff
From:	Sybil Montrose <smontrose@syracuse.com>
Subject:	Problematic Online Use by Employees
Cc:	
Attached:	E-Mail and Internet Policy

Once again I have the decidedly unpleasant task of reminding all employees that you may NOT utilize company computers or the Internet other than for work-related business and essential personal messages. Effective immediately a new policy must be implemented.

Our guys in IT tell me that our bandwidth is now seriously compromised by some of you boys and girls who are using company computers for Facebooking, blogging, shopping, chatting, gaming, and downloading streaming video. Yes, we have given you the right to use e-mail responsibly for essential personal messages. That does NOT, however, include checking your Facebook or other networking accounts during work hours or downloading your favorite shows or sharing music.

We distributed an e-mail policy a little while ago. We have now found it necessary to amplify and extrapolate that policy to include use of the Internet. If our company fails to control its e-mail and Internet use, you will continue to suffer slow downloads and virus intrusions. You may also lose the right to use e-mail altogether. In the past every employee has had the right to send a personal e-mail occasionally, but he must use that right carefully. We don't want to prohibit the personal use of e-mail entirely. Don't make me do this!

You will be expected to study the attached E-Mail and Internet policy and return the signed form with your agreement to adhere to this policy. You must return this form by March 1. No exceptions!

4.8 Channel Selection: Various Business Scenarios (Obj. 3)

‹ Communication Technology ›

YOUR TASK. Using Figure 4.5 on page 132, suggest the best communication channels for the following messages. Assume that all channels shown are available, ranging from face-to-face conversations to instant messages, blogs, and wikis. Be prepared to justify your choices considering the richness of each channel.

a. As part of a task force to investigate cell phone marketing, you need to establish a central location where each team member can see general information about the task as well as add comments for others to see. Task force members are located throughout the country.

b. You're sitting on the couch in the evening watching TV when you suddenly remember that you were to send Jeremy some information about a shared project. Should you text him right away before you forget?

c. As an event planner, you have been engaged to research the sites for a celebrity golf tournament. What is the best channel for conveying your findings to your boss or planning committee?

d. You want to persuade your manager to change your work schedule.

e. As a sales manager, you want to know which of your sales reps in the field are available immediately for a quick teleconference meeting.

f. You need to know whether Amanda in Reprographics can produce a rush job for you in two days.

g. Your firm must respond to a notice from the Internal Revenue Service announcing that the company owes a penalty because it underreported its income in the previous fiscal year.

4.9 Audience Analysis: Lord of the Online Rings (Obj. 3)

‹ Communication Technology ›

Would you buy an engagement ring from a website? Apparently, many customers, mostly men, do. Houston-based Whiteflash, crowned "Lord of the Online Rings" by *Kiplinger's* magazine, uses its website to sell engagement rings ranging in price to five figures without a face-to-face encounter. Whiteflash founder and chief executive Debi Wexler says that many of the company's customers are from Malaysia, Hong Kong, and Singapore. "A lot of them don't feel comfortable speaking on the phone, but they are very comfortable with technology." The site also attracts servicemen stationed overseas as well as stateside customers headed for the altar. Customers may zoom in on various diamond and ring choices before consulting with computer specialists in live chat sessions. Three to five chat sessions are usually required before a sale is completed.[25]

YOUR TASK. Discuss some of the factors involved in audience analysis and channel selection that helped Whiteflash decide that e-mail and chat were the best channels to communicate with their customers.

4.10 Analyzing Audiences (Obj. 3)

YOUR TASK. Using the questions in Figure 4.4 on page 130, write a brief analysis of the audience for each of the following communication tasks. What kind of reaction should you expect?

a. You are preparing a cover message to accompany your résumé for a job that you saw listed on a company website. You are confident that your qualifications match the job description.

b. You are about to send an e-mail to your regional sales manager describing your visit to a new customer who is demanding special discounts.

c. As an administrator at the municipal water department, you must write a letter to water users explaining that the tap water may taste and smell bad; however, it poses no threats to health.

d. You are planning to write an e-mail to your manager to try to persuade her to allow you to attend a computer workshop that will require you to leave work early two days a week for ten weeks.

e. You are preparing an unsolicited sales letter to a targeted group of executives promoting part-time ownership in a corporate jet plane.

4.11 Using Track Changes and Comment Features to Edit a Document (Obj. 5)

‹ Communication Technology › ‹ E-mail › ‹ Team ›

YOUR TASK. Organize into groups of three. Using the latest version of Word, copy and respond to the Document for Analysis in **Activity 4.7**. Set up a round-robin e-mail file exchange so that each member responds to the other group members' documents by using the **Comment** feature of Word to offer advice or suggestions for improvement. Submit a printout of the document with group comments, as well as a final edited document.

Chat About It

In each chapter you will find five discussion questions related to the chapter material. Your instructor may assign these topics for you to discuss in class, in an online chat room, or on an online discussion board. Some of the discussion topics may require outside research. You may also be asked to read and respond to postings made by your classmates.

Topic 1: To what extent is your place of work using technology? In your personal life, are the businesses you frequent digitally connected or off the grid? Share your experiences with your fellow students.

Topic 2: List and analyze the steps that you followed to write a document before you started this course. Based on what you are learning in this course, which steps were effective? Which were ineffective? How will you change your approach to writing?

Topic 3: After searching an alumni database, you decide to e-mail a professional who is working in the career you hope to enter. Your goal in writing this professional is to obtain firsthand information about this person's career and to receive career advice. However, you know nothing about this person. How could you profile the receiver to help you shape your message? What audience benefits could you use to persuade the receiver? What channel would you choose to deliver your message? What tone would you use?

Topic 4: Think back to the last time you were involved in a team project. What did the team do that resulted in an efficient working process and a successful product? What did the team do that resulted in an inefficient working process and an unsuccessful product?

Topic 5: Find a news article online that describes a company that used careless language in its communication with its customers, stockholders, or employees. Briefly explain what the company did and what it should have done instead.

C.L.U.E. Grammar & Mechanics | *Review 4*

Adjectives and Adverbs

Review Guides 19–20 about adjectives and adverbs in Appendix A, Grammar and Mechanics Guide, beginning on page A-9. On a separate sheet, revise the following sentences to correct errors in adjectives and adverbs. For each error that you locate, write the guide number that reflects this usage. Some sentences may have two errors. If a sentence is correct, write *C*. When you finish, check your answers on page Key-1.

1. A face to face conversation is a richer communication channel than an e-mail or letter.

2. Christie thought she had done good in her performance review.

3. Team members learned to use the wiki quicker than they expected.

4. Most of our team written documents could be posted quickly to the wiki.

5. We all felt badly when one member lost her laptop and had no backup.

6. The 3-x-3 writing process provides step by step instructions for preparing messages.

7. Everyone likes the newly-revamped website and its up-to-date links.

8. Our project ran smooth after Justin reorganized the team.

9. Locally-installed online collaboration tools are easy-to-use and work well.

10. Well written e-mail messages sound conversational but professional.

Notes

[1] Mycoskie, B. (2011, September 20). How I did it. Retrieved from http://www.entrepreneur.com/article/220350

[2] Cifnai, N., & Sternberg, A. (2010, September 26). TOMS shoes one millionth pair shoe drop. Retrieved from http://toms1m.wordpress.com

[3] Kirschner, A. (2012, March 6). Intern adventures: Meet the interns, part II. [Blog post]. Retrieved from http://www.toms.com/blog/taxonomy/term/4

[4] Maltby. E. (2010, January 19). Expanding abroad? Avoid cultural gaffes. *The Wall Street Journal*, p. B5.

[5] Foderaro, L. (2009, May 18). Psst! Need the answer to no. 7? Just click here. *The New York Times*, p. A17.

[6] Sullivan, J., Karmeda, N., & Nobu, T. (1992, January/February). Bypassing in managerial communication. *Business Horizons*, 34(1), 72.

[7] Brewer, E., & Holmes, T. (2009, October). Obfuscating the obvious: Miscommunication issues in the interpretation of common terms. *Journal of Business Communication*, 46(4), 480-496.

[8] Quoted in Bryant, A. (2011, July 9). Cultivating his plants, and his company. *The New York Times*. Retrieved from http://www.nytimes.com/2011/07/10/business/esris-chief-on-tending-his-plants-and-his-company.html?pagewanted=all&_r=0

[9] Photo essay based on Keim, B. (2009, August 24). Multitasking muddles brains, even when the computer is off. Wired. Retrieved from http://www.wired.com; Gorlick, A. (2009, August 24). Media multitaskers pay mental price, Stanford study shows. *Stanford News*. Retrieved from http://news.stanford.edu; Nauert, R. (2011, May 3). Multitasking is distracting. *Psych Central*. Retrieved from http://psychcentral.com

[10] McGirt, E. (2006, March 20). Getting out from under: Beset by interruptions, information overload, and irksome technology, knowledge workers need help: A survival guide. *Fortune*, p. 8. See also Simperl, E., Thurlow, I., et al. (2010, November 1). Overcoming information overload in the enterprise: The active approach. *Internet Computing*, 14(6). doi: 10.1109/MIC.2010.146

[11] Drucker, P. (1990). *Managing the non-profit organization: Practices and principles.* New York: HarperCollins, p. 46.

[12] Silverman, D. (2009, February 10). Why is business writing so bad? *Harvard Business Review*. Retrieved from http://blogs.hbr.org/silverman/2009/02/why-is-business-writing-so-bad.html

[13] Quoted in Middleton, D. (2011, March 3). Students struggle for words. *The Wall Street Journal*. Retrieved from http://online.wsj.com/article/SB1000142405274870340990457614651780110970.html?mod=WSJ_hpp_sections_careerjournal

[14] Photo essay based on Lashinsky, A. (2012, November 16). Amazon's Jeff Bezos: The ultimate disrupter. *Fortune*. Retrieved from http://management.fortune.cnn.com/2012/11/16/jeff-bezos-amazon

[15] Arnold, V. (1986, August). Benjamin Franklin on writing well. *Personnel Journal*, p. 17.

[16] Bacon, M. (1988, April). Quoted in Business writing: One-on-one speaks best to the masses. *Training*, p. 95.

[17] Clark, B. (n.d.). The two most important words in blogging. Retrieved from http://www.copyblogger.com/the-two-most-important-words-in-blogging

[18] Google. (2012, January 30). E-mail message to Mary Ellen Guffey.

[19] Be positive. (2009, March). *Communication Briefings*, p. 5. Adapted from Brandi, J. *Winning at customer retention* at http://www.customercarecoach.com

[20] Canavor, N. (2012). *Business writing in the digital age*. Thousand Oaks, CA: Sage, p. 52.

[21] Ibid.

[22] Link, S. (2012, May 2). Use 'person first' language. [Letter to editor]. *USA Today*, p. 6A.

[23] Figure 4.8 partially based on Higdon, J. (2006) What is a wiki? The Center for Scholarly Technology, University of Southern California. Retrieved from http://net.educause.edu/ir/library/pdf/ELI0626.pdf; also partially based on Zoho Wiki Collaboration at http://www.zoho.com/wiki/share-collaborate-wiki.html

[24] Web collaboration tools come in all shapes and sizes. (2011). Collaboration comparison chart. Retrieved from http://www.facilitate.com/collaboration-tools

[25] Grossmann, J. (2011, June 16). Connecting with clients through the power of tech. *The New York Times*, p. B5.

Organizing and Drafting Business Messages

OBJECTIVES

After studying this chapter, you should be able to

1 Apply Phase 2 of the 3-x-3 writing process, which begins with formal and informal research to collect background information.

2 Explain how to generate ideas and organize information to show relationships.

3 Compose the first draft of a message using a variety of sentence types and avoiding sentence fragments, run-on sentences, and comma splices.

4 Improve your writing techniques by emphasizing important ideas, employing the active and passive voice effectively, using parallelism, and preventing dangling and misplaced modifiers.

5 Draft effective paragraphs using three classic paragraph plans and techniques for achieving paragraph coherence.

Remember When the Gap Was Cool?

Formerly, retailer Gap enjoyed cult status and "had the market cornered on belonging."[1] Despite its astounding growth to become the largest clothing chain in the United States, it now struggles to regain its mojo. Critics accused it of making every bad move a retailer could. Besides major misses in fashion, the company failed to differentiate among its three major brands—Banana Republic, Gap, and Old Navy—and it opened too many stores.

Instead of dictating taste, the company that formerly pioneered the casual, cool look with fitted jeans, khakis, and simple T-shirts now appears to have lost its fashion compass. Once the king of casual but classic clothing, Gap has been stung by retailing upstarts that woo young people with trendy fashions at affordable prices. Retailers such as Zara, Mango, Hot Topic, and Hollister are snagging customers with chic styles and competitive pricing.

Further compounding its woes, Gap has saturated the market. Its stores are almost as ubiquitous as Starbucks. In the fashion business, bigness isn't necessarily a plus. With outlets in nearly every shopping center, Gap has overexposed the brand. Customers are staying away because its styles no longer seem unique or special.

Constantly changing designers and management, Gap strains to improve its merchandise mix, shrink its square footage in North America, and enhance its online and global presence. By tripling the number of outlets in China and expanding into emerging markets in Europe and South Africa, Gap optimistically looks forward to powerful growth potential.[2] Although opening outlets in new markets, it is closing stores in North America. Ultimately, Gap, Old Navy, and Banana Republic must find a way to lure customers back to its home country market.

You will learn more about Gap and be asked to complete a relevant task at the end of this chapter.

Critical Thinking

- In what ways would research (gathering information) be important to Gap, Old Navy, and Banana Republic in coaxing their customers back?

- What must Gap managers, and all business communicators, do before making management decisions?

- What techniques can business communicators at Gap and other companies use to generate ideas for new products as well as to improve business processes?

Getting Started Requires Researching Background Information

LEARNING OBJECTIVE 1
Apply Phase 2 of the 3-x-3 writing process, which begins with formal and informal research to collect background information.

Managers at Gap face significant challenges in restoring this retailing powerhouse to its former fashion pinnacle. Like other business leaders, Gap executives strive to solve problems and make decisions by gathering information, generating ideas, and organizing those ideas into logical messages that guide their organizations. These activities are part of the second phase of the 3-x-3 writing process. You will recall that the 3-x-3 writing process, reviewed in Figure 5.1, involves three phases. This chapter focuses on the second phase of the process: researching, organizing, and drafting.

No smart businessperson would begin drafting a message before gathering background information. We call this process *research*, a rather formal-sounding term. For our purposes, however, *research* simply means collecting information about a certain topic. This is an important step in the writing process because that information helps the writer shape the message. Discovering significant information after a message is half completed often means having to start over and reorganize. To avoid frustration and inaccurate messages, writers collect information that answers several questions:

- What does the receiver need to know about this topic?

- What is the receiver to do?

Figure **5.1** The 3-x-3 Writing Process

1 Prewriting

Analyze: Decide on the message purpose. What do you want the receiver to do or believe?

Anticipate: What does the audience already know? How will it receive this message?

Adapt: Think about techniques to present this message most effectively. Consider how to elicit feedback.

2 Drafting

Research: Gather background data by searching files and the Internet.

Organize: Arrange direct messages with the big idea first. For persuasive or negative messages, use an indirect, problem-solving strategy.

Compose: Prepare the first draft, using active-voice sentences, coherent paragraphs, and appropriate transitional expressions.

3 Revising

Edit: Eliminate wordy fillers, long lead-ins, redundancies, and trite business phrases. Strive for parallelism, clarity, conciseness, and readability.

Proofread: Check carefully for errors in spelling, grammar, punctuation, and format.

Evaluate: Will this message achieve your purpose? Is the tone pleasant? Did you encourage feedback?

© Cengage Learning 2015

- How is the receiver to do it?
- When must the receiver do it?
- What will happen if the receiver doesn't do it?

Whenever your communication problem requires more information than you have in your head or at your fingertips, you must conduct research. This research may be informal or formal.

Informal Research Methods

Many routine tasks—such as drafting e-mails, memos, letters, informational reports, and oral presentations—require information that you can collect informally. Where can you find information before starting a project? The following techniques are useful in informal research:

- **Search your company's files.** If you are responding to an inquiry or drafting a routine message, you often can find background information such as previous correspondence in your own files or those of the company. You might consult the company wiki or other digital and manual files. You might also consult colleagues.

- **Talk with the boss.** Get information from the individual making the assignment. What does that person know about the topic? What slant should you take? What other sources would that person suggest?

- **Interview the target audience.** Consider talking with individuals at whom the message is aimed. They can provide clarifying information that tells you what they want to know and how you should shape your remarks. Suggestions for conducting more formal interviews are presented in Chapter 11.

- **Conduct an informal survey.** Gather unscientific but helpful information through questionnaires, telephone surveys, or online surveys. In preparing a report predicting the success of a proposed company fitness center, for example, circulate a questionnaire asking for employee reactions.

Formal Research Methods

Long reports and complex business problems generally require formal research methods. Let's say you are part of the management team at Gap and you have been asked to help launch a new store in Canada. Or, let's assume you must write a term paper for a college class. Both tasks require more data than you have in your head or at your fingertips. To conduct formal research, consider the following research options:

- **Access electronic sources.** College and public libraries provide retrieval services that permit access to a wide array of books, journals, magazines, newspapers, and other online literature. In addition, you could conduct an online Google search turning up thousands of hits, which can be overwhelming. Expect to be deluged with torrents of information, presenting a troubling paradox: research seems to be far more difficult to conduct in the digital age than in previous times.[3] With so much data drowning today's researchers, they struggle to sort through it all, trying to decide what is current, relevant, and credible. Help is on the way, however! You'll learn more about researching and using electronic sources effectively in Chapter 11.

- **Search manually.** Valuable background and supplementary information is available through manual searching of resources in public and college libraries. These traditional sources include books and newspaper, magazine, and journal articles. Other sources are encyclopedias, reference books, handbooks, dictionaries, directories, and almanacs.

- **Investigate primary sources.** To develop firsthand, primary information for a project, go directly to the source. In helping to launch a Gap store in Canada, you might travel to possible sites and check them out. If you need information about how many shoppers pass by a location or visit a shopping center, you might conduct a traffic count. If you needed information about consumers, you could search blogs, Twitter, wikis, and Facebook fan pages. To learn more about specific shoppers, you could use questionnaires, interviews, or focus groups. Formal research often includes scientific sampling methods that enable investigators to make accurate judgments and valid predictions.

- **Conduct scientific experiments.** Another source of primary data is experimentation. Instead of merely asking for the target audience's opinion, scientific researchers present choices with controlled variables. Assume, for example, that the management team at Gap wants to know at what price and under what circumstances consumers would purchase jeans from Gap instead of from Abercrombie & Fitch. Instead of jeans, let's say that management wants to study the time of year and type of weather conditions that motivate consumers to begin purchasing sweaters, jackets, and cold-weather gear. The results of such experimentation would provide valuable data for managerial decision making. Because formal research techniques are particularly necessary for reports, you will study resources and techniques more extensively in Unit 4.

Courtesy of JUMP Associates

At Jump Associates, a San Francisco growth strategy firm, brainstorming may devolve into a kind of competitive-idea tennis match. One "Jumpster" starts with the first idea, and the next Jumpster says, "Yes, and?" which leads to another "Yes, and?" bouncing around its Black Box idea room. Once a storytelling method, this technique became an effective collaboration procedure and a core element of scrum, a daily standing meeting where the same "yes, and" principle is applied in improv games that prepare the company for its unique approach to brainstorming. For its megaclient Target, Jump helped create a product called "Kitchen in a Box," which became a phenomenal success. How does the "Yes, and" concept improve brainstorming?[4]

Generating Ideas and Organizing Information

Not all information for making decisions is available through research. Often fresh ideas must be generated. The most common method for groups to generate ideas at companies around the world is brainstorming.[5] Right up front, however, we should point out that some critics argue that brainstorming groups "produce fewer and poorer quality ideas than the same number of individuals working alone."[6] Even brainstorming proponents agree that, done poorly, it can be a waste of time. However, when experts manage the sessions and skillfully link them to other work practices, brainstorming can "unleash remarkable innovation."[7] The following steps generally produce the best results:

- Define the problem and create an agenda that outlines the topics to be covered.
- Establish time limits, remembering that short sessions are best.
- Set a quota, such as a minimum of 100 ideas. The goal is quantity, not quality.
- Require every participant to contribute ideas, accept the ideas of others, or improve on ideas.
- Encourage wild thinking. Allow no one to criticize or evaluate ideas.
- Write ideas on flipcharts or on sheets of paper hung around the room.
- Organize and classify the ideas, retaining the best.

Once participants have generated many ideas, they can be organized into a diagram such as that shown in Figure 5.2. This brainstorming session focused on developing ideas for a Gap recruiting brochure to draw new employees.

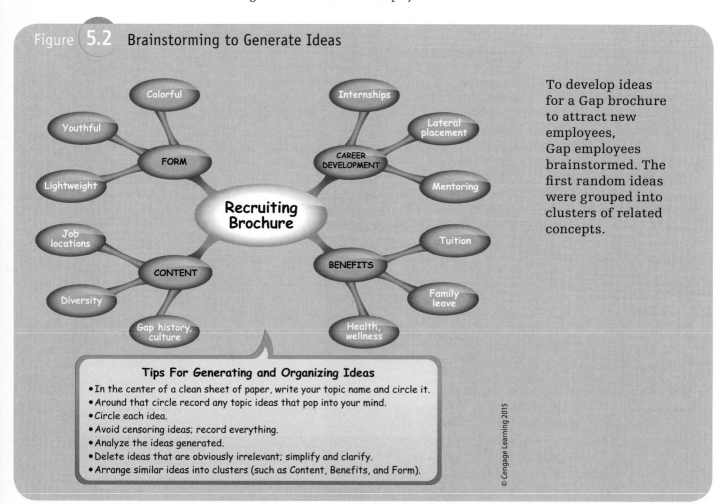

Figure 5.2   Brainstorming to Generate Ideas

To develop ideas for a Gap brochure to attract new employees, Gap employees brainstormed. The first random ideas were grouped into clusters of related concepts.

Tips For Generating and Organizing Ideas
- In the center of a clean sheet of paper, write your topic name and circle it.
- Around that circle record any topic ideas that pop into your mind.
- Circle each idea.
- Avoid censoring ideas; record everything.
- Analyze the ideas generated.
- Delete ideas that are obviously irrelevant; simplify and clarify.
- Arrange similar ideas into clusters (such as Content, Benefits, and Form).

© Cengage Learning 2015

Toy developers at Disney use systematic brainstorming to overhaul its toy lineup every six months. A diverse group of designers, engineers, artists, animators, video game designers, marketers, and theme park employees gather 20 to 30 times a year. They meet for two- or three-day brainstorming sessions at hotels around the world. Three elements are crucial to their success: (a) icebreaker activities from 10 minutes to a half hour, (b) 45- to 60-minute brainstorming sessions in which teams list as many ideas as they can and then vote for their favorites, and (c) a product pitch including a storyboard record of the best toy ideas. When people have tried to ignore the icebreaker segment and jump right into brainstorming, toy developer Chris Heatherly says, "It just doesn't work. . . . You have to have some decompression time to be creative."[8]

Disney developers use creative brainstorming, including an icebreaker segment, to develop top-selling toys.

Grouping Ideas to Show Relationships

After collecting data and generating ideas, writers must find some way to organize their information. Organizing includes two processes: grouping and strategizing. Skilled writers group similar items together. Then they place ideas in a strategic sequence that helps the reader understand relationships and accept the writer's views. Unorganized messages proceed freeform, jumping from one thought to another. Such messages fail to emphasize important points. Puzzled readers can't see how the pieces fit together, and they become frustrated and irritated. Many communication experts regard poor organization as the greatest failing of business writers. Two simple techniques can help writers organize data: the scratch list and the outline.

Using Lists and Outlines.   In developing simple messages, some writers make a quick scratch list of the topics they wish to cover. Next they compose a message at their computers directly from the scratch list. Most writers, though, need to organize their ideas—especially if the project is complex—into a hierarchy, such as an outline. The beauty of preparing an outline is that it gives writers a chance to organize their thoughts before becoming bogged down in word choice and sentence structure. Figure 5.3 shows the format for a typical outline.

Figure 5.3 Format for an Outline

Title: Major Idea or Purpose

```
I.  First major component
    A.  First subpoint
        1.  Detail, illustration, evidence
        2.  Detail, illustration, evidence
        3.  Detail, illustration, evidence
    B.  Second subpoint
        1.
        2.
II. Second major component
    A.  First subpoint
        1.
        2.
    B.  Second subpoint
        1.
        2.
        3.
```

Tips for Making Outlines

- Define the main topic in the title.
- Divide the main topic into major components or classifications (preferably three to five).
- Break the components into subpoints.
- Don't put a single item under a major component; if you have only one subpoint, integrate it with the main item above it or reorganize.
- Strive to make each component exclusive (no overlapping).
- Use details, illustrations, and evidence to support subpoints.

© Cengage Learning 2015

Figure **5.4** Typical Major Components in Business Outlines

E-mail, Memo, Letter

I. Opening
II. Body
III. Closing

Procedure

I. Step 1
II. Step 2
III. Step 3
IV. Step 4

Informational Report

I. Introduction
II. Facts
III. Summary

Analytical Report

I. Introduction/ problem
II. Facts/findings
III. Conclusions
IV. Recommendations (if requested)

Proposal

I. Introduction
II. Proposed solution
III. Staffing
IV. Schedule, costs
V. Authorization

© Cengage Learning 2015

Typical Document Components. How you group ideas into components depends on your topic and your channel of communication. Business documents usually contain typical components arranged in traditional strategies, as shown in Figure 5.4. Notice that an e-mail, memo, or letter generally is organized with an opening, body, and closing. Instructions for writing a procedure, such as how to use the company wiki, would proceed through a number of steps. The organizational plan for an informational report usually includes an introduction, facts, and a summary. However, the plan for an analytical report includes an introduction/problem, facts/findings, conclusions, and recommendations (if requested). The plan for a proposal includes an introduction, a proposed solution, staffing, a schedule and/or costs, and authorization.

These document outlines must seem like a lot to absorb at this time. Later in this book, you will be introduced to all of the business documents outlined here, and you will learn how to expertly draft all of their parts.

Organizing Ideas Into Strategies

Thus far, you have seen how to collect information, generate ideas, and prepare an outline. How you order the information in your outline, though, depends on the strategy you choose.

Two organizational strategies provide plans of action for typical business messages: the direct strategy and the indirect strategy. The primary difference between the two strategies is where the main idea is placed. In the direct strategy, the main idea comes first, followed by details, explanation, or evidence. In the indirect strategy, the main idea follows the details, explanation, and evidence. The strategy you select is determined by how you expect the audience to react to the message.

Direct Strategy for Receptive Audiences. In preparing to write any message, you need to anticipate the audience's reaction to your ideas and frame your message accordingly. When you expect the reader to be pleased, mildly interested, or, at worst, neutral—use the direct strategy. That is, put your main point—the purpose of your message—in

© iStockphoto.com/Andrew Johnson

> The primary difference between the direct and indirect strategies is where the main idea is placed.

the first or second sentence. Dianna Booher, renowned writing consultant, pointed out that typical readers begin any message by saying, "So what am I supposed to do with this information?" In business writing you have to say, "Reader, here is my point!"[9] As quickly as possible, tell why you are writing. Compare the direct and indirect strategies in the following e-mail openings. Notice how long it takes to get to the main idea in the indirect opening.

Indirect Opening	Direct Opening
Our company has been concerned with attracting better-qualified prospective job candidates. For this reason, the Management Council has been gathering information about an internship program for college students. After considerable investigation, we have voted to begin a pilot program starting next fall.	The Management Council has voted to begin a college internship pilot program next fall.

Explanations and details follow the direct opening. What's important is getting to the main idea quickly. This direct method, also called *frontloading*, has at least three advantages:

- **Saves the reader's time.** Many of today's businesspeople can devote only a few moments to each message. Messages that take too long to get to the point may lose their readers along the way.
- **Sets a proper frame of mind.** Learning the purpose up front helps the reader put the subsequent details and explanations in perspective. Without a clear opening, the reader may be thinking, "Why am I being told this?"
- **Reduces frustration.** Readers forced to struggle through excessive verbiage before reaching the main idea become frustrated. They resent the writer. Poorly organized messages create a negative impression of the writer.

© ZUMA Press, Inc./Alamy

In a recent high-profile cyberheist, hackers breached the networks of shoe retailer Zappos and stole the account data of more than 24 million customers. The ensuing email apology from CEO Tony Hsieh opened, "First, the bad news" and proceeded to inform customers that their personal data was compromised. The second paragraph was titled "The Better News," and it assured customers that their credit card data was unaffected. Did Zappos do the right thing by leading with the bad news?[10]

Typical business messages that follow the direct strategy include routine requests and responses, orders and acknowledgments, nonsensitive memos, e-mails, informational reports, and informational oral presentations. All these tasks have one element in common: none has a sensitive subject that will upset the reader. It should be noted, however, that some business communicators prefer to use the direct strategy for nearly all messages.

Indirect Strategy for Unreceptive Audiences. When you expect the audience to be uninterested, unwilling, displeased, or perhaps even hostile, the indirect strategy is more appropriate. In this strategy you reveal the main idea only after you have offered an explanation and evidence. This approach works well with three kinds of messages: (a) bad news, (b) ideas that require persuasion, and (c) sensitive news, especially when being transmitted to superiors. The indirect strategy has these benefits:

- **Respects the feelings of the audience.** Bad news is always painful, but the trauma can be lessened by preparing the receiver for it.
- **Facilitates a fair hearing.** Messages that may upset the reader are more likely to be read when the main idea is delayed. Beginning immediately with a piece of bad news or a persuasive request, for example, may cause the receiver to stop reading or listening.
- **Minimizes a negative reaction.** A reader's overall reaction to a negative message is generally improved if the news is delivered gently.

Typical business messages that could be developed indirectly include e-mails, memos, and letters that refuse requests, deny claims, and disapprove credit. Persuasive requests, sales letters, sensitive messages, and some reports and oral presentations may also benefit from the indirect strategy. You will learn more about using the indirect strategy in Chapters 9 and 10.

In summary, business messages may be organized directly, with the main idea first, or indirectly, with the main idea delayed, as illustrated in Figure 5.5. Although these two strategies cover many communication problems, they should be considered neither universal nor inviolate. Every business transaction is distinct. Some messages are mixed: part good news, part bad; part goodwill, part persuasion. In upcoming chapters you will practice applying the

Figure 5.5 Audience Response Determines Direct or Indirect Strategy

If pleased
If somewhat interested
If neutral

Direct Strategy

Message
- **Good news or main idea**
- ------------------
- ------------------
- ------------------

If uninterested
If displeased
If disappointed
If hostile

Indirect Strategy

Message
- ------------------
- ------------------
- **Bad news or main idea**
- ------------------

© Cengage Learning 2015

direct and indirect strategies in typical situations. Then, you will have the skills and confidence to evaluate communication problems and vary these strategies depending on the goals you wish to achieve.

Composing the First Draft With Effective Sentences

LEARNING OBJECTIVE **3**
Compose the first draft of a message using a variety of sentence types and avoiding sentence fragments, run-on sentences, and comma splices.

Once you have researched your topic, organized the data, and selected a strategy, you're ready to begin drafting. Many writers have trouble getting started, especially if they haven't completed the preparatory work. Organizing your ideas and working from an outline are very helpful in overcoming writer's block. Composition is also easier if you have a quiet environment in which to concentrate. Businesspeople with messages to compose set aside a given time and allow no calls, visitors, or other interruptions. This is a good technique for students as well.

As you begin writing, think about what style fits you best. Some experts suggest that you write quickly (*freewriting*). Get your thoughts down now and refine them in later versions. As you take up each idea, imagine that you are talking to the reader. Don't let yourself get bogged down. If you can't think of the right word, insert a substitute or type *find perfect word later*. Freewriting works well for some writers, but others prefer to move more slowly and think through their ideas more deliberately. Whether you are a speedy or a deliberate writer, keep in mind that you are writing the first draft. You will have time later to revise and polish your sentences.

Achieving Variety With Four Sentence Types

Messages that repeat the same sentence pattern soon become boring. To avoid monotony and to add spark to your writing, use a variety of sentence types. You have four sentence types from which to choose: simple, compound, complex, and compound-complex.

Simple Sentence

Contains one complete thought (an independent clause) with a subject and predicate verb:

The entrepreneur saw an opportunity.

Compound Sentence

Contains two complete but related thoughts. May be joined by (a) a conjunction such as *and, but,* or *or;* (b) a semicolon; or (c) a conjunctive adverb such as *however, consequently,* and *therefore:*

The entrepreneur saw an opportunity, and she responded immediately.
The entrepreneur saw an opportunity; she responded immediately.
The entrepreneur saw an opportunity; consequently, she responded immediately.

Complex Sentence

Contains an independent clause (a complete thought) and a dependent clause (a thought that cannot stand by itself). Dependent clauses are often introduced by words such as *although, since, because, when,* and *if.* When dependent clauses precede independent clauses, they always are followed by a comma:

When the entrepreneur saw the opportunity, she responded immediately.

Compound-Complex Sentence

Contains at least two independent clauses and one dependent clause:

When the entrepreneur saw the opportunity, she responded immediately; however, she needed capital.

Avoiding Three Common Sentence Faults

As you craft your sentences, beware of three common traps: fragments, run-on (fused) sentences, and comma-splice sentences. If any of these faults appears in a business message, the writer immediately loses credibility.

One of the most serious errors a writer can make is punctuating a **fragment** as if it were a complete sentence. A fragment is usually a broken-off part of a complex sentence. Fragments often can be identified by the words that introduce them—words such as *although, as, because, even, except, for example, if, instead of, since, such as, that, which*, and *when*. These words introduce dependent clauses. Make sure such clauses always connect to independent clauses.

Fragment	Revision
Because most transactions require a permanent record. Good writing skills are critical.	Because most transactions require a permanent record, good writing skills are critical.
The recruiter requested a writing sample. Even though the candidate seemed to communicate well.	The recruiter requested a writing sample even though the candidate seemed to communicate well.

A second serious writing fault is the **run-on (fused)** sentence. A sentence with two independent clauses must be joined by a coordinating conjunction (*and, or, nor, but*) or by a semicolon (;) or separated into two sentences. Without a conjunction or a semicolon, a run-on sentence results.

Run-On Sentence	Revision
Many job seekers prepare traditional résumés some also use websites as electronic portfolios.	Many job seekers prepare traditional résumés. Some also use websites as electronic portfolios.
One candidate sent an e-mail résumé another sent a link to her Web portfolio.	One candidate sent an e-mail résumé; another sent a link to her Web portfolio.

A third sentence fault is a **comma splice.** It results when a writer joins (splices together) two independent clauses with a comma. Independent clauses may be joined with a coordinating conjunction (*and, or, nor, but*) or a conjunctive adverb (*however, consequently, therefore*, and others). Notice that clauses joined by coordinating conjunctions require only a comma. Clauses joined by a coordinating adverb require a semicolon. To rectify a comma splice, try one of the possible revisions shown here:

Comma Splice	Revisions
Some employees prefer their desktop computers, others prefer their tablets.	Some employees prefer their desktop computers, but others prefer their tablets.
	Some employees prefer their desktop computers; however, others prefer their tablets.
	Some employees prefer their desktop computers; others prefer their tablets.

REALITY CHECK: What's the Appeal of Comma Splices?

On the topic of comma splices, one well-known writing coach says, "Why do intelligent people make the error? I think people worry that they will come across too informally or too plainly if they use [two] short sentences. They believe using 4-to-6-word sentences, especially two of them in a row, can't be professional. But two short, crisp, clear sentences in a row are professional and punchy."

—**LYNN GAERTNER-JOHNSTON,** business writing trainer, coach, blogger

Favoring Short Sentences

Because your goal is to communicate clearly, you should strive for sentences that average 20 words. Some sentences will be shorter; some will be longer. The American Press Institute reports that reader comprehension drops off markedly as sentences become longer.[12] Therefore, in crafting your sentences, think about the relationship between sentence length and comprehension.

Sentence Length	Comprehension Rate
8 words	100%
15 words	90%
19 words	80%
28 words	50%

Instead of stringing together clauses with *and, but,* and *however,* break some of those complex sentences into separate segments. Business readers want to grasp ideas immediately. They can do that best when thoughts are separated into short sentences. On the other hand, too many monotonous short sentences will sound "grammar schoolish" and may bore or even annoy the reader. Strive for a balance between longer sentences and shorter ones. Your grammar- and spell-checker can show you readability statistics that flag long sentences and give you an average sentence length.

Improving Writing Techniques

LEARNING OBJECTIVE **4**
Improve your writing techniques by emphasizing important ideas, employing the active and passive voice effectively, using parallelism, and preventing dangling and misplaced modifiers.

You can significantly improve your messages by working on a few writing techniques. These techniques are emphasizing important ideas, employing the active and passive voice effectively, using parallelism, and preventing dangling and misplaced modifiers.

Stressing Important Ideas

Some ideas are more important than others. You can stress prominent ideas *mechanically* by underscoring, italicizing, or boldfacing. You can also stress important ideas *stylistically* by employing one of the following methods:

- **Use vivid words.** Vivid words are emphatic because the reader can picture ideas clearly.

General	Vivid
The way we socialize is changing.	Facebook has dramatically changed the way people socialize on the Web.

- **Label the main idea.** If an idea is significant, tell the reader.

Unlabeled	Labeled
Explore the possibility of a Facebook fan page but also consider security.	Explore the possibility of a Facebook fan page, but, *most important*, consider security.

- **Place the important idea first or last in the sentence.** Ideas have less competition from surrounding words when they appear first or last in a sentence.

Unemphatic	Emphatic
All production and administrative personnel will meet on May 23, at which time we will introduce Asana, a new software program that keeps employees informed. (Date of meeting is de-emphasized.)	On May 23 all personnel will meet to learn about the new software program Asana that keeps employees informed. (Date of meeting is emphasized.)

- **Place the important idea in a simple sentence or in an independent clause.** Don't dilute the effect of the idea by making it share the spotlight with other words and clauses.

Unemphatic	Emphatic
Although you are the first trainee that we have hired for this program, we have interviewed many candidates and expect to expand the program in the future. (Main idea lost in introductory dependent clause.)	You are the first trainee that we have hired for this program. (Simple sentence contains main idea.)

- **Make sure the important idea is the sentence subject.** You will learn more about active and passive voice shortly, but at this point just focus on making the important idea the subject.

Unemphatic	Emphatic
The social networking report was written by Courtney. (De-emphasizes *Courtney*; emphasizes the report.)	Courtney wrote the social networking report. (Emphasizes *Courtney*.)

Using the Active and Passive Voice Effectively

In active-voice sentences, the subject, the actor, performs the action. In passive-voice sentences, the subject receives the action. Active-voice sentences are more direct because they reveal the performer immediately. They are easier to understand and usually shorter. Most business writing should be in the active voice. However, passive voice is useful to (a) emphasize an action rather than a person, (b) de-emphasize negative news, and (c) conceal the doer of an action.

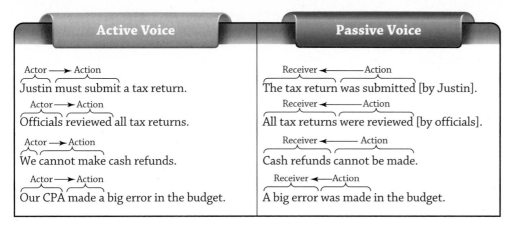

Active Voice	Passive Voice
Actor → Action Justin must submit a tax return.	Receiver ← Action The tax return was submitted [by Justin].
Actor → Action Officials reviewed all tax returns.	Receiver ← Action All tax returns were reviewed [by officials].
Actor → Action We cannot make cash refunds.	Receiver ← Action Cash refunds cannot be made.
Actor → Action Our CPA made a big error in the budget.	Receiver ← Action A big error was made in the budget.

Using Parallelism

Parallelism is a skillful writing technique that involves balanced writing. Sentences written so that their parts are balanced or parallel are easy to read and understand. To achieve parallel construction, use similar structures to express similar ideas. For example, the words *computing, coding, recording,* and *storing* are parallel because the words all end in *-ing*. To express the list as *computing, coding, recording,* and *storage* is disturbing because the last item is not what the reader expects. Try to match nouns with nouns, verbs with verbs, and clauses with clauses. Avoid mixing active-voice verbs with passive-voice verbs. Your goal is to keep the wording balanced in expressing similar ideas.

Lacks Parallelism	Illustrates Parallelism
The policy affected all vendors, suppliers, and *those involved with consulting.*	The policy affected all vendors, suppliers, and *consultants.* (Matches nouns.)
Our primary goals are to increase productivity, reduce costs, and *the improvement of product quality.*	Our primary goals are to increase productivity, reduce costs, and *improve product quality.* (Matches verbs.)
We are scheduled to meet in Atlanta on January 5, *we are meeting in Montreal on the 15th of March,* and in Chicago on June 3.	We are scheduled to meet in Atlanta on January 5, *in Montreal on March 15,* and in Chicago on June 3. (Matches phrases.)
Shelby audits all accounts lettered A through L; accounts lettered M through Z are audited by Andrew.	Shelby audits all accounts lettered A through L; Andrew audits accounts lettered M through Z. (Matches clauses.)
Our Super Bowl ads have three objectives: 1. We want to increase product use. 2. Introduce complementary products. 3. Our corporate image will be enhanced.	Our Super Bowl ads have three objectives: 1. Increase product use 2. Introduce complementary products 3. Enhance our corporate image (Matches verbs in listed items.)

REALITY CHECK: Good Writers Don't Let Their Modifiers Dangle in Public

"Always suspect an -ing word of dangling if it's near the front of a sentence; consider it guilty until proved innocent."

—**PATRICIA T. O'CONNER,** *author,* Woe Is I: The Grammarphobe's Guide to Better English in Plain English.[13]

Escaping Dangling and Misplaced Modifiers

For clarity, modifiers must be close to the words they describe or limit. A modifier dangles when the word or phrase it describes is missing from its sentence—for example, *After working overtime, the report was finally finished*. This sentence says the report was working overtime. Revised, the sentence contains a logical subject: *After working overtime, we finally finished the report*.

A modifier is misplaced when the word or phrase it describes is not close enough to be clear—for example, *Firefighters rescued a dog from a burning car that had a broken leg*. Obviously, the car did not have a broken leg. The solution is to position the modifier closer to the word(s) it describes or limits: *Firefighters rescued a dog with a broken leg from a burning car*.

Introductory verbal phrases are particularly dangerous; be sure to follow them immediately with the words they logically describe or modify. Try this trick for detecting and remedying many dangling modifiers. Ask the question *Who?* or *What?* after any introductory phrase. The words immediately following should tell the reader who or what is performing the action. Try the *Who?* test on the first three danglers here:

Dangling or Misplaced Modifier	Clear Modification
Skilled at graphic design, the contract went to DesignOne.	Skilled at graphic design, DesignOne won the contract.
Working together as a team, the project was finally completed.	Working together as a team, we finally completed the project.
To meet the deadline, your Excel figures must be sent by May 1.	To meet the deadline, you must send us your Excel figures by May 1.
The recruiter interviewed candidates who had excellent computer skills in the morning.	In the morning the recruiter interviewed candidates with excellent computer skills.
As an important customer to us, we invite you to our spring open house.	As you are an important customer to us, we invite you to our spring open house. *OR:* As an important customer to us, you are invited to our spring open house.

CHECKLIST ▸▸
Drafting Effective Sentences

For Effective Sentences

- **Use a variety of sentence types.** To avoid monotony, include simple, compound, complex, and occasionally compound-complex sentences in your writing.

- **Avoid common sentence faults.** To avoid run-on sentences, do not join two clauses without appropriate punctuation. To avoid comma splices, do not join two clauses with a comma. To avoid fragments, be sure to use periods only after complete sentences.

- **Control sentence length.** Use longer sentences occasionally, but rely primarily on short and medium-length sentences.

- **Emphasize important ideas.** Place main ideas at the beginning of short sentences for emphasis.

- **Apply active- and passive-voice verbs strategically.** Use active-voice verbs (*She sent the e-mail* instead of *The e-mail was sent by her*) most frequently; they immediately identify the doer. Use passive-voice verbs to emphasize an action, to be tactful, or to conceal the performer.

- **Employ parallelism.** Balance similar ideas (*biking, jogging, and walking* instead of *biking, jogging, and to walk*).

- **Eliminate misplaced modifiers.** Be sure that introductory verbal phrases are followed by the words that can logically be modified. To check the placement of modifiers, ask *Who?* or *What?* after such phrases.

Building Well-Organized Paragraphs

LEARNING OBJECTIVE **5**
Draft effective paragraphs using three classic paragraph plans and techniques for achieving paragraph coherence.

A paragraph is a group of sentences about one idea. To avoid muddled paragraphs, writers should be able to recognize basic paragraph elements, conventional sentence patterns, and ways to organize sentences using one of three classic paragraph plans. They must also be able to polish their paragraphs by building coherence and using transitional expressions.

Well-constructed paragraphs discuss only one topic. A *topic sentence* reveals the primary idea in a paragraph and usually, but not always, appears first. Paragraphs may be composed of three kinds of sentences:

Topic Sentence	Expresses the primary idea of the paragraph.
Supporting Sentence	Illustrates, explains, or strengthens the primary idea.
Limiting Sentence	Opposes the primary idea by suggesting a negative or contrasting thought; may precede or follow the topic sentence.

These sentences may be arranged in any of three classic paragraph plans: direct, pivoting, and indirect.

Using the Direct Paragraph Plan to Define, Classify, Illustrate, or Describe

Paragraphs using the direct plan begin with the topic sentence, followed by supporting sentences. Most business messages use this paragraph plan because it clarifies the subject immediately. This plan is useful whenever you must define (a new product or procedure), classify (parts of a whole), illustrate (an idea), or describe (a process). Start with the topic sentence; then strengthen and amplify that idea with supporting ideas, as shown here:

Topic Sentence	A social audit is a report on the social performance of a company.
Supporting Sentences	Such an audit may be conducted by the company itself or by outsiders who evaluate the company's efforts to produce safe products, engage in socially responsible activities, and protect the environment. Many companies publish the results of their social audits in their annual reports. Ben & Jerry's Homemade, for example, devotes a major portion of its annual report to its social audit. The report discusses Ben & Jerry's efforts to support environmental restoration. Moreover, it describes workplace safety, employment equality, and peace programs.

You can alter the direct plan by adding a limiting sentence if necessary. Be sure, though, that you follow with sentences that return to the main idea and support it, as shown here:

Topic Sentence	Flexible work scheduling could immediately increase productivity and enhance employee satisfaction in our entire organization.
Limiting Sentence	Such scheduling, however, is impossible for all employees.
Supporting Sentences	Managers would be required to maintain their regular hours. For many other employees, though, flexible scheduling permits extra time to manage family responsibilities. Feeling less stress, employees are able to focus their attention better at work; hence they become more relaxed and more productive.

Using the Pivoting Paragraph Plan to Compare and Contrast

Paragraphs using the pivoting plan start with a limiting sentence that offers a contrasting or negative idea before delivering the topic sentence. Notice in the following example how two limiting sentences about drawbacks to foreign service careers open the paragraph; only then do the topic and supporting sentences describing rewards in foreign service appear. The pivoting plan is especially useful for comparing and contrasting ideas. In using the pivoting plan, be sure to emphasize the turn in direction with an obvious *but* or *however*.

Limiting Sentences	<u>Foreign service careers are certainly not for everyone. Many representatives are stationed in remote countries where harsh climates, health hazards, security risks, and other discomforts exist.</u>
Topic Sentence	<u>However, careers in the foreign service offer special rewards for the special people who qualify.</u>
Supporting Sentences	Foreign service employees enjoy the pride and satisfaction of representing the United States abroad. They enjoy frequent travel, enriching cultural and social experiences in living abroad, and action-oriented work.

Using the Indirect Paragraph Plan to Explain and Persuade

Paragraphs using the indirect plan start with the supporting sentences and conclude with the topic sentence. This useful plan enables you to build a rationale, a foundation of reasons, before hitting the audience with a big idea—possibly one that is bad news. It enables you to explain your reasons and then in the final sentence draw a conclusion from them. In the following example, the vice president of a large accounting firm begins by describing the trend toward casual dress and concludes with a recommendation that his firm change its dress code. The indirect plan works well for describing causes followed by an effect.

Supporting Sentences	According to a recent poll, more than half of all white-collar workers are now dressing casually at work. Many high-tech engineers and professional specialists have given up suits and ties, favoring khakis and sweaters instead. In our own business, our consultants say they stand out like "sore thumbs" because they are attired in traditional buttoned-down styles, while the businesspeople they visit are usually wearing comfortable, casual clothing.
Topic Sentence	<u>Therefore, I recommend that we establish an optional business casual policy allowing consultants to dress down, if they wish, as they perform their duties both in and out of the office.</u>

You will learn more techniques for implementing direct and indirect writing strategies when you draft e-mails, memos, letters, reports, and other business messages as well as prepare oral presentations in coming chapters.

Developing Paragraph Coherence

Paragraphs are coherent when ideas cohere—that is, when the ideas stick together and when one idea logically leads to the next. Well-written paragraphs take the reader through a number of steps. When the author skips from Step 1 to Step 3 and forgets Step 2, the reader is lost. Several techniques will help you keep the reader in step with your ideas.

Sustaining the Key Idea.   Repeating a key expression or using a similar one throughout a paragraph helps sustain a key idea. In the following example, notice that the repetition of *guest* and *VIP* connects ideas.

Our philosophy holds that every customer is really a guest. *All new employees are trained to treat* guests *in our theme parks as VIPs. We take great pride in respecting our guests. As VIPs, they are never told what they can or cannot do.*

Dovetailing Sentences.

Sentences are "dovetailed" when an idea at the end of one connects with an idea at the beginning of the next. Dovetailing sentences is especially helpful with dense, difficult topics. It is also helpful with ordinary paragraphs, such as the following.

New hosts and hostesses learn about the theme park and its facilities. *These* facilities *include telephones, food services, bathrooms, and attractions, as well as the location of* offices. *Knowledge of* offices *and the internal workings of the company is required of all staffers.*

Including Pronouns.

Familiar pronouns, such as *we, they, he, she,* and *it,* help build continuity, as do demonstrative pronouns, such as *this, that, these,* and *those.* These words confirm that something under discussion is still being discussed. However, be careful with such pronouns. They often need a noun with them to make their meaning clear. In the following example, notice how confusing the pronoun *this* would be if the word *training* were omitted.

All new park employees receive a two-week orientation. They learn that every staffer has a vital role in preparing for the show. This training includes how to maintain enthusiasm.

Employing Transitional Expressions.

Transitional expressions are another excellent device for showing connections and achieving paragraph coherence. These words, some of which are shown in Figure 5.6, act as verbal road signs to readers and listeners. Transitional expressions enable the receiver to anticipate what's coming, reduce uncertainty, and speed comprehension. They signal that a train of thought is moving forward, being developed, possibly detouring, or ending. As Figure 5.6 shows, transitions can add or strengthen a thought, show time or order, clarify ideas, show cause and effect, contradict thoughts, and contrast ideas. Look back at the examples of direct, pivoting, and indirect paragraphs to see how transitional expressions and other techniques build paragraph coherence. Remember that coherence in communication rarely happens spontaneously; it requires effort and skill.

Drafting Short Paragraphs for Readability

Although no rule regulates the length of paragraphs, business writers recognize that short paragraphs are more attractive and readable than longer ones. Paragraphs with eight or fewer lines look inviting. If a topic can't be covered in eight or fewer printed lines (not sentences), consider breaking it up into smaller segments.

The following figure shows transitional expressions, and on the next page is a checklist summarizing key points in preparing meaningful paragraphs.

Figure 5.6 Transitional Expressions That Build Coherence

To Add or Strengthen	To Show Time or Order	To Clarify	To Show Cause and Effect	To Contradict	To Contrast
additionally	after	for example	accordingly	actually	as opposed to
accordingly	before	for instance	as a result	but	at the same time
again	earlier	I mean	consequently	however	by contrast
also	finally	in other words	for this reason	in fact	conversely
beside	first	put another way	hence	instead	on the contrary
indeed	meanwhile	that is	so	rather	on the other hand
likewise	next	this means	therefore	still	previously
moreover	now	thus	thus	yet	similarly

© Cengage Learning 2015

CHECKLIST ▶▶
Preparing Meaningful Paragraphs

- **Develop one idea.** Each paragraph should include a topic sentence plus supporting and limiting sentences to develop a single idea.

- **Use the direct plan.** To define, classify, illustrate, and describe, start with the topic sentence followed by supporting sentences.

- **Use the pivoting plan.** To compare and contrast ideas, start with a limiting sentence; then, present the topic sentence followed by supporting sentences.

- **Use the indirect plan.** To explain reasons or causes first, start with supporting sentences. Build to the conclusion with the topic sentence at the end of the paragraph.

- **Build coherence with linking techniques.** Hold ideas together by repeating key words, dovetailing sentences (beginning one sentence with an idea from the end of the previous sentence), and using appropriate pronouns.

- **Provide road signs with transitional expressions.** Use verbal signals to help the audience know where the idea is going. Words and phrases such as *moreover, accordingly, as a result,* and *therefore* function as idea pointers.

- **Limit paragraph length.** Remember that paragraphs with eight or fewer printed lines look inviting. Consider breaking up longer paragraphs if necessary.

© Daniilantiq/Shutterstock.com

© Africa Studio/Shutterstock.com;
© ra2studio/Shutterstock.com

Your Turn: Applying Your Skills at Gap

The management team at Gap is struggling to regain its premier position in retailing. As part of a focus group, you and your team have been asked to brainstorm ideas that will help turn around its fortunes. Your team members are to visit a Gap or Old Navy store and take notes on store appearance, merchandise selection, and customer service. Team members should also look at the Gap website to learn about the company's commitment to social responsibility.

YOUR TASK. Form teams of four or five people. Discuss your task and decide on a goal. Make assignments. Who will visit stores? Who will investigate Gap's website? Who will lead the brainstorming session? Hold a 10-minute brainstorming session following the suggestions in this chapter for generating ideas. What could be changed to attract more customers in your age group to Gap and Old Navy? Set a quota of at least 50 suggestions. Take notes on all suggestions. After 10 minutes, organize and clas-

© AP Images/Paul Sakuma

sify the ideas, retaining the best. Organize the ideas into an outline and submit it to your instructor. Your instructor may ask for individual or team submissions.

Summary of Learning Objectives

1 Apply Phase 2 of the 3-x-3 writing process, which begins with formal and informal research to collect background information. The second phase of the writing process includes researching, organizing, and drafting. Researching means collecting information using formal or informal techniques. Informal research for routine tasks may include looking in the company's digital and other files, talking with your boss, interviewing the target audience, and conducting informal surveys. Formal research for long reports and complex problems may involve searching electronically or manually, investigating primary sources, and conducting scientific experiments.

2 Explain how to generate ideas and organize information to show relationships. Fresh ideas may be generated by brainstorming, a technique that involves encouraging a group of people to unleash "out-of-the-box" ideas, which are then grouped into outlines. Ideas for simple messages may be organized in a quick scratch list of topics. More complex messages may require an outline. To prepare an outline, divide the main topic into three to five major components. Break the components into subpoints consisting of details, illustrations, and evidence. Organizing information with the main idea first is called the direct strategy. This strategy is useful when audiences will be pleased, mildly interested, or neutral. The indirect strategy places the main idea after explanations. This strategy is useful for audiences that will be unwilling, displeased, or hostile.

3 Compose the first draft of a message using a variety of sentence types and avoiding sentence fragments, run-on sentences, and comma splices. Choose a quiet environment to compose the first draft of a message. Compose quickly but plan to revise. Employ a variety of sentence types including simple (one independent clause), complex (one independent and one dependent clause), compound (two independent clauses), and compound-complex (two independent clauses and one dependent clause). Avoid fragments (broken-off parts of sentences), comma splices (joining two clauses improperly), and run-on sentences (fusing two clauses improperly). Remember that sentences are most effective when they are short (20 or fewer words).

4 Improve your writing techniques by emphasizing important ideas, employing the active and passive voice effectively, using parallelism, and preventing dangling and misplaced modifiers. You can emphasize an idea by making it the sentence subject, placing it first, and removing competing ideas. Effective sentences use the active and passive voice strategically. In the active voice, the subject is the doer of the action (*She hired the student*). Most sentences should be in the active voice. In the passive voice, the subject receives the action (*The student was hired*). The passive voice is useful to de-emphasize negative news, to emphasize an action rather than the doer, and to conceal the doer of an action. Parallelism is a skillful writing technique that uses balanced construction (*jogging, hiking, and biking* rather than *jogging, hiking, and to bike*). Skillful writing avoids dangling modifiers (*sitting at my computer, the words would not come*) and misplaced modifiers (*I have the report you wrote in my office*).

5 Draft effective paragraphs using three classic paragraph plans and techniques for achieving paragraph coherence. Typical paragraphs follow one of three plans. Direct paragraphs (topic sentence followed by supporting sentences) are useful to define, classify, illustrate, and describe. Pivoting paragraphs (limiting sentence followed by a topic sentence and supporting sentences) are useful to compare and contrast. Indirect paragraphs (supporting sentences followed by a topic sentence) build a rationale and foundation of ideas before presenting the main idea. Paragraphs are more coherent when the writer links ideas by (a) sustaining a key thought, (b) dovetailing sentences, (c) using pronouns effectively and (d) employing transitional expressions. Paragraphs with eight or fewer lines look most attractive.

Chapter Review

1. Describe the three parts of the second phase of the writing process. (Obj. 1)

2. What is *research* and why is it important for business writers? (Obj. 1)

3. Compare informal and formal research methods. (Obj. 1)

4. Name seven specific techniques for a productive group brainstorming session. (Obj. 2)

5. What is the difference between a list and an outline? (Obj. 2)

6. When is the indirect strategy appropriate, and what are the benefits of using it? (Obj. 2)

7. What is the difference between a compound and a complex sentence? Provide an original example of each. (Obj. 3)

8. What writing fault is illustrated in the following sentence, and how can it be remedied? *In the United States, services dominate the economy, however, many worry about the loss of manufacturing jobs.* (Obj. 3)

9. What writing fault is illustrated in the following groups of words, and how can it be remedied? *Because they have been hobbled by government regulations, privacy issues, and internal bureaucracy. Giant banks are struggling to find the magic formula for using social media.* (Obj. 3)

10. List four techniques for emphasizing important ideas in sentences. (Obj. 4)

11. When should business writers use active-voice sentences? When should they use passive-voice sentences? Give an original example of each. (Obj. 4)

12. Explain the writing fault in the following sentence and how to remedy it. *To meet the deadline, your Excel figures must be received before May 1.* (Obj. 4)

13. What is a topic sentence and where is it usually found? (Obj. 5)

14. What is paragraph coherence and how is it achieved? (Obj. 5)

15. How can writers avoid *writer's block*? (Obj. 5)

Critical Thinking

1. Do you agree or disagree with critics who contend that brainstorming is not the best way to foster creativity in large groups? (Obj. 2)

2. Why is audience analysis so important in the selection of the direct or indirect strategy of organization for a business message? (Obj. 2)

3. How are speakers different from writers in the way they emphasize ideas? (Obj. 4)

4. Why are short sentences and short paragraphs appropriate for business communication? (Objs. 4, 5)

5. **Ethical Issue:** Discuss the ethics of the indirect strategy of organization. Is it manipulative to delay the presentation of the main idea in a message?

Activities

Note: All Documents for Analysis are provided at **www.cengagebrain.com** for you to download and revise.

5.1 Sentence Types (Obj. 3)

YOUR TASK. For each of the following sentences, select the number that identifies its type:

1. Simple sentence
2. Compound sentence
3. Complex sentence
4. Compound-complex sentence

a. Americans pride themselves on their informality.

b. When Americans travel abroad on business, their informality may be viewed negatively.

c. Informality in Asia often equals disrespect; it is not seen as a virtue.

d. The order of first and last names in Asia may be reversed, and this causes confusion to Americans and Europeans.

e. When you are addressing someone, ask which name a person would prefer to use; however, be sure you can pronounce it correctly.

5.2 Sentence Faults (Obj. 3)

YOUR TASK. In the following, identify the sentence fault (fragment, run-on, comma splice). Then revise to remedy the fault.

a. Although they began as a side business for Disney. Destination weddings now represent a major income source.

b. About 2,000 weddings are held yearly. Which is twice the number just ten years ago.

c. Weddings may take place in less than one hour, however the complete cost may be as much as $20,000.

d. Limousines line up outside Disney's wedding pavilion, ceremonies are scheduled in two-hour intervals.

e. Many couples prefer a traditional wedding others request a fantasy experience.

5.3 Emphasis (Obj. 4)

YOUR TASK. For each of the following sentences, circle (1) or (2). Be prepared to justify your choice.

a. Which is more emphatic?
   1. They offer a lot of products.
   2. CyberGuys offers computer, travel, and office accessories.

b. Which is more emphatic?
   1. Increased online advertising would improve sales.
   2. Adding $50,000 in online advertising would double our sales.

c. Which is more emphatic?
   1. We must consider several factors.
   2. We must consider cost, staff, and safety.

d. Which sentence places more emphasis on product loyalty?
   1. Product loyalty is the primary motivation for advertising.
   2. The primary motivation for advertising is loyalty to the product, although other purposes are also served.

e. Which sentence places more emphasis on the seminar?
   1. An executive training seminar that starts June 1 will include four candidates.
   2. Four candidates will be able to participate in an executive training seminar that we feel will provide a valuable learning experience.

f. Which sentence places more emphasis on the date?
   1. The deadline is April 1 for summer vacation reservations.
   2. April 1 is the deadline for summer vacation reservations.

g. Which is less emphatic?
   1. One division's profits increased last quarter.
   2. Profits in consumer electronics soared 15 percent last quarter.

h. Which sentence de-emphasizes the credit refusal?
   1. We cannot grant you credit at this time, but we welcome your cash business and encouage you to reapply in the future.
   2. Although credit cannot be granted at this time, we welcome your cash business and encourage you to reapply in the future.

i. Which sentence gives more emphasis to leadership?
   1. She has many admirable qualities, but most important is her leadership skill.
   2. She has many admirable qualities, including leadership skill, good judgment, and patience.

j. Which is more emphatic?
   1. We notified three departments: (1) Marketing, (2) Accounting, and (3) Distribution.
   2. We notified the following departments:
      a. Marketing
      b. Accounting
      c. Distribution

5.4 Active Voice (Obj. 4)

YOUR TASK. Business writing is more forceful when it uses active-voice verbs. Revise the following sentences so that verbs are in the active voice. Put the emphasis on the doer of the action. Add subjects if necessary.

> **Example** Antivirus software was installed on her computer.
>
> **Revision** Madison installed antivirus software on her computer.

a. To protect students, laws were passed in many states that prohibited the use of social security numbers as identification.

b. Software was installed to track how much time employees spend surfing the Web.

c. Checks are processed more quickly by banks because of new regulations.

d. Millions of packages are scanned by FedEx every night as packages stream through its Memphis hub.

e. Companies are being advised by analysts that tablet computers have to be replaced more often than PCs.

5.5 Passive Voice (Obj. 4)

YOUR TASK. When indirectness or tact is required, use passive-voice verbs. Revise the following sentences so that they are in the passive voice.

> **Example** Travis did not submit the proposal before the deadline.
>
> **Revision** The proposal was not submitted before the deadline.

a. Accounting seems to have made a serious error in this report.

b. We cannot ship your order for smart surge protectors until May 5.

c. The government first issued a warning regarding the use of this pesticide more than 15 months ago.

d. Your insurance policy does not automatically cover damage to rental cars.

e. We cannot provide patient care unless patients show proof of insurance.

5.6 Parallelism (Obj. 4)

YOUR TASK. Revise the following sentences so that their parts are balanced.

a. (**Hint:** Match verbs.) To improve your listening skills, you should stop talking, your surroundings should be controlled, be listening for main points, and an open mind must be kept.

b. (**Hint:** Match active voice of verbs.) Paula Day, director of the Okefenokee branch, will now supervise all Eastern Division operations; the Western Division will be supervised by our Oroville branch director, Reggie Kostiz.

c. (**Hint:** Match verb phrases.) Our newly hired employee has started using her computer and to learn her coworkers' names.

d. (**Hint:** Match adjectives.) Training seminars must be stimulating and a challenge.

e. Our telecommunications software allows you to meet with customers over the Internet for training, Web-based meetings can be held, and other online collaboration within virtual teams is also facilitated.

f. We need more trained staff members, office space is limited, and the budget for overtime is too small.

g. The application for a grant asks for this information: funds required for employee salaries, how much we expect to spend on equipment, and what is the length of the project.

h. Sending an e-mail or letter establishes a more permanent record than to make a telephone call.

5.7 Dangling and Misplaced Modifiers (Obj. 4)

YOUR TASK. Revise the following sentences to avoid dangling and misplaced modifiers.

a. When collecting information before purchasing a tablet, the Web proved to be my best resource.

b. To win the lottery, a ticket must be purchased.

c. Angered by slow computer service, complaints were called in by hundreds of unhappy users.

d. The exciting Cosmopolitan is just one of the fabulous hotels you see strolling along the Las Vegas strip.

e. Walking into the hotel lobby, the artwork was stunning.

5.8 Organizing Paragraph Sentences (Obj. 5)

YOUR TASK. Study the following list of sentences from an interoffice memo to hospital staff.

1. The old incident report form caused numerous problems and confusion.

2. One problem was that employees often omitted important information.

3. The Hospital Safety Committee has revised the form used for incident reports.

4. Another problem was that inappropriate information was often included that might expose the hospital to liability.

5. The Hospital Safety Committee has scheduled a lunchtime speaker to discuss prevention of medication mistakes.

6. Factual details about the time and place of the incident are important, but speculation on causes is inappropriate.

7. The new form will be available on April 1.

a. Which sentence should be the topic sentence? _____

b. Which sentence(s) should be developed in a separate paragraph? _____

c. Which sentences should become support sentences? _____

5.9 Building Coherent Paragraphs (Obj. 5)

YOUR TASK. Use the following facts to construct a coherent paragraph with a topic sentence and appropriate transitional expressions in the supporting sentences.

- The federal government will penalize medical practices that don't adopt electronic medical records (EMRs).

- Valley Medical Center is considering beginning converting soon.

- Converting paper-based records to EMRs will be complex.

- Converting will be technically challenging. It will probably be time-consuming and labor-intensive.

- Converting should bring better patient care and maybe even lower costs in the long run.

- The federal government provides funds to reimburse the cost of adopting the technology.

5.10 Building Coherent Paragraphs (Obj. 5)

YOUR TASK. Improve the organization, coherence, and correctness of the following paragraph.

We feel that the "extreme" strategy has not been developed fully in the fast-food market. Pizza Hut is considering launching a new product called The Extreme. We plan to price this new pizza at $19.99. It will be the largest pizza on the market. It will have double the cheese. It will also have double the toppings.

The plan is to target the X and Y Generations. The same target audience that would respond to an extreme product also reacts to low prices. The X and Y Generations are the fastest-growing segments in the fast-food market. These population segments have responded well to other marketing plans using the extreme strategy.

5.11 Building Coherent Paragraphs (Obj. 5)

YOUR TASK. Use the following facts to construct a coherent paragraph with a topic sentence and appropriate transitional expressions in the supporting sentences.

- Nearly all teams experience conflict. They should recognize and expect it.

- The most effective teams strive to eliminate destructive conflict and develop constructive conflict.

- Destructive conflict arises when team members take criticism personally.

- Destructive conflict poisons teamwork.

- Conflict can become constructive.

- Teams that encourage members to express their opinions may seem to be experiencing conflict when the opinions differ.

- Better decisions often result when teams listen to and discuss many views.

5.12 Document for Analysis: Faulty E-Mail Message (Objs. 3–5)

E-mail   **Team**

YOUR TASK. The following e-mail suffers from numerous writing faults such as dangling modifiers, overuse of the passive voice, and fragments. Notice that small superscript numbers identify each sentence or group of words. Individually or in a group, analyze this message and list the faulty sentences or groups of words. You should find three sentences with dangling modifiers, seven with passive voice, and three fragments. Be sure your group agrees on its analysis. Your instructor may ask you to revise the message to remedy its faults.

To: Tyler.Long@cox.org

From: Janice Rivera <jrivera@24hourgym.com>

Subject: Expanding Your Workouts at 24-Hour Gym

Cc:

Bcc:

Dear Mr. Long,

[1]24-Hour Gym here in Seattle was probably selected by you because it is one of the top-rated gyms in the Northwest. [2]Our principal goal has always been making your workouts productive. [3]To continue to provide you with the best equipment and programs, your feedback is needed.

[4]An outstanding program with quality equipment and excellent trainers has been provided by 24-Hour Gym. [5]However, more individual attention could be given by us to our customers if our peak usage time could be extended. [6]You have probably noticed that attendance at the gym increases from 4 p.m. to 8 p.m. [7]We wish it were possible to accommodate all our customers on their favorite equipment during those hours. [8]Although we can't stretch an hour. [9]We would like to make better use of the time between 8 p.m. and 11 p.m. [10]If more members came later, the gym would have less crush from 4 p.m. to 8 p.m.

11To encourage you to stay later, security cameras for our parking area are being considered by my partner and me. **12**Cameras for some inside facilities may also be added. **13**This matter has been given considerable thought. **14**Although 24-Hour Gym has never previously had an incident that endangered a member.

15Please fill in the attached interactive questionnaire. **16**Which will give us instant feedback about scheduling your workouts. **17**By completing this questionnaire, your workouts and training sessions can be better planned so that you can enjoy exactly the equipment and trainers you prefer.

Cordially,

5.13 Brainstorming: Solving a Problem on Campus (Objs. 1, 2)

< Team >

YOUR TASK. In teams of three to five, analyze a problem on your campus such as the following: unavailable classes, unrealistic degree requirements, a lack of student intern programs, poor parking facilities, an inadequate registration process, a lack of diversity among students on campus, and so forth. Use brainstorming techniques to generate ideas that clarify the problem and explore its solutions. Either individually or as a team, organize the ideas into an outline with three to five main points and numerous subpoints. Assume that your ideas will become part of a message to be sent to an appropriate campus official or to your campus newspaper discussing the problem and your proposed solution. Remember, however, your role as a student. Be polite, positive, and constructive—not negative, hostile, or aggressive.

5.14 Brainstorming: Solving a Problem at Work (Objs. 1, 2)

< E-mail >

YOUR TASK. Analyze a problem that exists where you work or go to school such as noisy work areas, an overuse of express mail services, understaffing during peak customer-service hours, poor scheduling of employees, inappropriate cell phone use, an inferior or inflexible benefits package, outdated equipment, or one of the campus problems listed in **Activity 5.13.** Select a problem about which you have some knowledge. Organize the ideas into an outline with three to five main points and numerous subpoints. Be polite, positive, and constructive. E-mail the outline to your boss (your instructor). Include an introduction (such as, *Here is the outline you requested in regard to . . .*). Include a closing that offers to share your outline if your boss would like to see it.

5.15 Research: Tips for Productive Brainstorming Sessions (Objs. 1, 2)

< Web >

Michelle M., your supervisor at Gap, has been asked to lead a brainstorming group in an effort to generate new ideas for the company's product line. Although Michelle knows a great deal about the company and its products, she doesn't know much about brainstorming. She asks you to research the topic quickly and give her a concise guide on how to brainstorm. One other thing—Michelle doesn't want to read a lot of articles. She wants you to outline tips for productive brainstorming.

YOUR TASK. Conduct an Internet or database keyword search for brainstorming tips. Locate a number of articles with helpful tips. Prepare an outline that tells how to (a) prepare for a brainstorming session, (b) conduct the session, and (c) follow up after the meeting. Submit your outline in a memo or an e-mail to your supervisor (your instructor).

5.16 Brainstorming: Are Ethics Programs Helpful? (Objs. 1–5)

< Ethics > < Team > < Web >

In the wake of the mortgage meltdown and numerous banking scandals, more companies are hiring ethics officers—sometimes called "ethics cops." Companies are also investing in expensive interactive Web-based ethics training. You have been named to a team to discuss ethics compliance in your company, a large firm with thousands of employees. It has no current program. Other companies have ethics codes, conflict-of-interest policies, ethics officers, training programs, and hotlines. Some authorities, however, say that ethics failures are usually not the result of ignorance of laws or regulations.[15] A variety of pressures may cause ethics lapses.

YOUR TASK. Your boss, the Human Resources vice president, wants to learn more about employee feelings in regard to ethics programs. In teams, brainstorm to find reactions to these questions. What kinds of ethical dilemmas do typical entry-level and midlevel managerial employees face? Do you think ethics codes help employees be more ethical? What conditions might force employees to steal, lie, or break the rules? Can ethics be taught? What kind of workplace ethics program would you personally find helpful? Before your brainstorming session, you might want to investigate the topic of ethics programs on the Web. Record your ideas during the session. Then organize the best ones into an outline to be presented to Rita Romano, Human Resources Vice President. Your instructor might make this the topic of a long report.

Chat About It

In each chapter you will find five discussion questions related to the chapter material. Your instructor may assign these topics for you to discuss in class, in an online chat room, or on an online discussion board. Some of the discussion topics may require outside research. You may also be asked to read and respond to postings made by your classmates.

Topic 1: Applicants for graduate schools or scholarships often have to sign the following statement at the end of the application essay: *I certify that this essay is original work prepared by me, the author.*[16] What is your opinion of such a requirement, aside from the redundancy (*prepared by me, the author*)? Would such a requirement make you angry?

Topic 2: This chapter describes brainstorming as a technique for generating ideas. Explore the Internet for other methods such as *freewriting, looping, listing, clustering,* and *reporters' questions.* Select a method that appeals to you and explain why it would be effective.

Topic 3: Some writers have trouble writing the opening sentence of a message. Occasionally, a quotation makes for an appropriate opening. Assume that you need to motivate an employee to achieve more at work. Find a famous quotation online about motivation that might be an appropriate opening for such a message. In addition, write a sentence that would effectively transition from this opening.

Topic 4: In your opinion, how many business managers know what a comma splice is? If some managers don't know what a comma splice is, then is it critical that you avoid comma splices in your writing?

Topic 5: Why is it important for writers to think about how long their sentences are? Learn how to display the average sentence length in a document using Microsoft Word. Explain the process briefly.

C.L.U.E. Grammar & Mechanics | *Review 5*

Commas

Review Guides 21–26 about commas in Appendix A, Grammar and Mechanics Guide, beginning on page A-10. On a separate sheet, revise the following sentences to correct errors in comma usage. For each error that you locate, write the guide number and abbreviation that reflects this usage. The more you recognize the reasons, the better you will learn these punctuation guidelines. If a sentence is correct, write *C.* When you finish, check your answers on page Key-1.

Guide 21, CmSer (Comma series)

Guide 22, CmIntr (Comma introductory, addresses, geographical names, etc.)

Guide 23, CmConj (Comma conjunction)

Guide 24, CmDate (Comma, dates)

Guide 26, CmNo (Unnecessary comma)

EXAMPLE: When we use company e-mail we know our messages are monitored.

REVISION: When we use company e-mail, we know our messages are monitored. [Guide 22, CmIntr]

1. Informal research methods include looking in the files talking with your boss and interviewing the target audience.

2. When you prepare to write any message you need to anticipate the audience's reaction.

3. By learning to distinguish between dependent and independent clauses you will be able to avoid serious sentence faults.

4. Some business messages require sensitivity and writers may prefer to use passive-voice instead of active-voice verbs.

5. We hired Davida Michaels who was the applicant with the best qualifications as our new marketing manager.

6. Our business was incorporated on August 1, 2008 in Phoenix Arizona.

7. The new online business by the way is flourishing and is expected to show a profit soon.

8. After he graduates Dustin plans to move to Atlanta and find work there.

9. Last fall our company introduced policies regulating the use of cell phones instant messaging and e-mail on the job.

10. The problem with many company telecommunication policies is that the policies are self-policed and never enforced.

Notes

[1] Caramanica, J. (2011, May 18). Do my high school jeans still fit? *The New York Times*. Retrieved from http://www.nytimes.com/2011/05/19/fashion/gap-now-casts-a-wide-net-critical-shopper.html?ref=gaptheinc

[2] Birkner, C. (2011, December 1). Gap looks abroad as struggles continue at home. *Marketing News*. Retrieved from AMA Access at http://www.marketingpower.com/ResourceLibrary/Documents/newsletters/mne/2011/12/mne_gap_sales.pdf

[3] Head, A., & Eisenberg, M. (2009, February 4). What today's college students say about conducting research in the digital age. Project Information Literacy Progress Report, University of Washington. Retrieved from http://projectinfolit.org/pdfs/PIL_ProgressReport_2_2009.pdf

[4] Photo essay based on Segal, D. (2010, December 16). In pursuit of the perfect brainstorm. *The New York Times*. Retrieved from http://www.nytimes.com

[5] Coyne, K., & Coyne, S. (2011). Seven steps to better brainstorming. *McKinsey Quarterly*, 00475394, Issue 2.

[6] Sutton, R. I. (2006, September 5). The truth about brainstorming. *BusinessWeek*, p. 17. Retrieved from http://www.businessweek.com/magazine/content/06_39/b4002410.htm

[7] Ibid.

[8] Damian, J. (2009, July 2). Inside Disney's toy factory. *BusinessWeek*. Retrieved from http://www.businessweek.com/innovate/content/jul2009/id2009071_592328.htm

[9] Rindegard, J. (1999, November 22). Use clear writing to show you mean business. *InfoWorld*, p. 78.

[10] Photo essay based on Goldman, D. (2012, January 16). Zappos hacked, 24 million accounts accessed. *CNNMoney*. Retrieved from

http://money.cnn.com/2012/01/16/technology/zappos_hack/index.htm; Tony Hsieh. (2012, January 15). Security email. [Zappos Web log post]. Retrieved from http://www.zappos.com/securityemail

[11] Hull, J. S. (2007). Splenda hearings. Retrieved from http://www.janethull.com/newsletter/0607/splenda_hearings.php

[12] Goddard, R. W. (1989, April). Communication: Use language effectively. *Personnel Journal*, 32.

[13] O'Connor, P. (1996). *Woe is I*. New York: Putnam's, p. 161.

[14] Boris, C. (2011, August 26). Nearly half of all marketers are willing to pay for a post. Retrieved from http://www.marketingpilgrim.com/2011/08/nearly-half-of-all-marketers-are-willing-to-pay-for-a-post.html

[15] Toffler, B. quoted in Schmitt, R. B. (2002, November 5). Companies add ethics training: Will it work? *The Wall Street Journal*, p. Bl.

[16] Schall, J. (2008). Student writing and ethics. PennState, College of Earth and Mineral Sciences. Retrieved from https://www.e-education.psu.edu/writingpersonalstatementsonline/p1_p4.html

Revising Business Messages

1 Complete business messages by revising for conciseness, which includes eliminating flabby expressions, long lead-ins, *there is/are* and *it is/was* fillers, redundancies, and empty words, as well as condensing for microblogging.

2 Improve clarity in business messages by keeping the ideas simple, dumping trite business phrases, dropping clichés, avoiding slang and buzzwords, rescuing buried verbs, and controlling exuberance.

3 Enhance readability by understanding document design including the use of white space, margins, typefaces, fonts, numbered and bulleted lists, and headings.

4 Recognize proofreading problem areas, and apply effective techniques to catch mistakes in both routine and complex documents.

5 Evaluate a message to judge its effectiveness.

Taco Bell and Doritos: A Marriage Made in "Belly-Busting Heaven"

With Doritos on the outside and Taco Bell on the inside, the newly launched "Locos Tacos" might just rescue a brand wounded by bad publicity. Taco Bell recently partnered with Frito-Lay to offer a cheese-flavored shell stuffed with spicy beef filling. This big hit may be exactly what Taco Bell needs to get back on track after a devastating lawsuit falsely accused the fast-food chain of adulterating its beef with binders and extenders.[1]

NEW!

Doritos
LOCOS TACOS

© AP Images/Taco Bell

Yum Brands—owner of Taco Bell, Pizza Hut, and KFC—is the world's largest restaurant company, with 18,000 U.S. restaurants and more than 37,000 world-wide.[2] Although Taco Bell has the most restaurants, it continues to suffer from a serious image problem. Several years ago it endured an *E. coli* outbreak, and more recently it was "skewered by a viral video" showing rats scampering about one of its Manhattan stores. Then the sky nearly fell in with the beef accusations.[3]

Yum CEO David Novak admitted that "the lawsuit took the fun out of our business."[4] However, he is very upbeat about the brand's growth overseas and a new line of products. "We're positioning the brand around the notion that fresh is better. People don't realize the product we have come to our stores [is] delivered fresh every day."[5] Stinging from criticism that fast food contributes to the worldwide obesity epidemic, Taco Bell is also looking for nutritious as well as fresh menu choices.[6]

In the increasingly crowded fast-food market, customers are shifting away from the traditional burger and chicken fast foods. One food industry executive said, "Burgers are your dad's food, and Mexican is the choice of the new generation."[7] Poised to capitalize on this movement, Taco Bell remains keenly aware that (a) it sells a quasi-Mexican food, and (b) its customers are changing. Although its products cannot veer too far from what appeals to the masses, Taco Bell must also compete with new flavors and fresh ingredients.

You will learn more about Taco Bell and be asked to complete a relevant task at the end of this chapter.

Critical Thinking

- Assume that a recently hired culinary product manager is charged with generating and implementing new menu suggestions. What role do communication skills play in this person's effectiveness in completing this task?

- Do you think a culinary product manager would make an oral or a written presentation of new menu ideas?

- Why is a writing process helpful in developing a presentation of new ideas?

Taking Time to Revise: Applying Phase 3 of the Writing Process

LEARNING OBJECTIVE 1
Complete business messages by revising for conciseness, which includes eliminating flabby expressions, long lead-ins, *there is/are* and *it is/was* fillers, redundancies, and empty words, as well as condensing for microblogging.

In this digital age of e-mailing, texting, and tweeting, the idea of stopping to revise a message seems almost alien to productivity. What? Stop to proofread? Crazy idea! No time! However, sending quickie but sloppy business messages not only fails to enhance productivity but also often produces the opposite result. Those quickie messages can be confusing and frustrating. They often set into motion a maddening ping-pong series of back-and-forth queries and responses seeking clarification. To avoid messages that waste time, create confusion, and reduce your credibility, take time to slow down and revise—even for short messages.

The final phase of the 3-x-3 writing process focuses on editing, proofreading, and evaluating. Editing means improving the content and sentence structure of your message. Proofreading involves correcting its grammar, spelling, punctuation, format, and mechanics. Evaluating is the process of analyzing whether your message achieves its purpose. One would not expect people in the restaurant business to require these kinds of skills. However, the new culinary product manager at Taco Bell—and many similar businesspeople—realize that bright ideas are worth little unless they can be communicated effectively to fellow workers and to management. In the communication process, the techniques of revision can often mean the difference between the acceptance or rejection of ideas.

Although the drafting process differs depending on the person and the situation, this final phase should occupy a significant share of the total time you spend on a message. As you learned earlier, some experts recommend devoting about half the total writing time to the third phase of the writing process.[8]

Rarely is the first or even second version of a message satisfactory. Only amateurs expect writing perfection on the first try. The revision stage is your chance to make sure your message says what you mean and makes you look good. Many professional writers compose the first draft quickly without worrying about language, precision, or correctness. Then they revise and polish extensively. Other writers, however, prefer to revise as they go—particularly for shorter business documents.

Whether you revise immediately or after a break, you will want to examine your message critically. You should be especially concerned with ways to improve its conciseness, clarity, and readability.

Tightening Your Message by Revising for Conciseness

In business, time is indeed money. Translated into writing, this means that concise messages save reading time and, thus, money. In addition, messages that are written directly and efficiently are easier to read and comprehend. In the revision process, look for shorter ways to say what you mean. Examine every sentence that you write. Could the thought be conveyed in fewer words? Your writing will be more concise if you eliminate flabby expressions, drop unnecessary introductory words, get rid of redundancies, and purge empty words.

Eliminating Flabby Expressions

As you revise, focus on eliminating flabby expressions. This takes conscious effort. As one expert copyeditor observed, "Trim sentences, like trim bodies, usually require far more effort than flabby ones."[9] Turning out slim sentences and lean messages means that you will strive to "trim the fat." For example, notice the flabbiness in this sentence: *Due to the fact that sales are booming, profits are good*. It could be said more concisely: *Because sales are booming, profits are good*. Many flabby expressions can be shortened to one concise word as shown here and illustrated in Figure 6.1. Notice in this figure how you can revise digital documents with strike-through formatting and color. If you are revising print documents, use popular proofreading marks.

Flabby	Concise
as a general rule	generally
at a later date	later
at this point in time	now, presently
despite the fact that	although
due to the fact that, inasmuch as, in view of the fact that	because
feel free to	please
for the period of	for
in addition to the above	also
in all probability	probably
in the event that	if
in the near future	soon
in very few cases	seldom
until such time as	until
with regard to	about

Figure **6.1** Revising Digital and Print Documents

Revising Digital Documents Using Strikethrough and Color

~~This is a short note to let you know that, as~~ As you requested, I ~~made an investigation of~~ investigated several of our competitors' websites. Attached ~~hereto~~ is a summary of my findings. ~~of my investigation.~~ I was ~~really~~ most interested in ~~making a comparison of the employment of strategies for~~ comparing marketing ~~strategies~~ as well as ~~the use of~~ navigational graphics ~~used~~ to guide visitors through the sites. ~~In view of the fact that~~ Because we will be revising our own website ~~in the near future~~ soon, I was ~~extremely~~ intrigued by the organization, ~~kind of~~ marketing tactics, and navigation at each ~~and every~~ site I visited.

When revising digital documents, you can use simple word processing tools such as strikethrough and color. In this example, strikethroughs in red identify passages to be deleted. The strikethrough function is located on the **Font** tab. We used blue to show inserted words, but you may choose any color you prefer.

Revising Printed Documents Using Proofreading Symbols

When revising printed documents, use standard symbols to manually show your revisions.

~~This is a short note to let you know that,~~ as you requested, I ~~made an~~ investigation ~~of~~ (ed) several of our competitors' websites. Attached ~~hereto~~ is a summary of my findings ~~of my investigation.~~ I was ~~really~~ most interested in ~~making a comparison of the employment of~~ (comparing) strategies ~~for marketing~~ (marketing) as well as ~~the use of~~ navigational graphics ~~used~~ to guide visitors through the sites. ~~In view of the fact that~~ (Because) we will be revising our own website ~~in the near~~ (soon) future, I was ~~extremely~~ intrigued by the organization, ~~kind of~~ marketing tactics, and navigation at ~~each and~~ every site I visited.

Popular Proofreading Symbols

Delete	ℒ
Capitalize	≡
Insert	∧
Insert comma	⋏
Insert period	⊙
Start paragraph	¶

Limiting Long Lead-Ins

Concise sentences avoid long lead-ins with unnecessary introductory words. Consider this sentence: *I am sending you this e-mail to announce that we have hired a new manager.* It's more concise and direct without the long lead-in: *We have hired a new manager.* The meat of the sentence often follows the words *that* or *because*, as shown in the following:

Wordy	Concise
We are sending this announcement to let everyone know that we expect to change Internet service providers within six weeks.	We expect to change Internet service providers within six weeks.
This is to inform you that you may find lower airfares at our website.	You may find lower airfares at our website.
I am writing this letter because Professor Jim Dubinsky suggested that your organization was hiring trainees.	Professor Jim Dubinsky suggested that your organization was hiring trainees.

Dropping Unnecessary *there is/are* and *it is/was* Fillers

In many sentences the expressions *there is/are* and *it is/was* function as unnecessary fillers. In addition to taking up space, these fillers delay getting to the point of the sentence. Eliminate them by recasting the sentence. Many—but not all—sentences can be revised so that fillers are unnecessary.

Wordy	Concise
There are more women than men enrolled in college today.	More women than men are enrolled in college today.
There is an aggregator that collects and organizes blogs.	An aggregator collects and organizes blogs.
It was a Facebook post that revealed the news.	A Facebook post revealed the news.

Rejecting Redundancies

Expressions that repeat meaning or include unnecessary words are redundant. Saying *unexpected surprise* is like saying *surprise surprise* because *unexpected* carries the same meaning as *surprise*. Excessive adjectives, adverbs, and phrases often create redundancies and wordiness. Redundancies do not add emphasis, as some people think. Instead, they identify a writer as careless. As you revise, look for redundant expressions such as the following:

Redundant	Concise
absolutely essential	essential
adequate enough	adequate
basic fundamentals	fundamentals *or* basics
big in size	big
combined together	combined
exactly identical	identical
each and every	each *or* every
necessary prerequisite	prerequisite
new beginning	beginning
refer back	refer
repeat again	repeat
true facts	facts

Purging Empty Words

Familiar phrases roll off the tongue easily, but many contain expendable parts. Be alert to these empty words and phrases: *case, degree, the fact that, factor, instance, nature,* and *quality.* Notice how much better the following sentences sound when we remove all the empty words:

> ~~In the case of~~ Facebook, ~~it~~ increased users but lost share value.

> Because of ~~the degree of~~ support from upper management, the plan worked.

> We are aware ~~of the fact~~ that new products soar when pushed by social networking.

> Except for ~~the instance of~~ Toyota, Japanese imports sagged.

She chose a career in a field that was analytical ~~in nature~~. [OR: She chose a career in an analytical field.]

Student writing in that class is excellent ~~in quality~~.

Also avoid saying the obvious. In the following examples, notice how many unnecessary words we can omit through revision:

~~When it arrived~~, I cashed your check immediately. (Announcing the check's arrival is unnecessary. That fact is assumed in its cashing.)

As consumers learn more about ingredients ~~and as they become more knowledgeable~~, they are demanding fresher foods. (Avoid repeating information.)

Look carefully at clauses beginning with *that, which,* and *who*. They can often be shortened without loss of clarity. Search for phrases such as *it appears that*. These phrases often can be reduced to a single adjective or adverb, such as *apparently*.

Changing the name of a ^successful^ company ~~that is successful~~ is always risky.

All employees ~~who are among those~~ completing the course will be reimbursed.

Our ^final^ proposal, ~~which was~~ slightly altered ~~in its final form~~, won approval.

We plan to schedule ^weekly^ meetings ~~on a weekly basis~~.

Conciseness and other writing skills are particularly important in live chat sessions. These digital conversations are rapidly replacing telephone inquiries for customer service, as shown in Figure 6.2.

Figure 6.2 Live Chat Connects Service Reps and Customers

© Courtesy of clickandchat.com

Customer-service reps in chat sessions require exceptional writing skills to answer questions concisely, clearly, and conversationally. It takes special talent to be able to think and key immediate responses that are spelled correctly and are error free. One company found that it could not easily convert its telephone customer-service people to chat representatives because many lacked the language skills necessary to write clear and correct messages. They were good at talking but not at writing, again making the point that the Internet has increased the need for superior writing skills.

Writing Concisely for Microblogging on Social Media Networks

Concise expression is especially important in microblogging. As its name suggests, *microblogging* consists of short messages exchanged on social media networks such as Twitter, Facebook, and Tumblr. Many businesses are eagerly joining these microblogging networks to hear what is being said about them and their products. When they hear complaints, they can respond immediately and often solve customer problems. Companies are also using microblogging to make announcements, promote goodwill, and sell their products.

Microblogging may be public or private. Twitter and similar social networks are public channels with messages broadcast externally to the world. Twitter limits each post ("tweet") to 140 characters, including spaces, punctuation, and links. Recognizing the usefulness of microblogging but desiring more confidentiality and security, some companies prefer to keep their messages internal. IBM, for example, employs BlueTwit, a tool that enables IBMers to share real-time news and get help from colleagues without going outside the organization. BlueTwit extends the length of messages to 400 characters.

Regardless of the microblogging network, conciseness is critical. Your messages must be short—without straying too far from conventional spelling, grammar, and punctuation. Sound difficult? It is, but it can be done, as shown in the following 140-character examples of workplace tweets:

Sample Response to Customer Complaint

@complainer Our manual can be confusing about that problem. Call me at 800-123-4567 or see http://bit.ly/xx for easy fix. Thanks, Henry[11]

To find out what makes a tweet good or bad, university researchers recently asked 1,400 Twitter users to rate thousands of tweets. The study found that tweets rated as good typically conveyed useful information or humor, or even posed questions to followers. Tweets rated as bad typically contained status updates, cryptic messages, negativity, or hashtag clutter. All in all, survey respondents said just 36 percent of tweets were worth reading. What guidelines should business communicators follow to help ensure that their microblogging messages are engaging yet professional?[12]

Zappos CEO Announces Meeting

Livestreaming the Zappos Family quarterly all hands meeting 1-5 PM Pacific today! Tune in: http://on.fb.me/allhandslive[13]

Southwest Airlines Explains

Southwest Airlines responds to loss of pressurization event on flight from PHX to SMF [with a link to a Southwest statement about the event][14]

Starbucks Thanks Customers

Throughout April, you contributed 231,000+ hours of community service in 34 countries across five continents. Thank You! #monthofservice[15]

When you are microblogging, (a) include only main ideas, (b) choose descriptive but short words, (c) personalize your message if possible, and (d) be prepared to write several versions striving for conciseness, clarity, and, yes, even correctness. It's like playing a game: can you get your message across in only 140 characters?

Making Your Message Clear

A major revision task involves assessing the clarity of your message. A clear message is one that is immediately understood. Employees, customers, and investors increasingly want to be addressed in a clear and genuine way. Fuzzy, long-winded, and unclear writing prevents comprehension. Readers understand better when information is presented clearly and concisely, as a Dartmouth study illustrates in Figure 6.3. Three techniques can improve the clarity of your writing: applying the KISS formula (Keep It Short and Simple), dumping trite business phrases, and avoiding clichés and slang.

LEARNING OBJECTIVE **2**
Improve clarity in business messages by keeping the ideas simple, dumping trite business phrases, dropping clichés, avoiding slang and buzzwords, rescuing buried verbs, and controlling exuberance.

REALITY CHECK: Even a Cartoonist Must Learn to Write Directly and Simply

Scott Adams, creator of the Dilbert cartoon, knows that even cartoonists must learn to write directly and simply. "I took a two-day class in business writing that taught me how to write direct sentences and to avoid extra words. Simplicity makes ideas powerful. Want examples? Read anything by Steve Jobs or Warren Buffet."[16]

—**SCOTT ADAMS,** *Dilbert cartoonist*

Figure **6.3** Conciseness Improves Clarity in Understanding Drug Facts

Consumers understand drug effects better when the information is presented concisely and clearly. A Dartmouth University study revealed that concise fact boxes were superior to the tiny-type, full-page DTC (direct-to-consumer) advertisements that drug manufacturers usually publish.

People who correctly quantified a heart drug's benefits after reading concise fact box.

People who correctly quantified a heart drug's benefits after reading the company's long ad.

Source: Based on Rubin, R. (2009, February 7). Concise drug-facts boxes vs. "brief" summaries, *USA Today*, p. D7.

Keep It Short and Simple

To achieve clarity, resist the urge to show off or be fancy. Remember that your goal is not to impress a reader. As a business writer, your goal is to *express*, not *impress*. One way to achieve clear writing is to apply the familiar KISS formula. Use active-voice sentences that avoid indirect, pompous language.

Wordy and Unclear	Improved
Employees have not been made sufficiently aware of the potentially adverse consequences regarding the use of these perilous chemicals.	Warn your employees about these dangerous chemicals.
In regard to the matter of obtaining optimal results, it is essential that employees be given the implements that are necessary for jobs to be completed satisfactorily.	To get the best results, give employees the tools they need to do the job.

Dumping Trite Business Phrases

To sound "businesslike," some business writers repeat the same stale expressions that others have used over the years. Your writing will sound fresher and more vigorous if you eliminate these trite phrases or find more original ways to convey the idea.

Trite Phrase	Improved
as per your request	as you request
pursuant to your request	at your request
enclosed please find	enclosed is
every effort will be made	we'll try
in accordance with your wishes	as you wish
in receipt of	have received
please do not hesitate to	please
respond forthwith	respond immediately
thank you in advance	thank you
under separate cover	separately
with reference to	about

Dropping Clichés

Clichés are expressions that have become exhausted by overuse. Many cannot be explained, especially to those who are new to our culture. Clichés lack not only freshness but also clarity. Instead of repeating clichés such as the following, try to find another way to say what you mean.

Clichés	
below the belt	last but not least
better than new	make a bundle
beyond a shadow of a doubt	pass with flying colors
easier said than done	quick as a flash
exception to the rule	shoot from the hip
fill the bill	stand your ground
first and foremost	think outside the box
good to go	true to form

REALITY CHECK: What's Bad, Boring, and Barely Read All Over?

"If you could taste words, most corporate websites, brochures, and sales materials would remind you of stale, soggy rice cakes: nearly calorie free, devoid of nutrition, and completely unsatisfying.... Unfortunately, years of language dilution by lawyers, marketers, executives, and HR departments have turned the powerful, descriptive sentence into an empty vessel optimized for buzzwords, jargon, and vapid expressions."[17]

—**JASON FRIED,** *software developer and cofounder of 37 signals*

Avoiding Slang and Buzzwords

Slang is composed of informal words with arbitrary and extravagantly changed meanings. Slang words quickly go out of fashion because they are no longer appealing when everyone begins to understand them. If you want to sound professional, avoid expressions such as *snarky, lousy, blowing the budget, bombed, getting burned,* and other slangy expressions.

Buzzwords are technical expressions that have become fashionable and often are meant to impress rather than express. Business buzzwords include empty terms such as *optimize, incentivize, innovative, leveraging, right-size,* and *paradigm shift.* Countless businesses today use vague rhetoric such as *cost effective, positioned to perform, solutions-oriented,* and *value-added services with end-to-end fulfillment.*

Consider the following statement of a government official who had been asked why his department was dropping a proposal to lease offshore oil lands: *The Administration has an awful lot of other things in the pipeline, and this has more wiggle room so they just moved it down the totem pole.* He added, however, that the proposal might be offered again since *there is no pulling back because of hot-potato factors.* What exactly does this mean?

Rescuing Buried Verbs

Buried verbs are those that are needlessly converted to wordy noun expressions. This happens when verbs such as *acquire, establish,* and *develop* are made into nouns such as *acquisition, establishment,* and *development.* Such nouns often end in *-tion, -ment,* and *-ance.* Sometimes called *zombie nouns* because they cannibalize and suck the life out of active verbs,[18] these nouns increase sentence length, slow the reader, and muddy the thought. Notice how you can make your writing cleaner and more forceful by avoiding buried verbs and zombie nouns:

Buried Verbs	Unburied Verbs
conduct a discussion of	discuss
create a reduction in	reduce
engage in the preparation of	prepare
give consideration to	consider
make an assumption of	assume
make a discovery of	discover
perform an analysis of	analyze
reach a conclusion that	conclude
take action on	act

Controlling Exuberance

Occasionally, we show our exuberance with words such as *very, definitely, quite, completely, extremely, really, actually,* and *totally.* These intensifiers can emphasize and strengthen your meaning. Overuse, however, sounds unbusinesslike. Control your enthusiasm and guard against excessive use.

Excessive Exuberance	Businesslike
The manufacturer was *extremely* upset to learn that its smartphones were *definitely* being counterfeited.	The manufacturer was upset to learn that its smartphones were being counterfeited.
We *totally* agree that we *actually* did not give his proposal a *very* fair trial.	We agree that we did not give his proposal a fair trial.

© iStockphoto.com/Andrew Johnson

LEARNING OBJECTIVE **3**
Enhance readability by understanding document design including the use of white space, margins, typefaces, fonts, numbered and bulleted lists, and headings.

Enhancing Readability Through Document Design

Well-designed documents improve your messages in two important ways. First, they enhance readability and comprehension. Second, they make readers think you are a well-organized and intelligent person. When revising, you have a chance to adjust formatting and make other changes so that readers grasp your main points quickly. Significant design techniques to improve readability include the appropriate use of white space, margins, typefaces, numbered and bulleted lists, and headings for visual impact.

> When revising, you have a chance to adjust formatting and make other changes so that readers grasp your main points quickly.

Employing White Space

Empty space on a page is called *white space.* A page crammed full of text or graphics appears busy, cluttered, and unreadable. To increase white space, use headings, bulleted or numbered lists, and effective margins. Remember that short sentences (20 or fewer words) and short paragraphs (eight or fewer printed lines) improve readability and comprehension. As you revise, think about shortening long sentences. Consider breaking up long paragraphs into shorter chunks.

Understanding Margins and Text Alignment

Margins determine the white space on the left, right, top, and bottom of a block of type. They define the reading area and provide important visual relief. Business letters and memos usually have side margins of 1 to 1.5 inches.

Your word processing program probably offers four forms of margin alignment: (a) lines align only at the left, (b) lines align only at the right, (c) lines align at both left and right (*justified*), and (d) lines are centered. Nearly all text in Western cultures is aligned at the left and reads from left to right. The right margin may be either *justified* or *ragged right*. The text in books, magazines, and other long works is often justified on the left and right for a formal appearance.

Justified text, however, may require more attention to word spacing and hyphenation to avoid awkward empty spaces or "rivers" of spaces running through a document. When right margins are *ragged*—that is, without alignment or justification—they provide more white space and improve readability. Therefore, you are best served by using left-justified text and ragged-right margins without justification. Centered text is appropriate for headings and short invitations but not for complete messages.

Choosing Appropriate Typefaces

Business writers today may choose from a number of typefaces on their word processors. A typeface defines the shape of text characters. A wide range of typefaces, as shown in Figure 6.4, is available for various purposes. Some are decorative and useful for special purposes. For most business messages, however, you should choose from *serif* or *sans serif* categories.

Serif typefaces have small features at the ends of strokes. The most common serif typeface is Times New Roman. Other popular serif typefaces are Century, Georgia, and Palatino. Serif typefaces suggest tradition, maturity, and formality. They are frequently used for body text in business messages and longer documents. Because books, newspapers, and magazines favor serif typefaces, readers are familiar with them.

Sans serif typefaces include Arial, Calibri, Gothic, Tahoma, Helvetica, and Univers. These clean characters are widely used for headings, signs, and material that does not require continuous reading. Web designers often prefer sans serif typefaces for simple, pure pages. For longer documents, however, sans serif typefaces may seem colder and less accessible than familiar serif typefaces.

For less formal messages or special decorative effects, you might choose one of the happy fonts such as Comic Sans or a bold typeface such as Impact. You can simulate handwriting with a script typeface. Despite the wonderful possibilities available on your word processor, don't get carried away with fancy typefaces. All-purpose sans serif and traditional serif typefaces are most appropriate for your business messages. Generally, use no more than two typefaces within one document.

Figure **6.4** Typefaces With Different Personalities for Different Purposes

All-Purpose Sans Serif	Traditional Serif	Happy, Creative Script/Funny	Assertive, Bold Modern Display	Plain Monospaced
Arial	Century	Brush Script	Britannic Bold	Courier
Calibri	Garamond	Comic Sans	Broadway	Letter Gothic
Helvetica	Georgia	Gigi	Elephant	Monaco
Tahoma	Goudy	Jokerman	Impact	Prestige Elite
Univers	Palatino	Lucinda	Bauhaus 93	
Verdana	Times New Roman	Kristen	SHOWCARD	

© Cengage Learning 2015

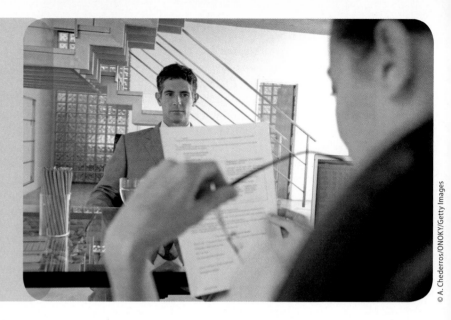
© A. Chederros/ONOKY/Getty Images

For most individuals, choosing a font is a matter of personal taste. But for today's job seekers, choosing a font is increasingly about selecting a typeface that meets the requirements of computer scanning and filtering software. To automate the task of job recruiting, businesses use computers that scan and sort résumés based on descriptive keywords. Résumés and other documents that fail to comply with the system's preferred fonts and formatting face instant rejection. What principles of document design can help guide business writers in their choice of fonts and typefaces?[19]

Capitalizing on Type Fonts and Sizes

Font refers to a specific style (such as *italic*) within a typeface family (such as Times New Roman). Most typeface families offer various fonts such as CAPITALIZATION, SMALL CAPS, **boldface**, *italic*, and underline, as well as less common fonts such as outline and shadow.

Font styles are a mechanical means of adding emphasis to your words. ALL CAPS, SMALL CAPS, and **bold** are useful for headings, subheadings, and single words or short phrases in the text. ALL CAPS, HOWEVER, SHOULD NEVER BE USED FOR LONG STRETCHES OF TEXT BECAUSE ALL THE LETTERS ARE THE SAME HEIGHT, MAKING IT DIFFICULT FOR READERS TO DIFFERENTIATE WORDS. In addition, excessive use of all caps feels like shouting and irritates readers. **Boldface,** *italics*, and underlining are effective for calling attention to important points and terms. Be cautious, however, when using fancy or an excessive number of font styles. Don't use them if they will confuse, annoy, or delay readers.

During the revision process, think about type size. Readers are generally most comfortable with 10- to 12-point type for body text. Smaller type enables you to fit more words into a space. Tiny type, however, makes text look dense and unappealing. Slightly larger type makes material more readable. Overly large type (14 points or more) looks amateurish and out of place for body text in business messages. Larger type, however, is appropriate for headings.

Numbering and Bulleting Lists for Quick Comprehension

One of the best ways to ensure rapid comprehension of ideas is through the use of numbered or bulleted lists. Lists provide high "skim value." This means that readers can browse quickly and grasp main ideas. By breaking up complex information into smaller chunks, lists improve readability, understanding, and retention. They also force the writer to organize ideas and write efficiently.

In the revision process, look for ideas that could be converted to lists, and follow these techniques to make your lists look professional:

- **Numbered lists:** Use for items that represent a sequence or reflect a numbering system.
- **Bulleted lists:** Use to highlight items that don't necessarily show a chronology.
- **Capitalization:** Capitalize the initial word of each line.
- **Punctuation:** Add end punctuation only if the listed items are complete sentences.
- **Parallelism:** Make all the lines consistent; for example, start each with a verb.

In the following examples, notice that the list on the left presents a sequence of steps with numbers. The bulleted list does not show a sequence of ideas; therefore, bullets are appropriate. Also notice the parallelism in each example. In the numbered list, each item begins with a verb. In the bulleted list, each item follows an adjective/noun sequence. Business readers appreciate lists because they focus attention. Be careful, however, not to use so many that your messages look like grocery lists.

Numbered List	Bulleted List
Our recruiters follow these steps when hiring applicants: 1. Examine the application. 2. Interview the applicant. 3. Check the applicant's references.	To attract upscale customers, we feature the following: • Quality fashions • Personalized service • Generous return policy

REALITY CHECK: Complaining of an Avalanche of Impenetrable Verbiage

An advocate for plain English, Arthur Levitt champions readability in investor documents. He advocates using the active voice, familiar words, and graphic techniques such as boldface, headings, and lists. However, he has been only partially successful, he complains, because such efforts "get tugged into the ditch by the irresistible pull of legal jargon" with documents "buried in an avalanche of impenetrable verbiage."[20]

—**ARTHUR LEVITT,** *former chair, U.S. Securities and Exchange Commission*

Adding Headings for Visual Impact

Headings are an effective tool for highlighting information and improving readability. They encourage the writer to group similar material together. Headings help the reader separate major ideas from details. They enable a busy reader to skim familiar or less important information. They also provide a quick preview or review. Headings appear most often in reports, which you will study in greater detail in Chapters 11, 12, and 13. However, main headings, subheadings, and category headings can also improve readability in e-mails, memos, and letters. In the following example, they are used with bullets to summarize categories:

Category Headings

Our company focuses on the following areas in the employment process:

- **Attracting applicants.** We advertise for qualified applicants, and we also encourage current employees to recommend good people.

- **Interviewing applicants.** Our specialized interviews include simulated customer encounters as well as scrutiny by supervisors.

- **Checking references.** We investigate every applicant thoroughly. We contact former employers and all listed references.

In Figure 6.5 the writer was able to convert a dense, unappealing e-mail message into an easier-to-read version by applying document design. Notice that the all-caps font in the first paragraph makes its meaning difficult to decipher. Justified margins and lack of white space further reduce readability. In the revised version, the writer changed the all-caps font to upper- and lowercase and also used ragged-right margins to enhance visual appeal. One of the best document design techniques in this message is the use of headings and bullets to help the reader see chunks of information in similar groups. All of these improvements are made in the revision process. You can make any message more readable by applying the document design techniques presented here.

ETHICS CHECK:

Costly Writing

Bad writing can be expensive: A Philadelphia lawyer was charged with malpractice to the tune of $6.6 million for drafting a poor commercial lease. The judge in Los Angeles said the draft was "inartfully written and done so in a confusing fashion, which lends itself to ambiguities and disagreements."[21] Can you think of other situations in which writing can be deliberately or accidentally misleading and expensive?

Figure **6.5** Document Design Improves Readability

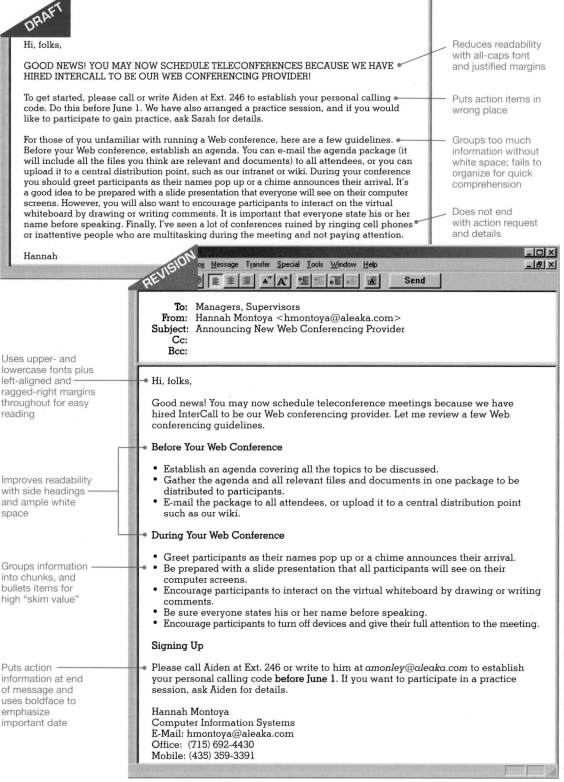

DRAFT

Hi, folks,

GOOD NEWS! YOU MAY NOW SCHEDULE TELECONFERENCES BECAUSE WE HAVE HIRED INTERCALL TO BE OUR WEB CONFERENCING PROVIDER!

To get started, please call or write Aiden at Ext. 246 to establish your personal calling code. Do this before June 1. We have also arranged a practice session, and if you would like to participate to gain practice, ask Sarah for details.

For those of you unfamiliar with running a Web conference, here are a few guidelines. Before your Web conference, establish an agenda. You can e-mail the agenda package (it will include all the files you think are relevant and documents) to all attendees, or you can upload it to a central distribution point, such as our intranet or wiki. During your conference you should greet participants as their names pop up or a chime announces their arrival. It's a good idea to be prepared with a slide presentation that everyone will see on their computer screens. However, you will also want to encourage participants to interact on the virtual whiteboard by drawing or writing comments. It is important that everyone state his or her name before speaking. Finally, I've seen a lot of conferences ruined by ringing cell phones or inattentive people who are multitasking during the meeting and not paying attention.

Hannah

Reduces readability with all-caps font and justified margins

Puts action items in wrong place

Groups too much information without white space; fails to organize for quick comprehension

Does not end with action request and details

REVISION

Message   Transfer   Special   Tools   Window   Help   **Send**

To: Managers, Supervisors
From: Hannah Montoya <hmontoya@aleaka.com>
Subject: Announcing New Web Conferencing Provider
Cc:
Bcc:

Hi, folks,

Good news! You may now schedule teleconference meetings because we have hired InterCall to be our Web conferencing provider. Let me review a few Web conferencing guidelines.

Before Your Web Conference

- Establish an agenda covering all the topics to be discussed.
- Gather the agenda and all relevant files and documents in one package to be distributed to participants.
- E-mail the package to all attendees, or upload it to a central distribution point such as our wiki.

During Your Web Conference

- Greet participants as their names pop up or a chime announces their arrival.
- Be prepared with a slide presentation that all participants will see on their computer screens.
- Encourage participants to interact on the virtual whiteboard by drawing or writing comments.
- Be sure everyone states his or her name before speaking.
- Encourage participants to turn off devices and give their full attention to the meeting.

Signing Up

Please call Aiden at Ext. 246 or write to him at *amonley@aleaka.com* to establish your personal calling code **before June 1**. If you want to participate in a practice session, ask Aiden for details.

Hannah Montoya
Computer Information Systems
E-Mail: hmontoya@aleaka.com
Office: (715) 692-4430
Mobile: (435) 359-3391

Uses upper- and lowercase fonts plus left-aligned and ragged-right margins throughout for easy reading

Improves readability with side headings and ample white space

Groups information into chunks, and bullets items for high "skim value"

Puts action information at end of message and uses boldface to emphasize important date

Proofreading to Catch Errors

Alas, none of us is perfect, and even the best writers sometimes make mistakes. The problem, however, is not making the mistakes; the real problem is not finding and correcting them. Documents with errors affect your credibility and the success of your organization, as illustrated in Figure 6.6.

Once you have the message in its final form, it's time to proofread. Don't proofread earlier because you may waste time checking items that eventually are changed or omitted. Important messages—such as those you send to management or to customers or turn in to instructors for grades—deserve careful revision and proofreading. When you finish a first draft, plan for a cooling-off period. Put the document aside and return to it after a break, preferably after 24 hours or longer. Proofreading is especially difficult because most of us read what we thought we wrote. That's why it's important to look for specific problem areas.

What to Watch for in Proofreading

Careful proofreaders check for problems in the following areas:

Spelling Now is the time to consult the dictionary. Is *recommend* spelled with one or two *c*'s? Do you mean *affect* or *effect*? Use your computer spell-checker, but don't rely on it totally.

Figure **6.6** Why Proofread? In Business, Accuracy Matters

Source: Based on PenroseMcNab Consulting. (2010) Poor grammar and business. Retrieved from http://www.penrosemcnab.com/theproblem.htm

Grammar Locate sentence subjects; do their verbs agree with them? Do pronouns agree with their antecedents? Review the grammar and mechanics principles in Appendix A if necessary. Use your computer's grammar-checker, but be suspicious because grammar checkers may mismark supposed "errors."

Punctuation Make sure that introductory clauses are followed by commas. In compound sentences put commas before coordinating conjunctions (*and, or, but, nor*). Double-check your use of semicolons and colons.

Names and numbers Compare all names and numbers with their sources because inaccuracies are not always visible. Especially verify the spelling of the names of individuals receiving the message. Most of us immediately dislike someone who misspells our name.

Format Be sure that your document looks balanced on the page. Compare its parts and format with those of standard documents shown in Appendix B. If you indent paragraphs, be certain that all are indented.

How to Proofread Routine Documents

Most routine documents require a light proofreading. If you read on screen, use the down arrow to reveal one line at a time. This focuses your attention at the bottom of the screen. A safer proofreading method, however, is reading from a printed copy. Regardless of which method you use, look for typos and misspellings. Search for easily confused words, such as *to* for *too* and *then* for *than*. Read for missing words and inconsistencies. For handwritten or printed messages, use standard proofreading marks, shown briefly in Figure 6.1 or completely in Appendix D. For digital documents and collaborative projects, use the simple word processing tools also shown in Figure 6.1 or use the **Comment** and **Track Changes** functions described in Chapter 4, Figure 4.10 on page 143.

How to Proofread Complex Documents

Long, complex, or important documents demand careful proofreading. Apply the previous suggestions but also add the following techniques:

- Print a copy, preferably double-spaced, and set it aside for at least a day. You will be more alert after a breather.
- Allow adequate time to proofread carefully. A common excuse for sloppy proofreading is lack of time.
- Be prepared to find errors. One student confessed, "I can find other people's errors, but I can't seem to locate my own." Psychologically, we don't expect to find errors, and we don't want to find them. You can overcome this obstacle by anticipating errors and congratulating, not criticizing, yourself each time you find one.
- Read the message at least twice—once for word meanings and once for grammar and mechanics. For very long documents (book chapters and long articles or reports), read a third time to verify consistency in formatting.
- Reduce your reading speed. Concentrate on individual words rather than ideas.
- For documents that must be perfect, enlist a proofreading buddy. Have someone read the message aloud. Spell names and difficult words, note capitalization, and read punctuation.
- Use the standard proofreading marks shown in Appendix D to indicate changes.

Many of us struggle with proofreading our own writing because we are seeing the same information over and over. We tend to see what we expect to see as our eyes race over the words without looking at each one carefully. We tend to know what is coming next and glide over it. To change the appearance of what you are reading, you might print it on a different colored paper or change the font. If you are proofing on screen, enlarge the page view or change the background color of the screen.

Evaluating the Effectiveness of Your Message

LEARNING OBJECTIVE **5**
Evaluate a message to judge its effectiveness.

As part of applying finishing touches, take a moment to evaluate your writing. Remember that everything you write, whether for yourself or someone else, takes the place of a personal appearance. If you were meeting in person, you would be certain to dress appropriately and professionally. The same standard applies to your writing. Evaluate what you have written to be certain that it attracts the reader's attention. Is it polished and clear enough to convince the reader that you are worth listening to? How successful will this message be? Does it say what you want it to? Will it achieve your purpose? How will you know whether it succeeds?

The best way to judge the success of your communication is through feedback. For this reason you should encourage the receiver to respond to your message. This feedback will tell you how to modify future efforts to improve your communication technique.

Your instructor will also be evaluating some of your writing. Although any criticism is painful, try not to be defensive. Look on these comments as valuable advice tailored to your specific writing weaknesses—and strengths. Many businesses today spend thousands of dollars bringing in communication consultants to improve employee writing skills. You are getting the same training in this course. Take advantage of this chance—one of the few you may have—to improve your skills. The best way to improve your skills, of course, is through instruction, practice, and evaluation.

In this class you have all three elements: instruction in the writing process, practice materials, and someone to guide you and evaluate your efforts. Those three elements are the reasons this book and this course may be the most valuable in your entire curriculum. Because it's almost impossible to improve your communication skills alone, take advantage of this opportunity.

The task of editing, proofreading, and evaluating, summarized in the following checklist, is hard work. It demands objectivity and a willingness to cut, cut, cut. Though painful, the process is also gratifying. It's a great feeling when you realize your finished message is clear, concise, and effective.

CHECKLIST ⏩
Editing, Proofreading, and Evaluating

- **Eliminate flabby expressions.** Strive to reduce wordy phrases to single words (*as a general rule* becomes *generally*; *at this point in time* becomes *now*).

- **Avoid opening fillers and long lead-ins.** Revise sentences so that they don't start with fillers (*there is, there are, it is, it was*) and long lead-ins (*this is to inform you that*).

- **Shun redundancies.** Eliminate words that repeat meanings, such as *refer back*. Watch for repetitious adjectives, adverbs, and phrases.

- **Tighten your writing.** Check phrases that include *case, degree, the fact that, factor,* and other words and phrases that unnecessarily increase wordiness. Avoid saying the obvious.

- **Write concisely for microblogging.** Keep your messages short without sacrificing proper spelling, grammar, and punctuation.

- **Keep the message simple.** Express ideas directly. Don't show off or use fancy language.

- **Avoid trite business phrases.** Keep your writing fresh, direct, and contemporary by skipping such expressions as *enclosed please find* and *pursuant to your request*.

- **Don't use clichés or slang.** Avoid expressions that are overused and unclear (*below the belt, shoot from the hip*). Don't use slang, which is not only unprofessional but also often unclear to a wide audience.

(Continued)

© Daniilantiq/Shutterstock.com

Editing, Proofreading, and Evaluating (continued)

- **Rescue buried verbs.** Keep your writing vigorous by not converting verbs to nouns (*analyze* not *make an analysis of*).

- **Control exuberance.** Avoid overusing intensifiers such as *really, very, definitely, quite, completely, extremely, actually,* and *totally.*

- **Improve readability through document design.** Use bullets, lists, headings, capital letters, underlining, boldface, italics, and blank space to spotlight ideas and organize them.

- **Proofread for correctness.** Check spelling, grammar, and punctuation. Compare names and numbers with their sources. Double-check the format to be sure you have been consistent.

- **Evaluate your final product.** Will your message achieve its purpose? Could it be improved? How will you know whether it is successful?

Your Turn: Applying Your Skills at Taco Bell

Assume that Taco Bell managers have asked the newly hired culinary product manager to anticipate trends in Mexican foods and improve the Taco Bell menu. Part of the challenge is recognizing trends that consumers haven't even picked up yet and then working these trends into restaurant products. The culinary product manager has prepared a rough draft of a memo summarizing her longer report, which will be presented at a management meeting next week.

Although exceptionally talented in cuisine, she realizes that her writing skills are not as well developed as her cooking skills. She comes to the corporate communication department and shows your boss the first draft of her memo. Your boss is a nice guy, and, as a favor, he revises the first two paragraphs, shown in Figure 6.7.

YOUR TASK. Your boss, the head of corporate communication, has many important tasks to oversee. He hands the product manager's memo to you, his assistant, and tells you to finish cleaning it up. He adds, "Her ideas are right on target, but the main points are totally lost in wordy sentences and dense paragraphs. Revise this and concentrate on conciseness, clarity, and readability. Don't you think some bulleted lists would help this memo a lot?" Revise the remaining four paragraphs of the memo using the techniques you learned in this chapter. Prepare a copy of the complete memo to submit to your boss (your instructor).

Figure **6.7** Partially Revised First Draft

DRAFT

Revises trite expression (*as per your request*) and uses first-person pronoun

Reduces wordiness throughout

Deletes *and foremost*; reduces excessive exuberance (*more*, *much more*, and *totally*)

Shortens *that I gained firsthand* to one word, *firsthand*, and deletes redundant *reading and*

Look for ways to reduce wordiness in headings and throughout

Improves subject line

Eliminates long lead in (*This is to inform you that*) and shortens *represents a summary* to the verb *summarizes*

Achieves parallelism

Unburies verb by changing *made an observation* to *observed*

Date: August 13, 2015
To: Taco Bell Management Council
From: Rosa Navarro, Culinary Product Manager
Subject: ~~My Menu Ideas~~ *Fast-Food Trends and New Menu Options*

~~As per~~ your request, ~~the writer is~~ *ed I am* submitting ~~herewith~~ the following ideas ~~that are~~ based on ~~her personal~~ *my* observation and research ~~in regard to~~ *about* eating trends ~~in relation to~~ restaurants ~~that serve~~ fast-food. ~~As you suggested, I am also offering~~ below *is* a rough outline of possible concepts to ~~upgrade and~~ enhance Taco Bell's menu. ~~This is to inform you that~~ this memo ~~represents a~~ summar*izes* ~~of~~ the findings ~~that I have extracted~~ from my longer report to be presented at your next Management Council meeting.

First ~~and foremost~~, I will ~~be~~ focus*ing* on ~~more~~ upscale menu items with ~~much more~~ sophisticated flavors and ~~totally~~ fresh ingredients. However, I know that ~~they~~ *the items* must also meet Taco Bell's strict criteria: high-quality flavor, ~~they must be portable~~ *portability*, and ~~they must be easily produced~~ *ease of production*. In an economy ~~that is~~ depressed, our restaurant can and ~~most certainly~~ should offer value as well as *tasty* food ~~that tastes very good~~. From my experience ~~that I gained~~ firsthand as a chef and from current ~~reading and~~ research, I have ~~made an~~ observ*ed* ~~ation of~~ numerous eating trends.

Currently What's Happening in Eating Trends

Low-fat, healthful choices are an important current trend. It's totally amazing that there are as many as one in five U.S. consumers on a diet. That's why our menu should reflect low-calorie, healthful options that still taste good. Spicy foods and freshness are additional trends. As consumers become more knowledgeable and as more knowledge is available to them, they are demanding ingredients that are fresher. A final trend is the demand for low prices. In an economic downturn, there are definitely consumers who want meals that won't break their budgets.

Use bulleted list with headings to improve readability

Convert noun phrase (*have a discussion*) to a verb (*discuss*) and reduce other wordiness

Summary of My Ideas for New Menu Concepts

Despite the fact that my full report contains a number of additional trends and menu ideas, I will concentrate below on three significant menu concepts that I think are important. First, I am of the opinion that we should add a new menu called **Cantina Bell**. This menu will offer exciting ingredients such as black beans, roasted corn salsa, and romaine lettuce with a cilantro-lime dressing. There will be chicken reformulated with a light citrus marinade, and our guacamole and pico di gallo will be tweaked with new seasonings and fresh cilantro.

A second idea involves a **Fresco Menu**. I would like to see us offer an entire menu of ten or more items that cater to dieters and customers who are health conscious. The Fresco menu might include Crunchy Beef Taco, Grilled Steak Taco, Blazing Bean Burrito, and Ranchero Chicken Soft Taco. These low-calorie items that are also low fat will contain fewer than 10 grams of fat, but they would be tasty, they would be filling, and they would be inexpensive. I would also like to recommend a **Self-Serve Salsa Bar**. In relation to this, we could offer exotic salsas that are fresh but with bold flavors and textures.

I would be more than delighted and happy to have a discussion of these ideas with you in greater detail and to have a demonstration of them in the test kitchen. Thanks for this opportunity to work with you in the expansion of our menu in a move to ensure that Taco Bell remains tops in Mexican cuisine.

© Cengage Learning 2015

Summary of Learning Objectives

1 Complete business messages by revising for conciseness, which includes eliminating flabby expressions, long lead-ins, *there is/are* and *it is/was* fillers, redundancies, and empty words, as well as condensing for microblogging. Concise messages make their points using the least number of words. Revising for conciseness involves eliminating flabby expressions (*as a general rule, at a later date, at this point in time*). Concise writing also excludes opening fillers (*there is, there are*), redundancies (*basic essentials*), and empty words (*in the case of, the fact that*). Conciseness is especially important in revising microblogging messages as short as 140 characters.

2 Improve clarity in business messages by keeping the ideas simple, dumping trite business phrases, dropping clichés, avoiding slang and buzzwords, rescuing buried verbs, and controlling exuberance. To be sure your messages are clear, apply the KISS formula: Keep It Short and Simple. Avoid foggy, indirect, and pompous language. Do not include trite business phrases (*as per your request, enclosed please find, pursuant to your request*), clichés (*better than new, beyond a shadow of a doubt, easier said than done*), slang (*snarky, lousy, bombed*), and buzzwords (*optimize, paradigm shift, incentivize*). Also avoid burying nouns (*to conduct an investigation* rather than *to investigate, to perform an analysis* rather than *to analyze*). Converting a verb into a noun lengthens the sentence, saps the force of the verb, and muddies the message. Finally, do not overuse intensifiers that show exuberance (*totally, actually, very, definitely*). These words can emphasize and strengthen meaning, but overusing them makes your messages sound unbusinesslike.

3 Enhance readability by understanding document design including the use of white space, margins, typefaces, fonts, numbered and bulleted lists, and headings. Well-designed messages enhance readability and comprehension. The most readable messages have ample white space, appropriate side margins, and ragged-right (not justified) margins. Serif typefaces (fonts with small features at the ends of strokes, such as Times New Roman, Century, and Palatino) are often used for body text. Sans serif typefaces (clean fonts without small features, such as Arial, Helvetica, and Tahoma) are often used for headings and signs. Numbered and bulleted lists provide high "skim value" in messages. Headings add visual impact and aid readability in business messages as well as in reports.

4 Recognize proofreading problem areas, and apply effective techniques to catch mistakes in both routine and complex documents. Proofreaders must be especially alert to spelling, grammar, punctuation, names, numbers, and document format. Routine documents may be proofread immediately after completion. They may be read line by line on the computer screen or, better yet, from a printed draft copy. More complex documents, however, should be proofread after a breather. To do a good job, you should read from a printed copy, allow adequate time, reduce your reading speed, and read the document at least three times—for word meanings, for grammar and mechanics, and for formatting.

5 Evaluate a message to judge its effectiveness. Encourage feedback from the receiver so that you can determine whether your communication achieved its goal. Try to welcome any advice from your instructor on how to improve your writing skills. Both techniques help you evaluate the effectiveness of a message.

Chapter Review

1. What's involved in the revision process? Is revision still necessary in a digital age when workplace messages fly back and forth in split seconds? (Obj. 1)

2. What's wrong with a message that begins, *I am writing this announcement to let everyone know that . . . ?* (Obj. 1)

3. What is *microblogging,* and why is conciseness especially important in microblogging messages? (Obj. 1)

4. Why would a good writer avoid this sentence? *When I received your message, I read your message and am now replying.* (Obj. 1)

5. What's wrong with familiar business phrases such as *as per your request* and *enclosed please find*? (Obj. 2)

6. Why should writers avoid expressions such as *first and foremost* and *think outside the box*? (Obj. 2)

7. What are buried verbs and zombie nouns? Give an original example showing each. Why should they be avoided? (Obj. 2)

8. What is *white space* and why is it important for readability? (Obj. 3)

9. How do bulleted and numbered lists improve readability? (Obj. 3)

10. Should headings be used in correspondence such as e-mail, memos, and letters? (Obj. 3)

11. What is the difference between serif and sans serif typefaces? What is the preferred use for each? (Obj. 3)

12. What are five specific items to check in proofreading? Be ready to discuss methods you find useful in spotting these errors. (Obj. 4)

13. In proofreading, why is it difficult to find your own errors? How can you overcome this barrier? (Obj. 4)

14. List four or more effective techniques for proofreading complex documents. (Obj. 4)

15. How can you overcome defensiveness when your writing is criticized constructively? (Obj. 5)

Critical Thinking

1. In this digital age of rapid communication, how can you justify the time it takes to stop and revise a message? (Objs. 1–5)

2. Assume you have started a new job in which you respond to customers by using boilerplate (previously constructed) paragraphs. Some of them contain clichés such as *pursuant to your request* or *in accordance with your wishes.* Other paragraphs are wordy and violate the principle of using concise and clear writing that you have learned. What should you do? (Obj. 2)

3. Because business writing should have high "skim value," why not write everything in bulleted lists? (Obj. 3)

4. Conciseness is valued in business. However, can messages be too short? (Obj. 1)

5. **Ethical Issue:** What advice would you give in this ethical dilemma? Brittani is serving as interim editor of the company newsletter. She receives an article written by the company president describing, in abstract and pompous language, the company's goals for the coming year. Brittani thinks the article will need considerable revising to make it readable. Attached to the president's article are complimentary comments by two of the company vice presidents. What action should Brittani take?

Writing Improvement Exercises

6.1 Flabby Expressions (Obj. 1)

YOUR TASK. Revise the following sentences to eliminate flabby expressions.

a. We are sending a revised proposal at this point in time due to the fact that building costs have jumped at a considerable rate.

b. In the normal course of events, we would seek additional funding; however, in view of the fact that rates have increased, we cannot.

c. In very few cases has it been advisable for us to borrow money for a period of 90 or fewer days.

d. Inasmuch as our Web advertising income is increasing in a gradual manner, we might seek a loan in the amount of $50,000.

e. Despite the fact that we have had no response to our bid, we are still available in the event that you wish to proceed with your building project.

6.2 Long Lead-Ins (Obj. 1)

YOUR TASK. Revise the following to eliminate long lead-ins.

a. This is an announcement to tell you that all computer passwords must be changed every six months for security purposes.

b. We are sending this memo to notify everyone that anyone who wants to apply for telecommuting may submit an application immediately.

c. I am writing this letter to inform you that your new account executive is Edward Ho.

d. This is to warn you that cyber criminals use sophisticated tools to decipher passwords rapidly.

e. This message is to let you know that social media services can position your company at the forefront of online marketing opportunities.

6.3 There *is/are* and *it is/was* Fillers (Obj. 1)

YOUR TASK. Revise the following to avoid unnecessary *there is/are* and *it is/was* fillers.

a. There is a password-checker that is now available that can automatically evaluate the strength of your password.

b. It is careless or uninformed individuals who are the most vulnerable to computer hackers.

c. There are computers in Internet cafes, at conferences, and in airport lounges that should be considered unsafe for any personal use.

d. A computer specialist told us that there are keystroke-logging devices that gather information typed on a computer, including passwords.

e. If there are any questions that you have about computer safety, please call us.

6.4 Redundancies (Obj. 1)

YOUR TASK. Revise the following to avoid redundancies.

a. Because his laptop was small in size, he could carry it everywhere.

b. A basic fundamental of computer safety is to avoid storing your password on a file in your computer because criminals will look there first.

c. The manager repeated again his warning that we must use strong passwords.

d. Although the two files seem exactly identical, we should proofread each and every page.

e. The computer specialist combined together a PowerPoint presentation and a handout.

6.5 Empty Words (Obj. 1)

YOUR TASK. Revise the following to eliminate empty words.

a. Are you aware of the fact that social media can drive brand awareness and customer loyalty?

b. Except for the instance of MySpace, social networking sites are booming.

c. If you seek to build an online community that will support your customers, social media services can help.

d. With such a degree of active participation in Facebook and Twitter, it's easy to understand why businesses are flocking to social sites.

e. We plan to schedule online meetings on a monthly basis.

6.6 Condensing for Microblogging (Obj. 1)

YOUR TASK. Read the following real Twitter messages and write a 140-character microblog reply to each. Be selective in what you include. Your instructor may show you the actual responses (in the Instructor's Manual) that the company wrote.

a. **@HTWilson94 asks whether grocer Whole Foods stocks Whole Trade certified flowers all year long.**[22] Prepare a response (140 or fewer characters) based on the following information. Yes, at Whole Foods stores we do indeed offer Whole Trade certified flowers the entire year. We strongly advocate and support the Whole Trade movement, which strives to promote quality, premium price to the producer, better wages and working conditions, and the environment. However, we can't tell you exactly which Whole Trade certified flowers will be available at our stores and when. You would have to check with your local store for its specific selection.

b. **@AmyJean64 sent Bank of America a tweet saying she was frustrated with a real estate short sale. "Have a contract on a house and cannot get them to return calls to finalize."**[23] Prepare a response based on the following information: You work for Bank of America, and you would very much like to help her, but you can't without certain information. You need her to send you the property address along with her name and phone number so that you can call to see how you can help. She should probably DM (direct message) you with this crucial information.

c. **@VickiK wrote to JetBlue: "I have booked a flt in July, CA-VT. Wondering about flying my wedding dress w/me. Is there a safe place to hang it on the plane?"**[24] Prepare a response based on the following information. We congratulate you on your coming wedding! We bet your wedding dress is beautiful. We don't have special closets on our planes and certainly nothing big enough for a wedding dress. But here's a suggestion. Have you considered having it shipped ahead of time? All the best wishes on your upcoming happy event!

d. **@ChrisC sent a message to Southwest Airlines saying, "This is extremely frustrating, how is it possible for your website to be down the entire day?"**[25] Prepare a response based on the following information. Southwest is very, very sorry! It's extremely frustrating to us also. We realize that you are accustomed to using this site to book flights. Our IT people tell us that the website functionality is getting better. We are not sure exactly what that means in terms of availability, but we are very hopeful that customers will be able to book their flights soon.

e. **@JamesR. sent a message to the delivery service UPS complaining, "Holy XXX. It's after 6 pm and UPS still hasn't delivered my pkg yet."** Prepare a response based on the following information. UPS makes every effort to deliver all packages promptly. For packages destined for offices, we must deliver by 3 p.m. However, for packages going to residences, our goal is to deliver by 7 p.m. But we can't always make it, so our drivers can sometimes run later. We're sorry about the wait.

f. **@calinelb sent a message to H&R Block: "YOU SUCK! I've been waiting for my return more than 3.5 months."**[26] Prepare a response based on the following: We are sorry that you feel that way. We certainly can't understand the reason for this long delay. We would like to look into the matter, but before we can respond, we need you to send a DM (direct mail) to our customer service desk at @HRBlockAnswers. We will definitely check on this and get back to you.

6.7 Trite Business Phrases (Obj. 2)

YOUR TASK. Revise the following sentences to eliminate trite business phrases.

a. Pursuant to your request, I will submit your repair request immediately.

b. Enclosed please find the list of customers to be used in our promotion.

c. As per your request, we are sending the contract under separate cover.

d. Every effort will be made to proceed in accordance with your wishes.

e. If we may help in any way, please do not hesitate to call.

6.8 Clichés, Slang, Buzzwords, and Wordiness

YOUR TASK. Revise the following sentences to avoid confusing clichés, slang, buzzwords, and wordiness.

a. Our manager insists that we must think outside the box in promoting our new kitchen tool.

b. Although we got burned in the last contract, you can be sure we will stand our ground this time.

c. Beyond the shadow of a doubt, our lousy competitor will make another snarky claim that is below the belt.

d. If you refer back to our five-year plan, you will see that there are provisions for preventing blowing the budget.

e. BTW, have you heard the latest buzz about hackers ripping off customer info from Best Buy?

6.9 Buried Verbs

YOUR TASK. Revise the following to recover buried verbs.

a. After making an investigation, the fire department reached the conclusion that the blaze was set intentionally.

b. Our committee made a promise to give consideration to your proposal at its next meeting.

c. When used properly, zero-based budgeting can bring about a reduction in overall costs.

d. Did our department put in an application for increased budget support?

e. The budget committee has not taken action on any projects yet.

f. Homeowners must make a determination of the total value of their furnishings.

6.10 Lists, Bullets, and Headings (Obj. 3)

YOUR TASK. Revise the following poorly written sentences and paragraphs using lists, bullets, and category headings, if appropriate. Improve parallel construction and reduce wordiness.

a. **Three Best Twitter Practices.** There are three simple ways you can build an online following, drive your reputation, and develop customers' trust by using these uncomplicated and simple Twitter practices. First off, share some of your photos and information about your business from behind the scenes.

Sharing is so important ! Next, listen. That is, you should regularly monitor the comments about your company, what's being said about your brand, and any chatter about your products. And, of course, you should respond. In real time it is necessary to respond to statements that are compliments and just general feedback.

b. Revise the following by incorporating a numbered list.

Computer passwords are a way of life at this point in time. In the creation of a strong password, you should remember a few things. First, you should come up with an eight-word phrase that is easy to remember, such as *my favorite uncle was a fireman in Cleveland*. Then take each of those words and the first letter should be selected, such as *mfuwafic*. The last step for creating a really strong password is to exchange—that is, swap out—some of those letters for characters and capital letters, such as *Mf@w&%iC*.

c. Revise the following by incorporating a bulleted list with category headings.

Auto accidents account for a high number of accidental deaths. The most common causes of these accidents are due to the following causes. In all probability, the most common cause is distracted drivers. Makeup, cell phones, texting, food, and the morning newspaper are all common ways that drivers are being distracted. Another cause is most assuredly impaired driving. Alcohol and drugs impair judgment and reaction times. This obviously results in accidents. Another cause has got to be aggressive drivers. Being an aggressive driver instead of a defensive driver puts you at risk for getting involved in an accident. Finally, road rage is a significant cause. Drivers who get angry easily and then take it out on other drivers are one of the leading causes of accidents.

d. Revise the following by incorporating a bulleted list with category headings.

There are many people today who want to improve their credit scores. Some simple tips for bumping up your score are obvious. For one thing, you should immediately fix mistakes. If you check your credit report (and you should at least once a year) and there are errors, you can dispute these and have them investigated. Another way to improve your credit score is to pay on time. At least 35 percent of your score is a direct result of your payment history. Next, you should make an effort to lower and reduce your balances. It may be difficult, but you should keep your personal credit balances as low as possible. The less you're using, the better for your score. Finally, making a habit of keeping older accounts will improve your score. This means that you should keep your older cards so that you have a longer history to share. It also shows stability.

Activities

Note: All Documents for Analysis may be downloaded from **www.cengagebrain.com** so that you do not have to rekey the entire message.

6.11 Document for Analysis: Ineffective E-Mail Suggestion to Boss

E-mail **Team**

YOUR TASK. Study the following poorly written e-mail message. In teams or in class discussion, list at least five specific weaknesses. If your instructor directs, revise to remedy flabby expressions, long lead-ins, *there is/there are* fillers, trite business expressions, clichés, buried verbs, lack of parallelism, lack of plain English, and other problems.

To: Roger M. Karjala <r.m.karjala@firstbank.com>

From: Keiko Kurtz <k.kurtz@firstbank.com>

Subject: Suggestion for Improvement of Customer Relations

Cc:

Bcc:

Roger,

Because of the fact that you asked for suggestions on how to improve customer relations, I am submitting my idea. I am writing you this message to let you know that I think we can improve customer satisfaction easy by making a change in our counters.

Last December glass barriers were installed at our branch. There are tellers on one side and customers on the other. The barriers have air vents to be able to allow us tellers to carry on communication with our customers. Management thought that these barriers that are bullet proof would prevent and stop thieves from catapulting over the counter.

However there were customers who were surprised by these large glass partitions. Communication through them is really extremely difficult and hard. Both the customer and the teller have to raise their voices to be heard. It's even more of an inconvenience when you are dealing with a person that is elderly or someone who happens to be from another country. Beyond a shadow of a doubt, these new barriers make customers feel that they are being treated impersonal.

I did research into the matter of these barriers and made the discovery that we are the only bank in town with them. There are many other banks that are trying casual kiosks and open counters to make customers feel that they are more at home.

Although it may be easier said than done, I suggest that we actually give serious consideration to the removal of these barriers as a beginning and initial step toward improving customer relations.

Keiko Kurtz_____

E-mail: k.kurtz@firstbank.com

Support Services

(455) 549-2201

6.12 Document for Analysis: Poor E-Mail Message Re: PowerPoint (Objs. 1–5)

E-mail   **Team**

YOUR TASK. Study the following message. In teams or in class discussion, list at least five specific weaknesses. If your instructor directs, revise to remedy these weaknesses. Look for ways to improve readability with bulleted or numbered points.

To: Sanders Watson <swatson@circa.com>

From: Monique Vance <mvance@circa.com>

Subject: Avoiding Death by PowerPoint

Cc:

Sanders,

This message is being written because, pursuant to your request, I attended a seminar about the use of PowerPoint in business presentations. You suggested that there might be tips that I would learn that we could share with other staff members, many of whom make presentations that almost always include PowerPoint. The speaker, Bret Rivera, made some very good points on the subject of PowerPoint. There were several points of an important nature that

are useful in avoiding what he called "Death by PowerPoint." Our staff members should give consideration to the following:

Create first the message, not the slide. Only after preparing the entire script should you think about how to make an illustration of it.

You should prepare slides with short lines. Your slides should have only four to six words per line. Short lines act as an encouragement to people to listen to you and not read the slide.

Don't put each and every thing on the slide. If you put too much on the slide, your audience will be reading Item C while you are still talking about Item A. As a last and final point, he suggested that presenters think in terms of headlines. What is the main point? What does it mean to the audience?

Please do not hesitate to let me know whether you want me to elaborate and expand on these presentation techniques subsequent to the next staff meeting.

Monique

6.13 Document for Analysis: Poor Response to Customer Inquiry Re: Improving Security (Objs. 1–5)

Team

YOUR TASK. Study the following message. In teams or in class discussion, list at least five specific weaknesses. If your instructor directs, revise to remedy those weaknesses. Look for ways to improve readability with bulleted or numbered points.

Dear Mr. Perez:

We are happy to have received your request for information. As per your request, the undersigned is transmitting to you the attached documents with regard to the improvement of security in your business. To ensure the improvement of your after-hours security, you should initially make a decision with regard to exactly what you contemplate must have protection. You are, in all probability, apprehensive not only about your electronic equipment and paraphernalia but also about your company records, information, and data.

Due to the fact that we feel you will want to obtain protection for both your equipment and data, we will make suggestions for taking a number of judicious steps to inhibit crime. First and foremost, we make a recommendation that you install defensive lighting. A consultant for lighting, currently on our staff, can design both outside and inside lighting, which brings me to my second point. Exhibit security signs, because of the fact that nonprofessional thieves are often deterred by posted signs on windows and doors.

As my last and final recommendation, you should install space alarms, which are sensors that look down over the areas that are to receive protection, and activate bells or additional lights, thus scaring off intruders.

After reading the materials that are attached, please call me to initiate a verbal discussion regarding protection of your business.

Sincerely,

6.14 Document for Analysis: Poor Response to Customer Inquiry About Social Media (Objs. 1–5)

YOUR TASK. Study the following message. In teams or in class discussion, list at least five specific weaknesses. If your instructor directs, revise to remedy those weaknesses. Look for ways to improve readability with bulleted or numbered points.

To: Melanie Jackson <mjackson @mediasolutions.com>

From: Dakota Dalquist <ddalquist@mediasolutions.com>

Subject: Expanding Your Marketing by Joining the Social Media Buzz

Cc:

This is a message to thank you for your inquiry regarding Media Solutions! Due to the fact that the buzz around social media is so loud, you're exceedingly smart to want to understand the paths to success before you jump in so that you can avoid mistakes.

Using social media tools and networks involves connecting people, it involves interacting, and being able to share online. There is hardly a day that goes by without hearing about success stories that are truly remarkable coming from businesses getting active on social media sites like Facebook and Twitter.

How can social media help your business? It can drive brand awareness and build customer loyalty. It can make it easy for you to listen to what consumers are saying. In addition to the above, it can create referral business for you. It provides you with an audience that is built in. Social media such as we see on the Web today is a logical extension of what people have been doing for centuries: communicating! Whether you are in the act of building a community to support your customers or whether you are thinking outside the box and want to create a blog to keep the public informed, Media Solutions can put your company in a position at the forefront of this fabulous marketing opportunity. Let us give your company the human touch with the creation of an online voice and personality just for you.

Thanking you in advance, please let me call you to provide more information on how to get your audience buzzing.

Socially yours,

6.15 How Much Do People in Your Field Write? (Objs. 1–5)

How much writing is required by people working in your career area? The best way to learn about on-the-job writing is to talk with someone who has a job similar to the one you hope to have one day.

YOUR TASK. Interview someone working in your field of study. Your instructor may ask you to present your findings orally or in a written report. Ask questions such as these:

What kind of writing do you do? What kind of planning do you do before writing? Where do you get information? Do you brainstorm? Make lists? Do you compose on a computer or on your iPad? How many e-mail messages do you typically write in a day? How long does it take you to compose a routine one- or two-page memo, e-mail, or letter? Do you revise? How often? Do you have a preferred method for proofreading? When you have questions about grammar and mechanics, what or whom do you consult? Does anyone read your drafts and make suggestions? Can you describe your entire composition process? Do you ever work with others to produce a document? How does this process work? What makes writing easier or harder for you? Have your writing methods and skills changed since you left school?

6.16 Pruning the Deadwood (Objs. 1, 2)

Team   Web

Many writers and speakers are unaware of "deadwood" phrases they use. Some of these are flabby expressions, redundancies, or trite business phrases.

YOUR TASK. Using your favorite Web browser, locate two or three sites devoted to deadwood phrases. Your instructor may ask you to (a) submit a list of ten deadwood phrases (and their preferred substitutes) not mentioned in this textbook, or (b) work in teams to prepare a comprehensive "Dictionary of Deadwood Phrases," including as many as you can find. Be sure to include a preferred substitute.

6.17 Analyzing the Readability of an Apartment Lease (Objs. 1–3)

E-mail   Ethics   Team

Have you read your apartment lease carefully? Did you understand it? Many students—and their friends and family members—are intimidated, frustrated, or just plain lost when they try to comprehend an apartment lease.

YOUR TASK. Locate an apartment lease —yours, a friend's, or a family member's. In teams, analyze its format and readability. What size is the paper? How large are the margins? Is the type large or small? How much white space appears on the page? Are paragraphs and sentences long or short? Does the lease contain legalese or obscure language? What makes it difficult to understand? In an e-mail message to your instructor, summarize your team's reaction to the lease. Your instructor may ask you to revise sections or the entire lease to make it more readable. In class, discuss how ethical it is for an apartment owner to expect a renter to read and comprehend a lease while sitting in the rental office.

Chat About It

In each chapter you will find five discussion questions related to the chapter material. Your instructor may assign these topics for you to discuss in class, in an online chat room, or on an online discussion board. Some of the discussion topics may require outside research. You may also be asked to read and respond to postings made by your classmates.

Topic 1: When you tackle a serious writing project, do you prefer freewriting, in which you rapidly record your thoughts, or do you prefer to polish and revise as you go? What are the advantages and disadvantages of each method for you? Do you use the same method for both short and long messages?

Topic 2: Think about your own speaking and writing. Do you recognize some favorite redundancies that you use in spoken or written messages? When did you realize that you could be more concise and precise by eliminating these expressions?

Topic 3: The default font in Microsoft Word used to be Times New Roman, a serif typeface. In recent Word versions, the default font is Calibri, a sans serif typeface. Why do you think Microsoft made the switch? In your opinion, is Calibri more readable than Times New Roman in (a) printed documents, (b) documents displayed on a computer screen, (c) both, or (d) neither?

Topic 4: What proofreading tasks can you safely ask a proofreading buddy to perform? What if that person is not a skilled writer?

Topic 5: Are you a good proofreader? Is it easier to find other people's errors than your own? Why? What are you good at finding? What do you frequently miss?

Grammar/Mechanics C.L.U.E. | *Review 6*

Semicolons, Colons

Review Guides 27–30 about semicolons and colons in Appendix A, Grammar and Mechanics Guide, beginning on page A-12. On a separate sheet, revise the following sentences to correct errors in semicolon and colon usage. Do not start new sentences. For each error that you locate, write the guide number that reflects this usage. The more you recognize the reasons, the better you will learn these punctuation guidelines. If a sentence is correct, write C. When you finish, check your answers on page Key-2.

EXAMPLE: Engineers produced a snazzy new product, however it had no exciting name.

REVISION: Engineers produced a snazzy new **product; however,** it had no exciting name. [Guide 27]

1. Companies find it difficult to name new products consequently they often hire specialists.

2. New product names must be interesting however many of the best names are already taken.

3. Branding a product is a creative endeavor, the name becomes a product's shorthand.

4. Global names must be appealing in such faraway places as Beijing China Montreal Canada and Dubai City United Arab Emirates.

5. One naming expert warned companies with the following comment "Be aware of global consequences. For example, Bimbo is the name of a Mexican baking conglomerate. However, the word in English has an unsavory meaning."

6. Product and company names are developed by combining the following three linguistic elements morphemes, phonemes, and syntax.

7. One of the reasons company names such as Google and Apple work is that they are catchy, however they are also backed by high-quality products.

8. Some English sounds (such as L, V, F, and W) are considered feminine, others (such as X, M, and Z) are viewed as masculine.

9. Among the company officers judging new names were Anthony Simmons, vice president, Rachel Lohr, CFO, and Lavonne Jones, manager.

10. Syntax, or word order, is key to consumers' perception, therefore, two-word product names must sound pleasing.

Notes

1. Horovitz, B. (2012, February 20). Taco Bell + Doritos = success? *USA Today*, pp. B1.
2. Yum financial data. (2011). Retrieved from http://www.yum.com/investors/restcounts.asp
3. Horovitz, B. (2012, February 20). Taco Bell + Doritos = success? *USA Today*, pp. B2.
4. Jargon, J. (2012, February 21). Yum's CEO serves up new taco, growth plans. *The Wall Street Journal*, p. B7.
5. Ibid.
6. Yum Brands: Taco Bell to expand. (2009, January). *MarketWatch: Food*, p. 16. Retrieved from http://connection.ebscohost.com/c/articles /36067179/yum-brands-taco-bell-expand
7. Brumback, N. (1998, September 1). Yo quiero Mexican food. *Restaurant Business*, pp. 43-44.
8. Elbow, P. (1998). *Writing with power: Techniques for mastering the writing process*. Oxford, UK: Oxford University Press, p. 30.
9. Cook, C. K. (1985). *Line by line*. Boston: Houghton Mifflin, p. 17.
10. Shankman, P. (2011, May 20). I will never hire a "social media expert," and neither should you. Retrieved from http://shankman.com/i-will -never-hire-a-social-media-expert-and-neither -should-you
11. Glassman, N. (2010, November 29). 6 tips for brands on responding to customer complaints on Twitter. Retrieved from http://socialtimes .com/responding-customer-complaints-twitter _b29179
12. Photo essay based on Fell, J. (2012, April 19). Want better Twitter results? Try these effective types of tweets. *Entrepreneur*. Retrieved from http://www.entrepreneur.com
13. Hsieh, T. (2011, May 11). Twitter. Retrieved from http://twitter.com/#!/zappos
14. Holmes, E. (2011, December 9). Tweeting without fear, *Wall Street Journal Online*. Retrieved from http://online.wsj.com/article/SB100014240529 7020431900457708614086507580.html
15. Starbucks . (2012, May 30). Retrieved from http://twitter.com/#!/Starbucks
16. Adams, S. (2011, April 9-10). How to get a real education. *The Wall Street Journal*, pp. C1-C2.
17. Fried, J. (2010, May 1). *Inc.* magazine. Retrieved from http://www.inc.com/magazine/20100501 /why-is-business-writing-so-awful.html
18. Sword, H. (2012, July 25). Zombie nouns. Retrieved from *NYTimes' Opinionator* at http://www.3quarksdaily.com/3quarksdaily /2012/07/zombie-nouns.html
19. Photo essay based on Giang, V. (2013, February 22). These formatting rules will get your resume through the screening system. Business Insider. Retrieved from http://www.businessinsider.com
20. Levitt, A. (2011, April 2). A word to Wall Street: 'Plain English,' please. Retrieved from *Wall Street Journal Online* at http://online.wsj.com/article /SB10001424052748704471904576231002037 599510.html
21. Duffy, S. P. (2007, April 23). Attorney hit with $6.6 million malpractice verdict. *The Legal Intelligencer*. Retrieved from http://www.law .com. Also available at http://www.cavignac .com/publications/publications-lawyers -perspectives/lawyers-perspective-confusion -and-contracts-dont-mix
22. Based on Van Grove, J. (2009, January 21). 40 of the best twitter brands and the people behind them. Retrieved from http://mashable .com/2009/01/21/best-twitter-brands
23. Based on Bank of America Twitter Help. (2012, June 3). @AmyJo 63Owen. Twitter. Retrieved from https://twitter.com/#!/BofA_Help
24. Based on JetBlue Twitter Help. (2012, June 4). VictoriaKlim @vikiybubbles. Twitter. Retrieved from https://twitter.com/#!/JetBlue
25. Based on Southwest Airlines Twitter. (2012, May 15). Chris Cichon@cichonship. Twitter. Retrieved from https://twitter.com/#!/SouthwestAir
26. Based on H&R Block. (2012, June 4). Carlos Noriega@calinelbarbaro. Twitter. Retrieved from https://twitter.com/#!/hrblock

Unit 3
Workplace Communication

Short Workplace Messages and Digital Media

OBJECTIVES

After studying this chapter, you should be able to

1 Understand e-mail and the professional standards for its usage, structure, and format in the digital-era workplace.

2 Explain workplace instant messaging and texting as well as their liabilities and best practices.

3 Identify professional applications of podcasts and wikis, and describe guidelines for their use.

4 Describe how businesses use blogs to connect with internal and external audiences, and list best practices for professional blogging.

5 Address business uses of social networking and the benefits of RSS feeds.

Twitter: From Fad to New Communication Channel for Business

Zooming in

Most large companies and increasingly also smaller businesses are using Twitter and other social media to build their brands, monitor what is being said about them, engage with customers, and market to other businesses. Take the airlines: @JetBlueCheeps is an account on Twitter solely dedicated to the carrier's special deals on domestic and international flights. Quirky Southwest Airlines uses

Twitter to drive traffic to its behind-the-scenes show *On the Fly* running on cable network TLC and to its popular blog Nuts About Southwest. Like American Airlines and United, Southwest mixes links to current best deals with company news items and customer interaction. JetBlue, United, Southwest, and others have appointed "tweet watchers" who troubleshoot air travelers' problems and may tweet right back when gripes are posted. American, Alaska, Air New Zealand, and the Virgin group also tweet actively.[1]

Social media such as Twitter also showcase a company's culture, for better or worse. Spirit Airlines was blasted for its "frat house style culture" nurtured by "spunky ole boys" after its hard-line stance on customer complaints became plain.[2] Positive standouts are companies such as Zappos, whose CEO Tony Hsieh is a Twitter powerhouse with 2.48 million followers. He credits the microblogging service with helping to forge a positive corporate culture. Hundreds of Zappos employees now tweet regularly.[3]

What seemed like a novelty for tech heads when the service first emerged a few years ago has become an Internet phenomenon. The ranks of Twitter users have been swelling so explosively—currently to about 500 million active users[4]—that some investors and businesses see huge opportunities. They speak of a new technological revolution, the "real-time Web."[5] High-speed Internet connections as well as smart mobile devices with messaging and social media applications have enabled easy around-the-clock, real-time communication.

Twitter today is yet another communication channel allowing businesses to reach customers, troubleshoot customer problems, and promote their brands. You will find advice on career-safe tweeting and a discussion of how businesses are handling Twitter later in this chapter.

Critical Thinking

- In what ways have social media and the real-time Web changed how Internet users communicate? Have services such as Twitter improved the way we exchange information?

- What trends have facilitated the emergence of social media, specifically Twitter?

- What could be advantages and drawbacks of using Twitter for business?

Preparing Digital-Age E-Mail Messages and Memos

LEARNING OBJECTIVE **1**

Understand e-mail and the professional standards for its usage, structure, and format in the digital-era workplace.

The world of communication is rapidly changing in this digital age. The Web has evolved from a mere repository of passively consumed information to Web 2.0—a dynamic, interactive, and highly networked environment. Users are empowered, active participants who create content, review products, and edit and share information. As discussed in previous chapters, communicators are increasingly switching to mobile devices. Messages are shorter and more frequent, and response time is much speedier. Social media networks such as Twitter have transformed communication from one-on-one conversations to one-to-many transmissions. For better or for worse, citizen journalists have the power to create and distribute miniature news programs to multitudes on the fly. In addition, social networking sites such as Facebook and Pinterest have revolutionized the way we keep in touch with friends and family.

Similarly, in the workplace new devices and technologies are transforming the way we exchange information and conduct business. Ever more data are stored on and accessed from remote networks, not individual computers. This storing and accessing of data along with software applications in remote networks, the "cloud," is called *cloud computing*. In many businesses desktop computers, once the mainstay of the office, are becoming obsolete. They're being replaced with ever-smaller laptops, smartphones, tablets, and other amazingly compact and powerful mobile devices. Virtual private networks (VPN) offer secure access to an organization's information from any location in the world that provides an Internet connection. Whether they like it or not, businesspeople are increasingly connected 24/7.

Doubtless you are already connecting digitally with your friends, family, and Internet pals. However, chances are that you need to understand how businesses transmit information electronically and how they use communication technologies. This chapter explores short forms of workplace communication, beginning with e-mail, which everyone loves to hate, and memos, which are disappearing but still necessary in many organizations. Moving on to newer media, you will learn about workplace functions of instant messaging, text messaging, corporate blogs, podcasts, wikis, and social networking sites. Learning these workplace technologies and best procedures can save you time, reduce blunders, and help you excel as a professional.

E-Mail: Love It or Hate It—But It's Not Going Away

Critics say that e-mail is outdated, inefficient, and slowly dying. They complain that it takes too much time, increases stress, and leaves a dangerous "paper" trail. However, e-mail in the workplace is here to stay. Despite the substantial attention that social media receives in the news, most business messages are still sent by e-mail.[7] In the next three to five years, we may see more business messages being sent by social media platforms, predicts Dr. Monica Seeley, author of *Brilliant Email*. "But email will remain a bedrock of businesses for some time to come," she maintains.[8] Typical businesspeople spend at least two hours a day—perhaps much more—writing and replying to e-mail.

E-mail has replaced paper memos for many messages inside organizations and some letters to external audiences. In addition to accessing e-mail in the office, increasing numbers of businesspeople check their e-mail on mobile devices. Because you can expect to use e-mail extensively to communicate at work, it's smart to learn how to do it efficiently and expertly. You may have to adjust your current texting and Facebook posting practices, but turning out professional e-mails is an easily attainable goal.

Why People Complain About E-Mail

Although e-mail is recognized as the mainstay of business communication, it's not always done well. In a recent study of 1,800 global knowledge workers, 40 percent confessed that "they had received e-mails that made no sense whatsoever."[9] A *Wall Street Journal* article reported that many business schools were ramping up their writing programs or hiring writing coaches because of complaints about their graduates' skills.[10] Adding to the complaints, Chris Carlson, recruiting officer at the consulting firm of Booz Allen Hamilton Inc., said that new MBA graduates exchange more than 200 e-mails a day, and some read like text messages. "They're not [even] in complete sentences," he said.[11]

In addition to the complaints about confusing and poorly written e-mails, many people are overwhelmed with too many messages. Some of those messages are unnecessary, such as those that merely confirm receipt of a message or ones that express thanks. The use of "Reply All" adds to the inbox, irritating those who have to plow through dozens of messages that barely relate to them. Others blame e-mail for eliminating the distinction between work life and home life. They feel an urgency to be available 24/7 and respond immediately.

REALITY CHECK: E-Mail = Smoking Gun

E-mail is the digital equivalent of DNA evidence, the smoking gun. "E-mail has become the place where everybody loves to look."[12]

—**IRWIN SCHWARTZ,** *president of the National Association of Criminal Defense Lawyers*

Still other e-mail senders fail to recognize how dangerous e-mail can be. After deletion, e-mail files still leave trails on servers within and outside organizations. Messages are also backed up on other servers, making them traceable and recoverable by forensic experts. Long-forgotten messages may turn up in court cases as damaging evidence. Even writers with nothing to hide should be concerned about what may come back to haunt them. Your best bet is to put nothing in an e-mail message that you wouldn't post on your office door. Also be sure that you know your organization's e-mail policy before sending personal messages. Estimates suggest that as many as a quarter of bosses have fired an employee for an e-mail violation.[13]

Despite its dark side, e-mail has many advantages and remains a prime communication channel. Therefore, it's to your advantage to learn when and how to use it efficiently and safely.

Knowing When E-Mail Is Appropriate

E-mail is appropriate for short, informal messages that request information and respond to inquiries. It is especially effective for messages to multiple receivers and messages that must be archived (saved). An e-mail is also appropriate as a cover document when sending longer attachments.

E-mail, however, is not a substitute for face-to-face conversations or telephone calls. These channels are much more successful if your goal is to convey enthusiasm or warmth, explain a complex situation, present a persuasive argument, or smooth over disagreements. One expert gives this wise advice: "Sometimes it's better to get off the computer and make a phone call. If e-mails are getting too complicated, if the tone is degenerating, if they're just not getting the job done, call or walk over to that colleague."[14] Managers and employees echo this advice, as revealed in recent research. They were adamant about using face-to-face contact, rather than e-mail, for critical work situations such as human resources annual reviews, discipline, and promotions.[15]

> E-mail is appropriate for short, informal messages that request information and respond to inquiries.

Drafting Professional E-Mails

Professional e-mails are quite different from messages you may send to friends. Instead of casual words tossed off in haste, professional e-mails are well-considered messages that involve all three stages of the writing process. They have compelling subject lines, appropriate greetings, well-organized bodies, and complete closing information.

Draft a Compelling Subject Line.   The most important part of an e-mail is its subject line. Avoid meaningless statements such as *Help, Important,* or *Meeting.* Summarize the purpose of the message clearly and make the receiver want to open the message. Try to include a verb (*Need You to Attend Las Vegas Trade Show*). Remember that in some instances the subject line can be the entire message (*Meeting Changed from May 3 to May 10*). Also be sure to adjust the subject line if the topic changes after repeated replies.

Include a Greeting. To help receivers see the beginning of a message and to help them recognize whether they are the primary or secondary receiver, include a greeting. The greeting sets the tone for the message and reflects your audience analysis. For friends and colleagues, try friendly greetings (*Hi, Julie, Thanks, Julie, Good morning, Julie,* or *Greetings, Julie*). For more formal messages and those to outsiders, include an honorific and last name (*Dear Ms. Stevens*).

Organize the Body for Readability and Tone. In the revision phase, ask yourself how you could make your message more readable. Did you start directly? Did you group similar topics together? Could some information be presented with bulleted or numbered lists? Could you add side headings—especially if the message is more than a few paragraphs? Do you see any phrases or sentences that could be condensed? Get rid of wordiness, but don't sacrifice clarity. If a longer sentence is necessary for comprehension, then keep it. To convey the best tone, read the message aloud. If it sounds curt, it probably is.

Close Effectively. At the end of your message, include an action statement with due dates and requests. Although complimentary closes are unnecessary, you might include a friendly closing such as *Many thanks* or *Warm regards*. Do include your name because messages without names become confusing when forwarded or when they are part of a long string of responses.

For most messages, include full contact information in a signature block that can be inserted automatically. Figure 7.1 illustrates a typical e-mail with proper formatting.

REALITY CHECK: E-Mail and Professionalism

"E-mail is today's version of a business letter or interoffice memo. "Think accordingly. Make it look professional."[16]

—**TENNILLE ROBINSON,** *Black Enterprise*

Controlling Your Inbox

Business communicators love to complain about e-mail, and some young people even deny its existence. In the business world, however, e-mail writing IS business writing.[17] Instead of letting your inbox consume your time and crimp your productivity, you can control it by observing a few time-management strategies.

The most important strategy is checking your e-mail at set times, such as first thing in the morning and again after lunch or at 4 p.m. To avoid being distracted, be sure to turn off your audio and visual alerts. No fair peeking! If mornings are your best working times, check your e-mail later in the day. Let your boss and colleagues know about your schedule for responding.

Another excellent time-saver is the "two-minute rule." If you can read and respond to a message within two minutes, then take care of it immediately. For messages that require more time, add them to your to-do list or schedule them on your calendar. To be polite, send a quick note telling the sender when you plan to respond.

Replying Efficiently With Down-Editing

When answering e-mail, a neat skill to develop is *down-editing*. This involves inserting your responses to parts of the incoming message. After a courteous opening, your reply message will include only the parts of the incoming message to which you are responding. Delete the sender's message headers, signature, and all unnecessary parts. Your responses can be identified with your initials, if more than one person will be seeing the response. Another efficient trick is to use a different color for your down-edits. It takes a little practice to develop this skill, but the down-edited reply reduces confusion, saves writing and reading time, and makes you look super savvy.

Figure 7.2 shows a number of additional best practices for managing your e-mail.

Figure 7.1 Formatting an E-Mail Message That Makes a Request

1 Prewriting

Analyze: The purpose of this e-mail is to solicit feedback regarding a casual-dress policy.

Anticipate: The message is going to a subordinate who is busy but probably eager to be consulted in this policy matter.

Adapt: Use a direct approach beginning with the most important question. Strive for a positive, professional tone rather than an autocratic, authoritative tone.

2 Drafting

Research: Collect secondary information about dress-down days in other organizations. Collect primary information by talking with company managers.

Organize: Begin with the main idea followed by a brief explanation and questions. Conclude with an end date and a reason.

Draft: Prepare the first draft remembering that the receiver is busy and appreciates brevity.

3 Revising

Edit: Rewrite questions to ensure that they are parallel and readable.

Proofread: Decide whether to hyphenate *casual-dress policy* and *dress-down days*. Be sure commas follow introductory clauses. Check question marks.

Evaluate: Does this message encourage participatory management? Will the receiver be able to answer the questions and respond easily?

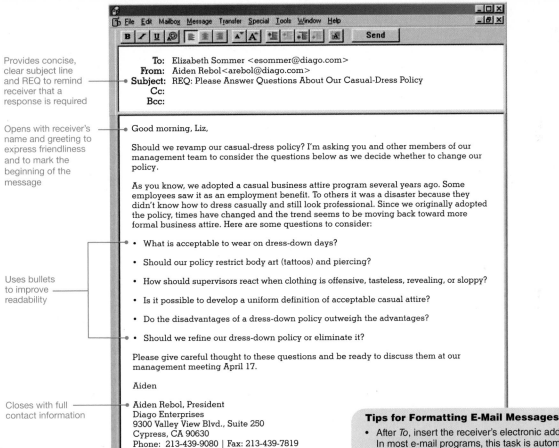

Provides concise, clear subject line and REQ to remind receiver that a response is required

Opens with receiver's name and greeting to express friendliness and to mark the beginning of the message

Uses bullets to improve readability

Closes with full contact information

To: Elizabeth Sommer <esommer@diago.com>
From: Aiden Rebol<arebol@diago.com>
Subject: REQ: Please Answer Questions About Our Casual-Dress Policy
Cc:
Bcc:

Good morning, Liz,

Should we revamp our casual-dress policy? I'm asking you and other members of our management team to consider the questions below as we decide whether to change our policy.

As you know, we adopted a casual business attire program several years ago. Some employees saw it as an employment benefit. To others it was a disaster because they didn't know how to dress casually and still look professional. Since we originally adopted the policy, times have changed and the trend seems to be moving back toward more formal business attire. Here are some questions to consider:

- What is acceptable to wear on dress-down days?
- Should our policy restrict body art (tattoos) and piercing?
- How should supervisors react when clothing is offensive, tasteless, revealing, or sloppy?
- Is it possible to develop a uniform definition of acceptable casual attire?
- Do the disadvantages of a dress-down policy outweigh the advantages?
- Should we refine our dress-down policy or eliminate it?

Please give careful thought to these questions and be ready to discuss them at our management meeting April 17.

Aiden

Aiden Rebol, President
Diago Enterprises
9300 Valley View Blvd., Suite 250
Cypress, CA 90630
Phone: 213-439-9080 | Fax: 213-439-7819

Tips for Formatting E-Mail Messages

- After *To*, insert the receiver's electronic address. In most e-mail programs, this task is automated. If done manually, enclose the receiver's address in angle brackets.
- After *From*, type your name and electronic address, if your program does not insert it automatically.
- After *Subject*, present a clear description of the message.
- Insert the addresses of anyone receiving courtesy or blind copies.
- Include a salutation (*Liz; Hi, Liz*) or honorific and last name (*Dear Ms. Sommer*), especially in messages to outsiders.
- Double-space (skip one line) between paragraphs.
- Do not type in all caps or in all lowercase letters.
- Include full contact information in the signature block.

Figure **7.2** Best Practices for Better E-Mail

Getting Started

- Don't write if another channel—such as IM, social media, or a phone call——might work better.
- Send only content you would want published.
- Write compelling subject lines, possibly with names and dates:
  Jake: Can You Present at January 10 Staff Meeting?

Replying

- Scan all e-mails, especially those from the same person. Answer within 24 hours or say when you will.
- Change the subject line if the topic changes. Check the threaded messages below yours.
- Practice down-editing; include only the parts from the incoming e-mail to which you are responding.
- Start with the main idea.
- Use headings and lists.

Observing E-Mail Etiquette

- Obtain approval before forwarding.
- Soften the tone by including a friendly opening and closing.
- Resist humor and sarcasm. Absent facial expression and tone of voice, humor can be misunderstood.
- Avoid writing in all caps, which is like SHOUTING.

Closing Effectively

- End with due dates, next steps to be taken, or a friendly remark.
- Add your full contact information including social media addresses.
- Edit your text for readability. Proofread for typos or unwanted auto-corrections.
- Double-check before hitting **Send.**

© Cengage Learning 2015

Writing Interoffice Memos

In addition to e-mail, you should be familiar with another workplace document type, the interoffice memorandum. Although e-mail has largely replaced memos, you may still be called on to use the memo format in specific instances. Memos are necessary for important internal messages that (a) are too long for e-mail, (b) require a permanent record, (c) demand formality, or (d) inform employees who may not have access to e-mail. Within organizations, memos deliver changes in procedures, official instructions, and reports.

The memo format is particularly necessary for complex internal messages that are too long for e-mail. Prepared as memos, long messages are then delivered as attachments to e-mail cover messages. Memos seem to function better as permanent records than e-mail messages because the latter may be difficult to locate and may contain a trail of confusing replies. E-mails also may change the origination date whenever the file is accessed, thus making it impossible to know the original date of the message.

When preparing e-mail attachments, be sure that they carry sufficient identifying information. Because the cover e-mail message may become separated from the attachment, the attachment must be fully identified. Preparing the e-mail attachment as a memo provides a handy format that identifies the date, sender, receiver, and subject.

Similarities in Memos and E-Mails. Memos have much in common with e-mails. Both usually carry nonsensitive information that may be organized directly with the main idea first. Both have guide words calling for a subject line, a dateline, and the identification of the sender and receiver. To enhance readability, both should be organized with headings, bulleted lists, and enumerated items whenever possible.

E-mails and memos both generally close with (a) action information, dates, or deadlines; (b) a summary of the message; or (c) a closing thought. An effective memo or e-mail closing might be, *Please submit your written report to me by June 15 so that we can review your data before our July planning session.* In more detailed messages, a summary of main points may be an appropriate closing. If no action request is made and a closing summary is unnecessary, you might end with a simple concluding thought (*I'm glad to answer your questions* or *This sounds like a useful project*).

You need not close messages to coworkers with goodwill statements such as those found in letters to customers or clients. However, some closing thought is often necessary to avoid sounding abrupt. Closings can show gratitude or encourage feedback with remarks such as *I sincerely appreciate your help* or *What are your ideas on this proposal?* Other closings look forward to what's next, such as *How would you like to proceed?* Avoid closing with overused expressions such as *Please let me know if I may be of further assistance*. This ending sounds mechanical and insincere.

CHECKLIST ▶▶
Professional E-Mail and Memos

Subject Line

- **Summarize the central idea.** Express concisely what the message is about and how it relates to the reader.

- **Include labels if appropriate.** Labels such as *FYI* (*for your information*) and *REQ* (*required*) help receivers recognize how to respond.

- **Avoid empty or dangerous words.** Don't write one-word subject lines such as *Help, Problem,* or *Free*.

Opening

- **State the purpose for writing.** Include the same information that is in the subject line, but expand it.

- **Highlight questions.** If you are requesting information, begin with the most important question, use a polite command (*Please answer the following questions about . . .*), or introduce your request courteously.

- **Supply information directly.** If responding to a request, give the reader the requested information immediately in the opening. Explain later.

Body

- **Explain details.** Arrange information logically. For detailed topics develop separate coherent paragraphs.

- **Enhance readability.** Use short sentences, short paragraphs, and parallel construction for similar ideas.

- **Apply document design.** If appropriate, provide bulleted or numbered lists, headings, tables, or other graphic devices to improve readability and comprehension.

- **Be cautious.** Remember that e-mail messages often travel far beyond their intended audiences.

Closing

- **Request action.** If appropriate, state specifically what you want the reader to do. Include a deadline, with reasons, if possible.

- **Provide a goodwill statement or a closing thought.** When communicating outside of the company or with management, include a positive goodwill statement such as *Our team enjoyed working on the feasibility report, and we look forward to your feedback*. If no action request is necessary, end with a closing thought.

- **Avoid cliché endings.** Use fresh remarks rather than overused expressions such as *If you have additional questions, please do not hesitate to call* or *Thank you for your cooperation*.

© Daniilantiq/Shutterstock.com

In Figure 7.3, notice how memos are formatted and how they can be created to improve readability with lists and white space. The Checklist on the previous page offers tips for including professional content in your e-mail messages and memos.

Figure **7.3** Formatting a Memo That Responds to a Request

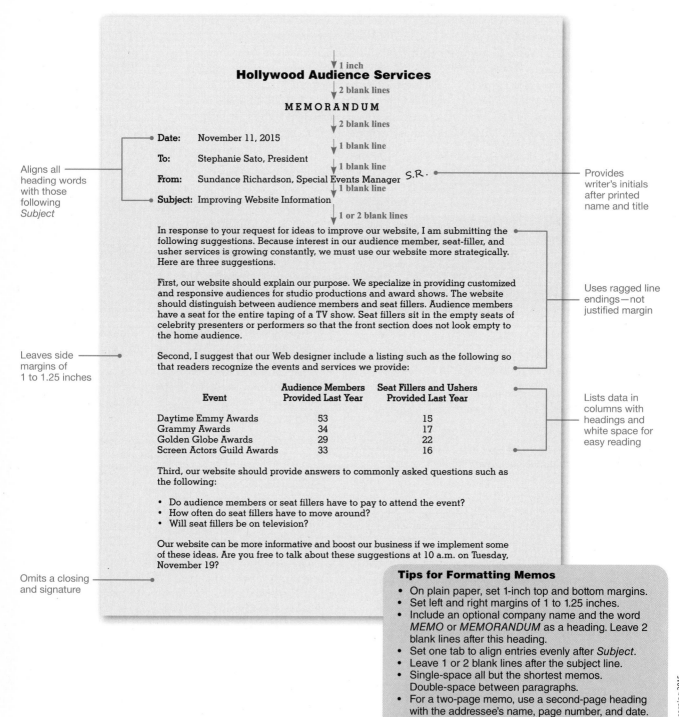

Aligns all heading words with those following *Subject*

Leaves side margins of 1 to 1.25 inches

Omits a closing and signature

Hollywood Audience Services

↓ 1 inch

↓ 2 blank lines

MEMORANDUM

↓ 2 blank lines

Date: November 11, 2015

↓ 1 blank line

To: Stephanie Sato, President

↓ 1 blank line

From: Sundance Richardson, Special Events Manager *S.R.*

↓ 1 blank line

Subject: Improving Website Information

↓ 1 or 2 blank lines

In response to your request for ideas to improve our website, I am submitting the following suggestions. Because interest in our audience member, seat-filler, and usher services is growing constantly, we must use our website more strategically. Here are three suggestions.

First, our website should explain our purpose. We specialize in providing customized and responsive audiences for studio productions and award shows. The website should distinguish between audience members and seat fillers. Audience members have a seat for the entire taping of a TV show. Seat fillers sit in the empty seats of celebrity presenters or performers so that the front section does not look empty to the home audience.

Second, I suggest that our Web designer include a listing such as the following so that readers recognize the events and services we provide:

	Audience Members	Seat Fillers and Ushers
Event	Provided Last Year	Provided Last Year
Daytime Emmy Awards	53	15
Grammy Awards	34	17
Golden Globe Awards	29	22
Screen Actors Guild Awards	33	16

Third, our website should provide answers to commonly asked questions such as the following:

• Do audience members or seat fillers have to pay to attend the event?
• How often do seat fillers have to move around?
• Will seat fillers be on television?

Our website can be more informative and boost our business if we implement some of these ideas. Are you free to talk about these suggestions at 10 a.m. on Tuesday, November 19?

Provides writer's initials after printed name and title

Uses ragged line endings—not justified margin

Lists data in columns with headings and white space for easy reading

Tips for Formatting Memos
• On plain paper, set 1-inch top and bottom margins.
• Set left and right margins of 1 to 1.25 inches.
• Include an optional company name and the word *MEMO* or *MEMORANDUM* as a heading. Leave 2 blank lines after this heading.
• Set one tab to align entries evenly after *Subject*.
• Leave 1 or 2 blank lines after the subject line.
• Single-space all but the shortest memos. Double-space between paragraphs.
• For a two-page memo, use a second-page heading with the addressee's name, page number, and date.
• Handwrite your initials after your typed name.
• Place bulleted or numbered lists flush left or indent them 0.5 inches.

© Cengage Learning 2015

Workplace Messaging and Texting

LEARNING OBJECTIVE **2**
Explain workplace instant messaging and texting as well as their liabilities and best practices.

Instant messaging (IM) and text messaging have become powerful communication tools, not only among teens and twentysomethings. IM enables two or more individuals to use the Internet or an intranet (an internal corporate communication platform) to "chat" in real time by exchanging brief text-based messages. Companies large and small now provide live online chats with customer-service representatives during business hours, in addition to the usual contact options, such as telephone and e-mail. Academic libraries in the United States staff a Web-based Ask a Librarian chat with trained reference librarians available 24/7. Facebook, Skype, and some browsers have built-in IM (chat) functions.

Text messaging, or texting, is another popular means for exchanging brief messages in real time. Usually delivered by or to a smartphone, texting requires a short message service (SMS) supplied by a cell phone service provider or a voice over Internet protocol (VoIP) service. Increasingly, both instant and text messages are sent by smart handheld electronic devices as the use of such devices is skyrocketing.

Fueled by online security and legal compliance concerns, the other huge trend in business enterprises is the integration of multiple communication functions behind corporate firewalls. For example, Adobe Systems has developed Unicom. The Unified Communications Tool is an all-in-one internal communication platform that connects coworkers by chat, Twitter-like microblogging, and employee directory access, as well as by e-mail and phone. Unicom is used in the office or remotely, in one easy-to-use interface.

Web 2.0 social media campaigns are also usually integrated, meaning that they employ several social networks at once to increase the effectiveness of an appeal. For the sake of simplicity, however, we will examine the short-form functions separately.

Technology Behind Instant Messaging and Texting

Many large companies provide enterprise-grade IM secured by a firewall. However, smaller companies and most of us might use a free public IM service, called a client, such as AOL Instant Messenger, Google Talk, Windows Live Messenger, and Yahoo Messenger. Once the client is installed, you enter your name and password to log on. The software checks whether any of the users in your contact list are currently logged on. You can then exchange messages such as those shown in Figure 7.4.

Typically, IM communication is exchanged between two computers that are linked by servers. Increasingly, though, IM services are also Web based (e.g., Google Talk, Skype, and Facebook Chat), with no need to install an IM client. Most common applications allow people to use IM not only on their computers or in the cloud, but also on their handheld devices such as the iPhone, Android smartphone, or any number of tablets. Many smartphones and tablets work on a 3G or 4G cell phone network where they consume minutes, but they may also allow generally "free" Wi-Fi access where available.

Texting, on the other hand, usually requires a smartphone, and users pay for the service, often a flat rate for a certain number of text or media messages per month. Lately, VoIP providers such as Skype offer texting. For a small fee, Skype subscribers can send text messages to SMS-enabled phones in the United States and instant messages both domestically and internationally. Again, Skype and other formerly computer-based applications are simultaneously available on mobile devices and are making communication on the go more convenient than ever before.

Impact of Instant Messaging and Texting

Text messaging and IM are convenient alternatives to the telephone and are replacing e-mail for short internal communication. French IT giant Atos switched its in-house communication entirely from e-mail to a Facebook-style interface and instant messaging.[18] More than 2.6 billion IM accounts worldwide[19] attest to IM's popularity. Sixty-four percent of business professionals use IM.[20]

Figure **7.4** Instant Message for Brief, Fast Communication

Figure 7.4 shows a brief IM exchange between a supervisor and a subordinate. Both are using a computer-based IM program.

Ryan Mlodzik - Conversation

File   Edit   View   Actions   Help

To: Ryan Mlodzik <mlodzik@armour.com>

Start Camera
Start Talking
I Want To . .

Camille Montano says:
  Hi, Ryan, are you free for a quick question?

Ryan Mlodzik says:
  Sure thing. What have you got?

Camille Montano says:
  I just finished my meeting with the folks at Zymak Enterprises, and they've agreed to terms we discussed yesterday, but they want 45-day terms instead of 30.

Ryan Mlodzik says:
  Did they agree to a 2-year or 3-year contract?

Camille Montano says:
  3-year.

Ryan Mlodzik says:
  OK, let's go with it. I approve the 45-day adjustment. Good work!

Invite Someone to this Conversation
Send a File or Photo
Send E-mail
Ask for Remote Assistance
Start Application Sharing
Start Whiteboard

Block   **A** Font   ☺ ▾ Emoticons

Send

Last message received on 8/4/0x at 1:26 PM.

Courtesy of Mary Ellen Guffey and Dana Loewy; Used with permission from Microsoft.

Benefits of IM and Texting. The major attraction of instant messaging is real-time communication with colleagues anywhere in the world—so long as a cell phone signal or a Wi-Fi connection is available. Because IM allows people to share information immediately and make decisions quickly, its impact on business communication has been dramatic. Group online chat capabilities in enterprise-grade IM applications allow coworkers on far-flung project teams to communicate instantly. The popular Skype, the voice over Internet protocol powerhouse, is but one of many providers for small business and the general public.

Like IM, texting can be a low-cost substitute for voice calls, delivering a message between private mobile phone users quietly and discreetly. Organizations around the world provide news alerts, financial information, and promotions to customers via text. Credit card accounts can be set up to notify account holders by text or e-mail of approaching payment deadlines. Verizon Wireless sends automated texts helping customers track their data usage. The Centers for Disease Control started an SMS text messaging program that now has 15,000 participants receiving regular health alerts and tips on their mobile phones.[21] A few of these text alerts are shown in Figure 7.5.

The immediacy of instant and text messaging has created many fans. A user knows right away whether a message was delivered. Messaging avoids phone tag and eliminates the downtime associated with personal telephone conversations. Another benefit includes "presence functionality." Coworkers can locate each other online, thus avoiding wild goose chases hunting someone who is out of the office. Many people consider instant messaging and texting productivity boosters because they enable users to get answers quickly and allow multitasking.

Risks of IM and Texting. Despite their popularity among workers, some organizations forbid employees to use instant and text messaging for a number of reasons. Employers consider instant messaging yet another distraction in addition to the telephone, e-mail, and

Figure 7.5 Centers for Disease Control Text Alerts

Responding to the H1N1 flu virus threat, the Centers for Disease Control (CDC) launched a concerted Web 2.0 campaign employing several social networking channels, its website, and texting.

New Tobacco Regulations
CDC: What happened to light, low & mild? As of July 22, tobacco companies are no longer allowed to distribute products with these labels. http://m.cdc.gov/light

Safe Summer Travel
CDC: Summer trip? Get shots for int'l travel. Developing countries: stick to bottled water and fully cooked food, skip raw fruits/veggies unless you peel them.

Protect from Ticks
CDC: Protect yourself from ticks! Avoid high grasses & forests, wear light-colored clothes so you can see ticks, use repellent with 20-50% DEET. 800-232-4636

Prevent Rabies
CDC: Hiking outdoors? Avoid wild animals to prevent rabies. Report animals acting strangely (drooling, biting, trouble moving) to animal control. 800-232-4636

© Cengage Learning 2015

Based on information from http://www.cdc.gov/mobile and http://www.cdc.gov/widgets/SMS/alt/index.html.

the Web. Some organizations also fear that employees using free consumer-grade instant messaging systems will reveal privileged information and company records. One UK study found that 72 percent of businesses have banned IM, although 74 percent of the respondents believed that IM could boost collaboration in their organizations. IT directors in the United Kingdom worried about security risks posed by free consumer IM services, with loss of sensitive business data a primary concern (56 percent).[22] Large corporations are protecting themselves by taking instant messaging behind the firewall where they can log and archive traffic.

REALITY CHECK: IM Benefits vs. Network Security

"Clearly, everyone recognizes the benefits that IM can bring. However, the challenge will be for businesses to look for strategies that enable them to reap the rewards without putting themselves at risk of a security breach."[23]

—**Mickaël Rémond,** *CEO of ProcessOne, IM expert*

Courtesy of Mickaël Rémond

Liability Burden. A worker's improper use of mobile devices while on company business can expose the organization to staggering legal liability. A jury awarded $18 million to a victim struck by a transportation company's big rig whose driver had been checking text messages. Another case resulted in a $21 million verdict to a woman injured by a trucker who had used a cell phone while driving a company truck. A construction firm had to pay $4.75 million to a man injured by a driver using a company-provided cell phone.[24] Overall, as many as 34 percent of Americans admit to having texted while driving. Such DWI, or "driving while intexticated," is rampant. In one year alone, 1.3 million crashes, or 23 percent of all collisions, involved cell phones.[25] Unfortunately, 77 percent of young adults are confident that they can safely text and drive.[26]

Organizations are fighting back to raise awareness and diminish liability. They are instituting detailed digital-age e-policies, offering formal employee training, and using technology tools such as monitoring, filtering, and blocking. In one survey, more than half of employers stated that they monitor the Internet (66 percent), e-mail (43 percent), social media (36 percent), and blogs (12 percent). Personal use restrictions of e-mail are enforced by a full 83 percent of organizations; more than a third of businesses also enforce personal use rules for company IM and texting.[27]

Security and Legal Requirements. Companies also worry about *phishing* (fraudulent schemes), viruses, malware (malicious software programs), and *spim* (IM spam). Like e-mail, instant and text messages as well as all other electronic records are subject to discovery (disclosure); that is, they can become evidence in lawsuits. Wall Street regulatory agencies NASD, SEC, and NYSE require that IM exchanged between brokers and clients be retained for three years, much like e-mail and printed documents.[28] Moreover, companies fear instant messaging and texting because the services necessitate that businesses track and store messaging conversations to comply with legal requirements. This task may be overwhelming. Finally, IM and texting have been implicated in inappropriate uses such as bullying and the notorious *sexting*.

Best Practices for Instant Messaging and Texting

The effectiveness of short messaging for marketing is impressive if the appeal is done right. When UPS needed to hire 50,000 seasonal workers at the end of the year, its integrated social media effort drove over a million potential job candidates to view online videos about the shipping company, resulting in 150,000 applications. The SMS text campaign alone attracted more than 31,000 applicants and cost just $30,000, a respectable return on investment.[29]

Aside from digital marketing, instant messaging and texting can save time and simplify communication with coworkers and customers. Before using IM or text messaging on the job, be sure you have permission. Do not download and use software without checking with your supervisor. If your organization does allow IM or texting, you can use it efficiently and professionally by following these guidelines:

- Adhere to company policies at all times: netiquette rules, code of conduct, ethics guidelines, as well as harassment and discrimination policies.[30]

- Don't use IM or text messages to disclose sensitive information: financial, company, customer, employee, or executive data.

- Steer clear of harassment and discriminatory content against classes protected by law (race, color, religion, sex, sexual orientation, national origin, age, and disability).

Asked to provide just one attribute to describe their smartphones, mobile device owners' responses resulted in this word cloud. Word clouds are clusters of words, often in color; the size of each word depends on how often it appears in a text passage. Software can be used to turn any text passage into a word cloud. The adjectives in this word cloud attest to the popularity of smartphones. Pew Internet found that 42 percent of cell phones are smartphones. This means that 35 percent of American adults now own such a mobile device. Overall, mobile phone ownership stands at 83 percent of the U.S. population.[31]

- Be vigilant about the appropriateness of photos, videos, and art that you link to or forward.
- As with e-mail, don't say anything that would damage your reputation or that of your organization.
- Don't text or IM while driving a car. Pull over if you must read or send a message.
- Organize your contact lists to separate business contacts from family and friends.
- Avoid unnecessary chitchat, and know when to say goodbye. If personal messaging is allowed, keep it to a minimum.
- Keep your presence status up-to-date so that people trying to reach you don't waste their time. Make yourself unavailable when you need to meet a deadline.
- Beware of jargon, slang, and abbreviations, which, although they may reduce keystrokes, can be confusing and appear unprofessional.
- Use good grammar and proper spelling.

Text Messaging and Business Etiquette

Texting is quick and unobtrusive, and for routine messages it is often the best alternative to a phone call or e-mail. Given the popularity of text messaging, etiquette experts are taking note.[32] Figure 7.6 summarizes the suggestions they offer for the considerate and professional use of texting.

Figure 7.6 Texting Etiquette

Timing

- Don't text when calling would be inappropriate and rude, for example, at a performance, a restaurant, in a meeting, or a movie theater.
- Don't text or answer your phone during a face-to-face conversation. If others use their cell phones while talking to you, you may excuse yourself until they stop.

Addressing

- Check that you are texting to the correct phone number to avoid embarrassment. If you receive a message by mistake, alert the sender. No need to respond to the message itself.
- Avoid sending confidential, private, or potentially embarrassing texts. Someone might see your text at the recipient's end or the message might be sent to an unintended recipient.

Responding

Don't expect an instant reply. As with e-mail, we don't know when the recipient will read the message.

Introducing

Identify yourself when texting a new contact who doesn't have your phone number: "Hi—it's Erica (Office World). Your desk has arrived. Please call 877-322-8989."

Expressing

Don't use text messages to notify others of sad news, sensitive business matters, or urgent meetings, unless you wish to set up a phone call about that subject.

© Cengage Learning 2015

LEARNING OBJECTIVE **3**

Identify professional applications of podcasts and wikis, and describe guidelines for their use.

Making Podcasts and Wikis Work for Business

In the digital age, empowered by Web 2.0 interactivity, individuals wield enormous influence because they can potentially reach huge audiences. Far from being passive consumers, today's Internet users have the power to create Web content; interact with businesses and each other; review products, self-publish, or blog; contribute to wikis; or tag and share images and other files. Businesses often rightly fear the wrath of disgruntled employees and customers, or they curry favor with influential plugged-in opinion leaders, the so-called *influencers*. Like Twitter, other communication technologies such as podcasts and wikis are part of the new user-centered virtual environment called Web 2.0.

The democratization of the Web has meant that in the online world, Internet users can bypass gatekeepers who filter content in the traditional print and visual media. Hence, even extreme views often reach audiences of thousands or even millions. The dangers are obvious. Fact checking often falls by the wayside, buzz may become more important than truth, and a single keystroke can make or destroy a reputation. This section addresses prudent business uses of podcasts and wikis because you are likely to encounter these and other electronic communication tools on the job.

Business Podcasts or Webcasts

Perhaps because podcasts are more elaborate to produce and require quality hardware, their use is lagging behind other digital media. However, they have their place in the arsenal of Web 2.0 business communication strategies. Although the terms *podcast* and *podcasting* have caught on, they are somewhat misleading. The words *broadcasting* and *iPod* combined to create the word *podcast*; however, audio and video files can be played on any number of devices, not just Apple's iPod. *Webcasting* for audio and *vcasting* for video content would be more accurate. Podcasts can extend from short clips of a few minutes to 30-minute or longer digital files. Most are recorded, but some are live. Naturally, large video files gobble up a lot of memory, so they tend to be streamed on a website rather than downloaded.

How Organizations Use Podcasts.   Podcasting has found its place among various user groups online. Major news organizations and media outlets podcast radio shows (e.g., National Public Radio) and TV shows, from ABC to Fox. Some businesses have caught on. Vying to regain customers' trust after the banking crisis, Nicolet National Bank in Green Bay, Wisconsin, is using podcasts as part of its social media strategy to show transparency.[33] Podcasts are also common in education. Students can access instructors' lectures, interviews, sporting events, and other content. Apple's iTunes U is perhaps the best-known example of free educational podcasts from Berkeley, Stanford, and other universities. Podcasts encoded as MP3 files can be downloaded to a computer, a smartphone, or an MP3 player to be enjoyed on the go, often without subsequent Web access.

Delivering and Accessing Podcasts.   Businesses have embraced podcasting for audio and video messages that do not require a live presence yet offer a friendly human face. Because they can broadcast repetitive information that does not require interaction, podcasts can replace costlier live teleconferences. IBM is training its sales force with podcasts that are available anytime. The company also provides developerWorks video podcasts for software engineers and more. Real estate agents create podcasts to enable buyers to take virtual walking tours of available homes at their leisure. For example, The Corcoran Group's channel on YouTube features professionally produced videos of luxurious real estate properties in New York. HR policies can also be presented in the form of podcasts for unlimited viewing on demand. Podcasts are featured on media websites and company portals or shared on blogs and social networking sites, often with links to YouTube and Vimeo. They can usually be streamed or downloaded as media files. As

Figure **7.7** GreenTalk Radio Podcasts

In his audio podcasts, host Sean Daily examines eco-friendly lifestyles, discusses ecology-oriented products, and dispenses tips on becoming more "green."

we will see, really simple syndication (RSS) allows the distribution of current information published in podcasts, blogs, video files, and news items. GreenTalk Radio, shown in Figure 7.7, is just one example of a website that provides podcasts on many topics, such as green living and environmental stewardship. Frequently, business podcasts include short commercial segments. Podcasting is far from being a huge Internet phenomenon: in a Pew survey, 21 percent of Internet users stated they had downloaded a podcast to listen to or view later, yet only 3 percent stated that they did so daily.[34]

Experts advise business podcasters first to provide quality content with an authentic voice and consider money making second.[35] To browse and learn from popular favorites, search on *Podcast Awards* for podcasts in various categories, including business, science, and technology.

Collaborating With Wikis

Wikis are another important feature of the interactive, participatory Web 2.0 environment. As discussed in Chapter 4 on page 141, a wiki is a Web-based tool that employs easy-to-use collaborative software to allow multiple users collectively to create, access, and modify documents. Think Wikipedia, the well-known online encyclopedia. You will find wikis in numerous subject categories on the Internet. Wiki editors may be given varying access privileges and control over the cloud-based material; however, many public wikis are open to anyone.

Two major advantages of wikis come to mind. First, wikis capitalize on *crowdsourcing,* which can be defined as the practice of tapping into the combined knowledge of a large community to solve problems and complete assignments. Second, working on the same content jointly eliminates the infamous problem of version confusion. Most wikis store all changes and intermediate versions of files, so that users can return to a previous stage if necessary. A survey found that benefits of corporate wikis include enhancing the reputation of expert contributors, making work flow more easily, and improving an organization's processes.[36] IBM, for example, uses wikis to publish documentation for its WebSphere and Lotus products and to interact with the community of adopters.

How Businesses Use Wikis. Enterprises using wikis usually store their internal data on an intranet, a private network. An enterprise-level wiki serves as an easy-to-navigate, efficient central repository of company information, complete with hyperlinks and keywords pointing to related subjects and media. The four main uses of wikis in business, shown in Figure 7.8,[37] range from providing a shared internal knowledge base to storing templates for business documents.

Popular simple-to-use wiki hosting services, called *wiki farms,* are PBworks, Wetpaint Central, Wikia, and Wikispaces. Some are noncommercial. Consider starting a wiki for your next classroom project requiring teamwork. Alternatively, explore Google Docs and Google Sites, a page of which is shown in Figure 7.9.

Figure 7.8 Four Main Uses for Business Wikis

The global wiki

For companies with a global reach, a wiki is an ideal tool for information sharing between headquarters and satellite offices. Far-flung team members can easily edit their work and provide input to the home office and each other.

The wiki knowledge base

Teams or departments use wikis to collect and disseminate information to large audiences creating a database for knowledge management. For example, human resources managers may update employee policies, make announcements, and convey information about benefits.

Wikis for meetings

Wikis can facilitate feedback from employees before and after meetings and serve as repositories of meeting minutes. In fact, wikis may replace some meetings, yet still keep a project on track.

Wikis for project management

Wikis offer a highly interactive environment for project information with easy access and user input. All participants have the same information, templates, and documentation readily available.

© Cengage Learning 2015

Figure **7.9** Creating a Wiki With Google Sites and Google Docs

This screenshot of Organic City's intranet shows a template created in Google Sites, a free, user-friendly wiki and website creator. Google Sites and the document editing and revision tool Google Docs allow users to create, edit, share, and manage documents online in real time. Unlike in typical wikis, here multiple editors can modify files simultaneously.

REALITY CHECK: How Is Intel Socializing Its Brand?

"It is not about Intel broadcasting marketing talk. It is about bringing interesting content through that particular channel."[38]

—KATHLEEN C. MALONE, *senior social media strategist, Intel Corporation*

Blogging for Business

LEARNING OBJECTIVE **4**
Describe how businesses use blogs to connect with internal and external audiences, and list best practices for professional blogging.

The biggest advantage of business blogs is that they potentially reach a far-flung, vast audience. A blog is a website with journal entries on any imaginable topic usually written by one person, although most corporate blogs feature multiple contributors. Typically, readers leave comments. Businesses use blogs to keep customers, employees, and the public at large informed and to interact with them.

Marketing firms and their clients are looking closely at blogs because blogs can invite spontaneous consumer feedback faster and more cheaply than such staples of consumer research as focus groups and surveys. Employees and executives at companies such as Exxon, Walmart, Dell, and Xerox maintain blogs. They use blogs to communicate internally with employees and externally with the public. Currently, 114 of Fortune 500 companies (23 percent) are blogging, but researchers note a slight "leveling off and possibly retrenchment" in the adoption of social media among the Fortune 500.[39]

At this time, writers have posted an estimated 164 million blogs, up from only 3 million in 2004.[40] However, just about half of these blogs are active, meaning that posts were published within three months. A recent study pegged the number of domestic blog readers at more than 123 million, representing 53.5 percent of U.S. Internet users, or 39 percent of the population.[41] Although blogs may still be underused—for example, senior executives are largely absent from social media[42]—blogs do represent an amazing information stream if used wisely.

When Pei Wei Asian Diner needed bold new ideas for its menu, marketers at the fast-casual restaurant chain launched a high-profile social media event. The company sent writer Alice Shin and two executive chefs on an 18-day "culinary tour" across Thailand, Vietnam, Japan, China, and Korea. The purpose of the tour: get inspiration for new Pei Wei dishes. During the trip, the 27-year-old blogged daily about her Asian adventures, generating good publicity and tasty menu ideas for the restaurant. In your view, what are the characteristics of a good blog?[43]

Courtesy of Alice Shin/Pei Wei

How Companies Blog

Like other Web 2.0 phenomena, corporate blogs help create virtual communities, build brands, and develop relationships. Specifically, companies use blogs for public relations, customer relations, crisis communication, market research, viral marketing, internal communication, online communities, and recruiting.

Public Relations, Customer Relations, and Crisis Communication.   One of the prominent uses of blogs is to provide up-to-date company information to the press and the public. Blogs can be written by rank-and-file employees or by top managers. Executive chairman Bill Marriott is an avid and astute blogger. His Marriott on the Move blog feels personal and honest:

> *Five years ago, when I started this blog I wasn't sure what to expect. I love writing and sharing my thoughts with family, friends and talking to associates and customers. So I figured, well I guess so, why not? Through the years it's been a great outlet for me and I look forward to hearing from you every time I hit the "publish" button.[44]*

Just one of several General Electric blogs, Edison's Desk addresses industry insiders and the interested public. Under the heading Best Buy Unboxed, the electronics retailer operates five niche blogs targeting various constituencies and actively soliciting customer input. Again, engaging customers in this way by tapping into their collective wisdom is called crowdsourcing. Many companies now use crowdsourcing promotions to connect with their customers and generate buzz that they hope will go viral on the Internet. Frito-Lay is offering $1 million to the consumer who creates a winning home-made Doritos ad for the Super Bowl or comes up with a new potato chip flavor.[45]

A company blog is a natural forum for late-breaking news, especially when disaster strikes. Business bloggers can address rumors and combat misinformation. Tony "Frosty" Welch, top social media strategist at Hewlett-Packard, averted a crisis before a video tagged "HP Computers Are Racist" would explode on the Internet (currently at 2.9 million YouTube views). The webcam-made video demonstrated how HP's face-tracking software only registered light-skinned faces. In his blog response, Welch thanked the video creators, addressed the design flaw, and promised a remedy.[46]

Although a blog cannot replace other communication channels in a PR crisis or an emergency, it should be part of the overall effort to soothe the public's emotional reaction with a human voice of reason.

Market Research and Viral Marketing.   Because most blogs invite feedback, they can be invaluable sources of opinion and bright ideas from customers as well as industry experts. Starbucks is a Fortune 500 company that understands blogging and crowdsourcing in

Figure **7.10** Starbucks Blog Specializes in Crowdsourcing

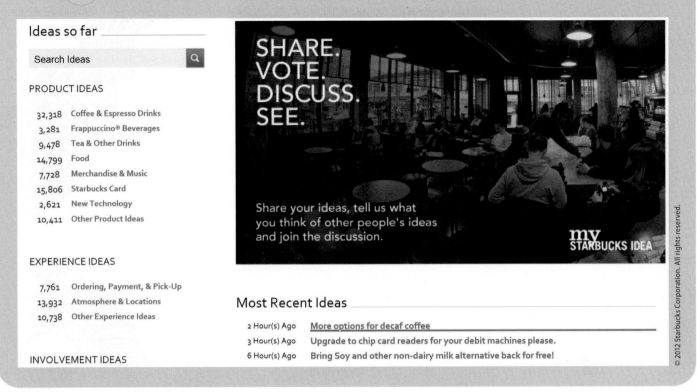

particular. My Starbucks Idea blog, depicted in Figure 7.10, is a public forum for the sharing of product ideas. Members vote and comment on the suggestions and eliminate poor ideas.

In addition to monitoring visitor comments on their corporate blogs, large companies employ teams of social media experts and marketers who scrutinize the blogosphere for buzz and positive or negative postings about their organization and products.

The term *viral marketing* refers to the rapid spread of messages online, much like infectious diseases that pass from person to person. Marketers realize the potential of getting the word out about their products and services in the blogosphere, where their messages are often picked up by well-connected bloggers, the so-called *influencers,* who boast large audiences. Viral messages must be authentic and elicit an emotional response, but for that very reason they are difficult to orchestrate. Online denizens resent being co-opted by companies using overt hard-sell tactics.

Experts say that marketers must provide content that will resonate with lots of people who will then share it in small networks. This buzz is comparable to word-of-mouth offline.[47] Nickelodeon chose the wildly popular annual Comic-Con convention in San Diego to unleash a viral campaign ahead of launching the animated *Teenage Mutant Ninja Turtles* series in the fall. Fans are asked to choose sides for or against the turtles and act out various missions. Enthusiasts can connect with the game through various social networks and can expect incentives.[48]

Online Communities. Like Twitter, which can draw a loyal core following to businesses and brands, company blogs can attract a devoted community of participants. Such followers want to keep informed about company events, product updates, and other news. In turn, those enthusiasts can contribute new ideas. Few companies enjoy the brand awareness and customer loyalty of Coca-Cola. With its blog Coca-Cola Conversations, the soft drink maker shares its rich past ("Life without Coca-Cola") and thus deepens Coke fans' loyalty. Coke's marketing is subtle; the blog is designed to provide a unique experience to fans.

Internal Communication and Recruiting. Blogs can be used to keep virtual teams on track and share updates on the road. Members in remote locations can stay in touch by smartphone and other devices, exchanging text, images, sound, and video clips. In many companies,

ETHICS CHECK:

Fired for Blogging

Former flight attendant Ellen Simonetti was fired by Delta Air Lines for posting on her blog Diary of a Flight Attendant photos showing her in provocative poses on Delta planes in uniform. Simonetti claims that her dismissal violated her free-speech rights and was an act of sexual discrimination.[49] After years of litigation against Delta, Simonetti was able to parlay her fame into a book and even a few talk show appearances. Whose rights take precedence, the employee's or the employer's?

blogs have replaced hard-copy publications in offering late-breaking news or tidbits of interest to employees. Blogs can create a sense of community and stimulate employee participation.

Blogs mirror the company culture and present an invaluable opportunity for job candidates to size up a potential employer and the people working there.

Blogging has grown up as a commercial activity and now offers sound business opportunities. To even have a shot at competing with established blogs, consider the guidelines[50] in Figure 7.11.

Figure 7.11 Creating a Professional Blog

Identify your audience.

As with any type of communication, you must know your audience to decide what to write to get people to read your blog. Will your blog stand out? Is it interesting?

Choose a hosting site.

WordPress, Tumblr, and Blogger are popular platforms. Templates and other options will help you attract traffic. You will be able to track recent posts and message threads.

Craft your message.

Showcase your expertise and insights. Offer a fresh, unique perspective on subjects your audience cares about. Your writing should be intriguing and sincere.

Pick the right keywords.

Emphasize potential search terms to rise to the top of search listings. An import business might stress the keywords *import, China, trade,* and industry-specific terms (*toys*).

Work the blogroll.

Provide links to other quality blogs relevant to your business or industry to boost traffic. Chances are those bloggers will link back to you, and their readers too may visit your blog.

Blog often.

Provide fresh content regularly. Stay current. Stale informations puts off visitors. Post short, concise messages, but do so often.

Monitor traffic.

If traffic slows, experiment with new topics while staying with your core business and expertise. Monitor the effectiveness of your hosting site in increasing your blog's visibility to search engines.

REALITY CHECK: Internal Blogs Track Intellectual Property at Google

"With a company like Google that's growing this fast, the verbal history can't be passed along fast enough. Our legal department loves the blogs, because it basically is a written-down, backed-up, permanent time-stamped version of the scientist's notebook. When you want to file a patent, you can now show in blogs where this idea happened."[51]

—**MARISSA MAYER,** *former vice president of location and local services at Google, now CEO at Yahoo*

Blog Best Practices: Eight Tips for Master Bloggers

Much advice is freely accessible on the Web, but this section offers guidelines culled from experienced bloggers and communication experts that will lead you to successful online writing. As with any public writing, your posts will be scrutinized; therefore, you want to make the best impression. Your blog posts can benefit from the journalistic pattern shown in Figure 7.12 by emphasizing the big news up front, supported with specifics and background information.

Craft a Catchy but Concise Title.   The headline is what draws online readers to even open your post. Some will be intriguing questions or promises. Online writers often use numbers to structure their posts. Here are some examples: *Six Apps You Don't Want to Miss; 5 Tips to Keep Spear Phishers Out of Your Inbox; How Many Lives Does a Brand Have?; Create Powerful Imagery in Your Writing; How Financially Sexy is Your Household?; The False Choice of Mediocrity.*

Ace the Opening Paragraph.   The lead must deliver on the promise of the headline. Identify a need and propose to solve the problem. Ask a relevant question. Say something startling. Tell an anecdote or use an analogy to connect with the reader. The author of *How Many Lives Does a Brand Have?* opened with this:

> *It's said that cats have nine lives, but how many lives does a brand have? The answer, it seems, is definitely more than one. Recently, in Shanghai, a friend took me to one of the city's most sophisticated luxury malls . . . .*[52]

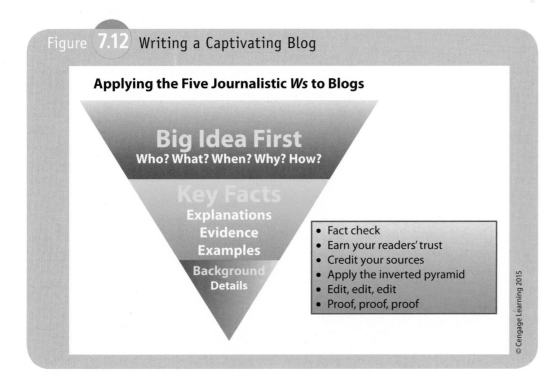

Figure **7.12** Writing a Captivating Blog

Applying the Five Journalistic *Ws* to Blogs

Big Idea First
Who? What? When? Why? How?

Key Facts
Explanations
Evidence
Examples
Background
Details

- Fact check
- Earn your readers' trust
- Credit your sources
- Apply the inverted pyramid
- Edit, edit, edit
- Proof, proof, proof

© Cengage Learning 2015

Provide Details in the Body.   Mind the *So what?* and *What's in it for me?* questions. Use vivid examples, quotations and testimonials, or statistics. Structure the body with numbers, bullets, and subheadings. Use expressive action verbs (*buy* for *get*; *own* for *have*; *to travel* or *to jet* for *go*). Use conversational language to sound warm and authentic. Use contractions (*can't* for *cannot*; *doesn't* for *does not*; *isn't* for *is not*).

Consider Visuals.   Add visual interest with relevant images and diagrams. Keep paragraphs short and use plenty of white space around them. Aim to make the look simple and easy to scan.

Include Calls to Action.   Call on readers in the title to do something or provide a take-away and gentle nudge at the end. Chris Brogan, writing in his blog Become a Dream Feeder, had this to say: *So, how will you make your blog into a dream feeder? Or do you do that already? What dreams do your readers have?* Ask open-ended questions or tell the reader what to do: *So, be sure to ask about 360-degree security tactics that aim to stop inbound attacks, but also to block outbound data theft attempts.*

Edit and Proofread.   Follow the revision tips in Chapter 6 of this book. Cut any unneeded words, sentences, and irrelevant ideas. Fix awkward, wordy, and repetitive sentences. Edit and proofread as if your life depended on it. Your reputation might. The best blogs are error free.

Respond to Posts Respectfully.   Build a positive image online by posting compelling comments on other bloggers' posts. Politely and promptly reply to comments on your site. This

CAREER COACH:
The Coolest (Social Media) Jobs

Travel, eat, and blog about it. Meet Alice Shin, "culinary ambassador" and winner of a contest from the Pei Wei Asian Diner chain, a P.F. Chang's property. For three weeks Alice crisscrossed five Asian countries with two chefs and blogged about her exploits. Check out the Pei Wei Blog. Her job skills? "A big appetite, no fear and the ability to capture your experience in a way that's relatable to the folks at home," Shin said. "Also, writing like the wind doesn't hurt either!"[53] In her day job, Alice writes advertising copy for SapientNitro.

Start a funny Web empire. After a stint as a journalist and a failed tech start-up later, Ben Huh saw the potential in I Can Has Cheezburger, a site featuring cute cat photos with "LOLspeak" captions. He nurtured it into a 40-website business with 53 employees. "I like to describe our business as party in the front, business in the back—it's a reverse mullet!" Huh said. "It's a big, giant lab for humor."[54]

Test honeymoon destinations. For six months Denise Duffield-Thomas and her husband Mark traveled to exotic locales for Irish company Runaway Bride & Groom after besting 30,000 applicants. They shot videos, uploaded photos, and blogged about experiences as varied as stays in luxury villas, desert camping trips, African tribal ceremonies, and camel rides in Jordan.[55]

Become a tourism ambassador. Ben Southall started out as an "island caretaker" in Queensland, Australia. His job duties? Going to the beach, snorkeling, diving, and exploring, and then blogging about it. His success landed Ben a full-time job as "tourism ambassador" for Queensland. He travels around the world to speak about his experience to audiences of 2,000 people at conferences, escorts visitors, or seeks out adventures at home to write about.[56]

Don't write off "old media." Not all the plum jobs are broadcast on the social Web. Kirsten Schimoler, ice cream developer/flavor guru at Ben & Jerry's, found her dream job advertised in a *print ad*! She grew up around food in her parents' restaurant. She holds a degree in food science from Cornell University and worked as a product developer at Unilever, Ben & Jerry's parent.[57]

reply to Guy Kawasaki's infographic makes a positive observation about the post and adds a valuable thought albeit with a glaring spelling error and missing commas:

> Great graphic portrayal of the human connection. Three other areas might include 1) use people's first name (something pretty basic but often forgotten) 2) listen before you talk (a great one for bosses when meeting with employees) and 3) don't be afraid to pay comple-ments [sic] when they are warranted.[58]

If you disagree with a post, do so respectfully. Don't ramble.

Learn From the Best. Visit the blogs of Seth Godin, Chris Brogan, Guy Kawasaki, Bill Marriott, and others. See what you can adopt and make work for yourself. You may decide to post a personal blog, as student Dana Schwartz did (see Figure 7.13). Just apply the same

---

Figure 7.13 Student Blog Article Illustrates Best Practices

ABOUT US | SERVICES & PRICING | HOW WE WORK | CASE STUDIES | BLOG | CONTACT US

Includes title with a number and with keywords to snag browsers

3 TIPS FOR MANAGING SOCIAL MEDIA IN THE WORKPLACE

by Dana Schwartz on February 10, 2012

Like 2 | 0 | Tweet 12 | Share 4

Provides appropriate graphic for visual appeal

This semester I'm taking a social media class. I've already learned much about how social media is changing society—from the way it changes relationships (are you Facebook official?) to how it impacts the workplace.

Many questions are troubling about the social media–work relationship. Are you allowed to use social media sites at work? Should you affiliate with your company online? What is appropriate to tweet from the company Twitter handle?

Mashable recently posted its top practices for social networking in the workplace. Here are the three tips I think are most important:

Lists important points in concise parallel form for quick readability and comprehension

1. **Understand company policy.** Be sure to understand fully the company's written policy but also the culture of the office. Know what sites are off limits. Also, just because something isn't forbidden in the official policy does not mean it is a good idea. If you can't find your company's written policy, ask about it. Not every company has one, and it might show initiative to inquire about it.

2. **Be wary of mixing the personal and the professional.** Be careful when using your company's digital channels. You're allowed to be yourself, but stick to the company's personality. The Time.com Twitter handle (@TIME) is my favorite example of this. The content it tweets is all *Time*-related, with a personality, thanks to *Time* social media editor, Allie Townsend (@Allie Townsend). Allie's personality comes out through the *Time* handle, but the content is all appropriate for the account.

3. *Private* **really doesn't mean private anymore.** Just because you have sent a private message to someone does not mean that it will stay private. The Mashable article mentions *The New York Times* test. Would you be comfortable seeing your message on the front page of *The New York Times*? This goes for public and private messages.

Concludes with important advice for social media users

A speaker I heard last year gave a great piece of advice for using social media: "Think twice, post once." It's definitely an important thing to remember when using social media sites in the workplace.

Calls on readers to respond

Do you use social media in the workplace? Do you have any tips to add?

Reblog This Article

You might also enjoy:

Provides links to related online articles of interest to readers

1. Study: How Do Employers Manage Social Media?
2. Staying Connected with Social Media
3. Social Networking At Work [INFOGRAPHIC]

Dana Schwartz

Dana Schwartz is a senior studying public relations and management at Syracuse University. She has previous internship experience with a small New York City public relations firm, as a communications intern for the Special Olympics in London, and in health care marketing. She is looking forward to starting a career in public relations upon her graduation.

With permission of Heather R. Huhman, http://comerecommended.com

© Cengage Learning 2015

best practices outlined here for professional business blogs. Notice that Dana's blog offers a catchy title with a number in it (*3 Tips for Managing Social Media in the Workplace*) on a popular topic that will attract browsers. She shares helpful advice in easy-to-read numbered items and provides links to other relevant articles. To motivate readers to respond, she asks questions (*Do you use social media in the workplace? Do you have any tips to add?*).

LEARNING OBJECTIVE **5**
Address business uses of social networking and the benefits of RSS feeds.

Web 2.0: Social Networking Sites

Popular social networking sites such as Facebook and Twitter are used by businesses for similar reasons and in much the same way as podcasts, blogs, and wikis. Social networking sites enable businesses to connect with customers and employees, share company news, and exchange ideas. Social online communities for professional audiences (e.g., LinkedIn), discussed in Chapter 15, help recruiters find talent and encounter potential employees before hiring them.

Tapping Into Social Networks

Business interest in social networking sites is not surprising if we consider that 83 percent of millennials, also called Generation Y, regularly socialize and chat online. They are most likely to access the Internet wirelessly with mobile phones and laptops. Millennials lead in instant messaging, blog reading, listening to music, playing online games, and participating in virtual worlds. However, those in older age groups are gaining on them and pulling ahead in some categories. The number of social media users seventy-four and older has quadrupled in four years to 16 percent.[59]

According to Nielsen, users over fifty-five are driving the growth of social networking via the mobile Internet. Social networks and blogs are the top destinations and dominate Americans' time spent online (23 percent), twice as much as online games (10 percent), the No. 2 category. As for Twitter, at 31 percent the heaviest users are people in the eighteen-to-twenty-four age bracket, followed by twenty-five- to thirty-four-year-olds (17 percent).[60]

Predictably, businesses are trying to adapt and tap the vast potential of social networking. Almost 60 percent of the Fortune 500 companies are now on Facebook, and 62 percent have corporate Twitter accounts. Google leads with 5.8 million Twitter followers, with Starbucks coming in second (3.7 million), and Whole Foods Market in third place (3.4 million).

How Businesses Use Social Networks.   The key to all the new media is that they thrive in a highly mobile and interactive Web 2.0 environment. However, the social Web has also spawned internal networking sites safely located behind corporate firewalls. For example, McDonald's has a strong presence on Facebook boasting more than 10.7 million "fans." In addition, the fast-food chain maintains a private networking site, StationM, for its 700,000 hourly employees across the United States. The vice president of human resources, Danitra Barnett, credits the crew site with reducing turnover. She says that the attrition rate is lower than the industry average and at its lowest in over 20 years.[61]

Adopting the Facebook Model.   Indeed, other companies too have found that the Facebook model can be adapted to internal networks, many of which run on the Chatter enterprise social networking platform. For one thing, staff members already intuitively understand how a corporate social network operates because they are familiar with Facebook. Red Robin's corporate social network, by allowing discussions and providing videos, helped cut the introduction of a new burger line from months to days.[62]

Connecting Far-Flung Workers.   Because social networks are about connections, they also enable companies to match up dispersed employees and their skills as needed, especially when managers in different divisions don't know each other. SUPERVALU supermarket chains built a Yammer-based network connecting 11,000 executives and store managers, eliminating the need for expensive travel. More than 1,000 groups emerged that provided creative solutions to specific problems.[63]

Crowdsourcing Customers.   Social networks and blogs also help companies to invite customer input at the product-design stage. On its IdeaStorm site, Dell has solicited over 17,000 new

Figure **7.14** Big Companies Rule on Facebook: Coca-Cola Is Number One

Facebook has reached 1 billion users. For comparison, LinkedIn has 200 million members, Twitter claims 200 million active users, and Google Plus has 500 registered users. Facebook allows registered users to create individual home pages as well as group pages based on their interests. Large corporations seem to thrive on Facebook. The top three companies with the most fans are Coca-Cola (64.1 million), Disney (44 million), and Starbucks (34.4 million).

product ideas and suggested improvements, including backlit keyboards that are ideal for working on airplanes.[64] As Figure 7.14 shows, large companies have established a successful social media presence.

Experts predict that social media will become as important for the economy as mobile phones and cloud computing: "Mobile is an extension of the cloud, because it lets you get your data wherever you are. And social is the layer on top of that, making it easier to cross-communicate," says California-based venture capitalist Stacey Bishop.[65]

Potential Risks of Social Networks for Businesses. Online public social networks hold great promise for businesses while also presenting some risk. Most managers want plugged-in employees with strong tech skills. They like to imagine their workers as brand ambassadors. They fantasize about their products becoming overnight sensations thanks to viral marketing. However, they also fret about incurring productivity losses, compromising trade secrets, attracting the wrath of huge Internet audiences, and facing embarrassment over inappropriate and damaging employee posts.[66]

Businesses take different approaches to the "dark side" of social networking. Some, such as Zappos.com, take a hands-off approach and encourage employee online activity. Others, such as IBM, have drafted detailed policies to cover all forms of self-expression online. According to one survey, 50 percent of businesses block Web access to social networking sites; 61 percent, to gaming sites; and 40 percent, to entertainment sites.[67] Several top German corporations, including Volkswagen and Porsche, have banned social media outright, fearing loss of productivity and industrial espionage.[68] However, experts believe that organizations should embrace positive word-of-mouth testimonials from employees about their jobs, not quash them with rigid policies.[69] In the United States, social media policies need to be guidelines, not rules, or they could violate labor laws under certain circumstances.[70]

Because the lines between work time and personal time are increasingly blurry, some organizations allow partial access by limiting what employees can do online. They may disable file sharing to protect sensitive information.

Using Social Networking Sites and Keeping Your Job. Experts agree that, as with any public online activity, users of social networking sites would do well to exercise caution.

ETHICS CHECK:

Pricing Blunder Broadcast Far and Wide via Social Media

Because of a software glitch, Tesco, the world's third-largest retailer based in the United Kingdom, offered a new iPad worth £659 ($1,021) for £49.99 ($77) on its website. Within hours the news exploded on Facebook and Twitter. Some customers ordered as many as 20 iPads and insisted that Tesco honor the advertised price. The company quickly corrected the online pricing error and would not accept orders at the incorrect price. Was Tesco obligated to honor the offer?

Figure **7.15** Guidelines for Safe Social Networking

Establish boundaries.

Don't share information, images, and media online that you would not be comfortable sharing openly in the office.

Distrust privacy settings.

Even privacy settings don't guarantee complete protection from prying eyes. Facebook has repeatedly come under fire for changing privacy settings and opening unwitting user's profiles for the world to see.

Rein in your friends.

One of your 500 Facebook friends may tag you in an inappropriate photograph. Tags make pictures searchable, so that an embarrassing college incident may resurface years later. Always ask before tagging someone.

Beware "friending."

Don't reject friend requests from some coworkers while accepting them from others. Snubbed workers may harbor ill feelings. Don't friend your boss unless he or she friends you first. Send friend requests only once.

Expect the unexpected.

Recruiters now routinely check applicants' online presence. Some employers have gone so far as to demand that candidates disclose their Facebook login information. Facebook and lawmakers have criticized the practice.

© Cengage Learning 2015

Privacy is a myth, and sensitive information should not be shared lightly, least of all risqué photographs. Furthermore, refusing "friend" requests or "unfriending" individuals could jeopardize professional relationships. Consider the tips in Figure 7.15 provided by career counselor Julie Powell[71] if you like to visit social networking sites and want to keep your job.

Navigating the Information Glut With RSS Feeds

Seeking relevant information on the Web can be time-consuming and sometimes tedious, especially if it means browsing many websites for updates. Really simple syndication, RSS for short, is a time-saver, allowing users to monitor many news sources in one convenient spot and receive targeted, personalized news.

RSS, a way to receive custom-tailored information from hundreds of sources, is a data file format capable of transmitting changing Web content. News organizations, bloggers, social networks, and other online information providers syndicate (i.e., publish and distribute) their content to subscribers. RSS documents are called feeds or channels, and they can be read most efficiently with a Web-based feed reader (also known as an aggregator) or a mobile app equivalent. Feeds alert subscribers about blog entries, news items, videos, and podcasts from various sources that interest them. The most popular news aggregator today is Google Reader. Increasingly, feed readers are available as apps and read on mobile devices, helping busy executives stay informed on the go. Besides Google Reader, popular RSS readers are Feedly, my6sense, Pulse, and Reeder.[72]

Content providers have a vital interest in providing RSS feeds. For one thing, feeds increase traffic to syndicated websites because they can be indexed in search engines and tagged to appear in feed lists, making them easier to find. This helps content providers stay ahead of the vast competition in cyberspace. Retailer Target, online travel sites such as Travelocity, and many airlines have been using RSS feeds to alert customers to weekly sales and special offers.

Perhaps you can see now how RSS feeds could help you stay abreast of breaking news from many sources and save you valuable time. Whether you wish to grab a broadcast from CNN.com, read a *Wall Street Journal* article, or check the most recent sports scores, look for the square orange RSS feed icon on your favorite websites or a rectangular button with the letters RSS.

The checklist that follows highlights some employee dos and don'ts that you should abide by to keep out of trouble on the job.

CHECKLIST ▶▶❙

Using Electronic Media Professionally: Dos and Don'ts

Dos: Know Workplace Policies and Avoid Private Use of Media at Work

- **Learn your company's rules.** Some companies require workers to sign that they have read and understand Internet and digital media use policies. Being informed is your best protection.

- **Avoid sending personal e-mail, instant messages, or texts from work.** Even if your company allows personal use during lunch or after hours, keep it to a minimum. Better yet, wait to use your own electronic devices away from work.

- **Separate work and personal data.** Keep information that could embarrass you or expose you to legal liability on your personal storage devices, on hard drives, or in the cloud, never on your office computer.

- **Be careful when blogging, tweeting, or posting on social networking sites.** Unhappy about not receiving a tip, a Beverly Hills waiter lost his job for tweeting disparaging remarks about an actress. Forgetting that his boss was his Facebook "friend," a British employee was fired after posting "OMG, I HATE MY JOB!" and calling his supervisor names.[73]

- **Keep sensitive information private.** Use privacy settings, but don't trust the "private" areas on Facebook, Twitter, Flickr, and other social networks.

- **Stay away from pornography, sexually explicit jokes, or inappropriate screen savers.** Anything that might "poison" the work environment is a harassment risk and, therefore, prohibited.

Don'ts: Avoid Questionable Content, Personal Documents, and File Sharing

- **Don't spread rumors, gossip, and negative, defamatory comments.** Because all digital information is subject to discovery in court, avoid unprofessional content and conduct, including complaints about your employer, customers, and employees.[74]

- **Don't download and share cartoons, video clips, photos, and art.** Businesses are liable for any recorded digital content regardless of the medium used.[75]

- **Don't open attachments sent by e-mail.** Attachments with executable files or video files may carry viruses, spyware, or other malware (malicious programs).

- **Don't download free software and utilities to company machines.** Employees can unwittingly introduce viruses, phishing schemes, and other cyber "bugs."

- **Don't store your music and photos on a company machine (or server), and don't watch streaming videos.** Capturing precious company bandwidth for personal use is a sure way to be shown the door.

- **Don't share files, and avoid file-sharing services.** Clarify whether you may use Google Docs and other services that offer optional file sharing. Stay away from distributors of pirated files such as LimeWire.

Zooming in

Your Turn: Applying Your Skills at Twitter

Many large companies monitor Twitter chatter and have discovered it as a tool to avert public relations disasters. Domino's Pizza deftly responded with a coordinated social media campaign to counter the fallout from a damaging prank. Two employees had posted a disgusting YouTube video showing them engaging in several health code violations.[76] Despite initial damage, the company was able to regain its customers' trust and even enlisted their help via social networking to improve the taste of its pizzas. Comcast, Coca-Cola, PepsiCo, and others are quick to apologize to irate customers and to correct problems that they discover on Twitter or other social media network sites. Southwest Airlines employs a six-member "emerging-media team." The former head of social media at Coke, Adam Brown, now at computer maker Dell, says: "We're getting to a point if you're not responding, you're not being seen as an authentic type of brand."[77]

YOUR TASK. You are one of three social media interns working for Adam Brown at Dell. Your job is to comb through tweets to find those that are both positive about and critical of your company and to inform your boss about any that could potentially end up hurting Dell's image. Deciding which post could cause trouble is difficult, given that even with tracking software, you may need to scan hundreds of posts every day. You know that if many users "retweet," or redistribute the news, the problem may get out of hand. Create a Twitter account and search for posts about Dell or any other company your instructor may assign. Make a list of three positive and three negative tweets. Recommend or draft responses to them. If you identify a trend, make a note of it and report it either in class or in writing as directed by your instructor. To review efficient microblogging, see Chapter 6 page 182.

Summary of Learning Objectives

1 Understand e-mail and the professional standards for its usage, structure, and format in the digital-era workplace. The exchange of information in organizations today is increasingly electronic and mobile although office workers still send paper-based messages when they need a permanent record; wish to maintain confidentiality; and need to convey formal, long, and important messages. E-mail is still the lifeblood of businesses today, but instant messaging is gaining popularity. Direct (nonsensitive) e-mails and memos begin with a subject line that summarizes the central idea. The opening repeats that idea and amplifies it. The body explains and provides more information. The closing includes (a) action information, dates, and deadlines; (b) a summary; and/or (c) a closing thought. Skilled e-mail writers take advantage of *down-editing*. After deleting all unnecessary parts of the sender's message, they insert their responses to the remaining parts of the incoming message. Careful e-mail users write concisely and don't send anything they wouldn't want published.

2 Explain workplace instant messaging and texting as well as their liabilities and best practices. Because they are fast, discreet, and inexpensive, instant messaging (IM) and text messaging have become increasingly relevant for businesses in communicating with customers, employees, and suppliers. Risks include productivity loss, leaked trade secrets, and legal liability from workers' improper use of digital media. Businesses also fear fraud, malware, and spam. Best practices include following company policies, avoiding sensitive information, not forwarding inappropriate links and other digital content, and using correct grammar and spelling. When texting, businesspeople should consider the proper timing, address their messages to the correct person, and identify themselves to the recipient. They should not use texting for sensitive news or expect an instant reply.

3 Identify professional applications of podcasts and wikis, and describe guidelines for their use. Business podcasts are digital audio or video files ranging from short clips to long media files. Any applications that do not require a human presence (e.g., certain training videos) lend themselves to podcast recordings that users can stream or download on demand. Wikis enable far-flung team members to share information and build a knowledge base, and can be used to replace meetings, manage projects, and document projects large and small.

4 Describe how businesses use blogs to connect with internal and external audiences, and list best practices for professional blogging. Blogs help businesses to keep customers, employees, and suppliers informed and to receive feedback. Online communities can form around blogs. Companies employ blogs for public relations and crisis communication, market research and viral marketing, internal communication, and recruiting. To create a professional blog, writers first identify their audience, choose a hosting site, craft their message, pick the right keywords, link to other bloggers to boost interest in their own sites, blog often, and monitor traffic to their posts.

5 Address business uses of social networking and the benefits of RSS feeds. Social networking sites such as Facebook and Twitter allow firms to share company news; exchange ideas; and connect with customers, employees, other stakeholders, and the public at large. Companies boost their brand recognition, troubleshoot customer problems, use crowdsourcing to engage customers, and participate in established social networks or by creating their own in-house communities. The downsides of social media at work are productivity losses, legal liability, leaking of trade secrets, and angry Internet users. Keep safe by sharing only information that you would openly discuss in the office. Be sure to activate your privacy options. Don't post questionable content. Really simple syndication allows users to navigate the huge resources on the Internet. RSS feeds are time-savers because they allow businesspeople to monitor many news sources in one convenient online location.

Chapter Review

1. How have social media sites such as Twitter changed communication? (Obj. 5)

2. What is cloud computing, and how is it changing business? (Obj. 1)

3. List and concisely describe at least six electronic communication channels used most commonly by businesspeople today. (Objs. 1–5)

4. List and briefly describe the four parts of typical e-mails. (Obj. 1)

5. Suggest at least ten pointers that you could give to a first-time e-mail user. (Obj. 1)

6. How can you use instant messaging and texting safely on the job? (Obj. 2)

7. Name at least five reasons some organizations forbid employees to use instant and text messaging. (Obj. 2)

8. How can you show professionalism and respect for your receivers in writing business instant messages and texts? (Obj. 2)

9. How do organizations use podcasts, and how are they accessed? (Obj. 3)

10. What is a wiki, and what are its advantages to businesses? (Obj. 3)

11. Explain why companies use blogs. (Obj. 4)

12. List the eight best practices for master bloggers. (Obj. 4)

13. How do businesses try to tap the vast potential of social networking? (Obj. 5)

14. Name a few of the potential risks that social networking sites may pose to business. (Obj. 5)

15. What is really simple syndication (RSS), and how is it helpful? (Obj. 5)

Critical Thinking

1. Journalist Bob Garfield, author of *The Chaos Scenario*, is concerned that privacy is increasingly a rare commodity in our hyperconnected world. He argues: "Google searches, Foursquare check-ins and even basic browsing leave a practically neon trail. And on Facebook, we trade privacy for a sense of community; we fear Big Brother, but we tell lots of 'little brothers' everything."[78] Discuss what seem to be contradictory sentiments. Are you concerned about disclosing personal matters online?

2. In her book *Alone Together*, MIT professor Sherry Turkle argues that increasing dependence on technology leads to a consequent diminution in personal connections. "Technology is seductive when what it offers meets our human vulnerabilities. And as it turns out, we are very vulnerable indeed. We are lonely but fearful of intimacy. Digital connections . . . may offer the illusion of companionship without the demands of friendship."[79] Do you agree that technology diminishes personal relationships rather than bringing us closer together? Do social media fool us into thinking that we are connected when in reality we bear none of the commitments and burdens of true friendship?

3. How could IM be useful in your career field? Does IM produce a permanent record? Do you think that common abbreviations such as *lol* and *imho* and all-lowercase writing are acceptable in text messages for business? Will the use of shorthand abbreviations as well as creative spelling negatively affect writing skills? (Obj. 2)

4. Tweeting, texting, and quickie e-mailing all may foster sloppy messages. Author Mark Garvey argued, "In business, in education, in the arts, in any writing that takes place outside the linguistic cul-de-sac of our close friends and relatives, writers are expected to reach for certain standards of clarity, concision and care."[80] What did Garvey mean? Do you agree? (Objs. 1, 2)

5. **Ethical Issue:** Aside from actually paying people to act as fans on social networks and entice their friends to do so as well, some marketers employ machines to inflate the number of their fans and followers online. Writing for *PC World*,[81] Dan Tynan describes how he discovered the activities of a so-called Facebook bot network that operates a large number of zombie accounts created in Bangladesh. Tynan had noticed that many obscure companies were suddenly experiencing wild surges in "likes." He cites Rent My Vacation Home, a rental agency based in Washington, DC, that went from two fans to almost 15,000 within a few days. Tynan counted about 70 other businesses and fan pages across the globe that were also flooded with suspicious "likes" from the same source. Tynan himself was able to create such a bot master with fake accounts in 10 minutes using minimal software and for under $70. Cheap software allows users to use proxies, trick Captcha programs that normally thwart bots, and add bogus friends and subscribers, Tynan writes. Why do some businesses resort to such measures? What might be the consequences of faking fans? How do you feel about companies and their brands pretending they have actual traffic on their sites?

Activities

Note: All Documents for Analysis are provided at **www.cengagebrain.com** for you to download and revise.

7.1 Document for Analysis: Wordy, Woeful E-Mail (Obj. 1)

> E-mail

YOUR TASK. The following poorly organized and poorly written e-mail message needs revision. Study the message and list its specific weaknesses. Then revise it to create a polite, concise, and readable message.

To: Department Managers
From: Mellanie Mankin <mmankin@rockstudios.com>
Subject: New People
Cc:
Bcc:

Department Managers,

This is to inform you that we are, after a long period in which we were forbidden to hire at all, considering hiring new employees. The economy seems to finally be improving (Yea!), and everyone is pleased that it might actually be looking up. We have five candidates lined up to be interviewed, and your presence is required to avoid making some bad decisions. Mark your calendars for three upcoming interviewing sessions. The first is May 5 in the Conference Room. The second meeting is scheduled for May 9 in Office 22 (the Conference Room was already scheduled). On May 12 we can finish up in the Conference Room.

Attached are résumés of the five candidates we have scheduled. As you will note, these are very promising candidates. In view of the fact that your projects need talented new team members, I should not have to urge you to attend and be well prepared. This is our chance to work together to hire the top people you select and need. For these interviews to be successful, you must examine all the candidates' résumés and send me your ranking lists.

Mellanie Mankin, Manager
[full contact information]

7.2 Document for Analysis: Poor Memo Describing Social Media Brown Bag Lunch Talk

Amy Thompson, a project manager at construction firm Acton, was asked to present a brief Brown Bag Lunch Talk to fellow employees about using social networking responsibly on the job. As an avid social media user, she has prepared a program and has written the following memo describing the proposed talk to her boss, who requested the Brown Bag talk. However, her message has many faults.

YOUR TASK. List the weaknesses of this message. Then revise it to improve organization, tone, and readability.

Date: May 12, 2014
To: Byron Hobbes
From: Amy Thompson
Subject: Social Media

As per your request, I have been slaving over the Brown Bag Lunch talk (for June 5) you requested. I appreciate this opportunity. If you can think of any points to add to the items I have already thought of, please feel free to let me know. What I have in mind is discussing about three major points related to using social media responsibly and hoping that these points will open up a broader discussion of proper practices. In a short presentation like this, I should not talk too much.

As you know, we do have an Internet policy here at Acton. But no mention of Facebook or any of the other social media because it was written ages ago. So, my three points will focus first on following existing company policy. Which has always allowed limited personal Internet use by employees. But, as I mentioned, does not spell out social media specifically. My advise is to stay away from social media on company computers. After all, we're not being paid to check our Facebook profile, peruse News Feeds, or send tweets.

Second, I would advice everyone to use a disclaimer if you have a personal blog and you mention where you work. A good one to use is *The opinions expressed are mine and do not reflect those of my employer.* Remember, you represent Acton no matter where you go.

My last point refers to badmouthing and negative references. You may think that your social media sites are really private and secure. Man, that's dreaming! Don't ever criticize the company, a colleague, or a customer on social media. This kind of backbiting makes you look bad. When applying for another job, the hiring manager may see your whining online and cross you off his list.

Hope this covers my main points.

7.3 Document for Analysis: Troubling Internship Program (Obj. 1)

<E-mail>

The following poorly written message from the human resources director to project director Joshua Turck suffers from disorganization and murky focus. It also suffers from many poor writing techniques that you have studied.

YOUR TASK. Analyze this message and list at least five faults. Then determine the main idea, organize the message to develop that idea, and remedy all the writing faults.

To: Joshua Turck <joshua.turck@bayside.com>
From: Sable Johnson <sable.johnson@bayside.com>
Subject: Interns
Cc:
Bcc:

I am writing in response to your recent inquiry. Thank you for your inquiry and for your concern. We do indeed want a strong internship program that can provide us with superior, well-trained personnel; however, the program must also, to the best of our abilities, meet government regulations.

Your inquiry about the status of our interns alarmed my staff and I. Which made us immediately begin to look into this matter more carefully. Our attorneys told us that all interns must be considered employees. They must be paid at least the minimum wage. Learning that college interns are legitimate only if they receive real training—and not merely doing busy work—is another major concern. Interns are not legitimate if they do any of the following: 1. If they displace a regular employee. 2. If they complete a client's work for which we bill. 3. If they are given the promise of full-time jobs at the end of training.

As mentioned earlier, I appreciate your bringing this to my attention. I would like to make arrangements for you to meet with the vice president and I to analyze this fall's internship program and give consideration to changes.

Having every single intern sign a contract saying that they are willing to accept college credit in place of wages does not provide legal protection. An intern must do more than busy work.

After reviewing our complete program, changes must be made. We believe that future interns must have a structured training program. Let's meet to discuss!

Sable Johnson, Director
Human Resources

7.4 Document for Analysis: Instant Messaging at a Local Auto Dealer (Obj. 2)

<Social Media> <Web>

Read the following log of a live IM chat between a customer-service representative and a visitor to an Orlando car dealership's website.

YOUR TASK. In class discuss how Mark could have made this interaction with a customer more effective. Is his IM chat with Mr. Kim professional, polite, and respectful? If your instructor directs, rewrite Mark's responses to Mr. Kim's queries.

Dealer rep: Hey, I'm Mark. How's it goin? Welcome to Fields BMW South Orlando!

Customer: ??

Dealer rep: Im supposed to provid live assistance. What can I do you for?

Customer: I want buy car.

Dealer rep: May I have your name fist?

Customer: Young Jae Kim

Dealer rep: Whoa! Is that a dude's name? Okay. What kind? New inventory or preowned?

Customer: BMW. 2014 model. for family, for business.

Dealer rep: New, then, huh? Where are you from?

Customer: What car you have?

Dealer rep: We got some that will knock your socks off.

Customer: I want green car, no high gasoline burn.

Service rep: My man, if you can't afford the gas on these puppies, you shouldn't buy a Beemer, you know what I mean? Or ya want green color?

Customer: ?

Dealer rep: Okeydoke, we got a full lineup. Which series, 3, 5, 6, or 7? Or an X3 or X5? A Z4 convertible?

Customer: BMW i ActiveE?

Dealer rep: Nope. Is that the electric car? Oh I dont recommend those. We got two regular 550i, one for $69,895 and one for 72,020

Customer: Eurepean delivery?

Dealer rep: Oh, I know zip about that. Let me find someone who does. Can I have your phone number and e-mail?

Customer: i prefer not get a phone call yet... but 407-484-6356 is phone numer and yjkim@t-tech.net email

Dealer rep: Awsome. Well give you a jingle back or shoot you an email pronto! Bye.

7.5 Reaching Consensus About Business Attire (Obj. 1)

< **E-mail** > < **Team** >

Casual dress in professional offices has been coming under attack. Your boss, Elizabeth Sommer, received the e-mail shown in Figure 7.1. She thinks it would be a good assignment for her group of management trainees to help her respond to that message. She asks your team to research answers to the first five questions in President Aiden Rebol's message. She doesn't expect you to answer the final question, but any information you can supply to the first questions would help him shape a response.

Diago Enterprises, LLC, is a public CPA firm with a staff of 90 CPAs, bookkeepers, managers, and support personnel. Located in Cypress, California, the plush offices on Valley View Boulevard overlook Oak Knoll Park. The firm performs general accounting and audit services as well as tax planning and preparation. Accountants visit clients in the field and also entertain them in the downtown office.

YOUR TASK. Decide whether the entire team will research each question in Figure 7.1 or whether team members will be assigned certain questions. Collect information, discuss it, and reach consensus on what you will report to Ms. Sommer. As a team write a concise one-page response. Your goal is to inform, not persuade. Remember that you represent management, not students or employees.

7.6 E-Mail Simulation: Writeaway Hotels (Obj. 1)

< **E-mail** >

At **www.cengagebrain.com**, you can build your e-mail skills in our Writeaway Hotels simulation. You will be reading, writing, and responding to messages in an exciting game that helps you make appropriate decisions about whether to respond to e-mail messages and how to write clear, concise messages under pressure. The game can be played in a computer lab, in a classroom, or even on your own computer and on your own time.

YOUR TASK. Check out the Writeaway Hotels simulation at your student site. If your instructor directs, follow the instructions to participate.

7.7 Chatting With Skyline Mobile Customer Service (Obj. 2)

< **Social Media** > < **Team** > < **Web** >

Read the following log of a live IM chat between a Skyline Mobile customer service representative and a customer inquiring about an unexpected added fee.

YOUR TASK. Evaluate the exchange based on word choice, grammar, tone, and professionalism. How well does the customer-service representative handle the customer's inquiry? Is it resolved fairly, and is it likely to foster a good business relationship?

Individually or in small groups, discuss alternative strategies for this online chat if applicable. Consider the organization's goals in providing live chat representatives; were those goals met? If your instructor directs, revise the dialogue.

Please hold for a Skyline Mobile sales representative to assist you with your order. Thank you for your patience. You are now chatting with "May D."

May D.: Hello. Thank you for visiting our chat service. May I help you with your order today?

Customer: Yes, I'm about to finish my order, but suddenly there's a $30 upgrade fee? What's that? I'm surprised. I thought I'm getting an upgrade discount.

May D.: Skyline Mobile implemented a $30 upgrade fee for existing customers purchasing new mobile equipment at a discounted price with a two-year contract. This fee will help us continue to provide customers with the level of service and support they have come to expect, which includes Wireless Workshops, online educational tools, and consultations with experts who provide advice and guidance on devices that are more sophisticated than ever.

Customer: Okay, so that means the phone advertised at $99.99 is really going to cost me $30 more?

May D.: Are you an existing customer?

May D.: You may have the option the $30 to your account.

Customer: Yes, I am. I have been for many years and each month I'm paying $130 for my service. I'm a bit taken aback by this last-minute charge. I have just chatted with another representative and that wasn't brought up.

Customer: It's not the additional charge, it's how "sneakily" it pops up at the end just as the customer is about to click "BUY."

May D.: Yes, I understand, it was just implemented last week on the 22nd.

Customer: Just my luck. Okay, I don't really need an upgrade. My Droid 2 is doing its work nicely and I have unlimited data. So I won't go through with it. You are losing my $175 business today.

May D.: I understand how you feel and appreciate your loyalty. In addition to receiving discounts on device prices when upgrading, we do from time to time send our loyal customers specials, offers and updates on new equipment, products, and price plans.

Customer: I know. I did get one such ad for Mother's day, the Droid Razr for $99.99. Okay, I'll wait until the price drops. No problem. Thank you.

May D.: Is there anything else I can help you with today?

Customer: No, thanks. Your customer service is getting worse.

Customer: Not you personally, but the "perks." Your company is adding hidden fees. Not cool. -- Have a good day.

7.8 Instant Messaging: Practicing Your Professional IM Skills (Obj. 2)

< **Social Media** > < **Team** > < **Web** >

Your instructor will direct this role-playing group activity. Using instant messaging, you will simulate one of several typical business scenarios—for example, responding to a product inquiry, training a new-hire, troubleshooting with a customer, or making an appointment. For each scenario, two or more students will chat professionally with only a minimal script to practice on-the-spot yet courteous professional interactions by IM. Your instructor will determine which software you will need and provide brief instructions to prepare you for your role in this exercise.

If you don't have instant messaging software on your computer or smart device yet, download the application first—for example, AOL's Instant Messenger, Yahoo Messenger, Microsoft's Windows Live Messenger, or Skype. Yahoo Messenger, for instance, allows you to IM your friends on Yahoo Messenger but also on Windows Live Messenger. You control who sees you online; if you don't wish to be interrupted, you can use stealth settings. All IM software enables users to share photos and large media files. You can make voice calls and use webcam video as well. These advanced features turn IM software into a simple conferencing tool and video phone. You can connect with users who have the same software all around the world. Contrary to calling landlines or cell phones, peer-to-peer voice calls are free. Most IM clients also offer mobile applications for your smartphone, so that you can IM or call other users while you are away from a computer.

YOUR TASK. Log on to the IM or chat program your instructor chooses. Follow your instructor's directions closely as you role-play the business situation you were assigned with your partner or team. The scenario will involve two or more people who will communicate by instant messaging in real time.

7.9 Analyzing a Podcast (Obj. 3)

> E-mail   Social Media

Browsing the podcasts at iTunes, you stumble across the Quick and Dirty Tips series, specifically Money Girl, who dispenses financial advice. You sign up for the free podcasts that cover a variety of business topics. You can also visit the website Quick and Dirty Tips or interact with Laura D. Adams on her Money Girl Facebook page. Alternatively, examine the advice conveyed via podcast, the Web, Facebook, and Twitter by clever Grammar Girl Mignon Fogarty.

YOUR TASK. Pick a Money Girl podcast that interests you. Listen to it or obtain a transcript on the website and study it for its structure. Is it direct or indirect? Informative or persuasive? How is it presented? What style does the speaker adopt? At your instructor's request, write an e-mail that discusses the podcast you analyzed. Alternatively, if your instructor allows, you could also send a very concise summary of the podcast by text message from your cell phone or tweet (140 characters or fewer) to your instructor.

7.10 Creating a Simple Business Podcast (Obj. 3)

> Communication Technology   Social Media   Web

Do you want to try your hand at producing a podcast? Businesses rely on a host of social media and communication technologies when reaching out to the public or internally to their workers. As you have seen, some companies produce such short audio or video clips on focused, poignant subjects. The following process describes how you can create a simple podcast:

Select software. Aside from offline software (e.g., Propaganda or Audacity), newer podcast creation software such as Hipcast, Yodio, and Podbean work in the cloud. They allow recordings within a Web browser or from a smartphone.

Obtain hardware. For high sound quality, you may need a sophisticated microphone and other equipment. The recording room must be properly shielded against noise, echo, and other interference. Many universities and some libraries provide recording booths.

Organize the message. Make sure your broadcast has a beginning, middle, and end. Build in some redundancy. Previews,

summaries, and transitions are important to help your audience follow the message.

Choose an extemporaneous or scripted delivery. Extemporaneous delivery means that you prepare, but you use only brief notes. It usually sounds more spontaneous and natural than reading from a script, but it can also lead to redundancy, repetition, and flubbed lines.

Prepare and practice. Practice before recording. Editing audio or video is difficult and time-consuming. Try to get your recording right, so that you won't have to edit much.

Publish your message. Once you post the MP3 podcast to your course website or blog, you can introduce it and request your audience's feedback.

YOUR TASK. Create a short podcast about a business-related subject you care about. Producing a simple podcast does not require sophisticated equipment. With free or inexpensive recording, editing, and publishing software such as the Propaganda, ePodcast Creator, or Audacity, you can inform customers, mix your own music, or host interviews. Any digital recorder can be used to create a no-frills podcast if the material is scripted and well rehearsed.

7.11 Podcast: Turning Text to Video in a Jiffy (Obj. 3)

> Web

Have you ever wondered how software converts text to video in a matter of minutes? Article Video Robot (AVR) is an application that automates the process of animating your text. You can create something resembling a simple podcast by inputting your text and letting the application do the rest. The AVR website provides an entertaining video with step-by-step instructions. To get a taste of creating an animated video from a text you prepare, use the free trial version. When you finish your trial video, you will see that the software makes distribution to about 17 websites very easy. Of course, this service may require a fee. Even though the voices sound a bit tinny and robotic, you will have created a rudimentary video in no time.

YOUR TASK. Write a page-long text that delivers information, provides instructions, or conveys a sales pitch. Go to Article Video Robot and view the introduction video. After that, you can register for the free trial. You can use the application only once at no cost, so prepare your text ahead of time. This video tool is suitable for informational, instructional, and persuasive messages.

7.12 Analyzing the Nuts About Southwest Blog (Obj. 4)

> E-mail   Social Media   Web

When you browse the Southwest Airlines blog, you will find the following terms of use:

> We want to build a personal relationship between our Team and you, and we need your participation. Everyone is encouraged to join in, and you don't need to register to read, watch, or comment. However, if you would like to share photos or videos or rate a post, among other things, you will need to complete a profile. . . .
>
> This is the point where we insert the "fine print" and discuss the guidelines for posting. Nuts About Southwest is a moderated site because we want to ensure that everyone stays on topic—or at least pretty close to it. We would LUV for you to

post your thoughts, comments, suggestions, and questions, but when you post, make sure that they are of general interest to most readers. Of course, profanity, racial and ethnic slurs, and rude behavior like disparaging personal remarks won't be tolerated nor published.

Even though Nuts About Southwest is moderated, we pledge to present opposing viewpoints as we have done since our blog first went "live" several years ago, and we will strive to keep posts interesting, diverse, and multi-sided. Our Team wants to engage in a conversation with you, but not every post will receive a response from us. . . .

YOUR TASK. Visit the Nuts About Southwest blog. Click **About** and read the entire User Guide. In class, discuss the tone of the guidelines. How are they presented? Who is authoring the blog, and what is its purpose? What assumptions can you make about the company culture when you read the guidelines and the blog entries? If your instructor directs, write a clear, direct memo, an e-mail message, or a discussion board post reporting your observations.

7.13 Reviewing Corporate Blogs (Obj. 4)

〈 E-mail 〉 〈 Social Media 〉 〈 Web 〉

Here is your opportunity to view and evaluate a corporate blog. As we have seen, about 23 percent of the primary Fortune 500 companies, or 116, have public blogs, and their growth has leveled off lately, mainly because businesses fear missteps and legal liability. However, the companies and their CEOs who do blog can impart valuable lessons.

YOUR TASK. Within your favorite browser, search for *CEO blogs, index of corporate blogs, index of CEO blogs,* and similar keywords . You will likely end up at Chief Executive.net, on Slideshare, and at other sites that may list the top 10 or so most popular corporate blogs, perhaps even one penned by a CEO. Select a corporate or CEO blog you find interesting, browse the posts, and read some of the contents. Furthermore, note how many of the points the blog makes match the guidelines in this book. If your instructor directs, write a brief informational memo or e-mail summarizing your observations about the business blog, its style, the subjects covered, and so forth.

7.14 Composing a Personal Blog Entry (Obj. 4)

〈 E-mail 〉 〈 Social Media 〉 〈 Web 〉

Review the guidelines for professional blogging in this chapter. Find a recent social media–related study or survey, and target an audience of business professionals who may wish to know more about social networking. Search for studies conducted by respected organizations and businesses such as Pew Internet, Robert Half International, Burson-Marsteller, ePolicy Institute, and U.S. government agencies as applicable. As you plan and outline your post, follow the advice provided in this chapter. Review the student blog post in Figure 7.13 for tips on how to convert ideas from your research into a suitable article. Although the goal is usually to offer advice, you could also weigh in with your opinion regarding a controversy. For example, do you agree with companies that forbid employees to use company computers for social networking? Do you agree that millennials are losing social skills because of excessive online connectivity?

YOUR TASK. Compose a one-page blog entry in MS Word and submit it in hard copy. Alternatively, post it to the discussion board on the class course-management platform, or e-mail it to your instructor as appropriate. Because you will be using outside sources, be careful to paraphrase correctly. Visit Chapter 11 to review how to put ideas into your own words with integrity.

7.15 Writing Superefficient Tweets (Obj. 5)

〈 Communication Technology 〉 〈 Social Media 〉

As you have seen in Chapter 6, Twitter forces its users to practice extreme conciseness. Some music reviewers have risen to the challenge and reviewed whole albums in no more than 140 characters. National Public Radio put Stephen Thompson, one of its music editors, to the test. "I approach Twitter as a science," Thompson says.[82] He sees well-designed tweets as online equivalents of haiku, a highly structured type of Japanese poetry. Thompson believes that tweets should be properly punctuated, be written in complete sentences, and of course, not exceed the 140-character limit. His rules also exclude abbreviations.

Here are two samples of Thompson's mini reviews: "Mos Def is a hip-hop renaissance man on smart songs that look to the whole world and its conflicts. Slick Rick's guest spot is a nice touch." The second one reads: "The Phenomenal Handclap Band: Chugging, timeless, jammy throwback from eight shaggy Brooklyn hipsters. Starts slowly, gets hypnotically fun."[83]

YOUR TASK. As an intern in Stephen Thompson's office, review your favorite album in 140 characters or fewer, following your boss's rules. After you have warmed up, your instructor may direct you to other concise writing tasks. Send a tweet to your instructor, if appropriate. Alternatively, practice writing Twitter posts in MS Word or on an online discussion board. The best tweets could be shared with the class.

7.16 Twitter Communication Audit (Obj. 5)

〈 Communication Technology 〉 〈 E-mail 〉 〈 Social Media 〉 〈 Web 〉

YOUR TASK. On Twitter read a number of business-related messages from reputable organizations such as GM, Ford Motor Company, Kia Motors, Pepsi, or Coca-Cola. Look for apparent examples of successful customer-service interventions, promotional appeals, and special deals. Conversely, copy or make screenshots of conversations on Twitter that you deem unprofessional based on the principles discussed in this chapter. If your instructor directs, submit your findings with a brief commentary in memo form, as an e-mail, or as a post on a discussion board you may be using in your course. You may be asked to edit and rewrite some of the tweets you find.

7.17 What? You Tweeted THAT? (Obj. 5)

〈 E-mail 〉 〈 Social Media 〉

The modern workplace is a potential digital minefield. The imprudent use of practically any online tool—whether e-mail, IM, texting, tweeting, blogging, or posting to Facebook—can land workers in hot water and even lead to dismissal. Here are five ways Twitter can get you canned for showing poor judgment:[84]

1. **Sending hate tweets about the boss.** Example: *My idiot boss said he put in for raises. I think he lies. He is known for that. His daddy owns the company.*

2. **Lying to the boss and bragging about it.** Example: *I so lied to my boss . . . I was late but I said I forgot my badge and got away with it.*

3. **Romancing the boss (kissing and telling).** Example: *I give the boss what he wants, and the fringe benefits are amazing.*

4. **Announcing the desire to quit.** Example: *So close to quitting my job right now. Sometimes I can't [expletive] stand this place [expletive] moron assistant plant manager I'm about to deck him.*

5. **Blocking your boss.** Example: *i kept my promise . . . my boss thought she was gonna follow me on here . . . i BLOCKED her [expletive] ASAP.*

YOUR TASK. Discuss each violation of Twitter best practices, or summarize in general why these tweets are potentially damaging to their authors. How could the Twitter users have handled their grievances more professionally? Comment on the style of these questionable tweets. If your instructor requests, summarize your observations in an e-mail message or an online post.

7.18 Creating a Twitter Group (Obj. 5)

`Social Media` `Web`

Tweetworks.com is designed to make microblogging useful for private individuals and businesses. The site is based on the premise that people like to talk with other like-minded people. Users come together in communities around specific topics (politics, sports, art, business, and so on). Tweetworks invites members to talk about the big news stories of the day, bounce ideas off other participants online, or just join the conversation—all in fewer than 140 characters. Your instructor may choose to create a public or private group for the class. Within this Tweetworks group for your course, you may be asked to complete short assignments in the form of tweets. Posts in a private group are not shared with other general users, yet they should be relevant to the class content and professional.

YOUR TASK. Use your Twitter username and password to log on at Tweetworks.com. Sign into and follow the group designated by your instructor. Your instructor may ask you to comment on a topic he or she assigns or may encourage you to enter into a freewheeling discussion with other members of your class online. Your instructor may act as a group moderator evaluating the frequency and quality of your contributions.

7.19 Building an Online Community on Facebook (Obj. 5)

`Social Media` `Team` `Web`

Chances are you already have a Facebook profile and communicate with friends and family. You may be a fan of a celebrity or a business. Now you can also become a fan of your business communication class if your instructor decides to create a course page on Facebook. The main purpose of such a social networking site for a class is to exchange links and interesting stories relevant to the material being learned. Intriguing tidbits and business news might also be posted on the "wall" to be shared by all signed-up fans. Everybody, even students who are quiet in class, could contribute. However, before you can become a fan of your business communication class, it needs to be created online.

YOUR TASK. If you have a profile on Facebook, all you need to do is search for the title of the newly created business communication Facebook page and become a fan. If you don't have a Facebook account yet, on-screen prompts will make it easy for you to build a profile.

7.20 The Dark Side: Hooked on Social Media? (Obj. 5)

`Social Media`

Could you give up your electronic toys for 24 hours without "withdrawal symptoms"? Would you be able to survive a full day unplugged from all media? A class of 200 students at the University of Maryland, College Park, went media free for 24 hours and then blogged about the experience.[85]

Some sounded like addicts going cold turkey: *In withdrawal. Frantically craving. Very anxious. Extremely antsy. Miserable. Jittery.*

Crazy. One student lamented: *I clearly am addicted and the dependency is sickening.* In the absence of technology that anchors them to friends and family, students felt bored and isolated. One wrote: *I felt quite alone and secluded from my life. Although I go to a school with thousands of students, the fact that I was not able to communicate with anyone via technology was almost unbearable.*

The study reveals a paradigm shift in human interaction. A completely digital generation is viscerally wedded to electronic toys, so much so that technology has become an indispensable part of the young people's lives.

Perceived advantages (duh?): Electronically abstinent students stated that they spent more time on course work, took better notes, and were more focused. As a result, they said they learned more and became more productive. They also reported that they spent more time with loved ones and friends face-to-face. Life slowed down and the day seemed much longer to some.

YOUR TASK. Discuss in class, in a chat, or in an online post the following questions: Have you ever unplugged? What was that experience like? Could you give up your cell phone, iPod, TV, car radio, magazines, newspapers, and computer (no texting, no Facebook or IM) for a day or longer? What would you be doing instead? Is there any harm in not being able to unplug?

7.21 Entrusting Your Data to the Cloud (Obj. 5)

`Communication Technology` `E-mail` `Social Media`

For businesses, cloud computing might as well mean "cloud nine."[86] Companies are increasingly relying on "cloud-based" computer applications that can be accessed by mobile phones, tablets, and PCs anytime and anywhere. Google is spearheading efforts to enable future consumers to use inexpensive gadgets to manage their files and media in huge data centers on the Internet. If you use Amazon, Flickr, Gmail, Facebook, or Dropbox, to name a few, you are already participating in cloud computing. Your photos and other data are stored in remote locations, and you can access them with your laptop, netbook, smartphone, or tablet.

Companies are lured to cloud computing by the promise of greater efficiency and higher profits. Blue Cross of Pennsylvania has enabled its 300,000 members to access medical histories and claims information with their smartphones. Like other tech companies, Serena Software has fully embraced the cloud, even using Facebook as the primary source of internal communication. Coca-Cola Enterprises has provided 40,000 sales reps, truck drivers, and other workers in the field with portable devices to connect with the home office instantly, allowing them to respond to changing customer needs and problems.

However, skeptics warn that caution about the risks of convenience is in order. For one thing, once the information leaves our electronic device for the cloud, we don't know who may intercept it. In addition to data security, networks must be reliable, so that users can access them anytime. Amazon's Elastic Cloud outages knocked out the websites of several organizations, including Reddit, Foursquare, Pfizer, Netflix, and Nasdaq, all of which were using Amazon's cloud-based technology.[87]

YOUR TASK. Which cloud services or applications are you already using? What are their advantages and disadvantages? Can you identify security risks that our desire for convenience may invite? Which data types are potentially most sensitive? Is convenience worth the risk? Should sensitive data and revealing information be entrusted to the cloud? If your instructor directs, write an e-mail briefly discussing the benefits and drawbacks of cloud storage, or post a short response to the discussion board of your learning-management system (Blackboard, Moodle, or other platforms).

7.22 Creating Fair Digital Media Policies (Obj. 5)

Communication Technology ▸ **E-mail** ▸ **Social Media** ▸ **Team**

As advances in computer technology continue to change the way we work and play, Internet use on and off the job has become a danger zone for employees and employers. Misuse costs employers millions of dollars in lost productivity and litigation, and it can cost employees their jobs. A survey by the American Management Association revealed that 26 percent of employers fired workers for e-mail misuse. In addition, 2 percent terminated employees for using instant messaging, and another 2 percent for posting offensive blog content from a company machine or, yes, the employee's own computer.[88] Companies struggle with fair Internet use policies knowing that over half of their employees with Web access shop online from the office.[89]

YOUR TASK. Your boss is aware of these numbers and is weighing whether to prohibit all personal use of the Internet at work, including IM, texting, visiting shopping websites, viewing YouTube videos, and so on. How would you justify keeping Internet access open? Alone or as a group, brainstorm arguments for allowing unlimited or partial access to the Web. If asked, develop your ideas into an e-mail, discussion board post, or blog entry that could sway your boss.

7.23 Discussing "Cool" Social Media Jobs (Obj. 5)

Social Media

YOUR TASK. Visit the Career Coach on page 226. Although undoubtedly fun, even glamorous, some of the social media jobs described there are short-lived affairs. However, several individuals were able to leverage their success into more lasting employment. Consider the skills needed for these types of jobs. What do you think made these young people successful? How could you parlay your skills into an exciting position with or without social media? Have you heard of similar work that required social media expertise? Are you interested? Why? Share your experience and views with a small group or in class. If called upon, craft a written response.

Chat About It

In each chapter you will find five discussion questions related to the chapter material. Your instructor may assign these topics for you to discuss in class, in an online chat room, or on an online discussion board. Some of the discussion topics may require outside research. You may also be asked to read and respond to postings made by your classmates.

Topic 1: How could dashing off quick e-mails, tweets, or instant messages with incorrect style, grammar, or mechanics hurt one's ability to write longer, more formal messages correctly?

Topic 2: Describe a time when you should have had a face-to-face meeting instead of sending an electronic message. Why would the face-to-face meeting have been better?

Topic 3: Find an example of an e-mail or text that caused a problem for the sender because the message found its way to an unintended recipient. What problem did the situation cause?

Topic 4: What is your strategy to avoid sending an IM, tweet, or text message that you might regret later?

Topic 5: Why do businesses host public blogs with negative postings of their products or services?

 C.L.U.E. Grammar & Mechanics | *Review 7*

Apostrophes and Other Punctuation

Review Guides 31–38 about apostrophes and other punctuation in Appendix A, Grammar and Mechanics Guide, beginning on page A-14. On a separate sheet or on your computer, revise the following sentences to correct errors in the use of apostrophes and other punctuation. For each error that you locate, write the guide number that reflects this usage. The more you recognize the reasons, the better you will learn these punctuation guidelines. If a sentence is correct, write C. When you finish, check your answers on page Key-2.

EXAMPLE: Facebook users accounts may be suspended if the rules are violated.

REVISION: Facebook **users'** accounts may be suspended if the rules are violated. [Guide 32]

1. Employees were asked not to use the companys computers to stream video.
2. James blog discussed the overuse of the *Reply All* button.
3. Would you please give me directions to your downtown headquarters?
4. Her colleagues resented Melissa copying everyone on her messages.
5. The three top sales reps, Erik, Rachel, and Erin received substantial bonuses.

6. You must replace the ink cartridge see page 8 in the manual, before printing.

7. Tyler wondered whether all sales managers databases needed to be updated.

8. (Direct quotation) The death of e-mail, said Mike Song, has been greatly exaggerated.

9. In just two years time, the number of people e-mailing on mobile devices nearly doubled.

10. The staffing meeting starts at 10 a.m. sharp, doesn't it.

Notes

[1] Gardner, T. (2009, September 13). It may pay to Twitter. *Los Angeles Times*, p. L8; King, R. (2008, September 6). How companies use Twitter to bolster their brands. Retrieved from http://www.businessweek.com

[2] Eliason, F. (2012, May 5). The good ole boys of Spirit Airlines. Retrieved from http://www.frankeliason.com

[3] King, R. (2008, September 6). How companies use Twitter to bolster their brands. Retrieved from http://www.businessweek.com

[4] Dugan, L. (2012, February 21). Twitter to surpass 500 million registered users on Wednesday. Retrieved from http://www.mediabistro.com/alltwitter/500-million-registered-users_b18842

[5] Hof, R. (2009, August 17). Betting on the real-time Web. *BusinessWeek*, p. 46.

[6] Song, M. quoted in Tugend, A. (2012, April 21). What to think about before you hit 'Send.' *The New York Times*, p. B5.

[7] Foster, D. (2010, November 10). How to write better emails. WebWorkerDaily. Retrieved from http://gigaom.com/collaboration/how-to-write-better-emails

[8] Seeley, M. quoted in Palmer, M. (2011, December 19). The end of email? *Financial Times* (ft.com/management). Retrieved from http://www.ft.com/intl/cms/s/0/5207b5d6-21cf-11e1-8b93-00144feabdc0.html#axzz1u7265yfu

[9] Plantronics. (2010). How we work: Communication trends of business professionals. Retrieved from http://www.plantronics.com/media/howwework/brochure-role-of-voice.pdf

[10] Middleton, D. (2011, March 3). Students struggle for words. *The Wall Street Journal*, Executive edition. Retrieved from http://online.wsj.com/article/SB10001424052748703409904576174651780110970.html

[11] Ibid.

[12] E-mail becoming crime's new smoking gun. (2002, August 15). USA Today.com. Retrieved from http://www.usatoday.com/tech/news/2002-08-15-email-evidence_x.htm

[13] Tugend, A. (2012, April 21). What to think about before you hit 'Send.' *The New York Times*, p. B5.

[14] Orrell, L. quoted in Tugend, A. (2012, April 21). What to think about before you hit 'Send.' *The New York Times*, p. B5.

[15] Kupritz, V. W., & Cowell, E. (2011, January). Productive management communication: Online and face-to-face. *Journal of Business Communication*, 48(1), 70-71.

[16] Robinson, T. quoted in Brown, P. (2008, January 26). Same office, different planets. *The New York Times*. Retrieved from http://www.nytimes.com/2008/01/26/business/26offline.html?_r=1

[17] Terk, N. (2012, January 18). E-mail education: Global headaches and universal best practices. Retrieved from http://www.newswiretoday.com/news/104276

[18] Blodget, H. (2011, December 4). Bombshell: Huge company bans internal email, switches totally to Facebook-type-stuff and instant messaging. *Business Insider*. Retrieved from http://articles.businessinsider.com/2011-12-04/tech/30473966_1_abc-news-internal-emails-messages-employees

[19] Pingdom. (2012, January 17). Internet 2011 in numbers. Retrieved from http://royal.pingdom.com/2012/01/17/internet-2011-in-numbers

[20] Plantronics study cited by Diana, A. (2010, September 30). Executives demand communications arsenal. InformationWeek. Retrieved from http://www.informationweek.com/news/smb/227501053

[21] Marketing News Staff. (2010, March 15). Digital dozen. AMA.org. Retrieved from http://www.marketingpower.com/resourceLibrary/Publications/MarketingNews/2010/3_15_10/Digital%20Dozen.pdf

[22] Skinner. C.-A. (2008, July 16). UK businesses ban IM over security concerns. *CIO*. Retrieved from http://www.cio.com/article/437910/UK_Businesses_Ban_IM_over_Security_Concerns

[23] Ibid.

[24] Flynn, N. (2012, May 23). Social media rules: Policies & best practices to effectively manage your presence, posts & potential risks. The ePolicy Institute. Retrieved from http://www.ohioscpa.com/docs/conference-outlines/8_social-media-rules.pdf?sfvrsn=4

[25] Marino, K. (2012, June 22). DWI: Driving while intexticated—infographic. OnlineSchools.com. Retrieved from http://www.onlineschools.com/in-focus/driving-while-intexticated

[26] Ibid.

[27] Flynn, N. (2012, May 23). Social media rules: Policies & best practices to effectively manage your presence, posts & potential risks. The ePolicy Institute. Retrieved from http://www.ohioscpa.com/docs/conference-outlines/8_social-media-rules.pdf?sfvrsn=4

[28] Flynn, N., & Kahn, R. (2004). *E-mail rules: A business guide to managing policies, security, and legal issues for e-mail and digital communication*. Columbus, OH: ePolicy Institute, pp. 153-154.

[29] Marketing News Staff. (2010, March 15). Digital dozen. AMA.org. Retrieved from http://www.marketingpower.com/resourceLibrary/Publications/MarketingNews/2010/3_15_10/Digital%20Dozen.pdf

[30] Flynn, N. (2012, May 23). Social media rules: Policies & best practices to effectively manage your presence, posts & potential risks. The ePolicy Institute. Retrieved from http://www.ohioscpa.com/docs/conference-outlines/8_social-media-rules.pdf?sfvrsn=4

[31] Pew Internet & American Life Project. (2011, July 11). How smartphone owners describe their phones. Retrieved from http://pewinternet.org/Infographics/2011/Smartphones.aspx

[32] Based on The Emily Post Institute. (n. d.) Text messaging: I love text messaging. Retrieved from http://www.emilypost.com/home-and-family-life/133/391-text-messaging

[33] Marketing News Staff. (2010, March 15). Digital dozen. AMA.org. Retrieved from http://www.marketingpower.com/resourceLibrary/Publications/MarketingNews/2010/3_15_10/Digital%20Dozen.pdf

[34] Pew Internet & American Life Project. (2012, February). Tracking survey: Trend data (adults). Retrieved from http://pewinternet.org/Trend-Data-%28Adults%29/Online-Activites-Total.aspx

[35] Casel, B. (2011, March 25). 7 Tips for launching a successful podcast. Mashable. http://mashable.com/2011/03/25/podcasting-tips

[36] Majchrzak, A., Wagner, C., & Yates, D. (2006). Corporate wiki users: Results of a survey. CiteSeer. Retrieved from http://citeseerx.ist.psu.edu/viewdoc/summary?doi=10.1.1.97.407

[37] The five main uses of wikis based on Nations, D. (2009). The business wiki: Wiki in the workplace. About .com: Web Trends. Retrieved from http://webtrends.about.com/od/wiki/a/business-wiki.htm

[38] Cited in State of the blogosphere 2011, Part 2. (2011, November 4). Technorati. Retrieved from http://technorati.com/social-media/article/state-of-the-blogosphere-2011-part2

[39] Barnes, N. G., & Andonian, J. (2011). The 2011 Fortune 500 and social media adoption: Have America's largest companies reached a social media plateau? Center for Marketing Research, Charlton College of Business, and University of Massachusetts Dartmouth. Retrieved from http://www.umassd.edu/cmr/studiesandresearch/bloggingtwitterandfacebookusage

[40] 2011 Blogging statistics. (2011, October 3). Right Mix Marketing. Retrieved from http://www.rightmixmarketing.com/right-mix-blog/blogging-statistics

[41] Reese, S. (2011, May 26). Quick stat: 53.5% of Internet users will read blogs this year. The eMarketer Blog. Retrieved from http://www.emarketer.com/blog/index.php/tag/number-of-people-who-read-blogs

[42] Gaskell, A. (2012, July 12). Executives don't give a damn about social media. Technorati. Retrieved from http://technorati.com/social-media/article/executives-dont-give-a-damn-about

[43] Photo essay based on Morrison, M. (2011, January 21). Pei Wei to drag copywriter around Asia to blog about food. *Advertising Age*. Retrieved from http://www.adage.com

[44] Marriott, Jr., J. W. "Bill." (2012, June 11). Five years blogging—Pen pals, pilates and hitting publish. Retrieved from http://www.blogs.marriott.com. Reprinted by permission.

[45] Horovitz, B. (2012, July 19). Lay's will give you $1 million if you win their Facebook competition to create a new flavor. Business Insider. Retrieved from http://www.businessinsider.com/lays-new-flavor-competition-2012-7; Doritos brand reveals five consumer-created commercial vying for $1 million payout and once-in-a-lifetime opportunity to work with the Lonely Island. (2012, January 4). [Press release]. Retrieved from http://www.fritolay.com/about-us/press-release-20120104.html

46 Marketing News Staff. (2010, March 15). Digital dozen. AMA.org. Retrieved from http://www.marketingpower.com/resourceLibrary/Publications/MarketingNews/2010/3_15_10/Digital%20Dozen.pdf

47 Kawczyk, J., & Steinberg, J. (2012, March 7). How content is really shared: Close friends, not "influencers." Ad Age Digital. Retrieved from http://adage.com/article/digitalnext/content-shared-close-friends-influencers/233147

48 Oldenburg, Z. (2012, July 12). Nickelodeon's "Teenage Mutant Ninja Turtles" viral campaign asks you to choose your side. Retrieved from http://www.movieviral.com/2012/07/12/nickelodeons-teenage-mutant-ninja-turtles-viral-campaign-asks-you-to-choose-your-side

49 Green, A. (2012, October 15). 6 flight attendants gone wild: To blog, or not to blog. Retrieved from http://www.mentalfloss.com/blogs/archives/146465

50 Tips for Creating a Professional Blog based on Wuorio, J. (n.d.). Blogging for business: 7 tips for getting started. Microsoft Small Business Center. Retrieved from http://www.microsoft.com/smallbusiness/resources/marketing/online-marketing/small-business-blog.aspx#Smallbusinessblog

51 Kirkpatrick, D. (2005, January 10). Why there's no escaping the blog. CNNMoney. Retrieved from http://money.cnn.com/magazines/fortune/fortune_archive/2005/01/10/8230982/index.htm

52 Lindstrom, M. (2012, July 3). How many lives does a brand have? Fast Company. Retrieved from http://www.fastcompany.com/1841927/buyology-martin-lindstrom-lives-of-brands-china-marketing

53 Perman, C. (2011, March 3). The world's coolest jobs 2011: Culinary ambassador. CNBC.com. Retrieved from http://www.cnbc.com/id/41889880/38044260?slide=4; Marketing News Staff. (2010, March 15). Digital dozen. AMA.org. Retrieved from http://www.marketingpower.com/resourceLibrary/Publications/MarketingNews/2010/3_15_10/Digital%20Dozen.pdf

54 Perman, C. (2011, March 3). The world's coolest jobs 2011: CEO of funny Web empire. CNBC.com. Retrieved from http://www.cnbc.com/id/41889880/38044260?slide=5

55 Perman, C. (2011, March 3). The world's coolest jobs 2011: Honeymoon testers. CNBC.com. http://www.cnbc.com/id/41889880/38044260?slide=6

56 Perman, C. (2011, March 3). The world's coolest jobs 2011: Tourism ambassador. CNBC.com. Retrieved from http://www.cnbc.com/id/41889880/38044260?slide=7

57 Perman, C. (2011, March 3). The world's coolest jobs 2011: Ice cream developer. CNBC.com. Retrieved from http://www.cnbc.com/id/41889880/38044260?slide=3

58 Cairns, B. (2012, January 24). Blog comment. Retrieved from http://blog.guykawasaki.com/2011/06/how-to-increase-your-likability.html#axzz20dk8CnTk

59 Zickuhr, K. (2010, December 16). Generations online in 2010. Pew Internet. Retrieved from http://pewinternet.org/Reports/2010/Generations-2010/Overview.aspx

60 Smith, A., & Brenner, J. (2012, May 31). Twitter use 2012. Pew Internet & American Life Project. Retrieved from http://pewinternet.org/~/media//Files/Reports/2012/PIP_Twitter_Use_2012.pdf

61 Cited in Patton, C. (2010, December 1). Tackling turnover. Human Resource Executive Online. Retrieved from http://www.hreonline.com/HRE/story.jsp?storyId=533326583

62 Mullaney, T. (2012, May 16). Social media is reinventing how business is done. USA Today. Retrieved from http://www.usatoday.com/money/economy/story/2012-05-14/social-media-economy-companies/55029088/1

63 Ibid.

64 Ibid.

65 Wasserman, T. (2012, January 12). Facebook to hit 1 billion user mark in August. Mashable. Retrieved from http://mashable.com/2012/01/12/facebook-1-billion-users

66 Conlin, M., & MacMillan, D. (2009, June 1). Managing the tweets. BusinessWeek, p. 20.

67 Flynn, N. (2012, May 23). Social media rules: Policies & best practices to effectively manage your presence, posts & potential risks. The ePolicy Institute. Retrieved from http://www.ohioscpa.com/docs/conference-outlines/8_social-media-rules.pdf?sfvrsn=4

68 Ibid.

69 Wright, A. D. (2012, February 3). Social media policies slowly catch on worldwide. Society for Human Resource Management. Retrieved from http://www.shrm.org/hrdisciplines/global/Articles/Pages/WorldwidePolicies.aspx

70 Ibid.

71 Villano, M. (2009, April 26). The online divide between work and play. The New York Times. Retrieved from http://www.nytimes.com

72 MacManus, R. (2011, March 30). Mobile RSS readers: What's popular & what works. ReadWriteWeb. Retrieved from http://www.readwriteweb.com/archives/mobile_rss_readers_whats_popular_what_works.php

73 Flynn, N. (2012, May 23). Social media rules: Policies & best practices to effectively manage your presence, posts & potential risks. The ePolicy Institute. Retrieved from http://www.ohioscpa.com/docs/conference-outlines/8_social-media-rules.pdf?sfvrsn=4

74 Ibid.

75 Ibid.

76 Thomas, A., & Applegate, J. (2010). Pay attention!: How to listen, respond, and profit from customer feedback. Hoboken, NJ: John Wiley & Sons, pp. 1-2.

77 Needleman, S. E. (2009, August 4). For companies, a tweet in time can avert PR mess. The Wall Street Journal. Retrieved from http://online.wsj.com

78 Weeks, L. (2011, April 27). Privacy 2.0: The Garbo economy. NPR.org. Retrieved from http://www.npr.org/2011/04/27/135623137/privacy-2-0-the-garbo-economy

79 Turkle. S. (2011). Alone together: Why we expect more from technology and less from each other. New York: Basic Books, p. 1.

80 Garvey, M. (2009, October 31). Fifth years of simplicity as style. The Wall Street Journal, p. A19.

81 Tynan, D. (2012, May 25). How companies buy Facebook friends, likes, and buzz. PC World. Retrieved from http://www.pcworld.com/article/256240/how_companies_buy_facebook_friends_likes_and_buzz.html

82 Greene, D. (Host). (2009, July 2). Twitter music reviews: Criticism as haiku. Morning Edition. Washington, DC: National Public Radio. Retrieved from http://www.npr.org/templates/story/story.php?storyId=106178234

83 Ibid.

84 5 ways Twitter can get you fired. (2009, October 8). Applicant.com. Retrieved from http://applicant.com/5-ways-twitter-can-get-you-fired

85 Moeller, S. D. (2010). 24 hours: Unplugged. Retrieved from http://withoutmedia.wordpress.com; The Associated Press. (2009, September 6). Center tries to treat Web addicts. The New York Times. Retrieved from http://www.nytimes.com

86 Activity based on based on Hamm, S. (2009, June 15). Cloud computing's big bang for business. BusinessWeek, pp. 43-44; Wildstrom, S. H. (2009, April 6). What to entrust to the cloud. BusinessWeek, pp. 89-90; Burrows, P. (2009, August 17). Apple and Google: Another step apart. BusinessWeek, pp. 24-25; and Hamm, S. (2009, April 6). IBM reaches for the clouds. BusinessWeek, p. 34.

87 Weissberger, A. (2011, April 22). Amazon's EC2 outage proves cloud failure recovery is a myth! The Viodi View. Retrieved from http://viodi.com/2011/04/22/amazons-ec2-outage-proves-cloud-failure-recovery-is-a-myth

88 Searcey, D. (2009, November 24). Some courts raise bar on reading employee email. The Wall Street Journal, p. A31. Retrieved from http://online.wsj.com/article/SB125859862658454923.html; and Na, G. (2006, October 17). Employee e-mail use: Big brother may be watching. Mondaq Business Briefing. Retrieved https://global.factiva.com

89 Klein, K. E. (2009, December 1). Putting a fair Internet use policy in place. BusinessWeek.com. Retrieved from http://www.businessweek.com/smallbiz/content/dec2009/sb2009121_245449.htm

CHAPTER 8

Positive Messages

OBJECTIVES

After studying this chapter, you should be able to

1 Understand the channels through which typical positive messages travel in the digital era—e-mails, memos, and business letters—and apply the 3-x-3 writing process.

2 Compose direct messages that make requests, respond to inquiries online and offline, and deliver step-by-step instructions.

3 Prepare contemporary messages that make direct claims and voice complaints, including those posted online.

4 Create adjustment messages that salvage customers' trust and promote further business.

5 Write special messages that convey kindness and goodwill.

© Lane Oatey/Blue Jean Images/Getty Images

Insurance Industry Indebted to Ink

The health insurance industry is subject to heavy oversight. When approving or denying coverage, health insurance companies must comply with the strict guidelines of the Health Insurance Portability and Accountability Act (HIPAA). Doing so requires a great deal of documentation.

Highmark Blue Shield of Pittsburgh, Pennsylvania, an independent licensee of the Blue Cross Blue Shield Association, provides health and related products to nearly 35 million customers.[1] Like

© AP Images/Victoria Arocho

many organizations, Highmark realizes that some customers still need written correspondence because they do not have Internet access. Others simply prefer to receive printed messages. However, letters do not necessarily have to be delivered by the U.S. Postal Service. Business writers frequently convert letters to portable document format (PDF) or scan them and then send them by e-mail. Still other businesses prefer to transmit their letters by fax.

In addition to allowing customers the choice of receiving documentation electronically or in print, Highmark executives recognize still *another* reason to write letters instead of e-mails—to show valuable customers a high level of commitment and service. Highpoint Vice President of Sales and Client Management Kelly Lieblein chose a letter as the best channel to communicate with the Harrisburg School District about its health plan coverage. Lieblein personalized her letter by addressing it to her contact in the administration, Jeffrey S. Bader.[2]

Lieblein's letter followed the direct strategy and employed a formal tone. To ensure eye appeal, she integrated headings, bullet points, and short, easy-to-read paragraphs into the three-page document. The letter would become a binding legal agreement when signed, and its careful wording and strict adherence to correctness helped convey its gravity.

Documenting specifics in a letter requires planning, accuracy, and thoughtful document design. The business letter remains a valuable communication channel that helps organizations land—and retain—business. Later in this chapter, you will have an opportunity to write a business letter.

Critical Thinking

- Why might receiving a letter make a customer feel valued?

- Which instances might call for a confidential letter?

- How does graphic highlighting help save readers' time?

Positive Messages and the Writing Process

In the workplace most messages are positive or neutral and, therefore, direct. Positive messages are routine and straightforward; they help workers in organizations conduct everyday business. Such routine messages include simple requests for information or action, replies to customers, and explanations to coworkers. Other types of positive messages are instructions, direct claims, and complaints.

E-mails, memos, and letters are the channels most frequently used. In addition, businesses today must listen and respond to social networks and the blogosphere. At the same time, in some industries, memos continue to be an important channel of communication within an organization, while letters are a vital paper-based external channel. As discussed in Chapter 7, e-mail and social media are used to communicate within organizations as well as with outside audiences. What do all these channels have in common? As shown in Chapter 1, they all require solid writing skills. In the glaring light of social media, writing skills—or the lack of them—are amplified mercilessly and can sink careers.

In this book we divide business messages into three content areas: (a) **positive** messages communicating straightforward requests, replies, and goodwill, covered in this chapter;

LEARNING OBJECTIVE **1**
Understand the channels through which typical positive messages travel in the digital era—e-mails, memos, and business letters—and apply the 3-x-3 writing process.

(b) **negative** messages delivering refusals and bad news, covered in Chapter 9; and (c) **persuasive** messages, including sales pitches, covered in Chapter 10. This chapter focuses on routine, positive messages. These will make up the bulk of your workplace communication. Here is a quick review of the 3-x-3 writing process to help you apply it to positive messages. You will also learn when to respond by business letter and how to format it.

Phase 1: Analysis, Anticipation, and Adaptation

In Phase 1, prewriting, you will need to spend some time analyzing your task. It is amazing how many of us are ready to put our pens or computers into gear before engaging our minds. Too often, writers start a message without enough preparation. As you begin the writing process, ask yourself these important questions:

- **Do I really need to write this e-mail, memo, or letter?** A phone call, an IM inquiry, or a quick visit to a nearby coworker might solve the problem—and save the time and expense of a written message. On the other hand, some written messages are needed to provide a permanent record or to develop a thoughtful plan.

- **Why am I writing?** Know why you are writing and what you hope to achieve. This will help you recognize what the important points are and where to place them.

- **How will the reader react?** Visualize the reader and the effect your message will have. Imagine that you are sitting and talking with your reader. Avoid speaking bluntly, failing to explain, or ignoring your reader's needs. Shape the message to benefit the reader. Remember that e-mails may very well be forwarded to someone else and that ill-conceived social media posts can trigger very public reactions.

- **What channel should I use?** It's tempting to use e-mail for much of your correspondence. However, a phone call or face-to-face visit is a better channel choice if you need to (a) convey enthusiasm, warmth, or another emotion; (b) supply a context; or (c) smooth over disagreements. A business letter is better when the matter requires (a) a permanent record, (b) confidentiality, or (c) formality. A social media response is needed to reply to certain public posts whenever time is of the essence.

- **How can I save my reader's time?** Think of ways that you can make your message easier to comprehend at a glance. Use bullets, asterisks, lists, headings, and white space to improve readability.

Understanding Business Letters.   Despite the advent of e-mail, social networking, and other electronic communication technologies, in certain situations letters are still the preferred channel of communication for delivering messages *outside* an organization. Such letters go to suppliers, government agencies, other businesses, and, most important, customers. You may think that everybody is online, but at an Internet penetration rate of 74 percent, more than a quarter of the U.S. population is still unplugged. Just as they are eager to connect with a majority of consumers online, businesses continue to give letters to customers a high priority because these messages, too, encourage product feedback, project a favorable image of the organization, and promote future business.

Whether you send a business letter will depend on the situation and the preference of your organization. Business letters are necessary when the situation calls for a permanent record. For example, when a company enters into an agreement with another company, business letters introduce the agreement and record decisions and points of understanding. Business letters deliver contracts, explain terms, exchange ideas, negotiate agreements, answer vendor questions, and maintain customer relations.

Business letters are confidential. They are less likely than electronic media to be intercepted, misdirected, forwarded, retrieved, or otherwise inspected by unintended recipients. Also, business letters presented on company stationery carry a sense of formality and importance not possible with e-mail. They look important, as illustrated in Figure 8.1, a customer-welcoming letter in the popular block format.

Finally, business letters deliver persuasive, well-considered messages. Letters can persuade people to change their actions, adopt new beliefs, make donations, contribute their time, and try new products. Direct-mail letters remain a powerful tool to promote services

Figure 8.1 Direct Letter Welcoming Customer—Block Style

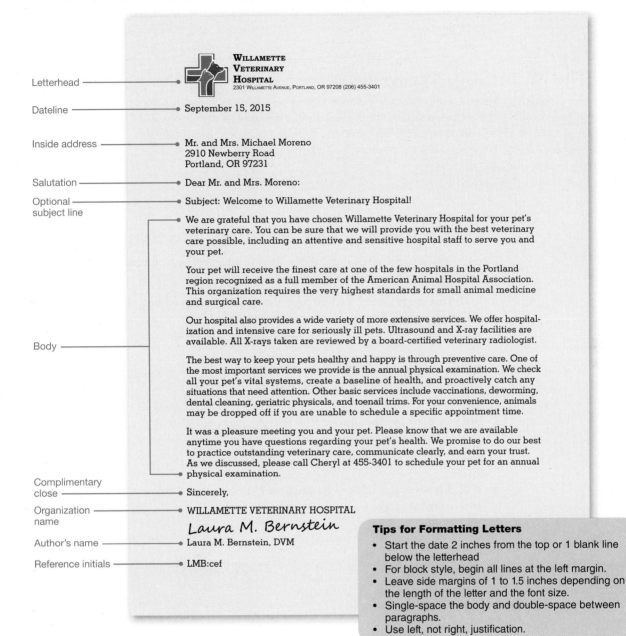

Letterhead

WILLAMETTE VETERINARY HOSPITAL
2301 WILLAMETTE AVENUE, PORTLAND, OR 97208 (206) 455-3401

Dateline

September 15, 2015

Inside address

Mr. and Mrs. Michael Moreno
2910 Newberry Road
Portland, OR 97231

Salutation

Dear Mr. and Mrs. Moreno:

Optional subject line

Subject: Welcome to Willamette Veterinary Hospital!

Body

We are grateful that you have chosen Willamette Veterinary Hospital for your pet's veterinary care. You can be sure that we will provide you with the best veterinary care possible, including an attentive and sensitive hospital staff to serve you and your pet.

Your pet will receive the finest care at one of the few hospitals in the Portland region recognized as a full member of the American Animal Hospital Association. This organization requires the very highest standards for small animal medicine and surgical care.

Our hospital also provides a wide variety of more extensive services. We offer hospitalization and intensive care for seriously ill pets. Ultrasound and X-ray facilities are available. All X-rays taken are reviewed by a board-certified veterinary radiologist.

The best way to keep your pets healthy and happy is through preventive care. One of the most important services we provide is the annual physical examination. We check all your pet's vital systems, create a baseline of health, and proactively catch any situations that need attention. Other basic services include vaccinations, deworming, dental cleaning, geriatric physicals, and toenail trims. For your convenience, animals may be dropped off if you are unable to schedule a specific appointment time.

It was a pleasure meeting you and your pet. Please know that we are available anytime you have questions regarding your pet's health. We promise to do our best to practice outstanding veterinary care, communicate clearly, and earn your trust. As we discussed, please call Cheryl at 455-3401 to schedule your pet for an annual physical examination.

Complimentary close

Sincerely,

Organization name

WILLAMETTE VETERINARY HOSPITAL

Laura M. Bernstein

Author's name

Laura M. Bernstein, DVM

Reference initials

LMB:cef

Tips for Formatting Letters

- Start the date 2 inches from the top or 1 blank line below the letterhead
- For block style, begin all lines at the left margin.
- Leave side margins of 1 to 1.5 inches depending on the length of the letter and the font size.
- Single-space the body and double-space between paragraphs.
- Use left, not right, justification.

© Cengage Learning 2015 ; Logo: © Kalavati/Shutterstock.com

and products, boost online and retail traffic, and enhance customer relations. You will learn more about writing persuasive and sales messages in Chapter 10.

Phase 2: Research, Organization, and Drafting

In Phase 2, drafting, you will first want to check the files, gather documentation, and prepare your message. Make an outline of the points you wish to cover. For short messages jot down notes on the document you are answering or make a scratch list at your computer.

For longer documents that require formal research, use the outlining techniques discussed in Chapter 5. As you compose your message, avoid amassing huge blocks of text. No one wants to read endless lines of type. Instead, group related information into paragraphs, preferably short ones. Paragraphs separated by white space look inviting. Be sure that each paragraph includes a topic sentence backed up by details and evidence. If you bury your main point in the middle of a paragraph, the reader may miss it. Also plan for revision, because excellence is rarely achieved on the first effort.

Phase 3: Editing, Proofreading, and Evaluating

Phase 3, revising, involves putting the final touches on your message. Careful and caring writers ask themselves the following questions:

- **Is the message clear?** Viewed from the receiver's perspective, are the ideas clear? Did you use plain English? If the message is passed on to others, will they need further explanation? Consider having a colleague critique your message if it is an important one.

- **Is the message correct?** Are the sentences complete and punctuated properly? Did you overlook any typos or misspelled words? Remember to use your spell-checker and grammar-checker to proofread your message before sending it.

- **Did you plan for feedback?** How will you know whether this message is successful? You can improve feedback by asking questions (such as *Are you comfortable with these suggestions?* or *What do you think?*). Remember to make it easy for the receiver to respond.

- **Will this message achieve its purpose?** The last step in the 3-x-3 writing process is evaluating the product.

To go green and save taxpayer money, governors from 13 states sent a joint letter to automakers expressing their intent to purchase natural gas vehicles for state and municipal fleets. The printed letter, which was addressed to 19 CEOs and emblazoned with official state seals, requested information regarding a procurement agreement that would enable states to meet their transportation needs using alternative fuel vehicles produced by the manufacturers. Why do you think the governors chose a business letter to make a request of automakers?[4]

© egd/Shutterstock.com

Typical Request, Response, and Instruction Messages

LEARNING OBJECTIVE **2**
Compose direct messages that make requests, respond to inquiries online and offline, and deliver step-by-step instructions.

In the workplace positive messages take the form of e-mails, memos, and letters. Brief positive messages are also delivered by instant messaging, texting, and social media. When you need information from a team member in another office, you might send an e-mail or use IM. If you must explain to employees a new procedure for ordering supplies and rank-and-file workers do not have company e-mail, you would write an interoffice memo. When you welcome a new customer or respond to a customer letter asking about your products, you would prepare a letter.

The majority of your business messages will involve routine requests and responses to requests, which are organized directly. Requests and replies may take the form of e-mails, memos, letters, or social media posts. You might, for example, receive an inquiry via Twitter or Facebook about an upcoming product launch. You may need to request information from a hotel as you plan a company conference. You might be answering an inquiry by e-mail from a customer about your services or products. These kinds of routine requests and replies follow a similar pattern.

Creating Request Messages

When you write messages that request information or action and you think your request will be received positively, start with the main idea first. The most emphatic positions in a message are the opening and closing. Readers tend to look at them first. You should capitalize on this tendency by putting the most significant statement first. The first sentence of an information request is usually a question or a polite command. It should not be an explanation or justification, unless resistance to the request is expected. When the information or action requested is likely to be forthcoming, immediately tell the reader what you want.

The e-mail in Figure 8.2 inquiring about hotel accommodations begins immediately with the most important idea: Can the hotel provide meeting rooms and accommodations for 250 people? Instead of opening with an explanation of who the writer is or why the writer happens to be writing this message, the e-mail begins directly.

If several questions must be asked, you have two choices. You can ask the most important question first, as shown in Figure 8.2, or you can begin with a summary statement, such as *Please answer the following questions about providing meeting rooms and accommodations for 250 people from September 23 through September 26.* Avoid beginning with *Will you please . . . .* Although such a statement sounds like a question, it is actually a disguised command. Because you expect an action rather than a reply, you should punctuate this polite command with a period instead of a question mark. To avoid having to choose between a period and a question mark, just omit *Will you* and start with *Please answer.*

Providing Details.   The body of a message that requests information or action provides necessary details. Remember that the quality of the information obtained from a request depends on the clarity of the inquiry. If you analyze your needs, organize your ideas, and frame your request logically, you are likely to receive a meaningful answer that doesn't require a follow-up message. Whenever possible, focus on benefits to the reader (*To ensure that you receive the exact sweater you want, send us your color choice*). To improve readability, itemize appropriate information in bulleted or numbered lists. Notice that the questions in Figure 8.2 are bulleted, and they are parallel. That is, they use the same balanced construction.

Closing With Appreciation and a Call for Action.   In the closing of your message, tell the reader courteously what is to be done. If a date is important, set an end date to take action and explain why. Some careless writers end request messages simply with *Thank you*, forcing the reader to review the contents to determine what is expected and when. You can save the readers' time by spelling out the action to be taken. Avoid other overused endings such as *Thank you for your cooperation* (trite), *Thank you in advance for . . .* (trite and presumptuous), and *If you have any questions, do not hesitate to call me* (suggests that you didn't make yourself clear).

ETHICS CHECK:

Surprising the Boss

Kyra Montes uses e-mail for nearly all messages. She is ecstatic over a new job offer and quickly sends an e-mail to her manager announcing that she is leaving. He did not know she was looking for a new position. Is this an appropriate use of e-mail?

Figure 8.2 Applying the Writing Process to a Direct Request E-Mail

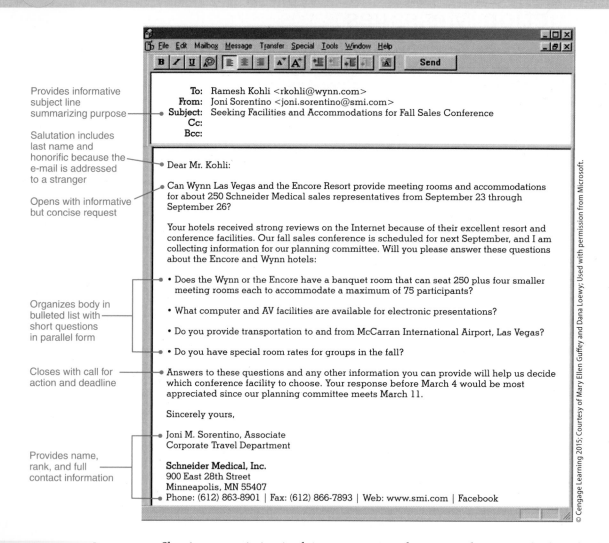

Provides informative subject line summarizing purpose

Salutation includes last name and honorific because the e-mail is addressed to a stranger

Opens with informative but concise request

Organizes body in bulleted list with short questions in parallel form

Closes with call for action and deadline

Provides name, rank, and full contact information

© Cengage Learning 2015; Courtesy of Mary Ellen Guffey and Dana Loewy; Used with permission from Microsoft.

Showing appreciation is always appropriate, but try to do so in a fresh and efficient manner. For example, you could hook your thanks to the end date (*Thanks for returning the questionnaire before May 5, when we will begin tabulation*). You might connect your appreciation to a statement developing reader benefits (*We are grateful for the information you will provide because it will help us serve you better*). You could briefly describe how the information will help you (*I appreciate this information, which will enable me to . . .*). When possible, make it easy for the reader to comply with your request (*Note your answers on this sheet and return it in the postage-paid envelope* or *Here is my e-mail address so that you can reach me quickly*).

Responding to Requests

Often, your messages will respond directly and favorably to requests for information or action. A customer wants information about a product, a supplier asks to arrange a meeting, an employee inquires about a procedure, or a manager requests your input on a marketing campaign. In complying with such requests, you will want to apply the same direct strategy you used in making requests.

A customer reply e-mail that starts with an effective subject line, as shown in Figure 8.3, helps the reader recognize the topic immediately. The subject line refers in abbreviated form to previous correspondence and/or summarizes a message (*Subject: Your July 12 Inquiry About WorkZone Software*). Knowledgeable business communicators use a subject line to refer to earlier correspondence so that in the first sentence, the most emphatic spot in a letter, they are free to emphasize the main idea.

Figure **8.3** Customer Response E-Mail

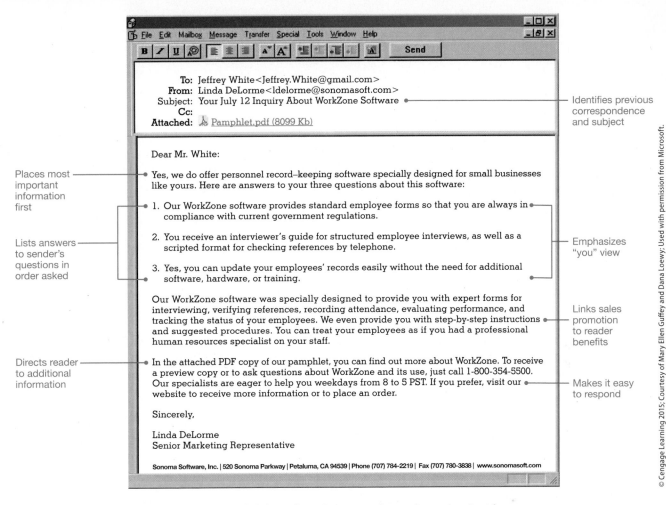

In the first sentence of a direct reply e-mail, deliver the information the reader wants. Avoid wordy, drawn-out openings (*I am responding to your e-mail of December 1, in which you request information about . . .*). More forceful and more efficient is an opener that answers the inquiry *(Here is the information you wanted about . . .).* When agreeing to a request for action, announce the good news promptly *(Yes, I will be happy to speak to your business communication class on the topic of . . .).*

In the body of your response, supply explanations and additional information. Because an e-mail, like any other document written for your company, may be considered a legally binding contract, be sure to check facts and figures carefully. Under certain circumstances in some U.S. states, an e-mail can also become an enforceable document; therefore, exercise caution when using a company e-mail address or anytime you are writing for your employer online. If a policy or procedure needs authorization, seek approval from a supervisor or executive before writing the message.

When customers or prospective customers inquire about products or services, your response should do more than merely supply answers. Try to promote your organization and products. Be sure to present the promotional material with attention to the "you" view and to reader benefits *(You can use our standardized tests to free you from time-consuming employment screening).*

In concluding a response message, refer to the information provided or to its use. *(The attached list summarizes our recommendations. We wish you all the best in redesigning your social media presence.)* If further action is required, help the reader with specifics *(The Small Business Administration publishes a number of helpful booklets. Its Web address is . . .).* Avoid signing off with clichés *(If I may be of further assistance, don't hesitate to . . .).*

The following checklist reviews the direct strategy for information or action requests and replies to such messages.

CHECKLIST ▶▶
Writing Direct Requests and Responses

Requesting Information or Action

- **Open by stating the main idea.** To elicit information, ask a question or issue a polite command (*Please answer the following questions . . .*).

- **Explain and justify the request.** In the body arrange questions or information logically in parallel, balanced form. Clarify and substantiate your request.

- **Request action in the closing.** Close a request by summarizing exactly what is to be done, including dates or deadlines. Express appreciation. Avoid clichés (*Thank you for your cooperation, Thanking you in advance*).

Responding to Requests

- **Open directly.** Immediately deliver the information the receiver wants. Avoid wordy, drawn-out openings (*I have before me your request of August 5*). When agreeing to a request, announce the good news immediately.

- **Supply additional information.** In the body provide explanations and expand initial statements. For customer letters, promote products and the organization.

- **Conclude with a cordial statement.** Refer to the information provided or its use. If further action is required, describe the procedures and give specifics. Avoid clichés (*If you have questions, please do not hesitate to let me know*).

Beware "Digital Waste": Can Brands Be Friends?

Plugged In

As businesses are racing online and spending big bucks to establish their social media presence, a sizable portion of that effort may be misguided, a global study has concluded.[5] Apparently more than half of consumers (57 percent) in highly connected markets resent major brands entering their social networks. Yet companies large and small are establishing profiles on social media networks such as Facebook and YouTube, wishing to connect with consumers quickly and inexpensively.

However, TNS's Digital Life study, based on in-depth interviews with over 72,000 people in 60 countries, found this aversion to brands on social networks to be even higher in the United States (60 percent) and the United Kingdom (61 percent).[6] This large survey reveals that unless businesses target their efforts well, they are wasting them on more than half of their intended audiences.

To be sure, when asked whether they want to engage with brands on social networking sites to find out more or make a purchase, 54 percent of users admit that social media are a good place to learn about new products.

Moreover, 47 percent of digital consumers comment about brands online. They say they are motivated by wanting to be helpful and dispense advice. However, 61 percent of such online commentators are driven to engage with brands by special offers or promotions.[7]

The researchers say that mounting consumer-generated content, coupled with poor digital strategies by businesses, are creating "mountains of digital waste," such as friendless Facebook accounts and unread blogs. Such "digital pollution" is making it harder for brands to be heard. To deepen their relationships with the public, brands must understand their target audience and consider the needs of various consumer groups, TNS[8] says.

REALITY CHECK: Developing a Comment Monitoring Policy

"If you're going to use social media, then embrace commenting. Don't just tolerate comments. Don't just accept comments. Interact. Comment back. If you are a company of one person, you may not need a policy for responding. Otherwise, before answering comments, develop some rules to live by."[9]

—**AMANDA FORD,** *Tymado Multimedia Solutions*

Responding to Customer Comments Online

We live in an age when vocal individuals can start a firestorm of criticism online or become powerful *brand ambassadors* who champion certain products. Therefore, businesses must listen to social media comments about themselves and, if necessary, respond. You may ask, how do companies know when to respond, and in what ways? This invaluable knowledge is an evolving field and, some would say, a minefield, littered with disastrous missteps and missed opportunities.

However, social media marketing experts are developing guidelines to provide organizations with tools for strategic decision making in various situations. Figure 8.4 shows a social media response flowchart, now increasingly common in for-profit and nonprofit organizations

Figure 8.4 Social Media Response Flowchart

To help their employees make a prudent decision about whether and how to respond to online posts, companies are creating decision trees and diagrams such as the one shown here.[10]

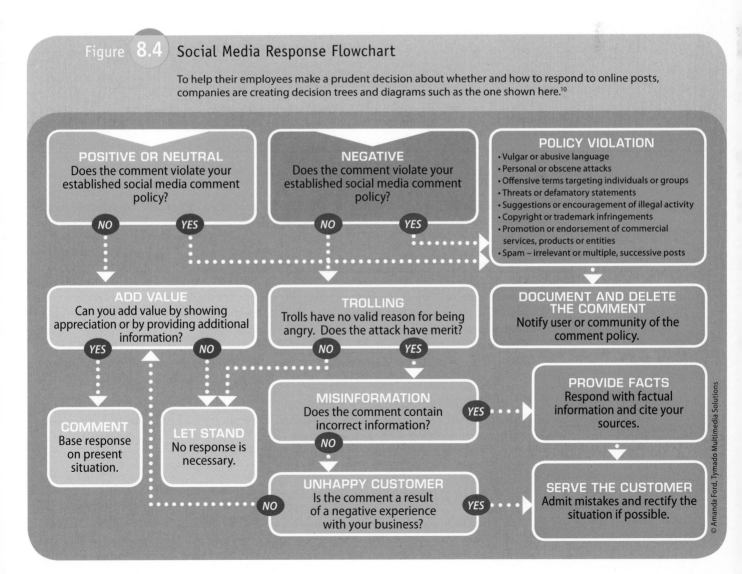

Figure **8.5** Responding to Customers Online

As businesses increasingly interact with their customers and the public online, they are developing "rules of engagement" and best practices.[11]

Be positive.

- Respond in a friendly, upbeat, yet professional tone.
- Correct mistakes politely.
- Do not argue, insult, or blame others.

Be transparent.

- State your name and position with the business.
- Personalize and humanize your business.

Be honest.

- Own up to problems and mistakes.
- Inform customers when and how you will improve the situation.

Be timely.

- Respond in less than 24 hours.

Be helpful.

- Point users to valuable information on your website or other approved websites.
- Follow up with users when new information is available.

© Amanda Ford, Tymado Multimedia Solutions

ETHICS CHECK:

How Authentic Are Customer Reviews Online?

As the value of social media buzz is steadily increasing, so are efforts to rig the system. Not all customer critiques on the Web can be trusted, particularly when so many are anonymous. Some businesses pay for positive online reviews or encourage their employees to sing the praises of their own products while knocking the competition.[12] How seriously should companies take the threat of potentially fraudulent reviews?

alike. Businesses can't control the conversation without disabling fans' comments on their Facebook walls or blogs, but they can respond in a way that benefits customers, prevents the problem from snowballing, and shines a positive light on the organization.

Embracing Customer Comments. Customer reviews online are opportunities for savvy businesses to improve their products or services and may serve as a free and efficient crowdsourced quality-control system. Retailers such as Walmart, Amazon, and L.L. Bean use powerful software to sift through billions of social media posts and product reviews. The data offer real-time feedback that may help clear up supply-chain bottlenecks, expose product flaws, and improve operating instructions.[13] For example, angry reviews on its website alerted Walmart to a problem with a prepaid wireless Internet stick the retailer was selling and prompted a remedy within two days.

Guidelines for Responding to Online Posts. Social media experts say that not every comment on the Web merits a response. They recommend responding to posts only when you can add value—for example, by correcting false information or providing customer service. Additional guidelines for professional responses to customer comments are summarized in Figure 8.5.

Instruction Messages

Instruction messages describe how to complete a task. You may be asked to write instructions about how to repair a paper jam in the photocopier, order supplies, file a grievance, or hire new employees. Instructions are different from policies and official procedures, which establish rules of conduct to be followed within an organization. We are most concerned with creating messages that clearly explain how to complete a task.

Like requests and responses, instruction messages follow a straightforward, direct approach. Before writing instructions for a process, be sure you understand the process completely. Practice doing it yourself. A message that delivers instructions should open with an explanation of why the procedure or set of instructions is necessary.

Dividing Instructions Into Steps.   The body of an instruction message should use plain English and familiar words to describe the process. Your messages explaining instructions will be most readable if you follow these guidelines:

- Divide the instructions into steps.
- List the steps in the order in which they are to be carried out.
- Arrange the items vertically with numbers.
- Begin each step with an action verb using the imperative (command) mood rather than the indicative mood.

Indicative Mood	Imperative Mood
The contract should be sent immediately.	Send the contract immediately.
The first step involves downloading the app.	Download the app first.
A survey of employees is necessary to learn what options they prefer.	Survey employees to learn the options they prefer.

In the closing of a message issuing instructions, try to tie following the instructions to benefits to the organization or individual.

If you are asked to prepare a list of instructions that is not part of a message, include a title such as *How to Clear Paper Jams*. Include an opening paragraph explaining why the instructions are needed.

Revising a Message Delivering Instructions.   Figure 8.6 shows the first draft of an interoffice memo written by Neil DeLuca. His memo was meant to announce a new method for employees to follow in advertising open positions. However, the tone was negative, the explanation of the problem rambled, and the new method was unclear. Notice, too, that Neil's first draft told readers what they *shouldn't* do (*Do not submit advertisements for new employees directly to an Internet job bank or a newspaper*). It is more helpful to tell readers what they *should* do. Finally, Neil's first memo closed with a threat instead of showing readers how this new practice will help them.

In the revision Neil improved the tone considerably. The subject line contains a *please*, which softens an order. The subject line also includes a verb and specifies the purpose of the memo. Instead of expressing his ideas with negative words and threats, Neil revised his message to explain objectively and concisely what went wrong.

Neil realized that his original explanation of the new procedure was vague. To clarify the instructions, he itemized and numbered the steps. Each step begins with an action verb in the imperative (command) mood (*Write, Bring, Let,* and *Pick up*). It is sometimes difficult to force all the steps in a list into this kind of command language. Neil struggled, but he finally found verbs that worked.

Why should you go to so much trouble to make lists and achieve parallelism? Because readers can comprehend what you have said much more quickly. Parallel language also makes you look professional and efficient.

In writing messages that deliver instructions, be careful of tone. Today's managers and team leaders seek employee participation and cooperation. These goals can't be achieved, though, if the writer sounds like a dictator or an autocrat. Avoid making accusations and fixing blame. Rather, explain changes, give reasons, and suggest benefits to the reader. Assume that

Figure 8.6   Memo Delivering Instructions

DRAFT

Date: January 5, 2015
To: Vicky Logan, Manager
From: Neil DeLuca, Human Resources
Subject: Job Advertisement Misunderstanding ●————————

We had no idea last month when we implemented a new hiring process that
major problems would result. Due to the fact that every department is now placing ●———
Internet advertisements for new-hires individually, the difficulties occurred. This
cannot continue. Perhaps we did not make it clear at the time, but all newly hired
employees who are hired for a position should be requested through this office.

Do not submit your advertisements for new employees directly to an Internet job ●———
bank or a newspaper. After you write them, they should be brought to Human
Resources, where they will be centralized. You should discuss each ad with one
of our counselors. Then we will place the ad at an appropriate Internet site or
other publication. If you do not follow these guidelines, chaos will result. You ●———
may pick up applicant folders from us the day after the closing date in the ad.

— Uses vague, negative
  subject line

— Fails to pinpoint main
  idea in opening

— New process is hard
  to follow

— Uses threats instead
  of showing benefits
  to reader

REVISION

MEMORANDUM

Date: January 5, 2015

To: Vicky Logan, Manager

From: Neil DeLuca, Human Resources *N.D.*

Subject: Please Follow New Job Advertisement Process

To find the right candidates for your open positions as fast as possible, we are
implementing a new routine. Effective today, all advertisements for departmental
job openings should be routed through the Human Resources Department.

A major problem resulted from the change in hiring procedures implemented last
month. Each department is placing job advertisements for new-hires individually,
when all such requests should be centralized in this office. To process applications
more efficiently, please follow these steps:

1. Write an advertisement for a position in your department.

2. Bring the ad to Human Resources and discuss it with one of our counselors.

3. Let Human Resources place the ad at an appropriate Internet job bank or
   submit it to a newspaper.

4. Pick up applicant folders from Human Resources the day following the closing
   date provided in the ad.

Following these guidelines will save you work and will also enable Human
Resources to help you fill your openings more quickly. Call Ann Edmonds at
Ext. 2505 if you have questions about this process.

Employs informative,
courteous, upbeat
subject line —

Combines "you" view
with main idea in —
opening

Explains why change
in procedures
is necessary —

Lists easy-to-follow
steps and starts each —
step with a verb

Closes by reinforcing
benefits to reader —

Tips for Writing Instructions
- Arrange steps in the order in which they should be
  completed.
- Start each step with an action verb in the imperative
  (command) mood.
- Be careful of tone in writing messages that give
  orders.
- Show reader benefits if you are encouraging the
  use of the procedure.

© Cengage Learning 2015

employees want to contribute to the success of the organization and to their own achievement. Notice in the Figure 8.6 revision that Neil tells readers that they will save time and have their open positions filled more quickly if they follow the new method.

Learning More About Writing Instructions.   The writing of instructions is so important that we have developed a special bonus online supplement called *How to Write Instructions*. It provides more examples and information. This online supplement at **www.cengagebrain.com** extends your textbook with in-depth material including links to real businesses showing you examples of well-written instructions.

Direct Claims and Complaints

LEARNING OBJECTIVE **3**
Prepare contemporary messages that make direct claims and voice complaints, including those posted online.

In business, things can and do go wrong—promised shipments are late, warrantied goods fail, and service is disappointing. When you as a customer must write to identify or correct a wrong, the message is called a *claim*. Straightforward claims are those to which you expect the receiver to agree readily.

Increasingly, consumers resort to telephone calls, they e-mail their claims, or—as we have seen—they vent their peeves in online posts. Large companies can afford to employ social media specialists who monitor and respond to comments. However, small and midsized businesses often have few options other than Google Alerts and their own limited forays into social networking.

This is why even in an age of digital communication, claims written as letters are taken more seriously than telephone calls or e-mails. Letters also more convincingly establish a record of what happened. Some business communicators opt for letters they can either fax or attach to e-mail messages. This option combines the advantages of fax and e-mail (speed) with the formality of a letter and the attention it commands. Regardless of channel, straightforward claims use a direct approach. Claims that require a persuasive response are presented in Chapter 10.

Opening a Claim With a Clear Statement

When you, as a customer, have a legitimate claim, you can expect a positive response from a company. Smart businesses want to hear from their customers. They know that retaining a customer is far less costly than recruiting a new customer.

Open your claim with a compliment, a point of agreement, a statement of the problem, a brief review of action you have taken to resolve the problem, or a clear statement of the action you want. You might expect a replacement, a refund, a new product, credit to your account, correction of a billing error, free repairs, free inspection, or cancellation of an order. When the remedy is obvious, state it immediately *(Please correct an erroneous double charge of $59 to my credit card for LapLink migration software. I accidentally clicked the Submit button twice)*. When the remedy is less obvious, you might ask for a change in policy or procedure or simply for an explanation *(Because three of our employees with confirmed reservations were refused rooms September 16 in your hotel, would you please clarify your policy regarding reservations and late arrivals)*.

> Smart businesses want to hear from their customers. They know that retaining a customer is far less costly than recruiting a new customer.

© iStockphoto.com/Andrew Johnson

Explaining and Justifying a Claim

In the body of a claim message, explain the problem and justify your request. Provide the necessary details so that the difficulty can be corrected without further correspondence. Avoid becoming angry or trying to fix blame. Bear in mind that the person reading your message is seldom responsible for the problem. Instead, state the facts logically, objectively, and unemotionally; let the reader decide on the causes. If you choose to send a letter by postal mail, include copies of all pertinent documents such as invoices, sales slips, catalog descriptions, and repair records. Of course, those receipts and other documents can also be scanned and attached to an e-mail.

If using paper mail, send copies and *not* your originals, which could be lost. When service is involved, cite the names of individuals you spoke to and the dates of calls. Assume that a company honestly wants to satisfy its customers—because most do. When an alternative remedy exists, spell it out (*If you are unable to offer store credit, please apply the second amount of $59 to your TurboSpeed software and a LapLink USB cable that I would like to buy too*).

Concluding a Claim With an Action Request

End a claim message with a courteous statement that promotes goodwill and summarizes your action request. If appropriate, include an end date (*I hope you understand that mistakes in ordering online sometimes occur. Because I have enjoyed your prompt service in the past, I hope that you will be able to issue a refund or store credit by May 2*).

Finally, in making claims, act promptly. Delaying claims makes them appear less important. Delayed claims are also more difficult to verify. By taking the time to put your claim in writing, you indicate your seriousness. A written claim starts a record of the problem, should later action be necessary. Be sure to save a copy of your message whether paper or electronic.

Putting It All Together and Revising

When Duncan Rabe received a statement showing a charge for a three-year service warranty that he did not purchase, he was furious. He called the store but failed to get satisfaction. He decided against voicing his complaint online because he wished for a quick resolution and doubted that a social media post would be noticed by the small business. He chose to write an e-mail to the customer-service address featured prominently on the Good Vibes website. You can see the first draft of his direct claim e-mail in Figure 8.7. This draft gave him a chance to vent his anger, but it accomplished little else. The tone was belligerent, and it assumed that the company intentionally mischarged him. Furthermore, it failed to tell the reader how to remedy the problem. The revision, also shown in Figure 8.7, tempered the tone, described the problem objectively, and provided facts and figures. Most important, it specified exactly what Duncan wanted to be done.

Courtesy of Mark Goldowitz

Posting Complaints and Reviews Online

Social media experts advise that consumers exhaust all other options for claims and complaints with the company before venting online.[16] Just as you probably wouldn't complain to the Better Business Bureau without giving a business at least one chance to respond, you shouldn't express dissatisfaction just to let off steam. Although it may feel good temporarily to rant, most businesses want to please their customers and welcome an opportunity to right a wrong. A well-considered message, whether a letter or an e-mail, allows you to tell the full story and is more likely to be heard. Moreover, businesses are still not monitoring social media enough; in one study of almost 1,300 Twitter complaints, less than a third of users received a reply from a company.[17]

Two other reasons may dissuade you from letting loose in ill-conceived online comments. First, social media posts have a way of ending up in the wrong hands, making vicious complainers seem irrational. As always, think whether people you respect and prospective employers would approve. Even anonymous posts can be tracked back to the writer. Moreover, nasty "cyber chest-pounding" might not be taken seriously, and your remarks could be deleted.[18] Second, businesses and professionals can take individuals to court for negative comments online. A chiropractor in San Francisco sued a patient for

Figure 8.7 Direct Claim E-Mail

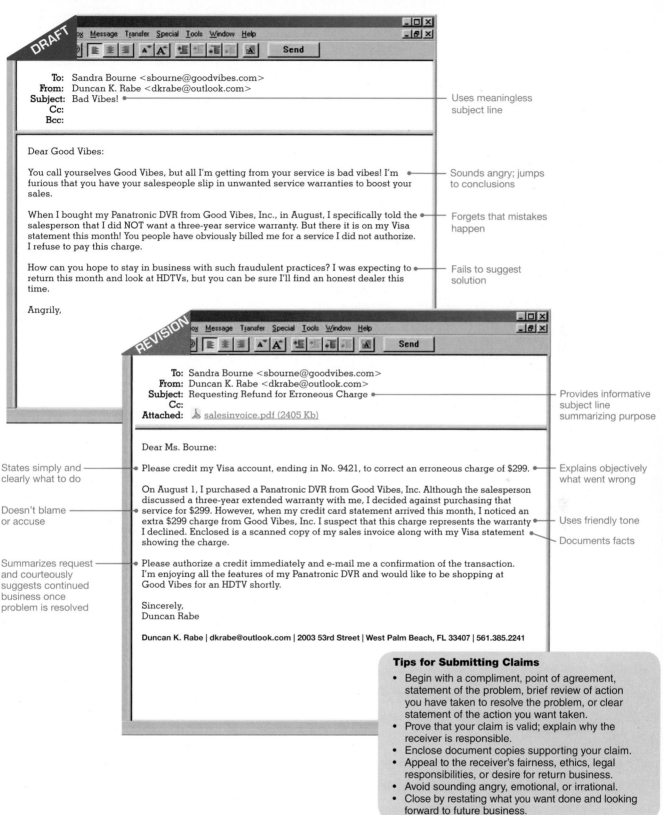

DRAFT

To: Sandra Bourne <sbourne@goodvibes.com>
From: Duncan K. Rabe <dkrabe@outlook.com>
Subject: Bad Vibes! •————— Uses meaningless subject line
Cc:
Bcc:

Dear Good Vibes:

You call yourselves Good Vibes, but all I'm getting from your service is bad vibes! I'm •——— Sounds angry; jumps to conclusions
furious that you have your salespeople slip in unwanted service warranties to boost your sales.

When I bought my Panatronic DVR from Good Vibes, Inc., in August, I specifically told the •——— Forgets that mistakes happen
salesperson that I did NOT want a three-year service warranty. But there it is on my Visa statement this month! You people have obviously billed me for a service I did not authorize. I refuse to pay this charge.

How can you hope to stay in business with such fraudulent practices? I was expecting to •——— Fails to suggest solution
return this month and look at HDTVs, but you can be sure I'll find an honest dealer this time.

Angrily,

REVISION

To: Sandra Bourne <sbourne@goodvibes.com>
From: Duncan K. Rabe <dkrabe@outlook.com>
Subject: Requesting Refund for Erroneous Charge •————— Provides informative subject line summarizing purpose
Cc:
Attached: salesinvoice.pdf (2405 Kb)

Dear Ms. Bourne:

States simply and —• Please credit my Visa account, ending in No. 9421, to correct an erroneous charge of $299. •——— Explains objectively what went wrong
clearly what to do

On August 1, I purchased a Panatronic DVR from Good Vibes, Inc. Although the salesperson
Doesn't blame —— discussed a three-year extended warranty with me, I decided against purchasing that
or accuse service for $299. However, when my credit card statement arrived this month, I noticed an
extra $299 charge from Good Vibes, Inc. I suspect that this charge represents the warranty •——— Uses friendly tone
I declined. Enclosed is a scanned copy of my sales invoice along with my Visa statement •——— Documents facts
showing the charge.

Summarizes request —• Please authorize a credit immediately and e-mail me a confirmation of the transaction.
and courteously I'm enjoying all the features of my Panatronic DVR and would like to be shopping at
suggests continued Good Vibes for an HDTV shortly.
business once
problem is resolved Sincerely,
Duncan Rabe

Duncan K. Rabe | dkrabe@outlook.com | 2003 53rd Street | West Palm Beach, FL 33407 | 561.385.2241

Tips for Submitting Claims
- Begin with a compliment, point of agreement, statement of the problem, brief review of action you have taken to resolve the problem, or clear statement of the action you want taken.
- Prove that your claim is valid; explain why the receiver is responsible.
- Enclose document copies supporting your claim.
- Appeal to the receiver's fairness, ethics, legal responsibilities, or desire for return business.
- Avoid sounding angry, emotional, or irrational.
- Close by restating what you want done and looking forward to future business.

criticizing his billing process on Yelp. The case was settled out of court. Also, libelous statements disguised as opinion (*In my view attorney Jack Miller is stealing $4,000 from his clients*) can get you in trouble.[19]

The tips in Figure 8.8, gleaned from *Consumer Reports,* will allow you to exercise your right to free speech while staying safe when critiquing a product or service online.

Shoppers read online comments on sites such as Yelp, TripAdvisor, Angie's List, and Amazon. In a *Consumer Reports* study of more than 4,000 online subscribers, 40 percent stated that they read user reviews when researching a product category.[20] Even if posting does not achieve your objective, your well-written complaint or review may help others. You have a responsibility. Use it wisely.

© Cengage Learning 2015

Figure **8.8** Guidelines for Writing Online Reviews and Complaints

Establish your credibility
- Zero in on your objective and make your comment as concise as possible.
- Focus only on the facts and be able to support them.

Check posting rules
- Understand what's allowed by reading the terms and conditions on the site.
- Keep your complaint clean, polite, and to the point.

Provide balanced reviews
- To be fair, offset criticism with positives to show that you are a legitimate consumer.
- Suggest improvements even in glowing reviews; all-out gushing is suspicious and not helpful.

Consider the Web's permanence
- Know that your review may be posted indefinitely, even if you change your mind and modify a post later.

Embrace transparency
- Be open; even anonymous comments can be tracked down. Privacy policies do not protect writers from subpoenas.

Accept offers to help
- Reply if a business offers to help or discuss the problem; update your original post as necessary.

Refuse payment for favorable critiques
- Never accept payment to change your opinion or your account of the facts.
- Comply with requests for a review if you are a satisfied customer.

Adjustment Messages

Even the best-run and best-loved businesses occasionally receive claims or complaints from consumers. When a company receives a claim and decides to respond favorably, the message is called an *adjustment*. Most businesses make adjustments promptly: they replace merchandise, refund money, extend discounts, send coupons, and repair goods. In fact, social media have shortened the response time drastically to mere hours, not days.

Businesses make favorable adjustments to legitimate claims for two reasons. First, consumers are protected by contractual and tort law for recovery of damages. If, for example, you find an insect in a package of frozen peas, the food processor of that package is bound by contractual law to replace it. If you suffer injury, the processor may be liable for damages. Second, and more obviously, most organizations genuinely want to satisfy their customers and retain their business.

In responding to customer claims, you must first decide whether to grant the claim. Unless the claim is obviously fraudulent or excessive, you will probably grant it. When you say *yes*, your adjustment message will be good news to the reader. Deliver that good news by using the direct strategy. When your response is *no*, the indirect strategy might be more appropriate. Chapter 9 discusses the indirect strategy for conveying negative news. You have three goals in adjustment messages:

- Rectifying the wrong, if one exists
- Regaining the confidence of the customer
- Promoting further business

Revealing Good News Up Front in an Adjustment Message

Instead of beginning with a review of what went wrong, present the good news in an adjustment message immediately. When Kathy Nguyen responded to the claim letter from customer Ultima Electronics about a missing shipment, her first draft, shown at the top of Figure 8.9, was angry. No wonder. Ultima Electronics apparently had provided the wrong shipping address, and the goods were returned. Once Kathy and her company

Courtesy of Brandon Stanton

Brandon Stanton's photo project "Humans of New York" has gone viral and earned rave reviews in *The Wall Street Journal* and *The Atlantic*. But when fashion-apparel label DKNY featured the photos in an in-store display without obtaining permission or offering compensation, Stanton's half-million Facebook followers protested through social media and on DKNY's Facebook site. Within hours of the stir, DKNY responded online saying, "We deeply regret this mistake. Accordingly, we are making a charitable donation of $25,000 to the YMCA in Bedford-Stuyvesant, Brooklyn, in Mr. Stanton's name." How do businesses generally handle consumer complaints?[21]

Figure 8.9 Customer Adjustment Letter

DRAFT

Dear Sir:

I have before me your recent complaint about a missing shipment. First, let me say that it's very difficult to deliver merchandise when we have been given the wrong address.

After receiving your complaint, our investigators looked into your problem shipment and determined that it was sent immediately after we received the order. According to the shipper's records, it was delivered to the warehouse address given on your stationery: 66B Industrial Lane, West Warwick, RI 02893. Unfortunately, no one at that address would accept delivery, so the shipment was returned to us. I see from your current stationery that your company has a new address. With the proper address, we probably could have delivered this shipment.

Although we feel that it is entirely appropriate to charge you shipping and restocking fees, as is our standard practice on returned goods, in this instance we will waive those fees. We hope this second shipment finally catches up with you at your current address.

Sincerely,

— Fails to reveal good news immediately and blames customer

— Creates ugly tone with negative words and sarcasm

— Sounds grudging and reluctant in granting claim

REVISION

DIGITAL WAREHOUSE
6 Business Park Drive
Branford, CT 06405

Phone: (203) 488-2202
Fax: (203) 489-3320
Web: www.dwarehouse.com

April 24, 2015

Mr. Robert Alarcon
Ultima Electronics
27 Wightman Street
West Warwick, RI 02893

Dear Mr. Alarcon:

Subject: Your April 19 Letter About Your Purchase Order

You should receive by April 26 a second shipment of the Blu-ray players, video game consoles, and other digital equipment that you ordered April 2.

The first shipment of this order was delivered April 10 to 66B Industrial Lane, West Warwick, RI. When no one at that address would accept the shipment, it was returned to us. Now that I have your letter, I see that the order should have been sent to 27 Wightman Street, West Warwick, RI 02893. When an order is undeliverable, we usually try to verify the shipping address by telephoning the customer. Somehow the return of this shipment was not caught by our normally painstaking shipping clerks. You can be sure that I will investigate shipping and return procedures with our clerks immediately to see if we can improve existing methods.

Your respect is important to us, Mr. Alarcon. Although our rock-bottom discount prices have enabled us to build a volume business, we don't want to be so large that we lose touch with valued customers like you. Over the years our customers' respect has made us successful, and we hope that the prompt delivery of this shipment will retain yours.

Sincerely,

Kathy Nguyen
Distribution Manager

cc Joe Gonzalez
    Shipping Department

Uses customer's name in salutation

Announces good news immediately

Regains confidence of customer by explaining what happened and by suggesting plans for improvement

Closes confidently with genuine appeal for customer's respect

© Cengage Learning 2015

decided to send a second shipment and comply with the customer's claim, however, she had to give up the anger. Her goal was to regain the goodwill and the business of this customer. The improved version of her letter announces that a new shipment will arrive shortly.

If you decide to comply with a customer's claim, let the receiver know immediately. Don't begin your letter with a negative statement (*We are very sorry to hear that you are having trouble with your dishwasher*). This approach reminds the reader of the problem and may rekindle the heated emotions or unhappy feelings experienced when the claim was written. Instead, focus on the good news. The following openings for various letters illustrate how to begin a message with good news:

> *You're right! We agree that the warranty on your American Standard Model UC600 dishwasher should be extended for six months.*

> *You will be receiving shortly a new slim Nokia smartphone to replace the one that shattered when dropped recently.*

> *Please take your portable Admiral microwave oven to A-1 Appliance Service, 200 Orange Street, Pasadena, where it will be repaired at no cost to you.*

> *The enclosed check for $325 demonstrates our desire to satisfy our customers and earn their confidence.*

In announcing that you will make an adjustment, do so without a grudging tone—even if you have reservations about whether the claim is legitimate. Once you decide to comply with the customer's request, do so happily. Avoid halfhearted or reluctant responses (*Although the American Standard dishwasher works well when used properly, we have decided to allow you to take yours to A-1 Appliance Service for repair at our expense*).

Explaining Compliance in the Body of an Adjustment Message

In responding to claims, most organizations sincerely want to correct a wrong. They want to do more than just make the customer happy. They want to stand behind their products and services; they want to do what is right.

In the body of the message, explain how you are complying with the claim. In all but the most routine claims, you should seek to regain the confidence of the customer. You might reasonably expect that a customer who has experienced difficulty with a product, with delivery, with billing, or with service has lost faith in your organization. Rebuilding that faith is important for future business.

How to rebuild lost confidence depends on the situation and the claim. If procedures need to be revised, explain what changes will be made. If a product has defective parts, tell how the product is being improved. If service is faulty, describe genuine efforts to improve it. Notice in Figure 8.9 that the writer promises to investigate shipping procedures to see whether improvements might prevent future mishaps.

Sometimes the problem is not with the product but with the way it is being used. In other instances customers misunderstand warranties or inadvertently cause delivery and billing mix-ups by supplying incorrect information. Remember that rational and sincere explanations will do much to regain the confidence of unhappy customers.

In your explanation avoid emphasizing negative words such as *trouble, regret, misunderstanding, fault, defective, error, inconvenience,* and *unfortunately.* Keep your message positive and upbeat.

Deciding Whether to Apologize

Whether to apologize is a debatable issue. Attorneys generally discourage apologies fearing that they admit responsibility and will trigger lawsuits. However, both judges and juries tend to look on apologies favorably. More than 20 U.S. states have passed some form of an "apology law" that allows an expression of regret without fear that such a statement will be used as a basis for liability in court.[22] Some business writing experts advise against apologies, contending that they are counterproductive and merely remind the customer of the unpleasantness related to the claim. If, however, apologizing seems natural, do so.

People like to hear apologies. It raises their self-esteem, shows the humility of the writer, and acts as a form of "psychological compensation."[23] Don't, however, fall back on the familiar phrase, *I'm sorry for any inconvenience we may have caused*. It sounds mechanical and insincere. Instead, try something like this: *We understand the frustration our delay has caused you, We're sorry you didn't receive better service*, or *You're right to be disappointed*. If you feel that an apology is appropriate, do it early and briefly. You will learn more about delivering effective apologies in Chapter 9 when we discuss negative messages.

The primary focus of an adjustment message is on how you are complying with the request, how the problem occurred, and how you are working to prevent its recurrence.

Using Sensitive Language in Adjustment Messages

The language of adjustment messages must be particularly sensitive, because customers are already upset. Here are some don'ts:

- Don't use negative words.
- Don't blame customers—even when they may be at fault.
- Don't blame individuals or departments within your organization; it's unprofessional.
- Don't make unrealistic promises; you can't guarantee that the situation will never recur.

To regain the confidence of your reader, consider including resale information. Describe a product's features and any special applications that might appeal to the reader. Promote a new product if it seems appropriate.

Showing Confidence in the Closing

End positively by expressing confidence that the problem has been resolved and that continued business relations will result. You might mention the product in a favorable light, suggest a new product, express your appreciation for the customer's business, or anticipate future business. It's often appropriate to refer to the desire to be of service and to satisfy customers. Notice how the following closings illustrate a positive, confident tone:

> *You were most helpful in informing us of this situation and permitting us to correct it. We appreciate your thoughtfulness in writing to us.*

> *Thanks for writing. Your satisfaction is important to us. We hope that this refund check convinces you that service to our customers is our No. 1 priority. Our goals are to earn your confidence and continue to justify that confidence with quality products and excellent service.*

> *For your patience and patronage, we are truly grateful.*

> *Your Asus Netbook will come in handy whether you are connecting with friends, surfing the net, listening to music, watching movies, or playing games. What's more, you can add an HDTV tuner and built-in GPS for a little more. Take a look at the enclosed booklet detailing the big savings for essential technology on a budget. We value your business and look forward to your future orders.*

Although the direct strategy works for many requests and replies, it obviously won't work for every situation. With more practice and experience, you will be able to alter the pattern and apply the writing process to other communication problems. See the checklist on the next page for a summary of what to do when you must write claim and adjustment messages.

Direct Claim, Complaint, and Adjustment Messages

Messages That Make Claims and Voice Complaints

- **Begin directly with the purpose.** Present a clear statement of the problem or the action requested such as a refund, a replacement, credit, an explanation, or the correction of an error. Add a compliment if you have been pleased in other respects.

- **Explain objectively.** In the body tell the specifics of the claim. Consider reminding the receiver of ethical and legal responsibilities, fairness, and a desire for return business. Provide copies of necessary documents.

- **Conclude by requesting action.** Include an end date, if important. Add a pleasant, forward-looking statement. Keep a copy of the message.

- **Exercise good judgment.** Online postings are permanent. Make your comments concise and focus only on the facts. Respect posting rules and be polite. Provide balanced reviews. Shun anonymity.

Messages That Make Adjustments

- **Open with approval.** Comply with the customer's claim immediately. Avoid sounding grudging or reluctant.

- **In the body win back the customer's confidence.** Explain the cause of the problem, or describe your ongoing efforts to avoid such difficulties. Apologize if you feel that you should, but do so early and briefly. Avoid negative words, accusations, and unrealistic promises. Consider including resale and sales promotion information.

- **Close positively.** Express appreciation to the customer for writing, extend thanks for past business, anticipate continued patronage, refer to your desire to be of service, and/or mention a new product if it seems appropriate.

Goodwill Messages

LEARNING OBJECTIVE **5**
Write special messages that convey kindness and goodwill.

Many communicators are intimidated when they must write goodwill messages expressing thanks, recognition, and sympathy. Finding the right words to express feelings is often more difficult than writing ordinary business documents. That is why writers tend to procrastinate when it comes to goodwill messages. Sending a ready-made card or picking up the telephone is easier than writing a message. Remember, though, that the personal sentiments of the sender are always more expressive and more meaningful to readers than are printed cards or oral messages. Taking the time to write gives more importance to our well-wishing. Personal notes also provide a record that can be reread, savored, and treasured.

In expressing thanks, recognition, or sympathy, you should always do so promptly. These messages are easier to write when the situation is fresh in your mind. They also mean more to the recipient. Don't forget that a prompt thank-you note carries the hidden message that you care and that you consider the event to be important. The best goodwill messages—whether thanks, congratulations, praise, or sympathy—concentrate on the five Ss. Goodwill messages should be

- **Selfless.** Focus the message solely on the receiver, not the sender. Don't talk about yourself; avoid such comments as *I remember when I . . . .*

- **Specific.** Personalize the message by mentioning specific incidents or characteristics of the receiver. Telling a colleague *Great speech* is much less effective than *Great story about McDonald's marketing in Moscow*. Take care to verify names and other facts.

- **Sincere.** Let your words show genuine feelings. Rehearse in your mind how you would express the message to the receiver orally. Then transform that conversational language to your written message. Avoid pretentious, formal, or flowery language (*It gives me great pleasure to extend felicitations on the occasion of your firm's twentieth anniversary*).

- **Spontaneous.** Keep the message fresh and enthusiastic. Avoid canned phrases (*Congratulations on your promotion, Good luck in the future*). Strive for directness and naturalness, not creative brilliance.
- **Short.** Although goodwill messages can be as long as needed, try to accomplish your purpose in only a few sentences. What is most important is remembering an individual. Such caring does not require documentation or wordiness. Individuals and business organizations often use special note cards or stationery for brief messages.

Saying Thank-You

When someone has done you a favor or when an action merits praise, you need to extend thanks or show appreciation. Letters of appreciation may be written to customers for their orders, to hosts for their hospitality, to individuals for kindnesses performed, to employees for a job well done, and especially to customers who complain. After all, whether in social media posts, by e-mail, or on paper, complaints are actually providing you with "free consulting reports from the field." Complainers who feel that their complaints were heard often become the greatest promoters of an organization.[24]

Because the receiver will be pleased to hear from you, you can open directly with the purpose of your message. The letter in Figure 8.10 thanks a speaker who addressed a group

---

Figure 8.10   Thank-You Letter for a Favor

International Marketing Association
225 West 17th Street
New York, New York 10029
http://www.ima.com

February 26, 2015

Mr. Michael T. Reese
Marketing Manager
Toys "R" Us, Inc.
One Geoffrey Way
Wayne, NJ 07470-2030

Dear Michael:

Thank you for providing the Manhattan chapter of the IMA with one of the best presentations our group has ever heard. — *Tells purpose and delivers praise*

Your description of the battle Toys "R" Us waged to begin marketing products in Japan was a genuine eye-opener for many of us. Nine years of preparation establishing connections and securing permissions seems an eternity, but obviously such persistence and patience pay off. We now understand better the need to learn local customs and nurture relationships when dealing in Japan or other Asian countries. — *Personalizes the message by using specifics rather than generalities*

In addition to your good advice, we particularly enjoyed your sense of humor and jokes—as you must have recognized from the uproarious laughter. What a great routine you do on faulty translations! — *Spotlights the reader's talents*

We're grateful, Michael, for the entertaining and instructive evening you provided our marketing professionals. — *Concludes with compliments and thanks*

Cordially,

Rosetta H. Johnson

Rosetta H. Johnson
Program Chair, IMA

RHJ: mef

© Cengage Learning 2015

of marketing professionals. Although such thank-you notes can be quite short, this one is a little longer because the writer wants to lend importance to the receiver's efforts. Notice that every sentence relates to the receiver and offers enthusiastic praise. By using the receiver's name along with contractions and positive words, the writer makes the letter sound warm and conversational.

Written notes that show appreciation and express thanks are significant to their receivers. In expressing thanks, you generally write a short note on special notepaper or heavy card stock. The following messages provide models for expressing thanks for a gift, for a favor, and for hospitality.

Expressing Thanks for a Gift.   When expressing thanks, tell what the gift means to you. Use sincere, simple statements.

Thanks, Laura, to you and the other members of the department for honoring me with the elegant Waterford crystal vase at the party celebrating my twentieth anniversary with the company. The height and shape of the vase are perfect to hold roses and other bouquets from my garden. Each time I fill it, I'll remember your thoughtfulness in choosing this lovely gift for me.

Sending Thanks for a Favor.   In showing appreciation for a favor, explain the importance of the gesture to you.

I sincerely appreciate your filling in for me last week when I was too ill to attend the planning committee meeting for the spring exhibition. Without your participation, much of my preparatory work would have been lost. Knowing that competent and generous individuals like you are part of our team, Mark, is a great comfort. Moreover, counting you as a friend is my very good fortune. I'm grateful to you.

Extending Thanks for Hospitality.   When you have been a guest, send a note that compliments the fine food, charming surroundings, warm hospitality, excellent host, and good company.

Jeffrey and I want you to know how much we enjoyed the dinner party for our department that you hosted Saturday evening. Your charming home and warm hospitality, along with the lovely dinner and sinfully delicious chocolate dessert, combined to create a truly memorable evening. Most of all, though, we appreciate your kindness in cultivating togetherness in our department. Thanks, Jennifer, for being such a special person.

Recognizing Employees for Their Contributions.   A letter that recognizes specific employee contributions makes the person feel appreciated even if it is not accompanied by a bonus check.

Jerry, I am truly impressed by how competently you shepherded your team through the complex Horizon project. Thanks to your leadership, team members stayed on target and met their objectives. Your adept meeting facilitation, use of an agenda, and quick turnaround of meeting minutes kept the project on track. However, most of all I appreciate the long hours you put in to hammer out the final report.

Replying to Goodwill Messages

Should you respond when you receive a congratulatory note or a written pat on the back? By all means! These messages are attempts to connect personally; they are efforts to reach out, to form professional and/or personal bonds. Failing to respond to notes of congratulations and most other goodwill messages is like failing to say *You're welcome* when someone says *Thank you.* Responding to such messages is simply the right thing to do. Do avoid, though, minimizing your achievements with comments that suggest you don't really deserve the praise or that the sender is exaggerating your good qualities.

Answering a Congratulatory Note.   In responding to congratulations, keep it short and simple.

> *Thanks for your kind words regarding my award, and thanks, too, for forwarding me the link to the article online. I truly appreciate your warm wishes.*

Responding to Praise.   When acknowledging a pat-on-the-back note, use simple words in conveying your appreciation.

> *Your note about my work made me feel good. I'm grateful for your thoughtfulness.*

Expressing Sympathy

Most of us can bear misfortune and grief more easily when we know that others care. Notes expressing sympathy, though, are probably more difficult to write than any other kind of message. Commercial "In sympathy" cards make the task easier—but they are far less meaningful than personal notes. Grieving friends want to know what you think—not what Hallmark's card writers think.

To help you get started, you can always glance through cards expressing sympathy. They will supply ideas about the kinds of thoughts you might wish to convey in your own words. In writing a sympathy note, (a) refer to the death or misfortune sensitively, using words that show you understand what a crushing blow it is; (b) in the case of a death, praise the deceased in a personal way; (c) offer assistance without going into excessive detail; and (d) end on a reassuring, forward-looking note. Sympathy messages may be typed, although handwriting seems more personal. In either case, use notepaper or personal stationery.

Sending Condolences.   Mention the loss tactfully, recognize good qualities of the deceased, assure the receiver of your concern, offer assistance, and conclude on a reassuring note.

> *We are deeply saddened, Gayle, to learn of the death of your husband. Warren's kind nature and friendly spirit endeared him to all who knew him. He will be missed. Although words seem empty in expressing our grief, we want you to know that your friends at QuadCom extend their profound sympathy to you. If we may help you or lighten your load in any way, you have but to call.*

> *We know that the treasured memories of your many happy years together, along with the support of your family and many friends, will provide strength and comfort in the months ahead.*

Is E-Mail Appropriate for Goodwill Messages?

In expressing thanks or responding to goodwill messages, handwritten notes are most impressive. However, if you frequently communicate with the receiver by e-mail and if you are sure your note will not get lost, then sending an e-mail goodwill message is acceptable, according to the Emily Post Institute.[25] To express sympathy immediately after learning of a death or accident, you might precede a phone call or a written condolence message with an e-mail. E-mail is a fast and nonintrusive way to show your feelings. However, advises the Emily Post Institute, immediately follow with a handwritten note. Remember that e-mail messages are quickly gone and forgotten. Handwritten or printed messages remain and can be savored. Your thoughtfulness is more lasting if you take the time to prepare a handwritten or printed message on notepaper or personal stationery.

Goodwill Messages

General Guidelines: The Five Ss

- **Be selfless.** Discuss the receiver, not the sender.

- **Be specific.** Instead of generic statements (*You did a good job*), include special details (*Your marketing strategy to target key customers proved to be outstanding*).

- **Be sincere.** Show your honest feelings with conversational, unpretentious language (*We are all very proud of your award*).

- **Be spontaneous.** Strive to make the message natural, fresh, and direct. Avoid canned phrases (*If I may be of service, please do not hesitate . . .*).

- **Keep the message short.** Remember that, although they may be as long as needed, most goodwill messages are fairly short.

Giving Thanks

- **Cover three points in gift thank-yous.** (a) Identify the gift, (b) tell why you appreciate it, and (c) explain how you will use it.

- **Be sincere in sending thanks for a favor.** Tell what the favor means to you. Avoid superlatives and gushiness. Maintain credibility with sincere, simple statements.

- **Offer praise in expressing thanks for hospitality.** Compliment, as appropriate, the (a) fine food, (b) charming surroundings, (c) warm hospitality, (d) excellent host, and (e) good company.

- **Be specific when recognizing employees.** To make a note of appreciation meaningful, succinctly sum up the accomplishments for which you are grateful.

Responding to Goodwill Messages

- **Respond to congratulations.** Send a brief note expressing your appreciation. Tell how good the message made you feel.

- **Accept praise gracefully.** Don't make belittling comments (*I'm not really all that good!*) to reduce awkwardness or embarrassment.

Extending Sympathy

- **Refer to the loss or tragedy directly but sensitively.** In the first sentence, mention the loss and your personal reaction.

- **For deaths, praise the deceased.** Describe positive personal characteristics (*Howard was a forceful but caring leader*).

- **Offer assistance.** Suggest your availability, especially if you can do something specific.

- **End on a reassuring, positive note.** Perhaps refer to the strength the receiver finds in friends, family, colleagues, or faith.

Your Turn: Applying Your Skills at Highpoint

Zooming in

Your supervisor at Highpoint Blue Shield, Ellen Feld, has asked that you draft a letter to Martin L. Pritchett, the president of Pritchett Consulting. Mr. Pritchett called today to ask about purchasing group health insurance coverage for his small business. Ms. Feld must respond immediately with a letter asking Mr. Pritchett for information before she can provide him with a quote. Specifically, she needs to know the number of employees requiring coverage; when coverage would begin; whether the policy would include dental coverage; and whether he would prefer to offer an HMO (health maintenance organization) or a PPO (preferred provider organization) style plan. Ms. Feld would also like to arrange an appointment with Mr. Pritchett to discuss a possible plan further. She needs all this information to prepare for a personal meeting with him.

YOUR TASK. Write a draft of the letter to Mr. Martin L. Pritchett, 114 Walnut Street, Harrisburg, PA 17101. Be sure to express Ms. Feld's gratitude for the opportunity to serve Mr. Pritchett and to include the questions your supervisor has specified. Decide whether graphic highlighting will make the letter more readable, and add a date by which you would like his response.

Summary of Learning Objectives

Go to
www.cengagebrain.com
and use your access code to unlock valuable student resources.

1 Understand the channels through which typical positive messages travel in the digital era—e-mails, memos, and business letters—and apply the 3-x-3 writing process. Positive messages—whether e-mails, interoffice memos, or business letters— can be straightforward and direct because they carry nonsensitive, routine information. In applying Phase 1 of the writing process for positive messages, you should determine your purpose, visualize the audience, and anticipate the reaction of the reader to your message. In Phase 2 you should collect information, make an outline of the points to cover, and write the first draft. In Phase 3 you should edit for clarity, proofread for correctness, and look for ways to promote "skim value." Finally, you should decide whether the message accomplishes its goal. Business letters are necessary when a permanent record is required; when confidentiality is critical; when formality and sensitivity are essential; and when a persuasive, well-considered presentation is important. Business letters written on company stationery often use block style with all lines starting at the left margin.

2 Compose direct messages that make requests, respond to inquiries online and offline, and deliver step-by-step instructions. In direct messages requesting information or action, the opening immediately states the purpose of the message. The body explains and justifies the request. If many questions are asked, they should be expressed in parallel form and balanced grammatically. The closing tells the reader courteously what to do and shows appreciation. In a message that replies directly and complies with a request, a subject line may identify previous correspondence, and the opening immediately delivers the good news. The body explains and provides additional information. The closing is cordial and personalized. If action is necessary, the ending tells the reader how to proceed and gives helpful details. When writing messages that explain instructions, (a) divide the instructions into steps, (b) list each step in the order in which it is to be carried out, (c) arrange the items vertically with bullets or numbers, and (d) begin each step with an action verb using the imperative (command) mood. Messages that give instructions should not sound dictatorial. When businesses respond online, they strive to be positive, transparent, honest, timely, and helpful.

3 Prepare contemporary messages that make direct claims and voice complaints, including those posted online. When a customer writes to identify a wrong and request a correction, the message is called a *claim*. A direct claim is one to which the receiver is expected to readily agree. A well-written claim begins by describing the problem clearly or telling what action is to be taken. The body of the claim explains and justifies the request without anger or emotion. The closing summarizes the request or action to be taken. It includes an end date, if appropriate, and courteously looks forward to continued business if the problem is resolved. Copies of relevant documents should be enclosed. Take your complaint online only after exhausting all other options with the business in question. Keep your post concise and clean. Focus on your objective and be prepared to support the facts.

4 Create adjustment messages that salvage customers' trust and promote further business. When a company grants a customer's claim, it is called an *adjustment*. An adjustment message has three goals: (a) rectifying the wrong, if one exists; (b) regaining the confidence of the customer; and (c) promoting further business. The opening immediately grants the claim without sounding grudging. To regain the confidence of the customer, the body may explain what went wrong and how the problem will be rectified. However, the writer may strive to avoid accepting responsibility for any problems. The closing expresses appreciation, extends thanks for past business, refers to a desire to be of service, and may mention a new product. If an apology is offered, it should be presented early and briefly.

5 Write special messages that convey kindness and goodwill. Messages that deliver thanks, praise, or sympathy should be selfless, specific, sincere, spontaneous, and short. Gift thank-yous should identify the gift, tell why you appreciate it, and explain how you will use it. Favor thank-yous should tell, without gushing, what the favor means to you. Expressions of sympathy should mention the loss tactfully; recognize good qualities in the deceased (in the case of a death); offer assistance; and conclude on a positive, reassuring note.

Chapter Review

1. Explain the types of positive messages and the strategy used when businesspeople write them. (Obj. 1)

2. What channels are used for routine messages in organizations today? (Obj. 1)

3. When are letters still the preferred channel of communication despite the advent of e-mail, social networking, and other electronic communication technologies? (Obj. 1)

4. What are the most emphatic positions in a message, and what goes there? (Obj. 2)

5. What should you include in the closing of a request message? (Obj. 2)

6. Why should businesses embrace customer comments online? (Obj. 2)

7. How should businesspeople respond to online posts? (Obj. 2)

8. How should instructions be written? Give a brief original example. (Obj. 2)

9. What is the imperative mood, and why is it important to use it in writing instructions? (Obj. 2)

10. What is a claim? When should it be straightforward? (Obj. 3)

11. Why should a direct claim be made by letter rather than by e-mail or a telephone call? (Obj. 3)

12. What is an adjustment message? (Obj. 4)

13. What are a writer's three goals in composing adjustment messages? (Obj. 4)

14. What are five characteristics of goodwill messages? (Obj. 5)

15. What are four groups of people to whom business communicators might write letters of appreciation? (Obj. 5)

Critical Thinking

1. What are the advantages of mailing a letter as opposed to sending an e-mail, making a phone call, or writing an online post? (Objs. 1, 2)

2. In promoting the value of letter writing, a well-known columnist recently wrote, "To trust confidential information to e-mail is to be a rube."[26] What did he mean? Do you agree? (Objs. 1, 3)

3. Why is it smart to keep your cool when making a claim, and how should you go about it? (Obj. 3)

4. Why is it important to regain the confidence of a customer in an adjustment message? How can it be done? (Obj. 4)

5. **Ethical Issue:** Credit repair companies are notorious for making grand promises that they can't legally fulfill. The Federal Trade Commission has warned that none of those companies are legitimate. Experts say that people with credit blemishes would be better off saving their money and trying to repair their bad credit themselves. One path to better credit involves the writing of so-called goodwill letters. A goodwill letter in this context is a formal message to individual creditors asking them for compassion and requesting that they stop reporting negative information such as late payments on one's credit report. Discuss why writing such goodwill letters instead of calling or sending an e-mail might be a good strategy.

Writing Improvement Exercises

8.1 Short Responses to Online Comments (Objs. 1–5)

YOUR TASK. Explain the positive and negative attributes of the following online posts.[27] Examine the companies' responses to them. Do they follow the guidelines in this chapter? How do the consumers' posts measure up?

a.

Heather Jones **really really poor customer service by you guys. i am now looking into a new auto insurance provider....**
Yesterday at 8:57 am • Like • Comment

👍 25 people **like this.**

GEICO **Hi Heather, is there something we can assist with? Please send us your contact info at facebook@geico.com if you would like follow up communication.**
22 hours ago × Like • Flag

Write a comment...

b.

JD Lopez **when is the LG BANTER coming out?**
11 hours ago • Like • Comment

Sky Horizon Wireless **Hi JD – Please continue visiting our page for the latest news on device launches. Stay tuned !**
about an hour ago • Like • Flag

Write a comment...

c.

Maria Daley **You should extend your 15% off since I tried to order things off the website and it crashed. Then I tried calling the 1 800 number and it is constantly busy. Very disappointed that I can not place my order!**
Monday at 11:09 pm • Like • Comment

👍 5 people **like this.**

Box and Barrel **Hi Maria. Thanks for bringing this to our attention. We hope that you were able to place your order but if not, please call us at 800.975.9969 – we'd like to help!**
Tuesday at 8:55 am • Like • Flag

Maria Daley **Thank you! I called the customer service department and they were able to help me. I might also add they were very nice.**
Tuesday at 11:14 am • Like • Flag

Write a comment...

d.

Dee Innes **Is there any hope that Turbotax could be written for Ubuntu Linux? It would be really great. I know I would appreciate it because I am moving away from windows and I am sure other Ubuntu users would like it too!**
October 28 at 11:57 pm • Like • Comment

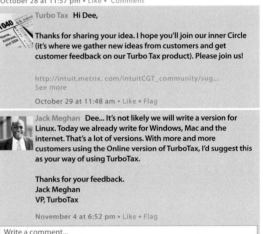

Turbo Tax **Hi Dee,**

Thanks for sharing your idea. I hope you'll join our inner Circle (it's where we gather new ideas from customers and get customer feedback on our Turbo Tax product). Please join us!

http://intuit.metrix.com/intuitCGT_community/sug...
See more

October 29 at 11:48 am • Like • Flag

Jack Meghan **Dee... It's not likely we will write a version for Linux. Today we already write for Windows, Mac and the internet. That's a lot of versions. With more and more customers using the Online version of TurboTax, I'd suggest this as your way of using TurboTax.**

Thanks for your feedback.
Jack Meghan
VP, TurboTax

November 4 at 6:52 pm • Like • Flag

Write a comment...

8.2 Writing Instructions (Obj. 2)

YOUR TASK. Revise each of the following wordy, dense paragraphs into a set of concise instructions. Include an introductory statement.

a. Obtaining credit and keeping good credit can be difficult, especially for young people. Here are five suggestions that will help you obtain credit and maintain a good credit score. One thing I like to suggest first is getting a gas store card. These cards are easier to get than regular credit cards. What's great about them is that you can establish a credit history by making small payments in full and on time. To maintain good credit, you should always pay your bills on time. Delinquencies are terrible. They create the biggest negative effect on a credit score. If you already have credit cards, your balance should be paid down. If you can't afford to do that, you might take a loan from a family member or friend. If you have unused credit card accounts, don't close them. I know it sounds as if you should, but actually, canceling a card can lower your score. Don't do it! Finally, never max out your credit cards. A good rule of thumb to follow is keeping your balance below 30 percent of your credit limit.

b. Orders may be placed at our website by following certain steps. Here they are. As a visitor to our site, you should first look over everything and find the items you want from our catalog. Then your shopping cart is important. You will add items to your shopping cart. When you are finished adding things to your shopping cart, the next step is to proceed to checkout. But wait! Have you created a new account? After creating a new account, we next need to know what shipping address to ship your items to. We will also need to have you choose a shipping method. Then you will be expected to provide payment information. Finally, you are nearly done! Now you are ready to review your order and submit it.

c. If you want to make a YouTube video, here are some important tips for those who have not done it before. First, you will need to obtain a video recording device such as a cell phone, webcam, or camcorder. Another thing you will have to do is make a decision on whether or not to make a video blog, comedy skit, how-to video, or a video that is about travel. Remember that your video must not be longer than 15 minutes. YouTube

members whose accounts are in good standing, without copyright violations, can upload files up to 20 GB in size. You will want to create a video with good light quality, and that usually means daytime recording. Finally, be sure to use computer editing software to change or delete anything.

d. A number of employees have asked about how to make two-sided copies. Here's what to do. Place Side 1 of the original face down on the document glass. Then the document cover should be closed. Next, you should select the quantity that you require. To copy Side 1, you should then press Start. Now you remove the first original and place the second original face down on the document glass. Then the document cover should be closed. Now you remove the Side 1 copy from the output tray. It should be inserted face down into the paper bypass tray. Then select the alternate paper tray and press Start.

Activities

Note: All Documents for Analysis are provided at **www .cengagebrain.com** for you to download and revise.

8.3. Document for Analysis: Poor Direct Request (Obj. 2)

YOUR TASK. Analyze the following poorly written message. List at least five weaknesses. If your instructor directs, revise the message using the suggestions you learned in this and previous chapters.

To:	ExEngine Manager List
From:	Paula Parker <paula.parker@exengine.com>
Subject:	E-Mail Problems
Cc:	
Bcc:	

As ExEngine vice president, this note is being written to ask for your help and advice to address an urgent problem—the problem of excessive e-mail. If you will do me the favor of answering the questions below, I'm sure your ideas will assist us in the development of a plan that should benefit your staff, yourself, and our organization will be improved. Your replies in writing to these questions (preferably by May 5) will help me prepare for our supervisory committee meeting on May 10.

Although e-mail is a great productivity tool, I'm afraid that its use is becoming extremely excessive. For our organization it is actually cutting into work time. Did you know that one study found that the average office worker is spending 3 hours a day on e-mail? In our organization we may be spending even more than this. It's exceedingly difficult to get any work done because of writing and answering an extraordinary number of e-mails coming in each and every day. Excessive e-mail is sapping the organization's strength and productivity. I would like to have your answers to some questions before the above-referenced dates to help us focus on the problem.

Can you give a ballpark figure for how many e-mails you receive and answer on a personal basis each day? Think about how many hours the staff members in your department spend on e-mail each day. Approximately how many hours would you estimate? Do you have any ideas about how we can make a reduction in the volume of e-mails being sent and received within our own organization? Do you think that e-mail is being used by our employees in an excessive manner?

I'm wondering what you think about an e-mail-free day once a week. How about Fridays? I appreciate your suggestions and advice

in developing a solution to the problem of controlling e-mail and making an improvement in productivity.

Paula Parker
Vice President, Operations

8.4 Document for Analysis: Poor Direct Response (Obj. 2)

YOUR TASK. Analyze the following poorly written memo about Chatter, a new application created by enterprise software leader Salesforce.com with headquarters in San Francisco.[28] List at least five weaknesses. If your instructor directs, revise the message.

Date:	March 4, 2015
To:	Helen Lazar, CEO
From:	Gilbert S. Luce
Subject:	Chatter

Thanks for asking me to research and investigate potential alternatives to Facebook and Twitter. I stumbled upon Chatter, a new social networking service provided to its customers by San Francisco–based Salesforce.com, a fast-growing upstart whose stock has more than doubled over the last year, to $120 per share. I had fun doing research and would welcome another opportunity anytime. Let me know if you want me to present my findings to you and other executives in greater detail. OK, back to Chatter and my report.

Imagine, a company that implements Chatter can expect its e-mail traffic to drop 40 percent as employees stay plugged in to the organization and remain connected. You can also track which workers add value to the company because you can keep an eye on deals being struck and monitor support staff members who excel at nipping problems in the butt.

The disadvantages of online social networks are obvious and clearly apparent. They sap and drain employees' time and productivity. Their openness creates a corporate security nightmare. Chatter, however, allows for virtual water cooler conversations but with limitations that are appropriate for business. Management can control and restrict access to sensitive information and records.

Salesforce.com is offering the Chatter service as part of its existing service to some 82,000 customers worldwide. Currently, about 20,000 companies have deployed Chatter, computer maker

Dell and advertising agency Saatchi & Saatchi among them. At Dell, some 20,000 workers are on Chatter, allowing managers to track deals. As for the cost, Chatter is included at no extra charge in the monthly fees of $65 to $125 for customer-relationship management and other Salesforce.com business software. As a stand-alone product, Chatter costs $15 a month per user.

Did I mention how Chatter works? It is a lot like Facebook and Twitter, but it asks what people are working on, not what is on their mind or what is happening. Salesforce.com calls Chatter a "real-time collaboration cloud," meaning that users need only a browser and an Internet connection to access it. Users create profiles, and their status updates center on questions, salient tidbits, and hyperlinks that are shared with coworkers in their personal networks. Together those comments and updates merge into a running feed. As on Twitter, employees can follow each other, their customers, and deals. Additional advantages are that (a) workers can connect with colleagues in the whole company, not just their work groups, and (b) profiles are searchable for needed skills, say, if you need someone who speaks Mandarin and so forth. Chatter also makes suggestions to account users about people they should follow based on their past activities and job needs. Pretty nifty, isn't it?

This is just a summary of what I learned. If you want to hear more, please do not hesitate to call.

8.5 Document for Analysis: Bewildering Instructions (Obj. 2)

The following actual message was sent to bewildered faculty and staff members of a large institution. The message warns of the use of "skimmers," small imaging devices attached to ATM machines and gas pumps to steal credit card information. Criminals place a skimmer over the normal card reading slot and record your card's magnetic data.

YOUR TASK. List its weaknesses and then revise with a proper set of instructions including an introduction, body, and conclusion.

To:	Faculty and Staff Members
From:	Michael Love <mlove@valleyviewpd.gov>
Subject:	ATM Safety
Cc:	
Bcc:	

Forgot to mention these prevention measures

1. Try to use ATMs that you are familiar with
2. Push pull the card slot and if it comes off, call 911. Skimmers are usually held on by double stick tape.
3. When punching in your PIN, cover the numbers you are punching in with you opposite hand or a sheet of paper
4. Gas pumps are also susceptible to skimming but usually the skimmer is inside so you cannot tell if a skimmer is present, so try to use a pump that is closest and in direct view of the attendance or go in and pay
5. Check your statement ASAP

Thank you for reading.

Detective Michael Love
Valley View Police Department

8.6 Document for Analysis: Weak Direct Claim Letter (Obj. 3)

YOUR TASK. Analyze the following poorly written claim letter. List at least five weaknesses. If your instructor directs, revise the document using the suggestions you learned in this chapter.

Current date

Mr. John Lear
Regional General Manager
Apex Car Rentals
4510 Cyprus Street
Denver, CO 80246

Dear Regional General Manager John Leer:

I have a horror story of gargantuan proportions to relate to you so that you know how incompetent the amateurish bozos are that work for you! You should fire the whole Colorado Springs Airport branch. I'm tired of lousy service and of being charged an arm and a leg for extras that end up not functioning properly. Calling your company is useless because no one answers the phone or returns calls!

In view of the fact that my colleague and I were forced to wait for an hour for a car at Colorado Springs Airport on August 15, your local branch people gave us a free navigation device. That would have been really nice in the event that the thing had actually worked, which it didn't. We advised the counter person that the GPS was broken, but it took another half hour to receive a new one and to finally start our business trip.

Imagine our surprise when the "free" GPS showed up on our bill apparently costing a whopping $180, plus tax! What came next would qualify as some dark Kafkaesque nightmare. I spent hours over the next three weeks talking to various employees of your questionable organization who swore that only "the manager" could help me, but this mysterious person was never available to talk. At this point in time, I called your Denver Airport location again and refused to get off the phone until I spoke to "the manager," and, lo and behold, he promised to credit the cost of the GPS to our corporate account. Was my nightmare over? No!

When we checked the status of the refund on our credit card statement, we noticed that he had forgotten to refund about $60 in taxes and surcharges that had also been assessed. So much for a full refund!

Inasmuch as my company is a new customer and inasmuch as we had hoped to use your agency for our future car rentals because of your competitive rates, I trust that you will give this matter your prompt attention.

Your very upset customer,

8.7 Responding to Posts Online (Obj. 2)

`Social Media`   `Web`

YOUR TASK. Decide whether to respond to the online posts shown below.[29] If you believe you should respond, compose a concise Facebook reply following the guidelines in this chapter. Your instructor may also direct that you rewrite some of the posts themselves, if necessary.

a. Amber posted this on the Sky Horizon Wireless website: *Hi I live in Texas & just bought the Samsung Freeform 2. And I keep getting the message that says unsupported content type on certain pages on the web. Also I uploaded a few pictures to my fb through my cell everyone can see them but me I also cant see pictures that my friends uploaded on here. I called customer service & they said they maintenced it but it didnt fix it. Please help me is it my phone or fb? If so do u know how to go about fixing this issue? Thanks Alot!*

b. Jamie posted this comment on the Zappos Facebook site: *I ordered a few things on the 20th and opted for next day shipping... but UPS says expected delivery date is the 30th! :-(*

c. Keith wrote the following to upscale men's clothing purveyor Brooks Brothers: *I first began shopping at Brooks Brothers about six years ago. I had read a book on menswear called "Style" by Russell Smith. He made mention to brass collar stays. I could not find them in Canada. I wandered into a Brooks Brothers store in Michigan and asked, "You don't sell brass collar stays do you?" The salesman said, "Of course." I bought collar stays, shirts and pajamas that day. A devoted customer I became. You can imagine how happy I am that Brooks Brothers has come to Canada. Bievenue! Welcome!*

d. Anita posted this message on Geico's Facebook page: *I just wanted to thank Geico for all your support on a claim I filed. The service was excellent at one of your body repair shops and also, you customer service is top notch: calls, emails, and not to mention the site which gives you all details possible like pictures, status of the claim, easy contact us section, upload of files. GREAT WEBSITE and SERVICE. Geico has me in GOOD HANDS, not Allstate :-)*

e. Mikaela posted this request for information on the Facebook page of her favorite resort hotel, Monte Carlo Resort & Casino in Las Vegas: *Will the pool still be opened this weekend?*

8.8 Direct Request: Searching for a Social Media Specialist (Obj. 2)

E-mail **Social Media**

Social media jobs are in great demand. Petco, supplier of pet supplies and services, recently hired Natalie Malaszenko as its director of social media and commerce. Her assignment at Petco was to envision and articulate the company's social media strategy for the future. To that end, she created fan pages on Facebook, opened several Twitter accounts, and wrote a company blog. In addition to Petco, other organizations have hired social media officers, including Sears Holdings, Panasonic, Citigroup, AT&T, Fiji Water, Go Daddy.com, and Harrah's Entertainment.

As the director of corporate communication for HomeCenter, a large home supply store, you are charged with looking into the possible hiring of a social media specialist. You know that other companies have both profited from and been hurt by fast-moving viral news. Social media experts, companies hope, can monitor cyberspace and be ready to respond to both negative and positive messages. They can help build a company's brand and promote its online reputation. They can also develop company guidelines for employee use and encourage staffers to spread the good word about the organization.

To learn more about social media jobs, you decide to go to Rick Trumka, who was recommended as a social media consultant by your CEO, David Seldenberg. You understand that Mr. Trumka has agreed to provide information and will be paid by HomeCenter. The CEO wants you to explore the possibilities. You decide that this is not a matter that can be handled quickly by a phone call. You want to get answers in writing.

Many issues concern you. For one thing, you are worried about the hiring process. You are not sure about a reasonable salary for a social media expert. You don't know where to place that person within your structure. Would the media expert operate out of corporate communications, marketing, customer service, or exactly where? Another thing that disturbs you is how to judge a candidate. What background would you require?

How will you know the best candidate? And what about salary? Should you be promising a full-time salary for doing what most people consider to be fun?[30]

YOUR TASK. Compose an e-mail inquiry to *rick.trumka@mediaresources.com*. Explain your situation and list specific questions. Mr. Trumka is not an employment source; he is a consultant who charges for his information and advice. Make your questions clear and concise. You realize that Mr. Trumka would probably like to talk on the phone or visit you, but make clear that you want a written response so that you can have a record of his information to share when you report to the CEO.

8.9 Direct Request: Planning a Winter Retreat in Jackson Hole, Wyoming (Obj. 2)

E-mail **Web**

Despite grim economic news, your employer, Stremer Media Group of Dallas, Texas, has had an excellent year and the CEO, Peter Stremer, would like to reward "the troops" for their hard work with a rustic yet plush winter retreat. The CEO wants his company to host a four-day combination conference/retreat/vacation for his 55 marketing and media professionals and their spouses or significant others at some spectacular winter resort.

One of the choices is Jackson Hole, Wyoming, a famous ski resort town with steep slopes and dramatic mountain views. The location is popular for its proximity to Grand Teton National Park, Yellowstone, and the National Elk Refuge. As the marketing manager, you will also look into winter resorts in Utah and Colorado. As you search the Web and investigate the options in Jackson Hole, you are captivated by the Four Seasons Resort, a five-star facility with outdoor pool, spa tub, ski in/ski out access, and an amply equipped gym and fitness room. Other amenities include an on-site spa with massage and treatment rooms, a sauna, and facial and body treatments.

The website of the Four Seasons Jackson Hole is not very explicit on the subject of business and event facilities, so you decide to jot down a few key questions. You estimate that your company will require about 50 rooms. You will also need two conference rooms (to accommodate 25 participants or more) for one and a half days. You want to know about room rates, conference facilities, A/V equipment in the conference rooms, and entertainment options for families. You have two periods that would be possible: December 15-19 or January 12-16. You realize that both are peak times, but you wonder whether you can get a discounted group rate. You are interested in entertainment on site, Jackson Hole, and tours to the nearby national parks. Jackson Hole airport is 4.5 miles away, and you would like to know whether the hotel operates a shuttle. Also, one evening the CEO will want to host a banquet for about 85 people. Mr. Stremer wants a report from you by September 15.

YOUR TASK. Write a well-organized direct request e-mail to Denise O'Handley, Sales Manager, Four Seasons Resort, 7680 Granite Loop Road, Teton Village, WY 83025. You might like to take a look at the Four Seasons Resort website at and search for general information about Jackson, Wyoming.

8.10 Direct Request: Pamper Palace Spa Worries About Duplicate Charges (Obj. 2)

E-mail

As an assistant to Donna K. Lilly, the busy proprietor of Pamper Palace Spa in Weymouth, Massachusetts, you have been asked to draft an e-mail to Virtual Treasures asking about an apparent duplicate charge for a small trial order of massage oils. The Weymouth location of Pamper Palace Spa, a professional spa franchise operating nationwide, wanted to try Virtual Treasures' exquisite Tahitian Monoi Tiare coconut oils. After reading a French magazine, your boss had ordered a few bottles and a bar of soap for $58.88 to test the product, but when Ms. Lilly checked Pamper Palace Spa's business account online, she found what she believed to be a duplicate order. She wants you to write to Virtual Treasures and ask about the apparent error.

Donna Lilly is suspicious because a few weeks earlier, she had ordered a French press coffee pot for $19 to use in her office and received two pots. Her account was charged $38. She did not take any action, making good use of the two French press coffee pots in her business. For both orders, Ms. Lilly had used Virtual Treasures' EasyPay feature, a one-click convenience tool online. Now she worries that future orders may lead to costly duplicate shipments and double charges. The order was divided into two shipments, each with a different order number: #502-3385779-9590624 and #502-8112203-6442608. Donna Lilly may order large quantities of Monoi Tiare oil after trying the pending shipment.

YOUR TASK. Write a direct request by e-mail to Virtual Treasures at *customer-care@virtualtreasures.com*. Inquire about the possible error stemming from the use of EasyPay. Format your e-mail correctly. Include Pamper Palace Spa's location and your business e-mail: *info@pamperpalacespa.com*

8.11 Direct Response: Virtual Treasures Reassures Business Customer (Obj. 2)

> **E-mail**

Online retailer Virtual Treasures has received the direct request from Donna K. Lilly (see **Activity 8.10**), who is concerned that her company, Pamper Palace Spa, is being charged twice for the same order whenever she uses the convenience feature EasyPay. As customer care representative at Virtual Treasures, you investigate the request and find that Ms. Lilly ordered five items on September 16, which were divided into two orders. The first, #502-3385779-9590624, was for Monoi Tiare Tahiti (Gardenia) Bar Soap, 4.6 oz., and three 4-ounce bottles of coconut oil, Monoi Coco (Natural Coconut Oil), Monoi Pitate (Coconut Oil w/ Jasmine) , and Monoi Santal (Coconut Oil w/ Sandalwood). Order #502-8112203-6442608 was for Monoi Tiare Tahiti (Coconut Oil w/ Gardenia), also 4 ounces. The invoice total accurately read $58.88; there were no duplicate charges.

When you talk to your technical team, however, you learn that occasionally customer account statements have shown duplicate orders when EasyPay was activated. The IT people assure you that the technical malfunction has been fixed. You are glad that, in turn, you can now reassure the customer.

Each e-mail you send out for Virtual Treasures contains two standard links allowing customers to click answers to the options "Did we solve your problem?" or "If not, we are very sorry. Please click the link below." This second option also suggests to the customer to contact Virtual Treasures by telephone. Soliciting feedback from customers in every message serves the purpose to "build America's Friendliest Company."

YOUR TASK. Write a direct reply e-mail to Donna K. Lilly. You may want to list the full order for reference. Ensure conciseness and readability when writing and formatting your message.

8.12 Direct Response: The Real-World Click Has Arrived (Obj. 2)

> **Communication Technology** ▸ **E-mail** ▸ **Team** ▸ **Web**

Online companies have enjoyed a distinct advantage over traditional brick-and-mortar retailers. On the Web, e-tailers can personalize deals to shoppers and allow instant price comparisons. They can establish a unique user profile based on the purchasing behavior of the customer and tailor special offers or recommendations to the shopper upon his or her next visit. Amazon.com and other e-commerce sites have mastered this technique.

Offline retailers, on the other hand, depend on foot traffic to make a sale and may never learn anything about a shopper who walks in, buys an item, and walks out again. Few visitors of websites actually make a purchase. However, traditional retailers experience a much higher "conversion rate," the percentage of patrons who walk into the store and actually buy an item. For example, about 20 percent of fashion shoppers buy a piece of clothing; in electronics, the percentage of store visitors who make purchases ranges from 40 to 60 percent.

New smartphone-centered services offered by cutting-edge tech entrepreneurs now promise to bridge the gap between e-commerce advantage and the traditional retail paradigm. Internet services such as Foursquare, Booyah, Shopkick, Gowalla, and, yes, Facebook, have begun to extend digital efficiencies to the physical retail world by enticing millions of consumers to digitally "check in" to real-world locations. With location-sensing technology, the visitor to a physical store is asked to open an app that sends this location information to selected friends. By checking in frequently, the user earns certain advantages such as gift certificates or a chance to win prizes. The services are designed to give brick-and-mortar businesses the opportunity to customize deals to patrons and to build enduring relationships with the otherwise anonymous walk-ins, potentially their best customers.

Big retailers are coming on board: Gap, Starbucks, Sephora, Best Buy, American Eagle, and Sports Authority all have forged partnerships with the upstart services. The digital check-in services try to make their interfaces interesting by using "game mechanics." In other words, they include gamelike features in their apps and help their retail partners—Sony and AT&T Wireless among them—to build game mechanics into their own websites as well. Traditional retailers are hoping that the services will catch on so that they will know—as an e-commerce website does—who their customers are, where they are, and even when they are nearby, potentially ready to spend.

Your boss, Jane McKinley, vice president of e-commerce and digital marketing at Verizon Wireless, heard that competitor AT&T Wireless is already using Scvngr. In groups or individually, research one of the following start-ups: Scvngr, Foursquare, Stickybits, Shopkick, or Booyah. Additionally, you could take a look at Barcode Hero and Facebook Places. Find out how they work, which retail partners they serve, how many users they have, and so forth.[31]

YOUR TASK. Ms. McKinley asked you, a group of interns at Verizon Wireless, to conduct research that would help her decide whether any of the current Internet check-in apps and services could benefit the company. She may request an e-mail or a memo about each service from the researcher or group assigned to it. If your instructor directs, the contributions of each researcher or group might be combined later in a direct response memo to Ms. McKinley.

8.13 Direct Response: Harbor Sail & Canvas Receives a Poor Customer Rating on Yelp

As you may know, Yelp is a social network for consumer reviews and local searches with approximately 78 million monthly unique visitors and 30 million local reviews at this time.[32] Many users rely on what they hope to be "real reviews" by "real people" as the company claims. They wish to make more informed buying decisions based on Yelp reviews. Businesses would do well to monitor their status on Yelp because anything less than a four- or five-star rating might be a blemish costing them sales.

Dan Wilcox, owner of Harbor Sail & Canvas in Long Beach, California, is not yet on Facebook, but he pays attention to Yelp reviews. Currently, he has six reviews, all five stars. Imagine his surprise when he recently received a rating of one star from Jenna K.:

> Harbor Custom Canvas does good work, but it seems to have become a casualty of its own success. The company is unresponsive when you call and e-mail. I will take my business elsewhere because after 3 weeks, I still haven't heard about that estimate for my marine canvas. I had left a voice mail message and sent an e-mail. No response. I called again and was received as if my request were outlandish when I expressed the hope of getting a quote that same week. Since then, silence. Not cool. And I am a repeat customer. . . . People, fortunately there are other businesses out there!

The writer says she is a returning customer. Dan sighs because he is really shorthanded. His secretary has been sick a lot lately and inquiries have gone unanswered; communication has not been flowing well. Business is booming and he does not have enough qualified installers; as a result, weeks elapse before his small crew gets around to completing a job. Dan searches his files and finds Jenna's job completed four years ago. Harbor had made a dodger, sail cover, and other smaller canvas items for Jenna's 30-foot Catalina sailboat.

YOUR TASK. Consider Dan's options. Should he respond to the one negative review? What could be the consequences of ignoring it? If you believe that Dan should respond, discuss first how. He has the disgruntled customer's e-mail, phone number, and street address. He could post a reply on Yelp to provide a commentary to the bad review. If your instructor directs, plan a strategy for Dan and respond to the customer in the way you believe is best for Dan and his business.

8.14 Direct Response: Telling Job Applicants How to Make a Résumé Scannable

As part of a team of interns at the outdoor e-tailer Campmor.com, you have been asked to write a form letter to send to job applicants who inquire about your résumé-scanning techniques. The following poorly written response to an inquiry was pulled from the file.

Dear Ms. Fratelli:

Your letter of April 11 has been referred to me for a response. We are pleased to learn that you are considering employment here at Campmor, and we look forward to receiving your résumé, should you decide to send same to us.

You ask if we scan incoming hard-copy résumés. Yes, we certainly do. Actually, we use SmartTrack, an automated résumé-tracking system. We sometimes receive as many as 300 résumés a day, and SmartTrack helps us sort, screen, filter, and separate the résumés. It also processes them, helps us organize them, and keeps a record of all of these résumés. Some of the résumés, however, cannot be scanned, so we have to return those—if we have time.

The reasons that résumés won't scan may surprise you. Some applicants send photocopies or faxed copies, and these can cause misreading, so don't do it. The best plan is to send an original copy. Some people use colored paper. Big mistake! White paper (8 1/2 x 11-inch) printed on one side is the best bet. Another big problem is unusual type fonts, such as script or fancy gothic or antique fonts. They don't seem to realize that scanners do best with plain, readable fonts such as Helvetica or Arial in a 10- to 14-point size.

Other problems occur when applicants use graphics, shading, italics, underlining, horizontal and vertical lines, parentheses, and brackets. Scanners like plain, unadorned résumés. Oh yes, staples can cause misreading. And folding of a résumé can also cause the scanners to foul up. To be safe, don't staple or fold, and be sure to use wide margins and a quality printer.

When a hiring manager within Campmor decides to look for an appropriate candidate, he is told to submit keywords to describe the candidate he has in mind for his opening. We tell him (or sometimes her) to zero in on nouns and phrases that best describe what they want. Thus, my advice to you is to try to include those words that highlight your technical and professional areas of expertise.

If you do decide to submit your résumé to us in hard copy, be sure you don't make any of the mistakes described herein that would cause the scanner to misread it. Of course, you can also submit your application to us by e-mail as a plain-text document.

Sincerely,

YOUR TASK. As a team, discuss how this letter could be improved. Decide what information is necessary to send to potential job applicants. Search the Web for additional information that might be helpful. Then, submit an improved version to your instructor. Although the form letter should be written so that it can be sent to anyone who inquires, address this one to Chiara Fratelli, 1019 University Drive, Boise, ID 83725.

8.15 Direct Response Memo: Interviewing at Becker & Associate Architects (Obj. 2)

James F. Becker, founder and CEO of Becker & Associate Architects, is a busy architect. As he expands his business, he is looking for ecologically conscious designers who can develop sustainable architecture that minimizes the negative environmental impact of buildings. His company has an open position for an environmental architect/designer. Three candidates were scheduled to be interviewed on March 14. However, Mr. Becker now finds he must be in Dallas during that week to consult with the builders of a 112-unit planned golf course community. He asks you, his office manager, to call the candidates, reschedule for March 28 or March 29, and prepare a memo with the new times as well as a brief summary of the candidates' backgrounds.

Fortunately, you were able to reschedule all three candidates. Scott Hogarth will come on March 29 at 11 a.m. Mr. Hogarth specializes in passive solar energy and has two years of experience with SolarPlus, Inc. He has a bachelor's degree from the University of Southern California. Amanda Froescher has a master's degree from

Boise State University and worked for five years as an architect planner for Boise Builders, with expertise in sustainable building materials. She will come on March 28 at 2 p.m. Without a degree but with ten years of building experience, Raul Ramirez is scheduled for March 28 at 10 a.m. He is the owner of Green Building Consulting and has experience with energy efficiency, sustainable materials, domes, and earth-friendly design. You are wondering whether Mr. Becker forgot to include Stanley Grafsky, his partner, who usually helps make personnel selections.

YOUR TASK. Prepare a memo (or e-mail if your instructor directs) to Mr. Becker with all the information he needs in the most readable format. Consider using a three-column table format for the candidate information.

8.16 Instruction Message: How to Copy Pictures and Text from PDF Documents (Obj. 2)

As a summer intern in the Marketing Department at Jovanovic Laboratory Supply, Inc., in Bozeman, Montana, you have been working on the company's annual catalog. You notice that staffers could save a lot of valuable time by copying and inserting images and text from the old edition into the new document. Your boss, Marketing Director Linda M. Trojner, has received numerous inquiries from staffers asking how to copy text and images from previous editions. You know that this can be done, and you show a fellow worker how to do it using a PDF feature called **Snapshot Tool**. Marketing Director Trojner decides that you are quite a tech-savvy student. Because she has so much confidence in you, she asks you to draft a memo detailing the steps for copying images and text passages from portable document format (PDF) files.

You start by viewing the **Tools** pull-down menu in an open PDF document. Depending on the Acrobat version, a feature called **Snapshot Tool** emerges either under **Basic** or under **Select & Zoom**. This feature is represented by a camera icon. To copy content, you need to select the part of the PDF document that you want to capture. The cursor will change its shape once the feature is activated. Check what shape it acquires. With the left mouse button, click the location where you want to insert the copied passage or image. At the same time, you need to drag the mouse over the page in the direction you want. A selected area appears that you can expand and reduce, but you can't let go of the left mouse button. Once you release the left mouse button, a copy of the selected area will be made. You can then paste the selected area into a blank Microsoft Office document, whether Word, Excel, or PowerPoint. You can also take a picture of an entire page.

YOUR TASK. Prepare a memo addressed to Marketing Department staff members for the signature of Linda M. Trojner. Practice the steps described here in abbreviated form, and arrange all necessary instructions in a logical sequence. You may need to add steps omitted here. Remember, too, that your audience may not be as computer literate as you are, so ensure that the steps are clear and easy to follow.

8.17 Instruction E-Mail Inviting Down-Editing Needs Revision (Obj. 2)

(E-mail)

The following message, which originated in an international technology company, was intended to inform new team members about their upcoming move to a different office location. But its stream-of-conscious thinking and jumbled connections leave the receiver confused as to what is expected and how to respond.

YOUR TASK. Study the complete message. Then revise it with (a) a clear introduction that states the purpose of the message, (b) a body with properly announced lists, and (c) a conclusion that includes a call to action and a deadline. Improve the organization by chunking similar material together. What questions must be answered? What tasks should be performed? Should this message show more "your" view? In addition, make it easy for receivers to respond. Receivers will be down-editing—that is, returning the message with their responses (in another color) interspersed among the listed items.

Hello everyone,

We'll be moving new team members into a new location next week so there are things we need you to do to be ready for the move. For one thing, let me know which Friday you want your personal items moved. The possibilities are November 9 and 16. Also, if you have an ergonomic desk or chair you want moved, let me know. By the way, we'll be sending boxes, labels, tape and a move map four or five days before the move date you choose, so let me know if this timeframe allows you enough time to pack your belongings. And if you are bringing office equipment from your current team to the new team, let me know. Remember that company policy allows you to take a workstation/laptop from your current team to the new workstation. So check with your admin and let me know what office equipment you will be bringing. Incidentally, your new workstation will have a monitor and peripherals.

You'll need to do some things before the movers arrive. Make sure you put foam pads around your valuable, fragile items and then box them up. This includes things such as IT plaques, glass, or anniversary glass sculptures. If the glass things break, replacing them is expensive and the cost center is responsible for replacement. You may want to move them yourself and not have the movers do it.

Another thing—make sure you pack up the contents of all gray filing cabinets because movers do not move those. Also, write on the move map the number and delivery location of whiteboards, corkboards, and rolling cabinets. Most important, make sure you add a name label to all your belongings, such as desk phones, docking stations, peripherals, monitors, tables, ergonomic desks, ergonomic chairs, etc. If you see old move labels on recycled boxes, remove them or cross them out.

Get back to me ASAP. And by the way, the movers will arrive between 4 p.m. and midnight on the move date.

Thank you

8.18 Instruction E-Mail or Memo: Describing a Workplace Procedure (Obj. 2)

(E-mail)

At your job or organization, assume that a new employee has joined the staff and the boss has asked you to write out a set of instructions for some task. It could be sending faxes, printing copies, answering the phone, setting up appointments, scheduling conferences, training employees, greeting customers, closing a cash register, opening the office, closing the office, or any other task that has at least five steps.

YOUR TASK. Prepare an e-mail or memo to your manager, Josh Washington, in response to his request for a set of instructions for the task.

8.19 Writing Clear Instructions (Obj. 2)

At **www.cengagebrain.com**, you will find a supplement devoted to writing instructions. It includes colorful examples and links to websites with examples of real sets of instructions from businesses.

YOUR TASK. Locate the section "How to Write Instructions," and study all of its sections. Then choose one of the following application activities: A-5, "Revising the Instructions for an Imported Fax Machine," or A-6, "Evaluation: Instructions for Dealing With Car Emergencies." Complete the assignment and submit it to your instructor.

8.20 Direct Claim: New Iron Gate Needs Work (Obj. 3)

You work for JPM, Johnson Property Management, in Portland, Oregon. Your employer specializes in commercial real estate. Yesterday one of your business tenants in the trendy NW 23rd neighborhood complained about problems with an iron gate you had installed by Chung Iron Works just six months earlier, on August 20. Apparently, the two doors of the gate have settled and don't match in height. The gate gets stuck. It takes much force to open, close, and lock the gate. The iron gate was painted, and in some spots rust is bleeding onto the previously pristine white paint. The tenant at 921 NW 23rd Ave., Portland, OR 97210 is a petite shop owner, who complained to you about struggling with the gate at least twice a day when opening and closing her store.

You realize that you will have to contact the installer, Chung Iron Works, and request that the company inspect the gate and remedy the problem. Only six months have passed, and you recall that the warranty for the gate was for one year. To have a formal record of the claim, and because Chung Iron Works does not use e-mail, you decide to write a claim letter.

YOUR TASK. Address your letter to Jin Ree at Chung Iron Works, 2255 NW Yeon Avenue in Portland, OR 97210. To jog his memory, you will enclose a copy of the company's proposal/invoice. Your business address is 1960 NE Irving Street, Portland, OR | 97209, phone (503) 335-5443 | and fax (503) 335-5001.

8.21 Direct Claim: Botched Valentine's Day Surprise (Obj. 3)

◀ E-mail ▶

Randy Pettit is very disappointed. He planned to surprise his girlfriend Sue at her workplace with beautiful roses and a vase for Valentine's Day. Sue works as an analyst for a major financial services company, and Randy knows that a generous bouquet sent there would impress not only Sue but also her colleagues and superiors. Randy had read favorable reviews on the Internet praising Bouquet International, a Swiss-based flower-delivery service operating worldwide. Because Valentine's Day was to fall on a Saturday, Randy requested that the flowers be sent a day before the big date.

Alas, upon the delivery of the bouquet in its flower-friendly packaging, Sue heard the sound of broken glass and refused the FedEx shipment. The delivery driver actually had advised Sue to return the package and took it back. Randy's surprise was ruined, and he was frustrated and angry with Bouquet International. On top of that, the same package with the identical tracking number was delivered to Sue's workplace again some three days after Valentine's Day. Sue was away, and a colleague signed for the package not knowing the history of the order. Sue later called FedEx to pick up the potentially less-than-fresh flowers.

However, about two weeks later, Randy's credit card statement showed the order number 106928959 and a charge of $73.25 from Bouquet International. Randy has friends and family on the East Coast and in Europe. He may potentially use Bouquet International's services to send flowers in the future. He decides to e-mail customer service to get his money back.

YOUR TASK. Imagine you are Randy but use your name when writing. Compose a direct claim by e-mail to Bouquet International at *info@bouquetinternational.com* requesting a refund. Include the necessary information and organize it logically in a well-formatted, professional e-mail.

8.22 Direct Claim: The Real Thing (Obj. 3)

Like most consumers, you have probably occasionally been unhappy with service or with products you have used.

YOUR TASK. Select a product or service that has disappointed you. Write a claim letter requesting a refund, replacement, explanation, or whatever seems reasonable. Generally, such letters are addressed to customer-service departments. For claims about food products, be sure to include bar code identification from the package, if possible. Your instructor may ask you to actually mail this letter. Remember that smart companies want to know what their customers think, especially if a product could be improved. Give your ideas for improvement. When you receive a response, share it with your class.

8.23 Direct Claim: But It Doesn't Work! (Obj. 3)

◀ E-mail ▶

After you receive an unexpected bonus, you decide to indulge and buy a new HDTV. You conduct research to compare prices and decide on a Panasonic 42-inch Plasma HDTV Model TC-P42X1. You find a great deal at Digital Depot for $599.95 plus tax. Although the closest store is a 45-minute drive, the price is so good you decide it's worth the trip. You sell your old TV to make room for the Panasonic and spend several hours installing the new set. It works perfectly, but the next day when you go to turn it on, nothing happens. You check everything, but no matter what you do, you can't get a picture. You're irritated! You are without a TV and have wasted hours hooking up the Panasonic. Assuming it's just a faulty set, you pack up the TV and drive back to Digital Depot. You have no trouble returning the item and come home with a second Panasonic.

Again you install the TV, and again you enjoy your new purchase. But the next day, you have no picture for a second time. Now you are fuming! Not looking forward to your third trip to Digital Depot, you repack the Panasonic and return it. The customer-service representative tries to offer you another Panasonic, but you decline. You point out all the trouble you have been through and say you would prefer a more reliable TV from a different manufacturer that is the same size and in the same price range as the Panasonic. Digital Depot carries a Samsung (Model PN42B450B1D) that fits your criteria, but at $729, it is more than you had budgeted. You feel that after all the problems you have endured, Digital Depot should sell you the Samsung at the same price as the Panasonic. However, when you called to discuss the matter, you were told to submit a written request.

YOUR TASK. Write a direct claim letter to Dennis Garcia, Manager, Digital Depot, 2300 Austin Street, Houston, TX 77074, asking him to sell you the TV for less than the advertised price.

8.24 Adjustment: Erroneous Charge for GPS Reversed (Obj. 4)

As assistant to John S. Lear, Regional General Manager at Apex Car Rentals, you read a shockingly irate complaint letter from a corporate customer (See **Activity 8.6**) addressed to your boss. Adriana Schuler-Reyes, Sales Manager for KDR Precision Components, Inc., in Phoenix, Arizona, has angrily detailed her tribulations with your company's Colorado Springs Airport branch.

Apparently, she and a colleague suffered long delays in obtaining their rental car. To compensate for the late car delivery, the customers received complimentary use of a navigation device, a $180 value plus taxes and surcharges that added up to another $60. However, at the end of their rental period, their bill reflected the full cost of the GPS. After multiple phone calls to the Colorado Springs Airport branch as well as to the Apex Car Rental corporate offices, Ms. Schuler-Reyes apparently was finally able to have the $180 credited to KDR's business account. However, soon she realized that the $60 levy had not been credited. She now wants the remainder of the refund. Ms. Schuler-Reyes has no confidence in the Colorado branch and is asking your boss to intervene on her behalf and reverse the remaining $60 charge.

Mr. Lear asks you to investigate what has gone so terribly wrong at the Colorado Springs Airport location. You learn that the branch is an independent franchisee, which may explain such a laxness in customer service that is unacceptable under corporate rules. In addition, you find out that the branch manager, Scott Brown, was traveling on company business during Ms. Schuler-Reyes' rental period and then left town to attend two management training seminars. Mr. Lear is concerned that Apex might lose this disappointed customer and decides to offer discount vouchers for KDR's next three rentals at 20 percent off each, valid at any U.S. branch. He wants you to draft the letter and enclose the discount vouchers.

YOUR TASK. Write a polite adjustment letter to Adriana Schuler-Reyes, KDR Precision Components, Inc., 2328 E Van Buren St., Phoenix, AZ 85006 to secure the customer's goodwill and future business.

8.25 Adjustment: We Can Restretch but Not Replace (Obj. 4)

E-mail

Your company, ArtWorkOnline, sells paintings through its website and catalogs. It specializes in workplace art intended for offices, executive suites, conference rooms, and common areas. To make shopping for office art easy, your art consultants preselect art, making sure that the finished product is framed and delivered in perfect shape. You are proud that ArtWorkOnline can offer fine works of original art at incredibly low prices.

Recently, you received an e-mail from Huntzinger Construction claiming that a large oil painting that your company sent had arrived in damaged condition. The e-mail said, "This painting sags, and we can't possibly hang it in our executive offices." You were surprised at this message because the customer had signed for delivery and not mentioned any damage. The e-mail went on to demand a replacement.

You find it difficult to believe that the painting is damaged because you are so careful about shipping. You give explicit instructions to shippers that large paintings must be shipped standing up, not lying down. You also make sure that every painting is wrapped in two layers of convoluted foam and one layer of Perf-Pack foam, which should be sufficient to withstand any bumps and scrapes that negligent shipping may cause. Nevertheless, you decide to immediately review your packing requirements with your shippers.

It's against your company policy to give refunds or replace paintings that the receiver found acceptable when delivered. However, you could offer Huntzinger Construction the opportunity to take the painting to a local framing shop for restretching at your expense. The company could send the restretching bill to ArtWorkOnline at 438 West 84th Street, New York, NY 10024.

YOUR TASK. Compose an e-mail adjustment message that regains the customer's confidence. Send it to Charles M. Huntzinger at *cmhuntzinger@huntzconstruction.com*.

8.26 Adjustment: Responding to Valentine's Day Bouquet Crisis (Obj. 4)

E-mail

Like your major competitor Fleurop Interflora, your employer, Swiss-based Bouquet International, offers same-day florist delivery of fresh flowers, plants, and gifts all over the world, aided by a global network of 20,000 associated florists. You like the company's cheerful motto: "Express yourself with a bouquet!"

You receive an e-mail from a frustrated Randy Pettit (See **Activity 8.21**), who requests a refund of $73.25 for a Valentine's Day bouquet that was delivered with a broken vase and subsequently refused only to be delivered again and sent back as before. You contact your shipping department about order number 106928959 to find out if more instances of broken vases have been reported or if this was an unfortunate but isolated incident. So far you haven't heard from your shipping department or from your contact at FedEx.

As an intern without your own e-mail account, you often write for your supervisor, Oksana Georgyevna Gotova, using her e-mail address, *oggotova@bouquetinternational.com*. You were tasked with delivering the good news to Randy Pettit at *rpettit@sbcglobal.net* that he will receive a credit of $73.25 and that his flower order was canceled. Tell him to check his next credit card statement for the refund. You know that all employees must always include the case ID number in every e-mail and encourage customers to do the same when contacting your company. Randy is a frequent customer.

YOUR TASK. Draft the e-mail to Randy Pettit for your supervisor. Try to rebuild Randy's trust in your services. For your electronic signature, you may want to indicate that the company is headquartered in Switzerland at Stiegengasse 5, CH-8065 Zurich, phone + 41 (0) 45 763 36 77 and fax + 41 (0) 45 763 25 70.

8.27 Thanks for a Favor: Glowing Letter of Recommendation (Obj. 5)

E-mail

One of your instructors has complied with your urgent request for a letter of recommendation and has given you an enthusiastic endorsement. Regardless of the outcome of your application, you owe thanks to all your supporters. Respond promptly after receiving this favor. Also, you can assume that your instructor is interested in your progress. Let him or her know whether your application was successful.

YOUR TASK. Write an e-mail or, better yet, a letter thanking your instructor. Remember to make your thanks specific so that your words are meaningful. Once you know the outcome of your application, use the opportunity to build more goodwill by writing to your recommender again.

8.28 Thanks for a Favor: Business Etiquette Training Session (Obj. 5)

`Team`   `Web`

Your business communication class was fortunate to have the etiquette and protocol expert Pamela Eyring speak to you. A sought-after TV commentator and media personality, she runs The Protocol School of Washington, a training center for etiquette consultants and protocol officers. Ms. Eyring emphasized the importance of soft skills. She talked about outclassing the competition and dining like a diplomat. She addressed topics such as business entertaining, invitations, introductions, greetings, seating arrangements, toasting, eye contact, remembering names, and conversation skills. In the table manners segment, among other topics, she discussed dining dos and don'ts, host and guest duties, seating and napkin placement, place settings and silverware savvy, eating various foods gracefully, and tipping. With characteristic poise but also humor, Ms. Eyring brought utensils, plates, and napkins to demonstrate correct table manners.

The class was thrilled to receive hands-on training from a nationally known business etiquette expert who was able to lessen their fears of making fools of themselves during business meals or at business mixers.

YOUR TASK. Individually or in groups, draft a thank-you letter to Pamela Eyring, director of The Protocol School of Washington, P.O. Box 676, Columbia, SC 29202.

Check out the company's website **http://www.psow.edu**, or find The Protocol School of Washington on Facebook, where you can follow Ms. Eyring's frequent media appearances, interviews, and etiquette advice.

8.29 Thanks for the Hospitality: Boat Party and Harbor Cruise (Obj. 5)

You and other members of your staff or organization were entertained at an elegant dinner during the winter holiday season on board a large ship that was cruising the harbor of Marina Del Rey in California. The posh pleasure boat featured a live band, ballroom dancing, and a casino.

YOUR TASK. Write a thank-you letter to your boss (supervisor, manager, vice president, president, or chief executive officer) or to the head of an organization to which you belong. Include specific details that will make your letter personal and sincere.

8.30 Responding to Good Wishes: Saying Thank You (Obj. 5)

YOUR TASK. Write a short note thanking a friend who sent you good wishes when you recently completed your degree.

8.31 Extending Sympathy: To a Spouse (Obj. 5)

YOUR TASK. Imagine that the spouse of a coworker recently died of cancer. Write the coworker a letter of sympathy.

8.32 Richard Branson Sends Goodwill Message to People of Ghana (Obj. 5)

`E-mail`   `Social Media`

It was with much regret and surprise that I learned about the passing of President John Evans Atta Mills of Ghana. I had the singular pleasure to spend some time with him at the Osu Castle when I visited Ghana on 24th May 2010. We were launching new flights to Accra and the warmth and hospitality which the President showed towards me and our entire delegation brought confidence and assurance that we were in good hands.

President Mills has served the country and the people of Ghana with a calm, peaceful hand and as a member of the Elders Organisation brought together by Nelson Mandela in 2007 I wish to state that I identify in President Mills many of our goals as I note him to be an elder statesman of Ghana, a follower of peace and an advocate for human rights and dignity.

I further laud the smooth transition of power to his immediate successor President John Dramani Mahama as I convey my thoughts to the family, the new Government and the people of Ghana at this difficult time.[33]

—Sir Richard Branson, the President of Virgin Group

YOUR TASK. In a concise social media post or an e-mail, examine the features in this goodwill message and evaluate whether they conform to the guidelines discussed in this chapter.

Chat About It

In each chapter you will find five discussion questions related to the chapter material. Your instructor may assign these topics for you to discuss in class, in an online chat room, or on an online discussion board. Some of the discussion topics may require outside research. You may also be asked to read and respond to postings made by your classmates.

Topic 1: In preparing to write a message, you learned that you should ask yourself (a) whether a written message is necessary, (b) what your goal is in writing, (c) how the reader might react, (d) what the best channel is, and (e) how you can write the message in a way that saves the reader's time. Which of these questions do you feel is most important, and why?

Topic 2: Do you write reviews on the Internet? Describe a situation in which you or someone you know wrote a review or complaint online. What was done first to "exhaust all other options," and did the post receive a reply? Were you satisfied with the response? Why or why not?

Topic 3: When responding favorably to a request that you are not thrilled to grant, why is it important in business to nevertheless sound gracious or even agreeable?

Topic 4: Conduct research regarding costly mistakes that resulted from unclear instructions. What is the most costly mistake you discovered?

Topic 5: Describe an occasion in which you should have written a goodwill message but failed to do so. Why was it difficult to write that message? What would make it easier for you to do so?

C.L.U.E. Grammar & Mechanics | *Review 8*

Capitalization

Review Guides 39–46 about capitalization in Appendix A, Grammar and Mechanics Guide, beginning on page A-16. On a separate sheet, revise the following sentences to correct capitalization errors. For each error that you locate, write the guide number that reflects this usage. Sentences may have more than one error. If a sentence is correct, write *C*. When you finish, check your answers on page Key-2.

EXAMPLE: Neither the Manager nor the Vice President would address hiring in the south.

REVISION: Neither the **manager** nor the **vice president** would address hiring in the **South**. [Guides 41, 43]

1. Our corporate Vice President and President met with several Directors on the west coast to discuss how to develop Apps for facebook.

2. All virgin atlantic airlines passengers must exit the plane at gate 2B in terminal 4 when they reach seattle-tacoma international airport.

3. The secretary of state of the united states urged members of the european union to continue to seek peace in the middle east.

4. My Cousin, who lives in the midwest, has a big mac and a dr. pepper for Lunch nearly every day.

5. Our Sales Manager and Director of Operations thought that the Company should purchase a new nordictrack treadmill for the Fitness room.

6. The World's Highest Tax Rate is in belgium, said professor du-babcock, who teaches at the city university of hong kong.

7. Rachel Warren, who heads our consumer services division, has a Master's Degree in Marketing from ohio university.

8. Please consult figure 2.3 in chapter 2 to obtain u.s. census bureau population figures for the northeast.

9. Last Summer did you see the article titled "the global consequences of using crops for fuel"?

10. Michael plans to take courses in Management, Economics, and History in the Spring.

Notes

[1] Highmark. (2012). Fast facts about Highmark. Retrieved from https://www.highmark.com /hmk2/newsroom/snapshot/fastfacts.shtml

[2] Lieblein, K. (2012, May 14). Item 9.6 insurances renewal. [PDF]. Retrieved from http://www.hbgsd.k12.pa.us/cms/lib /PA01000004/Centricity/Domain/3 /Item%209.6%20%20Insurances%20Renewal .pdf; note that the letter can also be found by searching the Harrisburg School District website at http://www.hbgsd.k12.pa.us/site /default.aspx?PageID=1

[3] Duarte, N. (2010, April 27). What's in the president's briefing book anyway? Retrieved from http://blog.duarte.com/2010/04 /what%E2%80%99s-in-the -president%E2%80%99s-briefing-book-anyway

[4] Photo essay based on Malewitz, J. (2012, May 1). Governors push natural gas-powered vehicles. *Stateline*. Retrieved from http://www.pewstates .org

[5] "Digital waste" pollutes the online world as brands fail to listen to what people want. (2011, November 10). TNS.com. [Press release]. Retrieved from http://www.tnsglobal .com/press-release/%E2%80%98digital -waste%E2%80%99-pollutes-online-world -brands-fail-listen-what-people-want

[6] Ibid.

[7] Ibid.

[8] TNS is part of the Kantar consultancy group owned by one of the world's largest advertising companies, UK-based WPP.

[9] Ford, A. (2011, June 28). Develop a comment monitoring policy... Or use this one. Tymado Multimedia Solutions. Retrieved from http://tymado.com/2011/06/develop-a -comment-monitoring-policy-or-use-this-one

[10] Ibid.

[11] Cited by permission from Ford, A. (2011, June 28). Develop a comment monitoring policy... Or use this one. Tymado Multimedia Solutions. Retrieved from http://tymado.com/2011/06/

develop-a-comment-monitoring-policy-or-use -this-one

[12] Banjo, S. (2012, July 29). Firm take online reviews to heart. *The Wall Street Journal*. Retrieved from http://online.wsj.com/article/SB1000142405270 23032922045775173940434318 9230.html

[13] Ibid.

[14] Based on An eagle eye on retail scams. (2005, August 8). *BusinessWeek*. Retrieved from http://www.businessweek.com

[15] Cited in New ways to complain: Airing your gripes can get you satisfaction—or trouble. (2011, August). Consumer Reports.org. Retrieved from http://www.consumerreports.org/cro/money /consumer-protection/new-ways-to-complain /overview/index.htm

[16] Pilon, M. (2009, August 5). How to complain about a company. *The Wall Street Journal*. Retrieved from http://blogs.wsj.com/wallet/2009/08/05/how-to -complain-about-a-company/tab/print; Torabi, F. (2011, July 28). Bad customer service? 3 smarter ways to complain. CBS News. Retrieved from http://www.cbsnews.com/8301-505144_162 -41542345/bad-customer-service -3-smarter-ways-to-complain

[17] Maritz Research and evolve—24 Twitter study. (2011, September). Retrieved from http://www.maritzresearch.com /~/media/Files/MaritzResearch/e24 /ExecutiveSummaryTwitterPoll.ashx

[18] New ways to complain: Airing your gripes can get you satisfaction—or trouble. (2011, August). Consumer Reports.org. Retrieved from http://www.consumerreports.org/cro/money /consumer-protection/new-ways-to-complain /overview/index.htm

[19] Ibid.

[20] Ibid.

[21] Photo essay based on Maloney, J. (2013, February 26). Photo use prompts DKNY apology. *The Wall Street Journal*. Retrieved from http://online.wsj .com; Griner, D. (2013, February 25). DKNY accused of stealing hundreds of images from

NYC photographer. *Adweek*. Retrieved from http://www.adweek.com

[22] Quinley, K. (2008, May). Apology programs. *Claims*, pp. 14-16. Retrieved from http://www.search .ebscohost.com; see also Runnels, M. (2009, Winter). Apologies all around: Advocating federal protection for the full apology in civil cases. *San Diego Law Review,46*(1), 137-160. Retrieved from http://www.search.ebscohost.com

[23] Davidow, M. (2003, February). Organizational responses to customer complaints: What works and what doesn't. *Journal of Service Research, 5*(3), 225. Retrieved from http://www.search .ebscohost.com; Blackburn-Brockman, E., & Belanger, K. (1993, June). You-attitude and positive emphasis: Testing received wisdom in business communication. *The Bulletin of the Association for Business Communication*, 1-5; Mascolini, M. (1994, June). Another look at teaching the external negative message. *The Bulletin of the Association for Business Communication*, 46.

[24] Liao, H. (2007, March). Do it right this time: The role of employee service recovery performance in customer-perceived justice and customer loyalty after service failures. *Journal of Applied Psychology, 92*(2), 475. Retrieved from http://www.search.ebscohost .com; Gilbert, P. (1996, December). Two words that can help a business thrive. *The Wall Street Journal*, p. A12.

[25] Emily Post Institute. (2008). Conveying sympathy Q & A. Retrieved from http://ww31.1800flowers .com/template.do?id=template8&page=4013&co nversionTag=true

[26] Fallows, J. (2005, June 12). Enough keyword searches. Just answer my question. *The New York Times*, p. BU3.

[27] Based on Buddy Media. (2010). How do I respond to that? The definitive guide to Facebook publishing & moderation. Retrieved from http://marketingcloud.buddymedia.com /whitepaper-form_the-definitive-guide-to -facebook-publishing-and-moderation_a

Chapter 8: Positive Messages

[28] Scenario partially based on Jaroslovsky, R. & Ricardela, A. (2010, August 30-September 5). Salesforce.com channels Facebook. *Bloomberg Businessweek*, pp. 34-35.

[29] Based on Buddy Media. (2010). How do I respond to that? The definitive guide to Facebook publishing & moderation. Retrieved from http://marketingcloud.buddymedia.com /whitepaper-form_the-definitive-guide-to -facebook-publishing-and-moderation_a

[30] Portions based on Gillette, F. (2010, July 19-25). Twitter, twitter, little stars. *Bloomberg Businessweek*, pp. 64-67.

[31] Portions based on Stone, B., & Sheridan, B. (2010, August 30-September 5). The retailer's clever little helper. *Bloomberg Businessweek*, pp. 31-32.

[32] Things you should know about Yelp. (2012, July). Retrieved from http://www.yelp.com /about

[33] Sir Richard Branson send [sic] goodwill message to Ghanaians. (2012, July 26). Retrieved from http://www.ghanamma.com/2012/07/sir-richard -branson-send-goodwill-message-to-ghanaians

Negative Messages

OBJECTIVES

After studying this chapter, you should be able to

1 Understand the strategies of business communicators in conveying negative news, apply the 3-x-3 writing process, and avoid legal liability.

2 Distinguish between the direct and indirect strategies in conveying unfavorable news.

3 Explain the components of effective negative messages, including opening with a buffer, apologizing, showing empathy, presenting the reasons, cushioning the bad news, and closing pleasantly.

4 Apply effective techniques for refusing typical requests or claims as well as for presenting bad news to customers in print or online.

5 Describe and apply effective techniques for delivering bad news within organizations.

Crises Rock Carnival Corporation and Rattle Cruise Passengers

"It's been like a nightmare!" That's how passenger Sahizah Alim of Sacramento described the situation aboard the Carnival Splendor cruise ship that became crippled after a fire in the engine room knocked out all systems. "There's been no food, no power, no electricity, no flushing toilets," she said.[1] For three days, nearly 3,300 passengers subsisted on Spam, Pop-Tarts, and canned food flown in by navy helicopters as the disabled ship was towed to San Diego. Fortunately, no one was hurt in the incident that upset passengers and the ship's operators alike. Carnival Cruise Lines, one of 10 subsidiaries of Carnival Corporation, responded fast. President and CEO of Carnival Cruise Lines, Gerry Cahill, won praise for sincerely apologizing at an early press conference: "Conditions on board the ship are very challenging and we sincerely apologize for the discomfort and inconvenience our guests are currently enduring. The safety of our passengers and crew is our top priority and we are working to get our guests home as quickly as possible."[2] The cruise line posted frequent updates on Twitter, Facebook, a popular blog, and its website.

© ZUMA Wire Service/Alamy

Such adroit communication with disappointed and distressed passengers was needed again when another Carnival ship, Costa Allegra, experienced an engine room fire and power blackout off the Seychelles Islands. This vessel, too, was towed to safety, and none of the 1,000 passengers and crew was injured.[3]

However, the Costa Concordia accident in Italy that killed 32 passengers reached a different scale, and no amount of apology or compensation is likely to turn the afflicted travelers into repeat customers. Although the world's largest cruise line will recover, in the short term it is facing staggering litigation, a falling stock price, and earnings losses. Micky Arison, chief executive of Costa Crociere parent Carnival Corporation, largely stayed out of the limelight, leaving the Italian Costa Crociere CEO, Pier Luigi Foschi, to fend for himself. Later, Arison told *The Miami Herald:* "Obviously, I am very sorry it happened. When you have 100 ships out there, sometimes unfortunate things happen, but as I said, it was an accident. We as a company do everything we can to encourage the highest of safety standards."[4] The top executive promised that Carnival would "take care" of passengers, crew, and victims.[5] You will learn more about this case on page 314.

Critical Thinking

- Suppose you made an honest mistake that could prove expensive for your employer or internship provider. Would you blurt out the bad news immediately or consider strategies to soften the blow somewhat?

- What are some of the techniques you could use if you had to deliver a bad-news message in print or online for a company such as Carnival Cruise Lines?

- Carnival Corporation's chairman and CEO, Micky Arison, was criticized by *The Wall Street Journal* and other commentators for remaining conspicuously silent during the extreme crisis unfolding in Italy. Arison was faulted for not exercising leadership from the top and instead leaving public appearances to Pier Luigi Foschi, the embattled CEO of Costa Crociere, Carnival Corporation's Italian subsidiary. Foschi was facing the news media virtually alone in the days and weeks after the Costa Concordia accident. What might explain Micky Arison's low profile, considering that he also let Gerry Cahill handle the Carnival Splendor crisis alone?

Communicating Negative News Effectively

LEARNING OBJECTIVE 1
Understand the strategies of business communicators in conveying negative news, apply the 3-x-3 writing process, and avoid legal liability.

Bad things happen in all businesses. At Carnival, technical trouble and human error, but also bad weather and virus outbreaks on board, can ruin cruises. In other businesses, goods are not delivered, products fail to perform as expected, service is poor, billing gets fouled up, or customers are misunderstood. You may have to write messages ending business relationships, declining proposals, explaining service outages, describing data breaches, announcing price increases, refusing requests for donations, terminating employees, turning down invitations, or responding to unhappy customers. You might have to apologize for mistakes in orders or

A horsemeat scandal that rocked Europe in 2013 affected Ikea when inspectors discovered traces of edible equine in the company's Swedish meatballs. The housewares giant quickly apologized: "We take this issue very seriously and apologize for the current situation. Horsemeat from authorized slaughter is in itself not dangerous. However, we do not tolerate any other ingredients than the ones stipulated in our recipes or specifications. It is important to us that customers can trust the products that we sell are high quality, safe, and healthy." What did Ikea hope to achieve by issuing this statement?[6]

pricing, the rudeness of employees, overlooked appointments, substandard service, faulty accounting, defective products, or jumbled instructions. As a company representative, you may have to respond to complaints voiced to the world on Twitter, Facebook, or complaint websites.

The truth is that everyone occasionally must deliver bad news in business. Because bad news disappoints, irritates, and sometimes angers the receiver, such messages must be written carefully. The bad feelings associated with disappointing news can generally be reduced if the receiver (a) knows the reasons for the rejection, (b) feels that the news was revealed sensitively, and (c) believes the matter was treated seriously and fairly.

In this chapter you will learn when to use the direct strategy and when to use the indirect strategy to deliver bad news. You will study the goals of business communicators in working with unfavorable news and learn techniques for achieving those goals.

Articulating Goals in Communicating Negative News

Delivering negative news is not the happiest communication task you may have, but it can be gratifying if you do it effectively. As a business communicator working with bad news, you will have many goals, the most important of which are summarized in Figure 9.1.

The goals outlined in Figure 9.1 are ambitious, and we are not always successful in achieving them all. However, many senders have found the strategies and techniques you are about to learn helpful in conveying disappointing news sensitively and safely. With experience, you will be able to vary these strategies and adapt them to your organization's specific communication tasks.

Applying the 3-x-3 Writing Process

Thinking through the entire writing process is especially important when writing bad-news messages because the way bad news is revealed often determines how it is accepted. You have probably heard people say, "I didn't mind the news so much, but I resented the way I was told!" Certain techniques can help you deliver bad news sensitively, beginning with the familiar 3-x-3 writing process.

Analysis, Anticipation, and Adaptation. In Phase 1 (prewriting), you need to analyze the bad news and anticipate its effect on the receiver. When Microsoft launched its first wide-scale layoff, an administrative glitch caused it to pay more severance than intended to some laid-off employees. After the mistake was discovered, Microsoft sent a bad-news letter bluntly asking the ex-workers to return the money. Employees not only suffered the loss

Figure **9.1** Goals in Conveying Unfavorable News

Explaining clearly and completely

- Readers understand and, in the best case, accept the bad news.
- Recipients do not have to call or write to clarify the message.

Projecting a professional image

- Writers stay calm, use polite language, and respond with clear explanations of why a negative message was necessary even when irate customers sound threatening and overstate their claims.

Conveying empathy and sensitivity

- Writers use language that respects the readers and attempts to reduce bad feelings.
- When appropriate, writers accept blame and apologize without creating legal liability for the organization or themselves.

Being fair

- Writers show that the decision was fair, impartial, and rational.

Maintaining friendly relations

- Writers demonstrate their desire to continue pleasant relations with the receivers and to regain their confidence.

© Cengage Learning 2015

of their jobs, but, adding insult to injury, Microsoft then demanded the return of $4,000 to $5,000 in severance pay. Some employees had already spent the money, and others were planning their futures with it. Obviously, the sender of the bad-news message had not considered the effect it would have on its readers. After the letters seeking repayment began to surface on the Web, Microsoft reversed course and allowed the workers to keep the overpayment.[7] However, the entire situation might have been handled better if Microsoft had given more thought to analyzing the situation and anticipating its effect.

When you have bad news to convey, one of your first considerations is how that message will affect its receiver. If the disappointment will be mild, announce it directly. For example, a small rate increase in a newspaper or Web subscription can be announced directly. If the bad news is serious or personal, consider techniques to reduce the pain. In the Microsoft situation, the bad-news letter should have prepared the reader, given reasons for the payback request, possibly offered alternatives, and sought the goodwill of the receiver.

Choose words that show that you respect the reader as a responsible, valuable person. Select the best channel to deliver the bad news. In many negative situations, you will be dealing with a customer. If your goal is retaining the goodwill of a customer, a letter on company stationery will be more impressive than an e-mail.

Research, Organization, and Composition.

In Phase 2 (drafting), you will gather information and brainstorm for ideas. Jot down all the reasons you have that explain the bad news. If four or five reasons prompted your negative decision, concentrate on the strongest and safest ones. Avoid presenting any weak reasons; readers may seize on them to reject the entire message. Include an ample explanation of the negative situation, and avoid fixing blame.

When the U.S. Post Office has to deliver damaged mail, it includes an explanation, such as the following: "Because the Post Office handles millions of pieces of mail daily, we must use mechanical methods to ensure prompt delivery. Damage can occur if mail is insecurely enveloped or bulky contents are enclosed. When this occurs and the machinery jams, it often causes damage to other mail that was properly prepared." Notice that the Post Office message offers the strongest reason for the problem, although other reasons may have been possible. Notice, too, that the explanation tactfully skirts the issue of who caused the problem.

In composing any negative message, conduct research if necessary to help you explain what went wrong and why a decision or action is necessary.

Editing, Proofreading, and Evaluating.

In Phase 3 (revising), you will read over your message carefully to ensure that it says what you intend. Check your wording to be sure you are concise without being brusque. If you find that you have overused certain words, click on your word processing thesaurus to find synonyms. Read your sentences to see if they sound like conversation and flow smoothly. This is the time to edit and improve coherence and tone. In bad-news messages, the tone is especially important. Readers are more likely to accept negative messages if the tone is friendly and respectful. Even when the bad news can't be changed, its effect can be reduced somewhat by the way it is presented.

In the last phase of the writing process, proofread to make sure your verbs agree with their subjects, your sentences are properly punctuated, and all words are spelled correctly. Pay attention to common mistakes (*its/it's; than/then; their/there*). If your word processing program checks grammar, be sure to investigate those squiggly underscores. Finally, evaluate your message. Is it too blunt? Too subtle? Have you delivered the bad news clearly but professionally?

Avoiding Legal Liability in Conveying Negative News

Before we examine the components of a negative message, let's look more closely at how you can avoid exposing yourself and your employer to legal liability in writing negative messages. Although we can't always anticipate the consequences of our words, we should be alert to three causes of legal difficulties: (a) abusive language, (b) careless language, and (c) the good-guy syndrome.

Abusive Language.

Calling people names (such as *deadbeat, crook*, or *quack*) can get you into trouble. *Defamation* is the legal term for any false statement that harms an individual's reputation. When the abusive language is written, it is called *libel*; when spoken, it is *slander*.

To be actionable (likely to result in a lawsuit), abusive language must be (a) false, (b) damaging to one's good name, and (c) "published"—that is, written or spoken within the presence of others. Therefore, if you were alone with Jane Doe and accused her of accepting bribes and selling company secrets to competitors, she couldn't sue because the defamation wasn't published. Her reputation was not damaged. However, if anyone heard the words or if they were written, you might be legally liable.

In a new wrinkle, you may now be prosecuted if you transmit a harassing or libelous message by e-mail or post it on social networking sites such as Facebook and Twitter.[8] Such electronic transmissions are considered to be published. Moreover, a company may incur liability for messages sent through its computer system by employees. That's why many companies are increasing their monitoring of both outgoing and internal messages. "Off-the-cuff, casual e-mail conversations among employees are exactly the type of messages that tend to trigger lawsuits and arm litigators with damaging evidence," says electronic communications guru Nancy Flynn.[9] Instant messaging adds another danger for companies. Whether your message is in print or electronic, avoid making unproven charges or letting your emotions prompt abusive language.

Careless Language.   As the marketplace becomes increasingly litigious, we must be certain that our words communicate only what we intend. Take the case of a factory worker injured on the job. His attorney subpoenaed company documents and discovered a seemingly harmless letter sent to a group regarding a plant tour. These words appeared in the letter: "Although we are honored at your interest in our company, we cannot give your group a tour of the plant operations as it would be too noisy and dangerous." The court found in favor of the worker, inferring from the letter that working conditions were indeed hazardous.[10] The letter writer did not intend to convey the impression of dangerous working conditions, but the court accepted that interpretation.

The Good-Guy Syndrome.   Most of us hate to have to reveal bad news—that is, to be the bad guy. To make ourselves look better, to make the receiver feel better, and to maintain good relations, we are tempted to make statements that are legally dangerous. Consider the case of a law firm interviewing job candidates. One of the firm's partners was asked to inform a candidate that she was not selected. The partner's letter said, "Although you were by far the most qualified candidate we interviewed, unfortunately, we have decided we do not have a position for a person of your talents at this time." To show that he personally had no reservations about this candidate and to bolster the candidate, the partner offered his own opinion. However, he differed from the majority of the recruiting committee. When the rejected interviewee learned later that the law firm had hired two male attorneys, she sued, charging sexual discrimination. The court found in favor of the rejected candidate. It agreed that a reasonable inference could be made from the partner's letter that she was the "most qualified candidate."[11]

Two important lessons emerge. First, business communicators act as agents of their organizations. Their words, decisions, and opinions are assumed to represent those of the organization. If you want to communicate your personal feelings or opinions, use your home computer or write on plain paper (rather than company letterhead) and sign your name without title or affiliation. Second, volunteering extra information can lead to trouble. Therefore, avoid supplying data that could be misused, and avoid making promises that can't be fulfilled. Don't admit or imply responsibility for conditions that caused damage or injury. Even some apologies (*We're sorry that a faulty bottle cap caused damage to your carpet*) may suggest liability.

Analyzing Negative-News Strategies

LEARNING OBJECTIVE **2**
Distinguish between the direct and indirect strategies in conveying unfavorable news.

Unfavorable news in business doesn't always fall into neat categories. To successfully convey bad news, writers must carefully consider the audience, purpose, and context. Experienced business communicators understand that their approaches to negative news must be flexible.[12] However, as a business writer in training, you have at your disposal two basic strategies for delivering negative news: direct and indirect.

Which approach is better suited for your particular message? One of the first steps you will take before delivering negative news is analyzing how your receiver will react to this news. In earlier chapters we discussed applying the direct strategy to positive messages. We suggested using the indirect strategy when the audience might be unwilling, uninterested, displeased, disappointed, or hostile. In this chapter we expand on that advice and suggest additional considerations that can help you decide which strategy to use.

When to Use the Direct Strategy

Many actual bad-news messages are organized indirectly, beginning with a buffer and reasons. Occasionally bad-news messages may be mixed, containing positive news as well, if available, to offset the unfavorable news. However, the direct strategy, with the bad news first, may be preferable in situations such as those shown in Figure 9.2.

Figure 9.2 Deciding When to Deliver Bad News Directly

When the bad news is not damaging

- Negative news is relatively minor (e.g., a small price increase).
- Bad news doesn't personally affect the receiver.

When the receiver may overlook the bad news

- Critical message requires attention (e.g., new policy requirements, legal announcements, changes in service) and should not be overlooked.

When the organization or receiver prefers directness

- Corporate culture favors direct messages even when conveying bad news.
- Individuals insist on a straightforward and no-frills presentation.

When firmness is necessary

- Messages must demonstrate determination and resolve (e.g., the last in a series of collection letters that seek payment on overdue accounts).
- Dire or extremely important situation involves someone who has ignored previous requests or appeals.

© Cengage Learning 2015

Notice in Figure 9.3 that the writer, Steven Ellis, is fairly direct in a letter announcing a security breach at Conectix Federal Credit Union. Although he does not blurt out "your information has been compromised," he does announce a potential identity theft problem in the first sentence. He then explains that a hacker attack has compromised roughly a quarter of customer accounts. In the second paragraph he recommends that credit union customer Michael Arnush take specific corrective action to protect his identity and offers helpful contact information. The tone is respectful and serious. The credit union's letter is modeled on an FTC template that was praised for achieving a balance between a direct and indirect opening.[13]

If you must write a security breach message, describe clearly what information was compromised, if known. Explain how the breach occurred, what data were stolen, and, if you know, how the thieves have used the information. Next, disclose what your company has done to repair the damage. Then list the recommended responses most appropriate for the type of data compromised. For instance, if social security numbers were stolen, urge victims to place fraud alerts on their credit reports; include the agencies' addresses. Designate a contact person in your organization, and work with law enforcement to ensure that your notification does not jeopardize the investigation in any way.

Security breach messages provide a good example of how to employ the direct strategy in delivering bad news. Let's now explore when and how to use the indirect strategy in delivering negative news.

When to Use the Indirect Strategy

Some writing experts suggest that the indirect strategy "ill suits today's skeptical, impatient, even cynical audience."[14] To be sure, in social media, bluntness seems to dominate the public discourse. Directness is equated with honesty; hedging, with deceit. However, many

Figure **9.3** Announcing Bad News Directly: Security Breach Letter

5234 PARK AVENUE, FAIRFIELD, CT 06825
www.conectix.com   203.448.2101

CONECTIX™
FEDERAL CREDIT UNION

September 5, 2015

Mr. Michael Arnush
15 Vanderbilt Avenue
Newton, MA 02459

Dear Mr. Arnush:

Uses modified direct strategy because urgent action is needed to prevent identity theft

We are contacting you about a potential problem involving identity theft. On August 30, names, encrypted social security numbers, birth dates, and e-mail addresses of fewer than 25 percent of accounts were compromised in an apparent hacker attack on our website. Outside data security experts are working tirelessly to identify the causes of the breach as well as prevent future intrusions into our system. Immediately upon detecting the attack, we notified the local police authorities as well as the FBI. We also alerted the three major credit-reporting agencies.

We recommend that you place a fraud alert on your credit file. A fraud alert tells creditors to contact you before they open any new accounts or change your existing accounts. Please call any one of the three major credit bureaus. As soon as one credit bureau confirms your fraud alert, the others are notified to place fraud alerts. All three credit reports will be sent to you, free of charge.

Suggests recommended steps and provides helpful information about credit-reporting agencies

Equifax	Experian	TransUnion
800-685-1111	888-397-3742	800-680-7289

Gives reasons for the recommended action, provides contact information, and offers additional pointers

Even if you do not find any suspicious activity on your initial credit reports, the Federal Trade Commission (FTC) recommends that you check your credit reports periodically. Victim information sometimes is held for use or shared among a group of thieves at different times. Checking your credit reports periodically can help you spot problems and address them quickly.

If you find suspicious activity on your credit reports or have reason to believe your information is being misused, call 518-584-5500 and file a police report. Get a copy of the report; many creditors want the information it contains to absolve you of the fraudulent debts. You also should file a complaint with the FTC at www.ftc.gov/idtheft or at 1-877-ID-THEFT (877-438-4338).

Please visit our website at www.conectix.com/databreach for updates on the investigation, or call our privacy hotline at 800-358-4422. Affected customers will receive free credit-monitoring services for one year.

Ends by providing more helpful information, company phone number, and offer of one-year free credit monitoring

Sincerely,

Steven Ellis

Steven Ellis
Customer Service

© Cengage Learning 2015

communicators prefer to use the indirect strategy to present negative news. Whereas good news can be revealed quickly, bad news may be easier to accept when broken gradually. Even a direct bad-news message can benefit from "sandwiching" the negative news between positive statements.[15] Figure 9.4 illustrates instances in which the indirect strategy works well.

REALITY CHECK: Don't Be a Scold!

"Any declarative sentence starting with 'you' when talking to a customer is best avoided—it comes across as shaking your finger at the customer, and no one wants to feel like we're talking to our mother! Better choices are 'We can' or 'Let's do this together' or 'What I could suggest is.'"[16]

—**KRISTIN ROBERTSON,** *executive coach, consultant, and author of* Spectacular Support Centers

Courtesy of Kristin Robertson

Figure **9.4** Deciding When to Deliver Bad News Indirectly

When the bad news is personally upsetting

- Negative news involves the receiver personally (e.g., refusal of a promotion request, rejection of a grant proposal, a layoff notice).
- An organization makes a mistake that inconveniences or disadvantages a customer.

When the bad news will provoke a hostile reaction

- Message will irritate or infuriate the recipient.
- Giving reasons before the bad news is likely to defuse and soothe.

When the bad news threatens the customer relationship

- Indirect presentation of bad news can salvage the customer bond.
- Unfavorable news is revealed slowly and with reasons that explain it.

When the bad news is unexpected

- Readers who are totally surprised by bad news have more negative reactions.

© Cengage Learning 2015

Whether to use the direct or indirect strategy depends largely on the situation, the reaction you expect from the audience, and your goals. The direct method saves time and is preferred by some who consider it more professional and even more ethical than the indirect method. Others think that revealing bad news slowly and indirectly shows sensitivity to the receiver. By preparing the receiver, you tend to soften the impact. Moreover, although social media users may favor the direct approach, the majority of negative

Just months into her new job as CEO, Marissa Mayer ended Yahoo's telecommuting policy, sparking a lively debate in the national media. A companywide memo instructing employees to return to the workplace opened with upbeat talk about new "energy and buzz" in Yahoo's offices. The memo's second paragraph touted the benefits of "physically being together." Then came the bad news: "Beginning in June, we're asking all employees with work-from-home arrangements to work in Yahoo offices." The message closed on a positive note: "The best is yet to come." What strategies can help communicators ease the impact of negative news?[17]

© ZUMA Wire Service/Alamy

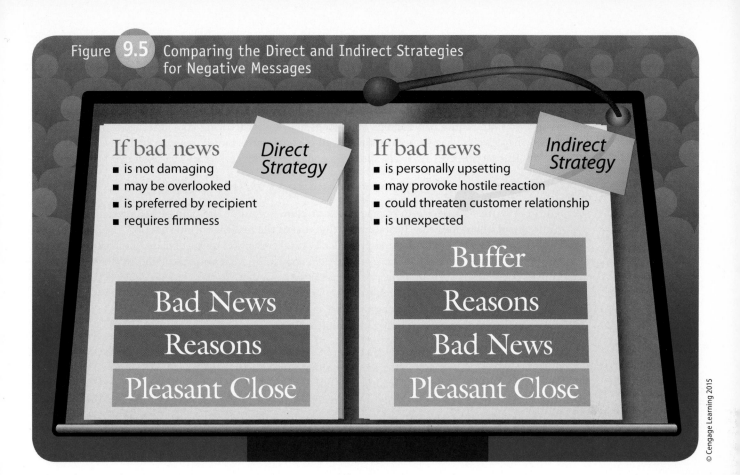

If bad news — *Direct Strategy*
- is not damaging
- may be overlooked
- is preferred by recipient
- requires firmness

Bad News
Reasons
Pleasant Close

If bad news — *Indirect Strategy*
- is personally upsetting
- may provoke hostile reaction
- could threaten customer relationship
- is unexpected

Buffer
Reasons
Bad News
Pleasant Close

© Cengage Learning 2015

messages are still conveyed indirectly. As you can see in Figure 9.5, the major differences between the two strategies are whether you start with a buffer and how early you explain the reasons for the negative news.

Keeping the Indirect Strategy Ethical

You may worry that the indirect organizational strategy is unethical or manipulative because the writer deliberately delays the main idea. Now, consider the alternative. Breaking bad news bluntly can cause pain and hard feelings. By delaying bad news, you soften the blow somewhat, as well as ensure that your reasoning will be read while the receiver is still receptive. One expert communicator recognized the significance of the indirect strategy when she said, "People must believe the reasons why before they will listen to the details of what and when."[18] In using the indirect strategy, your motives are not to deceive the reader or to hide the news. Rather, your goal is to be a compassionate, yet effective communicator.

The key to ethical communication lies in the motives of the sender. Unethical communicators *intend to deceive*. Although the indirect strategy provides a setting in which to announce bad news, it should not be used to avoid or misrepresent the truth. For example, the Internet is rife with bogus "free" trial offers for teeth whiteners and açaí supplements, to name just two of the current scams. Unscrupulous marketers advertise on trusted websites of national news organizations and falsely claim endorsements by Oprah Winfrey and Doctor Oz. Unsuspecting consumers end up paying hundreds of dollars, the Better Business Bureau reports.[19] As you will see in Chapter 10, misleading, deceptive, and unethical claims are never acceptable. In fact, many of them are simply illegal.

LEARNING OBJECTIVE **3**

Explain the components of effective negative messages, including opening with a buffer, apologizing, showing empathy, presenting the reasons, cushioning the bad news, and closing pleasantly.

Composing Effective Negative Messages

Even though it may be impossible to make the receiver happy when delivering negative news, you can reduce bad feelings and resentment by structuring your message sensitively. Most negative messages contain some or all of these parts: buffer, reasons, bad news, and closing. This section also discusses apologies and how to convey empathy in delivering bad news.

Opening Indirect Messages With a Buffer

A buffer is a device to reduce shock or pain. To buffer the pain of bad news, begin with a neutral but meaningful statement that makes the reader continue reading. The buffer should be relevant and concise and provide a natural transition to the explanation that follows. The individual situation, of course, will help determine what you should put in the buffer. Avoid trite buffers such as *Thank you for your letter*.

Not all business communication authors agree that buffers actually increase the effectiveness of negative messages. However, in many cultures softening bad news is appreciated. Following are various buffer possibilities.

Best News.   Start with the part of the message that represents the best news. For example, a message to workers announced new health plan rules limiting prescriptions to a 34-day supply and increasing co-payments. With home delivery, however, employees could save up to $24 on each prescription. To emphasize the good news, you might write, *You can now achieve significant savings and avoid trips to the drugstore by having your prescription drugs delivered to your home.*[20]

Compliment.   Praise the receiver's accomplishments, organization, or efforts, but do so with honesty and sincerity. For instance, in a letter declining an invitation to speak, you could write, *The Thalians have my sincere admiration for their fund-raising projects on behalf of hungry children. I am honored that you asked me to speak Friday, November 5.*

Appreciation.   Convey thanks for doing business, for sending something, for showing confidence in your organization, for expressing feelings, or simply for providing feedback. Suppose you had to draft a letter that refuses employment. You could say, *I appreciated learning about the hospitality management program at Cornell and about your qualifications in our interview last Friday.* Avoid thanking the reader, however, for something you are about to refuse.

Agreement.   Make a relevant statement with which both reader and receiver can agree. A letter that rejects a loan application might read, *We both realize how much the export business has been affected by the relative weakness of the dollar in the past two years.*

Facts.   Provide objective information that introduces the bad news. For example, in a memo announcing cutbacks in the hours of the employees' cafeteria, you might say, *During the past five years, the number of employees eating breakfast in our cafeteria has dropped from 32 percent to 12 percent.*

REALITY CHECK: Mending Fences and Restoring Trust With Effective Apologies

"These days, apologizing is a leadership skill. We see our decision makers dodging and weaving instead of accepting responsibility, and that disappoints us. We don't expect them to be perfect. Just willing to learn. In the long run apology leads to better outcomes and more durable relationships."[21]

—**JOHN KADOR,** *blogger and author of* Effective Apology

Courtesy of John Kador

Understanding. Show that you care about the reader. Notice how in this letter to customers announcing a product defect, the writer expresses concern: *We know that you expect superior performance from all the products you purchase from OfficeCity. That's why we're writing personally about the Omega printer cartridges you recently ordered.*

Apologizing

You learned about making apologies in adjustment messages discussed in Chapter 8. We expand that discussion here because apologies are often part of negative-news messages. The truth is that sincere apologies work. Peter Post, great-grandson of famed etiquette expert Emily Post and director of the Emily Post Institute, said that Americans love apologies. They will forgive almost anything if presented with a sincere apology.[22] An apology is defined as an "admission of blameworthiness and regret for an undesirable event."[23] Apologies to customers are especially important if you or your company erred. They cost nothing, and they go a long way in soothing hard feelings. Professional writer John Kador recommends what he calls "the 5Rs model" for effective apologies in business messages[24] summarized in Figure 9.6.

Figure 9.6 Apologizing Effectively in the Digital Age: The 5Rs

Recognition **Acknowledge the specific offense.**
- Organizations that apologize have better outcomes.
- Individuals who apologize well rise higher and have better relationships.

Responsibility **Accept personal responsibility.**
- Accountability means taking responsibility and rejecting defensiveness.
- Accountability is an important skill.
- The cover-up is always worse than the crime.

Remorse **Embrace "I apologize" and "I am sorry."**
- Apologies may become necessary unexpectedly.
- We can prevent automatic defensiveness by being prepared to apologize when the need arises.
- Apologies should be honest, sincere, and authentic.

Restitution **Explain what exactly you will do about it.**
- A concrete explanation of what you will do to make things right is best.
- The remedy should be appropriate, adequate, and satisfying.

Repeating **Promise it won't happen again and mean it.**
- Written apologies are more formal than spoken but work about the same.
- By communicating effectively over the long term, businesses gain the trust of employees, the public, as well as the media and are therefore well equipped to weather crises successfully.

© Cengage Learning 2015

Consider these poor and improved apologies:

Poor apology: We regret that you are unhappy with the price of frozen yogurt purchased at one of our self-serve scoop shops.

Improved apology: We are genuinely sorry that you were disappointed in the price of frozen yogurt recently purchased at one of our self-serve scoop shops. Your opinion is important to us, and we appreciate your giving us the opportunity to look into the problem you describe.

Poor apology: We apologize if anyone was affected.

Improved apology: I apologize for the frustration our delay caused you. As soon as I received your message, I began looking into the cause of the delay and realized that our delivery tracking system must be improved.

Poor apology: We are sorry that mistakes were made in filling your order.

Improved apology: You are right to be concerned. We sincerely apologize for the mistakes we made in filling your order. To prevent recurrence of this problem, we are . . . .

Showing Empathy

One of the hardest things to do in negative messages is to convey sympathy and empathy. As discussed in Chapter 3, *empathy* is the ability to understand and enter into the feelings of another. When ice storms trapped JetBlue Airways passengers on hot planes for hours, CEO Neeleman wrote a letter of apology that sounded as if it came from his heart. He said, "Dear JetBlue Customers: We are sorry and embarrassed. But most of all, we are deeply sorry." Later in his letter he said, "Words cannot express how truly sorry we are for the anxiety, frustration, and inconvenience that you, your family, friends, and colleagues experienced."[26] Neeleman put himself into the shoes of his customers and tried to experience their pain.

Here are other examples of ways to express empathy in written messages:

- In writing to an unhappy customer: *We did not intentionally delay the shipment, and we sincerely regret the disappointment and frustration you must have suffered.*

- In laying off employees: *It is with great regret that we must take this step. Rest assured that I will be more than happy to write letters of recommendation for anyone who asks.*

- In responding to a complaint: *I am deeply saddened that our service failure disrupted your sale, and we will do everything in our power to . . . .*

- In showing genuine feelings: *You have every right to be disappointed. I am truly sorry that . . . .*

Presenting the Reasons

Providing an explanation reduces feelings of ill will and improves the chances that readers will accept the bad news. Without sound reasons for denying a request, refusing a claim, or revealing other bad news, a message will fail, no matter how cleverly it is organized or written. For example, if you must deny a customer's request, as part of your planning before writing, you analyzed the request and decided to refuse it for specific reasons. Where do you place your reasons? In the indirect strategy, the reasons appear before the bad news. In the direct strategy, the reasons appear immediately after the bad news.

Explaining Clearly. If the reasons are not confidential and if they will not create legal liability, you can be specific: *Growers supplied us with a limited number of patio roses, and our demand this year was twice that of last year.* In responding to a billing error, explain what happened: *After you informed us of an error on your January bill, we investigated the matter and admit the mistake was ours. Until our new automated system is fully online, we are still subject to the*

frailties of human error. Rest assured that your account has been credited as you will see on your next bill. In refusing a speaking engagement, tell why the date is impossible: *On January 17 we have a board of directors meeting that I must attend.* Don't, however, make unrealistic or dangerous statements in an effort to be the "good guy."

Citing Reader or Other Benefits, if Plausible.   Readers are more open to bad news if in some way, even indirectly, it may help them. In refusing a customer's request for free hemming of skirts and slacks, Lands' End wrote: "We tested our ability to hem skirts a few months ago. This process proved to be very time-consuming. We have decided not to offer this service because the additional cost would have increased the selling price of our skirts substantially, and we did not want to impose that cost on all our customers."[27] Readers also accept bad news more readily if they recognize that someone or something else benefits, such as other workers or the environment: *Although we would like to consider your application, we prefer to fill managerial positions from within.* Avoid trying to show reader benefits, though, if they appear insincere: *To improve our service to you, we are increasing our brokerage fees.*

Explaining Company Policy.   Readers resent blanket policy statements prohibiting something: *Company policy prevents us from making cash refunds* or *Contract bids may be accepted from local companies only* or *Company policy requires us to promote from within.* Instead of hiding behind company policy, gently explain why the policy makes sense: *We prefer to promote from within because it rewards the loyalty of our employees. In addition, we have found that people familiar with our organization make the quickest contribution to our team effort.* By offering explanations, you demonstrate that you care about readers and are treating them as important individuals.

Choosing Positive Words.   Because the words you use can affect a reader's response, choose carefully. Remember that the objective of the indirect strategy is holding the reader's attention until you have had a chance to explain the reasons justifying the bad news. To keep the reader in a receptive mood, avoid expressions with punitive, demoralizing, or otherwise negative connotations. Stay away from such words as *cannot, claim, denied, error, failure, fault, impossible, mistaken, misunderstand, never, regret, rejected, unable, unwilling, unfortunately,* and *violate.*

Showing Fairness and Serious Intent.   In explaining reasons, show the reader that you take the matter seriously, have investigated carefully, and are making an unbiased decision. Receivers are more accepting of disappointing news when they feel that their requests have been heard and that they have been treated fairly. In canceling funding for a program, board members provided this explanation: *As you know, the publication of* Urban Artist *was funded by a renewable annual grant from the National Endowment for the Arts. Recent cutbacks in federally sponsored city arts programs have left us with few funds. Because our grant has been discontinued, we have no alternative but to cease publication of* Urban Artist. *You have my assurance that the board has searched long and hard for some other viable funding, but every avenue of recourse has been closed before us. Accordingly, June's issue will be our last.*

Cushioning the Bad News

Although you can't prevent the disappointment that bad news brings, you can reduce the pain somewhat by breaking the news sensitively. Be especially considerate when the reader will suffer personally from the bad news. A number of thoughtful techniques can cushion the blow.

Positioning the Bad News Strategically.   Instead of spotlighting it, sandwich the bad news between other sentences, perhaps among your reasons. Don't let the refusal begin or end a paragraph; the reader's eye will linger on these high-visibility spots. Another technique that reduces shock is putting a painful idea in a subordinate clause: *Although another candidate was hired, we appreciate your interest in our organization and wish you every success in your job search.* Subordinate clauses often begin with words such as *although, as, because, if,* and *since.*

George Hirsh displayed sensitivity when he announced the controversial decision to cancel the 2012 New York City Marathon because of storm damage from Hurricane Sandy. "It is with heavy hearts that we share the news that the 2012 ING New York City Marathon has been canceled," he explained. He then proceeded to explain that city services should focus on storm relief, not the marathon.

Using the Passive Voice.   Passive-voice verbs enable you to depersonalize an action. Whereas the active voice focuses attention on a person *(We don't give cash refunds),* the passive voice highlights the action *(Cash refunds are not given because . . .).* Use the passive voice for the bad news. In some instances you can combine passive-voice verbs and a subordinate clause: *Although franchise scoop shop owners cannot be required to lower their frozen yogurt prices, we are happy to pass along your comments for their consideration.*

Highlighting the Positive.   As you learned earlier, messages are far more effective when you describe what you can do instead of what you can't do. Rather than *We will no longer allow credit card purchases,* try a more positive appeal: *We are now selling gasoline at discount cash prices.*

Implying the Refusal.   It is sometimes possible to avoid a direct statement of refusal. Often, your reasons and explanations leave no doubt that a request has been denied. Explicit refusals may be unnecessary and at times cruel. In this refusal to contribute to a charity, for example, the writer never actually says *no: Because we will soon be moving into new offices in Glendale, all our funds are earmarked for relocation costs. We hope that next year we will be able to support your worthwhile charity.* The danger of an implied refusal, of course, is that it is so subtle that the reader misses it. Be certain that you make the bad news clear, thus preventing the need for further correspondence.

Suggesting a Compromise or an Alternative.   A refusal is not so depressing— for the sender or the receiver—if a suitable compromise, substitute, or alternative is available. In denying permission to a group of students to visit a historical private residence, for instance, this writer softens the bad news by proposing an alternative: *Although private tours of the grounds are not given, we do open the house and its gardens for one charitable event in the fall.* You can further reduce the impact of the bad news by refusing to dwell on it. Present it briefly (or imply it), and move on to your closing.

Closing Pleasantly

After explaining the bad news sensitively, close the message with a pleasant statement that promotes goodwill. The closing should be personalized and may include a forward look, an alternative, good wishes, freebies, resale information, or a sales promotion. *Resale* refers to mentioning a product or service favorably to reinforce the customer's choice. For example, *you chose our best-selling model.*

Forward Look.   Anticipate future relations or business. A letter that refuses a contract proposal might read: *Thanks for your bid. We look forward to working with your talented staff when future projects demand your special expertise.*

Alternative Follow-Up.   If an alternative exists, end your letter with follow-through advice. For example, in a letter rejecting a customer's demand for replacement of landscaping plants, you might say: *I will be happy to give you a free inspection and consultation. Please call 301-746-8112 to arrange a date for my visit.* In a message to a prospective home buyer: *Although the lot you saw last week is now sold, we do have two excellent view lots available at a slightly higher price.* In reacting to an Internet misprint: *Please note that our website contained an unfortunate misprint offering $850-per-night Bora Bora bungalows at $85. Although we cannot honor that rate, we are offering a special half-price rate of $425 to those who responded.*

Good Wishes.   A letter rejecting a job candidate might read: *We appreciate your interest in our company, and we extend to you our best wishes in your search to find the perfect match between your skills and job requirements.*

Freebies.   When customers complain—primarily about food products or small consumer items—companies often send coupons, samples, or gifts to restore confidence and to promote future business. In response to a customer's complaint about a frozen dinner, you could write: *Your loyalty and your concern about our frozen entrées are genuinely appreciated. Because we want you to continue enjoying our healthy and convenient dinners, we are enclosing a coupon that you can take to your local market to select your next Green Valley entrée.*

Figure 9.7 Delivering Bad News Sensitively

Buffer	Reasons	Bad News	Closing
• Best news • Compliment • Appreciation • Agreement • Facts • Understanding • Apology	• Cautious explanation • Reader or other benefits • Company policy explanation • Positive words • Evidence that matter was considered fairly and seriously	• Embedded placement • Passive voice • Implied refusal • Compromise • Alternative	• Forward look • Information about alternative • Good wishes • Freebies • Resale • Sales promotion

© Cengage Learning 2015

Resale or Sales Promotion.   When the bad news is not devastating or personal, references to resale information or promotion may be appropriate: *The computer workstations you ordered are unusually popular because of their stain-, heat-, and scratch-resistant finishes. To help you locate hard-to-find accessories for these workstations, we invite you to visit our website where our online catalog provides a huge selection of surge suppressors, multiple outlet strips, security devices, and PC tool kits.*

Avoid endings that sound canned, insincere, inappropriate, or self-serving. Don't invite further correspondence *(If you have any questions, do not hesitate . . .),* and don't refer to the bad news. Figure 9.7 reviews suggestions for delivering bad news sensitively.

Refusing Typical Requests and Claims

LEARNING OBJECTIVE **4**
Apply effective techniques for refusing typical requests or claims as well as for presenting bad news to customers in print or online.

When you must refuse typical requests, you will first think about how the receiver will react to your refusal and decide whether to use the direct or the indirect strategy. If you have any doubt, use the indirect strategy. As you move forward in your career and become a professional or a representative of an organization, you may receive requests for favors or contributions. You may also be invited to speak or give presentations.

Businesses must occasionally respond to disappointed customers in print and online. In many instances disappointed customers are turning to the Internet to air their grievances. Complaints about products and services now appear on sites such as Complaints.com and iRipoff.com as well as on Facebook, Twitter, and other social networks. Large companies have social media staff members who monitor negative messages online and solve problems whenever customers voice their discontent.

Rejecting Requests for Favors, Money, Information, and Action

Requests for favors, money, information, and action may come from charities, friends, or business partners. Many are from people representing commendable causes, and you may wish you could comply. However, resources are usually limited. In a letter from Heartland Management Associates, shown in Figure 9.8, the company must refuse a request for a donation to a charity. Following the indirect strategy, the letter begins with a buffer acknowledging the request. It also praises the good works of the charity and uses those words as a transition to the second paragraph. In the second paragraph, the writer explains why the company cannot donate. Notice that the writer reveals the refusal without actually stating it (*Because of internal restructuring and the economic downturn, we are forced to take a*

Large companies have social media staff members who monitor negative messages online and solve problems whenever customers voice their discontent.

© iStockphoto.com/Andrew Johnson

Figure **9.8** Refusing Donation Request

1 Prewriting

Analyze: The purpose of this letter is to reject the request for a monetary donation without causing ill will.

Anticipate: The reader is proud of her organization and the good work it pursues. She will appreciate recognition and praise for the Guide Dog Center's mission and achievements.

Adapt: The writer should strive to cushion the bad news and explain why it is necessary.

2 Drafting

Research: Collect information about the receiver's organization as well as reasons for the refusal.

Organize: Use the indirect strategy. Begin with complimentary comments, present reasons, and reveal the bad news gently or simply imply it. Close graciously.

Draft: Write the message and consider keeping a copy to serve as a form letter.

3 Revising

Edit: Be sure that the tone of the message is positive and that it suggests that the matter was taken seriously.

Proofread: Check the receiver's name and address to be sure that they are accurate. Check the letter's format.

Evaluate: Will this message retain the goodwill of the receiver despite its bad news?

Heartland
Management Associates

212 South Central Avenue
St. Louis, MO 631250
www.heartlandmanagement.com

February 12, 2015

Ms. Denise Moore
Guide Dog Center
2903 Market Street
St. Louis, MO 63103

Dear Ms. Moore:

Opens with praise and compliments →

Here at Heartland Management Associates, we are pleased that over the years we were able to partner with the Guide Dog Center and assist in its admirable program that provides guide and service dogs to blind or visually impaired individuals. We appreciate your recent letter describing the exceptionally worthwhile VetDogs program that offers trained animals to America's returning heroes in need of service dogs.

← *Doesn't say yes or no*

Transitions with repetition of key ideas (good work and worthy projects) →

Supporting the good work and worthy projects of your organization and others, although unrelated to our business, is a luxury we have enjoyed in the past. Because of internal restructuring and the economic downturn, we are forced to take a much harder look at funding requests that we receive this year. We feel that we must focus our charitable contributions on areas that relate more directly to our business.

← *Explains cutback in gifts, thus revealing refusal without actually stating it*

Closes graciously with praise and a forward look →

We are hopeful that the worst of the economic slump is now behind us and that in the future we will be able to again partner with the Guide Dog Center to help defray the costs of breeding, training, and placing guide and service dogs. You provide an admirable service, and Heartland salutes you.

Cordially,

HEARTLAND MANAGEMENT ASSOCIATES

Nelson M. Felton

Nelson M. Felton

much harder look at funding requests that we receive this year). This gentle refusal makes it unnecessary to be blunter in stating the denial.

In some donation refusal letters, the reasons may not be fully explained: *Although we can't provide financial support at this time, we all unanimously agree that the Make-A-Wish Foundation contributes a valuable service to sick children.* The emphasis is on the foundation's good deeds rather than on an explanation for the refusal.

Messages that refuse requests for favors, money, information, and action can often be tactfully handled by showing appreciation for the inquiry and respect for the writer. Businesses that are required to write frequent refusals might prepare a form letter, changing a few variables as needed.

Declining Invitations

When you must decline an invitation to speak or make a presentation, you generally try to provide a response that says more than *I can't* or *I don't want to.* Unless the reasons are confidential or business secrets, try to explain them. Because responses to invitations are often taken personally, make a special effort to soften the refusal. In the e-mail shown in Figure 9.9, an accountant must say *no* to the invitation from a friend's son to speak before the young man's college business club. This refusal starts with conviviality and compliments.

The writer then explains why he cannot accept. The refusal is embedded in a long paragraph and de-emphasized in a subordinate clause (*Although your invitation must be declined*). The reader naturally concentrates on the main clause that follows (*I would like to recommend . . .*). If no alternative is available, focus on something positive about the situation (*Although I'm not an expert, I commend your organization for selecting this topic*). Overall, the tone of this refusal is warm, upbeat, and positive.

Figure **9.9** Declining an Invitation

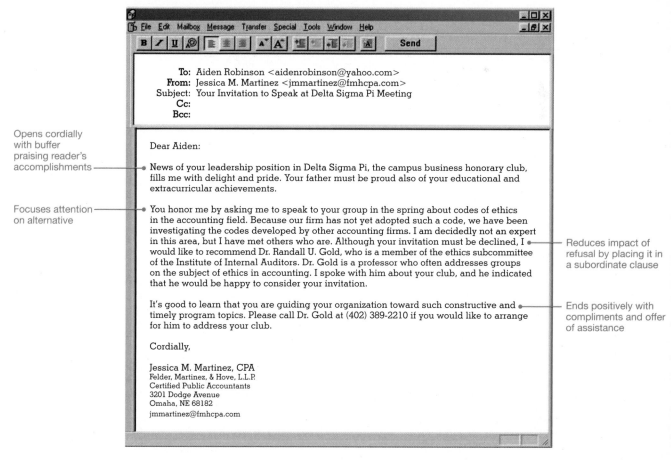

Opens cordially with buffer praising reader's accomplishments

Focuses attention on alternative

Reduces impact of refusal by placing it in a subordinate clause

Ends positively with compliments and offer of assistance

© Cengage Learning 2015; Courtesy of Mary Ellen Guffey and Dana Loewy; Used with permission from Microsoft.

Dealing With Disappointed Customers in Print and Online

All businesses offering products or services must sometimes deal with troublesome situations that cause unhappiness to customers. Merchandise is not delivered on time, a product fails to perform as expected, service is deficient, charges are erroneous, or customers are misunderstood. Whenever possible, these problems should be dealt with immediately and personally. Most business professionals strive to control the damage and resolve such problems in the following manner:[28]

- Call or e-mail the individual or reply to his or her online post within 24 hours.

- Describe the problem and apologize.

- Explain why the problem occurred, what you are doing to resolve it, and how you will prevent it from happening again.

- Promote goodwill by following up with a message that documents the phone call or acknowledges the online exchange of posts.

Responding by E-Mail and in Hard Copy.   Written messages are important (a) when personal contact is impossible, (b) to establish a record of the incident, (c) to formally confirm follow-up procedures, and (d) to promote good relations. Dealing with problems immediately is very important in resolving conflict and retaining goodwill.

A bad-news follow-up letter is shown in Figure 9.10. Consultant Eva Gonzalez Tejo found herself in the embarrassing position of explaining why she had given out the name of her client to a salesperson. The client, Accordia Resources International, had hired her firm, Azad Consulting Associates, to help find an appropriate service for outsourcing its payroll functions. Without realizing it, Eva had mentioned to a potential vendor (Payroll Services, Inc.) that her client was considering hiring an outside service to handle its payroll. An overeager salesperson from Payroll Services immediately called on Accordia, thus angering the client.

Eva Gonzalez Tejo first called her client to explain and apologize. She was careful to control her voice and rate of speaking. She also followed up with the letter shown in Figure 9.10. The letter not only confirms the telephone conversation but also adds the right touch of formality. It sends the nonverbal message that the writer takes the matter seriously and that it is important enough to warrant a hard-copy letter.

Many consumer problems are handled with letters, either written by consumers as complaints or by companies in response. However, e-mail and social networks are firmly established as channels for delivering complaints and negative messages.

Managing Negative News Online.   Today's impatient, hyperconnected consumers eagerly embrace the idea of delivering their complaints to social networking sites rather than calling customer-service departments. Why rely on word of mouth or send a letter to a company about poor service or a defective product when you can shout your grievance to the entire world? Internet sites such as Complaints.com, Ripoff Report, and MeasuredUp, and specialty message boards such as Cruise Critic encourage consumers to quickly share complaints about stores, products, and services that fall short of their standards. Twitter, Facebook, Angie's List, Yelp, and many more, are also favorite sites where consumers can make public their ire.

Complaint sites are gaining momentum for many reasons. Consumers may receive faster responses to tweets than to customer-service calls.[29] Airing gripes in public also helps other consumers avoid the same problems and may improve the complainer's leverage in solving the problem. In addition, sending a 140-word tweet is much easier than writing a complaint e-mail or letter to a customer-service department or navigating endless telephone menus to reach an agent. Businesses can employ some of the following effective strategies to manage negative news on social networking sites and blogs:

- **Recognize social networks as an important communication channel.** Instead of fearing social networks as a disruptive force, smart companies greet these channels as opportunities to look into the true mind-set of customers and receive free advice on how to improve.

- **Become proactive.** Company blogs and active websites with community forums help companies listen to their customers as well as to spread the word about their own good

Figure **9.10** Bad-News Follow-Up Message

AZAD CONSULTING ASSOCIATES

4350 Speedway Blvd.
Voice: (520) 259-0971
Tucson, AZ 85712
Web: www.azadassociates.com

May 7, 2015

Mr. Carl Bahadur
Director, Administrative Operations
Accordia Resources International
538 North Pima Road, Suite 1210
Phoenix, AZ 85001

Dear Mr. Bahadur:

Opens with agreement and apology → You have every right to expect complete confidentiality in your transactions with an independent consultant. As I explained in yesterday's telephone call, I am very distressed that you were called by a salesperson from Payroll Services, Inc. This should not have happened, and I apologize to you again for inadvertently mentioning your company's name in a conversation with a potential vendor, Payroll Services, Inc.

Takes responsibility and promises to prevent recurrence → All clients of Azad Consulting are assured that their dealings with our firm are held in the strictest confidence. Because your company's payroll needs are so individual and because you have so many contract workers, I was forced to explain how your employees differed from those of other companies. Revealing your company name was my error, and I take full responsibility for the lapse. I can assure you that it will not happen again. I have informed Payroll Services that it had no authorization to call you directly, and its actions have forced me to reconsider using its services for my future clients. ← *Explains what caused the problem and how it was resolved*

Closes with forward look → A number of other payroll services offer outstanding programs. I'm sure we can find the perfect partner to enable you to outsource your payroll responsibilities, thus allowing your company to focus its financial and human resources on its core business. I look forward to our next appointment when you may choose from a number of excellent payroll outsourcing firms.

Sincerely,

Eva Gonzales Tejo

Eva Gonzalez Tejo
Partner

Tips for Resolving Problems and Following Up

- Whenever possible, call or see the individual involved.
- Describe the problem and apologize.
- Explain why the problem occurred.
- Take responsibility, if appropriate.
- Explain what you are doing to resolve it.
- Explain what you are doing to prevent recurrence.
- Follow up with a message that documents the personal contact.
- Look forward to positive future relations.

© Cengage Learning 2015

deeds. Home Depot's site describing its foundation, workshops, and careers now outranks HomeDepotSucks.com, which used to rank No. 1 for searches on the keywords *home depot*.

- **Join the fun.** Wise companies have joined Twitter, Facebook, Flickr, YouTube, and LinkedIn so they can benefit from interacting with their customers and the public.

- **Monitor comments.** Many large companies employ social media managers and other digital media staff to monitor online traffic and respond immediately whenever possible. At Southwest Airlines and other carriers, teams listen online to what people are saying about their companies. Their policy is to engage the positive and address the negative—all within 24 hours.

When domain registrar and Internet hosting provider Go Daddy experienced a nearly six-hour-long service disruption that affected the websites of more than 10 million customers, the company responded swiftly. It took to social media and used multiple channels to reassure

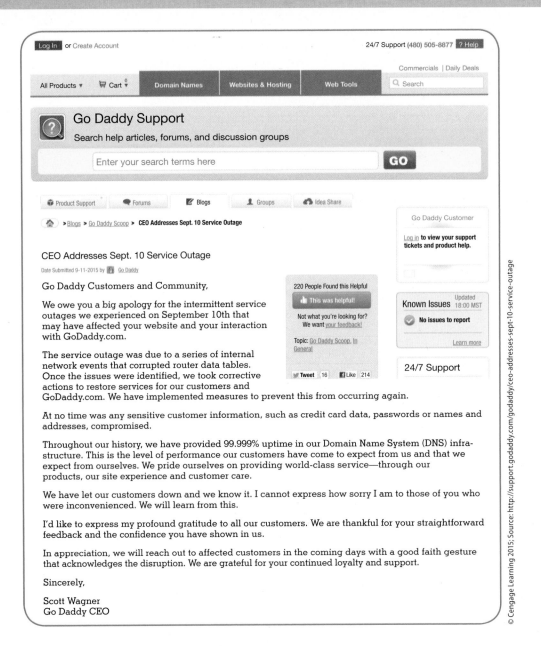

its users. Figure 9.11 shows a blog post by Go Daddy CEO Scott Wagner addressing the bad news head-on and apologizing to customers.[30]

An almost identical message went out by e-mail to all Go Daddy users offering a 30 percent discount on any new product or renewal to compensate for the loss of service. In addition, the company provided frequent Twitter updates. "Status Alert: Hey, all. We're aware of the trouble people are having with our site. We're working on it." Subsequently, @GoDaddy tweeted: "Update: Still working on it, but we're making progress. Some service has already been restored. Stick with us."[31] In a 24/7 news cycle and facing an Internet that never sleeps, companies lose if they snooze. Because the bad news didn't injure people's feelings, the company could afford to state the unfavorable news directly.

Handling Problems With Orders

Not all customer orders can be filled as received. Suppliers may be able to send only part of an order or none at all. Substitutions may be necessary, or the delivery date may be delayed.

Suppliers may suspect that all or part of the order is a mistake; the customer may actually want something else. In writing to customers about problem orders, it is generally wise to use the direct strategy if the message has some good-news elements. However, when the message is disappointing, the indirect strategy may be more appropriate.

Let's say you represent Live and Learn Toys, a large West Coast toy manufacturer, and you are scrambling for business in a slow year. A big customer, Child Land, calls in August and asks you to hold a block of your best-selling toy, the Space Station. Like most vendors, you require a deposit on large orders. September rolls around, and you still haven't received any money from Child Land. You must now write a tactful e-mail asking for the deposit—or else you will release the toy to other buyers. The problem, of course, is delivering the bad news without losing the customer's order and goodwill. Another challenge is making sure the reader understands the bad news. An effective message might begin with a positive statement that also reveals the facts:

> *You were smart to reserve a block of 500 Space Stations, which we have been holding for you since August. As the holidays approach, the demand for all our learning toys, including the Space Station, is rapidly increasing.*

Next, the message should explain why the payment is needed and what will happen if it is not received:

> *Toy stores from Florida to California are asking us to ship these Space Stations. One reason the Space Station is moving out of our warehouses so quickly is its assortment of gizmos that children love, including a land rover vehicle, a shuttle craft, a hovercraft, astronauts, and even a robotic arm. As soon as we receive your deposit of $4,000, we will have this popular item on its way to your stores. Without a deposit by September 20, though, we must release this block to other retailers.*

The closing makes it easy to respond and motivates action:

> *For expedited service, please call our sales department at 800-358-4488 and authorize the deposit using your business credit card. You can begin showing the fascinating Live and Learn toy in your stores by November 1.*

Announcing Rate Increases and Price Hikes

Informing customers and clients of rate increases or price hikes can be like handling a live grenade. These messages necessarily cause consumers to recoil. With skill, however, you can help your customers understand why the rate or price increase is necessary.

The important steps in these negative messages are explaining the reasons and hooking the increase to benefits. For example, a price increase might be necessitated by higher material costs, rising taxes, escalating insurance, driver pay increase—all reasons you cannot control. You might cite changing industry trends or technology innovations as causes of increased costs.

In developing audience benefits and building goodwill, think about how the increase will add new value or better features, make use more efficient, or make customers' lives easier. Whenever possible, give advance warning of rate increases—for example: *Because you are an important customer to us, I wanted to inform you about this right away. Our energy costs have almost doubled over the last year, forcing us to put through a 10 percent price increase effective July 1. You order these items regularly, so I thought I'd better check with you to see if it would make sense to reorder now to save you money and prevent last-minute surprises.*

In today's digital environment, rate and price increases may be announced by e-mail or online, as shown in Figure 9.12. DVD City had to increase the charge for access to Blu-ray movies by mail. In its blog it explained how Blu-ray discs are not only superior to DVDs but also more expensive. To provide its customers with a comprehensive library of Blu-ray movies, DVD City has to raise its rates. Notice that the rate increase is tied to benefits to customers.

Denying Claims

Customers occasionally want something they are not entitled to or that you can't grant. They may misunderstand warranties or make unreasonable demands. Because these customers are often unhappy with a product or service, they are emotionally involved. Messages that say *no*

Figure **9.12** E-Mail Announcing Price Increase With Audience Benefits

Explains expansion of Blu-ray DVD collection and describes how costly these films are, thus justifying a price increase

Provides name and number for more information

Connects increase in cost to bigger library and wider choice of movies

© Cengage Learning 2015; Courtesy of Mary Ellen Guffey and Dana Loewy; Used with permission from Microsoft.

to emotionally involved receivers will probably be your most challenging communication task. As publisher Malcolm Forbes observed, "To be agreeable while disagreeing—that's an art."[32]

Fortunately, the reasons-before-refusal plan helps you be empathic and artful in breaking bad news. Obviously, in denial letters you will need to adopt the proper tone. Don't blame customers, even if they are at fault. Avoid *you* statements that sound preachy *(You would have known that cash refunds are impossible if you had read your contract)*. Use neutral, objective language to explain why the claim must be refused. Consider offering resale information to rebuild the customer's confidence in your products or organization. In Figure 9.13 the writer denies a customer's claim for the difference between the price the customer paid for speakers and the price he saw advertised locally (which would have resulted in a cash refund of $100). Although the catalog service does match any advertised lower price, the price-matching policy applies *only* to exact models. This claim must be rejected because the advertisement the customer submitted showed a different, older speaker model.

The e-mail to Stephen Dominique opens with a buffer that agrees with a statement in the customer's e-mail. It repeats the key idea of product confidence as a transition to the second paragraph. Next comes an explanation of the price-matching policy. The writer does not assume that the customer is trying to pull a fast one. Nor does he suggest that the customer is a dummy who didn't read or understand the price-matching policy. The safest path is a neutral explanation of the policy along with precise distinctions between the customer's speakers and the older ones. The writer also gets a chance to resell the customer's speakers and demonstrate what a quality product they are. By the end of the third paragraph, it is evident to the reader that his claim is unjustified.

Figure **9.13** E-Mail Denying a Claim

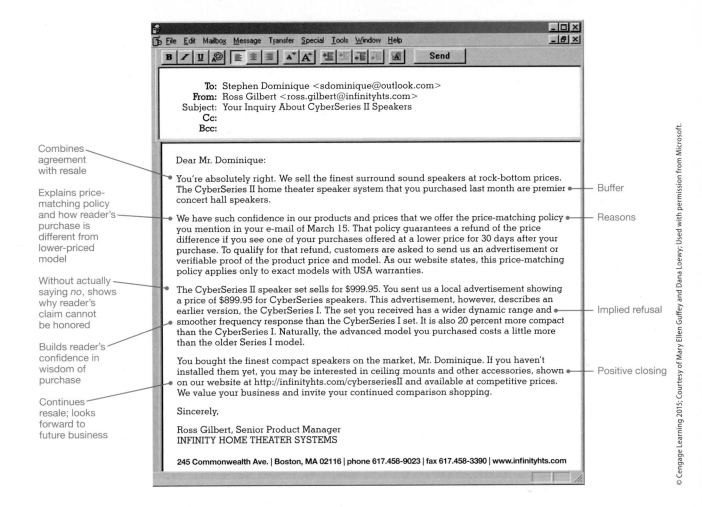

Combines agreement with resale

Explains price-matching policy and how reader's purchase is different from lower-priced model

Without actually saying *no*, shows why reader's claim cannot be honored

Builds reader's confidence in wisdom of purchase

Continues resale; looks forward to future business

To: Stephen Dominique <sdominique@outlook.com>
From: Ross Gilbert <ross.gilbert@infinityhts.com>
Subject: Your Inquiry About CyberSeries II Speakers
Cc:
Bcc:

Dear Mr. Dominique:

You're absolutely right. We sell the finest surround sound speakers at rock-bottom prices. The CyberSeries II home theater speaker system that you purchased last month are premier concert hall speakers. — Buffer

We have such confidence in our products and prices that we offer the price-matching policy you mention in your e-mail of March 15. That policy guarantees a refund of the price difference if you see one of your purchases offered at a lower price for 30 days after your purchase. To qualify for that refund, customers are asked to send us an advertisement or verifiable proof of the product price and model. As our website states, this price-matching policy applies only to exact models with USA warranties. — Reasons

The CyberSeries II speaker set sells for $999.95. You sent us a local advertisement showing a price of $899.95 for CyberSeries speakers. This advertisement, however, describes an earlier version, the CyberSeries I. The set you received has a wider dynamic range and smoother frequency response than the CyberSeries I set. It is also 20 percent more compact than the CyberSeries I. Naturally, the advanced model you purchased costs a little more than the older Series I model. — Implied refusal

You bought the finest compact speakers on the market, Mr. Dominique. If you haven't installed them yet, you may be interested in ceiling mounts and other accessories, shown on our website at http://infinityhts.com/cyberseriesII and available at competitive prices. We value your business and invite your continued comparison shopping. — Positive closing

Sincerely,

Ross Gilbert, Senior Product Manager
INFINITY HOME THEATER SYSTEMS

245 Commonwealth Ave. | Boston, MA 02116 | phone 617.458-9023 | fax 617.458-3390 | www.infinityhts.com

Refusing Credit

When customers apply for credit, they must be notified within 30 days if that application is rejected. The Fair Credit Reporting Act and Equal Credit Opportunity Act state that consumers who are denied loans must receive a notice of "adverse action" from the business explaining the decision. The business can refer the applicant to the credit-reporting agency, whether Experian, Equifax, or TransUnion, that provided the information upon which the negative decision was based. If you must write a letter to a customer denying credit, you have four goals in conveying the refusal:

- Avoiding language that causes hard feelings
- Retaining the customer on a cash basis
- Preparing for possible future credit without raising false expectations
- Avoiding disclosures that could cause a lawsuit

Because credit applicants are likely to continue to do business with an organization even if they are denied credit, you will want to do everything possible to encourage that patronage. Therefore, keep the refusal respectful, sensitive, and upbeat. A letter to a customer denying her credit application might begin as follows:

We genuinely appreciate your application of January 12 for a Fashion Express credit account.

To avoid possible litigation, many companies offer no explanation of the reasons for a credit refusal. Instead, they provide the name of the credit-reporting agency and suggest that inquiries be directed to it. In the following example, notice the use of passive voice (*credit cannot be extended*) and a long sentence to de-emphasize the bad news:

> *After we received a report of your current credit record from Experian, it is apparent that credit cannot be extended at this time. To learn more about your record, you may call an Experian credit counselor at (212) 356-0922.*

The cordial closing looks forward to the possibility of a future reapplication:

> *Thanks, Ms. Love, for the confidence you have shown in Fashion Express. We invite you to continue shopping at our stores, and we look forward to your reapplication in the future.*

Some businesses do provide reasons explaining credit denials (*Credit cannot be granted because your firm's current and long-term credit obligations are nearly twice as great as your firm's total assets*). They may also provide alternatives, such as deferred billing or cash discounts. When the letter denies a credit application that accompanies an order, the message may contain resale information. The writer tries to convert the order from credit to cash. For example, if a big order cannot be filled on a credit basis, perhaps part of the order could be filled on a cash basis.

Whatever form the bad-news message takes, it is a good idea to have the message reviewed by legal counsel because of the litigation land mines awaiting unwary communicators in this area.

LEARNING OBJECTIVE **5**
Describe and apply effective techniques for delivering bad news within organizations.

Managing Bad News Within Organizations

A tactful tone and a reasons-first approach help preserve friendly relations with customers. These same techniques are useful when delivering bad news within organizations. Interpersonal bad news might involve telling the boss that something went wrong or confronting an employee about poor performance. Organizational bad news might involve declining profits, lost contracts, harmful lawsuits, public relations controversies, and changes in policy. Whether you use a direct or an indirect strategy in delivering that news depends primarily on the anticipated reaction of the audience. Generally, bad news is better received when reasons are given first. Within organizations, you may find yourself giving bad news in person or in writing.

Delivering Bad News in Person

Whether you are an employee or a supervisor, you may have the unhappy responsibility of delivering bad news. First, decide whether the negative information is newsworthy. For example, trivial, noncriminal mistakes or one-time bad behaviors are best left alone. However, fraudulent travel claims, consistent hostile behavior, or failing projects must be reported.[33] For example, you might have to tell the boss that the team's computer crashed losing all its important files. Similarly, as a team leader or supervisor, you might be required to confront an underperforming employee. If you know that the news will upset the receiver, the reasons-first strategy is most effective. When the bad news involves one person or a small group nearby, you should generally deliver that news in person. Here are pointers on how to do so tactfully, professionally, and safely:[34]

- **Gather all the information.** Cool down and have all the facts before marching in on the boss or confronting someone. Remember that every story has two sides.
- **Prepare and rehearse.** Outline what you plan to say so that you are confident, coherent, and dispassionate.
- **Explain: past, present, future.** If you are telling the boss about a problem such as the computer crash, explain what caused the crash, the current situation, and how and when you plan to fix it.
- **Consider taking a partner.** If you fear a "shoot the messenger" reaction, especially from your boss, bring a colleague with you. Each person should have a consistent and credible part

in the presentation. If possible, take advantage of your organization's internal resources. To lend credibility to your view, call on auditors, inspectors, or human resources experts.

- **Think about timing.** Don't deliver bad news when someone is already stressed or grumpy. Experts also advise against giving bad news on Friday afternoon when people have the weekend to dwell on it.
- **Be patient with the reaction.** Give the receiver time to vent, think, recover, and act wisely.

Refusing Workplace Requests

Occasionally, managers must refuse requests from employees. In Figure 9.14 you see the first draft and revision of a message responding to a request from a key specialist, Donald Gantry. He wants permission to attend a conference. However, he can't attend the conference because the timing is bad; he must be present at budget planning meetings scheduled for the same two weeks. Normally, this matter would be discussed in person. However, Don has been traveling among branch offices, and he just hasn't been in the office recently.

Figure **9.14** Refusing an Internal Request

Announces the bad news too quickly and painfully

Overemphasizes the refusal and apology

Makes a promise that might be difficult to keep

Gives reasons, but includes a potentially dangerous statement about the "shaky" system

Buffer: Includes sincere praise

Transition: Uses date to move smoothly from buffer to reasons

Reasons: Explains why refusal is necessary

Bad news: Implies refusal

Closing: Contains realistic alternative

The vice president's first inclination was to dash off a quick e-mail, as shown in Figure 9.14 draft, and "tell it like it is." However, the vice president realized that this message was going to hurt and that it had possible danger areas. Moreover, the message misses a chance to give Don positive feedback. An improved version of the e-mail starts with a buffer that delivers honest praise (*pleased with the exceptional leadership you have provided* and *your genuine professional commitment*). By the way, don't be stingy with compliments; they cost you nothing. To paraphrase the motivational speaker Zig Ziglar, we don't live by bread alone. We need buttering up once in a while.[35] The buffer also includes the date of the meeting, used strategically to connect the reasons that follow.

The middle paragraph provides reasons for the refusal. Notice that they focus on positive elements: Don is the specialist; the company relies on his expertise; and everyone will benefit if he passes up the conference. In this section it becomes obvious that the request is being refused. The writer is not forced to say, *No, you may not attend.* Although the refusal is implied, the reader gets the message.

The closing suggests a qualified alternative (*if our workloads permit, we will try to send you then*). It also ends positively with gratitude for Don's contributions to the organization and with another compliment (*you're a valuable player*). The improved version focuses on explanations and praise rather than on refusals and apologies. The success of this message depends on attention to the entire writing process, not just on using a buffer or scattering a few compliments throughout.

REALITY CHECK: Tackling Tough Workplace Talks

"In difficult conversation, the keys to success are good strategy and tactics for handling the hard parts well; balance between extremes; and self-respect, respect for your counterpart and respect for the problem between you. That means breaking habits of mistaking tough conversations for warfare, getting caught up in emotional reactions and assuming that we know the unpredictable. It's not always easy, but it's better."[36]

—**HOLLY WEEKS,** *author of* Failure to Communicate: How Conversations Go Wrong and What You Can Do to Right Them

Courtesy of Holly Weeks

Announcing Bad News to Employees and the Public

In an age of social media, damaging information can rarely be contained for long. Executives can almost count on it to be leaked. Corporate officers who fail to communicate effectively and proactively may end up on the defensive and face an uphill battle trying to limit the damage. Many of the same techniques used to deliver bad news personally are useful when organizations face a crisis or must deliver bad news to various stakeholders. Smart organizations involved in a crisis prefer to communicate the news openly to employees and stockholders. A crisis might involve serious performance problems, a major relocation, massive layoffs, a management shakeup, or public controversy. Instead of letting rumors distort the truth, managers ought to explain the organization's side of the story honestly and promptly.

Morale can be destroyed when employees learn of major events affecting their jobs through the grapevine or from news accounts—rather than from management. When bad news must be delivered to individual employees, management may want to deliver the news personally. With large groups, however, this is generally impossible. Instead, organizations deliver bad news through multiple channels ranging from hard-copy memos, which are formal and create a permanent record, to digital media. Such electronic messages can take the form of intranet posts, e-mail, videos, webcasts, internal as well as external blogs, and voice mail.

The draft of the intranet blog post shown in Figure 9.15 announces a substantial increase in the cost of employee health care benefits. However, the message suffers from many problems. It announces jolting news bluntly in the first sentence. Worse, it offers little or no explanation for the steep increase in costs. It also sounds insincere (*We did everything possible . . .*) and arbitrary. In a final miscue, the writer fails to give credit to the company for absorbing previous health cost increases.

The revision of this bad-news message uses the indirect strategy and improves the tone considerably. Notice that it opens with a relevant, upbeat buffer regarding health care—but

Figure **9.15** Announcing Bad News to Employees

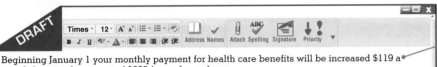

1 Prewriting

Analyze: The purpose of this intranet blog post is to tell employees that they must share with the company the cost of increasing health care costs.

Anticipate: The audience will be employees who are unaware of specific health care costs and, most likely, reluctant to pay more.

Adapt: Because the readers will be unhappy, use the indirect strategy. Choose to post the announcement on the company intranet, increasingly used to disseminate internal news in addition to e-mail.

2 Drafting

Research: Collect facts and statistics that document health care costs.

Organize: Begin with a buffer describing the company's commitment to health benefits. Provide an explanation of health care costs. Announce the bad news. In the closing, focus on the company's major share of the cost.

Draft: Draft the first version with the expectation to revise.

3 Revising

Edit: Remove negativity (*unfortunately, we can't, the company was forced, inadvisable*). Explain the increase with specific figures.

Proofread: Use quotation marks around *defensive* to show its special sense. Spell out *percent* after *300*.

Evaluate: Is there any other way to help readers accept this bad news?

DRAFT

Beginning January 1 your monthly payment for health care benefits will be increased $119 a month for a total payment of $639 for each employee. ← *Hits readers with bad news without any preparation*

Every year health care costs go up. Although we considered dropping other benefits, Northern decided that the best plan was to keep the present comprehensive package. Unfortunately, we can't do that unless we pass along some of the extra cost to you. Last year the company was forced to absorb the total increase in health care premiums. However, such a plan this year is inadvisable. ← *Offers no explanation for increase; sounds defensive and arbitrary*

We did everything possible to avoid the sharp increase in costs to you this year. A rate schedule describing the increases in payments for your family and dependents is enclosed. ← *Fails to take credit for absorbing previous increases*

REVISION

NORTHERN INDUSTRIES, INC.

Overview | Whiteboards | Tasks | Discussions | Files | Meetings | People | News

News From HR — Maintaining Quality Health Care

Begins with positive buffer → Health care programs have always been an important part of our commitment to employees at Northern Industries, Inc. We are proud that our total benefits package continues to rank among the best in the country.

Explains why costs are rising → Such a comprehensive package does not come cheaply. In the last decade, health care costs alone have risen over 300 percent. We are told that several factors fuel the cost spiral: an aging population, technology improvements, the increased cost of patient services, and "defensive" medicine practiced by doctors to prevent lawsuits.

Reveals bad news clearly but embeds it in paragraph → Just two years ago, our monthly health care cost for each employee was $515. It rose to $569 last year. We were able to absorb that jump without increasing your contribution. But this year's hike to $639 forces us to ask you to share the increase. To maintain your current health care benefits, you will be paying $119 a month. The enclosed rate schedule describes the costs for families and dependents.

Ends positively by stressing the company's major share of the costs → Northern continues to pay the major portion of your health care program ($520 each month). We think it's a wise investment.

Attachments (1)

☐ Health Care Rate Schedule.docx
132 Kb View Download

says nothing about increasing costs. For a smooth transition, the second paragraph begins with a key idea from the opening (*comprehensive package*). The reasons section discusses rising costs with explanations and figures. The bad news (*you will be paying $119 a month*) is clearly presented but embedded within the paragraph. Throughout, the writer strives to show the fairness of the company's position. The ending, which does not refer to the bad news, emphasizes how much the company is paying and what a wise investment it is.

Notice that the entire message demonstrates a kinder, gentler approach than that shown in the first draft. Of prime importance in breaking bad news to employees is providing clear, convincing reasons that explain the decision. Parallel to this internal blog post, the message was also sent by e-mail. In smaller companies in which some workers do not have company e-mail, a hard-copy memo would be posted prominently on bulletin boards and in the lunchroom.

Saying *No* to Job Applicants

Being refused a job is one of life's major rejections. Tactless letters intensify the blow (*Unfortunately, you were not among the candidates selected for . . .*).

You can reduce the receiver's disappointment somewhat by using the indirect strategy—with one important variation. In the reasons section, it is wise to be vague in explaining why the candidate was not selected. First, giving concrete reasons may be painful to the receiver (*Your grade point average of 2.7 was low compared with the GPAs of other candidates*). Second, and more important, providing extra information may prove fatal in a lawsuit. Hiring and firing decisions generate considerable litigation today. To avoid charges of discrimination or wrongful actions, legal advisors warn organizations to keep employment rejection letters general, simple, and short.

The job refusal letter shown in Figure 9.16 is tactful but intentionally vague. It implies that the applicant's qualifications don't match those needed for the position, but the letter

---

Figure 9.16 Saying *No* to Job Candidates

PIONEER CAPITAL

510 East 74th Street
212.445.9800

New York, NY 10021
www.pioneercapital.com

June 6, 2015

Ms. Maya Bostwick
3927 Juniper Avenue
Cherry Hill, NJ 08002

Dear Ms. Bostwick:

Thanks for letting us review your résumé submitted for our advertised management trainee opening.

We received a number of impressive résumés for this opening. Although another candidate was selected, your interest in our organization is appreciated. So that you may continue your search for a position at another organization, I am writing to you immediately.

With your credentials I am certain you will find a suitable position because you have a great deal to offer. Please accept my best wishes for the future.

Sincerely,

PIONEER CAPITAL

Malu Sun

Malu Sun
Director, Human Resources

Annotations:
- Doesn't indicate good or bad news
- To prevent possible lawsuits, gives no explanation
- Shows appreciation
- Places bad news in dependent clause
- Ends with best wishes

© Cengage Learning 2015

doesn't reveal anything specific. The writer could have included this alternate closing: *We wish you every success in finding a position that exactly fits your qualifications.*

The following checklist summarizes tips on how to communicate negative news inside and outside your organization.

CHECKLIST ▶▶|
Conveying Negative News

Prewrite

- Decide whether to use the direct or indirect strategy. If the bad news is minor and will not upset the receiver, open directly. If the message is personally damaging and will upset the receiver, consider techniques to reduce its pain.

- Think through the reasons for the bad news.

- Remember that your primary goal is to make the receiver understand and accept the bad news as well as to maintain a positive image of you and your organization.

Plan the Opening

- In the indirect strategy, start with a buffer. Pay a compliment to the reader, show appreciation for something done, or mention some mutual understanding. Avoid raising false hopes or thanking the reader for something you will refuse.

- In the direct strategy, begin with a straightforward statement of the bad news.

Provide Reasons in the Body

- Except in credit and job refusals, explain the reasons for the negative message.

- In customer mishaps, clarify what went wrong, what you are doing to resolve the problem, and how you will prevent it from happening again.

- Use objective, nonjudgmental, and nondiscriminatory language.

- Avoid negativity (e.g., words such as *unfortunately, unwilling,* and *impossible*) and potentially damaging statements.

- Show how your decision is fair and perhaps benefits the reader or others, if possible.

Soften the Bad News

- Reduce the impact of bad news by using (a) a subordinate clause, (b) the passive voice, (c) a long sentence, or (d) a long paragraph.

- Consider implying the refusal, but be certain it is clear.

- Suggest an alternative, such as a lower price, a different product, a longer payment period, or a substitute. Provide help in implementing an alternative.

- Offset disappointment by offering gifts, a reduced price, benefits, tokens of appreciation, or something appropriate.

Close Pleasantly

- Supply more information about an alternative, look forward to future relations, or offer good wishes and compliments.

- Maintain a bright, personal tone. Avoid referring to the refusal.

Zooming in

Your Turn: Applying Your Skills at Carnival Corporation

After the Costa Concordia shipwreck and several high-profile engine fires crippling cruise ships owned by Carnival or one of its ten subsidiaries, the company has embarked on a comprehensive safety overhaul. Among several initiatives, the cruise line is improving redundant systems. Each ship of the Splendor class has already been retrofitted with new equipment designed to activate more reliably the existing backup generator when the other fails. The company hopes that improvements to the two separate engine rooms will make devastating power blackouts at sea much less likely.

Unfortunately, the Carnival Starlight requires extensive repairs. Parts needed for the retrofit are made in Asia and will not arrive in time for the vessel's January voyages. Carnival must notify more than 10,000 passengers that they cannot sail on January 16, 23, and 30 as planned. Scrambling to offer remedies, the guest services staff identifies two choices. One is a full refund of the cruise fare, any air travel provided by Carnival, company-provided trip insurance, as well as government fees and taxes. The refund will be issued automatically within ten business days unless the traveler chooses the second option, rebooking the voyage.[37]

© ZUMA Wire Service/Alamy

Vacationers wishing to reschedule their trips must proceed to Carnival.com immediately. They can choose to sail on another ship in January or on the Carnival Starlight at a later date but must complete their voyage within 24 months after the original departure date. In both cases, the cruise rates will not increase. Alternatively, travelers choosing to rebook can opt for a 25 percent discount on any two- to nine-day Carnival cruise within 24 months. Change fees for independently purchased air travel will be reimbursed up to $200 in onboard credit. Proof of payment must be faxed to the Guest Services Department at 305-460-6744. Travelers can call the Guest Services Department at 1-877-CARNIVAL.

YOUR TASK. Assume that you are a trainee at Carnival. The assistant to the vice president of guest services asks you to draft the bad-news letter to 10,000 customers. Ponder your strategy. Will you use a direct or an indirect strategy? Decide whether you should apologize, but be sure to explain the options clearly to your disappointed readers.

Summary of Learning Objectives

1 Understand the strategies of business communicators in conveying negative news, apply the 3-x-3 writing process, and avoid legal liability. All businesses occasionally deal with problems. Experienced communicators have many goals in delivering unfavorable news: explaining clearly and completely, projecting a professional image, showing empathy, being fair, and maintaining friendly relations. Applying the 3-x-3 writing process helps you prepare, draft, and revise your message so that it accomplishes your purpose. Mindful communicators avoid careless and abusive language, which is actionable when it is false, damages a person's reputation, and is "published" (spoken within the presence of others or written).

2 Distinguish between the direct and indirect strategies in conveying unfavorable news. The direct strategy reveals the main idea immediately. It is preferable when the unfavorable news is not personally damaging, when the receiver could overlook the bad news, when the organizational culture favors directness, when the receiver prefers directness, and when firmness is necessary. The indirect strategy involves beginning with a buffer and delaying the bad news until reasons have been presented. The indirect strategy works well when the bad news is personally upsetting, may provoke a hostile reaction, threatens the customer relationship, or is unexpected.

3 Explain the components of effective negative messages, including opening with a buffer, apologizing, showing empathy, presenting the reasons, cushioning the bad news, and closing pleasantly. If you choose the indirect strategy for a negative message, begin with a buffer, such as a compliment, appreciation, a point of agreement, a statement of fact, understanding, or some part of the message that represents more favorable news. Then explain the reasons that necessitate the bad news, trying to cite benefits to the reader or others. If you use the direct strategy, begin directly with the bad news followed by the reasons. When apologizing, do so sincerely, accept responsibility, and use good judgment. Throughout a negative message, strive to cushion the bad news by positioning it strategically, using the passive voice, accentuating the positive, choosing positive words, and suggesting a compromise or alternative. Close pleasantly with a forward-looking goodwill statement.

4 Apply effective techniques for refusing typical requests or claims as well as for presenting bad news to customers in print or online. Typical requests ask for favors, money, information, action, and other items. When the answer will be disappointing, use the reasons-before-refusal pattern. When a company disappoints its customers, most organizations (a) call the individual involved, (b) describe the problem and apologize (when the company is to blame), (c) explain why the problem occurred and what is being done to prevent its recurrence, and (d) follow up with a message that documents the phone call and promotes goodwill. Many businesses engage with customers online by monitoring social networks for negative comments and troubleshooting as needed. In announcing rate increases, provide a plausible reason for the price hike. In denying claims, begin indirectly, provide reasons for the refusal, and close pleasantly, looking forward to future business. When refusing credit, avoid language that causes hard feelings, strive to retain the customer on a cash basis, prepare for possible future credit, and avoid disclosures that could cause a lawsuit.

5 Describe and apply effective techniques for delivering bad news within organizations. When delivering bad news personally to a superior, gather all the information, prepare and rehearse, explain what happened and how the problem will be fixed, consider taking a colleague with you, think about timing, and be patient with the reaction. In delivering bad news to groups of employees, use the indirect strategy but be sure to provide clear, convincing reasons that explain the decision. In refusing job applicants, however, keep letters short, general, and tactful.

Chapter Review

1. What are your most important goals in communicating negative news? (Obj. 1)

2. When delivering bad news, how can a communicator reduce the bad feelings of the receiver? (Obj. 1)

3. When is the direct strategy more effective than the indirect strategy in conveying negative news? (Obj. 1)

4. When is the indirect strategy in communicating bad news preferable? (Obj. 2)

5. What are the major differences between the direct and indirect strategies in delivering bad news? (Obj. 2)

6. What is a buffer? Name five or more techniques to buffer the opening of a bad-news message. (Obj. 3)

7. What are some tips for business writers wishing to apologize effectively? (Obj. 3)

8. What does conveying empathy mean in delivering apologies? (Obj. 3)

9. Name four or more techniques that cushion the delivery of bad news. (Obj. 3)

10. What are some strategies to manage adverse news on social networking sites and blogs effectively? (Obj. 4)

11. Identify a process used by a majority of business professionals in resolving problems with disappointed customers. (Obj.4)

12. If you must deny the claim of a customer who is clearly at fault, should you respond by putting the blame squarely on the customer? (Obj. 4)

13. What is an effective technique in announcing rate increases and price hikes? (Obj. 4)

14. How can a subordinate tactfully, professionally, and safely deliver upsetting news personally to a superior? (Obj. 5)

15. What are some channels that large organizations may use when delivering bad news to employees? (Obj. 5)

Critical Thinking

1. Robert Bies, professor of management at Georgetown University, believes that an important ethical guideline in dealing with bad news is never to shock the recipient: "Bad news should never come as a surprise. Failure to warn senior leadership of impending bad news, such as poor sales or a loss of a major client, is a cardinal sin. So is failure to warn subordinates about mistakes in their performance and provide an opportunity for them to make corrections and improve." Discuss the motivation of people who keep quiet and struggle with dispensing bad news. (Objs. 1–3)

2. Respected industry analyst Gartner Research issued a report naming social networking as one of the top ten disruptive (i.e., innovative) influences shaping information technology in the next five years.[38] Should organizations fear websites where consumers post negative messages about products and services? What actions can companies take in response to this disruptive influence? (Objs. 1–4)

3. Consider times when you have been aware that others were using the indirect strategy in writing or speaking to you. How did you react? (Obj. 2)

4. Living in Pittsburgh, Lauren Bossers worked virtually by e-mail and phone for a supply chain management software company in Dallas. She was laid off by phone, too. Bossers' manager had given her one day's notice; however, the news was still "shocking," and she responded with just *yes* or *no* to the HR officer who called: "I wasn't rude, but I didn't think it was my job to make them feel better," Bossers said. Software developer Jeff Langr was fired during a teleconference on Skype. What might be some advantages and disadvantages to being let go remotely, if any? Why might it be a good idea to rein in one's frustration and anger? (Objs. 1, 5)

5. **Ethical Issue:** You work for a large corporation with headquarters in a small town. Recently, you received shoddy repair work and a huge bill from a local garage. Your car's transmission has the same problems that it did before you took it in for repair. You know that a complaint letter written on your corporation's stationery would be much more authoritative than one written on plain stationery. Should you use corporation stationery? (Obj. 1)

Writing Improvement Exercises

9.1 Organizational Strategies (Objs. 1–3)

YOUR TASK. Identify which organizational strategy you would use for the following messages: direct or indirect.

a. E-commerce powerhouse Zappos must tell its 24 million customers that hackers gained access to critical information including their e-mail addresses, billing and shipping addresses, phone numbers, passwords, and the last four digits of their credit card numbers.

b. A letter from an insurance company announcing that customers' auto insurance will no longer include liability coverage unless they switch to a new plan.

c. An announcement at Amazon.com that prices will now include state taxes, as mandated by new laws.

d. A letter from a theme park refusing the request of a visitor who wants free tickets. The visitor was unhappy that he had to wait in line a very long time to ride a new thrill roller coaster.

e. An e-mail from a manager refusing an employee's request for funds and time off to attend a professional conference.

f. An e-mail from the manager denying an employee's request for special parking privileges. The employee works closely with the manager on many projects.

g. An announcement to employees that a fitness specialist has canceled a scheduled lunchtime talk and cannot reschedule.

h. A form letter from an insurance company announcing new policy requirements that many policyholders may resent. If policyholders do not indicate the plan they prefer, they may lose their insurance coverage.

i. An e-mail from an executive refusing a manager's proposal to upgrade the department's computers. The executive and the manager both appreciate efficient, straightforward messages.

9.2 Employing Passive-Voice Verbs (Obj. 3)

YOUR TASK. Revise the following sentences to present the bad news with passive-voice verbs.

a. We cannot offer free shipping for orders under $100.

b. This hospital has a strict policy of not admitting patients until we have verified their insurance coverage.

c. Because our liability insurance no longer covers visitors, we are postponing indefinitely requests for company tours.

d. Your car rental insurance coverage does not cover large SUVs.

e. Company policy prevents us from offering health and dental benefits until employees have been on the job for 12 months.

9.3 Subordinating Bad News (Obj. 3)

YOUR TASK. Revise the following sentences to position the bad news in a subordinate clause. (**Hint:** Consider beginning the clause with *Although*.) Use passive-voice verbs for the bad news.

a. A shipping strike makes it impossible for us to ship your complete order at this point in time. However, we are able to send two corner workstations now, and you should receive them within five days.

b. We were forced to stop taking orders for flowers the week before Mother's Day. To make up for this disappointment, we apologize and ask you to try again with free shipping for the next week.

c. We now offer all of our catalog choices at our website, which is always current. We are sorry to report that we no longer mail print catalogs. Our sustainability goals made it impossible for us to continue doing that.

d. We appreciate your interest in our organization, but we are unable to extend an employment offer to you at this time.

e. The shipment of your last order was late for a reason. We had some really large orders that had to be filled ahead of yours and tied up our facilities. After that tie-up, we realized we had to improve our shipping process. Your next order will arrive within a week. That's a promise.

9.4 Implying Bad News (Obj. 3)

YOUR TASK. Revise the following statements to *imply* the bad news. If possible, use passive-voice verbs and subordinate clauses to further de-emphasize the bad news.

a. Unfortunately, we find it impossible to contribute to your excellent and worthwhile fund-raising campaign this year. At present all the funds of our organization are needed to lease equipment and offices for our new branch in Hartford. We hope to be able to support this commendable endeavor in the future.

b. We cannot ship our fresh fruit baskets c.o.d. Your order was not accompanied by payment, so we are not shipping it. We have it ready, though, and will rush it to its destination as soon as you call us with your credit card number.

c. Because of the holiday period, all our billboard space was used this month. Therefore, we are sorry to say that we could not give your charitable group free display space. However, next month, after the holidays, we hope to display your message as we promised.

Activities

Note: All Documents for Analysis are provided at **www.cengagebrain.com** for you to download and revise.

9.5 Document for Analysis: Nuptials Nixed at Napa Inn (Objs. 1–4)

YOUR TASK. Analyze the following poorly written request refusal. List its weaknesses. If your instructor directs, revise it using the suggestions you learned in this chapter.

Current date

Ms. Heather Herreira
1180 Blossom Hill Road
San Jose, CA 95118

Dear Ms. Herreira:

Unfortunately, we must advise you that the wedding date you request in your letter of March 12 at the Napa Valley Inn is unavailable. Sadly, we are fully booked for all of the Saturdays in June, as you probably already suspected.

June is our busiest month, and smart brides make their reservations many months—even years—in advance. That's because the Napa Valley Inn is the ideal romantic getaway for weddings. With unparalleled cuisine and service, along with panoramic Napa Valley and vineyard views, our Inn offers unique, intimate ambiance in a breathtaking location for your special event.

We apologize in advance if we have caused you any inconvenience. However, if you could change your wedding date to the middle of the week, we would try to accommodate your party. We do have a few midweek spots open in June, but even those dates are rapidly filling up. With 45 Mediterranean-style rooms and suites, each with its own sunny private terrace, the Napa Valley Inn is the perfect location for you and your partner to begin your married lives. Afternoon ceremonies typically begin at 11 a.m., while golden sunsets at the Napa Valley Inn offer a romantic prelude of the evening to come. Evening ceremonies usually begin at 6 p.m. I'm available if you want to arrange something.

Sincerely,

9.6 Document for Analysis: Claim Denial—No New Droid for You (Objs. 1–4)

YOUR TASK. Analyze the following-mail. List its weaknesses. If your instructor directs, revise it using the suggestions you learned in this chapter. Add any needed information.

To: Lynda Brownsmith <lbrownsmith@aol.com>
From: Michael Quinn <mquinn@unitedservice.com>
Subject: Claim Refusal
Cc:
Bcc:

Dear Ms. Brownsmith:

This message is being sent to you to inform you that warranty repairs or replacements are not available for damage caused by operator fault. The dot inside your smartphone indicates in bright red that the device suffered prolonged exposure to liquid. The phone also shows signs of heavy external abuse—quite rightly excluded from coverage under your protection plan.

Your phone retailer, Premier Wireless, at 901 Saint Charles Avenue, forwarded your device to us. Our service technician made an inspection. That's when he made the discovery that your Droid had not been treated with proper caution and care. The inside was gunky and apparently the device had been subjected to blunt force. You are lucky that the touch screen did not crack or break and that you didn't lose all your data irretrievably since you apparently didn't bother to arrange for a backup. Today's smartphones are sophisticated high-tech devices. They must be handled with utmost respect.

Our Peace of Mind Plan gets rave reviews from users. They love the protection their expensive equipment enjoys at a low monthly cost of $5.99. However, the manufacturer's warranty on your Droid covers only this one thing: manufacturing defects. Your warranty has expired by now, but it wouldn't cover neglect and abuse anyway. Your Peace of Mind Plan is in effect but only covers you for theft, loss, and malfunction. It explicitly excludes liquid and physical damage. In any case, there is always a deductible of $89. We can't replace the Droid at no charge. But we could sell you a remanufactured model, at a cost of $49 plus tax. Your other option is to purchase a new device at full retail cost. Furthermore, since you have a two-year contract, you will be eligible for an upgrade as you are nearing month 20.

Let us know what you want to do. We pride ourselves on our unparalleled customer service.

Sincerely,

9.7 Document for Analysis: Saying *No* to Time Off for Newborns in Need (Objs. 1–5)

YOUR TASK. Analyze the following poorly written e-mail, and list its weaknesses. If your instructor directs, revise it using the suggestions you learned in this and previous chapters.

To: Amanda Fox <afox@financialsolutions.com>
From: Gabriel Lugo <glugo@financialsolutions.com>
Subject: Pulling Plug on Newborns in Need
Cc:
Bcc:

Hey, Foxie, you're one in a million. But we can't give you time off to work on that charity fashion show/luncheon thingy you want to coordinate. And Financial Solutions can't make a big contribution as we've done in previous years. It's no, no, no, all the way around.

Look, we admire the work you have done for the Newborns in Need Foundation. It has raised millions of dollars to make differences in the lives of babies, particularly premature ones. But we need you here! Hey, let's think about us.

With the upcoming release of our Planning Guide 3.0, we need you to interview clients. We need you to make video testimonials, and you are the one to search for stories about customer successes. Plus a zillion other tasks! Our new website will launch in just six short weeks, and all that killer content stuff must be in final form. With the economy in the tank and our bare-bones staff, you certainly must realize that each and every team member must be here and making a difference. If our Planning Guide 3.0 doesn't make a big splash, we'll all have a lot of time off.

Due to the fact that we're the worldwide leader in on-demand financial planning and reporting software, and in view of the fact that we are about to launch our most important new product ever, you just gotta understand our position. When things get better, we might be able to return back to our past practices. But not now!

Gabe

9.8 Document for Analysis: Hackers Hijack E-Mail Addresses (Objs. 1–4)

YOUR TASK. Analyze the following poorly written e-mail, and list at least seven weaknesses. If your instructor directs, revise it using the suggestions you learned in this and previous chapters.

To: Kara Khalial <kkhalial@coastal.net>
From: Justin Small <jsmall@princetonpayment.org>
Subject: Customer Security Incident at Princeton Payment Systems
Cc:

Companies and individuals across the country are experiencing more and more security breaches. This is to let you know that you are receiving this e-mail because of a recent unfortunate security breach at Princeton Payment Systems. Rest assured, however, that as a customer of Princeton, your privacy was never at risk. We promise to guard your privacy around the clock.

Hackers last week were able to maliciously exploit a new function that we were trying to use to make the customer log-in process faster for you and our other customers. The hackers were ingenious and malicious, going to extreme lengths to gain access to some customer addresses at Princeton. You should now beware of scams that may result from your address being used in phishing scams. To learn more, go to http://www.fdic.gov/consumers/consumer/alerts/phishing.html.

To provide even more information about this incident, the U.S. postal service will bring you a letter with more information. Taking your privacy very seriously, e-mail addresses are heavily protected here at Princeton. Within hours of the hacker break-in, the log-in mechanism was disabled and a new procedure was established. The user is now required to enter their e-mail address and their password before they can log in successfully. E-mail addresses were the only

information the hackers got. Other information such as account information and other personal information were never risked.

We appreciate you being a Princeton customer.

Sincerely,

9.9 Request Refusal: Try Applying Online and On Time (Objs. 1–4)

〈 **E-mail** 〉 〈 **Web** 〉

Adobe Systems Incorporated prides itself on its commitment to employees who receive generous benefits and enjoy a supportive corporate culture. This core value may have contributed to the company's ranking among the top 50 of *Fortune* magazine's 100 Best Companies to Work For. The software giant is also known for its community involvement and corporate social responsibility efforts. This is why, like most large companies, Adobe receives many requests for sponsorships of charity events and community projects. True to its innovative spirit, the software company has streamlined the application process by providing an online sponsorship request form at its website.

You work in Corporate Affairs/Community Relations at Adobe and periodically help decide which nonprofits will obtain support. Just yesterday you received an e-mail from the Pink Dragons of San Diego, a dragon boat racing team of breast cancer survivors. The ancient Chinese sport has spread around the globe with competitions held not only in Asia but also in many Western countries. Dragon boat racing has gained popularity in North America among breast cancer patients who bond with fellow survivors, engage in healthy competition, and exercise regularly on the water. Synchronicity and technique are more important than brute strength, which is the main reason even recreational paddlers enjoy this fast-growing water sport.

The newly formed survivor team would like Adobe to sponsor a dragon boat festival in San Diego in less than a month, an event potentially drawing at least 20 survivor teams that would compete against each other. Your company is already funding several cancer charities and has a policy of sponsoring many causes. Naturally, no corporate giving program has infinite funds, nor can it green-light every request. Adobe steers clear of religious, political, and "pornographic" events. The team judging the sponsorship entries wants to ensure that each proposal reaches audiences affiliated with Adobe. Most important, applicants must submit their requests at least six weeks before the event.

YOUR TASK. As a junior staff member in Corporate Affairs/Community Relations, write an e-mail to Pink Dragon captain Josephine Rosa (jrosa@pinkdragons.org) refusing her initial request and explaining the Adobe sponsorship philosophy and submission rules.

9.10 Request Refusal: Advocating for Abused Children (Objs. 1–4)

As a vice president of a financial services company, you serve many clients and they sometimes ask your company to contribute to their favorite charities. You recently received a letter from Paulina Ramirez asking for a substantial contribution to the National Court Appointed Special Advocate (CASA) Association. On visits to your office, she has told you about its programs to recruit, train, and support volunteers in their work with abused children. She herself is active in your town as a CASA volunteer, helping neglected children find safe, permanent homes. She told you that children with CASA volunteers are more likely to be adopted and are less likely to reenter the child welfare system. You have a soft spot in your heart for children and especially for those who are mistreated. You sincerely want to support CASA and its good work. But times are tough, and you can't be as generous as you have been in the past. Ms. Ramirez wrote a special letter to you asking you to become a Key contributor, with a pledge of $1,000.

YOUR TASK. Write a refusal letter that maintains good relations with your client. Address it to Ms. Paulina Ramirez, 4382 Congress Avenue, Austin, TX 78701.

9.11 Request Refusal: No Favors for Jamba Juice (Objs. 1–4)

In an aggressive expansion effort, Jamba Juice became a good customer of your software company. You have enjoyed the business it brought, and you are also quite fond of its products—especially Banana Berry and Mega Mango smoothies. Jamba Inc. is in the midst of expanding its menu with the goal of becoming the Starbucks of the smoothie. "Just as Starbucks defined the category of coffee, Jamba has the opportunity to define the category of the healthy snack," said analyst Brian Moore. One goal of Jamba is to boost the frequency of customer visits by offering some products that are more filling. Then it could attract hungry customers as well as thirsty ones. It was experimenting with adding grains such as oatmeal or nuts such as almonds so that a smoothie packs more substance and could substitute for a meal.

You receive a letter from Joe Wong, your business friend and contact at Jamba Juice. He asks you to do him and Jamba Juice a favor. He wants to set up a juice-tasting bar in your company cafeteria to test his new experimental drinks. All the drinks would be free, of course, but employees would have to fill out forms to evaluate each recipe. The details could be worked out later.

You definitely support healthy snacks, but you think this idea is terrible. First of all, your company doesn't even have a cafeteria. It has a small lunchroom, and employees bring their own food. Second, you would be embarrassed to ask your boss to do this favor for Jamba Juice, despite the business it has brought your company.

YOUR TASK. Write a letter that retains good customer relations with Jamba Juice but refuses this request. What reasons can you give, and what alternatives are available? Address your message to Joe Wong, Vice President, Product Development, Jamba Inc., 450 Golden Gate Avenue, San Francisco, CA 94102.[39]

9.12 Request Refusal: Party Over for 21 and Under (Objs. 1–4)

The world's largest cruise line finds itself in a difficult position. Carnival climbed to the No. 1 spot by promoting fun at sea and appealing to younger customers who were drawn to onboard discos, swim-up bars, and hassle-free partying. But apparently the partying of high school and college students went too far. Roving bands of teens had virtually taken over some cruises in recent years. Travel agents complained of "drunken, loud behavior," as reported by Mike Driscoll, editor of *Cruise Week*.

To crack down, Carnival raised the drinking age from 18 to 21 and required more chaperoning of school groups. However, young individual travelers were still unruly and disruptive. Therefore, Carnival instituted a new policy, effective immediately. No one under 21 may travel unless accompanied by an adult over 25. Vicki Freed, Carnival's vice president for marketing, said, "We will turn them back at the docks, and they will not get refunds." As Demetrice Hawkins, a Carnival marketing manager, you must respond to the inquiry of Elizabeth Neil, of Leisure World Travel, a Chicago travel agency that features special spring- and summer-break packages for college and high school students.

Leisure World Travel has been one of Carnival's best customers. However, Carnival no longer wants to encourage unaccompanied young people. You must refuse the request of Ms. Neil to help set up student tour packages. Carnival discourages even chaperoned tours. Its target market is now families. You must write to Leisure World Travel and break the bad news. Try to promote fun-filled, carefree cruises destined for sunny, exotic ports of call that remove guests from the stresses of everyday life. Despite its recent trouble, Carnival attracts more passengers than any other cruise line—nearly 4.4 million people a year from all over the world. Over 98 percent of Carnival's guests say that they were well satisfied.

YOUR TASK. Write your letter to Elizabeth Neil, Leisure World Travel, 480 West Harrison Street, Chicago, IL 60607. Send her a schedule for spring and summer Caribbean cruises. Tell her you will call during the week of January 15 to help her plan special family tour packages.[40]

9.13 Request Refusal: Learn to Live With a Noisy Tenant (Objs. 1–4)

Web

As the owner of Two Buckhead Plaza, you must respond to the request of Manuel Quinones, one of the tenants in your three-story office building. Mr. Quinones, a CPA, demands that you immediately evict a neighboring tenant who plays loud music throughout the day, interfering with Mr. Quinones' conversations with clients and with his concentration. The noisy tenant, Scott Eslan, seems to operate an entertainment booking agency and spends long hours in his office. You know you can't evict Mr. Eslan because, as a legal commercial tenant, he is entitled to conduct his business. However, you might consider adding soundproofing, an expense that you would prefer to share with Mr. Eslan and Mr. Quinones. You might also discuss limiting the time of day that Mr. Eslan could make noise.

YOUR TASK. Before responding to Mr. Quinones, you decide to find out more about commercial tenancy. Use the Web to search the keywords *commercial eviction*. Then develop a course of action. In a letter to Mr. Quinones, deny his request but retain his goodwill. Tell him how you plan to resolve the problem. Write to Manuel Quinones, CPA, Suite 300, Two Buckhead Plaza, 3050 Peachtree Rd., NW, Atlanta, GA 30305. Your instructor may also ask you to write an appropriate message to Mr. Scott Eslan, Suite 330.

9.14 Claim Denial: Complaining on the Web (Objs. 1–4)

Social Media **Web**

The growth of social networking has also spawned many websites dedicated to customer reviews and complaints—for example, Angie's List, which profiles local service companies, contractors, and professionals. More specifically, companies such as CruiseCritic.com focus solely on vacation travel by ship. Visit Complaints.com, Ripoff Report, or another complaint site. Study ten or more complaints about products or companies (e.g., iPod, Starbucks, Delta Air Lines).

YOUR TASK. Select one complaint and, as a company employee, respond to it employing some of the techniques presented in this chapter. Submit a copy of the complaint along with your response to your instructor. Your instructor may request that you write an e-mail or a letter.

9.15 Claim Denial: Going Ape After Botched Gorilla Party (Objs. 1–4)

E-mail **Web**

BuyCostumes, the world's largest online costume and accessories retailer, is proud of its extensive stock of costumes, its liberal return policy, and its many satisfied customers. But one day an e-mail arrived with a request that went beyond the company's ability to deliver. The customer said that he had ordered the Gorilla Blinky Eye With Chest costume. This popular gorilla costume comes with a unique gorilla mask, attractive suit with rubber chest, foot covers, and hands. The customer complained that the gorilla costume did not arrive until two days after his Halloween party. He planned an elaborate party with a gorilla theme, and he was extremely unhappy that he did not have his costume. He asks BuyCostumes to reimburse $300 that he spent on theme-related decorations, which he says were useless when he failed to receive his costume.

As a customer-service representative, you checked his order and found that it was not received until five days before Halloween, the busiest time of the year for your company. The order was filled the next day, but standard shipping requires three to six business days for delivery. The customer did not order express or premium delivery; his shipping option was marked "Standard."

You showed the e-mail to the owner, Mr. Getz, who said that this request was ludicrous. However, he wanted to retain the customer's goodwill. Obviously, BuyCostumes was not going to shell out $300 for late delivery of a costume. But Mr. Getz suggested that the company would allow the customer to return the costume (in its original packaging). In addition, BuyCostumes would send a digital coupon for $20 off the next costume purchase.

YOUR TASK. Mr. Getz asks you to write an e-mail that retains the goodwill of this customer. Address your e-mail to Christopher King. Check the BuyCostumes company website for more information.

9.16 Claim Denial: No Receipt, No Replacement! (Objs. 1–4)

E-mail   Web

As a customer-service team member for Schwenger, maker of fine Swiss luggage, you have exchanged a few e-mails with Bert Mayes of New Orleans, Louisiana, about his carry-on travel case. Mr. Mayes inquired about repairs to the wheels of his favorite travel bag. He wrote that the plastic tread was falling apart; to prove his point, he sent a few photos showing the bag. Schwenger has no repair facilities in the United States but would consider replacing the product under its limited lifetime warranty if certain conditions are met.

You notified Bert Mayes that to consider a warranty claim, you would need various items: a front and side view of the product and two or three images of the defect, the SKU number (e.g., WA-7853-02, GA-7305), and the PO number (e.g., ONJ1.4537, KNJ1.2486). You indicated where to find the manufacturer's fabric labels with the product information sewn into the seam. Furthermore, to comply with warranty claims, you require a brief description of the defect and a scan or fax of the dated sales receipt. You prefer e-mail or fax claims, but Schwenger does have a service location in St. Louis, Missouri, and you urge customers without access to e-mail or fax to ship their damaged items to that address along with the required documentation: GRT Group, Attn: Schwenger Warranty Claims, 4702 Eastport Center Drive, St. Louis, MO 63148.

Bert Mayes has e-mailed you the photos, a description of the defect, and his contact information; however, he insists he can find neither the proof of purchase nor the SKU or PO numbers. He seems to remember that he bought the bag at wholesaler Costco four years ago. You could suggest that Mr. Mayes ship the bag to your Missouri service address. To show goodwill, you do a quick Web search and find Militello's Shoe & Luggage Repair, 2413 Magazine St., New Orleans, LA 70114. Although not an official Schwenger repair facility, Militello's has received many favorable reviews on Angie's List. As a last resort, you could direct Mr. Mayes to this shop to inquire about a repair at his own expense.

YOUR TASK. You must deny this warranty claim unless Mr. Mayes produces the required items. Say *no* gently, and consider how you could keep the customer's goodwill. Draft an e-mail to Bert Mayes (*bmayes@outlook.com*).

9.17 Claim Denial: Expensive Eyeglasses Lost on Plane (Objs. 1–4)

Atlantic Northern Airlines (ANA) had an unhappy customer. Kristen Linder-Bowls flew from Washington, DC, to Los Angeles. The flight stopped briefly at Denver International Airport , where she got off the plane for half an hour. When she returned to her seat, her $400 prescription reading glasses were gone. She asked the flight attendant where the glasses were, and the attendant said they probably were thrown away since the cleaning crew had come in with big bags and tossed everything in them. Ms. Linder-Bowls tried to locate the glasses through the airline's lost-and-found service, but she failed.

Then she wrote a strong letter to the airline demanding reimbursement for the loss. She felt that it was obvious that she was returning to her seat. The airline, however, knows that an overwhelming number of passengers arriving at hubs switch planes for their connecting flights. The airline does not know who is returning. What's more, flight attendants usually announce that the plane is continuing to another city and that passengers who are returning should take their belongings. Cabin cleaning crews speed through planes removing newspapers, magazines, leftover foods, and trash. Airlines feel no responsibility for personal items left in cabins.[41]

YOUR TASK. As a staff member of the customer relations department of Atlantic Northern Airlines, deny the customer's claim but retain her goodwill using techniques learned in this chapter. The airline never refunds cash, but it might consider travel vouchers for the value of the glasses. Remember that apologies cost nothing. Write a claim denial to Mrs. Kristen Linder-Bowls, 534 Cadillac Avenue, Venice, CA 90034.

9.18 Claim Denial: Raising a Stink About Charge for Smoking in the Room (Objs. 1–4)

Recently, the Metropol Grand Hotel embarked on a two-year plan to provide enhanced value and improved product quality to its guests. It always strives to exceed guest expectations. As part of this effort, Metropol Grand Hotel has been refurbishing many rooms with updated finishes. The new carpet, paint, upholstery, and draperies, however, absorb the heavy odor of cigarette smoke. To protect the hotel's investment, Metropol Grand Hotel enforces a strict nonsmoking policy for its nonsmoking rooms.

Metropol Grand Hotel makes sure that guests know about its policy regarding smoking in nonsmoking rooms. It posts a notice in each nonsmoking room, and it gives guests a handout from the manager detailing its policy and the consequences for smoking in nonsmoking rooms. The handout clearly says, "Should a guest opt to disregard our nonsmoking policy, we will process a fee of $150 to the guest's account." For those guests who prefer to smoke, a smoking accommodation can be provided.

On May 10 Trevor H. Taylor was a guest in the hotel. He stayed in a room clearly marked "Nonsmoking." After he left, the room cleaners reported that the room smelled of smoke. According to hotel policy, a charge of $150 was processed to Mr. Taylor's credit card. Mr. Taylor has written to demand that the $150 charge be removed. He doesn't deny that he smoked in the room. He just thinks that he should not have to pay.

YOUR TASK. As hotel manager, deny Mr. Taylor's claim. You would certainly like to see Mr. Taylor return as a Metropol Grand Hotel guest, but you cannot budge on your smoking policy. Address your response to Mr. Trevor H. Taylor, 580 Lottie Street, Bellingham, WA 98225.

9.19 Bad News to Customers: Picking Perfect Stepper for Fit Power Gym (Objs. 1–4)

You are delighted to receive a large order from Phil Norton at Fit Power Gym. This order includes two Lifecycle Trainers (at $1,295 each), four Pro Abdominal Boards (at $295 each), three Tunturi Muscle Trainers (at $749 each), and three Dual-Action StairClimbers (at $1,545 each).

You could ship immediately except for one problem. The Dual-Action StairClimber is intended for home use, not for gym or club use. Customers like it because they say it is more like scaling a mountain than climbing a flight of stairs. With each step, users exercise their arms to pull or push themselves up. Its special cylinders absorb shock so that no harmful running impact results. However, this model is not what you would recommend for gym use. You feel Mr. Norton should order your premier stair climber, the LifeStep (at $2,395 each). This unit has sturdier construction and is meant for heavy use. Its sophisticated electronics provide a selection of customer-pleasing programs that challenge muscles progressively with a choice of workouts. It also quickly multiplies workout gains with computer-controlled interval training. Electronic monitors inform users of step height, calories burned, elapsed time, upcoming levels, and adherence to fitness goals. For gym use the LifeStep is clearly better than the StairClimber. The bad news is that the LifeStep is considerably more expensive.

You get no response when you try to telephone Mr. Norton to discuss the problem. Should you ship what you can, or hold the entire order until you learn whether he wants the StairClimber or the LifeStep? Or perhaps you should substitute the LifeStep and send only two of them.

YOUR TASK. Decide what to do and write a letter to be faxed to Phil Norton, Fit Power Gym, 359 Ridge Road, Parma, OH 44128.

9.20 Bad News to Customers: University Accidentally Admits All Who Applied (Objs. 1–4)

> **E-mail**

The University of California, San Diego, recently made a big mistake. It inadvertently invited all applicants to the LaJolla campus to an orientation—even those who had been rejected. The message said, "We're thrilled that you've been admitted to UC San Diego, and we're showcasing our beautiful campus on Admit Day." That message was intended to be sent to about 18,000 students who had been accepted. Instead, it went to all 47,000 students who applied. Admissions Director Mae Brown quickly realized the mistake. "The minute the e-mails were sent out, we noted that it was sent to a much larger pool than was admitted. We immediately recognized the error," she said.

What could the university do to correct this massive slip-up? One applicant, who had already received a rejection from UCSD, said she was confused. Her mother said, "It is adding insult to injury for kids who have already been through the wringer." When asked if anyone had been disciplined for the mistake, Brown said that the university was undertaking a complete review of the process.[42]

YOUR TASK. For Admissions Director Mae Brown, write an appropriate bad-news message to the students who received the message in error. Many applicants will be wondering what their real admission status is.

9.21 Bad News to Customers: Pick a Price Hike (Objs. 1–4)

Select a product or service that you now use (e.g., newspaper, Internet service, water or electricity, propane or natural gas, cell or landline phone, car insurance). Assume that the provider must raise its rates and that you are the employee who must notify customers. Should you use a letter, e-mail, company website, or blog? Decide whether you should use the direct or indirect strategy. Gather as much information as you can about the product or service. What, if anything, justifies the increase? What benefits can be cited?

YOUR TASK. Prepare a rate increase announcement. Submit it along with a memo explaining your rationale for the strategy you chose.

9.22 Bad News to Customers: Stuck in Berlin Without a Credit Card (Objs. 1–4)

Travel writer Blair Rhines was mystified when the sales clerk at a Berlin department store refused her credit card. "Sorry," the clerk said, "your credit card is not being accepted. I don't know why." Rhines found out soon enough. Her bank had frozen her account because of an "unusual" spending pattern. The problem? "We've never had a charge from you in Germany before," a bank official told her. The bank didn't seem to remember that Rhines had repeatedly used that card in cities ranging from Boston to Tokyo to Cape Town over the past six years, each time without incident.

Rhines was a victim of neural-network technology, a tool that is intended to protect credit cardholders from thieves who steal cards and immediately run up huge purchases. This technology tracks spending patterns. If it detects anything unusual—such as a sudden splurge on easy-to-fence items like jewelry—it sets off an alarm. Alan Rochester, senior vice president of fraud management at Conroy Credit Card Services, says that the system is "geared toward not declining any travel and entertainment expenses, like hotels, restaurants, or car rentals." But somehow it goofed and did not recognize that Blair Rhines was traveling, although she had used her card earlier to rent a car in Berlin, a sure sign that she was traveling.

Rhines was what the credit card industry calls a false positive—a legitimate cardholder inconvenienced by the hunt for fraudsters. What particularly riled her was finding out that 75 percent of the transactions caught in the neural network turn out to be legitimate. Yet the technology has been immensely successful for credit card companies. Since Visa started using the program, its fraud rate dropped from 15 cents to 6 cents per $100. To avoid inconveniencing cardholders, the company doesn't automatically suspend a card when it suspects fraud. Instead, it telephones the cardholder to verify purchases. Of course, cardholders who are traveling are impossible to reach.

Angry about the inconvenience and embarrassment she experienced, Rhines sent a letter to Visa demanding an explanation in writing.

YOUR TASK. As an assistant to the vice president in charge of fraud detection at Visa, you have been asked to draft a letter that can be used to respond to Blair Rhines as well as to other unhappy customers whose cards were wrongly refused by your software. You know that the program has been an overwhelming success. It can, however, inconvenience people, especially when they are traveling. You have heard your boss tell travelers that it is a good idea to touch base with the bank before leaving and take along the card's customer-service number (1-800-553-0321). Write a letter that explains what happened, retains the goodwill of the customer, and suggests reader benefits. Address your letter to Ms. Blair Rhines, 68 Riverside Drive, Apt. 35, New York, NY 10025.

9.23 Customer Bad News: Bike Is a Lemon (Obj. 4)

Social Media   Web

One of your job duties in Corporate Communications at Harley-Davidson is monitoring customer complaints on the Web and social media networks. You frequently check the various Harley-Davison forums on the Web and the occasional complaint site. Only yesterday you stumbled upon what sounds like a harrowing tale of woe involving a 2014 CVO Softail Convertible. The brand-new post is vitriolic and barely literate, and the emotion is raw. Worst of all, after only a day, "Anonymous" already scored over 500 hits and multiple sympathetic comments.

> Dont buy this piece of junk! I bought this lemon at the worst dealer in Michigan Wareford Harley-Davidson in November 2013. The 2014 CVO Softail Convertible is the hottest machine, but from the start this bike has been underpowered and a gas guzzler. Not much help from the Waterford dealer. The dealers general manger told me that my bike and I are no longer welcome. He said to break it in. Some chrome parts were defective, paint was rusty under clear coat, poor gas mileage, under 35, repairs really poor. Harely Davidson are not standing up to thier responsiblities. $29,600 bike, offered to trade-in for $19,000. that was supposed to be dealers best offer when I wanted to return the lemon.

Your detective work begins. You call up ABC Harley-Davidson, the only dealer in Waterford, Michigan, and inquire about a customer who had trouble with a 2014 CVO Softail Convertible. Sure enough, you obtain the contact information of the unhappy Harley owner. Before calling and writing to Pete Dix, however, you post a response to his scathing review online to limit further damage. You suggest he contact the Harley-Davidson customer-service department by calling (414) 343-4056 and indicate his name, address, phone number, and the bike's vehicle identification number (VIN) along with the dealer's name and location.

You find additional negative comments about ABC Harley-Davidson; therefore, you look up the next closest dealership that could inspect the bike, Motor City Harley-Davidson in Farmington Hills, Michigan. All dealerships are independent franchises; hence, their quality can vary considerably. You want to find out if anything is truly wrong with the motorcycle. After all, the bike is still under warranty. Jack Vroman, owner of Motor City Harley-Davidson, agrees to inspect the CVO free of charge to the customer. Jack Vroman has already called Pete Dix to offer him a free inspection. You have also called Pete and left a voice mail message. Pete Dix's problem does not sound as if the motorcycle would fit the legal definition of a "lemon" under Michigan law, and taking the bike back at full price is out of the question.

Starting at $29,599, the 2014 CVO Softail Convertible is the pride of Harley-Davidson's model lineup. Highly customizable, the bike is essentially two motorcycles. In a few simple steps, the fully dressed touring bike can be turned into a "naked," yet comfortable, cruiser. Unlike BMW and Japanese motorcycles, Harleys are not known for their speed or fuel economy. Buyers love the "retro" appeal of the legendary brand, the signature engine roar, and the laid-back riding style.

YOUR TASK. Use tact when writing a follow-up letter to Pete Dix at 30 Estes Court, Waterford, MI 48327. Your objective is to mollify his frustration by listening to him and helping him get to the bottom of the problems with his bike. Who knows; if you are successful, Pete may even withdraw his negative post. You may want to investigate the lemon laws in your state to better

understand the definition of this legal term. To view the CVO Softail, visit Harley-Davidson's official website.

9.24 Disappointed Customers: J. Crew Cashmere at Bargain Prices? (Objs. 1–4)

E-mail

Who wouldn't want a cashmere zip turtleneck sweater for $18? At the J. Crew website, many delighted shoppers scrambled to order the bargain cashmere. Unfortunately, the price should have been $218! Before J. Crew officials could correct the mistake, several hundred e-shoppers had bagged the bargain sweater for their digital shopping carts.

When the mistake was discovered, J. Crew immediately sent an e-mail to the soon-to-be disappointed shoppers. The subject line shouted "Big Mistake!" Emily Woods, chairwoman of J. Crew, began her message with this statement: "I wish we could sell such an amazing sweater for only $18. Our price mistake on your new cashmere zip turtleneck probably went right by you, but rather than charge you such a large difference, I'm writing to alert you that this item has been removed from your recent order."

As an assistant in the communication department at J. Crew, you saw the e-mail that was sent to customers and you tactfully suggested that the bad news might have been broken differently. Your boss says, "OK, hot stuff. Give it your best shot."

YOUR TASK. Although you have only a portion of the message, analyze the customer bad-news message sent by J. Crew. Using the principles suggested in this chapter, write an improved e-mail. In the end, J. Crew decided to allow customers who ordered the sweater at $18 to reorder it for $118.80 to $130.80, depending on the size. Customers were given a special website to go to, to reorder (make up an address). Remember that J. Crew customers are youthful and hip. Keep your message upbeat.[43]

9.25 Disappointed Customers: No Pay Day Without Checks (Objs. 1–4)

Team

Christopher Bale, a printing company sales manager, must tell one of his clients that the payroll checks his company ordered are not going to be ready by the date Bale had promised. The printing company's job scheduler overlooked the job and didn't get the checks into production in time to meet the deadline. As a result, Bale's client, a major insurance company, is going to miss its pay run.

Bale meets with internal department heads. They decide on the following plan to remedy the situation: (a) move the check order to the front of the production line; (b) make up for the late production date by shipping some of the checks—enough to meet their client's immediate payroll needs—by air freight; (c) deliver the remaining checks by truck.[44]

YOUR TASK. Form groups of three or four students. Discuss the following issues about how to present the bad news to Rachel Modleska, Bale's contact person at the insurance company.

a.   Should Bale call Modleska directly or delegate the task to his assistant?

b.   When should Modleska be informed of the problem?

c.   What is the best procedure for delivering the bad news?

d.   What follow-up would you recommend to Bale?

Be prepared to share your group's responses during a class discussion. Your instructor may ask two students to role-play the presentation of the bad news.

9.26 Disappointed Customers: Creepy Crawlies in PowerBars! (Objs. 1–4)

Web

In a recent trip to her local grocery store, Sandy Wheeler decided for the first time to stock up on PowerBars. These are low-fat, high-carbohydrate energy bars that are touted as a highly nutritious snack food specially formulated to deliver long-lasting energy. Since 1986, PowerBar has been dedicated to helping athletes and active people achieve peak performance. It claims to be "the fuel of choice" for top athletes around the world. Sandy is a serious runner and participates in many track meets every year.

On her way to a recent meet, Sandy grabbed a PowerBar and unwrapped it while driving. As she started to take her first bite, she noticed something white and shiny in the corner of the wrapping. An unexpected protein source wriggled out of her energy bar—a worm! Sandy's first inclination was to toss it out the window and never buy another PowerBar. On second thought, though, she decided to tell the company. When she called the toll-free number on the wrapper, Sophie, who answered the phone, was incredibly nice, extremely apologetic, and very informative about what happened. "I'm very sorry you experienced an infested product," said Sophie.

She explained that the infamous Indian meal moth is a pantry pest that causes millions of dollars in damage worldwide. It feeds on grains or grain-based products, such as cereal, flour, dry pasta, crackers, dried fruits, nuts, spices, and pet food. The tiny moth eggs lie dormant for some time or hatch quickly into tiny larvae (worms) that penetrate food wrappers and enter products.

At its manufacturing facilities, PowerBar takes stringent measures to protect against infestation. It inspects incoming grains, supplies proper ventilation, and shields all grain-storage areas with screens to prevent insects from entering. It also uses light traps and electrocuters; these devices eradicate moths with the least environmental impact.

PowerBar President Brian Maxwell makes sure every complaint is followed up immediately with a personal letter. His letters generally tell customers that it is rare for infestations like this to occur. Entomologists say that the worms are not toxic and will not harm humans. Nevertheless, as President Maxwell says, "It is extremely disgusting to find these worms in food."

YOUR TASK. For the signature of Brian Maxwell, PowerBar president, write a bad-news follow-up letter to Sandy Wheeler, 705 South Linn Street, Iowa City, IA 52240. Keep the letter informal and personal. Explain how pests get into grain-based products and what you are doing to prevent infestation. You can learn more about the Indian meal moth by searching the Web. In your letter include a brochure titled "Notes About the Indian Meal Moth," along with a kit for Sandy to use to mail the culprit PowerBar to the company for analysis in Boise, Idaho. Also send a check reimbursing Sandy $26.85 for her purchase.[45]

9.27 Disappointed Customers: Renting a Tank Can Cost You (Obj. 4)

Michael Lin, a consultant from San Mateo, California, was surprised when he picked up his rental car from Budget in Seattle over Easter weekend. He had reserved a full-size car, but the rental agent told him he could upgrade to a Ford Excursion for an additional $25 a day. "She told me it was easy to drive," Mr. Lin reported. "But when I saw it, I realized it was huge—like a tank. You could fit a full-size bed inside."

On his trip Mr. Lin managed to scratch the paint and damage the rear-door step. He didn't worry, though, because he thought the damage would be covered since he had charged the rental on his American Express card. He knew that the company offered backup car rental insurance coverage. To his dismay, he discovered that its car rental coverage excluded large SUVs. "I just assumed they'd cover it," he confessed. He wrote to Budget to complain about not being warned that certain credit cards may not cover damage to large SUVs or luxury cars.

Budget agents always encourage renters to sign up for Budget's own "risk product." But they don't feel that it is their responsibility to study the policies of customers' insurance carriers and explain what may or may not be covered. Moreover, they try to move customers into their rental cars as quickly as possible and avoid lengthy discussions of insurance coverage. Customers who do not purchase insurance are at risk. Mr. Lin does not make any claim against Budget, but he is upset about being "pitched" to upgrade to the larger SUV, which he didn't really want.[46]

YOUR TASK. As a member of the communication staff at Budget, respond to Mr. Lin's complaint. Budget obviously is not going to pay for the SUV repairs, but it does want to salvage his goodwill and future business. Offer him a coupon for two days' free rental of any full-size sedan. Write to Michael Lin, 801 Saratoga Dr., Apt. B, San Mateo, CA 94401.

9.28 Credit Refusal: Cash Is King at Twin Cities Athletic Club (Objs. 1–4)

As manager of the Twin Cities Athletic Club, you must refuse the application of Zoë Lanier for an Extended Membership. This is strictly a business decision. You liked Zoë very much when she applied, and she seems genuinely interested in fitness and a healthy lifestyle. However, your Extended Membership plan qualifies the member for all your testing, exercise, recreation, yoga, and aerobics programs. This multiservice program is expensive for the club to maintain because of the large staff required. Applicants must have a solid credit rating to join. To your disappointment, you learned that Zoë's credit rating is decidedly negative. Her credit report indicates that she is delinquent in payments to four businesses, including Total Body Fitness Center, your principal competitor.

You do have other programs, including your Drop In and Work Out plan, which offers the use of available facilities on a cash basis. This plan enables a member to reserve space on the racquetball and handball courts. The member can also sign up for yoga and exercise classes, space permitting. Since Zoë is far in debt, you would feel guilty allowing her to plunge in any more deeply.

YOUR TASK. Refuse Zoë Lanier's credit application, but encourage her cash business. Suggest that she make an inquiry to the credit-reporting company Experian to learn about her credit report. She is eligible to receive a free credit report if she mentions this application. Write to Zoë Lanier, 3100 South Vista Avenue, Apt. 310, Boise, ID 83705.

9.29 Bad News to Employees: Bonding Without Spouses and Friends (Objs. 1–3, 5)

E-mail

As director of Human Resources at Weyerman Paper Company, you received an unusual request. Several employees asked that their spouses or friends be allowed to participate in Weyerman intramural sports teams. Although the teams play only once a week during the season, these employees claim that they can't afford more time away from friends and family. Over 100 employees currently participate in the eight coed volleyball, softball, and tennis teams, which are open to company employees only. The teams were designed to improve employee friendships and to give employees a regular occasion to have fun together.

If nonemployees were to participate, you fear that employee interaction would be limited. Although some team members might have fun if spouses or friends were included, you are not so sure all employees would enjoy it. You are not interested in turning intramural sports into "date night." Furthermore, the company would have to create additional teams if many nonemployees joined, and you don't want the administrative or equipment costs of more teams. Adding teams also would require changes to team rosters and game schedules. This could create a problem for some employees. You do understand the need for social time with friends and families, but guests are welcome as spectators at all intramural games. Also, the company already sponsors a family holiday party and an annual company picnic.

YOUR TASK. Write an e-mail or hard-copy memo to the staff denying the request of several employees to include nonemployees on Weyerman's intramural sports teams.

9.30 Bad News to Employees: Rising Tuition? You're on Your Own (Objs. 1–3, 5)

Selma Ceviker, a hardworking bank teller, has sent a request asking that the company create a program to reimburse the tuition and book expenses for employees taking college courses. Although some companies have such a program, Middleton Bank has not felt that it could indulge in such an expensive employee perk. Moreover, the CEO is not convinced that companies see any direct benefit from such programs. Employees improve their educational credentials and skills, but what is to keep them from moving that education and those skill sets to other employers? Middleton Bank has over 200 employees. If even a fraction of them started classes, the company could see a huge bill for the cost of tuition and books. Because the bank is facing stiff competition and its profits are sinking, such a program is out of the question. In addition, it would involve administration—applications, monitoring, and record keeping. It is just too much of a hassle. When employees were hard to hire and retain, companies had to offer employment perks. But with a soft economy, such inducements are unnecessary.

YOUR TASK. As director of Human Resources, send an individual response to Selma Ceviker. The answer is a definite *no*, but you want to soften the blow and retain the loyalty of this conscientious employee.

Chat About It

In each chapter you will find five discussion questions related to the chapter material. Your instructor may assign these topics for you to discuss in class, in an online chat room, or on an online discussion board. Some of the discussion topics may require outside research. You may also be asked to read and respond to postings made by your classmates.

Topic 1: Describe a time when a company delivered negative news to you ineffectively; that is, you did not understand the news or could not accept the decision. Explain why the company's strategy was ineffective.

Topic 2: Many people say they prefer the direct approach when receiving bad news. What situational factors might cause you to use the indirect approach with these people?

Topic 3: Draft an effective buffer that you might use if you were a dean of a business college and must tell the business club president that you cannot fund the club's celebrity golf tournament event.

Topic 4: A flyer at a city bus stop announced a fare increase with the title *Rate Changes*. Was this title effective? If not, what title might have worked better?

Topic 5: You are an executive at a company that suddenly has to lay off 400 employees within three days or risk financial disaster. You have to make the cuts quickly, but you don't want to be impersonal by announcing the cuts by e-mail. How would you announce the bad news?

C.L.U.E. Grammar & Mechanics | *Review 9*

Confusing Words and Frequently Misspelled Words

Review the lists of confusing words and frequently misspelled words in Appendix A, Grammar and Mechanics Guide, beginning on page A-21. On a separate sheet, revise the following sentences to correct word usage errors. Sentences may have more than one error. If a sentence is correct, write *C*. When you finish, check your answers on page Key-2.

EXAMPLE: He complained that his capitol investments had been aversely effected.

REVISION: He complained that his **capital** investments had been **adversely affected.**

1. Did you allready respond to his request for a reccomendation?

2. The principle part of the manager's response contained a complement and valuable advise.

3. In responding to the irate customer, Rachel made a conscience effort to show patients and present creditable facts.

4. Even in every day business affairs, we strive to reach farther and go beyond what is expected.

5. Before you procede with the report, please check those suprising statistics.

6. It's usally better to de-emphasize bad news rather then to spotlight it.

7. Incidently, passive-voice verbs can help you make a statement less personnel when neccessary.

8. Customers are more excepting of disapointing news if they are ensured that there requests were heard and treated fairly.

9. The customer's complaint illicited an immediate response that analized the facts carefully but was not to long.

10. When delivering bad news, try to acomodate a disatisfied customer with a plausible alternative.

Notes

[1] Spagat, E. (2010, November 11). Stricken cruise ship reaches San Diego amid cheers. *Associated Press*. Retrieved from http://www.guardian.co.uk /world/feedarticle/9355810

[2] Crippled cruise ship returns, passengers recall "nightmare" trip. (2010, November 11). KTLA .com. Retrieved from http://www.ktla.com /news/landing/ktla-carnival-cruise-ship -fire,0,6826562.story

[3] Golden, F., & Lenhart, M. (2012, February 27). Carnival Corp. besieged by bad news. *Travel Market Report*. Retrieved from http://www .travelmarketreport.com/content/publiccontent .aspx?PageID=1365&articleid=6968&LP=1

[4] Conant, E., & Nadeau, B. L. (2012, July 30). The horror below decks. *Newsweek*. Retrieved from http://www.lexisnexis.com

[5] Esterl, M., & Lublin, J. S. (2012, January 23). Carnival CEO lies low after wreck. *The Wall Street Journal*. Retrieved from http://online.wsj.com /article/SB10001424052970204624204577177 131752006116.html

[6] Photo essay based on Higgins, H., & Castle, S. (2013, February 25). Ikea recalls meatballs after detection of horse meat. *The New York Times*. Retrieved from http://www.nytimes.com; Ikea News Room. (2013, February 28). Important customer information. Retrieved from http://www.ikea.com/gb/en/about_ikea /newsitem/customer_information

[7] Mintz, J. (2009, February 23). Microsoft: Laid-off can keep extra pay after all. *USA Today*. Retrieved from http://www.usatoday.com/tech/news /2009-02-23-microsoft-layoffs_N.htm

[8] Greenwald, J. (2009, June 1). Layoffs may spark defamation suits. Retrieved from businessinsurance .com

[9] American Management Association. (2004). 2004 survey on workplace e-mail and IM reveals unmanaged risks. Retrieved from http://www .epolicyinstitute.com/survey/survey04.pdf

[10] McCord, E. A. (1991, April). The business writer, the law, and routine business communication: A legal and rhetorical analysis. *Journal of Business and Technical Communication*, 183.

[11] Ibid.

[12] Creelman, V.(2012). The case for "living" models. *Business Communication Quarterly*, 75(2), 181.

[13] Veltsos, J. (2012). An analysis of data breach notifications as negative news. *Business Communication Quarterly*, 75(2), 198. doi: 10.1177/1080569912443081

[14] Canavor, N. (2012). *Business writing in the digital age*. Thousand Oaks, CA: Sage, p. 62.

[15] Ibid., p. 61.

[16] Robertson, K. (2004, April). Saying no: How to deliver bad news to a customer. Retrieved from http://www.krconsulting.com/saying-no-how -to-deliver-bad-news-to-a-customer

[17] Photo essay based on Smith, K. (2013, February 23). Here's the confidential memo Yahoo sent employees about working from home. *Business Insider*. Retrieved from http://www.businessinsider .com; MacMillan, D., & Baker, K. (2013, February 26). Yahoo CEO Mayer revives debate over work-from-home merits. *Bloomberg Businessweek*. Retrieved from http://www.businessweek.com /news/2013-02-25/yahoo-s-mayer-risks -productivity-with-work-from-home-restriction

[18] O'Neil, S. (2003, November). Quoted in Need to deliver bad news? How & why to tell it like it is. *HR Focus*, p. 3. Retrieved from http://search .ebscohost.com

[19] Council of Better Business Bureaus. (2010, January 5). BBB lists top 10 scams and rip-offs of 2009. Retrieved from http://www.buffalo.bbb.org

[20] Shuit, D. P. (2003, September). Do it right or risk getting burned. *Workforce Management*, p. 80.

[21] Cited in Canavor, N. (2012). *Business writing in the digital age*. Thousand Oaks, CA: Sage, p. 63.

[22] Brodkin, J. (2007, March 19). Corporate apologies don't mean much. *Networkworld, 24*(11), 8. Retrieved from Business Source Complete database.

[23] Schweitzer, M. (2006, December). Wise negotiators know when to say "I'm sorry." *Negotiation*, 4. Retrieved from Business Source Complete database.

[24] Cited in Canavor, N. (2012). *Business writing in the digital age*. Thousand Oaks, CA: Sage, p. 62.

[25] Hastings, R. (2011, September 18). An explanation and some reflections. The Official Netflix Blog. Retrieved from http://blog.netflix.com/2011/09 /explanation-and-some-reflections.html; Weissman, J. (2011, September 21). Netflix and politics. *Forbes*. Retrieved from http://www .forbes.com/sites/jerryweissman/2011/09/21 /netflix-and-politics; Phillips, B. (2011, September 19). Six reasons Netflix CEO Reed Hastings' apology failed. Retrieved from http://www.mrmediatraining.com/index .php/2011/09/19/six-reasons-netflix-ceo-reed -hastings-apology-failed

[26] Neeleman, D. (2007). An apology from David Neeleman. Retrieved from http://jetblue -happyjetting.blogspot.com/2009/12/apology -from-david-neeleman.html

[27] Letters to Lands' End. (1991, February). 1991 Lands' End Catalog. Dodgeville, WI: Lands' End, p. 100.

[28] Mowatt, J. (2002, February). Breaking bad news to customers. *Agency Sales*, p. 30; and Dorn, E. M. (1999, March). Case method instruction in the business writing classroom. *Business Communication Quarterly, 62*(1), 51-52.

[29] Kapner, S. (2012, October 5). Citi won't sleep on customer tweets. *The Wall Street Journal*, p. 1.

[30] Wagner, S. (2012, September 11). CEO addresses Sept. 10 service outage. Retrieved from http://support.godaddy.com/godaddy /ceo-addresses-sept-10-service-outage

[31] Ngak, C. (2012, September 10). GoDaddy goes down, Anonymous claims responsibility. CBSNews.com Retrieved from http://www.cbsnews.com/8301 -501465_162-57509744-501465/godaddy-goes -down-anonymous-claims-responsibility

[32] Forbes, M. (1999). How to write a business letter. In K. Harty (Ed.), *Strategies for business and technical writing*. Boston: Allyn & Bacon, p. 108.

[33] Browning, M. (2003, November 24). Work dilemma: Delivering bad news a good way. *Government Computer News*, p. 41; and Mowatt, J. (2002, February). Breaking bad news to customers. *Agency Sales*, p. 30.

[34] Ensall, S. (2007, January 30). Delivering bad news. *Personnel Today*, p. 31. Retrieved from Business Source Premier database; and Lewis, B. (1999, September 13). To be an effective leader, you need to perfect the art of delivering bad news. *InfoWorld*, p. 124.

[35] Ziglar, Z. (2011, January 18). Dad, you do choose your daughter's husband. Retrieved from http://www.ziglar.com/newsletter/?p=949

[36] Livingston, J. (2008, September 17). Author Holly Weeks talks communication. [Interview]. Retrieved from http://www.humanresourcesiq .com/business-strategies/articles/author -holly-weeks-talks-communication

[37] Based on Carnival cancellation notice. (2010, December 15). Retrieved from http://www .carnival.com/cms/fun/pdf/Splendor-Comp -Guidelines.pdf

[38] Gartner identifies top ten disruptive technologies for 2008-2012. (n.d.). Press release. Retrieved from https://www.gartner.com/it/page .jsp?id=681107

[39] Based on Lee, L. (2007, June 11). A smoothie you can chew on. *BusinessWeek*, p. 64.

[40] Based on Sloan, G. (1996, November 29). Under 21? Carnival says cruise is off. *USA Today*; Sieder, J. (1995, October 16). Full steam ahead: Carnival Cruise Line makes boatloads of money by selling fun. *U.S. News & World Report*, p. 72; Carnival Cruise Lines Fact Sheet. (2011, December 14). Retrieved from http://carnival-news .com/2011/12/14/carnival-cruise-lines-fact -sheet-2; and Schretter, N. (2012). Cruise line minimum age policies. Family Travel Network. Retrieved from http://www.familytravelnetwork .com/articles/cruise_line_minimum_age _policies.asp

[41] Based on Burbank, L. (2007, June 8). Personal items can be swept away between flights. *USA Today*, p. 3D.

[42] Kucher, K. (2009, March 31). UCSD email erroneously welcomes all who applied. Retrieved from http://www.utsandiego.com/news/2009/mar/31 /bn31letter114447

[43] Sorkin, A. R. (1999, November). J. Crew web goof results in discount. *The New York Times*, p. D3.

[44] Mishory, J. (2008, June). Don't shoot the messenger: How to deliver bad news and still keep customers satisfied. *Sales and Marketing Management*, p. 18.

[45] Based on Harari, O. (1999, July-August). The power of complaints. *Management Review*, p. 31.

[46] Based on SUV surprise. (2004, June 15). *The Wall Street Journal*, p. W7.

Persuasive and Sales Messages

OBJECTIVES

After studying this chapter, you should be able to

1 Explain digital-age persuasion, identify effective persuasive techniques, and apply the 3-x-3 writing process to persuasive messages in print and online.

2 Describe the traditional four-part AIDA strategy for creating successful persuasive messages, and apply the four elements to draft effective and ethical business messages.

3 Craft persuasive messages that request actions, make claims, and deliver complaints.

4 Understand interpersonal persuasion at work and write persuasive messages within organizations.

5 Create effective and ethical direct-mail and e-mail sales messages.

6 Apply basic techniques in developing persuasive press releases.

© Africa Studio/Shutterstock.com;
© ra2studio/Shutterstock.com

Labeled a "green business icon," L. Hunter Lovins has
dedicated her life to convincing large and small corporations, governments, and
educational institutions that sustainability makes good business sense. The founder of Natural
Capitalism Solutions, author of many books, and recipient of dozens of awards, Lovins is a
sought-after speaker and educator who appeals to her audience by effectively integrating the
techniques of persuasion.[1]

Her long list of clients and track record of nearly 40 years in the forefront of the sustainability movement establishes her credibility. Whether she addresses executives at retail giant

© Sarunyu_foto/Shutterstock.com

Walmart, leaders at the Pentagon, or owners of
small companies such as Clif Bar,[2] her recognized expertise helps make her case. To encourage businesses to implement sustainability
practices, she offers attainable requests. When
talking to small business owners, for example,
she presents reasonable solutions. "Putting in
more efficient lighting has a very quick return,"
she says.[3]

Tying facts to benefits lies at the heart of
persuasion and is the way successful communicators influence thought and promote desired actions. Lovins infuses her arguments with facts,
linking those facts to benefits. In a recent webinar, she talks about the importance of engaging
employees by creating a company that cares about the environment. "Engaged organizations have
almost four times the earnings per share growth rate," she says.[4] She uses statistics to persuade her
audience that sustainability is good business, and she wisely cites her sources to solidify her argument. "Ogilvy [& Mather] did a study of the U.S. consumer market and found that green consumers
are up to 80 percent of the market," she tells her audience.[5]

Another key element of effective persuasion is overcoming resistance by anticipating objections
and being ready to counter them with measured responses. When Lovins addresses skeptics about
climate change, she employs reason to avoid being summarily dismissed. "You don't have to believe
in the problem to believe in the solution," she tells doubters.[6]

As a result of her down-to-earth style, Lovins avoids sounding preachy. Her speaking style is
yet another persuasive technique that adds to her effectiveness as a communicator advocating
sustainability. It's little wonder *Time Magazine* named this master of persuasion "Hero for the
Planet."

Critical Thinking

- Why is using a moderate tone so important to persuasion?

- How do facts help make a convincing case?

- Why do good writers weave benefits into persuasive messages?

Understanding Persuasion in the Digital Age

In the digital age, businesses have moved toward leaner corporate hierarchies, simultaneously relying on teams, dismantling division walls, and blurring the lines of authority. This is
why persuasive skills are becoming ever more important at work, as teams and managers are
abandoning the traditional command structure. Instead, they must try to *influence* others.[7]
At Natural Capitalism Solutions, sustainability champion L. Hunter Lovins had to be very
convincing whether she was trying to win over skeptical corporate executives or raise funds to
support "green" projects. Unlike Lovins, however, many of us are poor persuaders or we don't
always recognize persuasive tactics directed at us.[8]

LEARNING OBJECTIVE **1**
Explain digital-age persuasion,
identify effective persuasive
techniques, and apply the 3-x-3
writing process to persuasive
messages in print and online.

Symbols, such as this recycling symbol, convey rich meaning to others and may be used to convey an organization's important values.

Although we are subjected daily to a barrage of print and electronic persuasive messages, many of us don't recognize the techniques of persuasion. To be smart consumers, we need to be alert to persuasive practices and how they influence behavior. Being informed is our best defense. Yet more than ever in today's digital world, we should also realize that persuasion has the power "to change attitudes and behaviors on a mass scale," as persuasion guru B. J. Fogg at Stanford puts it. Social networks enable individuals or groups to reach virtually limitless audiences and practice what Fogg calls "mass interpersonal persuasion."[9] This puts a lot of power into the hands of many.

You have already studied techniques for writing routine request messages that require minimal persuasion. However, this chapter focuses on messages that require deliberate and skilled persuasion in the workplace. This chapter also addresses selling, both offline and online.

What Is Persuasion?

As communication scholar Richard M. Perloff defines it, persuasion is "a symbolic process in which communicators try to convince other people to change their attitudes or behaviors regarding an issue through the transmission of a message in an atmosphere of free choice."[10] Helping us understand how persuasion works, this definition has five components, which are outlined in the following sections.

Persuasion Is a Symbolic Process. Symbols are meaningful words, signs, and images infused with rich meaning—for example, words such as *liberty*, signs such as national flags, and images such as the red cross for rescue or the apple for computers. An ethical persuader understands the power of symbols and does not use them to trick others. Because people's attitudes change slowly, persuasion takes time.

Persuasion Involves an Attempt to Influence. Persuasion involves a conscious effort to influence another person with the understanding that change is possible. For instance, when you ask your boss for permission to telecommute, you intend to achieve a specific outcome and assume that your boss can be swayed.

Persuasion Is Self-Persuasion. Ethical communicators give others the choice to accept their arguments by making compelling, honest cases to support them. They plant the seed but do not coerce. They leave it to others to "self-influence," that is, to decide whether to make the change. In the case of telecommuting, you would want to present to your boss clear benefits of working from home but definitely not push hard.

Persuasion Involves Transmitting a Message. Persuasive messages can be verbal or nonverbal, and they can be conveyed face-to-face or via the Internet, TV, radio, and other media. Persuasive messages are not always rational. They often appeal to our emotions. Consider the car commercial playing your favorite tune and showing pristine landscapes, not a gridlocked interstate during rush hour.

Persuasion Requires Free Choice. Although *free* is a difficult term to define, we can perhaps agree that people are free when they are not forced to comply, when they can refuse the idea suggested to them, and when they are not pressured to act against their own preferences.

Many smart thinkers have tried to explain how savvy persuaders influence others. One classic model illustrating persuasion is shown in Figure 10.1. In the classic book *Influence*,[11] Robert B. Cialdini outlined six psychological triggers that prompt us to act and to believe: reciprocation, commitment, social proof, liking, authority, and scarcity. Each "weapon of automatic influence" motivates us to say *yes* or *no* without much thinking or awareness. Our complex world forces us to resort to these shortcuts. Needless to say, such automatic responses make us vulnerable to manipulation.

ETHICS CHECK:

Subtle Use of Persuasion in an Age of Social Media and Information Overload

Professional persuaders try to generate "a distinct kind of automatic, mindless compliance" in people, a "willingness to say yes without thinking first," believes psychologist Robert B. Cialdini. The best-selling author of *Influence* cautions: "The ever-accelerating pace and informational crush of modern life will make . . . unthinking compliance more and more prevalent in the future. It will be increasingly important for the society, therefore, to understand the how and why of automatic influence." What does this mean for you as a consumer and participant in social media?[12]

Figure **10.1** Six Basic Principles That Direct Human Behavior

Reciprocation   **"The Old Give and Take … and Take"**

Humans seem to be hardwired to give and take. If someone does us a favor, most of us feel obligated to return the favor. This rule is so binding that it may lead to a *yes* to a request we might otherwise refuse. This explains the "gifts" that accompany requests for money.

Commitment   **"Hobgoblins of the Mind"**

We believe in the correctness of a difficult choice once we make it. We want to keep our thoughts and beliefs consistent with what we have already decided. Fund-raisers may ask for a small amount at first, knowing that we are likely to continue giving once we start.

Social Proof   **"Truths Are Us"**

To determine correct behavior, we try to find out what other people think is correct. We see an action as more acceptable when others are doing it. Advertisers like to tell us that a product is "best-selling"; the message is that it must be good because others think so.

Liking   **"The Friendly Thief"**

We are more likely to accept requests of people we know and like or those who say they like us. Tupperware capitalizes on this impulse to buy from a friend. Strangers are persuasive if they are likable and attractive. Also, we favor people who are or appear to be like us.

Authority   **"Directed Deference"**

We tend to obey authority because we learn that a widely accepted system of authority is beneficial to the orderly functioning of society. People exuding authority, even con artists, can trigger our mechanical, blind compliance. Testimonials bank on this response to authority.

Scarcity   **"The Rule of the Few"**

We tend to regard opportunities as more valuable when their availability is restricted. Scarce items seem more appealing to us. The idea of potential loss greatly affects our decisions. Marketers may urge customers not to miss out on a "limited-time offer."

© Cengage Learning 2015

If you become aware of these gut-level mechanisms that trigger decisions, you will be able to resist unethical and manipulative persuasion more easily. Conversely, this knowledge might make you a successful persuader.

How Has Persuasion Changed in the Digital Age?

The preoccupation with persuasion is not new. From the days of Aristotle in ancient Greece and Niccolò Machiavelli in Renaissance Italy, philosophers, politicians, and businesspeople have longed to understand the art of influencing others. However, persuasion in the twenty-first century is different from persuasion in previous historic periods in distinct ways.[13] The most striking developments are less than three decades old.

The Volume and Reach of Persuasive Messages Have Exploded. Experts say that the average American adult endures between 300 and 3,000 ads and other persuasive appeals a day.[14] TV, radio, the Internet, and mobile phones blast myriad messages to the far corners of the earth. A Pew Research study shows that American popular culture continues to soar abroad. Two thirds of people surveyed in 16 countries said they liked American music, films, and television—up 6 percent from five years earlier.[15]

Persuasive Messages Spread at Warp Speed. Popular TV shows such as *The X Factor* and their corporate sponsors use social media to engage the fans whose more than half a million social media comments instantly influence the contestants' dance routines, songs, and wardrobe. *American Idol* now clocks one million posts during a single show.[16] Election campaign buzz also travels at dizzying speed.

Organizations of All Stripes Are in the Persuasion Business. Companies, ad agencies, PR firms, social activists, lobbyists, marketers, and more, spew persuasive messages. Although outspent by corporations that can sink millions into image campaigns, activists use social networks to galvanize their followers.

Persuasive Techniques Are More Subtle and Misleading. Instead of a blunt, pushy hard-sell approach, persuaders play on emotions by using flattery, empathy, nonverbal cues, and likability appeals. They are selling an image or a lifestyle, not a product.[17] In this age of spin, the news media are increasingly infiltrated by partisan interests and spread messages masquerading as news.

Persuasion Is More Complex and Impersonal. American consumers are more diverse and don't necessarily think alike. To reach them, marketers carefully study various target groups and customize their appeals. Technology has increased the potential for distortion. People can "mash up" content, give it meanings the original source never intended, and blast it into the world in seconds.

You probably recognize how important it is not only to become a skilled persuader, but also to identify devious messages and manipulation attempts directed at you.

How to Persuade Effectively

When you want your ideas to prevail, start thinking about how to present them. Listeners and readers will be more inclined to accept what you are offering if you focus on important strategies, outlined in Figure 10.2 and further discussed throughout the chapter.

Applying the 3-x-3 Writing Process to Persuasive Messages

Changing people's views and overcoming their objections are difficult tasks. Pulling it off demands planning and perception. The 3-x-3 writing process provides a helpful structure for laying a foundation for persuasion. Of particular importance here are (a) analyzing the purpose, (b) adapting to the audience, (c) collecting information, and (d) organizing the message.

Analyzing the Purpose: Knowing What You Want to Achieve. The goal of a persuasive message is to convert the receiver to your ideas and motivate action. To accomplish this feat in the age of social media, persuaders seek to build relationships with their audiences. Even so, a message without a clear purpose is doomed. Too often, inexperienced writers reach the end of the first draft of a message before discovering exactly what they want the receiver to think or do.

Meet Chef James Barry. The owner of Wholesome2Go, an organic-food home-delivery service, understands contemporary persuasive techniques. A former personal chef for celebrities, Chef James is convinced that all his customers want to feel special. He knows that to achieve success today, he must cultivate relationships, not just push products.[18] He engages his clients by maintaining a website, tweeting updates, and posting on his Facebook and Pinterest pages. Wholesome2Go also has a YouTube channel. Frequently, Chef James sends persuasive e-mails such as the one shown in Figure 10.3 that spreads holiday cheer and creates buzz about an upcoming special offer.

Figure **10.2** Effective Persuasion Techniques

Establish credibility

- Show that you are truthful, experienced, and knowledgeable.
- Use others' expert opinions and research to support your position.

Make a reasonable, specific request

- Make your request realistic, doable, and attainable.
- Be clear about your objective. Vague requests are less effective.

Tie facts to benefits

- Line up plausible support such as statistics, reasons, and analogies.
- Convert the supporting facts into specific audience benefits.

Recognize the power of loss

- Show what others stand to lose if they don't agree.
- Know that people dread losing something they already possess.

Expect and overcome resistance

- Anticipate opposition from conflicting beliefs, values, and attitudes.
- Be prepared to counter with well-reasoned arguments and facts.

Share solutions and compromise

- Be flexible and aim for a solution that is acceptable to all parties.
- Listen to people and incorporate their input to create buy-in.

© Cengage Learning 2015

Adapting to the Audience to Make Your Message Heard. In addition to identifying the purpose of a persuasive message, you also need to concentrate on the receiver. Zorba the Greek wisely observed, "You can knock forever on a deaf man's door." A persuasive message is futile unless it meets the needs of its audience. In a broad sense, you want to show how your request helps the receiver achieve some of life's major goals or fulfills key needs: money, power, comfort, confidence, importance, friends, peace of mind, and recognition, to name a few.

On a more practical level, you want to show how your request solves a problem, achieves a personal or work objective, or just makes life easier for your audience. Chef James is planning his sugar detox offer for early January to help his established customers recover from the excesses of the holiday season. The health benefits and lower prices will appeal to his audience. When adapting persuasive requests to your audience, consider these questions that receivers will very likely be asking themselves:

Why should I?

What's in it for me?

What's in it for you?

Who cares?

Figure 10.3 Wholesome2Go Engages the Audience

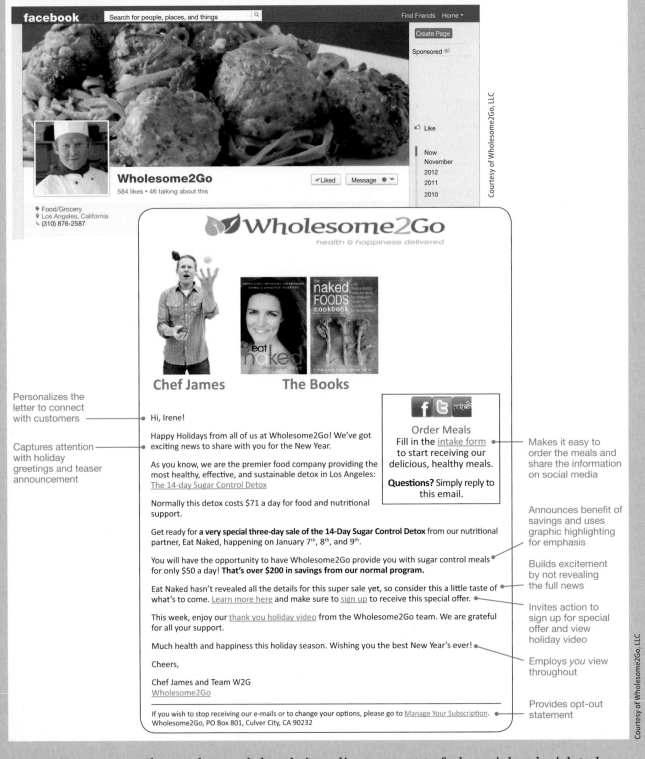

Personalizes the letter to connect with customers

Captures attention with holiday greetings and teaser announcement

Makes it easy to order the meals and share the information on social media

Announces benefit of savings and uses graphic highlighting for emphasis

Builds excitement by not revealing the full news

Invites action to sign up for special offer and view holiday video

Employs *you* **view throughout**

Provides opt-out statement

Facebook page

facebook | Search for people, places, and things | Find Friends Home ▾

Create Page
Sponsored

Wholesome2Go
584 likes • 46 talking about this

✓ Liked | Message ⚙ ▾

👍 Like

Now
November
2012
2011
2010

📍 Food/Grocery
📍 Los Angeles, California
📞 (310) 876-2587

Email content

Wholesome2Go
health & happiness delivered

Chef James   **The Books**

Order Meals
Fill in the intake form to start receiving our delicious, healthy meals.

Questions? Simply reply to this email.

Hi, Irene!

Happy Holidays from all of us at Wholesome2Go! We've got exciting news to share with you for the New Year.

As you know, we are the premier food company providing the most healthy, effective, and sustainable detox in Los Angeles: The 14-day Sugar Control Detox

Normally this detox costs $71 a day for food and nutritional support.

Get ready for **a very special three-day sale of the 14-Day Sugar Control Detox** from our nutritional partner, Eat Naked, happening on January 7th, 8th, and 9th.

You will have the opportunity to have Wholesome2Go provide you with sugar control meals for only $50 a day! **That's over $200 in savings from our normal program.**

Eat Naked hasn't revealed all the details for this super sale yet, so consider this a little taste of what's to come. Learn more here and make sure to sign up to receive this special offer.

This week, enjoy our thank you holiday video from the Wholesome2Go team. We are grateful for all your support.

Much health and happiness this holiday season. Wishing you the best New Year's ever!

Cheers,

Chef James and Team W2G
Wholesome2Go

If you wish to stop receiving our e-mails or to change your options, please go to Manage Your Subscription. Wholesome2Go, PO Box 801, Culver City, CA 90232

Contemporary persuaders understand that their audiences want to feel special and wish to have their needs met. Consumers today are savvy and know that they have many choices. Chef James uses all popular social networks to engage his customers and to build a sincere relationship with them.

Adapting to your audience means learning about audience members and analyzing why they might resist your proposal. It means searching for ways to connect your purpose with their needs. If completed before you begin writing, such analysis goes a long way toward overcoming resistance and achieving your goal.

Researching and Organizing Persuasive Data.   Once you have analyzed the audience and considered how to adapt your message to its needs, you are ready to collect data and organize it. You might brainstorm and prepare cluster diagrams to provide a rough outline of ideas. Chef James studies the competition and sets his sustainable whole food prices lower than most. However, he knows that price is not the first concern of his clients, who love the value and convenience of receiving tasty, healthy meals. Social media networks provide him with feedback. Chef James understands that New Year's resolutions to eat healthy food and lose weight might reduce resistance to his offer.

The next step in a persuasive message is organizing data into a logical sequence. If you are asking for something that you know will be approved, little persuasion is required. In that case, you would make a direct request, as you studied in Chapter 8. However, when you expect resistance or when you need to educate the receiver, the indirect strategy often works better. The classic indirect strategy known by the acronym AIDA works well for many persuasive requests, not just in selling. Figure 10.4 summarizes this four-part strategy for overcoming resistance and crafting successful persuasive messages. Chef James uses AIDA to create goodwill as he persuades his readers to view his cheerful holiday video and to consider an upcoming discounted offer.

Figure 10.4 The AIDA Strategy for Persuasive Messages

STRATEGY		CONTENT	SECTION
A	Attention	Captures attention, creates awareness, makes a sales proposition, prompts audience to read on	Opening
I	Interest	Describes central selling points, focuses not on features of product/service but on benefits relevant to the reader's needs	Body
D	Desire	Reduces resistance, reassures the reader, elicits the desire for ownership, motivates action	Body
A	Action	Offers an incentive or gift, limits the offer, sets a deadline, makes it easy for the reader to respond, closes the sale	Closing

From Guffey/Loewy, Essentials of Business Communication (with www.meguffey.com Printed Access Card), 9E. © 2013 Cengage Learning.

LEARNING OBJECTIVE **2**

Describe the traditional four-part AIDA strategy for creating successful persuasive messages, and apply the four elements to draft effective and ethical business messages.

Blending Four Major Elements in Successful Persuasive Messages

Although AIDA, the indirect strategy, appears to contain separate steps, successful persuasive messages actually blend the four steps into a seamless whole. Also, the sequence of the steps may change depending on the situation and the emphasis. Regardless of where they are placed, the key elements in persuasive requests are (a) gaining your audience's attention, (b) building interest by convincing your audience that your proposal is worthy, (c) eliciting desire for the offer and reducing resistance, and (d) prompting action. Figure 10.5 summarizes the specific tools that writers use when following the AIDA strategy.

Figure **10.5** Applying the Four-Part AIDA Strategy to Persuasive Documents

Attention	**I**nterest	**D**esire	**A**ction
Summary of problem	Facts, figures	Reduce resistance	Describe specific request
Unexpected statement	Expert opinions	Anticipate objections	Sound confident
Reader benefit	Examples	Offer counterarguments	Make action easy to take
Compliment	Specific details	Use *What if?* scenarios	Offer incentive or gift
Related facts	Direct benefits	Demonstrate competence	Don't provide excuses
Stimulating question	Indirect benefits	Show value of proposal	Repeat main benefits

From Guffey/Loewy, Essentials of Business Communication (with www.meguffey.com Printed Access Card), 9E. © 2013 Cengage Learning.

Gaining Attention in Persuasive Messages

To grab attention, the opening statement in a persuasive request should be brief, relevant, and engaging. When only mild persuasion is necessary, the opener can be low-key and factual. If, however, your request is substantial and you anticipate strong resistance, provide a thoughtful, provocative opening. Following are some examples.

- **Problem description.** In a recommendation to hire temporary employees: *Last month legal division staff members were forced to work 120 overtime hours, costing us $6,000 and causing considerable employee unhappiness.* With this opener you have presented a capsule of the problem your proposal will help solve.

- **Unexpected statement.** In a memo to encourage employees to attend an optional sensitivity seminar: *Men and women draw the line at decidedly different places in identifying what behavior constitutes sexual harassment.* Note how this opener gets readers thinking immediately.

- **Reader benefit.** In a letter promoting Clear Card, a service that helps employees make credit card purchases without paying interest: *The average employee carries nearly $13,000 in revolving debt and pays $2,800 in interest and late fees. The Clear Card charges zero percent interest.* Employers immediately see the benefit of this offer to employees.

- **Compliment.** In a letter inviting a business executive to speak: *Because our members admire your success and value your managerial expertise, they want you to be our speaker.* In offering praise or compliments, however, be careful to avoid obvious flattery. Be sincere.

- **Related facts.** In a message to company executives who are considering restricting cell phone use by employee drivers: *A recent study revealed that employers pay an average of $16,500 each time an employee is in a traffic accident.* This relevant fact sets the scene for the interest-building section that follows.

- **Stimulating question.** In a plea for funds to support environmental causes: *What do golden tortoise beetles, bark spiders, flounders, and Arctic foxes have in common?* Readers will be curious to find the answer to this intriguing question. [They all change color depending on their surroundings.]

© John Elk III/Alamy

Why would Patagonia run an expensive ad in *The New York Times* on Black Friday admonishing readers, "DON'T BUY THIS JACKET"? Known for its sustainability efforts, the outdoor outfitter self-critically lists the "astonishing cost" of, for example, its featured R2 Jacket: "To make it required 135 liters of water, enough to meet the daily needs (three glasses a day) of 45 people. . . . This jacket left behind, on its way to Reno, two-thirds its weight in waste."[20] Patagonia suggests that consumers not buy goods they don't need, and that businesses make products of higher quality and in environmentally sound ways. Is this hypocrisy, a brilliant marketing ploy, or a sincere attempt to influence consumer behavior?

Building Interest in Persuasive Messages

After capturing attention, a persuasive request must retain that attention and convince the audience that the request is reasonable. To justify your request, be prepared to invest in a few paragraphs of explanation. Persuasive requests are likely to be longer than direct requests because the audience must be convinced rather than simply instructed. You can build interest and conviction through the use of the following:

- Facts, statistics
- Examples
- Expert opinion
- Specific details
- Direct benefits
- Indirect benefits

Showing how your request can benefit the audience directly or indirectly is a key factor in persuasion. If you were asking alumni to contribute money to a college foundation, for example, you might promote *direct benefits* such as listing the donor's name in the college magazine or sending a sweatshirt with the college logo. Another direct benefit is a tax write-off for the contribution. An *indirect benefit* might be feeling good about helping the college and knowing that students will benefit from the gift. Nearly all charities rely in large part on indirect benefits to promote their causes.

REALITY CHECK: Feed a Cookie to the Monster

When Terry Tietzen, a developer of customer loyalty software, has a big idea that meets resistance, he imagines that the resistance is a monster. He must feed the monster cookies so that it will start liking the idea and not feel overwhelmed. "So I have to break it down into smaller steps," he explains. His feed-the-monster-a-cookie approach coaxes people to buy in to a new idea with little nibbles.[21]

—TERRY TIETZEN, *CEO of Edatanetworks*

© Librado Romero/The New York Times/Redux

Eliciting Desire and Reducing Resistance in Persuasive Requests

The best persuasive requests anticipate audience resistance. How will the receiver object to the request? When brainstorming, try *What if?* scenarios. Let's say you want to convince management that the employees' cafeteria should switch from disposable to ceramic dishes. What if managers say the change is too expensive? What if they argue that they recycle paper and plastic? What if they contend that ceramic dishes would increase cafeteria labor and energy costs? What if they protest that ceramic is less hygienic? For each of these *What if?* scenarios, you need a counterargument.

Countering resistance and prompting desire in the receiver is important, but you must do it with finesse *(Although ceramic dishes cost more at first, they actually save money over time)*. You can minimize objections by presenting your counterarguments in sentences that emphasize benefits: *Ceramic dishes may require a little more effort in cleaning, but they bring warmth and graciousness to meals. Most important, they help save the environment by requiring fewer resources and eliminating waste.* However, don't dwell on counterarguments, thus making them overly important. Finally, avoid bringing up objections that may never have occurred to the receiver in the first place.

Another factor that reduces resistance and elicits desire is credibility. Receivers are less resistant if your request is reasonable and if you are believable. When the receiver does not know you, you may have to establish your expertise, refer to your credentials, or demonstrate your competence. Even when you are known, you may have to establish your knowledge in a given area. If you are asking your manager for a snazzy tablet computer, you might have to establish your credibility by providing articles about the latest tablets, their portability, low cost, battery life, and so on. Some charities establish their credibility by displaying on their stationery the names of famous people who serve on their boards. The credibility of speakers making presentations is usually outlined by someone who introduces them.

Prompting Action in Persuasive Messages

After gaining attention, building interest, eliciting desire, and reducing resistance, you will want to inspire the newly receptive audience to act. Knowing exactly what action you favor before you start to write enables you to point your arguments toward this important final paragraph. Here you make your recommendation as specifically and confidently as possible—without seeming pushy. A proposal from one manager to another might conclude with, *So that we can begin using the employment assessment tests by May 1, please send a return e-mail immediately.* In making a request, don't sound apologetic *(I'm sorry to have to ask you this, but . . .)*, and don't supply excuses *(If you can spare the time, . . .).* Compare the following persuasive e-mail closings recommending training seminars in communication skills.

Too General

We are certain we can develop a series of training sessions that will improve the communication skills of your employees.

Too Timid

If you agree that our training proposal has merit, perhaps we could begin the series in June.

Too Pushy

Because we are convinced that you will want to begin improving the skills of your employees immediately, we have scheduled your series to begin in June.

Effective

You will see decided improvement in the communication skills of your employees. Please call me at 439-2201 by May 1 to give your approval so that training sessions may start in June, right after the completion of your internal restructuring.

Note how the last opening suggests a specific and easy-to-follow action. It also provides a deadline and a reason for that date.

Figure 10.6 exemplifies the AIDA persuasive strategy just discussed. Writing for her research firm, Sophia Tellez seeks to persuade other companies to complete a questionnaire revealing salary data. To most organizations, salary information is strictly confidential. What can she do to convince strangers to part with such private information?

Figure 10.6 Persuasive Request

1 Prewriting

Analyze: The purpose of this letter is to persuade the reader to complete and return a questionnaire.

Anticipate: Although the reader is busy, he may respond to appeals to his professionalism and to his need for salary data in his own business.

Adapt: Because the reader may be uninterested at first and require persuasion, use the indirect strategy.

2 Drafting

Research: Study the receiver's business and find ways to relate this request to company success.

Organize: Gain attention by opening with relevant questions. Build interest by showing how the reader's compliance will help his company and others. Reduce resistance by promising confidentiality and offering free data.

Draft: Prepare a first draft with the intention to revise.

3 Revising

Edit: Revise to show direct and indirect benefits more clearly. Make sure the message is as concise as possible.

Proofread: In the first sentence, spell out *percent* rather than using the symbol. Check the use of all question marks. Start all lines at the left for a block-style letter.

Evaluate: Will this letter convince the reader to complete and return the questionnaire?

© Cengage Learning 2015

HUNTER RESEARCH

599 Delaware Avenue, Buffalo, NY 14850 www.hunterresearch.com
PH 716.878.2300

FAX 716.878.4359

May 18, 2015

Mr. Brian H. Mosher
Walker Wealth Management
420 South Cayuga Street, Suite 250
Ithaca, NY 14850

Dear Mr. Mosher:

Poses two short questions related to the reader → Have you ever added a unique job title but had no idea what compensation the position demanded? Has your company ever lost a valued employee to another organization that offered 20 percent more in salary for the same position? ← *Gains attention*

Presents reader benefit tied to request explanation; establishes credibility → To remain competitive in hiring and to retain qualified workers, companies rely on survey data showing current salaries. Hunter Research has been collecting business data for a quarter century and has been honored by the American Management Association for its accurate data. We need your help in collecting salary data for today's workers. Information from the enclosed questionnaire will supply companies like yours with such data. ← *Builds interest*

Anticipates and counters resistance to confidentiality and time/effort objections → Your information, of course, will be treated confidentially. The questionnaire takes but a few moments to complete, and it can provide substantial dividends for professional organizations just like yours that need comparative salary data. ← *Elicits desire and reduces resistance*

Offers free salary data as a direct benefit → To show our gratitude for your participation, we will send you free comprehensive salary surveys for your industry and your metropolitan area. Not only will you find basic salaries, but you will also learn about bonus and incentive plans, special pay differentials, expense reimbursements, and perquisites such as a company car and credit card.

Comparative salary data are impossible to provide without the support of professionals like you. Please complete the questionnaire and return it in the prepaid envelope before June 1, our spring deadline. Participating in this survey means that you will no longer be in the dark about how much your employees earn compared with others in your industry. ← *Appeals to professionalism, an indirect benefit*

Provides deadline and a final benefit to prompt action ↗ ← *Motivates action*

Sincerely yours,

HUNTER RESEARCH

Sophia Tellez

Sophia Tellez
Director, Survey Research

Enclosures

© Cengage Learning 2015

To gain attention, Sophia poses two short questions that spotlight the need for salary information. To build interest and establish trust, she states that Hunter Research has been collecting business data for a quarter century and has received awards. She ties her reasonable request to audience benefits.

Being an Ethical Persuader

A persuader is effective only when he or she is believable. If receivers suspect that they are being manipulated or misled, or if they find any part of the argument untruthful, the total argument fails. Fudging on the facts, exaggerating a point, omitting something crucial, or providing deceptive emphasis may seem tempting to some business communicators, but such schemes usually backfire. Consider the case of a manager who sought to persuade employees to accept a change in insurance benefits. His memo emphasized a small perk (easier handling of claims) but de-emphasized a major reduction in total coverage. Some readers missed the main point—as the manager intended. Others recognized the deception, however, and before long the manager's credibility was lost.

Persuasion becomes unethical when facts are distorted, overlooked, or manipulated with an intent to deceive. Applied to language that manipulates, such distortion and twisting of the meaning is called *doublespeak*. Of course, persuaders naturally want to put forth their strongest case. However, that argument must be based on truth, objectivity, and fairness.

Consumers complain in blogs, tweets, and online posts about businesses resorting to aggressive sales tactics, manipulation, and downright lies.[22] Many such complaints point to car buying. The Federal Trade Commission recently stepped in to prevent five car dealers from falsely promising to pay off consumers' trade-in vehicles no matter how much the consumers still owed on their automobiles.[23] Honest business communicators would not sacrifice their good reputation for short-term gain. Once lost, credibility is difficult to regain.

REALITY CHECK: Teaching Students About Doublespeak

"These kids are growing up in a propaganda blitz unparalleled in human history. . . . Schools should shift their emphasis in order to train the larger segment of our population in a new kind of literacy so that more citizens can recognize the more sophisticated techniques of persuasion."[24]

—**HUGH RANK,** *researcher, commenting on the daily barrage of persuasive media messages in 1976, long before the rise of social networks.*

LEARNING OBJECTIVE **3**
Craft persuasive messages that request actions, make claims, and deliver complaints.

Writing Persuasive Requests, Making Claims, and Delivering Complaints

Convincing someone to change a belief or to perform an action when that person is reluctant requires planning and skill—and sometimes a little luck. A written, rather than face-to-face, request may require more preparation but can be more effective. For example, you may ask a businessperson to make a presentation to your club. You might ask a company to encourage its employees to participate in a charity drive. Another form of persuasion involves claims or complaints. All of these messages require skill in persuasion. Persuasion is often more precise and controlled when you can think through your purpose and prepare a thoughtful message in writing. AIDA, the indirect strategy, gives you an effective structure.

Writing Persuasive Requests

Persuading someone to do something that largely benefits you may not be the easiest task. Fortunately, many individuals and companies are willing to grant requests for time, money, information, cooperation, and special privileges. They comply for a variety of reasons. They may just happen to be interested in your project, or they may see goodwill potential for themselves. Professionals sometimes feel obligated to contribute their time or expertise to "give back." Often, though, businesses and individuals comply because they see that others will benefit from the request.

The persuasive action request shown in Figure 10.6 incorporates many of the techniques that are effective in persuasion: establishing credibility, making a reasonable and precise request, tying facts to benefits, and eliciting desire while overcoming resistance in the receiver.

Writing Persuasive Claims

Persuasive claims may involve damaged products, mistaken billing, inaccurate shipments, warranty problems, limited return policies, insurance snafus, faulty merchandise, and so on. Generally, the direct strategy is best for requesting straightforward adjustments (see Chapter 8). When you feel your request is justified and will be granted, the direct strategy is most efficient. However, if a past request has been refused or ignored, or if you anticipate reluctance, then the indirect strategy is appropriate.

Developing a Logical Persuasive Argument. Strive for logical development in a claim message. You might open with sincere praise, an objective statement of the problem, a point of agreement, or a quick review of what you have done to resolve the problem. Then you can explain precisely what happened or why your claim is legitimate. Don't provide a blow-by-blow chronology of details; just hit the highlights. Be sure to enclose copies of relevant invoices, shipping orders, warranties, and payments. Close with a clear statement of what you want done: a refund, replacement, credit to your account, or other action. Be sure to think through the possibilities and make your request reasonable.

Using a Moderate Tone. The tone of your message is important. Don't suggest that the receiver intentionally deceived you or intentionally created the problem. Rather, appeal to the receiver's sense of responsibility and pride in the company's good name. Calmly express your disappointment in view of your high expectations of the product and of the company. Communicating your feelings without rancor is often your strongest appeal.

Composing Effective Complaints

As their name suggests, complaints deliver bad news. Some complaint messages just vent anger. However, if the goal is to change something (and why bother to write except to motivate change?), then persuasion is necessary. An effective claim message makes a reasonable and valid request, presents a logical case with clear facts, and has a moderate tone. Anger and emotion are not effective persuaders.

Charlotte Piroska's e-mail, shown in Figure 10.7, follows the persuasive pattern as she seeks credit for two VoIP (voice over Internet protocol) systems. Actually, she was quite upset because her company was counting on these new Internet systems to reduce its phone bills. Instead, the handsets produced so much static that incoming and outgoing calls were all but impossible to hear.

ETHICS CHECK:

Complaint Bullying

As any salesperson will tell you, some customers seem to believe that if they vent their anger and make a scene at the store, bullying and intimidating a fearful sales representative, they are more likely to get their way. Indeed, some sales staff may cave in, wishing to defuse the ruckus. Is it fair to resort to such tactics to get what one wants? Does the end justify the means?

Figure **10.7** Persuasive Claim (Complaint) E-Mail

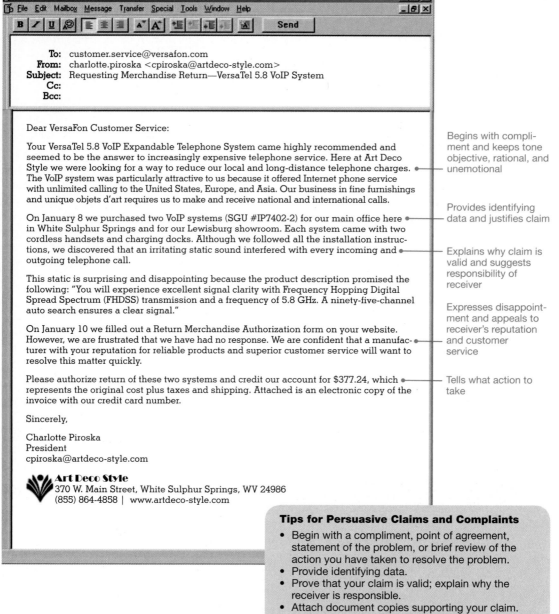

File Edit Mailbox Message Transfer Special Tools Window Help

Send

To: customer.service@versafon.com
From: charlotte.piroska <cpiroska@artdeco-style.com>
Subject: Requesting Merchandise Return—VersaTel 5.8 VoIP System
Cc:
Bcc:

Dear VersaFon Customer Service:

Your VersaTel 5.8 VoIP Expandable Telephone System came highly recommended and seemed to be the answer to increasingly expensive telephone service. Here at Art Deco Style we were looking for a way to reduce our local and long-distance telephone charges. The VoIP system was particularly attractive to us because it offered Internet phone service with unlimited calling to the United States, Europe, and Asia. Our business in fine furnishings and unique objets d'art requires us to make and receive national and international calls.

On January 8 we purchased two VoIP systems (SGU #IP7402-2) for our main office here in White Sulphur Springs and for our Lewisburg showroom. Each system came with two cordless handsets and charging docks. Although we followed all the installation instructions, we discovered that an irritating static sound interfered with every incoming and outgoing telephone call.

This static is surprising and disappointing because the product description promised the following: "You will experience excellent signal clarity with Frequency Hopping Digital Spread Spectrum (FHDSS) transmission and a frequency of 5.8 GHz. A ninety-five-channel auto search ensures a clear signal."

On January 10 we filled out a Return Merchandise Authorization form on your website. However, we are frustrated that we have had no response. We are confident that a manufacturer with your reputation for reliable products and superior customer service will want to resolve this matter quickly.

Please authorize return of these two systems and credit our account for $377.24, which represents the original cost plus taxes and shipping. Attached is an electronic copy of the invoice with our credit card number.

Sincerely,

Charlotte Piroska
President
cpiroska@artdeco-style.com

Art Deco Style
370 W. Main Street, White Sulphur Springs, WV 24986
(855) 864-4858 | www.artdeco-style.com

Begins with compliment and keeps tone objective, rational, and unemotional

Provides identifying data and justifies claim

Explains why claim is valid and suggests responsibility of receiver

Expresses disappointment and appeals to receiver's reputation and customer service

Tells what action to take

Tips for Persuasive Claims and Complaints
- Begin with a compliment, point of agreement, statement of the problem, or brief review of the action you have taken to resolve the problem.
- Provide identifying data.
- Prove that your claim is valid; explain why the receiver is responsible.
- Attach document copies supporting your claim.
- Appeal to the receiver's fairness, ethical and legal responsibilities, and desire for customer satisfaction.
- Describe your feelings and your disappointment.
- Avoid sounding angry, emotional, or irrational.
- Close by telling exactly what you want done.

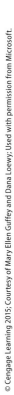
What's more, Charlotte was frustrated that the Return Merchandise Authorization form she filled out at the company's website seemed to sink into a dark hole in cyberspace. She had reason to be angry! However, she resolved to use a moderate tone in writing her complaint e-mail because she knew that a calm, unemotional tone would be more effective. She opted for a positive opening, a well-documented claim, and a request for specific action in the closing.

CHECKLIST ▶▶

Using the AIDA Strategy to Request Actions, Make Claims, and Deliver Complaints

Prewrite

- Determine your purpose. Know exactly what you want to achieve.

- Anticipate the reaction of your audience. Remember that the receiver is thinking, *Why should I? What's in it for me? What's in it for you? Who cares?*

Gain Attention

- Use the indirect strategy rather than blurting out the request immediately.

- Begin with a problem description, unexpected statement, reader benefit, compliment, related facts, or stimulating question to grab attention.

Build Interest

- Convince the audience that your request is reasonable.

- Develop interest by using facts, statistics, examples, testimonials, and specific details.

- Establish your credibility, if necessary, by explaining your background and expertise. Use testimonials, expert opinion, or research if necessary.

- Support your request by tying facts to direct benefits (increased profits, more efficient operations, better customer relations, money savings, a returned favor) or indirect benefits (improving the community, giving back to the profession, helping the environment).

- In claims and complaints, be objective but prove the validity of your request.

Elicit Desire and Reduce Resistance

- Anticipate objections to your request by using *What if?* scenarios and provide compelling counterarguments.

- Demonstrate credibility and competence.

- In claims and complaints, use a moderate, unemotional tone.

Motivate Action

- Make a precise request that spells out exactly what you want done. Add a deadline date if necessary.
- Repeat a key benefit, provide additional details, or offer an incentive. Express appreciation.
- Be confident without seeming pushy.

Writing Persuasive Messages in Digital-Age Organizations

LEARNING OBJECTIVE 4
Understand interpersonal persuasion at work and write persuasive messages within organizations.

As noted earlier, the lines of authority are blurry in today's information-age workplaces, and the roles of executives are changing. Technology has empowered rank-and-file employees who can turn to their companies' intranets and don't need their managers to be information providers—formerly a crucial managerial role. "Instead of being controllers or hoarders of knowledge," one top executive said, most contemporary managers "viewed themselves as collaborators and mentors, trusted for their experience—not their gigabytes of memory."[25]

This huge shift in authority is affecting the strategies for creating and the tone of workplace persuasive messages. You may still want to be indirect if you hope to persuade your boss to do something he or she will be reluctant to do; however, your boss, in turn, will be less likely to rely on the power of position and just issue commands. Rather, today's executives increasingly bank on persuasion to achieve buy-in from subordinates.[26]

This section focuses on messages flowing downward and upward within organizations. Horizontal messages exchanged among coworkers resemble those discussed earlier in requesting actions.

Persuading Employees: Messages Flowing Downward

Employees traditionally expected to be directed in how to perform their jobs; therefore, instructions or directives moving downward from superiors to subordinates usually required little persuasion. Messages such as information about procedures, equipment, or customer service still use the direct strategy, with the purpose immediately stated.

However, employees are sometimes asked to volunteer for projects such as tutoring disadvantaged children or helping at homeless shelters. Some organizations encourage employees to join programs to stop smoking, lose weight, or start exercising. Organizations may ask employees to participate in capacities outside their work roles—such as spending their free time volunteering for charity projects. In such cases, the four-part indirect AIDA strategy provides a helpful structure.

Because many executives today rely on buy-in instead of exercising raw power,[27] messages flowing downward require attention to tone. Warm words and a conversational tone convey a caring attitude. Persuasive requests coming from a trusted superior are more likely to be accepted than requests from a dictatorial executive who relies on threats and punishments to secure compliance. The proverbial carrot has always been more persuasive than the stick. Because the words *should* and *must* sometimes convey a negative tone, be careful in using them.

Figure 10.8 shows a memo e-mailed by Delia Ormod, director of HR Staffing and Training at a large bank. Her goal is to persuade employees to participate in Hands On Miami Day, a fund-raising and community service event that the bank sponsors. In addition to volunteering their services for a day, employees also have to pay $30 to register! You can see that this is no small persuasion task for Delia.

Delia decides to follow the AIDA four-part indirect strategy beginning with gaining attention. Notice, for example, that she strives to capture attention by describing specific benefits of volunteering in Miami. The second paragraph of this persuasive message builds interest by listing examples of what volunteers have accomplished during previous Hands On Miami events. To reduce resistance, the third paragraph explains why the $30 fee makes sense. To motivate action in the closing, Delia saved a strong indirect benefit. The bank will chip in $30 for every employee who volunteers before the deadline. This significant indirect benefit along with the direct benefits of having fun and joining colleagues in a community activity combine to create a strong persuasive message.

A successful CEO summed up the changing collaborative workplace by referring to himself as "the guy who is obsessed with enabling the employees to create value." He added self-deprecatingly: "I'm not the greatest and brightest leader born. My job is to make sure that all people are enabled to do what they do well."[28]

Persuading the Boss: Messages Flowing Upward

Convincing management to adopt a procedure or invest in a product or new equipment requires skillful communication. Managers are just as resistant to change as others are. Providing evidence is critical when submitting a recommendation to your boss. Be ready to back up your request with facts, figures, and evidence. When selling an idea to management, strive to make a strong dollars-and-cents case.[29] A request that emphasizes how the proposal saves money or benefits the business is more persuasive than one that simply announces a good deal or tells how a plan works.

In describing an idea to your boss, state it confidently and fairly. Don't undermine your suggestions with statements such as, *This may sound crazy* or, *I know we tried this once before but . . . .* Show that you have thought through the suggestion by describing the risks involved as well as the potential benefits. You may wonder whether you should even mention the downside of a suggestion. Most bosses will be relieved and impressed to know that you have considered the risks as well as the benefits to a proposal.[30] Two-sided arguments are generally more persuasive because they make you sound credible and fair. Presenting only one side of a proposal reduces its effectiveness because such a proposal seems biased, subjective, and flawed.

Figure **10.8** Persuasive Organizational Message Flowing Downward

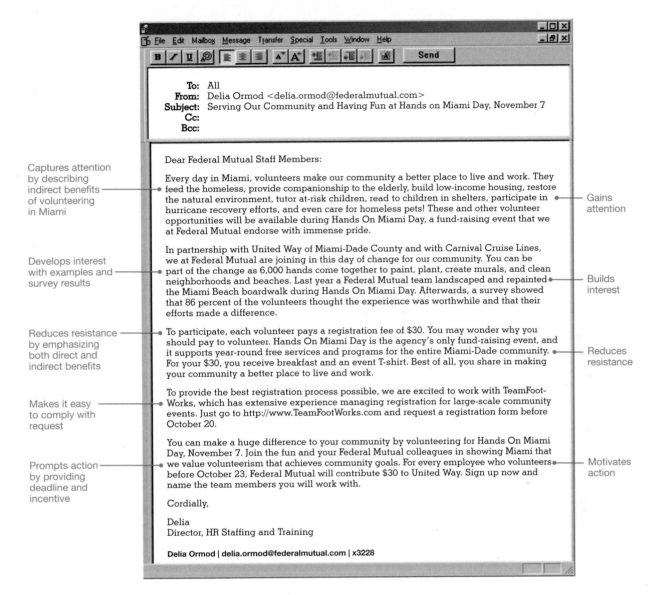

Captures attention by describing indirect benefits of volunteering in Miami

Develops interest with examples and survey results

Reduces resistance by emphasizing both direct and indirect benefits

Makes it easy to comply with request

Prompts action by providing deadline and incentive

Gains attention

Builds interest

Reduces resistance

Motivates action

To: All
From: Delia Ormod <delia.ormod@federalmutual.com>
Subject: Serving Our Community and Having Fun at Hands on Miami Day, November 7
Cc:
Bcc:

Dear Federal Mutual Staff Members:

Every day in Miami, volunteers make our community a better place to live and work. They feed the homeless, provide companionship to the elderly, build low-income housing, restore the natural environment, tutor at-risk children, read to children in shelters, participate in hurricane recovery efforts, and even care for homeless pets! These and other volunteer opportunities will be available during Hands On Miami Day, a fund-raising event that we at Federal Mutual endorse with immense pride.

In partnership with United Way of Miami-Dade County and with Carnival Cruise Lines, we at Federal Mutual are joining in this day of change for our community. You can be part of the change as 6,000 hands come together to paint, plant, create murals, and clean neighborhoods and beaches. Last year a Federal Mutual team landscaped and repainted the Miami Beach boardwalk during Hands On Miami Day. Afterwards, a survey showed that 86 percent of the volunteers thought the experience was worthwhile and that their efforts made a difference.

To participate, each volunteer pays a registration fee of $30. You may wonder why you should pay to volunteer. Hands On Miami Day is the agency's only fund-raising event, and it supports year-round free services and programs for the entire Miami-Dade community. For your $30, you receive breakfast and an event T-shirt. Best of all, you share in making your community a better place to live and work.

To provide the best registration process possible, we are excited to work with TeamFoot-Works, which has extensive experience managing registration for large-scale community events. Just go to http://www.TeamFootWorks.com and request a registration form before October 20.

You can make a huge difference to your community by volunteering for Hands On Miami Day, November 7. Join the fun and your Federal Mutual colleagues in showing Miami that we value volunteerism that achieves community goals. For every employee who volunteers before October 23, Federal Mutual will contribute $30 to United Way. Sign up now and name the team members you will work with.

Cordially,

Delia
Director, HR Staffing and Training

Delia Ormod | delia.ormod@federalmutual.com | x3228

Persuasive messages traveling upward require a special sensitivity to tone. When asking superiors to change views or take action, use words such as *suggest* and *recommend* rather than *you must* and *we should*. Avoid sounding pushy or argumentative. Strive for a conversational, yet professional, tone that conveys warmth, competence, and confidence.

When Marketing Manager Michael Cooper wanted his boss to authorize the purchase of a multifunction color laser copier, he knew he had to be persuasive. His memo, shown in Figure 10.9, illustrates an effective approach.

Notice that Michael's memo isn't short. A successful persuasive message typically takes more space than a direct message because proving a case requires evidence. In the end, Michael chose to send his memo as an e-mail attachment accompanied by a polite, short e-mail because he wanted to keep the document format in MS Word intact. He also felt that the message was too long to paste into his e-mail program. The subject line announces the purpose of the message but without disclosing the actual request. The strength of the persuasive document in Figure 10.9 is in the clear presentation of comparison figures showing how much money the company can save by purchasing a remanufactured copier.

Figure **10.9** Persuasive Message Flowing Upward

To: Gary Greer <gary.greer@smartmachinetools.com>
From: Michael Cooper <michael.cooper@smartmachinetools.com>
Subject: Saving Time and Money on Copying and Printing
Cc:
Attached: refurbished color copiers.docx (10 KB)

Gary,

Attached is a brief document that details our potential savings from purchasing a refurbished color laser copier. After doing some research, I discovered that these sophisticated machines aren't as expensive as one might think.

Please look at my calculations and let me know what you suggest that we to do improve our in-house production of print matter and reduce both time and cost for external copying.

Mike

Michael Cooper
Marketing Assistant * Smart Machine Tools, Inc.
800 S. Santa Fe Blvd. * City of Industry, CA 91715
213.680.3000 office / 213.680.3229 fax
michael.cooper@smartmachinetools.com

Serves as cover e-mail to introduce attached memo in MS Word

Opens with catchy subject line

Does not reveal recommendation but leaves request for action to the attached memo

Provides an electronic signature with contact information

↓ 1 inch
MEMORANDUM
↓ 2 blank lines

Date: April 8, 2015
↓ 1 blank line
To: Gary Greer, Vice President
↓ 1 blank line
From: Michael Cooper, Marketing
↓ 1 blank line
Subject: Saving Time and Money on Copying
↓ 1 or 2 blank lines

We are losing money on our current copy services and wasting the time of employees as well. Because our aging Canon copier is in use constantly and can't handle our growing printing volume, we find it increasingly necessary to send major jobs out to Copy Quick. Moreover, whenever we need color copies, we can't handle the work ourselves. Just take a look at how much we spend each month for outside copy service:

Copy Costs: Outside Service
10,000 B&W copies/month made at Copy Quick	$ 700.00
1,000 color copies/month, $0.25 per copy (avg.)	250.00
Salary costs for assistants to make 32 trips	480.00
Total	$1,430.00

To save time and money, I have been considering alternatives. Large-capacity color laser copiers with multiple features (copy, e-mail, fax, LAN fax, print, scan) are expensive. However, reconditioned copiers with all the features we need are available at attractive prices. From Copy City we can get a fully remanufactured Xerox copier that is guaranteed and provides further savings because solid-color ink sticks cost a fraction of laser toner cartridges. We could copy and print in color for roughly the same as black and white. After we make an initial payment of $300, our monthly costs would look like this:

Copy Costs: Remanufactured Copier:
Paper supplies for 11,000 copies	$160.00
Ink sticks and copy supplies	100.00
Labor of assistants to make copies	150.00
Monthly financing charge for copier (purchase price of $3,105 – $300 amortized at 10% with 36 payments)	93.74
Total	$503.74

As you can see, a remanufactured Xerox 8860MFP copier saves us more than $900 per month. For a limited time Copy City is offering a free 15-day trial offer, a free copier stand (a $250 value), free starter supplies, and free delivery and installation. We have office space available, and my staff is eager to add a second machine.

Please call me at Ext. 630 if you have questions. This copier is such a good opportunity that I have prepared a purchase requisition authorizing the agreement with Copy City. With your approval before May 1, we could have our machine by May 10 and start saving time and more than $900 every month. Fast action will also help us take advantage of Copy City's free start-up incentives.

Summarizes problem

Uses headings and columns for easy comprehension

Provides more benefits

Makes it easy to grant approval

Describes topic without revealing request

Proves credibility of request with facts and figures

Highlights most important benefit

Counters possible resistance

Repeats main benefit with motivation to act quickly

© Cengage Learning 2015

Creating Effective Sales Messages in Print and Online

LEARNING OBJECTIVE **5**
Create effective and ethical direct-mail and e-mail sales messages.

Sales messages use persuasion to promote specific products and services. In our coverage we are most concerned with sales messages delivered by postal mail or by e-mail. The best sales messages, whether delivered by direct mail or by e-mail, have much in common. In this section we look at how to apply the 3-x-3 writing process to sales messages. We also present techniques developed by experts to draft effective sales messages, both in print and online.

Applying the 3-x-3 Writing Process to Sales Messages

Marketing professionals analyze and perfect every aspect of a sales message to encourage consumers to read and act on the message. Like the experts, you will want to pay close attention to analysis and adaptation before writing the actual message.

Analyzing the Product and Purpose for Writing. Prior to sitting down to write a sales message promoting a product, you must study the item carefully. What can you learn about its design, construction, raw materials, and manufacturing process? What can you learn about its ease of use, efficiency, durability, and applications? Be sure to consider warranties, service, price, premiums, exclusivity, and special appeals. At the same time, evaluate the competition so that you can compare your product's strengths against the competitor's weaknesses.

Now you are ready to identify your central selling point, the main theme of your appeal. In its latest marketing campaign, the U.S. Marine Corps chose "chaos" as its central selling point. Dramatic footage focuses on Marines providing humanitarian aid in unstable regions around the world because many millennials find such service appealing.[31] Analyzing your product and studying the competition help you determine what to emphasize in your sales message.

Equally important is determining the specific purpose of your message. Do you want the reader to call for a free video and brochure? Listen to a podcast at your website? Fill out an order form? Send a credit card authorization? Before you write the first word of your message, know what response you want and what central selling point you will emphasize to achieve that purpose.

Adapting a Sales Message to Its Audience. Despite today's predominance of e-mail marketing over direct-mail letters, in terms of response rates, sales letters win. Direct mail achieves a 4.4 percent response rate to e-mail's paltry 0.12 percent.[32] The response rate can be increased dramatically by targeting the audience through selected database mailing lists. Let's say you are selling fitness equipment. A good mailing list might come from subscribers to fitness or exercise magazines, who you would expect to have similar interests, needs, and demographics (age, income, and other characteristics). With this knowledge you can adapt the sales message to a specific audience.

Crafting Successful Sales Letters

Sales letters are usually part of multichannel marketing campaigns. These letters are a powerful means to make sales, generate leads, boost retail traffic, solicit donations, and direct consumers to websites. Direct mail allows a personalized, tangible, three-dimensional message that is less invasive than telephone solicitations and less reviled than unsolicited e-mail. A recent study shows that tangible mail appears to have a greater emotional impact than virtual mail. MRI scans suggest that physical materials "leave a deeper footprint in the brain."[33] Figure 10.10 displays information about channel choice and consumer perceptions of the various marketing media.

Figure **10.10** Channel Choice: Direct Mail and Social Media

BUT: **80%** of U.S. consumers do not want location-based mobile offers after visiting a brick-and-mortar store.

The use of mobile devices is growing rapidly.

#1 e-mail marketing

#2 direct mail

Preferred channels for Americans to receive brand communication

- most used for written, personal communications (45%)
- influences purchases the most (66%)
- preferred even by teens for permission-based marketing communications (66%)

Percentage of Americans who prefer to receive direct mail for

42% health care information

36% insurance information

39% financial services information

26% retail information

E-MAIL VS. SNAIL MAIL

Mobile device users were 40%–50% more likely than nonusers to favor e-mail and communicate online.

73% of Americans receive a lot of e-mails that they do not open.
70% have received more e-mails in the past year than the previous year.
62% like checking the mailbox for postal mail.
51% say they pay more attention to postal mail than e-mail.
73% prefer direct mail for brand communication because they decide when they read it.

ON TRUST

55% of women trust word-of-mouth information from friends and family

47% of men do

78% of Americans trust doctors and nurses for healthcare information.

6% believe YouTube and Twitter.

www.Epsilon.com/channelpreference2012; Exact Target 2012 Channel Preference Survey; © Cengage Learning 2015

"Our study found that direct mail continues to be a highly trusted and preferred channel among American and Canadian consumers."

Professionals who specialize in traditional direct-mail services have made it a science. They analyze a market, develop an effective mailing list, study the product, prepare a sophisticated campaign aimed at a target audience, and motivate the reader to act. You have probably received many direct-mail packages, often called junk mail. These packages typically contain a sales letter, a brochure, a price list, illustrations of the product, testimonials, and other persuasive appeals.

We are most concerned here with the sales letter: its strategy, organization, and evidence. Because sales letters are generally written by specialists, you may never write one on the job. Why learn how to write a sales letter? Learning the techniques of sales writing will help you be more successful in any communication that requires persuasion and promotion. What's more, you will recognize sales strategies directed at you, which will make you a more perceptive consumer of ideas, products, and services.

Your primary goal in writing a sales message is to get someone to devote a few moments of attention to it. You may be promoting a product, a service, an idea, or yourself. In each case the most effective messages will follow the AIDA strategy and (a) gain attention, (b) build interest, (c) elicit desire and reduce resistance, and (d) motivate action. This is the same recipe we studied earlier, but the ingredients are different.

Gaining Attention in Sales Messages. One of the most critical elements of a sales message is its opening paragraph. This opener should be short (one to five lines), honest, relevant, and stimulating. Marketing pros have found that eye-catching typographical arrangements or provocative messages, such as the following, can hook a reader's attention:

- **Offer:** *A free trip to Hawaii is just the beginning!*
- **Promise:** *Now you can raise your sales income by 50 percent or even more with the proven techniques found in . . . .*
- **Question:** *Do you yearn for an honest, fulfilling relationship?*
- **Quotation or proverb:** *Necessity is the mother of invention.*
- **Fact:** *The Greenland Eskimos ate more fat than anyone in the world. And yet . . . they had virtually no heart disease.*
- **Product feature:** *Volvo's snazzy new convertible ensures your safety with a roll bar that pops out when the car tips 40 degrees to the side.*
- **Testimonial:** *My name is Sheldon Schulman. I am a practicing medical doctor. I am also a multimillionaire. I didn't make my millions by practicing medicine, though. I made them by investing in my spare time.*
- **Startling statement:** *Let the poor and hungry feed themselves! For just $100 they can.*
- **Personalized action setting:** *It's 4:30 p.m. and you've got to make a decision. You need everybody's opinion, no matter where they are. Before you pick up your phone to call them one at a time, pick up this card: WebEx Teleconference Services.*

Other openings calculated to capture attention might include a solution to a problem, an anecdote, a personalized statement using the receiver's name, or a relevant current event.

Building Interest With Rational and Emotional Appeals. In this phase of your sales message, you should describe clearly the product or service. In simple language emphasize the central selling points that you identified during your prewriting analysis. Those selling points can be developed using rational or emotional appeals.

Rational appeals are associated with reason and intellect. They translate selling points into references to making or saving money, increasing efficiency, or making the best use of resources. In general, rational appeals are appropriate when a product is expensive, long-lasting, or important to health, security, and financial success.

Emotional appeals relate to status, ego, and sensual feelings. Appealing to the emotions is sometimes effective when a product is inexpensive, short-lived, or nonessential. Many clever sales messages, however, combine emotional and rational strategies for a dual appeal. Consider these examples:

Rational Appeal

You can buy the things you need and want, pay household bills, and pay off higher-cost loans and credit cards—as soon as you are approved and your ChoiceCredit card account is opened.

With motorists at risk from texting while driving, highway safety groups are sending the message that texting kills. One police department in the United Kingdom sparked controversy by creating a Hollywood-styled PSA so disturbing that viewers complained it should not air on television. The graphic video, which follows three teenage girls as they text and drive their way into a head-on collision with another vehicle, left international viewers shocked and in tears. But one tracking firm found that 80 percent of viewers planned to quit texting while on the road. Are safety messages delivered best using emotional appeals?[35]

© iStockphoto.com/Steve Jacobs

Emotional Appeal

Leave the urban bustle behind and escape to sun-soaked Bermuda! To recharge your batteries with an injection of sun and surf, all you need are your bathing suit, a little suntan lotion, and your ChoiceCredit card.

Dual Appeal

New ChoiceCredit cardholders are immediately eligible for a $200 travel certificate and additional discounts at fun-filled resorts. Save up to 40 percent while lying on a beach in picturesque, sun-soaked Bermuda, the year-round resort island.

A physical description of your product is not enough, however. Zig Ziglar, thought by some to be America's greatest salesperson, pointed out that no matter how well you know your product, no one is persuaded by cold, hard facts alone. In the end, people buy because of product benefits.[36] Your job is to translate those cold facts into warm feelings and reader benefits. Let's say a sales message promotes a hand cream made with aloe and cocoa butter extracts, along with vitamin A. Those facts become, *Nature's hand helpers—including soothing aloe and cocoa extracts, along with firming vitamin A—form invisible gloves that protect your sensitive skin against the hardships of work, harsh detergents, and constant environmental assaults.* As the Plugged In feature shows, despite their popularity, social networks have been eluding marketers eager to increase sales.

Reducing Resistance and Building Desire. Marketing specialists use a number of techniques to overcome resistance and build desire. When price is an obstacle, consider these suggestions:

- Delay mentioning price until after you've created a desire for the product.
- Show the price in small units, such as the price per issue of a magazine.
- Demonstrate how the reader saves money—for instance, by subscribing for two or three years.
- Compare your prices with those of a competitor.

In addition, you need to anticipate other objections and questions the receiver may have. When possible, translate these objections into selling points (*If you are worried about training your staff members on the new software, remember that our offer includes $1,000 worth of on-site*

ETHICS CHECK:

Scare Tactics

Direct marketers sometimes resort to scare tactics—for example, to make us purchase alarm systems or subscribe to monitoring services. They may also appeal to our compassion and guilt before the holidays in soliciting money for the less fortunate. Are such emotional appeals ethical?

one-on-one instruction). Other techniques to overcome resistance and prove the credibility of the product include the following:

- **Testimonials:** *"I never stopped eating, yet I lost 107 pounds." — Tina Rivers, Greenwood, South Carolina*
- **Names of satisfied users** (with permission, of course): *Enclosed is a partial list of private pilots who enthusiastically subscribe to our service.*

Social Media vs. Junk Mail and Spam—Which Sells Better?

Plugged In

© iStockphoto/Thinkstock

Self-improvement legend Dale Carnegie believed that humans are not rational beings, as is commonly believed. Rather, he wrote in one of his best-selling books: "We are dealing with creatures of emotion, creatures bristling with prejudices and motivated by pride and vanity."[37] Similarly, salesmanship guru Zig Ziglar claimed, "People don't buy for logical reasons. They buy for emotional reasons."[38] This is hardly news to veteran salespeople; however, until recently, modern economic theory assumed that humans make logical decisions based on rational calculations. The influence of emotions on decision making was largely overlooked.[39]

Emotions Guide Decision Making. Recent neurological research supports the view that human decision making is a process guided by emotions. As Robert Cialdini and others have argued, people seem to make nearly automated, split-second decisions that they then justify with logical reasoning. We are not aware of our biases and influences and sometimes rationalize or even fictionalize our past behavior.[40] Human beings are also more likely to be persuaded by people or entities they like and know. These two insights have important implications for social media marketing. They explain why so much emphasis today is placed on customer *engagement,* mostly carried out through social networks.

Social Media Are for Engagement and Branding. Adobe CEO Shantanu Narayen calls engagement "the new business mandate." He believes that "the health of a company relies on the extent to which it creates meaningful and sustainable interactions" with customers.[41] Engaged customers are more loyal and willing to recommend products. Social media success depends on creating an emotional connection.[42] One expert likens social media to a cocktail party at which one mingles and networks but does not rudely hawk products and services.[43] Social media are for branding, not selling, claims another expert.[44]

Yet even consumers who are fans don't necessarily want to be friends with brands.[45]

Social Media Don't Drive Sales. Although people use social networks to connect with friends, find jobs, and evaluate brands, over 80 percent of consumers would not try to resolve customer-service problems through social media.[46] Nor do they go to social media sites for shopping.[47] Recent IBM data revealed a shocking truth: Facebook and Twitter were responsible for less than 1 percent of online sales on Black Friday and Cyber Monday.[48] Although Facebook ads at 17.1 percent represented nearly double the online advertising of Google, Facebook's revenue was just 10 percent of Google's take of $36.4 billion. Google earned ten times as much as Facebook with about half as many ads.[49] Digital advertising faces an uphill battle as 63 percent of consumers say they tend to disregard Internet ads the most, banner ads in particular.[50]

When It Comes to Sales, E-Mail and Direct-Mail Marketing Rule. A channel preference study found that 65 percent of people who received direct mail (i.e., postal mail) made a purchase or engaged in a different marketing channel prompted by the direct-mail sender. Direct mail is second only to e-mail marketing, which induces 66 percent of recipients to make purchases.[51] Even in the digital age, direct mail is thriving, despite the uncertain future of the U.S. Postal Service. In terms of triggering sales, e-mail and sales letters still outperform social media. Sellers use direct mail as "a foot in the door" to invite consumers to connect through other channels.[52] Marketers today understand that to send seamless messages, they must use multiple channels.

- **Money-back guarantee or warranty:** *We offer the longest warranties in the business—all parts and service on-site for five years!*
- **Free trial or sample:** *We are so confident that you will like our new accounting program that we want you to try it absolutely free.*
- **Performance tests, polls, or awards:** *Our TP-3000 was named Best Internet Phone, and Etown.com voted it Smartphone of the Year.*

Motivating Action at the Conclusion of a Sales Message.   All the effort put into a sales message goes to waste if the reader fails to act. To make it easy for readers to act, you can provide a reply card, a stamped and preaddressed envelope, a toll-free telephone number, an easy-to-scan website, or a promise of a follow-up call. Because readers often need an extra push, consider including additional motivators, such as the following:

- **Offer a gift:** *You will receive a free cell phone with the purchase of any new car.*
- **Promise an incentive:** *With every new, paid subscription, we will plant a tree in one of America's Heritage Forests.*
- **Limit the offer:** *Only the first 100 customers receive free travel mugs.*
- **Set a deadline:** *You must act before June 1 to get these low prices.*
- **Guarantee satisfaction:** *We will return your full payment if you are not entirely satisfied—no questions asked.*

The final paragraph of the sales letter carries the punch line. This is where you tell readers what you want them to do and give them reasons for doing it. Most sales letters also include postscripts because they make irresistible reading. Even readers who might skim over or bypass paragraphs are drawn to a P.S. Therefore, use a postscript to reveal your strongest motivator, to add a special inducement for a quick response, or to reemphasize a central selling point.

Although you want to be persuasive in sales letters, you must guard against overstepping legal and ethical boundaries. Information contained in sales letters has landed some writers in hot water. See the accompanying Ethical Insights box to learn how to stay out of trouble.

Putting Together All the Parts of a Sales Message.   A direct-mail sales letter is the number two preferred marketing medium right behind e-mail[53] because it can be personalized, directed to target audiences, and filled with a more complete message than other advertising media can. However, direct mail is expensive. That's why crafting and assembling all the parts of a sales message are so critical.

Figure 10.11 shows a sales letter addressed to individuals and families who may need health insurance. To prompt the reader to respond to the mailing, the letter incorporates the effective four-part AIDA strategy. The writer first establishes the need for health coverage. Then she develops a rational central selling point (a variety of affordable health plans for every budget offered without sales pressure and medical jargon) and repeats this selling point in all the components of the letter. This sales letter saves its strongest motivator—a free heart-rate monitor for the first 30 callers—for the high-impact P.S. line.

Writing Successful E-Mail Sales Messages

E-mail is the primary channel that consumers use to interact with brands today. It is the most used channel for written, personal communication (45 percent), and 77 percent of consumers prefer permission-based marketing through e-mail.[54] E-mails cost about $7 per consumer response versus about $48 per response for traditional direct mail.[55] Much like traditional direct mail, e-mail marketing can attract new customers, keep existing ones, encourage future sales, cross-sell, and cut costs. However, e-marketers can create and send a promotion in half the time it takes to print and distribute a traditional message. To reach today's consumer, marketers must target their e-mails well if they wish to even get their messages opened.

Figure **10.11** HealthSelect Sales Letter

351

1 Prewriting

Analyze: The purpose is to persuade the reader to respond by calling, chatting with a representative online, or returning a reply card to obtain information.

Anticipate: The audience is individuals and families who may be interested in health insurance. The central selling point is value and flexibility of the various health plans.

Adapt: Because readers will be reluctant, use the indirect pattern, AIDA.

2 Drafting

Research: Gather facts to promote your product and its benefits.

Organize: Gain attention by addressing the cost of health insurance. Emphasize that insurance protects assets, and focus on reader benefits. Motivate action by promising a no-obligation quote. Encourage a response with a toll-free number and an easy-reply card.

Draft: Prepare a first draft for a pilot study.

3 Revising

Edit: Use short paragraphs and short sentences. Replace *bankrupt you* with *break the bank*.

Proofread: Use bulleted list for features and benefits description. Set headings boldface and underscore other important information. Hyphenate *easy-to-understand*. Check for any medical or bureaucratic jargon.

Evaluate: Monitor the response rate to this letter to assess its effectiveness.

© Cengage Learning 2015

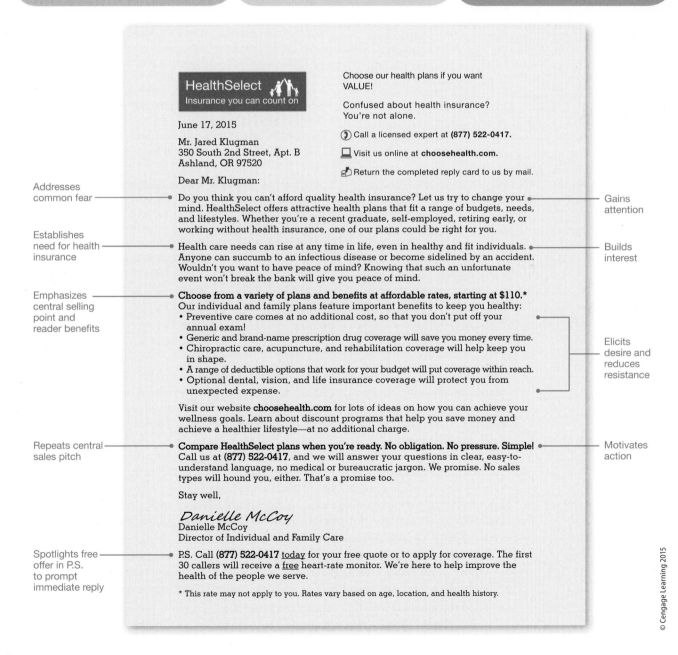

HealthSelect
Insurance you can count on

June 17, 2015

Mr. Jared Klugman
350 South 2nd Street, Apt. B
Ashland, OR 97520

Dear Mr. Klugman:

Choose our health plans if you want VALUE!

Confused about health insurance? You're not alone.

Call a licensed expert at **(877) 522-0417.**

Visit us online at **choosehealth.com.**

Return the completed reply card to us by mail.

Addresses common fear — Do you think you can't afford quality health insurance? Let us try to change your mind. HealthSelect offers attractive health plans that fit a range of budgets, needs, and lifestyles. Whether you're a recent graduate, self-employed, retiring early, or working without health insurance, one of our plans could be right for you. — *Gains attention*

Establishes need for health insurance — Health care needs can rise at any time in life, even in healthy and fit individuals. Anyone can succumb to an infectious disease or become sidelined by an accident. Wouldn't you want to have peace of mind? Knowing that such an unfortunate event won't break the bank will give you peace of mind. — *Builds interest*

Emphasizes central selling point and reader benefits — **Choose from a variety of plans and benefits at affordable rates, starting at $110.***
Our individual and family plans feature important benefits to keep you healthy:
- Preventive care comes at no additional cost, so that you don't put off your annual exam!
- Generic and brand-name prescription drug coverage will save you money every time.
- Chiropractic care, acupuncture, and rehabilitation coverage will help keep you in shape.
- A range of deductible options that work for your budget will put coverage within reach.
- Optional dental, vision, and life insurance coverage will protect you from unexpected expense.

— *Elicits desire and reduces resistance*

Visit our website **choosehealth.com** for lots of ideas on how you can achieve your wellness goals. Learn about discount programs that help you save money and achieve a healthier lifestyle—at no additional charge.

Repeats central sales pitch — **Compare HealthSelect plans when you're ready. No obligation. No pressure. Simple!** Call us at **(877) 522-0417,** and we will answer your questions in clear, easy-to-understand language, no medical or bureaucratic jargon. We promise. No sales types will hound you, either. That's a promise too. — *Motivates action*

Stay well,

Danielle McCoy
Danielle McCoy
Director of Individual and Family Care

Spotlights free offer in P.S. to prompt immediate reply — P.S. Call **(877) 522-0417** <u>today</u> for your free quote or to apply for coverage. The first 30 callers will receive a <u>free</u> heart-rate monitor. We're here to help improve the health of the people we serve.

* This rate may not apply to you. Rates vary based on age, location, and health history.

© Cengage Learning 2015

In promoting products and writing sales messages, be careful about the words you use and the claims you make. Avoid paid reviews. How far can you go in praising and selling your product?

- **Puffery.** In a sales message, you can write, *Hey, we've got something fantastic! It's the very best product on the market!* Called "puffery," such promotional claims are not taken literally by reasonable consumers. Dannon Yogurt settled a lawsuit for $45 million over allegedly deceptive claims that its Activia product was "clinically" and "scientifically" proven" to aid digestion.[56] What constitutes puffery is not always clear-cut.

- **Proving your claims.** If you write that *three out of four dentists recommend* your toothpaste, you had better have competent and reliable scientific evidence to support the claim. Such a claim goes beyond puffery and requires proof. According to a government report, as many as 20 percent of dietary supplements in the United States featured labels that made illegal claims to cure or treat diseases such as cancer or AIDS.[57] The $20 billion supplement industry is frequently in the sights of investigators and subject to litigation for misleading claims. Actress and *Dancing With the Stars* celebrity Kirstie Alley, whose struggle with weight loss is amply documented, is being sued for alleged deception over the Organic Liaison weight-loss program she touts.[58]

- **Celebrities.** The unauthorized use of a celebrity's name, likeness, or nickname is not permitted in sales messages. Hollywood stars George Clooney and Julia Roberts joined forces to sue two audiovisual companies for misusing their names and images in selling projectors and entertainment systems. Hilary Swank filed a lawsuit claiming unauthorized use of her film *Million Dollar Baby* in ads.[59] Similarly, the White House does not approve the use of the president's name and likeness for commercial purposes. Weatherproof Garment Company was asked to remove a billboard in Times Square that showed Barack Obama wearing one of its coats above the caption "A Leader in Style."[60]

- **Misleading statements.** You cannot tell people that they are winners or finalists in a sweepstake unless they actually are. American Family Publishers was found guilty of sending letters tricking people into buying magazine subscription in the belief that they had won $1.1 million. Sweepstakes scams prompted the Deceptive Mail Prevention and Enforcement Act that specifies numerous provisions and applies to all contests sent by U.S. postal mail.[61] Although POM Wonderful lost a lawsuit for exaggerating claims about the alleged health benefits of its pomegranate juice, the company continued selectively to use expert testimony from the very ruling it had lost.[62] Companies also may not misrepresent the nature, characteristics, qualities, or geographic origin of goods or services they are promoting.

- **Paying for favorable online reviews.** The Federal Trade Commission mandates full disclosure when a merchant and a promoter have a financial relationship. Legacy Learning Systems paid $250,000 to settle charges that it hired reviewers to recommend its videos on the Web.[63] Amazon and other online retailers have policies against buying positive reviews. Nonetheless, experts estimate that about one third of all Internet consumer reviews are fake.[64]

Selling by E-Mail.   If you will be writing online sales messages for your organization, try using the following techniques gleaned from the best-performing e-mails. Although much e-marketing dazzles receivers with colorful graphics, we focus on the words involved in persuasive sales messages. Earlier in the chapter, Figure 10.3 demonstrated many of the principles discussed here.

The first rule of e-marketing is to communicate only with those who have given permission. By sending messages only to "opt-in" folks, you greatly increase your "open rate"—those e-mails that will be opened. E-mail users detest spam. However, receivers are surprisingly receptive to offers tailored specifically for them. Remember that today's customer is somebody—not just anybody. Here are a few guidelines that will help you create effective e-mail sales messages:

- **Craft a catchy subject line.** Include an audience-specific location (*Emporium in Vegas Opens Soon!*); ask a meaningful question (*What's Your Dream Vacation?*); and use no more than 50 characters. Promise realistic solutions. Offer discounts or premiums.

- **Keep the main information "above the fold."** E-mails should be top heavy. Primary points should appear early in the message so that they capture the reader's attention.

- **Make the message short, conversational, and focused.** Because on-screen text is taxing to read, be brief. Focus on one or two central selling points only.
- **Sprinkle testimonials throughout the copy.** Consumers' own words are the best sales copy. These comments can serve as callouts or be integrated into the copy.
- **Provide a means for opting out.** It's polite and a good business tactic to include a statement that tells receivers how to be removed from the sender's mailing database.

Whether you actually write sales message on the job or merely receive them, you will better understand their organization and appeals by reviewing this chapter and the tips in the following checklist.

CHECKLIST ▶▶|
Preparing Persuasive Direct-Mail and E-Mail Sales Messages

Prewrite

- Analyze your product or service. What makes it special? What central selling points should you emphasize? How does it compare with the competition?
- Profile your audience. How will this product or service benefit this audience?
- Decide what you want the audience to do at the end of your message.
- For e-mails, send only to those who have opted in.

Gain Attention

- Describe a product feature, present a testimonial, make a startling statement, or show the reader in an action setting.
- Offer something valuable, promise the reader a result, or pose a stimulating question.
- Suggest a solution to a problem, offer a relevant anecdote, use the receiver's name, or mention a meaningful current event.

Build Interest

- Describe the product or service in terms of what it does for the reader. Connect cold facts with warm feelings and needs.
- Use rational appeals if the product or service is expensive, long-lasting, or important to health, security, or financial success. Use emotional appeals to suggest status, ego, or sensual feelings.
- Explain how the product or service can save or make money, reduce effort, improve health, produce pleasure, or boost status.

Elicit Desire and Reduce Resistance

- Counter anticipated reluctance with testimonials, money-back guarantees, attractive warranties, trial offers, or free samples.
- Build credibility with results of performance tests, polls, or awards.
- If price is not a selling feature, describe it in small units *(only 99 cents an issue)*, show it as savings, or tell how it compares favorably with that of the competition.

Motivate Action

- Close by repeating a central selling point and describing an easy-to-take action.
- Prompt the reader to act immediately with a gift, incentive, limited offer, deadline, or guarantee of satisfaction.
- Put the strongest motivator in a postscript.
- In e-mails include an opportunity to opt out.

In persuasive tweets and posts, writers try to pitch offers, prompt specific responses, or draw the attention of their audiences to interesting events and media links.

Writing Short Persuasive Messages Online

Increasingly, writers are turning to social network posts to promote their businesses, further their causes, and build their online personas. As we have seen, social media are not primarily suited for overt selling; however, tweets and other online posts can be used to influence others and to project a professional, positive social online presence.

Typically, organizations and individuals with followers post updates of their events, exploits, thoughts, and experiences. In persuasive tweets and posts, writers try to pitch offers, prompt specific responses, or draw the attention of their audiences to interesting events and media links. Figure 10.12 displays a sampling of persuasive tweets.

Figure 10.12 Analyzing Persuasive Tweets

Tweet promoting professional services by offering the reader a general benefit

Sandra Zimmer @sandrazimmer
Coaching for authentic presentations, public speaking & **persuasive messages** to help you shine. tinyurl.com/m5hrrx
Expand ← Reply ⊔ Retweet ★ Favorite

Tweet offering a freebie to promote a book and urging action by restricting the availability of the freebie

Jessica Brody @JessicaBrody
5 autographed copies of UNREMEMBERED (UK edition) are up for grabs on Free Book Friday teens this week! Check it out! ow.ly/k5k6M

Delta @Delta
Be sure to enter our Kick It in NYC contest before the curtain closes. Enter now! oak.ctx.ly/r/1nwv pic.twitter.com/CRHxOwKe
📷 View photo ← Reply ⊔ Retweet ★ Favorite

An airline creating urgency by suggesting that time to enter a contest is running out

James Barry @ChefJamesBarry
The Sugar Control Detox is coming and at an insanely low price! This opportunity is available to everyone, no... fb.me/S2XDfTXB
▶ View media ← Reply ⊔ Retweet ★ Favorite

Teaser tweet by a small business owner announcing an upcoming promotion

A notable public figure advocating action for a cause, to sign a petition

richardbranson @richardbranson
Make this holiday story have a happy ending – sign the petition to put #educationfirst for children around the world virg.in/hap
Expand

A nonprofit organization requesting political action of advocacy for a popular cause

Army of Women @ArmyofWomen
Think #breastcancer should be a Nat. priority? Tell the president HERE:ow.ly/dnMd3
Expand ← Reply ⊔ Retweet ★ Favorite

Prominent philanthropist tweeting to motivate giving by reassuring followers of charities' merit

Bill Gates @BillGates
Make your donations count. @CharityNav provides great information on the impact non-profits are actually having. b-gat.es/ThLBLJ
Expand

Mike Bloomberg @MikeBloomberg
I've joined @Instagram. Follow me here: instagram.com/mikebloomberg
Expand

Tweet by a notable public figure announcing his new social network account and inviting followers along

Guy Kawasaki @GuyKawasaki
Are you a writer? Here are some fantastic resources available free today as a download on the APE website.... fb.me/10bBh8apK
Expand ← Reply ⊔ Retweet ★ Favorite

Tweet by well-known businessperson offering a free resource using an attention-getter

Note that the compact format of a tweet requires extreme conciseness and efficiency. Don't expect the full four-part AIDA strategy to be represented in a 140-character Twitter message. Instead, you may see attention getters and calls for action, both of which must be catchy and intriguing. Regardless, many of the principles of persuasion apply even to micromessages.

Developing Persuasive Press Releases

LEARNING OBJECTIVE **6**

Apply basic techniques in developing persuasive press releases.

Press (news) releases announce important information to the media, whether traditional or digital. Such public announcements can feature new products, new managers, new facilities, sponsorships, participation in community projects, awards given or received, joint ventures, donations, or seminars and demonstrations. Naturally, organizations hope that the media will pick up this news and provide good publicity. However, purely self-serving or promotional information is not appealing to magazine and newspaper editors or to TV producers. To get them to read beyond the first sentence, press release writers follow these principles:

- Open with an attention-getting lead or a summary of the important facts.

- Include answers to the five *W*s and one *H* (*who, what, when, where, why*, and *how*) in the article—but not all in the first sentence!

- Appeal to the audience of the target media. Emphasize reader benefits written in the style of the focus publication or newscast.

- Present the most important information early, followed by supporting information. Don't put your best ideas last because they may be chopped off or ignored.

- Insert intriguing and informative quotations of chief decision makers to lend the news release credibility.

- Make the document readable and visually appealing. Limit the text to one or two double-spaced pages with attractive formatting.

- Look and sound credible—no typos, no imaginative spelling or punctuation, no factual errors.

The most important ingredient of a press release, of course, is *news*. Articles that merely plug products end up in the circular file, or they languish unread on a company website. The press release in Figure 10.13 announced the launch of a unique breast cancer research study conducted by two reputable medical organizations, Dr. Susan Love Research Foundation and City of Hope. The announcement provides an appealing headline and describes the purpose as well as the conduct of the massive, long-term research. The Health of Women Study is unusual in that it employs crowdsourcing and actively involves huge numbers of subjects online and by mobile devices. Moreover, data will be shared with all interested researchers and the participants themselves.

The best press releases focus on information that appeals to a targeted audience. A breast cancer study focusing on the potential causes and prevention of the disease is likely to generate keen and wide-ranging interest. The credibility of the study's sponsors discourages sensationalist coverage. Indirectly, the nonprofit organizations may also attract more research subjects and donations. Figure 10.13 illustrates many useful techniques for creating effective press releases.

Newspapers, magazines, and digital media are more likely to publish a press release that is informative, interesting, and helpful. The websites of many organizations today provide readily available media information including releases and photos.

Figure **10.13** Press Release With a Broad Appeal

Offers contacts for press inquiries

DR. SUSAN LOVE RESEARCH FOUNDATION
Act with Love™
FOR A FUTURE WITHOUT BREAST CANCER

FOR IMMEDIATE RELEASE

PRESS CONTACTS: Shirley Carr scarr@dslrf.org
Hanna Johnson hjohnson@dslrf.org
310-282-0600

"The key to ending breast cancer is to learn how to stop it before it starts."
--Dr. Susan Love, President, Dr. Susan Love Research Foundation

GROUNDBREAKING HEALTH OF WOMEN STUDY LAUNCHED

Provides optional headline

Opens by explaining who, what, when, where, why, and how

SANTA MONICA, Calif. – The Dr. Susan Love Research Foundation and Beckman Research Institute of City of Hope, today launch the Health of Women Study (HOW), a long-term cohort study tracking the health of women via online and mobile platforms. This new 21st-century research was designed to help find the root causes of breast cancer, leading to prevention. Any woman over 18 years old, as well as interested men, can join this revolutionary effort. HOW will study survivors and women who have not been diagnosed with breast cancer to investigate causes and new risk factors.

Announces populations targeted by the study

Quotes the chief investigators to add insight and credibility

"The majority of women who get breast cancer have none of the known clinical risk factors for the disease," said Susan Love, MD, president and founder of the Dr. Susan Love Research Foundation. "We have made strides in how we treat breast cancer, but we still don't know how to prevent it. We believe this new kind of study that traces and involves healthy women and breast cancer patients will give us the data we need to find the cause and develop prevention."

"Cohort studies are most valuable in epidemiology, but they are extremely costly and difficult to manage," said Leslie Bernstein, PhD, Beckman Research Institute of City of Hope. "The HOW Study uses economical technology and will capture behavior and lifestyle changes affecting women's cancer risk."

The HOW Study enables clinical researchers to pose questions rapidly, reaching a large sample population online and via mobile devices. Thus, researchers will capture more relevant data than has been feasible before and will empower consumers to become major stakeholders actively engaged in research. Study participants will be able to pose questions and play a tangible role in working to end breast cancer. "The important data collected as a part of HOW will be shared with researchers who can use it—a practice virtually unheard of in the research community," said Love.

Explains in detail the unique features and benefits of the study

Addresses the recruitment of study subjects

In 2008 the Dr. Susan Love Research Foundation introduced the Love/Avon Army of Women to participate in breast cancer research studies looking into causes and prevention of the disease. Today the Army of Women has nearly 370,000 women ready to participate in research studies.

About the Study Sponsors
The mission of Dr. Susan Love Research Foundation is to eradicate breast cancer and improve the quality of women's health through innovative research, education and advocacy. Beckman Research Institute of City of Hope is known worldwide for its outstanding basic, translational and epidemiological research. For details, visit www.healthofwomenstudy.org

Describes credentials of sponsoring organizations

Offers means of obtaining additional information

Uses pound symbols to signal end of release

Adapted from the press release found at www.armyofwomen.org. Adaption is copyrighted © Cengage Learning 2015.

Your Turn: Applying Your Skills at Natural Capitalism Solutions

YOUR TURN. As a business development and marketing intern at Natural Capitalism Solutions, you will be accompanying L. Hunter Lovins to a workshop she's giving on engaging employees in small businesses. After the talk, you will hand out memory sticks with ancillary materials (brochures, fact sheets, lists of resources) the attendees can take back to their workplaces. Your supervisor has asked you to draft a persuasive letter that thanks the attendees for coming, reminds them of a few points covered in the talk, and persuades them to implement the message.

YOUR TASK. In pairs, watch the first six minutes of the webinar "Engage Your Employees— Increase Your Profits" on YouTube. Then, with your partner, write a persuasive letter addressed to the business owner attendees. The letter should reiterate approximately five benefits to engaging employees and encourage the business owners to use some of the methods for increasing profits.

Summary of Learning Objectives

1 Explain digital-age persuasion, identify effective persuasive techniques, and apply the 3-x-3 writing process to persuasive messages in print and online. Persuasion may be defined as the ability to use words and other symbols to influence an individual's attitudes and behaviors. Six psychological triggers seem to prompt us to act and to believe: reciprocation, commitment, social proof, liking, authority, and scarcity. Digital-age persuasion is prolific, widespread, far-reaching, and fast-moving. Persuasive techniques today are more subtle and misleading than those used in the past, as well as more complex and impersonal. Effective persuaders establish credibility, make a specific request, tie facts to benefits, recognize the power of loss, expect and overcome resistance, share solutions, and compromise. Before writing a persuasive message, decide what you want the receiver to do or think. Adapt the message to the audience. Collect information and organize it into an appropriate strategy. Choose an indirect strategy if the audience might resist the request.

2 Describe the traditional four-part AIDA strategy for creating successful persuasive messages, and apply the four elements to draft effective and ethical business messages. The most effective persuasive messages include four major elements: gaining attention, building interest, eliciting desire while reducing resistance, and motivating action. Writers gain attention by opening with a problem, unexpected statement, reader benefit, compliment, related fact, or stimulating question. They build interest with facts, expert opinions, examples, details, and direct and indirect reader benefits. They elicit desire and reduce resistance by anticipating objections and presenting counterarguments. They conclude by motivating a specific action and making it easy for the reader to respond. Ethical communicators avoid distortion, exaggeration, and doublespeak when making persuasive arguments.

3 Craft persuasive messages that request actions, make claims, and deliver complaints. Persuasive requests are more effective if communicators think through their purpose and prepare a thoughtful message. Receivers tend to comply because they want to "give back" and because others may benefit. Persuasive claims involve damaged products, billing mistakes,

Go to
www.cengagebrain.com
and use your access code
to unlock valuable student
resources.

warranty problems, and so on. Claims and complaints require a logical argument, an objective, unemotional tone, and proof of the validity of the request. Open with sincere praise, an objective statement of the problem, a point of agreement, or a quick review of what you have done to resolve the problem. Elicit desire and reduce resistance by anticipating objections and providing counter-arguments. Motivate action by stating exactly what is to be done. Add a deadline if necessary and express appreciation.

4 Understand interpersonal persuasion at work and write persuasive messages within organizations. In today's workplace executives are more likely to rely on persuasion and employee buy-in than on the power of their position. When asking subordinates to volunteer for projects or to make lifestyle changes, organizations, too, may use the AIDA strategy to persuade. In messages flowing downward, good writers use a conversational tone and warm words. They focus on direct and indirect benefits. In messages flowing upward, such as recommendations from subordinates to supervisors, providing evidence is critical. Making a strong dollars-and-cents appeal whenever appropriate strengthens the argument. Two-sided arguments are more persuasive because they make writers sound credible and fair.

5 Create effective and ethical direct-mail and e-mail sales messages. Careful analysis of the product or service is necessary before you can compose a sales message. Identify the central selling point. Effective sales messages usually begin with a short, honest, and relevant attention getter. Simple language describing appropriate appeals builds interest. Testimonials, a money-back guarantee, or a free trial can reduce resistance and elicit desire. A gift, incentive, or deadline can motivate action. E-marketing messages should be sent only to opt-in receivers. Writers of effective e-mails begin with a catchy subject line, keep the main information "above the fold," make the message short and focused, convey urgency, include testimonials if available, and provide a means for opting out. Tweets and other short persuasive social media messages are used to influence others and to project a professional social online presence. Even brief persuasive posts may contain AIDA components.

6 Apply basic techniques in developing persuasive press releases. Press releases usually open with an attention-getting lead or summary of the important facts. They attempt to answer the questions *who, what, when, where, why*, and *how*. They are written carefully to appeal to the audience of the target media. The best press releases present the most important information early, are visually appealing, and look and sound credible.

Chapter Review

1. What is persuasion as defined by communication scholar Richard M. Perloff? (Obj. 1)

2. List and explain the five components that make up Richard M. Perloff's definition of persuasion. (Obj. 1)

3. List and explain the six psychological triggers that prompt us to act and believe. Include brief examples. (Obj. 1)

4. What is the AIDA strategy, and what does the acronym stand for? (Obj. 2)

5. List six elements that might help you build interest in a persuasive message and show that your request is reasonable. (Obj. 2)

6. What are *What if* scenarios, and how can they be used to reduce resistance in a persuasive request? (Obj. 2)

7. When does persuasion become unethical and what is *double-speak*? (Obj. 2)

8. Name five or more examples of typical situations requiring persuasive claim messages. (Obj. 3)

9. How have shifts in authority in digital-age organizations affected the strategies for creating goodwill and the tone of workplace persuasive messages? (Obj. 4)

10. When is persuasion necessary in business messages flowing downward in an organization? (Obj. 4)

11. When might persuasion be necessary in messages flowing upward? (Obj. 4)

12. Before composing a letter to sell a product, what should the writer do? (Obj. 5)

13. Name eight or more ways to attract attention in the opening of a sales message. (Obj. 5)

14. How can a writer motivate action in a sales letter? (Obj. 5)

15. List five or more topics that an organization might feature in a press release. (Obj. 6)

Critical Thinking

1. Reviewing a new critical marketing book, Adrian Wooldridge of *The Economist* cites these three examples of how today's "hidden persuaders" ply their trade:

   > Marketers have long known that the most powerful persuader is peer pressure. What is new is that the data revolution and social media have hugely increased their ability to start "social epidemics." They create outrageous videos that "go viral": Quiksilver, a company that sells surfing clothes, produced one about surfers hurling dynamite into a river and then surfing the resulting wave. . . .
   >
   > SAS, a software company, analyses social-media chatter to find people whose online comments influence others; companies can then target these "influentials."
   >
   > Firms such as Whole Foods turn anti-corporate fads such as organic food into marketing tools.[65]

   What is the author's objection? Can you find evidence of it in your own life? (Obj. 1)

2. What are some of the underlying motivations that prompt individuals to agree to requests that do not directly benefit themselves or their organizations? (Obj. 3)

3. How are direct-mail sales letters and e-mail sales messages similar, and how are they different? (Obj. 5)

4. Why are magazine and newspaper editors or TV producers wary of press (news) releases from businesses and reluctant to turn them into articles? (Obj. 6)

5. **Ethical Issue:** Two students at Cambridge University, England, were charging businesses to have their logos painted on their faces for a day. The students raised more than $40,000 toward their university tuition.[66] Companies such as Volvo adopted temporary tattoos in their promotions. Dunlop, however, went to the extreme by offering a set of free tires to those who would have the company's flying-D logo *permanently* tattooed somewhere on their bodies. Ninety-eight people complied.[67] Is it ethical for advertisers to resort to such extreme promotions dubbed "skinvertising"? Do you think it's even effective? Would you participate?

Activities

Note: All Documents for Analysis are provided at **www.cengagebrain.com** for you to download and revise.

10.1 Document for Analysis: Poor Persuasive Request Going to Texas 7-Eleven Owners (Objs. 1–3)

YOUR TASK. Analyze the following poorly written persuasive e-mail request. List its weaknesses. If your instructor directs, revise it using the suggestions you learned in this chapter.

To:	7-Eleven Franchise Owners Association of Texas
From:	Terry Navarro <terrynavarro@yahoo.com>
Subject:	Plastic-Wrapped Fruit Not for Us!
Cc:	
Bcc:	

Hey, have you heard about this new thing coming at us? As a 7-Eleven franchise owner and member of the 7-Eleven Franchise Owners Association of Texas, I am seriously put off about this move to wrap our bananas in plastic. Sure, it would extend their shelf life to five days. And I know that our customers want yellow–not brown—bananas. But wrapping them in plastic?? I mentioned this at home, and my teenage daughter immediately turned up her nose and said, "A banana wrapped in plastic? Eeeyooo! Do we really need more plastic clogging up the environment?" She's been studying sustainability and said that more plastic packaging is not a sustainable solution to our problem.

I realize that we 7-Eleven franchisees are increasingly dependent on fresh food sales as cigarette sales tank. But plastic-wrapped bananas is going too far, even if the wrapping slows ripening. As members of the 7-Eleven Franchise Owners Association, we have to do something. I think we could insist that our supplier Fresh Del Monte come up with a wrapper that's biodegradable. On the other hand, extending the shelf life of bananas cuts the carbon footprint by cutting down all those deliveries to our stores.

We have a meeting of franchisees coming up on February 1. Let's resist this banana thing!

Terry

10.2 Document for Analysis: Weak Persuasive Request Inviting Small Planet Speaker (Objs. 1–3)

YOUR TASK. Analyze the following poorly written request. List its weaknesses. If your instructor directs, revise the letter. Add appropriate information if needed.

Current date

Ms. Anna Lappe
418 North Jay Street
Brooklyn, NY 11212

Dear Ms. Lappe:

I am program chair for an upcoming member drive in Seattle. We would like very much to invite you to be our keynote speaker.

Our organization is called Sustainable Enterprises of Seattle, and we are a nonprofit dedicated to equipping the Northwest's citizens and decision makers with policy research and practical tools to advance long-term solutions to our region's most challenging challenges. We do many things including in-depth research. We offer commentary and analysis. All of these things we disseminate through e-mail, online, and in person.

We realize that you are extremely busy with your advocacy of the sustainability movement and as founding principal of the Small Planet Institute. But are you free on March 14? We are hoping you could address our group and talk about connecting the dots between the food on our plate and global warming—or do you call it global climate change? You have written that this country's food sector is both a central culprit in global warming and a key part of the solution. We would really like to learn how the world can be fed and the planet cooled through sustainable farming. We heard about you through your Facebook page and through your websites: Food MythBusters, Small Planet Fund, and Take a Bite Out of Climate Change.

We can offer only a small honorariam, although we could put you up at Seattle's eco-friendly Cedarbrook Lodge. Our mission is to make the Northwest a global model of sustainability. We envision sustainable communities, a green economy, and a healthy environment.

If you can speak to our group, we could, with your permission, possibly arrange to have copies of your latest book that you could sign.

Thank you and please let me know.

Sincerely,

10.3 Document for Analysis: Poor Claim Letter From Unhappy Copier Owner (Objs. 1–3)

YOUR TASK. Analyze the following poorly written claim letter. List its weaknesses. If your instructor directs, revise it.

Current date

Mr. Trenton Khalifa
VIP Copier Specialists
1532 Nashville Pike
Gallatin, TN 37012

Dear Ripoff Specialist:

Here are the dismal facts. My company recently purchased four of your BizStar C500 photocopiers, which sounded great at the time. They promised 2-sided copies, fax, printer, and color scanning to my computer. This was perfect for my health care office. Your salesperson Carol Finley assured us that the BizStar C500 could handle our high volume of 3,000 copies a day. This sounded unlikely since the sales brochure suggested that the C500 was meant for 500 copies a day. Regardless, we listened to what Ms. Finley told us. And that was our big mistake! Our four C500 copies are down every day, and my employees are screaming at me constantly. These machines are still under warranty, but I will admit that they do eventually get repaired. However, we can't get by with so much downtime.

Because I lost faith in your Ms. Finley, I telephoned the district manager, William Tanaka. I suggested that we trade in our BizStar C500 copiers (which cost us $2,300 each) on two BizStar C1000 models (at $12,500 each). However, Mr. Tanaka said he would have to charge 50 percent depreciation on our C500 copiers. What a major rip-off! I think that 20 percent depreciation is more reasonable since we've had the machines only three months. Mr. Finley said he would get back to me, and I haven't heard from him since.

Now I'm forced to write to your headquarters because I have had no luck with either Ms. Finley or Mr. Tanaka, and I need to see some action on these machines. If you understood anything about business, you would see what a sweet deal I'm offering you. I'm willing to stick with your company and purchase your most expensive model—but I can't take such a steep loss on the C500 copiers. These copiers are relatively new; you should be able to sell them with no trouble. And think of all the money you will save by not having your repair technicians making constant trips to service our underpowered BizStar C500copiers! Please let me hear from you immediately, or I may next turn to Yelp.

Sincerely yours,

10.4 Document for Analysis: Poor Persuasive E-Mail Flowing Upward—Miserable Meetings (Objs. 1, 2, and 4)

YOUR TASK. Analyze the following poorly written e-mail. List its weaknesses. If your instructor directs, revise it.

To: Charlotte Cohen <ccohen@mitenterprise>
From: Clint Johnson <cjohnson@mitenterprise>
Subject: Miserable Meetings
Cc:
Attached:

Good morning!

I wonder if you know how bad meetings are around here. We seem to have endless meetings that drag on and on forever. I myself attended five meetings within the building but also was forced to participate in three more conference call meetings. And that was just last week! Nearly every one of those meetings was poorly run. Some should never have been called because they merely announced information after a decision had already been made. Some could easily have been handled in an e-mail. Sometimes I think our meetings are really opportunities to socialize under the guise of "work." Our meetings are huge time suckers.

I'm going to level with you and tell it like it is. Something needs to be done about the lost productivity and sagging employee morale around here. No one likes to waste valuable time attending poorly run or unnecessary meetings. Apparently, our managers have not been trained in how to conduct meetings, although I realize that all of them are professional and have business training.

What we need is a meeting policy or something like that. We need some guidelines or training about how to conduct meetings. Has anyone thought of that? I can think of many ways to improve meetings. Could we please talk about this?

Clint Johnson
Project Manager

10.5 Understanding the Art of Persuasion— Aristotle's Rhetoric (Obj. 1)

`Social Media`   `Web`

Besides the persuasive models introduced in this chapter, many more exist. One of the oldest and best-known modes of persuasion comes from Aristotle (384–322 BC). The Greek philosopher identified three components of persuasion: *ethos, pathos,* and *logos.*

Ethos describes the merit, character, and expertise of a speaker. Persuasion is possible when the audience believes that the persuader is credible and has a good reputation. For instance, we tend to believe a successful coach speaking about training methods. Testimonials in advertising are an example of ethos.

Pathos describes an emotional appeal. It means the style of delivery—for example, when a speaker exhibits passion and uses colorful metaphors, language, attention getters, and more. When successful, pathos triggers feelings in the audience intended by the speaker, such as empathy or outrage.

Logos describes a rational appeal. It is the persuasive technique of an argument based in logic and appealing to the audience's intellect. Logos requires us to support our ideas with sound reasons, relevant statistics, and other solid evidence.

As experts point out, most persuaders skillfully weave all three tactics into a seamless, effective persuasive message.[68] In reputable publications such as *The Wall Street Journal* and *The New York Times,* and mainstream news media such as CBS, ABC, and CNN, expect logos to dominate the generally "civilized" debate. Contributors featured in these media generally rank high on ethos. On the political fringes, however, be they left- or right-leaning, pathos dominates over logos. Similarly, expect a lot more pathos than logos in advertising.

YOUR TASK. Look for persuasive messages: speeches on YouTube or opinion pieces such as editorials or blog entries. Examine them for ethos, pathos, and logos. The discussion of rational and emotional appeals in this chapter might be helpful. Jot down your observations and bring your notes to class. If your instructor directs, submit a written interpretation discussing the ethos, pathos, and logos of a speech, an ad, or an opinion piece.

10.6 Mastering the Strategies of Persuasion—Hugh Rank's Model (Obj. 1)

Theorist Hugh Rank created a relatively simple model of persuasion. He believed that persuaders resort to two main strategies to reach their goals. Figure 10.14 illustrates Rank's model. Simply put, persuaders intensify their own strong points and the weaknesses of their opponent or a competing idea. Second, they downplay their own weak points and the strengths of their opponent or a competing idea.

Intensifying is achieved by repetition, association, and composition. Words and visual patterns of a key ingredient of a persuasive message are repeated to become memorable. Think jingles, recurring images, key phrases, or slogans—"The Ultimate Driving Machine" (BMW), for example. Association works by linking the idea or product with something that has emotional appeal; for example, attractive, youthful people in their pristine kitchen. Composition can also enhance the message by contrasting it with an opposite (e.g., a cleaning product shown to work wonders on very dirty floors or clothes).

Downplaying is achieved with omission, diversion, and confusion. Omission means leaving out information that might contradict the positive message (e.g., ignoring high purchase and maintenance costs). Diversion is a tactic to cause the audience to overlook a certain negative aspect of the product or idea—for example, by pointing out fuel economy gear in a snazzy vehicle to reduce attention to its poor gas mileage overall. Confusion is used to cover up known weaknesses in one's own argument, idea, or product. In the case of a giant gas guzzler, the persuader might emphasize performance data, racing wins, and so on, to gloss over poor buyer satisfaction and a poor safety record.

YOUR TASK. Look for examples to test Rank's model. Find advertising, opinion pieces, speeches, and other persuasive messages to illustrate the intensify–downplay model. In class discussion or in an e-mail to your instructor, discuss whether it is unethical to intensify or downplay, and give examples.

10.7 Analyzing a Persuasive Appeal: From the Zappos Family to Yours (Objs. 1, 5)

Communication Technology   **Web**

Online shoe and apparel store Zappos seems to abide by a unique motto: "We are a service company that happens to sell." With a recent record-setting 10-hour customer service call,[69] Zappos bolstered its reputation for pleasing online shoppers. Therefore, it's perhaps not surprising that the online retailer sent this preholiday mailer with a coupon code to some of its less active customers:

It just wouldn't be the holidays without you!

We'd love to see you again . . .

That's why we're giving you **10% off** your next Zappos.com order!

These coupons are very rare, but then again, you are very special.

Here's your handy-dandy coupon code to use during checkout:

ZMDR-500012

Can't wait to see you!

XOXO,

The Zappos Family

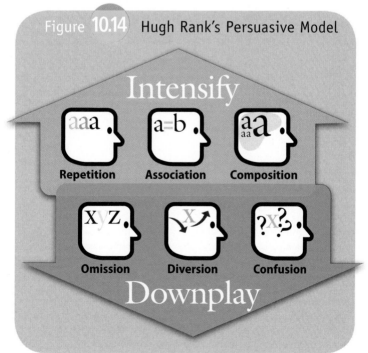

Figure **10.14** Hugh Rank's Persuasive Model

Intensify

Repetition   **Association**   **Composition**

Omission   **Diversion**   **Confusion**

Downplay

© Cengage Learning 2015

YOUR TASK. Evaluate the persuasive appeal of this message. Which needs does this message address? How does it try to accomplish its goal, to sell merchandise? Do you think it's effective? Can you point to similar examples of such an approach? Discuss in class or in writing. If your instructor directs, post your response and discuss it with peers on your course management system—Blackboard, Moodle, or similar platform.

10.8 Persuasive Request: Please Write Me a Letter of Recommendation (Obj. 3)

E-mail

As a student, you will need letters of recommendation to find a job, to apply for a scholarship or grant, or to enter graduate school. Naturally, you will consider asking one or several of your college instructors. You talk to a senior you know to find out how to get a busy professor to write you an effective letter. Your friend Paul has the following basic advice for you:

Ask only instructors who have had the opportunity to observe your performance and who may still remember you fondly. Two to five years after you attended a course of 20 to 40 students, your teachers may not recall you at all. Second, contact only professors who can sing your praises. If your grades were lackluster, don't expect a glowing endorsement. Some teachers may flatly refuse to write a recommendation that they cannot make wholeheartedly. Last, make it easy for them to agree to your request and to write a solid letter promptly by following these guidelines:

If possible, make the first request in person. This way, your former instructor will be more likely to remember you. Introduce yourself by name and try to point out something memorable you have done to help your professor recall your performance. Have a copy of the job description, scholarship information, grant requirements, or graduate school application ready. Carry a copy of a recent polished résumé. Alternatively, promise to e-mail these documents and any other information that will help your recommender recall you in a professional setting and understand the nature of the application process. Confirm any agreement by e-mail promptly, and set a firm yet reasonable deadline by which the letter must be received. Don't expect to get a letter if you ask at the last minute. On the other hand, if you give your instructor too much time, he or she may forget. In that case, don't be afraid gently to nudge by e-mail to remind the recommender when the deadline draws closer.

YOUR TASK. Write a persuasive request by e-mail asking your instructor (or supervisor or manager) to write you a letter of recommendation for a job application, grant, scholarship, or graduate school application. Provide all relevant information to make it easy for your reader to write a terrific letter. Explain any potential attachments.

10.9 Persuasive Request: Seeking Dumps for TV Makeovers (Obj. 3)

As an intern at a major cable network, you have been given a task associated with a new show. The network plans to introduce a home makeover show called *Hideous Houses*. It will feature not only homes in desperate need of repair but also dwellings deluged with accumulated junk or those with haphazard additions. Producers say they are particularly interested in homes decked out in horrific colors, leopard prints, or disco, goth, and 1950s looks.

In preparation for the show, producers conducted multiple searches in three major cities and located hundreds of possible homes for the show. They did, however, want to avoid homes with structural damage suggesting that the home needed to be torn

down. Instead, they focused on homes that were eyesores in the neighborhood and perhaps exhibited bad taste. In some cases, neighbors recommended a "hideous house" as a possibility for the upcoming show.

Homeowners could receive up to $20,000 worth of renovations as well as national exposure on a major cable network. Expert designers and contractors will be called in to renovate. To be eligible, participants must own the home, have a front yard, and provide two areas in need of major help. Producers recognize, however, that many people would be offended by being singled out for this program.[70] Should you reveal the name of the program?

YOUR TASK. As part of your internship program, the producers of *Hideous Houses* ask you to prepare a persuasive message or a telephone script inviting a prospective owner to participate in the show. The producer, who used to work with the *Oprah* show, cautions you to treat the owners with genuine respect. Your goal is to obtain a callback so that you can discuss details.

10.10 Persuasive Request: Making a Case for Tuition Reimbursement (Obj. 3)

Team

After working a few years, you would like to extend your college education on a part-time basis. You know that your education can benefit your employer, but you can't really afford the fees for tuition and books. You have heard that many companies offer reimbursement for fees and books when employees complete approved courses with a grade of *C* or higher.

YOUR TASK. In teams discuss the best way to approach an employer whom you wish to persuade to start a tuition/books reimbursement program. How could such a program help the employer? Remember that the most successful requests help receivers see what's in it for them. What objections might your employer raise? How can you counter them? After discussing strategies in teams, write a team memo or individual memos to your boss (for a company where you now work or one with which you are familiar). Persuade her or him to act on your persuasive request.

10.11 Persuasive Request: Junk Food Props Up School Budget (Obj. 3)

Team   Web

"If I start to get huge, then, yeah, I'll cut out the chips and Coke," says 17-year-old Nicole O'Neill, as she munches sour-cream-and-onion potato chips and downs a cold can of soda fresh from the snack machine. Most days her lunch comes from a vending machine. The trim high school junior, however, isn't too concerned about how junk food affects her weight or overall health. Although she admits she would prefer a granola bar or fruit, few healthy selections are available from school vending machines.

Vending machines loaded with soft drinks and snacks are increasingly under attack in schools and lunchrooms. Some school boards, however, see them as cash cows. In Gresham, Oregon, the school district is considering a lucrative soft drink contract. If it signs an exclusive 12-year agreement with Coca-Cola to allow vending machines at Gresham High School, the school district will receive $75,000 up front. Then it will receive an additional $75,000 three years later. Commission sales on the 75-cent drinks will bring in an additional $322,000 over the 12-year contract, provided the school sells 67,000 cans and bottles every year. In the past the vending machine payments supported student body activities such as sending students to choir concerts and paying athletic participation fees. Vending machine funds also paid for an electronic reader board in front of the school and a sound system for the gym. The latest contract would bring in $150,000, which is already earmarked for new artificial turf on the school athletic field.

Coca-Cola's vending machines would dispense soft drinks, Fruitopia, Minute Maid juices, Powerade, and Dasani water. The hands-down student favorite, of course, is calorie-laden Coke. Because increasing childhood and adolescent obesity across the nation is a major health concern, the Gresham Parent Teacher Association (PTA) decided to oppose the contract. The PTA realizes that the school board is heavily influenced by the income generated from the Coca-Cola contract. It wonders what other school districts are doing about their vending machine contracts.

YOUR TASK. As part of a PTA committee, you have been given the task of researching and composing a persuasive but concise (no more than one page) letter addressed to the school board. Use the Web or databases to locate articles that might help you develop arguments, alternatives, and counterarguments. Meet with your team to discuss your findings. Then, individually or as a group, write a letter to the Board of Directors, Gresham-Barlow School District, P.O. Box 310, Gresham, OR 97033.

10.12 Persuasive Claim: Pricey Hotel Breakfast (Obj. 3)

As regional manager for an electronics parts manufacturer, you and two other employees attended a conference in Nashville. You stayed at the Country Inn because your company recommends that employees use this hotel chain. Generally, your employees have liked their accommodations, and the rates have been within your company's budget.

Now, however, you are unhappy with the charges you see on your company's credit statement from Country Inn. When your department's administrative assistant made the reservations, she was assured that you would receive the weekend rates and that a hot breakfast—in the hotel restaurant, the Atrium—would be included in the rate. You hate those cold sweet rolls and instant coffee "continental" breakfasts, especially when you have to leave early and won't get another meal until afternoon. So you and the other two employees went to the restaurant and ordered a hot meal from the menu.

When you received the credit statement, though, you see a charge for $114 for three champagne buffet breakfasts in the Atrium. You hit the ceiling! For one thing, you didn't have a buffet breakfast and certainly no champagne. The three of you got there so early that no buffet had been set up. You ordered pancakes and sausage, and for this you were billed $35 each. You are outraged! What's worse, your company may charge you personally for exceeding the expected rates.

In looking back at this event, you remembered that other guests on your floor were having a "continental" breakfast in a lounge on your floor. Perhaps that's where the hotel expected all guests on the weekend rate to eat. However, your administrative assistant had specifically asked about this matter when she made the reservations, and she was told that you could order breakfast from the menu at the hotel's restaurant.

YOUR TASK. You want to straighten out this problem, and you can't do it by telephone because you suspect that you will need a written record of this entire mess. Write a persuasive claim to Customer Service, Country Inn, Inc., 428 Church Street, Nashville, TN 37219. Should you include a copy of the credit statement showing the charge?

10.13 Persuasive Claim: Anything but Heavenly Legal Fees (Obj. 3)

Originally a shipbuilding village, the town of Mystic, Connecticut, captures the spirit of the nineteenth-century seafaring era. But it is best known for Mystic Pizza, a bustling local pizzeria featured in a movie that launched the film career of Julia Roberts. Today, customers line the sidewalk waiting to taste its pizza, called by some "a slice of heaven."

Assume that you are the business manager for Mystic Pizza's owners. They were approached by an independent vendor who wants to use the Mystic Pizza name and secret recipes to distribute frozen pizza through grocery and convenience stores. As business manager, you worked with a law firm, Giordano, Murphy, and Associates. This firm was to draw up contracts regarding the use of Mystic Pizza's name and quality standards for the product. When you received the bill from Henry Giordano, you were flabbergasted. It itemized 38 hours of attorney preparation, at $400 per hour, and 55 hours of paralegal assistance, at $100 per hour. The bill also showed $415 for telephone calls, which might be accurate because Mr. Giordano had to talk with the owners, who were vacationing in Italy at the time. You seriously doubt, however, that an experienced attorney would require 38 hours to draw up the contracts in question. When you began checking, you discovered that excellent legal advice could be obtained for $200 an hour.

YOUR TASK. Decide what you want to request, and then write a persuasive request to Henry Giordano, Attorney at Law, Giordano, Murphy, and Associates, 254 Sherborn Street, Boston, MA 02215. Include an end date and a reason for it.

10.14 Persuasive Claim: Hawaiian Toner Scam (Obj. 3)

Heather W. was new to her job as administrative assistant at the Waialae Country Club in Honolulu. Alone in the office one morning, she answered a phone call from Rick, who said he was the country club's copier contractor. "Hey, look, Babydoll," Rick purred, "the price on the toner you use is about to go way up. I can offer you a great price on this toner if you order right now." Heather knew that the copy machine regularly needed toner, and she thought she should probably go ahead and place the order to save the country club some money. Ten days later two bottles of toner arrived, and Heather was pleased at the perfect timing. The copy machine needed it right away. Three weeks later Maureen, the bookkeeper, called to report a bill from Copy Machine Specialists for $960.43 for two bottles of toner. "What's going on here?" said Maureen. "We don't purchase supplies from this company, and this price is totally off the charts!"[71]

Heather spoke to the manager, Steven Tanaka, who immediately knew what had happened. He blamed himself for not training Heather. "Never, never order anything from a telephone solicitor, no matter how fast-talking or smooth he sounds," warned Steven. He outlined an office policy for future supplies purchases. Only certain people can authorize or finalize a purchase, and purchases require a confirmed price including shipping costs settled in advance. But what to do about this $960.43 bill? The country club had already begun to use the toner, although the current copies were looking faint and streaked.

YOUR TASK. As Steven Tanaka, decide how to respond to this obvious scam. Should you pay the bill? Should you return the unused bottle? Write a persuasive claim to Copy Machine Specialists, 4320 Admiralty Way, Honolulu, HI 96643. Supply any details necessary.

10.15 Persuasive Organizational Message Flowing Upward: Can We Create Our Own Business Podcasts? (Obj. 4)

`Communication Technology`   `E-mail`   `Web`

You are working for the small accounting firm, CPA Plus, and your boss, Bradford Trask, wonders whether your company could produce podcasts for its clients without professional help. He doesn't know how podcasting really works, nor what resources or costs would be required. However, he has read about the benefits of providing advice or sending promotional messages to customers who can download them from the company website or subscribe to them in a podcast directory.

Conduct some Web research to understand better how podcasting works and what hardware and software are needed. Visit podcast directories such as Podcast Alley or Podcast.com for some ideas, or search iTunes for business and investment podcasts. The U.S. Small Business Administration also offers Web pages devoted to the topic.

YOUR TASK. Consider your accounting firm's needs and its audience. Then write a memo addressed to Bradford Trask that you would send along with a brief e-mail cover message. In your memo argue for or against creating podcasts in-house. For professional podcasts listen to *The Wall Street Journal* podcasts. Search for podcasts at **http://online.wsj.com/home-page** or look for any number of business podcasts on iTunes.

10.16 Persuasive Organizational Message Flowing Upward: Combating "Mall Rat" Invasion (Obj. 4)

Emma Markham is general manager at Oak Park Town Center, a bustling shopping mall with a big problem. Large roaming groups of rowdy teenagers frighten families and elderly shoppers evenings and weekends but spend little money. On the contrary, shoplifting is common. Many businesses in the mall are losing revenue as typical shoppers are staying away after 5 p.m. and on Saturdays and Sundays when the "mall rats" descend on Oak Park Town Center.

Emma Markham wants to persuade Gerard Gordon, mall owner and president of Oak Park Associates, to restrict access of unchaperoned teenagers on weekends and evenings. Gerard Gordon is largely an absentee president and may not understand the gravity of the problem. The fighting and disruptions have become so common and disturbing that on some weekend nights as many as 750 teenagers had to be ejected from the mall by security guards and police. The mall had to hire seven off-duty police officers for weekend duty. The 21-screen movie theater has lost 40 percent of its visitors. Five of the largest businesses in the mall are experiencing huge drops in sales in the evenings and on weekends.

Emma understands that she also has to win the backing of community groups. School officials, local civil rights groups, and religious leaders would need to cooperate if policies restricting teen access were to work. Summer is coming, and Emma fears that the problem will only get worse. She draws up a detailed plan that she wants to attach to her persuasive memo. She would also like to speak to Mr. Gordon in person. She thinks that the benefits outweigh the drawbacks of the proposed teen restriction policy.

To find precedents to support her plan, Emma contacted the business association International Council of Shopping Centers. Luckily, the organization had just completed a survey of its 1,000 members. Almost a third of the survey participants had created policies to restrict teen access. For example,

Mall of America in Bloomington, Minnesota, bans unaccompanied teenagers under seventeen after 4 p.m. on weekends. In Massachusetts, two shopping centers, Holyoke Mall and Eastfield Mall, do not allow teenagers seventeen and under after 4 p.m. on Fridays and Saturdays unless escorted by an adult. In Michigan's Fairlane Town Center, teens younger than seventeen must be accompanied by a chaperone after 5 p.m. every day. This is good news for Emma, but she knows that she must convert these facts into benefits for her audience.

YOUR TASK. Draft the memo for Emma. Address it to Gerard B. Gordon. Gain attention with specific examples and data detailing the problem. Use a careful tone in your message to a manager. Include the benefits of limiting teen access, such as increased profits and savings in dollar terms, if possible. Address potential objections of the community. Use bullets with parallel items.

10.17 Persuasive Organizational Message Flowing Upward: Three-Day Weekends, Anyone? (Obj. 4)

`Team`   `Web`

Gas prices are skyrocketing, and many companies and municipalities are switching to a four-day workweek to reduce gas consumption and air pollution. Compressing the workweek into four 10-hour days sounds pretty good to you. You would much prefer having Friday free to schedule medical appointments and take care of family business, in addition to leisurely three-day weekends.

As a manager at Skin Essentials, a mineral-based skin care products and natural cosmetics company, you are convinced that the company's 400 employees could switch to a four-day workweek with many resulting benefits. For one thing, they would save on gasoline and commute time. You know that many cities and companies have already implemented a four-day workweek with considerable success. You took a quick poll of immediate employees and managers and found that 80 percent thought that a four-day workweek was a good idea. One said, "This would be great! Think of what I could save on babysitting and lunches!"

YOUR TASK. With a group of other managers, conduct research on the Web and discuss your findings. What are the advantages of a four-day workweek? What organizations have already tried it? What appeals could be used to persuade management to adopt a four-day workweek? What arguments could be expected, and how would you counter them? Individually or as a group, prepare a one-page persuasive memo addressed to Skin Essentials Management Council. Decide on a goal. Do you want to suggest a pilot study? Meet with management to present your ideas? Start a four-day workweek immediately?

10.18 Persuasive Organizational Message Flowing Upward: The End of Apples? (Obj. 4)

During the recent economic downturn, Omni Hotels looked for ways to slice expenses. Omni operates 43 luxury hotels and resorts in leading business gateways and leisure destinations across North America. From exceptional golf and spa retreats to dynamic business settings, each Omni showcases the local flavor of the destination while featuring four-diamond services.

Omni Hotels ranks at the top in "Highest in Guest Satisfaction Among Upscale Hotel Chains," according to J. D. Power. One signature amenity it has offered for years is a bowl of free apples in its lobbies. However, providing apples costs hundreds of thousands of dollars a year. They have to cut costs somewhere, and executives are debating whether to cut out apples as a way to save money with minimum impact on guests.

Omni Hotels prides itself on providing guests with superior service through The Power of One, a service program that offers associates the training and authority to make decisions that exceed the expectations of guests. The entire culture of the hotel provides a positive, supportive environment that rewards associates through the Omni Service Champions program. As an Omni associate, you are disturbed that the hotel is considering giving up its free apples. You hope that executives will find other ways to cut expenses, such as purchasing food in smaller amounts or reducing the hours of its lobby cafes.[72]

YOUR TASK. In the true sense of The Power of One, you decide to express your views to management. Write a persuasive message to Richard Johnson (*rjohnson@omni.com*), Vice President, Operations, Omni Hotels, 420 Decker Drive, Irving, TX 75062. Should you write a letter or an e-mail? In a separate note to your instructor, explain your rationale for your channel choice and your message strategy.

10.19 Persuasive Organizational Message Flowing Upward: How to Work From Home (Obj. 4)

E-mail **Team** **Web**

Jared Johnson arose from bed in his New Hampshire home and looked outside to see a heavy snowstorm creating a fairyland of white. But he felt none of the giddiness that usually accompanies a potential snow day. Such days were a gift from heaven when schools closed, businesses shut down, and the world ground to a halt. As an on-and-off telecommuter for many years, he knew that snow days were a thing of the past. These days, work for Jared Johnson and about 20 percent of other workers around the globe is no farther than their home offices.[73]

More and more employees are becoming telecommuters. They want to work at home, where they feel they can be more productive and avoid the hassle of driving to work. Some need to telecommute only temporarily, while they take care of family obligations, births, illnesses, or personal problems. Others are highly skilled individuals who can do their work at home as easily as in the office. Businesses definitely see advantages to telecommuting. They don't have to supply office space for workers. What's more, as businesses continue to flatten management structures, bosses no longer have time to micromanage employees. Increasingly, they are leaving workers to their own devices.

But the results have not been totally satisfactory. For one thing, in-house workers resent those who work at home. More important are problems of structure and feedback. Telecommuters don't always have the best work habits, and lack of communication is a major issue. Unless the telecommuter is expert at coordinating projects and leaving instructions, productivity can fizzle. Appreciating the freedom but recognizing that they need guidance, employees are saying, "Push me, but don't leave me out there all alone!"

As the human resources manager at your company, you already have 83 employees who are either full- or part-time telecommuters. With increasing numbers asking to work in remote locations, you decide that workers and their managers must receive training on how to do it effectively. You are considering hiring a consultant to train your prospective telecommuters and their managers. Another possibility is developing an in-house training program.

YOUR TASK. As the human resources manager, you must convince Chris Crittenden, vice president, that your company needs a training program for all workers who are currently telecommuting or who plan to do so. Their managers should also receive training. You decide to ask your staff of four to help you gather information. Using the Web, you and your team read several articles on what such training should include. Now you must decide what action you want the vice president

to take. Meet with you to discuss a training program? Commit to a budget item for future training? Hire a consultant or agency to come in and conduct training programs? Individually or as a team, write a convincing e-mail that describes the problem, suggests what the training should include, and asks for action by a specific date. Add any reasonable details necessary to build your case.

10.20 Persuasive Organizational Message Flowing Upward: Hey, Boss, I Have an Idea (Obj. 4)

E-mail

In your own work or organization experience, identify a problem for which you have a solution. Should a procedure be altered to improve performance? Would a new or different piece of equipment help you perform your work better? Could some tasks be scheduled more efficiently? Are employees being used most effectively? Could customers be better served by changing something? Do you want to work other hours or perform other tasks? Do you deserve a promotion? Do you have a suggestion to improve profitability?

YOUR TASK. Once you have identified a situation requiring persuasion, write a memo or an e-mail to your boss or organization head. Use actual names and facts. Employ the concepts and techniques in this chapter to help you convince your boss that your idea should prevail. Include concrete examples, anticipate objections, emphasize reader benefits, and end with a specific action to be taken.

10.21 Persuasive Organizational Message Flowing Upward: Tipping Not Optional (Obj. 4)

Team

Perched high atop a granite cliff overlooking the rugged Big Sur coastline sits Pacific's Edge Restaurant, where migrating whales may be seen from every table in the dining room. Sunsets here are so spectacular that the entire dining room often breaks out in spontaneous applause. You truly enjoy working in this magical Big Sur resort setting—except for one thing. You have occasionally been "stiffed" by a patron who left no tip. You know your service is excellent, but some customers just don't get it. They seem to think that tips are optional, a sign of appreciation. For servers, however, tips are 80 percent of their income.

In a recent *New York Times* article, you learned that some restaurants—such as the famous Coach House Restaurant in New York—automatically add a 15 percent tip to the bill. In Santa Monica the Lula restaurant prints "gratuity guidelines" on checks, showing customers what a 15 or 20 percent tip would be. You also know that American Express recently developed a gratuity calculation feature on its terminals. This means that diners don't even have to do the math!

YOUR TASK. Because they know you are studying business communication, your fellow servers have asked you to write a serious letter to Constantine Delmonico, General Manager, Big Sur Properties, 48130 California Highway 1, Big Sur, CA 93920. They think a letter will be more effective than a conversation. Persuade him to adopt mandatory tipping guidelines in the restaurant. Talk with fellow servers (your classmates) to develop logical persuasive arguments.

10.22 Persuasive Organizational Message Flowing Downward: Saving Cash on Shipping (Obj. 4)

As office manager of an East Coast software company, write a memo persuading your technicians, engineers, programmers, and other employees to reduce the number of overnight or second-day mail shipments. Your FedEx and other shipping bills have been sky high, and you feel that staff members are over-using these services.

You think employees should send messages by e-mail or fax. Sending a zipped file or PDF file as an e-mail attachment costs very little. What's more, a fax costs only about 35 cents a page to most long-distance areas and nothing to local areas. Compare this with $15 to $20 for FedEx service! Whenever possible, staff members should obtain the FedEx account number of the recipient and use it for charging the shipment. If staff members plan ahead and allow enough time, they can use UPS or FedEx ground service, which takes three to five days and is much cheaper. You wonder whether staff members consider whether the recipient is really going to use the message as soon as it arrives. Does it justify an overnight shipment? You would like to reduce overnight delivery services voluntarily by 50 percent over the next two months. Unless a sizable reduction occurs, the CEO threatens severe restrictions in the future.

YOUR TASK. Address your memo to all staff members. What other ways could employees reduce shipping costs?

10.23 Persuasive Organizational Message Flowing Downward: Fixing Atrocious Memo (Obj. 4)

The following memo (with names changed) was actually sent.

YOUR TASK. Based on what you have learned in this chapter, improve the memo. Expect the staff to be somewhat resistant because they have never before had meeting restrictions.

Date: Current
To: All Managers and Employees
From: Nancy Nelson, CEO
Subject: Scheduling Meetings

Please be reminded that travel in the greater Los Angeles area is time consuming. In the future we are asking that you set up meetings that

1. Are of critical importance
2. Consider travel time for the participants
3. Consider phone conferences (or video or e-mail) in lieu of face-to-face meetings
4. Meetings should be at the location where most of the participants work and at the most opportune travel times
5. Traveling together is another way to save time and resources.

We all have our traffic horror stories. A recent one is that a certain manager was asked to attend a one-hour meeting in Burbank. This required one hour travel in advance of the meeting, one hour for the meeting, and two and a half hours of travel through Los Angeles afterward. This meeting was scheduled for 4 p.m. Total time consumed by the manager for the one-hour meeting was four and a half hours.

Thank you for your consideration.

10.24 Identifying the AIDA Strategy in Sales Messages (Obj. 5)

> **E-mail**

YOUR TASK. Select a one- or two-page direct-mail sales letter, or pick a marketing e-mail with a substantial amount of text. If you don't have access to direct-mail pieces, ask friends or family. Study the structure of the sales message and then answer these questions:

a. What techniques capture the reader's attention?

b. Is the opening effective? Explain.

c. What is the central selling point?

d. Does the letter use rational, emotional, or a combination of appeals? Explain.

e. What reader benefits are suggested?

f. How does the letter build interest in the product or service?

g. How is price handled?

h. How does the letter anticipate reader resistance and offer counterarguments?

i. What action is the reader to take? How is the action made easy?

j. What motivators spur the reader to act quickly?

10.25 Examining Puffery in Advertising (Obj. 5)

> **Communication Technology** **Social Media** **Web**

As you have seen in this chapter, puffery in advertising may be tacky, but it is not illegal. Few of us take claims seriously that shout, *the best pizza in town*, *largest selection of electronics*, *the ultimate fresh breath*, *the world's juiciest hamburgers*, *the biggest pie money can buy*, or *coldest beer*. After all, such exaggerated claims cannot be proven and do not fool anyone.

Serious, quantifiable claims, however, must be backed up with evidence or they could mean litigation: "Our chicken has less fat than a hamburger. It's better for you."[74] This bold claim was investigated, and the fried chicken restaurant had to stop using it in its advertising. Yes, the fried chicken had a little less total fat than a hamburger, but it contained more harmful transfat, sodium, and cholesterol, making it higher in calories—a decidedly unhealthy alternative. As the FTC points out, a restaurant can compare itself to others, but it must tell the truth.

YOUR TASK. Look for examples of puffery and find ads that would need to prove their claims. How can you tell which is which? Discuss examples in class or in an online forum set up for your class.

10.26 Because I Said So? The Truth About Testimonials (Objs. 3, 5)

> **Social Media** **Web**

When Jamie Lee Curtis extols the virtues of digestive aid Activia, can we trust that she truly uses and likes the product? This nagging doubt may be what prompts many celebrities to collect hefty advertising dollars abroad, seemingly out of sight of their fans' penetrating gazes. In the age of YouTube, however, celebrity endorsements are now visible to anyone on the planet, regardless of where they play. You decide whether Tommy Lee Jones pushing Boss, a canned coffee drink popular in Japan, is credible as an "alien" bending forks. Does he really drink the beverage? His colleague Brad Pitt stars as a humble servant to a sumo wrestler in commercials for SoftBank, a Japanese telecom company. Does Pitt use SoftBank? Suave George Clooney sells Martini-brand vermouth in Italy. He is wearing a tux and looks dashing. Does he drink Martini vermouth?

YOUR TASK. Find an advertisement that contains an endorsement or testimonial. Do you believe the person in the ad uses and likes the product? Why or why not? Can you know with certainty? Does it matter?

10.27 Critiquing Persuasive Blog Post Headlines and Examining Bylines (Objs. 1, 5)

> **Social Media** **Web**

Many blog entries are by definition persuasive because they express a writer's view, be it personal experiences or perspectives on current events and other topics. In the parlance of traditional journalism, blogs most resemble opinion columns or editorials, not the generally objective news reporting pages. Nevertheless, many reputable blogs are valuable sources of information as long as the expertise of the authors is credible and we understand their biases. Some of the perceived credibility also stems from the authority a publication may enjoy. For example, blogs by *Businessweek, Forbes*, and *Harvard Business Review* contributors can be assumed to be more credible than an anonymous blog on the Web without a byline.

YOUR TASK. Visit business-related blogs—for example WSJ Blogs, HBR Blog Network, or opinion columns. Focus on the headlines and the bylines (name of author). What draws you to the article or blog entry? Are the headings credible, serious, playful, or funny? Look for puns, jingles, and other features that might prompt readers to click on the link and actually read the article. Pay attention to the authors. What can you learn about their credentials? Are they credible experts?

10.28 Turning Features Into Benefits (Objs. 1, 5)

Audience benefits sell. People are more likely to be persuaded when they see a direct or indirect benefit of a product, service, idea, or cause. Features may describe a product or service, but they don't tell a story. To be persuasive, writers must convert features into benefits. They must tell the audience how they can best use the item to benefit from it.

YOUR TASK. Find a product or service that you admire. Be sure to locate a detailed description of the item's unique features. Create a table and in the left column list the item's features. In the right column, convert the features into benefits, by matching them to the needs of your target audience.

10.29 Sales Letter: Pitaya—The Next "Superfruit"? (Obj. 5)

Eric Helms is the founder and CEO of Juice Generation, a chain of juice and smoothie bars in New York City. He bought the exclusive rights to a year's supply of pitaya, a little-known softball-sized fruit that grows from cacti found in Nicaragua. The Vietnamese dragonfruit is the pitaya's Asian cousin. To prevent agricultural pests from entering the United States, only the fruit's frozen pulp may be shipped from Central America. The pitaya reportedly tastes like a cross between strawberries and wheatgrass and is said to contain an antioxidant believed to protect from cancer-causing free radicals. David Wolfe, author of *Superfoods*, is enthusiastic: "It's one of my favorite fruits of all time. It's superhigh in vitamin C and superhydrating." Yet even within health food circles, the fruit is still largely unknown.

The "superpremium" juice business that focuses on healthy, exotic nectars (such as pomegranate and, most recently, the açaí berry) is a multibillion-dollar enterprise. The big players all have their brands—for example, Odwalla (Coca-Cola), Naked (PepsiCo), and Jamba Juice. Celebrities such as Russell Simmons and Gwyneth Paltrow have endorsed juicing. Selma Hayek, a longtime juicer, cofounded the Cooler Cleanse juice brand with Helms.

The term *superfruit* is a marketing term, referring to fruits heavy in antioxidants, but without any scientific or regulatory definition, says Jeffrey Blumberg, director of the U.S. Department of Agriculture's antioxidants research laboratory. "As most natural fruits contain one or more positive nutrient attributes," Blumberg explains, "any one might be considered by someone 'super' in its own way." An industry primer is blunt:

"Superfruits are the product of strategy, not something you find growing on a tree."[75] POM Wonderful lost a lawsuit to FTC for deceptive advertising of its pomegranate juice.

Helms' Juice Generation partnered with a factory in Nicaragua that employs only single mothers who scoop and blend the fruit. The women pour the pulp into 3.5-ounce packets that are frozen for shipping. The Pink Pitaya Coco Blend, a mix of coconut, banana, and pitaya, costs $8.45. "You have to give people what they want, but also what they should be trying," Helms believes.[76]

YOUR TASK. Write a sales letter or a marketing e-mail promoting the Pink Pitaya Coco Blend. Your audience in this campaign will probably be gyms with in-house juice bars. Introduce the exotic pitaya fruit and explain its benefits. Cull information from the scenario to include a testimonial. Make sure your claims are ethical and legal.

10.30 E-Mail Marketing Message or Direct-Mail Sales Letter: Promoting Products and Services (Obj. 5)

E-mail

Identify a situation in your current job or a previous one in which a sales letter is or was needed. Using suggestions from this chapter, write an appropriate sales message that promotes a product or service. Use actual names, information, and examples. If you have no work experience, imagine a business you would like to start: word processing, pet grooming, car detailing, tutoring, specialty knitting, balloon decorating, delivery service, child care, gardening, lawn care, or something else.

YOUR TASK. Write a sales letter or an e-mail marketing message selling your product or service to be distributed to your prospective customers. Be sure to tell them how to respond.

You don't need to know HTML or have a Constant Contact account to craft a concise and eye-catching online sales message. Try designing it in Microsoft Word and saving it as a Web page (go to the **File** tab and select **Save as**; then in the **Save as type** line, select **Web Page**). Consider adding graphics or photos—either your own or samples borrowed from the Internet. As long as you use them for this assignment and don't publish them online, you are not violating copyright laws.

10.31 Micromessages: Analyzing Twitter Feeds for AIDA Components (Objs. 1, 2, and 5)

Social Media   **Web**

People are increasingly sharing persuasive and promotional social media posts. Most of the persuasive micromessages incorporate some elements of sales techniques—individual AIDA components. Naturally, few of us would buy something solely on the basis of a tweet, but such micromessages are teasers or alerts, directing receivers to websites, video clips, and other media.

Tip: To find persuasive posts fast, view the ultra-brief LinkedIn member ads visible on the right side of most LinkedIn screens. Alternatively, visit the sponsored links at *Bloomberg Businessweek*. Determine whether tweets and posts ask questions, favor the "you" view, and use other features that are hallmarks of persuasion. Share your results in class. Analyze and critique each other's findings.

Examples:

Consider these LinkedIn posts with the commentary that follows:

> **Senior Women Executives. Apply now to the Association of Women in Business. Register free.** *Calls on a specific audience; uses "you" view; free registration encourages compliance.*
>
> **Spruce up Business Events. "Frank is fantastic." Skilled, fun, interactive musical entertainment.** *Opts for vivid language and attracts attention with benefit in the opening; includes a claim resembling a testimonial.*
>
> **Masters in Counseling. Earn a Chapman M.A. and jumpstart your career. Apply by Jan. 31.** *Advertises graduate program as beneficial to career advancement; uses limited-time offer.*

Consider these tweets and the accompanying comments as models:

> **With our updated Android app, share collections of photos with friends and family. Enjoy! http://wo.ly/gLknQ** *Offers a benefit; conveys warmth (Enjoy!); provides a useful hyperlink.*
>
> **Enjoy easier, smarter access to Delta with the new http://delta.com and Fly Delta apps for smartphones and iPad: http://oka.xtr.ly/m/1umh** *Employs "you" view, offers a benefit (easier, smarter access); prompts a response with convenient hyperlinks.*
>
> **Please donate to @RedCrossAU Tasmanian Bushfires Appeal http://bit.ly/Xs4l7g All donations over $2 are tax deductible #redcross #tasfires** *Starts with a direct call for action; points out the benefit that contributions are tax deductible.*

YOUR TASK. Examine a Twitter feed or other social media (e.g., LinkedIn) for persuasive micromessages that feature AIDA components such as attention getters, reader benefits, calls for action, limited-time offers, freebies, and so on. Arrange them in categories as shown in Figure 10.12.

10.32 Writing Persuasive Tweets and Posts (Objs. 1, 5)

Social Media ⟩ Web ⟩

Being able to compose effective and concise micromessages and posts will positively contribute to your professional online persona.

YOUR TASK. Brainstorm to identify a special skill you have, an event you want others to attend, a charitable cause dear to your heart, or a product you like. Applying what you have learned about short persuasive messages online, write your own 140-character persuasive tweets or posts. Use Figure 10.12 as a starting point and model.

10.33 Writing Newsworthy Press Releases (Obj. 6)

Web ⟩

You have been interviewed for a terrific job in corporate communications at an exciting organization. To test your writing skills, the organization asks you to rewrite one of its press releases for possible submission to your local newspaper. This means revising the information you find into a new press release that your local newspaper would be interested in publishing.

YOUR TASK. Select an organization and study its press releases. For example, search the Web for *Amazon Media Room: Press Releases, FBI press release, Ben & Jerry's press release, Mars candy press release, World Honda news release, Screen Actors Guild press release*, or an organization of your choice. Select one event or product that you think would interest your local newspaper. Although you can use the information from current press releases, don't copy the exact wording because the interviewer wants to see how you would present that information. Use the organization's format and submit the press release to your instructor with a cover note identifying the newspaper or other publication where you would like to see your press release published.

10.34 Press Release: I've Got News for You! (Obj. 6)

YOUR TASK. For a company where you now work or an organization you belong to, identify a product or service that could be publicized. Consider writing a press release announcing a new course at your college, a new president, new equipment, or a campaign to raise funds. The press release is intended for your local newspaper.

Chat About It

In each chapter you will find five discussion questions related to the chapter material. Your instructor may assign these topics for you to discuss in class, in an online chat room, or on an online discussion board. Some of the discussion topics may require outside research. You may also be asked to read and respond to postings made by your classmates.

Topic 1: Think of a successful viral campaign or crowdfunding venture you know or have heard about, whether on YouTube or any other social media. Can you identify reasons that explain the persuasiveness and popularity of your chosen social media phenomenon? Share your insights with your classmates.

Topic 2: When you think about persuasion, does the term suggest deception or dishonesty? Compare negative and positive aspects of persuasion. Share descriptions of when you have experienced both kinds of persuasion.

Topic 3: In your own experience, when have you had to persuade someone (boss, parent, instructor, friend, colleague) to do something or to change a belief? What strategies did you use? Were they successful? How could you improve your technique?

Topic 4: When have you had to complain to a company, organization, or person about something that went wrong or that offended you? Share your experience. What channel did you use for your complaint? How effective was your channel choice and strategy? What would you change in your method for future complaints?

Topic 5: Think of a product you have used and like. If you were trying to sell that product, what rational appeals would you use? What emotional appeals would you use? Try to sell that product to your classmates.

Number Use

Review Guides 47–50 about number usage in Appendix A, Grammar and Mechanics Guide, beginning on page A-1. On a separate sheet, revise the following sentences to correct number usage errors. For each error that you locate, write the guide number that reflects this usage. Sentences may have more than one error. If a sentence is correct, write *C*. When you finish, check your answers on page Key-1.

EXAMPLE: 18 people posted notes on the Small Planet Facebook page.

REVISION: Eighteen people posted notes on the Small Planet Facebook page. [Guide 47]

1. Our manager reported receiving 7 messages from customers with the same 2 complaints.

2. 33 companies indicated that they were participating in renewable energy programs.

3. Did Dakota request five hundred dollars to attend the 2-day seminar?

4. UPS strives to make important deliveries before 10:00 o'clock a.m.

5. The meeting was rescheduled for March 7th at 2:00 p.m.

6. Investors earned 3.5% dividends on each three thousand dollar investment.

7. With a birth occurring every 8 seconds, the U.S. population is currently estimated to be three hundred fifteen million.

8. One petition now has more than two hundred sixty thousand signatures, far and above the twenty-five thousand needed for an official White House response.

9. She bought the vintage item on eBay for two dollars and fifty cents and sold it for twenty dollars.

10. At least 9 prominent retail stores offer a thirty-day customer satisfaction return policy.

Notes

1. Lovins, L. H. (n.d.). Natural Capitalism Solutions. Retrieved from http://www.natcapsolutions.org /index.php?option=com_content&view=article& id=247&Itemid=53

2. Ibid.

3. Witkin, J. (2011, February 2). Convincing even the skeptics to go green. *The New York Times*. Retrieved from http://www.nytimes .com/2011/02/03/business /smallbusiness/03sbiz-conversation.html

4. Russell, T. (2012, March 16). Engage your employees—increase your profits. [Webinar]. Retrieved from http://www.youtube.com /watch?v=SpI_ksTWjU8

5. Russell, T. (2012, October 31). Making sustainability work for you. Retrieved from http://www.youtube.com/watch?v=VBfrERbdVK 8&feature=youtu.be

6. Witkin, J. (2011, February 2). Convincing even the skeptics to go green. *The New York Times*. Retrieved from http://www .nytimes.com/2011/02/03/business /smallbusiness/03sbiz-conversation.html

7. White, E. (2008, May 19). The art of persuasion becomes key. *The Wall Street Journal*. Retrieved from http://online.wsj.com/article /SB121115784262002373.html ; McIntosh, P., & Luecke, R. A. (2011). *Increase your influence at work*. New York: American Management Association, p. 4.

8. Hamilton, C. (2011). *Communicating for results* (9th ed.). Boston: Wadsworth, Cengage Learning, p. 373.

9. Fogg, B. J. (2008). Mass interpersonal persuasion: An early view of a new phenomenon. In: Proceedings. Third International Conference on Persuasive Technology, Persuasive 2008. Berlin, Germany: Springer.

10. Perloff, R. M. (2010). *The dynamics of persuasion: Communication and attitudes in the twenty-first century* (4th ed.). New York: Routledge, pp. 12–19.

11. Cialdini, R. B. (2009). *Influence: The psychology of persuasion*. New York: HarperCollins, p. xiv.

12. Cialdini, R. B. (2009). *Influence: The psychology of persuasion*. New York: HarperCollins e-books, p. x.

13. Discussion based on Perloff, R. M. (2010). *The dynamics of persuasion: Communication and attitudes in the twenty-first century* (4th ed.). New York: Routledge, pp. 4–5.

14. Cherry, K. (n. d.). What is persuasion? About.com. Retrieved from http://psychology.about.com/od /socialinfluence/f/what-is-persuasion.htm

15. Wike, R., & Krishnamurthy, V. (2012, June 13). Global opinion of Obama slips, international policies faulted. Pew Research Center. Retrieved from http://www.pewglobal.org/files/2012/06 /Pew-Global-Attitudes-U.S.-Image-Report -FINAL-June-13-2012.pdf

16. Halperin, S. (2012, December 19). "X Factor" sees significant social media strides. *The Hollywood Reporter*. Retrieved from http://www.hollywoodreporter.com /live-feed/x-factors-social-media-strategy-405485

17. Perloff, R. M. (2010). *The dynamics of persuasion: Communication and attitudes in the twenty-first century* (4th ed.). New York: Routledge, p. 9.

18. *Harvard Business Review on reinventing your marketing*. (2011, May 7). Boston: Harvard Business Press Books.

19. Nayar, V. (2010, June). How I did it: A maverick CEO explains how he persuaded his team to leap into the future. *Harvard Business Review*. Retrieved from http://hbr.org/2010/06 /how-i-did-it-a-maverick-ceo-explains-how-he -persuaded-his-team-to-leap-into-the-future /ar/1

20. Don't buy this jacket, Black Friday and the New York Times. (2011, November). The Cleanest Line. [Blog]. Retrieved from http://patagonia.typepad .com/files/nyt_11-25-11.pdf

21. Bryant, A. (2012, March 25). Want to innovate? Feed a cookie to the monster. *The New York Times*, p. Bu Y2.

22. James, G. (2010, March 11). Enterprise Rent-A-Car: When sales tactics backfire. CBSNews.com /Moneywatch. Retrieved from http://www .cbsnews.com/8301-505183_162-28548988 -10391735/enterprise-rent-a-car-when-sales -tactics-backfire; Strauss, S. (2010, May 24). Ask an expert: Do us a favor and avoid the hard sell, it's bad for business. USAToday.com. Retrieved from http://usatoday30.usatoday.com/money

/smallbusiness/columnist/strauss/2010-05-23 -hard-sell-tactics_N.htm; Salmon, J. (2010, May 12). Barclays hard sell tactics exposed. This is MONEY.co.uk. Retrieved from http://www .thisismoney.co.uk/money/saving /article-1693952/Barclays-hard-sell-tactics -exposed.html

23. Federal Trade Commission. (2012, March 14). FTC takes action to stop deceptive car dealership ads. [Press release]. Retrieved from http://www.ftc .gov/opa/2012/03/autoloans.shtm

24. Larson, C. U. (2013). *Persuasion: Reception and responsibility* (13th ed.). Boston: Wadsworth, Cengage Learning, p. 29.

25. Nayar, V. (2011, August 8). The manager's new role. HBR Blog Network. Retrieved from http://blogs .hbr.org/hbr/nayar/2011/08/the-manager-new -role.html

26. McIntosh, P., & Luecke, R. A. (2011). *Increase your influence at work*. New York: AMACOM, p. 2.

27. White, E. (2008, May 19). The art of persuasion becomes key. *The Wall Street Journal*. Retrieved from http://online.wsj.com/article /SB121115784262002373.html

28. Bryant, A. (2010, February 13). He's not Bill Gates, or Fred Astaire. *The New York Times*. Retrieved from http://www.nytimes .com/2010/02/14/business/14cornerweb .html?pagewanted=all&_r=0

29. Pollock, T. (2003, June). How to sell an idea. *SuperVision*, p. 15. Retrieved from http://search .proquest.com

30. Communicating with the boss. (2006, May). *Communication Briefings*, p. 8.

31. Dao, J. (2012, March 9). Ad campaign for Marines cites chaos as job perk. *The New York Times*. Retrieved from http://www.nytimes.com/2012/03/10/us /marines-marketing-campaign-uses-chaos-as-a -selling-point.html?_r=0

32. Schiff, A. (2012, June 14). DMA: Direct mail response rates beat digital. *Direct Marketing News*. Retrieved from http://www.dmnews.com /dma-direct-mail-response-rates-beat-digital /article/245780

33. Millward Brown. (2009). Using neuroscience to understand the role of direct mail, p. 2. Retrieved

from http://www.millwardbrown.com/Insights
/CaseStudies/NeuroscienceDirectMail.aspx

[34] Based on Krames, J. A. (2003, November).
Performance culture. *Executive Excellence*, p. 16;
and Kelleher, K. (1992). Beware the impossible
guarantee. *Inc.,* p. 30.

[35] Based on Kuang, C. (2009, August 17). Send this to
your kids: Horrifying PSA about texting while
driving. *Fast Company*. Retrieved from http://
www.fastcompany.com/1332273/send-your
-kids-horrifying-psa-about-texting-while-driving;
and British PSA texting while driving. (2009,
August 26). HCD Research. Retrieved from
http://www.mediacurves.com
/NationalMediaFocus/J7508-PSA/Index.cfm

[36] McLaughlin, K. (1990, October). Words of wisdom.
Entrepreneur, p. 101. See also Wastphal, L.
(2001, October). Empathy in sales letters. *Direct
Marketing*, p. 55.

[37] Carnegie, D. (2009). *How to win friends and influence
people*. New York: Simon & Schuster, p. 14.

[38] Kruse, K. (2012, November 28). Zig Ziglar:
10 quotes that can change your life.
Forbes. Retrieved from http://www.forbes
.com/sites/kevinkruse/2012/11/28/
zig-ziglar-10-quotes-that-can-change-your-life

[39] Bechara, A. (2002). Does emotion play a useful or
disruptive role in economic decisions? First
Conference on Neuroscience and Economics.
Retrieved from http://neuroeconomics.econ
.umn.edu/papers/Bechara%20Paper.doc

[40] Nahmias, E. (2012, August 13). Does contemporary
neuroscience support or challenge the reality of
free will? Big Questions Online. Retrieved from
https://www.bigquestionsonline.com/content
/does-contemporary-neuroscience-support-or
-challenge-reality-free-will

[41] Shantanu Narayen discusses customer engagement.
(2013). Retrieved from http://www.adobe.com
/engagement/q_and_a.html

[42] Huy, Q., & Shipilov, A. (2012, November 29). Use
social media to build emotional capital. HBR Blog
Network. Retrieved from http://blogs.hbr.org
/cs/2012/11/use_social_media_to_build_emot
.html

[43] Scott, D. M. (2011). *The new rules of marketing & PR*
(3rd ed.). Hoboken, NJ: John Wiley & Sons, p. 39.

[44] Kendall, J. C. (2012, November 30). Facebook is a
waste of time for advertisers. Retrieved from
http://www.tekpersona.ca/awasteoftime
.html#sthash.hgFMb0Bh.W1tyGYti.dpbs

[45] ExactTarget. (2012). The 2012 channel preference
survey. Retrieved from http://www.exacttarget
.com/subscribers-fans-followers/sff14.aspx

[46] Dixon, M., & Ponomareff, L. (2012, December 10).
Should you bother using social media to serve
customers? HBR Blog Network. Retrieved from
http://blogs.hbr.org/cs/2012/12/should_you
_bother_using_social.html; Wasserman, T. (2012,
November 28). Let's face it: Most social media
marketing is a waste of time. Mashable. Retrieved
from http://mashable.com/2012/11/28
/jerry-maguire-social-media-marketing

[47] Kendall, J. C. (2012, November 30). Facebook is a
waste of time for advertisers. Retrieved from

http://www.tekpersona.ca/awasteoftime
.html#sthash.hgFMb0Bh.W1tyGYti.dpbs

[48] Wasserman, T. (2012, November 28). Let's face it:
Most social media marketing is
a waste of time. Mashable. Retrieved
from http://mashable.com/2012/11/28
/jerry-maguire-social-media-marketing

[49] Kendall, J. C. (2012, November 30). Facebook is a
waste of time for advertisers. Retrieved from
http://www.tekpersona.ca/awasteoftime
.html#sthash.hgFMb0Bh.W1tyGYti.dpbs

[50] Harris Interactive. (2010, December 3). Are
advertisers wasting their money? Retrieved
from http://www.harrisinteractive.com
/NewsRoom/HarrisPolls/tabid/447/ctl
/ReadCustom%20Default/mid/1508
/ArticleId/649/Default.aspx

[51] ExactTarget. (2012). The 2012 channel preference
survey. Retrieved from http://www.exacttarget
.com/subscribers-fans-followers/sff14.aspx

[52] Ibid.

[53] ExactTarget. (2012). The 2012 channel preference
survey. Retrieved from http://www.exacttarget
.com/subscribers-fans-followers/sff14.aspx

[54] Ibid.

[55] Howard, T. (2008, November 28). E-mail grows as
direct-marketing tool. *USA Today*, p. 5B.

[56] Distinguishing puffery from deceptive advertising.
(2011, October 2). Consumer Fraud Online.
Retrieved from http://www
.consumerfraudonline.com/2011/10/02
/consumer-fraud/distinquishing-puffery-from
-deceptive-advertising

[57] Burke, G. (2012, October 3). Dietary supplements
illegally labeled: Dozens make false claims.
Huffpost Healthy. Retrieved from http://www
.huffingtonpost.com/2012/10/03/dietary
-supplements-illegally-labeled-weight-loss
-immune_n_1936670.html; U.S. Food and
Drug Administration. (2012, September
4). Tips for older dietary supplement users.
Retrieved from http://www.fda.gov/food
/dietarysupplements/ConsumerInformation
/ucm110493.htm

[58] Saad, N. (2012, July 25). Kirstie Alley sued for false
advertising over weight-loss program. *The Los
Angeles Times*. Retrieved from http://articles
.latimes.com/2012/jul/25/entertainment
/la-et-mg-kirstie-alley-lawsuit-weight
-loss-20120725

[59] Anand, S. (2012, June 19). George Clooney and Julia
Roberts sue for unauthorized use of their names
and images. Retrieved from http://www
.lfirm.com/blog/2012/06/george-clooney-and
-julia-roberts-sue-for-unauthorized-use-of-their
-names-and-images.shtml

[60] Clifford, S. (2010, January 6). Coat maker
transforms Obama photo into ad. *The New York
Times*. Retrieved from http://www.nytimes
.com/2010/01/07/business/media/07garment
.html

[61] Joerling, D. (2012, August 28). Does the Deceptive
Mail Prevention and Enforcement Act apply to
sweepstakes? [Blog]. Retrieved from http://www
.thompsoncoburn.com/news-and-information

/sweepstakes-law-blog/blog/12-08-28/does-the
-deceptive-mail-prevention-and-enforcement-act
-apply-to-your-sweepstakes.aspx

[62] Fereydouni, A. (2012, August 22). Misleading
advertising on the rise. Retrieved from
http://www.salon.com/2012/08/22
/misleading_advertising_salpart

[63] Streitfeld, D. (2012, January 26). For $2 a star, an
online retailer gets 5-star reviews. *The New York
Times*. Retrieved from http://www.nytimes
.com/2012/01/27/technology/for-2-a-star-a
-retailer-gets-5-star-reviews.html

[64] Streitfeld, D. (2012, August 25). The best
book reviews money can buy. *The New York
Times*. Retrieved from http://www.nytimes
.com/2012/08/26/business/book-reviewers-
for-hire-meet-a-demand-for-online-raves
.html?pagewanted=all&_r=0

[65] Wooldridge, A., aka Schumpeter. (2011, September
24). Hidden persuaders II. *The Economist*.
Retrieved from http://www.economist.com
/node/21530076

[66] Edwards, L. (2012, March 5). Are brands turning
people into adverts with social media?
Socialmedia Today. Retrieved from http://
socialmediatoday.com/laurahelen/462175
/are-brands-turning-people-adverts-social
-media

[67] Tong, V. (2007, November 26). Tattoos: A new
favorite of advertisers. Boston.com. Retrieved
from http://www.boston.com/news/education
/higher/articles/2007/11/26/tattoos_a_new
_favorite_of_advertisers/?page=full

[68] Larson, C. U. (2013). *Persuasion: Reception and
responsibility* (13th ed.). Boston: Wadsworth,
Cengage Learning, p. 17.

[69] Zappos' 10-hour long customer service call sets
record. (2012, December 21). *The Huffington Post*.
Retrieved from http://www.huffingtonpost
.com/2012/12/21/zappos-10-hour
-call_n_2345467.html?view=print

[70] Wadler, J. (2012, July 26). Home improvement,
whether you asked for it or not. *The New York
Times*, p. D2.

[71] Based on Fritscher-Porter, K. (2003, June/July).
Don't be duped by office supply scam artists.
OfficePro, pp. 9-10.

[72] Based on Yu, R. (2009, 13 March). Hotels take action
to pare down food, restaurant expenses. *USA
Today*, p. 3D.

[73] Reaney, P. (2012, January 24). About 20 percent of
global workers telecommute: Poll. Retrieved from
http://www.huffingtonpost.com/2012/01/24
/workers-telecommute_n_1228004.html

[74] Scenario based on Federal Trade Commission. (n.d.).
FTC fact sheet: It looks good . . . but is it true?
Retrieved from http://www.ftc.gov/bcp
/edu/microsites/youarehere/pages/pdf/FTC-Ad
-Marketing_Looks-Good.pdf

[75] Scenario based on Rubin, C. (2012, September 6).
Pitaya: The selling of a superfruit. *Bloomberg
Businessweek*. Retrieved from http://www
.businessweek.com/articles/2012-09-06
/pitaya-the-selling-of-a-superfruit

[76] Ibid.

Unit 4

Reports, Proposals, and Presentations

Reporting in the Digital-Age Workplace

OBJECTIVES

After studying this chapter, you should be able to

1 Explain report functions and types used in the digital-age workplace, understand direct and indirect organizational strategies, and describe report-writing style as well as typical report formats.

2 Apply the 3-x-3 writing process to contemporary business reports to create well-organized documents that show a firm grasp of audience and purpose.

3 Locate and evaluate secondary sources such as databases and Web resources, and understand how to conduct credible primary research.

4 Identify the purposes and techniques of citation and documentation in business reports, and avoid plagiarism.

5 Generate, use, and convert numerical data to visual aids, and create meaningful and attractive graphics.

Digging Into Research at Pew

Zooming in

Reports are vital to organizations both large and small. They allow supervisors to stay informed about projects. They provide data that help management answer questions. They synthesize information so that leaders can solve problems. Creating these important documents requires critical thinking as well as the ability to write clearly and correctly.

The Pew Research Center is a "fact tank" that conducts research and publishes the results in reports made free to the public.[1] Pew pollsters, demographers, and analysts create dozens of

reports yearly. Its recent report *How Much Protection Does a College Degree Afford?* is nearly 30 pages long, beginning with a detailed table of contents and ending with three pages of cited sources. Like all reports, it contains an introduction, a body, and a conclusion. To help readers visualize important information, the authors included nine figures and three tables throughout the text.

Reports as detailed as this are the result of a series of steps the writing team takes to complete the task, including (a) analyzing the problem, (b) conducting the research, (c) illustrating the data, (d) writing, and (e) revising and proofreading. Pew's polished end products, which reach thousands of readers across the globe, are easy to read and esthetically pleasing. Such professional documents, composed in an appropriate style and laid out according to the principles of good document design, show that the authors have a firm grasp of their audience and purpose.

It is not surprising that Pew demands excellence of its report writers. Team members must possess "top-notch copy editing, proofreading, and writing skills"[2] and "knowledge of how to display data in easy-to-understand ways in tables and charts."[3] Such skills are valued not just by Pew but by all organizations that must communicate in reports, both informal and formal.

Whether a report is seen by only a few key members of an organization or by thousands of readers around the world, good report-writing skills are essential for any business writer.

Critical Thinking

- What function does a detailed table of contents play in long reports such as those that Pew produces?

- Why do you suppose "top-notch copy editing and proofreading skills" are critical to Pew?

- Why do reports such as *How Much Protection Does a College Degree Afford?* contain graphics?

Reporting in the Digital-Age Workplace

LEARNING OBJECTIVE 1
Explain report functions and types used in the digital-age workplace, understand direct and indirect organizational strategies, and describe report-writing style as well as typical report formats.

Management decisions in many organizations are based on information submitted in the form of reports. Routine reports keep managers informed about completed tasks, projects, and work in progress. Reports help us understand and study systematically the challenges we encounter in business before we can outline the steps toward solving them. Historian and author David McCullough said it best: "Trying to plan for the future without a sense of the past is like trying to plant cut flowers."[4] Business solutions are unthinkable without a thorough examination of the problems that prompted them.

The larger an organization is, the more vital the exchange and flow of information becomes. To manage the avalanche of information that today's organizations amass, corporations and even some smaller companies are using enterprise-class *business intelligence* software that can analyze raw data. Such data management tools pull key information together in dashboards much like the one shown in Figure 11.1. For example, a restaurant chain can analyze consumer spending patterns to make key decisions, such as adjusting staff levels or changing menu items.[5]

Figure **11.1** Dashboard Showing Key Performance Indicators in Sales

Executive monitoring dashboards provide a real-time view of an organization and its performance. The control panel can be accessed by Web browser, desktop computer, tablet, or smartphone and aids decision making.

Courtesy of InetSoft Technology Corporation

Business reports range from informal bulleted lists and half-page trip reports to formal 200-page financial forecasts. Reports may be internal or external documents. Their findings may be presented orally in front of a group or electronically on a computer screen. In many organizations, reports still take the form of paper documents such as traditional memos and letters. Other reports, such as tax reports and profit-and-loss statements, present primarily numerical data.

Many reports today are delivered and presented digitally—for instance, as e-mail messages, PDF (portable document format) files, or slide decks. These files can then be e-mailed, distributed on the company intranet, or posted on the Internet.

This chapter examines the functions, strategies, writing style, and formats of typical business reports. It also introduces the report-writing process and discusses methods of collecting, documenting, and illustrating data. Some reports provide information only; others analyze and make recommendations. Although reports vary greatly in length, content, form, and formality level, they all have one or more of the following purposes: *to convey information, answer questions, and solve problems.*

Basic Report Functions and Types

In terms of what they do, most reports fit into one of two broad categories: informational reports and analytical reports.

Informational Reports.   Reports that present data without analysis or recommendations are primarily informational. For such reports, writers collect and organize facts, but they do not analyze the facts for readers. A trip report describing an employee's visit to a trade show, for example, presents information. Weekly bulleted status reports distributed by e-mail to a team record the activities of each group member and are shared with supervisors. Other reports that present information without analysis involve routine operations, compliance with regulations, and company policies and procedures.

Analytical Reports.   Reports that provide data or findings, analyses, and conclusions are analytical. If requested, writers also supply recommendations. Analytical reports may intend to persuade readers to act or change their beliefs. For example, if you were writing a yardstick report that compares several potential manufacturing locations for a new automobile plant, you might conclude by recommending one site after discussing several criteria. Alternatively, let's say you work for a company that is considering a specific building for a women-only gym, and you are asked to study the location's suitability. You may have to write a feasibility report, an analysis of alternatives, and a recommendation that attempts to persuade readers to accept that site.

To distinguish among findings, conclusions, and recommendations, consider the example of an audit report. The auditor compiles facts and figures—the findings of the report—to meet the purpose or objective of the audit. Drawing inferences from the findings, the auditor arrives at conclusions. With the audit objectives in mind, the auditor may then propose corrective steps or actions as part of the recommendations.

REALITY CHECK: Everything but the Kitchen Sink

"[Annual report] authors are unsure about what to include in their reports (or indeed where to put it) so they throw everything in. Consequently, such reports are often bursting to the gunnels with the minutiae of every forensic detail. No stone is left unturned, no waffle spared the result, reams and reams of paper. And the reward, for all this toil? Ninety percent of readers will just read the summary."[6]

—JULIE WALES, *senior training consultant, Impact Factory*

Courtesy of Julie Wales

Organizational Strategies

Like other business messages, reports may be organized directly or indirectly. The reader's expectations and the content of a report determine its development strategy, as illustrated in Figure 11.2. In long reports, such as corporate annual reports, some parts may be developed directly whereas other parts are arranged indirectly.

Figure **11.2** Audience Analysis and Report Organization

If readers are informed | If readers are eager to have results first | If readers are supportive | If readers need to be educated | If readers need to be persuaded | If readers may be disappointed or hostile

Direct Strategy

Informational Report
- Introduction/Background
- Facts/Findings
- Summary

Analytical Report
- Introduction/Problem
- Conclusions/Recommendations
- Facts/Findings
- Discussion/Analysis

Indirect Strategy

Analytical Report
- Introduction/Problem
- Facts/Findings
- Discussion/Analysis
- Conclusions/Recommendations

© Cengage Learning 2015

Direct Strategy.   When the purpose for writing is presented close to the beginning of a report, the organizational strategy is direct. Informational reports, such as the letter report shown in Figure 11.3, are usually arranged directly. They open with an introduction, which is followed by the facts and a summary. In Figure 11.3 the writer explains a legal services plan using a letter report. The report begins with an introduction. The facts, divided into three subtopics and identified by descriptive headings, follow. The report ends with a summary and a complimentary close.

Figure 11.3   Informational Report—Letter Format

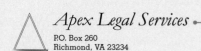

Apex Legal Services
P.O. Box 260
Richmond, VA 23234

(804) 248-8931
www.apexlegal.com

> Uses letterhead stationery for an informal report addressed to an outsider

September 17, 2015

Ms. Amanda Drew, Secretary
Lake Austin Homeowners
3902 Oak Hill Drive
Austin, TX 78134

Dear Ms. Drew:

As executive director of Apex Legal Services, I'm pleased to send you this information describing how your homeowners' association can sponsor a legal services plan for its members. After an introduction with background data, this report will discuss three steps necessary for your group to start its plan.

Introduction

> Presents introduction and facts without analysis or recommendations

A legal services plan promotes preventive law by letting members talk to attorneys whenever problems arise. Prompt legal advice often avoids or prevents expensive litigation. Because groups can supply a flow of business to the plan's attorneys, groups can negotiate free consultation, follow-up, and discounts.

Two kinds of plans are commonly available. The first, a free plan, offers free legal consultation along with discounts for services when the participating groups are sufficiently large to generate business for the plan's attorneys. These plans actually act as a substitute for advertising for the attorneys. The second common type is the prepaid plan. Prepaid plans provide more benefits, but members must pay annual fees, usually of $500 or more a year. Over 30 million people are covered by legal services plans today, and a majority belong to free plans.

Since you inquired about a free plan for your homeowners' association, the following information describes how to set up such a program.

Determine the Benefits Your Group Needs

> Arranges facts of report into sections with descriptive headings

The first step in establishing a free legal services plan is to meet with the members of your group to decide what benefits they want. Typical benefits include the following:

Free consultation. Members may consult a participating attorney—by phone or in the attorney's office—to discuss any matter. The number of consultations is unlimited, provided each is about a separate matter. Consultations are generally limited to 30 minutes, but they include substantive analysis and advice.

> Emphasizes benefits in paragraph headings with boldface type

Free document review. Important papers—such as leases, insurance policies, and installment sales contracts—may be reviewed with legal counsel. Members may ask questions and receive an explanation of terms.

Tips for Letter Reports
- Use letter format for short informal reports sent to outsiders.
- Organize the facts section into logical divisions identified by consistent headings.
- Single-space the body.
- Double-space between paragraphs.
- Leave two blank lines above each side heading.
- Create side margins of 1 to 1.25 inches.
- Add a second-page heading, if necessary, consisting of the addressee's name, the date, and the page number.

© Cengage Learning 2015

Figure **11.3** (Continued)

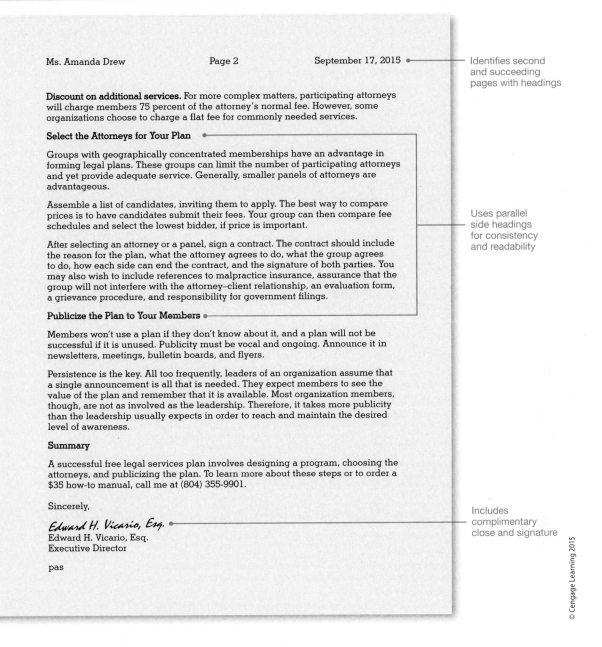

Ms. Amanda Drew   Page 2   September 17, 2015 ●━━ Identifies second
and succeeding
pages with headings

Discount on additional services. For more complex matters, participating attorneys
will charge members 75 percent of the attorney's normal fee. However, some
organizations choose to charge a flat fee for commonly needed services.

Select the Attorneys for Your Plan ●

Groups with geographically concentrated memberships have an advantage in
forming legal plans. These groups can limit the number of participating attorneys
and yet provide adequate service. Generally, smaller panels of attorneys are
advantageous.

Assemble a list of candidates, inviting them to apply. The best way to compare
prices is to have candidates submit their fees. Your group can then compare fee
schedules and select the lowest bidder, if price is important.   Uses parallel
side headings
for consistency
and readability

After selecting an attorney or a panel, sign a contract. The contract should include
the reason for the plan, what the attorney agrees to do, what the group agrees
to do, how each side can end the contract, and the signature of both parties. You
may also wish to include references to malpractice insurance, assurance that the
group will not interfere with the attorney–client relationship, an evaluation form,
a grievance procedure, and responsibility for government filings.

Publicize the Plan to Your Members ●

Members won't use a plan if they don't know about it, and a plan will not be
successful if it is unused. Publicity must be vocal and ongoing. Announce it in
newsletters, meetings, bulletin boards, and flyers.

Persistence is the key. All too frequently, leaders of an organization assume that
a single announcement is all that is needed. They expect members to see the
value of the plan and remember that it is available. Most organization members,
though, are not as involved as the leadership. Therefore, it takes more publicity
than the leadership usually expects in order to reach and maintain the desired
level of awareness.

Summary

A successful free legal services plan involves designing a program, choosing the
attorneys, and publicizing the plan. To learn more about these steps or to order a
$35 how-to manual, call me at (804) 355-9901.

Sincerely,

Edward H. Vicario, Esq. ●━━ Includes
complimentary
close and signature
Edward H. Vicario, Esq.
Executive Director

pas

Analytical reports may also be organized directly, especially when readers are
supportive of or familiar with the topic. Many busy executives prefer this strategy
because it gives them the results of the report immediately. They don't have to spend time
wading through the facts, findings, discussion, and analyses to get to the two items they
are most interested in—the conclusions and recommendations. Figure 11.4 illustrates
such an arrangement. This analytical memo report describes environmental hazards of
a property that a realtor has just listed. The realtor is familiar with the investigation and
eager to find out the recommendations. Therefore, the memo is organized directly. You
should be aware, though, that unless readers are familiar with the topic, they may find
the direct strategy confusing. Many readers prefer the indirect strategy because it seems
logical and mirrors the way they solve problems.

Indirect Strategy.   The organizational strategy is indirect when the conclusions and
recommendations, if requested, appear at the end of the report. Such reports usually

Figure **11.4** Analytical Report—Memo Format

Atlas Environmental, Inc.
Interoffice Memo

DATE: March 7, 2015

TO: Todd Linder, President

FROM: Bonnie Kalipha, Environmental Engineer *Bk*

SUBJECT: Investigation of Mountain Park Commercial Site

For New River Realty, Inc., I've completed a preliminary investigation of its Mountain Park property listing. The following recommendations are based on my physical inspection of the site, official records, and interviews with officials and persons knowledgeable about the site.

Recommendations

To reduce its potential environmental liability, New River Realty should take the following steps in regard to its Mountain Park listing:

- Conduct an immediate asbestos survey at the site, including inspection of ceiling insulation material, floor tiles, and insulation around a gas-fired heater vent pipe at 2539 Mountain View Drive.

- Prepare an environmental audit of the generators of hazardous waste currently operating at the site, including Mountain Technology.

- Obtain lids for the dumpsters situated in the parking areas and ensure that the lids are kept closed.

Findings and Analyses

My preliminary assessment of the site and its immediate vicinity revealed rooms with damaged floor tiles on the first and second floors of 2539 Mountain View Drive. Apparently, in recent remodeling efforts, these tiles had been cracked and broken. Examination of the ceiling and attic revealed further possible contamination from asbestos. The insulation for the hot-water tank was in poor condition.

Located on the property is Mountain Technology, a possible hazardous waste generator. Although I could not examine its interior, this company has the potential for producing hazardous material contamination.

In the parking area, large dumpsters collect trash and debris from several businesses. These dumpsters were uncovered, thus posing a risk to the general public.

In view of the construction date of the structures on this property, asbestos-containing building materials might be present. Moreover, this property is located in an industrial part of the city, further prompting my recommendation for a thorough investigation. New River Realty can act immediately to eliminate one environmental concern: covering the dumpsters in the parking area.

Side annotations:

Applies memo format for short, informal internal report

Presents recommendations first (direct pattern) because reader is supportive and familiar with topic

Combines findings and analyses in short report

Uses first paragraph as introduction

Tips for Memo Reports

- Use memo format for most short (ten or fewer pages) informal reports within an organization.
- Leave side margins of 1 to 1.25 inches.
- Sign your initials on the *From* line.
- Use an informal, conversational style.
- For direct analytical reports, put recommendations first.
- For indirect analytical reports, put recommendations last.

© Cengage Learning 2015

---

begin with an introduction or description of the problem, followed by facts and interpretations from the writer. They end with conclusions and recommendations. This strategy is helpful when readers are unfamiliar with the problem. This strategy is also useful when readers must be persuaded or when they may be disappointed in or hostile toward the report's findings. The writer is more likely to retain the reader's interest by first explaining, justifying, and analyzing the facts and then making recommendations. This strategy also seems most rational to readers because it follows the normal thought process: problem, alternatives (facts), solution.

Report-Writing Style

Like other business messages, reports can range from informal to formal, depending on their purpose, audience, and setting. Research reports from consultants to their clients tend to be rather formal. Such reports must project objectivity, authority, and impartiality. However, depending on the industry, a report to your boss describing a trip to a conference would probably be informal.

An office worker once called a grammar hotline service with this problem: "We've just sent a report to our headquarters, and it was returned with this comment, 'Put it in the third person.' What do they mean?" The hotline experts explained that management apparently wanted a more formal writing style, using third-person constructions (*the company* or *the researcher* instead of *we* and *I*). Figure 11.5, which compares the characteristics of formal and informal report-writing styles, can help you decide which style is appropriate for your reports. Note that, increasingly, formal reports are written with contractions and in the active voice. Today, report writers try to avoid awkward third-person references to themselves as *the researchers* or *the authors* because it sounds stilted and outdated.

Typical Report Formats

The format of a report depends on its length, topic, audience, and purpose. After considering these elements, you will probably choose from among the following formats.

Letter Format. Use letter format for short informal reports (usually eight or fewer pages) addressed outside an organization. Prepared on office stationery, a letter report contains a date, inside address, salutation, and complimentary close, as shown in Figure 11.3.

Figure 11.5 Report-Writing Styles

	Formal Writing Style	Informal Writing Style
Use	Theses Research studies Controversial or complex reports (especially to outsiders)	Short, routine reports Reports for familiar audiences Noncontroversial reports Most reports for company insiders
Effect	Impression of objectivity, accuracy, professionalism, fairness Distance created between writer and reader	Feeling of warmth, personal involvement, closeness
Characteristics	Traditionally, no first-person pronouns; use of third person (*the researcher, the writer*); increasingly, however, first-person pronouns and contractions are beginning to gain acceptance. Absence of contractions (*can't, don't*) Use of passive-voice verbs (*the study was conducted*) Complex sentences; long words Absence of humor and figures of speech Reduced use of colorful adjectives and adverbs Elimination of "editorializing" (author's opinions, perceptions)	Use of first-person pronouns (*I, we, me, my, us, our*) Use of contractions Emphasis on active-voice verbs (*I conducted the study*) Shorter sentences; familiar words Occasional use of humor, metaphors Occasional use of colorful speech Acceptance of author's opinions and ideas

© Cengage Learning 2015

Although they may carry information similar to that found in correspondence, letter reports usually are longer and show more careful organization than most letters. They also include headings.

Memo and E-Mail Formats.   For short informal reports that stay within organizations, the memo format is appropriate. Memo reports begin with essential background information, using standard headings: *Date, To, From,* and *Subject* (which may be all caps or lowercase), as shown in Figure 11.4. Like letter reports, memo reports differ from regular memos in length, use of headings, and deliberate organization. Today, memo reports are rarely distributed in hard copy; rather, they are attached to e-mails or, if short, contained in the body of e-mails.

Manuscript Format.   For longer, more formal reports, use the manuscript format. These reports are usually printed on plain paper instead of letterhead stationery or memo forms. They begin with a title followed by systematically displayed headings and subheadings. You will see examples of proposals and formal reports using the manuscript format in Chapter 13.

Forms and Templates.   Formerly, office workers used preprinted forms for repetitive data, such as monthly sales reports, performance appraisals, merchandise inventories, and personnel and financial reports. Today, such forms are available digitally. Employees can customize the templates and forms and print them out or distribute them electronically. Standardized headings on these forms save time for the writer. Forms make similar information easy to locate and ensure that all necessary information is provided.

Digital Format.   Digital media allow writers to produce and distribute reports in electronic form, not in hard copy. With Adobe Acrobat any report can be converted into a PDF document that retains its format and generally cannot be changed. Also, increasingly, reports are not static; instead, they can be presented with some animation or be converted to video. Today's communicators use not only Microsoft's PowerPoint or Apple's Keynote to create electronic presentations but also more dynamic and engaging cloud-based software solutions such as Prezi and SlideRocket, as presented in Chapter 14.

How digital reports are presented depends on their purpose. Many slide presentations today are not intended for verbal delivery. Rather, these *slide decks* may feature more text than traditional slides but are also heavy on meaningful graphics. As stand-alone reports, slide decks are often posted online or e-mailed to busy executives who can read quickly and comprehend content faster in this format than in traditional formal reports. See Figure 12.17 on p. 449 and Figure 14.11 on p. 530 for model slide decks.

LEARNING OBJECTIVE **2**

Apply the 3-x-3 writing process to contemporary business reports to create well-organized documents that show a firm grasp of audience and purpose.

Applying the 3-x-3 Writing Process to Contemporary Reports

Because business reports are systematic attempts to compile often complex information, answer questions, and solve problems, the best reports are developed methodically. In earlier chapters the 3-x-3 writing process was helpful in guiding short projects such as e-mails, memos, and letters. That same process is even more necessary when writers are preparing longer projects such as reports and proposals. After all, an extensive project poses a greater organizational challenge than a short one and, therefore, requires a rigorous structure to help readers grasp the message. Let's channel the writing process into seven specific steps:

Step 1: Analyze the problem and purpose.

Step 2: Anticipate the audience and issues.

Step 3: Prepare a work plan.

Step 4: Conduct research.

Step 5: Organize, analyze, interpret, and illustrate the data.

Step 6: Compose the first draft.

Step 7: Edit, proofread, and evaluate.

How much time you spend on each step depends on your report task. A short informational report on a familiar topic might require a brief work plan, little research, and no data analysis. A complex analytical report, on the other hand, might demand a comprehensive work plan, extensive research, and careful data analysis. In this section we consider the first three steps in the process—analyzing the problem and purpose, anticipating the audience and issues, and preparing a work plan.

To illustrate the planning stages of a report, we will watch Emily Mason develop a report she's preparing for her boss, Joshua Nichols, at Pharmgen Laboratories. Joshua asked Emily to investigate the problem of transportation for sales representatives. Currently, some Pharmgen reps visit customers (mostly doctors and hospitals) using company-leased cars. A few reps drive their own cars, receiving reimbursements for use. In three months Pharmgen leasing agreements for 14 cars expire, and Joshua is considering a major change. Emily's task is to investigate the choices and report her findings to Joshua.

Analyzing the Problem and Purpose

The first step in writing a report is understanding the problem or assignment clearly. For complex reports, prepare a written problem statement to clarify the task. In analyzing her report task, Emily had many questions: Is the problem that Pharmgen is spending too much money on leased cars? Does Pharmgen wish to invest in owning a fleet of cars? Is Joshua unhappy with the paperwork involved in reimbursing sales reps when they use their own cars? Does he suspect that reps are submitting inflated mileage figures? Before starting research for the report, Emily talked with Joshua to define the problem. She learned several dimensions of the situation and wrote the following statement to clarify the problem—both for herself and for Joshua.

> **Problem statement:** *The leases on all company cars will be expiring in three months. Pharmgen must decide whether to renew them or develop a new policy regarding transportation for sales reps. Expenses and paperwork for employee-owned cars seem excessive.*

Emily further defined the problem by writing a specific question that she would try to answer in her report:

> **Problem question:** *What plan should Pharmgen follow in providing transportation for its sales reps?*

Now Emily was ready to concentrate on the purpose of the report. Again, she had questions: Exactly what did Joshua expect? Did he want a comparison of costs for buying and leasing cars? Should she conduct research to pinpoint exact reimbursement costs when employees drive their own cars? Did he want her to do all the legwork, present her findings in a report, and let him make a decision? Or did he want her to evaluate the choices and recommend a course of action? After talking with Joshua, Emily was ready to write a simple purpose statement for this assignment.

> **Simple statement of purpose:** *To recommend a plan that provides sales reps with cars to be used in their calls.*

Preparing a written purpose statement is a good idea because it defines the focus of a report and provides a standard that keeps the project on target. In writing useful purpose statements, choose action verbs telling what you intend to do: *analyze, choose, investigate, compare, justify, evaluate, explain, establish, determine,* and so on. Notice that Emily's statement begins with the action verb *recommend.*

Some reports require only a simple statement of purpose: *to investigate expanded teller hours, to select a manager from among four candidates, to describe the position of accounts supervisor.* Many assignments,

> Preparing a written purpose statement is a good idea because it defines the focus of a report and provides a standard that keeps the project on target.

©iStockphoto.com/Andrew Johnson

though, demand additional focus to guide the project. An expanded statement of purpose considers three additional factors: scope, limitations, and significance.

Scope and Limitations.   What issues or elements will be investigated? The scope statement prepares the audience by clearly defining which problem or problems will be analyzed and solved. To determine the scope, Emily brainstormed with Joshua and others to pin down her task. She learned that Pharmgen currently had enough capital to consider purchasing a fleet of cars outright. Joshua also told her that employee satisfaction was almost as important as cost-effectiveness. Moreover, he disclosed his suspicion that employee-owned cars were costing Pharmgen more than leased cars. Emily had many issues to sort out in setting the boundaries of her report.

What conditions affect the generalizability and utility of a report's findings? As part of the scope statement, the limitations further narrow the subject by focusing on constraints or exclusions. For this report Emily realized that her conclusions and recommendations might apply only to reps in her Kansas City sales district. Her findings would probably not be reliable for reps in Seattle, Phoenix, or Atlanta. Another limitation for Emily was time. She had to complete the report in four weeks, thus restricting the thoroughness of her research.

Significance.   Why is the topic worth investigating at this time? Some topics, after initial examination, turn out to be less important than originally thought. Others involve problems that cannot be solved, making a study useless. For Emily and Joshua the problem had significance because Pharmgen's leasing agreement would expire shortly and decisions had to be made about a new policy for transportation of sales reps.

Emily decided to expand her statement of purpose to define the scope, describe the limitations of the report, and explain the significance of the problem.

> **Expanded statement of purpose:** *The purpose of this report is to recommend a plan that provides sales reps with cars to be used in their calls. The report will compare costs for three plans: outright ownership, leasing, and compensation for employee-owned cars. It will also measure employee reactions to each plan. The report is significant because Pharmgen's current leasing agreement expires March 31 and an improved plan could reduce costs and paperwork. The study is limited to costs for sales reps in the Kansas City district.*

After expanding her statement of purpose, Emily checked it with Joshua Nichols to be sure she was on target.

REALITY CHECK: I Love Writing, Even Report Writing

"My years at the United Nations made me the Grand Mistress of report writing. We wrote daily, weekly, monthly and annual reports. A couple of years in the UN and you can write reports in your sleep. Because I cared so deeply about the people I was writing about, I wanted to be sure the people in Kabul or New York who read my reports were paying attention. So I taught myself to tell a good story in every report. People pay attention and keep reading for a good story."[7]

—**MARIANNE ELLIOTT,** *writer and human rights advocate*

Photographer: Susannah Conway

Anticipating the Audience and Issues

After defining the purpose of a report, a writer must think carefully about who will read it. Concentrating solely on a primary reader is a major mistake. Although one individual may have solicited the report, others within the organization may eventually read it, including upper management and people in other departments. A report to an outside client may first be read by someone who is familiar with the problem and then be distributed to others less familiar with the topic. Moreover, candid statements to one audience may be offensive to another audience. Emily could make a major blunder, for instance, if she mentioned Joshua's suspicion that sales reps were padding their mileage statements. If the report were made public—as it probably would be to explain a new policy—the sales reps could feel insulted that their integrity was questioned.

As Emily considered her primary and secondary readers, she asked herself these questions:

- *What do my readers need to know about this topic?*
- *What do they already know?*
- *What is their educational level?*
- *How will they react to this information?*
- *Which sources will they trust?*
- *How can I make this information readable, believable, and memorable?*

Answers to these questions help writers determine how much background material to include, how much detail to add, whether to include jargon, what method of organization and presentation to follow, and what tone to use.

In the planning stages, a report writer must also break the major investigative problem into subproblems. This process, sometimes called *factoring*, identifies issues to be investigated or possible solutions to the main problem. In this case Pharmgen must figure out the best way to transport sales reps. Each possible solution or issue that Emily considers becomes a factor or subproblem to be investigated. Emily came up with three tentative solutions to provide transportation to sales reps: (a) purchase cars outright, (b) lease cars, or (c) compensate employees for using their own cars. These three factors form the outline of Emily's study.

Emily continued to factor these main points into the following subproblems for investigation:

What plan should Pharmgen use to transport its sales reps?

I.   Should Pharmgen purchase cars outright?

   A. How much capital would be required?

   B. How much would it cost to insure, operate, and maintain company-owned cars?

   C. Do employees prefer using company-owned cars?

II. Should Pharmgen lease cars?

   A. What is the best lease price available?

   B. How much would it cost to insure, operate, and maintain leased cars?

   C. Do employees prefer using leased cars?

III. Should Pharmgen compensate employees for using their own cars?

   A. How much has it cost in the past to compensate employees who used their own cars?

   B. How much paperwork is involved in reporting expenses?

   C. Do employees prefer being compensated for using their own cars?

Each subproblem would probably be further factored into additional subproblems. These issues may be phrased as questions, as Emily's are, or as statements. In factoring a complex problem, prepare an outline showing the initial problem and its breakdown into subproblems. Make sure your divisions are consistent (don't mix issues), exclusive (don't overlap categories), and complete (don't skip significant issues).

Preparing a Work Plan

After analyzing the problem, anticipating the audience, and factoring the problem, you are ready to prepare a work plan. A good work plan includes the following:

- Statement of the problem (based on key background/contextual information)
- Statement of the purpose including scope with limitations and significance
- Research strategy including a description of potential sources and methods of collecting data

- Tentative outline that factors the problem into manageable chunks
- Work schedule

Preparing a plan encourages you to evaluate your resources, set priorities, outline a course of action, and establish a schedule. Having a plan keeps you on track and provides management a means of measuring your progress.

A work plan gives a complete picture of a project. Because the usefulness and quality of any report rest primarily on its data, you will want to develop a clear research strategy, which includes allocating plenty of time to locate sources of information. For firsthand information you might interview people, prepare a survey, or even conduct a scientific experiment. For secondary information you will probably search electronic materials on the Internet and printed materials such as books and magazines. Your work plan describes how you expect to generate or collect data. Because data collection is a major part of report writing, the next section of this chapter treats the topic more fully.

Figure 11.6 shows a complete work plan for a proposal pitched by social marketing company BzzAgent's advertising executive Dave Balter to his client Lee Jeans. A work plan is useful because it outlines the issues to be investigated. Notice that considerable thought and discussion and even some preliminary research are necessary to be able to develop a useful work plan.

Although this tentative outline guides the investigation, it does not determine the content or order of the final report. You may, for example, study five possible solutions to a problem. If two prove to be useless, your report may discuss only the three winners. Moreover, you will organize the report to accomplish your goal and satisfy the audience. A busy executive who is familiar with a topic may prefer to read the conclusions and recommendations before a discussion of the findings. If someone authorizes the report, be sure to review the work plan with that person (your manager, client, or professor, for example) before proceeding with the project.

Identifying Secondary Sources and Conducting Primary Research

Research, or the gathering of information, is one of the most important steps in writing a report. As the philosopher Goethe once said: "The greater part of all mischief in the world arises

Chicago is the "Windy City" and New Orleans is the "Big Easy," but what is Glendale, California? Boring. That's what municipal branding firm North Star Destination Strategies found after conducting a yearlong study on the inconspicuous neighbor of Pasadena and Burbank. To improve Glendale's image, North Star recommended that city council leaders adopt "Your Life. Animated," a marketing-and-development campaign designed to rebrand Glendale as the home of DreamWorks Animation, the creative studio behind such delightful movies as *Shrek* and *Kung Fu Panda*. Which type of research data would be best at helping cities evaluate their strengths and weaknesses?[9]

© Photos 12/Alamy

Figure 11.6 Work Plan for a Formal Report

Statement of Problem

Many women between the ages of 18 and 34 have trouble finding jeans that fit. Lee Jeans hopes to remedy that situation with its One True Fit line. We want to demonstrate to Lee that we can create a word-of-mouth campaign that will help it reach its target audience.

Statement of Purpose

Defines purpose, scope, limits, and significance of report

The purpose of this report is to secure an advertising contract from Lee Jeans. We will examine published accounts about the jeans industry and Lee Jeans in particular. In addition, we will examine published results of Lee's current marketing strategy. We will conduct focus groups of women in our company to generate campaign strategies for our pilot study of 100 BzzAgents. The report will persuade Lee Jeans that word-of-mouth advertising is an effective strategy to reach women in this demographic group and that BzzAgent is the right company to hire. The report is significant because an advertising contract with Lee Jeans would help our company grow significantly in size and stature.

Research Strategy (Sources and Methods of Data Collection)

Describes primary and secondary data

We will gather information about Lee Jeans and the product line by examining published marketing data and conducting focus group surveys of our employees. In addition, we will gather data about the added value of word-of-mouth advertising by examining published accounts and interpreting data from previous marketing campaigns, particularly those targeted toward similar age groups. Finally, we will conduct a pilot study of 100 BzzAgents in the target demographic.

Tentative Outline

Factors problem into manageable chunks

I. How effectively has Lee Jeans marketed to the target population?
  A. Historically, who has typically bought Lee Jeans products? How often? Where?
  B. How effective are the current marketing strategies for the One True Fit line?
II. Is this product a good fit for our marketing strategy and our company?
  A. What do our staff members and our sample survey of BzzAgents say about this product?
  B. How well does our pool of BzzAgents correspond to the target demographic in terms of age and geographic distribution?
III. Why should Lee Jeans engage BzzAgent to advertise its One True Fit line?
  A. What are the benefits of word of mouth in general and for this demographic in particular?
  B. What previous campaigns have we engaged in that demonstrate our company's credibility?

Work Schedule

Estimates time needed to complete report tasks

Investigate Lee Jeans and One True Fit line's current marketing strategy	July 15–25
Test product using focus groups	July 15–22
Create campaign materials for BzzAgents	July 18–31
Run a pilot test with a selected pool of 100 BzzAgents	August 1–21
Evaluate and interpret findings	August 22–25
Compose draft of report	August 26–28
Revise draft	August 28–30
Submit final report	September 1

Tips for Preparing a Work Plan

- Start early; allow plenty of time for brainstorming and preliminary research.
- Describe the problem motivating the report.
- Write a purpose statement that includes the report's scope, significance, and limitations.
- Describe the research strategy including data collection sources and methods.
- Divide the major problem into subproblems stated as questions to be answered.
- Develop a realistic work schedule citing dates for the completion of major tasks.
- Review the work plan with whoever authorized the report.

© Cengage Learning 2015

Figure **11.7** Gathering and Selecting Report Data

Form of Data	Questions to Ask
Background or historical	How much do my readers know about the problem? Has this topic/issue been investigated before? Are those sources current, relevant, and/or credible? Will I need to add to the available data?
Statistical	What or who is the source? How recent are the data? How were the figures derived? Will this data be useful in this form?
Expert opinion	Who are the experts? What are their biases? Are their opinions in print? Are they available for interviewing? Do we have in-house experts?
Individual or group opinion	Whose opinion(s) would the readers value? Have surveys or interviews been conducted on this topic? If not, do questionnaires or surveys exist that I can modify and/or use? Would focus groups provide useful information?
Organizational	What are the proper channels for obtaining in-house data? Are permissions required? How can I learn about public and private companies?

© Cengage Learning 2015

from the fact that men do not sufficiently understand their own aims. They have undertaken to build a tower, and spend no more labor on the foundation than would be necessary to erect a hut." Think of your report as a tower. Because a report is only as good as its foundation—the questions you ask and the data you gather to answer those questions—the remainder of this chapter describes the fundamental work of finding, documenting, and illustrating data.

As you analyze a report's purpose and audience and prepare your research strategy, you will identify and assess the data you need to support your argument or explain your topic. As you do, you will answer questions about your objectives and audience: Will the audience need a lot of background or contextual information? Will your readers value or trust statistics, case studies, or expert opinions? Will they want to see data from interviews or surveys? Will summaries of focus groups be useful? Should you rely on organizational data? Figure 11.7 lists five forms of data and provides questions to guide you in making your research accurate and productive.

Locating Secondary Sources

Data fall into two broad categories: primary and secondary. Primary data result from firsthand experience and observation. Secondary data come from reading what others have experienced or observed and written down. Red Bull, Monster Energy, Rockstar, and other top energy drink brands may be forced by the government to produce primary data on ingredients and marketing claims in an investigation of energy drink health risks.[8] These same sets of data become secondary after they have been published and, let's say, a newspaper reporter uses them in an article about energy drinks. Secondary data are easier and cheaper to gather than primary data, which might involve interviewing large groups or sending out questionnaires.

We discuss secondary data first because that is where nearly every research project should begin. Often, something has already been written about your topic. Reviewing secondary sources can save time and effort and prevent you from reinventing the wheel. Most secondary material is available either in print or electronically.

© Skylines/Shutterstock.com

REALITY CHECK: Modern Librarians as Information Curators

"It used to be there was a little information out there and librarians helped you find it. Now, there is tons of information out there and librarians help you sift through and determine what's relevant. Librarians help people understand information literacy, how to discern if the information online is accurate and if it's from a responsible provider. . . . There's a lot of junk out there now that people didn't run into before."[10]

—GWEN ALEXANDER, *dean of Emporia (Kansas) State University's School of Library and Information*

Print Resources. Although we are seeing a steady movement away from print data and toward electronic data, print sources are still the most visible part of most libraries. Much information is available only in print.

By the way, if you are an infrequent library user, begin your research by talking with a reference librarian about your project. Librarians won't do your research for you, but they will steer you in the right direction. Many librarians help you understand their computer, cataloging, and retrieval systems by providing advice, brochures, handouts, and workshops.

Books. Although quickly outdated, books provide excellent historical, in-depth data. Like most contemporary sources, books can be located through online listings.

- **Card catalogs.** Very few libraries still maintain card catalogs with all books indexed on 3-by-5 cards alphabetized by author, title, and subject.
- **Online catalogs.** Most libraries today have computerized their card catalogs. Some systems are fully automated, thus allowing users to learn not only whether a book is located in the library but also whether it is currently available. Moreover, online catalogs can help you trace and borrow items from other area libraries if your college doesn't own them.

Periodicals. Magazines, pamphlets, and journals are called *periodicals* because of their recurrent, or periodic, publication. Journals are compilations of scholarly articles. Articles in journals and other periodicals are extremely useful because they are concise, limited in scope, and current and can supplement information in books. Current publications are digitized and available in full text online, often as PDF documents.

Indexes. University libraries today offer online access to *The Readers' Guide to Periodical Literature*, an index now offered by EBSCO, a major provider of online databases. Contemporary business writers rely almost totally on electronic indexes and research databases to locate references, abstracts, and full-text articles from magazines, journals, and newspapers, such as *The New York Times*.

When using Web-based online indexes, follow the on-screen instructions or ask for assistance from a librarian. Beginning with a subject search such as *manufacturers' recalls* is helpful because it generally turns up more relevant citations than keyword searches—especially when searching for names of people (*Akio Toyoda*) or companies (*Toyota*). Once you locate usable references, print a copy of your findings, save them to a portable flash memory device or in a cloud-based storage location such as Dropbox, or send them to your e-mail address.

Research Databases.   As a writer of business reports today, you will probably begin your secondary research with electronic resources. Online databases have become the staple of secondary research. Most writers turn to them first because they are fast and easy to use. You can conduct detailed searches without ever leaving your office, home, or dorm room.

A *database* is a collection of information stored digitally so that it is accessible by computer or mobile electronic devices and searchable. Databases provide bibliographic information (titles of documents and brief abstracts) and full-text documents. Various databases contain a rich array of magazine, newspaper, and journal articles, as well as newsletters, business reports, company profiles, government data, reviews, and directories. The five databases most useful to business writers are ABI/INFORM Complete (ProQuest), Business Source Premier (EBSCO), JSTOR Business, Factiva (Dow Jones), and LexisNexis Academic. Figure 11.8 shows the ABI/INFORM Complete search menu.

Developing a search strategy and narrowing your search can save time. Think about the time frame for your search, the language of publication, and the types of materials you will need. Most databases enable you to focus a search easily. For example, if you were researching the Great Recession and wanted to look at articles published in a specific year, most search tools would enable you to limit your search to that period. All databases and search engines allow you to refine your search and increase the precision of your hits.

Efficient search strategies take time to master. Therefore, before wasting time and retrieving lots of useless material, talk to a university librarian. College and public libraries as well as some employers offer free access to several commercial databases, sparing you the high cost of individual subscriptions.

Figure 11.8   ABI/INFORM Complete (ProQuest) Search Result

ABI/INFORM (ProQuest) indexes over 4,000 journals and features more than 2,900 full-text documents about business topics. Users can access newspapers, magazines, reports, dissertations, book reviews, scholarly journals, and trade publications. Figure 11.8 shows that the search terms *sustainable development* and *energy efficiency* brought up 912 full-text search results. Savvy researchers further narrow their search to a more manageable number.

Source: http://search.proquest.com

The Web

If you are like most adults today, you probably use the Web for entertainment and work every day. Chances are you have a Facebook or Pinterest page, and perhaps you play one of the countless free online games. You have probably looked up directions on Google Maps and may have bid on or sold items on eBay. You are likely to download ringtones for your smartphone, and perhaps you obtain your favorite music from iTunes, not some illegal file-sharing site. In short, you rely on the Internet daily for information and entertainment. In this section we examine the Web as an effective research tool.

Web Search Tools.   Finding what you are looking for on the Web is hopeless without powerful, specialized search tools, such as Google, Bing, Yahoo Search, and Ask.com. These search tools can be divided into two types: subject (or Web) directories and search engines. In addition, some search engines specialize in "metasearching." This means they combine several powerful search engines into one (e.g., Infosearch, Dogpile, and Search.com).

Search engines differ in the way they trawl the vast amount of data on the Web. Google uses automated software, "spiders" or bots, that crawl across the Web at regular intervals to collect and index the information from each location visited. Some search tools (e.g., Ask.com) use natural-language-processing technology to enable you to ask questions to gather information. Both search engines and subject directories will help you find specific information. Figure 11.9 shows Business.com, a business search engine and subject directory in one. To compare the quality of results, or "hits," try the same keyword or query using various search sites.

Figure 11.9 Business.com

Source: http://www.business.com/business-planning/it-consulting/

Business.com is a resource that indexes any imaginable business-related topic and is very useful to business communicators and researchers.

Applying Internet Search Strategies and Techniques.   To conduct a thorough search for the information you need, build a (re)search strategy by understanding the tools available. Figure 11.10 outlines several effective search techniques.

Figure **11.10**   Useful Internet Search Techniques

Use two or three search tools.
- Conduct a topic search using a subject directory such as Yahoo, About.com, or Open Directory Project (dmoz.org).
- Switch to a search engine or metasearch engine once you have narrowed your topic.

Know your search tool.
- Always read the description of each new search site you visit, including the FAQs, Help, and How to Search sections.
- Take advantage of special features, e.g., the News, Images, Video, Books, and other categories on Google, that can speed up your search.

Understand case sensitivity.
- Use lowercase, unless you are looking for a term that is usually written in upper- and lowercase, such as a person's name.

Use nouns as search words.
- The right keywords, up to eight words in a query, can narrow the search effectively.

Combine keywords into phrases.
- Phrases, marked by the use of quotation marks (e.g., "business ethics"), will limit results to specific matches.

Omit articles and prepositions.
- Known as stop words, articles and prepositions do not add value to a search. Instead of *request for proposal*, use *proposal request*.

Use wild cards.
- Try wildcards, such as asterisks, because most search engines support them. The search term *cent** will retrieve cents, while *cent*** will retrieve both *center* and *centre*.

Bookmark the best.
- Keep track of your favorite Internet sites by saving them as bookmarks or favorites.

© Cengage Learning 2015

To improve your odds of discovering more relevant sources, try these additional research strategies used by successful Internet sleuths:

- **Learn basic Boolean search strategies.** You can save yourself a lot of time and frustration by narrowing your search with the following Boolean operators:

AND   Identifies only documents containing all of the specified words: **employee AND productivity AND morale**

OR   Identifies documents containing at least one of the specified words: **employee OR productivity OR morale**

NOT   Excludes documents containing the specified word: **employee productivity NOT morale**

NEAR   Finds documents containing target words or phrases within a specified distance, for instance, within ten words: **employee NEAR productivity**.

- **Keep trying.** If a search produces no results, check your spelling. If you are using Boolean operators, check the syntax of your queries. Try synonyms and variations on words. Try to be less specific in your search term. If your search produces too many hits, try to be more specific. Use the Advanced feature of your search engine to narrow your search. Think of words that uniquely identify what you are looking for. Use as many relevant keywords as possible.

- **Repeat your search a week later.** For the best results, return to your search a couple of days or a week later. The same keywords will probably produce additional results. That's because millions of new pages are being added to the Web every day. The ranking of hits can also change depending on how often a link is accessed by Internet users.

Staying on Top of Research Data

Plugged In

© iStockphoto/Thinkstock

In collecting search results, you can easily lose track of websites and articles you quoted. To document Web data that may change, as well as to manage all your other sources, you need a specific plan for saving the information. At the very least, you will want to create a *working bibliography* or list of *references* in which you record the URL of each electronic source. These techniques can help you stay in control of your data:

- **Saving sources to a local drive or USB flash drive** has advantages, including being able to open the document in a browser even if you don't have access to the Internet. More important, saving sources to disk or memory stick preserves information that may not be available later. Using either the **File** and **Save As** or the **File** and **Save Page** As menu command in your browser, you will be able to store the information permanently. Save images and other kinds of media by either right-clicking or command-clicking on the item, and selecting **Save Picture As** or **Save Image As**.

- **Copying and pasting** information you find on the Web into MS Word is an easy way to save and store it. Copy and paste the URL into the file as well, and record the URL in your working bibliography. If you invest in Adobe's PDF Converter, you can save most files in the portable document format simply by choosing the **Print** command and selecting Adobe PDF in the **Printer** window of the **Print** menu. The URL, access date, and time stamp will be automatically saved on the document. You can keep your PDF documents as electronic files or print out paper copies later.

- **Printing** pages is a handy way to gather and store information. Doing so enables you to have copies of important data that you can annotate or highlight. Make sure the URL prints with the document (usually on the bottom of the page). If not, write it on the page.

- **Bookmarking favorites** is an option within browsers to enable you to record and store the URLs of important sources. The key to using this option is creating folders with relevant names and choosing concise and descriptive names for bookmarks.

- **Cloud storage and e-mailing** documents, URLs, or messages to yourself are also useful strategies. Many databases and online magazines permit you to e-mail information and sometimes the entire article to your account. A cloud storage account such as Dropbox or iCloud lets you access your files from any electronic device.

Credibility of Web Sources.   Most Web users tend to assume that any information turned up by a search engine has somehow been evaluated as part of a valid selection process. Wrong! Unlike library-based research, information at many sites has not undergone the editing or scrutiny of scholarly publication procedures. The information we read in journals and most reputable magazines is reviewed, authenticated, and evaluated.

Information on the Web is much less reliable than data from traditional sources. Wikis, blogs, and discussion forum entries illustrate this problem. They change constantly and may disappear fast, so that your source can't be verified. Many don't provide any references or reveal sources that are either obscure or suspect. Academic researchers prefer lasting, scholarly sources.

Wikipedia and Other Encyclopedias.   College-level research requires you to use general encyclopedia information only as a starting point for more in-depth research. That means you will not cite Wikipedia, Ask.com, general encyclopedias, search engines, or similar reference works in your writing. Their information is too fluid and too general. However, these information-packed sites often provide their own references (bibliographies) that you can employ in your research. Locate the original sources of information rather than the condensed reference articles. Both the American Psychological Association (APA) and the Modern Language Association (MLA) favor the use of original source material.

To use the Web meaningfully, you must scrutinize what you find and check who authored and published it. Here are specific criteria to consider as you examine a site:

- **Currency.** What is the date of the Web page? Is some of the information obviously out-of-date? If the information is time sensitive and the site has not been updated recently, the site is probably not reliable.

- **Authority.** Who publishes or sponsors this Web page? What makes the presenter an authority? Is information about the author or creator available? Is a contact address available for the presenter? Learn to be skeptical about data and assertions from individuals and organizations whose credentials are not verifiable.

- **Content.** Is the purpose of the page to entertain, inform, convince, or sell? How would you classify this page (e.g., news, personal, advocacy, reference)? Who is the intended audience, based on content, tone, and style? Can you judge the overall value of the content compared with the other resources on this topic?

- **Accuracy.** Do the facts that are presented seem reliable? Do you find errors in spelling, grammar, or usage? Do you see any evidence of bias? Are references provided? Errors and missing references should alert you that the data may be questionable.

Conducting Primary Research

Although you will start nearly every business report assignment by sifting through secondary sources, you will probably need primary data to give a complete picture. Business reports that solve specific current problems typically rely on primary, firsthand data. If, for example, management wants to discover the cause of increased employee turnover in its Seattle office, it must investigate conditions in Seattle by collecting recent information. Providing answers to business problems often means generating primary data through surveys, interviews, observation, or experimentation.

Surveys.   Surveys collect data from groups of people. Before developing new products, for example, companies often survey consumers to learn their needs. The advantages of surveys are that they gather data economically and efficiently. Snail-mailed or e-mailed surveys reach big groups nearby or at great distances. Moreover, people responding to mailed or e-mailed surveys have time to consider their answers, thus improving the accuracy of the data.

Mailed or e-mailed surveys, of course, have disadvantages. Because most of us rank them with junk mail or spam, response rates may be low. Furthermore, respondents may not represent an accurate sample of the overall population, thus invalidating generalizations from the group. Let's say, for example, that an insurance company sends out a questionnaire asking about provisions in a new policy. If only older people respond, the questionnaire data cannot be used to generalize what people in other age groups might think. If a survey is only e-mailed, it may miss audiences that do not use the Internet.

A final problem with surveys has to do with truthfulness. Some respondents exaggerate their incomes or distort other facts, thus causing the results to be unreliable. Nevertheless, surveys may be the best way to generate data for business and student reports. In preparing print or electronic surveys, consider these pointers:

- **Select the survey population carefully.** Many surveys question a small group of people (a sample) and project the findings to a larger population. Let's say that a survey of your class reveals that the majority prefer *phở*, the Vietnamese beef and rice noodle soup. Can you then say that all students on your campus (or in the nation) prefer pho? To be able to generalize from a survey, you need to make the sample large enough. In addition, you need to determine whether the sample represents the larger population. For important surveys you will want to learn sampling techniques. As for pho, in a Sodexo survey the soup ranked among the top three comfort foods favored by American college students.[11]

- **Explain why the survey is necessary.** In a cover letter or an opening paragraph, describe the need for the survey. Suggest how someone or something other than you will benefit. If appropriate, offer to send recipients a copy of the findings.

- **Consider incentives.** If the survey is long, persuasive techniques may be necessary. Response rates can be increased by offering money (such as a $1 bill), coupons, gift certificates, books, or other gifts.

- **Limit the number of questions.** Resist the temptation to ask for too much. Request only information you will use. Don't, for example, include demographic questions (income, gender, age, and so forth) unless the information is necessary to evaluate responses.

- **Use questions that produce quantifiable answers.** Check-off, multiple-choice, yes-no, and scale (or rank-order) questions, illustrated in Figure 11.11, provide quantifiable data that are easily tabulated. Responses to open-ended questions (*What should the bookstore do about plastic bags?*) reveal interesting, but difficult-to-quantify perceptions.[12] To obtain workable data, give interviewees a list of possible responses, as shown in items 5 through 8 of Figure 11.11. For scale and multiple-choice questions, try to present all the possible answer choices. To be safe, add an *Other* or *Don't know* category in case the choices seem insufficient to the respondent. Many surveys use scale questions because they capture degrees of feelings. Typical scale headings are *Agree strongly, Agree somewhat, Neutral, Disagree somewhat,* and *Disagree strongly.*

- **Avoid leading or ambiguous questions.** The wording of a question can dramatically affect responses to it.[13] When respondents were asked, "Are we spending too much, too little, or about the right amount on *assistance to the poor?*" 13 percent responded *Too much.* When the same respondents were asked, "Are we spending too much, too little, or about the right amount on *welfare?*" 44 percent responded *Too much.* Because words have different meanings for different people, you must strive to use objective language and pilot test your questions with typical respondents. Ask neutral questions (*Do CEOs earn too much, too little, or about the right amount?*). Also, avoid queries that really ask two or more things (*Should the salaries of CEOs be reduced or regulated by government legislation?*). Instead, break them into separate questions (*Should the salaries of CEOs be reduced by government legislation? Should the salaries of CEOs be regulated by government legislation?*).

- **Make it easy for respondents to return the survey.** Researchers often provide prepaid self-addressed envelopes or business-reply envelopes. Low-cost Web survey software such as SurveyMonkey and Zoomerang help users develop simple, template-driven questions and allow survey takers to follow a link to take the survey.

- **Conduct a pilot study.** Try the questionnaire with a small group so that you can remedy any problems. In the survey shown in Figure 11.11, students generally favored cloth

Figure **11.11** Preparing a Survey

1 Prewriting

Analyze: The purpose is to help the bookstore decide whether it should replace plastic bags with cloth bags for customer purchases.

Anticipate: The audience will be busy students who will be initially uninterested.

Adapt: Because students will be unwilling to participate, the survey must be short and simple. Its purpose must be significant and clear.

2 Drafting

Research: Ask students how they would react to cloth bags. Use their answers to form question response choices.

Organize: Open by explaining the survey's purpose and importance. In the body ask clear questions that produce quantifiable answers. Conclude with appreciation and instructions.

Draft: Write the first draft of the questionnaire.

3 Revising

Edit: Try out the questionnaire with a small representative group. Revise unclear questions.

Proofread: Read for correctness. Be sure that answer choices do not overlap and that they are complete. Provide an *Other* category if appropriate (as in No. 9).

Evaluate: Is the survey clear, attractive, and easy to complete?

© Cengage Learning 2015

Shoreline College Bookstore
STUDENT SURVEY

The Shoreline College Bookstore wants to do its part in protecting the environment. Each year we give away 45,000 plastic bags for students to carry off their purchases. We are considering changing from plastic to cloth bags or some other alternative, but we need your views.

— Explains need for survey (use cover letter for longer surveys)

Please place checks below to indicate your responses.

Uses groupings that do not overlap (not *9 to 15* and *15 or more*)

1. How many units are you presently carrying?
   ___ 15 or more units   ___ Male
   ___ 9 to 14 units   ___ Female
   ___ 8 or fewer units

2. How many times have you visited the bookstore this semester?
   ___ 0 times ___ 1 time ___ 2 times ___ 3 times ___ 4 or more times

3. Indicate your concern for the environment.
   ___ Very concerned ___ Concerned ___ Unconcerned

4. To protect the environment, would you be willing to change to another type of bag when buying books?
   ___ Yes
   ___ No

Indicate your feeling about the following alternatives.

	Agree	Undecided	Disagree
For major purchases the bookstore should			
5. Continue to provide plastic bags.	___	___	___
6. Provide no bags; encourage students to bring their own bags.	___	___	___
7. Provide no bags; offer cloth bags at reduced price (about $3).	___	___	___
8. Give a cloth bag with each major purchase, the cost to be included in registration fees.	___	___	___

Uses scale questions to channel responses into quantifiable alternatives, as opposed to open-ended questions

Allows respondent to add an answer in case choices provided seem insufficient

9. Consider another alternative, such as_____

Please return the completed survey form to your instructor or to the survey box at the Shoreline College Bookstore exit. Your opinion counts.

— Tells how to return survey form

Thanks for your help!

© Cengage Learning 2015

bags and were willing to pay for them. Male students opposed purchasing cloth bags. By adding a gender category, researchers could verify this finding. The pilot study also revealed the need to ensure an appropriate representation of male and female students in the survey.

Interviews.   Some of the best report information, particularly on topics about which little has been written, comes from individuals. These individuals are usually experts or veterans in their fields. Consider both in-house and outside experts for business reports. Tapping these sources will call for in-person, telephone, or online interviews. To elicit the most useful data, try these techniques:

- **Locate an expert.** Ask managers and individuals who are considered to be most knowledgeable in their areas. Check membership lists of professional organizations, and consult articles about the topic. Most people enjoy being experts or at least recommending them. You could also *crowdsource* your question in social media; that is, you could pose the query to your network to get input from your contacts.

- **Prepare for the interview.** Learn about the individual you are interviewing, and make sure you can pronounce the interviewee's name. Research the background and terminology of the topic. Let's say you are interviewing a corporate communication expert about producing an in-house newsletter. You ought to be familiar with terms such as *font* and software such as PagePlus and InDesign. In addition, be prepared by making a list of questions that pinpoint your focus on the topic. Ask the interviewee if you may record the talk. Familiarize yourself with the recording device beforehand.

- **Maintain a professional attitude.** Call before the interview to confirm the arrangements, and then arrive on time. Be prepared to take notes if your recorder fails (and remember to ask permission beforehand if you want to record). Use your body language to convey respect.

- **Make your questions objective and friendly.** Adopt a courteous and respectful attitude. Don't get into a debating match with the interviewee, and don't interrupt. Remember that you are there to listen, not to talk! Use open-ended questions to draw experts out.

- **Watch the time.** Tell interviewees in advance how much time you expect to need for the interview. Don't overstay your appointment. If your subject rambles, gently try to draw him or her back to the topic; otherwise, you may run out of time before asking all your questions.

- **End graciously.** Conclude the interview with a general question, such as *Is there anything you would like to add?* Express your appreciation, and ask permission to telephone later if you need to verify points.

REALITY CHECK: Analyzing Primary and Secondary Data to Win

Experts such as Tom Peters recognize the value of ongoing primary and secondary research to gain a competitive advantage: "Even gross indicators, such as market share by segment, relative revenue, and relative earnings, can give you a good start on competitive analysis. These are crude measures, yet I am surprised at how few (1) collect the data, (2) update them regularly, and (3) share them widely within the firm. Every person in the company should have ready, visible access to the numbers on market share—yours and your competitors'—updated weekly."[14]

—**Tom Peters,** *prominent management consultant and best-selling author*

© AP Images/Toby Talbot

LEARNING OBJECTIVE **4**

Identify the purposes and techniques of citation and documentation in business reports, and avoid plagiarism.

Observation and Experimentation.   Some kinds of primary data can be obtained only through firsthand observation and investigation. If you determine that you need observational data, then you need to plan carefully. Most important is deciding what or whom you are observing and how often those observations are necessary. For example, if you want to learn more about an organization's telephone customer service, you probably need to conduct an observation (along with interviews and perhaps even surveys). You will want to answer questions such as *How long does a typical caller wait before a customer-service rep answers the call?* and *Is the service consistent?* Recording 60-minute periods at various times throughout a week will give you a better picture than just observing for an hour on a Friday before a holiday.

To observe, arrive early enough to introduce yourself and set up any equipment. If you are recording, secure permissions beforehand. In addition, take notes, not only of the events or actions but also of the settings. Changes in environment often have an effect on actions. Starbucks chief Howard Schultz frowns on research, advertising, and customer surveys. Instead of relying on sophisticated marketing research, Schultz visits 25 Starbucks locations a week to learn about his customers.[15]

Experimentation produces data suggesting causes and effects. Informal experimentation might be as simple as a pretest and posttest in a college course. Did students learn in the course? Scientists and professional researchers undertake more formal experimentation. They control variables to test their effects. Assume, for example, that Hershey's wants to test the hypothesis (a tentative assumption) that chocolate provides an emotional lift. An experiment testing the hypothesis would separate depressed people into two groups: the chocolate eaters (the experimental group) and the chocolate deprived (the control group). Such experiments are not done haphazardly, however. Valid experiments require sophisticated research designs.

Documenting Information

In writing business reports, you will often build on the ideas and words of others. In Western culture, whenever you "borrow" the ideas of others, you must give credit to your information sources. This is called *documentation*.

The Purposes of Documentation

As a careful writer, you should take pains to document report data properly for the following reasons:

- **To strengthen your argument.** Including good data from reputable sources will convince readers of your credibility and the logic of your reasoning.
- **To protect yourself against charges of plagiarism.** Acknowledging your sources keeps you honest. *Plagiarism*, which is unethical and in some cases illegal, is the act of using others' ideas without proper documentation.
- **To instruct the reader.** Citing references enables readers to pursue a topic further and make use of the information themselves.
- **To save time.** The world of business moves so quickly that words and ideas must often be borrowed—which is very acceptable when you give credit to your sources.

Intellectual Theft: Plagiarism

Plagiarism of words or ideas is a serious offense and can lead to loss of a job. Famous historians, several high-level journalists, and even college professors[16] have suffered grave consequences for copying from unnamed sources. Your instructor may use a commercial plagiarism detection service such as Turnitin.com, which cross-references much of the information on the Web, looking for documents with identical phrasing. The result, an "originality report," shows the instructor whether you have been accurate and honest.

You can avoid charges of plagiarism as well as add clarity to your work by knowing what to document and by developing good research habits. First, however, let's consider the differences between business and academic writing with respect to documentation.

Academic Documentation and Business Practices

In the academic world, documentation is critical. Especially in the humanities and sciences, students are taught to cite sources by using quotation marks, parenthetical citations, footnotes, and bibliographies. College term papers require full documentation to demonstrate that a student has become familiar with respected sources and can cite them properly in developing an argument. Giving credit to the authors is extremely important. Students who plagiarize risk a failing grade in a class and even expulsion from school.

In business, however, documentation and authorship are sometimes viewed differently. Business communicators on the job may find that much of what is written does not follow the standards they learned in school. In many instances, individual authorship is unimportant. For example, employees may write for the signature of their bosses. The writer receives no credit. Similarly, teams turn out documents for which none of the team members receive individual credit. Internal business reports, which often include chunks of information from previous reports, also don't give credit. Even information from outside sources may lack detailed documentation. However, if facts are questioned, business writers must be able to produce their source materials.

Although both internal and external business reports are not as heavily documented as school assignments or term papers, business communication students are well advised to learn proper documentation methods. In the workplace, stealing the ideas of others and passing them off as one's own can be corrosive to the business because it leads to resentment and worse. One writer suggests that the wronged employee may quit and speak out about the unethical behavior, destroying the integrity of the business.[17]

REALITY CHECK: Intellectual Theft on the Internet

In academic circles, plagiarism remains a serious offense, yet many see the Internet as a free-for-all. A Pew Research study found that nearly half of all bloggers have admitted to having appropriated text, images, and other media without attributing them to their original sources. One expert claims: "People are incredibly sloppy. It's like the Wild West out there."

—**JIM BERKOWITZ,** *technology coach, blogger, CRM Mastery, Inc.*

© iStockphoto.com/Brasil2

What to Document

When you write reports, especially in college, you are continually dealing with other people's ideas. You are expected to conduct research, synthesize ideas, and build on the work of others. But you are also expected to give proper credit for borrowed material. To avoid plagiarism, you must give credit whenever you use the following:[18]

- Another person's ideas, opinions, examples, or theory
- Any facts, statistics, graphs, and drawings that are not common knowledge
- Quotations of another person's actual spoken or written words
- Paraphrases of another person's spoken or written words
- Visuals, images, and any kind of electronic media

Information that is common knowledge requires no documentation. For example, the statement *The Wall Street Journal is a popular business newspaper* would require no citation. Statements that are not common knowledge, however, must be documented. For example, the following statement would require a citation because most people do not know these facts: *Texas is home to two of the nation's top ten fastest-growing large cities (100,000 or more population): Austin and San Antonio also ranked first and second in jobs.*[19] More important, someone went through the trouble and expense of assembling this original work and now *owns* it. Cite sources for such proprietary information—in this case, statistics reported by a newspaper or magazine. You probably know to use citations to document direct quotations, but you must also cite ideas that you summarize in your own words.

When in doubt about common knowledge, check to see whether the same piece of information is available in at least three sources in your topic's specific field and appears without citation. If what you borrow doesn't fall into one of the five categories listed earlier, for which you must give credit, you are safe in assuming it is common knowledge. Copyright and intellectual property are discussed in greater detail later in this chapter.

Good Research Habits

As they gather sources, report writers have two methods available for recording the information they find. The time-honored manual method of notetaking works well because information is recorded on separate cards, which can then be conveniently arranged in the order needed to develop a thesis or argument. Today, however, writers prefer to do their research online. Traditional notetaking may seem antiquated and laborious in comparison. Let's explore both methods.

Paper Note Cards.   To make sure you know whose ideas you are using, train yourself to take excellent notes. If possible, know what you intend to find before you begin your research so that you won't waste time on unnecessary notes. Here are some pointers on taking good notes:

- Record all major ideas from various sources on separate note cards.
- Include all publication information (author, date, title, and so forth) along with precise quotations.
- Consider using one card color for direct quotes and a different color for your paraphrases and summaries.
- Put the original source material aside when you are summarizing or paraphrasing.

Digital Records.   Instead of recording facts on note cards, savvy researchers today take advantage of digital media tools, as noted in the accompanying Plugged In box. Beware, however, of the risk of cutting and pasting your way into plagiarism. Here are some pointers on taking good virtual notes:

- Begin your research by setting up a folder on your local drive or cloud-based storage site. On the go, you can access these files with any mobile electronic device or you can use a USB flash drive to carry your data.
- Create subfolders for major sections, such as introduction, body, and closing.
- When you find facts on the Web or in research databases, highlight the material you want to record, copy it, and paste it into a document in an appropriate folder.
- Be sure to include all publication information in your references or works-cited lists.
- As discussed in the section on managing research data, consider archiving on a USB flash drive or external disk drive those Web pages or articles used in your research in case the data must be verified.

The Fine Art of Paraphrasing

In writing reports and using the ideas of others, you will probably rely heavily on *paraphrasing*, which means restating an original passage in your own words and in your own style. To do a good job of paraphrasing, follow these steps:

1. Read the original material intently to comprehend its full meaning.
2. Write your own version without looking at the original.
3. Avoid repeating the grammatical structure of the original and merely replacing words with synonyms.

4. Reread the original to be sure you covered the main points but did not borrow specific language.

To better understand the difference between plagiarizing and paraphrasing, study the following passages. Notice that the writer of the plagiarized version uses the same grammatical construction as the source and often merely replaces words with synonyms. Even the acceptable version, however, requires a reference to the source author.

Source
We have seen, in a short amount of time, the disappearance of a large number of household brands that failed to take sufficient and early heed of the software revolution that is upending traditional brick-and-mortar businesses and creating a globally pervasive digital economy.[20]

Plagiarized version
Many trusted household name brands disappeared very swiftly because they did not sufficiently and early pay attention to the software revolution that is toppling traditional physical businesses and creating a global digital economy. (Saylor, 2012)

Acceptable paraphrase
Digital technology has allowed a whole new virtual global economy to blossom and very swiftly wipe out some formerly powerful companies that responded too late or inadequately to the disruptive force that has swept the globe. (Saylor, 2012)

When and How to Quote

On occasion, you will want to use the exact words of a source, but beware of overusing quotations. Documents that contain pages of spliced-together quotations suggest that writers have few ideas of their own. Wise writers and speakers use direct quotations for three purposes only:

- To provide objective background data and establish the severity of a problem as seen by experts
- To repeat identical phrasing because of its precision, clarity, or aptness
- To duplicate exact wording before criticizing

When you must use a long quotation, try to summarize and introduce it in your own words. Readers want to know the gist of a quotation before they tackle it. For example, to introduce a quotation discussing the shrinking staffs of large companies, you could precede it with your words: *In predicting employment trends, Charles Waller believes the corporation of the future will depend on a small core of full-time employees.* To introduce quotations or paraphrases, use wording such as the following:

According to Waller, ...

Waller argues that . . . .

In his recent study, Waller reported . . . .

Use quotation marks to enclose exact quotations, as shown in the following: *"The current image," says Charles Waller, "of a big glass-and-steel corporate headquarters on landscaped grounds directing a worldwide army of tens of thousands of employees may soon be a thing of the past" (2013, p. 51).*

Copyright Information

The Copyright Act of 1976 protects authors—literary, dramatic, and artistic—of published and unpublished works. The word *copyright* refers to "the right to copy," and a key provision is *fair use*. Under fair use, individuals have limited use of copyrighted material without requiring permission. These uses are for criticism, comment, news reporting, teaching, scholarship, and research. Unfortunately, the distinctions between fair use and infringement are not clearly defined.

Four-Factor Test to Assess Fair Use.   What is fair use? Actually, it is a shadowy territory with vague and often disputed boundaries—now even more so with the addition of cyberspace. Courts use four factors as a test in deciding disputes over fair use:

- **Purpose and character of the use, particularly whether for profit.** Courts are more likely to allow fair use for nonprofit educational purposes than for commercial ventures.

- **Nature of the copyrighted work.** When information is necessary for the public good—such as medical news—courts are more likely to support fair use.

- **Amount and substantiality of portion used.** Copying a 200-word passage from a 200,000-word book might be allowed but not 200 words from a 1,000-word article or a substantial part of a shorter work. A total of 300 words is mistakenly thought by many to be an acceptable limit for fair use, but courts have not upheld this figure. Don't rely on it.

- **Effect of the use on the potential market.** If use of the work may interfere with the author's potential profit from the original, fair use copying would not be allowed.

How to Avoid Copyright Infringement.   Whenever you borrow words, charts, graphs, photos, music, and other media—in short, any *intellectual property*—be sure you know what is legal and acceptable. The following guidelines will help:

- **Assume that all intellectual property is copyrighted.** Nearly everything created privately and originally after 1989 is copyrighted and protected whether or not it has a copyright notice.

- **Realize that Internet items and resources are NOT in the public domain.** No modern intellectual or artistic creation is in the public domain (free to be used by anyone) unless the owner explicitly says so.

- **Observe fair-use restrictions.** Be aware of the four-factor test. Avoid appropriating large amounts of outside material.

- **Ask for permission.** You are always safe if you obtain permission. Write to the source, identify the material you wish to include, and explain where it will be used. Expect to pay for permission.

- **Don't assume that a footnote is all that is needed.** Including a footnote to a source prevents plagiarism but not copyright infringement. Anything copied beyond the boundaries of fair use requires permission.

For more information about *copyright law, fair use, public domain,* and *work for hire,* you can search the Web with these keywords.

Citation Formats

You can direct readers to your sources with parenthetical notes inserted into the text and with bibliographies. The most common citation formats are those presented by the Modern Language Association (MLA) and the American Psychological Association (APA). Learn more about how to use these formats in Appendix C.

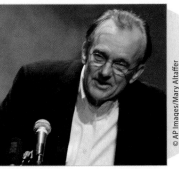

REALITY CHECK: Clarity and Simplicity in Information Design

"The interior decoration of graphics generates a lot of ink that does not tell the viewer anything new. The purpose of decoration varies—to make the graphic appear more scientific and precise, to enliven the display, to give the designer an opportunity to exercise artistic skills. Regardless of its cause, it is all non-data-ink or redundant data-ink, and it is often chartjunk."[21]

—**EDWARD TUFTE**, *statistician and pioneer of data visualization*

© AP Images/Mary Altaffer

© iStockphoto/Thinkstock

Telling a Story With Infographics

Plugged In

Although infographics seem to have burst onto the scene within the last decade, Edward Tufte, a pioneer of data visualization, has introduced brilliant 19th-century examples. One strikingly depicts Napoleon's ill-fated Russian campaign of 1812—the diminishing numbers of soldiers, their movements, and even the temperatures during their retreat.[22] Pictograms and ideograms (images and symbols visualizing an idea or action) date back thousands of years to cave paintings, hieroglyphs, and other writing systems.[23]

Contemporary infographics "gurus" include Ryan Case and Nicholas Felton, known for turning ordinary details of everyday life into strikingly expressive charts. Felton is credited with inspiring Facebook's Timeline feature.[24] An information design wiz, Felton once charted a year of his life in an annual report format. With Case, he created Daytum, an app that allows users to visualize their own personal statistics.

- **Purpose.** Good infographics tell a story and allow the reader to make sense of ever-growing amounts of data. The purpose of the best infographics, it has been said, is to "add intelligence and insight to the digital noise buzzing around us every day."[25] Information design master Francesco Franchi claims that "infographic thinking" is not just pretty images; rather, it means creating a new, nonlinear reading experience and encouraging critical thought. Franchi believes that the best infographic design is informative and entertaining. It invites the reader to participate in the process of interpretation, he says.[26] Well-executed infographics illustrate often complex topics and data almost at one glance. Substituted for ho-hum, conventional visuals, good infographics can be stunning.

- **Infographics Software.** Today even amateur designers can create captivating infographics. Any software that can merge text and visuals can help create infographics. However, no single piece of software is the ultimate tool.[27] Some come with a steep learning curve (e.g., Adobe Illustrator and Photoshop), whereas others are easier to use (Apple iWorks and MS Office). Some are cloud-based; others can be downloaded. Try out Visual.ly, Google Public Data Explorer, StatSilk, Many Eyes, Hohli, or Creately.

- **Popular Uses.** A few innovative companies have turned some reports and executive summaries into infographics. Résumés, advocacy documents such as white papers, decision trees, maps, flowcharts, instructions, rankings, brand messages, and more have been presented as infographics. Although infographics can tell a story with images and entertain while doing so, they can take up a lot of space and, therefore, are most appropriate online. There, viewers and readers can scroll unconstrained by the printed page. Not all businesses have embraced the sometimes whimsical infographics. Apple Inc. sticks with a plain-vanilla Form 10-K and does not produce a glossy annual report, but many corporations do. Smartphone apps allow users to track and share the numbers in their lives by creating personal infographics.

Courtesy of Michael Anderson

The key to infographics is to present a concise and compelling story through images and graphical elements that encourages the reader or viewer to actively participate in the interpretation. One newly popular application of infographics is visual résumés.

Creating Effective Graphics

After collecting and interpreting information, you need to consider how best to present it. If your report contains complex data and numbers, you may want to consider graphics such as tables and charts. These graphics clarify data, create visual interest, and make numerical data meaningful. By simplifying complex ideas and emphasizing key data, well-constructed graphics make key information easier to remember. However, the same data can be shown in many forms; for example, in a chart, table, or graph. That's why you need to know how to match the appropriate graphic with your objective and how to incorporate it into your report.

Matching Graphics and Objectives

In developing the best graphics, you must decide what data you want to highlight and which graphics are most appropriate for use with your objectives. Tables? Bar charts? Pie charts? Line charts? Surface charts? Flowcharts? Organization charts? Pictures? Figure 11.12 summarizes appropriate uses for each type of graphic. The following sections discuss each type in more detail.

Tables.   Probably the most frequently used graphic in reports is the table. Because a table presents quantitative or verbal information in systematic columns and rows, it can clarify large quantities of data in small spaces. The disadvantage is that tables do not readily display trends. You may have made rough tables to help you organize the raw data collected from questionnaires or interviews. In preparing tables for your readers or listeners, however, you need to pay more attention to clarity and emphasis. Here are tips for making good tables, one of which is provided in Figure 11.13:

- Place titles and labels at the top of the table.
- Arrange items in a logical order (alphabetical, chronological, geographical, highest to lowest), depending on what you need to emphasize.

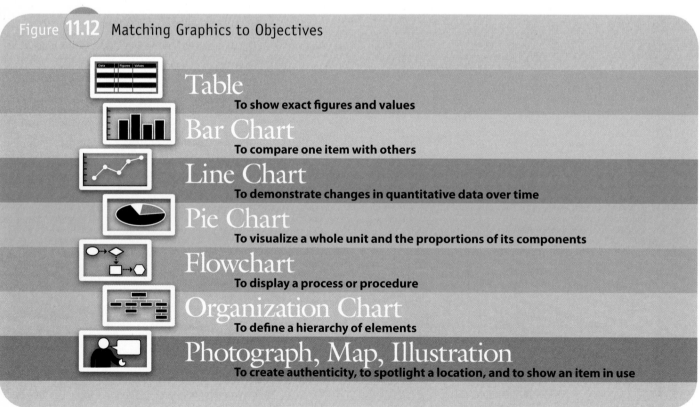

Figure **11.12** Matching Graphics to Objectives

Table
To show exact figures and values

Bar Chart
To compare one item with others

Line Chart
To demonstrate changes in quantitative data over time

Pie Chart
To visualize a whole unit and the proportions of its components

Flowchart
To display a process or procedure

Organization Chart
To define a hierarchy of elements

Photograph, Map, Illustration
To create authenticity, to spotlight a location, and to show an item in use

Figure 11.13 Table Summarizing Precise Data

Figure 1 MPM ENTERTAINMENT COMPANY Income by Division (in millions of dollars)				
	Theme Parks	Motion Pictures	DVDs & Blu-ray Discs	Total
2011	$15.8	$39.3	$11.2	$66.3
2012	18.1	17.5	15.3	50.9
2013	23.8	21.1	22.7	67.6
2014	32.2	22.0	24.3	78.5
2015 (projected)	35.1	21.0	26.1	82.2

Source: *Industry Profiles* (New York: DataPro, 2014) 225.

- Provide clear headings for the rows and columns.
- Identify the units in which figures are given (percentages, dollars, units per worker hour) in the table title, in the column or row heading, with the first item in a column, or in a note at the bottom.
- Use *N/A* (*not available*) for missing data.
- Make long tables easier to read by shading alternate lines or by leaving a blank line after groups of five.
- Place tables as close as possible to the place where they are mentioned in the text.

Figure 11.12 shows the purposes of various graphics. Tables, as illustrated in Figure 11.13, are especially suitable for illustrating exact figures in systematic rows and columns. The table in our figure is particularly useful because it presents data about the MPM Entertainment Company over several years, making it easy to compare several divisions. Figures 11.14 through 11.17 highlight some of the data shown in the MPM Entertainment Company table, illustrating vertical, horizontal, grouped, and segmented 100 percent bar charts, each of which creates a unique effect.

Bar Charts.   Although they lack the precision of tables, bar charts enable you to make emphatic visual comparisons by using horizontal or vertical bars of varying lengths. Bar charts are useful for comparing related items, illustrating changes in data over time, and showing segments as a part of the whole. Note how the varied bar charts present information in differing ways.

Many techniques for constructing tables also hold true for bar charts. Here are a few additional tips:

- Keep the length and width of each bar and segment proportional.
- Include a total figure in the middle of the bar or at its end if the figure helps the reader and does not clutter the chart.
- Start dollar or percentage amounts at zero.
- Place the first bar at some distance (usually half the amount of space between bars) from the *y* axis.
- Avoid showing too much information, thus avoiding clutter and confusion.
- Place each bar chart as close as possible to the place where it is mentioned in the text.

Line Charts.   The major advantage of line charts is that they show changes over time, thus indicating trends. The vertical axis is typically the dependent variable; and the horizontal axis, the independent one. Simple line charts (Figure 11.18) show just one variable. Multiple line charts compare items, such as two or more data sets, using the same variable (Figure 11.19). Segmented line charts (Figure 11.20), also called surface

Figure 11.14 Vertical Bar Chart

Figure 1
2014 MPM INCOME BY DIVISION

Source: *Industry Profiles* (New York: DataPro, 2014), 225.

© Cengage Learning 2015

Figure 11.15 Horizontal Bar Chart

Figure 2
TOTAL MPM INCOME, 2011 TO 2015

*Projected
Source: *Industry Profiles* (New York: DataPro, 2014), 225.

© Cengage Learning 2015

Figure 11.16 Grouped Bar Chart

Figure 3
MPM INCOME BY DIVISION 2011, 2013, AND 2015

*Projected
Source: *Industry Profiles*

© Cengage Learning 2015

Figure 11.17 Segmented 100 Percent Bar Chart

Figure 4
PERCENTAGE OF TOTAL INCOME BY DIVISION
2011, 2013, 2015

*Projected
Source: *Industry Profiles*

© Cengage Learning 2015

charts, illustrate how the components of a whole change over time. To prepare a line chart, remember these tips:

- Begin with a grid divided into squares.
- Arrange the time component (usually years) horizontally across the bottom; arrange values for the other variable vertically.
- Draw small dots at the intersections to indicate each value at a given year.
- Connect the dots and add color if desired.
- To prepare a segmented (surface) chart, plot the first value (say, DVD and Blu-ray disc income) across the bottom; add the next item (say, motion picture income) to

the first figures for every increment; for the third item (say, theme park income), add its value to the total for the first two items. The top line indicates the total of the three values.

Pie Charts.   Pie charts, or circle graphs, enable readers to see a whole and the proportion of its components, or wedges. Although less flexible than bar or line charts, pie charts are useful for showing percentages, as Figure 11.21 illustrates. They are very effective for lay, or nonexpert, audiences. Notice that a wedge can be "exploded," or popped out, for special emphasis, as seen in Figure 11.21. MS Excel and other spreadsheet programs

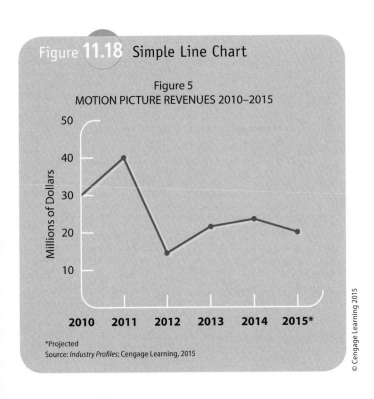

Figure **11.18** Simple Line Chart

Figure 5
MOTION PICTURE REVENUES 2010–2015

*Projected
Source: *Industry Profiles*; Cengage Learning, 2015

© Cengage Learning 2015

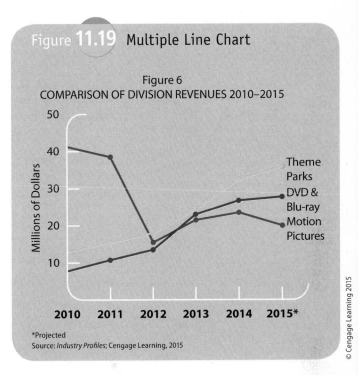

Figure **11.19** Multiple Line Chart

Figure 6
COMPARISON OF DIVISION REVENUES 2010–2015

*Projected
Source: *Industry Profiles*; Cengage Learning, 2015

© Cengage Learning 2015

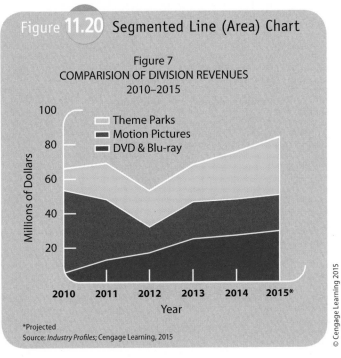

Figure **11.20** Segmented Line (Area) Chart

Figure 7
COMPARISION OF DIVISION REVENUES
2010–2015

*Projected
Source: *Industry Profiles*; Cengage Learning, 2015

© Cengage Learning 2015

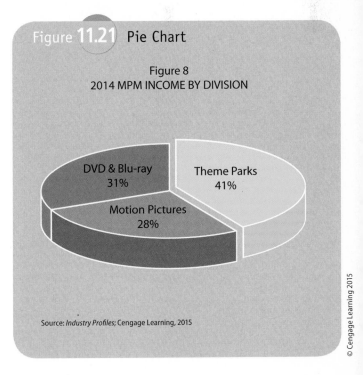

Figure **11.21** Pie Chart

Figure 8
2014 MPM INCOME BY DIVISION

DVD & Blu-ray
31%

Theme Parks
41%

Motion Pictures
28%

Source: *Industry Profiles*; Cengage Learning, 2015

© Cengage Learning 2015

provide a selection of three-dimensional pie charts. For the most effective pie charts, follow these suggestions:

- Make the biggest wedge appear first. Computer spreadsheet programs correctly assign the biggest wedge first (beginning at the 12 o'clock position) and arrange the others in order of decreasing size as long as you list the data representing each wedge on the spreadsheet in descending order.
- Include, if possible, the actual percentage or absolute value for each wedge.
- Use four to six segments for best results; if necessary, group small portions into a wedge called *Other*.
- Draw radii from the center.
- Distinguish wedges with color, shading, or cross-hatching.
- Keep all the labels horizontal.

Flowcharts. Procedures are simplified and clarified by diagramming them in a flowchart, as shown in Figure 11.22. Whether you need to describe the procedure for handling a customer's purchase, highlight steps in solving a problem, or display a problem with a process, flowcharts help the reader visualize the process. Traditional flowcharts use the following symbols:

- Ovals to designate the beginning and end of a process
- Diamonds to designate decision points
- Rectangles to represent major activities or steps

Organization Charts. Many large organizations are so complex that they need charts to show the chain of command, from the boss down to the line managers and employees.

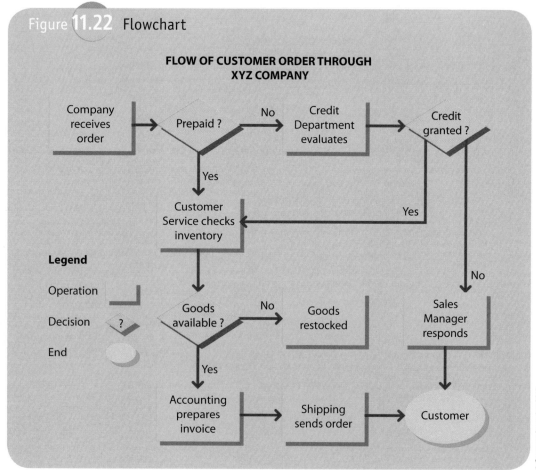

Figure 11.22 Flowchart

© Cengage Learning 2015

Organization charts provide such information as who reports to whom, how many subordinates work for each manager (the span of control), and what channels of official communication exist. These charts may illustrate a company's structure—for example, by function, customer, or product. They may also be organized by the work being performed in each job or by the hierarchy of decision making.

Photographs, Maps, and Illustrations.   Some business reports include photographs, maps, and illustrations to serve specific purposes. Photos, for example, add authenticity and provide a visual record. An environmental engineer may use photos to document hazardous waste sites. Maps enable report writers to depict activities or concentrations geographically, such as dots indicating sales reps in states across the country. Illustrations and diagrams are useful in indicating how an object looks or operates. A drawing showing the parts of a printer with labels describing their functions, for example, is more instructive than a photograph or verbal description.

With today's smart visualization tools as described in the Plugged In box on page 401, high-resolution photographs, maps, and illustrations can be inserted into business reports, or accessed through hyperlinks within electronically delivered documents. Online they can be animated or appear in clusters as they do in infographics.

Incorporating Graphics in Reports

Used appropriately, graphics make reports more interesting and easier to understand. In putting graphics into your reports, follow these suggestions for best effects:

- **Evaluate the audience.** Consider the reader, the content, your schedule, and your budget. Graphics take time and can be costly to print in color, so think carefully before deciding how many graphics to use. Six charts in an internal report to an executive may seem like overkill; however, in a long technical report to outsiders, six may be too few.

- **Use restraint.** Don't overuse color or decorations. Although color can effectively distinguish bars or segments in charts, too much color can be distracting and confusing. Remember, too, that colors themselves sometimes convey meaning: reds suggest deficits or negative values; blues suggest calmness and authority; and yellow may suggest warning.

- **Be accurate and ethical.** Double-check all graphics for accuracy of figures and calculations. Be certain that your visuals aren't misleading—either accidentally or intentionally. Manipulation of a chart scale can make trends look steeper and more dramatic than they really are. Moreover, be sure to cite sources when you use someone else's facts. The accompanying Ethical Insights box discusses in more detail how to make ethical charts and graphs.

- **Introduce a graph meaningfully.** Refer to every graphic in the text, and place the graphic close to the point where it is mentioned. Most important, though, help the reader understand the significance of the graphic. You can do this by telling your audience what to look for or by summarizing the main point of the graphic. Don't assume the reader will automatically draw the same conclusions you reached from a set of data. Instead of saying, *The findings are shown in Figure 3,* tell the reader what to look for: *Two thirds of the responding employees, as shown in Figure 3, favor a flextime schedule.* The best introductions for graphics interpret them for readers.

- **Choose an appropriate caption or title style.** Like reports, graphics may use "talking" titles or generic, descriptive titles. Talking titles are more persuasive; they tell the reader what to think. Descriptive titles describe the facts more objectively.

Talking Title	Descriptive Title
Rising Workplace Drug Testing Unfair and Inaccurate	Workplace Drug Testing Up 277 Percent
College Students' Diets Clogged With Fat	College Students and Nutrition

Making Ethical Charts and Graphics

ETHICAL insights

Business communicators must present graphical data in the same ethical, honest manner required for all other messages. Remember that the information shown in your charts and graphics will be used to inform others or help them make decisions. If this information is not represented accurately, the reader will be incorrectly informed; any decisions based on the data are likely to be faulty. In addition, mistakes in interpreting such information may have serious and long-lasting consequences.

Chart data can be distorted in many ways. Figure 1 shows advertising expenses displayed on an appropriate scale. Figure 2 shows the same information, but the horizontal scale, from 2010 to 2015, has been lengthened. Notice that the data have not changed, but the increases and decreases are smoothed out, so changes in expenses appear to be slight. In Figure 3 the vertical scale is taller and the horizontal scale is shortened, resulting in what appear to be sharp increases and decreases in expenses.

To avoid misrepresenting data, keep the following pointers in mind when designing your graphics:

- Use an appropriate type of chart or graphic for the message you wish to convey.

- Design the chart so that it focuses on the appropriate information.

- Include all relevant or important data; don't arbitrarily leave out necessary information.

- Don't hide critical information by including too much data in one graphic.

- Use appropriate scales with equal intervals for the data you present.

CAREER APPLICATION

Locate one or two graphics in a newspaper, magazine article, or annual report. Analyze the strengths and weaknesses of each graphic. Is the information presented accurately? Select a bar or line chart. Sketch the same chart but change the vertical or horizontal scales on the graphic. How does the message of the chart change?

Figure 1
ADVERTISING EXPENSES

Figure 2
ADVERTISING EXPENSES

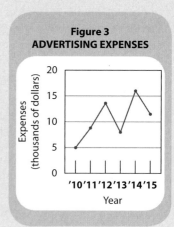

Figure 3
ADVERTISING EXPENSES

© Cengage Learning 2015

Your Turn: Applying Your Skills at Pew Research Center

Zooming in

You are excited about the possibility of becoming an intern for the Pew Economic Mobility Project, the division of the Pew Research Center that published *How Much Protection Does a College Degree Afford?* Although you cannot find evidence that Pew is looking for interns, you decide to send a letter to show your interest in obtaining an internship. You know that successful persuasive writing is genuine and sincere and uses the AIDA organizational strategy discussed in Chapter 10. You also think your letter should illustrate your knowledge of report writing as well as your skill as a writer.

© AP Images/Lauren Victoria Burke

YOUR TASK. Visit the Pew Research Center's website (**http://www.pewresearch.org**) to learn more about the organization and read *How Much Protection Does a College Degree Afford?* Write an unsolicited job request letter that uses the AIDA persuasive organizational strategy and ask to be considered for an internship. Address the letter to Ms. Erin Currier, Director, Economic Mobility Project, 901 E Street NW, Washington, DC 20004.

Summary of Learning Objectives

1 Explain report functions and types used in the digital-age workplace, understand direct and indirect organizational strategies, and describe report-writing style as well as typical report formats. The smooth flow and exchange of information are the lifeblood of digital-age business. The ever-greater complexity of data amassed by large organizations requires so-called business intelligence tools to display and analyze key performance indicators. Business reports generally function either as informational reports (without analysis or recommendations) or as analytical reports (with analysis, conclusions, and possibly recommendations). Reports organized directly present the purpose and conclusions immediately. This strategy is appropriate when the audience is supportive and familiar with the topic. Reports organized indirectly provide the conclusions and recommendations last. This strategy is helpful when the audience is unfamiliar with the problem or may be disappointed or hostile. Reports written in a formal style use third-person constructions (*the researcher* instead of *I*), avoid contractions (*do not* instead of *don't*), and may include passive-voice verbs (*the findings were analyzed*). Reports written informally use first-person constructions, contractions, shorter sentences, familiar words, and active-voice verbs. Reports may be formatted as letters, memos, e-mails, manuscripts, hard-copy or digital forms, or electronic slide decks.

2 Apply the 3-x-3 writing process to contemporary business reports to create well-organized documents that show a firm grasp of audience and purpose. Report writers begin by analyzing a problem and writing a problem statement, which may include the scope, significance, and limitations of the project. Writers then analyze the audience and define major issues. They prepare a work plan, including a tentative outline and work schedule. They collect, organize, interpret, and illustrate their data. Then they compose the first draft. Finally, they edit (often many times), proofread, and evaluate.

Go to
www.cengagebrain.com
and use your access code to unlock valuable student resources.

3 Locate and evaluate secondary sources such as databases and Web resources, and understand how to conduct credible primary research. Secondary data may be located by searching for books, periodicals, and newspapers, mostly through electronic indexes. Writers can look for information using research databases such as ABI/INFORM and EBSCO. They may also find information on the Internet, but searching for it requires a knowledge of search tools and techniques. Popular search tools include Google, Yahoo, and Bing. Once found, however, information obtained on the Internet should be scrutinized for currency, authority, content, and accuracy. Researchers generate firsthand, primary data through surveys (in-person, print, and online), interviews, observation, and experimentation. Surveys are most economical and efficient for gathering information from large groups of people. Interviews are useful when working with experts in a field. Firsthand observation can produce rich data, but they must be objective. Experimentation produces data suggesting causes and effects. Valid experiments require sophisticated research designs and careful attention to matching the experimental and control groups.

4 Identify the purposes and techniques of citation and documentation in business reports, and avoid plagiarism. Documentation means giving credit to information sources. Careful writers document data to strengthen an argument, protect against charges of plagiarism, instruct readers, and save time. Although documentation is less strict in business reports than in academic reports, business writers should learn proper techniques to verify their sources and avoid charges of plagiarism. Report writers should document others' ideas, facts that are not common knowledge, quotations, and paraphrases. Good notetaking, either manual or electronic, enables writers to give accurate credit to sources. Paraphrasing involves putting another's ideas into one's own words. Quotations may be used to provide objective background data, to repeat memorable phrasing, and to duplicate exact wording before criticizing.

5 Generate, use, and convert numerical data to visual aids, and create meaningful and attractive graphics. Good graphics improve reports by clarifying, simplifying, and emphasizing data. Tables organize precise data into rows and columns. Bar and line charts enable data to be compared visually. Line charts are especially helpful in showing changes over time. Pie charts show a whole and the proportion of its components. Organization charts, pictures, maps, and illustrations serve specific purposes. In choosing or crafting graphics, effective communicators evaluate their audience, purpose, topic, and budget to determine the number and kind of graphics. They write "talking" titles (telling readers what to think about the graphic) or descriptive titles (summarizing the topic objectively). Finally, they work carefully to avoid distorting visual aids.

Chapter Review

1. In terms of analysis, what are the two broad report functions or types? (Obj. 1)

2. Explain the rationale behind the direct and indirect strategies when organizing reports. (Obj.1)

3. Name five common report formats. (Obj. 1)

4. List the seven steps in the report-writing process. (Obj. 2)

5. What is a problem statement, and what function does it serve? (Obj. 2)

6. What is a work plan, and why is it used? (Obj. 2)

7. Compare primary data and secondary data. Give an original example of each. (Obj. 3)

8. Name at least two of the top four business databases and identify their chief strengths. (Obj. 3)

9. List four major sources of primary information. (Obj. 3)

10. How can you ensure that your survey will be effective and appeal to as many respondents as possible? (Obj. 3)

11. Describe what documentation is and why it is necessary in reports. (Obj. 4)

12. In what way is documentation of sources different in colleges and universities than in business? (Obj. 4)

13. How can you ensure that you do a good job of paraphrasing? (Obj. 4)

14. Briefly compare the advantages and disadvantages of illustrating data with charts (bar and line) versus tables. (Obj. 5)

15. Name five techniques you can use to ensure that visual aids do not distort graphic information. (Obj. 5)

Critical Thinking

1. Explain why good research habits are important and how they relate to personal integrity and ethics. (Obj. 4)

2. Howard Schultz, Starbucks president and CEO, has been described as a "classic entrepreneur: optimistic, relentless, mercurial, and eager to prove people wrong."[28] Schultz has followed his gut instinct mostly to success while scoffing at established management practices. Unlike other executives, until the Great Recession hit, he was not interested in cost control, advertising, and customer research. "I despise research," he said. "I think it's a crutch. But people smarter than me pushed me in this direction, and I've gone along."[29] Starbucks continues to be one of the most followed companies on Facebook. For the most recent year on record, Starbucks' net income reached $359 million.[30] What do you think Howard Schultz meant when he called consumer research a "crutch"? Can you explain why the corporate maverick hates it so much? (Obj. 3)

3. Is information obtained on the Web as reliable as information obtained from journals, newspapers, and magazines? How about information derived from Wikipedia and blogs? (Obj. 3)

4. Some people say that business reports never contain footnotes. If you were writing your first report for a business and you did considerable research, what would you do about documenting your sources? (Obj. 4)

5. **Ethical Issue:** Consider this logical appeal under the heading "Reasons Students Hate Writing Essays or Term Papers" and evaluate its validity and ethics:

   > Three term papers due tomorrow with three major tests from three of the classes as well as a long math assignment. What should a student do? This problem while in [sic] exaggeration often happens to students. It is like all the teachers decide to overwhelm the students in their classes with not only tests on the same day but also term papers, essays, or other writing assignments. This is the reason most students hate writing term papers or other types of writing. Other reasons for disliking writing assignments are poor English classes in high school, often instructors fail to explain different writing styles, unsure of topics to write, and instructors fail to read the writing assignments.[...] Don't be afraid to reach out and get help if it's needed! CustomPapers.com can assist you.[31]

Activities

11.1 Report Functions, Strategies, and Formats (Obj. 1)

YOUR TASK. For the following reports, (a) name the report's primary function (informational or analytical), (b) recommend the direct or indirect strategy of development, and (c) select a report format (memo or e-mail, letter, or manuscript).

a. A proposal from a group of citizens to the federal government asking to designate several tracts of public lands as wilderness under the 1964 Wilderness Act.

b. A report submitted by a sales rep to her manager describing her attendance at a consumer electronics trade show, including interviews with industry insiders and attendees.

c. A yardstick report in the leisure industry put together by consultants who compare the potential of a future theme park at three different sites.

d. A report prepared by an outside consultant reviewing proposed components of a virtual state library and recommending the launch of its initial components.

e. A progress report from an intern at NASA's Employee and Organizational Excellence Branch to her mentor and the management.

f. A report from a national shipping company telling state authorities how it has improved its safety program so that its trucks now comply with state regulations. The report describes but doesn't interpret the program.

g. A feasibility report from an administrative assistant to his boss exploring the savings from buying aftermarket ink-jet cartridges as opposed to the original refills recommended by the manufacturer.

11.2 Collaborative Project: Looking Closely at Annual Reports (Obj. 1)

Team

YOUR TASK. In teams of three or four, collect several corporate annual reports. For each report identify and discuss the following characteristics:

a. Function (informational or analytical)

b. Strategy (primarily direct or indirect)

c. Writing style (formal or informal)

d. Format (memo or e-mail, letter, manuscript, preprinted form, digital form)

e. Effectiveness (clarity, accuracy, expression)

In an informational memo report to your instructor, describe your findings.

11.3 Types of Data and Research Questions (Obj. 3)

Researchers must identify or generate credible but also relevant data that will be suitable for their research task.

YOUR TASK. In conducting research for the following reports, name at least one form of data you will need and questions you should ask to determine whether that set of data is appropriate (see Figure 11.7).

a. A report about the feasibility of a student gym and recreation center.

b. A report by a state department of parks and recreation providing information on the state park system as it was operated during the most recent fiscal year.

c. A report on business attire in banking that you must submit to your company's executives, who want to issue a formal professional dress code on the job.

d. A report by the Agricultural Research Service of the U.S. Department of Agriculture on the nutritional value of oats.

e. A report examining the effectiveness of technology use policies in American businesses.

11.4 Problem, Purpose, and Scope Statements (Obj. 2)

YOUR TASK. The following situations require reports. For each situation write (a) a concise problem question, (b) a simple statement of purpose, and (c) a scope statement with limitations if appropriate.

a. AlphaCore Company is a midsized specialized cutting tools manufacturer. The company is growing slowly but steadily, and its current computer network system is inefficient. Worse yet, it cannot be upgraded. Quick fixes and temporary patches are increasingly getting costly and frustrate the users, who suffer frequent down times. The company does not have a highly qualified in-house IT staff.

b. Car buyers regularly complain in postpurchase surveys about the persuasive tactics of the so-called closers (salespeople trained to finalize the deal). Your car dealership wishes to improve customer satisfaction in the stressful price negotiation process.

c. An AAA survey found that 35 percent of drivers felt less safe on the road than they did five years ago. A third of those respondents blamed distracted driving. State legislators and national safety organizations have taken notice and focused on cell phone use in general and texting in particular as major causes of distracted driving. Several states have issued hand-held cell phone bans.

d. Cities around the country enacted strict regulations banning trans fats in restaurant fare. Food processors nationwide are wondering whether they need to make changes before being forced to switch to nonhydrogenated fats by law. Food and Drug Administration regulations have already changed the definitions of common terms such as *fresh, fat free, low in cholesterol,* and *light.* The Old World Bakery worries that it may have to change its production process and rewrite all its package labels. Old World doesn't know whether to hire a laboratory or a consultant for this project.

e. Customers placing telephone orders for outdoor clothing and leisure wear with Eddie Bauer typically order only one or two items. The company wonders whether it can train telephone service reps to motivate customers to increase the number of items ordered per call.

11.5 Problem and Purpose Statements (Obj. 2)

YOUR TASK. Identify a problem in your current job or a previous job, such as inadequate use of technology, inefficient procedures, spotty customer service, poor product quality, low morale, or a personnel problem. Assume your boss agrees with your criticism and asks you to prepare a report. Write (a) a two- or three-sentence statement describing the problem, (b) a problem question, and (c) a simple statement of purpose for your report.

11.6 Plagiarism, Paraphrasing, and Citing Sources (Obj. 4)

One of the biggest challenges for student writers is paraphrasing secondary sources correctly to avoid plagiarism.

YOUR TASK. For each of the following, read the original passage. Analyze the paraphrased version. List the weaknesses in relation to what you have learned about plagiarism and the use of references. Then write an improved version.

a. **Original Passage**

Lurking behind chartjunk is contempt both for the information and for the audience. Chartjunk promoters imagine that numbers and details are boring, dull, and tedious, requiring ornament to enliven. Cosmetic decoration, which frequently distorts the data, will never salvage an underlying lack of content. If the numbers are boring, then you've got the wrong numbers. Credibility vanishes in clouds of chartjunk; who would trust a chart that looks like a video game?[32]

Paraphrased Passage

Chartjunk creators hold the information they are conveying and their audience in contempt because they believe that statistical details are dull, unimaginative, and tedious and need to be spruced up with decorations. Purely ornamental design elements distort the data and cannot cover up a lack of content. If the statistics are boring, then they are the wrong statistics. Chartjunk kills credibility. Readers cannot trust a chart that looks like a video game.

b. **Original Passage**

Developing casual online game titles can be much less risky than trying to create a game that runs on a console such as an Xbox. Casual games typically cost less than $200,000 to produce, and production cycles are only six months to a year. There's no shelf space, packaging, or CD production to pay for. Best of all, there's more room for innovation.[33]

Paraphrased Passage

The development of casual online games offers less risk than creating games running on Xbox and other consoles. Usually, casual games are cheaper, costing under $200,000 to create and 6 to 12 months to produce. Developers save on shelf space, packaging, and CD production too. Moreover, they have more freedom to innovate.

c. **Original Passage**

The collapse in the cost of computing has made cellular communication economically viable. Worldwide, one in two new phone subscriptions is cellular. The digital revolution in telephony is most advanced in poorer countries because they have been able to skip the outdated technological step of relying on landlines.

Paraphrased Passage

The drop in computing costs now makes cellular communication affordable around the world. In fact, one out of every two new phones is cellular. The digital revolution in cellular telephones is developing faster in poorer countries because they can skip the outdated technological process of using landlines (Henderson 44).

11.7 Factoring and Outlining a Problem (Obj. 2)

Virgin America has asked your company, Connections International, to prepare a proposal for a training school for tour operators. Virgin America wants to know whether Burbank would be a good spot for its school. Burbank interests Virgin America, but only if nearby entertainment facilities can be used for tour training. The airline also needs an advisory committee consisting, if possible, of representatives of the travel community and perhaps executives of other major airlines. The real problem is how to motivate these people to cooperate with Virgin America.

You have heard that NBC Studios in Burbank offers training seminars, guest speakers, and other resources for tour operators. You wonder whether Magic Mountain in Valencia would also be willing to cooperate with the proposed school. Moreover, you remember that Griffith Park is nearby and might make a good tour training spot. Before Virgin America will settle on Burbank as its choice, it wants to know whether access to air travel is adequate. Virgin America's management team is also concerned about available school building space. Moreover, the carrier wants to know whether city officials in Burbank would be receptive to this tour training school proposal.

YOUR TASK. To guide your thinking and research, factor this problem into an outline with several areas to investigate. Further divide the problem into subproblems, phrasing each entry as a question. For example, *Should the Virgin America tour training program be located in Burbank?* (See the work plan model in Figure 11.6.)

11.8 Preparing a Work Plan (Obj. 2)

Any long report project requires a structured work plan.

YOUR TASK. Select a report topic from activities presented at the end of Chapters 12 and 13 or from a comprehensive list of report topics at **www.cengagebrain.com**. For that report prepare a work plan that includes the following:

a. Statement of the problem

b. Expanded statement of purpose (including scope, limitations, and significance)

c. Research strategy to answer the questions

d. Tentative outline of key questions to answer

e. Work schedule (with projected completion dates)

11.9 Experimenting With Secondary Sources (Obj. 3)

Web

Secondary sources can provide quite different information depending on your mode of inquiry.

YOUR TASK. Use Google or another search engine that supports Boolean searches to investigate a topic such as carbon footprint or sustainability or any other business topic of interest to you. Explore the same topic using (a) keywords and (b) Boolean operators. Which method produces more relevant hits? Save two relevant sources from each search using two or more of the strategies presented in this chapter. Remember to include the URL for each article. Alternatively, compare your Google search results with those from a metasearch site such as Dogpile, Search.com, or InfoSpace.

In a memo to your instructor, list the bibliographical information from all sources and explain briefly which method was most productive.

11.10 Exploring Culinary Trends With SurveyMonkey or Zoomerang (Obj. 3)

E-mail   Team   Web

Your University Business Club (UBC) is abuzz about a Sodexo study that surveyed American college students regarding their favorite comfort foods. Food service provider Sodexo tracks flavor trends, holds taste test focus groups with students, and consults with top-notch chefs to identify students' favorite college foods. The current top three items are grilled chicken souvlaki kabob, paella, and spanakopita. Overwhelmingly, current students crave Mediterranean fare, whether Greek, Spanish, Italian, North African, or Middle Eastern. You read the Sodexo press release and decide to use this quotation in your report:

Mediterranean fare is heart-healthy, exotic, and appeals to vegetarians and omnivores alike. Sodexo's main resident dining menu offering will highlight Mediterranean cuisine. Other trends include stealth health—maintaining traditional flavors while substituting healthier ingredients. That trend is making popular gluten-free pasta and whole wheat and brown rice offerings. Students continue to insist on locally-sourced ingredients.[34]

UBC wants to advocate for a new, small student-run restaurant in the campus food court. Your club colleagues have chosen you to create an online survey to poll fellow students, staff, and faculty about their preferences. You hope to generate data that will support the feasibility of the eatery.

The two main providers of online survey software, SurveyMonkey and Zoomerang, make creating questionnaires fast, fun, and easy. After signing up for the free no-frills basic plans, you can create brief online questionnaires and e-mail the links to your targeted respondents. The programs analyze and display the results for you—at no charge.

YOUR TASK. In pairs or teams of three, design a questionnaire to survey students on your campus about comfort food options in the campus cafeteria. Visit SurveyMonkey or Zoomerang, and sign up for the basic plan. You may also want to view the Sodexo website. After creating the online survey, e-mail the survey link to as many members of the campus community as possible. Interpret the results. As a team, write a memo to the campus food services administrator advocating for a student-run eatery featuring the top-scoring national or regional comfort food.

Your instructor may ask you to complete this activity as a report or proposal assignment after you study Chapter 12. If so, write a feasibility report or proposal for the campus food services and support your advocacy with the survey results.

11.11 Time for Research! Studying Teen and Young Adult Media Use (Obj. 3)

E-mail   Web

You know what you do online or how much TV you watch, but what does everybody else do? We tend to judge others by our own preferences and by behaviors we observe among our family, friends, and acquaintances. In marketing, however, hunches are not enough.

Your boss, Alice Takagi, doesn't believe in stereotyping. She encourages her market researchers to be wary of all data. She asked you to explore so-called niche marketing opportunities in targeting teens, a notoriously fickle consumer group. Primarily, Ms. Takagi wants to know how teenagers communicate and, more specifically, how they use social media and e-mail. Understanding teen behavior is invaluable for the success of any promotional or ad campaign.

For a full picture to emerge, you will need to consult several recent studies. The best candidates for your research are surveys by the Nielsen Company, Pew Research Center's Internet & American Life Project, Common Sense Media, and similar reputable sources of data. While Nielsen is a for-profit global market research company, Pew Internet and Common Sense Media are nonprofit organizations.

YOUR TASK. Ms. Takagi requested a brief informational e-mail report summarizing the main findings. Paraphrase correctly and don't just copy from the online source. Ms. Takagi may ask you later to analyze more comprehensive data in an analytical report and create a media use profile of U.S. teens and young adults. You may be called on to create various graphs to illustrate your findings.

11.12 Researching Data: Target Aims at Charitable Giving (Objs. 3–5)

E-mail　Team　Web

Lauren Bacall and Robert Redford have both promoted it. And Oprah Winfrey thinks it is so chic that she pronounces its name in mock French (*Tar-jay*). Unlike its big-box competitors, Target is an American discount retailer that appeals to many female shoppers with trendy and edgy but affordable fashions. However, Target is also proud of its positive corporate image. The company has been praised for giving back to the community with higher-than-usual charitable contributions. At 5 percent of pretax earnings, Target's annual donations are more than double the national average among big corporations (in absolute dollars recently as high as $157 million a year).[35]

Such civic and social advocacy is not without its controversies. Target was criticized for a $150,000 donation to a Minnesota gubernatorial candidate opposing gay marriage. Subsequently, the company took heat over selling T-shirts benefiting a gay-rights group. In a less divisive move, Target has pledged to give $1 billion to education causes by 2015.

YOUR TASK. Select one of the following tasks.

a. As a summer intern at Walmart, you are asked to prepare an informational memo to your boss, Martin Chavez, about Target's charitable practices. Walmart is seeking greater community involvement to boost its public image. What types of projects does the Target Corporation fund? What other policies set this company apart from its competitors when it comes to giving back to the community? Write an individual informational e-mail or memo or one collaborative e-mail or memo as a team of summer interns. Alternatively, Martin Chavez could ask you to write an e-mail or memo describing how Target handled controversies in its past and what its actions say about the company's management and its philosophy.

b. As a team of summer interns for Walmart, research charitable giving of Target and other major corporations. Prepare an informational memo comparing and contrasting corporate practices. Target ranks fourth behind Walmart, Home Depot, and Lowe's in size. How much of their pretax earnings are these and other big chain stores spending on philanthropy? What types of causes do they embrace, and why? Do their policies seem consistent and purposeful over the long term? How do they justify charitable giving to their shareholders?

In each case, compile a bibliography of sources you used. Whenever appropriate, display numbers visually by creating charts, graphs, and tables.

You may want to start by viewing company mission statements and annual reports for discussions of corporate social responsibility, charitable giving, and worthy causes companies support. Then, go to independent sources for a more detached, objective perspective.

11.13 Gathering Data: Fortune 100 Best Companies to Work For (Objs. 3, 4)

Web

Even in tough economic times, some companies continue to spend lavishly on unusual employee perks such as massages and sauna visits, hold on to generous compensation and benefits, and don't lay off workers as a matter of principle. At the same time, they remain profitable. Chances are that you haven't heard of three among the top five of *Fortune*'s 100 Best Companies to Work For—tech giant SAS Institute, New York–based Wegmans Food Market, and investment advisor Edward Jones. The perennial favorite, Google, has again clinched the top spot. Eighth-ranked outdoor powerhouse REI attracts active types who may bring their dogs to work, go on a midday bike ride, and test the products they sell. Sound nice? Just as companies have their distinctive corporate cultures, they also differ in why they are perceived as ideal employers.

YOUR TASK. Visit the *Fortune* magazine website for the most current 100 Best Companies to Work For. Examine the information about the top 20 or 25 highest-ranked companies. Watch the short video clips profiling each business. After studying the information, identify factors that attract and please workers. Take note of features shared across the board, but don't overlook quirky, unusual benefits. Summarize these trends in an informational memo report. Alternatively, prepare an analytical report investigating employee satisfaction gleaned from the secondary data obtained on the *Fortune* site.

11.14 Who Gets Hurt? Examining Infamous Plagiarism Scandals (Obj. 4)

Team　Web

Have you ever wondered who gets hurt when students, teachers, journalists, scientists, and other authors are dishonest researchers and writers? Occasionally we read about people who plagiarize their work, try to cheat their way through college, invent news features, copy from others, or fabricate research results. Earlier in the chapter you learned about anesthesiologist Yoshitaka Fujii, who wrote 172 bogus scientific papers, 126 of which were based on imaginary research studies. Two shocking cases in medical research rival Fujii's fabrications in gravity and scope.

Former British surgeon Andrew Wakefield published an article in the reputable medical journal *The Lancet* that seemed to provide evidence that a common immunization against measles, mumps, and rubella (MMR) could cause autism. Wakefield had fabricated evidence and was found guilty of professional misconduct. He lost his license to practice as a medical doctor. His fraudulent research, however, caused a precipitous drop in vaccinations in the United Kingdom and Ireland. In the words of one pediatrician, "That paper killed children."[36]

German anesthesiologist Joachim Boldt was fired from his professorship and is being investigated for allegedly manipulating data in his drug trials that led to more than 90 now suspect papers. Although no research subjects were directly harmed, Boldt's fraudulent drug research could have put millions of patients at risk.[37]

YOUR TASK. If your instructor directs, individually or as a team, investigate the cases of Andrew Wakefield, Joachim Boldt, Stephen Ambrose, Jayson Blair, Doris Kearns Goodwin, Jonah Lehrer, Kaavya Viswanathan, or other infamous plagiarists. Consider these authors' transgressions, their excuses, and the consequences of their actions. As a team, gather your individual research results, compare notes, and summarize your insights in a memo report to your instructor. This assignment could also be turned into a long report as presented in Chapter 12 if the investigation is expanded to include more detailed discussions and more cases.

11.15 Selecting Graphics (Obj. 5)

YOUR TASK. Identify the best graphics forms to illustrate the following data.

a. Commercial real estate in an industrial park

b. Month-to-month retail store sales figures

c. Government unemployment data by industry and sector, in percentages

d. Figures showing the distribution of the H3N2 strain of type A flu virus in humans by state

e. Figures showing the process of delivering water to a metropolitan area

f. Areas in the United States most likely to have earthquakes

g. Figures showing what proportion of every state tax dollar is spent on education, social services, transportation, debt, and other expenses

h. Academic, administrative, and operation divisions of a college, from the president to department chairs and division managers

i. Figures comparing the sales of smartphones, tablets, and laptops over the past five years

11.16 Evaluating Graphics (Obj. 5)

E-mail

YOUR TASK. Select four graphics from newspapers or magazines, in hard copy or online. Look in *The Wall Street Journal, USA Today, Bloomberg Businessweek, U.S. News & World Report, Fortune,* or other business news publications. In an e-mail or memo to your instructor, critique each graphic based on what you have learned in this chapter. What is correctly shown? What is incorrectly shown? How could the graphics be improved?

11.17 Creating a Bar Chart (Obj. 5)

The ability to create appropriate and relevant graphics is a sought-after skill in today's information-age workplace. Spreadsheet programs such as Excel make it easy to generate appealing visuals.

YOUR TASK. Based on the statistics that follow, prepare (a) a bar chart comparing the latest tax rates in eight industrial countries and (b) a bar chart that shows the change from the previous year to the current year. The past-year data follow the current statistics in parentheses: Canada, 39 (33) percent; France, 52 (45) percent; Germany, 45 (41) percent; Japan, 34 (28) percent; Netherlands, 46 (38) percent; Sweden, 52 (49) percent; United Kingdom, 41 (38) percent; United States, 22 (28) percent. These figures represent a percentage of the gross domestic product for each country. The current figures are largely estimates by the Central Intelligence Agency. The previous-year statistics were compiled by the Heritage Foundation. What should you emphasize in the chart and title? What trends do you recognize?

11.18 Creating a Line Chart (Obj. 5)

YOUR TASK. Prepare a line chart showing the sales of Sidekick Athletic Shoes, Inc., for these years: 2014, $6.7 million; 2013, $5.4 million; 2012, $3.2 million; 2011, $2.1 million; 2010, $2.6 million; 2009, $3.6 million. In the chart title, highlight the trend you see in the data.

11.19 Searching for Data Visualization and Infographics in Annual Reports (Obj. 5)

Annual reports are infamous for being anything but fascinating reading even for the most ardent investors.

E-mail   **Web**

YOUR TASK. Search annual reports filed by Fortune 500 companies and examine to what extent they have embraced infographics. Critique their readability, clarity, and effectiveness in visualizing data. How were the visuals introduced in the text? What suggestions would you make to improve them? Can you detect any effort to present financials and other data in visually appealing,

unconventional ways? In an e-mail or memo to your instructor, evaluate the use and effectiveness of graphics in three to five corporate annual reports.

11.20 Seeking Business Infographics (Obj. 5)

Web

YOUR TASK. On the Web or in print, find an infographic that visualizes intriguing business-relevant data. Look for sources within or below the infographic. Are they indicated? If yes, are they credible? How much hard statistical information is provided in relation to the space the infographic occupies? Does the infographic meet its objective: is the information clearly presented, easy to read, and insightful? Report your findings orally or in writing. Be prepared to show your chosen infographic to the class.

11.21 Learning From the Titans of Infographic Design (Obj. 5)

E-mail   **Team**   **Web**

To familiarize yourself with the contemporary trend toward infographics, research the ideas and design work of Edward Tufte, Ryan Case and Nicholas Felton, Ben Fry, or Francesco Franchi.

YOUR TASK. Individually or in teams, share with your class samples of the work created by these influential infographics designers, whether digitally or in hard copy. Explain what makes these designers highly respected practitioners of their art. If your instructor requests, summarize your findings in a concise yet informative short memo report that can be submitted in hard copy or sent by e-mail.

11.22 Creating Meaningful Infographics—Making Statistics Come Alive (Obj. 5)

Web

The process of creating infographics is illustrated by the community platform for data visualization, Visual.ly, as follows:

> **idea → research → data → analysis → story → design → creation**

This means that a writer must (a) find a subject worthy of exploring numerically and visually, (b) conduct research, (c) locate or generate data, (d) analyze the data, (e) create a story to best convey the meaning of the information, (f) plan how to design this story idea, and (g) create the visualization with the appropriate software tools.[38]

YOUR TASK. Using the Visual.ly cloud-based tool or any number of other applications (e.g., Excel, PowerPoint, Adobe Illustrator, Photoshop, Many Eyes, Hohli, and StatSilk), create an informative and visually arresting infographic. The statistics you use should be meaningful, intriguing, and clear. To view examples on the Internet, simply input the search term *infographic* into your favorite browser.

11.23 Avoiding Huge Credit Card Debt for College Students (Objs. 3, 4)

E-mail   **Web**

College students represent a new push for credit card companies. An amazing 84 percent of students carried at least one credit card in the most recent study of undergraduate card use, and half of college students had four or more cards.[39] Credit cards are a factor when students graduate with an average of $27,000 in loan debt. Because they can't buy cars, rent homes, or purchase insurance, graduates with big credit debt see a bleak future for themselves.

A local newspaper plans to run a self-help story about college students and credit cards. The editor asks you, a young part-time reporter, to prepare a memo with information that could be turned into an article. The article would focus on parents of students who are about to leave for college. What can parents do to help students avoid sinking deeply into credit card debt?

YOUR TASK. Using ABI/INFORM Complete, EBSCO, Factiva, or LexisNexis and the Web, locate basic information about student credit card options. In an e-mail or memo, discuss shared credit cards and other options. Your goal is to be informative, not to reach conclusions or make recommendations. Use one or more of the techniques discussed in this chapter to track your sources. Address your memo to Paula Parks, editor.

11.24 Netflix & Co.: After DVD and Blu-ray
(Objs. 3, 4)

E-mail   Team   Web

The competition for DVD home media rental and Internet video streaming dollars is fierce. A 2,350-employee company, Netflix still offers online flat rates for DVD and Blu-ray disc rentals

by mail. Separately, users can also subscribe to stream certain movie titles on the Web and view them on their computers, tablets, and smartphones. Netflix is racing against Apple iTunes, Amazon Instant Video, Hulu, Redbox, and the cable companies—all of which are jostling to become the leading provider of online films.

YOUR TASK. As a team or individually, use ABI/INFORM Complete, EBSCO, Factiva, or LexisNexis and the Web to find information about the movie rental and video-on-demand market today. Research the latest trends in the use of DVD/Blu-ray discs and Web streaming. Focus on Netflix's competitors, new and old. In a memo or e-mail report, discuss the future of this important entertainment sector. Based on your research, expert opinion, and other resources, reach conclusions about the current state and future prospects of the movie rental and streaming business. If possible, make recommendations detailing how the business model could be modified to help Netflix survive the cutthroat competition. Use one or more of the techniques discussed in this chapter to track your sources. Address your memo or e-mail to Netflix CEO Reed Hastings.

Chat About It

In each chapter you will find five discussion questions related to the chapter material. Your instructor may assign these topics for you to discuss in class, in an online chat room, or on an online discussion board. Some of the discussion topics may require outside research. You may also be asked to read and respond to postings made by your classmates.

Topic 1: Writing experts say that good planning at the beginning of your project is an investment that pays off later. If you don't plan, you pay for it in the middle of your project.[40] What is your experience with planning and drafting your individual or team reports?

Topic 2: What are some business topics that you would like to research and perhaps even enjoy writing about? Please explain and compare notes with your peers.

Topic 3: What questions would you ask to factor the problem for a report about improving the course registration process at your college or university?

Topic 4: Why is it important for a nonexpert on a topic to use professional journals as report sources?

Topic 5: Is plagiarism worth the risk of being caught? Why or why not?

C.L.U.E. Grammar & Mechanics | *Review 11*

Total Review

The first ten chapters reviewed specific guides from Appendix A: Grammar and Mechanics Guide. The exercises in this and the remaining chapters are total reviews, covering all of the grammar and mechanics guides plus confusing words and frequently misspelled words.

Each of the following sentences has **three** errors in grammar, punctuation, capitalization, usage, or spelling. On a separate sheet, write a correct version. Avoid adding new phrases, starting new sentences, or rewriting in your own words. When finished, compare your responses with the key beginning on page Key-1.

EXAMPLE: Many jobs in todays digital workplace are never advertised, there part of the hidden job market.

REVISION: Many jobs in **today's** digital workplace are never **advertised; they're** part of the hidden job market.

1. One creditable study revealed that thirty percent of jobs go to companies inside candidates.

2. Networking is said to be the key to finding a job, however, its easier said then done.

3. Some job seekers paid five hundred dollars each to attend twelve sessions that promised expert job-searching advise.

4. To excel at networking an easy to remember e-mail address is a must for a candidate.

5. My friend asked me if I had all ready prepared a thirty second elevator speech?

6. When Rachel and myself were collecting data for the report we realized that twitter and Facebook could be significant.

7. Todays workers must brush up their marketable skills otherwise they may not find another job after being laid off.

8. Being active on LinkedIn and building an impressive internet presence is important, but the looseness of these connections mean you shouldn't expect much from them.

9. Just between you and I, one of the best strategys in networking are distributing business cards with your personal tagline.

10. On February 1st our company President revealed that we would be hiring thirty new employees, which was excellent news for everyone.

Notes

[1] About Pew Research Center. http://www.pewresearch.org/about

[2] Assistant Editor, Pew Research Center's Forum on Religion & Public Life. http://www.pewresearch.org/about/career s/assistant-editor-pew-research-centers-forum-on-religion-public-life

[3] Research Assistant, Pew Research Center's Pew Hispanic Center and Social & Demographic Trends Project. http://www.pewresearch.org/about/careers /research-assistant-pew-research-centers-pew-hispanic-center-and-social-demographic-trends-project

[4] Questions for David McCullough. (2006, July 7). *Workforce Management*, p. 9.

[5] King, R. (2009, March 2). Business intelligence software's time is now. *Bloomberg Businessweek*. Retrieved from http://www.businessweek.com

[6] Wales, J. (n. d.). Most people hate official reports—Effective report writing and creative business writing. Impact Factory. Retrieved from http://www .impactfactory.com. Reprinted by permission of the author.

[7] Elliott, M. (2010-2013). Writing. Retrieved from http://marianne-elliott.com /writing

[8] Meier, B. (2013, January 17). Officials seek energy drink information. *The New York Times*. Retrieved from http://www.nytimes .com/2013/01/18/business/lawmakers-seek-data-on-energy-drinks .html; "Stand and deliver" Dick Durbin and co. tell Red Bull, Rockstar, Monster . . . . (2013, January 18). BeverageDaily.com. Retrieved from http://www.beveragedaily.com/Trends/Energy-Drinks-Beyond /Stand-and-deliver-Dick-Durbin-and-co.-tell-Red-Bull-Rockstar-Monster

[9] Photo essay based on Levine, B. (2011, November 30). Glendale to get 'animated' in image makeover. *Glendale News-Press*. Retrieved from http://www .glendalenewspress.com; North Star Destination Strategies. Independent Research Products. Retrieved from http://www.northstarideas.com

[10] Lapan, T. (2012, April 11). Libraries reinvent themselves for the digital age. *Las Vegas Sun*. Retrieved from http://www.lasvegassun.com

[11] Cohen, J. S. (2009, December 28). Top 10 favorite foods preferred by college students. *Chicago Tribune*. Retrieved from http://www.inyork.com /ci_14080691?source=most_viewed

[12] Giorgetti, D., & Sebastiani, F. (2003, December). Automating survey coding by multiclass text categories. *Journal of the American Society for Information Science and Technology*, 54(14), 1269. Retrieved from http://search.proquest.com

[13] Goldsmith, B. (2002, June). The awesome power of asking the right questions. *OfficeSolutions*, 52; and Bracey, G. W. (2001, November). Research-question authority. *Phi Delta Kappan*, 191.

[14] Peters, T. (1991). *Thriving on chaos*. New York: HarperCollins, pp. 281–282.

[15] Berfield, S. (2009, August 17). Howard Schultz versus Howard Schultz. *BusinessWeek*, p. 31.

[16] Arenson, K. W., & Gootman, E. (2008, February 21). Columbia cites plagiarism by a professor. *The New York Times*. Retrieved from http://www.nytimes .com/2008/02/21/education/21prof.html; and Bartlett, T. (2006, September 8). Professor faces firing for plagiarism. *Chronicle of Higher Education*, p. 11. Retrieved from http://search.ebscohost.com

[17] Vincent, J. (2012, May 26). Write or wrong: Thoughts on plagiarism. Helium.com. Retrieved from http://www.helium.com/items/982257-thoughts-on-plagiarism

[18] Writing Tutorial Services, Indiana University. *Plagiarism: What it is and how to recognize and avoid it*. Retrieved from http://www.indiana.edu/~wts /pamphlets/plagiarism.shtml

[19] Kotkin, J. (2010, October 10). The fastest-growing cities in the U.S. Forbes. Retrieved from http://www.forbes.com/2010/10/11/cities-innovation-texas-great-plains-indianapolis-opinions-columnists-joel-kotkin_2.html

[20] Saylor, M. (2012). *The mobile wave: How mobile intelligence will change everything*. New York: Vanguard Press, p. ix.

[21] Tufte, E. R. (1983). *The visual display of quantitative information*. Cheshire, CT: Graphics Press, p. 107.

[22] Tufte, E. (n. d.) Poster: Napoleon's march. Retrieved from http://www.edwardtufte .com/tufte/posters

[23] Arafah, B. (2010, May 21). Huge infographics design resources: Overview, principles, tips and examples. Onextrapixel.com. Retrieved from http://www.onextrapixel .com/2010/05/21/huge-infographics-design-resources-overview-principles-tips-and-examples

[24] Labarre, S. (2012, January). How infographics guru Nicholas Felton inspired Facebook's Timeline. Co.DESIGN. Retrieved from http://www.fastcodesign .com/1665062/how-infographics-guru-nicholas-felton-inspired-facebooks-timeline

[25] Kuang, C. (2011, December). 2 GE infographics offer hints about the future of data-driven management. Co.DESIGN. Retrieved from http://www .fastcodesign.com/1669049/2-infographics-from-ge-offer-hints-about-future-of-data-driven-management#1

[26] Pavlus, J. (2011, December). Why "infographic thinking" is the future, not a fad. Co.DESIGN. Retrieved from http://www.fastcodesign.com/1668987 /why-infographic-thinking-is-the-future-not-a-fad

[27] Visually, Inc. (2012). Infographics software. Retrieved from http://visual.ly /learn/infographics-software

[28] Berfield, S. (2009, August 17). Howard Schultz versus Howard Schultz. *BusinessWeek*, p. 33.

[29] Ibid.

[30] Patton, L. (2012, November 2). Starbucks jumps as profit increases on U.S. sales gain. Bloomberg.com. Retrieved from http://www.bloomberg.com/news /2012-11-01/starbucks-fourth-quarter-profit-climbs-as-u-s-sales-gain.html

[31] Reasons students hate writing essays or term papers. (n. d.) CustomPapers.com. Retrieved from http://custompapers.com/essay-not

[32] Tufte, E. (1990). *Envisioning information*. Cheshire, CT: Graphics Press, 1990, p. 34.

[33] Reena, J. (2006, October 16). Enough with the shoot-'em-ups. *BusinessWeek*, p. 92.

[34] 2011 College food trends: Students crave Mediterranean, made-to-order fare, stealth health, global flavors and apps. (2011, February 7). SodexoUSA.com. Retrieved from http://www.sodexousa.com/usen/newsroom/press /press11/2011collegefoodtrends.asp

[35] Barton, N., Di Mento, M., Flandez, R., & López-Rivera, M. (2012, July 22). 10 companies that gave the most cash in 2011. *The Chronicle of Philanthropy*. Retrieved from http://philanthropy.com/article/10-Companies-That-Gave-the/132991; Naughton, K. (2006, July 3). Corporate giant. *Newsweek*, p. 74. Retrieved from http://search.ebscohost.com

[36] Park, A. (2011, January 6). Study linking vaccines to autism is "fraudulent." *Time*. Retrieved from http://healthland.time.com/2011/01/06 /study-linking-vaccines-to-autism-is-fraudulent

[37] Blake, H. (2011, March 3). Millions of surgery patients at risk in drug research fraud scandal. *The Telegraph*. Retrieved from http://www.telegraph.co.uk /health/8360667/Millions-of-surgery-patients-at-risk-in-drug-research-fraud-scandal.html

[38] Visually, Inc. (2012). Infographics software. Retrieved from http://visual.ly/learn /infographics-software

[39] How undergraduate students use credit cards. (2009). Sallie Mae. Retrieved from http://www.salliemae.com

[40] O'Keefe, S., & Pringle, A. S. (2009). *Technical Writing 101: A real-world guide to planning and writing technical content* (3rd ed.). Research Triangle Park, NC: Scriptorium, pp. 47–48.

Informal Business Reports

© iStockphoto.com/Neustockimages

Starbucks: The Global Chain That Wants to Remain "a Neighborhood Gathering Place"

Despite epic setbacks that prompted chairman and CEO Howard Schultz to return to the helm at Starbucks, the company continues to reign as the world's largest coffee shop chain. After a recessionary slump, Starbucks has soared to more than 18,000 retail locations in 61 countries.[1] The specialty coffee roaster and retailer has bolstered its presence in China, its fastest-growing market.

Recently, it has entered India, a traditionally tea-loving country. In its own words, Starbucks set out to be "a different kind of company"[2] by providing a unique experience to customers and trying to create a connection "one person, one cup, and one neighborhood at a time."[3] Yet the global behemoth serves a whopping 70 million customers a week and employs over 200,000 people.[4] With annual sales of $11.7 billion and a market value of $40 billion, the company has returned to record performance.[5]

Adding to its accolades, Starbucks consistently ranks among the top ten in the *Fortune* magazine list of America's Most Admired Companies. It is known for its social responsibility initiatives such as fair-trade coffee sourcing, energy conservation, farmer loans, and ethical employment practices. Moreover, the retailer is regularly named among *Fortune's* 100 Best Companies to Work For, not least because Starbucks gives health insurance and stock options to all employees, whom it calls partners.[6]

Howard Schultz successfully bucked traditional retail wisdom, for example, by locating stores so densely together that they cannibalized each other's sales. He famously relied on his entrepreneurial instinct and scorned conventional market research. Yet although he is one of the most admired corporate executives of our time, Howard Schultz suffered a few flops, too. His headlong introduction of Sorbetto failed miserably, and Starbucks had to abandon the sugary beverage.[7] The company also has had mixed results with its music and film offerings. Moreover, Schultz himself admits that he misread the depth of the recession and its impact on his business. However, he scored a winner with Via, Starbucks' instant coffee, because this time he embraced focus groups and listened to his executives, who advocated a slow, methodical introduction.

Now the company wants to replicate in India what it considers its unique and exciting Starbucks experience—connecting with customers and creating a sense of community. Such large-scale ventures in vastly different cultures are fraught with peril, and Starbucks has conducted plenty of research. The company also decided not to go it alone. Instead, it allied itself with Indian giant Tata Global Beverages. The joint venture is designed to help Starbucks establish a foothold in India's potentially giant market. You will learn more about this case on page 450.

Critical Thinking

- What kind of information should Starbucks gather to help it decide whether and how to introduce a new product to avoid pitfalls such as the failed Sorbetto beverage?

- How could Howard Schultz test his assumption that the intimate communal coffee-drinking experience is intact at Starbucks?

- How can collected information be transmitted to Starbucks' decision makers?

Interpreting Digital-Age Data

LEARNING OBJECTIVE 1
Analyze, sort, and interpret statistical data and other information using tables, measures of central tendency (mean, median, and mode), and decision matrices.

Much of the information that allows decision makers to run their organizations efficiently in this digital age comes to them in the form of reports. To respond nimbly to changing economic times, Starbucks and other businesses need information to stay abreast of what is happening inside and outside of their firms. This chapter focuses on interpreting and organizing data, drawing conclusions, providing reader cues, and writing informal business reports.

Given the easy access to research databases, the Web, and other sources of digitized information, collecting information is nearly effortless today. However, making sense of the massive amounts of data you may collect is much harder. You may feel overwhelmed as you look at a jumble of digital files, printouts, note cards, articles, interview notes, questionnaire results, and statistics. Unprocessed data become meaningful information through skillful and accurate sorting, analysis, combination, and recombination. You will be examining each item to see what it means by itself and what it means when connected with other data. You are looking for meanings, relationships, and answers to the research questions posed in your work plan.

REALITY CHECK: Have a Plan and Do Research

"Failure to do market research before you begin a business venture or during its operation is like driving a car from Texas to New York without a map or street signs. You have to know which direction to travel and how fast to go. A good market research plan indicates where and who your customers are. It will also tell you when they are most likely and willing to purchase your goods or use your services."

—**WILLIAM BILL,** *Wealth Design Group LLC, Houston, Texas*

ETHICS CHECK:

Starbucks CEO Howard Schultz explains his company's Shared Planet initiative: "We feel now is the time to invest—truly and authentically—in ways to help create a better future for the world we share."[8] Starbucks also teamed up with Product Red, the global anti-AIDS project spearheaded by U2's front man and activist Bono. The coffee chain wishes to pursue its vision of community involvement, commitment to the environment, and ethical sourcing of coffee. Do you view favorably companies that are "green" and wish to appear ethical? Do such considerations influence your buying decisions?

Tabulating and Analyzing Data

After collecting numerical data and other information, you must tabulate and analyze them. Fortunately, several techniques can help you simplify, summarize, and classify large amounts of data. The most helpful summarizing techniques are tables, statistical concepts (mean, median, and mode), correlations, grids, and decision matrices.

Tables. Tables usually help researchers summarize and simplify data. Using columns and rows, tables make quantitative information easier to comprehend. After assembling your data, you will want to prepare preliminary tables to enable you to see what the information means. Here is a table summarizing the response to one question from a campus survey about student parking:

Question: Should student fees be increased to build parking lots?

	Number	Percentage	
Strongly agree	76	11.5	To simplify the table, combine these items.
Agree	255	38.5	50 percent support the proposal
No opinion	22	3.3	
Disagree	107	16.1	To simplify the table, combine these items.
Strongly disagree	203	30.6	46.7 (nearly 47) percent oppose the proposal
Total	**663**	**100.0**	

Notice that this preliminary table includes a total number of responses and a percentage for each response. (To calculate a percentage, divide the figure for each response by the total number of responses times 100.)

Sometimes data become more meaningful when cross-tabulated. This process allows analysis of two or more variables together. By breaking down our student survey data into male and female responses, shown in the following table, we make an interesting discovery.

Question: Should student fees be increased to build parking lots?

	Total		Male			Female		
	Number	Percentage	Number	Percentage		Number	Percentage	
Strongly agree	76	11.5	8	2.2	= 17.5 percent	68	22.0	= 87 percent SUPPORT
Agree	255	38.5	54	15.3		201	65.0	
No opinion	22	3.3	12	3.4		10	3.2	
Disagree	107	16.1	89	25.1	= 79.1 percent	18	5.8	= 9.8 percent OPPOSE
Strongly disagree	203	30.6	191	54.0		12	4.0	
Total	**663**	**100.0**	**354**	**100.0**		**309**	**100.0**	

Although 50 percent of all student respondents supported the proposal, among females the approval rating was much stronger. You naturally wonder why such a disparity exists. Are female students unhappier than male students with the current parking situation? If so, why? Is safety a reason? Are male students more concerned with increased fees than female students are?

By cross-tabulating the findings, you sometimes uncover data that may help answer your problem question or that may prompt you to explore other possibilities. Do not, however, undertake cross-tabulation unless it serves more than merely satisfying your curiosity. Tables also help you compare multiple data collected from questionnaires and surveys. Figure 12.1 shows, in raw form, responses to several survey items. To convert these data into a more usable form, you need to calculate percentages for each item. Then you can arrange the responses in some rational sequence, such as largest percentage to smallest.

Once the data are displayed in a table, you can more easily draw conclusions. As Figure 12.1 shows, South Bay College students apparently are not interested in public transportation or shuttle buses from satellite lots. They want to park on campus and restrict visitor parking; and only half are willing to pay for new parking lots.

Figure 12.1   Converting Survey Data Into Finished Tables

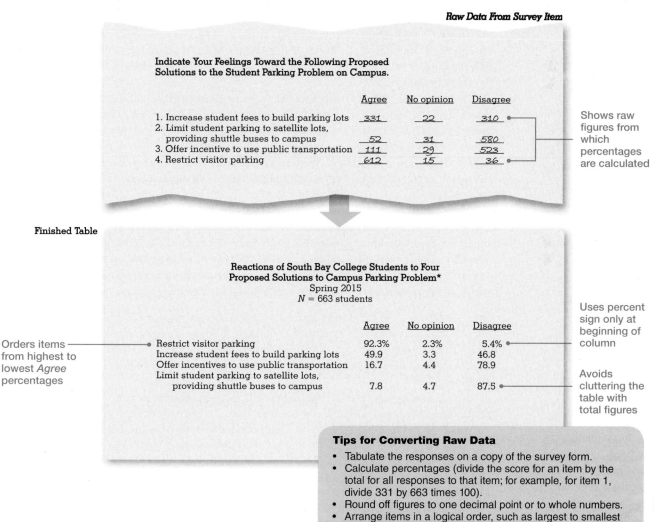

Raw Data From Survey Item

Indicate Your Feelings Toward the Following Proposed Solutions to the Student Parking Problem on Campus.

	Agree	No opinion	Disagree
1. Increase student fees to build parking lots	331	22	310
2. Limit student parking to satellite lots, providing shuttle buses to campus	52	31	580
3. Offer incentive to use public transportation	111	29	523
4. Restrict visitor parking	612	15	36

Shows raw figures from which percentages are calculated

Finished Table

Reactions of South Bay College Students to Four Proposed Solutions to Campus Parking Problem*
Spring 2015
N = 663 students

	Agree	No opinion	Disagree
Restrict visitor parking	92.3%	2.3%	5.4%
Increase student fees to build parking lots	49.9	3.3	46.8
Offer incentives to use public transportation	16.7	4.4	78.9
Limit student parking to satellite lots, providing shuttle buses to campus	7.8	4.7	87.5

Orders items from highest to lowest *Agree* percentages

Uses percent sign only at beginning of column

Avoids cluttering the table with total figures

Tips for Converting Raw Data
- Tabulate the responses on a copy of the survey form.
- Calculate percentages (divide the score for an item by the total for all responses to that item; for example, for item 1, divide 331 by 663 times 100).
- Round off figures to one decimal point or to whole numbers.
- Arrange items in a logical order, such as largest to smallest percentage.
- Prepare a table with a title that tells such things as who, what, when, where, and why.
- Include the total number of respondents (the *N* figure).

© Cengage Learning 2015

Measures of Central Tendency. Tables help you organize data, and the three Ms—mean, median, and mode—help you describe data. These statistical terms are all occasionally used loosely to mean "average." To be safe, though, you should learn to apply these statistical terms precisely.

When people say *average*, they usually intend to indicate the *mean*, or arithmetic average. Let's say that you are studying the estimated starting salaries of graduates from various disciplines, ranging from education to medicine:

Education	$ 47,000	*Mode (figure occurring most frequently)*
Sociology	47,000	
Humanities	47,000	
Biology	53,000	
Health sciences	63,000	*Median (middle point in continuum)*
Business	66,000	*Mean (arithmetic average)*
Law	74,000	
Engineering	82,000	
Medicine	114,000	

To find the mean, you simply add all the salaries and divide by the total number of items. Therefore, the mean salary is $65,800 (almost $66,000). Means are very useful to indicate central tendencies of figures, but they have one major flaw: extremes at either end cause distortion. Notice that the $114,000 figure makes the mean salary of $66,000 deceptively high. Use means only when extreme figures do not distort the result.

The *median* represents the midpoint in a group of figures arranged from lowest to highest (or vice versa). In our list of salaries, the median is $63,000 (health sciences). In other words, half the salaries are above this point and half are below it. The median is useful when extreme figures may warp the mean.

The *mode* is simply the value that occurs most frequently. In our list $47,000 (for education, sociology, and the humanities) represents the mode because it occurs three times. The mode has the advantage of being easily determined—just a quick glance at a list of arranged values reveals it. Although researchers use mode infrequently, knowing the mode is useful in some situations; for example, if we wish to determine a group's preferences. To remember the meaning of *mode*, think about fashion: the most frequent response, the mode, is the most fashionable.

Mean, median, and mode figures are especially helpful when the range of values is also known. Range represents the span between the highest and lowest values. To calculate the range, you simply subtract the lowest figure from the highest. In starting salaries for graduates, the range is $67,000 (114,000 – 47,000). Knowing the range enables readers to put mean and median figures into perspective. This knowledge also prompts researchers to wonder why such a range exists, thus stimulating hunches and further investigation to solve problems.

Correlations. In tabulating and analyzing data, you may see relationships among two or more variables that help explain the findings. If your data for graduates' starting salaries also included years of education, you would doubtless notice that graduates with more years of education received higher salaries. A correlation may exist between years of education and starting salary.

Intuition suggests correlations that may or may not prove to be accurate. Is there a causal relationship between studying and good grades? Between electronic gadget use by supervising adults and increased injuries of children? Between the rise and fall of hemlines and the rise and fall of the stock market (as some newspaper writers have suggested)? The business researcher who sees a correlation needs to ask why and how the two variables are related. In this way, apparent correlations stimulate investigation and present possible solutions to be explored.

In reporting correlations, you should avoid suggesting that a cause-and-effect relationship exists when none can be proved. Only sophisticated research methods can statistically prove correlations. Instead, present a correlation as a possible relationship (*The data suggest that beginning salaries are related to years of education*). Cautious statements followed by explanations gain you credibility and allow readers to make their own decisions.

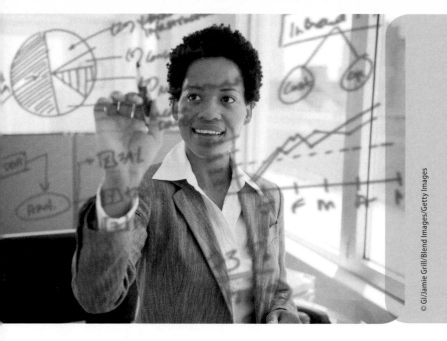

Research errors over the years have given rise to an important maxim: "correlation does not imply causation." Whether investigating the link between depression and Internet use or studying the tenuous relationship between shoe size and reading skills, researchers caution that data correlations do not mean that one variable is the cause of the other. In one recent eyebrow-raising study, a researcher claimed that the decline in violent crime during the 1990s was caused by the declining use of leaded gasoline. How should business writers present correlations in reports?[9]

© GI/Jamie Grill/Blend Images/Getty Images

Grids.   Another technique for analyzing raw data—especially verbal data—is the grid. Let's say you have been asked by the CEO to collect opinions from all vice presidents about the CEO's four-point plan to build cash reserves. The grid shown in Figure 12.2 enables you to summarize the vice presidents' reactions to each point. Notice how this complex verbal information is transformed into concise, manageable data; readers can see immediately which points are supported and which are opposed. Imagine how long you could have struggled to comprehend the meaning of this verbal information without a grid.

Arranging data in a grid also works for projects such as feasibility studies and yardstick reports that compare many variables. *Consumer Reports* often uses grids to show information. In addition, grids help classify employment data. For example, suppose your boss asks you to recommend one individual from among many job candidates. You could arrange a grid with names across the top and distinguishing characteristics—experience, skills, education, and other employment interests—down the left side. Summarizing each candidate's points offers a helpful tool for drawing conclusions and writing a report.

Figure 12.2 Grid to Analyze Complex Verbal Data About Building Cash Reserves

	Point 1	Point 2	Point 3	Point 4	Overall Reaction
VICE PRESIDENT 1	Disapproves. "Too little, too late."	Strong support. "Best of all points."	Mixed opinion. "Must wait and see market."	Indifferent.	Optimistic, but "hates to delay expansion for six months."
VICE PRESIDENT 2	Disapproves. "Creates credit trap."	Approves.	Strong disapproval.	Approves. "Must improve receivable collections."	Mixed support. "Good self-defense plan."
VICE PRESIDENT 3	Strong disapproval.	Approves. "Key to entire plan."	Indifferent.	Approves, but with "caveats."	"Will work only with sale of unproductive fixed assets."
VICE PRESIDENT 4	Disapproves. "Too risky now."	Strong support. "Start immediately."	Approves, "but may damage image."	Approves. "Benefits far outweigh costs."	Supports plan. Suggests focus on Pacific Rim markets.

© Cengage Learning 2015

Decision Matrices. A decision matrix is a special grid that helps managers make the best choice among complex options. Designed to eliminate bias and poor judgment, decision matrices are helpful in many fields. Assume you need to choose the most appropriate laptop for your sales representatives. You are most interested in weight, battery life, price, and hard drive size. You want to compare these features in four highly rated business laptop models. Figure 12.3 shows a simple decision matrix to help you make the choice. In Table 1, you evaluate each of the desired features on a scale of 1 to 5. Because the Lenovo ThinkPad X1 weighs in at a very light 2.93 pounds, you give it a score of 5 for weight. However, its hard drive capacity is much less desirable, and you give it a score of 1 for hard drive.

After you have evaluated all of the laptop models in Table 1, you assign relative weights to each feature. You decide to assign a factor of 5 to weight as well as to unit price because these two aspects are of average importance. However, your field sales reps want laptops

Figure 12.3 Decision Matrix Used to Choose a Business Laptop for Sales Reps

Unweighted Decision Matrix—Table 1					
Features:	Weight	Battery Life	Price	Hard Drive	Total
Laptop Options					
Apple MacBook: 2.5 GHz, 3.57 lbs, 10 hrs, $1,500, 256 GB	4	5	1	3	
Dell Latitude: 2.9 GHz, 6.3 lbs, 9 hrs, $1,199, 256 GB	1	4	3	3	
Lenovo ThinkPad X1: 1.8 GHz, 2.93 lbs, 8 hrs, $1,364, 128 GB	5	3	2	1	
Lenovo ThinkPad X230: 2.6 GHz, 3.7 lbs, 6 hrs, $1,126, 320 GB	3	2	4	4	

Weighted Decision Matrix—Table 2					
Features:	Weight	Battery Life	Price	Hard Drive	Total
Laptop Options Weights:	5	10	5	7	
Apple MacBook: 2.5 GHz, 3.57 lbs, 10 hrs, $1,500, 256 GB	20	50	5	21	96
Dell Latitude: 2.9 GHz, 6.3 lbs, 9 hrs, $1,199, 256 GB	5	40	15	21	81
Lenovo ThinkPad X1: 1.8 GHz, 2.93 lbs, 8 hrs, $1,364, 128 GB	25	30	10	7	72
Lenovo ThinkPad X230: 2.6 GHz, 3.7 lbs, 6 hrs, $1,126, 320 GB	15	20	20	28	73

Tips for Creating a Decision Matrix

- **Select the most important criteria.** For a laptop computer, the criteria were weight, battery life, price, and hard drive size.
- **Create a matrix.** List each laptop model (Apple, Dell, and others) down the left side. Place the features across the top of the columns.
- **Evaluate the criteria.** Use a scale of 1 (lowest) to 5 (highest). Rate each feature for each option, as shown in Table 1.
- **Assign relative weights.** Decide how important each feature is and give it a weight.
- **Multiply the scores.** For each feature in Table 1, multiply by the weights in Table 2 and write the score in the box.
- **Total the scores.** The total reveals the best choice.

with batteries that last. Therefore, battery life is twice as important; you assign it a factor of 10. You assign a factor of 7 to the size of the hard drive because this option is slightly more important than price, but somewhat less important than battery life. Then you multiply the scores in Table 1 with the weights and total them, as shown in Table 2. According to the weighted matrix and the rating system used, the Apple MacBook should be purchased for the sales reps because it received the highest score of 96 points, closely followed by the Dell Latitude with 81 points.

Drawing Conclusions and Making Recommendations

LEARNING OBJECTIVE **2**
Draw meaningful conclusions and make practical report recommendations after sound and valid analysis.

The sections devoted to conclusions and recommendations are the most widely read portions of a report. Knowledgeable readers go straight to the conclusions to see what the report writer thinks the data mean. Because conclusions summarize and explain the findings, they represent the heart of a report.

Your value in an organization rises considerably if you can draw conclusions that analyze information logically and show how the data answer questions and solve problems. Responding to a growing demand for sustainable electronics, Dutch entrepreneur Bas van Abel is developing the FairPhone, a fair-trade device. "It is an alternative for a growing group of aware consumers," van Abel said, "but it's also a way to prepare the industry and to inspire the industry to do [things] differently." The raw materials used in smartphones often come from war-torn countries and are extracted under dangerous working conditions, frequently by children. The mining of these "conflict metals" releases toxins that poison the environment.[10] Solving such problems requires research. Drawing logical conclusions from data is crucial to business success.

> Your value in an organization rises considerably if you can draw conclusions that analyze information logically and show how the data answer questions and solve problems.

Analyzing Data to Arrive at Conclusions

Any set of data can produce a variety of meaningful conclusions. Always bear in mind, though, that the audience for a report wants to know how these data relate to the problem being studied. What do the findings mean in terms of solving the original report problem?

For example, the Marriott Corporation recognized a serious problem among its employees. Conflicting home and work requirements seemed to be causing excessive employee turnover and decreased productivity. To learn the extent of the problem and to consider solutions, Marriott hired Hospitality Consultants to survey its staff. The hotel chain learned, among other things, that nearly 35 percent of its employees had children under age twelve, and 15 percent had children under age five. Other findings, shown in Figure 12.4, indicated that one third of its staff with young children took time off because of child-care difficulties. Moreover, many current employees left previous jobs because of work and family conflicts. The survey also showed that managers did not consider child-care or family problems to be appropriate topics for discussion at work.

A sample of possible conclusions that a writer might draw from these findings is shown in Figure 12.4. Notice that each conclusion relates to the initial report problem. Although only a few possible findings and conclusions are shown here, you can see that the conclusions try to explain the causes for the home/work conflict among employees. Many report writers would expand the conclusion section by explaining each item and citing supporting evidence. Even for simplified conclusions, such as those shown in Figure 12.4, you will want to list each item separately and use parallel construction (balanced sentence structure).

Although your goal is to remain objective, drawing conclusions naturally involves a degree of subjectivity. Your goals, background, and frame of reference all color the inferences you make. All writers interpret findings from their own perspectives, but they should not manipulate them to achieve a preconceived purpose. You can make your report conclusions more objective by using consistent evaluation criteria. Let's say you are comparing computers for an office equipment purchase. If you evaluate each by the same criteria (such as price, specifications, service, and warranty), your conclusions are more likely to be bias-free.

You also need to avoid the temptation to sensationalize or exaggerate your findings or conclusions. Be careful of words such as *many, most*, and *all*. Instead of *many of the respondents felt . . .* , you might more accurately write *some of the respondents felt . . . .* Examine your motives before drawing conclusions. Do not let preconceptions or wishful thinking color your reasoning.

Preparing Report Recommendations

Conclusions explain what the problem is, whereas recommendations tell how to solve it. Typically, business readers prefer specific, practical recommendations. They want to know exactly how to implement the suggestions. The specificity of your recommendations depends on your authorization. What are you commissioned to do, and what does the reader expect? In the planning stages of your report project, you anticipate what the reader wants in the report.

Figure 12.4 Report Conclusions and Recommendations in Intranet Screen View

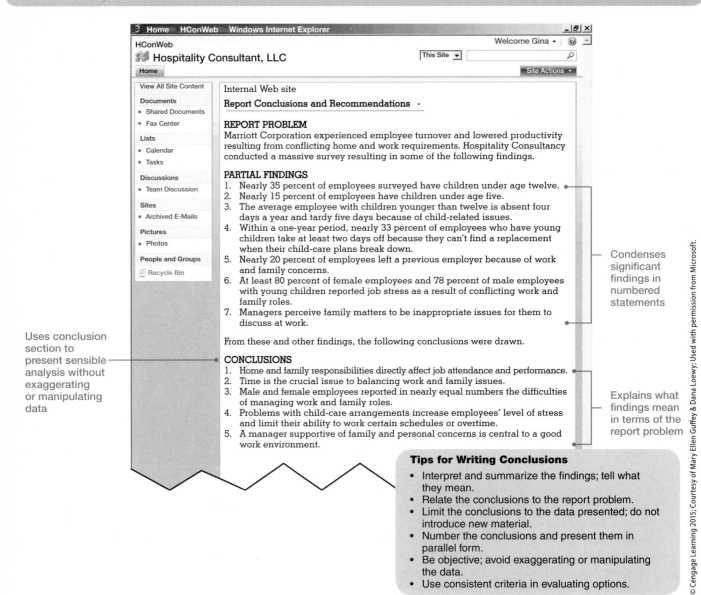

Uses conclusion section to present sensible analysis without exaggerating or manipulating data

Condenses significant findings in numbered statements

Explains what findings mean in terms of the report problem

Tips for Writing Conclusions
- Interpret and summarize the findings; tell what they mean.
- Relate the conclusions to the report problem.
- Limit the conclusions to the data presented; do not introduce new material.
- Number the conclusions and present them in parallel form.
- Be objective; avoid exaggerating or manipulating the data.
- Use consistent criteria in evaluating options.

Figure **12.4** (Continued)

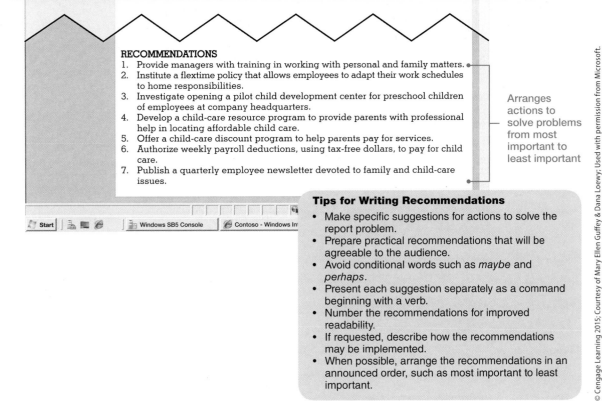

RECOMMENDATIONS
1. Provide managers with training in working with personal and family matters.
2. Institute a flextime policy that allows employees to adapt their work schedules to home responsibilities.
3. Investigate opening a pilot child development center for preschool children of employees at company headquarters.
4. Develop a child-care resource program to provide parents with professional help in locating affordable child care.
5. Offer a child-care discount program to help parents pay for services.
6. Authorize weekly payroll deductions, using tax-free dollars, to pay for child care.
7. Publish a quarterly employee newsletter devoted to family and child-care issues.

Arranges actions to solve problems from most important to least important

Tips for Writing Recommendations
- Make specific suggestions for actions to solve the report problem.
- Prepare practical recommendations that will be agreeable to the audience.
- Avoid conditional words such as *maybe* and *perhaps*.
- Present each suggestion separately as a command beginning with a verb.
- Number the recommendations for improved readability.
- If requested, describe how the recommendations may be implemented.
- When possible, arrange the recommendations in an announced order, such as most important to least important.

© Cengage Learning 2015; Courtesy of Mary Ellen Guffey & Dana Loewy; Used with permission from Microsoft.

Your intuition and your knowledge of the audience indicate how far you should develop your recommendations.

In the recommendations section of the Marriott employee survey, shown in Figure 12.4, the consultants summarized their recommendations. In the actual report, the consultants would back up each recommendation with specifics and ideas for implementing them. For example, the child-care resource recommendation would be explained: it provides parents with names of agencies and professionals who specialize in locating child care across the country.

A good report provides practical recommendations that are agreeable to the audience. In the Marriott survey, for example, the consulting company knew that the company wanted to help employees cope with conflicts between family and work obligations. As a result, the report's conclusions and recommendations focused on ways to resolve the conflict. If Marriott's goal had been merely to save money by reducing employee absenteeism, the recommendations would have been quite different.

If possible, make each recommendation a command. Note in Figure 12.4 that each recommendation begins with a verb. This structure sounds forceful and confident and helps the reader comprehend the information quickly. Avoid hedging words such as *maybe* and *perhaps*; they reduce the strength of recommendations.

Experienced writers may combine recommendations and conclusions. In short reports writers may omit conclusions and move straight to recommendations. An important point about recommendations is that they include practical suggestions for solving the report problem. Furthermore, they are always the result of prior logical analysis.

Moving From Findings to Recommendations

Recommendations evolve from the interpretation of the findings and conclusions. Consider the examples from the Marriott survey summarized in Figure 12.5.

Figure **12.5** Understanding Findings, Conclusions, and Recommendations

Finding

Managers perceive family matters to be inappropriate issues to discuss at work.

Conclusion

Managers are neither willing nor trained to discuss family matters that may cause employees to miss work.

Recommendation

Provide managers with training in recognizing and working with personal and family matters that affect work.

Finding

Within a one-year period, nearly 33 percent of employees with young children take at least two days off because they can't find a replacement when their child-care plans break down.

Conclusion

Problems with child-care arrangements increase employees' level of stress and limit their ability to work certain schedules or overtime.

Recommendation

Develop a child-care resource program to provide parents with professional help in locating affordable child care.

© Cengage Learning 2015

LEARNING OBJECTIVE 3
Organize report data logically and provide reader cues to aid comprehension.

Organizing Data

After collecting sets of data, interpreting them, drawing conclusions, and thinking about the recommendations, you are ready to organize the parts of the report into a logical framework. Poorly organized reports lead to frustration. Readers will not understand, remember, or be persuaded. Wise writers know that reports rarely "just organize themselves." Instead, organization must be imposed on the data, and cues must be provided so the reader can follow the logic of the writer.

Informational reports, as you learned in Chapter 11, generally present data without interpretation. As shown in Figure 12.6, informational reports typically consist of three parts. Analytical reports, which generally analyze data and draw conclusions, typically contain four parts. However, the parts in analytical reports do not always follow this sequence. For readers who know about the project, are supportive, or are eager to learn the results quickly, the direct strategy is appropriate. Conclusions and recommendations, if requested, appear up front. For readers who must be educated or persuaded, the indirect strategy works better. Conclusions and recommendations appear last, after the findings have been presented and analyzed.

Informational Reports	Analytical Reports	
Direct Strategy	**Direct Strategy**	**Indirect Strategy**
I. Introduction/background	I. Introduction/problem	I. Introduction/problem
II. Facts/findings	II. Conclusions/recommendations	II. Facts/findings
III. Summary/conclusion	III. Facts/findings	III. Discussion/analysis
	IV. Discussion/analysis	IV. Conclusions/recommendations

© Cengage Learning 2015

Although every report is unique, the overall organizational strategies described here generally hold true. The real challenge, though, lies in (a) organizing the facts/findings and discussion/analysis sections and (b) providing reader cues.

Ordering Information Logically

Whether you are writing informational or analytical reports, you must structure the data you have collected. Five common organizational methods are by time, component, importance, criteria, and convention. Regardless of the method you choose, be sure that it helps the reader understand the data. Reader comprehension, not writer convenience, should govern organization. For additional examples of organizational principles, please go to page 505 in Chapter 14.

Time.   Ordering data by time means establishing a chronology of events. Agendas, minutes of meetings, progress reports, and procedures are usually organized by time. For example, a report describing an eight-week training program would most likely be organized by weeks. A plan for the step-by-step improvement of customer service would be organized by steps. A monthly trip report submitted by a sales rep might describe customers visited during Week 1, Week 2, and so on.

Beware of overusing chronologies (time) as an organizing method for reports, however. Although this method is easy and often mirrors the way data are collected, chronologies—like the sales rep's trip report—tend to be boring, repetitive, and lacking in emphasis. Readers cannot always pick out what is important.

Component.   Especially for informational reports, data may be organized by components such as location, geography, division, product, or part. For instance, a report detailing company expansion might divide the plan into West Coast, East Coast, and Midwest expansion. The report could also be organized by divisions: personal products, consumer electronics, and household goods. A report comparing profits among makers of athletic shoes might group the data by company: Nike, Reebok, Adidas, and so forth. Organization by components works best when the classifications already exist.

Importance.   Organization by importance involves beginning with the most important item and proceeding to the least important—or vice versa. For example, a report discussing the reasons for declining product sales would present the most important reason first followed by less important ones. The Marriott consultants' report describing work/family conflicts might begin by discussing child care, if the writer considered it the most important issue. Using importance to structure findings involves a value judgment. The writer must decide what is most important, always keeping in mind the readers' priorities and expectations. Busy readers appreciate seeing important points first; they may skim or skip other points.

On the other hand, building to a climax by moving from least important to most important enables the writer to focus attention at the end. Thus, the reader is more likely to remember the most important item. Of course, the writer also risks losing the reader's attention along the way.

Criteria.   Establishing criteria by which to judge helps writers to treat topics consistently. Let's say your report compares health plans A, B, and C. For each plan you examine the same standards: cost per employee, amount of deductible, and patient benefits. The resulting data could then be organized either by plans or by criteria as Figure 12.7 illustrates:

Figure 12.7 Ordering Information Logically by Using Criteria

© Cengage Learning 2015

Although you might favor organizing the data by plans (because that is the way you collected the data), the better way is by criteria. When you discuss patient benefits, for example, you would examine all three plans' benefits together. Organizing a report around criteria helps readers make comparisons, instead of forcing them to search through the report for similar data.

Convention.   Many operational and recurring reports are structured according to convention. That is, they follow a prescribed plan that everyone understands. For example, an automotive parts manufacturer might ask all sales reps to prepare a weekly report with these headings: *Competitive observations* (competitors' price changes, discounts, new products, product problems, distributor changes, product promotions), *Product problems* (quality, performance, needs), and *Customer-service problems* (delivery, mailings, correspondence, social media, and Web traffic). Management gets exactly the information it needs in an easy-to-read form.

Like operating reports, proposals are often organized conventionally. They might use such groupings as background, problem, proposed solution, staffing, schedule, costs, and authorization. As you might expect, reports following these conventional, prescribed structures greatly simplify the task of organization. Proposals and long reports are presented in Chapter 13.

Providing Reader Cues

When you finish organizing a report, you probably see a neat outline in your mind: major points, supported by subpoints and details. Readers, however, do not know the material as well as you do; they cannot see your outline. To guide them through the data, you need to provide the equivalent of a map and road signs. For both formal and informal reports, devices such as introductions, transitions, and headings prevent readers from getting lost.

Introduction.   One of the best ways to point a reader in the right direction is to provide a report introduction that does three things:

■ Tells the purpose of the report

■ Describes the significance of the topic

■ Previews the main points and the order in which they will be developed

The following paragraph includes all three elements in introducing a report on computer security:

This report examines the security of our current computer operations and presents suggestions for improving security. Lax computer security could mean loss of information, loss of business, and damage to our equipment and systems. Because many former employees released during recent downsizing efforts know our systems, we must make major changes. To improve security, I will present three recommendations: (a) begin using dongles that limit access to our computer system, (b) alter log-on and log-off procedures, and (c) move central computer operations to a more secure area.

This opener tells the purpose (examining computer security), describes its significance (loss of information and business, damage to equipment and systems), and outlines how the report is organized (three recommendations). Good openers in effect set up a contract with the reader. The writer promises to cover certain topics in a specified order. Readers expect the writer to fulfill the contract. They want the topics to be developed as promised—using the same wording and presented in the order mentioned. For example, if in your introduction you state that you will discuss the use of *dongles* (a small plug-in security device), do not change the heading for that section to *security tokens*. Remember that the introduction provides a map to a report; switching the names on the map will ensure that readers get lost. To maintain consistency, delay writing the introduction until after you have completed the report. Long, complex reports may require introductions, brief internal summaries, and previews for each section.

Transitions.   Expressions such as *on the contrary, at the same time*, and *however* show relationships and help reveal the logical flow of ideas in a report. These transitional expressions enable writers to tell readers where ideas are headed and how they relate. Notice how abrupt the following three sentences sound without any transition: *The iPad was the first mainstream tablet. [In fact] Reviewers say the iPad with Retina Display is still the best. [However] The display of the Google Nexus tablet trumps even the iPad's stunning screen.*

The following transitional expressions (see Chapter 5, Figure 5.6 for a complete list) enable you to show readers how you are developing your ideas:

To present additional thoughts: *additionally, again, also, moreover, furthermore*

To suggest cause and effect: *accordingly, as a result, consequently, therefore*

To contrast ideas: *at the same time, but, however, on the contrary, though, yet*

To show time and order: *after, before, first, finally, now, previously, then, to conclude*

To clarify points: *for example, for instance, in other words, that is, thus*

In using these expressions, recognize that they do not have to sit at the head of a sentence. Listen to the rhythm of the sentence, and place the expression where a natural pause occurs. If you are unsure about the placement of a transitional expression, position it at the beginning of the sentence. Used appropriately, transitional expressions serve readers as guides; misused or overused, they can be as distracting and frustrating as too many road signs on a highway.

Headings.   Good headings are another structural cue that assists readers in comprehending the organization of a report. They highlight major ideas, allowing busy readers to see the big picture at a glance. Moreover, headings provide resting points for the mind and for the eye, breaking up large chunks of text into manageable and inviting segments.

Report writers may use functional or talking headings, examples of which are summarized in Figure 12.8. Functional headings show the outline of a report but provide little insight for readers. Functional headings are useful for routine reports. They are also appropriate for sensitive topics that might provoke emotional reactions. By keeping the headings general, experienced writers hope to minimize reader opposition or response to controversial subjects.

Talking headings provide more information and spark interest. Unless carefully written, however, talking headings can fail to reveal the organization of a report. With some planning, though, headings can combine the best attributes of both functional and talking, as Figure 12.8 shows.

The best strategy for creating helpful talking headings is to write a few paragraphs first and then generate a talking heading that covers both paragraphs. To create the most effective headings, follow a few basic guidelines:

- **Use appropriate heading levels.** The position and format of a heading indicate its level of importance and relationship to other points. Figure 12.9 illustrates and discusses a commonly used heading format for business reports. For an overview of alphanumeric and decimal outlines, please see page 155.

- **Capitalize and emphasize carefully**. Most writers use all capital letters (without underlines) for main titles, such as the report, chapter, and unit titles. For first- and second-level headings, they capitalize only the first letter of main words such as nouns, verbs, adjectives, adverbs, names, and so on. Articles (*a, an, the*), conjunctions (*and, but, or, nor*), and prepositions with three or fewer letters (*in, to, by, for*) are not capitalized unless they appear at the beginning or ending of the heading. For additional emphasis, most writers use a bold font, as shown in Figure 12.9.

- **Try to balance headings within levels.** Although it may not be always possible, attempt to create headings that are grammatically similar at a given level. For example, *Developing Product Teams* and *Presenting Plan to Management* are balanced, but *Development of Product Teams* and *Presenting Plan to Management* are not.

- **For short reports use first-level or first- and second-level headings.** Many business reports contain only one or two levels of headings. For such reports use first-level headings (centered, bolded) and, if needed, second-level headings (flush left, bolded). See Figure 12.9.

- **Include at least one heading per report page, but don't end the page with a heading.** Headings increase the readability and attractiveness of report pages. Use at least one per page to break up blocks of text. Move a heading that is separated from the text that follows from the bottom of the page to the top of the following page.

- **Apply punctuation correctly.** Omit end punctuation in first- and second-level headings. End punctuation is required in third-level headings because they are capitalized and punctuated like sentences. Proper nouns (names) are capitalized in third-level headings as they would be in a sentence.

- **Keep headings short but clear.** One-word headings are emphatic but not always clear. For example, the heading *Budget* does not adequately describe figures for a summer project involving student interns for an oil company in Texas. Try to keep your headings brief (no more than eight words), but make sure they are understandable. Experiment with headings that concisely tell who, what, when, where, and why.

Figure 12.9 | Levels of Headings in Reports

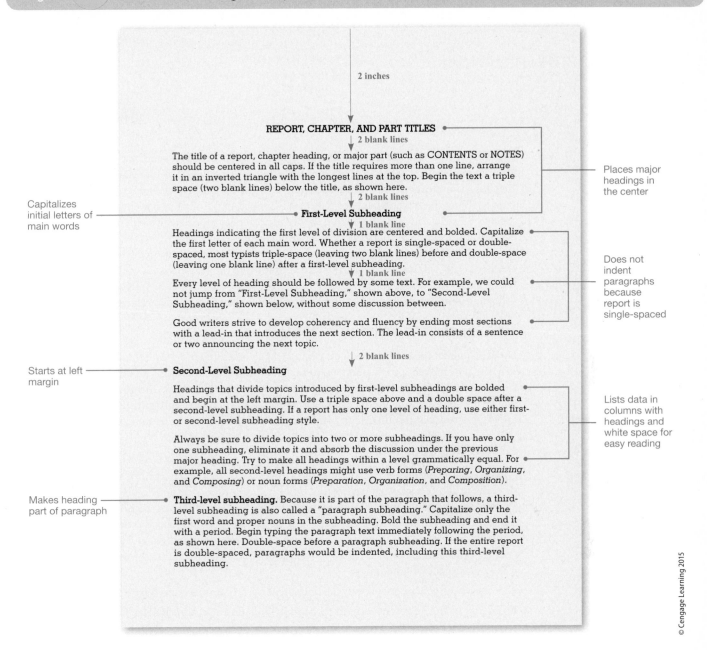

Capitalizes initial letters of main words

Starts at left margin

Makes heading part of paragraph

2 inches

REPORT, CHAPTER, AND PART TITLES
2 blank lines

The title of a report, chapter heading, or major part (such as CONTENTS or NOTES) should be centered in all caps. If the title requires more than one line, arrange it in an inverted triangle with the longest lines at the top. Begin the text a triple space (two blank lines) below the title, as shown here.
2 blank lines

First-Level Subheading
1 blank line

Headings indicating the first level of division are centered and bolded. Capitalize the first letter of each main word. Whether a report is single-spaced or double-spaced, most typists triple-space (leaving two blank lines) before and double-space (leaving one blank line) after a first-level subheading.
1 blank line

Every level of heading should be followed by some text. For example, we could not jump from "First-Level Subheading," shown above, to "Second-Level Subheading," shown below, without some discussion between.

Good writers strive to develop coherency and fluency by ending most sections with a lead-in that introduces the next section. The lead-in consists of a sentence or two announcing the next topic.
2 blank lines

Second-Level Subheading

Headings that divide topics introduced by first-level subheadings are bolded and begin at the left margin. Use a triple space above and a double space after a second-level subheading. If a report has only one level of heading, use either first- or second-level subheading style.

Always be sure to divide topics into two or more subheadings. If you have only one subheading, eliminate it and absorb the discussion under the previous major heading. Try to make all headings within a level grammatically equal. For example, all second-level headings might use verb forms (*Preparing*, *Organizing*, and *Composing*) or noun forms (*Preparation*, *Organization*, and *Composition*).

Third-level subheading. Because it is part of the paragraph that follows, a third-level subheading is also called a "paragraph subheading." Capitalize only the first word and proper nouns in the subheading. Bold the subheading and end it with a period. Begin typing the paragraph text immediately following the period, as shown here. Double-space before a paragraph subheading. If the entire report is double-spaced, paragraphs would be indented, including this third-level subheading.

Places major headings in the center

Does not indent paragraphs because report is single-spaced

Lists data in columns with headings and white space for easy reading

© Cengage Learning 2015

Writing Short Informational Reports

LEARNING OBJECTIVE **4**
Write short informational reports that describe routine tasks.

Now that we have covered the basics of gathering, interpreting, and organizing data, we are ready to put it all together into short informational or analytical reports. Informational reports often describe periodic, recurring activities (such as monthly sales or weekly customer calls) as well as situational, nonrecurring events (such as trips, conferences, and progress on special projects). Short informational reports may also include summaries of longer publications. What all these reports have in common is delivering information to readers who do not have to be persuaded. Informational report readers usually are neutral or receptive.

You can expect to write many informational reports as an entry-level or middle-management employee. Because these reports generally deliver nonsensitive data and,

"We believe that the traditional methods of communicating government financial information—through reams of audited financial statements that have little relevance to the taxpayer—must be supplemented by government financial reporting that expresses complex financial details in an understandable form."[11]

—RELMOND VAN DANIKER, *executive director of the Association of Government Accountants (AGA)*

therefore, will not upset the reader, they are organized directly. Often, they need little background material or introductory comments because readers are familiar with the topics. Although they are generally conversational and informal, informational reports should not be so casual that the reader struggles to find the important points. Main points must be immediately visible. Headings, lists, bulleted items, and other graphic design elements, as well as clear organization, enable readers to grasp major ideas immediately.

The lessons that you have learned about conciseness, clarity, courtesy, and effective writing in general throughout earlier chapters apply to report writing as well. After all, competent reports can boost your visibility in the company and promote your advancement. The following pointers on design features and techniques can assist you in improving your reports.

Effective Document Design

Desktop publishing packages, sophisticated word processing programs, and high-quality laser printers now make it possible for you to turn out professional-looking documents and promotional materials. Resist the temptation, however, to overdo it by incorporating too many features in one document. The top ten design tips summarized in Figure 12.10 will help you apply good sense and solid design principles in "publishing" your documents.

Summaries

A summary compresses the main points from a book, report, article, website, meeting, or convention. A summary saves time by reducing a report or article by 85 to 95 percent. Employees are sometimes asked to write summaries that condense technical reports, periodical articles, or books so that their staff or superiors may grasp the main ideas quickly. Students may be asked to write summaries of articles, chapters, or books to sharpen their writing skills and to confirm their knowledge of reading assignments. In writing a summary, follow these general guidelines:

- Present the goal or purpose of the document being summarized. Why was it written?
- Highlight the research methods (if appropriate), findings, conclusions, and recommendations.
- Omit illustrations, examples, and references.
- Organize for readability by including headings and bulleted or enumerated lists.
- Include your reactions or an overall evaluation of the document if asked to do so.

An *executive summary* summarizes a long report, proposal, or business plan. It concentrates on what management needs to know from a longer report. How to prepare an executive summary is covered in Chapter 13 on p. 470.

Periodic (Activity) Reports

Most businesses—especially larger ones—require *periodic reports* (sometimes called *activity reports*) to keep management informed of operations. These recurring reports are written at regular intervals—weekly, monthly, yearly—so that management can monitor business strategies and, if necessary, remedy any problems. Some periodic reports simply contain figures, such as sales volume, number and kind of customer-service calls, shipments delivered, accounts payable, and personnel data. More challenging periodic reports require descriptions

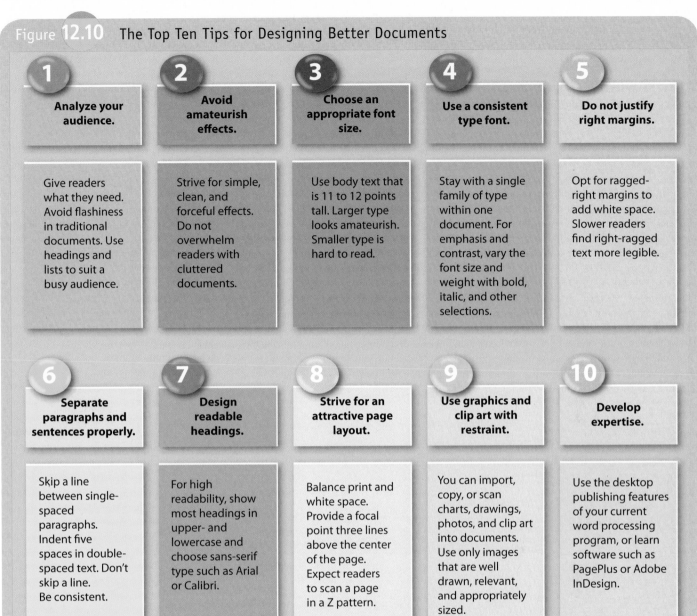

Figure 12.10 The Top Ten Tips for Designing Better Documents

1
Analyze your audience.

Give readers what they need. Avoid flashiness in traditional documents. Use headings and lists to suit a busy audience.

2
Avoid amateurish effects.

Strive for simple, clean, and forceful effects. Do not overwhelm readers with cluttered documents.

3
Choose an appropriate font size.

Use body text that is 11 to 12 points tall. Larger type looks amateurish. Smaller type is hard to read.

4
Use a consistent type font.

Stay with a single family of type within one document. For emphasis and contrast, vary the font size and weight with bold, italic, and other selections.

5
Do not justify right margins.

Opt for ragged-right margins to add white space. Slower readers find right-ragged text more legible.

6
Separate paragraphs and sentences properly.

Skip a line between single-spaced paragraphs. Indent five spaces in double-spaced text. Don't skip a line. Be consistent.

7
Design readable headings.

For high readability, show most headings in upper- and lowercase and choose sans-serif type such as Arial or Calibri.

8
Strive for an attractive page layout.

Balance print and white space. Provide a focal point three lines above the center of the page. Expect readers to scan a page in a Z pattern.

9
Use graphics and clip art with restraint.

You can import, copy, or scan charts, drawings, photos, and clip art into documents. Use only images that are well drawn, relevant, and appropriately sized.

10
Develop expertise.

Use the desktop publishing features of your current word processing program, or learn software such as PagePlus or Adobe InDesign.

© Cengage Learning 2015

and discussions of activities. In preparing a narrative description of their activities, employees writing periodic reports usually do the following:

- Summarize regular activities and events performed during the reporting period
- Describe irregular events deserving the attention of management
- Highlight special needs and problems

Managers naturally want to know that routine activities are progressing normally. Employees today enjoy a great deal of independence and shoulder much responsibility due to flattened hierarchies on the job. They often work flexible hours in far-flung locations. Keeping track of their activities and the tasks they were assigned is crucial in such an environment. Routine reports are typically sent by e-mail and may take the form of efficient bulleted lists without commentary.

Figure 12.11 shows a weekly activity report prepared by Siddharth Singh, a senior Web producer at the information technology firm Sygnal Macro in Silicon Valley. Sid is responsible for his firm's Web presence in Asian countries or territories, mainly Japan, China,

Figure **12.11** Periodic (Activity) Report

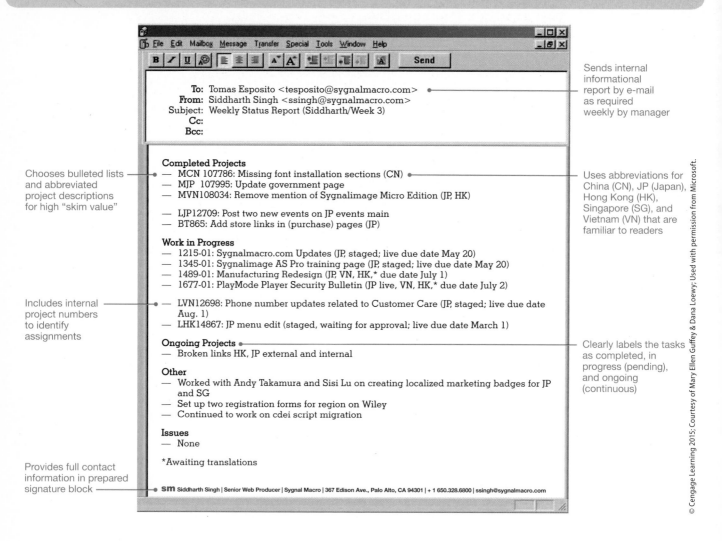

Sends internal informational report by e-mail as required weekly by manager

Chooses bulleted lists and abbreviated project descriptions for high "skim value"

Uses abbreviations for China (CN), JP (Japan), Hong Kong (HK), Singapore (SG), and Vietnam (VN) that are familiar to readers

Includes internal project numbers to identify assignments

Clearly labels the tasks as completed, in progress (pending), and ongoing (continuous)

Provides full contact information in prepared signature block

© Cengage Learning 2015; Courtesy of Mary Ellen Guffey & Dana Loewy; Used with permission from Microsoft.

To: Tomas Esposito <tesposito@sygnalmacro.com>
From: Siddharth Singh <ssingh@sygnalmacro.com>
Subject: Weekly Status Report (Siddharth/Week 3)
Cc:
Bcc:

Completed Projects
— MCN 107786: Missing font installation sections (CN)
— MJP 107995: Update government page
— MVN108034: Remove mention of Sygnalimage Micro Edition (JP, HK)

— LJP12709: Post two new events on JP events main
— BT865: Add store links in (purchase) pages (JP)

Work in Progress
— 1215-01: Sygnalmacro.com Updates (JP, staged; live due date May 20)
— 1345-01: Sygnalimage AS Pro training page (JP, staged; live due date May 20)
— 1489-01: Manufacturing Redesign (JP, VN, HK,* due date July 1)
— 1677-01: PlayMode Player Security Bulletin (JP live, VN, HK,* due date July 2)

— LVN12698: Phone number updates related to Customer Care (JP, staged; live due date Aug. 1)
— LHK14867: JP menu edit (staged, waiting for approval; live due date March 1)

Ongoing Projects
— Broken links HK, JP external and internal

Other
— Worked with Andy Takamura and Sisi Lu on creating localized marketing badges for JP and SG
— Set up two registration forms for region on Wiley
— Continued to work on cdei script migration

Issues
— None

*Awaiting translations

sm Siddharth Singh | Senior Web Producer | Sygnal Macro | 367 Edison Ave., Palo Alto, CA 94301 | + 1 650.328.6800 | ssingh@sygnalmacro.com

---

Hong Kong, and Vietnam. In his weekly reports to his supervisor, Tomas Esposito, Sid neatly divides his projects into three categories: *completed*, *in progress*, and *ongoing*. *In progress* means the task is not yet completed, or pending. *Ongoing* refers to continuous tasks such as regular maintenance. Tomas, the manager, then combines the activity reports from all his subordinates into a separate periodic report detailing the department's activities to send to his superiors.

Sid justifies the use of jargon, the lack of a salutation and complimentary close, and ultrashort bulleted items as follows: "We e-mail our reports internally, so some IT jargon can be expected. The readers will understand it. Tomas and upper management all want reporting to be brief and to the point. Bullets fit us just fine." Periodic reports ensure that information within the company flows steadily and that supervisors know the status of current and pending projects. This efficient information flow is all the more important because Sid works at home two days a week to spend time with his young children. Several of his coworkers also telecommute.

Trip, Convention, and Conference Reports

Employees sent on business trips or to conventions and conferences typically must submit reports when they return. Organizations want to know that their money was well spent in funding the travel. These reports inform management about new procedures, equipment, and laws as well as supply information affecting products, operations, and service.

© Richard Levine/Alamy

Online music service Pandora has revolutionized radio by playing only the tunes that listeners want. The company's high-tech Music Genome Project acts as a personalized music search engine, churning out playlists that match the artists and genres that users say they like. Simply enter the name of a favorite song or artist, and Pandora plays hundreds of similar-sounding tunes and bands, guaranteeing total radio listening satisfaction. To keep investors informed on the company's growth, managers at Pandora issue monthly progress reports. What information might business communicators want to include in a periodic activity report for Pandora investors?[12]

The hardest parts of writing these reports are selecting the most relevant material and organizing it coherently. Generally, it is best not to use chronological sequencing (*in the morning we did X, at lunch we heard Y, and in the afternoon we did Z*). Instead, you should focus on three to five topics in which your reader will be interested. These items become the body of the report. Then simply add an introduction and a closing, and your report is organized. Here is a general outline for trip, conference, and convention reports:

- Begin by identifying the event (exact date, name, and location) and previewing the topics to be discussed.

- Summarize in the body three to five main points that might benefit the reader.

- Itemize your expenses, if requested, on a separate sheet.

- Close by expressing appreciation, suggesting action to be taken, or synthesizing the value of the trip or event.

Joshua Maddison was recently named employment coordinator in the Human Resources Department of an electronics appliance manufacturer headquartered in central Ohio. Recognizing his lack of experience in interviewing job applicants, he asked permission to attend a one-day conference on the topic. His boss, Emma Paige, encouraged Joshua to attend, saying, "We all need to brush up on our interviewing techniques. Come back and tell us what you learned." When he returned, Joshua wrote the conference report shown in Figure 12.12. Here is how he described its preparation: "I know my boss values brevity, so I worked hard to make my report no more than a page and a quarter. The conference saturated me with great ideas, far too many to cover in one brief report. So, I decided to discuss three topics that would be most useful to our staff. Although I had to be brief, I nonetheless wanted to provide as many details—especially about common interviewing mistakes—as possible. By the third draft, I had compressed my ideas into a manageable size without sacrificing any of the meaning."

Progress and Interim Reports

Continuing projects often require progress or interim reports to describe their status. These reports may be external (advising customers regarding the headway of their projects) or internal (informing management of the status of activities). Progress reports typically follow this pattern of development:

- Specify in the opening the purpose and nature of the project.

- Provide background information if the audience requires filling in.

- Describe the work completed.

Figure **12.12** Conference Report

//TriCom
Total HR Services
Interoffice Memo

DATE: April 22, 2015

TO: Emma Paige

FROM: Joshua Maddison *J.M.*

SUBJECT: Conference on Employment Interviews

I enjoyed attending the "Interviewing People" training conference sponsored by the National Business Foundation. This one-day meeting, held in Columbus on April 19, provided excellent advice that will help us strengthen our interviewing techniques. Although the conference covered many topics, this report concentrates on three areas: structuring the interview, avoiding common mistakes, and responding to new legislation.

Identifies topic and previews how the report is organized

Structuring the Interview

Job interviews usually have three parts. The opening establishes a friendly rapport with introductions, a few polite questions, and an explanation of the purpose for the interview. The body of the interview consists of questions controlled by the interviewer. The interviewer has three goals: (a) educating the applicant about the job, (b) eliciting information about the applicant's suitability for the job, and (c) promoting goodwill about the organization. In closing, the interviewer should encourage the applicant to ask questions, summarize main points, and indicate what actions will follow.

Sets off major topics with centered headings

Avoiding Common Mistakes

Probably the most interesting and practical part of the conference centered on common mistakes made by interviewers, some of which I summarize here:

1. <u>Not taking notes at each interview.</u> Recording important facts enables you to remember the first candidate as easily as you remember the last—and all those in between.

2. <u>Not testing the candidate's communication skills.</u> To be able to evaluate a candidate's ability to express ideas, ask the individual to explain some technical jargon from his or her current position.

3. <u>Having departing employees conduct the interviews for their replacements.</u> Departing employees may be unreliable as interviewers because they tend to hire candidates not quite as strong as they are.

4. <u>Failing to check references.</u> As many as 45 percent of all résumés may contain falsified data. The best way to check references is to network: ask the person whose name has been given to suggest the name of another person.

Covers facts that will most interest and help reader

Emma Paige   Page 2   April 22, 2015

Responding to New Legislation

Current federal provisions of the Americans With Disabilities Act prohibit interviewers from asking candidates—or even their references—about candidates' disabilities. A question we frequently asked ("Do you have any physical limitations which would prevent you from performing the job for which you are applying?") would now break the law. Interviewers must also avoid asking about medical history; prescription drug use; prior workers' compensation claims; work absenteeism due to illness; and past treatment for alcoholism, drug use, or mental illness.

Sharing This Information

Concludes with offer to share information

This conference provided me with valuable training that I would like to share with other department members at a future staff meeting. Let me know when it can be scheduled.

© Cengage Learning 2015

- Explain the work currently in progress, including personnel, activities, methods, and locations.
- Describe current problems and anticipate future problems and possible remedies.
- Discuss future activities and provide the expected completion date.

As a location manager for Eagle Video Productions, Olivia Nevaeh frequently writes progress reports, such as the one shown in Figure 12.13. Producers want to know what she is doing, and a phone call does not provide a permanent record. Here is how she described the reasoning behind her progress report: "I usually include background information in my reports because a director does not always know or remember exactly what specifications I was given for a location search. Then I try to hit the high points of what I have completed and what I plan to do next, without getting bogged down in tiny details. Although it would be easier to skip them, I have learned to be up front with any problems that I anticipate. I do not tell how to solve the problems, but I feel duty-bound to at least mention them."

Figure **12.13** Progress Report

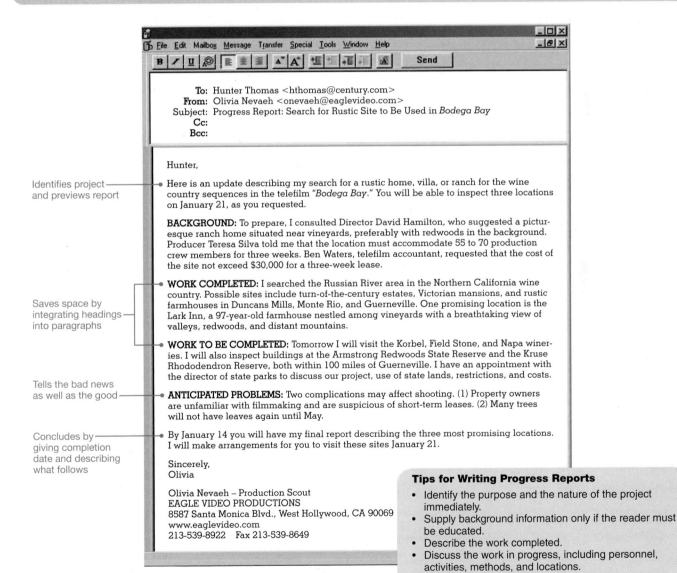

Identifies project and previews report

Saves space by integrating headings into paragraphs

Tells the bad news as well as the good

Concludes by giving completion date and describing what follows

Tips for Writing Progress Reports
- Identify the purpose and the nature of the project immediately.
- Supply background information only if the reader must be educated.
- Describe the work completed.
- Discuss the work in progress, including personnel, activities, methods, and locations.
- Identify problems and possible remedies.
- Consider future activities.
- Close by telling the expected date of completion.

Investigative Reports

Investigative reports deliver data for specific situations—without offering interpretations or recommendations. These nonrecurring reports are generally arranged using the direct strategy with three segments: introduction, body, and summary. The body—which includes the facts, findings, or discussion—may be organized by time, component, importance, criteria, or convention. What is important is dividing the topic into logical segments—say, three to five areas that are roughly equal and do not overlap.

The subject matter of the report usually suggests the best way to divide or organize it. Abby Gabriel, an information specialist for a Minneapolis health care consulting firm, was given the task of researching and writing an investigative report for St. John's Hospital. Her assignment: study the award-winning patient service program at Good Samaritan Hospital and report how it improved its patient satisfaction rating from 6.2 to 7.8 in just one year. Abby collected data and then organized her findings into four parts: management training, employee training, patient services, and follow-up program. Although we do not show Abby's complete report here, you can see a similar informational report in Chapter 11, Figure 11.3.

Whether you are writing a periodic, trip, conference, progress, or investigative report, you will want to review the suggestions found in the following checklist.

CHECKLIST ▶▶
Writing Informational Reports

Introduction

- **Begin directly.** Identify the report and its purpose.

- **Provide a preview.** If the report is over a page long, give the reader a brief overview of its organization.

- **Supply background data selectively.** When readers are unfamiliar with the topic, briefly fill in the necessary details.

- **Divide the topic.** Strive to group the facts or findings into three to five roughly equal segments that do not overlap.

Body

- **Arrange the subtopics logically.** Consider organizing by time, component, importance, criteria, or convention.

- **Use clear headings.** Supply functional or talking headings (at least one per page) that describe each important section.

- **Determine degree of formality.** Use an informal, conversational writing style unless the audience expects a more formal tone.

- **Enhance readability with graphic highlighting.** Make liberal use of bullets, numbered and lettered lists, headings, underlined items, and white space.

Summary/Concluding Remarks

- **When necessary, summarize the report.** Briefly review the main points and discuss what action will follow.

- **Offer a concluding thought.** If relevant, express appreciation or describe your willingness to provide further information.

REALITY CHECK: **Love It or Hate It, Skillful Report Writing Is Essential**

"Report-writing skills are crucial to communicating your research, ideas, and recommendations. Losing the gems of months of research in confusing, convoluted prose helps neither you nor your readers. The way you write can be more important than what you write. An instantly readable report will usually have more impact than one that is difficult to decipher."[13]

—ROB ASHTON, *CEO of Emphasis, report-writing expert and coach*

Preparing Short Analytical Reports

Analytical reports differ significantly from informational reports. Although both seek to collect and present data clearly, analytical reports also evaluate the data and typically try to persuade the reader to accept the conclusions and act on the recommendations. Informational reports emphasize facts; analytical reports emphasize reasoning and conclusions.

For some readers you may organize analytical reports directly with the conclusions and recommendations near the beginning. Directness is appropriate when the reader has confidence in the writer, based on either experience or credentials. Frontloading the recommendations also works when the topic is routine or familiar and the reader is supportive.

Directness can backfire, though. If you announce the recommendations too quickly, the reader may immediately object to a single idea. You may have had no suspicion that this idea would trigger a negative reaction. Once the reader is opposed, changing an unfavorable mindset may be difficult or impossible. A reader may also believe that you have oversimplified or overlooked something significant if you lay out all the recommendations before explaining how you arrived at them. When you must lead the reader through the process of discovering the solution or recommendation, use the indirect strategy: present conclusions and recommendations last.

Most analytical reports answer questions about specific problems and aid in decision making. How can we use social media most effectively? Should we close the El Paso plant? Should we buy or lease company cars? How can we improve customer service? Three categories of analytical reports answer business questions: justification/recommendation reports, feasibility reports, and yardstick reports. Because these reports all solve problems, the categories are not mutually exclusive. What distinguishes them are their goals and organization.

Justification/Recommendation Reports

Both managers and employees must occasionally write reports that justify or recommend something, such as buying equipment, changing a procedure, hiring an employee, consolidating departments, or investing funds. These reports may also be called *internal proposals* because their persuasive nature is similar to that of external proposals (presented in Chapter 13). Large organizations sometimes prescribe how these reports should be organized; they use forms with conventional headings. When you are free to select an organizational plan yourself, however, let your audience and topic determine your choice of the direct or indirect strategy.

Direct Strategy. For nonsensitive topics and recommendations that will be agreeable to readers, you can organize directly according to the following sequence:

- Identify the problem or need briefly.
- Announce the recommendation, solution, or action concisely and with action verbs.

- Explain more fully the benefits of the recommendation or steps necessary to solve the problem.

- Include a discussion of pros, cons, and costs.

- Conclude with a summary specifying the recommendation and necessary action.

Indirect Strategy.   When a reader may oppose a recommendation or when circumstances suggest caution, do not rush to reveal your recommendation. Consider using the following sequence for an indirect approach to your recommendations:

- Refer to the problem in general terms, not to your recommendation, in the subject line.

- Describe the problem or need your recommendation addresses. Use specific examples, supporting statistics, and authoritative quotes to lend credibility to the seriousness of the problem.

- Discuss alternative solutions, beginning with the least likely to succeed.

- Present the most promising alternative (your recommendation) last.

- Show how the advantages of your recommendation outweigh its disadvantages.

- Summarize your recommendation. If appropriate, specify the action it requires.

- Ask for authorization to proceed if necessary.

Alexis D'Amico, an executive assistant at a large petroleum and mining company in Grand Prairie, Texas, received a challenging research assignment. Her boss, the director of Human Resources, asked her to investigate ways to persuade employees to quit smoking. Here is how she described her task: "We banned smoking many years ago inside our buildings and on the premises, but we never tried very hard to get smokers to actually kick their habits. My job was to gather information about the problem and learn how other companies have helped workers stop smoking. The report would go to my boss, but I knew he would pass it along to the management council for approval."

Continuing her explanation, Alexis said, "If the report were just for my boss, I would put my recommendation right up front, because I'm sure he would support it. But the management council is another story. They need persuasion because of the costs involved—and because some of them are smokers. Therefore, I put the alternative I favored last. To gain credibility, I footnoted my sources. I had enough material for a ten-page report, but I kept it to two pages in keeping with our company report policy." Alexis chose MLA style to document her sources. A long report that uses the APA style is shown in Chapter 13.

Alexis single-spaced her report, shown in Figure 12.14, because her company prefers this style. Some companies prefer the readability of double spacing. Be sure to check with your organization for its preference before printing your reports.

Feasibility Reports

Feasibility reports examine the practicality and advisability of following a course of action. They answer this question: Will this plan or proposal work? Feasibility reports typically are internal reports written to advise on matters such as consolidating departments, offering a wellness program to employees, or hiring an outside firm to handle a company's accounting or social media presence. These reports may also be written by consultants called in to investigate a problem. The focus of these reports is on the decision: rejecting or proceeding with the proposed option. Because your role is not to persuade the reader to accept the decision, you will want to present the decision immediately. In writing feasibility reports, consider these suggestions:

- Announce your decision immediately.

- Provide a description of the background and problem necessitating the proposal.

- Discuss the benefits of the proposal.

- Describe the problems that may result.

- Calculate the costs associated with the proposal, if appropriate.

- Show the time frame necessary for implementing the proposal.

Figure 12.14 Justification/Recommendation Report, MLA Style

DATE: October 11, 2015

TO: Jackson Gill, Director, Human Resources

FROM: Alexis D'Amico, Executive Assistant A.D

SUBJECT: Smoking Cessation Programs for Employees

At your request, I have examined measures that encourage employees to quit smoking. As company records show, approximately 23 percent of our employees still smoke, despite the antismoking and clean-air policies we adopted in 2013. To collect data for this report, I studied professional and government publications; I also inquired at companies and clinics about stop-smoking programs.

This report presents data describing the significance of the problem, three alternative solutions, and a recommendation based on my investigation.

Significance of Problem: Health Care and Productivity Losses

Employees who smoke are costly to any organization. The following statistics show the effects of smoking for workers and for organizations:

- Absenteeism is 40 to 50 percent greater among smoking employees.
- Accidents are two to three times greater among smokers.
- Bronchitis, lung and heart disease, cancer, and early death are more frequent among smokers (Arhelger 4).

Although our clean-air policy prohibits smoking in the building, shop, and office, we have done little to encourage employees to stop smoking. Many workers still go outside to smoke at lunch and breaks. Other companies have been far more proactive in their attempts to stop employee smoking. Many companies have found that persuading employees to stop smoking was a decisive factor in reducing their health insurance premiums. Below is a discussion of three common stop-smoking measures tried by other companies, along with a projected cost factor for each (Rindfleisch 4).

Alternative 1: Literature and Events

The least expensive and easiest stop-smoking measure involves the distribution of literature, such as "The Ten-Step Plan" from Smokefree Enterprises and government pamphlets citing smoking dangers. Some companies have also sponsored events such as the Great American Smoke-Out, a one-day occasion intended to develop group spirit in spurring smokers to quit. "Studies show, however," says one expert, "that literature and company-sponsored events have little permanent effect in helping smokers quit" (Mendel 108).

    Cost: Negligible

Annotations (left margin):
- Avoids revealing recommendation immediately
- Uses headings that combine function and description
- Discusses least effective alternative first

Annotations (right margin):
- Introduces purpose of report, tells method of data collection, and previews organization
- Documents data sources for credibility, uses MLA style citing author and page number in the text

© Cengage Learning 2015

Daisy Manaia-Payton, human resources manager for a large public accounting firm in San Antonio, Texas, wrote the feasibility report shown in Figure 12.15 on page 445. Because she discovered that the company was losing time and money as a result of personal e-mail and Internet use by employees, she talked with the vice president, Ariana Devin, about the problem. Ariana didn't want Daisy to take time away from her job to investigate what other companies were doing to prevent this type of problem. Instead, she suggested that they hire a consultant to investigate what other companies were doing to prevent or limit personal e-mail and Internet use. The vice president then wanted to know whether the consultant's plan was feasible. Although Daisy's report is only one page long, it provides all the necessary information: background, benefits, employee acceptance, costs, and time frame.

Figure 12.14 (Continued)

Jackson Gill   October 11, 2015   Page 2

Alternative 2: Stop-Smoking Programs Outside the Workplace

Local clinics provide treatment programs in classes at their centers. Here in Houston we have the Smokers' Treatment Center, ACC Motivation Center, and New-Choice Program for Stopping Smoking. These behavior-modification stop-smoking programs are acknowledged to be more effective than literature distribution or incentive programs. However, studies of companies using off-workplace programs show that many employees fail to attend regularly and do not complete the programs.

Cost: $1,200 per employee, three-month individual program
       (New-Choice Program)
       $900 per employee, three-month group session

Highlights costs for easy comparison

Alternative 3: Stop-Smoking Programs at the Workplace

Many clinics offer workplace programs with counselors meeting employees in company conference rooms. These programs have the advantage of keeping a firm's employees together so that they develop a group spirit and exert pressure on each other to succeed. The most successful programs are on company premises and also on company time. Employees participating in such programs had a 72 percent greater success record than employees attending the same stop-smoking program at an outside clinic (Honda 35). A disadvantage of this arrangement, of course, is lost work time—amounting to about two hours a week for three months.

Arranges alternatives so that most effective is last

Cost: $900 per employee, two hours per week of release time for three months

Conclusions and Recommendation

Summarizes findings and ends with specific recommendation

Smokers require discipline, counseling, and professional assistance in kicking the nicotine habit, as explained at the American Cancer Society Web site ("Guide to Quitting Smoking"). Workplace stop-smoking programs on company time are more effective than literature, incentives, and off-workplace programs. If our goal is to reduce health care costs and lead our employees to healthful lives, we should invest in a workplace stop-smoking program with release time for smokers. Although the program temporarily reduces productivity, we can expect to recapture that loss in lower health care premiums and healthier employees.

Therefore, I recommend that we begin a stop-smoking treatment program on company premises with two hours per week of release time for participants for three months.

Reveals recommendation only after discussing all alternatives

---

Page 3

Lists all referen[ces] in MLA Style

Works Cited

Magazine — Arhelger, Zack. "The End of Smoking." *The World of Business* 5 Nov. 2014: 3-8. Print.

Website article — "Guide to Quitting Smoking." *The American Cancer Society.org.* Web. 27 Oct. 2014.

Journal article, database — Honda, Emeline Maude. "Managing Anti-Smoking Campaigns: The Case for Company Programs." *Management Quarterly* 32 (2013): 29-47. Web. 25 Oct. 2010.

Book — Mendel, I. A. *The Puff Stops Here.* Chicago: Science Publications, 2013. Print.

Newspaper article — Rindfleisch, Terry. "Smoke-Free Workplaces Can Help Smokers Quit, Expert Says." *Evening Chronicle* 4 Dec. 2014: 4+. Print.

© Cengage Learning 2015

Note: A long report showing APA citation style appears in Chapter 13.

Figure **12.15** Feasibility Report

DONALDSON CPA SERVICES LLP
MEMORANDUM

Date: May 12, 2015

To: Ariana Devin, Vice President

From: Daisy Manaia-Payton, Human Resources Manager *DMP*

Subject: Feasibility of a Social Media and Internet Monitoring Program

The plan calling for implementing an employee social media and Internet monitoring program is workable and could be fully implemented by July 1. This report discusses the background, benefits, problems, costs, and time frame.

Background: Current Misuse of Social Media and the Internet. We allow employees Internet access for job-related tasks. Many of us use social media, specifically Facebook, Twitter, and MySpace to communicate with our clients and the public. However, we know that many employees are using their access for personal reasons, resulting in lowered productivity, higher costs, and a strain on our network. We hired an outside consultant who suggested an Internet monitoring program.

Benefits of Plan: Appropriate Use of Social Media and the Internet. The proposed plan calls for installing Internet monitoring software such as EmployeeMonitoring, Perfect Keylogger, or Spector CNE. We would fully disclose to employees that this software will be tracking their online activity. We will also teach employees what social media and Internet use is appropriate. In addition to increased productivity, lowered costs, and improved network performance, this software will produce numerous other benefits. It can help protect our company against loss of intellectual property, trade secrets, and confidential information. The software will limit any liability for sexual harassment, workplace harassment, or cyberstalking. It will shield us against copyright infringement from employees who illegally download digital content.

Employee Acceptance. One of the biggest problems will be convincing employees to accept this new policy without feeling as if their privacy is being violated. However, our consultant can help us communicate the reasons for this policy in a way that employees will understand. In addition, adequate training will help employees understand the appropriate use of social media and the Internet.

Costs. Implementing the monitoring plan involves two direct costs. The first is the initial software cost of $400 to $900, depending on the package we choose. The second cost involves employee training and trainer fees. Initial training will cost about $1,000. However, the expenditures are within the project's budget.

Time Frame. Selecting the software package will take about two weeks. Preparing a training program will require another three weeks. Once the program is started, I expect a breaking-in period of at least three months. By July 1 the Internet monitoring program will be fully functional resulting in increased productivity, decreased costs, lowered liability, and improved network performance.

Please let me know by May 20 whether you would like additional information about social media and Internet monitoring programs.

Callouts (left):
Outlines organization of the report

Evaluates positive and negative aspects of proposal objectively

Callouts (right):
Reveals decision immediately

Describes problem and background

Presents costs and schedule; omits unnecessary summary

© Cengage Learning 2015

Yardstick Reports

Yardstick reports examine problems with two or more solutions. To determine the best solution, the writer establishes criteria by which to compare the alternatives. The criteria then act as a yardstick against which all the alternatives are measured, as shown in Figure 12.16. The yardstick approach is effective for companies that must establish specifications for equipment purchases and then compare each manufacturer's product with the established specs. The yardstick approach is also effective when exact specifications cannot be established.

For example, before Nissan Motor Company decided to produce a new Infiniti luxury SUV model in its existing plant in Smyrna (Tennessee), the auto manufacturer conducted an internal competition to find a suitable location. The No. 6 global carmaker evaluated several sites, including one in Japan. Nissan considered important criteria such as manufacturing

Figure **12.16** Yardstick Report

DATE: April 28, 2015

TO: Tony Marshall, Vice President

FROM: Maria Rios, Benefits Administrator *M.R.*

SUBJECT: Selecting Outplacement Services

Here is the report you requested April 1 investigating the possibility of CompuTech's use of outplacement services. It discusses the problem of counseling services for discharged staff and establishes criteria for selecting an outplacement agency. It then evaluates three prospective agencies and presents a recommendation based on that evaluation.

Introduces purpose and gives overview of report organization

Problem: Counseling Discharged Staff

Discusses background briefly because readers already know the problem

In an effort to reduce costs and increase competitiveness, CompuTech will begin a program of staff reduction that will involve releasing up to 20 percent of our workforce over the next 12 to 24 months. Many of these employees have been with us for ten or more years, and they are not being released for performance faults. These employees deserve a severance package that includes counseling and assistance in finding new careers.

Uses dual headings, giving function and description

Solution and Alternatives: Outplacement Agencies

Numerous outplacement agencies offer discharged employees counseling and assistance in locating new careers. This assistance minimizes not only the negative feelings related to job loss but also the very real possibility of litigation. Potentially expensive lawsuits have been lodged against some companies by unhappy employees who felt they were unfairly released.

Announces solution and the alternatives it presents

In seeking an outplacement agency, we should find one that offers advice to the sponsoring company as well as to dischargees. The law now requires certain procedures, especially in releasing employees over forty. CompuTech could unwittingly become liable to lawsuits because our managers are uninformed of these procedures. I have located three potential outplacement agencies appropriate to serve our needs: Gray & Associates, Right Access, and Careers Plus.

Establishing Criteria for Selecting Agency

Tells how criteria were selected

In order to choose among the three agencies, I established criteria based on professional articles, discussions with officials at other companies using outplacement agencies, and interviews with agencies. Here are the four groups of criteria I used in evaluating the three agencies:

Creates four criteria for use as yardstick in evaluating alternatives

1. Counseling services—including job search advice, résumé help, crisis management, corporate counseling, and availability of full-time counselors

2. Administrative and research assistance—including availability of administrative staff, librarian, and personal computers

3. Reputation—based on a telephone survey of former clients and listing with a professional association

4. Costs—for both group programs and executive services

© Cengage Learning 2015

costs (including currency fluctuations), the potential for high product quality, and the proximity to the market in the United States.[14]

The real advantage to yardstick reports is that alternatives can be measured consistently using the same criteria. Writers using a yardstick approach typically do the following:

- Begin by describing the problem or need.

- Explain possible solutions and alternatives.

- Establish criteria for comparing the alternatives; tell how the criteria were selected or developed.

- Discuss and evaluate each alternative in terms of the criteria.

- Draw conclusions and make recommendations.

Figure **12.16** (Continued)

Vice President Marshall   Page 2   April 28, 2015

Discussion: Evaluating Agencies by Criteria

Each agency was evaluated using the four criteria just described. Data comparing the first three criteria are summarized in Table 1.

Table 1

A COMPARISON OF SERVICES AND REPUTATIONS
FOR THREE LOCAL OUTPLACEMENT AGENCIES

	Gray & Associates	Right Access	Careers Plus
Counseling services			
Résumé advice	Yes	Yes	Yes
Crisis management	Yes	No	Yes
Corporate counseling	Yes	No	No
Full-time counselors	Yes	No	Yes
Administrative, research assistance			
Administrative staff	Yes	Yes	Yes
Librarian, research library	Yes	No	Yes
Personal computers	Yes	No	Yes
Listed by National Association of Career Consultants	Yes	No	Yes
Reputation (telephone survey of former clients)	Excellent	Good	Excellent

(annotation: Places table close to spot where it is first mentioned)

(annotation: Summarizes complex data in table for easy reading and reference)

Counseling Services

All three agencies offered similar basic counseling services with job-search and résumé advice. They differed, however, in three significant areas.

Right Access does not offer crisis management, a service that puts the discharged employee in contact with a counselor the same day the employee is released. Experts in the field consider this service especially important to help the dischargee begin "bonding" with the counselor immediately. Immediate counseling also helps the dischargee learn how to break the news to family members. Crisis management can be instrumental in reducing lawsuits because dischargees immediately begin to focus on career planning instead of concentrating on their pain and need for revenge. Moreover, Right Access does not employ full-time counselors; it hires part-timers according to demand. Industry authorities advise against using agencies whose staff members are inexperienced and employed on an "as-needed" basis.

(annotation: Highlights the similarities and differences among the alternatives)

In addition, neither Right Access nor Careers Plus offers regular corporate counseling, which I feel is critical in training our managers to conduct terminal interviews. Careers Plus, however, suggested that it could schedule special workshops if desired.

Administrative and Research Assistance

Both Gray & Associates and Careers Plus offer complete administrative services and personal computers. Dischargees have access to staff and equipment to assist them in their job searches. These agencies also provide research libraries, librarians, and databases of company information to help in securing interviews.

(annotation: Does not repeat obvious data from table)

© Cengage Learning 2015

Maria Rios, benefits administrator for computer manufacturer CompuTech, was called on to write the report in Figure 12.16 comparing outplacement agencies. These agencies counsel discharged employees and help them find new positions; fees are paid by the former employer. Maria knew that times were bad for CompuTech and that extensive downsizing would take place in the next two years. Her task was to compare outplacement agencies and recommend one to CompuTech.

After collecting information, Maria found that her biggest problem was organizing the data and developing a system for making comparisons. All the outplacement agencies she investigated seemed to offer the same basic package of services.

With the information she gathered about three outplacement agencies, she made a big grid listing the names of the agencies across the top. Down the side she listed general

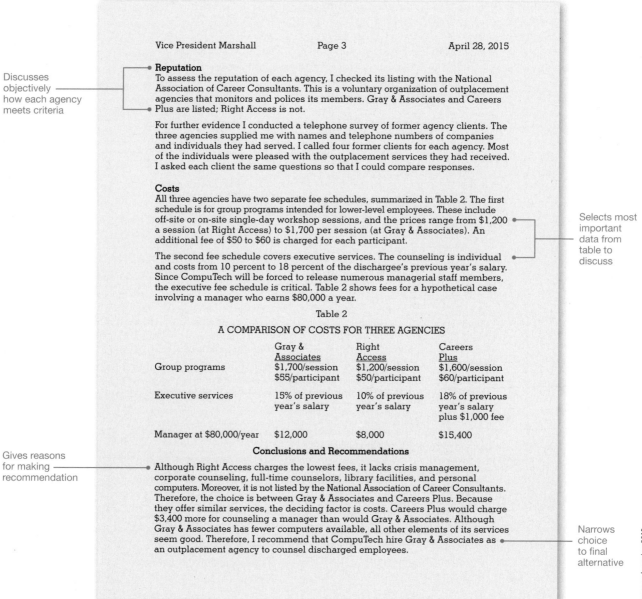

Figure 12.16 (Continued)

Discusses objectively how each agency meets criteria

Vice President Marshall   Page 3   April 28, 2015

Reputation

To assess the reputation of each agency, I checked its listing with the National Association of Career Consultants. This is a voluntary organization of outplacement agencies that monitors and polices its members. Gray & Associates and Careers Plus are listed; Right Access is not.

For further evidence I conducted a telephone survey of former agency clients. The three agencies supplied me with names and telephone numbers of companies and individuals they had served. I called four former clients for each agency. Most of the individuals were pleased with the outplacement services they had received. I asked each client the same questions so that I could compare responses.

Costs

All three agencies have two separate fee schedules, summarized in Table 2. The first schedule is for group programs intended for lower-level employees. These include off-site or on-site single-day workshop sessions, and the prices range from $1,200 a session (at Right Access) to $1,700 per session (at Gray & Associates). An additional fee of $50 to $60 is charged for each participant.

Selects most important data from table to discuss

The second fee schedule covers executive services. The counseling is individual and costs from 10 percent to 18 percent of the dischargee's previous year's salary. Since CompuTech will be forced to release numerous managerial staff members, the executive fee schedule is critical. Table 2 shows fees for a hypothetical case involving a manager who earns $80,000 a year.

Table 2

A COMPARISON OF COSTS FOR THREE AGENCIES

	Gray & Associates	Right Access	Careers Plus
Group programs	$1,700/session $55/participant	$1,200/session $50/participant	$1,600/session $60/participant
Executive services	15% of previous year's salary	10% of previous year's salary	18% of previous year's salary plus $1,000 fee
Manager at $80,000/year	$12,000	$8,000	$15,400

Gives reasons for making recommendation

Conclusions and Recommendations

Although Right Access charges the lowest fees, it lacks crisis management, corporate counseling, full-time counselors, library facilities, and personal computers. Moreover, it is not listed by the National Association of Career Consultants. Therefore, the choice is between Gray & Associates and Careers Plus. Because they offer similar services, the deciding factor is costs. Careers Plus would charge $3,400 more for counseling a manager than would Gray & Associates. Although Gray & Associates has fewer computers available, all other elements of its services seem good. Therefore, I recommend that CompuTech hire Gray & Associates as an outplacement agency to counsel discharged employees.

Narrows choice to final alternative

© Cengage Learning 2015

categories—such as services, costs, and reputation. Then she filled in the information for each agency. This grid, which began to look like a table, helped her organize all the bits and pieces of information. After studying the grid, she saw that all the information could be grouped into four categories: counseling services, administrative and research assistance, reputation, and costs. She made these the criteria she would use to compare agencies.

Next, Maria divided her grid into two parts, which became Table 1 and Table 2. In writing the report, she could have made each agency a separate heading, followed by a discussion of how it measured up to the criteria. Immediately, though, she saw how repetitious that would become. Therefore, she used the criteria as headings and discussed how each agency met each criterion—or failed to meet it. Making a recommendation was easy once Maria had made the tables and could see how the agencies compared.

Digital Slide Decks

In addition to print, many business writers deliver their reports as digital slideshows, also called slide decks. These slides can be sent by e-mail, embedded on the Web, or posted on a company intranet. If you research business topics online, look up Internet statistics, or, for example, visit certain WordPress blogs, you may see slide decks or sliders. When used in reporting, slide decks are heavier on text than bulleted presentation slides. However, any text typically appears in small chunks and in large print. Lively, copious photographs and other visuals make slide decks more inviting to read than print pages of dense report text are. See Chapter 14 for a discussion of slide presentations delivered orally.

Not surprisingly, communicators in marketing, tech fields, media, entertainment, and consulting are fond of using slide deck reports to summarize their statistics and other findings. Figure 12.17 shows several slides from global marketing company ExactTarget analyzing the Internet market in Germany. In their simplest form, slide decks can be PowerPoint, Keynote, and other presentation software files. The resulting documents can be exported as PDF, HTML, or image files, or animated and run as video clips. You may never need to produce slick slide decks like the ones created by ExactTarget because they require advanced expertise in graphic art design. However, you will encounter them more and more online.

Figure 12.17 Informal Reports Delivered as Slide Decks

Source: http://www.exacttarget.com/resource-center/digital-marketing/infographics/sff-german-digital-republic

© Cengage Learning 2015

CHECKLIST ▶▶

Writing Analytical Reports

Introduction

- **Identify the purpose of the report.** Explain why the report is being written.

- **Describe the significance of the topic.** Explain why the report is important.

- **Preview the organization of the report.** Especially for long reports, explain how the report will be organized.

- **Summarize the conclusions and recommendations for receptive audiences.** Use the direct strategy only if you have the confidence of the reader.

Findings

- **Discuss pros and cons.** In recommendation/justification reports, evaluate the advantages and disadvantages of each alternative. For unreceptive audiences consider placing the recommended alternative last.

- **Establish criteria to evaluate alternatives.** In yardstick reports, create criteria to use in measuring each alternative consistently.

- **Support the findings with evidence.** Supply facts, statistics, expert opinion, survey data, and other proof from which you can draw logical conclusions.

- **Organize the findings for logic and readability.** Arrange the findings around the alternatives or the reasons leading to the conclusion. Use headings, enumerations, lists, tables, and graphics to focus emphasis.

Conclusions/Recommendations

- **Draw reasonable conclusions from the findings.** Develop conclusions that answer the research question. Justify the conclusions with highlights from the findings.

- **Make recommendations, if asked.** For multiple recommendations prepare a list. Use action verbs. Explain fully the benefits of the recommendation or steps necessary to solve the problem or answer the question.

Your Turn: Applying Your Skills at Starbucks

Starbucks' success is due in no small measure to its CEO's unflagging drive to reinvent the company while mimicking an edgy "indie feel" of local coffeehouses.[15] To weather the economic crisis, Starbucks CEO Howard Schultz went back to basics. He turned to current Starbucks "partners" (employees) and asked them to envision a new, improved coffeehouse with a distinct neighborhood vibe. This experiment resulted in several Seattle concept stores under different names, not the famous Starbucks banner. These coffeehouses featured reused, recycled, and locally sourced design elements and furnishings. They were inspired by Starbucks and sold Starbucks brand products, but the materials were raw and repurposed to create the vibe of a neighborhood store. Three years later, it turns out the coffee giant used these overhauled neighborhood coffeehouses in Seattle as a "learning environment" to invigorate its core brand and returned at least one of them, 15th Ave Coffee & Tea, to the Starbucks fold.[16]

However, this concept of tailored, locally relevant stores that are intriguing yet also sustainable has culminated in Starbucks' latest "pilot program." The company, which designs all store locations strictly in-house, once again experimented with reclaimed materials and prefabricated components. The result? Starbucks' first modular drive-through and walk-up store was rolled out in Colorado.[17] The project combines environmental concern, "localism," and market growth while offering a low-cost, expandable platform.[18] Although the materials are standardized and prefabricated, the exterior materials are intended to blend into each particular environment. At 500 square feet, the diminutive building is designed to provide full Starbucks functionality and convenience. Best of all, it is LEED-certified. LEED, short for Leadership in Energy and Environmental Design, was established by the U.S. Green Building Council and applied originally to energy-efficient office buildings. Starbucks seems bent on leading the field in environmental stewardship.

© iStockphoto.com/Jeff Whyte

YOUR TASK. As assistant to Howard Schultz, you are asked to form a research team. Its purpose is to study the feasibility of new prefabricated LEED-certified Starbucks stores beyond Colorado. Prepare a feasibility report addressed to Howard Schultz that analyzes the suitability of a modular "mini Starbucks" in your town, city, or region. You would want to consider how such a new type of Starbucks could fit into a neighborhood you know well. The small modular stores could help Starbucks save power and decrease its carbon footprint. Some speculate that the company might eventually be able to move off the power grid in some locations.[19] Alternatively, you could explore Starbucks' Shared Planet initiatives and write an informational report that focuses on the company's environmental record.

Summary of Learning Objectives

1 Analyze, sort, and interpret statistical data and other information using tables, measures of central tendency (mean, median, and mode), and decision matrices. Report data are more meaningful when sorted into tables or when analyzed by mean (the arithmetic average), median (the midpoint in a group of figures), and mode (the most frequent response). Range represents a span between the highest and lowest figures. Grids help organize complex data into rows and columns. Decision matrices employ a special grid with weights to help decision makers choose objectively among complex options. Accuracy in applying statistical techniques is crucial to gain and maintain credibility with the reader.

Go to
www.cengagebrain.com
and use your access code to unlock valuable student resources.

2 Draw meaningful conclusions and make practical report recommendations after sound and valid analysis. Conclusions tell what the survey data mean—especially in relation to the original report problem. They interpret key findings and may attempt to explain what caused the report problem. They are usually enumerated. In reports that call for recommendations, writers make specific suggestions for actions that can solve the report problem. Recommendations should be feasible, practical, and potentially agreeable to the audience. They should all relate to the initial problem. Recommendations may be combined with conclusions.

3 Organize report data logically and provide reader cues to aid comprehension. Reports may be organized in many ways, including by (a) time (establishing a chronology or history of events), (b) component (discussing a problem by geography, division, or product), (c) importance (arranging data from most important to least important, or vice versa), (d) criteria (comparing items by standards), or (e) convention (using an already established grouping). To help guide the reader through the text, introductions, transitions, and headings serve as cues.

4 Write short informational reports that describe routine tasks. Periodic, trip, convention, progress, and investigative reports are examples of typical informational reports. Such reports include an introduction that may preview the report purpose and supply background data if necessary. The body of the report is generally divided into three to five segments that may be organized by time, component, importance, criteria, or convention. The body should include clear headings and may use an informal, conversational style unless the audience expects a more formal tone. The summary or conclusion reviews the main points and discusses the action that will follow. The conclusion may offer a final thought, express appreciation, or signal a willingness to provide further information. Like all professional business documents, a clear, concise, well-written report cements the writer's credibility with the audience. Because they are so important, reports require writers to apply all the writing techniques addressed in Chapters 4, 5, and 6.

5 Prepare short analytical reports that solve business problems. Typical analytical reports include justification/recommendation reports, feasibility reports, and yardstick reports. Justification/recommendation reports organized directly identify a problem, immediately announce a recommendation or solution, explain and discuss its merits, and summarize the action to be taken. Justification/recommendation reports organized indirectly describe a problem, discuss alternative solutions, prove the superiority of one solution, and ask for authorization to proceed with that solution. Feasibility reports study the advisability of following a course of action. They generally announce the author's proposal immediately. Then they describe the background of, advantages and disadvantages of, costs of, and time frame for implementing the proposal. Yardstick reports compare two or more solutions to a problem by measuring each against a set of established criteria. They usually describe a problem, explain possible solutions, establish criteria for comparing alternatives, evaluate each alternative in terms of the criteria, draw conclusions, and make recommendations. The advantage to yardstick reports is consistency in comparing alternatives. Increasingly, digital-age reports are delivered as slide decks rich in graphics and more text-dense than typical presentation slides. Most reports serve as a basis for decision making in business.

Chapter Review

1. What are the advantages of tables? (Obj. 1)

2. Calculate the mean, median, and mode for these figures: 4, 12, 12, 12, 20. (Obj. 1)

3. What are correlations? (Obj. 1)

4. Why is a decision matrix a valuable managerial tool? (Obj. 1)

5. How can you make your report conclusions as objective and bias-free as possible? (Obj. 2)

6. What is the difference between conclusions and recommendations, and what do business readers expect from a report writer's recommendations? (Obj. 2)

7. Name five methods for organizing report data. Be prepared to discuss each. (Obj. 3)

8. What three devices can report writers use to prevent readers from getting lost in the text? (Obj. 3)

9. Explain three types of report headings as well as their characteristics and uses. (Obj. 3)

10. Name at least four guidelines for creating effective headings, and be prepared to explain them (Obj. 3)

11. Name typical short informational reports and their overall purpose. (Obj. 4)

12. What should progress reports include? (Obj. 4)

13. When is the indirect strategy appropriate for justification/recommendation reports? (Obj. 5)

14. What is a feasibility report? Are such reports generally intended for internal or external audiences? (Obj. 5)

15. What are digital slide decks, and why are they becoming popular? (Obj. 5)

Critical Thinking

1. Paid survey sites such as Opinion Outpost and Ipsos i-Say offer gift cards and cash rewards to users for taking surveys about retailers, services, and products. MySurvey.com, Toluna.com, and others are even social networks. Users register, create a profile, and submit opinion surveys to earn points. How would you rate the value and credibility of such survey results? (Obj. 1)

2. When tabulating and analyzing data, you may discover relationships among two or more variables that help explain the findings. Can you trust these correlations and assume that their relationship is one of cause and effect? (Obj. 1)

3. How can you increase your chances that your report recommendations will be implemented? (Obj. 2)

4. What are the major differences between informational and analytical reports? (Objs. 4, 5)

5. **Ethical Issue:** You have learned that drawing conclusions involves subjectivity, although your goal is to remain objective. Even the most even-handed researchers bring their goals, background, and frame of reference to bear on the inferences they make. Consider the contentious issue of climate change. Some mainstream scientists now believe climate change to be real and induced by human activity. However, other scientists cast doubt on the extent to which global warming is the result of human activity and constitutes an imminent threat. How can something seemingly objectively measurable be so contentious? (Obj. 2)

Activities

12.1 Making Sense of the Three Ms (Obj. 1)

Nine homes recently sold in your community in the following order and for these amounts: $260,000; $360,000; $260,000; $280,000; $260,000; $320,000; $280,000; $420,000; and $260,000. Your boss, Tom DiFranco, a realtor with Sanford & Associates, wants you to compute the mean, median, and mode for this real estate market.

YOUR TASK. Compute the mean, median, and mode for the recently sold homes. Explain your analysis as well as the characteristics of each type of "average."

12.2 Analyzing Survey Results (Obj. 1)

Team

Your business communication class at South Bay College was asked by the college bookstore manager, Jim Duff, to conduct a survey. Concerned about the environment, Duff wants to learn students' reactions to eliminating plastic bags, of which the bookstore gives away 45,000 annually. Students answered questions about a number of proposals, resulting in the following raw data:

For major purchases the bookstore should:

	Agree	Undecided	Disagree
1. Continue to provide plastic bags	132	17	411
2. Provide no bags; encourage students to bring their own bags	414	25	121
3. Provide no bags; offer cloth bags at a reduced price (about $3)	357	19	184
4. Give a cloth bag with each major purchase, the cost to be included in registration fees	63	15	482

YOUR TASK. In groups of four or five, do the following:

a. Convert the data into a table (see Figure 12.1) with a descriptive title. Arrange the items in a logical sequence.

b. How could these survey data be cross-tabulated? Would cross-tabulation serve any purpose?

c. Given the conditions of this survey, name at least three conclusions that researchers could draw from the data.

d. Prepare three to five recommendations to be submitted to Mr. Duff. How could the bookstore implement them?

e. Role-play a meeting in which the recommendations and implementation plan are presented to Mr. Duff. One student plays the role of Mr. Duff; the remaining students play the role of the presenters.

12.3 Discerning Conclusions From Recommendations (Obj. 2)

A study led by psychologists at Kent State University examined empirical research on ten common learning techniques, such as highlighting text with markers and practice tests. For each technique, the researchers explored the assumptions underlying the strategy. They studied what empirical research has to teach us about actual effectiveness. They found that despite the prevalence of various study techniques such as highlighting text and writing summaries, many of these student-preferred strategies do not work very well.[20]

YOUR TASK. Based on the preceding facts, indicate whether the following statements are conclusions or recommendations:

a. Students are generally overconfident that their study strategies are effective.

b. Although it is a typical learning technique, writing summaries of assigned reading is not always a reliable study tool.

c. Instructors need to teach study skills to help students maximize their time and outcomes.

d. Highlighting text has little to offer in the way of subsequent performance.

e. Students should identify the main ideas in the text *before* highlighting to benefit from this technique.

f. Researchers found that many typical student study techniques were ineffective.

g. Students should consider techniques they have never tried before; for example, *interleaved practice,* which mixes different types of material or problems in a single study session.

12.4 Unsure About Which Laptop to Buy? Try a Decision Matrix (Objs. 1, 2)

You want to buy a low-cost laptop for your college work and consider price the most important feature. The sheer number of options in countless laptops overwhelms you.

YOUR TASK. Study Figure 12.3 on page 424 and change the weights in Table 2 to reflect your emphasis on low price, to which you will assign a factor of 10 because it is twice as important to you as unit weight, which receives a factor of 5. The hard drive size is likewise secondary to you, so you give it a 5 also. Last, you change battery life to a factor of 7 from 10 because it is less important than price, but more important than unit weight and hard drive size. Calculate the new scores. Which low-budget computer wins this time?

12.5 Buying Cool Wheels? Take a Decision Matrix for a Spin (Objs. 1, 2)

David, an outrigger canoe racer, needs to buy a new car. He wants a vehicle that will carry his disassembled boat and outrigger.

At the same time, he will need to travel long distances on business. His passion is soft-top sports cars, but he is also concerned about gas mileage. These four criteria are impossible to find in one vehicle.

David has the following choices:

- Station wagon
- SUV with or without a sunroof
- Four-door sedan, a high-miles-per-gallon "family car"
- Sports car, convertible

He wants to consider the following criteria:

- Price
- Ability to carry cargo such as a canoe
- Fuel efficiency
- Comfort over long distances
- Good looks and fun
- Quality build/manufacturer's reputation

YOUR TASK. Follow the steps outlined in Figure 12.3 to determine an assessment scale and to assign a score to each feature. Then, consider which weights are probably most important to David, given his needs. Calculate the totals to find the vehicle that's most suitable for David.

12.6 Organizing Data (Obj. 3)

Team

YOUR TASK. In groups of three to five, discuss how the findings in the following reports could be best organized. Consider these methods: time, component, importance, criteria, and convention.

a. A set of instructions described in a recommendation report about improved maintenance procedures on a highly sophisticated production line.

b. A weekly bulleted activity report sent by e-mail to a supervisor.

c. A report comparing the benefits of buying or leasing a fleet of electric vehicles. The report presents data on depreciation, upfront cost, maintenance, battery life, range on one charge, and other factors.

d. A progress report written by a team of researchers to their supervisor to keep the boss informed at each of the five project stages.

e. A report comparing the sales volume among the agents of a large national realtor based on the number of listings taken, number of listings sold, total sales in the agents' market areas, and more.

f. A recommendation report to be submitted to management presenting four building plans to improve access to your building, in compliance with federal regulations. The plans range considerably in feasibility and cost.

g. An investigative report describing a company's expansion plans in South America, Europe, Australia, and Southeast Asia.

h. An employee performance appraisal submitted annually.

12.7 Evaluating Headings and Titles (Obj. 3)

YOUR TASK. Identify the following report headings and titles as *functional*, *talking*, or *combination*. Discuss the usefulness and effectiveness of each.

a. Findings

b. How to Block Unwanted Calls to Smartphones

c. Disadvantages

d. Balancing Worker Productivity and Social Media Use

e. Case Study: America's Most Sustainable Company

f. Recommendations: Solving Our Applicant-Tracking Problem

g. Comparing Costs of Hiring Exempt and Nonexempt Employees

h. Budget

12.8 Executive Summary: Boiling Down the Facts for Your Boss (Obj. 4)

Web

Like many executives, your boss is too rushed to read long journal articles. However, she is eager to keep up with developments in her field. Assume she has asked you to help her stay abreast of research in her field. She asks you to submit to her one summary every month on an article of interest.

YOUR TASK. In your field of study, select a professional journal, such as the *Journal of Management*. Using an electronic database search or a Web search, look for articles in your target journal. Select an article that is at least five pages long and is interesting to you. Write an executive summary in memo format. Include an introduction that might begin with *As you requested, I am submitting this executive summary of . . . .* Identify the author, article title, journal, and date of publication. Explain what the author intended to do in the study or article. Summarize three or four of the most important findings of the study or article. Use descriptive rather than functional headings. Summarize any recommendations you make. Your boss would also like a concluding statement indicating your reaction to the article. Address your memo to Susan Wright.

12.9 Periodic Report: Keeping the Boss in the Loop (Obj. 4)

E-mail

You work hard at your job, but you rarely see your boss. He or she has asked to be informed of your activities and accomplishments and any problems you are encountering.

YOUR TASK. For a job that you currently hold or a previous one, describe your regular activities, discuss irregular events that management should be aware of, and highlight any special needs or problems you are having. If you don't have a job, communicate to your instructor your weekly or monthly activities as they are tied to your classes, homework, and writing assignments. Establish components or criteria such as those in the bulleted e-mail in Figure 12.11. Use the memo format or write an e-mail report in bullet form as shown in Figure 12.11. Address the memo or the e-mail report to your boss or, alternatively, to your instructor.

12.10 Progress Report: Providing a Project Update (Obj. 4)

E-mail

If you are writing a long report either for another course or for the long report assignment described in Chapter 13, you will want to keep your instructor informed of your progress.

YOUR TASK. Write a progress report informing your instructor of your work. Briefly describe the project (its purpose, scope, limitations, and methodology), work completed, work yet to be completed, problems encountered, future activities, and expected completion date. Address the e-mail report to your instructor. If your instructor allows, try your hand at the bulleted e-mail report introduced in Figure 12.11.

12.11 Progress Report: Is the End Near? (Obj. 4)

You have made an agreement with your parents (or spouse, partner, relative, or friend) that you would submit a progress report at this time.

YOUR TASK. Prepare a progress report in letter format. (a) Describe your headway toward your educational goal (such as employment, degree, or certificate); (b) summarize the work you have completed thus far; (c) discuss the work currently in progress, including your successes and anticipated obstacles; and (d) outline what you have left to complete.

12.12 Conference or Trip Report: Business and Pleasure (Obj. 4)

You have been sent to a meeting, conference, or seminar in an exotic spot at company expense.

YOUR TASK. From a business periodical, select an article describing a conference or meeting connected with your major area of study. The article must be at least 500 words long. Assume that you attended the meeting. Prepare a memo report to your supervisor.

12.13 Investigative Report: Attracting Newbie Bikers (Obj. 4)

[Web]

As a junior sales associate working for Chicago BMW Motorcycle, you are concerned about the economy. Following the economic crisis, sales of motorcycles took a huge hit industry-wide (41 percent!). Obviously, when money is tight, consumers tend to cut back on luxurious "toys" such as expensive bikes. However, sales are bouncing back, especially wherever the economy is humming. BMW relies on a well-heeled clientele, much of it composed of middle-aged men. However, the German motorcycle manufacturer has not been able to capture a share of the market larger than the 2.6 percent it has in the United States as opposed to 25 percent in Germany.

The ever-popular Harley-Davidson bike sales are rebounding, too. The manufacturer's core target audience has likewise traditionally been white and middle-aged. This is why Harley-Davidson is now trying to appeal to women riders and to a younger generation of would-be bikers. You bring up this topic with your boss, Dale Bell, and he asks you to find out what exactly Harley-Davidson is doing.

YOUR TASK. Visit the Harley-Davidson USA website and study how the legendary motorcycle manufacturer is targeting females and younger riders. Write an informational report in memo form addressed to Dale Bell. Which of its motorcycles does your competitor promote as ideal for women and why? How about apparel? What other ways has Harley-Davidson found to attract female riders and younger bikers?

12.14 Investigative Report: Prospecting for Global Business (Obj. 4)

[Intercultural] [Web]

You have been asked to prepare a training program for U.S. companies doing business outside the country.

YOUR TASK. Select a country to investigate. Collect data from the CountryWatch website, the Central Intelligence Agency's (CIA)

The World Factbook, or from the country's embassy in Washington. Interview on-campus international students. Use the Web to discover data about the country. See **Activity 13.13** and Figure 13.6 in Chapter 13 for additional ideas on gathering information on intercultural communication. Collect information about formats for written communication, observance of holidays, customary greetings, business ethics, and other topics of interest to businesspeople. Remember that your report should promote business, not tourism. Prepare a memo report addressed to Mia Alexander, editor for the training program materials.

12.15 Investigative Report: Studying International Business Etiquette (Obj. 4)

[Intercultural] [Team] [Web]

Your boss, Chloe Daniels, wants to know more about intercultural and international business etiquette. Today, most managers recognize that they need to be polished and professional to earn the respect of diverse audiences. Assume that your boss will assign various countries to several interns and recent hires. Choose a country that interests you and conduct a Web search. For example, in a Google search, input terms such as *business etiquette*, *business etiquette abroad*, and *intercultural communication*. You could visit websites such as the popular, informative etiquette and business guides for specific countries by Kwintessential Ltd. Also consider CountryWatch and the Central Intelligence Agency's (CIA) *The World Factbook*.

YOUR TASK. As an intern or a new-hire, write a memo report about one country that is considerably different from the United States and that offers new business opportunities. Address your report to Chloe Daniels, president of Cronos CompuTec. Confine your research to what U.S. managers need to know about business etiquette in that culture. You should investigate social customs such as greetings, attire, gift giving, formality, business meals, attitudes toward time, and communication styles to help your boss avoid etiquette blunders. The purpose of your report is to promote business, not tourism. Compare your results with those of other students and, if directed, compile them in an informational team report.

12.16 Informational or Analytical Report: Examining Tweets and Other Social Media Posts (Objs. 4, 5)

[E-mail] [Social Media] [Web]

Select a Fortune 500 company that appeals to you and search recent tweets and Facebook posts about it. Soon you will recognize trends and topic clusters that may help you organize the report content by criteria. For example, if you use the hashtag to conduct a subject search for *#Coca-Cola*, you will obtain a huge number of tweets about the company and brand. They will range from fan posts, buying tips, exhortations to recycle plastic, and specious cleaning tips involving Coke all the way to urban legends (e.g., the acid in Coke will completely dissolve a T-bone steak in two days). Many returned tweets will be only marginally interesting because they show up just because *#Coca-Cola* is mentioned.

If you explore Facebook, you will mostly find official pages and fan sites, most of which display favorable posts. You would have to look hard to find negative posts, partly also because companies moderate discussions and often remove offensive posts according to their user agreements.

YOUR TASK. Write either an informational or analytical report about the company you chose. In an informational report to your instructor, you could summarize your findings in memo form or as an e-mail. Describe how the tweets about the company are trending. Are they overwhelmingly positive or negative? Organize the report around the subject areas you identify (criteria). Alternatively, you could write an analytical report analyzing the strategies your chosen company adopts in responding to tweets and Facebook posts. Your analytical report would evaluate the organization's social media responses and provide specific examples to support your claims.

12.17 Informational Report: Charting Your Career Path (Obj. 4)

> Web

Gather information about a career or position in which you might be interested. Learn about the nature of the job. Discover whether certification, a license, or experience is required. One of the best places to search is the latest *Occupational Outlook Handbook* compiled by the U.S. Bureau of Labor Statistics. Google the latest *Handbook* and either input your desired occupation using the Search box or click an A-Z Index link.

YOUR TASK. Write an informational report to your instructor that describes your target career area. Discuss the nature of the work, working conditions, necessary qualifications, and the future job outlook for the occupation. Include information about typical salary ranges and career paths. If your instructor wants an extended report, collect information about two companies to which you might apply. Investigate each company's history, products and/or services, size, earnings, reputation, and number of employees. Describe the functions of an employee working in the position you have investigated. To do this, interview one or more individuals who are working in that position. Devote several sections of your report to the specific tasks, functions, duties, and opinions of these individuals. You can make this into a recommendation report by drawing conclusions and making recommendations. One conclusion that you could draw relates to success in this career area. Who might be successful in this field?

12.18 Informational Report: Prospecting for Potential Employers (Obj. 4)

> Web

You are considering jobs with a Fortune 500 company, and you want to learn as much as possible about it.

YOUR TASK. Select a Fortune 500 company and collect information about it on the Web. If available, use your library's ProQuest subscription to access Hoover's company records for basic facts. Then take a look at the company's website; check its background, news releases, and annual report. Learn about its major product, service, or emphasis. Find its Fortune 500 ranking, its current stock price (if listed), and its high and low range for the year. Look up its profit-to-earnings ratio. Track its latest marketing plan, promotion, or product. Identify its home office, major officers, and number of employees. In a memo report to your instructor, summarize your research findings. Explain why this company would be a good or bad employment choice.

12.19 Justification/Recommendation Report: Money to Burn for a Good Cause (Obj. 5)

> Web

Great news! MegaTech, the start-up company where you work, has become enormously successful. Now the owner wants to support

some kind of philanthropic program. He does not have time to check out the possibilities, so he asks you, his assistant, to conduct research and report to him and the board of directors.

YOUR TASK. The owner wants you to investigate the philanthropic projects at 20 high-profile companies of your choice. Visit their websites and study programs such as volunteerism, cause-related marketing, matching funds, and charitable donations. In a recommendation report, discuss five of the best programs and recommend one that could serve as a philanthropic project model for your company.

12.20 Justification/Recommendation Report: Considering an Organizational Social Media Use Policy (Obj. 5)

> Social Media   > Team   > Web

As a manager in a midsized engineering firm, you are aware that members of your department frequently use e-mail, social networking sites, instant messaging, and texting for private messages, shopping, and games. In addition to the strain on computer facilities, you worry about declining productivity as well as security problems. When you walked by one worker's computer and saw inappropriate content on the screen, you knew you had to do something. Although workplace privacy is a hot-button issue for unions and employee rights groups, employers have legitimate reasons for wanting to know what is happening on their computers or during the time they are paying their employees to work. A high percentage of lawsuits involve the use and abuse of e-mail and social media. You think that the executive council should establish a comprehensive media use policy. The council is generally receptive to sound suggestions, especially if they are inexpensive. At present no explicit media use policy exists, and you fear that the executive council is not fully aware of the dangers. You decide to talk with other managers about the problem and write a justification/recommendation report.

YOUR TASK. In teams discuss the need for a comprehensive media use policy. Using the Web and electronic databases, find information about other firms' adoption of such policies. Look for examples of companies struggling with lawsuits over abuse of technology on the job. In your report, should you describe suitable policies? Should you recommend computer monitoring and surveillance software? Should the policy cover instant messaging, social networking sites, blogging, and smartphone use? Each member of the team should present and support his or her ideas regarding what should be included in the report. Individually or as a team, write a convincing justification/recommendation report to the executive council based on the conclusions you draw from your research and discussion. Decide whether you should be direct or indirect.

12.21 Feasibility Report: Analyzing the Need for an International Student Association (Obj. 5)

> Intercultural

To fulfill a senior project in your department, you have been asked to submit a letter report to the dean evaluating the feasibility of starting an organization of international students on campus.

YOUR TASK. Find out how many international students are on your campus, what nations they represent, how one goes about starting an organization, and whether a faculty sponsor is needed. Assume that you conducted an informal survey of international students. Of the 39 who filled out the survey, 31 said they would be interested in joining.

12.22 Feasibility Report: Motivating Employees to Get off the Couch (Obj. 5)

Your company is considering ways to promote employee fitness and morale.

YOUR TASK. Select a fitness program that seems reasonable for your company. Consider a softball league, bowling teams, a basketball league, lunchtime walks, lunchtime fitness speakers and demos, company-sponsored health club memberships, a workout room, a fitness center, or a fitness director. Assume that your boss has tentatively agreed to the program you select and has asked you to write a memo report investigating its feasibility.

12.23 Yardstick Report: Shopping for Big-Ticket Office Equipment (Obj. 5)

You recently complained to your boss that you were unhappy with a piece of equipment you use (printer, computer, copier, fax, or the like). After some thought, the boss decided that your complaint was valid and told you to go shopping.

YOUR TASK. Compare at least three manufacturers' models and recommend one. Because the company will be purchasing ten or more units and because several managers must approve the purchase, write a careful report documenting your findings. Establish at least five criteria for comparing the models. Submit a memo report to your boss. If your instructor directs, prepare a decision matrix with reasonable weights assigned to significant attributes.

12.24 Yardstick Report: Fixing Workplace Procedures (Obj. 5)

YOUR TASK. Identify a problem or procedure that must be changed at your work or in an organization you know. Consider challenges such as poor scheduling of employees, outdated equipment, slow order processing, failure to encourage employees to participate fully, restrictive rules, inadequate training, or disappointed customers. Consider several solutions or courses of action (retaining the present status could be one alternative). Develop criteria that you could use to evaluate each alternative. Write a report measuring each alternative by the yardstick you have created. Recommend a course of action to your boss or to the organization head.

Self-Contained Report Activities

No Additional Research Required

12.25 Justification/Recommendation Report: Speedier Service at Stellato Family Pizza* (Obj. 5)

You work for Carmine Stellato, the owner of Stellato Family Pizza, a small, casual pizza shop he founded 33 years ago. Its signature items are eight-inch-diameter individual pizzas. The pizza shop also serves mozzarella sticks, wings, and assorted beverages.

The pizza shop is located in the warehouse district of Indianapolis, where it originally served truckers who delivered their meat, fruits, and vegetables in the middle of the night and then whisked off to the next city. Truckers loved the satisfying and filling pizza because it provided them with lots of energy on those tedious late-night runs. Later the pizza shop caught on with the nightclub crowd and with students who studied late. The shop opens at 10 p.m. and closes at 6 a.m.

The concept was a resounding success. However, success brings competition. Three imitators opened their pizza shops within a five-mile radius of Stellato Family Pizza. You know that the family has been using the same delivery system for years, and you know service could be faster. You also notice that new pizza shops are receiving orders via smartphones.

The current system at Stellato's begins with a counter clerk recording the customer's order and table number on a ticket. The customer pays, and the counter person gives the order to the pizza makers. The pizza makers remove the dough from the refrigerator, shape it, add the sauce and other ingredients, put the pie in the oven, and remove it from the oven when baked. The counter clerk then takes the order to the customer's table. Stellato Family Pizza has three counter clerks, two pizza makers, and one cash register that the counter clerks share. It takes two minutes to prep a pizza before it can go in the oven. The pizza shop uses an outdated Rankin Model D85 pizza deck oven, which cooks a pizza in seven minutes.

You think the entire system is inefficient, and when you discuss the problem with Mr. Stellato, he says, "Although the original ways are familiar to me, I see that the time for improvement has come."

You suggest observing the three competitors' systems of serving customers to understand why their service is faster. Currently, the average time it takes a customer to receive an order at Stellato Family Pizza is 16 minutes. The following are notes from your observations of the competitors.

DeNunzio Pizza
- Similar menu
- Orders are taken using an electronic system that includes the customer's number
- Customers pay immediately
- Customers pick up their orders after their numbers have been called
- Two counter clerks at one register; two pizza makers
- Preprepared dough; prep time: one minute
- One state-of-the art Elite Chef Model BFE-28 convection oven—five minutes to cook a pizza
- Average time a customer waits to receive an order: ten minutes

Capriotti's
- Similar menu
- Order takers call out the menu item as the order is taken
- Customers pay immediately
- Customers wait at the counter to pick up their orders
- Three counter employees at three registers; two pizza makers
- Preprepared dough; prep time: one minute
- One state-of-the art Elite Chef Model BFE-28 convection oven—five minutes to cook a pizza
- Average time a customer waits to receive an order: eight minutes

Hip Hop Pizza Shop
- Similar menu
- Tickets are used to record the customers' orders
- Customers pay immediately

---

*Instructors: See the Instructor's Manual for additional report-writing resources.

- Counter staff employees take the order to customers' tables
- Three counter staff employees, two pizza makers, and one cash register
- Pizza prep the same as Stellato Family Pizza: two minutes
- One DeLong Model FC30 pizza deck oven—six minutes to cook a pizza
- Average time a customer waits to receive an order: 15 minutes

YOUR TASK. Now it is up to you to analyze the data you have collected. In a short memo report to Carmine Stellato, present your findings, discuss your conclusions, and make recommendations, including a recommendation on how Stellato's might gain a competitive edge by enabling its customers to use some of the most recent technology to order their food. You may want to present the data using visual aids, but you also realize that you must emphasize the important findings by presenting them in an easy-to-read list.

12.26 Justification/Recommendation Report: Drunk-Driver Service for Hockey Players (Obj. 5)

As the public relations executive for the Smithville Ice Rockets, a minor league hockey team, you become involved in a number of team problems. Recently, one of the team's players was driving drunk and injured himself. This accident is an extremely worrisome and painful reminder to the organization that people die in drunk-driving accidents, including players on other professional sports teams who have injured or killed themselves and others.

You are well aware of the other consequences of drunk driving. They include negative publicity for the league, a bad example to young fans, distractions that cause lost games, and lower attendance. Drunk driving also results in the possible "release" (jargon in professional sports for firing a player) of players who are cited, which also hurts the team. Additionally, you're aware that the penalty for drunk-driving vehicular homicide in the team's home state is up to 15 years in prison.

Team newcomers must take a course about the dangers of alcohol consumption. Course topics include the risk of accidental injury and death, increased danger of violent behavior, and negative effects on player conditioning and performance. Although this course has reduced drunk-driving incidents, some players still drink and drive.

After drinking, players often try to drive themselves home instead of calling a cab or a friend. Although calling a cab seems an easy solution, many players drive expensive cars and don't want to abandon them by taking a cab or having a friend drive them home. According to designated driver service Zingo,[21] not wanting to leave their cars is the top reason people avoid calling cabs or friends. In addition, most drunk drivers arrive home safely despite their hazardous decision to drive drunk, making it more likely that they will do it again. Greg Davis, owner of the Ice Rockets, said that he would rather a player call him in the middle of the night and ask for a ride home after a night of drinking than drive himself.

Mr. Davis asks you to decide whether the team should implement a service to drive its players home when they have been out drinking. He wants you to weigh the pros and cons of implementing the service, by comparing the service to its alternatives: increased education, incentives for players who don't drive drunk, and stiffer punishment for players who do.

You conduct primary and secondary research, and then categorize your findings into the pros and cons of operating the service.

Pros of Implementing the Player Drunk-Driving Service.

The estimated financial cost to a player of a drunk-driving vehicular homicide case, excluding lawsuits, is $9,000 to $45,000. The survivors of a drunk-driving accident can sue the driver and anyone else who might have contributed to the accident. If a court finds the team negligent, the team would have to pay damages. Recent out-of-court settlements for drunk-driving lawsuits average $1.5 million, and the estimated cost of lost ticket sales from the negative publicity is $15,000.

The estimated annual cost to operate the service (wages, vehicles, fuel, maintenance, and insurance) is $16,000, a fraction of the cost of a drunk-driving vehicular homicide. The team could legally operate the service as a separate nonprofit company.

Data from the Substance Abuse and Mental Health Services Administration (SAMHSA), the Centers for Disease Control and Prevention (CDC), and CNN indicate that men in the age range of many professional hockey players (21 to 25) are much more likely to binge drink and have drunk-driving accidents than those in other demographic groups. These data suggest the need for a "safety net."

Cons of Implementing the Player Drunk-Driving Service.

The course about the dangers of alcohol consumption that newcomers take could be more effective. For instance, players don't realize the potential financial costs of a drunk-driving vehicular homicide conviction, and a discussion of these costs is not included in the course.

Offering a drunk-driving service doesn't address the core problem: binge drinking. In fact, the service might send the wrong message to players. It might suggest that the organization tacitly condones drinking, and the service may be seen as enabling this behavior. By contrast, education, incentives, and disciplinary action address the core problem more directly.

A team can force its players to comply with its behavioral policies or lose their jobs through morals clauses in their contracts. The Pittsburgh Steelers, one of the most respected and winning professional sport organizations, is well-known for its refusal to tolerate player behavioral problems. In a four-year span, the Steelers swiftly released and traded four players (all of whom were top players or top draft picks) for drunk driving and violence against women. Many professional sport teams suspend or release players who drive drunk, and the careers of many players have ended prematurely because of unacceptable off-the-field behavior.

However, players are grown men. They should be responsible for their behavior, and other members of the organization can't babysit them. Player interviews show that they generally agree with this view. Finally, although this service costs an estimated $16,000 annually, it's unclear whether players would use it.

YOUR TASK. Write a three- to five-page memo report with your analysis and recommendations. Address your report to Mr. Davis.

12.27 Feasibility Report: Advisability of Hiring a Social Media Consultant (Obj. 5)

Social Media

You are the vice president of marketing for Scents Are Us, a manufacturer and distributor of scented flameless candles and candle warmers. The president, Tracie Johnson, feels that the company could do a better job of listening to and connecting with its customers. Tracie knows that the company's two main competitors are gaining ground in brand awareness and sales. She also knows that although Scents Are Us created a Facebook page, she wants the company to develop a broader social media strategy. Tracie thinks it might be wise to hire a social media consultant to help Scents Are Us in this effort, and she wants your advice.

To provide Tracie with an informed recommendation, you decide to conduct research to answer the following questions:

1. Is the company collecting social media data (tracking number of mentions, number of followers, and so on), and is the company using the data?

2. Does the Marketing Department have employees with the talent to implement this strategy without a consultant's help?

3. If it has the talent, does the department have the time to implement this strategy?

4. How long will it take to implement this strategy?

5. What social media tools should the company use? What services do consultants provide?

6. What is the cost of hiring a social media expert?

7. What are the disadvantages of hiring a consultant?

8. What could go wrong if the company hires a consultant?

As vice president of marketing, you already know answers to many of these questions, but Tracie, understandably, does not.

Following are the results of your research. The company collects data from Facebook, but it doesn't analyze that data for decision making. Two of the Marketing Department's 12 employees have some social media knowledge and skills, but no employee has enough knowledge and skill to implement a social media strategy. What's more, none of your employees is able to devote 40 hours a week to such an effort.

The estimated implementation time for a social media strategy is two months. Many social media consultants recommend implementing a wide range of tools, including Facebook, Twitter, Pinterest, Google Plus, and blogging. The average fees for these social media consulting services appear in the following table.

Average Fees for Social Media Consulting Services

Tool	Setup Charge	Monthly Charges
Facebook	$950 for initial page setup	$1,450 for monthly content management
Twitter	$800 for account setup	$950 for monthly account management
Pinterest	$800 for account setup	$950 for monthly account management
Google Plus	$800 for account setup	$950 for monthly account management
Blogging	$1,950 for design and template creation	$1,850 per month for writing and editing content for the blog (one post per week)

A consultant also has the time to uncover what social media tools and strategies other companies are using.

You have identified two main disadvantages of hiring a social media consultant. First, the consultant will not be an expert in your company or its products. You'll have to combine the consultant's knowledge of social media tools with your knowledge of the scented candle business. Second, it's impossible to accurately predict the return on investment of these services. The best you can do is monitor costs and make sure you receive the services the company has paid for.

Reading about the Ragu Spaghetti Sauce and ChapStick lip balm social media fiascos taught you that remaining silent in a Twitter conversation, not planning for problems, alienating customers by not targeting them and removing negative Facebook comments are major blunders in a social media campaign. To avoid these problems, the company can make one employee responsible for participating in Twitter conversations, hold worst-case scenario meetings, remind the consultant that men use the products too, and prohibit the removal of negative comments without permission.

YOUR TASK. Write a one- to three-page memo report to the president. Make clear your decision regarding whether to hire a consultant, and determine where in the report to announce it. Include all the results of your research in the report, condensing it to stay within the page-length limit. Format the report for easy reading.

12.28 Yardstick Report: Comparing Textbook Options (Obj. 5)

Play the part of the treasurer for Delta Chi Kappa, a business association at your college or university. After some members bought textbooks at the campus bookstore recently, they complained about how expensive they were. Some members said that because of the expense, they didn't buy some of the textbooks they needed last semester, which hurt their grades. Lower grades could lead to the loss of scholarships and reduced job opportunities.

The executive committee of Delta Chi Kappa asks you to identify alternatives to buying full-priced hard-copy books at the campus bookstore. What criteria are most important? The committee is most interested in the best price (including shipping charges) and availability. Even a low price is useless if the book is not readily available.

One option for students, of course, is to continue buying books at the campus bookstore. Some instructors and students, however, are buying books for the Chronos Player. The Chronos Player is a hardware/software device for reading a proprietary e-book file format—that is, books that play only on this device. Some publishers and bookstores are now renting books, which is a distinct possibility. Students can also buy books online, or they can download e-books as PDF files for a fee. All of these options seem like reasonable alternatives to buying full-priced hard-copy books at the campus bookstore. A few students love e-books because they are instantly accessible and cost much less up front than their print counterparts. However, some complain about the poor readability of textbooks accessed on mobile devices.

For the study, you choose a representative sample of four textbooks: *Modern Perspectives on World History*, *Case Studies in Business Writing*, *Abstract Algebra: Theory and Practice*, and *Astronomy for Non-Majors*. You check the prices and availability of the books at the campus bookstore, on websites that specialize in renting textbooks, on websites that sell hard-copy books, and on websites that sell e-books. You check the price of the Chronos Player and the prices and availability of books that play on this device. You evaluate readability by seeing how easy a textbook is to read (only a concern with e-books and the Chronos Player). Delivery times for books purchased and rented online are less important because most online vendors deliver books in three to five business days.

Price is by far the most important criterion, so you assign it a weight of 6. You assign availability a weight of 3 and readability a weight of 1.

Average Price. At the campus bookstore, the average price of each book is $130 and the average buyback price is $50, making the average net price $80. The better the condition of the book is when you return it, the more the campus bookstore pays. The average price on the Chronos Player is $148, and the average price of its books is $9, making the average price of a book $148 ÷ 4 + $9 = $46. The average price to rent the four books for one semester is $23 per book. The average price is $37 per book to buy the four books online. None of the online booksellers has a buyback option. The average price of the four books as e-books is $49 per book, which the following chart shows.

Availability. The campus bookstore has all four of the books in stock. Only one of the four books is available for the Chronos Player. A wider selection of books for the Chronos Player is available for the mass market than for the college market. Textbookheaven claims it has over 2.1 million textbooks for rent and offers prepaid return shipping. Three of the four books are available on this site, which consistently offered the lowest prices on book rentals. Two

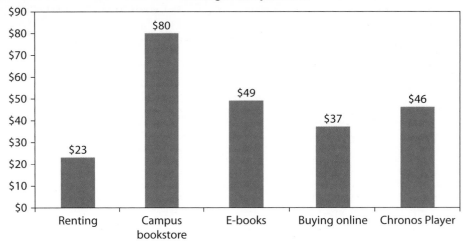

Average Price per Book

Renting	$23
Campus bookstore	$80
E-books	$49
Buying online	$37
Chronos Player	$46

online booksellers, Dirtcheap and Slickshopper, each had three of the four books. Geniusbooks had two of the four books as e-books. Other e-booksellers had smaller selections.

Readability. You judge all hard-copy books as most readable. Formatting issues and small print on small screens, especially on smartphones and small tablets, make e-books the least readable. Although books on the Chronos Player are easier to read than typical e-books, the device is relatively hard to use.

YOUR TASK. Write a memo report of five or fewer pages and address it to the organization's members. Include conclusions and recommendations, a bar chart showing the availability of books, and a decision matrix.

12.29 Yardstick Report: Jobless Young Worker Starts a Business (Obj. 5)

Four months ago, as a recent graduate, you lost your job with Focal Lens Corporation when the contact lens manufacturer downsized. After four months of trying to find full-time employment with another company, you are running out of money.

You decide to take control of your own destiny by becoming an entrepreneur. You evaluate your interests and skills, and ponder the following four potential services:

- A pet-sitting business (you'll do the sitting at customers' homes)
- A yard work company (weeding, planting, leaf raking, snow shoveling, and possibly hanging and removing holiday decorations)
- An errand service (including dropping off dry cleaning, paying bills, and grocery shopping)
- An aquarium maintenance service (residential and commercial)

Next you need to decide how to evaluate each of the four options fairly, and to do that, you choose to create a decision matrix. You must select criteria to evaluate the four potential ventures. Because you need time to continue seeking full-time employment (unless the new business really takes off), the most important criterion is the time per week the business will require and the schedule flexibility it offers. Hence, you assign this criterion a weight of 8.

Because you are running out of money, start-up costs are important, and each option has relatively low start-up costs. Therefore, you assign this criterion a weight of 6. Each business you're considering is likely to meet with at least some demand. You want a business with enough demand to make money, which is why you assign demand a weight of 4. Moreover, the degree

of competition is important because you want to able to make a reasonable profit, and more competitors means more competition based on price. You give competition a weight of 3. Of course, legal and safety considerations are important with every business. However, you judge the liability and safety risks to be about equal for all options, so you omit these criteria from the evaluation.

Time per Week and Schedule Flexibility. Pet sitting requires the least amount of time and offers the greatest schedule flexibility per week. Once you get the pet(s) situated, you can use your laptop to look for other jobs. Aquarium maintenance is second best in terms of time and schedule flexibility. This business will demand less time per week than yard work would require. The third best option is yard work because you believe it offers more schedule flexibility than running an errand service would. With an errand service, you are at the mercy of your customers. You must be available whenever the customer needs you and work for as long as the customer wants.

Start-Up Costs. Compared to the other three options, pet sitting requires minimal start-up costs. The most significant outlays include pet-sitter insurance, website creation, and a pet first-aid class. An errand service generates the next lowest start-up costs because you already have a car. The only other major expenditures are gas, car maintenance, and a navigation system. As for aquarium maintenance, you would have to buy an aquarium cleaning siphon, an algae scraper, water test kits, filter media, fish medication, replacement fish (in case the meds don't work), fish food, and a portable filter for "polishing" your customers' aquarium water. Of the four options, yard work comes with the steepest start-up costs. Unless you want to wear yourself out in a hurry, you'll need to buy a riding lawnmower, so that you can handle big jobs. You will also need a trimmer/edger, a trailer, and eventually a pickup truck.

Demand for the Service. Some people love to do yard work, but many hate it. Some loathe it so much that they find a way to pay for yard service even when their income is low. You judge the demand for yard work as highest of the four options. The next highest demand is for pet sitting. Boarding a pet at a kennel is very expensive, and it can be traumatic to take a pet from its home. You judge the demand for an errand service as having the next highest demand. The idea of using a personal assistant is starting to catch on, especially because the population is aging and consequently less mobile. An aquarium maintenance service has the least demand because few homes and businesses have aquariums.

Degree of Competition. The advantage of lackluster demand for acquarium maintenance is that it attracts the least competition of the four business options. Next, the errand service has relatively little competition followed by pet sitting, which draws less competition than yard service but faces more competition than the other options. Yard service is a very competitive business—the most competitive of the four.

YOUR TASK. Write a letter report of five or fewer pages. Include conclusions, recommendations, and a two-part decision matrix with the rankings in the first matrix and the weighted rankings in the second matrix. Using the decision matrix as a basis for your conclusions and recommendations will make writing this report easier.

12.30 Yardstick Report: Parking Problem at Caputi's Italian Restaurant (Obj. 5)

You have always enjoyed the great food at Caputi's Italian Restaurant, owned by your uncle Guido. Caputi's is a formal, upscale dining Italian restaurant in downtown Tempe, Arizona, near the campus of a major university where you are a student. Because of its steadily increasing business, Caputi's has outgrown its small parking lot, which has only 20 parking spaces.

Frustrated over their inability to park in the restaurant's lot, some potential customers give up and go elsewhere to eat. Some of the regulars have also disappeared. Caputi's cannot add parking spaces because adjacent land is unavailable. However, according to Guido, "The problem is not a lack of parking spaces; it's a lack of willingness on the part of customers to walk from where they parked to the restaurant." To pay its debts, the restaurant needs to continue to grow. Guido says, "Relocation is out of the question—this spot is too good!"

Guido wants you to evaluate options to ease the parking problem, using criteria that he and you develop. The options are to (a) use a valet service with attendants who park and later retrieve cars for patrons, (b) run a free shuttle service between the restaurant and a nearby parking garage, and (c) advertise the availability of nearby parking garages and bus routes on the restaurant's website and in the restaurant. The criteria are (a) the cost to the restaurant to implement the solution, (b) the cost to the customer to use the solution, (c) the ease of implementation for the restaurant, and (d) convenience to the customer.

Besides talking to Guido, you interview a valet parking company about its services and fees, and you interview the managers of the nearby parking garages about availability and prices. You survey 40 of the restaurant's customers about their willingness to use a valet service and the price they would be willing to pay for the service.

You explain what a decision matrix is to Guido, and together you decide on the weights of the criteria. The net profit (or loss) to the restaurant to implement the solution receives a weight of 10.

The cost to the customer to use the solution receives a weight of 6. The ease of implementation for the restaurant receives a weight of 4. The convenience to the customer receives a weight of 8.

Cost to the Restaurant to Implement a Solution. The least expensive valet service in town sent you a quotation that pegs a patron's charge at $7 per car, an amount that includes a $2 flat fee for parking at a nearby parking garage. The valet parking company has offered its service free of charge to the restaurant.

The major costs of operating a shuttle service are about $1,500 to buy a van and $200 per week to pay an employee to drive the van between the garage and the restaurant during dinner hours. Costs to advertise available parking options on the restaurant's website and at the restaurant are about $200.

Cost to the Customer. The per-vehicle charge of $7 plus a customer tips for valet service of about $3 makes the valet service the costliest option. The shuttle service is free to customers. Similarly, learning about the availability of nearby parking garages and bus routes on the restaurant's website and at the restaurant is free to customers.

Ease of Implementation. Advertising parking options is the most convenient option for the restaurant because it takes the least amount of time and effort. Offering a valet service is the second most convenient option for the restaurant. Although the valet service does most of the work, this option requires more weekly administrative work for the restaurant than advertising requires. Caputi's may also need to provide food and beverages for valets. Operating a shuttle service is the least convenient option for the restaurant because it requires the restaurant to buy a van; pay a driver; and provide fuel, maintenance, and insurance.

Convenience to the Customer. A valet service is the most convenient option for customers because this option results in the fastest entry into the restaurant. Your survey shows that 90 percent of the customers are willing to use the service. A shuttle service is the second most convenient option for customers. It is not as convenient as driving to the restaurant entrance and leaving a car with a valet. Advertising offers information to customers but not any significant convenience, making it the least convenient option.

YOUR TASK. Guido is relying on you to analyze the data and help him make a decision. Write a memo report of three or fewer pages. Prepare a decision matrix with the weights provided. For each criterion in the decision matrix, give the option that ranks highest a ranking of 3, the option that ranks second highest a ranking of 2, and the option that ranks lowest a ranking of 1. Multiply each weight by the ranking, repeat for the other criteria, and then sum up the results to compute a total. From your decision matrix, draw conclusions and then make recommendations. Overall, which option is best? Should you still recommend advertising the parking options?

Chat About It

In each chapter you will find five discussion questions related to the chapter material. Your instructor may assign these topics for you to discuss in class, in an online chat room, or on an online discussion board. Some of the discussion topics may require outside research. You may also be asked to read and respond to postings made by your classmates.

Topic 1: Some recent research studies have revealed that young people experience anxiety or estrangement from family and friends as a result of their social media use. Other studies report that young people believe that social media use has helped them make connections and has led to great accomplishments. How do you view social media use? Do you believe that it connects people or isolates people?

Topic 2: If you were asked to study the relationship between traffic speeds and traffic accidents, what statistic might be most useful: the mean, median, or mode? Why?

Topic 3: Provide a simple example that illustrates the differences among findings, conclusions, and recommendations.

Topic 4: What do you think might be a good rule of thumb regarding the number of graphics (charts, tables, and so on) to put in a report and the size of the graphics? Why?

Topic 5: This is how one participant in a recent study of college students' research strategies characterized *procrastination*, a habit embraced by 80 percent of the respondents: "Procrastination, for me, is about the adrenaline rush. . . . It's always just like a race. . . . Oh, look, I need to get this done in 20 minutes and turn it in. And once you know you can do it and get a good grade, you do it, especially if you can get away with it."[22] Does procrastination help or hinder your academic work?

C.L.U.E. Grammar & Mechanics | *Review 12*

Total Review

The first ten chapters reviewed specific guides from Appendix A, Grammar and Mechanics Guide. The exercises in this and the remaining chapters are total reviews, covering all of the grammar and mechanics guides plus confusing words and frequently misspelled words.

Each of the following sentences has a total of **three** errors in grammar, punctuation, capitalization, usage, or spelling. On a separate sheet, write a correct version. Avoid adding new phrases, starting new sentences, or rewriting in your own words. When finished, compare your responses with the key beginning on page Key-3.

EXAMPLE: The auditors report, which my boss and myself read very closely, contained three main flaws, factual inaccuracies, omissions, and incomprehensible language.

REVISION: The **auditor's** report, which my boss and **I** read very closely, contained three main **flaws:** factual inaccuracies, omissions, and incomprehensible language.

1. After our supervisor and her returned from their meeting at 2:00 p.m. we were able to sort the customers names more quickly.

2. 6 of the 18 workers in my department were released, as a result we had to work harder to achieve our goals.

3. Toyota, the market-leading japanese carmaker continued to enjoy strong positive ratings despite a string of much publicized recalls.

4. Michaels presentation to a nonprofit group netted him only three hundred dollars, a tenth of his usual honorarium but he believes in pro bono work.

5. To reflect our guiding principals and our commitment to executive education we offer financial support to more than sixty percent of our current MBA candidates.

6. Our latest press release which was written in our Corporate Communication Department announces the opening of three asian offices.

7. In his justification report dated September first, Justin argued that expansion to twelve branch offices could boost annual revenue to 22 million dollars.

8. The practicality and advisability of opening 12 branch offices is what will be discussed in the consultants feasability report.

9. The President, who had went to a meeting in the Midwest, delivered a report to Jeff and I when he returned.

10. Because some organizations prefer single spaced reports be sure to check with your organization to learn it's preference.

Notes

[1] Krishna, S. (2012, October 25). India's coffee market competition is ferocious: Howard Schultz, Starbucks. *The Economic Times*. Retrieved from http://articles.economictimes.indiatimes.com/2012-10-25/news/34729911_1_starbucks-howard-schultz-tatas

[2] Kapur, M. (2012, November 9). Interview with Starbucks CEO Howard Schultz. [Transcript of video]. CNN.com. Retrieved from http://transcripts.cnn.com/TRANSCRIPTS/1211/09/ta.01.html

[3] Our Starbucks mission statement. (n. d.). Retrieved from http://www.starbucks.com/about-us/company-information/mission-statement

[4] Krishna, S. (2012, October 25). India's coffee market competition is ferocious: Howard Schultz, Starbucks. *The Economic Times*. Retrieved from http://articles.economictimes.indiatimes.com/2012-10-25/news/34729911_1_starbucks-howard-schultz-tatas

[5] The 12 greatest entrepreneurs of our time – 6. Howard Schultz. (2012). *CNN Money*. Retrieved from http://money.cnn.com/galleries/2012/news/companies/1203/gallery.greatest-entrepreneurs.fortune/7.html

[6] Kapur, M. (2012, November 9). Interview with Starbucks CEO Howard Schultz. [Transcript of video]. CNN.com. Retrieved from http://transcripts.cnn.com/TRANSCRIPTS/1211/09/ta.01.html

[7] Miller, C. C. (2011, March 13). A changed Starbucks. A changed C.E.O. *The New York Times*. Retrieved from http://www.nytimes.com

[8] Schultz, H. (2008). Global responsibility report. Retrieved from http://globalassets.starbucks.com/assets/76f95d923db341fe9237a3360e0d03e3.pdf

[9] Photo essay based on Mullholland, A. (2013, March 7). How leaded gasoline could be linked to crime rates. CTV News. Retrieved from http://www.ctvnews.ca/

[10] Lütticke, M. (2013, January 24). FairPhone—A smartphone for a good conscience. DW.de. Retrieved from http://www.dw.de/fairphone-a-smartphone-for-a-good-conscience/a-16544455

[11] Quoted in Association of Government Accountants. (2010). Current government financial reporting leaves taxpayers dissatisfied and distrustful. Retrieved from http://finance.paidcontent.org/paidcontent/news/read/11936770/current_government_financial_reporting_leaves_taxpayers_dissatisfied_and_distrustful

[12] Photo essay based on Pandora. (2013, March 7). Pandora announces February 2013 audience metrics. [Press release]. Retrieved from http://www.prnewswire.com/news-releases/pandora-announces-february-2013-audience-metrics-196067481.html

[13] Ashton, R. (n. d.). Top ten writing tips for scientists. Sciencebase. Retrieved from http://www.sciencebase.com/science-blog/writing-tips-for-scientists

[14] Vlasic, B., Tabuchi, H., & Duhigg, C. (2012, August 4). pursuit of Nissan, a jobs lesson for the tech industry? *The New York Times*. Retrieved from http://www.nytimes.com; Infiniti game on for big 2012. (2012, February 20). Nissan Reports. Retrieved from http://reports.nissan-global.com/EN/?p=3320

[15] "Jseattle." (2011, January 7). Starbucks returns: The 15th Ave Coffee & Tea experiment is over. CHS Capitol Hill Seattle Blog. Retrieved from http://www.capitolhillseattle.com/2011/01/07/starbucks-returns-the-15th-ave-coffee-tea-experiment-is-over

[16] Ibid.

[17] Wilson, M. (2012, October 8). An experimental new Starbucks store: Tiny, portable, and hyper local. Yahoo Finance. Retrieved from http://finance.yahoo.com/news/an-experimental-new-starbucks-store--tiny--portable--and-hyper-local.html?page=all

[18] Ibid.

[19] Ibid.

[20] Based on Sommers, S. (2013, January 31). Highlight this blog post at your own risk. The Huffington Post. Retrieved from http://www.huffingtonpost.com/sam-sommers/highlight-this-blog-post-_b_2587017.html?utm_hp_ref=education

[21] Ehlers, M. (2009). Zingo Raleigh, sober saviors. Zingo Raleigh Press Releases. Retrieved from http://zingoraleigh.com

[22] Head, A. J., & Eisenberg, M. B. (2009, February 4). Finding context: What today's college students say about conducting research in the digital age. Project Information Literacy Progress Report. The Information School, University of Washington. Retrieved from http://projectinfolit.org/pdfs/PIL_ProgressReport_2_2009.pdf

Proposals, Business Plans, and Formal Business Reports

© Tony Metaxas/AsiaImages/Getty Images

Proposals a Matter of Life and Death at Raytheon

Zooming in

© Africa Studio/Shutterstock.com;
© ra2studio/Shutterstock.com

`It all started on a sunny November morning in Southern California. The director of operations at Raytheon Company's Santa Barbara business unit stood in front of an audience of about 20 engineers and managers—the individuals selected by management to write a proposal for the Aerosol Polarimetry Sensor on the National Polar-Orbiting Operational Environmental Satellite System. He began by telling them, "The request for proposal (RFP) has finally arrived. I know that many of you have been thinking about how to win this contract for more than a year. Now it's time to turn that thinking into words—time to write the proposal!"[1]

He then introduced the proposal team's newest member, Dr. Mark Grinyer. As a Raytheon proposal specialist, he was named to write the vitally important executive summary. The director closed with a final comment: "Remember, everyone, we're on the clock now. We've got less than 60 days to build a winning proposal for almost $100 million in new business."

© AP Images/PRNewsFoto/Raytheon Company, New York Stock Exchange

As Dr. Grinyer listened, he thought, "It'll be a busy holiday season." Such schedules, however, are typical for aerospace industry proposals. Several big companies were competing for this contract, and only one proposal would win.

A leading aerospace company, Raytheon is a Fortune 500 giant with about 75,000 employees worldwide. Most are technicians, engineers, scientists, and managers involved in high-technology military and government programs. Raytheon's Remote Sensing business unit in Santa Barbara specializes in high-quality electro-optical sensor systems for weather satellites and other space-based vehicles. The company's sensors on weather satellites provide images seen on TV every day and enable quality weather predictions around the world.

Like most aerospace companies and other companies, Raytheon's success depends on its ability to produce winning proposals selling complex systems that must meet the needs of its customers.

Critical Thinking

- Why are proposals vitally important to a company like Raytheon?

- How are Raytheon proposals similar to and different from proposals or long reports written by students?

- How do you think team members maintain consistency and meet deadlines when writing important, time-constrained, multi-volume documents such as this proposal?

Developing Informal Proposals

LEARNING OBJECTIVE 1
Understand the importance and purpose of proposals, and name the basic components of informal proposals.

Proposals can mean life or death for an organization. Why are they so important? Let's begin by defining what they are. A *proposal* may be defined as a written offer to solve problems, provide services, or sell equipment. Profit-making organizations, such as Raytheon, depend on proposals to compete for business. A well-written proposal can generate millions of dollars of income. Smaller organizations also depend on proposals to sell their products and services. Equally dependent on proposals are many nonprofit organizations. Their funding depends on grant proposals, to be discussed shortly.

Some proposals are internal, often taking the form of justification and recommendation reports. You learned about these persuasive reports in Chapter 12. Most proposals, however, are external, such as those written at Raytheon. These proposals respond to requests for proposals (RFPs). When government organizations or businesses know exactly what they want, they prepare a *request for proposal* (RFP), specifying their requirements. Government agencies as well as private businesses use RFPs to solicit competitive bids from vendors. RFPs ensure that bids are comparable and that funds are awarded fairly, using consistent criteria.

Proposals may be further divided into two categories: solicited and unsolicited. Most proposals are solicited. For example, the city of Las Vegas published a 30-page RFP seeking proposal bids for a new parking structure from public and private funding sources.[2] Enterprising companies looking for work or a special challenge might submit an unsolicited proposal. For example, the world-renowned architect I. M. Pei, who designed the Louvre Museum pyramid in Paris, was so intrigued by a new biomedical research facility of Novato, California, that he submitted an unsolicited proposal to design the building.[3] Although many kinds of proposals exist, we'll focus on informal, formal, and grant proposals.

Components of Informal Proposals

Informal proposals may be presented in short (two- to four-page) letters. Sometimes called *letter proposals*, they usually contain six principal components: introduction, background, proposal, staffing, budget, and authorization request. As you can see in Figure 13.1, both informal and formal proposals contain these six basic parts.

Figure 13.2 illustrates a letter proposal to a Florida dentist who sought to improve patient satisfaction. Notice that this letter proposal contains all six components of an informal proposal.

Figure 13.1   Components of Informal and Formal Proposals

Informal Proposals	Formal Proposals
Introduction	Copy of RFP (optional)
Background, problem, purpose	Letter of transmittal
Proposal, plan, schedule	Abstract or summary
Staffing	Title page
Budget	Table of contents
Authorization	List of figures
	Introduction
	Background, problem, purpose
	Proposal, plan, schedule
	Staffing
	Budget
	Authorization
	Appendix

© Cengage Learning 2015

Figure **13.2** Informal Letter Proposal

1 Prewriting

Analyze: The purpose of this letter proposal is to persuade the reader to accept this proposal.

Anticipate: The reader expects this proposal but must be convinced that this survey project is worth its hefty price.

Adapt: Because the reader will be resistant at first, use a persuasive approach that emphasizes benefits.

2 Drafting

Research: Collect data about the reader's practice and other surveys of patient satisfaction.

Organize: Identify four specific purposes (benefits) of this proposal. Specify the survey plan. Promote the staff, itemize the budget, and ask for approval.

Draft: Prepare a first draft, expecting to improve it later.

3 Revising

Edit: Revise to emphasize benefits. Improve readability with functional headings and lists. Remove jargon and wordiness.

Proofread: Check spelling of client's name. Verify dates and calculation of budget figures. Recheck all punctuation.

Evaluate: Is this proposal convincing enough to sell the client?

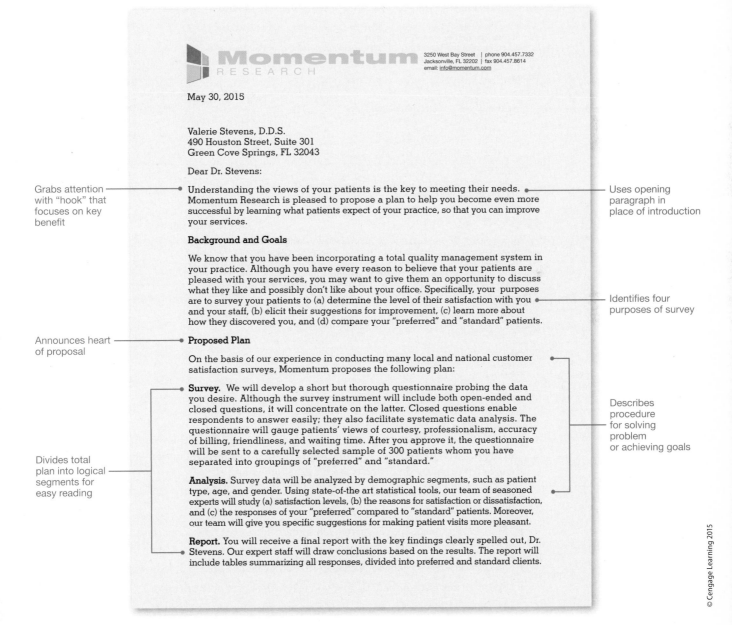

Grabs attention with "hook" that focuses on key benefit

Uses opening paragraph in place of introduction

Announces heart of proposal

Identifies four purposes of survey

Divides total plan into logical segments for easy reading

Describes procedure for solving problem or achieving goals

© Cengage Learning 2015

Figure **13.2** (Continued)

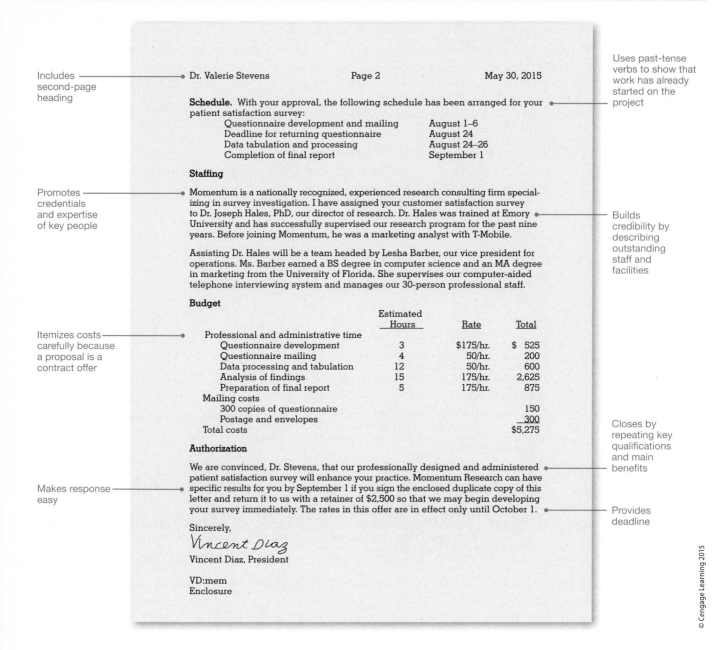

Includes second-page heading

Uses past-tense verbs to show that work has already started on the project

Dr. Valerie Stevens   Page 2   May 30, 2015

Schedule. With your approval, the following schedule has been arranged for your patient satisfaction survey:

Questionnaire development and mailing	August 1–6
Deadline for returning questionnaire	August 24
Data tabulation and processing	August 24–26
Completion of final report	September 1

Staffing

Promotes credentials and expertise of key people

Momentum is a nationally recognized, experienced research consulting firm specializing in survey investigation. I have assigned your customer satisfaction survey to Dr. Joseph Hales, PhD, our director of research. Dr. Hales was trained at Emory University and has successfully supervised our research program for the past nine years. Before joining Momentum, he was a marketing analyst with T-Mobile.

Builds credibility by describing outstanding staff and facilities

Assisting Dr. Hales will be a team headed by Lesha Barber, our vice president for operations. Ms. Barber earned a BS degree in computer science and an MA degree in marketing from the University of Florida. She supervises our computer-aided telephone interviewing system and manages our 30-person professional staff.

Budget

Itemizes costs carefully because a proposal is a contract offer

	Estimated Hours	Rate	Total
Professional and administrative time			
Questionnaire development	3	$175/hr.	$ 525
Questionnaire mailing	4	50/hr.	200
Data processing and tabulation	12	50/hr.	600
Analysis of findings	15	175/hr.	2,625
Preparation of final report	5	175/hr.	875
Mailing costs			
300 copies of questionnaire			150
Postage and envelopes			300
Total costs			$5,275

Authorization

Closes by repeating key qualifications and main benefits

Makes response easy

We are convinced, Dr. Stevens, that our professionally designed and administered patient satisfaction survey will enhance your practice. Momentum Research can have specific results for you by September 1 if you sign the enclosed duplicate copy of this letter and return it to us with a retainer of $2,500 so that we may begin developing your survey immediately. The rates in this offer are in effect only until October 1.

Provides deadline

Sincerely,

Vincent Diaz

Vincent Diaz, President

VD:mem
Enclosure

© Cengage Learning 2015

Introduction. Most proposals begin by briefly explaining the reasons for the proposal and highlighting the writer's qualifications. To make your introduction more persuasive, you should strive to provide a "hook," such as the following:

- Hint at extraordinary results with details to be revealed shortly.

- Promise low costs or speedy results.

- Mention a remarkable resource (well-known authority, new computer program, well-trained staff) available exclusively to you.

- Identify a serious problem (worry item) and promise a solution, to be explained later.

- Specify a key issue or benefit that you feel is the heart of the proposal.

Although writers may know what goes into the proposal introduction, many face writer's block before they can get started. Proposal expert Tom Sant recommends a method he calls *cognitive webbing* to overcome the paralyzing effects of writer's block and arrive at a proposal writing plan. Dr. Sant tells proposal writers to (a) identify the outcome the client seeks, (b) brainstorm by writing down every idea and detail that will help the client achieve that objective, and (c) prioritize by focusing on the client's most pressing needs.[4] You may have brainstormed using a similar technique, sometimes called *mind mapping*, to generate ideas for your papers. Like brainstorming, mind mapping involves generating ideas around a single word and grouping those ideas into major and minor categories, thus creating a web of relationships.

In the proposal introduction shown in Figure 13.2, Vincent Diaz focused on what the customer wanted. The researcher analyzed the request of Florida dentist, Dr. Valerie Stevens, and decided that she was most interested in specific recommendations for improving service to her patients. However, Vincent did not hit on this hook until he had written a first draft and had come back to it later. It's not a bad idea to put off writing the proposal introduction until after you have completed other parts. In longer proposals the introduction also describes the scope and limitations of the project, as well as outlining the organization of the material to come.

Background, Problem, and Purpose. The background section identifies the problem and discusses the goals or purposes of the project. In an unsolicited proposal, your goal is to convince the reader that a problem exists. Therefore, you must present the problem in detail, discussing such factors as monetary losses, failure to comply with government regulations, or loss of customers. In a solicited proposal, your aim is to persuade the reader that you understand the problem completely. Therefore, if you are responding to an RFP, this means repeating its language. For example, if the RFP asks for the *design of a maintenance program for mobile communication equipment*, you would use the same language in explaining the purpose of your proposal. This section might include segments titled Basic Requirements, Most Critical Tasks, or Most Important Secondary Problems.

Proposal, Plan, and Schedule. In the proposal section itself, you should discuss your plan for solving the problem. In some proposals this is tricky because you want to disclose enough of your plan to secure the contract without giving away so much information that your services aren't needed. Without specifics, though, your proposal has little chance, so you must decide how much to reveal. Tell what you propose to do and how it will benefit the reader. Remember, however, that a proposal is a sales presentation. Sell your methods, product, and *deliverables* (items that will be left with the client). In this section some writers specify how the project will be managed and how its progress will be audited. Most writers also include a schedule of activities or timetable showing when events will take place.

REALITY CHECK: But Will They Steal My Ideas?

"You may fear that revealing your ideas about how to solve a problem during the proposal process could result in clients taking those ideas and completing the project themselves. In rare cases, that may happen. But you'll have more success if you don't hoard your ideas."[5]

—MICHAEL W. MCLAUGHLIN, *consultant and coauthor of* Guerilla Marketing for Consultants

Staffing. The staffing section of a proposal describes the credentials and expertise of the project leaders. It may also identify the size and qualifications of the support staff, along with other resources such as computer facilities and special programs for analyzing statistics. The staffing section is a good place to endorse and promote your staff and to demonstrate to the client that your company can do the job. Some firms, like Raytheon, follow industry standards and include staff qualifications in an appendix. Raytheon features the résumés of the major project participants, such as the program manager, the technical director, and team leaders. If key contributors must be replaced in the course of the project, Raytheon commits to providing only individuals with equivalent qualifications. The first rule is to give clients exactly what they asked for regarding staff qualifications, the number of project participants, and proposal details.

Budget.   A central item in most proposals is the budget, a list of proposed project costs. You need to prepare this section carefully because it represents a contract; you cannot raise the price later—even if your costs increase. You can—and should—protect yourself from rising costs with a deadline for acceptance. In the budget section, some writers itemize hours and costs; others present a total sum only. A proposal to install a complex system of interactive office equipment might, for example, contain a detailed line-by-line budget. Similarly, Vincent Diaz felt that he needed to justify the budget for his firm's patient satisfaction survey, so he itemized the costs, as shown in Figure 13.2. However, the budget for a proposal to conduct a one-day seminar to improve employee communication skills might be a lump sum only. Your analysis of the project will help you decide what kind of budget to prepare.

Authorization Request.   Informal proposals often close with a request for approval or authorization. In addition, the closing should remind the reader of key benefits and motivate action. It might also include a deadline beyond which the offer is invalid. At Raytheon authorization information can be as simple as naming in the letter of transmittal the company official who would approve the contract resulting from the proposal. However, in most cases, a *model contract* is sent along that responds to the requirements specified by the RFP. This model contract almost always results in negotiations before the final project contract is awarded.

LEARNING OBJECTIVE **2**

Discuss the components of formal and grant proposals.

Preparing Formal Proposals

Formal proposals differ from informal proposals not in style but in size and format. Formal proposals respond to big projects and may range from 5 to 200 or more pages. Because proposals are vital to the success of many organizations, larger businesses may maintain specialists who do nothing but write proposals. Smaller firms rely on in-house staff to develop proposals. Proposals use standard components that enable companies receiving bids to compare "apples with apples." Writers must know the parts of proposals and how to develop those parts effectively.

Components of Formal Proposals

To help readers understand and locate the parts of a formal proposal, writers organize the project into a typical structure, as shown in Figure 13.1. In addition to the six basic components described for informal proposals, formal proposals may contain some or all of the following front matter and back matter components.

Copy of the RFP.   A copy of the request for proposal may be included in the front matter of a formal proposal. Large organizations may have more than one RFP circulating, and identification is necessary.

Letter of Transmittal.   A letter of transmittal, usually bound inside formal proposals, addresses the person who is designated to receive the proposal or who will make the final decision. The letter describes how you learned about the problem or confirms that the proposal responds to the enclosed RFP. This persuasive letter briefly presents the major features and benefits of your proposal. Here, you should assure the reader that you are authorized to make the bid and mention the time limit for which the bid stands. You may also offer to provide additional information and ask for action, if appropriate.

Abstract or Executive Summary.   An abstract is a brief summary (typically one page) of a proposal's highlights intended for specialists or technical readers. An executive summary also reviews the proposal's highlights, but it is written for managers and should be less technically oriented. An executive summary tends to be longer than an abstract, up to 10 percent of the original text. In reports and proposals, the executive summary typically represents a nutshell version of the entire document and addresses all its sections or chapters. Formal proposals may contain either an abstract or an executive summary, or both. For more information about writing executive summaries in formal reports, see the discussion on page 477.

Title Page.   The title page includes the following items, generally in this order: title of proposal, name of client organization, RFP number or other announcement, date of submission, and the authors' names and/or the name of their organization.

Table of Contents.   Because most proposals do not contain an index, the table of contents becomes quite important. A table of contents should include all headings and their beginning page numbers. Items that appear before the contents (copy of RFP, letter of transmittal, abstract, and title page) typically are not listed in the contents. However, any appendixes should be listed.

List of Illustrations.   Proposals with many tables and figures often contain a list of illustrations. This list includes each figure or table title and its page number. If you have just a few figures or tables, however, you may omit this list.

Appendix(es).   Ancillary material of interest to only some readers goes in appendixes. Appendix A might include résumés of the principal investigators or testimonial letters. Appendix B might include examples or a listing of previous projects. Other appendixes could include audit procedures, technical graphics, or professional papers cited in the body of the proposal.

Grant Proposals

A *grant proposal* is a formal proposal submitted to a government or civilian organization that explains a project, outlines its budget, and requests money in the form of a grant. Every year the U.S. government, private foundations, and public corporations make available billions of dollars in funding for special projects. These funds, or grants, require no repayment, but the funds must be used for the purposes outlined in the proposal. Grants are often made to charities, educational facilities, and especially to nonprofits. Securing funding can mean life or death for nonprofits and other organizations.

Organizations such as McDonald's offer millions of dollars in grants to support health care. This past year one of the many grants from Ronald McDonald House Charities focused on Project C.U.R.E. The grant provided funds for clinic teams to travel to Belize, Mexico, Peru, Ghana, Tanzania, India, and Papua New Guinea. The overall goal of Project C.U.R.E. was reducing birth asphyxia and mortality rates in babies.[6]

Many of the parts of a grant proposal are similar to those of a formal proposal. A grant proposal includes an abstract and a needs statement that explains a problem or situation that the grant project proposes to address. The body of the proposal explains that the problem is significant enough to warrant funding and that the proposal can solve the problem. The body also describes short- and long-term goals, which must be reasonable, measurable, and attainable within a specific time frame. An action plan tells what will be done by whom and when. The budget outlines how the money will be spent. Finally, a grant proposal presents a plan for measuring progress toward completion of its goal.

Skilled grant writers are among the most in-demand professionals today. A grant writer is the vital connecting link between a funder and the grant seeker. Large projects may require a team of writers to produce various sections of a grant proposal. Then one person does the final editing and proofreading. Effective grant proposals require careful organization, planning, and writing. Skillful writing is particularly important because funding organizations may receive thousands of applications for a single award.

© iStockphoto.com/Bartosz Hadyniak

Ronald McDonald House Charities provided a grant for health workers to focus on reducing infant mortality rates in remote locations.

Well-written proposals win contracts and sustain the business life of many companies, individuals, and nonprofit organizations. The following checklist summarizes key elements to remember in writing proposals.

Writing Proposals

Introduction

- **Indicate the purpose.** Specify why you are making the proposal.
- **Develop a persuasive "hook."** Suggest excellent results, low costs, or exclusive resources. Identify a serious problem or name a key issue or benefit.

Background, Problem, Purpose

- **Provide necessary background.** Discuss the significance of the proposal and the goals or purposes that matter to the client.
- **Introduce the problem.** For unsolicited proposals convince the reader that a problem exists. For solicited proposals show that you fully understand the customer's problem and its ramifications.

Proposal, Plan, Schedule

- **Explain the proposal.** Present your plan for solving the problem or meeting the need.
- **Discuss plan management and evaluation.** If appropriate, tell how the plan will be implemented and evaluated.

- **Outline a timetable.** Furnish a schedule showing what will be done and when.

Staffing

- **Promote the qualifications of your staff.** Explain the specific credentials and expertise of the key personnel for the project.
- **Mention special resources and equipment.** Show how your support staff and resources are superior to those of the competition.

Budget

- **Show project costs.** For most projects itemize costs. Remember, however, that proposals are contracts.
- **Include a deadline.** Here or in the conclusion, present a date beyond which the bid figures are no longer valid.

Authorization

- **Ask for approval.** Make it easy for the reader to authorize the project (for example, *Sign and return the duplicate copy*).

© Daniilantiq/Shutterstock.com

LEARNING OBJECTIVE 3
Identify the components of typical business plans.

Creating Effective Business Plans

Another form of proposal is a business plan. Let's say you want to start your own business. Unless you can count on the Bank of Mom and Dad, you will need financial backing such as a bank loan, seed money from an individual angel investor, or funds supplied by venture capitalists. A business plan is critical for securing financial support of any kind. Such a plan also ensures that you have done your homework and know what you are doing in launching your business. It provides you with a detailed road map to chart a course to success.

Creating a business plan for an entirely new concept takes time. Estimates range from 160 to 640 hours to research and write a start-up plan.[7] Consultants can probably do it in less time, but they may be pricy. Budding entrepreneurs often prefer to save the cash and do it themselves. Classic software such as Business Plan Pro can help those who have done their research, assembled the relevant data, and just want formatting help. Enloop, a more recent business plan app, makes it quick and easy to provide a financial forecast for bankers and investors.[8] However, no business plan app can provide a cookie-cutter plan that works for everyone.

Components of Typical Business Plans

For people who are serious about starting a business, the importance of a comprehensive, thoughtful business plan cannot be overemphasized, says the Small Business

While winners of business plan competitions rarely get beyond the planning phase of starting a business, Chapman University student Matt Kanne succeeded at turning his first-prize business plan into Open Gym, a million-dollar four-court basketball training center in Anaheim, California. For years Kanne had dreamed about his Open Gym concept, but writing down ideas in an organized business plan helped make the dream a reality, as abstract visions of leagues and tournaments quickly transformed into moneymaking strategies in the minds of interested investors. What purposes do business plans serve?[9]

Administration. A *business plan* may be defined as a description of a proposed company that explains how it expects to achieve its marketing, financial, and operational goals. If you are considering becoming an entrepreneur, your business plan is more likely to secure the funds it needs if it is carefully written and includes the following elements.

Letter of Transmittal.   A letter of transmittal provides contact information for all principals and explains your reason for writing. If you are seeking venture capital or an angel investor, the transmittal letter may become a pitch letter. In that case you would want to include a simple description of your idea and a clear statement of what's in it for the investor. The letter should include a summary of the market, a brief note about the competition, and an explanation of why your business plan is worthy of investment.

> For people who are serious about starting a business, the importance of a comprehensive, thoughtful business plan cannot be overemphasized, says the Small Business Administration.

Mission Statement.   A business plan mission statement explains the purpose of your business and why it will succeed. Because potential investors will be looking for this mission statement, consider highlighting it with a paragraph heading (*Mission Statement*) or use bolding or italics. Some consultants say that you should be able to write your mission statement in eight or fewer words.[10] Others think that one or two short paragraphs might be more realistic. Many Fortune 500 companies have created mission statements that are both inspirational and concrete. For example, Starbucks states its mission simply but graphically: "To inspire and nurture the human spirit—one person, one cup and one neighborhood at a time." As illustrated in Figure 13.3, mission statements should be simple, concise, memorable, and unique.

REALITY CHECK: The Eight-Word Mission Statement

Advocating for very concise mission statements, Kevin Starr says, "We've found the eight-word mission a crucial tool for funding decisions. . . . As investors in impact, we—the Mulago Foundation—don't want to wade through a bunch of verbiage about 'empowerment,' 'capacity-building,' and 'sustainability'—we want to know exactly [what] you're trying to accomplish. We want to cut to the chase, and the tool that works for us is the eight-word mission statement."

—**KEVIN STARR,** *social entrepreneur and managing director, the Mulago Foundation*

Figure **13.3** Creating Winning Mission Statements

Definition

A mission statement describes the reason an organization or program exists.

GOALS should be:

- Easily understood
- Free of complex words and buzz words
- Concise, memorable, and simple
- Unique in distinguishing a business or program

QUESTIONS TO PONDER

What do we do?

Why and how do we serve our clients?

What image do we want to convey?

Why did we start this business?

What is the broadest way to describe our work?

EXAMPLES

Nonprofit Organizations

Wounded Warrior Project: To honor and empower wounded warriors

The Humane Society: Celebrating Animals, Confronting Cruelty

Charity Water: We're a nonprofit organization bringing clean, safe drinking water to people in developing countries.

Make-A-Wish: We grant the wishes of children with life-threatening medical conditions to enrich the human experience with hope, strength and joy.

Fortune 500 Companies

Nike: To bring inspiration and innovation to every athlete in the world

ADM: To unlock the potential of nature to improve the quality of life

Gap, Inc. is a brand-builder. We create emotional connections with customers around the world through inspiring product design, unique store experiences, and compelling marketing.

Amazon: To be the most customer-centric company in the world, where people can find and discover anything they want to buy online

© Cengage Learning 2015

Executive Summary. Your executive summary, which is written last, highlights the main points of your business plan and should not exceed two pages. It should conclude by introducing the parts of the plan and asking for financial backing. Some business plans combine the mission statement and executive summary.

Table of Contents and Company Description. List the page numbers and topics included in your plan. Identify the form of your business (proprietorship, partnership, or corporation) and its type (merchandising, manufacturing, or service). For existing companies, describe the company's founding, growth, sales, and profit.

Product or Service Description. In jargon-free language, explain what you are providing, how it will benefit customers, and why it is better than existing products or services. For start-ups, explain why the business will be profitable. Investors aren't always looking for a unique product or service. Instead, they are searching for a concept whose growth potential distinguishes it from others competing for funds.

Market Analysis.   Discuss market characteristics, trends, projected growth, customer behavior, complementary products and services, and barriers to entry. Identify your customers and how you will attract, hold, and increase your market share. Discuss the strengths and weaknesses of your direct and indirect competitors.

Operations and Management.   Explain specifically how you will run your business, including location, equipment, personnel, and management. Highlight experienced and well-trained members of the management team and your advisors. Many investors consider this the most important factor in assessing business potential. Can your management team implement this business plan?

Financial Analysis.   Outline a realistic start-up budget that includes fees for legal and professional services, occupancy, licenses and permits, equipment, insurance, supplies, advertising and promotions, salaries and wages, accounting, income, and utilities. Also present an operating budget that projects costs for personnel, insurance, rent, depreciation, loan payments, salaries, taxes, repairs, and so on. Explain how much money you have, how much you will need to start up, and how much you will need to stay in business.

Appendixes.   Provide necessary extras such as managers' résumés, promotional materials, and product photos. Most appendixes contain tables that exhibit the sales forecast, a personnel plan, anticipated cash flow, profit and loss, and a balance sheet.

Sample Business Plans on the Web

Writing a business plan is easier if you can see examples and learn from experts' suggestions. On the Web you will find many sites devoted to business plans. Some sites want to sell you something; others offer free advice. One of the best sites (**http://www.bplans .com/samples/sba.cfm**) does try to sell business plans and software. However, in addition to useful advice and blogs from experts, the site provides over 100 free samples of business plans ranging from aircraft rental to wedding consultant businesses. These simple but helpful plans, provided by Palo Alto Software, Inc., illustrate diverse business start-ups.

At the Small Business Administration (SBA) site (**http://www.sba.gov/business -plan/1**), you will find more business plan advice. By registering with the SBA, you can access an eight-step plan for building a business plan. The SBA site provides helpful business start-up information about financing, marketing, employees, taxes, and legal matters.

Writing Formal Business Reports

A *formal report* may be defined as a document in which a writer analyzes findings, draws conclusions, and makes recommendations intended to solve a problem. Formal business reports are similar to formal proposals in length, organization, and serious tone. Instead of making an offer, however, formal reports represent the end product of thorough investigation and analysis. They present ordered information to decision makers in business, industry, government, and education. In many ways formal business reports are extended versions of the analytical business reports presented in Chapter 12. If you are preparing a formal business report, be sure to review the work plan that appears in Figure 11.6 on page 385 in Chapter 11.

Informal and formal business reports have similar components, as shown in Figure 13.4, but, as might be expected, formal reports have more sections.

Front Matter Components of Formal Business Reports

A number of front matter and back matter items lengthen formal reports but enhance their professional tone and serve their multiple audiences. Formal reports may be read by many levels of managers, along with technical specialists and financial consultants. Therefore,

LEARNING OBJECTIVE **4**
Describe the components of the front matter in formal business reports, and show how they further the purpose of the report.

Figure **13.4** Components of Informal and Formal Reports

Informal Business Reports

Introduction
Body
Conclusions
Recommendations (if requested)

Formal Business Reports

Cover
Title page
Letter of transmittal
Table of contents
List of figures
Executive summary
Introduction
Body
Conclusions
Recommendations (if requested)
Appendix
References

© Cengage Learning 2015

breaking a long, formal report into small segments makes its information more accessible and easier to understand for all readers. The segments in the front of the report, called front matter or preliminaries, are discussed in this section. They are also illustrated in Figure 13.5, the model formal report shown later in the chapter. This analytical report studies the economic impact of an industrial park on Flagstaff, Arizona, and makes recommendations for increasing the city's revenues.

Cover.   Traditional formal reports are usually enclosed in vinyl or heavy paper binders to protect the pages and to give a professional, finished appearance. Some companies have binders imprinted with their name and logo. The title of the report may appear through a cut-out window or may be applied with an adhesive label. Electronic formal reports may present an attractive title with the company logo.

Title Page.   A report title page, as illustrated in the Figure 13.5 model report, begins with the name of the report typed in uppercase letters (no underscore and no quotation marks). Next comes *Presented to* (or *Submitted to*) and the name, title, and organization of the individual receiving the report. Lower on the page is *Prepared by* (or *Submitted by*) and the author's name plus any necessary identification. The last item on the title page is the date of submission. All items after the title are typed in a combination of upper- and lowercase letters.

Letter or Memo of Transmittal.   Generally written on organization stationery, a letter or memorandum of transmittal introduces a formal report. You will recall that letters are sent to outsiders and memos to insiders. A transmittal letter or memo uses the direct strategy and is usually less formal than the report itself (for example, the letter or memo may use contractions and the first-person pronouns *I* and *we*). The transmittal letter or memo typically (a) announces the topic of the report and tells how it was authorized; (b) briefly describes the project; (c) highlights the report's findings, conclusions, and recommendations, if the reader is expected to be supportive; and (d) closes with appreciation for the assignment, instruction for the reader's follow-up actions, acknowledgement of help from others, or offers of assistance in answering questions. If a report is going to various readers, a special transmittal letter or memo should be prepared for each, anticipating how each reader will use the report.

Table of Contents. The table of contents shows the headings in the report and their page numbers. It gives an overview of the report topics and helps readers locate them. You should wait to prepare the table of contents until after you have completed the report. For short reports you should include all headings. For longer reports you might want to list only first- and second-level headings. Leaders (spaced or unspaced dots) help guide the eye from the heading to the page number. Items may be indented in outline form or typed flush with the left margin.

List of Illustrations. For reports with several figures or tables, you may wish to include a list to help readers locate them. This list may appear on the same page as the table of contents, space permitting. For each figure or table, include a title and page number. Some writers distinguish between tables and all other illustrations, which they call figures. If you make the distinction, you should prepare separate lists of tables and figures. Because the model report in Figure 13.5 has few illustrations, the writer labeled them all *figures*, a method that simplifies numbering.

Executive Summary. The purpose of an executive summary is to present an overview of a longer report to people who may not have time to read the entire document. Generally, an executive summary is prepared by the author of the report. However, occasionally you may be asked to write an executive summary of a published report or article written by someone else. In either case, your goal will be to summarize the important points. The best way to prepare an executive summary is to do the following:

- **Look for strategic words and sentences.** Read the completed report carefully. Pay special attention to the first and last sentences of paragraphs, which often contain summary statements. Look for words that enumerate (*first, next, finally*) and words that express causation (*therefore, as a result*). Also, look for words that signal essentials (*basically, central, leading, principal, major*) and words that contrast ideas (*however, consequently*).

- **Prepare an outline with headings.** At a minimum, include headings for the purpose, findings, and conclusions/recommendations. What kernels of information would your reader want to know about these topics?

- **Fill in your outline.** Some writers cut and paste important parts of the text. Then they condense with careful editing. Others find it more efficient to create new sentences as they prepare the executive summary.

- **Begin with the purpose.** The easiest way to begin an executive summary is with the words *The purpose of this report is to . . . .* Experienced writers may be more creative.

- **Follow the report sequence.** Present all your information in the order in which it is found in the report.

- **Eliminate nonessential details.** Include only main points. Do not include anything not in the original report. Use minimal technical language.

- **Control the length.** An executive summary is usually no longer than 10 percent of the original document. Thus, a 100-page report might require a 10-page summary. A 10-page report might need only a 1-page summary—or no summary at all. The executive summary for a long report may also include graphics to adequately highlight main points.

To see a representative executive summary, look at Figure 13.5 on page 481. Although it is only one page long, this executive summary includes headings to help the reader see the main divisions immediately. Let your organization's practices guide you in determining the length and format of an executive summary.

Introduction.   Formal reports begin with an introduction that sets the scene and announces the subject. Because they contain many parts that serve different purposes, formal reports are somewhat redundant. The same information may be included in the letter of transmittal, summary, and introduction. To avoid sounding repetitious, try to present the data slightly differently. However, do not skip the introduction because you have included some of its information elsewhere. You cannot be sure that your reader saw the information earlier. A good report introduction typically covers the following elements, although not necessarily in this order:

- **Background.** Describe events leading up to the problem or need.

- **Problem or purpose.** Explain the report topic and specify the problem or need that motivated the report.

- **Significance.** Tell why the topic is important. You may wish to quote experts or cite newspapers, journals, books, Web resources, and other secondary sources to establish the importance of the topic.

- **Scope.** Clarify the boundaries of the report, defining what will be included or excluded.

- **Organization.** Orient readers by giving them a road map that previews the structure of the report.

Beyond these minimal introductory elements, consider adding any of the following information that may be relevant to your readers:

- **Authorization.** Identify who commissioned the report. If no letter of transmittal is included, also tell why, when, by whom, and to whom the report was written.

- **Literature review.** Summarize what other authors and researchers have published on this topic, especially for academic and scientific reports.

- **Sources and methods.** Describe your secondary sources (periodicals, books, databases). Also explain how you collected primary data, including the survey size, sample design, and statistical programs you used.

- **Definitions of key terms.** Define words that may be unfamiliar to the audience. Also define terms with special meanings, such as *small businesses* when it specifically means businesses with fewer than 30 employees.

LEARNING OBJECTIVE **5**
Understand the body and back matter of formal business reports and how they serve the purpose of the report.

Body and Back Matter Components of Formal Business Reports

The body of a formal business report is the "meat" of the document. In this longest and most substantive section of the text, the author or team discusses the problem and findings, before reaching conclusions and making recommendations. Extensive and bulky materials that don't fit in the text belong in the appendix. Although some very long reports may have additional components, the back matter usually concludes with a list of sources. The body and back matter of formal business reports are discussed in this section. Figure 13.4 shows the parts of typical reports, the order in which they appear, and elements usually found only in formal reports.

Because formal business reports can be long and complex, they usually include more sections than routine informal business reports do. These components are standard and conventional; that is, the audience expects to see them in a professional report. Documents that conform to such expectations are easier to read and deliver their message more effectively. You will find most of the components addressed here in the model report in Figure 13.5, the formal analytical report studying the economic impact of an industrial park on Flagstaff, Arizona.

Body.   The principal section in a formal report is the body. It discusses, analyzes, interprets, and evaluates the research findings or solution to the initial problem. This is where you show the evidence that justifies your conclusions. Organize the body into main categories following your original outline or using one of the organizational methods described in Chapter 12 (i.e., time, component, importance, criteria, or convention).

Although we refer to this section as the body, it does not carry that heading. Instead, it contains clear headings that explain each major section. Headings may be functional or talking. Functional heads (such as *Results of the Survey, Analysis of Findings,* or *Discussion*) help readers identify the purpose of the section but do not reveal what is in it. Such headings are useful for routine reports or for sensitive topics that may upset readers. Talking heads (for example, *Findings Reveal Revenue and Employment Benefits*) are more informative and interesting, but they do not help readers see the organization of the report. The model report in Figure 13.5 uses combination headings; as the name suggests, they combine functional heads for organizational sections (*Introduction, Conclusions and Recommendations*) with talking heads that reveal the content. The headings divide the body into smaller parts.

Conclusions.   This important section tells what the findings mean, particularly in terms of solving the original problem. Some writers prefer to intermix their conclusions with the analysis of the findings—instead of presenting the conclusions separately. Other writers place the conclusions before the body so that busy readers can examine the significant information immediately. Still others combine the conclusions and recommendations. Most writers, though, present the conclusions after the body because readers expect this structure. In long reports this section may include a summary of the findings. To improve comprehension, you may present the conclusions in a numbered or bulleted list. See Chapter 12 for more suggestions on drawing conclusions.

Recommendations.   When asked, you should submit recommendations that make precise suggestions for actions to solve the report problem. Recommendations are most helpful when they are practical, reasonable, feasible, and ethical. Naturally, they should evolve from the findings and conclusions. Do not introduce new information in the conclusions or recommendations sections. As with conclusions, the position of recommendations is somewhat flexible. They may be combined with conclusions, or they may be presented before the body, especially when the audience is eager and supportive. Generally, though, in formal reports they come last.

Recommendations require an appropriate introductory sentence, such as *The findings and conclusions in this study support the following recommendations*. When making many recommendations, number them and phrase each as a command, such as *Begin an employee fitness program with a workout room available five days a week*. If appropriate, add information describing how to implement each recommendation. Some reports include a timetable describing the who, what, when, where, why, and how for putting each recommendation into operation. Chapter 12 provides more information about writing recommendations.

Appendix(es).   Incidental or supporting materials belong in appendixes at the end of a formal report. These materials are relevant to some readers but not to all. They may also be too bulky to include in the text. Appendixes may include survey forms, copies of other reports, tables of data, large graphics, and related correspondence. If multiple appendixes are necessary, they are named *Appendix A, Appendix B*, and so forth.

Works Cited or References.   If you use the MLA (Modern Language Association) referencing format, list all sources of information alphabetically in a section titled *Works Cited*. If you use the APA (American Psychological Association) format, your list is called *References*. Your listed sources must correspond to in-text citations in the report whenever you are borrowing words or ideas from published and unpublished resources.

Regardless of the documentation format, you must include the author, title, publication, date of publication, page number, and other significant data for all ideas or quotations used in your report. For electronic references include the preceding information plus the Internet address or URL leading to the citation. For model electronic and other citations, examine the list of references at the end of Figure 13.5. Appendix C of this textbook contains additional documentation models and information.

Final Writing Tips

Formal business reports are not undertaken lightly. They involve considerable effort in all three phases of writing, beginning with analysis of the problem and anticipation of the audience (as discussed in Chapter 4). Researching the data, organizing it into a logical presentation, and composing the first draft (Chapter 5) make up the second phase of writing. Editing, proofreading, and evaluating (Chapter 6) are completed in the third phase. Although everyone

LEARNING OBJECTIVE **6**
Specify final writing tips that aid authors of formal business reports.

approaches the writing process somewhat differently, the following tips offer advice in problem areas faced by most writers of formal reports:

- **Allow sufficient time.** The main reason given by writers who are disappointed with their reports is "I just ran out of time." Develop a realistic timetable and stick to it.

- **Finish data collection.** Do not begin writing until you have collected all the data and drawn the primary conclusions. Starting too early often means backtracking. For reports based on survey data, complete the tables and figures first.

- **Work from a good outline.** A big project such as a formal report needs the order and direction provided by a clear outline, even if the outline has to be revised as the project unfolds.

- **Create a proper writing environment.** You will need a quiet spot where you can spread out your materials and work without interruption. Formal reports demand blocks of concentration time.

- **Use the features of your computer wisely.** Your word processor enables you to keyboard quickly; revise easily; and check spelling, grammar, and synonyms readily. A word of warning, though: save your document often and keep backup copies on disks or other devices. Print out important materials so that you have a hard copy. Take these precautions to guard against the grief caused by lost files, power outages, and computer malfunctions.

- **Write rapidly; revise later.** Some experts advise writers to record their ideas quickly and save revision until after the first draft is completed. They say that quick writing avoids wasted effort spent in polishing sentences or even sections that may be cut later. Moreover, rapid writing encourages fluency and creativity. However, a quick-and-dirty first draft does not work for everyone. Many business writers prefer a more deliberate writing style, so consider this advice selectively and experiment to find the method that works best for you.

- **Save difficult sections.** If some sections are harder to write than others, save them until you have developed confidence and a rhythm from working on easier topics.

- **Be consistent in verb tense.** Use past-tense verbs to describe completed actions (for example, *the respondents said* or *the survey showed*). Use present-tense verbs, however, to explain current actions (*the purpose of the report is, this report examines, the table shows*). When citing references, use past-tense verbs (*Jones reported that*). Do not switch back and forth between present- and past-tense verbs in describing related data.

- **Generally avoid *I* and *we*.** To make formal reports seem as objective and credible as possible, most writers omit first-person pronouns. This formal style sometimes results in the overuse of passive-voice verbs (for example, *periodicals were consulted* and *the study was conducted*). Look for alternative constructions (*periodicals indicated* and *the study revealed*). It is also possible that your organization may allow first-person pronouns, so check before starting your report.

- **Let the first draft sit.** After completing the first version, put it aside for a day or two. Return to it with the expectation of revising and improving it. Do not be afraid to make major changes.

- **Revise for clarity, coherence, and conciseness.** Read a printed copy out loud. Do the sentences make sense? Do the ideas flow together naturally? Can wordiness and flabbiness be cut out? Make sure that your writing is so clear that a busy manager does not have to reread any part. See Chapter 6 for specific revision suggestions.

- **Proofread the final copy three times.** First, read a printed copy slowly for word meanings and content. Then read the copy again for spelling, punctuation, grammar, and other mechanical errors. Finally, scan the entire report to check its formatting and consistency (page numbering, indenting, spacing, headings, and so forth).

Putting It All Together

Formal reports in business generally aim to study problems and recommend solutions. Martha Montoya, senior research consultant with Sedona Development Company, was asked to study the economic impact of a local industrial park on the city of Flagstaff, Arizona, resulting in the formal report shown in Figure 13.5.

Figure **13.5** Model Formal Report With APA Citation Style 481

Includes report title in all caps with longer line above shorter line

2 inches

**ECONOMIC IMPACT OF COCONINO INDUSTRIAL PARK
ON THE CITY OF FLAGSTAFF**

Highlights name of report recipient

Prepared for
The Flagstaff City Council
Flagstaff, Arizona

Divide blank lines equally to separate the sections

Identifies report writer

Prepared by
Martha E. Montoya
Senior Research Consultant
Sedona Development Company

January 12, 2015

Omits page number

2 inches

© Cengage Learning 2015

The title page is usually arranged in four evenly balanced areas. If the report is to be bound on the left, move the left margin and center point ¼ inch to the right (i.e., set the left margin to 1.25 inches). Notice that no page number appears on the title page, although it counts as page i. In designing the title page, be careful to avoid anything unprofessional—such as too many type fonts, italics, oversized print, and inappropriate graphics. Keep the title page simple and professional.

This model report uses APA documentation style. However, it does not use double-spacing, the recommended format for research papers using APA style. Instead, this model uses single-spacing, which saves space and is more appropriate for business reports.

Figure **13.5** (Continued) Letter of Transmittal

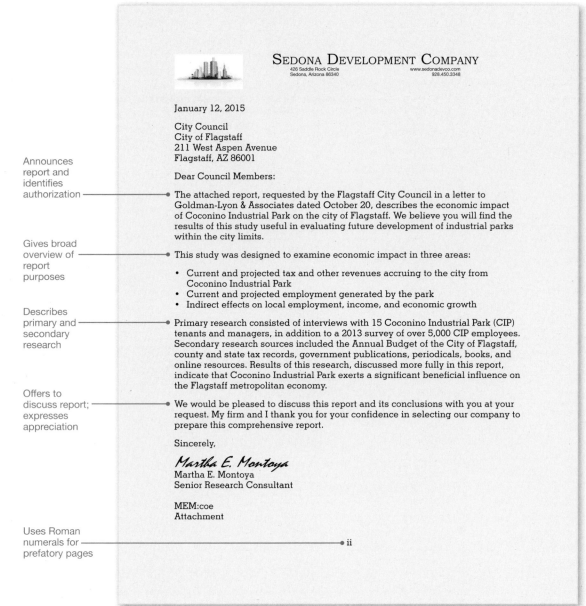

Announces report and identifies authorization

Gives broad overview of report purposes

Describes primary and secondary research

Offers to discuss report; expresses appreciation

Uses Roman numerals for prefatory pages

SEDONA DEVELOPMENT COMPANY
426 Saddle Rock Circle
Sedona, Arizona 86340
www.sedonadevco.com
928.450.3348

January 12, 2015

City Council
City of Flagstaff
211 West Aspen Avenue
Flagstaff, AZ 86001

Dear Council Members:

The attached report, requested by the Flagstaff City Council in a letter to Goldman-Lyon & Associates dated October 20, describes the economic impact of Coconino Industrial Park on the city of Flagstaff. We believe you will find the results of this study useful in evaluating future development of industrial parks within the city limits.

This study was designed to examine economic impact in three areas:

- Current and projected tax and other revenues accruing to the city from Coconino Industrial Park
- Current and projected employment generated by the park
- Indirect effects on local employment, income, and economic growth

Primary research consisted of interviews with 15 Coconino Industrial Park (CIP) tenants and managers, in addition to a 2013 survey of over 5,000 CIP employees. Secondary research sources included the Annual Budget of the City of Flagstaff, county and state tax records, government publications, periodicals, books, and online resources. Results of this research, discussed more fully in this report, indicate that Coconino Industrial Park exerts a significant beneficial influence on the Flagstaff metropolitan economy.

We would be pleased to discuss this report and its conclusions with you at your request. My firm and I thank you for your confidence in selecting our company to prepare this comprehensive report.

Sincerely,

Martha E. Montoya

Martha E. Montoya
Senior Research Consultant

MEM:coe
Attachment

ii

© Cengage Learning 2015

A letter or memo of transmittal announces the report topic and explains who authorized it. It briefly describes the project and previews the conclusions, if the reader is supportive. Such messages generally close by expressing appreciation for the assignment, suggesting follow-up actions, acknowledging the help of others, or offering to answer questions. The margins for the transmittal should be the same as for the report, about 1 to 1¼ inches on all sides. The letter should be left-justified. A page number is optional.

Figure **13.5** (Continued) Table of Contents and List of Figures

483

TABLE OF CONTENTS

Uses leaders to guide eye from heading to page number

Indents secondary headings to show levels of outline

LIST OF FIGURES

Includes tables and figures in one list for simplified numbering

iii

© Cengage Learning 2015

Because the table of contents and the list of figures for this report are small, they are combined on one page. Notice that the titles of major report parts are in all caps, while other headings are a combination of upper- and lowercase letters. This duplicates the style within the report. Advanced word processing capabilities enable you to generate a contents page automatically, including leaders and accurate page numbering—no matter how many times you revise. Notice that the page numbers are right-justified. Multiple-digit page numbers must line up properly (say, the number 9 under the 0 of 10).

Figure **13.5** (Continued) Executive Summary

EXECUTIVE SUMMARY

Opens directly with major research findings

The city of Flagstaff can benefit from the development of industrial parks like the Coconino Industrial Park. Both direct and indirect economic benefits result, as shown by this in-depth study conducted by Sedona Development Company. The study was authorized by the Flagstaff City Council when Goldman-Lyon & Associates sought the City Council's approval for the proposed construction of a G-L industrial park. The City Council requested evidence demonstrating that an existing development could actually benefit the city.

Identifies data sources

Our conclusion that the city of Flagstaff benefits from industrial parks is based on data supplied by a survey of 5,000 Coconino Industrial Park employees, personal interviews with managers and tenants of CIP, city and state documents, and professional literature.

Summarizes organization of report

Analysis of the data revealed benefits in three areas:

- **Revenues.** The city of Flagstaff earned over $3 million in tax and other revenues from the Coconino Industrial Park in 2013. By 2020 this income is expected to reach $5.4 million (in constant 2013 dollars).

- **Employment.** In 2013, CIP businesses employed a total of 7,035 workers, who earned an average wage of $56,579. By 2020, CIP businesses are expected to employ directly nearly 15,000 employees who will earn salaries totaling over $998 million.

- **Indirect benefits.** Because of the multiplier effect, by 2020 Coconino Industrial Park will directly and indirectly generate a total of 38,362 jobs in the Flagstaff metropolitan area.

Condenses recommendations

On the basis of these findings, it is recommended that development of additional industrial parks be encouraged to stimulate local economic growth. The city would increase its tax revenues significantly, create much-needed jobs, and thus help stimulate the local economy in and around Flagstaff.

iv

© Cengage Learning 2015

For readers who want a quick overview of the report, the executive summary presents its most important elements. Executive summaries focus on the information the reader requires for making a decision related to the issues discussed in the report. The summary may include some or all of the following elements: purpose, scope, research methods, findings, conclusions, and recommendations. Its length depends on the report it summarizes. A 100-page report might require a 10-page summary. Shorter reports may contain one-page summaries, as shown here. Unlike letters of transmittal (which may contain personal pronouns and references to the writer), the executive summary of a long report is formal and impersonal. It uses the same margins as the body of the report. See the discussion of executive summaries in this chapter.

Figure **13.5** (Continued) Page 1

INTRODUCTION: COCONINO AND THE LOCAL ECONOMY

This study was designed to analyze the direct and indirect economic impact of Coconino Industrial Park on the city of Flagstaff. Specifically, the study seeks answers to these questions:

- What current tax and other revenues result directly from this park? What tax and other revenues may be expected in the future?

- How many and what kinds of jobs are directly attributable to the park? What is the employment picture for the future?

- What indirect effects has Coconino Industrial Park had on local employment, incomes, and economic growth?

BACKGROUND: THE ROLE OF CIP IN COMMERCIAL DEVELOPMENT

The development firm of Goldman-Lyon & Associates commissioned this study of Coconino Industrial Park at the request of the Flagstaff City Council. Before authorizing the development of a proposed Goldman-Lyon industrial park, the city council requested a study examining the economic effects of an existing park. Members of the city council wanted to determine to what extent industrial parks benefit the local community, and they chose Coconino Industrial Park as an example.

For those who are unfamiliar with it, Coconino Industrial Park is a 400-acre industrial park located in the city of Flagstaff about 4 miles from the center of the city. Most of the land lies within a specially designated area known as Redevelopment Project No. 2, which is under the jurisdiction of the Flagstaff Redevelopment Agency. Planning for the park began in 1999; construction started in 2001.

The original goal for Coconino Industrial Park was development for light industrial users. Land in this area was zoned for uses such as warehousing, research and development, and distribution. Like other communities, Flagstaff was eager to attract light industrial users because such businesses tend to employ a highly educated workforce, are relatively quiet, and do not pollute the environment (Cohen, 2014). The city of Flagstaff recognized the need for light industrial users and widened an adjacent highway to accommodate trucks and facilitate travel by workers and customers coming from Flagstaff.

1

Annotations (left margin):

Uses a bulleted list for clarity and ease of reading

Lists three problem questions

Describes authorization for report and background of study

Includes APA citation with author name and date

© Cengage Learning 2015

Titles for major parts of a report are centered in all caps. In this model document we show several combination headings. As the name suggests, combination heads are a mix of functional headings, such as *INTRODUCTION, BACKGROUND, DISCUSSION,* and *CONCLUSIONS,* and talking heads that reveal the content. Most business reports would use talking heads or a combination, such as *FINDINGS REVEAL REVENUE* and *EMPLOYMENT BENEFITS*. First-level headings (such as Revenues on page 2) are printed with bold upper- and lowercase letters. Second-level headings (such as Distribution on page 3) begin at the side, are bolded, and are written in upper- and lowercase letters. See Figure 12.9 for an illustration of heading formats. This business report is shown with single-spacing, although some research reports might be double-spaced. Always check with your organization to learn its preferred style.

Figure 13.5 (Continued) Page 2

The park now contains 14 building complexes with over 1.25 million square feet of completed building space. The majority of the buildings are used for office, research and development, marketing and distribution, or manufacturing uses. Approximately 50 acres of the original area are yet to be developed.

Provides specifics for data sources

Data for this report came from a 2013 survey of over 5,000 Coconino Industrial Park employees; interviews with 15 CIP tenants and managers; the annual budget of the city of Flagstaff; county and state tax records; and current books, articles, journals, and online resources. Projections for future revenues resulted from analysis of past trends and "Estimates of Revenues for Debt Service Coverage, Redevelopment Project Area 2" (Miller, 2013, p. 79).

Uses combination heads

DISCUSSION: REVENUES, EMPLOYMENT, AND INDIRECT BENEFITS

Previews organization of report

The results of this research indicate that major direct and indirect benefits have accrued to the city of Flagstaff and surrounding metropolitan areas as a result of the development of Coconino Industrial Park. The research findings presented here fall into three categories: (a) revenues, (b) employment, and (c) indirect benefits.

Revenues

Coconino Industrial Park contributes a variety of tax and other revenues to the city of Flagstaff, as summarized in Figure 1. Current revenues are shown, along with projections to the year 2020. At a time when the economy is unstable, revenues from an industrial park such as Coconino can become a reliable income stream for the city of Flagstaff.

Places figure close to textual reference

Figure 1

REVENUES RECEIVED BY THE CITY OF FLAGSTAFF FROM COCONINO INDUSTRIAL PARK

Current Revenues and Projections to 2020

	2013	2020
Sales and use taxes	$1,966,021	$3,604,500
Revenues from licenses	532,802	962,410
Franchise taxes	195,682	220,424
State gas tax receipts	159,420	211,134
Licenses and permits	86,213	201,413
Other revenues	75,180	206,020
Total	$3,015,318	$5,405,901

Source: Arizona State Board of Equalization Bulletin. Phoenix: State Printing Office, 2014, p. 28.

2

© Cengage Learning 2015

Notice that this formal report is single-spaced. Many businesses prefer this space-saving format. However, some organizations prefer double-spacing, especially for preliminary drafts. If you single-space, do not indent paragraphs. If you double-space, do indent the paragraphs. Page numbers may be centered 1 inch from the bottom of the page or placed 1 inch from the upper right corner at the margin. Your word processor can insert page numbers automatically. Strive to leave a minimum of 1 inch for top, bottom, and side margins. References follow the parenthetical citation style (or in-text citation style) of the American Psychological Association (APA). Notice that the author's name, the year of publication, and page number appear in parentheses. The complete bibliographic entry for any in-text citation appears at the end of report in the references section.

Figure **13.5** (Continued) Page 3

Sales and Use Revenues

As shown in Figure 1, the city's largest source of revenues from CIP is the sales and use tax. Revenues from this source totaled $1,966,021 in 2013, according to figures provided by the Arizona State Board of Equalization (2014, p. 28). Sales and use taxes accounted for more than half of the park's total contribution to the total income of $3,015,318.

Other Revenues

Other major sources of city revenues from CIP in 2013 include alcohol licenses, motor vehicle in lieu fees, trailer coach licenses ($532,802), franchise taxes ($195,682), and state gas tax receipts ($159,420). Although not shown in Figure 1, other revenues may be expected from the development of recently acquired property. The U.S. Economic Development Administration has approved a grant worth $975,000 to assist in expanding the current park eastward on an undeveloped parcel purchased last year. Revenues from leasing this property may be sizable.

Projections

Total city revenues from CIP will nearly double by 2020, producing an income of $5.4 million. This estimate is based on an annual growth rate of 0.65 percent, as projected by the Bureau of Labor Statistics.

Employment

One of the most important factors to consider in the overall effect of an industrial park is employment. In Coconino Industrial Park the distribution, number, and wages of people employed will change considerably in the next six years.

Distribution

A total of 7,035 employees currently work in various industry groups at Coconino Industrial Park. The distribution of employees is shown in Figure 2. The largest number of workers (58 percent) is employed in manufacturing and assembly operations. The next largest category, computer and electronics, employs 24 percent of the workers. Some overlap probably exists because electronics assembly could be included in either group. Employees also work in publishing (9 percent), warehousing and storage (5 percent), and other industries (4 percent).

Although the distribution of employees at Coconino Industrial Park shows a wide range of employment categories, it must be noted that other industrial parks would likely generate an entirely different range of job categories.

3

Continues interpreting figures in table

Includes ample description of electronic reference

Sets stage for next topic to be discussed

© Cengage Learning 2015

Only the most important research findings are interpreted and discussed for readers. The depth of discussion depends on the intended length of the report, the goal of the writer, and the expectations of the reader. Because the writer wants this report to be formal in tone, she avoids *I* and *we* in all discussions.

As you type a report, avoid widows and orphans (ending a page with the first line of a paragraph or carrying a single line of a paragraph to a new page). Strive to start and end pages with at least two lines of a paragraph, even if a slightly larger bottom margin results.

Figure **13.5** (Continued) Page 4

Pie chart shows proportion of a whole and includes percentage figures for clarity

Figure 2

EMPLOYMENT DISTRIBUTION OF INDUSTRY GROUPS

Other (4%)
Warehousing and storage (5%)
Publishing (9%)
Computer and electronics (24%)
Manufacturing and assembly (58%)

Source: 2013 survey of CIP employees

Wages

Places figure close to textual reference

In 2013 employees at CIP earned a total of $398 million in wages, as shown in Figure 3. The average employee in that year earned $56,579. The highest average wages were paid to employees in white-collar fields, such as computer and electronics ($65,200) and publishing ($61,100). Average wages for workers in blue-collar fields ranged from $48,500 in warehousing and storage to $53,400 in manufacturing and assembly.

Figure 3

AVERAGE ANNUAL WAGES BY INDUSTRY GROUPS

Coconino Industrial Park, 2013

Aligns figures on the right and centers headings over columns

Industry Group	Employees	Annual Wages	Total
Manufacturing and assembly	4,073	$53,400	$217,498,200
Computer and electronics	1,657	65,200	108,036,400
Publishing	672	61,100	41,059,200
Warehousing and storage	370	48,500	17,945,000
Othe	263	51,300	13,491,900
	7,035		$398,030,700

Source: 2013 Survey of CIP employees

4

© Cengage Learning 2015

If you use figures or tables, be sure to introduce them in the text (for example, *as shown in Figure 3*). Although it is not always possible, try to place them close to the spot where they are first mentioned. To save space, you can print the title of a figure at its side. Because this report contains few tables and figures, the writer named them all "Figures" and numbered them consecutively. Graphics that serve for reference only and aren't discussed in the text belong in the appendix.

Figure **13.5** (Continued) Page 5

Projections

By 2020 Coconino Industrial Park is expected to more than double its number of employees, bringing the total to over 15,000 workers. The total payroll in 2020 will also more than double, producing over $998 million (using constant 2013 dollars) in salaries to CIP employees. These projections are based on a 9 percent growth rate (Miller, 2013, p. 78), along with anticipated increased employment as the park reaches its capacity.

Clarifies information and tells what it means in relation to original research questions

Future development in the park will influence employment and payrolls. One CIP project manager stated in an interview that much of the remaining 50 acres is planned for medium-rise office buildings, garden offices, and other structures for commercial, professional, and personal services (I. M. Novak, personal communication, November 30, 2013). Average wages for employees are expected to increase because of an anticipated shift to higher-paying white-collar jobs. Industrial parks often follow a similar pattern of evolution (Badri, Rivera, & Kusak, 2011, p. 41). Like many industrial parks, CIP evolved from a warehousing center into a manufacturing complex.

Combines conclusions and recommendations

CONCLUSIONS AND RECOMMENDATIONS

Analysis of tax revenues, employment data, personal interviews, and professional literature leads to the following conclusions and recommendations about the economic impact of Coconino Industrial Park on the city of Flagstaff:

1. Sales tax and other revenues produced over $3 million in income to the city of Flagstaff in 2013. By 2020 sales tax and other revenues are expected to produce $5.4 million in city income.

Uses a numbered list for clarity and ease of reading

2. CIP currently employs 7,035 employees, the majority of whom are working in manufacturing and assembly. The average employee in 2013 earned $56,579.

3. By 2020 CIP is expected to employ more than 15,000 workers producing a total payroll of over $998 million.

4. Employment trends indicate that by 2020 more CIP employees will be engaged in higher-paying white-collar positions.

On the basis of these findings, we recommend that the City Council of Flagstaff authorize the development of additional industrial parks to stimulate local economic growth. The direct and indirect benefits of Coconino Industrial Park strongly suggest that future commercial development would have a positive impact on the Flagstaff community and the surrounding region as population growth and resulting greater purchasing power would trigger higher demand.

As the Coconino example shows, gains in tax revenue, job creation, and other direct and indirect benefits would follow the creation of additional industrial parks in and around Flagstaff.

5

© Cengage Learning 2015

After discussing and interpreting the research findings, the writer articulates what she considers the most important conclusions and recommendations. Longer, more complex reports may have separate sections for conclusions and resulting recommendations. In this report they are combined. Notice that it is unnecessary to start a new page for the conclusions.

Figure **13.5** (Continued) References

Arranges references in alphabetical order

Brochure

Journal with doi

Newspaper article

Website without author or date

Book

Online newspaper article

Online government publication

Follows American Psychological Association documentation style

REFERENCES

Arizona State Board of Equalization Bulletin. (2014). Phoenix: State Printing Office, 26-29.

Badri, J., Rivera, H., & Kusak, M. (2011). A comparison of sustainability and economic development in urban industrial parks. *Journal of Industrial Ecology, 24*(4), 233-268. doi: 10.1078/0366-6133.25.335

Cohen, A. P. (2014, December 14). Industrial parks invade suburbia. *The New York Times*, p. C1.

Fighting poverty and protecting the environment: Development of a sustainable technologies industrial park. (n.d.). Retrieved from http://www.smart-communities.ncat.org/success/northam.shtml

Miller, A. M. (2013). *Redevelopment projects: Future prospects.* New York: Rincon Press.

Pearson, S. (2013, June 30). Travel to work characteristics for the 50 largest metropolitan areas by population in the United States. *The Wall Street Journal.* Retrieved from http://www.wsj.com/article130630

U.S. Department of Labor, Bureau of Labor Statistics. (2014). *Overview of the 2010-2020 Projections.* Retrieved from http://www.bls.gov/ooh/About/Projections-Overview.htm

© Cengage Learning 2015

On this page the writer lists all references cited in the text as well as others that she examined during her research. The writer lists these citations following the APA referencing style. Notice that all entries are arranged alphabetically. Book and periodical titles are italicized, but they could be underlined. When referring to online items, she shows the full name of the citation and then identifies the URL as well as the date on which she accessed the electronic reference. This references page is shown with single-spacing, which is preferable for business reports. However, APA style recommends double-spacing for research reports, including the references page. APA style also shows "References" in upper- and lowercase letters. However, the writer preferred to use all caps to be consistent with other headings in this business report.

As shown in Figure 13.5, the Flagstaff City Council hired consultants to evaluate Coconino Industrial Park and to assess whether future commercial development would stimulate further economic growth. Martha Montoya subdivided the economic impact into three aspects: Revenues, Employment, and Indirect Benefits. The report was compiled from survey data as well as from secondary sources that Martha consulted.

Martha's report illustrates many of the points discussed in this chapter. Although it is a good example of the typical report format and style, it should not be viewed as the only way to present a report. Wide variation exists in business and academic reports.

The checklist on the next page summarizes the report process and report components in one handy list.

Report Process

- **Analyze the report and purpose.** Develop a problem question (*Could expanded development of the Coconino Industrial Park benefit the city of Flagstaff?*) and a purpose statement (*The purpose of this report is to investigate the expansion of Coconino Industrial Park and possible benefits accruing to the city of Flagstaff in the area of revenues, employment, and other indirect benefits*).

- **Anticipate the audience and issues.** Consider primary and secondary audiences. What do they already know? What do they need to know? Divide the major problem into subproblems for investigation.

- **Prepare a work plan.** Include problem and purpose statements, as well as a description of the sources and methods of collecting data. Prepare a tentative project outline and work schedule with anticipated dates of completion for all segments of the project.

- **Collect data.** Begin by searching secondary sources (electronic sources, books, magazines, journals, newspapers) for information on your topic. Then, if necessary, gather primary data by surveying, interviewing, observing, and experimenting.

- **Document data sources.** Establish a system for keeping track of your sources. When saving files from business databases or the Internet, be sure to record the complete publication information. Some researchers prepare electronic folders or note cards citing all references (author, date, source, page, and quotation). Select a documentation format and use it consistently.

- **Interpret and organize the data.** Arrange the collected information in tables, grids, or outlines to help you visualize relationships and interpret meanings. Organize the data into an outline (see Chapter 5).

- **Prepare graphics.** Make tables, charts, graphs, and illustrations—but only if they serve a function. Use graphics to help clarify, condense, simplify, or emphasize your data.

- **Compose the first draft.** At a computer write the first draft from your outline. Use appropriate headings as well as transitional expressions (such as *however, on the contrary,* and *in addition*) to guide the reader through the report.

- **Revise and proofread.** Revise to eliminate wordiness, ambiguity, and redundancy. Look for ways to improve readability, such as bulleted or numbered lists. Proofread three times for (a) word and content meaning; (b) grammar, punctuation, and usage errors; and (c) formatting.

- **Evaluate the product.** Examine the final report. Will it achieve its purpose? Encourage feedback so that you can learn how to improve future reports.

Report Components

- **Title page.** Balance the following lines on the title page: (a) name of the report (in all caps); (b) name, title, and organization of the individual receiving the report; (c) author's name, title, and organization; and (d) date submitted.

- **Letter of transmittal.** Announce the report topic and explain who authorized it. Briefly describe the project and preview the conclusions, if the reader is supportive. Close by expressing appreciation for the assignment, suggesting follow-up actions, acknowledging the help of others, or offering to answer questions.

- **Table of contents.** Show the page number where each report heading appears in the report. Connect the page numbers and headings with leaders (spaced dots) using your word processing software.

- **List of illustrations.** Include a list of tables, illustrations, or figures showing the title of the item and its page number. If space permits, put these lists on the same page with the table of contents.

- **Executive summary.** Summarize the report purpose, findings, conclusions, and recommendations. Gauge the length of the summary by the length of the report and by your organization's practices.

- **Introduction.** Explain the problem motivating the report; describe its background and significance. Clarify the scope and limitations of the report. Optional items include a review of the relevant literature and a description of data sources, methods, and key terms. Close by previewing the report's organization.

- **Body.** Discuss, analyze, and interpret the research findings or the proposed solution to the problem. Arrange the findings in logical segments following your outline. Use clear, descriptive headings.

- **Conclusions and recommendations.** Explain what the findings mean in relation to the original problem. If requested, make enumerated recommendations that suggest actions for solving the problem.

- **Appendix(es).** Include items of interest to some, but not all, readers, such as questionnaires, transcripts of interviews, data sheets, and other information that is not essential to explain your findings, but that supports your analysis. Add large graphics—pictures, maps, figures, tables, charts, and graphs—that are not discussed directly in the text.

- **Works cited or references.** If footnotes are not provided in the text, list all references in a section called *Works Cited* or *References*.

Zooming in

© Africa Studio/Shutterstock.com; © ra2studio/Shutterstock.com

Your Turn: Applying Your Skills at Raytheon

Proposals and reports are written, often in teams, to accomplish serious business purposes. Both require research, and sometimes resources are unavailable. As an intern for Dr. Grinyer at Raytheon, you have been given a task. He asks you to help him develop materials to improve Raytheon reports and proposals. He suggests two possible tasks:

© AP Images/PRNewsFoto/Raytheon Company, New York Stock Exchange

1. A short (three- to five-page) business report recommending a structured writing process to be used for team-written company documents

2. A memo evaluating several (two to four) proposal-consulting companies that might be able to help Raytheon teams write good proposals when the company's proposal specialists are unavailable

YOUR TASK. Select one of the suggested tasks. For Option 1, in a two- or three-person team, plan the required report and have each team member prepare an outline of his or her assigned section. As a team, review and improve the outlines with written comments and annotations. For Option 2, individually research, plan, and write the required one- to two-page memo for your instructor.

Summary of Learning Objectives

Go to

www.cengagebrain.com
and use your access code to unlock valuable student resources.

1 Understand the importance and purpose of proposals, and name the basic components of informal proposals. Proposals are extremely important to many organizations because they generate business or funding. A proposal is a written offer to solve problems, provide services, or sell equipment. Request for proposals (RFPs) specify what a proposal should include. Although they may vary, most proposals have certain standard parts in common. Informal proposals contain the following: a persuasive introduction that explains the purpose of the proposal and qualifies the writer; background material identifying the problem and project goals; a proposal, plan, or schedule outlining the project; a section describing staff qualifications; a budget showing expected costs; and a request for approval or authorization.

2 Discuss the components of formal and grant proposals. Beyond the six components generally contained in informal proposals, formal proposals may include these additional parts: a copy of the RFP (request for proposal), a letter of transmittal, an executive summary, a title page, a table of contents, a list of illustrations, and an appendix. A grant proposal is a formal proposal submitted to a government or civilian organization that explains a project, outlines its budget, and requests money in the form of a grant. These funds, or grants, require no repayment. Grants are made to charities, educational facilities, and especially to nonprofits.

3 Identify the components of typical business plans. A business plan is a description of a proposed company that explains how it expects to achieve its marketing, financial, and operational goals. Typical business plans include a letter of transmittal, mission statement, executive summary, table of contents, company description, product or service description, market analysis, description of operations and management, financial analysis, and appendixes. For start-up businesses seeking financial backing, the product or service description as well as the operations and management analyses are particularly important. They must exhibit growth potential and promise a management team capable of implementing the business plan.

4 Describe the components of the front matter in formal business reports, and show how they further the purpose of the report. A formal report is a document in which a writer analyzes findings, draws conclusions, and makes recommendations intended to solve a problem.

The front matter may include a cover, title page, letter or memo of transmittal, table of contents, and list of illustrations. The front matter may also include an executive summary that explains key points. The introduction sets the scene by discussing some or all of the following: the significance, scope, and organization of the report as well as its authorization, relevant literature, sources, methods of research, and definitions of key terms.

5 Understand the body and back matter of formal business reports and how they serve the purpose of the report. The body of a report discusses, analyzes, interprets, and evaluates the research findings or solution to a problem. The conclusion states what the findings mean and how they relate to the report's purpose. The recommendations tell how to solve the report problem. The last portions of a formal report are the appendix(es) and references or works cited.

6 Specify final writing tips that aid authors of formal business reports. Before writing, develop a realistic timetable and collect all necessary data. During the writing process, work from a good outline, compose in a quiet environment, and use the features of your computer wisely. Some writers like to write rapidly, intending to revise later. Other writers prefer a more deliberate writing style, perfecting as they go. While writing, use verb tenses consistently, and avoid *I* and *we*. A few days after completing the first draft, edit to improve clarity, coherence, and conciseness. Proofread the final copy three times.

Chapter Review

1. Why are formal and informal proposals written? (Objs. 1, 2)

2. Why do government agencies make requests for proposals (RFPs)? (Objs. 1, 2)

3. Why might you use a "hook" in a proposal, and what is an example? (Obj. 1)

4. What should be highlighted in the staffing section of a proposal? (Obj. 1)

5. In what two ways do formal and informal proposals differ? (Obj. 2)

6. Name eight components of typical business plans. (Obj. 3)

7. What should a business plan mission statement include, and how long should it be? (Obj. 3)

8. Why are formal reports written in business? Give an original example of a business-related formal report. (Obj. 4)

9. What is a letter or memorandum of transmittal, and what should it include? (Obj. 4)

10. How long should a typical executive summary be? (Obj. 4)

11. Describe how to write an executive summary for a formal business report. (Obj. 4)

12. What should be included in the introduction to a formal business report? (Obj. 4)

13. What should the writer strive to do in the body of a formal business report? (Obj. 5)

14. Why must writers list their sources and identify them in the text? (Obj. 5)

15. In your view, what are six of the most important tips for the writer of a formal report? Explain each of your choices. (Obj. 6)

Critical Thinking

1. Which category of proposal, solicited or unsolicited, is more likely to succeed, and why? (Obj. 1)

2. If you were about to launch a new business, would you write your business plan from scratch or use a software program to do it? What are the pros and cons of each method? (Obj. 3)

3. What is the purpose of a business plan, and what should it communicate to investors? (Obj. 3)

4. Compare these two very different mission statements: (a) An organization with five people said that its mission was "to eliminate hunger in the world." (b) Actor and social entrepreneur

Brad Pitt, appalled by the sorry progress of rebuilding in New Orleans after Hurricane Katrina, started a nonprofit organization with a mission "to build 150 affordable, green, storm-resistant homes for families living in the Lower 9th Ward."[11] What are the strengths and weaknesses of each mission statement? (Obj. 3)

5. **Ethical Issue:** How can a team of writers ensure that each member shoulders an equal or fair amount of the work on an extensive writing project, such as a formal proposal or business report?

Activities

13.1 Proposal: Businesses Built on Social Media (Obj. 1)

E-mail **Social Media** **Web**

Businesses both large and small are flocking to social media platforms to engage consumers in conversations and also to drive sales through deals and coupons. Small businesses have found that social media and the Internet help them to level the playing field. They can foster closer relationships with clients and identify potential customers. Flirty Cupcakes owner Tiffany Kurtz says that Facebook and Twitter greatly helped her with product innovation, market expansion, and customer service.[12] Many other entrepreneurs are using social media to launch and expand their businesses.

YOUR TASK. Using the Internet, search for small businesses that have used social media to start a business or expand their market share. Select four businesses to study. Analyze their use of social media. What do they have in common? When these companies were first launched, most of them probably needed to borrow money to get started. How might these companies have described the social media potential in writing a proposal seeking funding? In which of the proposal components would this information be best placed? In an e-mail or memo to your instructor, describe briefly the four companies you selected. Then, for one company write a portion of the proposal in which the entrepreneur explains how he or she plans to use social media to promote the business. How much time do you think the entrepreneur would need to devote to social media weekly? What platforms would be most useful?

13.2 Proposal: What Workplace Problem Deserves Serious Investigation? (Obj. 1)

The ability to spot problems before they turn into serious risks is prized by most managers. Draw on your internship and work experience. Can you identify a problem that could be solved with a small to moderate financial investment? Look for issues such as missing lunch or break rooms for staff; badly needed health initiatives such as gyms or sport club memberships; low-gas-mileage, high-emission company vehicles; or a lack of recycling efforts.

YOUR TASK. Discuss with your instructor the workplace problem that you have identified. Make sure you choose a relatively weighty problem that can be lessened or eliminated with a minor expenditure. Be sure to include a cost–benefit analysis. Address your unsolicited letter or memo proposal to your current or former boss and copy your instructor.

13.3 Proposal: Starting Your Own Business (Obj. 1)

Web

Perhaps you have fantasized about one day owning your own company, or maybe you have already started a business. Proposals are offers to a very specific audience whose business you are soliciting. Think of a product or service that you like or know something about. On the Web or in electronic databases, research the market so that you understand going rates, prices, and costs. Search the Small Business Administration's website for valuable tips on how to launch and manage a business.

YOUR TASK. Choose a product or service you would like to offer to a particular audience, such as a dating consulting service, a window cleaning business, a bakery specializing in your favorite cakes, an online photography business, or a new Asian or European hair care line. Discuss products and services as well as target audiences with your instructor. Write an informal letter proposal promoting your chosen product or service.

13.4 Proposal: Offering Assistance in Writing a Proposal (Objs. 1, 2)

Web

Many new companies with services or products to offer would like to land corporate or government contracts. However, they are intimidated by the proposal and RFP processes. Your friend Teresa, who has started her own designer uniform company, has asked you for help. Her goal is to offer her colorful yet functional uniforms to hospitals and clinics. Before writing a proposal, however, she wants to see examples and learn more about the process.

YOUR TASK. Use the Web to find at least two examples of business proposals. Don't waste time on sites that want to sell templates or books. Find actual examples. Try **http://www.bplans.com /samples/sba.cfm.** Then prepare a memo to Teresa in which you do the following:

a. Identify two sample business proposals.

b. Outline the parts of each proposal.

c. Compare the strengths and weaknesses of each proposal.

d. Draw conclusions. What can Teresa learn from these examples?

13.5 Proposal: BioMed Sports Medicine Comes to Town (Obj. 1)

Team

Sports medicine is increasingly popular, especially in university towns. A new medical clinic, BioMed Sports Medicine, is opening its doors in your community. A friend recommended your small business to the administrator of the clinic, and you received a letter asking you to provide information about your service. The new medical clinic specializes in sports medicine, physical therapy, and cardiac rehabilitation services. It is interested in retaining your company, rather than hiring its own employees to perform the service your company offers.

YOUR TASK. Working in teams, first decide what service you offer. It could be landscaping, uniforms, uniform laundering, general cleaning, computerized no-paper filing systems, online medical supplies, patient transportation, supplemental hospice care, temporary office support, social media guidance, or food service. As a team, develop a letter proposal outlining your plan, staffing, and budget. Use persuasion to show why contracting your services is better than hiring in-house employees. In the proposal letter, request a meeting with the administrative board. In addition to a written proposal, you may be expected to make an oral presentation that includes visual aids and/or handouts. Send your proposal to Dr. Tim Krahnke, Director, BioMed Sports Medicine. Supply a local address.

13.6 Grant Writing: Building Your Skills With Nonprofits (Objs. 1, 2)

Web

Nonprofit organizations are always seeking grant writers, and you would like to gain experience in this area. You've heard that they pull down good salaries, and one day you might even decide to become a professional grant/proposal writer. However, you first need experience. You saw a Web listing from The Actors Theatre Workshop advertising for a grant writer to "seek funding for general operating expenses and program-related funding." A grant writer would "develop proposals, generate boilerplates for future applications, and oversee a writing team." This listing sounds good, but you need a local position.

YOUR TASK. Search the Web for local nonprofits. Alternatively, your instructor may already know of local groups seeking grant writers, such as a United Way member agency, an educational institution, or a faith-based organization. Talk with your instructor about an assignment. Your instructor may ask you to submit a preliminary memo report outlining ten or more guidelines you expect to follow when writing proposals and grants for nonprofit organizations.

13.7 Service Learning and Writing: A Happy Marriage (Objs. 1, 2, 4, and 5)

<E-mail> <Web>

Your school may be one that encourages service learning, a form of experiential learning. You could receive credit for a project that bridges academic and nonacademic communities. Because writing skills are in wide demand, you may have an opportunity to simultaneously apply your skills, contribute to the community, and expand your résumé. The National Service-Learning Clearinghouse describes service learning as "a teaching and learning strategy that integrates meaningful community service with instruction and reflection to enrich the learning experience, teach civic responsibility, and strengthen communities."[13] The Web offers many sites devoted to examples of students engaging in service-learning projects.

YOUR TASK. Research possible service-learning projects in this class or another. Your instructor may ask you to submit a memo or e-mail message analyzing your findings. Describe at least four completed service-learning projects that you found on the Web. Draw conclusions about what made them successful or beneficial. What kinds of similar projects might be possible for you or students in your class? Your instructor may use this as a research project or turn it into a hands-on project by having you find a service organization in your community in need of trained writers.

13.8 Business Plans: Analyzing Mission Statements (Obj. 3)

<E-mail>

Large and small businesses develop mission statements to explain their purposes. Some statements are excellent; others, less so.

YOUR TASK. Analyze the following selection of Fortune 500 company descriptions and mission statements.[14] In a class discussion or an e-mail to your instructor, (a) list four goals of mission statements (see Figure 13.3), (b) list five questions to be answered in preparing mission statements, (c) explain which of the following statements fulfill the goals of winning mission statements discussed in Figure 13.3, and (d) tell how the following statements could be improved.

Company	Mission Statement
1. AGCO manufactures and distributes agricultural equipment such as replacement parts, tractors, hay tools, and implements.	Profitable growth through superior customer service, innovation, quality, and commitment.
2. Dover Corporation manufactures equipment such as garbage trucks and electronic equipment such as ink-jet printers and circuit board assemblies.	To be the leader in every market we serve, to the benefit of our customers and our shareholders.
3. Eaton Corporation supplies parts for fluid power, electrical systems, automobiles, and trucks.	We are committed to attracting, developing, and keeping a diverse workforce that reflects the nature of our global business.
4. Graybar Electric Company acquires, stores, and distributes electrical, data, and communication components such as wire, cable, and lighting products.	We are a vital link in the supply chain, adding value with efficient and cost-effective service and solutions for our customers and our suppliers.
5. Harley-Davidson, Inc., manufactures motorcycles with over 32 models of touring and custom Harleys plus motorcycle accessories, motorcycle clothing apparel, and engines.	We fulfill dreams through the experience of motorcycling, by providing to motorcyclists and to the general public an expanding line of motorcycles and branded products and services in selected market segments.
6. IBM provides computer hardware such as mainframes, servers, storage systems, printing systems, and semiconductors, as well as software related to business integration, networking, operating systems, systems management, and so forth.	Operating a safe and secure government.

13.9 Business Plan: Can Your Team Write a Winning Business Plan? (Obj. 3)

<Team> <Web>

Business plans at many schools are more than classroom writing exercises. They have won regional, national, and worldwide prizes. Although some contests are part of MBA programs, other contests are available for undergraduates. As part of a business plan project, you and your team are challenged to come up with an idea for a new business or service. For example, you might want to offer a lunch service with fresh sandwiches or salads delivered to office workers' desks. You might propose building a better website for an organization. You might want to start a document preparation business that offers production, editing, and printing services. You might have a terrific idea for an existing business to expand with a new product or service.

YOUR TASK. Working in teams, explore entrepreneurial ventures based on your experience and expertise. Conduct team meetings to decide on a product or service, develop a work plan, assign responsibilities, and create a schedule. Your goal is to write a business plan that will convince potential investors (sometimes your own management) that you have an excellent business idea and that you can pull it off. Check out sample business plans on the Web. The two "deliverables" from your project will be your written business plan and an oral presentation. Your written report should include a cover, transmittal document (letter or memo), title page, table of contents, executive summary, proposal (including introduction, body, and conclusion), appendix items, glossary (optional), and sources. In the body of the proposal, be sure to explain your mission and vision, the market, your marketing strategy, operations, and financials. Address your business plan to your instructor.*

13.10 Executive Summary: Reviewing Articles (Objs. 2, 5)

> E-mail > Web >

Many managers and executives are too rushed to read long journal articles, but they are eager to stay current in their fields. Assume your boss has asked you to help him stay abreast of research in his field. He asks you to submit to him one executive summary every month on an article of interest.

YOUR TASK. In your field of study, select a professional journal, such as the *Journal of Management*. Using ProQuest, Factiva, EBSCO, or some other database, look for articles in your target journal. Select an article that is at least five pages long and is interesting to you. Write an executive summary in a memo format. Include an introduction that might begin with *As you requested, I am submitting this executive summary of . . . .* Identify the author, article title, journal, and date of publication. Explain what the author intended to do in the study or article. Summarize three or four of the most important findings of the study or article. Use descriptive, or "talking," headings rather than functional headings. Summarize any recommendations made. Your boss would also like a concluding statement indicating your reaction to the article. Address your memo to Marcus E. Fratelli. Alternatively, your instructor may ask you to e-mail your executive summary in the body of a properly formatted message or as an MS Word attachment in correct memo format.

13.11 Unsolicited Proposal: Requesting Funding for Your Campus Business Organization (Obj. 1)

Let's say you are a member of a campus business club, such as the Society for the Advancement of Management (SAM), the American Marketing Association (AMA), the American Management Association (AMA), the Accounting Society (AS), the Finance Association (FA), or the Association of Information Technology Professionals (AITP). Your organization has managed its finances well, and therefore, it is able to fund monthly activities. However, membership dues are insufficient to cover any extras. Identify a need such as for a hardware or software purchase, a special one-time event that would benefit a great number of students, or officer training.

YOUR TASK. Request one-time funding to cover what you need by writing an unsolicited letter or memo proposal to your assistant dean, who oversees student business clubs. Identify your need or problem, show the benefit of your request, support your claims with evidence, and provide a budget (if necessary).

13.12 Unsolicited Proposal: Protecting Digital Doodads in Dorms (Objs. 1, 2)

> Team > Web >

As an enterprising college student, you recognized a problem as soon as you arrived on campus. Dorm rooms filled with pricey digital doodads were very attractive to thieves. Some students move in with more than $3,000 in gear, including laptops, tablets, flat-screen TVs, digital cameras, MP3 players, video game consoles, smartphones, and hoards of other digital delights. You solved the problem by buying an extra-large steel footlocker to lock away your valuables. However, shipping the footlocker was expensive (nearly $100), and you had to wait for it to arrive from a catalog company. Your bright idea is to propose to the Associated Student Organization (ASO) that it allow you to offer these steel footlockers to students at a reduced price and with campus delivery. Your footlocker, which you found by searching the Web, is extremely durable and works great as a coffee table, nightstand, or card table. It comes with a smooth interior liner and two compartments.

YOUR TASK. Working individually or with a team, imagine that you have made arrangements with a manufacturer to act as an intermediary selling footlockers on your campus at a reduced price. Consult the Web for manufacturers and make up your own figures. How can you get the ASO's permission to proceed? Give that organization a cut? Use your imagination in deciding how this plan might work on a college campus. Then prepare an unsolicited proposal to your ASO. Outline the problem and your goals of protecting students' valuables and providing convenience. Check the Web for statistics regarding on-campus burglaries. Such figures should help you develop one or more persuasive "hooks." Then explain your proposal, project possible sales, discuss a timetable, and describe your staffing. Submit your proposal to Anthony Johnson, president, Associated Student Organization.

13.13 Formal Business Report: Gathering Data for Expansion Into Another Country (Objs. 4–6)

> Intercultural > Team > Web >

U.S. businesses are expanding into foreign markets with manufacturing plants, sales offices, and branches abroad. Many Americans, however, have little knowledge of or experience with people from other cultures. To prepare for participation in the global marketplace, you are to collect information for a report focused on an Asian, Latin American, European, or African country where English is not regularly spoken. Before selecting the country, though, consult your campus international student program for volunteers who are willing to be interviewed. Your instructor may make advance arrangements with international student volunteers.

YOUR TASK. In teams of three to five, collect information about your target country from electronic databases, the Web, and other sources. Then invite an international student representing your target country to be interviewed by your group. As you conduct primary and secondary research, investigate the topics listed in Figure 13.6. Confirm what you learn in your secondary research by talking with your interviewee. When you complete your research, write a report for the CEO of your company (make up a name and company). Assume that your company plans to expand

---

*A complete instructional module for this activity is available at the instructor premium website. Under the tab Teaching Modules, click Business Plan.

Figure **13.6** Intercultural Interview Topics and Questions

Social Customs

- How do people react to strangers? Are they friendly? Hostile? Reserved?
- How do people greet each other?
- What are the appropriate manners when you enter a room? Bow? Nod? Shake hands with everyone?
- How are names used for introductions? Is it appropriate to inquire about one's occupation or family?
- What are the attitudes toward touching?
- How does one express appreciation for an invitation to another's home? Bring a gift? Send flowers? Write a thank-you note? Are any gifts taboo?
- Are there any customs related to how or where one sits?
- Are any facial expressions or gestures considered rude?
- How close do people stand when talking?
- What is the attitude toward punctuality in social situations? In business situations?
- What are acceptable eye contact patterns?
- What gestures indicate agreement? Disagreement?

Family Life

- What is the basic unit of social organization? Basic family? Extended family?
- Do women work outside of the home? In what occupations?

Housing, Clothing, and Food

- Are there differences in the kinds of housing used by different social groups? Differences in location? Differences in furnishings?
- What occasions require special clothing?
- Are some types of clothing considered taboo?
- What is appropriate business attire for men? For women?
- How many times a day do people eat?
- What types of places, food, and drink are appropriate for business entertainment? Where is the seat of honor at a table?

Class Structure

- Into what classes is society organized?
- Do racial, religious, or economic factors determine social status?
- Are there any minority groups? What is their social standing?

Political Patterns

- Are there any immediate threats to the political survival of the country?
- How is political power manifested?
- What channels are used for expressing political opinions?
- What information media are important?
- Is it appropriate to talk politics in social situations?

Religion and Folk Beliefs

- To which religious groups do people belong? Is one predominant?
- Do religious beliefs influence daily activities?
- Which places are considered sacred? Which objects? Which events?
- How do religious holidays affect business activities?

Economic Institutions

- What are the country's principal products?
- Are workers organized in unions?
- How are businesses owned? By family units? By large public corporations? By the government?
- What is the standard work schedule?
- Is it appropriate to do business by telephone? By computer?
- How has technology affected business procedures?
- Is participatory management used?
- Are there any customs related to exchanging business cards?
- How is status shown in an organization? Private office? Secretary? Furniture?
- Are businesspeople expected to socialize before conducting business?

Value Systems

- Is competitiveness or cooperation more prized?
- Is thrift or enjoyment of the moment more valued?
- Is politeness more important than honesty?
- What are the attitudes toward education?
- Do women own or manage businesses? If so, how are they treated?
- What are your people's perceptions of Americans? Do Americans offend you? What has been hardest for you to adjust to in America? How could Americans make this adjustment easier for you?

its operations abroad. Your report should advise the company's executives of the social customs, family life, attitudes, religions, education, and values of the target country. Remember that your company's interests are business oriented; do not dwell on tourist information. Write your report individually or in teams.

13.14 Report Topics for Proposals, Business Plans, and Formal Reports (Objs. 1–6)

> Team   Web

A list of nearly 100 report topics is available at the premium student site accessed at **www.cengagebrain.com**. The topics are divided into the following categories: accounting, finance, personnel/human resources, marketing, information systems, management, and general business/education/campus issues. You can collect information for many of these reports by using electronic databases and the Web. Your instructor may assign them as individual or team projects. All involve critical thinking in organizing information, drawing conclusions, and making recommendations. The topics are appropriate for proposals, business plans, and formal business reports. Also, a number of self-contained report activities that require no additional research are provided at the end of Chapter 12.

YOUR TASK. As directed by your instructor, select a topic from the report list at **www.cengagebrain.com**.

Chat About It

In each chapter you will find five discussion questions related to the chapter material. Your instructor may assign these topics for you to discuss in class, in an online chat room, or on an online discussion board. Some of the discussion topics may require outside research. You may also be asked to read and respond to postings made by your classmates.

Topic 1: How would you feel about offering your writing skills to a nonprofit to gain experience if you knew you would earn nothing for your effort?

Topic 2: A member of your family coaches or plays on a sport team that badly needs uniforms and equipment. When you attend one of the games, a coach recognizes you as a college business student and asks you to help write a grant proposal for funds to support the team. After some coercion, you agree to do it. Where would you begin, and what would you need to do to get the team the funds it needs?

Topic 3: Some consulting firms use experienced managers, but they also employ inexperienced, lower-paid staff to lower costs. How would you write the staffing section of a proposal with experienced managers but inexperienced staff?

Topic 4: Discuss the pros and cons of the following two methods for completing the outline of the executive summary of a formal report: (a) cutting and pasting existing report sentences, or (b) creating new sentences.

Topic 5: Is it ethical for a student team to "borrow" and then substantially revise a report from a team that wrote about the same topic during the previous semester? What does your school say about such a practice?

 # Grammar & Mechanics | *Review 13*

TOTAL REVIEW

Each of the following sentences has a total of **three** errors in grammar, punctuation, capitalization, usage, or spelling. On a separate sheet, write a correct version. Avoid adding new phrases, starting new sentences, or rewriting in your own words. When finished, compare your responses with the key beginning on page Key-3.

EXAMPLE: If you face writers block you should review the 3 main reasons for writing.

REVISION: If you face **writer's block,** you should review the **three** main reasons for writing.

1. Our CEO and President both worked on the thirty page proposal. Which was due immediately.

2. Managers in 2 departments' complained that there departments should have been consulted.

3. The RFP and it's attachments arrived to late for my manager and I to complete the necessary research.

4. Although we worked everyday on the proposal, we felt badly that we could not meet the May 15th deadline.

5. If the program and staff is to run smooth we must submit an effective grant proposal.

6. Although short a successful mission statement should capture the businesses goals and values. In a few succinct sentences.

7. A proposal budget cannot be changed if costs raise later, consequently, it must be written careful.

8. A good eight-word mission statement is a critical tool for funding, it helps start-up company's evolve there big idea without being pulled off track.

9. Entrepreneur Stephanie Rivera publisher of a urban event callendar, relies on social media to broadcast her message.

10. Stephanie asked Jake and myself to help her write a business plan. That would guide her new company and garner perminent funding.

Notes

[1] Based on Grinyer, M., Raytheon proposal consultant (personal communication with Mary Ellen Guffey, July 23, 2007).

[2] City of Las Vegas. (2010, January 4). RFP for public private partnership parking initiative. Onvia DemandStar. Retrieved from http://www .lasvegasnevada.gov/Business/5990.htm?ID

[3] Buck Institute for Age Research. (n.d.). Architecture. Retrieved from http://www.buckinstitute.org /architecture

[4] Sant, T. (2004). *Persuasive business proposals.* New York: AMACOM, pp. 99-100.

[5] McLaughlin, M. W. (n.d.). 12 tips for writing a winning proposal. Retrieved from http://office .microsoft.com/en-us/word-help/12-tips-for -writing-a-winning-proposal-HA010024506 .aspx

[6] Ronald McDonald House Charities. (2012). Grants in action. Retrieved from http://rmhc.org /what-we-do/grants/grants-in-action

[7] Answers. (n.d.). Retrieved from http://wiki.answers .com/Q/How_long_will_it_take_to_write_a _business_plan

[8] Lewis, H. (2013, January 5). Hassle-free business plans. *New York Post.* Retrieved from http://www.nypost.com/p/news /business/hassle_free_business_plans _4tqWOfXU9hmWrsLUKgFECO

[9] Photo essay based on Norman, J. (2012, June 8). Winning business plan becomes reality. *Orange County Register.* Retrieved from http://www.ocregister.com

[10] Starr, K. (2012, September 18). The eight-word mission statement. *Stanford Social Innovation Review.* Retrieved from http://www .ssireview.org/blog/entry/the_eight _word_mission_statement

[11] McKeown, G. (2012, October 4). If I read one more platitude-filled mission statement, I'll scream. HBR Blog Network. Retrieved from http:// blogs.hbr.org/cs/2012/10/if_i_read_one_more _platitude_filled_mission_statement.html

[12] Ratner, H. M. (2012, March 1). 9 businesses that social media built. *Today's Chicago Woman.* Retrieved from http://www.tcwmag .com/9-businesses-social-media-built

[13] Corporation for National and Community Service. (2013). What is service learning? Retrieved from http://www.servicelearning.org /what-is-service-learning

[14] Partially based on McKeown, G. (2012, October 4). If I read one more platitude-filled mission statement, I'll scream. HBR Blog Network. Retrieved from http://blogs.hbr.org/cs/2012/10 /if_i_read_one_more_platitude_filled _mission_statement.html. Also partially based on Missionstatements.com. Ideas and inspirations for defining your own mission statement. (n.d.). Retrieved from http://www.missionstatements .com/fortune_500_mission_statements.html

OBJECTIVES

After studying this chapter, you should be able to

1 Recognize various types of business presentations, and discuss two important first steps in preparing for any of these presentations.

2 Explain how to organize the introduction, body, and conclusion as well as how to build audience rapport in a presentation.

3 Create effective visual aids and handouts using today's multimedia presentation technology.

4 Specify delivery techniques for use before, during, and after a presentation.

5 Organize presentations for intercultural audiences, in teams, and as slide decks.

6 List techniques for improving telephone skills to project a positive image.

© Pressmaster/Shutterstock.com

Guy Kawasaki and the 10/20/30 Rule of Presenting

Zooming in

© Amy E. Price/Getty Images for SXSW

Presenting—speaking to an audience of one or one thousand, often with accompanying graphic support— does not come naturally to most people. In fact, so many businesspeople find presenting a daunting task that an entire industry has grown up around helping presenters improve their skills.

However, presentations are simply another communication mode with the same goals as written communication. They must be purpose driven and appeal to the needs of a specific audience. Like many modes of communication, presentations are organized into recognizable sections—introduction, body, and conclusion. One way business presentations differ from written communication is that they must use visual aids effectively, especially multimedia presentations created using software such as PowerPoint and Prezi.

Guy Kawasaki—popular speaker, best-selling author, and former Apple evangelist—has been called a "presenter extraordinaire."[1] He has employed his dynamic presenting skills at various organizations such as Audi, Hewlett Packard, and countless start-ups[2] and has condensed his presentation advice into a simple formula admirers dub "The Kawasaki Method."[3]

Kawasaki himself calls this method the "10/20/30 Rule of PowerPoint." First, he says, no presentation should contain more than 10 slides. "Ten is the optimal number of slides in a PowerPoint presentation because a normal human being cannot comprehend more than ten concepts in a meeting," he explains.[4]

Next, Kawasaki advocates limiting the length of a presentation to 20 minutes. He says that speakers who drone on for longer will bore *and* alienate their audiences. His third rule—the 30—refers to slide font size. He is adamant that presenters use no less than a 30-point font for two reasons. One, a large font makes it impossible to include too much on a slide. By limiting words, the writer must focus on the core of an idea. Second, "A lot less text forces you to actually know your presentation," Kawasaki says. He considers a lack of preparation, especially as exemplified in reading slides, among the worst presenting sins. "If you start reading your material because you don't know your material, the audience is very quickly going to figure out you're a bozo," he quips.[5]

This last piece of tongue-in-cheek advice is really at the heart of business presentations. Effective presenters are always polished, prepared, and professional. Anything else would make them "bozos." At the end of this chapter, you will have a chance to learn more about Guy Kawasaki and apply your skills in a related task.

Critical Thinking

- What kinds of oral presentations might you have to make in your chosen career field? Would Kawasaki's 10/20/30 rule work for the presentations you anticipate?

- Why are most people fearful of making presentations?

- How do you think people become effective speakers?

Preparing Effective Oral Presentations

Perhaps you have admired the speaking skills of such well-known orators as venture capitalist Guy Kawasaki, motivational expert Anthony Robbins, the late self-help guru Zig Ziglar, activist Martin Luther King, Jr., and former Apple CEO Steve Jobs. Few of us will ever talk to an audience of millions—whether face-to-face or aided by technology. We won't be introducing a spectacular new product or motivating millions. At some point, however, all businesspeople have to inform others or sell an idea. Such information and persuasion are often conveyed in person and involve audiences of various sizes. If you are like most people, you have some apprehension when speaking in public. That's normal. Good speakers are made, not born. The good news is that you can conquer the fear of public speaking and hone your skills with instruction and practice.

LEARNING OBJECTIVE 1
Recognize various types of business presentations, and discuss two important first steps in preparing for any of these presentations.

Speaking Skills and Your Career

The savviest future businesspeople take advantage of opportunities in college to develop their speaking skills. Such skills often play an important role in a successful career. In fact, the No. 1 predictor of success and upward mobility, according to an AT&T and Stanford University study, is how much you enjoy public speaking and how effective you are at it.[6] Speaking skills are useful at every career stage. You might, for example, have to make a sales pitch before customers or speak to a professional gathering. You might need to describe your company's expansion plans to your banker, or you might need to persuade management to support your proposed marketing strategy.

When you are in the job market, remember that speaking skills rank high on recruiters' wish lists. In a survey of employers, spoken communication took the top spot as the most desirable "soft skill" sought in job candidates. It even ranks above a strong work ethic, teamwork, analytical skills, and initiative.[7] Another employer study reported that 70 percent of executives considered oral communication skills very important for high school graduates entering the job market; 82 percent for two-year college graduates, and a whopping 95 percent for four-year college graduates.[8]

This chapter prepares you to use speaking skills in making effective oral presentations, whether alone or as part of a team, whether face-to-face or virtually. You will learn what to do before, during, and after your presentation, as well as how to design effective visual aids and multimedia presentations. Before diving into specifics on how to become an excellent presenter, consider the types of business presentations you may encounter in your career.

REALITY CHECK: How to Boost Your Career

"Presentation skills are a primary differentiator among you and your peers. Master your presentation skills, and become the master of your career options."[9]

—**ANDREW DLUGAN**, *communication coach, public speaker*

Types of Business Presentations

A common part of a business professional's life is making presentations. Some presentations are informative while others may be persuasive. Some face to face; others, virtual. Some are performed before big audiences, whereas others are given to smaller groups. Some presentations are elaborate; others, simple. Here is a sampling of business presentations you may encounter in your career.

Briefings.   As its name suggests, a briefing is a concise overview or summary of an issue, proposal, or problem. Team briefings bring managers together with their teams so that information can be delivered, questions asked, and feedback collected. Nurses may get together at the beginning of every shift to sort out duties. Military officers use briefings to outline missions. Marketing managers meet frequently to brief sales reps about goals and accomplishments.

Reports.   Businesspeople often present progress reports, status reports, convention reports, and other similar informative accounts orally. In Chapters 12 and 13, you learned to prepare such reports in writing. You may be invited to present that same information before internal or external groups. In some organizations reports are expected to be simple, off-the-cuff presentations. Other organizations expect more elaborate presentations with visuals, multimedia technology, and question-and-answer periods.

Podcasts.   A podcast is an online, prerecorded audio clip delivered over the Web. Chapter 7 describes how to make podcasts and discusses their uses. In this chapter you learn how to make all presentations, including podcasts, more effective by focusing on preparation, organization, and delivery. Podcasts are now used by companies to launch products, introduce employees, train employees, and sell products and services.

Virtual Presentations. Team members in this digital age are increasingly separated geographically and must meet virtually. That is, they use information technology to accomplish shared tasks online. If you participate in a collaborative effort with remote colleagues, you may make a virtual presentation. Fortunately, the keys to a successful virtual presentation are similar to those of other presentations and will be covered in this chapter. You can find more information about participating in virtual meetings in Chapter 2.

Webinars. A webinar is a Web-based presentation, lecture, workshop, or seminar that is transmitted digitally, with or without video. Much like podcasts, webinars may be used to train employees, interact with customers, and promote products. Tips for delivering successful webinars and other virtual presentations appear later in this chapter.

Knowing Your Purpose

Regardless of the type of presentation, you must prepare carefully if you expect it to be effective. The most important part of your preparation is deciding what you want to accomplish. Do you want to sell a health care program to a prospective client? Do you want to persuade management to increase the marketing budget? Do you want to inform customer-service reps of three important ways to prevent miscommunication? Whether your goal is to persuade or to inform, you must have a clear idea of where you are going. At the end of your presentation, what do you want your listeners to remember or do?

Sandra Castillo, a loan officer at First Fidelity Trust, faced such questions as she planned a talk for a class in small business management. Sandra's former business professor had asked her to return to campus and give the class advice about borrowing money from banks in order to start new businesses. Because Sandra knew so much about this topic, she found it difficult to extract a specific purpose statement for her presentation. After much thought she narrowed her purpose to this: *To inform potential entrepreneurs about three important factors that loan officers consider before granting start-up loans to launch small businesses.* Her entire presentation focused on ensuring that the class members understood and remembered three principal ideas.

Knowing Your Audience

A second key element in preparation is analyzing your audience, anticipating its reactions, and adjusting to its needs if necessary. Audiences may fall into four categories, as summarized in Figure 14.1. By anticipating your audience, you have a better idea of how to organize your presentation. A friendly audience, for example, will respond to humor and personal experiences. A neutral audience requires an even, controlled delivery style. You would want to fill the talk with facts, statistics, and expert opinions. An uninterested audience that is forced to attend requires a brief presentation. Such an audience might respond best to humor, cartoons, colorful visuals, and startling statistics. A hostile audience demands a calm, controlled delivery style with objective data and expert opinion. Regardless of the type of audience, remember to plan your presentation so that it focuses on audience benefits. The members of your audience will want to know what's in it for them.

> Regardless of the type of audience, remember to plan your presentation so that it focuses on audience benefits.

Other elements, such as age, education, experience, and the size of the audience will affect your style and message. Analyze the following questions to determine your organizational pattern, delivery style, and supporting material.

- How will this topic appeal to this audience?
- How can I relate this information to my listeners' needs?
- How can I earn respect so that they accept my message?
- What would be most effective in making my point? Facts? Statistics? Personal experiences? Expert opinion? Humor? Cartoons? Graphic illustrations? Demonstrations? Case histories? Analogies?
- What measures must I take to ensure that this audience remembers my main points?

Figure **14.1** Succeeding With Four Audience Types

Audience Members	Organizational Pattern	Delivery Style	Supporting Material
Friendly			
They like you and your topic.	Use any pattern. Try something new. Involve the audience.	Be warm, pleasant, and open. Use lots of eye contact and smiles.	Include humor, personal examples, and experiences.
Neutral			
They are calm, rational; their minds are made up, but they think they are objective.	Present both sides of the issue. Use pro/con or problem/solution patterns. Save time for audience questions.	Be controlled. Do nothing showy. Use confident, small gestures.	Use facts, statistics, expert opinion, and comparison and contrast. Avoid humor, personal stories, and flashy visuals.
Uninterested			
They have short attention spans; they may be there against their will.	Be brief—no more than three points. Avoid topical and pro/con patterns that seem lengthy to the audience.	Be dynamic and entertaining. Move around. Use large gestures.	Use humor, cartoons, colorful visuals, powerful quotations, and startling statistics.

Avoid darkening the room, standing motionless, passing out handouts, using boring visuals, or expecting the audience to participate.

Hostile			
They want to take charge or to ridicule the speaker; they may be defensive, emotional.	Organize using a noncontroversial pattern, such as a topical, chronological, or geographical strategy.	Be calm and controlled. Speak evenly and slowly.	Include objective data and expert opinion. Avoid anecdotes and humor.

Avoid a question-and-answer period, if possible; otherwise, use a moderator or accept only written questions.

© Cengage Learning 2015

If you have agreed to speak to an audience with which you are unfamiliar, ask for the names of a half dozen people who will be in the audience. Contact them and learn about their backgrounds and expectations for the presentation. This information can help you answer questions about what they want to hear and how deeply you should explore the subject. You will want to thank these people when you start your speech. Doing this kind of homework will impress the audience.

LEARNING OBJECTIVE 2

Explain how to organize the introduction, body, and conclusion as well as how to build audience rapport in a presentation.

Organizing Content for Impact and Audience Rapport

Once you have determined your purpose and analyzed the audience, you are ready to collect information and organize it logically. Good organization and intentional repetition are the two most powerful keys to audience comprehension and retention. In fact, many speech experts recommend the following admittedly repetitious, but effective, plan:

- **Step 1:** Tell them what you are going to tell them.
- **Step 2:** Tell them.
- **Step 3:** Tell them what you have told them.

In other words, repeat your main points in the introduction, body, and conclusion of your presentation. Although it is redundant, this strategy is necessary in oral presentations. Let's examine how to construct the three parts of an effective presentation: introduction, body, and conclusion.

Capturing Attention in the Introduction

How many times have you heard a speaker begin with, *It's a pleasure to be here.* Or, *I'm honored to be asked to speak.* Or the all-too-common, *Today I'm going to talk about . . . .* Boring openings such as these get speakers off to a dull start. Avoid such banalities by striving to accomplish three goals in the introduction to your presentation:

- Capture listeners' attention and get them involved.
- Identify yourself and establish your credibility.
- Preview your main points.

If you are able to appeal to listeners and involve them in your presentation right from the start, you are more likely to hold their attention until the finish. Consider some of the same techniques that you used to open sales letters: a question, a startling fact, a joke, a story, or a quotation. Some speakers achieve involvement by opening with a question or command that requires audience members to raise their hands or stand up. Additional techniques to gain and keep audience attention are presented in the accompanying Career Coach box.

To establish your credibility, you need to describe your position, knowledge, education, or experience—whatever qualifies you to speak. The way you dress, the self-confidence you display, and your direct eye contact can also build credibility. In addition, try to connect with your audience. Listeners respond particularly well to speakers who reveal something of themselves and identify with them. A consultant addressing office workers might reminisce about how she started as an administrative assistant; a CEO might tell a funny story in which the joke is on him. Use humor if you can pull it off (not everyone can); self-effacing humor may work best for you.

After capturing your audience's attention and effectively establishing your credibility using humor or some other technique, you will want to preview the main points of your topic, perhaps with a visual aid.

Take a look at Sandra Castillo's introduction, shown in Figure 14.2, to see how she integrated all the elements necessary for a good opening.

Organizing the Body

The most effective oral presentations focus on a few principal ideas. Therefore, the body of your short presentation (20 or fewer minutes) should include a limited number of main points, say, two to four. Develop each main point with adequate, but not excessive, explanation and details. Too many details can obscure the main message, so keep your presentation simple and logical. Remember, listeners have no pages to refer to should they become confused.

When Sandra Castillo began planning her presentation, she realized immediately that she could talk for hours on her topic. She also knew that listeners are not good at separating major and minor points. Therefore, instead of submerging her listeners in a sea of information, she sorted out a few main ideas. In the banking industry, loan officers generally ask the following three questions of each applicant for a small business loan: (a) Are you ready to "hit the ground running" in starting your business? (b) Have you done your homework? and (c) Have you made realistic projections of potential sales, cash flow, and equity investment? These questions would become her main points, but Sandra wanted to streamline them further so that her audience would be sure to remember them. She encapsulated the questions in three words: *experience, preparation,* and *projection.* As you can see in Figure 14.2, Sandra prepared a sentence outline showing these three main ideas. Each is supported by examples and explanations.

How to organize and sequence main ideas may not be immediately obvious when you begin working on a presentation. The following methods, which review and amplify those discussed in Chapter 12, provide many possible strategies and examples to help you organize a presentation:

- **Chronology.** Example: A presentation describing the history of a problem, organized from the first sign of trouble to the present.
- **Geography/space.** Example: A presentation about the changing diversity of the workforce, organized by regions in the country (East Coast, West Coast, and so forth).

CAREER COACH:

Gaining and Keeping Audience Attention

Experienced speakers know how to capture the attention of an audience and how to maintain that attention throughout a presentation. You can spruce up your presentations by trying these twelve proven techniques.

- **A promise.** Begin with a realistic promise that keeps the audience expectant (for example, *By the end of this presentation, you will know how you can increase your sales by 50 percent!*).

- **Drama.** Open by telling an emotionally moving story or by describing a serious problem that involves the audience. Throughout your talk include other dramatic elements, such as a long pause after a key statement. Change your vocal tone or pitch. Professionals use high-intensity emotions such as anger, joy, sadness, and excitement.

- **Eye contact.** As you begin, command attention by surveying the entire audience to take in all listeners. Give yourself two to five seconds to linger on individuals to avoid fleeting, unconvincing eye contact. Don't just sweep the room and the crowd.

- **Movement.** Leave the lectern area whenever possible. Walk around the conference table or down the aisles of the presentation room. Try to move toward your audience, especially at the beginning and end of your talk.

- **Questions.** Keep listeners active and involved with rhetorical questions. Ask for a show of hands to get each listener thinking. The response will also give you a quick gauge of audience attention.

- **Demonstrations.** Include a member of the audience in a demonstration (for example, *I'm going to show you exactly how to implement our four-step customer courtesy process, but I need a volunteer from the audience to help me*).

- **Samples/props.** If you are promoting a product, consider using items to toss out to the audience or to award as prizes to volunteer participants. You can also pass around product samples or promotional literature. Be careful, though, to maintain control.

- **Visuals.** Give your audience something to look at besides yourself. Use a variety of visual aids in a single session. Also consider writing the concerns expressed by your audience on a flipchart or on a whiteboard or smart board as you go along.

- **Dress.** Enhance your credibility with your audience by dressing professionally for your presentation. Professional attire will help you look competent and qualified, making your audience more likely to listen and take you seriously.

- **Current events/statistics.** Mention a current event or statistic (the more startling, the better) that is relevant to your topic and to which the audience can relate.

- **A quote.** Quotations, especially those made by well-known individuals, can be powerful attention-getting devices. The quotation should be pertinent to your topic, short, and interesting.

- **Self-interest.** Review your entire presentation to ensure that it meets the critical *What's-in-it-for-me* audience test. Remember that people are most interested in things that benefit them.

- **Topic/function/conventional grouping.** Example: A report discussing mishandled airline baggage, organized by names of airlines.

- **Comparison/contrast (pro/con).** Example: A report comparing organic farming methods with those of modern industrial farming.

- **Journalistic pattern (the five Ws and an H).** Example: A report describing how identity thieves can ruin your good name. Organized by *who, what, when, where, why,* and *how.*

- **Value/size.** Example: A report describing fluctuations in housing costs, organized by prices of homes.

- **Importance.** Example: A report describing five reasons a company should move its headquarters to a specific city, organized from the most important reason to the least important.

Chapter 14: Business Presentations

- **Problem/solution.** Example: A company faces a problem such as declining sales. A solution such as reducing the staff is offered.
- **Simple/complex.** Example: A report explaining genetic modification of plants such as corn, organized from simple seed production to complex gene introduction.
- **Best case/worst case.** Example: A report analyzing whether two companies should merge, organized by the best-case result (improved market share, profitability, employee morale) as opposed to the worst-case result (devalued stock, lost market share, employee malaise).

In the presentation shown in Figure 14.2, Sandra arranged the main points by importance, placing the most important point last where it had maximum effect. When organizing any presentation, prepare a little more material than you think you will actually need. Savvy speakers always have something useful in reserve such as an extra handout, slide, or idea—just

Figure 14.2 Outlining an Oral Presentation

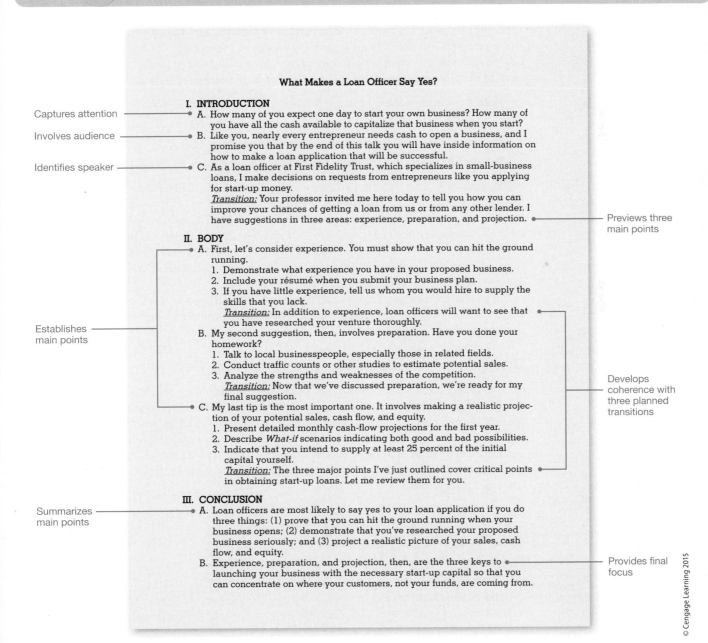

in case they finish early. At the same time, most speakers go about 25 percent over the allotted time as opposed to their practice runs at home in front of the mirror. If your speaking time is limited, as it usually is in your classes, aim for less than the limit when rehearsing, so that you don't take time away from the next presenters.

Summarizing in the Conclusion

Nervous speakers often rush to wrap up their presentations because they can't wait to flee the stage. However, listeners will remember the conclusion more than any other part of a speech. That's why you should spend some time to make it most effective. Strive to achieve three goals:

- Summarize the main themes of the presentation.
- Leave the audience with a specific and noteworthy take-away.
- Include a statement that allows you to leave the podium gracefully.

A conclusion is akin to a punch line and must be memorable. Think of it as the high point of your presentation, a valuable kernel of information to take away. The valuable kernel of information, or take-away, should tie in with the opening or present a forward-looking idea. Avoid merely rehashing, in the same words, what you said before, but ensure that the audience will take away very specific information or benefits and a positive impression of you and your company. The take-away is the value of the presentation to the audience and the benefit audience members believe they have received. The tension that you built in the early parts of the talk now culminates in the close. Compare these poor and improved conclusions:

Poor Conclusion: Well, I guess that's about all I have to say. Thanks for your time.

Improved: In bringing my presentation to a close, I will restate my major purpose . . . .

Improved: In summary, my major purpose has been to . . . .

Improved: In conclusion, let me review my three major points. They are . . . .

Notice how Sandra Castillo, in the conclusion shown in Figure 14.2, summarized her three main points and provided a final focus to listeners.

If you are promoting a recommendation, you might end as follows: *In conclusion, I recommend that we retain Matrixx Marketing to conduct a telemarketing campaign beginning September 1 at a cost of X dollars. To complete this recommendation, I suggest that we (a) finance this campaign from our operations budget, (b) develop a persuasive message describing our new product, and (c) name Lisa Beck to oversee the project.*

In your conclusion you could use an anecdote, an inspiring quotation, or a statement that ties in the opener and offers a new insight. Whatever you choose, be sure to include a closing thought that indicates you are finished.

Building Audience Rapport Like a Pro

Good speakers are adept at building audience rapport, and they think about how they are going to build that rapport as they organize their presentations. Building rapport means that speakers form a bond with the audience; they entertain as well as inform. How do they do it? Based on observations of successful and unsuccessful speakers, we learn that the good ones use a number of verbal and nonverbal techniques to connect with the audience. Their helpful techniques include providing effective imagery, supplying verbal signposts, and using body language strategically.

Courtesy of Susan Dugdale

Effective Imagery. You will lose your audience quickly if you fill your talk with abstractions, generalities, and dry facts. To enliven your presentation and enhance comprehension, try using some of the techniques shown in Figure 14.3. However, beware of exaggeration or distortion. Keep your imagery realistic and credible.

Verbal Signposts. Speakers must remember that listeners, unlike readers of a report, cannot control the rate of presentation or read back through pages to review main points. As a result, listeners get lost easily. Knowledgeable speakers help the audience recognize the organization and main points in an oral message with verbal signposts. They keep listeners on track by including helpful previews, summaries, and transitions such as these:

- **Previewing**

  The next segment of my talk presents three reasons for . . . .
  Let's now consider the causes of . . . .

- **Summarizing**

  Let me review with you the major problems I have just discussed . . . .
  You see, then, that the most significant factors are . . . .

- **Switching directions**

  Thus far we have talked solely about . . . ; now let's move to . . . .
  I have argued that . . . and . . . , but an alternate view holds that . . . .

You can further improve any oral presentation by including appropriate transitional expressions such as *first, second, next, then, therefore, moreover, on the other hand, on the contrary,* and *in conclusion.* These transitional expressions, which you learned about in Figure 5.6 on page 167, build coherence, lend emphasis, and tell listeners where you are headed. Notice in Sandra Castillo's outline, in Figure 14.2, the specific transitional elements designed to help listeners recognize each new principal point.

Nonverbal Messages. Although what you say is most important, the nonverbal messages you send can also have a potent effect on how well your audience receives your message. How you look, how you move, and how you speak can make or break your presentation. The following suggestions focus on nonverbal tips to ensure that your verbal message resonates with your audience.

- **Look terrific!** Like it or not, you will be judged by your appearance. For everything but small in-house presentations, be sure you dress professionally. The rule of thumb is that you should dress at least as well as the best-dressed person in the audience.

- **Animate your body.** Be enthusiastic and let your body show it. Emphasize ideas to enhance points about size, number, and direction. Use a variety of gestures, but don't consciously plan them in advance.

- **Speak extemporaneously.** Do not read from notes, a manuscript, or your presentation slides. Instead, speak freely, maintaining eye contact with your audience. Use your presentation slides to guide your talk and jog your memory, and use note cards or a paper outline only if presenting without an electronic slideshow. You will come across as more competent, prepared, and enthusiastic if you do not have to rely on your notes, manuscript, or slides.

- **Punctuate your words.** You can keep your audience interested by varying your tone, volume, pitch, and pace. Use pauses before and after important points. Allow the audience to take in your ideas.

- **Get out from behind the podium.** Avoid standing rigidly behind a podium. Movement makes you look natural and comfortable. You might pick a few places in the room to walk

Figure **14.3** Effective Imagery Engages the Audience

Analogy — **Comparison of similar traits between dissimilar things**

- Product development is similar to the process of conceiving, carrying, and delivering a baby.
- Downsizing or restructuring is comparable to an overweight person undergoing a regimen of dieting, habit changing, and exercising.

Simile — **Comparison that includes the words *like* or *as***

- Our critics used our background report like a drunk uses a lamppost–for support rather than for illumination.
- She's as happy as someone who just won the lottery.

Metaphor — **Comparison between otherwise dissimilar things without using the words *like* or *as***

- Our competitor's CEO is a snake when it comes to negotiating.
- My desk is a garbage dump.

Personal Anecdote — **A personal story**

- Let me tell you about a few personal blunders I made when using social media and what I learned from these mistakes.
- I could never take vacations because I couldn't find anyone to take care of my pets while I was away. That's when I decided to start a pet hotel.

Personalized Statistics — **Statistics that relate directly to the audience**

- Look around the room. Only three out of five graduates will find a job immediately after graduation.
- The sales of Coca-Cola totaled 26.7 billion cases last year worldwide. That equates to every man, woman, and child in the world consuming 3.8 cases of Coke.

Worst-or-Best-Case Scenario — **The worst or best that could happen**

- If we do nothing about our computer backup system now, it's just a matter of time before the entire system crashes and we lose all of our customer contact information. Can you imagine starting from scratch in building all of your customer files again? However, if we fix the system now, we can expand our customer files and actually increase sales at the same time.

© Cengage Learning 2015

to. Even if you must stay close to your visual aids, make a point of leaving them occasionally so that the audience can see your whole body.

- **Vary your facial expression.** Begin with a smile, but change your expressions to correspond with the thoughts you are voicing. You can shake your head to show disagreement, roll your eyes to show disdain, look heavenward for guidance, or wrinkle your brow to show concern or dismay.

Whenever possible, beginning presenters should have an experienced speaker watch them and give them tips as they rehearse. Your instructor is an important coach who can provide you with invaluable feedback. In the absence of helpers, record yourself and watch your nonverbal behavior on camera. Are you doing what it takes to build rapport?

Planning Visual Aids and Multimedia Presentations

LEARNING OBJECTIVE **3**
Create effective visual aids and handouts using today's multimedia presentation technology.

Before you make a business presentation, consider this wise proverb: "Tell me, I forget. Show me, I remember. Involve me, I understand." Your goals as a speaker are to make listeners understand, remember, and act on your ideas. To get them interested and involved, include effective visual aids. Some experts claim that we acquire 85 percent of all our knowledge visually: "Professionals everywhere need to know about the incredible inefficiency of text-based information and the incredible effects of images," says developmental molecular biologist John Medina.[11] Therefore, an oral presentation that incorporates visual aids is far more likely to be understood and retained than one lacking visual enhancement.

Good visual aids serve many purposes. They emphasize and clarify main points, thus improving comprehension and retention. They increase audience interest, and they make the presenter appear more professional, better prepared, and more persuasive. Well-designed visual aids illustrate and emphasize your message more effectively than words alone; therefore, they may help shorten a meeting or achieve your goal faster. Visual aids are particularly helpful for inexperienced speakers because the audience concentrates on the visual aid rather than on the speaker. However, experienced speakers work hard at not being eclipsed or upstaged by their slideshows. Good visual aids also serve to jog the memory of a speaker, thus improving self-confidence, poise, and delivery.

Types of Visual Aids

Speakers have many forms of visual media at their fingertips if they wish to enhance their presentations. Figure 14.4 describes the pros and cons of a number of visual aids, both high-tech and low-tech, that can guide you in selecting the best one for any speaking occasion. Two of the most popular visuals for business presentations are multimedia slides and handouts. Zoom presentations, an alternative to multimedia slides, are also growing in popularity.

Multimedia Slides. With today's excellent software programs—such as Microsoft PowerPoint, Apple Keynote, Apache OpenOffice Impress, Google Quickpoint, Corel Presentations, and Adobe Presenter—you can create dynamic, colorful presentations with your desktop, laptop, tablet, or smartphone. The output from these programs is generally shown on a computer screen, a TV monitor, an LCD (liquid crystal display) panel, or a screen. With a little expertise and the right equipment, you can create multimedia presentations that include audio, videos, images, animation, and hyperlinks, as described shortly in the discussion of multimedia presentations. Multimedia slides can also be uploaded to a website or broadcast live over the Web.

Handouts. You can enhance and complement your presentations by distributing pictures, outlines, brochures, articles, charts, summaries, or other supplements. Speakers who use

---

REALITY CHECK: Zooming in on Your Ideas

"New, dynamic presentation tools like Prezi allow us to communicate design ideas with our clients in highly engaging and dynamic ways, liberating interesting conversations from the boredom of one-way presentations."[12]

—**RANDY HOWDER,** *design strategist with Gensler*

Figure **14.4** Pros and Cons of High-Tech and Low-Tech Visual Aid Options

High Tech	Pros	Cons
Multimedia slides	Create professional appearance with many color, art, graphic, and font options. Ability to incorporate video, audio, and hyperlinks. Easy to use and transport via removable storage media, Web download, or e-mail attachment. Inexpensive to update.	Present potential incompatibility issues. Require costly projection equipment and practice for smooth delivery. Tempt user to include razzle-dazzle features that may fail to add value. Too one-dimensional and linear.
Zoom presentations	Nonlinear, 3D quality allows presenter to zoom in and out of content to show the "big picture" or specific details. Attractive templates. Ability to insert rich media. Presentations are interactive, cinematic, and dynamic.	Cloud-based, so Internet access is required. No way to edit images. Limited font choices. Because there are no separate slides, some users find it difficult to move around the canvas. Zooming can be distracting and even nauseating.
Video	Gives an accurate representation of the content; strong indication of forethought and preparation.	Creates potential for compatibility issues related to computer video formats. Expensive to create and update.
Low Tech		
Handouts	Encourage audience participation. Easy to maintain and update. Enhance recall because audience keeps reference material.	Increase risk of unauthorized duplication of speaker's material. Can be difficult to transport. May cause speaker to lose audience's attention.
Flipcharts or whiteboards	Provide inexpensive option available at most sites. Easy to (a) create, (b) modify or customize on the spot, (c) record comments from the audience, and (d) combine with more high-tech visuals in the same presentation.	Require graphics talent. Difficult for larger audiences to see. Prepared flipcharts are cumbersome to transport and easily worn with use.
Props	Offer a realistic reinforcement of message content. Increase audience participation with close observation.	Lead to extra work and expense in transporting and replacing worn objects. Limited use with larger audiences.

presentation software often prepare a set of their slides along with notes to hand out to viewers. Timing the distribution of any handout, though, is tricky. If given out during a presentation, your handouts tend to distract the audience, causing you to lose control. Therefore, you should discuss handouts during the presentation but delay distributing them until after you finish. If you do this, tell audience members at the beginning of your presentation that you will be distributing handouts at the end.

Zoom Presentations.   Many business presenters feel limited by multimedia slides, which tend to be too linear. As a result, some communicators are starting to create more dynamic visual aids. Using software such as Prezi, which is a cloud-based presentation and storytelling tool, businesspeople can design 3D presentations. These 3D presentations allow the speaker to zoom out and in of images to help the audience better understand and remember content,

Figure **14.5** Prezi Zoom Presentation 513

http://prezi-a.akamaihd.net/presskit/Prezi%20Desktop/PreziDesktop_Windows.png

Prezi uses one canvas for a presentation rather than individual slides. Here is an example of the main canvas of a zoom presentation. Clicking on any section of this canvas will zoom in on detailed information. For example, if you click on the area around the tree roots, you will zoom in on a quote about thinking positively, as shown in the thumbnail images in the left pane.

details, and relationships.[13] Zoom presentations allow presenters to communicate their ideas in a more exciting, creative way. Audience members also seem to appreciate the cinematic, interactive quality of these presentations. Figure 14.5 shows what a typical Prezi canvas looks like during the design process.

Designing an Impressive Multimedia Presentation

Few businesspeople or entrepreneurs would do without the razzle-dazzle of colorful images to make their points. Electronic slideshows, created using PowerPoint in particular, have become a staple of business presentations, although zoom presentations and other media-rich Web-based presentations are gaining in popularity. However, overuse or misuse may be the downside of the ever-present multimedia slideshow. Over the two decades of the software program's existence, millions of poorly created and badly delivered PowerPoint presentations have tarnished PowerPoint's reputation as an effective communication tool. Tools are helpful only when used properly.

In the last few years, several communication consultants have tried to show business how it can move "beyond bullet points." The experts recommend creating slideshows that tell a story and send a powerful message with much less text and more images.[14] Presentation guru Garr Reynolds urges readers to unleash their creativity: "Do not rely on Microsoft or Apple or anyone else to dictate your choices. Most of all, do not let mere habit—and the habits of others—dictate your decisions on how you prepare and design and deliver your presentations."[15] Some businesspeople who are ready to explore highly visual, less text-laden design choices are turning to zoom presentations and other media-rich presentations designed using software such as Prezi and SlideRocket. Figure 14.6 shows some of the tools that SlideRocket provides to create a visually rich presentation.

In the sections that follow, you will learn to create an impressive multimedia presentation using the most widely used presentation software program, PowerPoint. You will also learn how Prezi can be used to create zoom presentations as an alternative to PowerPoint slides.

Figure **14.6** SlideRocket Presentation

SlideRocket is a cloud-based presentation software. Like PowerPoint, it allows users to create slides, but it takes the emphasis off bullet points. Instead, SlideRocket offers numerous tools to help users create visually rich slides: stock photos, flash animation, 2D and 3D transitional effects, tables, and charts.

http://www.sliderocket.com/product/

With any software program, of course, gaining expertise requires an investment of time and effort. You could take a course, or you could teach yourself through an online tutorial. Another way to master PowerPoint or Prezi is to read a book such as Faithe Wempen's *PowerPoint 2013 Bible* or Russell Anderson-Williams's *Mastering Prezi for Business Presentations*. When operated by proficient designers and skillful presenters, both PowerPoint and Prezi can add visual impact to any presentation.

Applying the 3-x-3 Writing Process to Multimedia Presentations

Some presenters prefer to create their visuals first and then develop the narrative around their visuals. Others prefer to prepare their content first and then create the visual component. The risk associated with the first approach is that you may be tempted to spend too much time making your visuals look good and not enough time preparing your content. Remember that great-looking visuals never compensate for thin content. In the following discussion, we review the three phases of the writing process and show how they help you develop a visually appealing PowerPoint, SlideRocket, or Prezi presentation. In the first phase (prewriting), you analyze, anticipate, and adapt. In the second phase, you research, organize, compose, and design. In the third phase, you edit, proofread, and evaluate.

Analyzing the Situation.   Making the best content and design choices for your presentation depends greatly on your analysis of the situation. Will your slides be used during a live presentation? Will they be part of a self-running presentation such as in a store kiosk? Will they be saved on a server so that those with Web access can watch the presentation at their convenience? Will they be sent as a PowerPoint show or a PDF document to a client instead of a hard-copy report? Are you converting your presentation for viewing on smartphones or tablets?

If you are e-mailing the presentation or posting it online as a self-contained file, or slide deck, it will typically feature more text than if you were delivering it orally. If, on the other hand, you are creating slides for a live presentation, you will likely rely more on images than on text.

Anticipating Your Audience.   Think about how you can design your presentation to get the most positive response from your audience. Audiences respond, for example, to the colors you use. Primary ideas are generally best conveyed with bold colors such as blue, green, and purple. Because the messages that colors convey can vary from culture to culture, colors must be chosen carefully. In the United States, blue is the color of credibility, tranquility, conservatism, and trust. Therefore, it is the background color of choice for many business presentations. Green relates to interaction, growth, money, and stability. It can work well as a background or an accent color. Purple can also work as a background or accent color. It conveys spirituality, royalty, dreams, and humor.[16] As for text, adjust the color in such a way that it provides high contrast and is readable as a result. White or yellow, for example, usually works well on dark backgrounds.

Just as you anticipate audience members' reactions to color, you can usually anticipate their reactions to special effects. Using animation and sound effects—flying objects, swirling text, clashing cymbals, and the like—only because they are available is not a good idea. Special effects distract your audience, drawing attention away from your main points. You should add animation features only if doing so helps convey your message or adds interest to the content. When your audience members leave, they should be commenting on the ideas you conveyed—not the cool swivels and sound effects. The zooming effect of Prezi presentations can add value to your presentation as long as it can make your audience understand connections and remember content.

Adapting Text and Color Selections.

Adapt the amount of text on your slide to how your audience will use the slides. As a general guideline, most graphic designers encourage the 6-x-6 rule: "Six bullets per screen, max; six words per bullet, max."[17] You may find, however, that breaking this rule is sometimes necessary, particularly when your users will be viewing the presentation on their own with no speaker assistance. For most purposes, though, strive to break free from bulleted lists whenever possible and minimize the use of text.

Adapt the colors based on where the presentation will be given. Use light text on a dark background for presentations in darkened rooms. Use dark text on a light background for presentations in lighted rooms. Avoid using a dark font on a dark background, such as red text on a dark blue background. In the same way, avoid using a light font on a light background, such as white text on a pale blue background.

Researching Your Presentation Options.

If you need to present a complicated idea, you may have to learn more about PowerPoint, SlideRocket, or Prezi to determine the best way to clarify and simplify the software's visual presentation. Besides using online tutorials and studying books on the subject, be on the lookout as you view other people's presentations to learn fresh ways to illustrate your content more effectively. Chances are you will learn the most from fellow students and team members who have truly mastered presentation tools.

Organizing Your Presentations.

When you prepare your presentation, translate the major headings in your outline into titles for slides. Then build bullet points using short phrases. In Chapter 5 you learned to improve readability by using graphic highlighting techniques, including bullets, numbers, and headings. In preparing a PowerPoint, SlideRocket, or Prezi presentation, you will use those same techniques.

The slides (or canvas) you create to accompany your spoken ideas can be organized with visual elements that will help your audience understand and remember what you want to communicate. Let's say, for example, that you have three points in your presentation. You can create a blueprint slide that captures the three points in a visually appealing way, and then you can use that slide several times throughout your presentation. Near the beginning, the blueprint slide provides an overview of your points. Later, it will provide transitions as you move from point to point. For transitions, you can direct your audience's attention by highlighting the next point you will be talking about. Finally, the blueprint slide can be used near the end to provide a review of your key points.

Working With Templates.

All presentation programs require you to (a) select or create a template that will serve as the background for your presentation and (b) make each individual slide by selecting a layout that best conveys your message. Novice and even advanced users often use existing templates because they are designed by professionals who know how to combine harmonious colors, borders, bullet styles, and fonts for pleasing visual effects. If you prefer, you can alter existing templates so they better suit your needs. Adding a corporate logo, adjusting the color scheme to better match the colors used on your organization's website, or selecting a different font are just some of the ways you can customize existing templates. One big advantage of templates is that they get you started quickly.

Be careful, though, of what one expert has labeled "visual clichés."[18] Overused templates and even clip art that come preinstalled with PowerPoint, SlideRocket, and Prezi can weary viewers who have seen them repeatedly in presentations. Instead of using a standard template, search for *PowerPoint template, SlideRocket template,* or *Prezi template* in your favorite search tool. You will see hundreds of template options available as free downloads. Unless your employer requires that presentations all have the same look, your audience will appreciate fresh templates that complement the purpose of your presentation and provide visual variety.

Composing Your Presentation.   During the composition stage, many users fall into the trap of excessive formatting and programming. They fritter away precious time fine-tuning their slides or canvas. They don't spend enough time on what they are going to say and how they will say it. To avoid this trap, set a limit for how much time you will spend making your slides or canvas visually appealing. Your time limit will be based on how many "bells and whistles" (a) your audience expects and (b) your content requires to make it understandable. Remember that not every point nor every thought requires a visual. In fact, it's smart to switch off the presentation occasionally and direct the focus to yourself. Darkening the screen while you discuss a point, tell a story, give an example, or involve the audience will add variety to your presentation.

Create a slide or canvas only if it accomplishes at least one of the following purposes:

- Generates interest in what you are saying and helps the audience follow your ideas
- Highlights points you want your audience to remember
- Introduces or reviews your key points
- Provides a transition from one major point to the next
- Illustrates and simplifies complex ideas

In a later section of this chapter, you will find very specific steps to follow as you create your presentation.

Designing for Optimal Effect.   When using PowerPoint or other presentation software, try to avoid long, boring bulleted lists. You can alter layouts by repositioning, resizing, or changing the fonts for the placeholders in which your title, bulleted list, organization chart, video clip, photograph, or other elements appear. Figure 14.7 shows how to make your slides visually more appealing and memorable even with relatively small changes.

Notice that the bulleted items on the Before slide in Figure 14.7 are not parallel. The wording looks as if the author had been brainstorming or freewriting a first draft. The second and sixth bullet points express the same thought, that shopping online is convenient and easy for customers. Some bullet points are too long. The bullets on the After slide are short and well within the 6-x-6 rule, although they are complete sentences. The illustrations in the revised slide add interest and illustrate the points. You may use stock photos that you can download from the Web for personal or school use without penalty, or consider taking your own digital pictures. You can also use other PowerPoint features, such as SmartArt, to add variety and pizzazz to your slides. Converting pure text and bullet points to graphics, charts, and other images will keep your audience interested and help them retain the information you are presenting.

Editing, Proofreading, and Evaluating Your Presentation.   Use the PowerPoint slide sorter view to rearrange, insert, and delete slides during the revision process. You can also use the Prezi editor to make any necessary changes to your canvas. This is the time to focus on making your presentation as clear and concise as possible. If you are listing items, be sure that they all use parallel grammatical form. Figure 14.8 shows how to revise a PowerPoint slide to improve it for conciseness, parallelism, and other features. Study the design tips described in the first slide and determine which suggestions were not followed. Then compare it with the revised slide.

As you are revising, check carefully to find spelling, grammar, punctuation, and other errors. Use the PowerPoint, SlideRocket, or Prezi spell-check feature, but don't rely on it without careful proofing, preferably from a printed copy of the slideshow.

Figure **14.7** Revising and Enhancing Slides for Greater Impact

Before Revision

Reasons for Selling Online

- Your online business can grow globally.
- Customer convenience.
- You can conduct your business 24/7.
- No need for renting a retail store or hiring employees.
- Reduce inquiries by providing policies and a privacy statement.
- Customers can buy quickly and easily.

After Revision

Why You Should Sell Online

Grow business globally.

Offer convenience to customers.

Conduct business 24/7.

Save on rent and staff.

Create policies to reduce inquiries.

© denis_pc/Fotolia

The slide on the left contains bullet points that are not parallel and that overlap in meaning. The second and sixth bullet points say the same thing. Moreover, some bullet points are too long. After revision, the slide on the right has a more convincing title illustrating the "you" view. The bullet points are shorter, and each begins with a verb for parallelism and an emphasis on action. The illustrations add interest.

Nothing is as embarrassing as projecting errors on a huge screen in front of an audience. Also, check for consistency in how you capitalize and punctuate points throughout the presentation.

The final stage in applying the 3-x-3 writing process to developing a PowerPoint, SlideRocket, or Prezi presentation involves evaluation. Is your message presented in a visually appealing way? Have you tested your presentation on the equipment and in the room you will be using during your presentation? Do the colors you selected work in this new setting? Are the font styles and sizes readable from the back of the room? Figure 14.9 shows examples of PowerPoint slides that incorporate what you have learned in this discussion.

The dark purple background and the complementary hues in the slideshow shown in Figure 14.9 are standard choices for many business presentations. With an unobtrusive dark background, white fonts are a good option for maximum contrast and, hence, readability. The creator of the presentation varied the slide design to break the monotony of bulleted or numbered lists. Images and animated diagrams add interest and zing to the slides.

Practicing and Preparing

Solid preparation and practice are crucial. One expert advises presenters to complete their PowerPoint slides, SlideRocket slides, or Prezi canvases a week before the actual talk and rehearse several times each day before the presentation.[19] Allow plenty of time before your presentation to set up and test your equipment. Confirm that the places you plan to stand are not in the line of the projected image. Audience members don't appreciate having part of the slide displayed on your body. Make sure that all video or Web links are working and that you know how to operate all features the first time you try. No matter how much time you put into preshow setup and testing, you still have no guarantee that all will go

Figure 14.8 Designing More Effective Slides

Before Revision

DESIGN TIPS FOR SLIDE TEXT

1. STRIVE TO HAVE NO MORE THAN SIX BULLETS PER SLIDE AND NO MORE THAN SIX WORDS PER BULLET.
2. IF YOU USE UPPER- AND LOWERCASE TEXT, IT IS EASIER TO READ.
3. IT IS BETTER TO USE PHRASES RATHER THAN SENTENCES.
4. USING A SIMPLE HIGH-CONTRAST TYPE FACE IS EASIER TO READ AND DOES NOT DISTRACT FROM YOUR PRESENTATION.
5. BE CONSISTENT IN YOUR SPACING, CAPITALIZATION, AND PUNCTUATION.

After Revision

Design Tips for Slide Text

- Six or fewer bullets per slide
- Six or fewer words per bullet
- Concise phrases, not sentences
- Simple typeface
- Consistent spacing, capitalization, punctuation

© Cengage Learning 2015

The slide on the left uses a difficult-to-read font style. In addition, the slide includes too many words per bullet and violates most of the slide-making rules it covers. After revision, the slide on the right provides a pleasing color combination, uses short bullet points in a readable font style, and creates an attractive list using PowerPoint SmartArt features.

smoothly. Therefore, you should always bring backups of your presentation. Overhead transparencies and handouts of your presentation provide good substitutes. Transferring your presentation to a CD or a USB flash drive that could run from any available computer might prove useful as well. Transferring your presentation to the cloud (e.g., Dropbox or Google Drive) can also prove beneficial.

Keeping Your Audience Engaged

In addition to using technology to enhance and enrich your message, here are additional tips for performing like a professional and keeping the audience engaged:

- Know your material. This will free you to look at your audience and gaze at the screen, not your practice notes. Maintain genuine eye contact to connect with individuals in the room.

- As you show new elements on a slide or canvas, allow the audience time to absorb the information. Then paraphrase and elaborate on what the listeners have seen. Don't insult your audience's intelligence by reading verbatim from a slide or canvas.

- Leave the lights as bright as you can. Make sure the audience can see your face and eyes.

- Use a remote clicker so you can move freely rather than having to remain tethered to your computer. Remote clickers work with both PowerPoint and Prezi.

- Maintain a connection with the audience by using a laser pointer to highlight slide or canvas items to discuss. Be aware, however, that a dancing laser point in a shaky hand may make you appear nervous. Steady your hand.

- Don't leave a slide on the screen when you have finished discussing it. In Slide Show view on the View tab in PowerPoint, strike *B* on the keyboard to turn on or off the screen image by blackening it. Pushing *W* will turn the screen white. When giving a Prezi zoom presentation, remember to zoom back out when necessary.

Some presenters allow their PowerPoint slides, SlideRocket slides, or Prezi canvases to steal their thunder. One expert urges speakers to "use their PowerPresence in preference to

Figure 14.9 PowerPoint Slides That Summarize and Illustrate Multimedia Presentations

Business Presentations and the 3-x-3 Writing Process

PREWRITING
Analyzing
Anticipating
Adapting

DRAFTING
Researching
Organizing
Composing

REVISING
Editing
Proofreading
Evaluating

① PREWRITING

PREWRITING
Analyzing
Anticipating
Adapting

- Identify purpose of presentation.
- Find suitable colors.
- Create effective animations.
- Choose images over text.

② DRAFTING

DRAFTING
Researching
Organizing
Composing

- Illustrate content in fresh ways.
- Use blueprint slides.
- Follow six steps in your presentation.

Creating a Multimedia Presentation

Start with the text
Select background and fonts
Choose images
Create graphics
Add special effects
Include interactive elements

Develop Content With Templates and Themes

Click to add title

Before Delivering Your Multimedia Presentation

- Create visual interest.
- Highlight memorable points.
- Introduce or review key points.
- Provide transitions.
- Illustrate ideas.
- Simplify complex thoughts.

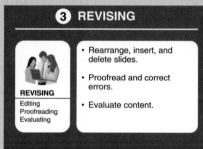

③ REVISING

REVISING
Editing
Proofreading
Evaluating

- Rearrange, insert, and delete slides.
- Proofread and correct errors.
- Evaluate content.

Before Delivering Your Multimedia Presentation

Set up and test equipment

Bring backups in case of equipment failure.

During Your Multimedia Presentation

Address the audience, not slides.

Paraphrase, don't read.

Keep room lights fairly bright.

Strike B to toggle image off.

Supplement with other visual aids.

their PowerPoint."[20] Although multimedia presentations supply terrific sizzle, they cannot replace the steak. In developing a presentation, don't expect your visuals to carry the show. Avoid being upstaged by not relying totally on your slides or canvas. Remember that you are the main attraction!

When the founders of the microlending nonprofit organization Kiva make business presentations around the world, audiences respond with enthusiastic applause and even tears. Kiva's online lending platform connects personal lenders with poverty-stricken individuals in developing nations, enabling villagers to start tomato farms, carpet kiosks, and other small ventures that improve their lives. Kiva's presentations include heartwarming stories and videos about village entrepreneurs to show that small loans can make a big difference. What tips can communicators follow to deliver powerful, inspirational presentations?

Seven Steps to a Powerful Multimedia Presentation

We have now discussed many suggestions for making effective PowerPoint, SlideRocket, and Prezi presentations, but you may still be wondering how to put it all together. Figure 14.10 presents a step-by-step process for creating a powerful multimedia presentation:

Figure **14.10** Seven Steps to a Powerful Multimedia Presentation

1 Start with the text.

What do you want your audience to believe, do, or remember? Organize your ideas into an outline with major and minor points.

2 Select background and fonts.

Choose a template or create your own. Focus on consistent font styles, sizes, colors, and backgrounds. Try to use no more than two font styles in your presentation. The point size should be between 24 and 36, and title fonts should be larger than text font.

3 Choose images that help communicate your message.

Use relevant clip art, infographics, photographs, maps, or drawings to illustrate ideas. Microsoft Office Online is accessed in PowerPoint and contains thousands of clip art images and photographs, most of which are in the public domain and require no copyright permissions. Before using images from other sources, determine whether permission from the copyright holder is required.

4 Create graphics.

Use software tools to transform boring bulleted items into appealing graphics and charts. PowerPoint's SmartArt feature can be used to create organization charts, cycles and radials, time lines, pyramids, matrixes, and Venn diagrams. Use PowerPoint's Chart feature to develop various types of charts including line, pie, and bar charts. But don't overdo the graphics!

5 Add special effects.

To keep the audience focused, use animation and transition features to control when objects or text appear. With motion paths, 3D, and other animation options, you can move objects to various positions on the slide and zoom in and out of images and text on your canvas; or to minimize clutter, you can dim or remove them once they have served their purpose.

6 Create hyperlinks.

Make your presentation more interactive and intriguing by connecting to videos, spreadsheets, or websites.

7 Move your presentation online.

Make your presentation available by posting it to the Internet or an organization's intranet. Even if you are giving a face-to-face presentation, attendees appreciate these electronic handouts. The most complex option for moving your multimedia presentation to the Web involves a Web conference or broadcast. You can convert your presentations to PDF documents or send them via e-mail as files that open directly in PowerPoint or Prezi. SlideRocket presentations can be embedded in a website or blog to be viewed by anyone who visits the site.

Polishing Your Delivery and Following Up

LEARNING OBJECTIVE **4**
Specify delivery techniques for use before, during, and after a presentation.

Once you have organized your presentation and prepared visuals, you are ready to practice delivering it. You will feel more confident and appear more professional if you know more about various delivery methods and techniques to use before, during, and after your presentation.

Choosing a Delivery Method

Inexperienced speakers often feel that they must memorize an entire presentation to be effective. Unless you are an experienced performer, however, you will sound robotic and unnatural. What's more, forgetting your place can be disastrous! That is why we don't recommend memorizing an entire oral presentation. However, memorizing significant parts—the introduction, the conclusion, and perhaps a meaningful quotation—can be dramatic and impressive.

If memorizing your business presentation won't work, is reading from a manuscript or your notes the best plan? Definitely not! Reading to an audience is boring and ineffective. Because reading suggests that you don't know your topic very well, the audience loses confidence in your expertise. Reading also prevents you from maintaining eye contact. You can't see audience reactions; consequently, you can't benefit from feedback.

Neither memorizing nor reading creates very convincing business presentations. The best plan, by far, is to present *extemporaneously,* especially when you are displaying a multimedia presentation such as a PowerPoint slideshow, SlideRocket slideshow, or Prezi canvas. Extemporaneous delivery means speaking freely, generally without notes, after preparing and rehearsing. It means that in your talk you comment on the multimedia visuals you have prepared and rehearsed several times. Remember, PowerPoint, SlideRocket, Prezi, and other presentation software platforms have replaced traditional outlines and notes. Reading notes or a manuscript in addition to PowerPoint slides, SlideRocket slides, or a Prezi canvas will damage your credibility.

If you give a talk without multimedia technology, however, you may use note cards or an outline containing key sentences and major ideas, but beware of reading from a script. By preparing and then practicing with your notes, you can talk to your audience in a conversational manner. Your notes should be neither entire paragraphs nor single words. Instead, they should contain a complete sentence or two to introduce each major idea. Below the topic sentence(s), outline subpoints and illustrations. Note cards will keep you on track and prompt your memory, but only if you have rehearsed the presentation thoroughly.

Combating Stage Fright

Nearly everyone experiences some degree of stage fright when speaking before a group. "If you hear someone say he or she isn't nervous before a speech, you're talking either to a liar or a very boring speaker," says corporate speech consultant Dianna Booher.[21] Being afraid is quite natural and results from actual physiological changes occurring in your body. Faced with a frightening situation, your body responds with the fight-or-flight response, discussed more fully in the accompanying Career Coach box. You can learn to control and reduce stage fright, as well as to incorporate techniques for effective speaking, by using the following strategies and techniques before, during, and after your presentation.

Before Your Presentation

Speaking in front of a group will become less daunting if you allow for adequate preparation, sufficient practice, and rehearsals. Interacting with the audience and limiting surprises such as malfunctioning equipment will also enhance your peace of mind. Review the following tips for a smooth start:

- **Prepare thoroughly.** One of the most effective strategies for reducing stage fright is knowing your subject thoroughly. Research your topic diligently and prepare a careful sentence outline. Those who try to "wing it" usually suffer the worst butterflies—and make the worst presentations.

CAREER COACH:

How to Avoid Stage Fright

Ever get nervous before making a presentation? Everyone does! And it's not all in your head, either. When you face something threatening or challenging, your body reacts in what psychologists call the fight-or-flight response. This physical reflex provides your body with increased energy to deal with threatening situations. It also creates those sensations—dry mouth, sweaty hands, increased heartbeat, and stomach butterflies—that we associate with stage fright. The fight-or-flight response arouses your body for action—in this case, making a presentation.

Because everyone feels some form of apprehension before speaking, it's impossible to eliminate the physiological symptoms altogether. However, you can reduce their effects with the following techniques:

- **Breathe deeply.** Use deep breathing to ease your fight-or-flight symptoms. Inhale to a count of ten, hold this breath to a count of ten, and exhale to a count of ten. Concentrate on your counting and your breathing; both activities reduce your stress.

- **Convert your fear.** Don't view your sweaty palms and dry mouth as evidence of fear. Interpret them as symptoms of exuberance, excitement, and enthusiasm to share your ideas.

- **Know your topic and come prepared.** Feel confident about your topic. Select a topic that you know well and that is relevant to your audience. Prepare thoroughly and practice extensively.

- **Use positive self-talk.** Remind yourself that you know your topic and are prepared. Tell yourself that the

audience is on your side—because it is! Moreover, most speakers appear to be more confident than they feel. Make this apparent confidence work for you.

- **Take a sip of water.** Drink some water to alleviate your dry mouth and constricted voice box, especially if you're talking for more than 15 minutes.

- **Shift the spotlight to your visuals.** At least some of the time the audience will be focusing on your slides, transparencies, handouts, or whatever you have prepared—and not totally on you.

- **Ignore any stumbles.** Realize that it is okay to make an occasional mistake. Don't apologize or confess your nervousness. If you make a mistake, ignore the stumble and keep going. The audience will forget any mistakes quickly.

- **Feel proud when you finish.** You will be surprised at how good you feel when you finish. Take pride in what you have accomplished, and your audience will reward you with applause and congratulations. Your body, of course, will call off the fight-or-flight response and return to normal!

- **Rehearse repeatedly.** When you rehearse, practice your entire presentation, not just the first half. In PowerPoint you may print out speaker's notes, an outline, or a handout featuring miniature slides, which are excellent for practice. If you don't use an electronic slideshow, place your outline sentences on separate note cards. You may also wish to include transitional sentences to help you move to the next topic as you practice. Rehearse alone or before friends and family. Also consider making an audio or video recording of your rehearsals so you can evaluate your effectiveness.

- **Time yourself.** Most audiences tend to get restless during longer talks. Therefore, try to complete your presentation in no more than 20 minutes. If you have a time limit, don't go over it. Set a simple kitchen timer during your rehearsal to keep track of time. Better yet, PowerPoint offers a function called Rehearse Timings in the Slide Show tab that can measure the length of your talk as you practice. Other presentation software packages offer similar features.

- **Dress professionally.** Dressing professionally for a presentation will make you look more credible to your audience. You will also feel more confident. If you are not used to professional attire, practice wearing it or you may appear uncomfortable in formal wear.

- **Request a lectern.** Every beginning speaker needs the security of a high desk or lectern from which to deliver a presentation. It serves as a note holder and a convenient place to rest wandering hands and arms. Don't, however, lean on it. Eventually you will want to interact with the audience without any physical barriers.

- **Check the room.** If you are using a computer, a projector, or sound equipment, be certain they are operational. Before you start, check electrical outlets and the position of the viewing screen. Ensure that the seating arrangement is appropriate to your needs.

- **Greet members of the audience.** Try to make contact with a few members of the audience when you enter the room, while you are waiting to be introduced, or when you walk to the podium. Your body language should convey friendliness, confidence, and enjoyment.

- **Practice stress reduction.** If you feel tension and fear while you are waiting your turn to speak, use stress-reduction techniques, such as deep breathing. Additional techniques to help you conquer stage fright are presented in the accompanying Career Coach box.

During Your Presentation

To stay in control during your talk, to build credibility, and to engage your audience, follow these time-tested guidelines for effective speaking:

- **Begin with a pause.** When you first approach the audience, take a moment to make yourself comfortable. Establish your control of the situation.

- **Present your first sentence from memory.** By memorizing your opening, you can immediately establish rapport with the audience through eye contact. You will also sound confident and knowledgeable.

- **Maintain eye contact.** If the size of the audience overwhelms you, pick out two individuals on the right and two on the left. Talk directly to these people. Don't ignore listeners in the back of the room. Scan the room to make all audience members feel included. If you are presenting to a smaller audience, try to make genuine, not fleeting, eye contact with everyone in the room at least once during your presentation.

- **Don't read from your notes.** Reading from your notes is boring, and your audience will quickly lose interest. Reading from notes also suggests that you are not prepared or knowledgeable about your topic, which will harm your credibility.

- **Control your voice and vocabulary.** This means speaking in moderated tones but loudly enough to be heard. Eliminate verbal static, such as *ah, er, like, you know,* and *um.* Silence is preferable to meaningless fillers when you are thinking of your next idea.

- **Show enthusiasm.** If you are not excited about your topic, how can you expect your audience to be? Show passion for your topic through your tone, facial expressions, and gestures. Adding variety to your voice also helps to keep your audience alert and interested.

- **Skip the apologies.** Don't begin with a weak opening, such as *I will not take much time. I know you are busy.* Or: *I know you have heard this before, but we need to review it anyway.* Or: *I had trouble with my computer and the slides, so bear with me.* Unless the issue is blatant, such as not being able to load the presentation or make the projector work, apologies are counterproductive. Focus on your presentation. Dynamic speakers never say they are sorry.

- **Put the brakes on.** Many novice speakers talk too rapidly, displaying their nervousness and making it very difficult for audience members to understand their ideas. Slow down and listen to what you are saying.

- **Incorporate pauses when appropriate.** Silence can be effective especially when you are transitioning from one point to another. Pauses are also effective in giving the audience time to absorb an important point.

- **Move naturally.** If you have a lectern, don't remain standing stiffly behind it. Move about casually and naturally. Avoid fidgeting with your clothing, hair, or items in your pockets. Do not roll up your sleeves or put your hands in your pockets. Learn to use your body to express a point.

- **Use visual aids effectively.** You should discuss and interpret each visual aid for the audience. Move aside as you describe it so that it can be seen fully. Use a pointer if necessary, but steady your hand if it is shaking.
- **Avoid digressions.** Stick to your outline and notes. Don't suddenly include clever little anecdotes or digressions that occur to you on the spot. If it is not part of your rehearsed material, leave it out so you can finish on time. Remember, too, that your audience may not be as enthralled with your topic as you are.
- **Summarize your main points and arrive at the high point of your talk.** Conclude your presentation by reiterating your main points or by emphasizing what you want the audience to think or do. Once you have announced your conclusion, proceed to it directly.

After Your Presentation

As you are concluding your presentation, handle questions and answers competently and provide handouts if appropriate. Try the following techniques:

- **Distribute handouts.** If you prepared handouts with data the audience will need, pass them out when you finish.
- **Encourage questions.** If the situation permits a question-and-answer period, announce it at the beginning of your presentation. Then, when you finish, ask for questions. Set a time limit for questions and answers.
- **Repeat questions.** Although the speaker may hear the question, audience members often do not. Begin each answer with a repetition of the question. This also gives you thinking time. Then, direct your answer to the entire audience.
- **Reinforce your main points.** You can use your answers to restate your primary ideas (*I'm glad you brought that up because it gives me a chance to elaborate on . . .*). In answering questions, avoid becoming defensive or debating the questioner.
- **Keep control.** Don't allow one individual to take over. Keep the entire audience involved.
- **Avoid *Yes, but* answers.** The word *but* immediately cancels any preceding message. Try replacing it with *and*. For example, *Yes, X has been tried. And Y works even better because . . . .*
- **End with a summary and appreciation.** To signal the end of the session before you take the last question, say something like, *We have time for just one more question.* As you answer the last question, try to work it into a summary of your main points. Then, express appreciation to the audience for the opportunity to talk with them.

LEARNING OBJECTIVE **5**
Organize presentations for intercultural audiences, in teams, and as slide decks.

Developing Special Presentations: Intercultural, Collaborative, and Slide Decks

Most of the information presented thus far assumes you are a single presenter before a traditional audience. However, in this increasingly digital and global workplace, presentations take on myriad forms and purposes. Now we'll explore effective techniques for adapting presentations to intercultural audiences, participating in team-based presentations, and designing slide decks.

Adapting Presentations to Intercultural Audiences

Every good speaker adapts to the audience, and intercultural presentations call for special adjustments and sensitivity. Most people understand that they must speak slowly, choose simple English, avoid jargon and clichés, use short sentences, and pause frequently when communicating with nonnative speakers of English.

Preparing and Organizing Oral Presentations

Getting Ready to Speak

- **Identify your purpose.** Decide what you want your audience to believe, remember, or do when you finish. Aim all parts of your talk toward this purpose.

- **Analyze the audience.** Consider how to adapt your message (its organization, appeals, and examples) to your audience's knowledge and needs.

Organizing the Introduction

- **Get the audience involved.** Capture the audience's attention by opening with a promise, story, startling fact, question, quote, relevant problem, or self-effacing joke.

- **Establish your authority.** Demonstrate your credibility by identifying your position, expertise, knowledge, or qualifications.

- **Preview your main points.** Introduce your topic and summarize its principal parts.

Organizing the Body

- **Develop two to four main points.** Streamline your topic so that you can concentrate on its major issues.

- **Arrange the points logically.** Sequence your points chronologically, from most important to least important, by comparison and contrast, or by some other strategy.

- **Prepare transitions.** Between major points write "bridge" statements that connect the previous item to the next one. Use transitional expressions as verbal signposts (*first, second, then, however, consequently, on the contrary,* and so forth).

- **Have extra material ready.** Be prepared with more information and visuals in case you have additional time to fill.

Organizing the Conclusion

- **Review your main points.** Emphasize your main ideas in the closing so your audience will remember them.

- **Provide a strong, final focus.** Tell how your listeners can use this information, why you have spoken, or what you want them to do. End with a specific audience benefit or thought-provoking thought (a take-away), not just a lame rehash.

Designing Visual Aids

- **Select your medium carefully.** Consider the pros and cons of each alternative.

- **Highlight main ideas.** Use visual aids to illustrate major concepts only. Keep them brief and simple.

- **Try to replace bullets whenever possible.** Use flowcharts, diagrams, time lines, images, and so forth, to substitute for bulleted lists when suitable.

- **Use aids skillfully.** Talk to the audience, not to the visuals. Paraphrase their content.

Developing Multimedia Presentations

- **Learn to use your software program.** Study template and layout designs to see how you can adapt them to your purposes.

- **Select colors based on the light level in the room.** Consider how mixing light and dark fonts and backgrounds affects their visibility. Use templates and preset layouts if you are new to your presentation software.

- **Use bulleted points for major ideas.** Make sure your points are all parallel, and observe the 6-x-6 rule.

- **Include multimedia options that will help you convey your message.** Use moderate animation features and hyperlinks to make your talk more interesting and to link to files with related content in the same document, in other documents, or on the Internet. Use Prezi's zooming feature to help audience members narrow in on details.

- **Make speaker's notes.** Jot down the narrative supporting each visual, and use these notes to practice your presentation. Do not read from notes while speaking to an audience, however.

- **Maintain control.** Don't let your slides or canvas upstage you. Engage your audience by using additional techniques to help them visualize your points.

© Daniilantiq/Shutterstock.com

Beyond these basic language adaptations, however, more fundamental sensitivity is often necessary. In organizing a presentation for an intercultural audience, you may need to anticipate and adapt to various speaking conventions, values, and nonverbal behaviors. You may also need to contend with limited language skills and a certain reluctance to voice opinions openly.

REALITY CHECK: Presenting Internationally

Courtesy of Rana Sinha

"When the audience is international, you'll need to step out of your own frame of reference and focus on making communication relevant for your target group. The aim is to 'localize.' By focusing on the audiences' own frames of reference, you acknowledge their importance and pave the way for them to come closer to you."[22]

—RANA SINHA, *cross-cultural trainer, consultant*

Understanding Different Values and Nonverbal Behaviors. In addressing intercultural audiences, anticipate expectations and perceptions that may differ significantly from what you may consider normal. Remember, for example, that the North American emphasis on getting to the point quickly is not equally prized across the globe. Therefore, think twice about delivering your main idea up front. Many people (notably those in Japanese, Latin American, and Arabic cultures) consider such directness to be brash and inappropriate. Others may not share our cultural emphasis on straightforwardness.

When working with an interpreter or speaking before individuals whose English is limited, you must be very careful about your language. For example, you will need to express ideas in small chunks to give the interpreter time to translate. You may need to slow down as you speak and stop after each thought to allow time for the translation that will follow. Even if your presentation or speech is being translated simultaneously, remember to speak slowly and to pause after each sentence to ensure that your message is rendered correctly in the target language.

The same advice is useful in organizing presentations. You may want to divide your talk into distinct topics, developing each separately and encouraging a discussion period after each one. Such organization enables participants to ask questions and digest what has been presented. This technique is especially effective in cultures in which people communicate in "loops." In the Middle East, for example, Arab speakers "mix circuitous, irrelevant (by American standards) conversations with short dashes of information that go directly to the point." Presenters who are patient, tolerant, and "mature" (in the eyes of the audience) will make the sale or win the contract.[23]

Match your presentation and your nonverbal messages to the expectations of your audience. In Germany, for instance, successful presentations tend to be dense with facts and precise statistics. Americans might say "around 30 percent," whereas a German presenter might say "30.4271 percent." Similarly, constant smiling is not as valued in Europe as it is in North America. Many Europeans distrust a speaker who is cracking jokes, smiling, or laughing in a business presentation. Rather, many expect a rational—that is, "serious"— fact-based delivery. American-style enthusiasm is often interpreted abroad as hyperbolic exaggeration or, worse, as dishonesty and can lead to misunderstandings. If an American says "Great job!" to offer praise, a Spanish counterpart might believe that the American has approved the project. "When Europeans realize there's no commitment implied," warned an intercultural consultant, "they might feel deceived or that the American is being superficial."[24]

Remember, too, that some cultures prefer greater formality than Americans exercise. When communicating with people from such cultures, instead of first names, use only honorifics (*Mr.* or *Ms.*) and last names, as well as academic or business titles—such as *Doctor* or *Director*. Writing on a flipchart or transparency seems natural and spontaneous in this country. Abroad, though, such informal techniques may suggest that the speaker does not value the audience enough to prepare proper visual aids in advance.[25]

Adjusting Visual Aids to Intercultural Audiences.   Although you may have to exercise greater caution with culturally diverse audiences, you still want to use visual aids to help communicate your message. Find out from your international contact whether you can present in English or will need an interpreter. In many countries listeners are too polite or too proud to speak up when they don't understand you. One expert advises explaining important concepts in several ways using different words and then requesting members of the audience to relay their understanding of what you have just said back to you. Another expert suggests packing more text on PowerPoint slides and staying closer to its literal meaning. After all, most nonnative speakers of English understand written text much better than they comprehend spoken English. In the United States, presenters may spend 90 seconds on a slide, whereas in other countries they may need to slow down to two minutes per slide.[26]

To ensure clarity and show courtesy, provide handouts in English and the target language. Never use numbers without projecting or writing them out for all to see. If possible, say numbers in both languages, but only if you can pronounce or even speak the target language well enough to avoid embarrassment. Distribute translated handouts, summarizing your important information, when you finish.

Preparing Collaborative Presentations With Teams

For many reasons increasing numbers of organizations are using teams, as discussed in Chapter 2. The goal of some teams is an oral presentation to pitch a new product or to win a high-stakes contract. Before Apple CEO Tim Cook and his team roll out one of their hotly anticipated new electronic gadgets, you can bet that team members spend months preparing so that the presentation flows smoothly. The same is true of most new product launches or major announcements. Teams collaborate to make sure the presentation meets its objectives.

The goal of other teams is to investigate a problem and submit recommendations to decision makers in a report. At BMW, for example, nimble cross-functional teams excel at problem solving across divisions. Such teams speed innovation and the development of new products such as the electronics that now comprise about 20 percent of a new vehicle's value.[27] The outcome of any team effort is often (a) a written report; (b) a multimedia slideshow or presentation; or (c) an oral presentation delivered live. The boundaries are becoming increasingly blurred between flat, two-dimensional hard-copy reports and multimedia, hyperlinked slideshows, and zoom presentations. Both hard-copy reports and multimedia presentations are delivered to clients in business today.

Whether your team's project produces written reports, multimedia presentations, or oral presentations, you generally have considerable control over how the project is organized and completed. If you have been part of any team efforts before, you also know that such projects can be very frustrating—particularly when some team members don't carry their weight or when members cannot resolve conflict. On the other hand, team projects can be harmonious and productive when members establish ground rules and follow guidelines related to preparing, planning, and collecting information as well as for organizing, rehearsing, and evaluating team projects.

Preparing to Work Together.   Before any group begins to talk about a specific project, members should get together and establish basic ground rules. One of the first tasks is naming a meeting leader to conduct meetings, a recorder to keep a record of group decisions, and an evaluator to determine whether the group is on target and meeting its goals. The group should decide whether it will be governed by consensus (everyone must agree), by majority rule, or by some other method.

When teams first organize, they should also consider the value of conflict. By bringing conflict into the open and encouraging confrontation, teams can prevent personal resentment and group dysfunction. Confrontation can actually create better final products by promoting new ideas and avoiding groupthink. Conflict is most beneficial when team members can air their views fully. Another important topic to discuss during team formation is how to deal with team members who are not pulling their share of the load. Teams should decide whether they will "fire" members who are not contributing or take some other action in dealing with slackers.

The most successful teams make meetings a top priority. They compare schedules to set up the best meeting times, and they meet often, either in person or virtually. They avoid other responsibilities that might disrupt these meetings. Today's software makes meeting and collaborating online efficient and productive. Team members can use tools such as Google Drive or SlideRocket to collaboratively create and edit documents and presentations. Prezi offers a tool called Meeting that allows team members to collaborate live on a Prezi canvas. Team members who learn to use these tools can work on presentations with others from anywhere in the world at any time of day, synchronously or asynchronously.

Planning and Preparing the Document or Presentation.   Once teams have established ground rules, members are ready to discuss the target document or presentation. During these discussions, they must be sure to keep a record of all decisions. They should establish the specific purpose for the document or presentation and identify the main issues involved. They must decide on the final format. For a collaborative business report, they should determine what parts it will include, such as an executive summary, figures, and an appendix. They should consider how the report or presentation will be delivered—in person, online, or by e-mail. For a team oral presentation, they should decide on its parts, length, and graphics. For either written or oral projects, they should profile the audience and focus on the questions audience members would want answered. If the report or presentation involves persuasion, they must decide what appeals would achieve the team's purpose.

Next the team should develop a work plan (see Chapter 11), assign jobs, and set deadlines. If time is short, members should work backward from the due date. For oral presentations, teams must schedule time for content and creative development as well as for a series of rehearsals. The best-planned presentations can fall apart if they are poorly rehearsed.

For oral presentations, all team members should have written assignments. These assignments should detail each member's specific responsibilities for researching content, producing visuals, developing handout materials, building transitions between segments, and showing up for rehearsals. For written reports, members must decide how the final document will be composed: individuals working separately on assigned portions, one person writing the first draft, the entire group writing the complete document together, or some other method. Team members will be responsible for collecting information; organizing, writing, and revising; and editing, rehearsing, and evaluating the document or presentation.

Collecting Information.   One of the most challenging jobs for team projects is generating and collecting information. Unless facts are accurate, the most beautiful report or the most high-powered presentation will fail. Brainstorm for ideas, assign topics, and decide who will be responsible for gathering what information. Establishing deadlines for collecting information is important if a team is to remain on schedule. Team members should also discuss ways to ensure the accuracy of the information collected.

Organizing, Writing, and Revising.   When a project progresses into the organizing and writing stages, a team may need to modify some of its earlier decisions. Team members may review the proposed organization of the final document or presentation and adjust it if necessary. In composing the first draft of a written report or presentation, team members will probably write separate segments. As they work on these segments, they should use the same version of a word processing or presentation graphics program to facilitate combining files. They can also use tools such as Google Drive or SlideRocket to edit documents.

As individuals work on separate parts of a written report, the team should decide on one person (probably the best writer) to coordinate all the parts. The writer strives for a consistent style, format, and feel in the final product. For oral presentations, team members must try to make logical connections between segments. Each presenter builds a bridge to the next member's topic to create a smooth transition. Team members should also agree to use the same template, and they should allow only one person to make global changes in color, font, and other formatting on the slide and title masters.

REALITY CHECK: Presenting as a Team

"Anytime you present with another person, you need to plan for at least double--and perhaps even triple–the time it normally takes to prepare and practice a presentation you deliver on your own. When presenting as a team, every team member should at least understand all of the material and possibly even be able to present ALL of the material—and that takes time!"[28]

—LISA B. MARSHALL, *consultant, author, host and creator of The Public Speaker podcast*

Editing, Rehearsing, and Evaluating. The last stage in a collaborative project involves editing, rehearsing, and evaluating. For a written report, one person should assume the task of merging the various files, running a spell-checker, and examining the entire document for consistency of design, format, and vocabulary. That person is responsible for finding and correcting grammatical and mechanical errors. Then the entire group meets as a whole to evaluate the final document. Does it fulfill its purpose and meet the needs of the audience?

For oral presentations, one person should also merge all the files and be certain that they are consistent in design, format, and vocabulary. Teams making presentations should practice together several times. If that is not feasible, experts say that teams must schedule at least one full real-time rehearsal with the entire group.[29] Whenever possible, practice in a room that is similar to the location of your talk. Consider video recording one of the rehearsals so that each presenter can critique his or her own performance. Schedule a dress rehearsal with an audience at least two days before the actual presentation. Practice fielding questions.

Successful group documents emerge from thoughtful preparation, clear definitions of contributors' roles, commitment to a group-approved plan, and a willingness to take responsibility for the final product. More information about writing business reports appeared in previous chapters of this book.

Using Presentation Software to Present Slide Decks

Business communicators primarily use PowerPoint, Prezi, and other presentation programs to deliver multimedia presentations before an audience. However, these programs can also be used to create slide decks to be viewed, for example, by busy managers who don't want to listen to a presentation or read a long report. Such visual reports can effectively deliver data, research findings, and proposals to receivers who may not be able to attend a meeting and who find them easier to read and comprehend than traditional reports. Slide decks are also easy to share and to reference.[30]

Although many presentation programs can deliver slide decks, we'll focus on the most popular, PowerPoint. Slide decks differ from slides in that slides in a deck typically contain more text than slides in a presentation. The 10/20/30 rule and the 6-x-6 rule don't apply with slide decks. In addition, slides in a slide deck generally contain more complex figures, charts, and graphics than slides in a presentation. Figure 14.11 shows a slide deck from Sudio Sudarsan exploring innovative options for delivering products and services through digital channels and social media outlets. Easy to read and comprehend, this slide deck helps busy managers absorb key ideas quickly.

Figure **14.11** Using Presentation Software for Slide Decks

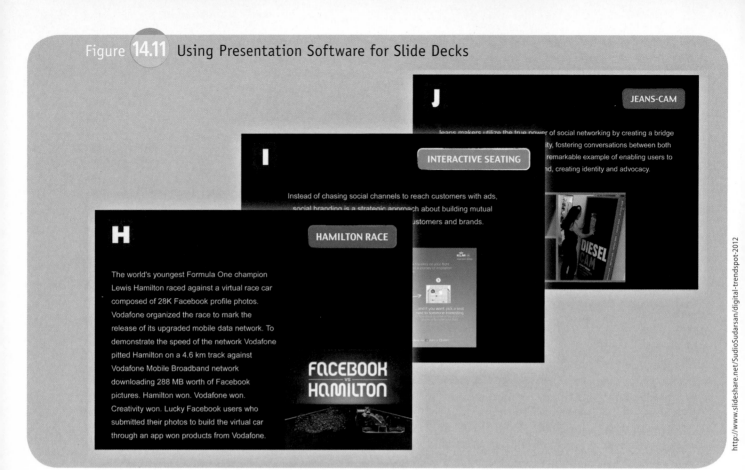

LEARNING OBJECTIVE 6

List techniques for improving telephone skills to project a positive image.

Improving Telephone Skills

One form of business presentation involves presenting yourself on the telephone, a skill that is still very important in today's workplace. Despite the heavy reliance on e-mail, the telephone remains an extremely important piece of equipment in offices. With today's wireless technology, it doesn't matter whether you are in or out of the office. You can always be reached by phone. This section focuses on traditional telephone techniques as well as smartphone use and voice mail—all opportunities for making a good impression. As a business communicator, you can be more productive, efficient, and professional by following some simple suggestions.

Making Telephone Calls Professionally

Before making a telephone call, decide whether the intended call is really necessary. Could you find the information yourself? If you wait a while, will the problem resolve itself? Perhaps your message could be delivered more efficiently by some other means. Some companies have found that telephone calls are often less important than the work they interrupt. Alternatives to telephone calls include instant messaging, texting, e-mail, memos, and calls to automated voice mail systems. If you must make a telephone call, consider using the following suggestions to make it fully productive:

- **Plan a mini-agenda.** Have you ever been embarrassed when you had to make a second telephone call because you forgot an important point the first time? Before placing a call, jot down notes regarding all the topics you need to discuss.

- **Use a three-point introduction.** When placing a call, immediately (a) name the person you are calling, (b) identify yourself and your affiliation, and (c) give a brief explanation of your reason for calling. For example: *May I speak to Larry Lopez? This is Hillary Dahl of Sebastian Enterprises, and I'm seeking information about a software program called ZoneAlarm Internet Security.*

- **Be brisk if you are rushed.** For business calls when your time is limited, avoid questions such as *How are you?* Instead, say, *Lisa, I knew you would be the only one who could answer these two questions for me.* Another efficient strategy is to set a contract with the caller: *Look, Lisa, I have only ten minutes, but I really wanted to get back to you.*

- **Be cheerful and accurate.** Let your voice show the same kind of animation that you radiate when you greet people in person. In your mind try to envision the individual answering the telephone. A smile can certainly affect the tone of your voice, so smile at that person.

- **Be professional and courteous.** Remember that you are representing yourself and your company when you make phone calls. Use professional vocabulary and courteous language. Say *thank you* and *please* during your conversations. Don't eat, drink, or chew gum while talking on the phone, which can often be heard on the other end.

- **Bring it to a close.** The responsibility for ending a call lies with the caller. This is sometimes difficult to do if the other person rambles on. You may need to use suggestive closing language, such as the following: (a) *I have certainly enjoyed talking with you;* (b) *I have learned what I needed to know, and now I can proceed with my work;* (c) *Thanks for your help;* (d) *I must go now, but may I call you again in the future if I need . . . ?* or (e) *Should we talk again in a few weeks?*

- **Avoid telephone tag.** If you call someone who's not in, ask when it would be best to call again. State that you will call at a specific time—and do it. If you ask a person to call you, give a time when you can be reached—and then be sure you are available at that time.

- **Leave complete voice mail messages.** Always enunciate clearly and speak slowly when giving your telephone number or spelling your name. Be sure to provide a complete message, including your name, telephone number, and the time and date of your call. Explain your purpose so that the receiver can be ready with the required information when returning your call.

Receiving Telephone Calls Professionally

With a little forethought you can project a professional image and make your telephone a productive, efficient work tool. Developing good telephone manners and techniques, such as the following, will also reflect well on you and on your organization.

- **Identify yourself immediately.** In answering your telephone or someone else's, provide your name, title or affiliation, and, possibly, a greeting. For example, *Larry Lopez, Digital Imaging Corporation. How may I help you?* Force yourself to speak clearly and slowly. Remember that the caller may be unfamiliar with what you are saying and fail to recognize slurred syllables.

- **Be responsive and helpful.** If you are in a support role, be sympathetic to callers' needs. Instead of *I don't know,* try *That's a good question; let me investigate.* Instead of *We can't do that,* try *That's a tough one; let's see what we can do.* Avoid *No* at the beginning of a sentence. It sounds especially abrasive and displeasing because it suggests total rejection.

- **Practice telephone confidentiality.** When answering calls for others, be courteous and helpful, but don't give out confidential information. Better to say, *She's away from her desk* or *He's out of the office* than to report a colleague's exact whereabouts. Also, be tight-lipped about sharing company information with strangers.

- **Take messages carefully.** Few things are as frustrating as receiving a potentially important phone message that is illegible. Repeat the spelling of names and verify telephone numbers. Write messages legibly and record their time and date. Promise to give the messages to intended recipients, but don't guarantee return calls.

- **Leave the line respectfully.** If you must put a call on hold, let the caller know and give an estimate of how long you expect the call to be on hold. Give the caller the option of holding. Say, *Would you prefer to hold, or would you like me to call you back?*

ETHICS CHECK:

Telling White Lies

Obviously, you wouldn't want to tell callers that your colleague went to the restroom or that your boss is responding to e-mail from a golf course in Hilo, Hawaii. But what about people who, for instance, hide behind voice mail and want you to lie about it? When is it acceptable to tell white lies on the phone to maintain confidentiality and decorum, and when is lying for others wrong?

REALITY CHECK: Have We Lost All Decency?

"It's a matter of priorities. When you have your phone on the table, you're communicating to the person in front of you that they are [*sic*] important, until something more important, whether it's a text message or a Twitter notification, comes up on your phone."[31]

—**MINDY LOCKARD**, *etiquette consultant (aka, The Gracious Girl)*

Using Smartphones for Business

Today's smartphones are very sophisticated mobile devices. They enable you to conduct business from virtually anywhere at any time. The smartphone has become an essential part of communication in the workplace. For a number of years now, the number of U.S. cellular phone users has outpaced the number of landline telephone users, and the number of people using mobile electronic devices and tablet computers keeps growing.[32] More than 88 percent of Americans own a cell phone,[33] and more than one third of wireless customers live without landlines.[34]

Today's highly capable smartphones can do much more than make and receive calls. High-end smartphones function much like laptops or tablets. They can be used to store contact information, make to-do lists, keep track of appointments and important dates, send and receive e-mail and text messages, search the Web, get news and stock quotes, take pictures and videos, synchronize with Outlook and other software applications, and perform many other functions.

Because so many people depend on their smartphones, it is important to understand proper use and etiquette. Most of us have experienced thoughtless and rude smartphone behavior. Researchers say that the rampant use of mobile electronic devices has increased workplace incivility. Some employees consider texting and compulsive e-mail checking while working and during meetings disruptive, even insulting. To avoid offending, smart business communicators practice smartphone etiquette, as outlined in Figure 14.12.

Making the Best Use of Voice Mail

Because telephone calls can be disruptive, many businesspeople make extensive use of voice mail to intercept and screen incoming calls on their landlines and smartphones. Here are some ways to make voice mail work most effectively for you.

On the Receiver's End. Your voice mail should project professionalism and should provide an easy way for your callers to leave messages for you. Here are some voice mail etiquette tips:

- **Don't overuse voice mail.** Don't use voice mail to avoid taking phone calls. It is better to answer calls yourself than to let voice mail messages build up.

- **Prepare a professional, concise, friendly greeting.** Make your voice mail greeting sound warm and inviting, both in tone and content. Identify yourself, thank the caller, and briefly explain that you are unavailable. Invite the caller to leave a message or, if appropriate, call back. Here's a typical voice mail greeting: *Hi! This is Larry Lopez of Proteus Software, and I appreciate your call. You have reached my voice mail because I'm either working with customers or talking on another line at the moment. Please leave your name, number, and reason for calling so that I can be prepared when I return your call.*

- **Respond to messages promptly.** Check your messages regularly, and try to return all voice mail messages within one business day.

- **Plan for vacations and other extended absences.** If you will not be picking up voice mail messages for an extended period, let callers know how they can reach someone else if needed.

Business communicators find smartphones to be enormously convenient and real time-savers. But rude users have generated a backlash against inconsiderate callers. Here are specific suggestions for using smartphones safely and responsibly:

Be courteous to those around you.

Don't force those near you to hear your business. Don't step up to a service counter, such as at a restaurant, bank, or post office, while talking on your smartphone. Don't carry on a smartphone conversation while someone is waiting on you. Think first of those in close proximity instead of those on the other end of the phone. Apologize and make amends gracefully for occasional smartphone blunders.

Observe wireless-free quiet areas.

Don't allow your smartphone to ring in theaters, restaurants, museums, churches, classrooms, important meetings, and similar places and situations. Use the smartphone's silent/vibrating ring option. A majority of travelers prefer that smartphone conversations not be held on most forms of public transportation.

Speak in low, conversational tones.

Microphones on smartphones are quite sensitive, therefore making it unnecessary to talk loudly. Avoid "cell yell."

Take only urgent calls.

Make full use of your smartphone's caller ID feature to screen incoming calls. Let voice mail take those calls that are not pressing.

Drive now, talk later.

Pull over if you must make a call. Talking while driving increases the chance of accidents fourfold, about the same as driving while intoxicated. Some companies are implementing policies that prohibit employees from using smartphones while driving for company business.

Choose a professional ringtone.

These days you can download a variety of ringtones, from classical to rap to the *Star Wars* theme. Choose a ringtone that sounds professional.

Text with caution.

Don't text while driving, cycling, or walking down a sidewalk; all can be extremely dangerous. Don't text during meetings or while conversing with others; your attention should be on your counterparts.

© Cengage Learning 2015

On the Caller's End. When leaving a voice mail message, you should follow these tips:

- **Be prepared to leave a message.** Before calling someone, be prepared for voice mail. Decide what you are going to say and what information you are going to include in your message. If necessary, write your message down before calling.

- **Leave a concise, thorough message.** When leaving a message, always identify yourself using your complete name and affiliation. Mention the date and time you called and a brief explanation of your reason for calling. Always leave a complete phone number, including the area code. Tell the receiver the best time to return your call. Don't ramble.

- **Speak slowly and articulate.** You want to make sure that your receiver will be able to understand your message. Speak slowly and pronounce your words carefully, especially when providing your phone number. The receiver should be able to write information down without having to replay your message.

- **Be careful with confidential information.** Don't leave confidential or private information in a voice mail message. Remember that anyone could gain access to this information.

© Africa Studio/Shutterstock.com;
© ra2studio/Shutterstock.com

Your Turn: Applying Your Skills

As an intern at a tech start-up, you have been asked to suggest a speaker who can discuss social media at an upcoming gathering of the firm's 100+ employees. You have seen Guy Kawasaki on YouTube and know he's written a book about Google+. You think he's the perfect fit for your organization. You research Mr. Kawasaki and decide to supplement your oral presentation with PowerPoint slides to persuade your supervisor that Kawasaki would make a dynamic speaker.

© Amy E. Price/Getty Images for SXSW

YOUR TASK. With a classmate, create no more than ten slides highlighting Kawasaki's draw as a speaker. Remember to anticipate your audience (your supervisor) and to organize your slides with headings. Use parallelism in your bulleted points and integrate graphics such as photos for visual interest.

Summary of Learning Objectives

1 Recognize various types of business presentations, and discuss two important first steps in preparing for any of these presentations. Business professionals give a variety of business presentations including briefings, reports, podcasts, virtual presentations, and webinars. Once you know how a report will be delivered, you must first identify what the purpose is and what you want the audience to believe or do so that you can aim the entire presentation toward your goal. Second, you must know your audience so that you can adjust your message and style to its knowledge and needs.

2 Explain how to organize the introduction, body, and conclusion as well as how to build audience rapport in a presentation. The introduction of a good presentation should capture the listener's attention, identify the speaker, establish credibility, and preview the main points. The body should discuss two to four main points, with appropriate explanations, details, and verbal signposts to guide listeners. The conclusion should review the main points, provide a final focus or take-away, and allow the speaker to leave the podium gracefully. Throughout your presentation, you can improve audience rapport by using effective imagery including analogies, metaphors, similes, personal anecdotes, statistics, and worst case/best-case scenarios. Rapport is also gained by including verbal signposts that tell the audience when you are previewing, summarizing, and switching directions. Nonverbal messages have a powerful effect on the way your message is received. You should look terrific, animate your body, punctuate your words, get out from behind the podium, and vary your facial expressions.

3 Create effective visual aids and handouts using today's multimedia presentation technology. Use simple, easily understood visual aids to emphasize and clarify main points. Choose multimedia slides, zoom presentations, transparencies, flipcharts, or other visuals. Generally, it is best to distribute handouts after a presentation. Speakers employing a program such as PowerPoint or Prezi use templates, layout designs, and bullet points to produce effective slides or canvases. A presentation may be enhanced with slide transitions, hyperlinks, sound, animation, video elements, and other multimedia effects. Speaker's notes and handouts may be generated from slides. Web-based presentations allow speakers to narrate and show slides and canvases without leaving their home bases. Increasing numbers of speakers are using the Web to e-mail or post their slides and canvases as electronic shows or report deliverables instead of generating paper copies.

4 Specify delivery techniques for use before, during, and after a presentation. Before your talk, prepare a sentence outline on note cards or speaker's notes and rehearse repeatedly. Check the room, lectern, and equipment. During the presentation, consider beginning with a pause and presenting your first sentence from memory. Speak freely and extemporaneously, commenting on your slides or canvas but using no other notes. Make eye contact, control your voice, speak and move naturally, and avoid digressions. After your talk, distribute handouts and answer questions. End gracefully and express appreciation.

5 Organize presentations for intercultural audiences, in teams, and as slide decks. Business professionals must know how to organize presentations for intercultural audiences and how to prepare collaborative, virtual, and slide deck presentations. In presentations before groups whose English is limited, presenters should speak slowly, use simple English, avoid jargon and clichés, opt for short sentences, build up to the main idea rather than announcing it immediately, break the presentation into short segments to allow participants to ask questions and digest small parts separately, beware of appearing too spontaneous and informal, and use visual aids to help communicate the message. In preparing to work together on a collaborate presentation, teams should name a leader; decide how they will make decisions; work out a schedule; discuss the benefits of conflict; determine how they will deal with members who fail to pull their share; and decide on the purpose, form, and procedures for preparing the final document or presentation. They must brainstorm ideas, assign topics, establish deadlines, and meet to discuss the drafts and rehearsals. Business communicators must also know how to use PowerPoint or other presentation software to prepare slide decks that will be read online.

6 List techniques for improving telephone skills to project a positive image. You can improve your telephone calls by planning a mini-agenda and using a three-point introduction (name, affiliation, and purpose). Be cheerful and responsive, and use closing language to end a conversation. Avoid telephone tag by leaving complete messages. In answering calls, identify yourself immediately, avoid giving out confidential information when answering for others, and take careful messages. For your own message, prepare a warm and informative greeting. Tell when you will be available. Evaluate your message by listening to it. Use proper etiquette when using your smartphone for business.

Chapter Review

1. How do speaking skills affect promotions and career success? (Obj. 1)

2. List and describe five types of presentations a business professional might make. (Obj. 1)

3. Why are analyzing an audience and anticipating its reactions particularly important before business presentations, and how would you adapt to the four categories of listeners? (Obj. 1)

4. In the introduction of an oral presentation, you can establish your credibility by using what two methods? (Obj. 2)

5. What are the three main goals of the conclusion of your presentation? (Obj. 2)

6. List six techniques for creating effective imagery in a presentation. Be prepared to discuss each. (Obj. 2)

7. List suggestions that would ensure that your nonverbal messages reinforce your verbal messages effectively. (Obj. 2)

8. Good visual aids have many purposes. List five of these purposes. (Obj. 3)

9. Name specific advantages and disadvantages of multimedia presentation software such as PowerPoint, SlideRocket, and Prezi. (Obj. 3)

10. How is the 6-x-6 rule applied in preparing bulleted points in a multimedia slideshow? (Obj. 3)

11. What delivery method is most effective for speakers? (Obj. 4)

12. Why should speakers deliver the first sentence from memory? (Obj. 4)

13. How might presentations before intercultural audiences be altered to be most effective? (Obj. 5)

14. What five issues should be resolved before a team can collaborate productively? (Obj. 5)

15. Discuss five tips for using smartphones courteously, safely, and responsibly. (Obj. 6)

Critical Thinking

1. Communication expert Dianna Booher claims that enthusiasm is infectious and "boredom is contagious."[35] What does this mean for you as a presenter? How can you avoid being a boring speaker? (Obj. 2)

2. "Communicate—don't decorate." This principle is one of 20 rules that graphic designer and educator Timothy Samara discusses in his classic book *Design Elements: A Graphic Style Manual*. How could you apply this principle

to the design of your PowerPoint, SlideRocket, or Prezi presentations? (Obj. 3)

3. How can speakers prevent multimedia presentation software from stealing their thunder? (Obj. 3)

4. Discuss effective techniques for reducing stage fright. (Obj. 4)

5. **Ethical Issue:** Critics of PowerPoint claim that flashy graphics, sound effects, and animation often conceal thin content. Consider, for example, the findings regarding the space shuttle *Challenger* accident that killed seven astronauts. Report authors charged that NASA scientists had used PowerPoint presentations to make it look as though they had done analyses that they hadn't. An overreliance on presentations instead of focusing on analysis may have contributed to the shuttle disaster.[36] What lessons about ethical responsibilities when using PowerPoint can be learned from this catastrophe in communication? (Objs. 1–3)

Activities

14.1 Evaluating a Speech (Objs. 1–3)

E-mail　Web

YOUR TASK. Search online for a speech that was delivered by a significant businessperson or a well-known political figure. Consider watching President Barack Obama's 2013 inauguration speech or Steve Jobs's "Stay Hungry, Stay Foolish" 2005 commencement speech at Stanford University on YouTube. Write an e-mail or memo report to your instructor critiquing the speech in terms of the following:

a. Effectiveness of the introduction, body, and conclusion

b. Evidence of effective overall organization

c. Use of verbal signposts to create coherence

d. Emphasis of two to four main points

e. Effectiveness of supporting facts (use of examples, statistics, quotations, and so forth)

f. Focus on audience needs and benefits

g. Enthusiasm for the topic

h. Effectiveness of visual aids (if applicable)

14.2 Analyzing the Needs of an Audience (Objs. 1, 2)

YOUR TASK. Select a recent issue of *Fortune, Fast Company, BusinessWeek,* or another business periodical approved by your instructor. Based on an analysis of your classmates, select an article that will appeal to them and that you can relate to their needs. Submit to your instructor a one-page summary that includes (a) the author, article title, source, issue date, and page reference; (b) a one-paragraph article summary; (c) a description of why you believe the article will appeal to your classmates; and (d) a summary of how you can relate the article to their needs. Your instructor may make this a topic for a class presentation.

14.3 Hiring a Business Tycoon Who Is an Accomplished Public Speaker (Obj. 1)

Social Media　Team　Web

YOUR TASK. Have you ever wondered why famous businesspeople, politicians, athletes, and other celebrities can command high speaking fees? How much are they really making per appearance, and what factors may justify their sometimes exorbitant fees? You may also wonder how a motivational speaker or corporate trainer might benefit you and your class or your campus community. Searching for and selecting an expert is easy online with several commercial speaker bureaus vying for clients. All services provide detailed speaker bios, areas of expertise, and fees. One agency even features video previews of its clients.

The three preeminent agencies for booking talent are All American Talent & Celebrity Network, BigSpeak, and Brooks International Speakers & Entertainment Bureau. All American represents, for example, Nouriel Roubini, Donald Trump, Jack Welch, Richard Branson, and Suze Orman. BigSpeak standouts are Deepak Chopra, Dr. Susan Love, and Diana Nyad. Brooks International features financier and philanthropist Mike Milken and TV commentator and personal finance expert Terry Savage, among others. Imagine that you have a budget of up to $100,000 to hire a well-known public speaker.

YOUR TASK. In teams or individually, select a business-related category of speaker by visiting one of the speaker bureaus online. For example, choose several prominent personal finance gurus (Orman, Savage, and others) or successful entrepreneurs and venture capitalists (Branson, Trump, Jack Welch, and so forth). Other categories could include motivational speakers, philanthropists, or famous economists. Study their bios for clues to their expertise and accomplishments. Comparing at least three, come up with a set of qualities that apparently make these individuals sought-after speakers. Consider how those qualities could enlighten you and your peers. To enrich your experience and enhance your knowledge, watch videos of your chosen speakers on YouTube, if available. Check talent agencies, personal websites, and Facebook for further information. Write a memo report about the speakers you chose, or present your findings orally, with or without visual aids. If your instructor directs, recommend your favorite speaker and give reasons for your decision.

14.4 Twitter: Follow Your Favorite Entrepreneur or Tycoon (Obj. 1)

Communication Technology　Social Media　Web

YOUR TASK. Sign up for a Twitter account if you don't have one yet, so that you can follow businesspeople and examine the topics they like to tweet about. In the Search window on top of the page, enter the name of the businessperson whose tweets you wish to follow. Donald Trump, Jack Welch, Richard Branson, Suze Orman, and other well-known businesspeople are avid Twitter users. Over the course of a few days, read the tweets of your favorite expert. After a while, you should be able to discern certain trends and areas of interest. Note whether and how your subject responds to queries from followers. What are his or her favorite topics? Report your findings to the class, verbally with notes or using PowerPoint or Prezi. If you find particularly intriguing tweets and links, share them with the class.

14.5 Overcoming Stage Fright (Obj. 4)

E-mail ▸ **Team** ▸

What makes you most nervous when making a presentation before class? Being afraid of becoming tongue-tied? Having all eyes on you? Messing up? Forgetting your ideas and looking unprofessional?

YOUR TASK. Discuss the previous questions as a class. Then, in groups of three or four, talk about ways to overcome these fears. Your instructor may ask you to write a memo, an e-mail, or a discussion board post (individually or collectively) summarizing your suggestions, or you may break out of your small groups and report your best ideas to the entire class.

14.6 The Importance of Oral Communication Skills in Your Field (Objs. 1, 4)

YOUR TASK. Interview one or two individuals in your professional field. How is oral communication important in this profession? Does the need for oral skills change as one advances? What suggestions can these people make to newcomers to the field for developing proficient oral communication skills? Discuss your findings with your class.

14.7 Outlining an Oral Presentation (Objs. 1, 2)

One of the hardest parts of preparing an oral presentation is developing the outline.

YOUR TASK. Select an oral presentation topic from the list in **Activity 14.16,** or suggest an original topic. Prepare an outline for your presentation using the following format:

Title
Purpose

	I. INTRODUCTION
State your name	A.
Gain attention and involve audience	B.
Establish credibility	C.
Preview main points	D.
Transition	
	II. BODY
Main point	A.
Illustrate, clarify, contrast	1.
	2.
	3.
Transition	
Main point	B.
Illustrate, clarify, contrast	1.
	2.
	3.
Transition	
Main point	C.
Illustrate, clarify, contrast	1.
	2.
	3.
Transition	
	III. CONCLUSION
Summarize main points	A.
Provide final focus or take-away	B.
Encourage questions	C.

14.8 Critiquing a Satirical Clip Lampooning PowerPoint (Objs. 1–3)

Web ▸

YOUR TASK. Watch Don McMillan's now famous YouTube hit "Life After Death by PowerPoint 2012." Which specific PowerPoint ills is McMillan satirizing? Write a brief summary of the short clip for discussion in class. With your peers discuss whether the bad habits the YouTube video parodies correspond with design issues addressed in this chapter. Is this satire still valid today?

14.9 Crafting a Multimedia Presentation: Outline Your Job Duties (Objs. 1–3)

Communication Technology ▸

What if you had to create a presentation for your classmates and instructor, or perhaps a potential recruiter, that describes the multiple tasks you perform at work? Could you do it in a five-minute PowerPoint, SlideRocket, or Prezi presentation?

Your instructor, for example, may wear many hats. Most academics (a) teach; (b) conduct research to publish; and (c) provide services to the department, college, university, and the community. Can you see how those aspects of the profession lend themselves to an outline of primary slides (teaching, publishing, service) and second-level slides (instructing undergraduate and graduate classes, presenting workshops, and giving lectures under the *teaching* label)?

YOUR TASK. Now it's your turn to introduce the duties of a current position or a past job, volunteer activity, or internship in a brief, simple, yet well-designed PowerPoint or Prezi presentation. Your goal is to inform your audience of your job duties in a three- to five-minute talk. Use animation features and graphics where appropriate.

14.10 Selling an Idea in an Impromptu Speech (Objs. 1–3)

"Can you pass the elevator test?" asks presentation whiz Garr Reynolds in a new twist on the familiar scenario.[37] He suggests this technique as an aid in sharpening your core message. In this exercise you need to pitch your idea in a few brief moments instead of the 20 minutes you had been granted with your vice president of product marketing. You arrive at her door for your appointment as she is leaving, coat and briefcase in hand. Something has come up. This meeting is a huge opportunity for you if you want to get the OK from the executive team. Could you sell your idea during the elevator ride and the walk to the parking lot? Reynolds asks. Although this scenario may never happen, you will possibly be asked to shorten a presentation, say, from an hour to 30 minutes or from 20 minutes to 5 minutes. Could you make your message tighter and clearer?

YOUR TASK. Take a business idea you may have, a familiar business topic you care about, or a promotion or raise you wish to request in a time of tight budgets. Create a spontaneous two- to five-minute speech making a good case for your core message. Even though you won't have much time to think about the details of your speech, you should be sufficiently familiar with the topic to boil it down and yet be persuasive.

14.11 *Fortune* Lists: How Are They Compiled? (Objs. 1–4)

Web ▸

YOUR TASK. Using an electronic database, perform a search to learn how *Fortune* magazine determines which companies make its annual lists. Research the following lists. Then organize and present a five- to ten-minute informative talk to your class.

a. Fortune 500

b. Global 500

c. 100 Best Companies to Work For

d. America's Most Admired Companies

e. Global Most Admired Companies

14.12 What Is My Credit Score and What Does It Mean? (Objs. 1–4)

Web

The program chair for the campus business club has asked you to present a talk to the group about consumer credit. He saw a newspaper article saying that only 10 percent of Americans know their credit scores. Many consumers, including students, have dangerous misconceptions about their scores. Not knowing your score could result in a denial of credit as well as difficulty obtaining needed services and even a job.

YOUR TASK. Using electronic databases and the Web, learn more about credit scores and typical misconceptions. For example, is a higher or lower credit score better? Can you improve your credit score by marrying well? If you earn more money, will you improve your score? If you have a low score, is it impossible to raise it? Can you raise your score by maxing out all your credit cards? (One survey reported that 28 percent of consumers believed the latter statement was true!) Prepare an oral presentation appropriate for a student audience. Conclude with appropriate recommendations.

14.13 Improving Telephone Skills by Role-Playing (Obj. 6)

YOUR TASK. Your instructor will divide the class into pairs. For each scenario take a moment to read and rehearse your role silently. Then play the role with your partner. If time permits, repeat the scenarios, changing roles.

Prepare a mini-agenda before you call. Introduce yourself. If necessary, spell your name and indicate the course and section. Speak slowly and clearly, especially when leaving your phone number. Think of a comment you could make about an intriguing fact, a peer discussion, or your business communication class.

14.15 Presenting Yourself Professionally When Texting (Obj. 6)

Communication Technology

Your phone skills extend not only to voice mail but also to the brief text messages you send to your boss and coworkers. Such *professional* texts are often markedly different in style and tone from the messages you may be exchanging with friends.

YOUR TASK. Send a professional text message to your instructor or to another designated partner in class responding to one of the following scenarios: (a) Explain why you must be late to an important meeting; (b) request permission to purchase a piece of important equipment for the office; or (c) briefly summarize what you have learned in your latest staff development seminar (use a key concept from one of your business classes). Use the recipient's e-mail address to send your text. Do not use abbreviations or smiley faces.

14.16 Choosing a Topic for an Oral Presentation (Objs. 1–5)

Team

YOUR TASK. Select a topic from the following list or from the report topics in the activities at the ends of Chapters 11 and 12. For an expanded list of report topics, go to the student premium site at **www.cengagebrain.com** and look under "Writing Resources." Individually or as a team, prepare a five- to ten-minute oral presentation. Consider yourself an expert or a team of experts called in to explain some aspect of the topic before a group of interested people. Because your time is limited, prepare a concise yet forceful presentation with effective visual aids.

Partner 1	Partner 2
a. You are the personnel manager of Datatronics, Inc. Call Elizabeth Franklin, office manager at Computers Plus. Inquire about a job applicant, Chelsea Chavez, who listed Ms. Franklin as a reference. Respond to Partner 2.	a. You are the receptionist for Computers Plus. The caller asks for Elizabeth Franklin, who is home sick today. You don't know when she will be able to return. Answer the call appropriately.
b. Call Ms. Franklin again the following day to inquire about the same job applicant, Chelsea Chavez. Ms. Franklin answers today, but she talks on and on, describing the applicant in great detail. Tactfully end the conversation.	b. You are now Ms. Franklin, office manager. Describe Chelsea Chavez, an imaginary employee. Think of someone with whom you have worked. Include many details, such as her ability to work with others, her appearance, her skills at computing, her schooling, her ambition, and so forth.
c. You are now the receptionist for Tom Wing, of Wing Imports. Answer a call for Mr. Wing, who is working in another office, at Extension 134, where he will accept calls.	c. You are now an administrative assistant for attorney Michael Murphy. Call Tom Wing to verify a meeting date Mr. Murphy has with Mr. Wing. Use your own name in identifying yourself.
d. You are now Tom Wing, owner of Wing Imports. Call your attorney, Michael Murphy, about a legal problem. Leave a brief, incomplete message.	d. You are now the receptionist for attorney Michael Murphy. Mr. Murphy is skiing in Aspen and will return in two days, but he doesn't want his clients to know where he is. Take a message.
e. Call Mr. Murphy again. Leave a message that will prevent telephone tag.	e. Take a message again as the receptionist for attorney Michael Murphy.

14.14 Presenting Yourself Professionally on the Telephone and in Voice Mail (Obj. 6)

YOUR TASK. Practice the phone skills you learned in this chapter. Leave your instructor a professional voice mail message.

If this is a group presentation, form a team of three or four members and conduct thorough research on one of the following topics, as directed by your instructor. Follow the tips on team presentations in this chapter. Divide the tasks fairly, meet for discussions and rehearsals, and crown your achievement with a 15- to 20-minute presentation to your class. Make your multimedia presentation interesting and dynamic.

a. How can businesses benefit from Twitter, LinkedIn, or Facebook? Cite specific examples in your chosen field.

b. Which is financially more beneficial to a business, leasing or buying company cars?

c. Tablet computers and other devices are eroding the market share previously held by laptops and netbooks. Which brands are businesses embracing and why? Which features are a must-have for businesspeople?

d. What kind of marketing works with students on college campuses? Word of mouth? Internet advertising? Free samples? How do students prefer to get information about goods and services?

e. How can consumers protect themselves from becoming victims of identity theft?

f. Companies usually do not admit shortcomings. However, some admit previous failures and use them to strategic advantage. For example, Domino's Pizza ran a commercial in which its customers said that its pizza tasted like ketchup and cardboard. Find three or more examples of companies admitting weaknesses and draw conclusions from their strategies. Would you recommend this as a sound marketing ploy?

g. How can students and other citizens contribute to conserving gasoline and other fossil fuel in order to save money and help slow global climate change?

h. What is the career outlook in a field of your choice? Consider job growth, compensation, and benefits. What kind of academic or other experience is typically required in your field?

i. What is the economic outlook for a given product, such as hybrid cars, laptop computers, digital cameras, fitness equipment, or a product of your choice?

j. What is telecommuting, and for what kinds of workers is it an appropriate work alternative?

k. What are the Webby Awards, and what criteria do the judges use to evaluate websites?

l. What franchise would offer the best investment opportunity for an entrepreneur in your area?

m. What should a guide to proper smartphone etiquette include?

n. Why should a company have a written e-mail, Web use, and social media policy?

o. Where should your organization hold its next convention?

p. What is the outlook for real estate (commercial or residential) investment in your area?

q. What do the personal assistants for celebrities do, and how does one become a personal assistant? (Investigate the Association of Celebrity Personal Assistants.)

r. What kinds of gifts are appropriate for businesses to give clients and customers during the holiday season?

s. What scams are on the Federal Trade Commission's list of top 10 consumer scams, and how can consumers avoid falling for them?

t. How can your organization or institution improve its image?

u. What are the pros and cons of using Prezi zoom presentations? Would they be appropriate in your field?

v. How can consumers protect themselves against identity theft?

w. What franchise would offer the best investment opportunity for an entrepreneur in your area?

x. What are the differences among casual, business casual, and business formal attire?

y. What is a sustainable business? What can companies do to become sustainable?

z. What smartphone apps are available that will improve a businessperson's productivity?

Chat About It

In each chapter you will find five discussion questions related to the chapter material. Your instructor may assign these topics for you to discuss in class, in an online chat room, or on an online discussion board. Some of the discussion topics may require outside research. You may also be asked to read and respond to postings made by your classmates.

Topic 1: What are your pet peeves about smartphone use? Share specific examples of rude, unsafe, or irresponsible smartphone behavior that you have experienced or observed.

Topic 2: How would you classify your classmates as an audience for student presentations: friendly, neutral, uninterested, or hostile? Why?

Topic 3: Why do some presenters avoid making steady eye contact? What might these individuals do to correct this problem?

Topic 4: Do some research to determine what made the "I Have a Dream" speech by Dr. Martin Luther King Jr. so memorable.

Topic 5: When is it acceptable not to return a call when a callback was requested?

Grammar & Mechanics | *Review 14*

Total Review

Each of the following sentences has a total of **three** errors in grammar, punctuation, capitalization, usage, or spelling. On a separate sheet, write a correct version. Avoid adding new phrases, starting new sentences, or rewriting in your own words. When finished, compare your responses with the key beginning on page Key-3.

EXAMPLE: My accountant and me are greatful to be asked to make a short presentation, however, we may not be able to cover the entire budget.

REVISION: My accountant and **I** are **grateful** to be asked to make a short **presentation;** however, we may not be able to cover the entire budget.

1. The CEOs assistant scheduled my colleague and I for a twenty minute presentation to explain the new workplace sustainability initiative.

2. PowerPoint presentations, claims one expert should be no longer then twenty minutes and have no more than ten slides.

3. The introduction to a presentation should accomplish 3 goals, (a) capture attention, (b) establish credibility and (c) preview main points.

4. In the body of a short presentation speakers should focus on no more than 3 principle points.

5. A poll of two thousand employees revealed that 4/5 of them said they feared giving a presentation more then anything else they could think of.

6. A good list of tips for inexperienced speakers are found in the article titled "Forty Quick Tips For Speakers."

7. The Director of operations made a fifteen-minute presentation giving step by step instructions on achieving our sustainability goals.

8. In the Spring our companies stock value is expected to raise at least 10 percent.

9. The appearance and mannerisms of a speaker definately effects a listeners evaluation of the message.

10. Because the bosses daughter was a dynamic speaker who had founded a successful company she earned at least twenty thousand dollars for each presentation.

Notes

[1] Reynolds, G. (2005, September 8). Guy Kawasaki: Presenter extraordinaire. Presentation Zen. Retrieved from http://www.presentationzen.com

[2] Kawasaki, G. (n.d.). Speaking. Guy Kawasaki. Retrieved from http://www.guykawasaki.com

[3] Reynolds, G. (2005, September 21). The Kawasaki method: An enlightened presentation. Presentation Zen. Retrieved from http://www.presentationzen.com/presentationzen

[4] Good, R. (2006, August 8). Guy Kawasaki 10-20-30 presentation rule. Retrieved from http://www.youtube.com/watch?v=liQLdRk0Ziw

[5] Ibid.

[6] Hooey, B. (2005). Speaking for success! Toastmasters International. Retrieved from http://members.shaw.ca/toasted/speaking_success.htm

[7] Korn, M. (2010, December 3). Wanted: Good speaking skills. The Wall Street Journal. Retrieved from Hire Education blog at http://blogs.wsj.com/hire-education/2010/12/03/wanted-good-speaking-skills

[8] Barrington, L., Casner-Lotto, J., & Wright, M. (2008, May). Are they really ready to work? The Conference Board. Retrieved from http://www.conference-board.org/pdf_free/BED-06-Workforce.pdf

[9] Dlugan, A. (2008, April 8). 10 ways your presentation skills generate career promotions. Retrieved from http://sixminutes.dlugan.com/career-promotions-presentation-skills

[10] Dugdale, S. (n.d.). Building rapport—building harmony. Write-out-loud.com. Retrieved from http://www.write-out-loud.com/building-rapport.html

[11] Dr. John J. Medina as quoted by Reynolds, G. (2010). Presentation zen design. Berkeley, CA: New Riders, p. 97.

[12] Howder, R. (n.d.). About Prezi. Retrieved from http://prezi.com/about

[13] The Basics. (2012). Retrieved from http://prezi.com/the-basics

[14] Atkinson, C. (2008). Beyond bullet points (2nd ed.). Redmond, WA: Microsoft Press.

[15] Reynolds, G. (2008). Presentation Zen. Berkeley, CA: New Riders, p. 220. See also Reynolds, G. (2010). Presentation Zen design. Berkeley, CA: New Riders.

[16] Booher, D. (2003). Speak with confidence: Powerful presentations that inform, inspire, and persuade. New York: McGraw-Hill Professional, p. 126; see

also Paradi, D. (2009, March 3). Choosing colors for your presentation slides. Indezine. Retrieved from http://www.indezine.com/ideas/prescolors.html

[17] Bates, S. (2005). Speak like a CEO: Secrets for commanding attention and getting results. New York: McGraw-Hill Professional, p. 113.

[18] Sommerville, J. (n.d.). The seven deadly sins of PowerPoint presentations. About.com. Retrieved from http://entrepreneurs.about.com/cs/marketing/a/7sinsofppt.htm

[19] Kupsh, J. (2011, January 21). Presentation delivery guidelines to remember. Training. Retrieved from http://www.trainingmag.com/article/presentation-delivery-guidelines-remember

[20] Ellwood, J. (2004, August 4). Less PowerPoint, more powerful points, The Times (London), p. 6.

[21] Booher, D. (2003). Speak with confidence. New York: McGraw-Hill Professional, p. 14; and Booher, D. (1991). Executive's portfolio of model speeches for all occasions. Englewood Cliffs, NJ: Prentice Hall, p. 259.

[22] Sinha, R. (n.d.). Making a presentation in front of international audiences. Dot-Connect. Retrieved from http://www.dot-connect.com/Making_a_presentation_in_front_of_international_audiences.html

[23] Wunderle, W. (2007, March/April). How to negotiate in the Middle East. The U.S. Army Professional Writing Collection, 5(7). Retrieved from http://www.army.mil/professionalwriting/volumes/volume5/july_2007/7_07_4.html; see also Marks, S. J. (2001, September). Nurturing global workplace connections. Workforce, p. 76.

[24] Brandel, M. (2006, February 20). Sidebar: Don't be the ugly American. Computerworld. Retrieved from http://www.computerworld.com/s/article/108772Sidebar_Don_t_Be_the_Ugly_American

[25] Dulek, R. E., Fielden, J. S., & Hill, J. S. (1991, January/February). International communication: An executive primer. Business Horizons, p. 22.

[26] Davidson, R., & Rosen, M. Cited in Brandel, M. (2006, February 20). Sidebar: Don't be the ugly American. Computerworld. Retrieved from http://www.computerworld.com/s/article/108772/Sidebar_Don_t_Be_the_Ugly_American

[27] Edmondson, G. (2006, October 16). The secret of BMW's success. Bloomberg Businessweek.

Retrieved from http://www.businessweek.com/magazine/content/06_42/b4005078.htm

[28] Marshall, L. B. (2010, April 23). How to present with another speaker. Quick and Dirty Tips. Retrieved from http://publicspeaker.quickanddirtytips.com/How-To-Present-With-Another-Speaker.aspx

[29] Peterson, R. (n.d.). Presentations: Are you getting paid for overtime? Presentation Coaching Institute. Retrieved from http://www.passociates.com/getting_paid_for_overtime.shtml; The sales presentation: The bottom line is selling. (2001, March 14). Marken Communications. Retrieved from http://www.markencom.com/docs/01mar14.htm

[30] Research Rockstar. (2012, March 25). PowerPoint-based reports: Overused or just abused? Retrieved from http://www.researchrockstar.com/powerpoint-based-reports-overused-or-just-abused

[31] Lockard, M. (2012, May 11) Smartphone etiquette: Have we lost all dignity? Retrieved from http://conversations.nokia.com/2012/05/11/smartphone-etiquette-have-we-lost-all-decency

[32] Smith, A. (2010, July 7). Mobile access 2010. Pew Internet. Retrieved from http://www.pewinternet.com/Reports/2010/Mobile-Access-2010.aspx; Lanman, S. (2005, July 9). Mobile-phone users become a majority. San Francisco Chronicle, p. C1.

[33] Zickuhr, K., & Smith, A. (2012, April 13). Digital differences. Pew Internet. Retrieved from http://pewinternet.org/Reports/2012/Digital-differences/Main-Report/The-power-of-mobile.aspx

[34] Higginbotham, S. (2012, December 26). Over half of American home don't have or use their landline. Nielsen Wire. Retrieved from http://gigaom.com/2012/12/26/over-half-of-american-homes-dont-have-or-use-their-landline

[35] Ibid., p. 9.

[36] Vergano, D. (2004, August 31). Computers: Scientific friend or foe? USA Today, p. D6.

[37] Reynolds, G. (2008). Presentation Zen. Berkeley, CA: New Riders, pp. 64 ff.

Unit 5

Employment Communication

economist

writer teacher

programmer

journalist photographer

scientist

manager doctor

designer

banker lawyer

© Haglog Group Production Studio/Shutterstock.com

The Job Search and Résumés in the Digital Age

OBJECTIVES

After studying this chapter, you should be able to

1 Prepare to search for a job in the digital age by understanding the changing job market, identifying your interests, assessing your qualifications, and exploring career opportunities.

2 Develop savvy search strategies by recognizing job sources and using digital tools to explore the open job market.

3 Expand your job-search strategies by using both traditional and digital tools in pursuing the hidden job market.

4 Organize your qualifications and information into effective résumé segments to create a winning, customized résumé.

5 Optimize your job search and résumé by taking advantage of today's digital tools.

6 Draft and submit a customized cover message to accompany a print or digital résumé.

Stepping Out of the Classroom and Into a Career

You've been in school for a long time, but the end is in sight. Now, however, you begin to worry about the job market and how to land a dream job.

"Hiring managers expect young professionals to be job-hunting experts," observes Gen Y career expert and experienced hiring manager Heather Huhman in her ebook *#ENTRYLEVELtweet: Taking Your Career From Classroom to Cubicle*.[1] The truth is, however, that most college students and recent grads don't know how to search for a job or what to expect. It's easy to be misled by misconceptions and myths.

With permission of Heather R. Huhman, http://comerecommended.com

In a recent blog,[2] Huhman dispels popular hiring myths that job seekers should know about. The first myth assumes that all job openings are posted on job boards. This is definitely not true, she says. Many hiring managers refuse to post job openings because they fear receiving too many applications from unqualified candidates. Instead, huge numbers of positions become part of the hidden job market, which is why Huhman passionately encourages recent grads to vigorously network. She agrees with other job-search experts who claim that as many as 80 percent of jobs are found through networking.[3]

Another myth holds that no one will read your cover letter. Huhman knows, however, that many recruiters read the cover letter first to learn whether the applicant is truly interested in the job and is a good fit for the organization. A third myth assumes that simply applying to jobs will land an interview. In today's tough job market, candidates must actively network and maintain a positive presence online.[4]

In discussing résumés, Huhman cautions against using a generic single résumé. Although this advice gets drilled into the heads of new grads, she says that such advice is often overlooked because it's more convenient for candidates to make one all-purpose résumé. Instead, she advises job seekers to know what makes them valuable, carefully research each targeted company, and then tailor every résumé to the targeted company. "Think of it this way," she says. "Why would an organization want to invest time in you if you haven't invested any time in them? Small details like personalized résumés, cover letters, and thank-you notes can go a long way."[5]

Critical Thinking

- **What do you know about the hidden job market, and how does networking help a new grad find a job in this elusive market?**

- **How can professional networking tools such as LinkedIn help job seekers get a foot in the door of a favorite company?**

- **How many résumés should a recent grad prepare? What format is preferable?**

Job Searching in the Digital Age

There's no doubt about it. The job market has become increasingly complex, and it's not just the poor economy, offshoring, outsourcing, and globalization that are creating the complexity. In this digital age, the Internet has fundamentally changed the way we search for jobs. Job boards, search engines, and social networks have all become indispensable tools in hunting for a job. Surprisingly, however, even in this digital age, personal networking and referrals continue to be the primary route to hiring.[6]

This chapter presents cutting-edge digital and personal networking strategies to help you land a job. Although these are difficult times and you may be depressed about your job search, you have a lot going for you. As a college student, think about your recent training, current skills, and enthusiasm. Remember, too, that in a depressed economy, you are less expensive to hire than older, experienced candidates. In addition, you have this book with the latest research, invaluable advice, and perfect model documents to guide you in your job search. Think positively! The more you understand the changing job market, the better equipped you will be to enter it wisely.

LEARNING OBJECTIVE 1
Prepare to search for a job in the digital age by understanding the changing job market, identifying your interests, assessing your qualifications, and exploring career opportunities.

Understanding the Changing Job Market

Today, the major emphasis of the job search has changed. In years past the emphasis was on what the applicant wanted. Today it's on what the employer wants.[7] Employers are most interested in how a candidate will add value to the hiring organization. That's why today's most successful candidates customize their résumés to highlight their qualifications for each opening. In addition, career paths are no longer linear; most new-hires will not start in a job and steadily rise through the ranks. Jobs are more short-lived and people are constantly relearning and retraining.

The résumé is still important, but it may not be the document that introduces the job seeker these days. Instead, the résumé may come only after the candidate establishes a real-world relationship. What's more, chances are that your résumé and cover message will be read digitally rather than in print. However, although some attention-grabbing publications scream that the "print résumé is dead," the truth is that every job hunter needs one. Whether offered online or in print, your résumé should be always available and current.

It's natural to think that the first step in finding a job is writing a résumé. But that's a mistake. The job-search process actually begins long before you are ready to prepare your résumé. Regardless of the kind of employment you seek, you must invest time and effort in getting ready. Your best plan for landing the job of your dreams involves (a) analyzing yourself, (b) developing a job-search strategy, (c) preparing a résumé, and (d) knowing the hiring process, as illustrated in Figure 15.1.

Beginning Your Job Search With Self-Analysis

The first step in a job search is analyzing your interests and goals and evaluating your qualifications. This means looking inside yourself to explore what you like and dislike so that you can make good employment choices. Career counselors charge large sums for helping individuals learn about themselves. You can do the same self-examination—without spending a dime. For guidance in choosing a career that eventually proves to be satisfying, consider the following questions:

- What are you passionate about? Can you turn this passion into a career?
- Do you enjoy working with people, data, or things?
- Would you like to work for someone else or be your own boss?
- How important are salary, benefits, technology support, and job stability?

Figure **15.1** Job Searching in the Digital Age

Analyze Yourself
- Identify your interests and goals.
- Assess your qualifications.
- Explore career opportunities.

Develop a Job-Search Strategy
- Search the open job market.
- Pursue the hidden job market.
- Cultivate your online presence.
- Build your personal brand.
- Network, network, network!

Create a Customized Résumé
- Choose a résumé style.
- Organize your info concisely.
- Tailor your résumé to each position.
- Optimize for digital technology.

Know the Hiring Process
- Submit a résumé, application, or e-portfolio.
- Undergo screening and hiring interviews.
- Accept an offer or reevaluate your progress.

- How important are working environment, colleagues, and job stimulation?

- Must you work in a specific city, geographical area, or climate?

- Are you looking for security, travel opportunities, money, power, or prestige?

- How would you describe the perfect job, boss, and coworkers?

Assessing Your Qualifications

Beyond your interests and goals, take a good look at your qualifications. Remember that today's job market is not so much about what you want, but what the employer wants. What assets do you have to offer? Your responses to the following questions will target your thinking as well as prepare a foundation for your résumé. Always keep in mind, though, that employers seek more than empty assurances; they will want proof of your qualifications.

- What technology skills can you present? What specific software programs are you familiar with, what Web experience do you have, and what social media skills can you offer?

- Do you communicate well in speech and in writing? How can you verify these talents?

- What other skills have you acquired in school, on the job, or through activities? How can you demonstrate these skills?

- Do you work well with people? Do you enjoy teamwork? What proof can you offer? Consider extracurricular activities, clubs, class projects, and jobs.

- Are you a leader, self-starter, or manager? What evidence can you offer? What leadership roles have you held?

- Do you speak, write, or understand another language?

- Do you learn quickly? Are you creative? How can you demonstrate these characteristics?

- What unique qualifications can you offer that make you stand out among candidates?

Exploring Career Opportunities

The job picture in the United States is extraordinarily dynamic and flexible. On average, workers between ages eighteen and thirty-eight in the United States will have ten different employers over the course of their careers. The median job tenure of wage earners and salaried workers is 4.4 years with a single employer.[8] Although you may be frequently changing jobs in the future (especially before you reach age forty), you still need to train for a specific career now. In exploring job opportunities, you will make the best decisions when you can match your interests and qualifications with the requirements and rewards of specific careers. Where can you find the best career data? Here are some suggestions:

- **Visit your campus career center.** Most campus career centers have literature, inventories, career-related software programs, and employment or internship databases that allow you to explore such fields as accounting, finance, office technology, information systems, hotel management, and so forth. Some have well-trained job counselors who can tailor their resources to your needs. They may also offer career exploration workshops, job skills seminars, career days with visiting companies, assistance with résumé preparation, and mock interviews.

- **Search the Web.** Many job-search sites—such as Monster, CareerBuilder, and CollegeGrad—offer career-planning information and resources. You will learn about some of the best career sites in the next section.

- **Use your library.** Print and online resources in your library are especially helpful. Consult *O*NET Occupational Information Network, Dictionary of Occupational Titles, Occupational Outlook Handbook,* and *Jobs Rated Almanac* for information about job requirements, qualifications, salaries, and employment trends.

- **Take a summer job, internship, or part-time position in your field.** Nothing is better than trying out a career by actually working in it or in a related area. Many companies offer internships and temporary or part-time jobs to begin training college students and to develop relationships with them. Unsurprisingly, lots of those internships turn into full-time positions. One recent study revealed that 60 percent of students who completed paid internships were offered full-time jobs.[9]

- **Interview someone in your chosen field.** People are usually flattered when asked to describe their careers. Inquire about needed skills, required courses, financial and other rewards, benefits, working conditions, future trends, and entry requirements.

- **Volunteer with a nonprofit organization.** Many colleges and universities encourage service learning. In volunteering their services, students gain valuable experience, and nonprofits appreciate the expertise and fresh ideas that students bring.

- **Monitor the classified ads.** Early in your college career, begin monitoring want ads and the websites of companies in your career area. Check job availability, qualifications sought, duties, and salary ranges. Don't wait until you are about to graduate to see how the job market looks.

- **Join professional organizations in your field.** Frequently, professional organizations offer student memberships at reduced rates. Such memberships can provide inside information on issues, career news, and jobs. Student business clubs and organization such as Phi Beta Lambda can also provide leadership development trainings, career tips, and networking opportunities.

LEARNING OBJECTIVE **2**
Develop savvy search strategies by recognizing job sources and using digital tools to explore the open job market.

Developing a Job-Search Strategy Focused on the Open Job Market

Once you have analyzed what you want in a job and what you have to offer, you are ready to focus on a job-search strategy. You're probably most interested in the sources of today's jobs. Figure 15.2 shows the job source trends revealed by a Right Management survey of between 46,000 and 55,000 job seekers over a period of six years. Surprisingly, despite the explosion of digital job sources, person-to-person networking remains the No. 1 tool for finding a position. The job search, however, is changing, as the figure shows. The line between online and traditional networking blurs as technology plays an increasingly significant role. Carly McVey, Right Management executive, says, "Online social networking may not always be separate from traditional networking since one so often leads to the other."[10]

Both networking and online searching are essential tools in locating jobs. But where are those jobs? The *open job market* consists of jobs that are advertised or listed. The *hidden job market* consists of jobs that are never advertised or listed. Some analysts and authors claim that between 50 and 80 percent of all jobs are filled before they even make it to online job boards or advertisements.[11] Those openings are part of the hidden job market, which we will explore shortly. First, let's start where most job seekers start—in the open job market.

Searching the Open Job Market

The open job market consists of positions that are advertised or listed publicly. Most job seekers start searching the open job market by using the Internet. Searching online is a common, but not always fruitful, approach. Both recruiters and job seekers complain about online job boards. Corporate recruiters say that the big job boards bring a flood of candidates, many of whom are not suited for the listed jobs. Job candidates grumble that listings are frequently outdated and fail to produce leads. Some career advisors call these sites black holes, into which résumés vanish without a trace. Almost as worrisome is the fear that an applicant's identity may be stolen through information posted at big boards.

Although the Internet may seem like a giant swamp where résumés disappear into oblivion, many job counselors encourage job seekers to spend a few minutes each day tracking online openings in their fields and locales. Moreover, job boards provide valuable job-search information such as résumé, interviewing, and salary tips. Job boards also serve as a jumping-off point in most searches. They inform candidates about the kinds of jobs that are available and the skill sets required.

Figure **15.2** Trends in Sources of New Jobs

	2008	2010	2012
Networking (person-to-person contacts)	41%	47%	**46%**
Internet job boards (such as Monster, CollegeGrad, and company websites)	19%	24%	**25%**
Agencies (search firms placing candidates for a fee)	12%	10%	**14%**
Direct approach (cold calling)	9%	8%	**7%**
Newspapers/periodicals (classified ads)	7%	2%	**1%**
Other (combination of above, direct referral, and luck)	12%	9%	**7%**

© Cengage Learning 2015; © Yuriy Rudyy/Shutterstock.com

Source: Based on a Right Management (ManpowerGroup) Survey of 46,000–55,000 job seekers[12]

However, job searching online can also be a huge time waster. Probably the most important tip you can apply is staying focused. In the hyperlinked utopia of endlessly fascinating sites, it's too easy to mindlessly follow link after link. Staying focused on a specific goal is critical. When you focus on the open job market, you will probably be checking advertised jobs on the big boards, company career sites, niche sites, LinkedIn, and other social networking sites.

Exploring the Big Boards.   As Figure 15.2 indicates, the number of jobs found through all job boards is increasing; therefore, it makes sense to check them out. However, with tens of thousands of job boards and employment websites deluging the Internet, it's hard to know where to start. We suggest a few general sites as well as sites for college grads.

- **CareerBuilder** claims to be the largest online career site with more than 1 million jobs and 49 million résumés.

- **Monster** offers access to information on millions of jobs worldwide. It uses a search technology called 6Sense to match applicants with the best job opportunities. Many consider Monster.com to be the Web's premier job site.

- **CollegeGrad** describes itself as the "number one entry-level job site" for students and graduates. Applicants can search for entry-level jobs, internships, summer jobs, and jobs requiring one or more years of work experience.

- **Indeed** aggregates job listings from thousands of websites including company career pages, job boards, newspaper advertisements, associations, and blogs.

Exploring Company Websites.   Probably the best way to find a job online is at a company's own website. Many companies now post job openings only at their own sites to avoid being inundated by the volume of applicants responding to postings at online job boards. A company's website is the first place to go if you have a specific employer in mind. You might

ETHICS CHECK:

Are Phantom Job Listings Ethical?

Some jobs are advertised even when a leading candidate has the position nailed down. The candidate could be an internal applicant or someone else with an inside track. Although not required by law, management policies and human resources departments at many companies demand that hiring managers list all openings on job boards or career sites. Often, hiring managers have already selected candidates for these "phantom" jobs. Is it ethical to advertise jobs that are not really available?[13]

find vision and mission statements, a history of the organization, and names of key hiring managers. Possibly you will see a listing for a position that doesn't fit your qualifications. Even though you're not right for this job, you have discovered that the company is hiring. Don't be afraid to send a résumé and cover message expressing your desire to be considered for future jobs. Rather than seeking individual company sites, you might prefer to visit aggregator LinkUp. It shows constantly updated job listings from small, midsized, and large companies.

Checking Niche Sites. If you seek a job in a specialized field, look for a niche site, such as Dice for technology jobs, Advance for Healthcare Careers for jobs in the medical field, and Accountemps for temporary accounting positions. Niche websites also exist for job seekers with special backgrounds or needs, such as GettingHired for disabled workers and Workforce50 for older workers. If you are looking for short-term jobs, check out CoolWorks, specializing in seasonal employment. Are you interested in living or working abroad? iHipo, the "high potential network," assists students and graduates in finding international internships, jobs, and graduate programs at businesses around the world. If you yearn for a government job, try USA Student Jobs, a website for students and recent graduates interested in federal service.

Using LinkedIn and Social Networking Sites. LinkedIn continues to dominate professional recruiting. Increasing numbers of hiring managers and recruiters employ this site to hunt for candidates. Job seekers can search for job openings directly, and they can also follow companies for the latest news and current job openings. (You will learn more about using LinkedIn effectively when we discuss networking.) Beyond LinkedIn, other social networking sites such as Facebook and Twitter also advertise job openings and recruit potential employees. On company Web pages you will find general company information, job postings, advice for applying, and information about what it's like to work there. Because organizations may post open jobs to their Facebook or Twitter pages prior to advertising them elsewhere, you might gain a head start on submitting an application.

When posting job-search information online, it's natural to want to put your best foot forward and openly share information that will get you a job. The challenge is striking a balance between supplying enough information and protecting your privacy. To avoid some of the risks involved, see Figure 15.3.

Figure 15.3 Protecting Yourself When Posting at Online Job Boards

- **Use reputable, well-known sites** and never pay to post your résumé.

- **Don't divulge personal data** such as your date of birth, social security number, or home address. Use your city and state or region in place of your home address.

- **Set up a separate e-mail account** with a professional-sounding e-mail address for your job search.

- **Post privately** if possible. Doing so means that you can control who has access to your e-mail address and other information.

- **Keep careful records** of every site on which you posted. At the end of your job search, remove all posted résumés.

- **Don't include your references** or reveal their contact information without permission.

- **Don't respond to "blind" job postings** (those without company names or addresses). Unfortunately, scammers use online job boards to post fake job ads to gather your personal information.

© Cengage Learning 2015

Checking Newspapers. Jobs in the open market may also be listed in local newspapers. Don't overlook this possibility, especially for local jobs. However, you don't have to buy a paper to see the listings. Most newspapers list their classified ads online.

Pursuing the Hidden Job Market With Networking

LEARNING OBJECTIVE **3**
Expand your job-search strategies by using both traditional and digital tools in pursuing the hidden job market.

Not all available positions are announced or advertised in the open job market. As mentioned earlier, between 50 and 80 percent of jobs may be part of the hidden job market.[14] Companies prefer not to openly advertise for a number of reasons. They don't welcome the deluge of unqualified candidates. What's more, companies dislike hiring unknown quantities. Career coach Donald Asher, author of *Cracking the Hidden Job Market*, sets this scene: Imagine you are a hiring manager facing hundreds of résumés on your desk and a coworker walks in with the résumé of someone she vouches for. Which résumé do you think hits the top of the stack?[15] Companies prefer known quantities.

The most successful job candidates seek to transform themselves from unknown into known quantities through networking. More jobs today are found through referrals and person-to-person contacts than through any other method. That's because people trust what they know. Therefore, your goal is to become known to a large network of people, and this means going beyond close friends.

> More jobs today are found through referrals and person-to-person contacts than through any other method. That's because people trust what they know.

© iStockphoto.com/Andrew Johnson

Building a Personal Network. Because most candidates find jobs today through networking, be prepared to work diligently to build your personal networks. This effort involves meeting people and talking to them about your field or industry so that you can gain information and locate possible job vacancies. Not only are many jobs never advertised, but some positions aren't even contemplated until the right person appears. One recent college grad underwent three interviews for a position, but the company hired someone else. After being turned down, the grad explained why he thought he was perfect for this company but perhaps in a different role. Apparently, the hiring manager agreed and decided to create a new job (in social media) because of the skills, personality, and perseverance of this determined young grad. Networking pays off, but it requires dedication. Here are three steps that will help you establish your own network:

Step 1. Develop a contact list. Make a list of anyone who would be willing to talk with you about finding a job. Figure 15.4 suggests possibilities. Even if you haven't talked with people in years, reach out to them in person or online. Consider asking your campus career center for alumni willing to talk with students. Also dig into your social networking circles, which we will discuss shortly.

Step 2. Make contacts in person and online. Call the people on your list or connect online. To set up a meeting in person, say, *Hi,_____. I'm looking for a job and I wonder if you could help me out. When could I come over to talk about it?* During your visit be friendly, well

---

Courtesy of Alexandra Engle

Figure **15.4** **Whom to Contact in Networking**

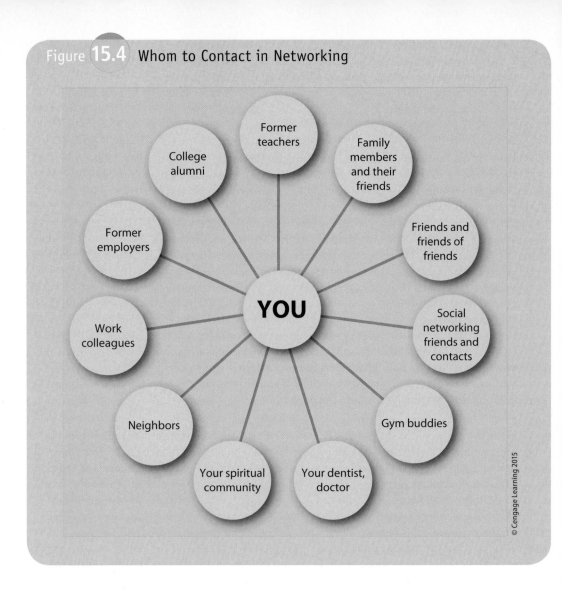

© Cengage Learning 2015

organized, polite, and interested in what your contact has to say. Provide a copy of your résumé, and try to keep the conversation centered on your job search. Your goal is to get two or more referrals. In pinpointing your request, ask, *Do you know of anyone who might have an opening for a person with my skills?* If the person does not, ask, *Do you know of anyone else who might know of someone who would?*

Step 3. Follow up on your referrals. Call or contact the people on your list. You might say something like, *Hello. I'm Stacy Rivera, a friend of Jason Tilden. He suggested that I ask you for help. I'm looking for a position as a marketing trainee, and he thought you might be willing to spare a few minutes and steer me in the right direction.* Don't ask for a job. During your referral interview, ask how the individual got started in this line of work, what he or she likes best (or least) about the work, what career paths exist in the field, and what problems must be overcome by a newcomer. Most important, ask how a person with your background and skills might get started in the field. Send an informal thank-you note to anyone who helps you in your job search, and stay in touch with the most promising people. Ask whether you could stay in contact every three weeks or so during your job search.

Using Social Media to Network.   As digital technology continues to change our lives, job candidates have a powerful new tool at their disposal: social media networks. These networks not only keep you in touch with friends, but they also function beautifully in a job search. If you just send out your résumé blindly, chances are good that not much will happen. However, if you have a referral, your chances of getting a job multiply. Today's expansion of online networks results in an additional path to developing coveted referrals. Job seekers today are increasingly expanding their networking strategies to include social media sites such as LinkedIn, Facebook, and Twitter.

Making the Most of LinkedIn to Search for a Job.   If you are looking for a job, LinkedIn is the No. 1 social media site for you to use. Although some young people have the impression that LinkedIn is for old fogies, that perception is changing as more and more college students and grads sign up. LinkedIn is where you can let recruiters know of your talents and where you begin your professional networking, as illustrated in Figure 15.5. For hiring managers to find your LinkedIn profile, however, you may need to customize your URL (uniform resource locator), which is the address of your page. To drive your name to the top of a Google search, advises career coach Susan Adams, scroll down to the LinkedIn "public profile" on your profile page, and edit the URL. Try your first and last name and then your last name and first name, and then add a middle initial, if necessary. Test a variety of combinations with punctuation and spacing until the combination leads directly to your profile.[16]

In writing your LinkedIn career summary, use keywords and phrases that might appear in job descriptions. Include quantifiable achievements and specifics that reveal your skills. You can borrow most of this from your résumé. In the Work Experience and Education fields, include all of your experience, not just your current position. For the Recommendations section, encourage instructors and employers to recommend you. Having more recommendations in your profile makes you look more credible, trustworthy, and reliable. Career coach Adams even encourages job seekers to offer to write the draft for the recommender; in the world of LinkedIn, she says, this is acceptable.[17]

One of the best ways to use LinkedIn is to search for a company in which you are interested. Try to find company employees who are connected to other people you know. Then use that contact as a referral when you apply. You can also send an e-mail to everyone in your LinkedIn network asking for help or for people they could put you in touch with. Don't be afraid to ask an online contact for advice on getting started in a career and for suggestions to help a newcomer break into that career. Another excellent way to use a contact is to have that person look at your résumé and help you tweak it. Like Facebook, LinkedIn has status updates, and it's a good idea to update yours regularly so that your connections know what is happening in your career search.

Enlisting Other Social Networks in Job Hunting.   In addition to LinkedIn, job seekers can join Facebook, Twitter, and Google+ to find job opportunities, market themselves to companies, showcase their skills, highlight their experience, and possibly land that dream job. However, some career experts think that social media sites such as Facebook do not mix well with

Figure **15.5** Harnessing the Power of LinkedIn

Five Ways College Students Can Use LinkedIn

1. **Receiving Job Alerts.** LinkedIn sends notifications of recommended jobs.
2. **Leveraging Your Network.** You may start with two connections but you can leverage those connections to thousands.
3. **Researching a Company.** Before applying to a company, you can check it out on LinkedIn and locate valuable inside information.
4. **Getting Recommendations.** LinkedIn takes the awkwardness out of asking for recommendations. It's so easy!
5. **Helping Companies Find You.** Many companies are looking for skilled college grads, and a strong profile on LinkedIn can result in inquiries.

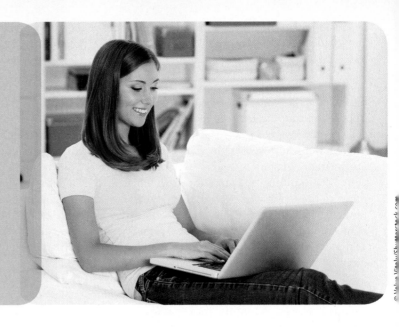

When people think of online job-search tools, they typically think of Monster or LinkedIn. But career analysts say job-hunters should add Facebook to that list. A recent study conducted by researchers at Carnegie Mellon University found that sharing one's employment interests on Facebook generates useful job leads. Moreover, the survey discovered that networking on Facebook had a positive impact on job-seekers' moods, although some users said sharing job woes on the site added to their stress. What are pros and cons of using social media to network professionally?[18]

business.[19] If you decide to use Facebook for professional networking, examine your profile and decide what you want prospective employers to see—or not see. Create a simple profile with minimal graphics, widgets, and photos. Post only content relevant to your job search or career, and choose your friends wisely.[20]

Employers often use these social media sites to check the online presence of a candidate. In fact, one report claimed that 91 percent of employers check Facebook, Twitter, and LinkedIn to filter out applicants.[21] Make sure your social networking accounts represent you professionally. You can make it easy for your potential employer to learn more about you by including an informative bio in your Twitter or Facebook profile that has a link to your LinkedIn profile. You can also make yourself more discoverable by posting thoughtful blog posts and tweets on topics related to your career goal.

Building Your Personal Brand

A large part of your job-search strategy involves building a brand for yourself. You may be thinking, *Who me? A brand?* Yes, absolutely! Even college grads should seriously consider branding because finding a job today is tough. Before you get into the thick of the job hunt, focus on developing your brand so that you know what you want to emphasize.

Personal branding involves deciding what makes you special and desirable in the job market. What is your unique selling point? What special skill set makes you stand out among all job applicants? What would your instructors or employers say is your greatest strength? Think about your intended audience. What are you promoting about yourself?

Try to come up with a tagline that describes what you do and who you are. Ask yourself questions such as these: Do you follow through with every promise? Are you a fast learner? Hardworking? What can you take credit for? It's OK to shed a little modesty and strut your stuff. However, do keep your tagline simple, short, and truthful so that it's easy to remember. See Figure 15.6 for some sample taglines appropriate for new grads.

Once you have a tagline, prepare a professional-looking business card with your name and tagline. Include an easy-to-remember e-mail address such as *firstname.lastname@ domain.com*.

Now that you have your tagline and business card, work on an elevator speech. This is a pitch that you can give in 60 seconds or less describing who you are and what you can offer. Tweak your speech for your audience, and practice until you can say it naturally. Here's an example:[22]

Possible Elevator Speech for New Grad

Hi, my name is _____. I will be graduating from _____ with a degree in _____. I'm looking to _____. I recently _____. May I take you out for coffee sometime to get your advice?

Figure **15.6** Developing Your Own Brand

4 Ways for Grads to Stand Out
Branding You

Create your own tagline.

Briefly describe what distinguishes you, such as *Talented at the Internet; Working harder, smarter; Super student, super worker; Love everything digital; Ready for a challenge; Enthusiasm plus fresh skills.*

Distribute a business card.

Include your name, tagline, and an easy-to-remember e-mail address. If you feel comfortable, include a professional headshot photo. Distribute it at all opportunities.

Prepare an elevator speech.

In 30 seconds, you need to be able to describe who you are and what problems your skills can solve. Tweak your speech for your audience, and practice until it feels natural.

Build a powerful online presence.

Prepare a strong LinkedIn profile dictating what comes up when people Google your name. Consider adding Facebook and Twitter profile pages. Be sure all sites promote your brand positively.

© Christoph Weihs/Shutterstock.com

Creating a Customized Résumé

LEARNING OBJECTIVE **4**
Organize your qualifications and information into effective résumé segments to create a winning, customized résumé.

In today's challenging and digital job market, the focus is not so much on what you want but on what the employer needs. That's why you will want to prepare a tailored résumé for every position you seek. The competition is so stiff today that you cannot get by with a generic, all-purpose résumé. Although you can start with a basic résumé, you should customize it to fit each company and position if you want it to stand out from the crowd.

The Web has made it so easy to apply for jobs that recruiters are swamped with applications. As a job seeker, you have about five seconds to catch the recruiter's eye—if your résumé is even read by a person. It may very well first encounter an *applicant tracking system* (ATS). This software helps businesses automatically post openings, screen résumés, rank candidates, and generate interview requests. These automated systems make writing your résumé doubly challenging. Although your goal is to satisfy a recruiter or hiring manager, that person will never see your résumé unless it is selected by the ATS. You will learn more about applicant tracking systems shortly.

You may not be in the job market at this moment, but preparing a résumé now has advantages. Having a current résumé makes you look well organized and professional should an unexpected employment opportunity arise. Moreover, preparing a résumé early may reveal weaknesses and give you time to address them. If you have accepted a position, it's still a good idea to keep your résumé up-to-date. You never know when an opportunity might come along!

Choosing a Résumé Style

Résumés usually fall into two categories: chronological and functional. In this section we present basic information as well as insider tips on how to choose an appropriate résumé style, determine its length, arrange its parts, and increase its chances of being selected by an applicant tracking system. You will also learn about adding a summary of qualifications, which busy recruiters welcome. Models of the résumés in the following discussion are shown in our comprehensive Résumé Gallery beginning on page 560.

Chronological.   The most popular résumé format is the chronological résumé, shown in Figures 15.9 through 15.11 in our Résumé Gallery. The chronological résumé lists work history job by job but in reverse order, starting with the most recent position. Recruiters favor the chronological format because they are familiar with it and because it quickly reveals a candidate's education and experience. The chronological style works well for candidates who have experience in their field of employment and for those who show steady career growth, but it is less appropriate for people who have changed jobs frequently or who have gaps in their employment records. For college students and others who lack extensive experience, the functional résumé format may be preferable.

Functional.   The functional résumé, shown in Figure 15.12 on page 563, focuses on a candidate's skills rather than on past employment. Like a chronological résumé, the functional résumé begins with the candidate's name, contact information, job objective, and education. Instead of listing jobs, though, the functional résumé groups skills and accomplishments in special categories, such as Supervisory and Management Skills or Retailing and Marketing Experience. This résumé style highlights accomplishments and can de-emphasize a negative employment history.

People who have changed jobs frequently, who have gaps in their employment records, or who are entering an entirely different field may prefer the functional résumé. Recent graduates with little or no related employment experience often find the functional résumé useful. Older job seekers who want to downplay a long job history and job hunters who are afraid of appearing overqualified may also prefer the functional format. Be aware, though, that online job boards may insist on the chronological format. In addition, some recruiters are suspicious of functional résumés, thinking the candidate is hiding something.

Deciding on Length

Experts disagree on how long a résumé should be. Conventional wisdom has always held that recruiters prefer one-page résumés. However, recruiters who are serious about candidates often prefer the kind of details that can be provided in a two-page or longer résumé. The best advice is to make your résumé as long as needed to present your skills to recruiters and hiring managers. Individuals with more experience will naturally have longer résumés. Those with fewer than ten years of experience, those making a major career change, and those who have had only one or two employers will likely have one-page résumés. Those with ten years or more of related experience may have two-page résumés. Finally, some senior-level managers and executives with a lengthy history of major accomplishments might have résumés that are three pages or longer.[23]

Organizing Your Information Into Effective Résumé Categories

Although résumés have standard categories, their arrangement and content should be strategically planned. A customized résumé emphasizes skills and achievements aimed at a particular job or company. It shows a candidate's most important qualifications first, and it de-emphasizes weaknesses. In organizing your qualifications and information, try to create as few headings as possible; more than six looks cluttered. No two résumés are ever exactly alike, but most writers consider including all or some of these categories: Main Heading, Career Objective, Summary of Qualifications, Education, Experience, Capabilities and Skills, Awards and Activities, Personal Information, and References.

Main Heading.   Your résumé, whether chronological or functional, should start with an uncluttered and simple main heading. The first line should always be your name; add your middle initial for an even more professional look. Format your name so that it stands out on the page. Following your name, list your contact information, including your complete address, area code and phone number, and e-mail address. Your telephone should be one where you can receive messages. The outgoing message at this number should be in your voice, it should state your full name, and it should be concise and professional. If you include your cell phone number and are expecting an important call from a recruiter, pick up only when you are in a quiet environment and can concentrate.

For your e-mail address, be sure it sounds professional instead of something like *toosexy4you@gmail.com* or *sixpackguy@yahoo.com*. Also be sure that you are using a personal e-mail address. Putting your work e-mail address on your résumé announces to prospective employers that you are using your current employer's resources to look for another job. If you have a website where an e-portfolio or samples of your work can be viewed, include the address in the main heading.

If you have an online presence, think about adding a *Quick Response* (QR) code to your résumé. This is a barcode that can be scanned by a smartphone, linking recruiters to your online portfolio or your LinkedIn profile page.

Career Objective.   Opinion is divided about the effectiveness of including a career objective on a résumé. Recruiters think such statements indicate that a candidate has made a commitment to a career and is sure about what he or she wants to do. Yet, some career coaches today say objectives "feel outdated" and too often are all about what the candidate wants instead of what the employer wants.[24] Regardless, a well-written objective—customized for the job opening—makes sense, especially for new grads with fresh training and relevant skills. The objective can include strategic keywords for applicant tracking systems. If you decide to include an objective, focus on what you can contribute to the organization, not on what the organization can do for you.

Poor objective: *To obtain a position with a well-established organization that will lead to a lasting relationship in the field of marketing. (Sounds vague and self-serving.)*

Improved objective: *To obtain a marketing position in which I use my recent training in writing and computer skills to increase customer contacts and expand brand penetration using social media. (Names specific skills and includes many nouns that might snag an applicant tracking system.)*

Avoid the words *entry-level* in your objective, as these words emphasize lack of experience. If you omit a career objective, be sure to discuss your career goals in your cover message.

Optional Summary of Qualifications.   "The biggest change in résumés over the last decade has been a switch from an objective to a summary at the top," says career expert Wendy Enelow.[25] Recruiters are busy, and smart job seekers add a summary of qualifications to their résumés to save the time of recruiters and hiring managers. Once a job is advertised, a hiring manager may get hundreds or even thousands of résumés in response. A summary at the top of your résumé makes it easier to read and ensures that your most impressive qualifications are not overlooked by a recruiter, who skims résumés quickly. In addition, because résumés today may be viewed on tablets and smartphones, make sure that the first third spotlights your most compelling qualifications.

A summary of qualifications (also called *career profile*, *job summary*, or *professional highlights*) should include three to eight bulleted statements that prove that you are the ideal candidate for the position. When formulating these statements, consider your experience in the field, your education, your unique skills, awards you have won, certifications, and any other accomplishments that you want to highlight. Include numbers wherever possible. Target the most important qualifications an employer will be looking for in the person hired for this position. Focus on nouns that might be selected as keywords by an applicant tracking system. Examples appear in Figures 15.9 and 15.11.

Education.   The next component in a chronological résumé is your education—if it is more noteworthy than your work experience. In this section you should include the name and location of schools, dates of attendance, major fields of study, and degrees received. By the way, once you have attended college, you don't need to list high school information on your résumé.

Your grade point average and/or class ranking may be important to prospective employers. One way to enhance your GPA is to calculate it in your major courses only (for example, *3.6/4.0 in major*). It is not unethical so long as you clearly show that that your GPA is in the major only. Looking to improve their hiring chances, some college grads are now offering an unusual credential: their scores on the Graduate Record Examination. Large companies and those specializing in computer software and financial services reportedly were most interested in their applicants' GRE scores.[26]

Under Education you might be tempted to list all the courses you took, but such a list makes for dull reading and consumes valuable space. Refer to courses only if you can relate them to the position sought. When relevant, include certificates earned, seminars attended, workshops completed, scholarships awarded, and honors earned. If your education is incomplete, include such statements as *BS degree expected 6/16* or *80 units completed in 120-unit program*. Title this section Education, Academic Preparation, or Professional Training. If you are preparing a functional résumé, you will probably put the Education section below your skills summaries, as Cooper Jackson has done in Figure 15.12.

REALITY CHECK: Make Your Case With Hard Facts and Figures

"Many résumé writers tend to aim for vague generalities and abstract attributes, focusing on their 'communication skills' and ability to work as a 'team player.' In a tough market, you need to move beyond these kinds of generic claims and focus on specifics. List each of your pertinent skills and responsibilities, and then back them up with fact-based bullets that explicitly prove your point."[27]

— **ROBERTA CHINSKY MATUSON,** *President of Matuson Consulting and Job Search Mentor*

Work Experience or Employment History. When your work experience is significant and relevant to the position sought, this information should appear before your education. List your most recent employment first and work backward, including only those jobs that you think will help you win the targeted position. A job application form may demand a full employment history, but your résumé may be selective. Be aware, though, that time gaps in your employment history will probably be questioned in the interview. For each position show the following:

- Employer's name, city, and state
- Dates of employment (month and year)
- Most important job title
- Significant duties, activities, accomplishments, and promotions

Your employment achievements and job duties will be easier to read if you place them in bulleted lists. Rather than list every single thing you have done, customize your information so that it relates to the target job. Your bullet points should be concise but not complete sentences, and they usually do not include personal pronouns (*I, me, my*). Strive to be specific:

Poor:	*Worked with customers*
Improved:	*Developed customer-service skills by successfully interacting with 40+ customers daily*

Whenever possible, quantify your achievements:

Poor:	*Did equipment study and report*
Improved:	*Conducted research and wrote final study analyzing equipment needs of 100 small businesses in Houston*
Poor:	*Was successful in sales*
Improved:	*Personally generated orders for sales of $90,000 annually*

In addition to technical skills, employers seek individuals with communication, management, and interpersonal capabilities. This means you will want to select work experiences and achievements that illustrate your initiative, dependability, responsibility, resourcefulness, flexibility, and leadership. Employers also want people who can work in teams.

Poor: *Worked effectively in teams*

Improved: *Collaborated with interdepartmental team in developing ten-page handbook for temporary workers*

Poor: *Joined in team effort on campus*

Improved: *Headed student government team that conducted most successful voter registration in campus history*

Statements describing your work experience should include many nouns relevant to the job you seek. These nouns may match keywords sought by the applicant tracking system. To appeal to human readers, your statements should also include action verbs, such as those in Figure 15.7. Starting each of your bullet points with an action verb will help ensure that your bulleted lists are parallel.

Capabilities and Skills.   Recruiters want to know specifically what you can do for their companies. Therefore, list your special skills. In this section be sure to include many nouns that relate to the targeted position. Include your ability to use the Web, software programs, social media, office equipment, and communication technology tools. Use expressions such as *proficient in, competent in, experienced in,* and *ability to* as illustrated in the following:

Poor: *Have payroll experience*

Improved: *Proficient in preparing federal, state, and local payroll tax returns as well as franchise and personal property tax returns*

Poor: *Trained in computer graphics*

Improved: *Certified in graphic design including infographics through an intensive 350-hour classroom program*

Figure 15.7 Action Verbs for Powerful Résumés

Communication Skills	Teamwork, Supervision Skills	Management, Leadership Skills	Research Skills	Clerical, Detail Skills	Creative Skills
clarified	advised	analyzed	assessed	activated	acted
collaborated	coordinated	authorized	collected	approved	conceptualized
explained	demonstrated	coordinated	critiqued	classified	designed
interpreted	developed	directed	diagnosed	edited	fashioned
integrated	evaluated	headed	formulated	generated	founded
persuaded	expedited	implemented	gathered	maintained	illustrated
promoted	facilitated	improved	interpreted	monitored	integrated
resolved	guided	increased	investigated	proofread	invented
summarized	motivated	organized	reviewed	recorded	originated
translated	set goals	scheduled	studied	streamlined	revitalized
wrote	trained	strengthened	systematized	updated	shaped

© Cengage Learning 2015

Poor:	*Have writing skills*
Improved:	*Competent in writing, editing, and proofreading reports, tables, letters, memos, e-mails, manuscripts, and business forms*

You will also want to highlight exceptional aptitudes, such as working well under stress, learning computer programs quickly, and interacting with customers. If possible, provide details and evidence that back up your assertions. Include examples of your writing, speaking, management, organizational, interpersonal, and presentation skills—particularly those talents that are relevant to your targeted job. For recent graduates, this section can be used to give recruiters evidence of your potential and to address successful college projects.

Awards, Honors, and Activities. If you have three or more awards or honors, highlight them by listing them under a separate heading. If not, put them in the Education or Work Experience section if appropriate. Include awards, scholarships (financial and other), fellowships, dean's list, honors, recognition, commendations, and certificates. Be sure to identify items clearly. Your reader may be unfamiliar, for example, with Greek organizations, honoraries, and awards; tell what they mean.

Poor:	*Recipient of Star award*
Improved:	*Recipient of Star award given by Pepperdine University to outstanding graduates who combine academic excellence and extracurricular activities*

It's also appropriate to include school, community, volunteer, and professional activities. Employers are interested in evidence that you are a well-rounded person. This section provides an opportunity to demonstrate leadership and interpersonal skills. Strive to use action statements.

Poor:	*Treasurer of business club*
Improved:	*Collected dues, kept financial records, and paid bills while serving as treasurer of 35-member business management club*

Personal Data. Résumés in the United States omit personal data, such as birth date, marital status, height, weight, national origin, health, disabilities, and religious affiliation. Such information doesn't relate to genuine occupational qualifications, and recruiters are legally barred from asking for such information. Some job seekers do, however, include hobbies or interests (such as skiing or photography) that might grab the recruiter's attention or serve as conversation starters. For example, let's say you learn that your hiring manager enjoys distance running. If you have run a marathon, you may want to mention it. Many executives practice tennis or golf, two sports highly suitable for networking. You could also indicate your willingness to travel or to relocate since many companies will be interested.

References. Listing references directly on a résumé takes up valuable space. Moreover, references are not normally instrumental in securing an interview—few companies check them before the interview. Instead, recruiters prefer that you bring to the interview a list of individuals willing to discuss your qualifications. Therefore, you should prepare a separate list, such as that in Figure 15.8, when you begin your job search. Consider three to five individuals, such as instructors, your current employer or previous employers, colleagues or subordinates, and other professional contacts. Ask whether they would be willing to answer inquiries regarding your qualifications for employment. Be sure, however, to provide them with an opportunity to refuse. No reference is better than a negative one. Better yet, to avoid rejection and embarrassment, ask only those contacts who will give you a glowing endorsement.

Figure **15.8** Sample Reference List

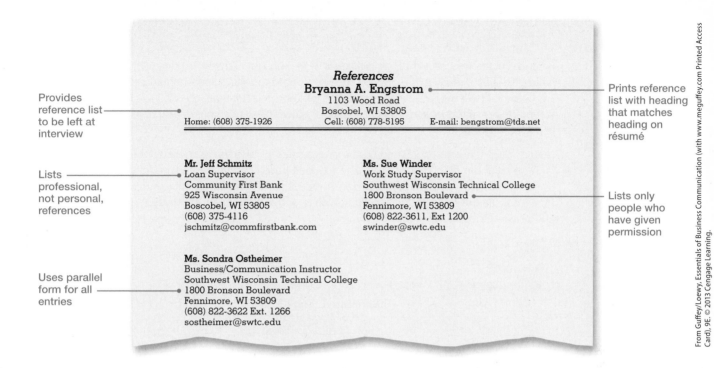

Provides reference list to be left at interview

Lists professional, not personal, references

Uses parallel form for all entries

References
Bryanna A. Engstrom
1103 Wood Road
Boscobel, WI 53805

Home: (608) 375-1926   Cell: (608) 778-5195   E-mail: bengstrom@tds.net

Mr. Jeff Schmitz
Loan Supervisor
Community First Bank
925 Wisconsin Avenue
Boscobel, WI 53805
(608) 375-4116
jschmitz@commfirstbank.com

Ms. Sue Winder
Work Study Supervisor
Southwest Wisconsin Technical College
1800 Bronson Boulevard
Fennimore, WI 53809
(608) 822-3611, Ext 1200
swinder@swtc.edu

Ms. Sondra Ostheimer
Business/Communication Instructor
Southwest Wisconsin Technical College
1800 Bronson Boulevard
Fennimore, WI 53809
(608) 822-3622 Ext. 1266
sostheimer@swtc.edu

Prints reference list with heading that matches heading on résumé

Lists only people who have given permission

From Guffey/Loewy, Essentials of Business Communication (with www.meguffey.com Printed Access Card), 9E. © 2013 Cengage Learning.

Do not include personal or character references, such as friends, family, or neighbors, because recruiters rarely consult them. Companies are more interested in the opinions of objective individuals who know how you perform professionally and academically. One final note: most recruiters see little reason for including the statement *References furnished upon request*. It is unnecessary and takes up precious space.

Polishing Your Résumé

As you continue to work on your résumé, look for ways to improve it. For example, consider consolidating headings. By condensing your information into as few headings as possible, you will produce a clean, professional-looking document. Study other résumés for valuable formatting ideas. Ask yourself what graphic highlighting techniques you can use to improve readability: capitalization, underlining, indenting, and bulleting. Experiment with headings and styles to achieve a pleasing, easy-to-read message. Moreover, look for ways to eliminate wordiness. For example, instead of *Supervised two employees who worked at the counter*, try *Supervised two counter employees*. Review Chapter 5 for more tips on writing concisely.

REALITY CHECK: Lasting and Permanent Damage

Executive Colleen McCreary says that job applicants must be aware of the long-term damage that can be done by lying on their résumés or "spamming" them (sending blanket copies everywhere). "You're going to be remembered—and not in a positive way," she cautions. McCreary warns applicants not to send the same messages to multiple firms. ATS systems recognize duplicates, and the applicant immediately loses credibility.[28]

—**COLLEEN MCCREARY,** *chief people officer, Zynga Inc.*

© Kevork Djansezian/Getty Images

Résumé Gallery

Bryanna Engstrom used a chronological résumé to highlight her work experience, most of which is related directly to the position she seeks. Although she is a recent graduate, she has accumulated experience in two part-time jobs and one full-time job. She included a summary of qualifications to highlight her skills, experience, and interpersonal traits aimed at a specific position.

Notice that Bryanna designed her résumé in two columns with the major categories listed in the left column. In the right column she included bulleted items for each of the four categories. Conciseness and parallelism are important in writing an effective résumé. In the *Experience* category, she started each item with an active verb, which improved readability and parallel form.

Bryanna A. Engstrom
1103 Wood Road
Boscobel, WI 53805

Home: (608) 375-1926   Cell: (608) 778-5195   E-mail: bengstrom@tds.net

Omits objective to keep all options open

SUMMARY OF QUALIFICATIONS
- Over three years' experience in administrative positions, working with business documents and interacting with customers
- Ability to keyboard (68 wpm) and use ten-key calculator (150 kpm)
- Proficient with Microsoft Word, Excel, Access, PowerPoint, SharePoint, and Publisher (passed MOS certification exam)

Focuses on skills and aptitudes that employers seek
- Competent in Web research, written and oral communication, records management, desktop publishing, and proofreading and editing business documents
- Trained in QuickBooks, Flash, Photoshop, Dreamweaver

EXPERIENCE

Administrative Assistant, Work Study
Southwest Wisconsin Technical College, Fennimore, Wisconsin
August 2012–present

Uses present-tense verb for current job
- Create letters, memos, reports, and forms in Microsoft Word
- Develop customized reports and labels using Microsoft Access
- Maintain departmental Microsoft Excel budget

Loan Support Specialist
Community First Bank, Boscobel, Wisconsin, May 2011–September 2012
- Prepared loan documents for consumer, residential, mortgage, agricultural, and commercial loans
- Ensured compliance with federal, state, and bank regulations
- Originated correspondence (oral and written) with customers and insurance agencies

Arranges employment by job title for easy recognition
- Ordered and interpreted appraisals, titles, and credit reports

Customer Sales Representative
Land's End, Dodgeville, Wisconsin, Winter seasons 2011–2012
- Developed customer-service skills by serving 40+ online customers a day
- Resolved customer problems
- Entered catalog orders into computer system

EDUCATION
Southwest Wisconsin Technical College, Fennimore, Wisconsin
Major: Administrative Assistant with Help Desk certificate
AA degree expected May 2014. GPA in major: 3.8 (4.0 = A)

Combines activities and awards to show extracurricular involvement

ACTIVITIES AND AWARDS
- Placed first in state BPA Administrative Assistant competition
- Served as SWTC Student Senate Representative
- Nominated for SWTC Ambassador Award (recognizes outstanding students for excellence in and out of classroom)

Hung-Wei Chun used Microsoft Word to design a traditional chronological print-based résumé that he plans to give to recruiters at the campus job fair or during interviews. Notice that he formatted his résumé in two columns. An easy way to do this is to use the Word table feature and remove the borders so that no lines show.

Although Hung-Wei has work experience unrelated to his future employment, his résumé looks impressive because he has transferable skills. His internship is related to his future career, and his language skills and study abroad experience will help him score points in competition with other applicants. Hung-Wei's volunteer experience is also attractive because it shows him to be a well-rounded, compassionate individual. Because his experience in his future field is limited, he omitted a summary of qualifications.

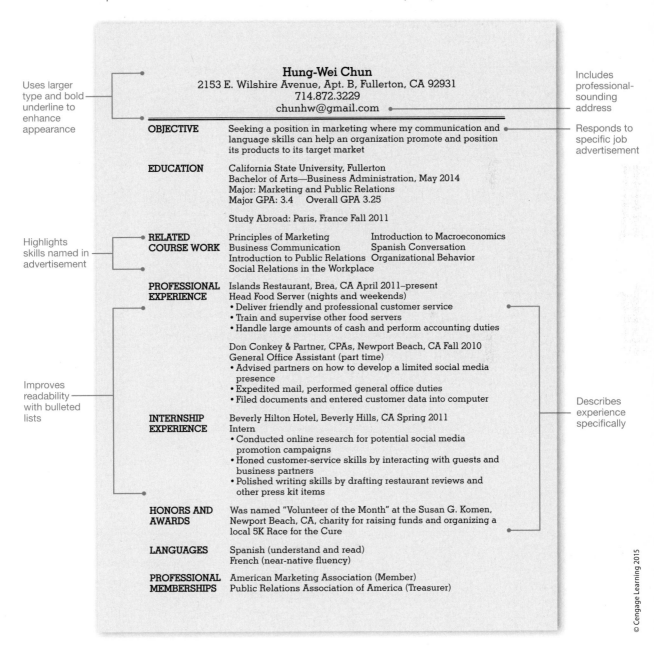

Uses larger type and bold underline to enhance appearance

Includes professional-sounding address

Responds to specific job advertisement

Highlights skills named in advertisement

Improves readability with bulleted lists

Describes experience specifically

Hung-Wei Chun
2153 E. Wilshire Avenue, Apt. B, Fullerton, CA 92931
714.872.3229
chunhw@gmail.com

OBJECTIVE — Seeking a position in marketing where my communication and language skills can help an organization promote and position its products to its target market

EDUCATION — California State University, Fullerton
Bachelor of Arts—Business Administration, May 2014
Major: Marketing and Public Relations
Major GPA: 3.4   Overall GPA 3.25

Study Abroad: Paris, France Fall 2011

RELATED COURSE WORK
Principles of Marketing   Introduction to Macroeconomics
Business Communication   Spanish Conversation
Introduction to Public Relations   Organizational Behavior
Social Relations in the Workplace

PROFESSIONAL EXPERIENCE
Islands Restaurant, Brea, CA April 2011–present
Head Food Server (nights and weekends)
• Deliver friendly and professional customer service
• Train and supervise other food servers
• Handle large amounts of cash and perform accounting duties

Don Conkey & Partner, CPAs, Newport Beach, CA Fall 2010
General Office Assistant (part time)
• Advised partners on how to develop a limited social media presence
• Expedited mail, performed general office duties
• Filed documents and entered customer data into computer

INTERNSHIP EXPERIENCE
Beverly Hilton Hotel, Beverly Hills, CA Spring 2011
Intern
• Conducted online research for potential social media promotion campaigns
• Honed customer-service skills by interacting with guests and business partners
• Polished writing skills by drafting restaurant reviews and other press kit items

HONORS AND AWARDS
Was named "Volunteer of the Month" at the Susan G. Komen, Newport Beach, CA, charity for raising funds and organizing a local 5K Race for the Cure

LANGUAGES
Spanish (understand and read)
French (near-native fluency)

PROFESSIONAL MEMBERSHIPS
American Marketing Association (Member)
Public Relations Association of America (Treasurer)

© Cengage Learning 2015

Because Rachel has many years of experience and seeks executive-level employment, she highlighted her experience by placing it before her education. Her summary of qualifications highlighted her most impressive experience and skills. This chronological two-page résumé shows the steady progression of her career to executive positions, a movement that impresses and reassures recruiters.

RACHEL M. CHOWDHRY
374 Cabot Drive
Thousand Oaks, CA 91359

E-Mail: rchowdhry@west.net
(805) 490-3310

OBJECTIVE Senior Financial Management Position

SUMMARY OF QUALIFICATIONS
- Over 12 years' comprehensive experience in accounting industry, including over 8 years as a controller
- Certified Public Accountant (CPA)
- Demonstrated ability to handle all accounting functions for large, midsized, and small firms
- Ability to isolate problems, reduce expenses, and improve the bottom line, resulting in substantial cost savings
- Proven talent for interacting professionally with individuals at all levels, as demonstrated by performance review comments
- Experienced in P&L, audits, taxation, internal control, inventory, management, A/P, A/R, and cash management

Lists most impressive credentials

PROFESSIONAL HISTORY AND ACHIEVEMENTS

11/11 to present CONTROLLER
United Plastics, Inc., Newbury Park, California (extruder of polyethylene film for plastic aprons and gloves)
- Direct all facets of accounting and cash management for 160-employee, $3 billion business
- Supervise inventory and production operations for tax compliance
- Talked owner into reducing sales prices, resulting in doubling first quarter 2013 sales
- Created cost accounting by product and pricing based on gross margin
- Increased line of credit with 12 major suppliers

Explains nature of employer's business because it is not immediately recognizable

Uses action verbs but includes many good nouns for possible computer scanning

1/09 to 10/11 CONTROLLER
Burgess Inc., Freeport, Illinois (major manufacturer of flashlight and lantern batteries)
- Managed all accounting, cash, payroll, credit, and collection operations for 175-employee business
- Implemented a new system for cost accounting, inventory control, and accounts payable, resulting in a $100,000 annual savings
- Reduced staff from 11 persons to 5 with no loss in productivity
- Successfully reduced inventory levels from $1.1 million to $600,000

Emphasizes steady employment history by listing dates FIRST

Describes and quantifies specific achievements

8/07 to 11/08 TREASURER/CONTROLLER
The Builders of Winter, Winter, Wisconsin (manufacturer of modular housing)
- Supervised accounts receivable/payable, cash management, payroll, insurance
- Directed monthly and year-end closings, banking relations, and product costing
- Refinanced company with long-term loan, ensuring stability

Rachel M. Chowdhry   Page 2

4/03 to 6/07 SUPERVISOR OF GENERAL ACCOUNTING
Levin National Batteries, St. Paul, Minnesota (local manufacturer of flashlight batteries)
- Completed monthly and year-end closing of ledgers for $2 million business
- Audited freight bills, acted as interdepartmental liaison, prepared financial reports

ADDITIONAL INFORMATION
Education: BBA degree, University of Minnesota, major: Accounting, 2002
Certification: Certified Public Accountant (CPA), 2004
Personal: Will travel and/or relocate

De-emphasizes education because work history is more important for mature candidates

© Cengage Learning 2015

Recent graduate Cooper Jackson chose this functional format to de-emphasize his meager work experience and emphasize his potential in sales and marketing. This version of his résumé is more generic than one targeted for a specific position. Nevertheless, it emphasizes his strong points with specific achievements and includes an employment section to satisfy recruiters. The functional format presents ability-focused topics. It illustrates what the job seeker can do for the employer instead of narrating a history of previous jobs. Although recruiters prefer chronological résumés, the functional format is a good choice for new graduates, career changers, and those with employment gaps.

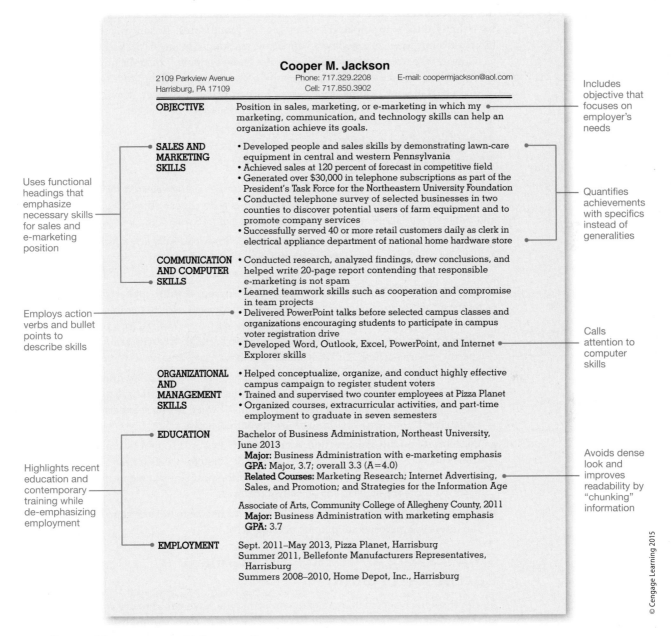

Includes objective that focuses on employer's needs

Uses functional headings that emphasize necessary skills for sales and e-marketing position

Employs action verbs and bullet points to describe skills

Highlights recent education and contemporary training while de-emphasizing employment

Quantifies achievements with specifics instead of generalities

Calls attention to computer skills

Avoids dense look and improves readability by "chunking" information

© Cengage Learning 2015

Cooper M. Jackson

2109 Parkview Avenue   Phone: 717.329.2208   E-mail: coopermjackson@aol.com
Harrisburg, PA 17109   Cell: 717.850.3902

OBJECTIVE — Position in sales, marketing, or e-marketing in which my marketing, communication, and technology skills can help an organization achieve its goals.

SALES AND MARKETING SKILLS
- Developed people and sales skills by demonstrating lawn-care equipment in central and western Pennsylvania
- Achieved sales at 120 percent of forecast in competitive field
- Generated over $30,000 in telephone subscriptions as part of the President's Task Force for the Northeastern University Foundation
- Conducted telephone survey of selected businesses in two counties to discover potential users of farm equipment and to promote company services
- Successfully served 40 or more retail customers daily as clerk in electrical appliance department of national home hardware store

COMMUNICATION AND COMPUTER SKILLS
- Conducted research, analyzed findings, drew conclusions, and helped write 20-page report contending that responsible e-marketing is not spam
- Learned teamwork skills such as cooperation and compromise in team projects
- Delivered PowerPoint talks before selected campus classes and organizations encouraging students to participate in campus voter registration drive
- Developed Word, Outlook, Excel, PowerPoint, and Internet Explorer skills

ORGANIZATIONAL AND MANAGEMENT SKILLS
- Helped conceptualize, organize, and conduct highly effective campus campaign to register student voters
- Trained and supervised two counter employees at Pizza Planet
- Organized courses, extracurricular activities, and part-time employment to graduate in seven semesters

EDUCATION Bachelor of Business Administration, Northeast University, June 2013
  Major: Business Administration with e-marketing emphasis
  GPA: Major, 3.7; overall 3.3 (A=4.0)
  Related Courses: Marketing Research; Internet Advertising, Sales, and Promotion; and Strategies for the Information Age

Associate of Arts, Community College of Allegheny County, 2011
  Major: Business Administration with marketing emphasis
  GPA: 3.7

EMPLOYMENT Sept. 2011–May 2013, Pizza Planet, Harrisburg
Summer 2011, Bellefonte Manufacturers Representatives, Harrisburg
Summers 2008–2010, Home Depot, Inc., Harrisburg

Proofreading Your Résumé

After revising your résumé, you must proofread, proofread, and proofread again for spelling, grammar, mechanics, content, and format. Then have a knowledgeable friend or relative proofread it yet again. This is one document that must be perfect. Because the job market is so competitive, one typo, misspelled word, or grammatical error could eliminate you from consideration.

By now you may be thinking that you'd like to hire someone to write your résumé. Don't! First, you know yourself better than anyone else could know you. Second, you will end up with either a generic or a one-time résumé. A generic résumé in today's highly competitive job market will lose out to a customized résumé nine times out of ten. Equally useless is a one-time résumé aimed at a single job. What if you don't get that job? Because you will need to revise your résumé many times as you seek a variety of jobs, be prepared to write (and rewrite) it yourself.

LEARNING OBJECTIVE **5**
Optimize your job search and résumé by taking advantage of today's digital tools.

Optimizing Your Job Search With Today's Digital Tools

Just as electronic media have changed the way candidates seek jobs, these same digital tools have changed the way employers select qualified candidates. This means that the first reader of your résumé may very well be an applicant tracking system (ATS). Estimates suggest that as many as 90 percent of large companies use these systems.[29] In addition, résumé databases such as Monster and CareerBuilder use similar screening techniques to filter applications. The primary goal of your résumé is pleasing a human reader. However, it must first get past the ATS gatekeeper to be selected and put in the right category, or "bucket."

Getting Your Résumé Selected: Maximizing Keyword "Hits"

Job hunters increase the probability of their résumés being selected by applicant tracking systems and put in the right bucket by the words they choose. The following techniques, in addition to those cited earlier, increase the chance of ATS selection:

- **Include specific keywords or keyword phrases.** Study carefully any advertisements and job descriptions for the position you want. Describe your experience, education, and qualifications in terms associated with the job advertisement or job description for this position.

- **Focus on nouns.** Although action verbs will make your résumé appeal to a recruiter, the applicant tracking system will often be looking for nouns in three categories: (a) a job title, position, or role (e.g., *accountant, Web developer, team leader*); (b) a technical skill or specialization (e.g., *Javascript, e-newsletter editor*); and (c) a certification, tool used, or specific experience (e.g., *Certified Financial Analyst, experience with WordPress*).[30]

- **Use variations of the job title.** Tracking systems may seek a slightly different job title from what you list. To be safe, include variations and abbreviations (e.g., *occupational therapist, certified occupational therapist*, or *cota)*. If you don't have experience in your targeted area, use the job title you seek in your objective.

- **Concentrate on the Skills section.** A majority of keywords sought by employees are for some specialized or technical skill requirement. Therefore, be sure the Skills section of your résumé is loaded with nouns that describe your skills and qualifications. See page 561 for more suggestions on skills categories.

- **Skip a keyword summary.** Avoid grouping nouns in a keyword summary because recruiters may perceive them to be manipulative.[31]

Showcasing Your Qualifications in a Career E-Portfolio

As the workplace becomes increasingly digital, you have yet another way to display your qualifications to prospective employers—the career e-portfolio. This is a collection of digital files that can be navigated with the help of menus and hyperlinks much like a personal website.

What Goes in a Career E-Portfolio?   An e-portfolio provides viewers with a snapshot of your talents, accomplishments, and technical skills. It may include a copy of your résumé, reference letters, commendations for special achievements, awards, certificates, work samples, a complete list of your courses, thank-you letters, and other items that tout your accomplishments. An e-portfolio could also offer links to digital copies of your artwork, film

Figure **15.13** Making a Career E-Portfolio

Why create a career e-portfolio?

- Demonstrate your technology skills.
- Support and extend your résumé.
- Present yourself in a lively format.
- Make data instantly accessible.
- Target a specific job.

What goes in it?

- Relevant course work
- Updated résumé, cover message
- Real work examples
- Recommendations
- Images, links, or whatever showcases your skills

How to make and publish it?

- Use a portfolio or blog template.
- Design your own website.
- Host at a university or private site.
- Publish its URL in your résumé and elsewhere.

projects, videos, blueprints, documents, photographs, multimedia files, and blog entries that might otherwise be difficult to share with potential employers.

Because e-portfolios offer a variety of resources in one place, they have many advantages, as seen in Figure 15.13. When they are posted on websites, they can be viewed at an employer's convenience. Let's say you are talking on the phone with an employer in another city who wants to see a copy of your résumé. You can simply refer the employer to the website where your résumé resides. E-portfolios can also be seen by many individuals in an organization without circulating a paper copy. However, the real reason for preparing an e-portfolio is that it shows off your talents and qualifications more thoroughly than a print résumé does.

Some recruiters may be skeptical about e-portfolios because they fear that such presentations will take more time to view than paper-based résumés do. Nontraditional job applications may end up at the bottom of the pile or be ignored. That's why some applicants submit a print résumé in addition to an e-portfolio.

How Are E-Portfolios Accessed? E-portfolios are generally accessed at websites, where they are available around the clock to employers. If the websites are not password protected, however, you should remove personal information. Some colleges and universities make website space available for student e-portfolios. In addition, institutions may provide instruction and resources for scanning photos, digitizing images, and preparing graphics. E-portfolios may also be burned onto CDs and DVDs to be mailed to prospective employers.

To learn more about making a career e-portfolio, take a look at a tutorial written by a recent university graduate who tells exactly how he did it. This tutorial is available under the Writing Resources tab at the student website for this book: **www.cengagebrain.com.**

Expanding Employment Chances With a Video Résumé

Still another way to expand your employment possibilities is with a video résumé. Video résumés enable job candidates to present their experience, qualifications, and interests in video form. This format has many benefits. It allows candidates to demonstrate their public speaking, interpersonal, and technical skills more impressively than they can in traditional print résumés. Both employers and applicants can save recruitment and travel costs by using video résumés. Instead of flying distant candidates to interviews, organizations can see them digitally.

Video résumés are becoming more prevalent with the emergence of YouTube, inexpensive webcams, and widespread broadband. With simple edits on a computer, you can customize a video message to a specific employer and tailor your résumé for a particular job opening. In making a video résumé, dress professionally in business attire, just as you would for an in-person interview. Keep your video to three minutes or less. Explain why you would be a good employee and what you can do for the company that hires you.

Before committing time and energy to a video résumé, decide whether it is appropriate for your career field. Such presentations make sense for online, media, social, and creative professions. Traditional organizations, however, may be less impressed. Done well, a video résumé might give you an edge. Done poorly, however, it could bounce you from contention.

Wowing Them With an Infographic Résumé

A hot trend among creative types is the infographic résumé. It uses colorful charts, graphics, and time lines to illustrate a candidate's work history and experience. No one could deny that an infographic résumé really stands out. "Anyone looking at it," effuses blogger Randy Krum, "is 650% more likely to remember it days later."[32] Those preparing infographic résumés are often in the field of graphic design or journalism. James Coleman, a graduating senior from the University of Houston, created an infographic résumé that secured a job. Shown in Figure 15.14, James' résumé uses a time line to track his experience and education. Colorful bubbles indicate his digital skills.

Figure **15.14** An Infographic Résumé That Snagged a Job

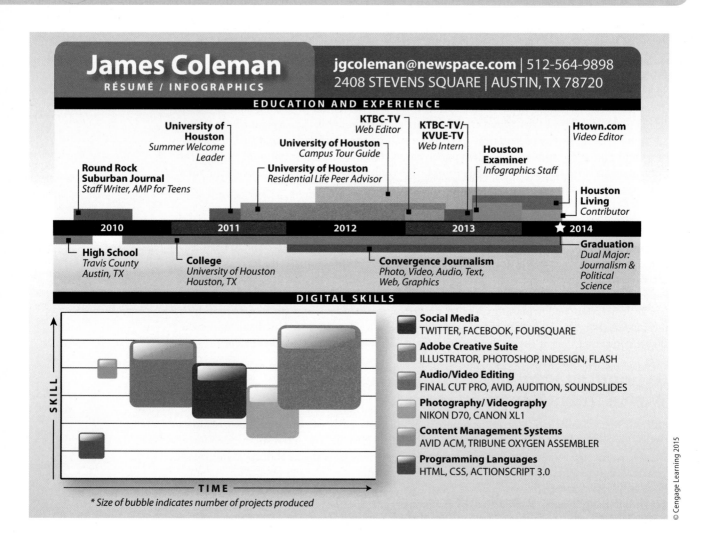

Most of us, however, are not talented enough to create professional-looking infographics. To the rescue are many companies that now offer infographic apps. Vizualize.me turns a user's LinkedIn profile information into a beautiful Web-based infographic. Re.vu also pulls in LinkedIn data to produce a stylish Web-based infographic. Brazen Careerist offers a Facebook application that generates an infographic résumé from a user's Facebook, Twitter, and LinkedIn information.

Will a dazzling infographic get you a job? Among hiring managers, the consensus is that infographic résumés help candidates set themselves apart, but such visual displays may not be appropriate for every kind of job.[33] In more traditional fields such as accounting and financial services, hiring managers want to see a standard print-based résumé. One hiring manager pointed out that traditional résumés evolved this way for a reason: they make comparison, evaluation, and selection easier for employers.[34]

How Many Résumés and What Format?

At this point you may be wondering how many résumés you should make, and what format they should follow. The good news is that you need only one basic résumé that you can customize for various job prospects and formats.

Preparing a Basic Print-Based Résumé.   The one basic résumé you should prepare is a print-based traditional résumé. It should be attractively formatted to maximize readability. This résumé is useful (a) during job interviews, (b) for person-to-person networking situations, (c) for recruiters at career fairs, and (d) when you are competing for a job that does not require an electronic submission.

You can create a basic, yet professional-looking, résumé by using your word processing program. The Résumé Gallery in this chapter provides ideas for simple layouts that are easily duplicated and adapted. You can also examine résumé templates for design and format ideas. Their inflexibility, however, may be frustrating as you try to force your skills and experience into a predetermined template sequence. What's more, recruiters who read hundreds of résumés can usually spot a template-based résumé. Instead, create your own original résumé that reflects your unique qualifications.

Converting to a Plain-Text Résumé for Digital Submission.   After preparing a basic résumé, you can convert it to a plain-text résumé so that it is available for e-mailing or pasting into online résumé submission forms. Employers prefer plain-text documents because they avoid possible e-mail viruses and word processing incompatibilities. Usually included in the body of an e-mail message, a plain-text résumé is immediately searchable. To make a plain-text résumé, create a new document, illustrated in Figure 15.15, in which you incorporate the following changes:

- Remove images, designs, colors, and any characters not on a standard keyboard.
- Remove page breaks, section breaks, tabs, and tables.
- Replace bullets with asterisks or plus signs.
- Consider using capital letters rather than boldface type—but don't overdo the caps.
- Use white space or a line of dashes or equal signs to separate sections.
- In Microsoft Word, save the document with *Plain Text* (*.txt*) as the file type.
- Send yourself a copy embedded within an e-mail message to check its appearance. Also send it to a friend to try it out.

Submitting Your Résumé

The format you choose for submitting your résumé depends on what is required. If you are responding to a job advertisement, be certain to read the listing carefully to learn how the employer wants you to submit your résumé. Not following the prospective employer's instructions can eliminate you from consideration before your résumé is even reviewed.

Figure **15.15** Portion of Plain-Text Résumé

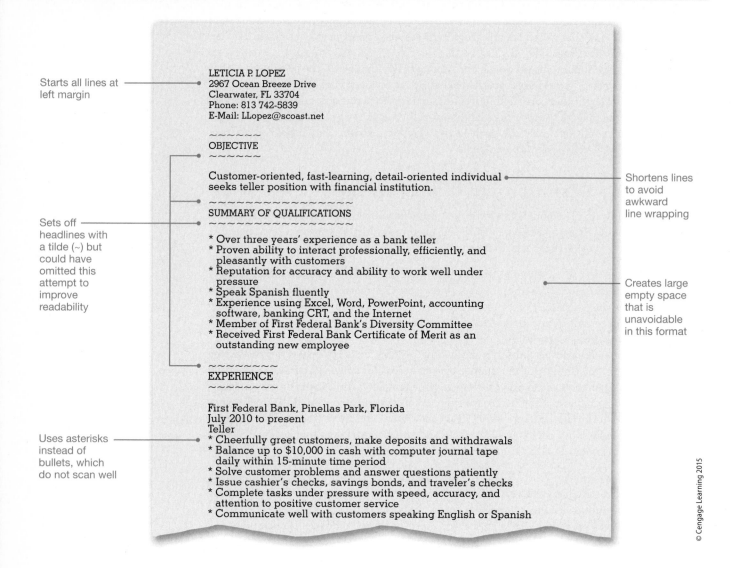

Starts all lines at left margin

LETICIA P. LOPEZ
2967 Ocean Breeze Drive
Clearwater, FL 33704
Phone: 813 742-5839
E-Mail: LLopez@scoast.net

~~~~~~
OBJECTIVE
~~~~~~

Customer-oriented, fast-learning, detail-oriented individual seeks teller position with financial institution.

Shortens lines to avoid awkward line wrapping

~~~~~~~~~~~~~~~~
SUMMARY OF QUALIFICATIONS
~~~~~~~~~~~~~~~~

Sets off headlines with a tilde (~) but could have omitted this attempt to improve readability

* Over three years' experience as a bank teller
* Proven ability to interact professionally, efficiently, and pleasantly with customers
* Reputation for accuracy and ability to work well under pressure
* Speak Spanish fluently
* Experience using Excel, Word, PowerPoint, accounting software, banking CRT, and the Internet
* Member of First Federal Bank's Diversity Committee
* Received First Federal Bank Certificate of Merit as an outstanding new employee

Creates large empty space that is unavoidable in this format

~~~~~~~~
EXPERIENCE
~~~~~~~~

First Federal Bank, Pinellas Park, Florida
July 2010 to present
Teller

Uses asterisks instead of bullets, which do not scan well

* Cheerfully greet customers, make deposits and withdrawals
* Balance up to $10,000 in cash with computer journal tape daily within 15-minute time period
* Solve customer problems and answer questions patiently
* Issue cashier's checks, savings bonds, and traveler's checks
* Complete tasks under pressure with speed, accuracy, and attention to positive customer service
* Communicate well with customers speaking English or Spanish

© Cengage Learning 2015

If you have any doubt about what format is desired, send an e-mail inquiry to a company representative or call and ask. Most organizations will request one of the following submission formats:

- **Word document.** Some organizations ask candidates to send their résumés and cover messages by surface mail. Organizations may request that résumés be submitted as Word documents attached to e-mail messages, despite the fear of viruses.

- **Plain-text document.** As discussed earlier, many employers expect applicants to submit résumés and cover letters as plain-text documents. This format is also widely used for posting to an online job board or for sending by e-mail. Plain-text résumés may be embedded within or attached to e-mail messages.

- **PDF document.** For safety reasons some employers prefer PDF (portable document format) files. A PDF résumé looks exactly like the original and cannot be altered. Most computers have Adobe Acrobat Reader installed for easy reading of PDF files. Converting your résumé to a PDF file can be easily done by saving it as a PDF file, which preserves all formatting.

- **Company database.** Larger organizations may prefer that you complete an online form with your résumé information. This enables them to plug your data into their formats for rapid searching. You might be able to cut and paste your information from your résumé into the form.

- **Fax.** Although fading in office use, fax transmission might be requested. Sending your résumé via fax gets your information to an employer safely and quickly. However, since print quality is often poor, use the fax method only if requested or if a submission deadline is upon you. Follow up with your polished, printed résumé.

Because your résumé is probably the most important message you will ever write, you will revise it many times. With so much information in concentrated form and with so much riding on its outcome, your résumé demands careful polishing, proofreading, and critiquing.

As you revise, be certain to verify all the facts, particularly those involving your previous employment and education. Don't be caught in a mistake, or worse, a distortion of previous jobs and dates of employment. These items likely will be checked, and the consequences of puffing up a résumé with deception or flat-out lies are simply not worth the risk. The accompanying Ethical Insights box outlines dangerous areas to avoid.

Are Inflated Résumés Worth the Risk?

ETHICAL insights

A résumé is expected to showcase a candidate's strengths and minimize weaknesses. For this reason, recruiters expect a certain degree of self-promotion. Some résumé writers, however, step over the line that separates honest self-marketing from deceptive half-truths and flat-out lies. Distorting facts on a résumé is unethical; lying may be illegal. Most important, either practice can destroy a career.

Given today's competitive job market, it might be tempting to puff up your résumé. You would not be alone in telling fibs or outright whoppers. A CareerBuilder survey of 8,700 workers found that 8 percent admitted to lying on their résumés; however, the same study found that of the 3,100 hiring managers surveyed, 49 percent caught a job applicant lying on some part of his or her résumé. Worse, 57 percent of employers will automatically dismiss applicants who lie on any part of their résumés.[35] Although recruiters can't check everything, most will verify previous employment and education before hiring candidates. Over half will require official transcripts.

After they have been hired, candidates may think they are safe—but organizations often continue the checking process. If hiring officials find a discrepancy in GPA or prior experience and the error is an honest mistake, they meet with the new-hire to hear an explanation. If the discrepancy wasn't a mistake, they will likely fire the person immediately.

No job seeker wants to be in the unhappy position of explaining résumé errors or defending misrepresentation. Avoiding the following problems can keep you off the hot seat:

- **Enhanced education, grades, or honors.** Some job candidates claim degrees from colleges or universities when in fact they merely attended classes. Others increase their grade point averages or claim fictitious honors. Any such dishonest reporting is grounds for dismissal when discovered.

- **Inflated job titles and salaries.** Wishing to elevate their status, some applicants misrepresent their titles or increase their past salaries. For example, one technician called himself a programmer when he had actually programmed only one project for his boss. A mail clerk who assumed added responsibilities conferred upon herself the title of supervisor.

- **Puffed-up accomplishments.** Some job seekers inflate their employment experience or achievements. One clerk, eager to make her photocopying duties sound more important, said that she assisted the *vice president in communicating and distributing employee directives.* In addition to avoiding puffery, guard against taking sole credit for achievements that required many people. When recruiters suspect dubious claims on résumés, they nail applicants with specific—and often embarrassing—questions during their interviews.

- **Altered employment dates.** Some candidates extend the dates of employment to hide unimpressive jobs or to cover up periods of unemployment and illness. Let's say that several years ago Sierra was unemployed for 14 months between working for Company A and being hired by Company B. To make her employment history look better, she adds seven months to her tenure with Company A and seven months to Company B. Now her employment history has no gaps, but her résumé is dishonest and represents a potential booby trap for her.

If your honest qualifications aren't good enough to get you the job you want, start working now to improve them. No job seeker should want to be hired based on lies.

Creating and Submitting a Customized Résumé

Preparation

- **Analyze your strengths.** Determine what aspects of your education, experience, and personal characteristics will be assets to prospective employers.

- **Research job listings.** Learn about available jobs, common qualifications, and potential employers. The best résumés are customized for specific jobs with specific companies.

Heading, Objective, and Summary of Qualifications

- **Identify yourself.** List your name, address, telephone numbers, and possibly a QR code.

- **Include a career objective for a targeted job.** Use an objective only if it is intended for a specific job (*Objective: Junior cost accountant position in the petroleum industry*).

- **Prepare a summary of qualifications.** Include a list of three to eight bulleted statements that highlight your qualifications for the targeted position.

Education

- **Name your degree, date of graduation, and institution.** Emphasize your education if your experience is limited.

- **List your major and GPA.** Give information about your studies, but don't inventory all your courses.

Work Experience

- **Itemize your jobs.** Start with your most recent job. Give the employer's name and city, dates of employment (month, year), and most significant job title.

- **Describe your experience.** Use action verbs and specific nouns to summarize achievements and skills relevant to your targeted job.

- **Promote your "soft" skills.** Give evidence of communication, management, and interpersonal talents. Employers want more than empty assurances; try to quantify your skills and accomplishments (*Developed teamwork skills while collaborating with six-member task force in producing 20-page mission statement*).

Special Skills, Achievements, and Awards

- **Highlight your technology skills.** Remember that nearly all employers seek employees who are proficient in using the Web, e-mail, word processing, databases, spreadsheets, and presentation programs.

- **Show that you are a well-rounded individual.** List awards, experiences, and extracurricular activities—particularly if they demonstrate leadership, teamwork, reliability, loyalty, industry, initiative, efficiency, and self-sufficiency.

Final Tips

- **Look for ways to condense your data.** Omit all street addresses except your own. Consolidate your headings. Study models and experiment with formats to find the most readable and efficient groupings.

- **Omit references.** Have a list of references available for the interview, but don't include them or refer to them on your résumé unless you have a specific reason to do so.

- **Resist the urge to inflate your qualifications.** Be accurate in listing your education, grades, honors, job titles, employment dates, and job experience.

- **Proofread, proofread, proofread!** Make this important document perfect by proofreading at least three times. Ask a friend to check it, too.

Submitting

- **Follow instructions for submitting.** Learn whether the employer wants candidates to send a print résumé, e-mail résumé, plain-text version, PDF file, fax, or some other format.

- **Practice sending a plain-text résumé.** Before submitting a plain-text résumé, try sending it to yourself or friends. Perfect your skill in achieving an attractive format.

Creating Customized Cover Messages

A cover message, also known as a *cover letter* or *letter of application,* is a graceful way of introducing your résumé. Job candidates often labor over their résumés but treat the cover message as an afterthought. Some candidates even question whether a cover message is necessary in today's digital world.

Are Cover Messages Still Important?

Although candidates may question the significance of cover messages, career advisors nearly unanimously support them. CareerBuilder specialist Anthony Balderrama asked those in the field whether cover messages were a waste of time, and he was surprised at the response. "Overwhelmingly," he reported, "hiring managers and human resources personnel view cover letters as a necessity in the job hunt."[36] Career coach Heather Huhman agrees: "Cover letters allow you—in narrative form—to tell the employer exactly why hiring you, instead of the numerous other candidates, is a good decision."[37]

Cover messages reveal to employers your ability to put together complete sentences and to sound intelligent. Corporate trainer Sue Thompson declares, "You can be the smartest person within 100 miles, and maybe the right person for the job, but you will knock yourself right out of the running with a poor cover letter."[38]

Given the stiff competition for jobs today, job candidates can set themselves apart with well-written cover messages. Yet, despite the vast support for them and information on how to write these cover messages, many job hunters don't submit them, reports *The Wall Street Journal.*[39]

Photo courtesy: Daniel Goodrich

REALITY CHECK: Missing Cover Message Raises Red Flag

"A résumé without a cover letter is a red flag," warns Angela Ruggiero, Account Manager with Stanton Communications. Shown here with former basketball star Shaq O'Neill at The Greenbrier Resort's Casino Club opening, Angela says, "The absence of cover letters [suggests] to me that the candidate is sending résumés in masses, rather than customizing or personalizing to each individual company of interest."[40]

—**ANGELA RUGGIERO,** *senior account executive, Stanton Communications. Shown here with one of Stanton's clients, former basketball star Shaq O'Neal.*

Although recruiting professionals favor cover messages, they disagree about their length. Some prefer short messages with no more than two paragraphs embedded in an e-mail message.[41] Other recruiters desire longer messages that supply more information, thus giving them a better opportunity to evaluate a candidate's qualifications and writing skills. These recruiters argue that hiring and training new employees is expensive and time consuming; therefore, they welcome extra data to guide them in making the best choice the first time. Follow your judgment in writing a brief or a longer cover message. If you feel, for example, that you need space to explain in more detail what you can do for a prospective employer, do so.

Regardless of its length, a cover message should have three primary parts: (a) an opening that captures attention, introduces the message, and identifies the position; (b) a body that sells the candidate and focuses on the employer's needs; and (c) a closing that requests an interview and motivates action. When putting your cover message together, remember that the biggest mistake job seekers make when writing cover messages is making them sound too generic. You should, therefore, write a personalized, customized cover message for every position that interests you.

Gaining Attention in the Opening

Your cover message will be more appealing—and more likely to be read—if it begins by addressing the reader by name. Rather than sending your letter to the *Hiring Manager* or *Human Resources Department,* try to identify the name of the appropriate individual. Kelly

Renz, vice president for a recruiting outsourcing firm, says that savvy job seekers "take control of their application's destiny." She suggests looking on the company's website, doing an Internet search for a name, or calling the human resources department and asking the receptionist the name of the person in charge of hiring. Ms. Renz also suggests using LinkedIn to find someone working in the same department as the position in the posted job. This person may know the name of the hiring manager.[42] If you still cannot find the name of any person to address, you might replace the salutation of your letter with a descriptive subject line such as *Application for Marketing Specialist Position*.

How you open your cover message depends largely on whether the application is solicited or unsolicited. If an employment position has been announced and applicants are being solicited, you can use a direct approach. If you do not know whether a position is open and you are prospecting for a job, use an indirect approach. Whether direct or indirect, the opening should attract the attention of the reader. Strive for openings that are more imaginative than *Please consider this letter an application for the position of . . . or I would like to apply for . . . .*

Openings for Solicited Jobs.   When applying for a job that has been announced, consider some of the following techniques to open your cover message:

- **Refer to the name of an employee in the company.** Remember that employers always hope to hire known quantities rather than complete strangers.

  Brendan Borello, a member of your Customer Service Department, told me that Alliance Resources is seeking an experienced customer-service representative. The enclosed summary of my qualifications demonstrates my preparation for this position.

  At the suggestion of Heather Bolger, in your Legal Services Department, I submit my qualifications for the position of staffing coordinator.

  Montana Morano, placement director at Southwest University, told me that Dynamic Industries has an opening for a technical writer with knowledge of Web design and graphics.

- **Refer to the source of your information precisely.** If you are answering an advertisement, include the exact position advertised and the name and date of the publication. If you are responding to a position listed on an online job board, include the website name and the date the position was posted.

  From your company's website, I learned about your need for a sales representative for the Ohio, Indiana, and Illinois regions. I am very interested in this position and am confident that my education and experience are appropriate for the opening.

  My talent for interacting with people, coupled with more than five years of customer service experience, make me an ideal candidate for the director of customer relations position you advertised on the CareerJournal website on August 3.

- **Refer to the job title and describe how your qualifications fit the requirements.** Hiring managers are looking for a match between an applicant's credentials and the job needs.

  Ceradyne Company's marketing assistant opening is an excellent match with my qualifications. As a recent graduate of Western University with a major in marketing, I offer solid academic credentials as well as industry experience gained from an internship at Flotek Industries.

  Will an honors graduate with a degree in recreation and two years of part-time experience organizing social activities for a convalescent hospital qualify for your position of activity director?

  Because of my specialized training in finance and accounting at Michigan State University, I am confident that I have the qualifications you described in your advertisement for a staff accountant trainee.

Openings for Unsolicited Jobs.   If you are unsure whether a position actually exists, you might use a more persuasive opening. Because your goal is to convince this person to read on, try one of the following techniques:

- **Demonstrate an interest in and knowledge of the reader's business.** Show the hiring manager that you have done your research and that this organization is more than a mere name to you.

    Because Signa HealthNet, Inc., is organizing a new information management team for its recently established group insurance division, could you use the services of a well-trained information systems graduate who seeks to become a professional systems analyst?

    I read with great interest the article in Forbes *announcing the upcoming launch of US Bank. Congratulations on this new venture and its notable $50 million in loans precharter! The possibility of helping your bank grow is exciting, and I would like to explore a potential employment match that I am confident will be mutually beneficial.*

- **Show how your special talents and background will benefit the company.** Human resources managers need to be convinced that you can do something for them.

    Could your rapidly expanding publications division use the services of an editorial assistant who offers exceptional language skills, an honors degree from the University of Mississippi, and two years' experience in producing a campus literary publication?

In applying for an advertised job, Tonya Powell wrote the solicited cover letter shown in Figure 15.16. Notice that her opening identifies the position advertised on the company's website so that the reader knows exactly what advertisement Tonya means. Using features on her word processing program, Tonya designed her own letterhead that uses her name and looks like professionally printed letterhead paper.

More challenging are unsolicited cover messages, such as the letter of Donald Vinton shown in Figure 15.17. Because he hopes to discover or create a job, his opening must grab the reader's attention immediately. To do that, he capitalizes on company information appearing in an online article. Donald purposely kept his cover letter short and to the point because he anticipated that a busy executive would be unwilling to read a long, detailed letter. Donald's unsolicited letter "prospects" for a job. Some job candidates feel that such letters may be even more productive than efforts to secure advertised jobs, since prospecting candidates face less competition and show initiative. Notice that Donald's letter uses a personal business letter format with his return address above the date.

Promoting Your Strengths in the Message Body

Once you have captured the attention of the reader and identified your purpose in the letter opening, you should use the body of the letter to plug your qualifications for this position. If you are responding to an advertisement, you will want to explain how your preparation and experience fulfill the stated requirements. If you are prospecting for a job, you may not know the exact requirements. Your employment research and knowledge of your field, however, should give you a reasonably good idea of what is expected for this position.

It is also important to stress reader benefits. In other words, you should describe your strong points in relation to the needs of the employer. Hiring officers want you to tell them what you can do for their organizations. This is more important than telling what courses you took in college or what duties you performed in your previous jobs.

Poor:	*I have completed courses in business communication, report writing, and technical writing,*
Improved:	*Courses in business communication, report writing, and technical writing have helped me develop the research and writing skills required of your technical writers.*

Figure **15.16** Solicited Cover Letter

Uses personally designed letterhead

Tonya L. Powell

1770 Hawthorne Place, Boulder CO 80304
(303) 492-1244, tpowell@yahoo.com

May 23, 2015

Ms. Courtney L. Donahue
Director, Human Resources
Del Rio Enterprises
4839 Mountain View Avenue
Denver, CO 82511

Addresses proper person by name and title

Dear Ms. Donahue:

Identifies job and exact page where ad appeared

Your advertisement for an assistant product manager, appearing May 22 in the employment section of your company web site, immediately caught my attention because my education and training closely parallel your needs.

According to your advertisement, the job includes "assisting in the coordination of a wide range of marketing programs as well as analyzing sales results and tracking marketing budgets." A recent internship at Ventana Corporation introduced me to similar tasks. Assisting the marketing manager enabled me to analyze the promotion, budget, and overall sales success of two products Ventana was evaluating. My ten-page report examined the nature of the current market, the products' life cycles, and their sales/profit return. In addition to this research, I helped formulate a product merchandising plan and answered consumers' questions at a local trade show.

Relates writer's experience to job requirements

Discusses schooling

Intensive course work in marketing and management, as well as proficiency in computer spreadsheets and databases, has given me the kind of marketing and computer training that Del Rio probably demands in a product manager. Moreover, my recent retail sales experience and participation in campus organizations have helped me develop the kind of customer service and interpersonal skills necessary for an effective product manager.

Discusses experience

After you have examined the enclosed résumé for details of my qualifications, I would be happy to answer questions. Please call me at (303) 492-1244 to arrange an interview at your convenience so that we may discuss how my marketing experience, computer training, and interpersonal skills could contribute to Del Rio Enterprises.

Refers reader to résumé

Asks for interview and repeats main qualifications

Sincerely

Tonya L. Powell

Tonya L. Powell

Enclosure

From Guffey/Loewy, Essentials of Business Communication (with www.meguffey.com Printed Access Card), 9E. (c) 2013 Cengage Learning.

Choose your strongest qualifications and show how they fit the targeted job. Remember that students with little experience are better off spotlighting their education and its practical applications:

Poor: *I have taken classes that prepare me to be an administrative assistant.*

Improved: *Composing e-mail messages, business letters, memos, and reports in my business communication and office technology courses helped me develop the writing, language, proofreading, and computer skills mentioned in your ad for an administrative assistant.*

In the body of your letter, you may choose to discuss relevant personal traits. Employers are looking for candidates who, among other things, are team players, take responsibility, show initiative, and learn easily. Don't just list several personal traits, though; instead, include

Figure 15.17 Unsolicited Cover Letter

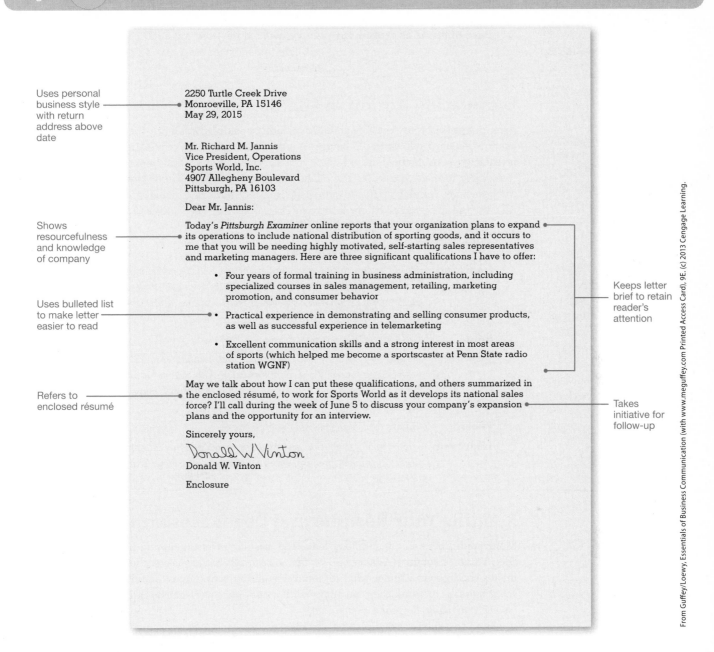

Uses personal business style with return address above date

Shows resourcefulness and knowledge of company

Uses bulleted list to make letter easier to read

Refers to enclosed résumé

Keeps letter brief to retain reader's attention

Takes initiative for follow-up

2250 Turtle Creek Drive
Monroeville, PA 15146
May 29, 2015

Mr. Richard M. Jannis
Vice President, Operations
Sports World, Inc.
4907 Allegheny Boulevard
Pittsburgh, PA 16103

Dear Mr. Jannis:

Today's *Pittsburgh Examiner* online reports that your organization plans to expand its operations to include national distribution of sporting goods, and it occurs to me that you will be needing highly motivated, self-starting sales representatives and marketing managers. Here are three significant qualifications I have to offer:

- Four years of formal training in business administration, including specialized courses in sales management, retailing, marketing promotion, and consumer behavior

- Practical experience in demonstrating and selling consumer products, as well as successful experience in telemarketing

- Excellent communication skills and a strong interest in most areas of sports (which helped me become a sportscaster at Penn State radio station WGNF)

May we talk about how I can put these qualifications, and others summarized in the enclosed résumé, to work for Sports World as it develops its national sales force? I'll call during the week of June 5 to discuss your company's expansion plans and the opportunity for an interview.

Sincerely yours,

Donald W. Vinton
Donald W. Vinton

Enclosure

From Guffey/Loewy, Essentials of Business Communication (with www.meguffey.com Printed Access Card), 9E. (c) 2013 Cengage Learning.

documentation that proves you possess these traits. Notice how the following paragraph uses action verbs to paint a picture of a promising candidate:

In addition to developing technical and academic skills at Florida Central University, I have gained interpersonal, leadership, and organizational skills. As vice president of the business students' organization, Gamma Alpha, I helped organize and supervise two successful fund-raising events. These activities involved conceptualizing the tasks, motivating others to help, scheduling work sessions, and coordinating the efforts of 35 diverse students in reaching our goal. I enjoyed my success with these activities and look forward to applying such experience in your management trainee program.

Finally, in this section or the next, refer the reader to your résumé. Do so directly or as part of another statement.

Direct reference to résumé: *Please refer to the attached résumé for additional information regarding my education, experience, and references.*

Part of another statement: *As you will notice from my enclosed résumé, I will graduate in June with a bachelor's degree in business administration.*

Motivating Action in the Closing

After presenting your case, you should conclude by asking confidently for an interview. Don't ask for the job. To do so would be presumptuous and naïve. In requesting an interview, you might suggest reader benefits or review your strongest points. Sound sincere and appreciative. Remember to make it easy for the reader to agree by supplying your telephone number and the best times to call you. In addition, keep in mind that some hiring officers prefer that you take the initiative to call them. Avoid expressions such as *I hope*, which weaken your closing. Here are possible endings:

Poor: *I hope to hear from you soon.*

Improved: *This brief description of my qualifications and the additional information on my résumé demonstrate my genuine desire to put my skills in accounting to work for McLellan and Associates. Please call me at (405) 488-2291 before 10 a.m. or after 3 p.m. to arrange an interview.*

Poor: *I look forward to a call from you.*

Improved: *To add to your staff an industrious, well-trained administrative assistant with proven Internet and communication skills, call me at (350) 492-1433 to arrange an interview. I look forward to meeting with you to discuss further my qualifications.*

Poor: *Thanks for looking over my qualifications.*

Improved: *I look forward to the opportunity to discuss my qualifications for the financial analyst position more fully in an interview. I can be reached at (213) 458-4030.*

Sending Your Résumé and Cover Message

Many applicants using technology make the mistake of not including cover messages with their résumés submitted by e-mail or fax. A résumé that arrives without a cover message makes the receiver wonder what it is and why it was sent. Some candidates either skip the cover message or think they can get by with a one-line cover such as this: *Please see attached résumé, and thanks for your consideration.*

How you submit your résumé depends on the employer's instructions, which usually involve one of the following methods:

- Submit both your cover letter and résumé in an e-mail message. Convert both to plain text.
- Send your cover letter as an e-mail message and attach your résumé (plain text, Word document, or PDF).
- Send a short e-mail message with both your cover letter and résumé attached.
- Send your cover letter and résumé as printed Word documents by U.S. mail.

If you are serious about landing the job, take the time to prepare a professional cover message. What if you are e-mailing your résumé? Just use the same cover message you would send by surface mail, but shorten it a bit. As illustrated in Figure 15.18, an inside address is unnecessary for an e-mail recipient. Also, move your return address from the top of the letter to just below your name. Include your e-mail address and phone number. Remove tabs, bullets, underlining, and italics that might be problematic in e-mail messages. For résumés submitted by fax, send the same cover message you would send by surface mail. For résumés submitted as PDF files, send the cover message as a PDF also.

Figure **15.18** E-Mail Cover Message

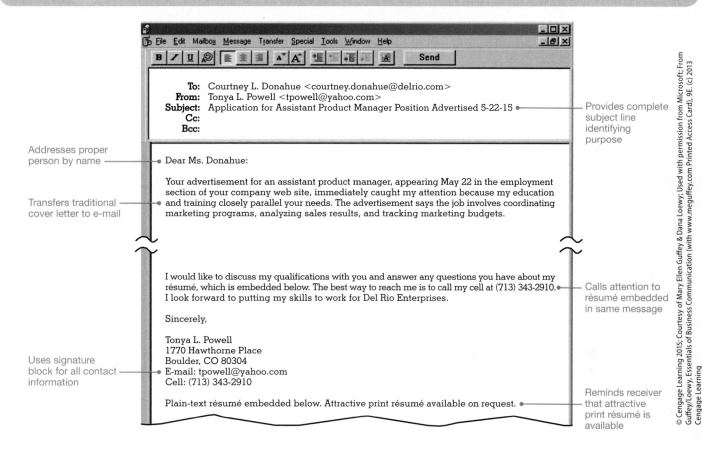

Addresses proper person by name

Transfers traditional cover letter to e-mail

Uses signature block for all contact information

Provides complete subject line identifying purpose

Calls attention to résumé embedded in same message

Reminds receiver that attractive print résumé is available

To: Courtney L. Donahue <courtney.donahue@delrio.com>
From: Tonya L. Powell <tpowell@yahoo.com>
Subject: Application for Assistant Product Manager Position Advertised 5-22-15
Cc:
Bcc:

Dear Ms. Donahue:

Your advertisement for an assistant product manager, appearing May 22 in the employment section of your company web site, immediately caught my attention because my education and training closely parallel your needs. The advertisement says the job involves coordinating marketing programs, analyzing sales results, and tracking marketing budgets.

I would like to discuss my qualifications with you and answer any questions you have about my résumé, which is embedded below. The best way to reach me is to call my cell at (713) 343-2910. I look forward to putting my skills to work for Del Rio Enterprises.

Sincerely,

Tonya L. Powell
1770 Hawthorne Place
Boulder, CO 80304
E-mail: tpowell@yahoo.com
Cell: (713) 343-2910

Plain-text résumé embedded below. Attractive print résumé available on request.

Final Tips for Successful Cover Messages

As you revise your cover message, notice how many sentences begin with *I*. Although it is impossible to talk about yourself without using *I*, you can reduce "I" domination with a number of thoughtful techniques. Make activities and outcomes, and not yourself, the subjects of sentences. Sometimes you can avoid *I* domination by focusing on the "you" view. Another way to avoid starting sentences with *I* is to move phrases from within the sentence to the beginning.

Poor: *I took classes in business communication and computer applications.*

Improved: *Classes in business communication and computer applications prepared me to . . . . (Make activities the subject.)*

Poor: *I enjoyed helping customers, which taught me to . . . .*

Improved: *Helping customers was a real pleasure and taught me to . . . . (Make outcomes the subject.)*

Poor: *I am a hardworking team player who . . . .*

Improved: *You are looking for a hardworking team player who . . . . (Use "you" view.)*

Poor: *I worked to support myself all through college, thus building . . . .*

Improved: *All through college, I worked to support myself, thus building . . . . (Move phrases to the beginning.)*

However, strive for a comfortable style. In your effort to avoid sounding self-centered, don't write unnaturally.

Like your résumé, your cover message must look professional and suggest quality. This means using a traditional letter style, such as block format. Also, be sure to print it on the same quality paper as your résumé. As with your résumé, proofread it several times yourself; then have a friend read it for content and mechanics. Don't rely on spell-check to find all the errors. Just like your résumé, your cover message must be perfect.

CHECKLIST ▶▶
Preparing and Sending a Customized Cover Letter

Opening

- **Use the receiver's name.** Whenever possible, address the proper individual by name.

- **Identify the position, where you found it, and your information source, if appropriate.** Specify the position advertised as well as the date and publication name. If someone referred you, name that person.

- **Gain the reader's attention.** Use one of these techniques: (a) tell how your qualifications fit the job specifications, (b) show knowledge of the reader's business, (c) describe how your special talents will be assets to the company, or (d) use an original and relevant expression.

Body

- **Describe what you can do for the reader.** Demonstrate how your background and training fill the job requirements.

- **Highlight your strengths.** Summarize your principal assets in terms of education, experience, and special skills. Avoid repeating specific wording from your résumé.

- **Refer to your résumé.** In this section or the closing, direct the reader to the attached résumé. Do so directly or incidentally as part of another statement.

Closing

- **Ask for an interview.** Also consider reviewing your strongest points or suggesting how your assets will benefit the company.

- **Make it easy to respond.** Tell when you can be reached during office hours, or announce when you will call the reader. Note that some recruiters prefer that you call them.

Sending

- **Include a cover message with your résumé.** Send your cover message along with your résumé as a Word attachment, embedded in an e-mail message, as a plain-text attachment, as a PDF file, or as a fax.

- **If you e-mail your cover message, put your contact information in the signature area.** Move your return address from the top of the letter to the signature block. Include your phone number and e-mail address.

Your Turn: Applying Your Job-Search Skills

As a new assistant to career advisor Heather Huhman, you are a good source of information about how first-time job seekers view the job search. She wants your input for an article she plans to write that targets recent college graduates, both young and more mature. She wonders about the following: Do students give much thought to job searching and résumé writing before they are graduate and enter the job market? How do students view networking in general and social networking sites in particular as they relate to finding jobs? Ms. Huhman suggests that you query your current and former classmates and get back to her. She would like to use the information you develop to write a meaningful article with advice for new grads.

YOUR TASK. In groups of three to four, address the topics Ms. Huhman has brought up. Ask each student to contribute at least two responses. Individually or as a group, summarize your findings in an e-mail report to <hhuhman@xxx.xxx> but delivered to your instructor. Treat this message as a short report, dividing it into logical sections with headings.

Summary of Learning Objectives

1 Prepare to search for a job in the digital age by understanding the changing job market, identifying your interests, assessing your qualifications, and exploring career opportunities. Searching for a job in this digital age has dramatically changed. Search engines, job boards, and social networks have all become indispensable tools in hunting for a job. Another change involves the emphasis today on what the employer wants, not what the candidate wants. Before drafting a résumé, job candidates should begin the job-search process by learning about themselves, their field of interest, and their qualifications. How do their skills match what employers seek? Candidates can find some of this information by searching the Web, visiting a campus career center, taking a summer job, interviewing someone in their field, volunteering, or joining professional organizations. This is the time to identify job availability, the skills and qualifications required, duties, and salaries.

2 Develop savvy search strategies by recognizing job sources and using digital tools to explore the open job market. The primary sources of jobs today are networking (46 percent), Internet job boards and company websites (25 percent), and agencies (14 percent). In searching the open job market—that is, jobs that are listed and advertised—candidates have numerous tools, many of which are digital. Candidates can study the big job boards, such as CareerBuilder, Monster, and CollegeGrad. However, if they have a specific company in mind, they should go directly to that company's website and check its openings and possibilities. An increasingly popular and effective website for professional recruiting is LinkedIn. Nearly all serious candidates post profiles there. Candidates seeking jobs in specialized fields should search some of the many niche sites, such as Accountemps for temporary accounting positions or Dice for technology positions.

Go to
www.cengagebrain.com and use your access code to unlock valuable student resources.

3 Expand your job-search strategies by using both traditional and digital tools in pursuing the hidden job market. Estimates suggest that as many as 80 percent of jobs are part of the hidden job market—that is, never advertised. Successful job candidates find jobs in the hidden market through networking. An effective networking procedure involves (a) developing a contact list, (b) reaching out to these contacts in person and online in search of referrals, and (c) following up on referrals. As electronic media and digital tools continue to change our lives, job candidates can use social media networks to extend their networking efforts. One of the most fruitful networking resources is LinkedIn. Other effective networking strategies involve building a personal brand, preparing a professional business card with a tagline, composing a 30- to 60-second elevator speech that describes what the candidate can offer, and developing a strong online presence.

4 Organize your qualifications and information into effective résumé segments to create a winning, customized résumé. Because of intense competition, candidates must customize their résumés for every position sought. Chronological résumés, which list work and education by dates, rank highest with recruiters. Functional résumés, which highlight skills instead of jobs, may be helpful for people with little experience, those changing careers, or those having negative employment histories. In preparing a résumé, candidates should organize their skills and achievements to aim at a particular job or company. Studying models helps candidates effectively arrange the résumé main heading and the optional career objective, summary of qualifications, education, work experience, capabilities, awards, and activities sections. The most effective résumés include action verbs to appeal to human readers and job-specific nouns that become keywords selected by applicant tracking systems.

5 Optimize your job search and résumé by taking advantage of today's digital tools. Many companies use automated applicant tracking systems to sort incoming résumés. To increase the probability of a résumé being selected by the system, candidates must include specific keywords, especially nouns that name job titles, technical skills, and tools used or specific experience. An additional tool to showcase a candidate's qualifications is a career e-portfolio. This collection of digital files can feature the candidate's talents, accomplishments, and technical skills. It may include examples of academic performance, photographs, multimedia files, and other items beyond what can be shown in a résumé. A video résumé enables candidates to present their experience, qualifications, and interests in video form. A hot trend among creative candidates is the infographic résumé, which provides charts, graphics, and time lines to illustrate a candidate's work history and experience. Most candidates, however, should start with a basic print-based résumé from which they can make a plain-text résumé stripped of formatting to be embedded within e-mail messages and submitted online.

6 Draft and submit a customized cover message to accompany a print or digital résumé. Although cover messages are questioned by some in today's digital world, recruiters and hiring managers overwhelmingly favor them. Cover messages help recruiters make decisions, and they enable candidates to set themselves apart from others. The opening of a cover message should gain attention by addressing the receiver by name and identifying the job. It may also identify a person who referred the applicant. The body of the message builds interest by stressing the candidate's strengths in relation to the stated requirements. It explains what the candidate can do for the targeted company. In the body or closing, the writer should refer to the résumé, request an interview, and make it easy for the receiver to respond. Cover messages sent by e-mail should be shortened a bit and include complete contact information in the signature block.

Chapter Review

1. In this digital age, what is the primary route to finding a job? (Obj. 1)

2. When preparing to search for a job, what should you do before writing a résumé? (Obj. 1)

3. List eight ways you can explore career opportunities while still in college. (Obj. 1)

4. What are the current trends in sources of new jobs? Which sources are trending upward and which are trending downward? (Obj. 2)

5. Although one may not actually find a job on the Internet, how can the big job boards be helpful to job hunters? (Obj. 2)

6. What is the hidden job market, and how can candidates find jobs in it? (Obj. 3)

7. In searching for a job, how can you build a personal brand, and why is it important to do so? (Obj. 3)

8. What is a customized résumé, and why should you have one? (Obj. 4)

9. How do chronological and functional résumés differ, and what are the advantages and disadvantages of each? (Obj. 4)

10. Describe a summary of qualifications, and explain why it is increasingly popular on résumés. (Obj. 4)

11. What is an ATS, and how does it affect the way you prepare a résumé? (Obj. 5)

12. How can you maximize the keyword hits in your résumé? What three categories are most important? (Obj. 5)

13. What is a career e-portfolio? How can having one benefit you? (Obj. 5)

14. What are the three parts of a cover message, and what is contained in each part? (Obj. 6)

15. Why is it important to include a cover message with all résumés you send, even if you send them by e-mail? (Obj. 6)

Critical Thinking

1. How has job searching for candidates and job placement for hiring managers changed in the digital age? In your opinion, have the changes had a positive or a negative effect? Why? (Obj. 1)

2. The authors of *Guerrilla Marketing for Job Hunters*[43] claim that every year 50 million U.S. jobs are filled, almost all without a job posting. Why do you think businesses avoid advertising job openings? If jobs are unlisted, how can a candidate locate them? (Obj. 3)

3. Some employment authors claim that the paper résumé is dead or dying. What's behind this assertion, and how should current job candidates respond? (Obj. 4)

4. Why might it be more effective to apply for unsolicited jobs than for advertised jobs? Discuss the advantages and disadvantages of letters that "prospect" for jobs. (Obj. 6)

5. **Ethical Issue:** After many months of job searching, recent grad Marcy finally found a job. On her résumé, she fudged a little by boosting her grade point average and by claiming an internship that she applied for but didn't actually get. These small white lies were absolutely necessary, she reasoned, in such a competitive and tough job market. She felt that she needed extra ammunition in her battle to edge out other job hunters. She breezed through the interview with no problems. Is Marcy justified in her actions, and is she home free now that she has been hired?

Activities

15.1 Document for Analysis: Poorly Written Résumé (Obj. 4)

One effective way to improve your writing skills is to critique and edit the résumé of someone else.

YOUR TASK. Analyze the following poorly organized résumé. List at least eight weaknesses. Your instructor may ask you to revise sections of this résumé before showing you an improved version.

Résumé of Isabella R. Jimenez

1340 East Phillips Ave., Apt. D Littleton, CO 80126
Phone 455-5182 • E-Mail: Hotchilibabe@gmail.com

OBJECTIVE

I'm dying to land a first job in the "real world" with a big profitable company that will help me get ahead in the accounting field.

SKILLS

Word processing, Internet browsers (Explorer and Google), Powerpoint, Excel, type 40 wpm, databases, spreadsheets; great composure in stressful situations; 3 years as leader and supervisor and 4 years in customer service

EDUCATION

Arapahoe Community College, Littleton, Colorado. AA degree Fall 2012

Now I am pursuing a BA in Accounting at CSU-Pueblo, majoring in Accounting; my minor is Finance. My expected degree date is June 2014; I recieved a Certificate of Completion in Entry Level Accounting in December 2011.

I graduated East High School, Denver, CO in 2007.

Highlights:

- Named Line Manger of the Month at Target, 08/2008 and 09/2009
- Obtained a Certificate in Entry Level Accounting, June 2012
- Chair of Accounting Society, Spring and fall 2012
- Dean's Honor List, Fall 2013
- Financial advisor training completed through Primerica (May 2013)
- Webmaster for M.E.Ch.A, Spring 2014

Part-Time Employment

Financial Consultant, 2013 to present
I worked only part-time (January 2013-present) for Primerica Financial Services, Pueblo, CO to assist clients in refinancing a mortgage or consolidating a current mortgage loan and also to advice clients in assessing their need for life insurance.

Target, Littleton, CO. As line manager, from September 2007-March 2011, I supervised 22 cashiers and front-end associates. I helped to write schedules, disciplinary action notices, and performance appraisals. I also kept track of change drawer and money exchanges; occasionally was manager on duty for entire store.

Mr. K's Floral Design of Denver. I taught flower design from August, 2007 to September, 2008. I supervised 5 florists, made floral arrangements for big events like weddings, send them to customers, and restocked flowers.

15.2 Document for Analysis: Poor Cover Letter (Obj. 6)

The following cover letter accompanies Isabella Jimenez's résumé **(Activity 15.1)**.

YOUR TASK. Analyze each section of the following cover letter and list its weaknesses. Your instructor may ask you to revise this letter before showing you an improved version.

To Whom It May Concern:

I saw your internship position yesterday and would like to apply right away. It would be so exiting to work for your esteemed firm!

An internship would really give me much needed real-world experience and help my career.

I have all the qualifications you require in your add and more. I am a junior at Colorado State University-Pueblo and an Accounting major (with a minor in Finance). Accounting and Finance are my passion and I want to become a CPA and a financial advisor. I have taken Intermediate I and II and now work as a financial advisor with Primerica Financial Services in Pueblo. I should also tell you that I was at Target for four years. I learned alot, but my heart is in accounting and finance.

I am a team player, a born leader, motivated, reliable, and I show excellent composure in stressful situation, for example, when customers complain. I put myself through school and always carry at least 15 units while working part time.

You will probably agree that I am a good candidate for your internship position, which should start July 1. I feel that my motivation, passion, and strong people skills will serve your company well.

Sincerely,

15.3 Beginning Your Job Search With Self-Analysis (Obj. 1)

E-mail

YOUR TASK. In an e-mail or a memo addressed to your instructor, answer the questions in the section "Beginning Your Job Search With Self-Analysis" on page 544. Draw a conclusion from your answers. What kind of career, company, position, and location seem to fit your self-analysis?

15.4 Evaluating Your Qualifications (Objs. 1–3)

YOUR TASK. Prepare four worksheets that inventory your qualifications in these areas: employment, education, capabilities and skills, and honors and activities. Use active verbs when appropriate and specific nouns that describe job titles and skills.

a. **Employment.** Begin with your most recent job or internship. For each position list the following information: employer; job title; dates of employment; and three to five duties, activities, or accomplishments. Emphasize activities related to your job goal. Strive to quantify your achievements.

b. **Education.** List degrees, certificates, and training accomplishments. Include courses, seminars, and skills that are relevant to your job goal. Calculate your grade point average in your major.

c. **Capabilities and skills.** List all capabilities and skills that qualify you for the job you seek. Use words and phrases such as *skilled, competent, trained, experienced,* and *ability to*. Also list five or more qualities or interpersonal skills necessary for success in your chosen field. Write action statements demonstrating that you possess some of these qualities. Empty assurances aren't good enough; try to show evidence (*Developed teamwork skills by working with a committee of eight to produce a . . .*).

d. **Awards, honors, and activities.** Explain any awards so that the reader will understand them. List campus, community, and professional activities that suggest you are a well-rounded individual or possess traits relevant to your target job.

15.5 Choosing a Career Path (Obj. 1)

Web

Many people know amazingly little about the work done in various occupations and the training requirements.

YOUR TASK. Use the online *Occupational Outlook Handbook* at **http://www.bls.gov/OCO**, prepared by the Bureau of Labor

Statistics (BLS), to learn more about an occupation of your choice. This is the nation's premier source for career information. The career profiles featured here cover hundreds of occupations and describe what people in these occupations do, the work environment, how to get these jobs, pay, and more. Each profile also includes BLS employment projections for the 2010–2020 decade.

Find the description of a position for which you could apply in two to five years. Learn about what workers do on the job, working conditions, training and education needed, earnings, and expected job prospects. Print the pages from the *Occupational Outlook Handbook* that describe employment in the area in which you are interested. If your instructor directs, attach these copies to the cover letter you will write in **Activity 15.10**.

15.6 Locating Salary Information (Obj. 1)

Web

What salary can you expect in your chosen career?

YOUR TASK. Visit **http://www.salary.com** and select an occupation based on the kind of employment you are seeking now or will be seeking after you graduate. Skip any advertisements that pop up. Use your current geographic area or the location where you would like to work after graduation. What wages can you expect in this occupation? Click to learn more about this occupation. Take notes on three or four interesting bits of information you uncovered about this career. Bring a printout of the wage information to class and be prepared to discuss what you learned.

15.7 Searching the Job Market (Obj. 1)

Web

Where are the jobs? Even though you may not be in the market at the moment, become familiar with the kinds of available positions because job awareness should be an important part of your education.

YOUR TASK. Clip or print a job advertisement or announcement from (a) the classified section of a newspaper, (b) a job board on the Web, (c) a company website, or (d) a professional association listing. Select an advertisement or announcement describing the kind of employment you are seeking now or plan to seek when you graduate. Save this advertisement or announcement to attach to the résumé you will write in **Activity 15.9**.

15.8 Posting a Résumé on the Web (Obj. 2)

Web

Learn about the procedure for posting résumés at job boards on the Web.

YOUR TASK. Prepare a list of three websites where you could post your résumé. In class discussion or in an e-mail to your instructor, describe the procedure involved in posting a résumé and the advantages for each site.

15.9 Writing Your Résumé (Obj. 4)

YOUR TASK. Using the data you developed in **Activity 15.4**, write your résumé. Aim it at the full-time job, part-time position, or internship that you located in **Activity 15.7**. Attach the job listing to your résumé. Also prepare a list of references. Revise your résumé until it is perfect.

15.10 Preparing Your Cover Message (Obj. 6)

YOUR TASK. Using the job listing you found for **Activity 15.7**, write a cover message introducing your résumé. Decide whether it should be a letter or an e-mail. Again, revise until it is perfect.

15.11 Using Social Media in the Job Search (Obj. 2)

Social Media

One of the fastest-growing trends in employment is using social media sites during the job search.

YOUR TASK. Locate one social media site and set up an account. Explore the site to discover how job seekers can use it to search for a job and how employers can use it to find job candidates. Be prepared to share your findings in class.

15.12 Tweeting to Find a Job (Obj. 5)

Social Media **Team** **Web**

Twitter résumés are a new twist on job hunting. While most job seekers struggle to contain their credentials on one page, others are tweeting their credentials in 140 characters or fewer! Here is an example from The Ladders.com:

RT #Susan Moline seeks a LEAD/SR QA ENG JOB http://bit.ly/1ThaW @TalentEvolution - http://bit.ly/QB5DC @TweetMyJobs.com #résumé #QA-Jobs-CA

Are you scratching your head? Let's translate: (a) RT stands for retweet, allowing your Twitter followers to repeat this message to their followers. (b) The hashtag (#) always means *subject;* prefacing your name, it makes you easy to find. (c) The uppercase abbreviations indicate the job title, here *Lead Senior Quality Assurance Engineer.* (d) The first link is a "tiny URL," a short, memorable Web address or alias provided free by TinyURL.com and other URL-shrinking services. The first short link reveals the job seeker's Talent Evolution profile page; the second directs viewers to a job seeker profile created on TweetMyJobs.com. (e) The hashtags indicate the search terms used as seen here: name, quality assurance jobs in California, and the broad term *résumé.* You may want to visit the career site The Ladders.com at **http://www .theladders.com** and view the many articles for job seekers listed under the category Career Advice. When doing research from within Twitter, use the @ symbol with a specific Twitter user name or the # symbol for a subject search.

YOUR TASK. As a team or individually, search the Web for *tweet résumé*. Pick one of the sites offering to tweet your résumé for you—for example, TweetMyJobs.com or Tweet My Résumé. Describe to your peers the job-search process via Twitter presented on that website. Some services are free, whereas others come with charges. If you select a commercial service, critically evaluate its sales pitch and its claims. Is it worthwhile to spend money on this service? Do clients find jobs? How does the service try to demonstrate that? As a group or individually, share the results with the class.

15.13 Analyzing and Building Student E-Portfolios (Obj. 5)

Communication Technology **Team** **Web**

Take a minute to conduct a Google search on your name. What comes up? Are you proud of what you see? If you want to change that information—and especially if you are in the job market—think about creating a career e-portfolio. Building such a portfolio has many benefits. It can give you an important digital tool to connect with a large audience. It can also help you expand your technology skills, confirm your strengths, realize areas for improvement, and establish goals for improvement. Many students are creating e-portfolios with the help of their schools.

YOUR TASK NO. 1. Before attempting to build your own career e-portfolio, take a look at those of other students. Use the Google search term *student career e-portfolio* to see lots of samples. For example, the New York City College of Technology (click **Student Samples**) provides many student e-portfolios. Your instructor may assign you individually or as a team to visit specific digital portfolio sites and summarize your findings in a memo or a brief oral presentation. You could focus on the composition of the site, page layout, links provided, software tools used, colors selected, or types of documents included.

YOUR TASK NO. 2. Next, examine websites that provide tutorials and tips on how to build career e-portfolios. One of the best sites is hosted by San Jose State University's School of Library and Information Science. Use Google to check its tutorial. Your instructor may have you individually or as team write a memo summarizing tips on how to create an e-portfolio and choose the types of documents to include. Alternatively, your instructor may ask you to actually create a career e-portfolio.

15.14 Exploring Infographic Résumés (Obj. 5)

The latest rage in résumés is infographics. However, are they appropriate for every field?

YOUR TASK. Using your favorite browser, locate 10 to 15 infographic résumés. Analyze them for readability, formatting, and color. How many use time lines? What other similarities do you see? What career fields do they represent? Do you find any in your career field? In terms of your career field, what are the pros and cons of creating an infographic résumé? Do you think an infographic résumé would improve your chances of securing an interview? In an e-mail to your instructor, summarize your findings and answers to these questions.

Chat About It

In each chapter you will find five discussion questions related to the chapter material. Your instructor may assign these topics for you to discuss in class, in an online chat room, or on an online discussion board. Some of the discussion topics may require outside research. You may also be asked to read and respond to postings made by your classmates.

Topic 1: In regard to hiring, conventional wisdom holds that it's all about whom you know. What advice would you give a friend in the job market who wants to use the Web to learn about specific companies and possibly pick up referrals from insiders?

Topic 2: In your opinion, what is the difference between honest self-marketing and deception? What are some examples from your experience?

Topic 3: Why do you think it is so important to customize your résumé for each employer and job for which you apply? How do you think employers will respond to a customized résumé versus a generic résumé? Is creating a customized résumé for each position worth your time and effort? Share your opinions with your classmates.

Topic 4: Assume you have decided to prepare a video résumé. What would you say and do in the video? What would you wear? What could you do in the video to impress potential employers?

Topic 5: Many employers will not even look at a résumé unless it is accompanied by a cover message. Why do you think cover messages are so important to potential employers? What would you include in a cover message to impress employers? Share your thoughts and ideas with your classmates.

C.L.U.E. Grammar & Mechanics | *Review 15*

Total Review

Each of the following sentences has a total of **three** errors in grammar, punctuation, capitalization, usage, or spelling. On a separate sheet, write a correct version. Avoid adding new phrases or rewriting sentences in your own words. When finished, compare your responses with the key beginning on page Key-3.

EXAMPLE: If you have 10 or fewer years' of experience, its customary to prepare a one-page résumé.

REVISION: If you have **ten** or fewer **years** of experience, **it's** customary to prepare a one-page résumé.

1. When searching for jobs candidates discovered that the résumé is more likely to be used to screen candidate's then for making hiring decisions.

2. Todays employers use sights such as Facebook to learn about potential employees. Which means that a job seeker must maintain a professional online presence.

3. To conduct a safe online job search, you should: (a) Use only reputable job boards, (2) keep careful records, and (c) limit the number of sites on which you post your résumé.

4. If I was you I would shorten my résumé to 1 page and include a summary of qualifications.

5. Mitchell wondered whether it was alright to ask his professor for employment advise?

6. At last months staff meeting team members examined several candidates résumés.

7. Rather then schedule face to face interviews the team investigated videoconferencing.

8. 11 applicants will be interviewed on April 10th, consequently, we may need to work late to accommodate them.

9. Although as many as twenty-five percent of jobs are found on the Internet the principle source of jobs still involves networking.

10. If Troy had went to the companies own website he might have seen the position posted immediately.

Notes

1. *#ENTRYLEVELtweet: Taking Your Career From Classroom to Cubicle.* (2010). Silicon Valley: Thinkhaha ebook.

2. Huhman, H. (2013). Five hiring myths you need to know. Retrieved from http://www.careerrealism.com/hiring-process-myths

3. Huhman, H. (n.d.). Networking 360: Coming full circle with networking. Retrieved from http://www.careerrealism.com/networking-360-coming-full-circle-networking

4. Huhman, H. (2013). Five hiring myths you need to know. Retrieved from http://www.careerrealism.com/hiring-process-myths

5. Huhman, H. (2009, March 12). Guest post from Heather Huhman: Impressing hiring managers to get your dream job. Retrieved from http://awesomeandunemployed.wordpress.com/2009/12/03/impress-hiring-mgrs

6. Adams, S. (2011, June 7). Networking is still the best way to find a job, survey says. Retrieved from http://www.forbes.com/sites/susanadams/2011/06/07/networking-is-still-the-best-way-to-find-a-job-survey-says

7. Waldman, J. (2012, February 26). 10 differences between the job search of today and of yesterday. Retrieved from http://www.careerrealism.com/job-search-differences

8. Bureau of Labor Statistics. (2010, September 14). Economic news release: Employee tenure summary. Retrieved from http://www.bls.gov/news.release/tenure.nr0.htm. See also Kimmit, R. M. (2007, January 23). Why job churn is good. *The Washington Post*, p. A17. Retrieved from http://www.washingtonpost.com/wp-dyn/content/article/2007/01/22/AR2007012201089.html

9. Adams, S. (2012, July 25). Odds are that your internship will get you a job. Retrieved from http://www.forbes.com/sites/susanadams/2012/07/25/odds-are-your-internship-will-get-you-a-job

10. Adams, S. (2011, June 7). Networking is still the best way to find a job, survey says. Retrieved from http://www.forbes.com/sites/susanadams/2011/06/07/networking-is-still-the-best-way-to-find-a-job-survey-says

11. Mathison, D., & Finney, M. I. (2009). *Unlock the hidden job market: 6 steps to a successful job search when times are tough.* Upper Saddle River, NJ: Pearson Education, Inc., FI Press. See also Poplinger, H., as reported by Jessica Dickler (2009, June 10) in The hidden job market. Retrieved from CNNMoney.com at http://money.cnn.com/2009/06/09/news/economy/hidden_jobs

12. Right Management. (2012, August 9). Networking, not Internet cruising, still lands most jobs. Retrieved from http://www.right.com/news-and-events/press-releases/2012-press-releases/item23658.aspx

13. Weber, L., & Kwoh, L. (2013, January 9). Beware the phantom job listing. *The Wall Street Journal*, pp. B1 and B6.

14. Mathison, D., & Finney, M. I. (2009). *Unlock the hidden job market: 6 steps to a successful job search when times are tough.* Upper Saddle River, NJ: Pearson Education, Inc., FI Press. See also Poplinger, H., as reported by Jessica Dickler (2009, June 10) in The hidden job market. Retrieved from CNNMoney.com at http://money.cnn.com/2009/06/09/news/economy/hidden_jobs

15. Richardson, V. (2011, March 16). Five ways inside the 'hidden job market.' Retrieved from http://www.dailyfinance.com/2011/03/16/five-ways-inside-the-hidden-job-market

16. Adams, S. (2012, March 27). Make LinkedIn help you find a job. Retrieved from http://www.forbes.com/sites/susanadams/2012/04/27/make-linkedin-help-you-find-a-job-2

17. Ibid.

18. Photo essay based on Albanesius, C. (2013, March 15). Need a job? Tap into your Facebook network, study finds. PC Mag. Retrieved from http://www.pcmag.com

19. Doyle, A. (n.d.). Facebook and professional networking. Retrieved from http://jobsearch.about.com/od/networking/a/facebook.htm

20. Ibid.

21. Parker, C. (2012, April 8). Silicon Alley: What's your Web presence? Retrieved from *New York Post* at http://www.nypost.com/p/news/business/digital_resume_f4bef9sMnoB77AhaOmKdeM

22. Hansen, K. (n.d.). From *Tell me about yourself: Storytelling that propels careers* (Ten Speed Press). Excerpt appearing in Heather Huhman's blog at http://www.personalbrandingblog.com/how-to-write-your-60-second-elevator-pitch

23. Isaacs, K. (2012). How to decide on résumé length. Retrieved from http://career-advice.monster.com/resumes-cover-letters/resume-writing-tips/how-to-decide-on-resume-length/article.aspx

24. Green, A. (2012, June 20). 10 things to leave off your résumé. Retrieved from http://money.usnews.com/money/blogs/outside-voices-careers/2012/06/20/10-things-to-leave-off-your-resume

25. Korkki, P. (2007, July 1). So easy to apply, so hard to be noticed. *The New York Times*. Retrieved from http://www.nytimes.com/2007/07/01/business/yourmoney/01career.html

26. Berrett, D. (2013, January 25). My GRE score says I'm smart. Hire me. *The Chronicle of Higher Education*, A4.

27. Matuson, R. C. (n.d.). Recession-proof your career. Retrieved from http://www.hcareers.com/us/resourcecenter/tabid/306/articleid/522/default.aspx

28. Based on Needleman, S. (2010, February 2). Job hunters, beware. *The Wall Street Journal*. Retrieved from http://online.wsj.com/article/SB10001424052748704107204575039361105870740.html?KEYWORDS=job+hunters+beware

29. Struzik, E., IBM expert quoted in Weber, L. (2012, January 24). Your résumé vs. oblivion. *The Wall Street Journal*, p. B6.

30. Optimalresume.com. (n.d.). Optimizing your résumé for scanning and tracking. Retrieved from http://www.montclair.edu/CareerServices/OptimalsScannedresumes.pdf

31. Ibid.

32. Krum, R. (2012, September 10). Is your résumé hopelessly out of date? Retrieved from http://infonewt.com/blog/2012/9/10/infographic-resumes-interview-by-the-art-of-doing.html

33. Larsen, M. (2011, Nov. 8). Infographic résumés: Fad or trend? Retrieved from http://www.recruiter.com/i/infographic-resumes

34. Ibid.

35. Zupek, R. (2008, March 27). Honesty is the best policy in résumés and interviews. Retrieved from Careerbuilder.com at http://msn.careerbuilder.com/Article/MSN-1854-Cover-Letters-Resumes-Honesty-is-the-Best-Policy-in-R%C3%A9sum%C3%A9s-and-Interviews

36. Balderrama, S. (2009, February 26). Do you still need a cover letter? Retrieved from http://msn.careerbuilder.com/Article/MSN-1811-Cover-Letters-Resumes-Do-You-Still-Need-a-Cover-Letter

37. Quoted in Doyle, A. (2012, July 14). Do you need a cover letter? Retrieved from http://jobsearch.about.com/b/2012/07/14/do-you-need-a-cover-letter.htm

38. Quoted in Balderrama, S. (2009, February 26). Do you still need a cover letter? Retrieved from http://msn.careerbuilder.com/Article/MSN-1811-Cover-Letters-Resumes-Do-You-Still-Need-a-Cover-Letter

39. Needleman, S. E. (2010, March 9). Standout letters to cover your bases. *The Wall Street Journal*, p. D4.

40. Ibid.

41. Balderrama, S. (2009, February 26). Do you still need a cover letter? Retrieved from http://msn.careerbuilder.com/Article/MSN-1811-Cover-Letters-Resumes-Do-You-Still-Need-a-Cover-Letter

42. Korkki, P. (2009, July 18). Where, oh where, has my application gone? *The New York Times*. Retrieved from http://www.nytimes.com/2009/07/19/jobs/19career.html?_r=1&scp=1&sq=Where,%20oh%20where,%20has%20my%20application%20gone&st=cse

43. Levinson, J. C., & Perry, D. (2011). *Guerrilla marketing for job hunters 3.0.* Hoboken, NJ: John Wiley & Sons.

Interviewing and Following Up

OBJECTIVES

After studying this chapter, you should be able to

1 Explain the purposes and types of job interviews, including screening, one-on-one, panel, group, sequential, stress, and online interviews.

2 Describe what to do *before* an interview, including ensuring professional phone techniques, researching the target company, rehearsing success stories, cleaning up digital dirt, and fighting fear.

3 Describe what to do *during* an interview, including controlling nonverbal messages and answering typical interview questions.

4 Describe what to do *after* an interview, including thanking the interviewer, contacting references, and writing follow-up messages.

5 Prepare additional employment documents such as applications, rejection follow-up messages, acceptance messages, and resignation letters.

© iStockphoto.com/sturti

Sharpening Job Interview Skills for Rookies

Everyone agrees that job interviews are stressful, especially for rookies and recent grads. If you are new to the job market or changing careers, Don Georgevich offers practical advice. A leading authority in job interviewing and résumé writing, Georgevich helps job candidates sharpen their skills so that they are hired for the jobs they want. The author of *The Complete Interview Answer Guide* and countless job-related YouTube

Courtesy of Don Georgevich

videos and Internet articles, Georgevich shares special advice for those who are new to the job search process.

"For new grads, preparation for the interview is crucial," he stressed in an e-mail interview with Mary Ellen Guffey.[1] "The more you study the company and the job description combined with how you believe your skills and experiences fit in, the more prepared you will be. You can even predict what to expect in a typical interview. After a few interviews, you will be able to identify key areas the interviewer will target and soon you'll be able to predict nearly every aspect of the interview, and even control it to a degree."

When asked how new grads and career changers can gain traction in a competitive job market, he stressed demonstrating transferable skills. For example, candidates can say, "I have [blank] skills and I can use them to do [blank] for you." Job seekers need to connect the dots for employers and show how their qualifications fit the targeted position. "All too often," he says, "job seekers leave it up to the interviewer to figure out what they are good at doing instead of taking a proactive stance."

Job seekers frequently ask Georgevich how to respond when the recruiter concludes the interview and asks, *Do you have any questions?* In an Internet article, Georgevich advised, "Many people make a critical mistake, believing they will save the interviewer's time by declining to ask anything. Unfortunately, this is itself a trap! If you fail to ask anything, it will seem that you have no further interest in the employer beyond what you can get for a paycheck. If you ask the wrong question, such as one about compensation, things become that much worse!"[2]

The best way to conclude an interview, says Georgevich, is to ask meaningful questions, such as *What is a typical week like?* or *Can you give me a six-month outlook on this position and where you see it going?* From the beginning of the interview to the end, the hiring manager wants to discover whether you are truly invested in the company.[3]

Critical Thinking

- Can novice job seekers predict what a job interview will involve?

- How is interviewing a two-way street? What does this mean for a job candidate?

- How can job seekers show recruiters or hiring managers that they are "invested" in a position during the job interview?

The Purposes and Types of Job Interviews

LEARNING OBJECTIVE **1**
Explain the purposes and types of job interviews, including screening, one-on-one, panel, group, sequential, stress, and online interviews.

Whether you are completing your education and searching for your first serious position or are in the workforce and striving to change jobs—a job interview can be life changing. Because employment is a major part of everyone's life, the job interview takes on enormous importance.

Most people consider job interviews extremely stressful, eliciting as much or more anxiety than first dates. However, the more you learn about the process and the more prepared you are, the less stress you will feel. Moreover, a job interview is a two-way street. It is not just about being judged by the employer. You, the applicant, will be using the job interview to evaluate the employer. Do you really want to work for this organization?

This chapter will increase your interviewing effectiveness and confidence by presenting the latest tips and trends in employment interviewing. You will be better prepared and feel much less stress if you know the purposes and kinds of interviews. This chapter teaches you how to gather information about a prospective employer, how to project a professional image, and how to reduce nervousness during an interview. You will learn about the tendency of today's recruiters to regularly check social media and the Internet to vet applicants in this digital age. This chapter presents favorite interview questions and possible responses. It even discusses how to cope with illegal inquiries and salary matters. Moreover, you will receive pointers on significant questions you can ask during an interview. Finally, you will learn how to follow up successfully after an interview.

Yes, job interviews can be intimidating and stressful. However, you can expect to ace an interview when you know what's coming and when you prepare thoroughly. Remember, preparation often determines who gets the job. First, though, you need to know the purposes of employment interviews and what types of interviews you might encounter in your job search.

Purposes of Employment Interviews

An interview has several purposes for you as a job candidate. It is an opportunity to (a) convince the employer of your potential, (b) learn more about the job and the company, and (c) expand on the information in your résumé. This is the time for you to gather information about whether you would fit into the company culture. You should also be thinking about whether this job suits your career goals.

From the employer's perspective, the interview is an opportunity to (a) assess your abilities in relation to the requirements for the position; (b) discuss your training, experience, knowledge, and abilities in more detail; (c) see what drives and motivates you; and (d) decide whether you would fit into the organization.

Types of Employment Interviews

Job applicants generally face two kinds of interviews: screening interviews and hiring/ placement interviews. You must succeed in the first to proceed to the second. Once you make it to the hiring/placement interview, you will find a variety of interview styles, including one-on-one, panel, group, sequential, stress, and online interviews. You will be better prepared if you know what to expect in each type of interview.

Screening Interviews.   Screening interviews do just that—they screen candidates to eliminate those who fail to meet minimum requirements. Companies use screening interviews to save time and money by weeding out lesser-qualified candidates before scheduling face-to-face interviews. Although some screening interviews are conducted during job fairs or on college campuses, many screening interviews take place on the telephone, and some take place online.[4]

Some companies computerize their screening interviews. For example, Lowe's Home Improvement has applicants access a website where they answer a series of ethics-related questions. Retail giant Walmart screens cashiers, stockers, and customer-service representatives with a multiple-choice questionnaire that applicants answer by pushing buttons on a phone keypad.[5]

During a screening interview, the interviewer will probably ask you to provide details about the education and experience listed on your résumé; therefore, you must be prepared to

Finding the right fit with an organization is about more than having the right technical skills and experience. For example, Chick-fil-A screens potential employees for values including loyalty, civic involvement, and adherence to the company's closed-on-Sundays policy. Zappos requires interviewees to participate in a zany team activity and attend happy hour with longtime employees. Some university academic departments judge professorial candidates based on their political leanings. How can job seekers determine if they are a good fit for an organization?[6]

© Mark Richards/PhotoEdit

promote your qualifications. Remember that the person conducting the screening interview is trying to determine whether you should move on to the next step in the interview process.

A screening interview may be as short as five minutes. Even though it may be short, don't treat it casually. If you don't perform well during the screening interview, it may be your last interview with that organization. You can use the tips that follow in this chapter to succeed during the screening process.

Hiring/Placement Interviews. The most promising candidates selected from screening interviews are invited to hiring/placement interviews. Hiring managers want to learn whether candidates are motivated, qualified, and a good fit for the position. Their goal is to learn how the candidate would fit into their organization. Conducted in depth, hiring/placement interviews take many forms.

One-on-One Interviews. In one-on-one interviews, which are the most common type, you can expect to sit down with a company representative and talk about the job and your qualifications. If the representative is the hiring manager, questions will be specific and job related. If the representative is from human resources, the questions will probably be more general.

Panel Interviews. Panel interviews are typically conducted by people who will be your supervisors and colleagues. Usually seated around a table, interviewers take turns asking questions. Panel interviews are advantageous because they save the company time and money, and they show you how the staff works together. If possible before these interviews, try to gather basic biographical information about each panel member. When answering questions, maintain eye contact with the questioner as well as with the others. Expect to repeat information you may have given in earlier interviews.[7] Try to take notes during the interview so that you can remember each person's questions and what was important to that individual.

Group Interviews. Group interviews occur when a company interviews several candidates for the same position at the same time. Some employers use this technique to measure leadership skills and communication styles. During a group interview, stay focused on the interviewer, and treat the other candidates with respect. Even if you are nervous, try to remain calm, take your time when responding, and express yourself clearly. The key during a group interview is to make yourself stand out from the other candidates in a positive way.[8]

Sequential Interviews. In a sequential interview, you meet individually with two or more interviewers one-on-one over the course of several hours or days. For example, you may meet with human resources representatives, your hiring manager, and potential future supervisors and colleagues in your division or department. You must listen carefully and respond positively to all interviewers. Promote your qualifications to each one; don't assume that any interviewer knows what was said in a previous interview. Keep your responses fresh, even when repeating yourself many times over. Subsequent interviews also tend to be more in-depth than first interviews, which means that you need to be even more prepared and know even more about the company. According to Chantal Verbeek Vingerhoed, head of enterprise talent for ING, during subsequent interviews, "They dig deeper into your technical skills, and make connections about how you'd add value and solve issues in the department. If you know the exact job requirements and expectations, you can really shine."[9]

Stress Interviews. Stress interviews are meant to test your reactions during nerve-racking situations and are common for jobs in which you will face significant stress. You may be forced to wait a long time before being greeted by the interviewer. You may be given a test with an impossible time limit, or one or more of the interviewers may treat you rudely. Another stress interview technique is to have interviewers ask questions at a rapid rate. If asked rapid-fire questions from many directions, take the time to slow things down. For example, you might say, *I would be happy to answer your question, Ms. X, but first I must finish responding to Mr. Z.* If greeted with silence (another stress technique), you might say, *Would you like me to begin the interview? Let me tell you about myself.* Or ask a question such as, *Can you give me more information about the position?* One career expert says, "The key to surviving stress interviews is to remain calm, keep a sense of humor, and avoid getting angry or defensive."[10]

Online, Video, and Virtual Interviews. Don't be surprised if you are asked to participate in a virtual interview for one or more of the positions in which you are interested. Many companies today use online and video technology to interview job candidates from a distance.[11] For example, savvy companies such as Zappos use webcams and videoconferencing software to conduct long-distance interviews. If an applicant doesn't have a webcam, Zappos sends one with a return label.[12] Virtual interviews save job applicants and companies time and money, especially when applicants are not in the same geographic location as the company. The same rules apply whether you are face-to-face with your interviewers or looking into a camera.

No matter what interview structure you encounter, you will feel more comfortable and be less stressed if you understand the anatomy of the interview process, as summarized in Figure 16.1. Following are specific tips on what to do before, during, and after the interview.

Figure **16.1** Anatomy of the Job Interview Process

Know the interviewing sequence.

- Expect a telephone screening interview.
- If you are successful, next comes the hiring interview.
- Be prepared to answer questions in a one-on-one, panel, group, or video interview.

ARE YOU READY?

© alexmillos/Shutterstock.com

Research the target company.

- Study the company's history, mission, goals, size, and management structure.
- Know its strengths and weaknesses.
- Try to connect with someone in the company.

Prepare thoroughly.

- Rehearse detailed but brief success stories.
- Practice stories that illustrate dealing with a crisis, handling tough situations, juggling priorities, and working on a team.
- Clean up your online presence.

Look sharp, be sharp.

- Suit up! Dress professionally to feel confident.
- Be ready for questions that gauge your interest, explore your experience, and reveal your skills.
- Practice using the STAR method to answer behavioral questions.

End positively.

- Summarize your strongest qualifications.
- Show enthusiasm; say that you want the job!
- Ask what happens next.

Follow up.

- Send a note thanking the interviewer.
- Contact your references.
- Check in with the interviewer if you hear nothing after five days.

© Cengage Learning 2015; © Minerva Studio/Shutterstock.com

Before the Interview

LEARNING OBJECTIVE **2**
Describe what to do *before* an interview, including ensuring professional phone techniques, researching the target company, rehearsing success stories, cleaning up digital dirt, and fighting fear.

Once you have sent out at least one résumé or filled out at least one job application, you must consider yourself an active job seeker. Being active in the job market means that you should be prepared to be contacted by potential employers. As discussed earlier, employers often use screening interviews to narrow the list of candidates. If you do well in the screening interview, you will be invited to an in-person or online meeting.

Ensuring Professional Phone Techniques

Even with the popularity of e-mail, most employers contact job applicants by phone to set up interviews. Employers can judge how well applicants communicate by hearing their voices and expressions over the phone. Therefore, once you are actively looking for a job, anytime the phone rings, it could be a potential employer. Don't make the mistake of letting an unprofessional voice mail message or a lazy roommate or a sloppy cell phone manner ruin your chances. To make the best impression, try these tips:

- On your answering machine device, make sure that your outgoing message is concise and professional, with no distracting background sounds. It should be in your own voice and include your full name for clarity. You can find more tips for creating professional telephone messages in Chapter 14.

- Tell those who might answer your phone at home about your job search. Explain to them the importance of acting professionally and taking complete messages. Family members or roommates can affect the first impression an employer has of you.

- If you have children, prevent them from answering the phone during your job search. Children of all ages are not known for taking good messages!

- If you have put your cell phone number on your résumé, don't answer unless you are in a good location to carry on a conversation with an employer. It is hard to pay close attention when you are driving down the highway or eating in a noisy restaurant!

- Use voice mail to screen calls. By screening incoming calls, you can be totally in control when you return a prospective employer's call. Organize your materials and ready yourself psychologically for the conversation.

Making the First Conversation Impressive

Whether you answer the phone directly or return an employer's call, make sure you are prepared for the conversation. Remember that this is the first time the employer has heard your voice. How you conduct yourself on the phone will create a lasting impression. To make that first impression a positive one, follow these tips:

- Keep a list on your cell phone or near the telephone of positions for which you have applied.

- Treat any call from an employer just like an interview. Use a professional tone and businesslike language. Be polite and enthusiastic, and sell your qualifications.

- If caught off guard by the call, ask whether you can call back in a few minutes. Take that time to organize your materials and yourself.

- Have a copy of your résumé available so that you can answer any questions that come up. Also have your list of references, a calendar, and a notepad handy.

- Be prepared for a screening interview. As discussed earlier, this might occur during the first phone call.

- Take good notes during the phone conversation. Obtain accurate directions, and verify the spelling of your interviewer's name. If you will be interviewed by more than one person, get all of their names.

- If given a chance, ask for an interview on Tuesday at 10:30 a.m. This is considered the most opportune time. Avoid the start of the day on Monday and the end of the day on Friday.[13]

- Before you hang up, reconfirm the date and time of your interview. You could say something like *I look forward to meeting with you next Wednesday at 2 p.m.*

"Whoever said 80 percent of success is just showing up wasn't thinking about job interviews. Thoroughly preparing for an interview makes a huge difference in how well you do. And it can also make you a lot less nervous."[14]

—**ALISON GREEN,** *management consultant and blogger, www.askamanager.org*

Researching the Target Company

Once you have scheduled an in-person or online interview, you need to start preparing for it. One of the most important steps in effective interviewing is gathering detailed information about a prospective employer. Never enter an interview cold. Recruiters are impressed by candidates who have done their homework.

Search the potential employer's website, news sources, trade journals, and industry directories. Unearth information about the job, the company, and the industry. Learn all you can about the company's history, mission and goals, size, geographic locations, and number of employees. Check out its customers, competitors, culture, management structure, reputation in the community, financial condition, strengths and weaknesses, and future plans, as well as the names of its leaders.

Analyze its advertising, including sales and marketing brochures. One candidate, a marketing major, spent a great deal of time poring over brochures from an aerospace contractor. During his initial interview, he shocked and impressed the recruiter with his knowledge of the company's guidance systems. The candidate had, in fact, relieved the interviewer of his least-favorite task—explaining the company's complicated technology.

To locate inside information, use social media sources such as LinkedIn and Twitter. "Like" the company on Facebook and comment shrewdly on the organization's status updates and other posts. Beyond these sites, check out employee review websites such as Glassdoor and TheFit to get the inside scoop on what it's like to work there. Online tools such as InTheDoor and LinkedIn's Job Insider toolbar can help you discover whether you know someone who already works at the company.

Try to connect with someone who is currently employed—but not working in the immediate area where you wish to be hired. Be sure to seek out someone who is discreet. Blogs are also excellent sources for insider information and company research. One marketing specialist calls them "job posting gold mines."[15] In addition, don't forget to google the interviewer.

As you learn about a company, you may uncover information that convinces you that this is not the company for you. It is always better to learn about negatives early in the process. More likely, though, the information you collect will help you tailor your interview responses to the organization's needs. You know how flattered you feel when an employer knows about you and your background. That feeling works both ways. Employers are pleased when job candidates take an interest in them.

Preparing and Practicing

After you have learned about the target organization, study the job description or job listing. The most successful job candidates rehearse success stories and practice answers to typical questions. They clean up digital dirt and plan their responses to any problem areas on their résumés. As part of their preparation before the interview, they decide what to wear, and they gather the items they plan to take with them.

Rehearsing Success Stories.   To feel confident and be ready to sell your qualifications, prepare and practice success stories. These stories are specific examples of your educational and work-related experience that demonstrate your qualifications and achievements. Look over the job description and your résumé to determine what skills, training, personal characteristics, and experience you want to emphasize during the interview. Then prepare a success story for each one. Incorporate numbers, such as dollars saved or percentage of sales increased, whenever possible. Your success stories should be detailed but brief. Think of them as 30-second sound bites.

Practice telling your success stories until they fluently roll off your tongue and sound natural. Then in the interview be certain to find places to insert them. Tell stories about (a) dealing with a crisis, (b) handling a tough interpersonal situation, (c) successfully juggling many priorities, (d) changing course to deal with changed circumstances, (e) learning from a mistake, (f) working on a team, and (g) going above and beyond expectations.[16]

> Potential employers definitely screen a candidate's online presence using Google and social media sites such as Facebook, LinkedIn, and Twitter.

Cleaning Up Digital Dirt.

Potential employers definitely screen a candidate's online presence using Google and social media sites such as Facebook, LinkedIn, and Twitter.[17] One study revealed that nearly 70 percent of recruiters found something online that caused them not to hire a candidate.[18] The top reasons cited for not considering an applicant after an online search were that the candidate (a) posted provocative or inappropriate photographs or information; (b) posted content about drinking or doing drugs; (c) talked negatively about current or previous employers, colleagues, or clients; (d) exhibited poor communication skills; (e) made discriminatory comments; (f) lied about qualifications; or (g) revealed a current or previous employer's confidential information.[19]

In Chicago the president of a small consulting company was about to hire a summer intern when he discovered the student's Facebook page. The candidate described his interests as "smokin' blunts [cigars hollowed out and stuffed with marijuana], shooting people and obsessive sex."[20] The executive quickly lost interest in this candidate. Even if the student was merely posturing, it showed poor judgment. Teasing photographs and provocative comments about drinking, drug use, and sexual exploits make students look immature and unprofessional. Think about cleaning up your online presence by following these steps:

- **Remove questionable content.** Remove any incriminating, provocative, or distasteful photos, content, and links that could make you look unprofessional to potential employers.

- **Stay positive.** Don't complain about things in your professional or personal life online. Even negative reviews you have written on sites such as Amazon.com can turn employers off.

- **Be selective about who is on your list of friends.** You don't want to miss out on an opportunity because you seem to associate with negative, immature, or unprofessional people. Your best bet is to make your personal social networking pages private.

Protecting yourself online may mean asking owners to remove offensive information about you. In serious cases you may require legal advice. Understand that digital dirt can persist on other websites even after it is removed on one. To prevent future problems, consider using nicknames or pseudonyms when starting a new profile on a social network. Know the privacy policy and be sure to view your profile before posting any text, images, or videos. Start with the strictest privacy settings. Accept "friend" requests only from people you know. What else can you do to protect your reputation in cyberspace?

- **Avoid joining groups or fan pages that may be viewed negatively.** Remember that online searches can turn up your online activities, including group memberships, blog postings, and so on. If you think any activity you are involved in might show poor judgment, remove yourself immediately.

- **Don't discuss your job search if you are still employed.** Employees can find themselves in trouble with their current employers by writing status updates or sending tweets about their job searches.

- **Set up a professional social networking page or create your own personal website.** Use Facebook, LinkedIn, or other social networking sites to create a professional page. Many employers actually find information during their online searches that convinces them to hire candidates. Make sure your professional page demonstrates creativity, strong communication skills, and well-roundedness.[21]

Traveling to and Arriving at Your Interview

The big day has arrived! Ideally, you are fully prepared for your interview. Now you need to make sure that everything goes smoothly. That means making sure the trip to the potential employer's office goes well and that you arrive on time.

On the morning of your interview, give yourself plenty of time to groom and dress. Then make sure you can arrive at the employer's office without being rushed. If something unexpected happens that will to cause you to be late, such as an accident or bridge closure, call the interviewer right away to explain what is happening. Most interviewers will be understanding, and your call will show that you are responsible. On the way to the interview, don't smoke, don't eat anything messy or smelly, and don't load up on perfume or cologne. Arrive at the interview five or ten minutes early, but not earlier. If you are very early, wait in the car or in a café nearby. If possible, check your appearance before going in.

When you enter the office, be courteous and congenial to everyone. Remember that you are being judged not only by the interviewer but also by the receptionist and anyone else who sees you before and after the interview. They will notice how you sit, what you read, and how you look. Introduce yourself to the receptionist, and wait to be invited to sit. You may be asked to fill out a job application while you are waiting. You will find tips for doing this effectively later in this chapter.

Greet the interviewer confidently, and don't be afraid to initiate a handshake. Doing so exhibits professionalism and confidence. Extend your hand, look the interviewer directly in the eye, smile pleasantly, and say, *I'm pleased to meet you, Mr. Thomas. I am Constance Ferraro.* In this culture a firm, not crushing, handshake sends a nonverbal message of poise and assurance. Once introductions have taken place, wait for the interviewer to offer you a chair. Make small talk with upbeat comments such as, *This is a beautiful headquarters* or *I'm very impressed with the facilities you have here.* Don't immediately begin rummaging in your briefcase for your résumé. Being at ease and unrushed suggest that you are self-confident.

Fighting Fear

Expect to be nervous before and during the interview. It's natural! One survey revealed that job interviews are more stressful than going on a blind date, being pulled over by the police, or taking a final exam without studying.[22] One of the best ways to overcome fear is to know what happens in a typical interview. You can further reduce your fears by following these suggestions:

- **Practice interviewing.** Try to get as much interviewing practice as you can—especially with real companies. The more times you experience the interview situation, the less nervous you will be. However, don't schedule interviews unless you are genuinely interested in the organization. If offered, campus mock interviews also provide excellent practice, and the interviewers will offer tips for improvement.

- **Prepare thoroughly.** Research the company. Know how you will answer the most frequently asked questions. Be ready with success stories. Rehearse your closing statement. Knowing that you have done all you can to be ready for the interview is a tremendous fear preventive.

- **Understand the process.** Find out ahead of time how the interview will be structured. Will you be meeting with an individual, or will you be interviewed by a panel? Is this the first of a series of interviews? Don't be afraid to ask about these details before the interview so that an unfamiliar situation won't catch you off guard.

- **Dress professionally.** If you know you look sharp, you will feel more confident.

- **Breathe deeply.** Plan to take deep breaths, particularly if you feel anxious while waiting for the interviewer. Deep breathing makes you concentrate on something other than the interview and also provides much-needed oxygen.

- **Know that you are not alone.** Everyone feels some anxiety during a job interview. Interviewers expect some nervousness, and a skilled interviewer will try to put you at ease.

- **Remember that an interview is a two-way street.** The interviewer isn't the only one who is gleaning information. You have come to learn about the job and the company. In fact, during some parts of the interview, you will be in charge. This should give you courage.

During the Interview

LEARNING OBJECTIVE **3**
Describe what to do *during* an interview, including controlling nonverbal messages and answering typical interview questions.

Throughout the interview you will be answering questions and asking your own questions. Your demeanor, body language, and other nonverbal cues will also be on display. The interviewer will be trying to learn more about you, and you should be learning more about the job and the organization. Although you may be asked some unique questions, many interviewers ask standard, time-proven questions, which means that you can prepare your answers ahead of time. You can also prepare by learning techniques to control those inevitable butterflies in the tummy.

REALITY CHECK: The Most Important Part of the Job-Search Process

"Most people, even after spending hours slaving over a perfect résumé, fail to put in the necessary preparation for the most important part of the process: the interview!"[23]

—**CAROLE MARTIN,** *interview coach and author of* Interview Fitness Training

Courtesy of Carole Martin

Sending Positive Nonverbal Messages and Acting Professionally

You have already sent nonverbal messages to your interviewer by arriving on time, being courteous, dressing professionally, and greeting the receptionist confidently. You will continue to send nonverbal messages throughout the interview. Remember that what comes out of your mouth and what is written on your résumé are not the only messages an interviewer receives from you. Nonverbal messages also create powerful impressions on people. You can send positive nonverbal messages during face-to-face and online interviews by following these tips:

- **Control your body movements.** Keep your hands, arms, and elbows to yourself. Don't lean on a desk. Keep your feet on the floor. Don't cross your arms in front of you. Keep your hands out of your pockets.

- **Exhibit good posture.** Sit erect, leaning forward slightly. Don't slouch in your chair; at the same time, don't look too stiff and uncomfortable. Good posture demonstrates confidence and interest.

- **Practice appropriate eye contact.** A direct eye gaze, at least in North America, suggests interest and trustworthiness. If you are being interviewed by a panel, remember to maintain eye contact with all interviewers.

- **Use gestures effectively.** Nod to show agreement and interest. Gestures should be used as needed, but not overused.

- **Smile enough to convey a positive attitude.** Have a friend give you honest feedback on whether you generally smile too much or not enough.

- **Listen attentively.** Show the interviewer you are interested and attentive by listening carefully to the questions being asked. This will also help you answer questions appropriately.

- **Turn off your cell phone or other electronic devices.** Avoid the embarrassment of having your iPhone or other smartphone ring, or even as much as buzz, during an interview. Turn off your electronic devices completely; don't just switch them to vibrate.

- **Don't chew gum.** Chewing gum during an interview is distracting and unprofessional.

- **Sound enthusiastic and interested—but sincere.** The tone of your voice has an enormous effect on the words you say. Avoid sounding bored, frustrated, or sarcastic during an interview. Employers want employees who are enthusiastic and interested.

- **Avoid empty words.** Filling your answers with verbal pauses such as *um*, *uh*, *like*, and *basically* communicates that you are not prepared. Also avoid annoying distractions such as clearing your throat repeatedly or sighing deeply.

- **Be confident, but not cocky.** Most recruiters want candidates who are self-assured but not too casual or even arrogant. Let your body language, posture, dress, and vocal tone prove your confidence. Speak at a normal volume and enunciate words clearly without mumbling.[24]

Recruiters may apply the airport test.

Naturally, hiring managers make subjective decisions based on intuition, but they need to ferret out pleasant people who fit in. To that end, some recruiters apply "the airport test" to candidates: "Would I want to be stuck in the airport for 12 hours with this person if my flight were delayed?"[25]

Practicing How to Answer Interview Questions

Although you can't anticipate precise questions, you can expect to be asked about your education, skills, experience, salary expectations, and availability. Recite answers to typical interview questions in front of a mirror, with a friend, while driving in your car, or in spare moments. Keep practicing until you have the best responses down pat. Consider recording a practice session to see and hear how you answer questions. Do you look and sound enthusiastic?

Remember that the way you answer questions can be almost as important as what you say. Use the interviewer's name and title from time to time when you answer. *Yes, Ms. Lyon, I would be pleased to tell you about* . . . . People like to hear their own names. Be sure you are pronouncing the name correctly, and don't overuse this technique. Avoid answering questions with a simple *yes* or *no*; elaborate on your answers to better promote yourself and your assets. Keep your answers positive; don't criticize anything or anyone.

During the interview it may be necessary to occasionally refocus and clarify vague questions. Some interviewers are inexperienced and ill at ease in the role. You may even have to ask your own question to understand what was asked, *By _____ , do you mean _____?* Consider closing out some of your responses with *Does that answer your question?* or *Would you like me to elaborate on any particular experience?*

Always aim your answers at the key characteristics interviewers seek: expertise, competence, motivation, interpersonal skills, decision-making skills, enthusiasm for the company and the job, and a pleasing personality. Remember to stay focused on your strengths. Don't reveal weaknesses, even if you think they make you look human. You won't be hired for your weaknesses, only for your strengths.

As you respond, be sure to use good English and enunciate clearly. Avoid slurred words such as *gonna* and *din't*, as well as slangy expressions such as *yeah, like*, and *ya know*. As you practice answering expected interview questions, it is always a good idea to make a recording. Is your speech filled with verbal static?

You can't expect to be perfect in an employment interview. No one is. But you can avert sure disaster by avoiding certain topics and behaviors such as those described in Figures 16.2 and 16.3.

Anticipating Typical Interview Questions

Employment interviews are all about questions, and many of the questions interviewers ask are not new. You can anticipate a large percentage of questions that will be asked before you ever walk into an interview room. Although you can't anticipate every question, you can prepare for various types.

This section presents questions that may be asked during employment interviews. Some questions are meant to help the interviewer become acquainted with you. Others are aimed at measuring your interest, experience, and accomplishments. Still others will probe your future plans and challenge your reactions. Some will inquire about your salary expectations. Your interviewer may use situational or behavioral questions and may even occasionally ask an illegal question.

To get you thinking about how to respond, we have provided an answer for, or a discussion of, one or more of the questions in each of the following groups. As you read the remaining questions in each group, think about how you could respond most effectively. For additional questions, contact your campus career center, or consult one of the career websites discussed in Chapter 15.

Figure **16.2** Ten Interview Actions to Avoid

1. Don't be late or too early. Arrive five to ten minutes before your scheduled interview.

2. Don't be rude or annoying. Treat everyone you come into contact with warmly and respectfully. Avoid limp handshakes, poor eye contact or staring, and verbal ticks such as *like*, *you know*, and *umm*.

3. Don't criticize anyone or anything. Avoid saying anything negative about your previous employer, supervisors, colleagues, or job. The tendency is for interviewers to wonder if you would speak about their companies similarly.

4. Don't act unprofessionally. Don't discuss controversial subjects, and don't use profanity. Don't answer your cell phone or fiddle with it. Silence all electronic devices so that they don't even buzz, or turn them off completely. Don't bring food or coffee.

5. Don't emphasize salary or benefits. Don't address salary, vacation, or benefits early in an interview. Let the interviewer set the pace; win him or her over first.

6. Don't focus on your imperfections. Never dwell on your liabilities or talk negatively about yourself.

7. Don't interrupt. Interrupting is not only impolite but also prevents you from hearing a complete question or remark. Don't talk too much or too little. Answer interview questions to the best of your ability, but avoid rambling as much as terseness.

8. Don't bring someone along. Don't bring a friend or relative with you to the interview. If someone must drive you, ask that person to drop you off and come back later.

9. Don't appear impatient or bored. Your entire focus should be on the interview. Don't glance at your watch, which can imply that you are late for another appointment. Be alert and show interest in the company and the position.

10. Don't act desperate. A sure way to turn off an interviewer is to appear desperate. Don't focus on why you need the job; focus on how you will add value to the organization.

© Cengage Learning 2015; © phil Holmes / Shutterstock 82655005

Figure **16.3** What Can Go Wrong in a Job Interview?

Most Common Interview Mistakes

71% Answering a cell phone or texting
69% Dressing inappropriately
69% Appearing uninterested
66% Appearing arrogant
63% Denigrating a former employer
59% Talking while chewing gum

Most Outrageous Interview Behavior

Providing a detailed listing of how the previous employer angered the candidate

Hugging the hiring manager at the end of the interview

Eating all the candy from the candy bowl while trying to answer questions

Blowing her nose and lining up the used tissues on the table in front of her

Throwing his beer can in the outside trash bin before coming into the office

Having a friend come in and say, "How much longer?"

Source: Based on CareerBuilder survey of more than 2,400 hiring managers. Retrieved from http://www.careerbuilder.com/share/aboutus/pressreleasesdetail.aspx?id=pr614&sd=1%2F12%2F2011&ed=12%2F31%2F2011

Questions to Get Acquainted. After opening introductions, recruiters generally try to start the interview with personal questions designed to put you at ease. They are also striving to gain an overview to see whether you will fit into the organization's culture. When answering these questions, keep the employer's needs in mind and try to incorporate your success stories.

1. Tell me about yourself.
   Experts agree that you must keep this answer short (one to two minutes tops) but on target. Use this chance to promote yourself. Stick to educational, professional, or business-related strengths; avoid personal or humorous references. Be ready with at least three success stories illustrating characteristics important to this job. Demonstrate responsibility you have been given; describe how you contributed as a team player. Try practicing this formula: *I have completed a _____ degree with a major in _____. Recently I worked for _____ as a _____. Before that I worked for _____ as a _____. My strengths are _____ (interpersonal) and _____ (technical).* Try rehearsing your response in 30-second segments devoted to your education, work experience, qualifications, and skills.

2. What are your greatest strengths?
   Stress your strengths that are related to the position, such as, *I am well organized, thorough, and attentive to detail.* Tell success stories and give examples that illustrate

these qualities: *My supervisor says that my research is exceptionally thorough. For example, I recently worked on a research project in which I . . . .*

3. Do you prefer to work by yourself or with others? Why?
   This question can be tricky. Provide a middle-of-the-road answer that not only suggests your interpersonal qualities but also reflects an ability to make independent decisions and work without supervision.

4. What was your major in college, and why did you choose it?

5. What are some things you do in your spare time?

Questions to Gauge Your Interest. Interviewers want to understand your motivation for applying for a position. Although they will realize that you are probably interviewing for other positions, they still want to know why you are interested in this particular position with this organization. These types of questions help them determine your level of interest.

1. Why do you want to work for [name of company]?
   Questions like this illustrate why you must research an organization thoroughly before the interview. The answer to this question must prove that you understand the company and its culture. This is the perfect place to bring up the company research you did before the interview. Show what you know about the company, and discuss why you want to become a part of this organization. Describe your desire to work for this organization not only from your perspective but also from its point of view. What do you have to offer that will benefit the organization?

2. Why are you interested in this position?

3. What do you know about our company?

4. Why do you want to work in the _____ industry?

5. What interests you about our products (or services)?

REALITY CHECK: Stretching the Truth

"Occasionally you bump into a talented and competent candidate . . . who's so lacking in the EQ components of humility and realness that you can't take a chance. This young man had a lot of the right stuff, but when he started telling us that he had never made a mistake in his life and didn't expect to, we knew we'd heard enough."[26]

—**JACK AND SUZY WELCH,** *MANAGEMENT CONSULTANTS AND AUTHORS*

© Joe Tabacca/Bloomberg via Getty Images

Questions About Your Experience and Accomplishments. After questions about your background and education and questions that measure your interest, the interview generally becomes more specific with questions about your experience and accomplishments. Remember to show confidence when you answer these questions. If you are not confident in your abilities, why should an employer be?

1. Why should we hire you when we have applicants with more experience or better credentials?

   In answering this question, remember that employers often hire people who present themselves well instead of others with better credentials. Emphasize your personal strengths that could be an advantage with this employer. Are you a hard worker? How can you demonstrate it? Have you had recent training? Some people have had more years of experience but actually have less knowledge because they have done the same thing over and over. Stress your experience using the latest methods and equipment. Be sure to mention your computer training and use of the Web. Tell success stories. Emphasize that you are open to new ideas and learn quickly. Above all, show that you are confident in your abilities.

2. Describe the most rewarding experience of your career so far.

3. How have your education and professional experiences prepared you for this position?

4. What were your major accomplishments in each of your past jobs?

5. What was a typical workday like?

6. What job functions did you enjoy most? Least? Why?

7. Tell me about your computer skills.

8. Who was the toughest boss you ever worked for and why?

9. What were your major achievements in college?

10. Why did you leave your last position? *OR:* Why are you leaving your current position?

Questions About the Future.   Questions that look into the future tend to stump some candidates, especially those who have not prepared adequately. Employers ask these questions to see whether you are goal oriented and to determine whether your goals are realistic.

1. Where do you expect to be five (or ten) years from now?

   Formulate a realistic plan with respect to your present age and situation. The important thing is to be prepared for this question. It is a sure kiss of death to respond that you would like to have the interviewer's job! Instead, show an interest in the current job and in making a contribution to the organization. Talk about the levels of responsibility you would like to achieve. One employment counselor suggests showing ambition but not committing to a specific job title. Suggest that you hope to have learned enough to have progressed to a position in which you will continue to grow. Keep your answer focused on educational and professional goals, not personal goals.

2. If you got this position, what would you do to be sure you fit in?

3. This is a large (or small) organization. Do you think you would like that environment?

4. Do you plan to continue your education?

5. What do you predict for the future of the _____ industry?

6. How do you think you can contribute to this company?

7. What would you most like to accomplish if you get this position?

8. How do you keep current with what is happening in your profession?

Challenging Questions.   The following questions may make you uncomfortable, but the important thing to remember is to answer truthfully without dwelling on your weaknesses. As quickly as possible, convert any negative response into a discussion of your strengths.

1. What is your greatest weakness?

   It is amazing how many candidates knock themselves out of the competition by answering this question poorly. Actually, you have many choices. You can present a strength as a weakness (Some people complain that I'm a workaholic or too attentive to details). *You can mention a corrected weakness* (Because I needed to learn about designing websites, I took a course.) *You could cite an unrelated skill* (I really need to brush up on my Spanish). *You can cite a learning objective* (One of my long-term goals is to learn more about international management. Does your company have any plans to expand overseas?). *Another possibility is to reaffirm your qualifications* (I have no weaknesses that affect my ability to do this job). *Be careful that your answer doesn't sound too cliché* (I tend to be a perfectionist) *and instead shows careful analysis of your abilities.*

2. What type of people do you have no patience for?

   Avoid letting yourself fall into the trap of sounding overly critical. One possible response is, I have always gotten along well with others. But I confess that I can be irritated by complainers who don't accept responsibility.

3. If you could live your life over, what would you change and why?

4. How would your former (or current) supervisor describe you as an employee?

5. What do you want the most from your job?

6. What is your grade point average, and does it accurately reflect your abilities?

7. Have you ever used drugs?

8. Who in your life has influenced you the most and why?

9. What are you reading right now?

10. Describe your ideal work environment.

11. Is the customer always right?

12. How do you define success?

Questions About Salary

Remember that nearly all salaries are negotiable, depending on your qualifications. Knowing the typical salary range for the target position is very important in this negotiation. The recruiter can tell you the salary ranges—but you will have to ask. If you have had little experience, you will probably be offered a salary somewhere between the low point and the midpoint in the range. With more experience, you can negotiate for a higher figure. A word of caution, though. One personnel manager warns that candidates who emphasize money are suspect because they may leave if offered a few thousand dollars more elsewhere. See the accompanying Career Coach box for dos and don'ts in negotiating a starting salary. Here are typical salary-related questions:

1. What salary are you looking for?

   One way to handle salary questions is to ask politely to defer the discussion until it is clear that a job will be offered to you (I'm sure when the time comes, we will be able to work out a fair compensation package. Right now, I'd rather focus on whether we have a match). Another possible response is to reply candidly that you can't know what to ask until you know more about the position and the company. If you continue to be pressed for a dollar figure, give a salary range with an annual dollar amount. Be sure to do research before the interview so that you know what similar jobs are paying in your geographic region. For example, check a website such as **http://www.salary.com**. *When citing salary expectations, you will sound more professional if you cite an annual salary range rather than a dollar-per-hour amount.*

2. How much are you presently earning?

3. How much do you think you are worth?

4. How much money do you expect to earn within the next ten years?

5. Are you willing to take a pay cut from your current (or previous) job?

Situational Questions.   Questions related to situations help employers test your thought processes and logical thinking. When using situational questions, interviewers describe a hypothetical situation and ask how you would handle it. Situational questions differ based on the type of position for which you are interviewing. Knowledge of the position and the company culture will help you respond favorably to these questions. Even if the situation sounds negative, keep your response positive. Here are just a few examples:

1. You receive a call from an irate customer who complains about the service she received last night at your restaurant. She is demanding her money back. How would you handle the situation?

2. If you were aware that a coworker was falsifying data, what would you do?

3. Your supervisor has just told you that she is dissatisfied with your work, but you think it is acceptable. How would you resolve the conflict?

4. Your supervisor has told you to do something a certain way, and you think that way is wrong and that you know a far better way to complete the task. What would you do?

5. Assume that you are hired for this position. You soon learn that one of the staff is extremely resentful because she applied for your position and was turned down. As a result, she is being unhelpful and obstructive. How would you handle the situation?

CAREER COACH:

Let's Talk Money: Salary Negotiation Dos and Don'ts

Nearly all salaries are negotiable. The following dos and don'ts can guide you to a better starting salary.

- **Do** make sure you have done your research on the salary you should expect for the position you are seeking. **Do** understand how geographic location affects salary ranges.

- **Don't** bring up salary before the employer does. **Do** delay salary negotiation until you know exactly what the position entails.

- **Do** be aware of your strengths and achievements. **Do** be sure to demonstrate the value you will bring to the employer.

- **Don't** tell the employer the salary you need to pay your bills or meet personal obligations.

- **Do** let the employer make the first salary offer. **Do**, if asked, say you expect a salary that is competitive with the market, or give a salary range that you find acceptable.

- **Don't** inflate your current earnings just to get a higher salary offer.

- **Don't** feel obligated to accept the first salary offer. **Do** negotiate salary if the offer made is inadequate.

- **Do** thank the employer for the offer when it is made. **Don't** try to negotiate right after the offer is made.

- **Do** take the time to consider all factors before making any job offer decisions.

- **Don't** be overly aggressive in negotiating the salary you want.

- **Don't** focus solely on salary. **Do** consider the entire compensation package.

- **Do** try to obtain other concessions (shorter review time, better title, better workspace) or benefits (bonuses, vacation time) if you aren't successful at negotiating a salary you want.

- **Don't** enter salary negotiations as part of an ego trip or game.

- **Don't** agree to the first acceptable salary offer you receive if you are not sure about the job or the company.

- **Do** get the offer in writing.

6. A colleague has told you in confidence that she suspects another colleague of stealing. What would your actions be?

7. You have noticed that communication between upper management and first-level employees is eroding. How would you solve this problem?

Behavioral Questions. Instead of traditional interview questions, you may be asked to tell stories. The interviewer may say, *Describe a time when . . .* or *Tell me about a time when . . . .* To respond effectively, learn to use the storytelling, or STAR, technique, as illustrated in Figure 16.4. Ask yourself what the **S**ituation or **T**ask was, what **A**ction you took, and what the **R**esults were.[27] Practice using this method to recall specific examples of your skills and accomplishments. To be fully prepared, develop a coherent and articulate STAR narrative for every bullet point on your résumé. When answering behavioral questions, describe only educational and work-related situations or tasks, and try to keep them as current as possible. Here are a few examples of behavioral questions:

1. Tell me about a time when you solved a difficult problem.

    Tell a concise story explaining the situation or task, what you did, and the result. For example, When I was at Ace Products, we continually had a problem of excessive back orders. After analyzing the situation, I discovered that orders went through many

Figure 16.4 Using the STAR Technique to Answer Behavioral Interview Questions

S Situation
Briefly explain the background and context of a situation. What happened? When? Where?

T Task
Describe the problem. What needed to be done? Why?

A Action
What did you do? How? What skills or tools did you use?

R Results
Explain the results (e.g., savings, greater efficiency). Try to quantify.

© Cengage Learning 2015

unnecessary steps. I suggested that we eliminate much paperwork. As a result, we reduced back orders by 30 percent. *Go on to emphasize what you learned and how you can apply that learning to this job. Practice your success stories in advance so that you will be ready.*

2. Describe a situation in which you were able to use persuasion to convince someone to see things your way.

The recruiter is interested in your leadership and teamwork skills. You might respond, I have learned to appreciate the fact that the way you present an idea is just as important as the idea itself. When trying to influence people, I put myself in their shoes and find some way to frame my idea from their perspective. I remember when I . . . .

3. Describe a time when you had to analyze information and make a recommendation.

4. Describe a time that you worked successfully as part of a team.

5. Tell me about a time that you dealt with confidential information.

6. Give me an example of a time when you were under stress to meet a deadline.

7. Tell me about a time when you had to go above and beyond the call of duty to get a job done.

8. Tell me about a time you were able to deal with another person successfully even though that individual did not like you personally (or vice versa).

9. Give me an example of when you showed initiative and took the lead.

10. Tell me about a recent situation in which you had to deal with an upset customer or coworker.

Illegal and Inappropriate Questions. Federal laws prohibit employment discrimination based on gender, age, religion, color, race, national origin, and disability. In addition, federal civil service statutes and many state and city laws prohibit employment discrimination based on factors such as sexual orientation.[28] Therefore, it is inappropriate for interviewers to ask any question related to these areas. These questions become illegal, though, only when a court of law determines that the employer is asking them with the intent to discriminate.[29] Most illegal interview questions are asked innocently by inexperienced interviewers. Some are only trying to be friendly when they inquire about your personal life or family. Regardless of the intent, how should you react?

If you find the question harmless and if you want the job, go ahead and answer it. If you think that answering it would damage your chance to be hired, try to deflect the question tactfully with a response such as, *Could you tell me how my marital status relates to the responsibilities of this position?* or, *I prefer to keep my personal and professional lives separate*. If you are uncomfortable answering a question, try to determine the reason behind it; you might answer, *I don't let my personal life interfere with my ability to do my job*, or, *Are you concerned with my availability to work overtime?* Another option, of course, is to respond to any inappropriate or illegal question by confronting the interviewer and threatening a lawsuit or refusing to answer. However, you could not expect to be hired under these circumstances. In any case, you might wish to reconsider working for an organization that sanctions such procedures.

Here are some inappropriate and illegal questions that you may or may not want to answer:[30]

1. What is your marital status? Are you married? Do you live with anyone? Do you have a boyfriend (or girlfriend)? (However, employers can ask your marital status after hiring for tax and insurance forms.)

2. Do you have any disabilities? Have you had any recent illnesses? (But it is legal to ask if the person can perform specific job duties, such as, *Can you carry a 50-pound sack up a 10-foot ladder five times daily?*)

3. I notice you have an accent. Where are you from? What is the origin of your last name? What is your native language? (However, it is legal to ask what languages you speak fluently if language ability is related to the job.)

4. Have you ever filed a workers' compensation claim or been injured on the job?

5. Have you ever had a drinking problem or been addicted to drugs? (But it is legal to ask if a person uses illegal drugs.)

6. Have you ever been arrested? (But it is legal to ask, *Have you ever been convicted of _____?* when the crime is related to the job.)

7. How old are you? What is your date of birth? When did you graduate from high school? (But it is legal to ask, *Are you 16 years [or 18 years or 21 years] old or older?* depending on the age requirements for the position.)

8. Of what country are you a citizen? Are you a U.S. citizen? Where were you born? (But it is legal to ask, *Are you authorized to work in the United States?*)

9. What is your maiden name? (But it is legal to ask, *What is your full name?* or, *Have you worked under another name?*)

10. Do you have any religious beliefs that would prevent you from working weekends or holidays? (An employer can, however, ask you if you are available to work weekends and holidays or otherwise within the company's required schedule.)

11. Do you have children? Do you plan to have children? Do you have adequate child-care arrangements? (However, employers can ask for dependent information for tax and insurance purposes after you are hired. Also, they can ask if you would be able to travel or work overtime on occasion.)

12. How much do you weigh? How tall are you? (However, employers can ask you about your height and weight if minimum standards are necessary to safely perform a job.)[31]

Asking Your Own Questions

At some point in the interview, usually near the end, you will be asked whether you have any questions. The worst thing you can do is say *No,* which suggests that you are not interested in the position. Instead, ask questions that will help you gain information and will impress the interviewer with your thoughtfulness and interest in the position. Remember that this interview is a two-way street. You must be happy with the prospect of working for this organization. You want a position that matches your skills and personality. Use this opportunity to learn whether this job is right for you. Be aware that you don't have to wait for the interviewer to ask you for questions. You can ask your own questions throughout the interview to learn more about the company and position. Here are some questions you might ask:

1. What will my duties be (if not already discussed)?
2. Tell me what it is like working here in terms of the people, management practices, workloads, expected performance, and rewards.
3. What training programs are available from this organization? What specific training will be given for this position?
4. Who would be my immediate supervisor?
5. What is the organizational structure, and where does this position fit in?
6. Is travel required in this position?
7. How is job performance evaluated?
8. Assuming my work is excellent, where do you see me in five years?
9. How long do employees generally stay with this organization?
10. What are the major challenges for a person in this position?
11. What do you see in the future of this organization?
12. What do you like best about working for this organization?
13. May I have a tour of the facilities?
14. When do you expect to make a decision?

Ending Positively

After you have asked your questions, the interviewer will signal the end of the interview, usually by standing up or by expressing appreciation that you came. If not addressed earlier, you should at this time find out what action will follow. Demonstrate your interest in the position by asking when it will be filled or what the next step will be. Too many candidates leave the interview without knowing their status or when they will hear from the recruiter. Don't be afraid to say that you want the job!

Before you leave, summarize your strongest qualifications, show your enthusiasm for obtaining this position, and thank the interviewer for a constructive interview and for considering you for the position. Ask the interviewer for a business card, which will provide the information you need to write a thank-you letter. You might also ask if you may stay in touch through LinkedIn.

Shake the interviewer's hand with confidence, and acknowledge anyone else you see on the way out. Be sure to thank the receptionist. Departing gracefully and enthusiastically will leave a lasting impression on those responsible for making the final hiring decision.

After the Interview

LEARNING OBJECTIVE 4
Describe what to do *after* an interview, including thanking the interviewer, contacting references, and writing follow-up messages.

After leaving the interview, immediately make notes of what was said in case you are called back for a second interview. Write down key points that were discussed, the names of people you spoke with, and other details of the interview. Ask yourself what went really well and what you could improve. Note your strengths and weaknesses during the interview so that you can work to improve in future interviews. Next, write down your follow-up plans. To whom should you send thank-you messages? Will you contact the employer by phone? By e-mail? If so, when? Then be sure to follow up on those plans, beginning with writing a thank-you e-mail or letter and contacting your references.

REALITY CHECK: Thanking the Interviewer From the Parking Lot

"Thank-you notes matter: They give you a terrific opportunity to follow up with the decision-maker right away. I encourage job seekers to get thank-you notes out (to each individual they've met in the interview process) immediately after the interview. Same day. From your laptop in the parking lot, if you really want to wow them."[32]

—**JENNY FOSS,** *job search strategist, career coach*

Thanking Your Interviewer

After a job interview, you should always send a thank-you note, e-mail, or letter. This courtesy sets you apart from other applicants, most of whom will not bother. Your message also reminds the interviewer of your visit and shows your good manners and genuine enthusiasm for the job.

Follow-up thank-you messages are most effective if sent immediately after the interview. Experts believe that a thoughtful follow-up note carries as much weight as the cover letter does. Almost nine out of ten senior executives admit that in their evaluation of a job candidate they are swayed by a written thank-you.[33] In your thank-you message, refer to the date of the interview, the exact job title for which you were interviewed, and specific topics discussed. "An effective thank-you letter should hit every one of the employer's hot buttons," says author and career consultant Wendy Enelow.[34]

Some employers are digitally inclined and prefer e-mail; more traditional recruiters may prefer handwritten notes or traditional letters.[35] In any case, avoid worn-out phrases, such as *Thank you for taking the time to interview me.* Be careful, too, about overusing *I*, especially to begin sentences. Most important, show that you really want the job and that you are qualified for it. Notice how the letter in Figure 16.5 conveys enthusiasm and confidence.

If you have been interviewed by more than one person, send a separate thank-you message to each interviewer. It is also a good idea to send a thank-you message to the receptionist and to the person who set up the interview. Your preparation and knowledge of the company culture will help you determine whether a traditional thank-you letter sent by mail or an e-mail is more appropriate. Make sure that you write your e-mail using professional language, standard capitalization, and proper punctuation. One job candidate makes a follow-up e-mail her standard practice. She summarizes what was discussed during the face-to-face interview and adds information that she had not thought to mention during the interview.[36]

Contacting Your References

Once you have thanked your interviewer, it is time to alert your references that they may be contacted by the employer. You might also have to request a letter of recommendation to be sent to the employer by a certain date. As discussed in Chapter 15, you should have already asked permission to use these individuals as references, and you should have supplied them with a copy of your résumé and information about the types of positions you are seeking

To provide the best possible recommendation, your references need information. What position have you applied for with what company? What should they stress to the prospective employer? Let's say you are applying for a specific job that requires a letter of recommendation. Professor Sherman has already agreed to be a reference for you. To get the best letter of recommendation from Professor Sherman, help her out. Write an e-mail or letter telling her about the position, its requirements, and the recommendation deadline. Include copies of your résumé, college transcript, and, if applicable, the job posting or ad with detailed information about the opening. You might remind her of a positive experience

Figure **16.5** Interview Follow-Up Message

Eugene H. Vincente

1308 Big Ridge Rd., Apt. 3, Biloxi, MS 39530
(228) 627-4362, evincente@gmail.com

May 28, 2015

Mr. André G. Mercier
3D Signs
5505 Industrial Parkway, Ste. 200
New Orleans, LA 70129

Dear Mr. Mercier:

Talking with you Thursday, May 27, about the graphic designer position was both informative and interesting.

Thanks for describing the position in such detail and for introducing me to Ms. Sasaki, the senior designer. Her current project designing an annual report in four colors sounds fascinating as well as quite challenging.

Now that I've learned in greater detail the specific tasks of your graphic designers, I'm more than ever convinced that my computer and creative skills can make a genuine contribution to your graphic productions. My training in design and layout using PhotoShop and InDesign ensures that I could be immediately productive on your staff.

You will find me an enthusiastic and hardworking member of any team effort. As you requested, I'm enclosing additional samples of my work. I'm eager to join the graphics staff at your New Orleans headquarters, and I look forward to hearing from you soon.

Sincerely,

Eugene H. Vincente

Eugene H. Vincente

Enclosures

Annotations (margin callouts):

- Uses customized lettherhead but could have merely typed street and city address above dateline
- Mentions the interview date and specific job title
- Personalizes the message by referring to topics discussed in the interview
- Highlights specific skills for the job
- Shows good manners, appreciation, and perseverance—traits that recruiters value
- Reminds reader of interpersonal skills as well as enthusiasm and eagerness for this job

© Cengage Learning 2015

with you that she could use in the recommendation. Remember that recommenders need evidence to support generalizations. Give them appropriate ammunition, as the student has done in the following request:

Dear Professor Sherman:

Recently I interviewed for the position of administrative assistant in the Human Resources Department of Host International. Because you kindly agreed to help me, I am now asking you to write a letter of recommendation to Host.

The position calls for good organizational, interpersonal, and writing skills, as well as computer experience. To help you review my skills and training, I enclose my résumé. As you

In a reference request letter, tell immediately why you are writing. Identify the target position and company.

Specify the job requirements so that the recommender knows what to stress.

Provide a stamped, addressed envelope.

may recall, I earned an A in your business communication class last fall; and you commended my long report for its clarity and organization.

Please send your letter to Mr. James Jenkins at Host International before July 1 in the enclosed stamped, addressed envelope. I'm grateful for your support and promise to let you know the results of my job search.

Sincerely,

Following Up

If you don't hear from the interviewer within five days, or at the specified time, consider following up. The standard advice to job candidates is to call a few days after the interview. However, some experts suggest that calling a hiring manager is fraught with risk. You may be putting a busy recruiter on the spot and force him or her to search for your application. In addition, don't assume you are the only candidate; multiply your phone call by the 200 applicants whom some hiring managers interview.[37] You don't want to be a pest! An e-mail to find out how the decision process is going may be your best bet because such a message is much less intrusive. If you asked about it in the interview, you might follow up with the interviewer through LinkedIn.

If you believe it is safe to follow up by phone or if the recruiter suggested it, practice saying something like, *I'm wondering what else I can do to convince you that I'm the right person for this job,* or, *I'm calling to find out the status of your search for the _____ position.* When following up, it is important to sound professional and courteous. Sounding desperate, angry, or frustrated that you have not been contacted can ruin your chances. The following follow-up e-mail message would impress the interviewer:

Dear Ms. Kahn:

I enjoyed my interview with you last Thursday for the project manager position. You should know that I'm very interested in this opportunity with Coastal Enterprises. Because you mentioned that you might have an answer this week, I'm eager to know how your decision process is coming along. I look forward to hearing from you.

Sincerely,

Depending on the response you get to your first follow-up request, you may have to follow up additional times.[38] Keep in mind, though, that some employers won't tell you about their hiring decision unless you are the one hired. Don't harass the interviewer, and don't force a decision. If you don't hear back from an employer within several weeks after following up, it is best to assume that you didn't get the job and to continue with your job search.

Preparing Additional Employment Documents

Although the résumé and cover letter are your major tasks, other important documents and messages are often required during the job-search process. You may need to complete an employment application form and write follow-up letters. You might also have to write a letter of resignation when leaving a job. Because each of these tasks reveals something about you and your communication skills, you will want to put your best foot forward. These documents often subtly influence company officials to offer a job.

Application Form

Some organizations require job candidates to fill out application forms instead of, or in addition to, submitting résumés. This practice permits them to gather and store standardized data about each applicant. Whether the application is on paper or online, follow the directions carefully and provide accurate information. The following suggestions can help you be prepared:

- Carry a card summarizing vital statistics not included on your résumé. If you are asked to fill out an application form in an employer's office, you will need a handy reference to the following data: graduation dates; beginning and ending dates of all employment; salary history; full names, titles, and present work addresses of former supervisors; full addresses and phone numbers of current and previous employers; and full names, occupational titles, occupational addresses, and telephone numbers of people who have agreed to serve as references.

- Look over all the questions before starting.

- Fill out the form neatly, using blue or black ink. Many career counselors recommend printing your responses; cursive handwriting can be difficult to read.

- Answer all questions honestly. Write *Not applicable* or *N/A* if appropriate. Don't leave any sections blank.

- Use accurate spelling, grammar, capitalization, and punctuation.

- If asked for the position desired, give a specific job title or type of position. Don't say, *Anything* or *Open*. These answers make you look unfocused; moreover, they make it difficult for employers to know what you are qualified for or interested in.

- Be prepared for a salary question. Unless you know what comparable employees are earning in the company, the best strategy is to suggest a salary range or to write *Negotiable* or *Open*.

- Be prepared to explain the reasons for leaving previous positions. Use positive or neutral phrases such as *Relocation, Seasonal, To accept a position with more responsibility, Temporary position, To continue education*, or *Career change*. Avoid words or phrases such as *Fired, Quit, Didn't get along with supervisor*, or *Pregnant*.

- Look over the application before submitting to make sure it is complete and that you have followed all instructions. Sign and date the application.

Application or Résumé Follow-Up Message

If your résumé or application generates no response within a reasonable time, you may decide to send a short follow-up e-mail or letter such as the following. Doing so (a) jogs the memory of the personnel officer, (b) demonstrates your serious interest, and (c) allows you to emphasize your qualifications or to add new information.

Dear Ms. Gutierrez:

Please know I am still interested in becoming an administrative support specialist with Quad, Inc.

Since submitting an application [or résumé] in May, I have completed my degree and have been employed as a summer replacement for office workers in several downtown offices. This experience has honed my word processing and communication skills. It has also introduced me to a wide range of office procedures.

Please keep my application in your active file and let me know when my formal training, technical skills, and practical experience can go to work for you.

Sincerely,

Open by reminding the reader of your interest.

Review your strengths or add new qualifications.

Close positively; avoid accusations that make the reader defensive.

Rejection Follow-Up Message

If you didn't get the job and you think it was perfect for you, don't give up. Employment specialists encourage applicants to respond to a rejection. The candidate who was offered the position may decline, or other positions may open up. In a rejection follow-up e-mail or letter, it is OK to admit that you are disappointed. Be sure to add, however, that you are still interested and will contact the company again in a month in case a job opens up. Then follow through for a couple of months—but don't overdo it. You should be professional and persistent, not annoying. Here is an example of an effective rejection follow-up message:

Dear Mr. O'Leary:

Although disappointed that someone else was selected for your accounting position, I appreciate your promptness and courtesy in notifying me.

Because I am confident that you would benefit from my technical and interpersonal skills in your fast-paced environment, please consider keeping my résumé in your active file. My desire to become a productive member of your Transamerica staff remains strong.

Our interview on _____ was very enjoyable, and I especially appreciate the time you and Ms. Goldstein spent describing your company's expansion into international markets. To enhance my qualifications, I have enrolled in a course in international accounting at CSU.

Should you have an opening for which I am qualified, you may reach me at (818) 719-3901. In the meantime, I will call you in a month to discuss employment possibilities.

Sincerely,

Subordinate your disappointment to your appreciation at being notified promptly and courteously.
Emphasize your continuing interest.

Refer to specifics of your interview.

Take the initiative; tell when you will call for an update.

Job Acceptance and Rejection Message

When all your hard work pays off, you will be offered the position you want. Although you will likely accept the position over the phone, it is a good idea to follow up with an acceptance e-mail or letter to confirm the details and to formalize the acceptance. Your acceptance message might look like this:

Dear Ms. Reed:

It was a pleasure talking with you earlier today. As I mentioned, I am delighted to accept the position of project manager with Innovative Creations, Inc., in your Seattle office. I look forward to becoming part of the IC team and starting work on a variety of exciting and innovative projects.

Confirm your acceptance of the position with enthusiasm.

As we agreed, my starting salary will be $46,000, with a full benefits package including health and life insurance, retirement plan, and two weeks of vacation per year.

Review salary and benefits details.

I look forward to starting my position with Innovative Creations on September 15, 2014. Before that date I will send you the completed tax and insurance forms you need. Thanks again for this opportunity, Ms. Reed.

Include the specific starting date.

Sincerely,

If you must turn down a job offer, show your professionalism by writing a sincere letter. This letter should thank the employer for the job offer and explain briefly that you are turning it down. Taking the time to extend this courtesy could help you in the future if this employer has a position you really want. Here's an example of a job rejection letter:

Dear Mr. Rosen:

Thank you very much for offering me the position of sales representative with Bendall Pharmaceuticals. It was a difficult decision to make, but I have accepted a position with another company.

Thank the employer for the job offer and decline the offer without giving specifics.

I appreciate your taking the time to interview me, and I wish Bendall much success in the future.

Express gratitude and best wishes for the future.

Sincerely,

REALITY CHECK: Don't Slam the Door When You Leave

"People spend much more time trying to find a new job than they do planning a proper exit. You can never be sure how secure any job is. It's important that you leave positive professional impressions with every employer so you can receive a good reference and keep the door open to returning if ever appropriate."[39]

—PATTY PROSSER, *chair, OI Partners, a global coaching, leadership development, and consulting firm*

Resignation Letter

After you have been in a position for a period of time, you may find it necessary to leave. Perhaps you have been offered a better position, or maybe you have decided to return to school full-time. Whatever the reason, you should leave your position gracefully and tactfully. Although you will likely discuss your resignation in person with your supervisor, it is a good idea to document your resignation by writing a formal letter. Some resignation letters are brief, while others contain great detail. Remember that many resignation letters are placed in personnel files; therefore, you should format and write yours using the professional business letter–writing techniques you learned earlier. Here is an example of a basic letter of resignation:

Dear Ms. Byrne:

This letter serves as formal notice of my resignation from Allied Corporation, effective Friday, August 15. I have enjoyed serving as your project manager for the past two years, and I am grateful for everything I have learned during my employment with Allied.

Confirm the exact date of resignation. Remind the employer of your contributions.

Please let me know what I can do over the next two weeks to help you prepare for my departure. I would be happy to help with finding and training my replacement.

Offer assistance to prepare for your resignation.

Thanks again for providing such a positive employment experience. I will long remember my time here.

End with thanks and a forward-looking statement.

Sincerely,

Although the employee who wrote the preceding resignation letter gave the standard two-week notice, you may find that a longer notice is necessary. The higher your position and the greater your responsibility, the longer the notice you give your employer should be. You should, however, always give some notice as a courtesy.

Writing job acceptance, job rejection, and resignation letters requires effort. That effort, however, is worth it because you are building bridges that may carry you to even better jobs in the future.

© Johannes Simon/Getty Images

Andrew Mason was once the admired founder and CEO of Groupon. But when the company's share price plummeted from $26 to $2.60 in a single year, calls for his resignation became fierce. Mason exited gracefully, writing, "After four-and-a-half intense and wonderful years as CEO of Groupon, I've decided that I'd like to spend more time with my family. Just kidding—I was fired today. If you're wondering why, you haven't been paying attention." Mason's memo took responsibility for failure, urged a renewed customer focus, and closed, "I will miss you terribly. Love, Andrew." One reporter hailed the exit as Mason's finest moment. Why are resignation letters important?[40]

Zooming in

© Africa Studio/Shutterstock.com; © ra2studio/Shutterstock.com

Your Turn: Applying Your Skills

You have begun to apply for internships in your chosen field and want to be prepared if one of the organizations contacts you for an interview. You decide to begin thinking about transferable skills you have developed in school. You also think you should develop success stories or illustrations of the three basic skills that career coach Don Georgevich says all employers want: communication skills, computer skills, and people skills.

YOUR TASK. List two or more anecdotes that illustrate each of the following: your communication skills, your computer skills, and your people skills. Think about experiences you have had at jobs, while volunteering, or in school that show you possess each characteristic. Prepare a list of success stories illustrating each. Remember that even entry-level or low-wage jobs such as babysitting or waiting tables provide opportunities to develop career-related skills. Then practice with a classmate until you can retell each story in an articulate and confident manner. Revise your list, improving the content and delivery. Your instructor may have you submit your list or perform your "interview" in class.

Courtesy of Don Georgevich

Summary of Learning Objectives

Go to
www.cengagebrain.com
and use your access code to unlock valuable student resources.

1 Explain the purposes and types of job interviews, including screening, one-on-one, panel, group, sequential, stress, and online interviews. Job interviews are extremely important because they can change your life. As a job candidate, you have the following purposes in an interview: (a) convince the employer of your potential, (b) find out more about the job and the company, and (c) expand on the information in your résumé. From the employer's perspective, the interview is an opportunity to (a) assess your abilities in relation to the requirements for the position; (b) discuss your training, experience, knowledge, and abilities in more detail; (c) see what drives and motives you; and (d) decide whether you would fit into the organization. Screening interviews seek to eliminate less qualified candidates. Hiring/placement interviews may be one-on-one, panel, group, sequential, stress, or online.

2 Describe what to do *before* an interview, including ensuring professional phone techniques, researching the target company, rehearsing success stories, cleaning up digital dirt, and fighting fear. If you are lucky enough to be selected for an interview, either in person or online, be prepared for a telephone screening interview so that you can respond professionally. Especially important before an interview is researching the target company by learning about its products, mission, customers, competitors, and finances. Before a hiring interview, prepare 30-second success stories that demonstrate your qualifications and achievements. Check your online presence and strive to clean up any digital dirt. Feeling fearful about an upcoming interview is natural. You can reduce fears, however, by knowing that you are thoroughly prepared and realizing that interviewing is a two-way street. If you are not sure where the employer is located, take a trial trip the day before your interview. Decide how to dress so that you will look qualified, competent, and professional. On the day of your interview, make sure you arrive on time and make a good first impression.

3 Describe what to do *during* an interview, including controlling nonverbal messages and answering typical interview questions. During your interview send positive nonverbal messages by controlling body movements, showing good posture, maintaining eye contact, using gestures effectively, and smiling enough to convey a positive attitude. Listen attentively, turn off your cell phone or other electronic devices, don't chew gum, and sound enthusiastic and sincere. Be prepared to respond to inquiries such as, *Tell me about yourself*. Practice answering questions about why you want to work for the organization, why you should be hired, how your education and experience have prepared you for the position, where you expect to be in five or ten years, what your greatest weaknesses are, and how much money you expect to earn. Be ready for situational questions that ask you to respond to hypothetical situations. Expect behavioral questions that begin with *Tell me about a time when you . . . .* Think about how you would respond to illegal or inappropriate questions, as well as questions you would ask about the job.

4 Describe what to do *after* an interview, including thanking the interviewer, contacting references, and writing follow-up messages. After leaving the interview, immediately make notes of the key points discussed. Note your strengths and weaknesses during the interview so that you can work to improve in future interviews. Write a thank-you letter including the date of the interview, the exact job title for which you were interviewed, and specific topics discussed. Show that you really want the job. Alert your references that they may be contacted. If you don't hear from the interviewer when expected, call or send an e-mail to follow up. Sound professional, not desperate, angry, or frustrated.

5 Prepare additional employment documents such as applications, rejection follow-up messages, acceptance messages, and resignation letters. If you are asked to fill out an application form, look over all the questions before starting. If asked for a salary figure, provide a salary range or write *Negotiable or Open*. If you don't get the job, consider writing a letter that expresses your disappointment but your desire to be contacted in case a job opens up. If you are offered a job, write a letter that confirms the details and formalizes your acceptance. If you decide not to accept a position, write a sincere letter turning down the job offer. Upon resigning from a position, write a letter that confirms the date of resignation, offers assistance to prepare for your resignation, and expresses thanks.

Chapter Review

1. During a job interview, do the interviewer and the interviewee want the same thing? How do their purposes differ? (Obj. 1)

2. Name the two main types of employment interviews, and explain how they differ. (Obj. 1)

3. Briefly describe the types of hiring/placement interviews candidates may encounter. (Obj. 1)

4. Career coaches warn candidates to never enter a job interview "cold." What does this mean, and how can a candidate heed the warning? (Obj. 2)

5. What are success stories, and how can candidates use them during job interviews? (Obj. 2)

6. What is digital dirt, and what should a candidate do to clean it up during the employment process? (Obj. 2)

7. When an interviewer asks, *Tell me about yourself*, what should a candidate do? (Obj. 3)

8. When an interviewer asks, *Where do you expect to be five (or ten) years from now*, what is a sure kiss of death in a candidate's response? How should a candidate respond? (Obj. 3)

9. Should candidates be candid with interviewers when asked about their weaknesses? (Obj. 3)

10. What are situational and behavioral interview questions, and how can a candidate craft responses that will make a favorable impression on the interviewer? (Obj. 3)

11. What kinds of questions should candidates ask during interviews? (Obj. 3)

12. List the steps candidates should take immediately following a job interview. (Obj. 4)

13. If a candidate is offered a position, why is it important for that person to write an acceptance letter, and what should it include? (Obj. 4)

14. When filling out an employment application form, how should a candidate respond when asked the reasons for leaving previous positions? (Obj. 5)

15. Is it a good idea to follow up after a job rejection? Why or why not? (Obj. 5)

Critical Thinking

1. "Like criminal background checks and drug tests, the social media check is quickly becoming an automatic part of the hiring process," asserts Melissa Bell, editor of BlogPost for *The Washington Post*.[41] Do you believe employers are justified or ethical in making these kinds of searches before hiring? Does this assume that candidates may be criminals? Isn't this similar to snooping?

2. Most job seekers are thrilled to be offered a job, and they fear haggling over salary. Yet, employment specialists say that failing to negotiate can be a mistake that reverberates for years. Do you agree or disagree with this statement? Why?

3. If you are asked an illegal interview question, why is it important to first assess the intentions of the interviewer?

4. Why is it a smart strategy to thank an interviewer, to follow up, and even to send a rejection follow-up message? Are any risks associated with this strategy?

5. **Ethical Issue.** A recruiter for an organization has an outstanding prospect for a position. As part of his screening process, the recruiter checks the online presence of the candidate and discovers from her social networks that she is 18 weeks pregnant—and happily so. He knows that the target position involves a big project that will go live just about the time she will be taking maternity leave. He decides not to continue the hiring process with this candidate. Is his action legal? Ethical? What lesson could be learned about posting private information online?

Activities

Note: All Documents for Analysis may be downloaded from **www.cengagebrain.com** so that you do not have to rekey the entire message.

16.1 Document for Analysis: Tracy's Poor Interview Follow-Up Letter (Obj. 4)

YOUR TASK. Study the following poorly written letter. In teams or in class discussion, list at least five specific weaknesses. It has problems with punctuation, wordiness, proofreading, capitalization, sentence structure, and other writing techniques you have studied. You may (a) use standard proofreading marks (see Appendix D) to correct the errors or (b) download the document from **www.cengagebrain.com** and revise at your computer.

3249 West Olive Avenue
Glendale, AZ 85302
June 17, 2015

Mr. Michael Searle
Vice President
Mariposa Agency
3021 East Van Buren Street
Phoenix, AZ 85022

Dear Mr. Searle:

It was extremely enjoyable to talk with you on tuesday about the Assistant Account Manager position at the Mariposa Agency. The position as you presented it seems to be a excelent match for my training and skills. The creative approach to Account Management that you described, confirmed my desire to work in a imaginative firm such as the Maraposa Agency.

In addition to an enthusiastic attitude I would bring to the position strong communication skills, and the ability to encourage others to work cooperatively within the department. My Graphic Arts training and experience will help me work with staff artists, and provide me with a understanding of the visual aspects of you work.

I certainly understand your departments need for strong support in the administrative area. My attention to detail and my organizational skills will help to free you to deal with more pressing issues in the management area. Despite the fact that it was on my résumé I neglected to emphasize during our interview that I had worked for 2 summers as a temporary office worker. This experience helped me to develop administrative support and clerical skills as well as to understand the every day demands of a busy office.

Thanks for taking the time to interview me, and explain the goals of your agency along with the dutys of this position. As I mentioned during the interview I am very interested in working for the Maraposa agency, and look forward to hearing from you about this position. In the event that you might possibly need additional information from me or facts about me, all you need to do is shoot me an e-mail at slinky.teslenko@hotmail.com.

Sincerely,

[signature]
Tracy A. Teslenko

16.2 Learning About the Target Organization (Obj. 2)

Web

One of the most important tasks of a job candidate is researching the target organization.

YOUR TASK. Select an organization where you would like to be employed. Assume you have been selected for an interview. Using resources described in this chapter, locate information about the organization's leaders and their business philosophies. Discover information about the organization's accomplishments, setbacks, finances, products, customers, competition, and advertising. Prepare a summary report documenting your findings.

16.3 Learning What Jobs Are Really About Through Blogs, Facebook, and Twitter (Obj. 2)

Social Media | **Web**

Blogs and social media sites such as Facebook and Twitter are becoming important tools in the job-search process. By accessing blogs, company Facebook pages, and Twitter feeds, job seekers can locate much insider information about a company's culture and day-to-day activities.

YOUR TASK. Using the Web, locate a blog that is maintained by an employee of a company where you might like to work. Monitor the blog for at least a week. Also, access the company's Facebook page and monitor Twitter feeds for at least a week. Prepare a short report summarizing what you learned about the company through reading the blog postings, status updates, and tweets. Include a statement of whether this information would be valuable during your job search.

16.4 Digging for Digital Dirt: Keeping a Low Profile Online (Obj. 2)

Social Media | **Web**

Before embarking on your job hunt, you should find out what employers might find if they searched your personal life in cyberspace, specifically on Facebook, Twitter, and so forth. Running your name through Google and other search engines, particularly enclosed in quotation marks to lower the number of hits, is usually the first step. To learn even more, try some of the people-search sites such as 123people, Snitch.name, and PeekYou. They collect information from a number of search engines, websites, and social networks.

YOUR TASK. Use Google, 123people, and another search tool to explore the Web for your full name, enclosed in quotation marks. In Google, don't forget to run an *Images* search at **http://www .google.com/images** to find any photos of questionable taste. If your instructor requests, share your insights with the class—not the salacious details, but general observations—or write a short memo summarizing the results.

16.5 Exploring Appropriate Interview Attire (Obj. 2)

Web

As you prepare for your interview by learning about the company and the industry, don't forget a key component of interview success: creating a favorable first impression by wearing appropriate business attire. Job seekers often have nebulous ideas about proper interview wear. Some wardrobe mishaps include choosing a conservative "power suit" but accessorizing it with beat-up casual shoes or a shabby bag. Grooming glitches include dandruff on dark suit fabric, dirty fingernails, or mothball odor. Women sometimes wrongly assume that any black clothing items are acceptable, even if they are too tight, revealing, sheer, or made of low-end fabrics. Most image consultants agree that workplace wardrobe falls into three main categories: business formal, business casual, and casual. Only business formal is considered proper interview apparel.

YOUR TASK. To prepare for your big day, search the Web for descriptions and images of *business formal*. You may research *business casual* and *casual* styles, but for an interview, always dress on the side of caution—conservatively. Compare prices and look for suit sales to buy one or two attractive interview outfits. Share your findings (notes, images, and a price range for suits, solid shoes, and accessories) with the class and your instructor.

16.6 Building Interview Skills With Worksheets (Obj. 3)

Successful interviews require diligent preparation and repeated practice. To be well prepared, you need to know what skills are required for your targeted position. In addition to computer and communication skills, employers generally want to know whether you work well with a team, accept responsibility, solve problems, are efficient, meet deadlines, show leadership, save time and money, and are a hard worker.

YOUR TASK. Consider a position for which you are eligible now or one for which you will be eligible when you complete your education. Identify the skills and traits necessary for this position. If you prepared a résumé in Chapter 15, be sure that it addresses these targeted areas. Now prepare interview worksheets listing at least ten technical and other skills or traits you think a recruiter will want to discuss in an interview for your targeted position.

16.7 Preparing Success Stories (Obj. 3)

You can best showcase your talents if you are ready with your own success stories that illustrate how you have developed the skills or traits required for your targeted position.

YOUR TASK. Using the worksheets you prepared in **Activity 16.6,** prepare success stories that highlight the required skills or traits. Select three to five stories to develop into answers to potential interview questions. For example, here is a typical question: *How does your background relate to the position we have open? A possible response: As you know, I have just completed an intensive training program in _____ . In addition, I have over three years of part-time work experience in a variety of business settings. In one position I was selected to manage a small business in the absence of the owner. I developed responsibility and customer-service skills in filling orders efficiently, resolving shipping problems, and monitoring key accounts. I also inventoried and organized products worth over $200,000. When the owner returned from a vacation to Florida, I was commended for increasing sales and was given a bonus in recognition of my efforts.* People relate to and remember stories. Try to shape your answers into memorable stories.

16.8 Polishing Answers to Interview Questions (Obj. 3)

Team

Practice makes perfect in interviewing. The more often you rehearse responses to typical interview questions, the closer you are to getting the job.

YOUR TASK. Select three questions from each of these question categories discussed in this chapter: questions to get acquainted, questions to gauge your interest, questions about your experience and accomplishments, questions about the future, and challenging questions. Write your answers to each set of questions. Try to incorporate skills and traits required for the targeted position, and include success stories where appropriate. Polish these answers and your delivery technique by practicing in front of a mirror or by making an audio or video recording. Your instructor may choose this assignment as a group activity in class.

16.9 Learning to Answer Situational Interview Questions (Obj. 3)

Team | **Web**

Situational interview questions can vary widely from position to position. You should know enough about a position to understand some of the typical situations you would encounter on a regular basis.

YOUR TASK. Use your favorite search tool to locate typical job descriptions of a position in which you are interested. Based on these descriptions, develop a list of six to eight typical situations someone in this position would face; then write situational interview questions for each of these scenarios. In pairs, role-play interviewer and interviewee, alternating with each question.

16.10 Developing Skills With Behavioral Interview Questions (Obj. 3)

> Team   Web

Behavioral interview questions are increasingly popular, and you will need a little practice before you can answer them easily.

YOUR TASK. Use your favorite search tool to locate lists of behavioral questions on the Web. Select five skills areas such as communication, teamwork, and decision making. For each skill area, find three behavioral questions that you think would be effective in an interview. In pairs, role-play interviewer and interviewee, alternating with your listed questions. You goal is to answer effectively in one or two minutes. Remember to use the STAR method when answering.

16.11 Negotiating a Salary (Obj. 3)

> Team

Negotiating a salary can be tricky. You want to get what you're worth, but you don't want to offend or scare off the recruiter—especially in a weak economy in which jobs are scarce. Worse yet, negotiating doesn't come naturally to Americans. "Most people in our country are not used to bargaining," says salary expert Matthew Deluca. "But if you don't bargain, you're not going to get all you should."[42]

YOUR TASK. To build your negotiating skills, reread the Career Coach box on page 602. Then, role-play a situation in which a hiring manager offers a candidate a starting salary of $44,500. The candidate wants $48,000 to start. The candidate responds to preliminary questions and negotiates the salary offer.

16.12 Creating an Interview "Cheat Sheet" (Obj. 3)

Even the best-rehearsed applicants sometimes forget to ask the questions they prepared, or they fail to stress their major accomplishments in job interviews. Sometimes applicants are so rattled they even forget the interviewer's name. To help you keep your wits during an interview, make a "cheat sheet" that summarizes key facts, answers, and questions. Review it before the interview and again as the interview is ending to be sure you have covered everything that is critical.

YOUR TASK. Prepare a cheat sheet with the following information:

Day and time of interview:

Meeting with: [Name of interviewer(s), title, company, city, state, zip, telephone, cell, fax, e-mail]

Major accomplishments (four to six):

Management or work style (four to six):

Things you need to know about me (three or four items):

Reason I left my last job:

Answers to difficult questions (four or five answers):

Questions to ask interviewer:

Things I can do for you:

16.13 Handling Inappropriate and Illegal Interview Questions (Obj. 3)

Although some questions are considered inappropriate and potentially illegal by the government, many interviewers will ask them anyway—whether intentionally or unknowingly. Being prepared is important.

YOUR TASK. How would you respond in the following scenario? Assume you are being interviewed at one of the top companies on your list of potential employers. The interviewing committee consists of a human resources manager and the supervising manager of the department where you would work. At various times during the interview, the supervising manager asks questions that make you feel uncomfortable. For example, he asks whether you are married. You know this question is inappropriate, but you see no harm in answering it. Then, however, he asks how old you are. Because you started college early and graduated in three and a half years, you are worried that you may not be considered mature enough for this position. However, you have most of the other qualifications required, and you are convinced you could succeed on the job. How should you answer this question?

16.14 Knowing What to Ask (Obj. 3)

When it is your turn to ask questions during the interview process, be ready.

YOUR TASK. Decide on three to five questions that you would like to ask during an interview. Write these questions down and practice asking them so that you sound confident and sincere.

16.15 Role-Playing in a Mock Interview (Obj. 3)

> Team

One of the best ways to understand interview dynamics and to develop confidence is to role-play the parts of interviewer and candidate in a mock interview.

YOUR TASK. Choose a partner for this activity. Each partner makes a list of two interview questions for each of the eight interview question categories presented in this chapter. In team sessions you and your partner will role-play an actual interview. One acts as interviewer; the other is the candidate. Prior to the interview, the candidate tells the interviewer the job he or she is applying for and the name of the company. For the interview, the interviewer and candidate should dress appropriately and sit in chairs facing each other. The interviewer greets the candidate and makes the candidate comfortable. The candidate gives the interviewer a copy of his or her résumé. The interviewer asks three (or more depending on your instructor's time schedule) questions from the candidate's list. The interviewer may also ask follow-up questions, if appropriate. When finished, the interviewer ends the meeting graciously. After one interview, partners reverse roles and repeat.

16.16 Recording an Interview (Obj. 3)

Seeing how you look and hearing how you sound during an interview can help you improve your body language and presentation style. Your instructor may act as an interviewer, or an outside businessperson may be asked to conduct mock interviews in your classroom.

YOUR TASK. Engage a student or campus specialist to prepare a video or audio recording of your interview. Review your performance and critique it looking for ways to improve. Your instructor may ask class members to offer comments and suggestions on individual interviews. Alternatively, visit your campus career center, if available, and sign up for a mock interview. Ask whether your session can be recorded for subsequent viewing.

16.17 YouTube: Critiquing Interview Skills (Obj. 3)

Web

The adage *Practice makes perfect* is especially true for interviewing. The more you confront your fears in mock or real interviews, the calmer and more confident you will be when your dream job is on the line. Short of undergoing your own interview, you can also learn from observation. The Web offers countless video clips showing examples of excellent, and poor, interviewing techniques.

YOUR TASK. In addition to the video accompanying this book, visit YouTube or search the Internet for other interview videos. Select a clip that you find particularly entertaining or informative. Watch it multiple times and jot down your observations. Then summarize the scenario in a paragraph or two. Provide examples of interview strategies that worked and those that didn't, applying the information you learned in this chapter. If required, share your insights about the video with the class.

16.18 Mastering Interviews Over Meals (Obj. 3)

Web

Although they are less likely for entry-level candidates, nevertheless, interviews over business meals are a popular means to size up the social skills of a job seeker, especially in second and subsequent interviews. Candidates coveting jobs with a lot of face-to-face contact with the public may be subjected to the ultimate test: table manners. Interviews are nerve-racking and intimidating enough, but imagine having to juggle silverware, wrangle potentially messy food, and keep your clothing stain-free—all this while listening carefully to what is being said around the table and giving thoughtful, confident answers.

YOUR TASK. Researching tips can help you avoid the most common pitfalls associated with interviews over meals. Use your favorite search engine and try queries such as *interview dining tips*, *interviewing over meals*, and so forth. Consider the credibility of your sources. Are they authorities on the subject? Compile a list of tips, and jot down your sources. Share the list with your peers. If you instructor directs, discuss the categories of advice provided. Then, as a class assemble a universal list of the most common interview tips.

16.19 Saying Thanks for the Interview (Obj. 4)

You have just completed an exciting employment interview, and you want the interviewer to remember you.

YOUR TASK. Write a follow-up thank-you letter to Ronald T. Ranson, Human Resources Development, Electronic Data Sources, 1328 Peachtree Plaza, Atlanta, GA 30314 (or a company of your choice). Make up any details needed.

16.20 Requesting a Reference (Obj. 4)

Your favorite professor has agreed to be one of your references. You have just arrived home from a job interview that went well, and you must ask your professor to write a letter of recommendation.

YOUR TASK. Write to the professor requesting that he or she send a letter of recommendation to the company at which you interviewed. Explain that the interviewer asked that the letter be sent directly to him. Provide information about the job and about yourself so that the professor can target its content.

16.21 Following Up After Submitting Your Résumé (Obj. 5)

E-mail

A month has passed since you sent your résumé and cover letter in response to a job advertisement. You are still interested in the position and would like to find out whether you still have a chance.

YOUR TASK. Write a follow-up e-mail or letter to an employer of your choice that does not offend the reader or damage your chances of employment.

16.22 Refusing to Take *No* for an Answer (Obj. 5)

After an excellent interview with Electronic Data Sources (or a company of your choice), you are disappointed to learn that someone else was hired. However, you really want to work for EDS.

YOUR TASK. Write a follow-up message to Ronald T. Ranson, Human Resources Development, Electronic Data Sources, 1328 Peachtree Plaza, Atlanta, GA 30314 (or a company of your choice). Indicate that you are disappointed but still interested.

16.23 Saying *Yes* to a Job Offer (Obj. 5)

Your dream has come true: you have just been offered an excellent position. Although you accepted the position on the phone, you want to send a formal acceptance letter.

YOUR TASK. Write a job acceptance letter to an employer of your choice. Include the specific job title, your starting date, and details about your compensation package. Make up any necessary details.

16.24 Searching for Advice (Objs. 1–5)

E-mail   **Web**

You can find wonderful, free, and sometimes entertaining job-search strategies and career tips, as well as interview advice, on the Web.

YOUR TASK. Use the Web to locate articles or links to sites with job-search, résumé, and interview information. Make a list of at least five good job-search pointers—ones that were not covered in this chapter. Send an e-mail to your instructor describing your findings, or post your findings to a class discussion board to share with your classmates.

16.25 Evaluating Your Course (Objs. 1–5)

Your boss has paid your tuition for this course. As you complete the course, he (or she) asks you for a letter about your experience in the course.

YOUR TASK. Write a letter to a boss in a real or imaginary organization explaining how this course made you more valuable to the organization.

Chat About It

In each chapter you will find five discussion questions related to the chapter material. Your instructor may assign these topics for you to discuss in class, in an online chat room, or on an online discussion board. Some of the discussion topics may require outside research. You may also be asked to read and respond to postings made by your classmates.

Topic 1: What is your greatest fear of what you might do or what might happen to you during an employment interview? How can you overcome your fears?

Topic 2: If you are interviewing for a company where most of the employees are dressed very casually, should you wear similar clothes to a job interview with that company? Why or why not?

Topic 3: You confide in a friend that you don't feel confident about going to job interviews. She tells you that you need more practice, and she suggests that you apply for jobs that you know you don't

want and accept interviews with companies in which you are not genuinely interested just so you can develop your interviewing skills. She says that interviewers expect some *shopping*. Do you agree? Would you take her advice? Why or why not?

Topic 4: Overprotective parents hovering over their millennial offspring have been dubbed *helicopter parents* by some human resources specialists. These take-charge parents now seem to extend their involvement into managing their adult children's job searches. Do you know of any parents that have been overinvolved, in your view? What did they do? How involved should parents be in their children's job efforts? Share your thoughts with your classmates.

Topic 5: Should job candidates be required to give their social media passwords to recruiters when asked? Explain your view. What does your state allow in this regard?

C.L.U.E. Grammar & Mechanics | *Review 16*

Total Review

Each of the following sentences has a total of **three** errors in grammar, punctuation, capitalization, usage, or spelling. On a separate sheet, write a correct version. Avoid adding new phrases, starting new sentences, or rewriting in your own words. When finished, compare your responses with those in the key beginning on page Key-3.

1. In interviewing job candidates recruiters have the following three purposes, assessing their skills, discussing their experience and deciding whether they are a good fit for the organization.

2. Jack wondered how many companys use the Internet to check candidates backgrounds?

3. Despite the heavy use of e-mail most employers' use the telephone to reach candidates and set up there interviews.

4. Most interviews usualy cover the same kinds of questions, therefore smart candidates prepare for them.

5. If your job history has gaps in it be prepared to explain what you did during this time, and how you kept up to date in your field.

6. Interviewing is a two way street and candidates should be prepared with there own meaningful questions.

7. Emma was asked whether she had a bachelors degree, and whether she had three years experience.

8. If you are consentious and want to create a good impression be sure to write a thank you message after a job interview.

9. When Marias interview was over she told friends that she had done good.

10. Maria was already to send a thank-you message, when she realized she could not spell the interviewers name.

Notes

[1] Georgevich, G. (2013, March 17). E-mail interview with Mary Ellen Guffey.

[2] Georgevich, G. (n.d.). Tough interview questions employers will ask. Retrieved from http://www.jobinterviewtools.com/blog/tough-interview-questions-employers-will-ask

[3] Ibid.

[4] Bergey, B. (2009, December 10). Online job interviews becoming more popular. WKOW.com. Retrieved from http://www.wkowtv.com/Global/story.asp?S=11655389; Kennedy, J. L. (2008). *Job interviews for dummies*. Hoboken, NJ: Wiley, p. 20.

[5] Wilmott, N. (n.d.). Interviewing styles: Tips for interview approaches. About.com: Human Resources. Retrieved from http://humanresources.about.com/cs/selectionstaffing/a/interviews.htm

[6] Photo essay based on Michelli, J. (2011, October 5). The Zappos experience: hiring for culture fit. [Web log post; Video file]. Retrieved from http://blogs.zappos.com/blogs/zappos-family/2011/10/05/zappos-experience-hiring-culture-fit; Sonnenberg, D. (2010, May 19). Religious CEOs: Chick-fil-A Founder, S. Truett Cathy. Minyanville. Retrieved from http://www.minyanville.com/special-features/articles/religious-ceos-s-truett-cathy-chickfila/5/19/2010/id/28281; Smith, E. (2012, August 1). Survey: Profs admit they'd discriminate against conservatives in hiring, advancement. *The Washington Times*. Retrieved from http://www.washingtontimes.com

[7] Proulx, L. S. (2012, May 26). How to ace the panel interview. Retrieved from http://www.careerrealism.com/interview-panel-ace

[8] Cristante, D. (2009, June 15). How to succeed in a group interview. CareerFAQs. Retrieved from http://www.careerfaqs.com.au/job-interview-tips/1116/How-to-succeed-in-a-group-interview

[9] Weiss, T. (2009, May 12). Going on the second interview. *Forbes*. Retrieved from http://www.forbes.com/2009/05/12/second-interview-advice-leadership-careers-basics.html

[10] Hansen, R. (2010). Situational interviews and stress interviews: What to make of them and how to succeed in them. Quintessential Careers. Retrieved from http://www.quintcareers.com /situational_stress_interviews.html

[11] Purdy, C. (2011, April 11). Job interviews: Tips for the virtual interview. Retrieved from http://www.monsterthinking.com/2011/04/18 /job-interviews-tips-for-the-virtual-interview

[12] Bergey, B. (2009, December 10). Online job interviews becoming more popular. WKOWTV. Retrieved from http://www.wkowtv.com/Global /story.asp?S=11655389

[13] Breslin, S. (2011, November 25). 7 weird job tips. Retrieved from http://www.forbes.com/sites /susannahbreslin/2012/11/25/7-weird-job -interview-tips

[14] Green, A. (2011, February 7). How to prepare for a job interview. US News.com. Retrieved from http://money.usnews.com/money /blogs/outside-voices-careers/2011/02/07 /how-to-prepare-for-a-job-interview

[15] Gold, T. (2010, November 28). How social media can get you a job. Marketing Trenches. Retrieved from http://www.marketingtrenches .com/marketing-careers/how-social-media -can-get-you-a-job

[16] Ryan, L. (2007, May 6). Job seekers: Prepare your stories. Ezine Articles. Retrieved from http://practicaljobsearchadvice.blogspot .com/2007/05/job-seekers-prepare-your -stories.html

[17] Haefner, R. (2009, June 10). More employers screening candidates via social networking sites. CareerBuilder. Retrieved from http://www .careerbuilder.com/Article/CB-1337-Getting -Hired-More-Employers-Screening-Candidates -via-Social-Networking-Sites

[18] Lynch, B. (2010, January 28). Online reputation in a connected world. [Presentation]. Data Privacy Day. Retrieved from http://www .microsoft.com

[19] Haefner, R. (2009, June 10). More employers screening candidates via social networking sites. CareerBuilder. Retrieved from http://www .careerbuilder.com/Article/CB-1337-Getting -Hired-More-Employers-Screening-Candidates -via-Social-Networking-Sites

[20] Finder, A. (2006, June 11). For some, online persona undermines a résumé. The New York Times. Retrieved from http://www.nytimes .com/2006/06/11/us/11recruit.html? _r=1&scp=1&sq=For%20some,%20online %20persona%20undermines&st= cse&oref=slogin

[21] Haefner, R. (2009, June 10). More employers screening candidates via social networking sites. CareerBuilder. Retrieved from http://www.careerbuilder.com/Article /CB-1337-Getting-Hired-More-Employers -Screening-Candidates-via-Social-Networking -Sites

[22] Active listening for interview success: How your ears can help you land the job. (n.d.). Hcareers.com. Retrieved from http://www.hcareers.com/us /resourcecenter/tabid/306/articleid/250/default .aspx

[23] Martin, C. (2001). Interview fitness training. San Ramon, CA: Interview Publishing.

[24] Korkki, P. (2009, September 13). Subtle cues can tell an interviewer "pick me." The New York Times. Retrieved from http://www.nytimes.com

[25] Susan L. Hodas cited in Korkki, P. (2009, September 13). Subtle cues can tell an interviewer "pick me." The New York Times. Retrieved from http://www .nytimes.com

[26] Welch, S., & Welch, J. (2008, July 7). Hiring is hard work. BusinessWeek, p. 80.

[27] Tyrell-Smith, T. (2011, January 25). Tell a story that will get you hired. Money/U.S. News & World Report. Retrieved from http://money .usnews.com/money/blogs/outside -voices-careers/2011/01/25/tell-a-story -that-will-get-you-hired

[28] The U.S. Equal Employment Opportunity Commission. (2009, November 21). Federal laws prohibiting job discrimination: Questions and answers. Retrieved from http://www.eeoc.gov /facts/qanda.html

[29] Doyle, A. (n.d.). Illegal interview questions. About. com. Retrieved from http://jobsearchtech.about .com/od/interview/l/aa022403.htm

[30] World HR editors. (n.d.) 30 interview questions you can't ask and 30 sneaky, legal alternatives to get the same info. HR World. Retrieved from http://www.hrworld.com /features/30-interview-questions-111507

[31] Ibid.

[32] Foss, J. (2012, May 12). 4 non-annoying ways to follow up after an interview. Forbes.com. Retrieved from http://www.forbes.com /sites/dailymuse/2012/05/30/4-non -annoying-ways-to-follow-up-after-an -interview/2

[33] Lublin, J. S. (2008, February 5). Notes to interviewers should go beyond a simple thank you. The Wall Street Journal, p. B1. Retrieved from http://online.wsj.com/article /SB120215930971242053.html

[34] Ibid.

[35] Korkki, P. (2009, September 13). Subtle cues can tell an interviewer "pick me." The New York Times. Retrieved from http://www.nytimes.com

[36] Olson, L. (2010, September 16). Why you should never skip the interview thank-you note. Money/U.S.News & World Report. Retrieved from http://money.usnews.com/money/blogs /outside-voices-careers/2010/09/16/why-you -should-always-send-an-interview-thankyou -note; Needleman, S. E. (2006, February 7). Be prepared when opportunity calls. The Wall Street Journal, p. B4.

[37] Green, A. (2010, December 27). How to follow up after applying for a job. Money/U.S.News & World Report. Retrieved from http://money .usnews.com/money/blogs/outside -voices-careers/2010/12/27/how-to-follow -up-after-applying-for-a-job

[38] Korkki, P. (2009, August 23). No response after an interview? What to do. The New York Times. Retrieved from http://www.nytimes.com

[39] Ford, S. (2012, March 7). The 10 biggest mistakes when leaving your job. Retrieved from http:// www.oipartners.net/news-detail/12-03-07 /The_10_Biggest_Mistakes_When_Leaving _Your_Job.aspx

[40] Photo essay based on Macke, J. (2013, February 28). Ousted Groupon CEO Andrew Mason writes the best exit memo ever. Breakout. Retrieved from http://finance.yahoo.com/blogs/breakout/one -thing-could-save-groupon-175358151.html

[41] Bell, M. (2011, July 15). More employers using firms that check applicants' social media history. Retrieved from http://www.washingtonpost .com/lifestyle/style/more-employers-using -firms-that-check-applicants-social-media -history/2011/07/12/gIQAxnJYGI_story.html

[42] Quoted in DeZube, D. (n.d.). Ten questions to ask when negotiating a salary. Monster.com. Retrieved from http://career-advice.monster .com/salary-benefits/negotiation-tips /10-salary-negotiation-questions/article.aspx

Appendix A
Grammar and Mechanics Guide

Competent Language Usage Essentials (C.L.U.E.)

C.L.U.E.

In the business world, people are often judged by the way they speak and write. Using the language competently can mean the difference between success and failure. Often a speaker sounds accomplished; but when that same individual puts ideas in print, errors in language usage destroy that person's credibility. One student observed, "When I talk, I get by on my personality; but when I write, the flaws in my communication show through. That's why I'm in this class."

How This Grammar and Mechanics Guide Can Help You

This grammar and mechanics guide contains 50 guidelines covering sentence structure, grammar, usage, punctuation, capitalization, and number style. These guidelines focus on the most frequently used—and abused—language elements. Frequent checkpoint exercises enable you to try your skills immediately. In addition to the 50 language guides in this appendix, you will find a list of 160 frequently misspelled words plus a quick review of selected confusing words.

The concentrated materials in this guide help novice business communicators focus on the major areas of language use. The guide is not meant to teach or review *all* the principles of English grammar and punctuation. It focuses on a limited number of language guidelines and troublesome words. Your objective should be mastery of these language principles and words, which represent a majority of the problems typically encountered by business writers.

How to Use This Grammar and Mechanics Guide

Your instructor may give you the short C.L.U.E. language diagnostic test (located in the Instructor's Manual) to help you assess your competency. A longer self-administered diagnostic test is available as part of Your Personal Language Trainer at **www.cengagebrain .com**. Either test will give you an idea of your language competence. After taking either diagnostic test, read and work your way through the 50 guidelines. You should also use the self-teaching Trainer exercises, all of which correlate with this Grammar and Mechanics Guide. Concentrate on areas in which you are weak. Memorize the spellings and definitions of the confusing words at the end of this appendix.

In this text you will find two kinds of exercises for your practice. (a) *Checkpoints,* located in this appendix, focus on a small group of language guidelines. Use them to test your comprehension as you complete each section. (b) *Grammar/Mechanics C.L.U.E. Review exercises*, located at the end of each chapter, help reinforce your language skills at the same time you are learning about the processes and products of business communication.

Many students want all the help they can get in improving their language skills. For additional assistance with grammar and language fundamentals, *Business Communication: Process and Product*, 8e, offers you unparalleled interactive and print resources:

- **Your Personal Language Trainer.** This self-paced learning tool is located at **www.cengagebrain.com**. Dr. Guffey acts as your personal trainer in helping you pump up your language muscles. Your Personal Language Trainer provides the rules plus hundreds of sentence applications so that you can test your knowledge and build your skills with immediate feedback and explanations.

- **Speak Right!**, found at **www.cengagebrain.com**, reviews frequently mispronounced words. You will hear correct pronunciations from Dr. Guffey so that you will never be embarrassed by mispronouncing these terms.
- **Spell Right!**, found at **www.cengagebrain.com**, presents frequently misspelled words along with exercises to help you improve your spelling.
- **Reference Books.** A more comprehensive treatment of grammar and punctuation guidelines can be found in Clark and Clark's *HOW: A Handbook for Office Professionals* and Guffey's *Business English*.

Grammar and Mechanics Guidelines

Sentence Structure

GUIDE 1: Avoid sentence fragments.   A fragment is an incomplete sentence. You can recognize a complete sentence because it (a) includes a subject (a noun or pronoun that interacts with a verb), (b) includes a verb (a word expressing action or describing a condition), and (c) makes sense (comes to a closure). A complete sentence is an independent clause. One of the most serious errors a writer can make is punctuating a fragment as if it were a complete sentence.

Fragment	Improved
Because 90 percent of all business transactions involve written messages. Good writing skills are critical.	Because 90 percent of all business transactions involve written messages, good writing skills are critical.
The recruiter requested a writing sample. Even though the candidate seemed to communicate well.	The recruiter requested a writing sample, even though the candidate seemed to communicate well.

Tip.   Fragments often can be identified by the words that introduce them—words such as *although, as, because, even, except, for example, if, instead of, since, so, such as, that, which,* and *when.* These words introduce dependent clauses. Make sure such clauses are always connected to independent clauses.

DEPENDENT CLAUSE   INDEPENDENT CLAUSE

Since she became supervisor, she had to write more memos and reports.

GUIDE 2: Avoid run-on (fused) sentences.   A sentence with two independent clauses must be joined by a coordinating conjunction (*and, or, nor, but*) or by a semicolon (;). Without a conjunction or a semicolon, a run-on sentence results.

Run-on	Improved
Rachel considered an internship she also thought about graduate school.	Rachel considered an internship, and she also thought about graduate school.
	Rachel considered an internship; she also thought about graduate school.

GUIDE 3: Avoid comma-splice sentences.   A comma splice results when a writer joins (splices together) two independent clauses—without using a coordinating conjunction (*and, or, nor, but*).

Comma Splice	Improved
Disney World operates in Orlando, EuroDisney serves Paris.	Disney World operates in Orlando; EuroDisney serves Paris.
	Disney World operates in Orlando, and EuroDisney serves Paris.
Visitors wanted a resort vacation, however they were disappointed.	Visitors wanted a resort vacation; however, they were disappointed.

Tip. In joining independent clauses, beware of using a comma and words such as *consequently, furthermore, however, therefore, then, thus,* and so on. These conjunctive adverbs require semicolons.

   Note: Sentence structure is also covered in Chapter 5.

✔ Checkpoint

Revise the following to rectify sentence fragments, comma splices, and run-ons.

1. Although it began as a side business for Disney. Destination weddings now represent a major income source.

2. About 2,000 weddings are held yearly. Which is twice the number just ten years ago.

3. Weddings may take place in less than one hour, however the cost may be as much as $5,000.

4. Limousines line up outside Disney's wedding pavilion, they are scheduled in two-hour intervals.

5. Most couples prefer a traditional wedding, others request a fantasy experience.

For all the Checkpoint sentences, compare your responses with the answers at the end of Appendix A.

Grammar

Verb Tense

GUIDE 4: Use present-tense, past-tense, and past-participle verb forms correctly.

Present Tense (Today I_____)	Past Tense (Yesterday I_____)	Past Participle (I have_____)
am	was	been
begin	began	begun
break	broke	broken
bring	brought	brought
choose	chose	chosen
come	came	come
do	did	done
give	gave	given
go	went	gone
know	knew	known
pay	paid	paid
see	saw	seen
steal	stole	stolen
take	took	taken
write	wrote	written

The package *came* yesterday, and Kevin *knew* what it contained.

If I *had seen* the shipper's bill, I *would have paid* it immediately.

I *know* the answer now; I wish I *had known* it yesterday.

Tip. Probably the most frequent mistake in tenses results from substituting the past-participle form for the past tense. Notice that the past-participle tense requires auxiliary verbs such as *has, had, have, would have,* and *could have.*

Faulty	Correct
When he *come* over last night, he *brung* pizza.	When he *came* over last night, he *brought* pizza.
If he *had came* earlier, we *could have saw* the video.	If he *had come* earlier, we *could have seen* the video.

Verb Mood

GUIDE 5: Use the subjunctive mood to express hypothetical (untrue) ideas.   The most frequent misuse of the subjunctive mood involves using *was* instead of *were* in clauses introduced by *if* and *as though* or containing *wish*.

> If I *were* (not *was*) you, I would take a business writing course.
>
> Sometimes I wish I *were* (not *was*) the manager of this department.
>
> He acts as though he *were* (not *was*) in charge of this department.

Tip.   If the statement could possibly be true, use *was*.

> If I *was* to blame, I accept the consequences.

✔ Checkpoint

Correct faults in verb tenses and mood.

6. If I was you, I would have went to the ten o'clock meeting.

7. Kevin could have wrote a better report if he had began earlier.

8. When the project manager seen the report, he immediately come to my office.

9. I wish the project manager was in my shoes for just one day.

10. If the manager had knew all that we do, I'm sure he would have gave us better reviews.

Verb Voice

For a discussion of active- and passive-voice verbs, see page 162 in Chapter 5.

Verb Agreement

GUIDE 6: Make subjects agree with verbs despite intervening phrases and clauses.   Become a detective in locating *true* subjects. Don't be deceived by prepositional phrases and parenthetic words that often disguise the true subject.

> Our study of annual budgets, five-year plans, and sales proposals *is* (not *are*) progressing on schedule. (The true subject is *study*.)
>
> The budgeted item, despite additions proposed yesterday, *remains* (not *remain*) as submitted. (The true subject is *item*.)
>
> A vendor's evaluation of the prospects for a sale, together with plans for follow-up action, *is* (not *are*) what we need. (The true subject is *evaluation*.)

Tip.   Subjects are nouns or pronouns that control verbs. To find subjects, cross out prepositional phrases beginning with words such as *about, at, by, for, from, of,* and *to*. Subjects of verbs are not found in prepositional phrases. Also, don't be tricked by expressions introduced by *together with, in addition to,* and *along with*.

GUIDE 7: Subjects joined by *and* require plural verbs. Watch for true subjects joined by the conjunction *and*. They require plural verbs.

> The CEO and one of his assistants *have* (not *has*) ordered a limo.

> Considerable time and money *were* (not *was*) spent on remodeling.

> Exercising in the gym and jogging every day *are* (not *is*) how he keeps fit.

GUIDE 8: Subjects joined by *or* or *nor* may require singular or plural verbs. The verb should agree with the closer subject.

> Either the software or the printer *is* (not *are*) causing the glitch. (The verb is controlled by the closer subject, *printer*.)

> Neither St. Louis nor Chicago *has* (not *have*) a chance of winning. (The verb is controlled by *Chicago*.)

Tip. In joining singular and plural subjects with *or* or *nor*, place the plural subject closer to the verb. Then, the plural verb sounds natural. For example, *Either the manufacturer or the distributors are responsible*.

GUIDE 9: Use singular verbs for most indefinite pronouns. The following pronouns all take singular verbs: *anyone, anybody, anything, each, either, every, everyone, everybody, everything, neither, nobody, nothing, someone, somebody*, and *something*.

> Everyone in both offices *was* (not *were*) given a bonus.

> Each of the employees *is* (not *are*) being interviewed.

GUIDE 10: Use singular or plural verbs for collective nouns, depending on whether the members of the group are operating as a unit or individually. Words such as *faculty, administration, class, crowd,* and *committee* are considered *collective* nouns. If the members of the collective are acting as a unit, treat them as singular subjects. If they are acting individually, it is usually better to add the word *members* and use a plural verb.

Correct

> The Finance Committee *is* working harmoniously. (*Committee* is singular because its action is unified.)

> The Planning Committee *are* having difficulty agreeing. (*Committee* is plural because its members are acting individually.)

Improved

> The Planning Committee members *are* having difficulty agreeing. (Add the word *members* if a plural meaning is intended.)

Tip. In the United States, collective nouns are generally considered singular. In Britain these collective nouns are generally considered plural.

✔ Checkpoint

Correct the errors in subject–verb agreement.

11. The agency's time and talent was spent trying to develop a blockbuster ad campaign.

12. Your e-mail message, along with both of its attachments, were not delivered to my computer.

13. Each of the Fortune 500 companies are being sent a survey regarding women in management.

14. A full list of names and addresses are necessary before we can begin.

15. Either the judge or the attorney have asked for a recess.

Pronoun Case

GUIDE 11: Learn the three cases of pronouns and how each is used. Pronouns are substitutes for nouns. Every business writer must know the following pronoun cases.

Subjective (Nominative) Case	Objective Case	Possessive Case
Used for subjects of verbs and subject complements	Used for objects of prepositions and objects of verbs	Used to show possession
we		
I	me	my, mine
us	our, ours	
you	you	you, yours
he	him	his
she	her	her, hers

Subjective (Nominative) Case	Objective Case	Possessive Case
Used for subjects of verbs and subject complements	Used for objects of prepositions and objects of verbs	Used to show possession
it	it	its
they	them	their, theirs
who, whoever	whom, whomever	whose

GUIDE 12: Use subjective-case pronouns as subjects of verbs and as complements. Complements are words that follow linking verbs (such as *am, is, are, was, were, be, being,* and *been*) and rename the words to which they refer.

> *Bryan and I* (not *Bryan and me*) are looking for entry-level jobs. (Use subjective-case pronouns as the subjects of the verb phrase *are looking.*)

> We hope that Marci and *he* (not *him*) will be hired. (Use a subjective-case pronoun as the subject of the verb phrase *will be hired.*)

> It must have been *she* (not *her*) who called last night. (Use a subjective-case pronoun as a subject complement.)

Tip. If you feel awkward using subjective pronouns after linking verbs, rephrase the sentence to avoid the dilemma. Instead of *It is she who is the boss,* say, *She is the boss.*

GUIDE 13: Use objective-case pronouns as objects of prepositions and verbs.

> Send the e-mail to *her* and *me* (not *she* and *I*). (The pronouns *her* and *me* are objects of the preposition *to.*)

> The CEO appointed Rick and *him* (not *he*) to the committee. (The pronoun *him* is the object of the verb *appointed.*)

Tip. When a pronoun appears in combination with a noun or another pronoun, ignore the extra noun or pronoun and its conjunction. Then, the case of the pronoun becomes more obvious.

> Jason asked Jennifer and *me* (not *I*) to lunch. (Ignore *Jennifer and.*)

> The waiter brought hamburgers to Jason and *me* (not *I*). (Ignore *Jason and.*)

Tip. Be especially alert to the following prepositions: *except, between, but,* and *like.* Be sure to use objective pronouns as their objects.

> Just between you and *me* (not *I*), that mineral water comes from the tap.

> Everyone except Robert and *him* (not *he*) responded to the invitation.

GUIDE 14: Use possessive pronouns to show ownership.

Possessive pronouns (such as *hers, yours, whose, ours, theirs,* and *its*) require no apostrophes.

> All reports except *yours* (not *your's*) have to be rewritten.

> The apartment and *its* (not *it's*) contents are *hers* (not *her's*) until June.

Tip. Don't confuse possessive pronouns and contractions. Contractions are shortened forms of subject–verb phrases (such as *it's* for *it is, there's* for *there is, who's* for *who is,* and *they're* for *they are*).

✔ Checkpoint

Correct errors in pronoun case.

16. My partner and me have looked at many apartments, but your's has the best location.

17. We thought the car was her's, but it's license plate does not match.

18. Just between you and I, do you think there printer is working?

19. Theres not much the boss or me can do if its broken, but its condition should have been reported to him or I earlier.

20. We received several applications, but your's and her's were missing.

GUIDE 15: Use pronouns ending in *self* only when they refer to previously mentioned nouns or pronouns.

> The president *himself* ate all the M&Ms.

> Send the package to Mike or *me* (not *myself*).

Tip. Trying to sound less egocentric, some radio and TV announcers incorrectly substitute *myself* when they should use *I.* For example, "Jimmy and *myself* (should be *I*) are cohosting the telethon."

GUIDE 16: Use *who* or *whoever* for subjective-case constructions and *whom* or *whomever* for objective-case constructions.

In determining the correct choice, it is helpful to substitute *he* for *who* or *whoever* and *him* for *whom* or *whomever*.

> For *whom* was this software ordered? (The software was ordered for *him*.)

> *Who* did you say called? (You did say *he* called?)

> Give the supplies to *whoever* asked for them. (In this sentence the clause *whoever asked for them* functions as the object of the preposition *to.* Within the clause *whoever* is the subject of the verb *asked.* Again, try substituting *he: he asked for them.*)

✔ Checkpoint

Correct any errors in the use of *self*-ending pronouns and *who/whom.*

21. The boss herself is willing to call whoever we decide to honor.

22. Who have you asked to develop ads for our new products?

23. I have a pizza for whomever placed the telephone order.

24. The meeting is set for Wednesday; however, Matt and myself cannot attend.

25. Incident reports must be submitted by whomever experiences a personnel problem.

Pronoun Reference

GUIDE 17: Make pronouns agree in number and gender with the words to which they refer (their antecedents). When the gender of the antecedent is obvious, pronoun references are simple.

> One of the men failed to fill in *his* (not *their*) name on the application. (The singular pronoun *his* refers to the singular *One*.)

> Each of the female nurses was escorted to *her car* (not *their cars*). (The singular pronoun *her* and singular noun *car* are necessary because they refer to the singular subject *Each*.)

> Somebody on the girls' team left *her* (not *their*) headlights on.

When the gender of the antecedent could be male or female, sensitive writers today have a number of options.

Faulty	Improved
Every employee should receive *their* check Friday. (The plural pronoun *their* does not agree with its singular antecedent *employee*.)	All employees should receive *their* checks Friday. (Make the subject plural so that the plural pronoun *their* is acceptable. This option is preferred by many writers today.)
	All employees should receive checks Friday. (Omit the possessive pronoun entirely.)
	Every employee should receive *a* check Friday. (Substitute *a* for a pronoun.)
	Every employee should receive *his or her* check Friday. (Use the combination *his or her*. However, this option is wordy and should be avoided.)

GUIDE 18: Be sure that pronouns such as *it, which, this,* and *that* refer to clear antecedents. Vague pronouns confuse the reader because they have no clear single antecedent. The most troublesome are *it, which, this,* and *that.* Replace vague pronouns with concrete nouns, or provide these pronouns with clear antecedents.

Faulty	Improved
Our office recycles as much paper as possible because *it* helps the environment. (Does *it* refer to *paper, recycling,* or *office?*)	Our office recycles as much paper as possible because *such an effort* helps the environment. (*Effort* supplies a concrete *noun* for the vague pronoun *it.*)
The disadvantages of some mobile apps can offset their advantages. *That* merits further evaluation. (What merits evaluation: advantages, disadvantages, or the offsetting of one by the other?)	The disadvantages of some mobile apps can offset their advantages. That fact merits further evaluation. (*Fact* supplies a concrete noun for the vague pronoun *that.*)
Negotiators announced an expanded wellness program, reductions in dental coverage, and a proposal to move child-care facilities off site. *This* ignited employee protests. (What exactly ignited employee protests?)	Negotiators announced an expanded wellness program, reductions in dental coverage, and a proposal to move child-care facilities off site. *This* change in child-care facilities ignited employee protests. (The pronoun *This* now has a clear reference.)

Tip. Whenever you use the words *this, that, these,* and *those* by themselves, a red flag should pop up. These words are dangerous when they stand alone. Inexperienced writers often use them to refer to an entire previous idea, rather than to a specific antecedent, as shown in the preceding examples. You can usually solve the problem by adding another idea to the pronoun (such as *this change*).

✔ Checkpoint

Correct the faulty and vague pronoun references in the following sentences. Numerous remedies exist.

26. Every employee must wear their picture identification badge.

27. Flexible working hours may mean slower career advancement, but it appeals to many workers.

28. Any renter must pay his rent by the first of the month.

29. Someone in this office reported that his computer had a virus.

30. Obtaining agreement on job standards, listening to coworkers, and encouraging employee suggestions all helped to open lines of communication. This is particularly important in team projects.

Adjectives and Adverbs

GUIDE 19: Use adverbs, not adjectives, to describe or limit the action of verbs. Use adjectives after linking verbs.

> Andrew said he did *well* (not *good*) on the exam. (The adverb *well* describes how he did.)
>
> After its tune-up, the engine is running *smoothly* (not *smooth*). (The adverb *smoothly* describes the verb *is running*.)
>
> Don't take the manager's criticism *personally* (not *personal*). (The adverb *personally* tells how to take the criticism.)
>
> She finished her homework *more quickly* (not *quicker*) than expected. (The adverb *more quickly* explains how she finished her homework.)
>
> Liam felt bad (not *badly*) after he heard the news. (The adjective *bad* follows the linking verb *felt*.)

GUIDE 20: Hyphenate two or more adjectives that are joined to create a compound modifier before a noun.

> You need an *easy-to-remember* e-mail address and a *one-page* résumé.
>
> *Person-to-person* networking continues to be the best way to find a job.

Tip. Don't confuse adverbs ending in *-ly* with compound adjectives: *newly enacted* law and *highly regarded* CEO would not be hyphenated.

✔ Checkpoint

Correct any problems in the use of pronouns, adjectives, and adverbs.

31. My manager and me could not resist the once in a lifetime opportunity.

32. Because John and him finished their task so quick, they made a fast trip to the recently opened snack bar.

33. If I do good on the exam, I qualify for many part time jobs and a few full time positions.

34. The vice president told him and I not to take the announcement personal.

35. In the not too distant future, we may enjoy more practical uses of robots.

Punctuation

Downward communication delivers job instructions, procedures, and appraisals.

In preparing your résumé, try to keep it brief, make it easy to read, and include only job-related information.

The new ice cream flavors include cookie dough, chocolate raspberry truffle, cappuccino, and almond amaretto.

Tip.   Some professional writers omit the comma before *and*. However, most business writers prefer to retain that comma because it prevents misreading the last two items as one item. Notice in the previous example how the final two ice cream flavors could have been misread if the comma had been omitted.

GUIDE 22: Use commas to separate introductory clauses and certain phrases from independent clauses (CmIntro).   This guideline describes the comma most often omitted by business writers. Sentences that open with dependent clauses (frequently introduced by words such as *since, when, if, as, although,* and *because*) require commas to separate them from the main idea. The comma helps readers recognize where the introduction ends and the big idea begins. Introductory phrases of four or more words or phrases containing verbal elements also require commas.

If you recognize introductory clauses, you will have no trouble placing the comma. (A comma separates the introductory dependent clause from the main clause.)

When you have mastered this rule, half the battle with commas will be won.

As expected, additional explanations are necessary. (Use a comma even if the introductory clause omits the understood subject: *As we expected*.)

In the spring of last year, we opened our franchise. (Use a comma after a phrase containing four or more words.)

Having considered several alternatives, we decided to invest. (Use a comma after an introductory verbal phrase.)

To invest, we needed $100,000. (Use a comma after an introductory verbal phrase, regardless of its length.)

Tip.   Short introductory prepositional phrases (three or fewer words) require no commas. Don't clutter your writing with unnecessary commas after introductory phrases such as *by 2015, in the fall,* or *at this time*.

GUIDE 23: Use a comma before the coordinating conjunction in a compound sentence (CmConj).   The most common coordinating conjunctions are *and, or, nor,* and *but*. Occasionally, *for, yet,* and *so* may also function as coordinating conjunctions. When coordinating conjunctions join two independent clauses, commas are needed.

The investment sounded too good to be true, *and* many investors were dubious about it. (Use a comma before the coordinating conjunction *and* in a compound sentence.)

Southern California is the financial fraud capital of the world, *but* some investors refuse to heed warning signs.

Tip.   Before inserting a comma, test the two clauses. Can each of them stand alone as a complete sentence? If either is incomplete, skip the comma.

Promoters said the investment offer was for a limited time and could not be extended even one day. (Omit a comma before *and* because the second part of the sentence is not a complete independent clause.)

Lease payments are based largely on your down payment and on the value of the car at the end of the lease. (Omit a comma before *and* because the second half of the sentence is not a complete clause.)

✔ Checkpoint

Add appropriate commas.

36. Before she enrolled in this class Erin used to sprinkle her writing with commas semicolons and dashes.

37. After studying punctuation she learned to use commas more carefully and to reduce her reliance on dashes.

38. At this time Erin is engaged in a serious yoga program but she also finds time to enlighten her mind.

39. Next fall Erin may enroll in communication and merchandising courses or she may work for a semester to earn money.

40. When she completes her junior year she plans to apply for an internship in Los Angeles Burbank or Long Beach.

GUIDE 24: Use commas appropriately in dates, addresses, geographical names, degrees, and long numbers (CmDate).

September 30, 1993, is his birthday. (For dates use commas before and after the year.)

Send the application to James Kirby, 20045 45th Avenue, Lynnwood, WA 98036, as soon as possible. (For addresses use commas to separate all units except the two-letter state abbreviation and the zip code.)

Lisa expects to move from Cupertino, California, to Sonoma, Arizona, next fall. (For geographical areas use commas to enclose the second element.)

Karen Munson, CPA, and Richard B. Larsen, PhD, were the speakers. (Use commas to enclose professional designations and academic degrees following names.)

The latest census figures show the city's population to be 342,000. (In figures use commas to separate every three digits, counting from the right.)

GUIDE 25: Use commas to set off internal sentence interrupters (CmIn). Sentence interrupters may be verbal phrases, dependent clauses, contrasting elements, or parenthetical expressions (also called transitional phrases). These interrupters often provide information that is not grammatically essential.

Harvard researchers, working steadily for 18 months, developed a new cancer therapy. (Use commas to set off an internal interrupting verbal phrase.)

The new therapy, which applies a genetically engineered virus, raises hopes among cancer specialists. (Use commas to set off nonessential dependent clauses.)

Dr. James C. Morrison, who is one of the researchers, made the announcement. (Use commas to set off nonessential dependent clauses.)

It was Dr. Morrison, not Dr. Arturo, who led the team effort. (Use commas to set off a contrasting element.)

This new therapy, by the way, was developed from a herpes virus. (Use commas to set off a parenthetical expression.)

Tip. Parenthetical (transitional) expressions are helpful words that guide the reader from one thought to the next. Here are typical parenthetical expressions that require commas:

as a matter of fact	in addition	of course
as a result	in the meantime	on the other hand
consequently	nevertheless	therefore
for example		

Tip. Always use *two* commas to set off an interrupter, unless it begins or ends a sentence.

✔ Checkpoint

Insert necessary commas.

41. James listed 1805 Martin Luther King Street San Antonio Texas 78220 as his forwarding address.

42. This report is not however one that must be classified.

43. Employment of paralegals which is expected to decrease 12 percent next year is contracting because of the slow economy.

44. The contract was signed May 15 2012 and remains in effect until May 15 2018.

45. As a matter of fact the average American drinks enough coffee to require 12 pounds of coffee beans annually.

GUIDE 26: Avoid unnecessary commas (CmNo).   Do not use commas between sentence elements that belong together. Do not automatically insert commas before every *and* or at points where your voice might drop if you were saying the sentence out loud.

Faulty

Growth will be spurred by the increasing complexity of business operations, and by large employment gains in trade and services. (A comma unnecessarily precedes *and*.)

All students with high grades, are eligible for the honor society. (A comma unnecessarily separates the subject and verb.)

One of the reasons for the success of the business honor society is, that it is very active. (A comma unnecessarily separates the verb and its complement.)

Our honor society has, at this time, over 50 members. (Commas unnecessarily separate a prepositional phrase from the sentence.)

✔ Checkpoint

Remove unnecessary commas. Add necessary ones.

46. Car companies promote leasing because it brings customers back into their showrooms sooner, and gives dealers a steady supply of late-model used cars.

47. When shopping for a car you may be offered a fantastic leasing deal.

48. The trouble with many leases is, that the value of the car at the end of the lease may be less than expected.

49. We think on the other hand, that you should compare the costs of leasing and buying, and that you should talk to a tax advisor.

50. American and Japanese automakers are, at this time, offering intriguing lease deals.

Semicolons, Colons

GUIDE 27: Use a semicolon to join closely related independent clauses. Experienced writers use semicolons to show readers that two thoughts are closely associated. If the ideas are not related, they should be expressed in separate sentences. Often, but not always, the second independent clause contains a conjunctive adverb (such as *however, consequently, therefore,* or *furthermore*) to show the relation between the two clauses. Use a semicolon before a conjunctive adverb of two or more syllables (such as *however, consequently, therefore,* or *furthermore*) and a comma after it.

Learning history is easy; learning its lessons is almost impossible. (A semicolon joins two independent clauses.)

He was determined to complete his degree; consequently, he studied diligently. (A semicolon precedes the conjunctive adverb, and a comma follows it.)

Serena wanted a luxury apartment located near campus; however, she couldn't afford the rent. (A semicolon precedes the conjunctive adverb, and a comma follows it.)

Tip. Don't use a semicolon unless each clause is truly independent. Try the sentence test. Omit the semicolon if each clause could not stand alone as a complete sentence.

Faulty	Improved
There is no point in speaking; unless you can improve on silence. (The second half of the sentence is a dependent clause. It could not stand alone as a sentence.)	There is no point in speaking unless you can improve on silence.
Although I cannot change the direction of the wind; I can adjust my sails to reach my destination. (The first clause could not stand alone.)	Although I cannot change the direction of the wind, I can adjust my sails to reach my destination.

GUIDE 28: Use a semicolon to separate items in a series when one or more of the items contains internal commas.

Representatives from as far away as Blue Bell, Pennsylvania; Bowling Green, Ohio; and Phoenix, Arizona, attended the conference.

Stories circulated about Henry Ford, founder, Ford Motor Company; Lee Iacocca, former CEO, Chrysler Motor Company; and Shoichiro Toyoda, founder, Toyota Motor Company.

GUIDE 29: Use a colon after a complete thought that introduces a list of items. Words such as *these, the following,* and *as follows* may introduce the list or they may be implied.

The following cities are on the tour: Louisville, Memphis, and New Orleans.

An alternate tour includes several West Coast cities: Seattle, San Francisco, and San Diego.

Tip. Be sure that the statement before a colon is grammatically complete. An introductory statement that ends with a preposition (such as *by, for, at,* and *to*) or a verb (such as *is, are,* or *were*) is incomplete. The list following a preposition or a verb actually functions as an object or as a complement to finish the sentence.

Faulty	Improved
Three Big Macs were ordered by: Pam, Jim, and Lee. (Do not use a colon after an incomplete statement.)	Three Big Macs were ordered by Pam, Jim, and Lee.
Other items that they ordered were: fries, Cokes, and salads. (Do not use a colon after an incomplete statement.)	Other items that they ordered were fries, Cokes, and salads.

GUIDE 30: Use a colon after business letter salutations and to introduce long quotations.

Dear Mr. Duran: Dear Lisa:

The Asian consultant bluntly said: "Americans tend to be too blabby, too impatient, and too informal for Asian tastes. To succeed in trade with Pacific Rim countries, Americans must become more willing to adapt to native cultures."

Tip. Use a comma to introduce short quotations. Use a colon to introduce long one-sentence quotations and quotations of two or more sentences.

✔ Checkpoint

Add appropriate semicolons and colons.

51. Marco's short-term goal is an entry-level job his long-term goal however is a management position.

52. Speakers included the following professors Rebecca Hilbrink University of Alaska Lora Lindsey Ohio University and Michael Malone Central Florida College.

53. The recruiter was looking for three qualities loyalty initiative and enthusiasm.

54. Microsoft seeks experienced individuals however it will hire recent graduates who are skilled.

55. South Florida is an expanding region therefore many business opportunities are available.

Apostrophe

GUIDE 31: If an ownership word does not end in an *s* sound, add an apostrophe and *s*, whether the word is singular or plural.

> We hope to show a profit in one year's time. (Add *'s* because the ownership word *year* is singular and does not end in *s*.)

> The children's teacher allowed free time on the computer. (Add *'s* because the ownership word *children*, although it is plural, does not end in *s*.)

GUIDE 32: If an ownership word does end in an *s* sound and is singular, add an apostrophe and *s*.

> The witness's testimony was critical. (Add *'s* because the ownership word *witness* is singular and ends in an *s*.)

> The boss's cell phone rang during the meeting. (Add *'s* because the ownership word *boss* is singular and ends in an *s*.

If the ownership words ends in an *s* sound and is plural, add only an apostrophe.

> Both investors' portfolios showed diversification. (Add only an apostrophe because the ownership word *investors* is plural and ends in *s*.)

> Some workers' benefits will cost more. (Add only an apostrophe because the ownership word *workers* is plural and ends in *s*.)

Tip. To determine whether an ownership word ends in *s*, use it in an *of* phrase. For example, *one month's salary* becomes *the salary of one month*. By isolating the ownership word without its apostrophe, you can decide whether it ends in *s*.

GUIDE 33: Use a possessive pronoun or add an apostrophe and *s* to make a noun possessive when it precedes a gerund (a verb form used as a noun).

> We all protested *Laura's* (not *Laura*) smoking. (Add an apostrophe and *s* to the noun preceding the gerund.)

> *His* (not *Him*) talking on his cell phone angered moviegoers. (Use a possessive pronoun before the gerund.)

> I appreciate *your* (not *you*) answering the telephone while I was gone. (Use a possessive pronoun before the gerund.)

✔ Checkpoint

Correct any problems with possessives.

56. Both companies executives received huge bonuses, even when employees salaries were falling.

57. In just one weeks time, we promise to verify all members names and addresses.

58. The manager and I certainly appreciate you bringing this matter to our CPAs attention.

59. All beneficiaries names must be revealed when insurance companies write policies.

60. Is your sister-in-laws job downtown?

Other Punctuation

GUIDE 34: Use one period to end a statement, command, indirect question, or polite request. Never use two periods.

> Matt worked at BioTech, Inc. (Statement. Use only one period.)
>
> Deliver it before 5 p.m. (Command. Use only one period.)
>
> Stacy asked whether she could use the car next weekend. (Indirect question)
>
> Will you please send me an employment application. (Polite request)

Tip. Polite requests often sound like questions. To determine the punctuation, apply the action test. If the request prompts an action, use a period. If it prompts a verbal response, use a question mark.

Faulty

Could you please correct the balance on my next statement? (This polite request prompts an action rather than a verbal response.)

Improved

Could you please correct the balance on my next statement.

Tip. To avoid the punctuation dilemma with polite requests, do not phrase the request as a question. Phrase it as a command: *Please correct the balance on my next statement*. It still sounds polite, and the punctuation problem disappears.

GUIDE 35: Use a question mark after a direct question and after statements with questions appended.

> Are they hiring at BioTech, Inc.?
>
> Most of their training is in-house, isn't it?

GUIDE 36: Use a dash to (a) set off parenthetical elements containing internal commas, (b) emphasize a sentence interruption, or (c) separate an introductory list from a summarizing statement. The dash has legitimate uses. However, some writers use it whenever they know that punctuation is necessary, but they are not sure exactly what. The dash can be very effective, if not misused.

> Three top students—Gene Engle, Donna Hersh, and Mika Sato—won awards. (Use dashes to set off elements with internal commas.)
>
> Executives at Apple—despite rampant rumors in the stock market—remained quiet regarding dividend earnings. (Use dashes to emphasize a sentence interruption.)
>
> Japan, Taiwan, and Turkey—these were areas hit by recent earthquakes. (Use a dash to separate an introductory list from a summarizing statement.)

GUIDE 37: Use parentheses to set off nonessential sentence elements, such as explanations, directions, questions, and references.

> Researchers find that the office grapevine (see Chapter 1 for more discussion) carries surprisingly accurate information.
>
> Only two dates (February 15 and March 1) are suitable for the meeting.

Tip. Careful writers use parentheses to de-emphasize and the dash to emphasize parenthetical information. One expert said, "Dashes shout the news; parentheses whisper it."

GUIDE 38: Use quotation marks to (a) enclose the exact words of a speaker; (b) enclose the titles of articles, chapters, or other short works; and (c) enclose specific definitions of words or expressions.

"If you make your job important," said the consultant, "it's quite likely to return the favor." (Quotation marks enclose the exact words of a speaker.)

The recruiter said that she was looking for candidates with good communication skills. (Omit quotation marks because the exact words of the speaker are not quoted.)

In *The Wall Street Journal*, I saw an article titled "Communication for Global Markets." (Quotation marks enclose the title of an article. Italics identify the name of newspapers, magazines, and books.)

The term *tweet* refers to "a post made on the microblogging site Twitter." (Quotation marks enclose the definition of a word.)

For jargon, slang, words used in a special sense such as humor, irony, and words following *Stamped* or *Marked*, some writers use italics. Other writers use quotation marks.

Computer criminals are often called *hackers* (OR "hackers"). (Jargon)

My teenager said that the film *The Hunger Games* is *sick* (OR "sick"). (Slang)

Justin claimed that he was *too ill* (OR "too ill") to come to work yesterday. (Irony)

The package was stamped *Fragile* (OR "Fragile"). (Words following *stamped*)

Tip. Never use quotation marks arbitrarily, as in *Our "spring" sale starts April 1.*

✔ Checkpoint

Add appropriate punctuation.

61. Will you please send your print catalog as soon as possible

62. (Direct quotation) Our Super Bowl promotion said the CEO will cost nearly $500,000

63. (De-emphasize) Two kinds of batteries see page 16 of the instruction booklet may be used in this camera.

64. Tim wondered whether sentences could end with two periods.

65. Stephanie plans to do a lot of chillaxing during her vacation.

Capitalization

GUIDE 39: Capitalize proper nouns and proper adjectives. Capitalize the *specific* names of persons, places, institutions, buildings, religions, holidays, months, organizations, laws, races, languages, and so forth. Do not capitalize seasons, and do not capitalize common nouns that make *general* references.

Proper Nouns	Common Nouns
Michelle Deluca	the manufacturer's rep
Everglades National Park	the wilderness park
College of the Redwoods	the community college
Empire State Building	the downtown building
Environmental Protection Agency	the federal agency
Persian, Armenian, Hindi	modern foreign languages
Annual Spring Festival	in the spring

Proper Adjectives

Hispanic markets

Xerox copy

Swiss chocolates

Italian dressing

Japanese executives

Reagan economics

GUIDE 40: Capitalize only specific academic courses and degrees.

Professor Donna Howard, PhD, will teach Accounting 121 next spring.

James Barker, who holds bachelor's and master's degrees, teaches marketing.

Jessica enrolled in classes in management, English, and business law.

GUIDE 41: Capitalize courtesy, professional, religious, government, family, and business titles when they precede names.

Mr. Jameson, Mrs. Alvarez, and Ms. Robinson (Courtesy titles)

Professor Andrews, Dr. Lee (Professional titles)

Rabbi Cohen, Pastor Williams, Pope Benedict (Religious titles)

Senator Tom Harrison, Mayor Jackson (Government titles)

Uncle Edward, Mother Teresa, Cousin Vinney (Family titles)

Vice President Morris, Budget Director Lopez (Business titles)

Do not capitalize a title when it is followed by an appositive (that is, when the title is followed by a noun that renames or explains it).

Only one professor, Jonathan Marcus, favored a tuition hike.

Local candidates counted on their governor, Lee Jones, to help raise funds.

Do not capitalize titles following names unless they are part of an address:

Mark Yoder, president of Yoder Enterprises, hired all employees.

Paula Beech, director of Human Resources, interviewed all candidates.

Send the package to Amanda Harr, Advertising Manager, Cambridge Publishers, 20 Park Plaza, Boston, MA 02116. (Title in an address)

Generally, do not capitalize a title that replaces a person's name.

Only the president, his chief of staff, and one senator made the trip.

The director of marketing and the sales manager will meet at 1 p.m.

Do not capitalize family titles used with possessive pronouns.

my mother, his father, your cousin

GUIDE 42: Capitalize the main words in titles, subject lines, and headings. *Main* words are all words except (a) the articles *a, an,* and *the;* (b) the conjunctions *and, but, or,* and *nor;* (c) prepositions containing two or three letters (e.g., *of, for, in, on, by*); (d) the word *to* in infinitives (such as *to work, to write,* and *to talk*); and (e) the word *as*—unless any of these words are the first or last words in the title, subject line, or heading.

I enjoyed the book *A Customer Is More Than a Name.* (Book title)

Team Meeting to Discuss Deadlines Rescheduled for Friday (Subject line)

We liked the article titled "Advice From a Pro: How to Say It With Pictures." (Article)

Check the Advice and Resources link at the *CareerBuilder* website.

(Note that the titles of books are italicized, but the titles of articles are enclosed in quotation marks.)

GUIDE 43: Capitalize names of geographic locations. Capitalize *north*, *south*, *east*, *west*, and their derivatives only when they represent specific geographical regions.

from the Pacific Northwest	heading northwest on the highway
living in the West	west of the city
Midwesterners, Southerners	western Oregon, southern Ohio
peace in the Middle East	a location east of the middle of the city

GUIDE 44: Capitalize the main words in the specific names of departments, divisions, or committees within business organizations. Do not capitalize general references.

All forms are available from our Department of Human Resources.

The Consumer Electronics Division launched an upbeat marketing campaign.

We volunteered for the Employee Social Responsibility Committee.

You might send an application to their personnel department.

GUIDE 45: Capitalize product names only when they refer to trademarked items. Do not capitalize the common names following manufacturers' names.

Dell laptop computer	Skippy peanut butter	NordicTrack treadmill
Eveready Energizer	Norelco razor	Canon color copier
Coca-Cola	Panasonic plasma television	Big Mac sandwich

GUIDE 46: Capitalize most nouns followed by numbers or letters (except in page, paragraph, line, and verse references).

Room 14	Exhibit A	Flight 12, Gate 43
Figure 2.1	Plan No. 1	Model Z2010

✔ Checkpoint

Capitalize all appropriate words.

66. vice president moore bought a new droid smartphone before leaving for the east coast.

67. when you come on tuesday, travel west on highway 5 and exit at mt. mckinley street.

68. The director of our human resources department called a meeting of the company's building security committee.

69. our manager and president are flying on american airlines flight 34 leaving from gate 69 at the las vegas international airport.

70. my father read a businessweek article titled can you build loyalty with bricks and mortar?

Number Usage

GUIDE 47: Use word form to express (a) numbers *ten* and under and (b) numbers beginning sentences.   General references to numbers *ten* and under should be expressed in word form. Also use word form for numbers that begin sentences. If the resulting number involves more than two words, however, recast the sentence so that the number does not fall at the beginning.

We answered *six* telephone calls for the *four* sales reps.

Fifteen customers responded to our *three* cell phone ads today.

A total of 155 smartphones were awarded as prizes. (Avoid beginning the sentence with a long number such as *one hundred fifty-five*.)

GUIDE 48: Use figures to express most references to numbers 11 and over.

Over *150* people from *53* companies attended the two-day workshop.

A four-ounce serving of Haagen-Dazs toffee crunch ice cream contains *300* calories and *19* grams of fat.

GUIDE 49: Use figures to express money, dates, clock time, decimals, and percentages.

One item costs only *$1.95*; most, however, were priced between *$10* and *$35*. (Omit the decimals and zeros in even sums of money.)

We scheduled a meeting for May 12. (Notice that we do NOT write May 12th.)

We expect deliveries at 10:15 a.m. and again at 4 p.m. (Use lowercase *a.m.* and *p.m.*)

All packages must be ready by 4 o'clock. (Do NOT write 4:00 o'clock.)

When U.S. sales dropped *4.7* percent, net income fell *9.8* percent. (In contextual material use the word *percent* instead of the symbol %.)

GUIDE 50. Use a combination of words and figures to express sums of 1 million and over. Use words for small fractions.

Orion lost *$62.9 million* in the latest fiscal year on revenues of *$584 million*. (Use a combination of words and figures for sums of 1 million and over.)

Only one half of the registered voters turned out. (Use words for small fractions.)

Tip. To ease your memory load, concentrate on the numbers normally expressed in words: numbers *ten* and under, numbers at the beginning of a sentence, and small fractions. Nearly everything else in business is generally written with figures.

✔ Checkpoint

Correct any inappropriate expression of numbers.

71. Although he budgeted fifty dollars, Jake spent 94 dollars and 34 cents for supplies.

72. Is the meeting on November 7th or November 14th?

73. UPS deliveries arrive at nine AM and again at four fifteen PM.

74. The company applied for a fifty thousand dollar loan at six%.

75. The U.S. population is just over 300,000,000, and the world population is estimated to be nearly 6,500,000,000.

Key to Grammar and Mechanics Checkpoint Exercises in Appendix A

This key shows all corrections. If you marked anything else, double-check the appropriate guideline.

1. Disney, destination

2. yearly, which

3. hour; however,

4. pavilion;

5. wedding;

6. If I *were* you, I would have *gone* . . .

7. could have *written* . . . had *begun* earlier.

8. project manager *saw* . . . immediately *came*

9. project manager *were*

10. manager had *known* . . . would have *given*

11. time and talent *were* spent (Note that two subjects require a plural verb.)

12. attachments, *was* (Note that the subject is *message*.)

13. Each of . . . companies *is* (Note that the subject is *Each*.)

14. list of names and addresses *is* (Note that the subject is *list*.)

15. attorney *has*

16. My partner and *I* . . . but *yours*

17. was *hers*, but *its*

18. you and *me* . . . *their* printer

19. *There's* not much the boss or *I* can do if *it's* broken, . . . reported to him or *me* earlier.

20. but *yours* and *hers*

21. *whomever*

22. *Whom* have you asked . . .

23. for *whoever*

24. Matt and *I*

25. by *whoever*

26. Every employee must wear *a* picture identification badge, *OR: All employees* must wear *picture identification badges.*

27. slower career advancement, but *flexible scheduling* appeals to many workers. (Revise to avoid the vague pronoun *it*.)

28. Any renter must pay *the* rent . . . *OR: All renters* must pay *their* rent . . .

29. reported that *a* computer . . . *OR:* reported that *his or her* computer . . .

30. communication. *These techniques are* particularly important (Revise to avoid the vague pronoun *This*.)

31. My manager and *I* could not resist the *once-in-a-lifetime* opportunity.

32. John and *he* finished their task so *quickly* (Do not hyphenate *recently opened*.)

33. do *well* . . . *part-time* jobs and a few *full-time*

34. told him and *me* . . . *personally.*

35. *not-too-distant* future

36. class, Erin . . . with commas, semicolons,

37. studying punctuation,

38. program,

39. merchandising courses,

40. junior year, . . . in Los Angeles, Burbank,

41. Street, San Antonio, Texas 78220,

42. not, however,

43. paralegals, . . . next year,

44. May 15, 2012, . . . May 15, 2018.

45. fact,

46. sooner [delete comma]

47. car,

48. is [delete comma]

49. think, on the other hand, . . . buying [delete comma]

50. automakers are [delete comma] at this time [delete comma]

51. entry-level job; his long-term goal, however,

52. professors: Rebecca Hilbrink, University of Alaska; Lora Lindsey, Ohio University; and Michael Malone, Central Florida College.

53. qualities: loyalty, initiative,

54. individuals; however,

55. region; therefore,

56. companies' . . . employees'

57. one week's time, . . . members'

58. appreciate *your* . . . CPA's

59. beneficiaries'

60. sister-in-law's

61. possible.

62. "Our Super Bowl promotion," said the CEO, "will cost nearly $500,000."

63. Two kinds of batteries (see page 16 of the instruction booklet)

64. two periods.

65. *chillaxing* or "chillaxing"

66. Vice President Moore . . . Droid . . . East Coast

67. When . . . Tuesday, . . . Highway 5 . . . Mt. McKinley Street.

68. Human Resources Department . . . Building Security Committee

69. Our . . . American Airlines Flight 34 . . . Gate 69 at the Las Vegas International Airport

70. My . . . *BusinessWeek* article titled "Can You Build Loyalty With Bricks and Mortar?"

71. $50 . . . $94.34

72. November 7 or November 14 [delete *th*]

73. 9 a.m. . . . 4:15 p.m. (Note only one period at the end of the sentence.)

74. $50,000 loan at 6 percent.

75. 300 million . . . 6.5 billion

Confusing Words

accede:	to agree or consent
exceed:	over a limit
accept:	to receive
except:	to exclude; (prep) but
adverse:	opposing; antagonistic
averse:	unwilling; reluctant
advice:	suggestion, opinion
advise:	to counsel or recommend
affect:	to influence
effect:	(n) outcome, result; (v) to bring about, to create
all ready:	prepared
already:	by this time
all right:	satisfactory
alright:	unacceptable variant spelling
altar:	structure for worship
alter:	to change
appraise:	to estimate
apprise:	to inform
ascent:	(n) rising or going up
assent:	(v) to agree or consent
assure:	to promise
ensure:	to make certain
insure:	to protect from loss
capital:	(n) city that is seat of government; wealth of an individual; (adj) chief
capitol:	building that houses state or national lawmakers
cereal:	breakfast food
serial:	arranged in sequence
cite:	to quote; to summon
site:	location
sight:	a view; to see
coarse:	rough texture
course:	a route; part of a meal; a unit of learning
complement:	that which completes
compliment:	(n) praise or flattery; (v) to praise or flatter
conscience:	regard for fairness

conscious:	aware
council:	governing body
counsel:	(n) advice, attorney, consultant; (v) to give advice
credible:	believable
creditable:	good enough for praise or esteem; reliable
desert:	(n) arid land; (v) to abandon
dessert:	sweet food
device:	invention or mechanism
devise:	to design or arrange
disburse:	to pay out
disperse:	to scatter widely
elicit:	to draw out
illicit:	unlawful
envelop:	(v) to wrap, surround, or conceal
envelope:	(n) a container for a written message
every day:	each single day
everyday:	ordinary
farther:	a greater distance
further:	additional
formally:	in a formal manner
formerly:	in the past
grate:	(v) to reduce to small particles; to cause irritation; (n) a frame of crossed bars blocking a passage
great:	(adj) large in size; numerous; eminent or distinguished
hole:	an opening
whole:	complete
imply:	to suggest indirectly
infer:	to reach a conclusion
lean:	(v) to rest against; (adj) not fat
lien:	(n) legal right or claim to property
liable:	legally responsible
libel:	damaging written statement
loose:	not fastened
lose:	to misplace
miner:	person working in a mine

minor:	(adj) lesser; (n) person under age	principle:	rule of action
patience:	calm perseverance	stationary:	immovable
patients:	people receiving medical treatment	stationery:	writing material
personal:	private, individual	than:	conjunction showing comparison
personnel:	employees	then:	adverb meaning "at that time"
plaintiff:	(n) one who initiates a lawsuit	their:	possessive form of they
plaintive:	(adj) expressive of suffering or woe	there:	at that place or point
populace:	(n) the masses; population of a place	they're:	contraction of they are
populous:	(adj) densely populated	to:	a preposition; the sign of the infinitive
precede:	to go before	too:	an adverb meaning "also" or "to an excessive extent"
proceed:	to continue		
precedence:	priority	two:	a number
precedents:	events used as an example	waiver:	abandonment of a claim
principal:	(n) capital sum; school official; (adj) chief	waver:	to shake or fluctuate

160 Frequently Misspelled Words

absence	courteous	fiscal	necessary	referred
accommodate	criticize	foreign	nevertheless	regarding
achieve	decision	forty	ninety	remittance
acknowledgment	deductible	fourth	ninth	representative
across	defendant	friend	noticeable	restaurant
adequate	definitely	genuine	occasionally	schedule
advisable	dependent	government	occurred	secretary
analyze	describe	grammar	offered	separate
annually	desirable	grateful	omission	similar
appointment	destroy	guarantee	omitted	sincerely
argument	development	harass	opportunity	software
automatically	disappoint	height	opposite	succeed
bankruptcy	dissatisfied	hoping	ordinarily	sufficient
becoming	division	immediate	paid	supervisor
beneficial	efficient	incidentally	pamphlet	surprise
budget	embarrass	incredible	permanent	tenant
business	emphasis	independent	permitted	therefore
calendar	emphasize	indispensable	pleasant	thorough
canceled	employee	interrupt	practical	though
catalog	envelope	irrelevant	prevalent	through
changeable	equipped	itinerary	privilege	truly
column	especially	judgment	probably	undoubtedly
committee	evidently	knowledge	procedure	unnecessarily
congratulate	exaggerate	legitimate	profited	usable
conscience	excellent	library	prominent	usage
conscious	exempt	license	quality	using
consecutive	existence	maintenance	quantity	usually
consensus	extraordinary	manageable	questionnaire	valuable
consistent	familiar	manufacturer	receipt	volume
control	fascinate	mileage	receive	weekday
convenient	feasible	miscellaneous	recognize	writing
correspondence	February	mortgage	recommendation	yield

Appendix B
Document Format Guide

Business communicators produce numerous documents that have standardized formats. Becoming familiar with these formats is important because business documents actually carry two kinds of messages. Verbal messages are conveyed by the words chosen to express the writer's ideas. Nonverbal messages are conveyed largely by the appearance of a document and its adherence to recognized formats. To ensure that your documents carry favorable nonverbal messages about you and your organization, you will want to give special attention to the appearance and formatting of your e-mails, letters, and envelopes.

E-Mail

E-mail continues to be a main communication channel in the workplace. Chapter 7 presented guidelines for preparing e-mails. This section provides additional information on formats and usage. The following suggestions, illustrated in Figure B.1 and also in Figure 7.1 on page 209, may guide you in setting up the parts of any e-mail. Always check, however, with your organization so that you can follow its practices.

Figure **B.1** Typical E-Mail

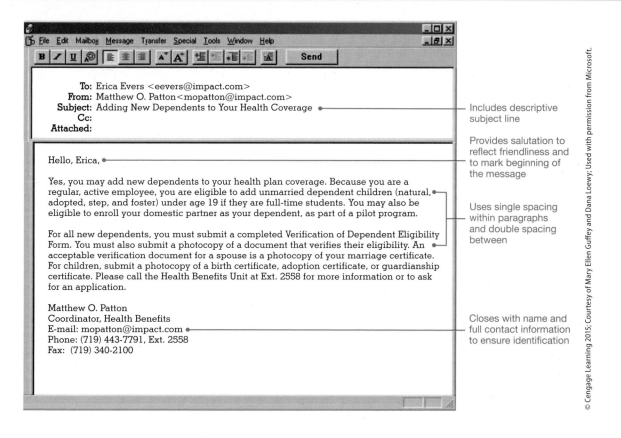

© Cengage Learning 2015; Courtesy of Mary Ellen Guffey and Dana Loewy; Used with permission from Microsoft.

To Line.   Include the receiver's e-mail address after *To*. If the receiver's address is recorded in your address book, you just have to click on it. Be sure to enter all addresses very carefully since one mistyped letter prevents delivery.

From Line.   Most mail programs automatically include your name and e-mail address after *From*.

Cc and *Bcc*.   Insert the e-mail address of anyone who is to receive a copy of the message. *Cc* stands for carbon copy or courtesy copy. Don't be tempted, though, to send needless copies just because it is easy. *Bcc* stands for blind carbon copy. Some writers use *bcc* to send a copy of the message without the addressee's knowledge. Writers also use the *bcc* line for mailing lists. When a message is sent to a number of people and their e-mail addresses should not be revealed, the *bcc* line works well to conceal the names and addresses of all receivers.

Subject.   Identify the subject of the e-mail with a brief but descriptive summary of the topic. Be sure to include enough information to be clear and compelling. Capitalize the initial letters of main words. Main words are all words except (a) the articles *a, an,* and *the*; (b) prepositions containing two or three letters (such as *at, to, on, by, for*); (c) the word *to* in an infinitive (*to work, to write*); and (d) the word *as*—unless any of these words are the first or last word in the subject line.

Salutation.   Include a brief greeting, if you like. Some writers use a salutation such as *Dear Erica* followed by a comma or a colon. Others are more informal with *Hi, Erica; Hello, Erica; Good morning;* or *Greetings*. See Chapter 7 for additional discussion of e-mail greetings.

Message.   Cover just one topic in your message, and try to keep your total message under three screens in length. Single-space and be sure to use both upper- and lowercase letters. Double-space between paragraphs.

Closing.   Conclude an e-mail, if you like, with *Cheers, Best wishes,* or *Warm regards,* followed by your name and complete contact information. Some people omit their e-mail address because they think it is provided automatically. However, programs and routers do not always transmit the address. Therefore, always include it along with other identifying information in the closing.

Attachment.   Use the attachment window or button to select the path and file name of any file you wish to send with your e-mail. You can also attach a Web page to your message.

Business Letters

Business communicators write business letters primarily to correspond with people outside the organization. Letters may go to customers, vendors, other businesses, and the government, as discussed in Chapters 8, 9, and 10. The following information will help you format your letters following conventional guidelines.

Conventional Letter Placement, Margins, and Line Spacing

To set up business letters using conventional guidelines, follow these steps:

- For a clean look, choose a sans serif font such as Arial, Calibri, Tahoma, or Verdana. For a more traditional look, choose a serif font such as Times New Roman. Use a 10-point, 11-point, or 12-point size.
- Use a 2-inch top margin for the first page of a letter printed on letterhead stationery. This will place the date on line 12. Use a 1-inch top margin for second and succeeding pages.
- Justify only the left margin. Set the line spacing to single.
- Choose side margins according to the length of your letter. Set 1.5-inch margins for short letters (under 200 words), and 1-inch margins for longer letters (200 or more words).
- Leave from 2 to 10 blank lines following the date to balance the message on the page. You can make this adjustment after keying your message.

Formatting Letters With Microsoft Word 2007 and 2010

If you are working with Microsoft Word 2007 or 2010, the default margins are set at 1 inch and the default font is 11-point Calibri. The default setting for line spacing is 1.15, and the paragraph default is 10 points of blank space following each paragraph or each tap of the Enter key. Many letter writers find this extra space excessive, especially after parts of the letter that are normally single-spaced. The model documents in this book show conventional single-spacing with one blank line between paragraphs.

To format your documents with conventional spacing and yet retain a clean look, we recommend that you change the Microsoft defaults to the following: Arial font set for 11 points, line spacing at 1.0, and spacing before and after paragraphs at 0.

Spacing and Punctuation

For some time typists left two spaces after end punctuation (periods, question marks, and so forth). This practice was necessary, it was thought, because typewriters did not have proportional spacing and sentences were easier to read when two spaces separated them. Professional typesetters, however, never followed this practice because they used proportional spacing, and readability was not a problem. Influenced by the look of typeset publications, many writers now leave only one space after end punctuation. As a practical matter, however, it is not wrong to use two spaces.

Business Letter Parts

Professional-looking business letters are arranged in a conventional sequence with standard parts. Following is a discussion of how to use these letter parts properly. Figure B.2 illustrates the parts of a block style letter. See Chapter 8 for additional discussion of letters and their parts.

Letterhead.   Most business organizations use 8½ x 11-inch paper printed with a letterhead displaying their official name, street address, Web address, e-mail address, and telephone and fax numbers. The letterhead may also include a logo and an advertising message.

Dateline.   On letterhead paper you should place the date one blank line below the last line of the letterhead or 2 inches from the top edge of the paper (line 12 or 13). On plain paper place the date immediately below your return address. Because the date goes on line 12 or 13, start the return address an appropriate number of lines above it. The most common dateline format is as follows: *June 9, 2015*. Don't use *th* (or *rd, nd* or *st*) when the date is written this way. For European or military correspondence, use the following dateline format: *9 June 2015*. Notice that no commas are used.

Addressee and Delivery Notations.   Delivery notations such as *E-MAIL TRANSMISSION, FEDEX, MESSENGER DELIVERY, CONFIDENTIAL,* or *CERTIFIED MAIL* are typed in all capital letters two blank lines above the inside address.

Inside Address.   Type the inside address—that is, the address of the organization or person receiving the letter—single-spaced, starting at the left margin. The number of lines between the dateline and the inside address depends on the size of the letter body, the type size (point or pitch size), and the length of the typing lines. Generally, one to nine blank lines are appropriate.

Be careful to duplicate the exact wording and spelling of the recipient's name and address on your documents. Usually, you can copy this information from the letterhead of the correspondence you are answering. If, for example, you are responding to *Jackson & Perkins Company*, do not address your letter to *Jackson and Perkins Corp.*

Always be sure to include a courtesy title such as *Mr., Ms., Mrs., Dr.,* or *Professor* before a person's name in the inside address—for both the letter and the envelope. Although many women in business today favor *Ms.*, you should use whatever title the addressee prefers.

In general, avoid abbreviations such as *Ave.* or *Co.* unless they appear in the printed letterhead of the document being answered.

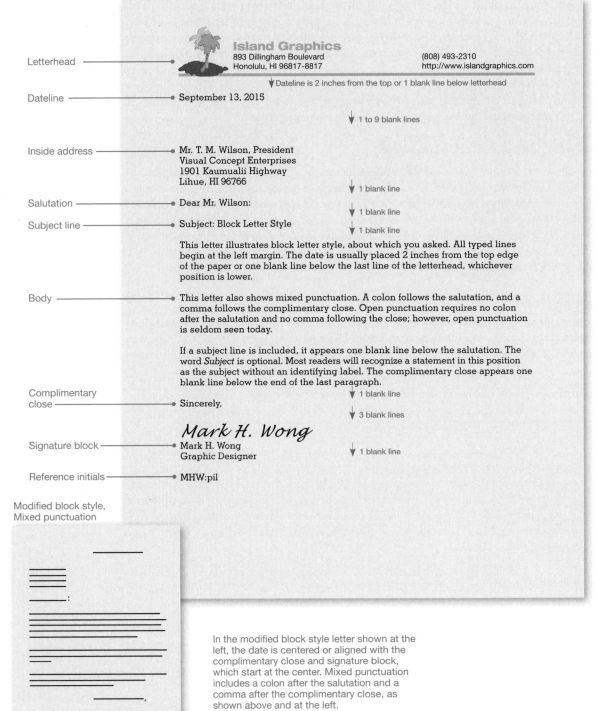

Letterhead

Island Graphics
893 Dillingham Boulevard
Honolulu, HI 96817-8817

(808) 493-2310
http://www.islandgraphics.com

⬇ Dateline is 2 inches from the top or 1 blank line below letterhead

Dateline

September 13, 2015

⬇ 1 to 9 blank lines

Inside address

Mr. T. M. Wilson, President
Visual Concept Enterprises
1901 Kaumualii Highway
Lihue, HI 96766

⬇ 1 blank line

Salutation

Dear Mr. Wilson:

⬇ 1 blank line

Subject line

Subject: Block Letter Style

⬇ 1 blank line

This letter illustrates block letter style, about which you asked. All typed lines begin at the left margin. The date is usually placed 2 inches from the top edge of the paper or one blank line below the last line of the letterhead, whichever position is lower.

Body

This letter also shows mixed punctuation. A colon follows the salutation, and a comma follows the complimentary close. Open punctuation requires no colon after the salutation and no comma following the close; however, open punctuation is seldom seen today.

If a subject line is included, it appears one blank line below the salutation. The word *Subject* is optional. Most readers will recognize a statement in this position as the subject without an identifying label. The complimentary close appears one blank line below the end of the last paragraph.

⬇ 1 blank line

Complimentary close

Sincerely,

⬇ 3 blank lines

Mark H. Wong

Signature block

Mark H. Wong
Graphic Designer

⬇ 1 blank line

Reference initials

MHW:pil

Modified block style,
Mixed punctuation

In the modified block style letter shown at the left, the date is centered or aligned with the complimentary close and signature block, which start at the center. Mixed punctuation includes a colon after the salutation and a comma after the complimentary close, as shown above and at the left.

Attention Line. An attention line allows you to send your message officially to an organization but to direct it to a specific individual, officer, or department. However, if you know an individual's complete name, it is always better to use it as the first line of the inside address and avoid an attention line. Placing an attention line first in the address block enables you to paste it directly onto the envelope:

Attention Marketing Director
The MultiMedia Company
931 Calkins Avenue
Rochester, NY 14301

Salutation. For most letter styles, place the letter greeting, or salutation, one blank line below the last line of the inside address or the attention line (if used). If the letter is addressed to an individual, use that person's courtesy title and last name (*Dear Mr. Lanham*). Even if you are on a first-name basis (*Dear Leslie*), be sure to add a colon (not a comma or a semicolon) after the salutation. Do not use an individual's full name in the salutation (not *Dear Mr. Leslie Lanham*) unless you are unsure of gender (*Dear Leslie Lanham*).

It's always best to address messages to people. However, if a message is addressed to an organization, consider these salutations: an organization of men (*Gentlemen*), an organization of women (*Ladies*), an organization of men and women (*Ladies and Gentlemen*). If a message is addressed to an undetermined individual, consider these salutations: a woman (*Dear Madam*), a man (*Dear Sir*), a title (*Dear Customer Service Representative*).

Subject and Reference Lines. Although experts suggest placing the subject line one blank line below the salutation, many businesses actually place it above the salutation. Use whatever style your organization prefers. Reference lines often show policy or file numbers; they generally appear one blank line above the salutation. Use initial capital letters for the main words or all capital letters.

Body. Most business letters and memorandums are single-spaced, with double-spacing between paragraphs. Very short messages may be double-spaced with indented paragraphs.

Complimentary Close. Typed one blank line below the last line of the letter, the complimentary close may be formal (*Very truly yours*) or informal (*Sincerely* or *Cordially*).

Signature Block. In most letter styles, the writer's typed name and optional identification appear three or four blank lines below the complimentary close. The combination of name, title, and organization information should be arranged to achieve a balanced look. The name and title may appear on the same line or on separate lines, depending on the length of each. Use commas to separate categories within the same line, but not to conclude a line.

Sincerely yours,   Cordially yours,

Jeremy M. Wood   *Casandra Baker-Murillo*

Jeremy M. Wood, Manager   Casandra Baker-Murillo
Technical Sales and Services   Executive Vice President

Some organizations include their names in the signature block. In such cases the organization name appears in all caps one blank line below the complimentary close, as shown here:

Cordially,

LIPTON COMPUTER SERVICES

Shelina A. Simpson

Shelina A. Simpson
Executive Assistant

Reference Initials. If used, the initials of the typist and writer are typed one blank line below the writer's name and title. Generally, the writer's initials are capitalized and the typist's are lowercased, but this format varies.

Enclosure Notation. When an enclosure or attachment accompanies a document, a notation to that effect appears one blank line below the reference initials. This notation reminds the typist to insert the enclosure in the envelope, and it reminds the recipient to look for the enclosure or attachment. The notation may be spelled out (*Enclosure, Attachment*), or it may be abbreviated (*Enc., Att.*). It may indicate the number of enclosures or attachments, and it may also identify a specific enclosure (*Enclosure: Form 1099*).

Copy Notation. If you make copies of correspondence for other individuals, you may use *cc* to indicate courtesy copy, *pc* to indicate photocopy, or merely *c* for any kind of copy. A colon following the initial(s) is optional.

Second-Page Heading. When a letter extends beyond one page, use plain paper of the same quality and color as the first page. Identify the second and succeeding pages with a heading consisting of the name of the addressee, the page number, and the date. Use the following format or the one shown in Figure B.3:

Ms. Sara Hendricks	2	May 3, 2015

Both headings appear six blank lines (1 inch) from the top edge of the paper followed by two blank lines to separate them from the continuing text. Avoid using a second page if you have only one line or the complimentary close and signature block to fill that page.

Plain-Paper Return Address. If you prepare a personal or business letter on plain paper, place your address immediately above the date. Do not include your name; you will type (and sign) your name at the end of your letter. If your return address contains two lines, begin typing so that the date appears 2 inches from the top. Avoid abbreviations except for a two-letter state abbreviation.

Figure B.3   Second-Page Heading

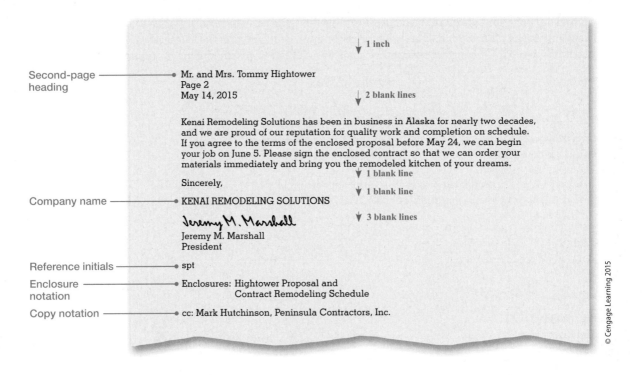

580 East Leffels Street
Springfield, OH 45501
December 14, 2015

Ms. Ellen Siemens
Escrow Department
TransOhio First Federal
1220 Wooster Boulevard
Columbus, OH 43218-2900

Dear Ms. Siemens:

The above return address and inside address illustrate the personal business style. For letters in the block style, type the return address at the left margin. For modified block style letters, start the return address at the center to align with the complimentary close.

Letter and Punctuation Styles

Most business letters today are prepared in either block or modified block style, and they generally use mixed punctuation.

Block Style.   In the block style, shown in Figure B.2, all lines begin at the left margin. This style is a favorite because it is easy to format.

Modified Block Style.   The modified block style differs from block style in that the date and closing lines appear in the center, as shown at the bottom of Figure B.2. The date may be (a) centered, (b) begun at the center of the page (to align with the closing lines), or (c) backspaced from the right margin. The signature block—including the complimentary close, writer's name and title, or organization identification—begins at the center. The first line of each paragraph may begin at the left margin or may be indented five or ten spaces. All other lines begin at the left margin.

Mixed Punctuation Style.   Most businesses today use mixed punctuation, shown in Figure B.2. It requires a colon after the salutation and a comma after the complimentary close. Even when the salutation is a first name, a colon is appropriate.

Envelopes

An envelope should be of the same quality and color of stationery as the letter it carries. Because the envelope introduces your message and makes the first impression, you need to be especially careful in addressing it. Moreover, how you fold the letter is important.

Return Address.   The return address is usually printed in the upper left corner of an envelope, as shown in Figure B.4. In large companies some form of identification (the writer's initials, name, or location) may be typed above the company name and address. This identification helps return the letter to the sender in case of nondelivery.

On an envelope without a printed return address, single-space the return address in the upper left corner. Beginning on line 3 on the fourth space (½ inch) from the left edge, type the writer's name, title, company, and mailing address. On a word processor, select the appropriate envelope size and make adjustments to approximate this return address location.

Mailing Address.   On legal-sized No. 10 envelopes (4⅛ x 9½ inches), begin the address on line 13 about 4¼ inches from the left edge, as shown in Figure B.4. For small envelopes (3⅝ x 6½ inches), begin typing on line 12 about 2½ inches from the left edge. On a word processor, select the correct envelope size and check to be sure your address falls in the desired location.

The U.S. Postal Service recommends that addresses be typed in all caps without any punctuation. This Postal Service style, shown in the small envelope in Figure B.4, was originally developed to facilitate scanning by optical character readers (OCRs). Today's OCRs, however, are so sophisticated that they scan upper- and lowercase letters easily. Many companies today do not follow the Postal Service format because they prefer to use the same format for the envelope as for the inside address. If the same format is used, writers can take advantage of word processing programs to copy the inside address to the envelope, thus saving keystrokes

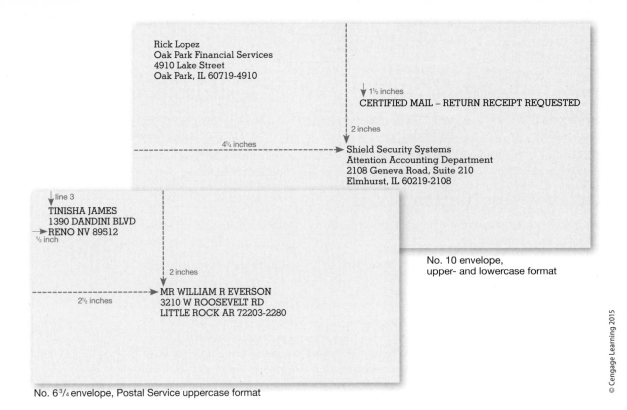

Rick Lopez
Oak Park Financial Services
4910 Lake Street
Oak Park, IL 60719-4910

↓ 1½ inches
CERTIFIED MAIL – RETURN RECEIPT REQUESTED

2 inches

4¼ inches ─────────►

Shield Security Systems
Attention Accounting Department
2108 Geneva Road, Suite 210
Elmhurst, IL 60219-2108

No. 10 envelope,
upper- and lowercase format

↓ line 3
TINISHA JAMES
1390 DANDINI BLVD
►RENO NV 89512
½ inch

2 inches

2½ inches ────────►

MR WILLIAM R EVERSON
3210 W ROOSEVELT RD
LITTLE ROCK AR 72203-2280

No. 6 ¾ envelope, Postal Service uppercase format

© Cengage Learning 2015

and reducing errors. Having the same format on both the inside address and the envelope also looks more professional and consistent. For those reasons you may choose to use the familiar upper- and lowercase combination format. But you will want to check with your organization to learn its preference.

In addressing your envelopes for delivery in this country or in Canada, use the two-letter state and province abbreviations shown in Figure B.5. Notice that these abbreviations are in capital letters without periods.

Folding.   The way a letter is folded and inserted into an envelope sends additional nonverbal messages about a writer's professionalism and carefulness. Most businesspeople follow the procedures shown here, which produce the least number of creases to distract readers.

For large No. 10 envelopes, begin with the letter face up. Fold slightly less than one-third of the sheet toward the top, as shown in the following diagram. Then fold down the top third to within ⅛ inch of the bottom fold. Insert the letter into the envelope with the last fold toward the bottom of the envelope.

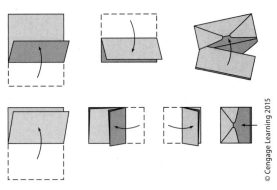

© Cengage Learning 2015

For small No. 6¾ envelopes, begin by folding the bottom up to within ⅓ inch of the top edge. Then fold the right third over to the left. Fold the left third to within ⅓ inch of the last fold. Insert the last fold into the envelope first.

Figure B.5 Abbreviations of States, Territories, and Provinces

State or Territory	Two-Letter Abbreviation	State or Territory	Two-Letter Abbreviation
Alabama	AL	North Carolina	NC
Alaska	AK	North Dakota	ND
Arizona	AZ	Ohio	OH
Arkansas	AR	Oklahoma	OK
California	CA	Oregon	OR
Canal Zone	CZ	Pennsylvania	PA
Colorado	CO	Puerto Rico	PR
Connecticut	CT	Rhode Island	RI
Delaware	DE	South Carolina	SC
District of Columbia	DC	South Dakota	SD
Florida	FL	Tennessee	TN
Georgia	GA	Texas	TX
Guam	GU	Utah	UT
Hawaii	HI	Vermont	VT
Idaho	ID	Virgin Islands	VI
Illinois	IL	Virginia	VA
Indiana	IN	Washington	WA
Iowa	IA	West Virginia	WV
Kansas	KS	Wisconsin	WI
Kentucky	KY	Wyoming	WY
Louisiana	LA	**Canadian Province**	
Maine	ME	Alberta	AB
Maryland	MD	British Columbia	BC
Massachusetts	MA	Labrador	LB
Michigan	MI	Manitoba	MB
Minnesota	MN	New Brunswick	NB
Mississippi	MS	Newfoundland	NF
Missouri	MO	Northwest Territories	NT
Montana	MT	Nova Scotia	NS
Nebraska	NE	Ontario	ON
Nevada	NV	Prince Edward Island	PE
New Hampshire	NH	Quebec	PQ
New Jersey	NJ	Saskatchewan	SK
New Mexico	NM	Yukon Territory	YT
New York	NY		

Appendix C
Documentation Formats

For many reasons business writers are careful to properly document report data. Citing sources strengthens a writer's argument, as you learned in Chapter 11 on page 396, while also shielding the writer from charges of plagiarism. Moreover, good references help readers pursue further research. As a business writer, you can expect to routinely borrow ideas and words to show that your ideas are in synch with the rest of the business world, to gain support from business leaders, or simply to save time in developing your ideas. To be ethical, however, you must show clearly what you borrowed and from whom.

Source notes tell where you found your information. For quotations, paraphrases, graphs, drawings, or online images you have borrowed, you need to cite the original authors' names, full titles, and the dates and facts of publication. The purpose of source notes, which appear at the end of your report, is to direct your readers to the complete references. Many systems of documentation are used by businesses, but they all have one goal: to provide clear, consistent documentation.

Rarely, business writers use content notes, which are identified with a raised number at the end of the quotation. At the bottom of the page, the number is repeated with a remark, clarification, or background information.

During your business career, you may use a variety of documentation systems. The two most common systems in the academic world are those of the American Psychological Association (APA) and the Modern Language Association (MLA). Each organization has its own style for text references and bibliographic lists. The APA style is increasingly the standard in business communication. This book uses a modified APA style. However, some business organizations use their own documentation systems.

Before starting any research project, whether for a class or in a business, inquire about the preferred documentation style. For school assignments ask about specifics. For example, should you include URLs and dates of retrieval for Web sources? For workplace assignments ask to see a previous report either in hard-copy version or as an e-mail attachment.

In your business and class writing, you will usually provide a brief citation in parentheses that refers readers to the complete reference that appears in a references or works-cited section at the end of your document. Following is a summary of APA and MLA formats with examples.

American Psychological Association Format

First used primarily in the social and physical sciences, the American Psychological Association (APA) documentation format uses the author-date method of citation. This method, with its emphasis on current information, is especially appropriate for business. Within the text, the date of publication of the referenced work appears immediately after the author's name (Rivera, 2014), as illustrated in the brief APA example in Figure C.1. At the end of the report, all references appear alphabetically on a page labeled "References." The APA format does not require a date of retrieval for online sources, but you should check with your instructor or supervisor about the preferred format for your class or organization. For more information about the APA format, see the *Publication Manual of the American Psychological Association,* Sixth Edition (Washington, DC: American Psychological Association, 2009).

Figure **C.1** Portions of APA Text Page and References

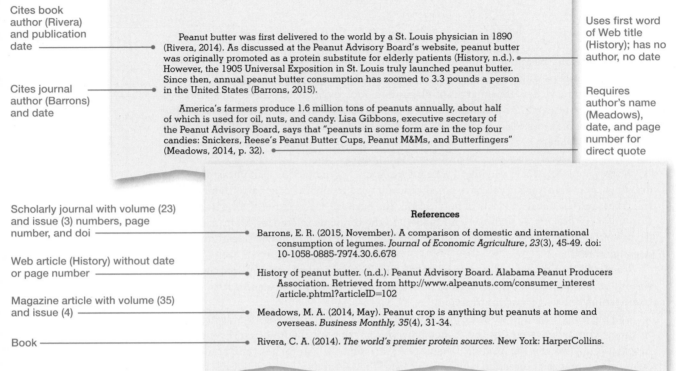

Cites book author (Rivera) and publication date

Cites journal author (Barrons) and date

Peanut butter was first delivered to the world by a St. Louis physician in 1890 (Rivera, 2014). As discussed at the Peanut Advisory Board's website, peanut butter was originally promoted as a protein substitute for elderly patients (History, n.d.). However, the 1905 Universal Exposition in St. Louis truly launched peanut butter. Since then, annual peanut butter consumption has zoomed to 3.3 pounds a person in the United States (Barrons, 2015).

America's farmers produce 1.6 million tons of peanuts annually, about half of which is used for oil, nuts, and candy. Lisa Gibbons, executive secretary of the Peanut Advisory Board, says that "peanuts in some form are in the top four candies: Snickers, Reese's Peanut Butter Cups, Peanut M&Ms, and Butterfingers" (Meadows, 2014, p. 32).

Uses first word of Web title (History); has no author, no date

Requires author's name (Meadows), date, and page number for direct quote

Scholarly journal with volume (23) and issue (3) numbers, page number, and doi

Web article (History) without date or page number

Magazine article with volume (35) and issue (4)

Book

References

Barrons, E. R. (2015, November). A comparison of domestic and international consumption of legumes. *Journal of Economic Agriculture, 23*(3), 45-49. doi: 10-1058-0885-7974.30.6.678

History of peanut butter. (n.d.). Peanut Advisory Board. Alabama Peanut Producers Association. Retrieved from http://www.alpeanuts.com/consumer_interest /article.phtml?articleID=102

Meadows, M. A. (2014, May). Peanut crop is anything but peanuts at home and overseas. *Business Monthly, 35*(4), 31-34.

Rivera, C. A. (2014). *The world's premier protein sources.* New York: HarperCollins.

APA In-Text Format. Within your text, document each text, figure, or personal source with a short description in parentheses. Following are selected guidelines summarizing the important elements of APA style.

■ For a direct quotation, include the last name of the author(s), if available, and the year of publication; for example, *(Meadows, 2014, p. 32).* If no author is shown in the text or on a website, use a shortened title or a heading that can be easily located on the References page; for example, *(History, n.d.).*

■ If you mention the author in the text, do not use the name again in the parenthetical reference. Just cite the date; for example, *According to Meadows (2014).*

■ Search for website dates on the home page or at the bottom of Web pages. If no date is available for a source, use *n.d.*

APA References Format. At the end of your report, in a section called "References," list all references alphabetically by author, or by title if no author is available. To better understand the anatomy of an APA scholarly journal article reference, see Figure C.2.

As with all documentation methods, APA has specific capitalization, punctuation, and sequencing rules, some of which are summarized here:

■ Include the last name of the author(s) followed by initials. APA is gender neutral, so first and middle names are not spelled out; for example, *(Martinez-Estrada, D. M.).*

■ Show the date of publication in parentheses immediately after the author's name. A magazine citation will also include the month and day in the parentheses.

■ Use sentence-style capitalization for all titles except journal article titles. Do not use quotation marks.

■ Italicize titles of magazines, newspapers, books, and journals.

Figure C.2 Anatomy of an APA Journal Article Reference

- Include the digital object identifier (DOI) when available for online periodicals. If no DOI is available, include the home page URL unless the source is difficult to retrieve without the entire URL.

- Break a URL or DOI only before a mark of punctuation such as a slash.

- If the website content may change, as in a wiki, include a retrieval date; for example, *Retrieved 7 July 2015 from http://www.encyclopediaofmath.org/index.php/Main_Page* Please note, however, that many instructors require that all Web references be identified by their URLs.

- For articles easily obtained from an online college database, provide the print information only. Do not include the database name or an accession number unless the article is discontinued or was never published.

For a comprehensive list of APA documentation format examples, see Figure C.3.

Modern Language Association Format

Writers in the humanities and the liberal arts frequently use the Modern Language Association (MLA) documentation format, illustrated briefly in Figure C.4. In parentheses close to the textual reference, include the author's name and page cited (Rivera 25). At the end of your writing on a page titled "Works Cited," list all the sources alphabetically. Some writers include all of the sources consulted. Differing from APA, MLA style does not require the URL if the source can be located with a keyword search. However, it's wise to check with your instructor or organization to see what is required. Another notable way MLA differs from APA is in the identification of the publication medium such as *Print* or *Web*. For more information, consult the *MLA Handbook for Writers of Research Papers*, Seventh Edition (New York: The Modern Language Association of America, 2009).

MLA In-Text Format.   Following any borrowed material in your text, provide a short parenthetical description. Here are selected guidelines summarizing important elements of MLA style:

- For a direct quotation, enclose in parentheses the last name of the author(s), if available, and the page number without a comma; for example, *(Rivera 25)*. If a website has no author, use a shortened title of the page or a heading that is easily found on the works-cited page; for example, ("History").

- If you mention the author in the text, do not use the name again in parentheses; for example, *According to Rivera (27)* . . .

- Search for website dates on the home page or on each Web page for use in the in-text citation. If no page number is available, use a paragraph number; for example, *(Killebrew par. 4)*. If neither a page number nor a paragraph number is available, cite the website in your text; for example, *The Inc. website about how to communicate with investors says that* . . .

Figure **C.3**   APA Sample References

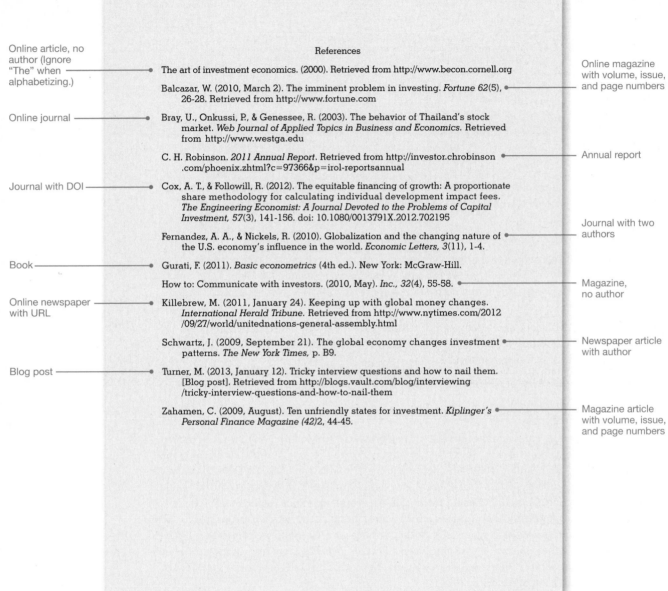

Online article, no author (Ignore "The" when alphabetizing.)

Online journal

Journal with DOI

Book

Online newspaper with URL

Blog post

References

The art of investment economics. (2000). Retrieved from http://www.becon.cornell.org

Balcazar, W. (2010, March 2). The imminent problem in investing. *Fortune 62*(5), 26-28. Retrieved from http://www.fortune.com

Bray, U., Onkussi, P., & Genessee, R. (2003). The behavior of Thailand's stock market. *Web Journal of Applied Topics in Business and Economics*. Retrieved from http://www.westga.edu

C. H. Robinson. *2011 Annual Report*. Retrieved from http://investor.chrobinson .com/phoenix.zhtml?c=97366&p=irol-reportsannual

Cox, A. T., & Followill, R. (2012). The equitable financing of growth: A proportionate share methodology for calculating individual development impact fees. *The Engineering Economist: A Journal Devoted to the Problems of Capital Investment, 57*(3), 141-156. doi: 10.1080/0013791X.2012.702195

Fernandez, A. A., & Nickels, R. (2010). Globalization and the changing nature of the U.S. economy's influence in the world. *Economic Letters, 3*(11), 1-4.

Gurati, F. (2011). *Basic econometrics* (4th ed.). New York: McGraw-Hill.

How to: Communicate with investors. (2010, May). *Inc., 32*(4), 55-58.

Killebrew, M. (2011, January 24). Keeping up with global money changes. *International Herald Tribune*. Retrieved from http://www.nytimes.com/2012 /09/27/world/unitednations-general-assembly.html

Schwartz, J. (2009, September 21). The global economy changes investment patterns. *The New York Times*, p. B9.

Turner, M. (2013, January 12). Tricky interview questions and how to nail them. [Blog post]. Retrieved from http://blogs.vault.com/blog/interviewing /tricky-interview-questions-and-how-to-nail-them

Zahamen, C. (2009, August). Ten unfriendly states for investment. *Kiplinger's Personal Finance Magazine (42)*2, 44-45.

Online magazine with volume, issue, and page numbers

Annual report

Journal with two authors

Magazine, no author

Newspaper article with author

Magazine article with volume, issue, and page numbers

Note: Although APA style prescribes double spacing for the references page, we show single spacing to conserve space and to represent preferred business usage.

MLA Works-Cited Format.   In a section called "Works Cited," list all references alphabetically by author or, if no author is available, by title. As with all documentation methods, MLA has specific capitalization and sequencing rules. Some of the most significant are summarized here:

- Include the author's last name first, followed by the first name and initial, as (Rivera, Charles A.).

- Enclose in quotation marks the titles of articles, essays, stories, chapters of books, pages in websites, individual episodes of television and radio broadcasts, and short musical compositions.

- Italicize the titles of books, magazines, newspapers, and journals.

Figure C.4   Portions of MLA Text Page and Works Cited

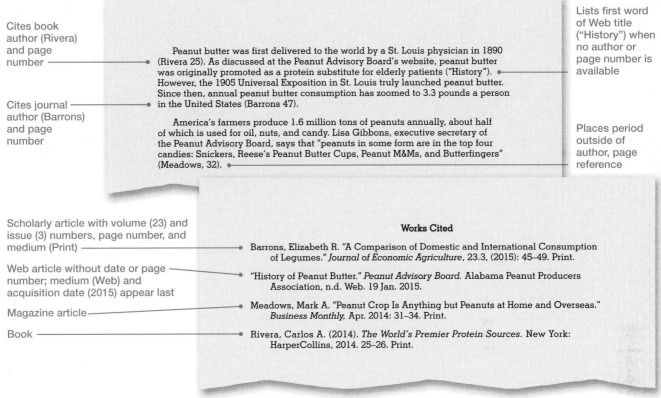

Cites book author (Rivera) and page number ———

Cites journal author (Barrons) and page number ———

Peanut butter was first delivered to the world by a St. Louis physician in 1890 (Rivera 25). As discussed at the Peanut Advisory Board's website, peanut butter was originally promoted as a protein substitute for elderly patients ("History"). However, the 1905 Universal Exposition in St. Louis truly launched peanut butter. Since then, annual peanut butter consumption has zoomed to 3.3 pounds a person in the United States (Barrons 47).

America's farmers produce 1.6 million tons of peanuts annually, about half of which is used for oil, nuts, and candy. Lisa Gibbons, executive secretary of the Peanut Advisory Board, says that "peanuts in some form are in the top four candies: Snickers, Reese's Peanut Butter Cups, Peanut M&Ms, and Butterfingers" (Meadows, 32).

Lists first word of Web title ("History") when no author or page number is available

Places period outside of author, page reference

Scholarly article with volume (23) and issue (3) numbers, page number, and medium (Print) ———

Web article without date or page number; medium (Web) and acquisition date (2015) appear last

Magazine article ———

Book ———

Works Cited

Barrons, Elizabeth R. "A Comparison of Domestic and International Consumption of Legumes." *Journal of Economic Agriculture*, 23.3, (2015): 45–49. Print.

"History of Peanut Butter." *Peanut Advisory Board.* Alabama Peanut Producers Association, n.d. Web. 19 Jan. 2015.

Meadows, Mark A. "Peanut Crop Is Anything but Peanuts at Home and Overseas." *Business Monthly,* Apr. 2014: 31–34. Print.

Rivera, Carlos A. (2014). *The World's Premier Protein Sources.* New York: HarperCollins, 2014. 25–26. Print.

© Cengage Learning 2015

- Include the medium of the publication, such as Web, *Print, Radio, Television, Film.*
- Include the URL only if the online site cannot be located by a keyword search. However, for class assignments, check to learn whether your instructor requires URLs, database names, and retrieval dates.

To better understand the anatomy of the format of an MLA scholarly journal article reference, see Figure C.5. For a comprehensive list of MLA documentation format examples, see Figure C.6.

Figure C.5   Anatomy of an MLA Journal Article Reference

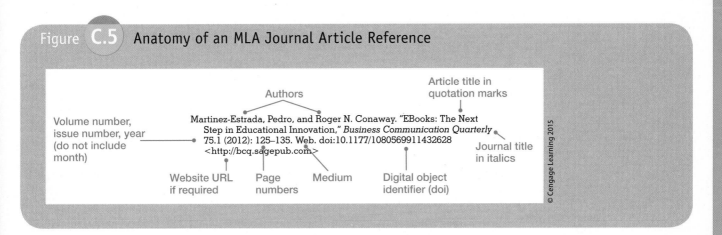

Authors

Article title in quotation marks

Volume number, issue number, year (do not include month)

Martinez-Estrada, Pedro, and Roger N. Conaway. "EBooks: The Next Step in Educational Innovation," *Business Communication Quarterly* 75.1 (2012): 125–135. Web. doi:10.1177/1080569911432628 <http://bcq.sagepub.com>

Journal title in italics

Website URL if required

Page numbers

Medium

Digital object identifier (doi)

© Cengage Learning 2015

Figure **C.6** MLA Sample References

Online magazine article. *Note:* Include date and page numbers but not volume or issue, even if available

Annual report from website

Journal article with two authors

Magazine article without author. No period after magazine title unless part of title

Newspaper article with author and edition

Blog post

Online journal without page, volume, or issue numbers

Online journal with volume (57) and issue (3) numbers

Book

Online newspaper

Unsigned online article with URL if required

Magazine article. Include date but not volume or issue numbers

Works Cited

Balcazar, William. "The Imminent Problem in Investing." *Fortune* 2 March 2010: 26–28. Web. 5 Jan. 2013.

Bray, Unoki, Peter Ohkussi, and Ronni Genessee. "The Behavior of Thailand's Stock Market." *Web Journal of Applied Topics in Business and Economics* (2003): n. pag. Web. 22 Dec. 2012.

C. H. Robinson. *2011 Annual Report*. Web. 22 Dec. 2012.

Cox, Arthlur T., and Robert Followill. "The Equitable Financing of Growth: A Proportionate Share Methodology for Calculating Individual Development Impact Fees." *The Engineering Economist: A Journal Devoted to the Problems of Capital Investment* 57.3 (2012): 141–156. Web. 6 Jan. 2013.

Fernandez, Anthony A., and Roberto Nickels. "Globalization and the Changing Nature of the U.S. Economy's Influence in the World." *Economic Letters* 3.11 (2010): 1–4. Print.

Gurati, Fredrik. *Basic Econometrics*. 4th ed. New York: McGraw-Hill, 2011. Print.

"How to: Communicate with Investors." *Inc.* May 2010: 55–58. Print.

Killebrew, Matthew. "Keeping Up with Global Money Changes." *International Herald Tribune* 24 Jan. 2011: 22+. Web. 24 Dec. 2012.

Schwartz, John. "The Global Economy Changes Investment Patterns." *The New York Times* 21 Sept. 2009, late ed.: B9. Print.

"The Art of Investment Economics." (2000): 1. Web. 24 Dec. 2012. <www.becon .cornell.org>.

Turner, Michelle. "Tricky Interview Questions and How to Nail Them." *Vault Blogs*. Vault Career Intelligence. Blog post. 12 Jan. 2013.

Zahamen, Cecil. "Ten Unfriendly States for Investment." *Kiplinger's Personal Finance Magazine* Aug. 2009: 44–45. Print.

Note: Check with your instructor about whether to cite URLs. Although MLA suggests using them only if necessary, many schools require students to include all URLs in their research papers.

Appendix D
Correction Symbols

In marking your papers, your instructor may use the following symbols or abbreviations to indicate writing or formatting weaknesses. You will find that studying these symbols and suggestions will help you understand your instructor's remarks. Knowing this information can also help you evaluate and improve your own letters, memos, e-mail messages, reports, and other writing. To improve your command of grammar and mechanics, please review the guides in the Grammar and Mechanics Guide in Appendix A. You can also build your skills by completing the exercises in Your Personal Language Trainer at **www.cengagebrain.com**.

Grammar and Mechanics

Act	Use active-voice verbs.
Apos	Use apostrophe correctly.
Art	Use a correct article (*a, an,* or *the*).
Cap	Correct capitalization error.
Cm	Insert a comma.
CmConj	Use a comma before a coordinating conjunction (*and, or, nor, but*) that joins independent clauses.
CmIntr	Use a comma after an introductory clause or a long phrase.
CmSer	Insert commas to separate items in a series.
CS	Correct a comma splice by separating clauses with a period or a semicolon.
DM	Correct a misplaced or dangling modifier by moving the modifier closer to the word it describes or by supplying a clear subject.
Exp	Eliminate expletives (*there is, there are,* and *it is*).
Frag	Revise sentence fragment to express a complete thought.
Num	Express numbers in appropriate word or figure form.
ProAgr	Make pronoun agree in number with its antecedent.
ProCase	Use appropriate nominative, objective, or possessive case.
Ref	Correct vague pronoun reference. Avoid pronoun that refers to a phrase, clause, sentence, or paragraph.
RO	Revise run-on or fused sentence by adding a period or a semicolon to separate independent clauses.
Sp	Correct spelling error.
S/V	Make verbs agree with their subjects.
Vb	Use correct verb tense.
V/Shift	Avoid unnecessary shifts in verb tense.
UnCm	Eliminate unnecessary comma.

Content, Organization, and Style

Asgn	Follow assignment instructions.
Awk	Recast to avoid awkward expression.
Ch	Use longer sentences to avoid choppiness. Vary sentence patterns.
Cl	Improve clarity of ideas or expression.
Coh	Develop coherence between ideas. Repeat key ideas, use pronouns, or add transitional expression.
Cop	Avoid copying textbook examples or wording.
DirSt	Start directly with the main idea.
Exp	Expand or explain an incomplete idea.
IS	Use indirect strategy by explaining before introducing main idea.
Log	Reconsider faulty logic.
Neg	Revise negative expression with more positive view.
Ob	Avoid stating the obvious.
Org	Improve organization by grouping similar ideas.
Par	Express ideas in parallel form.
Redun	Avoid redundant expression.
Tone	Use conversational, positive tone that promotes goodwill.
You	Emphasize the "you" view.
WC	Improve word choice.

Format

DS	Insert a double space.
F	Choose an appropriate format for this document.
GH	Use graphic highlighting (bullets, lists, indentions, or headings) to enhance readability.
Mar	Improve margins to fit document attractively on the page.
SS	Insert a single space.
TS	Insert a triple space.

Key to Grammar and Mechanics
C.L.U.E. Exercises

Chapter 1

1. Because you will be entering a fast-paced competitive, and highly connected digital **environment, communication** and technology skills are critical to your career success. [b, Guide 1, Fragment]
2. Such skills are particularly significant **now when** jobs are scarce and competition is keen. [b, Guide 1, Fragment]
3. During a recession many candidates vie for fewer **jobs; however,** candidates with exceptional communication skills will immediately stand out. [c, Guide 3, Comma splice. Use a semicolon or start a new sentence with *However*.]
4. Although we cannot predict the kinds of future jobs that will be available, they will undoubtedly require brainpower and education. [a, Correctly punctuated]
5. In traditional companies decisions must move through many levels of **managers; in** flat organizations decisions can be made more quickly. [c, Guide 3, Comma splice. Use a semicolon or start a new sentence with *In*.]
6. Millions of workers no longer report to nine-to-five **jobs thanks** largely to advances in high-speed and wireless Internet access. [b, Guide 1, Fragment]
7. Knowledge workers must be able to explain their **decisions; they** must be critical thinkers. [d, Guide 2, Run-on sentence. Use a semicolon or start a new sentence with *They*.]
8. The grapevine can be a powerful source of **information, although** it increasingly operates informally through social media. [b, Guide 1, Fragment]
9. Ethical companies experience less litigation, and they also are the target of less government regulation. [a, Correctly punctuated]
10. Ethics is a hot topic and trend in the **workplace; however,** making ethical decisions is not always easy. [c, Guide 3, Comma splice. Use a semicolon or start a new sentence with *However*.]

Chapter 2

1. Although three team members proofread the report, no one **saw** the error. [Guide 4]
2. During job interviews one of the most frequently requested soft skills **is** writing proficiency. [Guide 6]
3. Jeremy said he wished he **were** president for just one day. [Guide 5]
4. Better decisions and faster response time **explain** why companies are using teams. [Guide 7]
5. Either the team leader or the manager **is** going to schedule the meeting. [Guide 8]
6. Conflict and disagreement **are** normal and should be expected in team interactions. [Guide 7]
7. Everything in the company's e-mails and written records **was** made public during the trial. [Guide 9]
8. A committee of faculty and students **is** examining strategies to improve campus interviewing. [Guide 10]
9. Each of the employees was given the opportunity to **choose** a team to join. [Guide 4]
10. The appearance of e-mail messages, memos, and reports **has** a negative or positive effect on receivers. [Guide 6]

Chapter 3

1. Send all instructions to my manager and **me**; he and I will study them carefully. [Guide 13]
2. Except for Mark and **me,** all the sales reps attended the team meeting. [Guide 13]

3. In promoting **its** shoes to kids in Rome, Nike featured a Brazilian soccer star. [Guide 14]
4. Most of **us** consumers remember when fruits and vegetables were available only in season. [Guide 13]
5. The senior project manager and I are on call tonight, so please direct all calls to him or **me.** [Guide 15]
6. Every employee has a right to see **his or her** personnel folder. *OR:* All employees have a right to see **their** personnel **folders**. [Guide 17]
7. Lunches will be delivered to **whoever** ordered them. [Guide 16]
8. Most reservations were made in time, but **yours** and **hers** missed the deadline. [Guide 14]
9. *C* [Guide 13]
10. It must have been **she** who sent the e-mail to Jason and me. [Guide 12]

Chapter 4

1. A **face-to-face** conversation is a richer communication channel than an e-mail or letter. [Guide 20]
2. Christie thought she had done **well** in her performance review. [Guide 19]
3. Team members learned to use the wiki **more quickly** than they expected. [Guide 19]
4. Most of our **team-written** documents could be posted quickly to the wiki. [Guide 20]
5. We all felt **bad** when one member lost her laptop and had no backup. [Guide 19]
6. The 3-x-3 writing process provides **step-by-step** instructions for preparing messages. [Guide 20]
7. Everyone likes the **newly revamped** website and its up-to-date links. [Guide 20]
8. Our project ran **smoothly** after Justin reorganized the team. [Guide 19]
9. **Locally installed** online collaboration tools are **easy to use** and work well. [Guide 20]
10. **Well-written** e-mail messages sound conversational but professional. [Guide 20]

Chapter 5

1. Informal research methods include looking in the **files,** talking with your **boss,** and interviewing the target audience. [Guide 21, CmSer]
2. When you prepare to write any **message,** you need to anticipate the audience's reaction. [Guide 22, CmIntr]
3. By learning to distinguish between dependent and independent **clauses,** you will be able to avoid serious sentence faults. [Guide 22, CmIntr]
4. Some business messages require **sensitivity,** and writers may prefer to use passive-voice instead of active-voice verbs. [Guide 23, CmConj]
5. We hired Davida **Michaels,** who was the applicant with the best **qualifications,** as our new marketing manager. [Guide 25, CmIn]
6. Our business was incorporated on August 1, **2008,** in **Phoenix,** Arizona. [Guide 24, CmDate]
7. The new online **business,** by the **way,** is flourishing and is expected to show a profit soon. [Guide 25, CmIn]
8. After he **graduates,** Dustin plans to move to Atlanta and find work there. [Guide 22, CmIntr]
9. Last fall our company introduced policies regulating the use of cell **phones,** instant **messaging,** and e-mail on the job. [Guide 21, CmSer]
10. *C* [Guide 26, CmNo]

Chapter 6

1. Companies find it difficult to name new **products; consequently,** they often hire specialists. [Guide 27]
2. New product names must be **interesting; however,** many of the best names are already taken. [Guide 27]
3. Branding a product is a creative **endeavor;** the name becomes a product's shorthand. [Guide 27]
4. Global names must be appealing in such faraway places as **Beijing, China; Montreal, Canada;** and Dubai **City,** United Arab Emirates. [Guide 28]
5. One naming expert warned companies with the following **comment:** "Be aware of global consequences. For example, Bimbo is the name of a Mexican baking conglomerate. However, the word in English has an unsavory meaning." [Guide 30]
6. Product and company names are developed by combining the following three linguistic **elements:** morphemes, phonemes, and syntax. [Guide 29]
7. One of the reasons company names such as Google and Apple work is that they are **catchy; however,** they are also backed by high-quality products. [Guide 27]
8. Some English sounds (such as L, V, F, and W) are considered **feminine;** others (such as X, M, and Z) are viewed as masculine. [Guide 27]
9. Among the company officers judging new names were Anthony Simmons, vice **president;** Rachel Lohr, **CFO;** and Lavonne Jones, manager. [Guide 28]
10. Syntax, or word order, is key to consumers' **perception; therefore,** two-word product names must sound pleasing. [Guide 27]

Chapter 7

1. Employees were asked not to use the **company's** computers to stream video. [Guide 31]
2. **James's** blog discussed the overuse of the *Reply All* button. [Guide 32]
3. Would you please give me directions to your downtown **headquarters.** [Guide 34]
4. Her colleagues resented **Melissa's** copying everyone on her messages. [Guide 33]
5. The three top sales **reps**—Erik, Rachel, and **Erin**—received substantial bonuses. [Guide 36]
6. You must replace the ink cartridge **(see** page 8 in the **manual)** before printing. [Guide 37]
7. Tyler wondered whether all sales **managers'** databases needed to be updated. [Guide 32]
8. (Direct quotation) **"The** death of e-**mail,"** said Mike Song, **"has** been greatly **exaggerated."** [Guide 38]
9. In just two **years'** time, the number of people e-mailing on mobile devices nearly doubled. [Guide 32]
10. The staffing meeting starts at 10 a.m. sharp, doesn't **it?** [Guide 35]

Chapter 8

1. Our corporate **vice president** and **president** met with several **directors** on the **West Coast** to discuss how to develop **apps** for Facebook. [Guides 41, 43, 39]
2. All **Virgin Atlantic Airlines** passengers must exit the plane at **Gate** 2B in **Terminal** 4 when they reach **Seattle-Tacoma International Airport.** [Guides 39, 46]
3. The secretary of state of the **United States** urged members of the **European Union** to continue to seek peace in the **Middle East.** [Guides 39, 43]
4. My **cousin,** who lives in the **Midwest,** has a **Big Mac** and a **Dr. Pepper** for **lunch** nearly every day. [Guides 41, 43, 45]
5. Our **sales manager** and **director** of **operations** thought that the **company** should purchase a new **NordicTrack** treadmill for the **fitness** room. [Guides 41, 39, 45]
6. The **world's highest tax rate** is in **Belgium,** said **Professor Du-Babcock,** who teaches at the **City University** of **Hong Kong.** [Guides 39, 41]
7. Rachel Warren, who heads our **Consumer Services Division,** has a **master's degree** in **marketing** from **Ohio University.** [Guides 44, 40, 39]
8. Please consult **Figure** 2.3 in **Chapter** 2 to obtain **U.S. Census Bureau** population figures for the **Northeast.** [Guides 46, 39, 43]
9. Last **summer** did you see the article titled "**The Global Consequences of Using Crops for Fuel**"? [Guides 39, 42]
10. Michael plans to take courses in **management, economics,** and **history** in the **spring.** [Guides 40, 39]

Chapter 9

1. Did you **already** respond to his request for a **recommendation**?
2. The **principal** part of the manager's response contained a **compliment** and valuable **advice.**
3. In responding to the irate customer, Rachel made a **conscious** effort to show **patience** and present **credible** facts.
4. Even in **everyday** business affairs, we strive to reach **further** and go beyond what is expected.
5. Before you **proceed** with the report, please check those **surprising** statistics.
6. It's **usually** better to de-emphasize bad news rather **than** to spotlight it.
7. **Incidentally,** passive-voice verbs can help you make a statement less **personal** when **necessary.**
8. Customers are more **accepting** of **disappointing** news if they are **assured** that **their** requests were heard and treated fairly.
9. The customer's complaint **elicited** an immediate response that **analyzed** the facts carefully but was not **too** long.
10. When delivering bad news, try to **accommodate** a **dissatisfied** customer with a plausible alternative.

Chapter 10

1. Our manager reported receiving **seven** messages from customers with the same **two** complaints. [Guide 47]
2. **Thirty-three** companies indicated that they were participating in renewable energy programs. [Guide 47]
3. Did Dakota request **$500** to attend the **two**-day seminar? [Guides 49, 47]
4. UPS strives to make important deliveries before **10 a.m.** [Guide 49]
5. The meeting was rescheduled for **March 7** at **2 p.m.** [Guide 49]
6. Investors earned 3.5 **percent** dividends on each **$3,000** investment. [Guide 49]
7. With a birth occurring every **eight** seconds, the U.S. population is currently estimated to be **315 million.** [Guides 47, 50]
8. One petition now has more than **260,000** signatures, far and above the **25,000** needed for an official White House response. [Guide 48]
9. She bought the vintage item on eBay for **$2.50** and sold it for **$20.** [Guide 49]
10. At least **nine** prominent retail stores offer a **30-day** customer satisfaction return policy. [Guides 47, 48]

Chapter 11

1. One **credible** study revealed that **30** percent of jobs go to **companies'** inside candidates.
2. Networking is said to be the key to finding a **job;** however, **it's** easier said **than** done.
3. Some job seekers paid **$500** each to attend **12** sessions that promised expert job-searching **advice.**

4. To excel at **networking, a candidate** must have an **easy-to-remember** e-mail address.
5. My friend asked me if I had **already** prepared a **30-second** elevator **speech.**
6. When Rachel and **I** were collecting data for the **report,** we realized that **Twitter** and Facebook could be significant.
7. **Today's** workers must brush up their marketable **skills; otherwise,** they may not find another job after being laid off.
8. Being active on LinkedIn and building an impressive **Internet** presence **are** important, but the looseness of these connections **means** you shouldn't expect much from them.
9. Just between you and **me,** one of the best **strategies** in networking **is** distributing business cards with your personal tagline.
10. On **February 1** our company **president** revealed that we would be hiring **30** new employees, which was excellent news for everyone.

Chapter 12

1. After our supervisor and **she** returned from their meeting at **2 p.m.,** we were able to sort the **customers'** names more quickly.
2. **Six** of the 18 workers in my department were **released; as a result,** we had to work harder to achieve our goals.
3. Toyota, the market-leading **Japanese carmaker,** continued to enjoy strong positive ratings despite a string of **much-publicized** recalls.
4. **Michael's** presentation to a nonprofit group netted him only **$300,** a tenth of his usual **honorarium,** but he believes in pro bono work.
5. To reflect our guiding **principles** and our commitment to executive **education,** we offer financial support to more than **60** percent of our current MBA candidates.
6. Our latest press **release,** which was written in our Corporate Communication **Department,** announces the opening of three **Asian** offices.
7. In his justification report dated **September 1,** Justin argued that expansion to **12** branch offices could boost annual revenue to **$22 million.**
8. The practicality and advisability of opening 12 branch offices **are** what will be discussed in the **consultant's feasibility** report.
9. The **president,** who had **gone** to a meeting in the **Midwest,** delivered a report to Jeff and **me** when he returned.
10. Because some organizations prefer **single-spaced reports,** be sure to check with your organization to learn **its** preference.

Chapter 13

1. Our CEO and **president** both worked on the **30-page proposal,** which was due immediately.
2. Managers in **two departments** [delete apostrophe] complained that **their** departments should have been consulted.
3. The RFP and **its** attachments arrived **too** late for my manager and **me** to complete the necessary research.
4. Although we worked **every day** on the proposal, we felt **bad** that we could not meet the **May 15** deadline.
5. If the program and staff **are** to run **smoothly,** we must submit an effective grant proposal.
6. Although **short,** a successful mission statement should capture the **business's** goals and values [delete period] **in** a few succinct sentences.
7. A proposal budget cannot be changed if costs **rise later; consequently,** it must be written **carefully.**
8. A good eight-word mission statement is a critical tool for **funding;** it helps start-up **companies** evolve **their** big idea without being pulled off track.

9. Entrepreneur Stephanie **Rivera,** publisher of **an** urban event **calendar,** relies on social media to broadcast her message.
10. Stephanie asked Jake and **me** to help her write a business **plan that** would guide her new company and garner **permanent** funding.

Chapter 14

1. The **CEO's** assistant scheduled my colleague and **me** for a **20-**minute presentation to explain the new workplace sustainability initiative.
2. PowerPoint presentations, claims one **expert,** should be no longer **than 20** minutes and have no more than ten slides.
3. The introduction to a presentation should accomplish **three goals:** (a) capture attention, (b) establish **credibility,** and (c) preview main points.
4. In the body of a short **presentation,** speakers should focus on no more than **three principal** points.
5. A poll of **2,000** employees revealed that **four fifths** of them said they feared giving a presentation more **than** anything else they could think of.
6. A good list of tips for inexperienced speakers **is** found in the article titled "**40** Quick Tips **for** Speakers."
7. The **director** of operations made a **15-**minute presentation giving **step-by-step** instructions on achieving our sustainability goals.
8. In the **spring** our **company's** stock value is expected to **rise** at least 10 percent.
9. The appearance and mannerisms of a speaker **definitely affect** a **listener's** evaluation of the message.
10. Because the **boss's** daughter was a dynamic speaker who had founded a successful **company,** she earned at least **$20,000** for each presentation.

Chapter 15

1. When searching for **jobs,** candidates discovered that the résumé is more likely to be used to screen **candidates than** for making hiring decisions.
2. **Today's** employers use **sites** such as Facebook to learn about potential **employees,** which means that a job seeker must maintain a professional online presence.
3. To conduct a safe online job search, you **should** [delete colon] (a) **use** only reputable job boards, (**b**) keep careful records, and (c) limit the number of sites on which you post your résumé.
4. If I **were you,** I would shorten my résumé to **one** page and include a summary of qualifications.
5. Mitchell wondered whether it was **all right** to ask his professor for employment **advice.**
6. At last **month's** staff **meeting,** team members examined several **candidates'** résumés.
7. Rather **than** schedule **face-to-face interviews,** the team investigated videoconferencing.
8. **Eleven** applicants will be interviewed on **April 10; consequently,** we may need to work late to accommodate them.
9. Although as many as **25** percent of jobs are found on the **Internet,** the **principal** source of jobs still involves networking.
10. If Troy had **gone** to the **company's** own **website,** he might have seen the position posted immediately.

Chapter 16

1. In interviewing job **candidates,** recruiters have the following three **purposes:** assessing their skills, discussing their **experience,** and deciding whether they are a good fit for the organization.
2. Jack wondered how many **companies** use the Internet to check **candidates' backgrounds.**

3. Despite the heavy use of **e-mail,** most **employers** use the telephone to reach candidates and set up **their** interviews.
4. Most interviews **usually** cover the same kinds of **questions; therefore,** smart candidates prepare for them.
5. If your job history has gaps in **it,** be prepared to explain what you did during this **time** [delete comma] and how you kept **up-to-date** in your field.
6. Interviewing is a **two-way street,** and candidates should be prepared with **their** own meaningful questions.
7. Emma was asked whether she had a **bachelor's degree** [delete comma] and whether she had three **years'** experience.
8. If you are **conscientious** and want to create a good **impression,** be sure to write a **thank-you** message after a job interview.
9. When **Maria's** interview was **over,** she told friends that she had done **well**.
10. Maria was **all ready** to send a thank-you **message** [omit comma] when she realized she could not spell the **interviewer's** name.

Index

Italic page numbers indicate illustrative information in figures

Graphics, *488*
  creating effective, 402–408
  incorporating into reports, 407–408
  matching to objectives, 402–407
  multimedia presentation, *520*
Gray, Curt, 4
Grease payments to custom officials, 102
Green, Alison, 592
GreenTalk Radio podcasts, *219*
Greeting, professional e-mail, 208
Grid to analyze complex verbal data about building cash reserves, 423
Grids, tabulating and analyzing digital-age data, *423*
Grinyer, Dr. Mark, 465, 492
Group behaviors, positive and negative, 45
Group decisions, 46
Group interviews, 589
Grouped bar chart, *404*
Groupon, 611
Groupthink, 527
  combating, 45–46
Guess, 81
Guffey, Mary Ellen, 587

H

H&M, 11
Hackman, J. Richard, 43
Hall, Edward T., 64, 89
Hammer, M. R., 94–95
Handouts, 511–512
Hart Research Associates, 5
Hastings, Reed, 296
Hazards of courage, 45
Headings
  adding for visual impact 189–190
  apply punctuation correctly, 432
  balance within levels, 432
  capitalize and emphasize, 432
  distinguishing among functional, talking, and combination, 432
  first-level and second-level, 432, *485–490*
  include at least one per report page, 432
  keep short but clear, 432
  levels of in reports, *433*
  providing reader cues, 431–433
  use appropriate levels, 432
Health Insurance Portability and Accountability Act (HIPAA), 245
Health of Women Study, 355
Heatherly, Chris, 155
Hewlett-Packard, 23, 27, 501
Hidden job market, 546
  building personal network, 549–550
  making most of LinkedIn, 551–552
  pursuing with networking, 549–552
  using social media to network, 550–551
High potential network, iHipo, 548
High-context cultures, 89–90
Highpoint Blue Shield, 270
  of Pittsburgh, Pennsylvania, 245
Hiring/placement interviews, 589
Hirsh, George, 297
HMO (health maintenance organization), 270
Hofstede, Geert, 90
Hohli, 401
Hollister, 151

Home Depot, 82, 303
HomeDepotSucks.com, 303
Honesty is key, 475
Honors, organizing résumé information into categories, 558
Horizontal bar chart, *404*
Horizontal information flow, improving, 22
Hospitality, extending thanks for, 267
Hot desks, 17
Hot Topic, 151
Howder, Randy, 511
Hsieh, Tony, 157, 205
Huhman, Heather, 543, 571, 579
Human behavior, six basic principles that direct, *329*
Humane Society, mission statement, 474
Hyperlinks, multimedia presentation, *520*

I

IABC Code of Ethics for Professional Communicators, 28
IBM, 182, 218, 229
  Integrated Supply Chain Group, 104
ICT (Information and Communication Technologies), 85
Ideas
  generating, 154–159
  grouping to show relationships, 155–156
  make sure important idea is subject of sentence, 162
  organizing into strategies, 156–159
  place important idea either first or last in sentence, 162
  place important idea in simple sentence or an independent clause, 162
  stressing important ideas, 161–162
  sustaining key, 166–167
Ideograms, 401
iHipo, international internships, jobs and graduate programs, 548
IKEA, 100, 286
Illegal and inappropriate interview questions, 603–604
Illustrations, 407
IM (instant messaging), 132, 135
  benefits vs. network security, 215
Imagery, building audience rapport, 509
Images, multimedia presentation, *520*
Immelt, Jeffrey, 14
Immigration, 86
Impact, organizing content for 504–510
Impenetrable verbiage, complaining of an avalanche of, 189
Importance
  organizing data by, 429
  organizing the body of oral presentation, 506
In progress, periodic (activity) reports, 436
INC, 589
Inclusive language, 27
Indeed, 547
Indefinite pronouns, A-5
InDesign, 395
Indexes, secondary source, 387

Indirect benefit, building interest in persuasive messages, 335
Indirect negative messages, opening with a buffer, 294–295
Indirect paragraph plan, 166
Indirect strategy
  and direct strategy for negative messages, comparing, *293*
  for delivering negative news, 290–293
  for unreceptive audiences, 158–159
  justification/recommendation reports, 442
  organizational strategies for reports, 377–378
Individualism, 90
Inflated résumé, 569
Influence, 327
Influencers, 218, 223
Infographic résumé, 566–567
Infographics, telling story with, 401
Informal letter proposal, *467–468*
Informal proposals, 465–470
  authorization request, 470
  background, problem and purpose of, 469
  budget, 470
  components of, 466–470
  introduction, 468–469
  plan and schedule, 469
  staffing, 469
Informal reports
  components of, *476*
  delivered as slide decks, 449
Informal research methods, 152
  check company files, 152
  conduct informal survey, 152
  interview target audience, 152
  talk with boss, 152
Informal writing style, 379
Information
  documenting, 396–400
  formal communication channels, 21–22
  identifying secondary sources, 384–396
  improving downward flow of, 22
  improving horizontal flow of, 22
  improving upward flow of, 22
  informal communication channels, 23–24
  internal and external communication, 19–20
  making financial reader-friendly, 434
  media richness and social presence, 20–21
  networked workplace in hyperconnected world, 18
  ordering logically, 429–430
  organizing, 154–159
  rejecting requests for, 299–301
  researching background, 151–153
Information and communication technologies, globalization growing reach of, 85–86
Information collecting, collaborative teams, 528
Information curators, modern librarians as, 387
Information design, clarity and simplicity in, 400
Information flow
  and media choices in today's business world, 18–24
  in organizations, *21*
Information report
  letter format, *376–377*
  writing, 440

Information worker, 6
Informational reports, 374
  organizing data, 428
  writing short, 433–440
Infosearch, 389
Inside address, business letters, B-3
Instant message, 141, 214
Instant messaging (IM), 213
  benefits of, 214
  best practices for, 216–217
  impact of, 213–216
  risks of, 214–216
  technology behind, 213
Instruction messages, 249–257
  dividing instructions into steps, 255
  revising message delivering instructions, 255–257
Intel, 3, 23, 30
  Social Media Guidelines, 3
  socializing its brand, 221
Intellectual property, 400
Intellectual theft
  on the Internet, 397
  plagiarism, 396
Intercultural audiences
  adapting presentations to, 524–527
  understanding different values and nonverbal behavior, 526
Intercultural communication
  domestic workforce is becoming increasingly diverse, 86
  global businesses and social media use, 96
  growing importance of, 81–86
  how technology and social media affect, 95–96
  major trends fuel globalization, 83–86
  markets go global, 82
Intercultural e-mail message, 97–99
  effective, *98*
  ineffective, *98*
Intercultural environments
  enhancing oral communication in, 96–97
  improving conversations in intercultural environments, 96–97
  improving written communication, 97
Intercultural proficiency, achieving, 99
Interculturally proficient, 91–99
  how technology and social media affect intercultural communication, 95–96
  improving conversations in intercultural environments, 96–97
  intercultural e-mail message, 97–99
  strategies for improving your intercultural effectiveness, 91–93
  successful nonverbal intercultural communication, 93–95
Interest
  building in persuasive messages, 335
  building in sales messages, 347–348
Interim reports, 437–439
Internal blogs tract intellectual property at Google, 225
Internal communication, 19–20
  companies blog, 223–224
Internal proposals, 441

AN OVERVIEW OF CULTURE

All persons are puzzles until at last we find in some word
or act the key to the man, to the woman; straightway
all their past words and actions lie in light before us.

—Emerson[1]

What is culture? How do we identify, let alone define, something so complex and abstract? What are perceptions, and how do they shape our understanding of cross-cultural differences? How do stereotypes and ethnocentric thinking interfere with our understanding of culture and how we communicate with others? These are the key questions we will address in Chapter 1.

EVOLVING DEMOGRAPHICS IN THE GLOBAL VILLAGE

In today's global market and increasingly fast-paced society, we often hear people say that the world is shrinking. In the 1960s, media expert and social visionary Marshall McLuhan coined the term "global village," which accurately forecasted many of the changes we see today—changes that are the product of advances in technology through telecommunications, travel, and personal computing.[2] (See Figure 1.1.) New technologies have made it possible to rapidly move raw materials, capital, finished goods, and people across oceans, borders, and time zones. We can do that both physically and electronically, transporting whatever we may need from the far corners of the world into our offices, our classrooms, and our neighborhoods.[3]

In today's global market, chances are good that most of what you've worn, driven, operated, or eaten was designed, manufactured, and distributed by firms that are transnational in character, organization, and culture. Your pajamas were probably manufactured in China; your suit tailored in Italy; your cereal produced in the midwestern United States; your toothbrush made in Taiwan; your wristwatch manufactured in Switzerland. Our day-to-day lives are inextricably bound up with products, processes, and services from all over the world—something that, thirty years ago, was thought to be extraordinary. Imported goods were considered a luxury by your parents. That's no longer the case. Now Chinese factory workers wear New York Yankees ball caps; you wear gloves made in their factory.

We buy brand-name products from companies we think are American (Ford Motor Company, for example), only to discover that most of the component parts were manufactured in Brazil, Portugal, Ireland, or Canada. That German automobile in the neighbor's garage (think of a Volkswagen Jetta) was assembled entirely in Mexico. Your Dell computer was manufactured in Round Rock, Texas, but the tech support at the other end of their 1-800 line is in Bangalore, India. That cell phone made in Finland or Japan doubles as a camera, permitting you to e-mail vacation snapshots anywhere in less than a minute.

Those of us old enough to recall the 1970s and 1980s remember living in a world of rotary-dial telephones, electric typewriters, and manual transmissions. Fast forward to the twenty-first century, and we're awash in an explosion of broadband, digital technology that brings the world instantaneously to our desktops, laptops, and hand-held devices. It's changed the meaning of everything from "library research" to "chatting with a friend."

1

Figure 1.1   Welcome to Global Village

From David W. Johnson & Frank
P. Johnson, *Joining Together: Group
Theory and Group Skills*, 6th Ed.
Published by Allyn & Bacon, Boston,
MA. Copyright ©1997 by Pearson
Education.

As finished goods, capital, and the supply of labor move quickly around the world, so does the reality of workplace diversity. Through immigration, increased opportunities for education and advancement, and the upsurge of women and minorities in the workplace, the U.S. workforce is no longer a homogenous group of people who look, think, and behave in the same ways. According to the U.S. Census Bureau's Year 2000 Census, among the nearly 300 million people inhabiting the United States, about 200 million are classified as White, about 35 million are African American or Black, more than 35 million are Hispanic or Latino, and more than 10 million are Asian. Some 25 million more are of other races or mixed race.[4]

Also according to the Census Bureau, in the year 2003 there were approximately 32.5 million foreign-born residents in the United States.[5] *The Kiplinger Letter* reports that more than 1.5 million foreign-born people settle in the United States each year, a number that will reach 2 million per year by 2010.[6] In addition, a Northeastern University study reveals that immigrants have accounted for over half of the labor force growth between 1990 and 2001.[7] By 2003, many of the foreign-born residents living in the United States were working for one of the 2,800 foreign firms operating here. That figure doesn't include over 7,200 American subsidiaries, affiliates, or branches of firms from over 79 countries.[8] Statistics from the Institute of International Education also show that by 2003 there were approximately 600,000 international students studying in the United States, up by 6.4 percent from the previous year.[9]

McLuhan's global village is not composed of just those who come to North America. The issues inherent in intercultural communication are important for all those who leave the United States and Canada to live and work elsewhere. Kiplinger estimates that more Americans are living abroad than ever before—nearly four million, not including military and diplomats.[10] As of 2003, there were more than 3,000 American corporations operating overseas to support this large number of expatriates, along with 36,300 foreign subsidiaries, affiliates, or branches from over 187 countries.[11] With so many people coming and going, we have become a mobile, global culture of immense proportions.

At the same time, an image of a world growing smaller and more accessible, with a more-diverse population, working literally side by side in the marketplace, no longer brings to mind those nostalgic recollections of traveling abroad. The twentieth-century image of foreign travel is one of a tourist, intrigued by unusual or quaint customs as she samples interesting cuisine and buys colorful trinkets, all while conversing in an exotic language in some far-off land. Today, that image is as anachronistic as a steamer trunk. The global village is more than the superficial interaction of a tourist on vacation: It is the current-day reality of savvy business professionals, graduate business students, or the folks next door who interact each day with people from all over the world and from a variety of ethnicities and backgrounds.

As the pace of globalization and contact with other cultures increases, so does the probability that one language will not serve all of your needs. A recent study shows that, across the globe, more people are speaking two or more languages, and the percentage of the global population who learned English as their native language is on the decline.

While many have argued that English is and will continue to be the world language of the twenty-first century, certain researchers studying the future of languages argue that because of population growth in developing countries during the last century, a new "linguistic order" is coming. Studies

Figure 1.2   Demographic Redistribution in American Cities

Sources: S. Schifferes, "Hispanics Overtake Blacks in U.S." *BBC News Online*, June 19, 2003. Retrieved from http://www.bbcnews.com and "Whites a Minority in U.S. Cities," *BBC News Online*, April 30, 2003. Retrieved from http://www.bbcnews.com.

Hispanics, the fastest-growing ethnic group in the United States, have overtaken blacks to become the largest minority in the U.S., according to the U.S. Bureau of the Census. There are now nearly 38.8 million Hispanics, compared to 38.3 million blacks, and the Hispanic population is likely to grow very quickly. Since 2000, they have accounted for more than 50% of the total growth in the U.S. population.

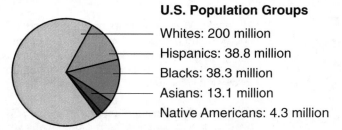

U.S. Population Groups

Whites: 200 million
Hispanics: 38.8 million
Blacks: 38.3 million
Asians: 13.1 million
Native Americans: 4.3 million

Nearly one-third of the U.S. population is now non-white, and some census projections suggest that by 2050, whites will become a minority. "This is an important event in this country," said Census Director Louis Kincannon, "an event that we know is the result of the growth of a vibrant and diverse population that is vital to America's future."

This demographic shift is more readily evident in large American cities, where white people now make up less than 50% of the population on the 100 largest cities in the U.S. for the first time in history. While they are a majority in 52 of the 100 largest cities, they make up only 44% of the total population of those cities.

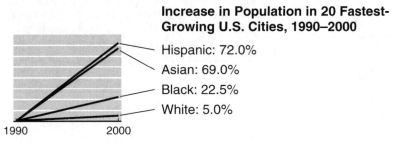

Increase in Population in 20 Fastest-Growing U.S. Cities, 1990–2000

Hispanic: 72.0%
Asian: 69.0%
Black: 22.5%
White: 5.0%

1990   2000

show that in the mid-twentieth century, about 9 percent of the world's population spoke English as their native language, but that number is expected to decline to about 5 percent by 2050.

Although more than 6,000 languages exist in the world today, more people speak Mandarin Chinese than any other, followed by English, Spanish, Hindi/Urdu, and Arabic. Those four languages will be spoken by roughly equal numbers of people by 2050. (See Figure 1.3.) That won't mean English will lose its cachet as a global language, though. English will continue to dominate the content of the Internet, the regulation of international finance markets, international aviation, and air-traffic control. Of course, where there is money, there is influence: English-speaking nations will continue to control a sizable fraction of the world's commerce, capital, and investments.[12]

Figure 1.3   Languages Other Than English Spoken in the United States

Source: Genaro C. Armas, "Census: Big Jump in Non-English Speakers." *The South Bend Tribune,* October 9, 2003, A1, A6.

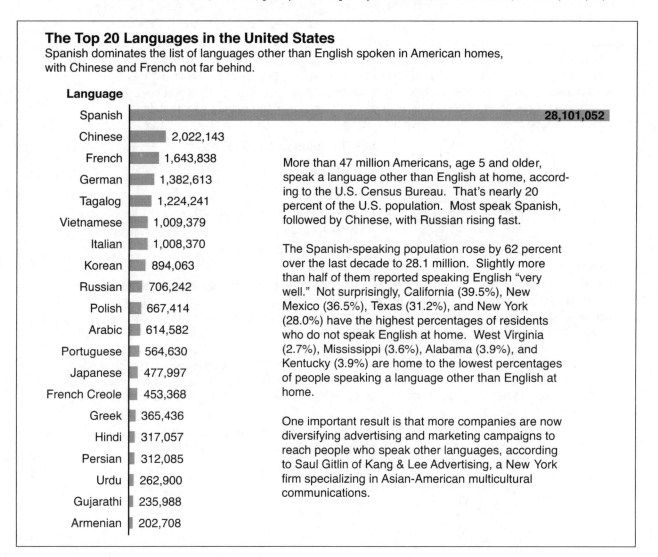

The Top 20 Languages in the United States

Spanish dominates the list of languages other than English spoken in American homes, with Chinese and French not far behind.

Language

Language	Count
Spanish	28,101,052
Chinese	2,022,143
French	1,643,838
German	1,382,613
Tagalog	1,224,241
Vietnamese	1,009,379
Italian	1,008,370
Korean	894,063
Russian	706,242
Polish	667,414
Arabic	614,582
Portuguese	564,630
Japanese	477,997
French Creole	453,368
Greek	365,436
Hindi	317,057
Persian	312,085
Urdu	262,900
Gujarathi	235,988
Armenian	202,708

More than 47 million Americans, age 5 and older, speak a language other than English at home, according to the U.S. Census Bureau. That's nearly 20 percent of the U.S. population. Most speak Spanish, followed by Chinese, with Russian rising fast.

The Spanish-speaking population rose by 62 percent over the last decade to 28.1 million. Slightly more than half of them reported speaking English "very well." Not surprisingly, California (39.5%), New Mexico (36.5%), Texas (31.2%), and New York (28.0%) have the highest percentages of residents who do not speak English at home. West Virginia (2.7%), Mississippi (3.6%), Alabama (3.9%), and Kentucky (3.9%) are home to the lowest percentages of people speaking a language other than English at home.

One important result is that more companies are now diversifying advertising and marketing campaigns to reach people who speak other languages, according to Saul Gitlin of Kang & Lee Advertising, a New York firm specializing in Asian-American multicultural communications.

A RATIONALE FOR CULTURE STUDY

Before we can understand what makes other people different, and before we can know what makes them tick, we must first understand the basic elements of culture. Those elements are the values, beliefs, and attitudes that serve as the basis for the norms and rules of social interaction, all of which translate into behavior. Knowing something about those will help us to understand another person's world view, and the most basic assumptions he or she holds about others who are different.

Our goal is to have more successful cross-cultural interactions, to become more culturally literate. This book is not a quick fix with instant recipes for success; rather, it is a blueprint. We lay the foundation by first discussing some basic concepts of culture, such as the effects of individual and collective identity; our use of time and personal space; and our use of language, gestures, and more. Once we have some sense of what these things mean and why we use them as we do, we can begin to build our understanding of other cultures. By examining the basic underpinnings of culture (looking at the general), we can translate this into everyday interactions (looking at specific instances). The aim is not just awareness of self and others, but to acquire and use information that will equip us to take action every time we interact with someone who approaches life from a different world view.

Interculturalist Marshall Singer believes that the goal for intercultural communication is not just better communication, since conflict and misunderstanding will always be a part of the human condition. While we can never eliminate misunderstandings because of cultural differences, misperception is less likely if we are aware of the tacit subtleties that create the potential for conflict.[13] By laying out the basic concepts of cultural differences, we hope you will look inward to understand yourself, and then look outward to interact successfully with people who come from different frames of reference.

DEFINING CULTURE

In order to discuss intercultural communication, we must first define the concept of culture. Culture dictates the norms of every group. These norms, or unstated rules, are the accepted and expected ways of behaving and interacting with other people. But culture is something that we don't always see. Culture is something that we learn. From infancy on, we are conditioned to act, react, and learn about how people in our world do things from watching them, conversing with them, and interacting with them. In sum, culture includes a group's communication patterns; how a group solves problems; and how a group perceives and passes on its shared values, beliefs, attitudes, and behaviors, including its perception of self, group, environment, authority, and power.

Over the last century, key thinkers on culture, including anthropologists, sociologists, psychologists, communication specialists, and business experts, have attempted to define culture from various perspectives, frameworks, and focal points. The notion of culture is so abstract and complex that over 160 more- or less-accepted definitions of the term are in common use.[14]

Anthropologist Edward T. Hall says that culture is about how we communicate, and that it's governed by hidden rules (the silent language and hidden dimension), which are reflected in both language and behavior. Dutch interculturalist Fons Trompenaars says that culture is reflected in how a group approaches problem-solving.[15] Sociologist Geert Hofstede argues by analogy that culture implies a kind of collective "software of the mind," learned over a lifetime of "programming" the way we do things.[16] Kluckhon and Strodbeck, well-known anthropologists of the 1960s, construct their definition of culture around six dimensions that delineate cultural differences. Their framework focuses on value orientations (environment, time, people, activity, responsibility, and space), which have become the basis for much of today's research in the area of intercultural communication.[17]

To complicate matters even further as we attempt to define culture, let's look at another perspective from Marshall Singer. He makes an interesting point regarding culture:

> *. . . because no person is a part of all, and only, the same groups as anyone else and because each person ranks the attitudes, values, and beliefs of the groups to which he or she belongs differently, each individual must be considered to be culturally unique . . . I am not arguing that every person is a culture unto herself or himself. Culture . . . is a group-related phenomenon . . . each individual in this world is a member of a unique collection of groups. No two humans share only and exactly the same group memberships, or exactly the same ranking of the importance, to themselves, of the group membership they do share. Thus, each person must be culturally unique.*[18]

This is an interesting concept: that each of us is culturally unique. While this key thinker on intercultural communication would not go so far as to say that each of us is his or her own culture, the thought of being culturally unique as individuals is provocative. As you can see, culture cannot be

Speaking of Culture ▼

From an anthropological perspective, every society has a culture and many subcultures. The questions are how to identify their components and how do they work?

– Melvyn Hammarberg Chair,
Department of Anthropology,
University of Pennsylvania ▲

neatly packaged into one definition, because it is as broad and complex as the number of people in this world. Culture is dynamic rather than static: it changes with people, geographical and historical events, and technological advances. For example, think about how cell phones and the Internet have changed the way we communicate, which amounts to less face-to-face interaction with other human beings. We now think twice about flying across the continent or to another country if we are able to save time, money, and resources by having a phone or video-conference. The way we communicate in the twenty-first century is evolving as new technologies come into existence and as we learn to use them in effective and socially responsible ways.

We learn about our culture as we interact with other people while sharing daily life, but we do not necessarily think about the fact that we are living out our particular lives, bound by culture. Most of our day-to-day activities are so natural to us that we have no need to think about why we behave, believe, or think the way we do. For example, we watch television commercials that stress self-actualization and individualism. "Be all you can be; join the army" coaxes young people to attain personal self-actualization. The newer slogan, "An army of one," implies that you can still maintain your individuality even though the purpose of joining the army is to become tightly interwoven in the fabric of the armed forces, with each man and woman depending on one another for their very lives. It is interesting to see how this slogan has evolved in the post-modern world where personal autonomy and self-identification have challenged the former mores of tradition and authority. We consider it natural to listen and accept such slogans without much reflection on or thought to the underlying values that shape these beliefs. We tend to take a more myopic view of culture and focus on what we can see and hear: the language we use, the clothes we wear, the food we eat, and the traditions and customs we uphold. But as we will see in the discussion that follows, there is much more to culture than meets the eye.

AN ANALOGY

An analogy may be appropriate at this point to help us visualize the concept of culture. Imagine that you are standing on the deck of a small tour ship making its way along the spectacular Alaskan coastline. It is close to dusk and you breathe deeply, the cold air filling your lungs as you watch the sun set. In the distance, you see majestic icebergs that ships pass at a respectful distance. Tall, jagged, foreboding clumps of ice float silently by as the sun reflects its late afternoon glow on a massive expanse of whiteness. You've never seen anything quite like it and the concerns of your day seem to fade along with the setting sun.

As spectacular as it is to see real icebergs up close, we only see—proverbial as it may sound—the very tip. An iceberg is actually an enormous mass of solid ice that has broken off from the polar icecap and, because of its density, floats independently like an ice cube in a glass of water. While what we see above the water level may seem to be massive, in actuality, what's below the water line is even bigger. On average, approximately seven-eighths of an iceberg's mass is submerged.

Culture is, in some ways, like an iceberg. (See Figure 1.4.) What we see on the surface is the most familiar and readily identifiable. As we've already seen, the usual associations with culture are a people's language, traditions, customs, food, dress, and more. Such things are noticeable, identifiable, and observable. What we can't see below the surface is what supports those external trappings. What we

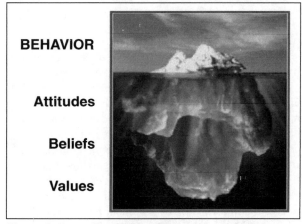

BEHAVIOR

Attitudes

Beliefs

Values

Figure 1.4   The Hidden Dimension of Culture

Ralph A. Clevenger/Corbis

can see is simply an outward manifestation of all of those underlying factors that inform our behavior and shape and our world view—our attitudes, beliefs, and values.

The most basic of those structures are our *values*: those fundamental, unmovable tenets that make us who we are and that shape all other structures in our attitudinal system. They're a psychological assessment, really, of those things, those concepts, those ideas most dear to us. We acquire them at an early age from people we trust, before rational thought begins to play a role in what we know and hold to be true. The world is a particular way for us because that's what our parents, our teachers, our coaches, and our religious figures have told us. We're not in a position to challenge such beliefs—we simply accept them for what they are. Such values can (and do) change, but they do so at glacial speed. Occasionally, as the result of trauma or some cataclysmic event in our lives—a divorce, the death of a child, the loss of a job, a particularly profound betrayal—we'll find that one or more of our basic values has changed. But it's a rare event for most people, and a good thing it doesn't happen more often. Those values serve as the foundation for everything else in our attitudinal system.

Values provide the basis for our *beliefs*: those truths we hold to be self-evident because they are based on our values. If friendship, for example, is a fundamental value for us, then we believe that genuine friends will behave in certain ways and will expect certain things of us. We, in turn, can expect certain things of them and will be more than willing to go out of our way to help our friends—because we believe in them.

Attitudes, in turn, arise from and are consistent with those beliefs. It's a navigational term, really, meaning orientation or position. Thus, an attitude gives some meaning and direction to our beliefs, serving as a guide to general thinking and our views of life over the near term. If a fundamental value of ours tells us that living a healthy lifestyle is important, then a consistent belief might be that smoking cigarettes is not a good idea. The attitude that arises from that belief would tell us, for example, that we not only shouldn't smoke, but that we should encourage others—our children, our employees, and our friends—not to smoke.

Behavior is the direct result of all these structures and is found at the uppermost level of our attitudinal system. It not only gives meaning and life to our more basic attitudes and beliefs, but it is the most visible portion of our system of beliefs. It may be hard to tell what a friend is thinking, but it's fairly easy to see what he or she is doing. We observe behaviors and infer the attitudes and beliefs that animate them. Behavior is often expressed in the form of *opinion*: for the moment, at least, it's our opinion that we will vote for this person, dine at that restaurant, or purchase a particular brand. It's all subject to change, of course, and is less predictable than the underlying attitudes, beliefs, and values that support it.

Becoming competent in another culture means looking beyond behavior to see if we can understand the attitudes, beliefs, and values that motivate what we observe. By looking only at the visible aspects of culture—customs, clothing, food, and language—we develop a myopic view of intercultural understanding—just the tip of the iceberg, really. If we are to be successful in our business interactions with people who have different values and beliefs about how the world is ordered, then we must go below the surface of what it means to understand culture and attempt to see what Edward Hall calls the "hidden dimensions." Those hidden aspects are the very foundation of culture and are the reason why culture is actually more than meets the eye. We tend not to notice those cultural norms until they violate what we deem to be common sense, good judgment, or the nature of things.

PERCEPTION

The core values that make up our world view also strongly shape our perceptions. Perception is a cognitive process in which we attach meaning to objects, symbols, people, and behavior in order to make sense of them. These mental categories are called *schema* or *schemata*[19] and help us categorize what we know, for example, about a certain cultural characteristic (such as the meaning behind greetings) in order to better understand it. We each go through a process of receiving, organizing, and translating external stimuli, which influence our behavior and attitudes. For example, in some cultures people shake hands as a means for greeting (the United States, for example), while in other cultures people bow (Japan), and in still others, they offer a kiss on both cheeks. We go through a cognitive process of receiving information or stimuli (e.g., being kissed on both cheeks) and attach meaning to this action in order to interpret or decode its meaning. During this process, we form mental categories (the schema) in order to help us organize the new information (e.g., the French greet us by kissing and the Japanese by bowing), so when we receive the stimuli, we process that information based on our perceptions and then categorize the information without even realizing it. Thus, it is an unconscious way of making sense out of the unfamiliar.

According to Jean Piaget, a twentieth-century Swiss psychologist who specialized in cognitive development, when we come into contact with something unfamiliar, in order to adapt to that situation, interaction, or environment, we must first assimilate and accommodate those external stimuli. Assimilation means that we process the information and mentally integrate it with our own existing knowledge—technically speaking, into our schema (mental categories). Accommodation means that we go through a process of adjustment or modification of these schema in order to make sense of this new information.[20]

For example, in the U.S. culture and in other cultures of the developed world, we normally shake hands and look a new business contact in the eye upon meeting and exchanging introductions. When we travel to Japan for the first time and experience our business counterparts bowing rather than shaking hands, we will try to assimilate or file away that information for future use. The next time we interact with a Japanese businessperson, we are more likely to adjust, or accommodate, our response by anticipating that the business contact will bow. The expectation, then, is that someone from Japan will probably greet others with a bow, so we need to be ready to bow in response.

An awareness of such norms, or unstated expectations of acceptable behavior, is just the beginning of successful intercultural encounters. Many more subtle nuances need to be learned. For example, let's return to the Japanese custom of bowing. While the Japanese are well-versed in U.S. culture and may very well initiate a greeting through a handshake, if they do choose to bow, there are nuances of how to bow appropriately that must be learned. For example, you only bow to the same depth that someone bows to you. Depth of the bow demonstrates the level, or depth, of the relationship and signifies the status of the initiator. If you observe carefully, you will also notice that you must lower your eyes, keeping the palms of your hands alongside your thighs.[21] Our own cultural norms are familiar to us, but often need to be explained to others because the behaviors carry different meaning.

Cultural norms are so pervasive because they are second nature to us, unless someone violates them. What makes understanding core cultural values difficult is that, even when we look below the surface and are aware of those cultural norms that define what people can and cannot do in their culture, our perception of those differences may not be accurate. For example, we may think that a handshake is quite appropriate in any situation and may be insulted if someone won't respond by shaking our hand. Consider the following: A number of years ago when I was a student in the Southwestern United States, I remember shaking the hand of a gentleman who was a Native American. My perception of the "normal" way to shake hands was that when you extend your hand both parties should grasp firmly and shake with an up and down motion. However, this man simply offered his hand, which remained limp; he did not shake my hand firmly. I was startled and almost insulted because his cultural norm violated my perception of what a handshake should be: both people participating with a vigorous and firm grasp. At first, I was a little concerned that perhaps I had said or done something wrong. Someone later explained that this is the way someone from his culture shakes hands. My new acquaintance was simply displaying a friendly and appropriate gesture in the way that he shook hands according to the implicit rules of his culture.

Another experience, years later, demonstrated an additional custom regarding how people shake hands—or don't. One of my students at the university had agreed to participate in some research I was conducting and, when I went to greet him and shake his hand, he pulled away from me apologetically, stating that since was a Hasidic Jew he could not shake hands with a woman. I suddenly recalled that I had heard of this tradition before (reaching back into the resources of my memory) so this time, I was not surprised at the response. I had reacted to these two separate instances based upon my own cultural conditioning and the perceptions about "normal" means of behavior. I internalized the data from my experience and was, as a result, able to adjust my expectations and reactions accordingly. The meaning each of these men attached to his style of handshake meant something to him, based on his cultural norms. Each was acting appropriately.

In sum, each of us has core values that affect how we look at the world—in essence, how we perceive ourselves and others. We constantly receive information (stimuli) through a mental (cognitive) process in which we simultaneously attach meaning—that makes sense to us—to that information. We then store away the information as we form mental categories (schema), which we can draw upon for future interactions with others whose actions and words hold different meanings than ours.

Where Big Macs Are Culturally Unacceptable, the Maharaja Mac Is Hot

In mostly Hindu Bombay, India, a tradition-steeped land with little taste for beef, what is one of the hottest eateries around? McDonald's.

On any given night, young adults in blue jeans join middle-class families with toddlers and the occasional grandmother—her head modestly covered with a sari—for a chance to chow down on beefless burgers. Here, the Golden Arches are a hot brand, but you can't find a Quarter Pounder or Big Mac anywhere. Out of respect for India's large Hindu population, which shuns the consumption of beef, the Big Mac was replaced by the Maharaja Mac—two all-lamb patties, special sauce, lettuce, cheese, pickles, and onions on a sesame seed bun.

It makes for quite a paradox. Here is the quintessential all-American hamburger joint without any hamburgers and with a decidedly Indian flavor, what with a menu that features lamb burgers, veggie burgers (potatoes, peas, sweet corn, carrots, onions, and spices), and Vegetable McNuggets with chili and masala dipping sauces.

No matter. Even if this is India's version of American fare, the crowds are eating it up.

"It's a new craze," said Dilip Odhrani, as his wife, children and friend's children gobbled McChicken burgers, fish filet sandwiches, Vegetable McNuggets, fries, sodas, and more. The first McDonald's franchises in India opened in 1997 in New Delhi and Bombay. Since then, New Delhi has added a dozen more and Bombay nearly that number, all told serving more than 50 million customers.

Local tastes and sensitivities are high on McDonald's list of priorities overseas. In Japan, McDonald's has the teriyaki burger, a sausage patty with teriyaki sauce. In New Zealand, it has the kiwi burger, which features a fried egg and slice of beet on top of a beef patty. In Manila, the company has a noodle dish. And in Norway, it has the McLox, a salmon sandwich.

"I don't think you'll find a more extreme example of cultural sensitivity by McDonald's than in India," said Brad Trask of McDonald's headquarters. "The very product we're known for can't be served there." Yet everything else about the experience speaks of America, or at least foreigners' impression of America, from the assembly-line efficiency of service to the broad smiles that accompany every "May I take your order, please?"

When asked if McDonald's considers itself to be a multi-national corporation, former Senior Vice President Dick Starmann responded by saying, "Oh, no. We're definitely not multi-national. We're multi-local." All but a few stores, he explained, are owned by local business partners, and everything from the menus to advertising is carefully tuned to local tastes.

Sources: Lini S Kadaba,. "Big Mac Nowhere to Be Seen in India, But Maharaja Mac Is One Hot Item," *The Philadelphia Inquirer*, March 9, 1998. Personal Interview, Richard G. Starmann, former Senior Vice President, Corporate Communications, McDonald's Corporation. Chicago, IL: November 12, 2003.

GENERALIZATION TRAPS

The idea of perceptions and attaching meaning in order to generalize the behavior of others can lead to a slippery slope if we are not careful how we go about doing this. Before we go much further, we should explain how an understanding of basic cultural dimensions is possible *without* stereotyping. Our goal is to identify basic core values of all cultures—that is, cultural dimensions—to provide a general understanding that we might apply to specific cultures.

As we have discussed, culture is complex, multifaceted, and dynamic. Various areas of culture overlap, such as how we define time, space, equality, achievement, activity, our relationship to people and the environment, and more. There are numerous ways in which to organize the various categories. Since we are drawing on the work of many different experts in the field, you will see a number of similar ideas and concepts in the pages that follow. We will first talk about what is both broad and general in order to highlight some specifics that have particular application to doing business in a global market.

The eight broad categories (also identified as dimensions of culture) we will discuss in subsequent chapters are:

- context in communication
- identity
- learning
- environment

- change
- time
- authority
- achievement

We will explore each of these in depth but, before we do, we should examine both the promises and the pitfalls of using our eight categories or dimensions of culture.

STEREOTYPES AND PROTOTYPES

Let's begin by thinking about how people talk about culture, about stereotyping, and culture-bound thinking. First, you should know that not all stereotypes are bad. Stereotypes are actually a way of mentally organizing what is familiar and unfamiliar to us so that we can compare what we do not yet understand with what we already know.

The term *stereotype* was coined by social scientist Walter Lippmann in 1921 when he wrote about why people so readily imagine how other people are, or why they behave as they do, even in the face of ready evidence to the contrary. In his landmark book *Public Opinion* he tells us that to stereotype is to ascribe to all members of a group or class those characteristics or behaviors observed in just one or a few members.[22]

Stereotypes can be grouped into positive, negative, and neutral categories. For example, we might say that the founders of the United States built their nation on the ideas of life, liberty, and the pursuit of happiness; or we might observe that Swedes are blonde; or that Scots wear traditional plaid for special occasions. We recognize that all cultures and subcultures exhibit certain behaviors or possess specific characteristics that are distinguishable from those of other cultures. This helps us sort out and categorize the world with mental processes that are predictable and easy to manage. One helpful way of distinguishing between negative and positive stereotypes is to focus on prototypes, which imply dynamic change, as opposed to stereotypes, which imply limitations. A prototype is an original model upon which we pattern something else. It is a springboard of identification that is the beginning of things yet to come.

For example, the following statement contains information gleaned from objective observations of the Chinese culture: "Building a business relationship may take considerable time with the Chinese." This is a neutral statement that contains information relating to specific cultural norms that have been empirically documented as identifiable patterns within the Chinese culture. After learning more about business practices in Chinese culture, you will come to understand that the Chinese place a very strong emphasis on developing trust over a long period of time and generally do not prefer to rush into business relationships only for the short-term. Further investigation will reveal that the Chinese generally have a long-term view of business; that is why developing relationships over time is so important—generally, the Chinese desire to create long-term relationships and not just focus on the task.

However, the traditional usage of the term "stereotype" sets up limitations for understanding because we can grow inflexible with the ways in which we categorize the behavior of someone from another culture. We run the risk, therefore, of assuming only similarities and may not acknowledge that cultures contain individuals who are capable of acting outside the typical cultural norms. While such generalizations are helpful, they do not take into account the many individual differences that vary from person to person within that culture. Do all U.S. citizens idealize such lofty pursuits? Are all Swedes blonde? Do all Scots adhere to the garb of their ancient clans? The obvious answer is no.

It is what we do with these generalizations that matters. While generalizations of this sort can be helpful in order for us to organize information, we risk becoming rigid in forming categories and assume that what applies to one applies to all. For example, if we use the concept of a family business, you probably think of a small organization employing fewer than a dozen people with annual revenues well below a half-million dollars. You probably also have an image in your mind of a middle-aged (or older) man opening the door in the morning and managing the facility with the assistance of his children or perhaps a few loyal employees. That's just one image of a family business.

In actuality, many family-owned businesses are as large as Campbell's Soup (the Dorrance family), Ford Motor Company (the Ford family), and Hyatt Hotels (the Pritzker family). Many employ professional executives who are unrelated to the owners, and have business interests that extend well beyond the founder's vision. Such businesses are atypical in other ways. Consider Johnson Publishing Company of Chicago, a family business headed by Linda Johnson Rice, an African American woman who became president and chief operating officer at age 27. She fits hardly *any* of the customary stereotypes of a family business owner.[23]

If we extend this analogy to culture, you will see that, just because a particular culture embraces a certain belief, such as Confucian philosophy, doesn't mean that all people of that culture, such as the Chinese, hold this belief. While it may be helpful to associate Confucianism with Eastern philosophy, we cannot accurately say that all Eastern cultures and their people embrace this philosophy. Therefore, using the term "prototype"[24] may be more helpful (and more accurate), because it focuses more on the dynamic changes and possibilities characteristic of any particular individual, rather than what is both fixed and universal to all in the group. A prototype has the connotation of a framework or a model we can build on. With a prototype view, then, we could say more accurately (and confidently) that while many Eastern cultures, such as the Chinese, may have a belief system founded on Confucian philosophy, others within that culture look to Taoism, Buddhism, or other philosophies—or perhaps nothing at all—because people are both individual and mutable in their beliefs and behaviors.[25]

All cultures have a way of organizing their time, space, social relationships, power, and reactions to uncertainty. Each individual within a culture, however, will behave in his or her own unique ways, which is why we underscore the idea of prototypes. Yet we have a realistic and human need to categorize behaviors and actions that are unfamiliar to us in order to make sense of them. How do we reconcile the two opposing needs of categorization and assumption? The answer isn't simple and this is where it will be important for us to move beyond a superficial awareness of intercultural differences toward action.

We can begin to reconcile these aspects of cultural understanding as long as we don't blindly group all people into one category. Let's say, for example, that you are negotiating a large contract for manufacturing equipment parts from a Chinese vendor. You are aware that, generally as a culture, the Chinese pay specific attention to establishing social relationships as an important part of the negotiation process. Knowing this, you might expect your business client from China to work very hard to establish a relationship through special outings, events, and dinners (as opposed to your own culture's practice of "getting right down to business"). This much is derived from a stereotype of the Chinese. But a prototype approach might also tell you to examine your client's other business relationships, history of business practice in North America, shareholder base, and reputation. Businesspeople behave as individuals and many of them adapt their practices according to the expectations and interests of their customers.

This stereotype-to-prototype model can allow us to use general cultural knowledge as a beginning point in our dealings with others, but to modify our approach as we acquire information specific to the individuals we're hoping to do business with. It becomes a way to recognize the many hidden dimensions that implicitly guide our behaviors. This model can also provide us with an opportunity to correct misperceptions, mistaken impressions, and outdated stereotypes that are based on archaic or anachronistic information.

We should also address the problem of approaching intercultural communication from a culture-bound perspective. As we proceed, you'll notice that much of the cross-cultural literature deals with dichotomies, creating polar opposites in order to compare one cultural dimension with another. Various cultures are being held up against one another for the purpose of making comparisons. Since much of the research conducted by the various authors (previously mentioned) is based on a western thought process and world view, it is important to note that such work is unquestionably culture-bound. It is written primarily by scholars and practitioners from the United States and Western Europe, whose perspectives are informed by Western-style thought and perception. This lens or filter through which these scholars and practitioners view the world is biased because it uses its own culture as the standard or basis for understanding other cultures. With this caveat in mind, we recognize that our basis for understanding others comes largely from a Western perspective. This doesn't mean that Western cultures are dominant; it is simply the perspective through which we will begin to explore differences in intercultural communication. We invite you to explore your own cultural background and experience and bring those perspectives and knowledge to the discussion.

Geert Hofstede, a Dutch social philosopher, has done seminal work in the area of categorizing specific cultural dimensions. Using decades of observational data, his defining research looks at the employees in a multinational company that spans forty countries.[26] While Hofstede's work has been widely cited and is closely associated with intercultural studies, it was never meant to be the final word on identifying certain cultural dimensions and he, himself, has suggested that his work was meant to be a catalyst for other follow-up research. Nevertheless, Hofstede identified five dimensions that describe how the national culture is organized:

- collectivism/individualism
- uncertainty avoidance
- long-term/short-term orientation
- power distance
- masculinity/femininity

While Hofstede's research is unquestionably culture-bound, he offers both pragmatic and realistic advice for approaching intercultural interactions. He warns us that statements about culture are not necessarily statements about individuals since any of the data he collected specific to each country in the survey is meant to describe the social system. For example, we can be cautious about assumptions regarding values, beliefs, attitudes, and behaviors that say *all* Korean students act a certain way (e.g., they are inscrutable) or that *all* teenagers from the United States who have body piercing are renegades and their behavior will show it.

WHEN SLOGANS GO WRONG

Communicating with a target market means more than tossing out catchy slogans. A few companies learned this the hard way when they tried to translate their catchy English slogans directly into Spanish.

Braniff beckoned its passengers to "Fly in Leather" and Eastern Airlines proclaimed that "We Earn Our Wings Daily" Both of these now-defunct airlines were terribly mistaken. A Spanish speaker would think Braniff was asking its riders to "Fly Naked" and a Spanish translation of the Eastern slogan evoked a final destination in heaven, following death.

A few classic marketing blunders: General Motors discovered too late that "Nova" literally means "doesn't go" in Spanish. Coors encouraged its English-speaking customers to "Turn It Loose" but the phrased in Spanish meant "Suffer from Diarrhea." Budweiser's "King of Beers" became "Queen of Beers" in Spanish because the Spanish word for beer, "cerveza" has a feminine ending. And when Frank Perdue said, "It Takes a Tough Man to Make a Tender Chicken" Spanish speakers heard "It Takes a Sexually Stimulated Man to Make a Chicken Affectionate."

These examples show how dangerous it is to assume a good English slogan will be the same in Spanish. But it also shows how important it is for a company to become attuned to the cultural differences within the rapidly growing Hispanic market.

Some companies are now making honest efforts to learn about this growing consumer segment. These efforts create a niche for Hispanic marketing consultants who can design more sophisticated pitches to a Hispanic audience.

Toyota Motor Sales USA, for example, ran a campaign in 1987 asking, "Who Could Ask for Anything More?" The slogan was changed to a more straightforward meaning in Spanish: "Toyota Siempre Le Da Mas" or "Toyota Always Gives You More" McDonald's ran a campaign directly aimed at the Hispanic family, showing three generations of a family that speaks both English and Spanish. McDonald's also used strong community involvement to build up its Hispanic following. McDonald's and Toyota are paying attention to Hispanic cultural nuances. That is the key to reaching this thriving but fragmented market.

Source: David, Helin, "When Slogans Go Wrong," *American Demographics*, February 1992, Vol. 14, Issue 2, pp. 14–17.

Discussion

1. What were some of the generalization traps made by these companies about doing business in another culture.
2. Identify language or marketing challenges other companies have faced as they go global.

ETHNOCENTRISM

It is human nature to think that all people are just like us. We often assume we are similar rather than different and expect that others will think the same way, perceive the same way, and behave the same way we do. While this is a natural assumption, this way of thinking is actually a form of ethnocentrism. Ethnocentrism is a form of superiority in which you believe your way of doing things is the right and preferable way. It is a way of negatively evaluating other cultures based on your particular cultural standards. While it may be human nature to do this, becoming an effective intercultural communicator requires that we understand people generally. Hofstede says we may have "different minds but common problems."[27] It is when we project our superiority onto others and judge their "different minds" as inferior that we block the process of understanding intercultural differences. Let's examine one way of looking at ethnocentrism.

Interculturalist Milton Bennett invites us to think about both the visible and invisible markers of culture as we begin to understand differences.

> ***Cross-cultural problems arise from differences in behavior, thinking, assumptions, and values between U.S. people and those from other countries and cultures with whom they associate. These cultural differences often produce misunderstandings and lead to ineffectiveness in face-to-face communication. A deeper understanding of the nature of cultural differences would increase the effectiveness of U.S. people in cross-cultural situations. But to reach this goal, Americans must first become more conscious and knowledgeable about how their own culture has conditioned their ways of thinking and planted within them the values and assumptions that govern their behavior.***[28]

Cross-cultural problems arise from differences in behavior, thinking, assumptions, and values between U.S. residents and those from other countries and cultures with whom they associate. These cultural differences often produce misunderstandings and lead to ineffectiveness in face-to-face communication. A deeper understanding of the nature of cultural differences would increase the effectiveness of U.S. residents in cross-cultural situations. But to reach this goal, Americans must first become more conscious and knowledgeable about how their own culture has conditioned their ways of thinking and planted within them the values and assumptions that govern their behavior.[29]

Bennett's framework can help us to become more conscious and knowledgeable about our ways of thinking interculturally. His developmental model walks us through six stages of the process, each representing one aspect of experiencing difference. (See Figure 1.7) This model is set on a continuum in which moving from left to right through the six stages of ***denial, defense, minimization, acceptance, adaptation, and integration*** will bring us to a more interculturally sensitive position.[30] This model is bent toward linear thinking (which we will discuss in Chapter 3), since Bennett stresses that in order to achieve the ultimate goal of "integration," we must move through each stage, one at a time. While a rigid model such as this has its limitations, it is nevertheless helpful to expand on the discussion of stereotypes and ethnocentric thinking. These phases are based on theoretical ideas taken from Bennett's years of teaching in intercultural training programs and are meant simply as a reference to help us analyze ethnocentricity. By identifying particular areas for self-centered thinking as related to cultural perspectives (hence, ethnocentricity), we can examine each of these stages to see where we may be affected. Bennett emphasizes action preceded by self-awareness to correct ethnocentric views and move us towards communication competence.

The first stage is ***denial***. Denial means that we see no difference at all, viewing all things from our own world view or experience. It is easy, for example, to lump people into a single category, such as ***Asians*** or ***Americans***. The former means that ***all*** Asians, whether Chinese, Taiwanese, Japanese, or Vietnamese, belong to the same culture. The latter usually means residents of the United States and neglects the fact that Canadians and South Americans are, in fact, Americans, as well.

Heaven
The cooks are French,
The mechanics are German,
The lovers are Italian,
The police are British,
And it's all organized by the Swiss.

Hell
The cooks are British,
The mechanics are French,
The lovers are Swiss,
The police are German,
And it's all organized by the Italians.

Figure 1.5   **If heaven and hell were seen from a cultural viewpoint, would we bring our preconceptions and stereotypes with us?**

Figure 1.6   **A driver makes an assumption about a policeman because of his last name**

Figure 1.7   **Stages of Intercultural Sensitivity**[31]

The second stage is ***defense***. This stage is characterized by excessive hostility against another culture or excessive pride in one's own. This is a stage in which we realize that there are differences but feel threatened by them, so we may insult, antagonize, or diminish others.

The third stage moves to ***minimization***. This acknowledges the existence of cultural differences but claims such differences are superficial at best. While we acknowledge differences, we experience a need to maintain our feelings of cultural superiority, so we look for similarities to assuage our fears of difference. For example, if our culture celebrates birthdays in a particular way, we look for similarities in how people from another culture celebrate birthdays. It's clearly superficial, but it makes us feel better.

Moving from the third stage of minimization to the fourth, ***acceptance*** is the beginning of intercultural understanding. Acceptance recognizes and explores cultural differences by identifying them both by behavior, such as language, styles of verbal communication and nonverbal communication, and by the tacit values of a given culture. These include cultural norms of interdependence and collective work products versus independent and individualistic achievement.

According to Bennett, once we move toward the acceptance stage, we can begin to adapt, the fifth stage. *Adaptation* is the point at which we see and begin to embrace a different frame of reference (we'll talk about this more in Chapter 2). Empathy is a big part of adaptation. We move from simply recognizing and respecting that others are different to sympathizing and then empathizing with them. We try to walk in their shoes and experience (limited as this may be) things from their perspective.

Finally, *integration* is the point at which we all recognize and adapt to the differences, case by case. This final stage is not about simply being sensitive to people from another cultural perspective; it involves building skills and a deeper awareness of what it means to be someone else.

SUMMARY

This first chapter has provided a somewhat broad view of culture to get you thinking about how your own values, beliefs, attitudes, and behaviors may differ from those of the people with whom you interact each day. Using the example of the iceberg, you have seen how behavior is noticeable at the surface, but the reasons for that behavior are submerged deep below. We have examined the nature of perception and how people naturally create mental images that help to sort out interactions, situations, and environments that are unfamiliar to them. We have also discussed the problematic nature of examining culture because each of us approaches life with culture-bound perspectives and sees the world from our naturally biased frame of reference.

The goal for every professional who hopes to be successful in the global market should be to develop a deep understanding of the major cultural dimensions that affect our values, beliefs, attitudes, and behaviors, and which ultimately set cultures and people apart. The explosion of the information age and the interconnectivity that brings people together from the far reaches of the Earth necessitate such an understanding. In the pages ahead, we will examine key cultural dimensions and plumb what lies beneath the waterline in the attempt to understand the tacit, subtle, and often confounding issues that remain hidden from our cultural consciousness.

APPLICATIONS IN THE GLOBAL MARKETPLACE

Culture can affect us in the workplace:

- When stereotypes affect impressions;
- When ethnocentrism interferes with understanding;
- When identifying and communicating differences;
- When trust is not readily established.

Can you think of a situation in which you encountered difficulties communicating with someone from a different background? What happened and how did you resolve it?

SELF-AWARENESS AND OTHER-AWARENESS

- What defines you as an individual?
- What are the differences among people in your current work group?
- What makes each person in your work group unique?
- What defines the groups to which you belong?

WHEN STEREOTYPES AFFECT IMPRESSIONS

- Have you ever evaluated someone else according to just one characteristic?
- Can you think of a situation in which you or someone you know has been evaluated according to a stereotype?
- When are we most likely to perceive others selectively? What characteristics are we most likely to focus on in such perceptions?
- Do people you know ever evaluate others based on limited evidence? When are such evaluations most likely to occur? Are they *always* bad?

INVENTORY 1.1: ASSESSING YOUR ETHNOCENTRISM

The purpose of this questionnaire is to assess your ethnocentrism. Respond to each statement by writing the number that corresponds to the degree to which the statement is true regarding the way you typically think about yourself. When you think about yourself, is the statement Always False (1), Mostly False (2), Sometimes True and Sometimes False (3), Mostly True (4), or Always True (5)? Answer honestly, not how you think you should be or how others might want you to be.

_____ 1. I do not apply my values when judging strangers.

_____ 2. I see people who are similar to me as virtuous.

_____ 3. I cooperate with strangers.

_____ 4. I prefer to associate with people who are like me.

_____ 5. I trust strangers.

_____ 6. I am obedient to authorities.

_____ 7. I do not fear strangers.

_____ 8. I try to maintain distance from members of other groups.

_____ 9. I do not blame strangers for troubles I have.

_____ 10. I believe that my values are universal values.

To find your score, first reverse the responses for the odd numbered items (i.e., if you wrote 1, make it 5; if you wrote 2, make it 4; if you wrote 3, leave it as 3; if you wrote 4, make it 2; and if you wrote 5, make it 1). Next, add the numbers next to each of the statements. Scores range from 10 to 50. The higher the score, the more ethnocentric you are.[32]

INVENTORY 1.2: ASSESSING YOUR KNOWLEDGE OF ANOTHER GROUP

The purpose of this questionnaire is to help you assess your knowledge of another culture or ethnic group. The statements in this questionnaire contain a blank space. Think of a specific culture or ethnic group when you are reading the statements. Respond to each statement by writing the number that corresponds to the degree to which the statement is true regarding your knowledge: Always False (1), Usually False (2), Sometimes True and Sometimes False (3), Usually True (4), or Always True (5).

_____ 1. I understand the norms of _____.

_____ 2. I do not understand how _____ manage conflict.

_____ **3.** I understand the customs of _____.

_____ **4.** I do not understand how _____ support each other's self-concepts.

_____ **5.** I understand the values of _____.

_____ **6.** I do not understand how _____ persuade each other.

_____ **7.** I understand the communication rules of _____.

_____ **8.** I do not understand how _____ comfort each other.

_____ **9.** I understand the language (or dialect) of _____.

_____ **10.** I do not understand how _____ joke with each other.

To find your score, first reverse your answers for the even numbered items (i.e., if you answered 1, make it a 5; if you answered 2, make it a 4; if you answered 3, leave it as 3; if you ansered 4, make it a 2; and if you answered 5, make it a 1). Once you have reversed the even-numbered items, add the numbers you wrote next to each statement. Scores range from 10 to 50. The higher your score, the greater your knowledge of the group.[33]

For both of these inventories, consider asking someone else (perhaps someone in your learning team or work group, or a supervisor who knows you well and could assess your performance) to rate you on this inventory. Where did you agree and disagree? Discuss your findings and develop an action plan for improving your intercultural communication competence.

ENDNOTES

1. Ralph Waldo Emerson cited in Lawrence A. Samovar and Richard E. Porter, *Intercultural Communication: A Reader,* 4th ed. (Belmont, CA: Wadsworth Publishing Company, 1994), 71.
2. *Ibid.,* 4.
3. *Ibid.,* 27.
4. "U.S. Census Bureau. Population Profile of the United States: 2000 (Internet Release)." Retrieved August 10, 2004, from http://www.census.gov/population/www/index.html.
5. *Ibid.*
6. *Kiplinger Letter,* vol. 79, no. 52 (December 27, 2002).
7. Northeastern University study, retrieved March 10, 2003, from http://www.cnn.com.
8. Uniworld Business Publications, Inc., "Directory of Foreign Firms Operating in the U.S., 11th ed., 2002." Retrieved August 10, 2004, from http://www.uniworldbp.com.
9. "Open Doors 2002, Institute of International Education, November 18, 2002." Retrieved August 10, 2004, from http://opendoors.iienetwork.org.
10. *Kiplinger Letter, supra* n.6.
11. Uniworld Business Publications, Inc., "Directory of Foreign Firms Operating in the U.S., 11th ed., 2002." Retrieved August 10, 2004, from http://www.uniworldbp.com.
12. Stefan Lovgren for *National Geographic News,* retrieved February 26, 2004, http://news.nationalgeographic.com/news/2004/02/0226_040226_language.html
13. Marshall R. Singer, *Intercultural Communication: A Perceptual Approach* (Englewood Cliffs, NJ: Prentice-Hall, Inc., 1987), 3.
14. A. L. Kroeber and Clyde Kluckhohn, "Culture: A Critical Review of Concepts and Definitions," *Papers of the Peabody Museum of American Archaeology and Ethnology* 47, no. 1 (1952).
15. Fons Trompenaars and Charles Hampden-Turner, *Riding the Waves of Culture: Understanding Cultural Diversity in Global Business* (New York, NY: McGraw-Hill, 1998).
16. Geert Hofstede, *Cultures and Organizations: Software of the Mind* (New York, NY: McGraw-Hill, 1997).
17. Singer, *supra* n.13.
18. *Ibid.*
19. Concept developed by Jean Piaget in Harry W. Gardiner, Jay D. Mutter, and Corinne Kosmitzki, *Lives Across Cultures: Cross-Cultural Human Development* (Needham Heights, MA: Allyn & Bacon, 1998), 81.
20. *Ibid.*

21. Terry Morrison, Wayne A. Conaway, and George A. Borden, *Kiss, Bow or Shake Hands* (Avon, MA: Adams Media Corporation, 1994), 207.

22. Walter Lippmann, *Public Opinion* (New York, NY: The Free Press, 1965), 53–68.

23. Randel S. Carlock and John L. Ward, *Strategic Planning for the Family Business* (New York, NY: Plagrave Macmillan, 2001).

24. Linda Beamer and Iris Varner, *Intercultural Communication in the Global Workplace* (Boston, MA: McGraw-Hill Irwin, 2001), 18–19.

25. Harry W. Gardiner, Jay D. Mutter, and Corinne Kosmitzki, *Lives Across Cultures: Cross-Cultural Human Development.* (Needham Heights, MA: Allyn & Bacon, 1998), 188.

26. Hofstede, *supra* n.16.

27. *Ibid.,* 3.

28. Edward C. Stewart & Milton J. Bennett, *American Cultural Patterns.* (Yarmouth, ME: Intercultural Press, Inc. 1991), x, xii.

29. *Ibid.,* x.

30. Milton J. Bennett, "A Developmental Approach to Training for Intercultural Sensitivity," *International Journal of Intercultural Relations,* 10 (1986), 179–196.

31. As conceptualized by Chris Maxwell and Anne M. Greenhalgh, Undergraduate Leadership Program, The Wharton School, University of Pennsylvania.

32. Used by permission. William B. Gudykunst, *Bridging Differences: Effective Intergroup Communication* 4e (Thousand Oaks, CA: Sage Publications, 1998), p. 110.

33. Used by permission. *Ibid.,* p. 222.

Dewey Ballantine, LLP: Cultural Stereotypes and an Interoffice E-Mail

It began, like so many office controversies, with an e-mail message. Responding to a note seeking someone to adopt a puppy, a partner in the London office of the law firm of Dewey Ballantine wrote, "Please don't let these puppies go to a Chinese restaurant!"

Some of the firm's associates found the message offensive and said so; dozens of Asian-American law student associations and bar associations stepped forward to criticize it as well. Senior partners in the firm apologized almost immediately, sending out a firmwide apology. So did the author of the message.[1]

The firm had already put its lawyers through sensitivity training in the wake of a skit performed at a dinner the year before when lawyers infuriated members of the Asian American community. Their after-dinner parody mocked stereotypical Asian accents to the tune of "Hello, Dolly," singing that they were "so solly" that the firm was closing its Hong Kong office. The firm now no longer even holds that annual dinner. "Somebody made a mistake, and they've apologized," said Morton A. Pierce, a co-chairman at the firm, adding that the partner would be disciplined. "And we keep apologizing," he added.[2]

It is rare but not unheard-of for dog to appear on the menu in a restaurant in rural China, though dog meat is much less likely to be offered by Chinese restaurants in other parts of the world. The message was offensive, associates at the firm say, because it seemed to mock Chinese people. "People say, 'Oh, you're just being over-sensitive,' but I think it's a symptom of something underlying," said Karen Y. Tu, a second-year law student at Columbia who is co-chairwoman of the Asian Pacific American Law Students Association. She later said, "What is going to change this environment? What is going to make it easier? What is going to make Asian Americans comfortable about going back to Dewey?"[3]

Dewey Ballantine, LLP

Founded in 1909, Dewey Ballantine, LLP is an international law firm with offices in key financial centers around the world. For nearly a century, they have provided guidance, experience, and insight to clients on a wide range of complex legal matters. The firm employs 582 attorneys worldwide and specializes in more than 40 separate practice areas, including litigation, taxation, mergers and acquisitions, intellectual property, and banking.[4]

Dewey Ballantine established its London office in 1991. The London office consists of more than 40 attorneys, including 14 partners, qualified in the United Kingdom and the United States, as well as in France, Germany, Ireland, Israel, Italy, Kazakhstan, Russia, and the Ukraine. They provide clients in Europe, the Middle East, and Africa with advice under the laws of those jurisdictions with a focus on capital markets, mergers and acquisitions, private equity, project finance, securitization, structured finance, and international tax. The firm's clients include FTSE 100 and Fortune 100 companies with commercial interests in consumer goods, financial services, infrastructure, oil and gas, power, technology, telecommunication, and transportation.[5]

The company's web site describes the firm as one that "serves a sophisticated and diverse client base."[6] Of 582 lawyers at Dewey Ballantine, 41 are Asian Americans, according to the firm.[7]

The Infamous Dinner Skit

The firm issued an apology nearly six weeks after the *New York Law Journal* reported that, at a January 31, 2003 annual dinner, the firm had parodied the closing of its Hong Kong office with a version of "Hello Dolly" re-titled "The Dirge of Long Duck Dong," an apparent reference to the stereotyped Chinese exchange student in the movie *Sixteen Candles*.

The song said the seven-lawyer office, which closed at the end of March 2003, was "chow mein" and would get "the gong." "You were the firm's folly," the song intoned, "and now we so solly to be cutting off your source of livelihood." The annual black-tie dinner and its anonymously penned parodies were a longstanding tradition at the firm. Sanford Morhouse and Morton Pierce discontinued the dinner shortly after becoming the firm's co-chairs in October of 2003.[8]

"It was a party culture that had outlived its usefulness," Mr. Morhouse told reporters. But he stressed that neither the dinner nor the e-mail incident in January 2004 should be taken as representative of the firm's character. He said Asian and Asian-American lawyers were "tremendously well-regarded" and "highly valued at the firm."[9]

An E-Mail to Regret

On the afternoon of Monday, January 26, 2004, Douglas L. Getter, the head of Dewey Ballantine's European mergers and acquisitions practice, returned from lunch to the firm's offices at 1 Undershaft in London's East End near Lincoln's Inn and the famed Old Bailey courthouse. As he opened his e-mail, Mr. Getter discovered a firm-wide memo in his inbox advertising the availability of some puppies for adoption. He quickly composed a firm-wide reply with the concluding line: "Please don't let these puppies go to a Chinese restaurant!"[10]

By clicking the "reply all" button on the e-mail server, Getter set off a firestorm of criticism, much of which began inside the firm. Within minutes, senior partners began hearing from irate associates and others. Following a brief conversation with Getter, co-chairs Sanford Morhouse and Morton Pierce issued a response. "This afternoon an offensive e-mail was circulated by a partner," they wrote. "Comments of this nature are inconsistent with the values of this firm and will not be tolerated. We extend our immediate apologies to the entire Dewey Ballantine community."[11]

In a press interview the next day, Mr. Morhouse said the firm's executive committee would be meeting shortly to determine what further action to take.

Opposition Begins to Emerge

Shortly after news of the e-mail message began making its way around the Internet to law firms, law students, public interest groups, and various Internet message boards, a group of Asian American law student organizations sent a letter to Dewey Ballantine asking what proactive steps the firm intended to take to prevent the recurrence of such an incident.

Mr. Pierce responded to critics by saying that it was not clear what the firm should do other than to keep apologizing. "I wish that there were some way we could convince them very easily and quickly that this was truly aberrational with respect to our culture," he said. "But clearly that's not going to happen." Several associates at the firm said they were thinking of leaving to work elsewhere but added that they had already decided to move on before this particular e-mail message was sent. One executive recruiter said that his firm had noted an increase in resumes from Dewey Ballantine associates over the preceding several months, but noted that the trend predated the e-mail message.[12]

News of the incident, however, along with a careful recounting of the dinner skit a year earlier, moved quickly across the Internet and onto a number of weblogs devoted to legal issues and Asian American concerns. One blog poster at *Angry Asian Man* wrote:

> It's got to be the world's worst luck for one firm to make national news twice in a twelve-month period for the same kind of incident, and against the same racial group. Various national Asian groups are lining up to excoriate the law firm. I, however, have some mixed feelings. Obviously, Getter's e-mail is more than tasteless and obnoxious; it's culturally insensitive and borderline bigoted. But it's hard to find any criticism of the law firm's response.[13]

Another poster on the same web site disagreed:

> As another American of Asian descent who continues to hear the same questions / remarks 'Where

are you from . . . . No, I mean your nationality. . . . No, I mean . . . .' And, 'You speak English so well!' . . . The Dewey Ballantine story does not surprise me. Though for the chairman to say this 'may' have been in bad taste? There is NO 'may be' about it. If the parody was made of African-Americans—use your imagination—there is no way the chairman would have simply said this 'may' have been in bad taste.[14]

And yet another shared his personal frustration:

The funny thing is that one of my good friends from law school—also of Asian descent—worked for Dewey as an associate out of law school. (He left long ago). I don't mean to blow this out of proportion, however. Maybe the associates who planned that skit simply lacked decent taste (or sobriety). And to be fair, the firm's chairman did agree that song was 'maybe' in bad taste. Still, this incident reminds me of the many times I've been told, 'Oh, you speak English so well.' I do not have an Americanized given name. But why should it be so surprising?[15]

An Offer to Talk

Senior partners at the law firm met with Asian American associates on the afternoon of Thursday, February 5, 2004, to talk about the incident. The message, according to Mr. Pierce, was simple: "This isn't Dewey Ballantine; this isn't who we are. This isn't the firm that they joined. It's not emblematic or symptomatic of who we are." The firm said it would hold a special round of sensitivity training in its London office in addition to its twice-yearly firmwide training.[16]

"There is no defense in these situations," said Roger Cramton, a law professor at Cornell University. He added that law professors have had to rethink the examples they use to illustrate legal issues in classes. "This is such a politically correct world."[17]

Several Asian American lawyers and law students said that the problem was not the e-mail message itself but the fact that the partner who sent it did not stop to think first. "What scares the rest of us," said Andrew Thomas Hahn, a partner at Seyfarth Shaw, LLP in New York, "is [whether] it is pervasive at law firms generally or corporations generally that Asians can be mocked with impunity." Mr. Hahn is president of the Asian American Bar Association of New York. At law firms generally, he thinks, Asians worry that they may be stereotyped as passive and are steered out of certain areas of practice.

Ms. Tu, the law student at Columbia, said that Asian American law students there were meeting to discuss how to respond. One possible step, she said, would be to boycott Dewey Ballantine during the fall recruiting season—something that might happen informally anyway. "Not as a statement," she said, "but because they don't want to work in that environment." Ms. Tu said that working at big firms can already be difficult for nonwhite lawyers, given their small numbers.

John C. Liu, a member of the New York City Council who has received numerous complaints about the e-mail message, had one suggestion in particular about what Dewey Ballantine could do to assuage concerned Asian Americans, both within and outside of the firm: "I would like to see them take up a case involving bias against Asian Americans pro bono. And I have one or two specific cases that I would like to see them take up."

Questions

1. From Dewey Ballantine's point of view, what are the critical issues in this case? Which among them are most important?
2. Who are the principal stakeholders here? What's at stake for each of them?
3. Is this just a temporary matter for the firm, or are complaints and animosity likely to persist? Can Dewey Ballantine take a low profile on this issue and simply wait for the controversy to pass?
4. From a reputation-management point of view, what sort of problems does the firm face?
5. What actions are available to the managing partners? Which actions would you advise they take first?
6. Does Dewey Ballantine need outside communications-management counsel for this matter, or can they reliably handle this with existing staff?
7. Is this, as some observers have said, simply a case of overreaction or political correctness taken to an extreme? Would be it helpful if the firm were to position these events in the context of "good-natured" humor?

Case Sources

1. Jonathan D. Glater, "Asian-Americans Take Offense at a Law Firm Memo," *The New York Times* (February 7, 2004): B1.
2. *Ibid.*
3. *Ibid.*
4. Dewey Ballantine, LLP web page. Retrieved February 11, 2004, from http://www.deweyballantine.com.
5. *Ibid.*
6. *Ibid.*
7. Glater, *supra* n.1, B14.

8. Anthony Lin, "Dewey Partner's E-Mail Causes Upset Over Racial Insensitivity," *New York Law Journal* (January 28, 2004): 1, 2.

9. *Ibid.,* 2.

10. Anthony Lin, "Dewey Partner's E-Mail Causes Upset Over Racial Insensitivity," Law.com. Retrieved February 12, 2004, from http://www.law.com.

11. *Ibid.*

12. Glater, *supra* n.1, B14.

13. *Angry Asian Man* weblog. Retrieved on February 10, 2004, from http://yin.blog-city.com/read/460931.htm.

14. *Ibid.*

15. *Ibid.*

16. Anthony Lin, "Dewey Ballantine Makes Commitment to Sensitivity Training, Working for Diversity," *New York Lawyer* (February 6, 2004). Retrieved February 11, 2004, from http://www.nylawyer.com/news/04/02/020604d.html.

17. Glater, *supra* n.1, B14.

Sources: This case was prepared by James S. O'Rourke, Concurrent Professor of Management, as the basis for class discussion rather than to illustrate either effective or ineffective handling of an administrative situation. Information was gathered entirely from public sources. Copyright ©2004.

CHALLENGES AND SOLUTIONS

STUMBLING BLOCKS TO INTERCULTURAL COMMUNICATION

LaRay Barna, Professor of Communication at Portland State University, has identified a number of stumbling blocks to intercultural communication, four of which we will examine as we conclude our discussion here. These stumbling blocks include assumptions of similarities, language differences, nonverbal misinterpretations, and stereotypes.[3] We will look first at what these stumbling blocks are and follow with a discussion of Fons Trompenaars' ideas associated with reconciling intercultural differences.

Speaking of Culture ▼

Human beings draw close to one another by their common nature, but habits and customs keep them apart.

– Confucius[4] ▲

ASSUMPTIONS OF SIMILARITIES

Can you remember a time when you encountered a new situation, whether starting a new job, moving to an unfamiliar city or neighborhood, becoming active in a new professional or civic association, or even just signing up for a membership in a new gym? Among the things you probably did first was to look for someone familiar to make that initial connection to ease the awkward transition. It is what we do as the "new kid on the block:" We look for people who are most like us. This is human nature because, in order to assuage our nervousness regarding uncertainty, we need to find familiar ground, something like getting our bearings or "sea legs." Although this is a natural part of humanity, when applied to cross-cultural situations, it can prove problematic. One of the most common stumbling blocks to intercultural communication is that we make *assumptions of similarities*. We assume that what we say or do, think or believe, is shared by everyone, which is a form of ethnocentrism. For example, one of the biggest mistakes for English speakers (whether from Canada, the United States, or Australia) is to assume that since English is the most popular and sought-after language of business, everyone naturally speaks English. Another example is the frequent assumption that other countries have the same amenities that we are accustomed to in our homelands. For example, in the United States, U.S. Americans expect to have hotels complete with private bathroom, air-conditioning, television, and popular fast-food restaurant chains readily available with familiar food. This is not the case when traveling abroad. Often hotels will not have private baths, air-conditioning is not standard, and even a Big Mac or a Coke *will* taste different.

For an example that could have more far-reaching consequences than simply not enjoying your room or food "just like home," we could turn to the significant ritual of exchanging business cards with the Japanese. In the United States it is customary to hand out business cards to just about anyone who asks for one. Most people, after shaking hands and greeting someone, will quickly find a place to stash the card—the focus is on the interpersonal interaction and not much thought is given to that small piece of cardstock. Unless you are aware of cultural practices regarding the ritual of business card exchanges in other cultures, you will probably assume that all cultures simply shake (or bow), greet, and put away the card. Not so. As explained in Chapter 4, simply putting the card away would be a big mistake in Asian cultures such as Japan, where the exchange of business cards (*meishi*) is a ritual and demonstrates respect for the status of others. *How* you receive and hold the business card as well as *where* you place it (never in a wallet or back pocket) have significant meanings and are potential stumbling blocks for communicating goodwill. Simply taking the card and placing it in your pocket would be a bad omen and signal a lack of respect for or trust with your Asian counterpart. You would unintentionally insult them, and this faux pas could have negative consequences on any business transaction you are conducting.

You won't find any cookbook of communication recipes that will help you to communicate perfectly in all intercultural encounters by providing you with prescriptive do's and don'ts for the customs and rituals in any given culture. Our goal is to help you be aware of possible differences that will surely occur. We hope that you will learn more about the specifics of the cultures in which you will interact so you put into practice what you have learned.

LANGUAGE DIFFERENCES

Another common stumbling block is to assume that similar words have similar meanings in different cultures. George Bernard Shaw (among others) is thought to have said, "England and America are two great nations separated by a common language."[5] He may have been right. In the United States, for example, business leaders will speak about the "exciting changes" happening in their organizations. Using this term with business leaders in Great Britain may bring you some quizzical looks since people use this word in connection with things that children rather than adults might do (e.g., "The children's trip to the zoo was exciting.")[6] Or, in Latin countries, what U.S. Americans call soccer is known as football. If an associate in Great Britain were to say, "A couple of messages, sir. Miss Norris called this morning, saying she'd like to speak with you," a U.S. American would assume that was a phone call. A British subject would more properly assume that Miss Norris appeared in person. Had she phoned in, your associate would have said she "rang." While these particular examples of differences in word usage would not necessarily lead to hard feelings during an intercultural encounter, they do highlight the opportunity for misunderstanding if you are not astute enough to check for clarification of meanings while communicating.

Other mishaps could damage your reputation with advertising campaigns that are not carefully researched. One legendary advertising debacle was the 1965 Pepsi-Cola campaign urging readers to "Come alive with the Pepsi Generation." In the Taiwanese market, however, that slogan translated as, "Pepsi brings your ancestors back from the grave." Since there is a strong following of Shintoistic beliefs where ancestors are revered and worshiped, the meaning in this translation was not only confusing but insulting to many people. Pepsi's competitor, Coca-Cola, has had its share of translation problems as well. Since Chinese is a tonal language, the phonetic equivalent in Chinese /ke-kou-ke-la/ is translated as "bite the wax tadpole." A careful review of more than 40,000 Chinese characters with a better phonetic translation produced a better slogan /ko-kou-ko-le/, which more appropriately meant "happiness in the mouth."

Speaking of Culture ▼

Be cautious in asking an Indonesian Chinese a question. English speakers would give a negative answer to the question "Isn't my order ready yet?" by responding, "No." (Meaning, "No, it's not ready."). The Chinese pattern is the opposite: "Yes" (meaning, "Yes, it is not ready.").

– Terry Morrison, Wayne A. Conaway and George A. Borden, Kiss, Bow, or *Shake Hands*[7] ▲

We must always be aware that what we say may have different connotations in another language and culture. It is important to obtain expert, local advice; perform clarification checks: asking directly or observing indirectly the reactions of conversation partners. Most importantly, keep your sense of humor and don't be afraid to laugh at yourself (but never at someone else because of the importance saving face). Don't be reluctant to apologize for a misstatement. Showing humility and a sense of humor can produce goodwill as you use the language and customs of another culture.

NONVERBAL MISINTERPRETATIONS

Nonverbal mishaps are among the most common stumbling blocks to intercultural communication. We are often unaware of our facial expressions or gestures as we use them, especially if we've been raised in a low-context culture. Roger Axtell is a former vice president of worldwide marketing for the Parker Pen Company who spent more than thirty years living and working abroad. He captured his experiences in several best-selling books that illustrate specific differences in cultural behavior around the world. "Gestures pack the power to punctuate, to dramatize, to speak a more colorful language than mere words," he writes. "You may discover that . . . innocent winks and well-meaning nods are anything but universal."[8]

For example, a familiar gesture using the thumb and forefinger to form a circle will mean "OK" in the United States, while in Latin American cultures, along with those in Russia and Arab countries, it is considered an obscene gesture. In Japan it means "money," and in France, "worthless."[9] The most common affect display, the smile, has numerous cultural norms attached to it. In the United States, it can be considered appropriate in many areas of the country to smile and look at someone you do not know (either male-to-female or vice versa). In Asian or Arab cultures, however, a female making eye contact and smiling at a man would hint of innuendo. Another common form of nonverbal confusion is whether to kiss, bow, or shake hands.[10] Naturally, each culture has its own way of demonstrating a welcome, and because touch and personal space come into play, there is great potential for mishaps and misunderstanding. In Western cultures it is customary to shake hands while maintaining a comfortable distance; in Asian cultures one bows (and *how* one does this depends on status and superiority); in Latin cultures one gives an *abrazo,* or strong hug; in French culture it is customary to greet one another with a light kiss on each cheek.

Speaking of Culture ▼

In Moscow, restaurant employees had to be specially trained to smile in the friendly McDonald's way because Russians do not feel comfortable smiling at strangers.

– Richard R. Gesteland,
Cross-Cultural Business Behavior[11] ▲

Speaking of Culture ▼

The causes of friction in communication between two cultures lie not in the shortcomings of either culture but rather in their interaction.

– John C. Condon and Fathi S. Yousef,
An Introduction to Intercultural Communication[13] ▲

As such, it's good to have an idea of what behavior is most common and how gender, age, and status might affect the reactions you receive. You need not sit on your hands when interacting with people from other cultures, nor is it necessary to know every type of gesture and their variations in meaning. It *is* necessary, however, to understand that the meanings we attach to certain gestures are symbolic and will evoke different meanings in different cultures.[12]

STEREOTYPES

In Chapter 1, we examined a cognitive process known as *stereotyping,* in which we develop mental categories or schemata that help us to make sense of unfamiliar behavior and align it with our own frame of reference. Creating mental categories can be a positive process to help us identify and respond to unfamiliar behavior, but it may become counterproductive if we then judge all members of a group or class by the characteristics or behaviors we observe in just one or a few. Stereotyping is the final stumbling block to intercultural communication.

Our aim all along is to provide broad exposure to various dimensions of culture in order to foster insight and encourage understanding of intercultural communication and interaction, rather than to provide a comprehensive checklist of cultural do's and don'ts. Think of our examples as signposts along the trail as you embark on your journey with intercultural communication. Not all trails have the same signposts. If we visit a national park for a hike, depending on what part of the country and what type of park it is, there inevitably will be different markers along the path. The examples we have used in this chapter will provide the foundation for our discussion of the various stumbling blocks to intercultural communication and will illustrate various negative, neutral, and positive generalizations. For example, while some U.S. Americans might assume that there will be McDonald's or Burger King restaurants in most other countries, others will not. To say that all U.S. Americans are culturally illiterate is a gross generalization and, therefore, a negative stereotype. To say that *all* Japanese will *always* bow and will *certainly* be offended if you don't do so correctly would also be a stereotype—but it's neutral rather than negative, since there are no harmful meanings associated with it. A more positive stereotype would be the assertion that *all* Brazilians will give you a big, squeezing hug, or *abrazo,* upon meeting you. A hug is usually a positive interaction, showing warmth and affection between friends, but not all Brazilians will hug in every circumstance. Keeping an open mind about this and seeking clarification about an *individual*'s expectations and behaviors can turn a potential stumbling block into a stepping stone.

Assumptions of similarities, language differences, nonverbal misinterpretations, and stereotypes are just a few of the stumbling blocks that can hinder our journey as we seek to understand the ways and behaviors of people from other cultures. But stumbling blocks are not the end of the road; they *can* be overcome. We have to remain alert to potential potholes and obstacles, and maintain the agility to step over and around them with finesse. The next section offers a few simple yet practical applications for succeeding in the global marketplace.

DEVELOPING INTERCULTURAL COMPETENCE

As we move toward intercultural competence by turning stumbling blocks into stepping stones, we must consider three specific skill sets: an awareness of cultural differences, respect for those differences, and the ability to reconcile them.[14]

Perception Check—Just Say No to Stereotypes

Re-examine Milton Bennett's "Stages for Intercultural Sensitivity" (see Chapter 1) and think of an example for each of those six stages from your own experience. The stages are: denial, defense, minimization, acceptance, adaptation and integration. Now that you are more aware of the hidden dimensions of culture, how might you do things differently next time a similar situation arises?

As you talk with others, analyze what you say and pinpoint the attitudes that motivate your comments. For example, what sort of stereotypes do you find useful? When do you use them? Can you think of a recent incident when you stereotyped someone or something? Remember, stereotypes can be positive, neutral, or negative.

What are your perceptions of others? What behaviors make you uncomfortable? What beliefs or attitudes to do you attach to them? How can you move more toward an understanding of the attitudes that motivate others' behaviors?

AWARENESS OF CULTURAL DIFFERENCES

It would be naïve to say that all intercultural misunderstandings could be avoided if only we were aware of the differences. Still, we have to start somewhere. Our discussions have done just this by examining various cultural dimensions and providing examples for each. Understanding the many intricacies of human interaction is difficult, but we can begin with the basics by understanding the *states of mind* [15] or *programming of the mind.*[16] You now understand a number of different cultural dimensions that will permit you to assess how the people of various cultures believe, think, and behave. Understanding the motivation for your own values, beliefs, attitudes, and behaviors will provide you with the ability to compare them with those of people from other cultures. Most of what we believe, and certainly much of what motivates our behavior, is not immediately self-evident. A good deal of it is where we have always said: below the waterline. Awareness is the first step in understanding and reconciling those differences that separate us from the inhabitants of other cultures.

Identifying Values
This exercise is about exploration. It might help to reference a current or previous situation or encounter with someone in your learning team or work team.

Values are the most basic and fundamental, unmovable tenets that make us who we are and which shape all other structures in our attitudinal system, a psychological assessment of the things, those concepts, those ideas we hold dear.

Think about some of the common values shared by members of your culture (e.g., freedom, self-reliance, group consensus, spirituality). Then do the same for another culture. Consider potential points of conflict or discord.

My Cultural Values	Values of Culture A	Values of Culture B	Differences
_____	_____	_____	_____
_____	_____	_____	_____
_____	_____	_____	_____
_____	_____	_____	_____

Now rank the priority of the values across cultures. What does this tell you about yourself? What might this tell you about someone from another culture? Discuss these priorities with your peers/coworkers and talk about what is culturally important to each of you regarding culture. What assumptions have you made? How might these assumptions affect your interaction with someone from a different culture?

RESPECTING CULTURAL DIFFERENCES

As we discussed in Chapter 1, our goal is to move away from a self-centered view of intercultural issues toward an *other*-centered perspective. Rather than *denying* that there are any differences, being *defensive* about the actions and behaviors of others, or trying to *minimize* differences as merely superficial, we must work toward *integrating* or recognizing and understanding differences by being adaptive. The goal is to *empathize* with others as we learn to *accept* and explore the many differences (some good, some not) that exist.[17] It is better to assume differences rather than similarities so that we can proceed cautiously, keeping an open mind, taking in feedback, and seeking understanding. Once we're aware of and have some understanding of fundamental differences, the next step is to demonstrate an openness to learning about the business customs and practices of others. This, in turn, can lead to the establishment of credibility and identification of common ground.

RECONCILING CULTURAL DIFFERENCES

There are many practical ways to reconcile cultural dilemmas. Once we are aware of the differences and have developed both respect and empathy for the ways of others, we can take practical steps to bridge the gap toward better—not perfect or flawless, but better—understanding and more-successful interactions. Saint Ambrose's admonition to St. Augustine of Hippo, "When in Rome, do as the Romans do," is basically good advice. If we're genuinely interested in doing business globally, whether we go abroad and become the foreigner, or welcome others who come to us, we should be responsible for taking the initiative to learn about other cultural practices. We can familiarize ourselves with the hidden dimensions of culture and begin to learn even more about specific cultural attributes. We can look inward for those natural ethnocentric perspectives that we each hold and be willing to alter them, trying to put things into perspective from someone else's viewpoint rather than our own. We can look for assumptions and seek clarification about our own communication and behaviors. We can keep an open mind so that we're less evaluative, judging others less by those norms and standards that make sense only to us. By doing so, we have a much better chance of treating others as individuals and not as stereotypical caricatures of another cultural group. We can reverse the situation and try to put ourselves in *their* shoes, thinking about the assumptions and stereotypes that they may have of *us*. Most importantly, we can be flexible by keeping our sense of humor, even in the midst of ambiguous situations. If we are open-minded, rather than defensive, and seek to understand our business counterparts—sincerely expressing this desire—we can open many doors, developing the potential for trust and healthy intercultural business relationships.

REVIEW: DIMENSIONS OF CULTURE

It is human nature to make assumptions about other people's actions and behaviors based upon what we know or assume to be the "right" way of doing things. Our various cultures dictate the norms of any given group and provide us with our beliefs, values, attitudes, and behaviors. These norms, or unstated rules, are the accepted and expected ways of behaving and interacting with other people. Culture is something that we learn—from infancy on we are conditioned and learn about how people in our "world" do things from watching them, conversing with them, and interacting with them.

The following is a summary of the various cultural dimensions that have been discussed in this book. You may want to use these as a springboard for discussion with your peers/coworkers about any personal intercultural encounters that you have experienced. As always, our goal is *not* to make gross overgeneralizations about any one culture or cultures but to merely define key dimensions that every culture possesses. These ideas are supported by leading anthropologists, interculturalists, and sociologists and are placed on a continuum that is intended to allow people to reflect on the degree to which they have experienced these aspects of intercultural encounters.

(See Figure 5.1 for a reminder of the major crosscultural dimensions discussed in this book.)

Cultural Dimension Summary

Context in communication: Do we derive meaning mostly from the non-verbal or through the words?

Identity: Do we tend to interact collectively as a group or on our own as an individual?

Learning: Do we "speak up" in class and participate assertively or do we listen respectfully?

Environment: Do we live in harmony with or try to control our surroundings?

Change/Ambiguity: Do we tend to avoid what is uncertain or do we accept it?

Time: Do we view time as scarce or plentiful?

Space: Do we tend to stand/interact in close proximity with others or do we stand/interact farther away?

Authority/Power: Is power something that is ascribed or is it earned?

Achievement: Do we behave competitively or cooperatively?

Doing or Being: Do we live to work or work to live?

Respect: Do we bestow more formal respect on those who are older, more experienced, etc. or do we tend to be more informal in our interactions?

Emotional expression: Do we express our emotions openly or do we control outward displays of emotion?

Persuasion: Do we tend to reason deductively—giving the main point and *then* giving the facts; or inductively—giving facts and *then* getting to the main point?

Problem Solving and Reasoning: Do we tend to be linear in our thinking or more circular?

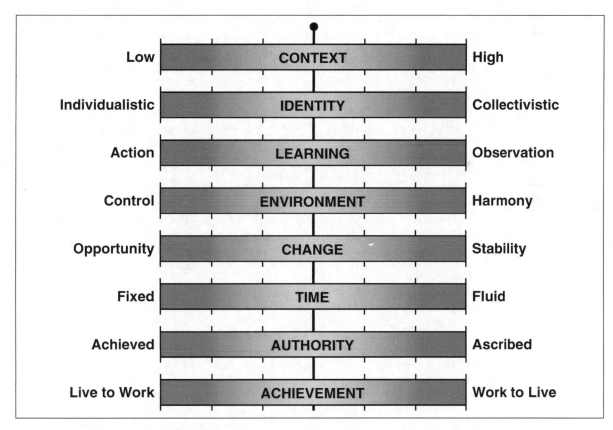

Figure 5.1   The Eight Dimensions of Culture

Adapted from Meena S. Wilson, Michael H. Hoppe, and Leonard R. Sayles, *Managing Across Cultures: A Learning Framework.* (Greensboro, NC: Center for Creative Leadership, 2002). (With emphasis drawn by Monica McGrath, The Wharton School, University of Pennsylvania).

SUMMARY

The quote at the beginning of this chapter, which acknowledges that sellers should adapt to buyers, and visitors should observe local customs in the global marketplace, helps us connect with the central point throughout this text: developing strong intercultural communicative competence means that we have to open our eyes to the tacit differences (hidden dimensions) of intercultural encounters in order to understand *why* we want to say something, *what* to say, *how* to say it, *when* it is an appropriate time to say it, and to *whom* we should say it. If we are to be effective as intercultural communicators, we must first understand ourselves and then act on that understanding as we share similar meanings in our interactions with others. We must be aware of our own cultures: the values, beliefs, attitudes, and behaviors based on our family and social relationships. We must also be aware of the power relationships that exist in national culture. Understanding how our nonverbal behavior can affect our interactions is a first step. People have different ways of processing and organizing information, and we must be open to and patient with these ways of interaction. Finally, we must understand that there are many different views of how we, as humans, should interact with the world and deal with change and uncertainty. Being aware of these differing viewpoints and then *acting* on this knowledge and learning from our experiences can help us to improve our communicative competence.

Culture might well be compared to the Great Wall of China. It is expansive and seemingly goes on forever, far beyond what the human eye can see. There are many parts to it as it twists and winds its way throughout the landscape, and it would surely take many visits for you to feel as if you had grasped even a portion of its magnificence. What we have attempted to do here is to introduce you to the Wall of Culture by taking several snapshots of various important parts that will give you a limited but useful sense of its splendor.[18] Our goal has been to provide you with a framework for thinking about intercultural communication in the global marketplace so that you can place these snapshots together to get the big picture. We have presented a number of pictures from different angles to give you an idea of the major themes and dimensions that characterize intercultural communication in order to build your awareness. The task now is to put this awareness into practice, counteracting the normal human tendency toward ethnocentric thinking. The rest is up to you: to take your own journey to explore other cultures and see where they take you. We encourage you to write your own stories to record, share, and compare with your colleagues as you become more aware of the many hidden dimensions of intercultural communication that lie behind every human interaction.

ENDNOTES

1. Richard R. Gesteland, Cross-Cultural Business Behavior: Marketing, Negotiating, Sourcing, and Managing Across Cultures (Copenhagen, Denmark: Copenhagen Business School Press, 2002).
2. James Downs, *"Psychocultural Influences on the Process,"* in William Gudykunst and Young Yun Kim, Communicating with Strangers: An Approach to Intercultural Communication (Reading, MA: Addison-Wesley Publishing Co., 1984), 83.
3. LaRay M. Barna, *"Stumbling Blocks in Intercultural Communication,"* in Larry A. Samovar and Richard E. Porter, Intercultural Communication: A Reader, 4th ed. (Belmont, CA: Wadsworth Publishing Company, 1994), 337–346.
4. Larry A. Samovar and Richard E. Porter, Intercultural Communication: A Reader, 9th ed (Belmont, CA: Wadsworth Publishing Company, 2000), 5.
5. "The Most-Quoted Remarks." Retrieved 18August, 2004, from http://www1c.btwebworld.com/quote-unquote/p0000149.htm.
6. Linel Laroche, "Managing Cross-Cultural Differences in International Projects." Retrieved 18 August 2004, from http://www.itapintl.com/mngdifintproj.htm.
7. Terry Morrison, Wayne A. Conaway, and George A. Borden, Kiss, Bow or Shake Hands (Avon, MA: Adams Media Corporation, 1994), 180–81.
8. *Ibid.,* 41.
9. *Ibid.,* 47.
10. *Ibid.*

11. Gesteland, supra n.1, 114.
12. For a comprehensive illustration of the full range of human gestures, see Desmond Morris, Bodytalk (New York, NY: Crown Trade Paperbacks, 1994).
13. John C. Condon and Fathi S. Yousef, An Introduction to Intercultural Communication (Indianapolis, IN: The Bobbs-Merrill Company, Inc., 1975).
14. Fons Trompenaars and Charles Hampden-Turner, Riding the Waves of Culture: Understanding Cultural Diversity in Global Business (New York, NY: McGraw-Hill, 1998).
15. Ibid., 201.
16. Geert Hofstede, Cultures and Organizations: Software of the Mind: Intercultural Cooperation and Its Importance for Survival (New York: NY, McGraw-Hill, 1997), 4.
17. Milton J. Bennett, "A Developmental Approach to Training for Intercultural Sensitivity," International Journal of Intercultural Relations 10 (1986), 179–96.
18. Conversation with Jim O'Rourke (September 2003).

Canwall Paper, Ltd.: Canadian and Chinese Negotiations

A Canadian team of two men representing Canwall, a wallpaper printing equipment manufacturer, went to a town north of Shanghai in the province of Jiangsu, China, to negotiate a sale to a new wallpaper production company. Charlie Burton, president of Canwall, traveled with his marketing director, Phil Raines. The company had never before sold its equipment outside Canada, and the two Canadians were delighted with the warm reception they enjoyed in China.

This wasn't the first meeting between the Canadian company and the Chinese wallpaper factory. The manager of the Chinese company, Mr. Li, had been a member of a delegation to Canada. He had met with one of Canwall's senior salespersons and the director of manufacturing. Subsequently, a trade representative from Canada had been in China representing Canwall's interests to the Chinese manager. After these meetings and numerous letters and faxes, Canwall's top people were now ready to negotiate the sale.

The day they arrived they were met at the airport in Shanghai by manager Li himself and transported in a chauffeur-driven car 90 miles to the town. Their accommodation was in a newly built hotel, and while it was not luxurious, it was certainly comfortable. A few hours after their arrival, they were treated to a 12-course banquet given by their host, with several high-level municipal officials present. This red-carpet treatment made them feel optimistic about the sale.

The next day they were taken to see the sights nearby: large, new port for container ships and several factories indicted the prosperity of the region. They were eager begin discussing the sale, but after lunch they were given time to rest. In the late afternoon one of the manager's English-speaking employees came by with the news they would be taken to see a local dance company's performance that night.

The third day they finally sat down to meetings. Progress seemed very slow—each side giving generalizations about itself that seemed unrelated to the sale. The Canadians used an interpreter, supplied by the Chinese, who was eager to please them, so the Canadians felt comfortable with her, but translation slowed down communication. Their interpreter seemed to be unfamiliar with technological terms since she and the interpreter from the factory spent some time discussing the terms between themselves. After listening to various apparently unrelated points, the Canadians thought, "So what?" The Chinese also spent a lot of time talking about the Canadian trade agent who had been in their town earlier. Burton wasn't able to tell them much about that person, since he had never met him personally.

When the Canadians at last were able to make the presentation they had prepared, they were surprised at the number of people who showed up. There were two of them, but there were ten Chinese facing them across the table. Still, the Chinese frequently nodded and smiled, and said yes. Burton and Raines had prepared sales data and showed—effectively, they thought—that within five years the factory could double its present production. At the end of the day, the jubilant Canadians returned to their hotel rooms confident they had sold the equipment.

The next day they were asked to explain once again things they thought had been covered already to a Chinese team with four new faces in it. They were confused about who their negotiating counterparts really were. Their jubilation began to evaporate. They were asked to explain the technology in minute detail. Neither Burton nor Raines had been involved in the engineering of the high-tech component that was the heart of the equipment. After doing the best they could, they returned to the hotel exhausted.

The next day, the Canwell negotiators were asked again about the technological details of the equipment. This time one member of the first-day team pointed out discrepancies between what they had said and what the manufacturing director, an engineer, had told them in Canada. Burton and Raines were chagrined. The Chinese were reproachful about the discrepancies, as if the Canadians had been caught in a shameful act. At lunchtime the two Canadians quickly faxed Canada for specifications and explanations. The afternoon session was uncomfortable although everyone was polite. Burton and Raines were a bit unsettled when a middle-aged woman suddenly burst into the negotiating room and whispered in the ear of one of the key Chinese speakers, who immediately got up and left the room. The Canadians expected some explanation for the emergency, but none ever came.

The next day, because of the time difference, the Canadians received some of the documentation they needed by fax, and discussions resumed with the same questions being asked yet again. It all went very slowly. The Chinese appreciated the high quality of the Canadian product but worried they wouldn't be able to fix the equipment if it broke down. They suggested (delicately, so as not to imply they *expected* breakdowns) that perhaps the Canadians could give them some help with maintenance training. The Canadians pointed out the expense and difficulty of keeping someone in their city for several weeks or months and expressed confidence that there wouldn't be any problems the manual didn't cover. The Chinese would be able to look after the equipment just fine.

Finally, the technical discussions gave way to the issue central to most negotiations in most countries: price. This proved to be the most difficult of all. The Chinese began by asking for a 20 percent price discount. The Canadians thought this was a simply outrageous negotiating ploy; they stuck to their price, which they knew to be fair, and offered a 3 percent discount on the printing cylinders.

Although Burton and Raines had heard that negotiations took time in China, they had thought a week would be ample. Now time was running out and they were due in Beijing in two days. They already had learned that getting plane tickets wasn't easy, so they were anxious to be on the plane as previously arranged. The Canadians began to ask pointed questions about what the Chinese were unhappy with and in which areas they needed to review issues again. During the last two sessions, the Canadians tried to get the Chinese to focus on the unresolved points, but the Chinese seemed reluctant to do so.

A number of issues remained unresolved when the farewell banquet was held the following noon. The question of price seemed near solution, but not the method of payment. That was the final apparently insurmountable hurdle since the Chinese couldn't guarantee the payment schedule; it seemed tied to deadlines and requirements of the municipal officials. Nevertheless, Manager Li smiled and spoke of mutual cooperation for the future, past Chinese-Canadian relations, and the great amount he and his factory could learn from the Canadians. They signed an expanded version of the letter of intent that had been signed nine months earlier in Canada. The Canadians left with expressions on both sides of willingness to continue to discuss the sale through mail and fax.

The Canadians were stunned to learn two weeks later that the factory had decided to buy from a Japanese equipment manufacturer. They knew their product was good and their price was fair. What had happened to derail their sale?

In discussing what had happened to derail their sale, consider the following cross-cultural dimensions that came into play regarding this transaction:

context	environment	authority
identity	change/ambiguity	achievement
learning	time	other

Adapted from Linda Beamer and Iris Varner, *Intercultural Communication in the Global Workplace* (Boston, MA: McGraw-Hill, 1995).